The Journal and Letters of

FRANCIS ASBURY

Illustrator

Erle Prior

Maps by

Lewis Akin
Thoburn Lyon

FRANCIS ASBURY, PROPHET OF THE LONG ROAD
Portrait by Frank O. Salisbury, C.V.O., R.P.S., LL.D., D.F.A., in the World Methodist Building at Lake Junaluska, North Carolina, U.S.A.

Frontispiece

The Journal and Letters of
FRANCIS ASBURY

In Three Volumes

VOLUME II

The Journal

1794 to 1816

ELMER T. CLARK *Editor-in-Chief*

J. MANNING POTTS

JACOB S. PAYTON

Published Jointly By

EPWORTH PRESS
London

ABINGDON PRESS
Nashville

FIRST PUBLISHED IN 1958

PRINTED IN GREAT BRITAIN BY
HAZELL WATSON AND VINEY LTD
AYLESBURY AND SLOUGH

1794

1794

Asbury at the Cokesbury School, on the Yadkin, in North Carolina

CHAPTER TWENTY-THREE

South Carolina

Wednesday, January 1, 1794. We removed brother Bruce into a room without fire. We hastened the business of our conference as fast as we could. After sitting in a close room with a very large fire, I retired into the woods nearly an hour, and was seized with a severe chill, an inveterate cough and fever, with a sick stomach: with difficulty I sat in conference the following day; and I could get but little rest; brother Bruce's moving so frequently, and the brethren's talking, disturbed me. Sick as I was, I had to ordain four elders and six deacons; never did I perform with such a burden. I took a powerful emetic. I was attended by Doctor D——.

I found I must go somewhere to get rest. The day was cloudy, and threatened snow; however, brother Reuben Ellis and myself made out to get seven miles to dear old brother Andrew Yeargan's house.[1] The next day came on a heavy fall of snow, which continued two days, and was from six to ten inches deep. I had to let some blood: I made use of flax seed, and afterward of betony tea,[2] both which were of use to me. I must be humbled before the Lord, and have great searching of heart.

[1] Andrew Yeargan came from Wales to Virginia in 1735, and Yeargan's Chapel in Brunswick County was the first in that state. In 1779 he was on the Tar River Circuit in North Carolina. He located and settled in Newberry County, South Carolina, as a local preacher soon after 1790. The Yeargan's had ten sons and one daughter. One son was the Rev. John Yeargan, a prominent local preacher in South Carolina. Tranquil Church near Joanna, South Carolina, organized in 1799, was the outgrowth of Yeargan's labors. (Sednum, *op. cit.*, 140).

[2] Betony is any plant of the mint family.

Monday, 13. Rode thirty miles, although the weather was damp and unpromising, and came to Herbert's store, on Broad River. I was so weak that my exercise and clothing almost overcame me. The next day we passed Connelly's Ferry; and got nothing for ourselves until we had ridden forty-six miles to Colonel Jacob Rumph's,[3] where we had everything, and were free and comfortable.

Sunday, 19. Rode to Cypress,[4] where I could not rest without giving them a little sermon.

Monday, 20. I reached the city of Charleston.[5] Here I began to rest: my cold grew better. Doctor Ramsey directed me to the use of laudanum, nitre and bark, after cleansing the stomach with an emetic. The kindness of sister Hughes was very great. I have written largely to the West, and declined visiting those parts this year. The American Alps, the deep snows and great rains, swimming the creeks and rivers, riding in the night, sleeping on the earthen floors, more or less of which I must experience, if I go to the Western country, might at this time cost me my life. I have only been able to preach four times in three weeks.

I have had sweet peace at times since I have been here: the love of meetings (especially those for prayer); the increase of hearers; the attention of the people; my own better feelings; and the increasing hope of good that prevails among the preachers, lead me to think that "the needy shall not always be forgotten, nor the expectation of the poor fail." I have been pleased in reading Prince's Christian History, of about four hundred pages: it was a cordial to my soul in the time of my affliction. It is Methodism in all its parts. I have a great desire to reprint an abridgment of it, to show the apostolic children what their fathers were. I have read Gordon's History of the American Revolution: here we view the suffering straits of the American army; and, what is greatly interesting, General Washington's taking his farewell of his officers—what an affecting scene! I could not but feel through the whole of the description. What, then, was the sight! O how minds are made great with affliction and suffering! Poor Beverly Allen, who has been going from bad to worse these seven or eight years—speaking against me to preachers and people, and writing to Mr. Wesley and Doctor Coke, and being thereby the source of most of the mischief that has followed; and lastly, having been agent for Mr. ——, is now secured in jail for shooting Major Forsyth through the head. The Major was marshal for the federal court in Georgia, and was about to serve a writ upon Beverly Allen: the master-piece of all is, a petition is prepared, declaring him to have shown marks of insanity pre-

[3] Colonel Jacob Rumph, where Asbury preached on other occasions (March 17, 1788), lived in Orangeburg County, above Orangeburg.

[4] This was the Cypress Swamp and Church. Latera Campground is still in operation there.

[5] See letter to John Kobler, January 22, 1794.

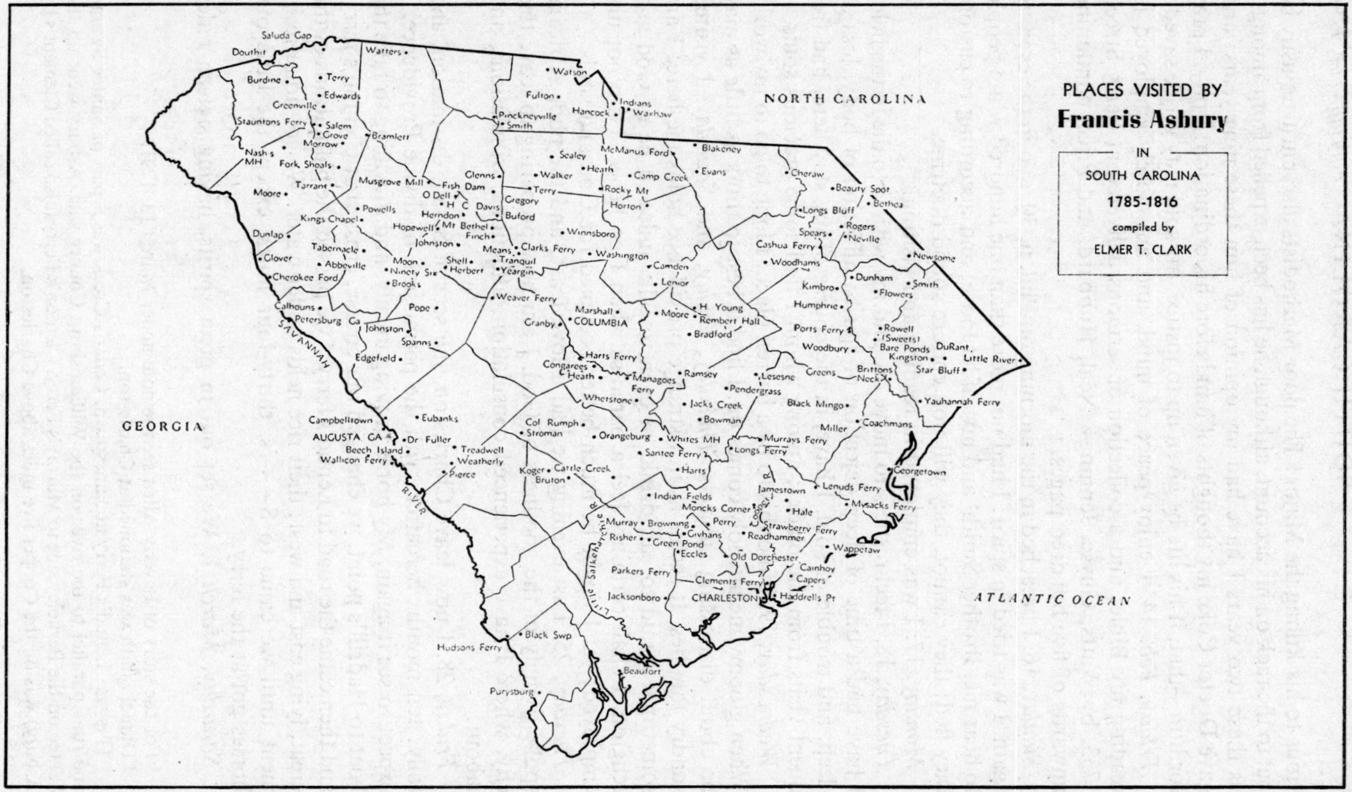
PLACES VISITED BY
Francis Asbury
IN
SOUTH CAROLINA
1785-1816
compiled by
ELMER T. CLARK
NORTH CAROLINA
GEORGIA
ATLANTIC OCEAN
SAVANNAH
RIVER
Little Salkehatchie R
Cooper R
Saluda Gap
Douthit
Watters
Watson
Burdine
Terry
Edwards
Fulton
Indians
Hancock
Waxhaw
Greenville
Pinckneyville
Smith
Stauntons Ferry
Salem
Grove
Morrow
Bramlett
Nash's MH
Fork Shoals
McManus Ford
Blakeney
Sealey
Heath
Evans
Glenns
Walker
Camp Creek
Cheraw
Moore
Tarrant
Musgrove Mill
Fish Dam
Terry
Rocky Mt
Beauty Spot
O Dell
H C
Gregory
Horton
Bethea
Powells
Herndon
Davis
Longs Bluff
Kings Chapel
Buford
Spears
Rogers
Hopewell
Mt Bethel
Winnsboro
Neville
Dunlap
Finch
Johnston
Means
Clarks Ferry
Cashua Ferry
Tabernacle
Newsome
Glover
Washington
Moon
Tranquil
Abbeville
Shell
Ninety Six
Herbert
Camden
Woodhams
Yeargin
Cherokee Ford
Brooks
Lenior
Kimbro
Dunham
Smith
Flowers
Weaver Ferry
Calhouns
Pope
H Young
Marshall
Humphrie
Moore
Rembert Hall
Petersburg Ga
Granby
COLUMBIA
Johnston
Bradford
Ports Ferry
Rowell
(Sweets)
Spanns
Woodbury
Bare Ponds
DuRant
Kingston
Little River
Harts Ferry
Edgefield
Greens
Brittons
Neck
Star Bluff
Congarees
Ramsey
Lesesne
Heath
Managoes
Ferry
Pendergrass
Whetstone
Yauhannah Ferry
Jacks Creek
Black Mingo
Campbelltown
Eubanks
Bowman
Miller
Coachmans
Col Rumph
Stroman
AUGUSTA GA
Dr Fuller
Orangeburg
Whites MH
Murrays Ferry
Treadwell
Beech Island
Longs Ferry
Santee Ferry
Wallicon Ferry
Weatherly
Georgetown
Pierce
Koger
Cattle Creek
Harts
Bruton
Lenuds Ferry
Jamestown
Indian Fields
Mysacks Ferry
Moncks Corner
Hale
Murray
Browning
Perry
Givhans
Strawberry Ferry
Risher
Green Pond
Readhammer
Eccles
Old Dorchester
Wappetaw
Parkers Ferry
Cainhoy
Clements Ferry
Capers
Jacksonboro
CHARLESTON
Haddrells Pt
Black Swp
Hudsons Ferry
Beaufort
Purysburg

vious to his killing the Major! The poor Methodists also must unjustly be put to the rack on his account, although he has been expelled from amongst us these two years I have had my opinion of him these nine years; and gave Doctor Coke my thoughts of him before his ordination: I pity, I pray for him—that, if his life be given up to justice, his soul may yet be saved.[6]

Friday, Feb. 14. I enjoy peace of mind, and am closely employed in reading my Bible; and a collection of sermons delivered at Berry Street, 1733, by Watts, Guyse, Jennings, Neal, Hubbard, and Price, containing upwards of five hundred pages.

Sunday, 16. I preached in the morning on Phil. ii, 30, and in the evening again. I was tried in spirit: I had not more than one hundred white people to hear me. Brother Smith[7] and myself let loose; and according to custom they fled: they cannot, they will not, endure sound doctrine.

Monday, 17. I was employed in reading and visiting.

Tuesday, 18. I feel restless to move on, and my wish is to die in the field. I have had a time of deep dejection of spirits, affliction of body, loss of sleep, and trouble of soul. I have, in the course of my stay here, had frequent visits from the blacks; among whom I find some gracious souls.

Wednesday, 19. I find this to be a barren place; I long to go to my work. When gloomy melancholy comes on, I find it best to think as little as may be about distressing subjects. *Thursday*, *Friday*, and *Saturday*, I visited sundry families. It seems as if a strange providence holds me here: I am sometimes afraid to eat, drink, or even to talk, unless it be of God and religion. I shall certainly feel a paradise when I go hence. I am not unemployed; yet I might be much better occupied for God and souls.

Tuesday, 25. Last evening we had a love feast; and the poor Africans spoke livingly of the goodness of God. I am now preparing to leave this city, where I have experienced consolation, afflictions, tribulations, and labour.

Friday, 28. I now leave Charleston, the seat of Satan, dissipation, and folly: ten months hereafter, with the permission of divine Providence, I expect to see it again. My horse proving unruly, and unwilling to take the boat to Hadrill's point, we changed our course, crossed at Clemon's ferry, and then came the road to Lenud's ferry:[8] we passed the plantations of the great, lying east and west; their rice fields under water. We got no refreshment until we came to S——'s, thirty-four miles, except the little our horses got at the ferry.

Saturday, March 1. We set out in great spirits, having sixteen miles

[6] For the story of Beverly Allen see the note under March 13, 1791.

[7] Daniel Smith was stationed at Charleston.

[8] This was Lenud's Ferry at Jamestown. Cedar's Creek was a part of Santee Swamp and runs parallel to the river on the Williamsburg County side. Asbury went up the Santee on the Berkeley side to Murray's Ferry. Clemon's Ferry (also called Clement's by Asbury) was on the Cooper five miles above Charleston.

to the ferry; where we were detained six hours. We hoped to have been in Georgetown by sunset. Now we thought of travelling until midnight: we came to Cedar Creek, which we found in a bad state. We stayed at the ferry; being persuaded we could not reach Georgetown time enough for meeting.

Sabbath morning. We directed our course westward, and came along, drooping and solitary, to Murray's ferry,[9] about twenty-five miles. We rode up to a large house, and were asked in to drink brandy: three men and two women appeared to be set in to drink the *pure stuff*, glass after glass; we were glad to retreat. There came on a storm of rain, with thunder and lightning. I was unwilling to go to ——, expecting the same kind of Sabbath devotion there. We travelled a most dreadful road to Black River, and had plenty of water above and below us. After riding fifteen miles, we came to the widow Bowman's,[10] where we got a shelter; still we had our fears: there is such a quantity of water in the swamp and low lands, that our feet are kept very uncomfortable, and some places are impassable. Isaac Smith, in all these difficulties and trials of swamps, colds, rains, and starvation, was my faithful companion.

After riding twenty-seven miles without eating, how good were the potatoes and fried gammon![11] We then had only ten miles to brother Rembert's; where we arrived about seven o'clock. I confess my soul and body have been sorely tried. What blanks are in this country—and how much worse are rice plantations! If a man-of-war is "a floating hell," these are standing ones: wicked masters, overseers, and Negroes—cursing, drinking—no Sabbaths, no sermons. But hush! perhaps my journal will never see the light; and if it does, matters may mend before that time; and it is probable I shall be beyond their envy or good-will. O wretched priests, thus to lead the people on in blindness!

Thursday, 6. We had family meeting at brother Rembert's: I gave them a long discourse on the last words of David, 2 Sam. xxiii, 5: "Although my house be not so with God, yet he hath made with me an everlasting covenant, ordered in all things and sure, for this is all my salvation and all my desire (pleasure or delight), although he make it not to grow." 1. I considered how we enter into covenant with God. 2. On man's part it is ordered to repent, believe, love, obey, suffer, &c., and in a word, to attend to every duty God hath enjoined. 3. That this is all the delight of a gracious soul, that his eternal all is rested upon the covenant relations he bears to the Lord. David appears, 1. To have been looking to Solomon's peaceable kingdom. 2. To Christ who was to come to David's seed. 3. Parents and gracious souls may say, the commonwealth, the Church, their families, &c., are not as they could wish; yet God is their portion,

[9] Murray's Ferry was at the point where present Highway 52 crosses the Santee.
[10] Mrs. Bowman may have lived near Manning in Clarendon County.
[11] Gammon was fried smoked or dried bacon or ham.

What distresses were experienced in the families of ancient saints! See the history of the families of Adam, Noah, Abraham, Isaac, Jacob, Eli, Samuel, David, and others of whom we read. My time is short—this may be my last to speak, or theirs to hear: we are not only creatures of a year, but of a day, an hour.

Sunday, 9. I preached on Romans v, 20, 21.

Monday, 10. We held a little conference to provide for Charleston, Georgetown, Edisto, and Santee: some are afraid that if we retain none among us who trade in slaves, the preachers will not be supported, but my fear is that we shall not be able to supply this State with preachers.

Tuesday, 11. I had to preach to the respectable people of Camden—where I suppose I had two hundred hearers in the court house. It was heavy work, my body and faith being both weak—some trifled; some felt; and perhaps more understood.

Wednesday, 12. We missed our way to the chapel called Grannies Quarter;[12] and made it thirty miles to Horton's, at the Hanging Rock, on a very warm day, without any refreshment except a little biscuit.

North Carolina

Thursday, 13. Rode thirty miles more to the Waxhaw,[13] after preaching at the chapel in the woods. I went to brother T——'s, where we had a room to ourselves; and our horses were richly fed: this was a great favour—such as we do not generally receive in this country.

Saturday, 15. We set out under discouraging prospects; having had a heavy rain the night before. We came to Shepherds;[14] where we had to swim our horses alongside a canoe, and had they not struggled powerfully and freed themselves, from among the bushes and grape-vines, they had certainly drowned: we returned across the stream, and then brought them down the creek, to a place where there were no trees in the way, and we got safe across.

Sunday, 16. The waters being still high, our passage difficult, and having no inclination to travel on the Sabbath, we continued at Shepherd's, where we stayed the night before. Notice we circulated through the neighbourhood, and by eleven o'clock there was collected a congregation of sixty or seventy people.

Monday, 17. We set out, and passed Charlotte, in Mecklenburg; here I learned that meeting was appointed for me at A——'s. I came to L. Hill's,

[12] Granny's Quarter was a creek, now called Sanders Creek, ten miles north of Camden. The chapel was evidently on a plantation located on that creek. It is no longer in existence.

[13] Waxhaw was across the line in Union County, North Carolina. Asbury had followed a familiar route from Remberts through Camden and Hanging Rock.

[14] Mr. Shepherd probably lived near the Union-Mecklenburg county line.

where I met with Nicholas Watters and Daniel Asbury,[15] having ridden thirty-four miles. By the time I reach Justice White's I shall make out to have ridden about one thousand miles in three months; and to have stopped six weeks of the time with great reluctance. I preached at —— on 2 Tim. ii, 12–17. I gave, 1. The marks of a Christian; one of which is, that he suffers persecution. 2. The marks of heretics and schismatics; the former oppose the established doctrines of the Gospel—the latter will divide Christians. 3. That we must continue in what we have been taught by the word, the Spirit, and faithful ministers of Christ. 4. That the Holy Scriptures are the standard sufficient for ministers and people to furnish them to every good work.

Thursday, 20. I directed my course, in company with my faithful fellow-labourer, Tobias Gibson, up the Catawba, settled mostly by the Dutch. A barren spot for religion. Having ridden in pain twenty-four miles we came, weary and hungry, to O——'s tavern; and were glad to take what came to hand. Four miles forward we came to Howes Ford, upon Catawba River, where we could neither get a canoe nor guide. We entered the water in an improper place, and were soon among the rocks and in the whirlpools: my head swam, and my horse was affrighted: the water was to my knees, and it was with difficulty we retreated to the same shore. We then called to a man on the other side, who came and piloted us across for which I paid him well. My horse being afraid to take the water a second time, brother Gibson crossed, and sent me his; and our guide took mine across. We went on, but our troubles were not at an end: night came on, and it was very dark. It rained heavily, with powerful lightning and thunder. We could not find the path that turned out to Connell's. In this situation we continued until midnight or past; at last we found a path which we followed till we came to dear old father Harper's plantation; we made for the house, and called; he answered, but wondered who it could be; he inquired whence we came; I told him we would tell that when we came in, for it was raining so powerfully we had not much time to talk: when I came dripping into the house, he cried, "God bless your soul, is it brother Asbury? wife, get up." Having had my feet and legs wet for six or seven hours, causes me to feel very stiff.

Friday, 21. We set forward towards brother White's, and took our time to ride twelve miles.

Saturday, 22. My soul enjoys peace; but O! for more of God! This campaign has made me "groan, being burdened." Bad news on my coming to the mountains; neither preachers nor elders have visited Swannanoah since last October; poor people—poor preachers that are

[15] Nicholas Watters was on the Union Circuit with Tobias Gibson, who was Asbury's traveling companion, and William McKendree. Daniel Asbury had been on the French Broad Circuit in 1788 but was now located. He began traveling again in 1803 and served the Union Circuit. (*Minutes.*) He lived at Rehobeth, the present Terrell.

not more stable: but all flesh is grass, and I am grass. I have provided brothers Gibson and Lurton[16] for the westward. I wrote a plan for stationing; and desired the dear preachers to be as I am in the work: I have no interest, no passions, in their appointments; my only aim is to care and provide for the flock of Christ. I see I must not leave Charleston till the third or fourth week in March; then the rains will subside, and the creeks and rivers be passable; and so shall we escape the danger of drowning ourselves and horses. I feel that my sufferings have been good preaching to me—especially in crossing the waters. I am solemnly moved in not visiting my Holston and Kentucky brethren. It may be their interest to desire the preservation of my life: while living I may supply them with preachers, and with men and money. I feel resolved to be wholly the Lord's, weak as I am; I have done nothing, I am nothing, only for Christ! or I had long since been cut off as an unfaithful servant; Christ is all, and in all I do, or it had not been done; or when done, had by no means been acceptable.

Sunday, 23. My subject at Justice White's was Heb. ii, 1–3; I had more people than I expected. I have visited this place once a year; but Mr. Kobler and Lowe[17] have both failed coming at all; I pity them and the people. If I could think myself of any account, I might say, with Mr. Wesley, "If it be so while I am alive, what will it be after my death?" I have written several letters to the westward to supply my lack of service. I am mightily wrought upon for New Hampshire, Province of Maine, Vermont, and Lower Canada.

Saturday, 29. Started for Nolenten's, and came part of the way alone. After winding about the creeks and hills, I came to a cabin: here I found a few serious people, to whom I preached on 1 Tim. iv, 8; after which I spent the evening with dear brother S. in his clean cabin

Sunday, 30. After riding about five miles, I came to a meeting house: it was a cabin half floored, with long open windows between the logs.

Monday, 31. I had the house filled with serious people, and found much to say on Ruth i, 16, 17: whatever weight there might have been in the discourse, I was happy in my own soul.

Tuesday, *April* 1. I was very happy whilst riding alone down to Doctor Brown's: on my way, I saw Babel, the Baptist-Methodist house, about which there has been so much quarrelling: it is made of logs and is no great matter. I am astonished at professors, old professors, neglecting family and private prayer; Lord, help! for there is but little genuine religion in the world.

Wednesday, 2. Came to E.'s meeting house, hear Hunting Creek, in

[16] Tobias Gibson went to Lexington in Kentucky, and Jacob Lurton went to the Cumberland Circuit in Tennessee. (See *Minutes*, 1794.)

[17] John Kobler and Isaac Lowe were the elders over the circuits in North Carolina and Holston. (See *Minutes*, 1794; letter to John Kobler, March 23, 1794.)

Surry county: here I met with some old disciples from Maryland, Delaware, and Virginia, who have known me these twenty-two years. Our meeting was attended with mutual pleasure: my soul enjoyed much sweetness with these people. There has been some trouble amongst them; but I know God is with them. I was secretly led to treat on sanctification at W.'s; and if the Lord will help me, I am resolved to speak more on this blessed doctrine. After preaching, I came to Cokesbury school,[18] at Hardy Jones's: it is twenty feet square, two stories high, well set out with doors and windows; this house is not too large, as some others are: it stands on a beautiful eminence, and overlooks the Lowlands, and river Yadkin.

Monday, 7. I set out alone, and missing my way, got entangled in the bush and thickets, and made it about twenty miles: although it was a trial to me, it might be intended to prevent the poor people from being disappointed who came late.

I had the pleasure of dining and drinking tea with a Moravian minister, who has the charge of the congregation at Muddy Creek. Next day I called at Salem.[19]

I rode twenty miles to Levin Ward's, on the head waters of Dan River, Stokes county. I was greatly fatigued; but having no appointment to preach, after a good night's rest, I was much refreshed. Having little opportunity of being alone, I wandered into the field for solitude. I met with Philip Sands,[20] from old Lynn, a child of Providence: after passing solemn scenes at sea, he was taken and left in the Lowlands of North Carolina. First a Christian, then a preacher. He was stationed in Guilford; but offered himself a volunteer for Swannanoa; which station hath been vacant near six months; one of the preachers appointed there being sick, and the other married; and now because I have power to send a preacher

[18] Cokesbury School was located on the Yadkin River near Phelp's Ferry in the lower end of present Davie County. This was doubtless the school for which John Dickins made the plan and for which Mr. Long and Mr. Bustian gave some money in 1780. (See *Journal* entry and notes for June 19, 1780.) The money was doubtless used for Cokesbury College in Maryland. Cokesbury School was the first Methodist conference school in America. James Parkes, the son-in-law of Hardy Jones, was taken from the district and became principal of the school this year. (Cummings, *op. cit.*, 71, 72; Grissom, *op. cit.*, 134–38; Turner and Bridgers, *op. cit.*, 468.) There is some confusion in the *Journal*, which indicates that Asbury preached in Surry County before reaching the school; he was traveling northward and would have passed the school long before reaching Surry County.

[19] The Moravian community of Salem, later united in Winston-Salem, was in Forsyth County. The confusion in the account continues. Salem was southeast of the meeting-house in Surry County, north of Cokesbury School, and directly south of Stokes County to which he proceeded. Asbury either entered his exact route incorrectly or doubled back on his trail during the five-day hiatus in the *Journal* between April 2 and April 7.

[20] Philip Sands was on the Roanoke Circuit and was sent to the Swannanoa with Josiah Cole, to change after six months with Christopher S. Mooring and Pemberton Smith, who were on the Yadkin Circuit. (See *Minutes*.)

to these poor people, some are pleased to account me and call me a despot.

Friday, 11. I went to Simpson's house. I was greatly chilled, and unable to preach. The house was very open, but brother Bird[21] sounded away bravely. It appeared as if my fingers were nearly frozen. I went home with brother C. and had everything comfortable.

Saturday, 12. I had a small congregation, but a good time with some feeling souls at brother J.'s, on my choice subject, Heb. iii, 12. We have rumours of war with England. But the Lord reigneth, although the earth be so much disquieted. I spent the evening with brothers Bird and Sands.

I was in the clouds on *Sunday*, 13; my body was full of pain, and my mind much dejected. I came through Rockingham, and saw my old friends: lodged with father Low, who is seventy-six years of age, and happy in God.

Monday, 14. Brother Sands set out for Swannanoah. Had I ventured to Kentucky, how should I have stood the wilderness, with four or five days of such cold, rainy weather as we have lately had? I was thankful to God that I changed my course.[22] I feel wholly devoted to God, and greatly wish to see more fruit of my labour.

Virginia

Friday, 18. I rose early; crossed Pudding Creek, Banister, and Bearskin, and came to brother C——'s, five miles from Pittsylvania court house. I met with my old friends Jones and W. D., and had a comfortable meeting.

Monday, 21. Rode with brothers Bruce and Mead[23] (who met me the day before) to brother Landrum's, and gave them a short sermon. I was happy in the company of the dear preachers. O! my soul, trust thou in the Lord! O for Zion's glory! Come, Lord Jesus, come quickly!

Wednesday, 23. I attended the funeral of R. Owen; who, I learn, died of a consumption, in the fear and love of God. I was too systematical for my congregation, who were wild and unawakened. I baptized a few children, then crossed Symes Ferry, and came twelve miles to brother Spencer's, in Charlotte county: here report saith, that there is sad work with those who have left us, and who are now exerting themselves to form as strong a party as they can; the principal of these are J. O'Kelly, Edward

[21] Jonathan Bird was on the Tar River Circuit.

[22] The Kentucky Conference was then in session at Bethel Academy. Thomas Scott joined the conference that year, and during the session he was lodged at the home of Captain John Lewis. He served circuits from 1789 to 1795. (See Scott's *Journal, op. cit.*, and his "Memoirs" in *Western Christian Advocate*, 1851–54; also notes under May 13 and 17, 1790.)

[23] See Bennett, *op. cit.*, 334.

Almond, J. K., and Jeremiah Cosden.[24] I learn by a letter from Ira Ellis, that matters are not desperate: this letter, with some others, I shall reserve for a future day. If the real cause of this division was known, I think it would appear, that one wanted to be immovably fixed in a district; another wanted money; a third wanted ordination; a fourth wanted liberty to do as he pleased about slaves, and not to be called to an account, &c.

Thursday, *Friday*, and *Saturday*, I spent in private application.

Sunday, 27. I had a crowded congregation at Reeve's chapel; those who had just left us appeared very shy. I was very unwell, and said but little on the division: I told them how long I had been in the country, how I had laboured, and what I had gained. After all we shall see what the end of all this work will be.

Wednesday, 30. I preached (though not of choice) at Charlotte court house: here Mr. ——[25] met me, and charged me with saying at —— "that they would take off my head." I told him I did not remember to have said so, but if I did, I must certainly have meant the Episcopacy of our Church; he answered, that in that I was very right, he strove to do it with all his might; yet he talked of *union*, and hoped I would do my part —At what? Why, to destroy; first, the Episcopacy, and then the conference —or at least its power and authority. I went to Major R.'s, and was treated very kindly.

Saturday, *May* 3. I had a serious congregation, and a good meeting at Crawley's.[26] Came to Pride's Church, in Amelia county, where there are no very great prospects. I was at the kind widow Coleman's,[27] on Appomattox River, thence to brother Hobson's[28]; where I was attended by brothers Foster, Mead, Bruce, Thompson, and Whatcoat.[29] I learn I am set forth as an enemy to the country; that I am laying up money to carry away to England, or elsewhere; but in the midst of all, I bless God for peace in my spirit. Let them curse, but God will bless, and his faithful preachers will love and pity me.

[24] Edward Almond was one of the O'Kelly preachers at the Charlotte Conference and was one of the messengers who took the petition from the Pine Grove Conference to Asbury. He held to the Republican Methodist name and refused to give it up. (MacClenny, *op. cit.*, 131, 136.) Since K is frequently confused with H, J. K. is probably John Hayes, who walked out of the Baltimore Conference with O'Kelly and who probably took the twelve-mile walk "to where they had left their horses." Hayes labored in North Carolina after the separation. Jeremiah Cosden withdrew from the connection in 1794. (See *Minutes.*)

[25] This was probably John Robertson, who withdrew with James O'Kelly and who preached in that locality. (William Spencer's *Journal.*)

[26] See Bennett, *op. cit.*, 250.

[27] Thrift: *Memoirs of the Reverend Jesse Lee*, 57.

[28] Hobson lived in Cumberland County.

[29] Bennett, *op. cit.*, 334. David Thompson and Stith Mead were on the Bedford Circuit. Richard Whatcoat was elder over the circuits in Delaware and Maryland. Philip Bruce was elder in South Carolina. (See *Minutes.*)

Friday, 9. After preaching at Spain's[30] chapel on Peter's denial, I rode to brother G——'s, twenty miles; my mind was heavy, my body weak and feeble. O that I had in the wilderness a lodging place! I ordained brother G. and baptized his son Philip; a dreadful rumour followed me from last Sabbath. I felt humble and thankful that I could suffer; I think more of religion now than ever. O, my God, I am thine; glory to Christ forever!

Monday, 12. Rode forty miles to Swiney's,[31] and preached the next day; but it seemed as if my discourse had almost as well have been Greek, such spiritual death prevails among the people. After preaching brothers Hunter,[32] Bruce, Whatcoat, and myself rode to brother Wilson's,[33] in Campbell County.

I preached in the court house at New London,[34] where I had a large, serious, and polite congregation; I dined with my old friend, countryman, and neighbour, Joseph Perkins, who is superintendent of the armoury. In this county (Bedford) there are thirteen societies of Methodists, three or four of which are large; there are about ten local preachers, who labour for Christ and souls.

Saturday and *Sunday*, 17 and 18. Was quarterly meeting at Wilson's chapel. The first day I gave place to brother Bruce. Sabbath day, after sacrament and love feast, I preached on Rev. iii, 20. The people within were serious, those without had their own talk and entertainment. I kept the Sabbath in the crowd in the best manner I could. I came off under rain and clouds to a town called Liberty:[35] and preached in the court house, but did not find freedom to eat bread or drink water in that place. Why should I receive aught from those who renounce my service? I went to friend S——'s, who has a godly wife, and was kindly entertained; I wish to serve the Methodists who can hear with candour, but I am not fond of preaching at places where the prejudices of the people run so high.

Tuesday, 20. I had about one hundred and fifty hearers at Edson's, and had liberty in preaching; brothers Mead and Bruce[36] assisted me. My soul is in peace and perfect love. I purpose to preach present conviction, conversion, and sanctification. I might do many things better than I do; but this I discover not till afterward. Christ is all to my soul; if my labours are not blessed, yet my soul shall rejoice in the Lord and be blessed.

[30] Thrift, *op. cit.*, 57.

[31] See *Journal* entry for July 3, 1790.

[32] This was probably James Hunter, pastor of Bottetourt Circuit. (See *Minutes*.)

[33] The quarterly meeting was at Wilson's Chapel. (See *Journal* entries for May 17, 18, below.)

[34] New London was the county seat of Bedford County. The county was divided in 1781, and Campbell County was formed. The present courthouse of Campbell County is at Rustburg.

[35] Liberty was the present Bedford.

[36] Bennett, *op. cit.*, 334; see also *Minutes*.

Thursday, 22. Came to Mitchell's,[37] on the Mill Creek, in Botetourt county, where I was met by brother Ira Ellis,[38] who assisted me next day in preparing the Minutes.

Saturday, 24. Preached at Fincastle, and had a very few to hear, except our own people; came the same evening to Edward Mitchell's,[39] where we were to hold our conference: here I met the brethren from Kentucky, and received a number of letters.

Sunday, 25. I was enabled to preach a searching discourse to near one thousand souls, on Isa. lii, 8.

Monday, 26. We were closely employed in the business of the conference.

Wednesday, 28. We went over the mountain to Rockbridge county. We crossed the north branch of James River, half a mile from the town of Lexington; dined at the Red House, and came to Mr. F——'s on the south branch of Shenandoah. Thence I urged my way by Stanton through the rain, without any boots; and having sold my oil cloth a few days before, I was wet from head to foot. My mind is in peace, waiting till my change come, hanging on Jesus for everlasting rest. We have a valuable house here (Newtown)[40] and three local preachers; at Charlestown[41] a good house and one local preacher;[42] I feel as though it would be a long time before I go through this country again. For some days I have had an inflammatory complaint in my ear, it is now removed into my mouth.

I spent *Monday*, 26th, and *Tuesday*, 27th, at brother Elijah Phelps's, and was very much indisposed. Came to Winchester; here is a good meeting house. I had many to hear my very feeble testimony on Romans v, 10. Doctor Tiffin[43] made a gargle of rose leaves, nitre, and spirits of vitriol, which was of use to my throat. I came on *Thursday*, to John Hite's, and employed brother Anderson[44] to preach, my throat continuing very

[37] This was probably the Rev. Samuel Mitchell.

[38] Ira Ellis was the presiding elder in Virginia. (See *Minutes*.)

[39] (Tipple, *op. cit.*, 379.) Mr. Mitchell lived on Craig's Creek.

[40] Newtown was the present Stephen's City near Winchester, Virginia.

[41] Charlestown was in present West Virginia. Asbury crossed and recrossed the Virginia–West Virginia line in the next several days, and it is difficult to trace his exact movements.

[42] This local preacher was Dr. Edward Tiffin. (See below.)

[43] Edward Tiffin, M.D. (1766–?), came with his parents from Carlisle, England, in 1784 and settled at Charlestown, in present Jefferson County, West Virginia. He was a local preacher whom Asbury ordained on November 19, 1792. He later moved to Ohio, where he became the first governor of that state in 1803. He held many other important offices, including that of United States Senator, and was active as a local preacher until his death. (Gilmore: *Life of Edward Tiffin, First Governor of Ohio*; see various *Journal* entries.)

[44] John Hite was a prominent Methodist who lived near Charlestown, in present West Virginia. Thomas Anderson was pastor at Leesburg.

bad. I found my mind greatly resigned to the will of God under my affliction.

Sick, wet, and weary, I found a comfortable retreat in the house of R. Harrison;[45] I have not been so thoroughly soaked in two years; I think I have need of a leathern coat that will stand all weathers. I got two men to *canoe* me across the river; they brought me over safe, and appeared to be satisfied with a quarter of a dollar each. *Saturday* was an awful day to me; my ear was exceedingly painful.

Sunday, June 1. I ventured to the church in the rain, and bore a feeble testimony for nearly an hour on 2 Pet. i, 4.

It was with difficulty I could attend the conference:[46] my throat and passage to the ear being inflamed, and I had also a chill and high fever. We had preaching morning, noon, and night, and had peace and consolation in our deliberations. On the last day of the conference I delivered a discourse on 1 Cor. i, 5, and we concluded with a solemn sacrament.

I next came to Shenandoah county. We have had awful rains for about two weeks; to these I have been exposed in my afflicted state.

Sunday, 8. Preached at Newtown, little notice being given, and few people attending.

Monday, 9. Rested at brother Phelp's. My mind is in peace, but I feel the spiritual death of the people; they are not what they were in religion.

West Virginia

I am now on the head branches of Opecken. I stopped awhile at John Hite's, and then came on to Shepherdstown. It was a very instructing time to me; I cannot pretend to preach, yet I talk a little to the dear people, who flock to see and hear me by hundreds. I hope to be as much resigned to a life of affliction as a life of health; and thus may I be perfect in love and wholly crucified with Christ! I concluded, after my high fever, and my being forced to bed, that it was out of the question for me to attempt to speak; but when I saw the people coming on every side, and thought "this may be the last time," and considered I had not been there for nearly five years, I took my staff, faintly ascended the hill, and held forth on 1 John i, 6, 7, and felt strengthened, having a clear view of the word of God. After meeting we administered the sacrament, and I then returned to my bed.

[45] In the *Journal* edition of 1821 this name was Hamson, but it was probably Harrison.

[46] The conference was held at Harrisonburg, in Rockingham County, Virginia. The sessions were probably held in the log church on the hill, though the tradition is that they were held in the stone house of Thomas Harrison on Bruce Street. Harrisonburg was also called Rockingham or Rockingham Court House from the county and also Rocktown.

Maryland

I preached at Fredericktown. Rode to Liberty: when I came there, I was so faint, and my strength so spent, that I felt as if I could by no means attempt to preach; but after brother R.[47] had sung a hymn and prayed, I made a feeble attempt on Gal. i, 11, 12.

Tuesday, 17. I rode twenty-three miles to the Stone Chapel, where I preached on Peter's denial of his Lord.

Wednesday, 18. I once more came to Baltimore; where, after having rested a little, I submitted to have my likeness taken:[48] it seems they will want a copy; if they wait longer, perhaps they may miss it. Those who have gone from us in Virginia,[49] have drawn a picture of me, which is not *taken from the life*. We called a meeting at Cokesbury, and made some regulations relative to the salaries of the teachers and the board of the students. I returned to Baltimore, and spent *Sabbath day*, 22d, there, and found the people but dull. Brother McClaskey[50] took his stand at the windmill between town and Point. My soul was quickened whilst applying these words, "Every knee shall bow, of things in heaven, things on earth, and things under the earth, and every tongue shall confess that Jesus Christ is Lord to the glory of God the Father:" I was grieved to find the hearts of the people so cold in religion; the world is a thief, stealing the heart from God.

Monday, 23. Set out for Philadelphia. Spent a day at college.

Delaware

Wednesday, 25. I reached John Hersey's, very unwell with bodily infirmities, but I found Christ with me.

Next day we breakfasted with brother John Miller, at Newport.

Pennsylvania

Dined at Chester, and preached in the evening at Philadelphia, after riding forty miles. I was weak and heavy in body and soul. I spent *Friday* in writing to my brethren in various parts who called for my advice.

[47] This was either Benton Riggin or Joseph Rowen.

[48] This portrait by Polk, in the possession of the Baltimore Conference Historical Society, was lost for many years and was recovered by Dr. George C. M. Roberts. It is now in Lovely Lane Meeting House, Baltimore. (See article by Thomas E. Bond, *The Christian Advocate and Journal*, 1854; *Methodist Quarterly Review*, 1831, 206; Wakeley: *Heroes of Methodism*, 40–42, 469, 470; *Methodist Sesqui-Centennial*, 34; Roberts: *Centenary Pictorial Album*, 16–19; Clark, *op. cit.*, 161–63.)

[49] These were the followers of James O'Kelly.

[50] John McClaskey (1756–1814), a native of Ireland who began his itinerant labors in 1785, was then stationed on the Baltimore Circuit. (*General Minutes* for 1815, I, 257.)

Sunday, 29. I preached at the new African church.[51] Our coloured brethren are to be governed by the doctrine and discipline of the Methodists. We had some stir among the people at Ebenezer. In the evening we had a cold time at the great church on Amos iv, 11. This has been a hard day's work.

New Jersey

Monday, 30. I rode to Trenton, an exceedingly warm day and preached in the evening. We rode to Kingston; thence to New Brunswick; thence to Bonhamtown,[52] and were weary enough when we got to Mr. Brown's.[53] Poor brother Swain[54] almost fainted, and went, outdone, to bed.

Came to Elizabethtown, and was grieved at the conduct of some of the preachers. O, how careful should each one be lest he become a stumbling block and destroy precious souls! As I cannot help, so neither am I to answer for other men's sins.

Wednesday, July 2. I gave them a close discourse on 2 Cor. vii, 1. I had four Methodist and one Presbyterian minister to hear me, and we had some life in our souls.

Thursday, 3. Came faint and weary to Powles Hook,[55] and felt my mind solemn and devoted to God. Thence crossed over to New York, and found my friends kind and full of the world.

New York

Friday, 4. Was the anniversary of Independence: I preached on 2 Pet. ii, 20, 21, wherein—

I. I showed that all real Christians had escaped the pollutions of the world.

II. That it is possible for them to be entangled therein again and overcome.

[51] This was the Bethel Church at Sixth and Lombard streets, Philadelphia, the first Methodist chapel built for the exclusive use of Negroes. It was a preaching point on the Philadelphia Circuit until 1816 and was served by Richard Allen, a Negro local preacher of St. George's Church. The Independent African Methodist Episcopal Church was organized here in 1816. (See *Journal* entries for October 11, 1795; June 8, 1800; March 19, 1808.)

[52] Bonhamtown is five miles northeast of New Brunswick in Middlesex County on the road to Woodbridge. It is the present-day location of the United States Army's Raritan Arsenal. (Gordon, *op. cit.*, 106; *New Jersey Guide*, 424.)

[53] Silas Brown lived at Browntown, New Jersey, about eight miles from Bonghamtown. (Phoebus, *op. cit.*, 74.)

[54] Probably Richard Swain, who had lately had the Flanders Circuit.

[55] Powles, or Paulus, Hook was the present Jersey City.

III. That when this is the case they turn from the holy commandments delivered unto them.

IV. That the last state of such is worse than the first: for God is provoked, Christ slighted, the Spirit grieved, religion dishonoured, their understanding is darkened, the will is perverted, the conscience becomes insensible, and all the affections unmoved under the means of grace; they keep the wisdom of the serpent, but lose the harmlessness of the dove.

At dinner Mr. Pilmoor spoke a word in favour of Mr. Glendenning (who was once with us, as also *he* had been); this brought on an explanation of matters: my answer was, 1. That I did not make rules, but had to execute them. 2. That any one who desired me to act unconstitutionally, either insulted me as an individual, or the conference as a body of men. I hardly knew sometimes where to set my foot; I must be always on my guard, and take heed to what I say of and before any one. Lord, make me upright in heart and life before thee and all men!

Sunday, 6. My mind was much agitated about trifles. I preached in the morning on Heb. xiii, 12, and we had a little move at the sacrament. At three I preached in the new house, and again in the evening at the old house, and gave a close exhortation to the society.

Monday, 7. Came to Berrien's,[56] near Kingsbridge, and thence to the White Plains, and dined with Lawyer H——, a member of our society. I preached at Chester court house[57] to about one hundred people: here are some living, gracious souls. Came in the evening to King street.[58] I am not conscious of having sinned, but I feel the infirmities of flesh and blood, and am in continual heaviness through manifold temptations. We had a sultry afternoon, and a rough ride over the rocks and hills to Bedford, where I had a feeble time in the town house, on the fall of Peter. I was sick, sore, tempted, and grieved:—and bade Bedford farewell!

Connecticut

Thursday, 10. Came to Norwich (Norwalk), sixteen miles; thence to Fairfield, twelve miles; and in the evening reached Poquonack, making nearly forty miles, in very great debility of body.

Friday, 11. We came to New Haven; thence to North Haven; thence to Middlefields: the rain took us as we crossed the mountains, and made it

[56] Samuel Berrien had recently inherited a large tract of farm land a short distance west of the village of Kingsbridge, on the shore of Spuyten Duyvil Creek as it moved west from the bridge to the Hudson River.

[57] This was the Westchester courthouse at White Plains.

[58] This chapel had been erected at a crossroads four miles southeast of White Plains; one of the roads running north from Rye was called King Street. Garrettson also mentions this preaching place, which was probably at or near the present community of Purchase. (See Scharf, *op. cit.*, II, maps.)

heavy work. We found it poor times. Were I to be paid by man for my services, I should rate them very high; it is so painful at present for me to ride, that a small sum would not tempt me to travel forty miles a day. I bless the Lord for daily afflictions of body and mind: O may these things terminate in my total resignation to the will of God!

Saturday, 12. The rain detained us till noon; I then came to Middletown, and preached at three o'clock in the Separate meeting house with some life. I lodged with the old prophet, Frothingham. After this dear old man had laboured and suffered many years, and had been imprisoned three times for the cause of Christ; after he grew old and his memory failed, and he could not receive the *new divinity*, they mistook and wrested his words; and his congregation turned him out to starve:—but the Lord will provide.

Sunday, 13. Was a great day—we had a love feast, and I preached in the court house, morning and evening, and brother S—— in the afternoon.

Monday, 14. Rode fourteen miles to the city of Hartford; and preached once more in Strong's church[59]—and I roared out wonderfully on Matt. xi, 28–30. Next day we came five miles to Spencer's, in Hartford; where we have a neat house, forty by thirty-four feet.[60] Thence I rode fifteen miles to Coventry, where I had a large congregation, and a comfortable meeting.

Wednesday, 16. We had to make our way through heat, rocks, and dust, to Cargill's at the wonderful water-works[61] erected on the falls of the river; and thence to Pomfret's; making in all thirty-three miles.

Massachusetts

Thursday, 17. We came a very rough path of five miles, to Douglass; then hasted twelve miles to Mendon; thence to Milford, three miles: we stopped at Mr. ——'s, and brother Roberts[62] went forward to supply my

[59] Nathan Strong was the minister of First Congregational Church at Hartford, 1774–1816. He studied law but was ordained in 1774. He published a volume of sermons in 1796 entitled *The Doctrine of Eternal Misery Reconcilable with the Benevolence of God.* He was the ninth minister of the First Church, the first being Thomas Hooker, who was installed in 1633.

[60] Spencer's was the Methodist society in what is now Manchester, Connecticut. It was near the home of Thomas Spencer on Spencer Street. At first this church was included in the Hartford Circuit.

[61] At Putnam there were two waterfalls, Bundy's and Cargill's. At the latter, on the Pomfret side of the river, the Rev. John Allen preached the first Methodist sermon in this region by permission of the owner, Captain Benjamin Cargill. (Perrin: *An Epitome History of the Inception of Methodism in Northeastern Connecticut.*)

[62] Asbury was accompanied by George Roberts, elder of the New York District. Roberts traveled six years in New England and later in New York, Baltimore, and Philadelphia. At the last-named place he became acquainted with the famous Dr. Benjamin Rush and studied and engaged in the practice of medicine. He died in Baltimore in 1827. (Stevens, *op. cit.*, 316; Simpson: *Cyclopedia of Methodism*, 758.)

place: I was not able, nor was there time to speak much after he had done: the heat was intense—and there was very little shade, this country being long since untimbered.

Friday, 18. Rode nineteen miles to Needham: if possible the heat and dust were greater than before, so that by the time we reached the appointment, we were nearly spent; here we met with brother Thompson,[63] and were grieved at the account of the improper conduct of ——, which causes noise, smoke, and fire enough.

Saturday, 19. Came to Waltham to a quarterly meeting: at three o'clock I gave them a discourse on *the little flock*, to comfort the affrighted sheep. *Sabbath day*, we had love feast at eight o'clock, sermon at half-past ten o'clock, and again in the afternoon: there was some life in the love feast, and sacrament also.

Monday, 21. I came to Boston unwell in body, and with a heavy heart. I passed the road and bridge from the University to Boston. A noble road and grand bridge. We have very agreeable lodging in this town: but have to preach, as did our Lord, in an upper room. We had a prayer meeting, and the Lord was present to bless us.

Labour, and affliction of body and mind, make my poor heart sad, and spirits sink. Why art thou cast down, O my soul, and why art thou disquieted within me? hope thou in God; thou shalt yet praise him!

Tuesday, 22. I took up my cross and preached in a large room, which was full enough, and warm enough; I stood over the street; the boys and Jack-tars made a noise, but mine was the loudest; there was fire in the smoke; some, I think, felt the word, and we shall yet have a work in Boston: my talk was strange and true to some.

Wednesday, 23. I now go hence to Lynn; once the joy, now the grief of our hearts: but we must go through all for Christ and souls.

Sunday, 27. I gave them a sermon in the forenoon, and another in the afternoon. I could but rejoice in the prospect of leaving Lynn on *Monday morning*. The society here began in union. It is now incorporated in order to prevent the Methodists from being obliged, by law, to pay congregational tax.

I left Boston, and passed Roxbury, Dorchester, Milton, Stoughton, and Easton; making it upwards of forty miles.

Rhode Island

Tuesday, 29. Rode through Attleboro to Providence—I had no freedom to eat bread or drink water in that place. I found a calm retreat at Gen. Christopher Lippett's, where we can rest ourselves: the Lord is in this family; I am content to stay a day, and give them a sermon.

Thursday, 31. I left Gen. Lippett's and set out for New London.

[63] The Rev. Amos G. Thompson was appointed to Needham in 1794.

Connecticut

Friday, August 1. Brother George Roberts preached in the evening in New London.

Saturday, 2. I made my appearance in the court house, and preached to about seven hundred people with considerable freedom.

Sunday, 3. We had love feast in the upper room of the court house; where some spoke feelingly: our sermon and sacrament took up three hours. God is certainly among these people. We have set on foot a subscription to build a house of worship, and have appointed seven trustees.

Monday, 4. Was one of the warmest days we have known. We left New London, and came through Norwich, twelve miles: this is a well-improved country; producing fine clover, oats, and flax.

We passed Windham and Mansfield. We were met by a powerful thunder-gust; but stepping into a house, escaped its effects: this is one advantage which we have in travelling in the eastern, rather than the western country; in the latter, oftentimes there is not a house for miles—in the former there are houses always in sight. We passed fine streams and excellent meadows; but the heat was excessive, and we had no shade except now and then a spreading tree: our horses were as though they had been ridden through a brook of water. We purchased our dinner on the way, and it was sweet: we laboured hard till eight o'clock, and came sick and weary to father P——'s, not less, in my judgment, than forty miles.

Thursday, 7. A day of rest and affliction of body: came to Tolland very unwell. I find my soul stayed upon God in perfect love, and wait his holy will in all things.

Saturday, 9. I preached in a school house at the north end of Tolland, and had the house filled.

Sunday, 10. Brother Roberts, though sick, went to Coventry, and I was left alone at Tolland; where I preached in the forenoon, on Acts ii, 37, 38, with some freedom; and in the afternoon on Colossians ii, 6, and found it heavy work. After meeting I was taken with a dysentery (attended with great sinking of bodily powers), which held me most of the night. *Monday* I was better, and preached in a school house at Ellington. I felt great dejection of spirit, but no guilt or condemnation. Ah! here are the iron walls of prejudice; but God can break them down. Out of fifteen United States, thirteen are free; but two are fettered with ecclesiastical chains—taxed to support ministers, who are chosen by a small committee, and settled for life. My simple prophecy is, that this must come to an end with the present century. The Rhode Islanders began in time, and are free:—hail, sons of liberty! Who first began the war? Was it not Connecticut and Massachusetts? and priests are now saddled upon them. O what a happy people would these be if they were not thus priest-ridden! It is well for me that I am not stretching along, while my body is so weak and the heat so intense; brother Roberts is with me, and we both only do the work of one man in public. I heard —— read a most severe letter from a citizen of Vermont, to the clergy and Christians of Connecticut, striking at the foundation and principle of the hierarchy, and the policy of Yale College, and the Independent order. It was expressive of the determination of the Vermonters to continue free from ecclesiastical fetters, to follow the Bible, and give liberty, equal liberty, to all denominations of professing Christians. If so, why may not the Methodists (who have been repeatedly solicited) visit these people also?

Tuesday, 12. I rode over the rocks to the Square Ponds, and found our meeting house as I left it two years ago, open and unfinished. We have here a few gracious souls: I preached on Luke xiii, 24, and lodged with brother C——, who was exceedingly kind to man and horse.

Wednesday, 13. Came to brother M——'s, on a branch of the Alemantick. Our friends and the people in North Stafford had appointed for me to preach in Mr. ——'s meeting house: to this I submitted, but it was not my choice: I was loud, plain, and pointed on Rom. viii, 6, 7. Mr. —— was present, and after meeting kindly invited me to his house. The soil of this country is naturally poor, but made rich by cultivation: it is blessed with good stone to build chimneys, and to make walls or fences, that may boast of strength and duration to the end of time.

I went beyond my strength at brother M——'s; we had a crowd of hearers, and some melting among the people. I felt myself so moved that I could not be calm. I gave them a sermon in West Stafford, on Heb. iii, 12–14. I am awfully afraid many in these parts have departed from the love, favour, and fear of God. I was led to treat particularly on unbelief, as the soul-destroying sin: it keepeth men from turning to God; and it is by this sin that the heart first departs from God; to prevent which, Christians ought to exhort one another daily, lest they be hardened through the deceitfulness thereof, and so become castaways. Came to Squire S——'s. In the evening, I felt much hurt by the exertions I had made for precious souls.

Massachusetts

Saturday, 16. I rode up the hills, where we had some close talk; I observed there was good attention, and some melting in the congregation. I came to L. S.'s; here some of the young people are with us, and the old people prefer hearing the Methodists preach to hearing sermons read.

Sunday, 17. I came to the new chapel in Wilbraham,[64] forty by thirty-

[64] The chapel in Wilbraham was built in 1794 on the property of Charles Brewer, who gave the lease to the Methodist society for "one pepper corn" annually. It was turned into a residence in 1832. It still stands at 450 Main Street. (Peck: *History of Wilbraham*, 190–97.)

four feet, neatly designed on the Episcopal plan. I was unwell and under heaviness of mind. I preached to about four hundred people, who were very attentive, but appeared to be very little moved. The standing order have moved their house into the street, not far from ours; and they think, and say, they can make the Methodist people pay them: but I presume in this they are mistaken.

Monday, 18. Came to Silas Bliss's[65]—and was at home, feeling comfortable in body and mind.

Tuesday, 19. I preached at Mr. Russell's;[66] and was led on a sudden to open and apply Phil. ii, 12, 13: 1. Who are addressed? Christian believers. 2. The leading subject—future and eternal salvation; to avoid legality, Antinomianism, and lukewarmness. 3. That he hath, and doth work in them to will and to do; to resist temptation; to be sanctified; and to be finally saved. 4. They should work out their own salvation, by being found in every means of grace; attending to mercy, justice, truth, and love. 5. With fear, where many have failed; with trembling, where many have fallen. Some were not well pleased at this anti-Calvinistic doctrine; but I cannot help that. I have been much tried, and much blessed; weak in body, but, I trust, happy in Christ—in the precious love of Jesus.

Wednesday, 20. I had a quiet retreat at brother W.'s. My mind enjoys peace; and my soul shall breathe after the salvation of dearly-bought souls. Mr. S., a minister of the standing order, held a meeting near us at the same time: whether this were in opposition or not, he knoweth. I preached on "Seek the Lord, and ye shall live." 1. The death to which those are exposed who have not found the Lord. 2. The life those do and shall enjoy who have found, and do live to the Lord—a life of faith, love, and holiness here, and glory hereafter. 3. We must seek him in all the means of grace. Rode in the evening to father A.'s, in Springfield; a kind family. Here I gave them a short sermon on Acts ii, 22: I showed, 1. What we must be saved from. 2. That we cannot save ourselves. 3. On whom we must call for salvation. 4. That whosoever thus calls on the name of the Lord, without distinction of age, nation, or character, shall be saved.

Connecticut

Friday, 22. We came to mother K.'s, in Enfield, a capital town in Massachusetts.[67] The inhabitants, one hundred and fifty miles up the river, send down the white pine logs by means of the freshets at the breaking

[65] Silas Bliss's name appeared on the petition for the incorporation of the Methodist society to the state legislature in 1795.

[66] This was probably John Russell, who seems to have been a very prominent Methodist in the early days. (Peck: *History of Wilbraham*, 193–94.)

[67] Enfield is not in Massachusetts but in Connecticut. Here on July 8, 1741, Jonathan Edwards preached his famous sermon on "Sinners in the Hands of an Angry God."

up of the winter and frost: the people up the stream mark them; and the people here take them up, and are paid for it, or purchase the logs. It is said, that if the proprietor is paid for two-thirds of those he puts into the river, he is content, and well rewarded for his labour.

Sunday, 24. I was well attended at the Separate meeting house,[68] where I applied Acts v, 29–33. We had a solemn sacrament; but O! my soul is distressed at the formality of these people. Brother Roberts preached in the afternoon to a crowded house, and at five o'clock I had to preach to a few sermon-stupefied hearers of different denominations. O my Lord! when wilt thou again visit the people of this place? I have read Lowman on the Jewish Government: strange that it should be so much like the British Government, and ancient New England; but the wonder ceases when we know the writer was an Englishman. Now I suppose I have found out how the Bostonians were moved to call the General Assembly a court, and their members deputies; they followed Lowman.

Tuesday, 26. I rode twelve miles to Wapping. I was happy to have an opportunity of retreating a little into much-loved solitude at Capt. Stoughton's,[69] a man of good sense and great kindness. I had some enlargement on Isa. lv, 6–9, and was enabled to speak with power and demonstration. I preached at T. Stoughton's[70] barn: my spirits were sunk at the wickedness of the people of this place. My subject was Isa. lxiv, 1–7. O what mountains are in the way! Idolatry, superstition, prejudice of education, infidelity, riches, honours, and the pleasures of the world. Ver. 7: "None calleth." Prayer of every kind is almost wholly neglected. "That stirreth up himself." O! how might men address their own souls!—as, O! my soul, hast thou had conviction, penitence, faith, regeneration? Art thou ready to enter the unseen, unknown state of happiness, and stand before God? or wilt thou be content to make thy bed in hell?

I lodged at the oldest house in Windsor,[71] with another brother Stoughton, not unlike the captain. Notwithstanding his certificate from the Methodists he has been taxed to pay a minister he heareth not. O liberty! O priestcraft! So all that withdraw must pay the ministry.

I can scarcely find a breath of living, holy, spiritual religion here, except amongst a few women in East Hartford. If there should continue to be peace in America, yet I am afraid that God will punish the people him-

[68] The Separate meetinghouse was the New Light Baptist Church.

[69] Captain Jonathan Stoughton was a man of exemplary life and never-tiring energy in Christian work, who with "Father Drake" "did much to prepare the way for the Methodist Society." (Miller: *Souvenir History of the New England Southern Conference*, II, 185.)

[70] The T should probably be J, for Jonathan Stoughton.

[71] "This home on Palisado Avenue was built by F. Sergeant Walter Fyler as early as 1640 and is the oldest dwelling house in Windsor." (Howard: *A New History of Old Windsor, Connecticut*, 189, 190.)

self for their wickedness; it may be by pestilence, or civil discord, or internal plague.

Saturday, 30. We were called upon to baptize a child, which Mr. —— refused to do, because the parents owned the covenant and have now broken it. This is the way to bind people to the good old Church.

Sunday, 31. My affliction of body and mind was great at Spencertown,[72] yet I had a solemn time in preaching in the new tabernacle[73] to about four hundred people on Luke xxiv, 45–48. After an hour's recess we came together again, and some were offended, and others convicted, while I enlarged on "The promise is to you and your children." I was in public exercise about five hours, including sacrament, and was so outdone with heat, labour, and sickness, that I could take but little rest that night.

Massachusetts

Monday, *September* 1. I rode to the plains of Ellington,[74] and next day to Wilbraham, and was kindly treated by S. S——. I preached at the next house, and we had a dreadful talk to a miserable, faithless people. We rode two miles in the heat, and I was near fainting, and felt almost like Jonah.

Thursday, 4. We opened our conference with what preachers were present. I was still weak in body. I lodged with Abel Bliss, whose son was educated, *and not spoiled*, at Cokesbury.

Friday, 5. We had a full house, and hasted through much business.

Saturday, 6. Brother L. Roberts[75] and myself preached. My subject was Mal. iii, 1–4. I treated on the coming and work of John the Baptist; the coming, work, and doctrine of Christ, and his changing the ordinances and priesthood, with the ministry and discipline of the Church.

Sunday, 7. We spent from eight to nine o'clock in prayer: a sermon, three exhortations, and the sacrament followed.

Connecticut

We parted at three o'clock, and I came to Enfield, and got my dinner at seven o'clock, in the evening.

[72] Spencertown was in what is now Manchester, Connecticut.

[73] The new tabernacle was "quite a pretentious meeting-house for the Methodists." (*History of the New England Southern Conference*; see note under July 14, 1794.)

[74] Ellington is located in Tolland County, Connecticut. Originally this section was a part of the township of East Windsor called the "Great Marsh." (Barber: *Connecticut Historical Collections.*)

[75] George Roberts was traveling with Asbury. The L. may have been an error of the transcriber of Asbury's notes. Jesse Lee was this year the elder over circuits in New Hampshire, Massachusetts, and Maine. (See *Journal* for August 10, 1794.)

Monday, 8. We spent this day on the road, passing Windsor and East Hartford, and came to the city. The next day we reached Middletown, where I was taken ill. We have a call for preachers to go to New Hampshire and to the Province of Maine.

Wednesday, 10. We rose at three, and set out at five o'clock, and breakfasted at North Haven. We came in the evening to Stratford, and had a little meeting, although I was heavy, sick, and sleepy.

Thursday, 11. We rode to General Waterbury's.[76] Here I learn they guard Kingsbridge,[77] and will not suffer any one to pass from New Haven. It is also said, the pestilential fever prevails in the city of New York, having been brought there by a brig from the Islands. I thought it best to stop, and consult the preachers in the Albany district, before I go into the city. As the yellow fever is so prevalent in the West Indies, and our vessels continually trading there, the United States will partake, I fear, of their plagues; and so the Lord will punish us for our sins and prodigality. I only wish to be holy; and then let come whatever the Lord pleases. I came through Poquonnock, Fairfield, and Norwalk; but there is no room for the Methodists in those places.

New York

We had a pleasant ride, within sight of Long Island, on the salt-water creeks, where there are tide mills which work very swiftly and powerfully. Brothers Roberts and Pickering[78] left me to attend the quarterly meeting at Dan Town,[79] and I spent my time in retirement.

Friday, 12. I filled my minute book, and read freely in the Bible: this book is so much hated by some; as for me, I will love and read it more than ever.

Saturday, 13. Very warm, and I was very faint. I preached in a new open house, and had a sweet comforting time, on Luke xii, 31, 32. Here I met brother Dunham from Upper Canada,[80] who wants more preachers in that province.

[76] General David Waterbury (1722–1801) of Stamford was a veteran of the French and Indian and Revolutionary wars, and he served twenty-three successive terms in the Connecticut legislature. He entertained Jesse Lee on December 21, 1789, according to Lee's *Journal* for that date.

[77] The Kingsbridge over Spuyten Duyvil Creek in New York was guarded because of the yellow-fever epidemic which raged through 1793 in New York and especially in Philadelphia.

[78] George Roberts was the elder over the circuits in Connecticut, Rhode Island, and Vermont, and George Pickering was at Tolland.

[79] Dan Town was a small community in Poundridge Township, Westchester County, New York, very near the Connecticut line. Methodist preaching began there in 1786 at the home of Captain Joseph Lockwood. Squire Dan gave land for a chapel. (Scharf, *op. cit.*, II, 572.)

[80] Darius Dunham was the elder in charge of the Upper Canada District.

Sunday, 14. Although very unwell, I crept out to administer the sacrament, and preached a little on Rom. xiii, 11. I must needs go through Bedford. O! how should I learn, whatever I think, to say but little; it was the sin of meek Moses, when pressed hard, to speak unadvisedly with his lips. This country is so rough and ridgy that we cannot get forwards except it be along the road to the landing, or to some capital place.

My horse having wandered and left me, I borrowed a horse, and on *Monday* rode to lawyer H.'s; and the next day came in a carriage to New Rochelle: after preaching on Heb. iii, 12, I lodged near the place I preached at twenty-three years ago.

Wednesday, 17. I came near Kingsbridge, and found that it was not as had been reported concerning the malignant fever in New York: perhaps a dozen might have taken the infection from a vessel but it hath not spread, and the weather became propitious by rain and pure winds. On *Thursday*, the 18th, I came into the city.

Sunday, 21. I preached in the old house, on Psalm cxxxii; at the new church in the afternoon on Psalm i; and at Brooklyn in the evening.[81] Here our brethren have built a very good house. The labours of the day, pain of body, and my concern for the peace of the Church, tended to keep me from proper rest, and caused an awful night.

Monday, 22. We opened conference, and sat closely to our business. Several of our preachers want to know what they shall do when they grow old; I might also ask, what shall I do? Perhaps many of them will not live to grow old.

Tuesday, 23. I preached with liberty: but on *Thursday* night I had a powerful temptation before I went into the church, which sat so heavily on me that I could not preach; yet I trust I was kept from sin. My sleep is so little, that my head becomes dizzy, and distresses me much: four hours' sleep in the night is as much as I can obtain. We concluded our work; and observed *Friday* as a day of abstinence and prayer, and had a good time at our love feast.

Sunday, 28. Preached at ten o'clock at Brooklyn. In the afternoon at the new church, on, "Woe to them that are at ease in Zion!" I ordained seven deacons and five elders; and in the evening, at the old church I preached again: we had the best time at the last, at least it was so to me. All day I was straitened in my throat, and in my heart. We collected two hundred and fifty dollars for the relief of the preachers in distress.

This has been a serious week to me: money could not purchase the

[81] In 1790 the work had developed in Brooklyn so that it was separated from New York and was made a point on the Long Island Circuit. Early in 1794 property was secured on Sands Street, and the cornerstone of the new church was laid by Dr. William Phoebus. The building was dedicated by Joseph Totten on June 1, 1794. A much larger church was built in 1811, in which Asbury preached on Sunday, May 17, 1812, during the General Conference in session at John Street Church.

labour and exercise I have gone through. At this conference it was resolved, that nothing but an English free day school should be kept at Cokesbury.

Monday, 29. I did not sleep after three o'clock in the morning. Came to the boat at seven o'clock, but could not get across till one o'clock; which, to my no small grief, prevented my attending my appointment on Staten Island.

New Jersey

Tuesday, 30. Rose at three o'clock. Set out at five o'clock, and rode forty-two miles to Milford, and preached; but I found this heavy work.

Wednesday, *October* 1. I had some life in preaching at Crosswick's meeting house.[82] I then came to brother Hancocks,[83] and took sweet counsel with my old friend, whose wife I received as a member of society twenty-two years ago. I was in suspense about going through Philadelphia, lest I should not reach Baltimore in due time. Now report saith that they have stopped the Baltimore stage on account of the malignant fever, which rages powerfully at the Point. There is a great stir among the people concerning the western insurrection; the people have risen up against government on account of the excise law relative to the distillation of spirits. A number of the militia are called out: thus trouble comes on in Church and state. O, my Lord, give us help; for vain is the help of man!

Thursday, 2. I came to Burlington; and as I had not had a day to myself for some time, I took one now, to read, write, and fill up my journal, &c. I feel for the Church and continent: but the Lord sitteth above the water floods, and remaineth a King forever. I preached at Burlington, and the people were serious.

Pennsylvania

Saturday, 4. Brother Morrell and myself came to Philadelphia; and on *Sunday*, 5, I preached three times; and was not a little fatigued with this day's labour: I felt assisted, and had some openings in preaching.

Monday, 6. Our conference began, and our matters were talked over freely. Our session continued until *Friday*, by which time I felt tired of the city, and had a desire to be on horseback. I have felt liberty in preaching

[82] The Crosswick's meetinghouse was built by the Quaker's about 1750, and it is significant that Asbury was permitted to preach there. Ezekiel Cooper's diary shows that preaching at Crosswicks was ordinarily at a Mr. Smith's. (Cawley: *Historic New Jersey in Pictures*, 36; Phoebus, *op. cit.*, 70, 71.)

[83] Hulitt Hancock was the son of Godfrey Hanock, who died in 1777. He inherited the plantation of his father at Mansfield, Burlington County, and also a valuable cedar swamp. (See *Journal* entry for October 2, 1798; Phoebus, *op. cit.*, 70.)

to the citizens, and indulge some hope of a revival of religion among them.

Saturday, 11. Rode thirty-five miles to sister Grace's,[84] at Coventry, who, with her daughter and granddaugher, is, I trust, happy in God. I visited this house twenty years ago. Sister Grace, when in a delirium, was singing and talking about God. I spent a solitary Sabbath at her house, and was happy in speaking at her door (she being sick).

Delaware

Monday, 13. Brother Cook[85] and myself had a heavy ride of nearly fifty miles to John Hersey's, which we accomplished by travelling a little in the night.

Maryland

Tuesday, 14. I preached at Bethel, on Back Creek; and on *Wednesday*, 15, crossed Elk River and came to quarterly meeting at Hart's meeting house.[86] I spent the evening with my dear son in Jesus, Daniel Sheredine:[87] I cannot give him up.

Thursday, 16. Crossed Susquehanna, and came to Cokesbury college. I found it £1,200 in debt, and that there were between £500 and £600 due us; £300 of what we owe ought now to be paid.

Saturday, 18. We came to Perry Hall. The preachers were afraid to go into Baltimore, but the brethren from there came out to calm their fears and invited them in. I have been hurried, and have not as much time for retirement as my soul panteth for—yet I desire nothing but Christ.

Monday, 20. We rode to Baltimore; and in the afternoon opened our conference: we had about fifty preachers, including probationers: our business was conducted in peace and love. Myself and others being unwell, we sat only six hours in the day.

Tuesday, 21. I gave them a sermon, on Exod. xxxii, 26. We had a list of names from Fairfax, who required an explanation of a minute in our form of discipline, relative to the trial of members; inquiring whether the

[84] See *Journal* entries for May 23, 1776; July 4, 1787.

[85] This was the Rev. Valentine Cook, who was the elder over the circuits in the region.

[86] Hart's Meeting House was located between the Elk and the Susquehanna rivers in Cecil County. An earlier church stood at the head of Piney Creek. (Johnston: *History of Cecil County, Maryland*, 448; Hallman, *op. cit.*, 294, 295, 298, 299.)

[87] Daniel Sheredine resided in Principio Furnace, Cecil County. He married the widow of Thomas Russell, manager of the Principio Iron Works, one of the largest in America. In 1802 Sheredine and his stepson established iron smelting at North East. (Hallman, *op. cit.*, 120.)

"select members were as witnesses, or judges, and had power to vote members in or out of society." We answered them.

Our collegiate matters now come to a crisis.[88] We now make a sudden and dead pause;—we mean to incorporate, and breathe, and take some better plan. If we cannot have a Christian school (that is, a school under Christian discipline and pious teachers) we will have none. I had peace of mind, but not much rest.

Sunday, 26. We had a comfortable love feast, but were prevented from attending our other meetings by the excessive rains. The next day I came to Elk Ridge; where I saw, after twenty-two years' labour, a well-designed frame of a new house for public worship;[89] a few good women are trustees. The storm prevented me from having a congregation here also. Came to John Holland's, where I had a few hearers, and had a comfortable time; it was like paradise regained among the old Methodists.

Virginia

Thursday, 30. Crossed the Potomac, at the mouth of Goose Creek; and came, unexpected by the brethren, to Leesburg. Thence we journeyed on through Prince William and Fauquier counties. We passed Germantown, and came along Rogues Road, to Norman's Ferry, on Rappahannock. After a disagreeable journey, and being exposed to uncomfortable weather, on *Tuesday*, the 4th of *November*, we came safe to father Kobler's in Culpepper county. Thank the Lord, there is here and there a house for God. At father Kobler's I had many women and but few men to hear. Some of the men are gone to war, some to their sports, and some have no desire to hear.

We rode ten miles to brother Fry's,[90] after a long absence of ten years I am here again. My mind is in great peace, and the preachers and people appear pleased to see me. I learn that about the month of June last died the great politician, Richard Henry Lee, of Westmoreland county; one who took an active part in promoting the independence of the United States of America. O, when will liberty be extended to the sable sons of

[88] Aside from the financial difficulties to which Asbury refers on his return to the college the previous Thursday, his correspondence reveals a continued suspicion that bad conduct in the student body was caused by the failure of the teachers to emphasize religion. The following year the college department was suspended. (See letter of November 10, 1793, to Dr. Jacob Hall, president of Cokesbury College, and letter dated October 23, 1794.)

[89] In his brief history of the Melville Methodist Church, Carlyle Earp says that this building was demolished when the Baltimore and Ohio railway laid its first tracks through Elkridge.

[90] Asbury was at Fry's on April 17, 1784, and on January 8, 1785.

Africa? We trust the happy period will come, when universal light shall shine through all the earth and Jesus shall reign—

————"Where'er the sun
Does his successive journeys run;
His kingdom spread from shore to shore,
Till moons shall wax and wane no more."

Thursday, 6. I had some life, and there was a small stir on the minds of some at Fry's where we had a crowd of preachers and people.

Friday, 7. Crossed one of the south branches of Rappahannock, called the Rapidan[91] and came thirty miles to J. Lastley's, in Louisa county.

Saturday and *Sunday*, 8, 9. Attended the quarterly meeting at Lastley's meeting house: we had a large congregation, a quickening sacrament, and life in the love feast. I feel it necessary to retire and humble myself before the Lord: I have been crowded with company, and have had much talk, and I find a solitary walk very agreeable.

I attended a few appointments in Hanover and Goochland counties; and on *Saturday*, 15, came to the city of Richmond, about five o'clock, and preached to a few people in Mr. Parrot's storehouse.

Sunday, 16. We came to a church near brother Baugh's, where were gathered many people, among whom were some sons of division.[92] Here were many pale faces, and (as I was told afterward) some who had been making solemn promises in their affliction, wondered how I should know, and speak so pertinently on that subject. Thence we came to brother I. Maxey's, in Chesterfield; and the next day crossed Appomattox and Nottoway rivers, and reached to B. Jones, in Brunswick county, on our way to Brunswick quarterly meeting at Merritt's chapel. It was rather a dull time, although I had some freedom in speaking, and we had a good love feast.

Saturday and *Sunday*, 22, 23. Attended a quarterly meeting at Jones's chapel in Sussex county, where we had many people: I preached on Deut. ix, 12; too applicable to many of these souls. The rumour of the small-pox being at Petersburg, and only ten or twelve, out of seventy or eighty, of the preachers having had it, it caused us to think of holding our conference at sister Mabry's, in Greenville county, where there are fifteen or sixteen houses that will receive and entertain the preachers. After sending brother

[91] Rapidan is spelled Rapid Anne on some old maps.

[92] The division was that led by James O'Kelley. (See *Journal* entry for September 4, 1799.) The division had reached into and around Richmond. Bennett refers to this visit of Asbury to Richmond. No church was built in Richmond until 1799. The first preaching, much earlier than this, was in the county courthouse. Parrot was an Englishman. He had not been a Wesleyan, but his wife had been. His storehouse seems to have been at first a stable, since Parrot's stable church is referred to earlier. The society outgrew the storehouse, and they went back to the courthouse. The Manchester (South Richmond) society was also affected by the division. Asbury and O'Kelly had one of their few meetings in Manchester.

Hutt to Petersburg, it was, by a majority of the preachers present, judged most prudent to hold the conference at the place just mentioned.

Monday, 24. About thirty preachers were collected together. I am crowded too much for my head and heart: when I sit and hear people talk on unprofitable subjects, it clouds my head and grieves my spirit, even if I say nothing.

Tuesday, 25. We opened our conference, and had great siftings and searchings especially on the subject of slavery. The preachers, almost unanimously, entered into an agreement and resolution not to hold slaves in any State where the law will allow them to manumit them, on pain of forfeiture of their honour and their place in the itinerant connexion; and in any State where the law will not admit of manumission, they agreed to pay them the worth of their labour, and when they die to leave them to some person or persons, or society, in trust, to bring about their liberty. After raising and applying what money we could (which was about £50), we calculated that one-fourth of the preachers at this conference had received for their salary the past year about £10; one-half from about £12 to £15, and one-fourth their full quarterage (sixty-four dollars). We had great peace, and not one preacher objected to his station. We sent an apology to our brethren in Petersburg for not having held conference there, according to appointment, for reasons already assigned. We were greatly obliged to our friends in Greenville for accommodating the conference. Men and horses were well entertained—all for love.

Monday, *December* 1. I rode twenty-seven miles, and on *Tuesday*, 2, I preached at F. Bonner's, twelve miles from Petersburg.

Wednesday, 3. Came to J. Smith's, and had a comfortable season. Brother Smith has been on the verge of eternity, and was blessed with delightful prospects of glory, but the Lord has raised him up again.

Thursday, 4. Came to Graves' chapel, very unwell; here lived brother Lewis Lloyd, who left this world this year. He was an old preacher, and professed perfect love fifteen years before his death, and finally departed in the triumphs of faith.

Friday, 5. I preached at Rivers's chapel,[93] and made it twenty miles by the time I reached brother Petham's in Greenville. I was heavy in body and spirit. I am not conscious of having sinned, yet I suffer on account of the people. I delighted myself in reading some of Doddridge's Sermons to Young People. To the young persons present I preached at brother Pelham's on *Saturday*; and on *Sunday*, 7, rode twenty-eight or thirty miles to brother Paup's, on Roses Creek, where I enlarged on Peter's fall. Our burdensome stone, Ebenezer, now gives us some trouble and care.[94]

[93] Rivers Chapel was in Greensville County. (*Heads of Families*, 54.)

[94] The Virginia Assembly in 1796 received a petition from a number of inhabitants of Brunswick County for the incorporation of an academy. The names of John Easter

If we can employ good men, keep up discipline, and maintain credit, it may come to something.

Monday, 8. I performed the funeral rites of sister Walker, on Waquae Creek, Brunswick county. We had a full house of unfeeling people, and the word of the Lord was a burden. I opened the Bible on Jer. xiv, 10. Let any one read it as an awful portion; it may be it is as true to these people as it was to Israel. I had a meeting with the trustees of Ebenezer school. Matters are very discouraging; people in general care too little for the education of their children.

Tuesday, 9. Preached at Williams's meeting house. These are a poor people, not impoverished with slaves; but they have a good meeting house, with a glass window behind the pulpit, so that we can see to read without raising a shutter and receiving all the wind that comes, though this is in Lunenburg county, near Mother Ogburn's, where we used to have our melting seasons twenty years ago. We dined with the gracious aged people, and in the evening crossed Meherrin, and came to S. Holmes's, an ancient stand in Mecklenburg. Next day I preached at Salem, where there is the best house we have in the country part of Virginia. In this neighbourhood there has been a society standing for twenty-one years. Rode in the evening to brother Speed's—rich and full, and a friend of freedom.

Thursday, 11. Preached and administered the sacrament at Young's chapel; and came in the evening to Tignal Jones's. Dear sister Jones is gone to rest, after two years of deep affliction. She has had a painful journey through life; but her persecutions and troubles are now at an end, and heaven will compensate for all. She made choice of Job iii, 17, for her funeral text; and with great deliberation disposed of her property. I preached her funeral on *Friday*, 12th, and found it a serious day to me. I never saw her more than twice or thrice, and we have interchanged a few letters. She was doubtless a woman of sense, vivacity, and grace. She wrote to admiration—all in raptures. She would pray in any place, and before any people; she reproved with pointed severity, and sung with great sweetness.

North Carolina

Saturday, 13. We crossed Roanoak, and came to Mr. Smith's, in Granville county. On *Sunday*, 14th, crossed Mountain and Grassy Creeks, and came to brother Owens's, whose wife is a true daughter of Daniel

and Edward Drumgoole were among the trustees. The school, called Ebenezer, was said to have opened in 1784 near Merritt's meetinghouse. Ebenezer Academy has been listed as the first Methodist school in America, even antedating Cokesbury College. It is said to be the forerunner of Randolph-Macon College and was in the beginning a day school. (Cummings: *Early Schools of Methodism*, 426; Duvall: *Methodist Church and Education up to* 1869, 28.)

Grant,[95] my dear old friend in Georgia. He was among the last fruits of that great man Mr. Davies, when he laboured in Hanover, in Virginia, forty years ago.

Monday, 15. Crossed the head streams of Tar River, which are only small branches, and rode on to R——'s (where I had an appointment); and found I had another twenty-five miles forward at L——'s: so I left brother C—— to fill up my place, and went forward to the latter; where I preached to about two hundred people. I feel weak in body and mind, yet find my soul stayed upon God. "Still onwards I go," fainting yet fighting.

Thursday, 18. I have a long journey to Charleston (S. C.), and but thirteen days to perform it; having appointed to be there the 1st of January.

Friday, 19. We rode twenty-five miles through a powerful fall of rain; but we wrought our way through the swamps, floating and sinking as we went.

Saturday, 20. It snowed as powerfully as it rained yesterday: however, we set out for Salem about nine o'clock, and forded two creeks; but the third we swam. Brother Ward went in, and after a pause I followed; but being cloaked up, my horse nearly slipped from under me: one foot was *properly* soaked. I walked about one mile and rode another, and reached the town about twelve o'clock, just as they were ringing the bell. Feeling the want of a fire, I went to the tavern; but I found but one fire-place there; I sat down with the company, and dried my feet a little, until my companions came along. I have need of power (and I am accused of having too much) to stand such days as this: my soul is kept in peace and communion with God; and, through grace, I will not murmur at my sufferings whilst the salvation of souls is my end and aim. We found a home at father Hill's, from Maryland, about three o'clock, having ridden nineteen miles today, and thirty yesterday. I was thankful for a house and friends, and an opportunity of putting into port. It is a comfort to remember there remaineth a rest for the people of God.

Sunday, 21. I came to Cokesbury school; and after preaching on 1 Cor. xv, 58, I rode down to brother Charles Caton's. Here a few souls have been brought to God since I was in these parts in May last.

Monday, 22. We were detained some time at Long's Ferry by a wagon, and a number of horses. Mrs. —— entertained us very kindly, and her husband gave us a hearty welcome when he came home, and found out

[95] Daniel Grant (d. 1793) and his brother Thomas built in Wilkes County, near Washington, the first Methodist meetinghouse in Georgia. The conference met there in 1789 and 1790. (See *Journal* entry, notes, and references for March 8, 1789.) The Davies referred to here is Samuel Davies, the great Presbyterian preacher. In Hanover, Davies was a correspondent of John Wesley (*The Letters of John Wesley*). Davies went to New Jersey to be president of the Log College. He and Tennent visited Whitefield and Wesley in England, where they solicited funds for the Log College. The Log College became Princeton University.

who we were. It was expected by some that I should preach at Salisbury, but I did not; so we rode on and reached the widow B's about eight o'clock at night, having ridden thirty miles.

Tuesday, 23. We set out at sunrise: the morning was cold and frosty. We rode ten miles and fed at A.'s; thence we hasted twenty-five miles to J. R.'s, took a late dinner, and rode to W. R.'s, making upwards of forty miles. Next day we had to swim Rocky River; we then passed Newtown, and made it thirty miles to Jackson's.

South Carolina

Thursday, 25. Christmas day. We changed our course, and took the grand Camden road to great Lynch's Creek, thirty miles. When I came to Mr. Evans's[96] and told my name, I was invited to stay; and it was well for us that we did.

Friday, 26. I came off about sunrise; and made forty miles to Publius James Rembert's: I was hungry, sore, and very low-spirited; here we found a warm house, comfortable table (which was very acceptable), good bed and fire, with very kind friends. Lord, dispose us to humility before Thee, and bless our benefactors! James Rogers and Samuel Cowls were my faithful attendants. I hear my friend John Hughes, of Charleston, is dead. From what I learn of him in his last illness, I trust the dear old man is gone safe. William Adams and Captain Darrell of the same place, have been cast away and drowned; strange changes take place in a very short time. O my God! help me to be each moment on my guard, ready for death and judgment. The land we came through yesterday is poor, and but thinly settled—a plantation once in three or four miles. The long-leaved lofty pines have a grand appearance.

Sunday evening, 28. Rode after preaching to brother Bradford's.[97] *Monday*, 29th, to Bowman's.[98] *Tuesday*, 30th, we had to wrestle with Santee Swamp for three hours, having to wade the flat ground then under water; but through mercy we got safe over at last. We hasted on, and came in the evening to the house of a very kind Frenchman, who entertained us gratis.

Wednesday, 31. Myself with the main body of the preachers came into the city of Charleston.[99] I felt faint and unwell after the fatigues I had passed through on my journey.

[96] This was probably William Evans, who lived between Pageland and Jefferson near Lynch's Creek.

[97] Bradford lived about four miles northwest of the present Sumter.

[98] Bowman lived near the present Summerton in Clarendon County. Asbury had come from Sumter by way of Manning.

[99] Asbury had come to Charleston across the Santee Ferry by way of the present Santee, Vance, Holly Hill, and the old state road.

1795

1795 *Asbury at Mary Withy's tavern in Chester, Pennsylvania*

CHAPTER TWENTY-FOUR

South Carolina

Thursday, *January* 1, 1795. Being New Year's day, I was called upon to preach, unwell as I was, which I did on Psalm xc, 12. We entered on the business of our conference, and continued until *Wednesday*, 7th. We had preaching every night during the sitting of conference. It was the request of the conference that I should preach them a sermon on *Tuesday* night; with which I complied, and made choice of Jer. xxiii, 29–32. In times past I have endeavoured to keep on travelling all the year, but I now judge it meet to stay in Charleston a little longer and then take the field: yet it is with fear and trembling.

Sunday, 11. Brothers I. C. and G.[1] being about to leave the city, I gave place to them to perform the services of the Sabbath. I heard part of a discourse by Mr. Furman[2] on partial and total backsliding: I thought he spoke well, and that it was an excellent sermon; I doubt if he had more than seventy white hearers. A vast number in the city do not attend to the worship of God anywhere.

Monday, 12. The remaining members of the conference left the city. Brother Bruce[3] and myself must now lay our shoulders to the work. I have

[1] I. C. was probably Joshua Cannon, who had been on the Edisto Circuit, having changed from Charleston at the end of the first half of the conference year and was now appointed to Georgetown. G. may have been Enoch George or Tobias Gibson. (See *Minutes*.)

[2] The Rev. Richard Furman was the Baptist pastor at Charleston. (Betts, *op. cit.*, 482.)

[3] Philip Bruce was pastor at Charleston and elder of the Charleston, Georgetown, and Edisto circuits. (See *Minutes*.)

my feelings and fears about staying in Charleston; but grace is sufficient: I wish to give my all to God; and whether I read, write, preach, or visit, to do it all to his glory; and to employ my precious time profitably.

And am I yet alive, with death so near? How many of my friends in this city, and in other places, are gone into eternity! I hear very little from the preachers in the north.

Tuesday, 13. I had a comfortable season in the church, on the words of St. Paul to the Galatians: "Am I therefore become your enemy because I tell you the truth?" In this discourse I observed, how great was the affection between the Christian societies in ancient Galatia and St. Paul, until the Judaizing teachers came in among them. The province of Galatia was in Lesser Asia; and when the ancient Gauls, or Galatæ, wanted to extend their province, they penetrated through Italy and Greece, and went into Asia, and pillaged the country as far south as Babylon: but one hundred and twenty thousand being defeated by a handful of Jews; and Attalus, king of Pergamus, having forced them from his territory, they settled here. Among these the Gospel was planted by St. Paul, Acts xvi, 6; who had but just left the country when the schism began by means of the teachers of the ceremonial law. In this Church there have been a great number of bishops, and some councils, and Synods; but for near eight hundred years the tyranny of the Mohammedans, Saracens, and Turks, hath almost exterminated the very name of Christianity. I observed, 1. That there is a proper portion of truth which is applicable to every one's case; 2. That it is a bad sign when a man is esteemed an enemy for telling the truth, as if falsehood alone were pleasing.

Wednesday, 14. I preached at brother Wells's,[4] on, "It is good for me that I have been afflicted, that I might learn thy statutes": this cannot be the language of any but gracious souls. Sinners think all these things are against them, and wonder what they have done more than others, that they are thus afflicted. I treated of afflictions of body and mind; personal and family; in the Church and in the state. Ah! my Lord, by whom shall Jacob arise, for he is very small?

Sunday, 18. I preached in the morning on Exod. xx, the first and second commandments. In the afternoon, on the affliction and conversion of Manasseh, 2 Chron. xxxiii, 12, 13. One young man behaved amiss, for which I reproved him: perhaps he might be among those in the evening who made a riot, broke the windows, and beat open the doors.

Tuesday, 20. I read Mr. Flavel on keeping the heart; where I found some weighty sayings. I preached in the evening and brother Bruce exhorted. Mr. —— came home with me, pleading and crying to God, and acknowledging his sin: who knoweth but he will turn, repent, and find mercy? The desperate wickedness of this people grieves and distresses my soul, so

[4] Edgar Wells was the Charleston merchant who entertained Asbury on his first visit in 1785.

that I am almost in continual heaviness; yet, through grace, I trust I am kept from sin. I spent part of this week in writing and reviewing some explanatory notes on our form of discipline.

Sunday, 25. I preached morning and afternoon. My soul, at seasons, wadeth through deep waters for this city and society; it cannot, in my opinion, continue long in its present situation—perhaps a dispensation of mercy or judgment is near.

Wednesday, 28. I finished reading the History of the French Revolution, containing about eight hundred pages; and a surprising history it is. They have had heavy struggles with monarchy, aristocracy, and democracy; and have had martyrs of each and every form.

Thursday, 29. I am sensible of not being enough in prayer; this gives me pain. There came on a violent, awful storm of rain, and what should I do upon the road in such weather? Charleston is, to me, one of the most serious places I ever was in.

Saturday, 31. I was in a most distressed, gloomy state of body and mind. I employed myself in reading, writing, and prayer—but very uncomfortably.

Sunday, February 1.

> "Still heavy is my heart,
> Still sink my spirits down."

I went to the church, and lectured on the second table of the law; attending particularly to our Lord's comment on each precept. In the afternoon I enlarged on Jer. xxxi, 33; and I do hope there was some stir in the hearts of the people: I had an afflictive night, by the labours of the day. I began reading "Berridge's Christian World Unmasked." How like the man and his conversation, which I heard by the hour thirty years ago! I think there is some tartness in his Christian remarks on the Checks, and dear Mr. Fletcher, of whom I have heard Mr. Berridge speak in terms of very great respect. I was insulted on the pavement with some as horrible sayings as could come out of a creature's mouth on this side of hell. When I pray in my room with a few poor old women, those who walk the streets will shout at me. The unparalleled wickedness of the people of this place, and the spirit of contention among the professors of religion, most severely agitate my mind. I now spend my time in running hastily through the first volume of the Hebrew Bible.

Thursday, 5. I was deeply dejected. I have been lately more subject to melancholy than for many years past; and how can I help it: the white and worldly people are intolerably ignorant of God; playing, dancing, swearing, racing; these are their common practices and pursuits. Our few male members do not attend preaching; and I fear there is hardly one who walks with God: the women and Africans attend our meetings, and some few strangers also. Perhaps it may be necessary for me to know how wicked the world is, in order that I may do more as a president minister. There is some similarity between my stay here and at Bath in Virginia. O how I should prize a quiet retreat in the woods!

In Mr. Wesley's Journal, Vol. I, page 154, I find he observes, "I set myself carefully to read N. Machiavel's celebrated book. I began," says Mr. Wesley, "with a prejudice in his favour, having been often informed he had been misunderstood and greatly misrepresented; I weighed the sentiments it contained; compared one passage with another, and endeavoured to form a cool, impartial judgment; and my most deliberate judgment is, that if all the other doctrines of devils which have been committed to writing since letters were in the world were collected together in one volume, it would fall short of this; and should a prince form himself by this book, so openly recommending hypocrisy, treachery, lying, robbery, oppression, adultery, and murder of all kinds, Domitian or Nero would be angels of light compared to that man." No wonder that Doctor —— should say that the Methodist preachers were men of true Machiavelian principles: *judge, reader*. This is the justice, this is the mercy, we are to expect from some priests: and why? because we spoil their reading trade.

Sunday, 8. I preached on Psalm viii, 4. Brother Bruce entertained us on, "That your faith should not stand in the wisdom of men, but in the power of God." I met the society, read the Rules of Discipline, and gave a close talk about conformity to the world. I have now finished the first volume of Mr. Wesley's Journal. I admire his candour and the soundness of his sentiments; but I need say but little, as it will be shortly published and speak for itself.

Monday, 9. The people have high work below stairs laid off for each day this week. The western regiment parades to-day, the eastern tomorrow; *Wednesday* is the President's birth-day; *Thursday*, *Friday*, and *Saturday*, come on the races. I intend to keep close to my room, except when attending meetings in the evenings. I am in the furnace; may I come out purified like gold! It is a dark Providence holds me here. Mr. Phillips is here, and in want of money. Our friends opened their hearts and gave him twenty or thirty dollars. He is not clear on Original Sin; so that we cannot, and dare not employ him; yet, notwithstanding his sentiments, I hope he is a good man: but, good or bad, he ought not to starve.

Monday, 16. I rode out to take the air; and saw the wandering air-balloon. I am persuaded there are gracious souls among Mr. Hammett's people; some of whom have left him, and will, perhaps, return. I was employed in reading Mr. Wesley's Journal; and I am now convinced of the great difficulty of journalizing. Mr. Wesley was, doubtless, a man of very general knowledge, learning, and reading, to which we may add a lively wit and humour; yet, I think I see too much credulity, long, flat narrations, and coarse letters taken from others, in his Journal: but when I come to his own thoughts, they are lively, sentimental, interesting, and instructing. The Journal of a minister of the Gospel should be theological:

only it will be well to wink at many things we see and hear, since men's feelings grow more and more refined.

Sunday, 22. I had no small inflammation in my ear; yet after I got to preaching, I was long and loud, warm, and very pointed: our congregations are uncommonly large. I was recollecting by the help of Mr. Wesley's Journal, how long it had been since I became acquainted with the Methodists. I was awakened (as I think), when about thirteen years six months old; at the age of sixteen I began to read and pray, in the public congregation; one year six months after this, publicly to exhort and expound God's holy word; at twenty-one I travelled much; and in the beginning of my twenty-second year, I travelled altogether. I was nine months in Staffordshire, and other adjoining shires; two years in Bedfordshire circuit, and two in Salisbury circuit.

Mr. Wesley, in his Journal, seems to think that the cause of the hindrance of the work of God is wholly and entirely in man. But may we not ask, with reverence, hath not God sometimes, for his own purposes, withheld his power, that no flesh might glory in his sight, but feel that he is all in all?

Wednesday, 25. We had a love feast for the Africans, and many gave in their experiences with life.

In the evening we had a love feast for the whites. I have had a long stay here, and now rejoice in the hope of going again into the field to work. Nothing would have kept me here but the hope of preserving my health the other ten months of the year; which will enable me to run through North and South Carolina, the New Territory, Virginia, Maryland, Delaware, Pennsylvania, Jersey, New York, Connecticut, Rhode Island, Massachusetts, Province of Maine, New Hampshire, Vermont, and sometimes Kentucky.

Friday, 27, we observed as a general fast. I was weak in body and afflicted with the headache; yet I met the people in the church, and read Joel ii, 12–18. I prayed; I wept before the Lord. I fasted from two o'clock on Thursday until half-past five on Friday. I wish we could have solemn monthly fasts, and love feasts before sacrament. I hope the Lord will look upon us generally throughout the continent, and take away our reproach.

Mr. Wesley lived to see two general revivals of religion—one at the beginning, the other about thirty-six years ago; though, doubtless, they had generally a gradual growth of religion. We also have had two revivals—one at the beginning, the other about seven years ago. The third revival has now taken place in England, and I hope ours will soon follow.

Saturday, 28. I attended the meeting of the stewards, and directed that each of the three stewards, in rotation, should receive and pay all moneys, for one third of the year, and then give place to another for the same time. I also appointed a clerk to attend particularly to the books.

Sunday, March 1. I preached in the forenoon and afternoon; and it was thought the arrows of the Almighty flew abroad. We had a melting sacrament with white and coloured people: about half a dozen of Mr. Hammett's people from Trinity attended. The people have had much dust cast in their eyes in this place, but now they begin to see more clearly.

I am now about packing up in order to take my leave of this city. I am sure faithful preaching will be blest. I have effectually worn myself out, and I feared we should not have strength to ride over the barren sands. We accordingly set out, and rode twenty-two miles to G.'s; tried it since I have been here. My parting subject was 1 Cor. xvi, 23, 24: the congregation was very large; and if the people are prudent and the preachers faithful, we shall have a work in this place. The poor Africans brought their blessings, and wishes, and prayers. Dear souls! May the Lord provide them pastors after his own heart!

Thursday, 5. I left this seat of wickedness, not without both grief and joy. I never saw so great a prospect here, and doubt if there hath been such an one since the place was first settled. We crossed Ashly River about ten miles from town. Here was a bridge of value, which was so damaged by the worms and barnacles, that it stood only two years. Sister G., her family, and a wagon were on it when it gave way; it sunk with them into the water, but they received no injury. We rode thirty-five miles, eating some biscuit with a little wine and water, and came to Mr. Eccles's,[5] Beach Hill, near Edisto River. I was somewhat wearied, but happy in my solitary retreat. I think I have not spent my time in vain in Charleston. First, I have had near as many hearers as I could have found in the country. Secondly, there hath been real fruit among the white and coloured people; and such as may, with care, be preserved. I gave them a sermon at Squire Eccles's near two hours long. My soul has peace; and by the help of God I must hasten eastward and heavenward.

Saturday, 7. We came to Lindsey's;[6] and after preaching to about sixty people, had to ride twelve miles to Cattle Creek after four o'clock. Nor was that the worst. A storm of thunder and rain came on, and had we not stopped, we should have been steeped from head to foot.

Sunday, 8. We had about four hundred people at the church, among whom were a few that loved and feared God; and many that are stupid, and have become hardened under the preaching of the gospel. I spent *Monday*, 9, at brother Moss's,[7] and felt the society in the city near my heart.

Wednesday, 11. We rode to Stroman's,[8] where I gave them a long talk on, "The grace of God that bringeth salvation," &c. I thought the weather was too fine to continue so long; so we made a push and rode eighteen

[5] Squire Eccles lived below Givhan's Ferry.

[6] Mr. Lindsey lived between Reesville and Branchville.

[7] Mr. Moss lived at Orangeburg.

[8] Mr. Stroman lived near Springfield.

miles to P.'s at the Ponds[9]; where we supped and breakfasted at our own expense, and bought provision for our horses. About midnight the rain began to patter on the long shingles. What could we do? If we stayed, our provision would be where we stopped to eat and feed; and then rode eighteen miles more to the widow Pope's,[10] on Little Saluda.

Saturday, 14. I came to A.'s chapel; but the weather was so exceedingly cold, and the house so open, that we went to the dwelling house, where I preached and prayed, and (the people said) stormed and scolded. When meeting was over, I saw the new still house, which, as George Fox said, "struck at my life"; and we found it necessary to deal plainly with brother —— about his distillery, and to tell him what we apprehended would be the consequence if persisted in. Its natural tendency would be to corrupt his family, and the neighbourhood; and to destroy the society. O, that the snare of Satan may be forever broken! We came to G.'s meeting house, where we had as wild and disorderly a congregation as could well be without words and blows. I preached a little, and stormed a great deal; but all would not do. It was an awful day to me; but I hope my labour was not wholly in vain. I lodged at D. Earpes's,[11] who came from Berkley to Seleuda, and has been a preacher twenty years. I ordained him deacon, and joined his daughter to a husband. Thence I came to Johnston's, where was another wedding. I had work enough—the bishop—the wedding. I could hardly keep them serious. I preached on Isa. xxxv, 3–7, and had an open time.

Wednesday, 18. I rode to Ruff's, and preached.

Thursday, 19, and the two following days, we had work enough to write subscription papers, to be sent abroad for the purpose of collecting one hundred pounds to finish Bethel school,[12] and secure the land: but my expectations are small; the people have so little sense of God and religion. *Saturday*, I opened the new house on 1 Thess. v, 14; and on *Sunday* we had a sermon and love feast.

[9] J. P. Pond lived in Lexington County near Gilbert, where Pond Branch Church is now located.

[10] Mrs. Pope lived in Saluda County near the present town of Saluda.

[11] Mr. Earpes lived in the lower part of Newberry County. Asbury had crossed the main Saluda River.

[12] The Mount Bethel Academy was opened on this visit by Asbury. It was located in a section of Newberry County where several Methodist families from Virginia had settled, among them being the Finches, Crenshaws, and Malones, and it was the first Methodist educational venture in South Carolina. Edward Finch gave thirty acres of land for a site. The main building was 20 × 40 feet, built of rough stone, with chimneys at each end. The second floor was used for students' lodgings, and several cabins were built for teachers and boarding houses. The Rev. Mark Moore, who entered the itinerary in 1786, was the first principal or rector. The school was attended by many persons who became prominent in the Carolinas and Georgia. It ceased to operate about 1820 and was superseded by the Mount Ariel and Cokesbury schools. Remains of the school, the Finch home, and the cemetery can still be discerned. (Chreitzberg: *Early Methodism in the Carolinas*, 62, 63; Betts, *op. cit.*, 91.)

Tuesday, 24. Crossed Enoree, at Anderson's Ford, in a canoe; and Tyger at Crenshaw's Ford, and came to brother Gregory's,[13] near the Fish Dam ford, on Broad River. What a confluence of waters flows into the Santee in about two hundred miles, on a straight line, from the mouth; and in its meanders, three hundred or more!

Wednesday, 25. I preached and administered the sacrament at a store near the Fish Dam ford. This part of the country hath been settled about forty years.

Thursday, 26. I found some assistance on Jer. xxxi, 34, 35, at Gregory's meeting house, in the woods; and I hope it was not altogether in vain. Last night I spent an hour with the blacks in their quarters, and it was well received by them. It will never do to meet them with the whites. By this means our preachers lose all their fruit. Many reasons might be assigned for this. O, my soul, rest in the Lord from moment to moment! All the places I have visited this week are new, and I hope the Lord will work at some, or all of them. I exhorted our people to teach their slaves to read; (this is greatly wanting); they would then understand preaching much better. We crossed Pacolet, and came to P——'s.[14] My mind was under deep exercises on account of the state of religion in this neighbourhood.

Sunday, 29. Was an awful day—perhaps the most awful I shall ever spend in this place. My comfort was in the woods with the Lord.

North Carolina

Monday, 30. I rode forty miles to Moore's. My body is weak, and so is my faith for this part of the vineyard. God is my portion, saith my soul. This country improves in cultivation, wickedness, mills, and stills; a *prophet of strong drink* would be acceptable to many of these people. I believe that the Methodist preachers keep clear, both by precept and example; would to God the members did so too! Lord, have pity on weeping, bleeding Zion!

Wednesday, *April* 1. We rode thirty miles through a barren country, and came, weak and hungry to brother B——'s clean, comfortable house; and had all things agreeable. I find it hard to ride eight or nine hours without any other nourishment but a little bread and tea.

Friday, 3. Was a rainy day. I had some talk with a few blacks, and was comfortable and happy. We lose much by not meeting these people alone. I find, generally, that those who are held by professors of religion are hard to move.

Saturday and *Sunday*, 4, 5. Quarterly meeting at Daniel Asbury's meeting

[13] Gregory lived in Union County at Fish Dam, now Carlisle.

[14] Asbury crossed the Pacolet River at Pinckneyville.

house. I notice many attend preaching at such times as these, who appear wild, and do not know how to behave themselves. In the afternoon I met the poor blacks by themselves, and was greatly blessed.

Monday, 6. We crossed Catawba, rode thirty-five miles, and came to brother Fitzhugh's, where we met with kind treatment to sweeten the bitter cup of a hard and hungry day's ride.

Thursday, 9. Crossed Hunting Creek, and came to Arnette's meeting house in Surry county. Here I had near three hundred hearers, to whom I preached on Heb. v, 12–14, and had more enlarged views of this subject than I ever had before. We have had a good work here; fifty souls are lately brought in; appearances are greatly changed for the better since I was here eleven months ago.

Friday, 10. We came to Gordon's, in Wilkes county. I feel awful; I fear lest darkness should be felt here. Ah, Lord, help me to go through good and evil report; prosperity and adversity; storms and calms; kindness and unkindness; friends and enemies; life and death, in the spirit and practice of the Gospel of Jesus Christ!

Sunday, 12. I preached the funeral of grandmother Gordon, aged eighty-seven or eighty-eight years.

Monday, 13. We took our acceptable departure; I cannot live where God is not acknowledged. I passed through the heart of Wilkes county. Here is a poor prospect of religion among all sects. We came in the evening to the house of a poor, honest man. Bless God! we can embrace the poor cabins, and find shelter. The people are kind and free with what they have.

Wednesday, 15. I preached on Heb. iv, 1, to many people, collected from various parts, at brother White's, on John's River, and was greatly assisted.

Thursday, 16. We had preaching, and were engaged in writing letters and copying the minutes. My soul enjoys sweet peace; but I see an awful danger of losing that simple walking and living in the enjoyment of God.

Friday, 17. I observed as a day of rigid fasting; this I cannot do more than once a month. I am frequently obliged to go on three cups of tea, with a little bread, for eight or nine hours, and to ride many miles, and preach, and perform my other ministerial labours.

Sunday, 19. We had a crowded congregation, and a moving season at the sacrament. *Monday* and *Tuesday* we directed our course up John's River.

Wednesday, 22. Crossed the Ridge, and kept on to the westward. We went Major J. White's path, and found it abundantly better than the old one. We reached the top of the Ridge in about six miles—here we found ourselves among fruitful hills; then we had a good path for six miles more, except where there were some laurel branches and roots. We stopped at

S——'s; and it was well we did, or we should have been well-nigh starved, both man and horse.

Tennessee

I went on to Julius Dugger's, and thence to William Nelson's,[15] where I met with brothers Stephen Brooks, Acuff, and Wilkerson,[16] ancient men among us. I stood the fatigue, and sleeping three in a bed, better than I expected. From White's to Nelson's is eighty miles. We crossed the Watauga about twenty times. At supper we ate of the perch that are taken in great plenty from Smith's fish spring.[17] I judge there must be a subterraneous communication from that to the river. I felt uncomfortable in my mind, as I feared the Lord had left this place. I was led to speak with life and power on, "Will ye also go away?" I spent a night with brother Whitaker,[18] I wish his wife may not love him to death.

Monday, 27. We hasted to Felix Earnest's,[19] on Nolachucky River; where we hold our western conference. Here six brethren from Kentucky met us, and we opened our conference with twenty-three preachers, fifteen of whom were members. We received every man's account of himself and his late labours; and inquired of each man's character among his brethren. Our business was conducted with great love and harmony. Our brethren have built a meeting house,[20] and I must needs preach the first sermon; which I did on Exod. xx, 24. Notwithstanding it was a time of great scarcity, we were well and most kindly entertained.

Friday, *May* 1. We rode thirty miles to Holston without food for man or horse: but when we came to brother Charles Baker's we had food and friendship. My feelings were disagreeable. In addition to the heat of the weather and the fatigue I have gone through, I have not slept five hours a night, one night with another, for five nights past.

[15] William Nelson lived near Jonesboro, the present Johnson City. (See note under May 10, 1788.) Julius Dugger, an early settler, lived fourteen miles above Elizabethton. (Ramsay: *Annals of Tennessee*, 142.)

[16] Francis Acuff was admitted to the conference in 1793 and died at Danville, Kentucky, in August, 1795. (See note under May 2, 1795.) Thomas Wilkerson was born in April 27, 1772, and joined the conference in 1792.

[17] The fish springs flowed out of the bank at the edge of Watauga River. (Williams: *Early Travels*, 302.)

[18] Mark Whitaker had been a traveling preacher, but he located in 1793 and lived at Castle's Wood near Bickley's Station in Russell County, Virginia. (Price: *Holston Methodism*, I, 163, 164.) Asbury's remark reveals his opposition to the marriage of his preachers.

[19] Felix Earnest lived in Green County, Tennessee, a few miles east of Greenville. He was converted in July, 1792, and became an outstanding Methodist. (McFerrin: *Methodism in Tennessee*, I, 90, 91; Price, *op. cit.*, 184, 185.)

[20] This was the Ebenezer Church in the Earnest community. It is still in existence.

Virginia

Saturday, 2. On our way we called to see father Acuff,[21] where we fed and prayed; and in the evening reached Abingdon, being the time and place of the sitting of the district court.

Sunday, 3. I gave them a sermon, and although it was so public a time, we had great decency in the congregation. Rode thirteen miles in the evening.

Monday, 4. We rode thirty-five miles to the head branches of the main Holston, and the next day reached Alfred's, on New River.[22]

Wednesday, 6. We rode to Pepper's ferry, and made it thirty-five miles to M'Daniel's. *Thursday*, we rode to brother W.'s, near Fincastle, thirty-eight miles: the toils of this journey have been great, the weather sultry, the rides long, and roads rough. We suffered from irregularity in food and lodging; although the people are very kind, and give us the best they have, and that without fee or reward, so that I have only spent about two shillings in riding about two hundred miles. I hope prosperity will be bettered by my feeble efforts. I have ridden two hundred and twenty miles in seven days and a half, and am so exceedingly outdone and oppressed with pain, weariness, and want of sleep, that I have hardly courage to do anything. Hail, happy day of rest! It draws nigh, and this labour and toil will soon be at an end!

Saturday, 9. I conferred with the travelling and local preachers at E. Mitchell's. *Sunday*, 10, the preachers and people were solemn whilst I enforced "Grieve not the Holy Spirit of God."

Monday, 11. I rode forty miles to Mr. Baker's at the Calf Pasture, and the next day thirty-five to Moore's. *Wednesday*, 13, rode twenty-four miles to Rocktown,[23] and preached at three o'clock; and again the next day. Here I met the trustees of our school,[24] to whom I read my Thoughts on

[21] Timothy Acuff (1735–1823) was a Revolutionary soldier from Virginia who lived in Sullivan County, Tennessee. He was the father of the Rev. Francis Acuff, and he gave the land on which was erected the first Methodist meetinghouse in Tennessee. (Price, *op. cit.*, 148, 149.)

[22] In Summers, *Annals of Southwest Virginia*, 936, Early Land Surveys, Montgomery County, appears an entry as follows: "1795, Sept. 19, Page, Alexander (Grantor) to Methodist Society on New River waters (Grantee) consideration (Love) 2 (acres) Location—New River waters."

[23] Rocktown was the present Harrisonburg.

[24] A school was established at Harrisonburg under Asbury's direction in 1794, and the "meeting house on the hill" (see note under June 1, 1794) was adapted for its use. The teacher was John Walsh, and the school was to be in operation all the year round; a Mr. Spencer became a teacher the second year. The school continued at least intermittently, since a quarterly conference met there on January 15, 1820. The students were limited to forty, and none "was to be permitted on any account to wear ruffles or powder his hair." (Wayland: *Historic Harrisonburg*, 99, and *A History of Rockingham County*, 283–87.)

Education. In the evening I left the town; and on *Friday*, 15, rode forty miles.

Saturday, 16. I had a hard push to Newtown[25] quarterly meeting, where, after delivering a short discourse, I held a conference with the local preachers and leaders. I enjoyed myself among these people; they are not quite as lively as heretofore, but God is still with them. *Sabbath day*, after sacrament, love feast, and ordination, I preached with some freedom on 2 Peter iii, 17, 18. Upon the whole, my soul is refreshed; although I have been on the run, and have written none in my Journal for more than a week.

West Virginia

Monday, 18. We rode to Charlestown, Jefferson county, and lodged with a pious physician.[26] Next morning breakfasted with John Hite,[27] and then came to Harper's Ferry, where the impending rocks impress the mind of the traveller with terror; and should they fall would crush him to pieces: this scene is truly awful and romantic.

Maryland

We came to Samuel Phillip's, but were not expected until next week: so I directed my course to Baltimore.

Wednesday, 20. I passed Frederick; thence to Liberty, where I stopped, conversed, and prayed, and then came on to brother Alexander Warfield's, thirty miles.

Thursday, 21. We set out for Baltimore; the rain came on very heavily; I have not felt, nor seen such, since the sixth of March, since which time I have ridden about one thousand two hundred miles. This day I heard of the death of one, among my best friends in America—Judge Thomas White, of Kent county, in the state of Delaware. This news was attended with an awful shock to me. I have met with nothing like it in the death of any friend on the continent. Lord, help us all to live out our short day to thy glory! I have lived days, weeks, and months in his house. O that his removal may be sanctified to my good and the good of the family! He was about sixty-five years of age. He was a friend to the poor and oppressed; he had been a professed Churchman, and was united to the Methodist connexion about seventeen or eighteen years. His house and heart were always open; and he was a faithful friend to liberty in spirit and practice; he was a most indulgent husband, a tender father, and an affectionate friend. He professed perfect love, and great peace, living and dying.

[25] Newtown was the present Stephens City, Virginia.

[26] This was Dr. Edward Tiffin. (See note under June 27, 1794.)

[27] See *Journal* entry and note for May 26–27, 1794.

Sunday, 24. I preached twice in town (Baltimore) and was delivered from my gloomy state of mind. I spent part of the week in visiting from house to house. I feel happy in speaking to all I find, whether parents, children, or servants; I see no other way; the common means will not do; Baxter, Wesley, and our Form of Discipline, say, "Go into every house": I would go farther, and say, go into every kitchen and shop; address all, aged and young, on the salvation of their souls.

Wednesday, 27. I read "The Dawn of Universal Peace"; and the second and third volumes of Walker's Sermons. *Thursday*, my mind was under deep exercises, unknown to all but God alone.

Saturday, 30. I met the Africans, to consult about building a house, and forming a distinct African, yet Methodist Church.

Friday, *June* 5. I came in peace to Cokesbury. Stayed on *Saturday*; and gave them a sermon *on the shortness of time*:—thence came through dust and heat to North East. *Sunday*. I preached within the frame of a house that is begun,[28] to a number of sinners.

Monday, 8. I preached twice; and came in the evening to Mr. Richard Bassett's, on the Manor. I have great inward distress in my soul. I felt when in prayer, as if the Lord would restore sister Moore[29] to health; time will determine whether the impression is of the Lord.

Tuesday, 9. We hasted on to Georgetown. Some are of opinion that ——[30] will receive £200 per annum or more, glebe subscriptions, &c.: this is more than sixty-four dollars; and even that he seldom received among us. He was always very generous, and did not serve us for money. He did certainly run well. I was low in body and mind; and very flat in preaching. Dear brother Bowie, who attended me with his carriage to North East the last time I was here, is now gone to rest. O! how short is the life of man! We must needs come on to Chestertown; still languid in body, and my spirits under an awful fit of dejection at reviewing the state of persons and things. I was quite unwell, and crowded with company: my subject in town was Psalm li, 9–13. We then rode fifteen miles home

[28] On August 2, 1801, Asbury locates the "chapel opposite the church, so called" at Northeast, Cecil County. This was St. Mary's Protestant Episcopal Church on South Main Street built about 1700. (Maryland: *A Guide to the Old Line State*, 321; Hallman, *op. cit.*, 118, 296.) Between 1793 and 1815 Asbury visited Northeast thirteen times. There he found the Cook, the George, the Howell, and the Sheridan families. Of the head of the last named, Daniel, he wrote: "He is one of my spiritual children, and has remained a disciple forty years." In 1804 the congregation built one of the earliest Methodist parsonages in the United States.

[29] This may have been the wife of James Moore, who was then the junior preacher on the Cecil Circuit.

[30] This was possibly Jeremiah Cosdon, who withdrew from the Methodist ministry in 1794 and succeeded the Rev. George Ralph as rector of North Sassafras Parish, Cecil County. (See *General Minutes*, I, 54; Johnston: *History of Cecil County, Maryland*, 453.)

with brother Causey;[31] my body and spirit still very low. O! my Lord, help me through all my afflictions. Ah! what a comfortable thing it is to be among the ancient Methodists! But this is not always my place; indeed, it cannot be.

Thursday, 11. Still under awful depression. I am not conscious of any sin, even in thought; but the imprudence and unfaithfulness of others bear heavily on my heart; I feel a degree of willingness to decline, die, and enter into rest. For the first time, I visited Centreville,[32] and preached in the new house: some of the people felt awful. I saw Doctor Benjamin Hall, who is greatly changed since 1792, and under deep exercise about preaching; so that he cannot attend to his practice, and appears to be lost in thought. I wrote to him to try Baltimore: it is a pity such a man of sentiment, learning, and fine feeling, should be lost. I rode home with Robert Wright[33]: he is rich in the world, but wants more of the life of religion; he appears still to love the preachers, and the cause of God. I received information that Doctor M——'s wife, before she died, manumitted her favourite servant-maid: not long after, the Doctor himself was called away; but before his removal he manumitted all his slaves. This man claimed no high Gospel light, and professed no more religion than the generality of the world among us do. I have a hope that God is preparing me for greater usefulness in my latter days. O how happy should I be, if after labouring thirty years, as I sometimes fear, to very little profit, it should hereafter appear that hundreds have been converted by my ministry! Of late I have had but little to do, but pray, preach, ride, converse, and take my necessary refreshment.

Saturday, 13. We crossed Choptank River at Ennall's Ferry: we had nine men, three horses, and a carriage on board, and a very indifferent boat; but through a kind Providence we got safe over. When I first landed I felt a damp on my spirits, which I feared was ominous of persons and things. Our friends were loving at the Dorchester quarterly meeting, but not very lively; however, there was some stir in the love feast. At eleven o'clock we had nearly a thousand people collected, but they are awfully

[31] Peter T. Causey was a resident of Church Hill, Queen Annes County, Maryland, until 1816 when he moved to Milford, Delaware. Asbury was the guest of Causey on May 11, 1799, and April 12, 1813. (Emory: *Queen Anne's County*, Maryland, 324; Hallman, *op. cit.*, 9, 324; Memoir of Mrs. Tamzey Causey, *The Methodist Magazine*, V, 306–10; Scharf: *History of Delaware* II, 1198.)

[32] This society, organized in 1773, met in the home of Colonel William Hopper, Hall's Cross Roads, until 1794 when the first chapel was built. By this society Bishop John Emory was given his license to exhort. Epworth Church, Centerville, Queen Annes County, is the descendant of this organization. (Emory, *op. cit.*, 175, 231, 369; Hallman, *op. cit.*, 325; Emory: *Life of Bishop Emory*, 34.)

[33] This was probably Robert Wright, thirteenth governor of Maryland (1806–9) and the brother of Thomas Wright, a trustee of the first Methodist chapel in Centerville, Queen Annes County. (*National Cyclopaedia of American Biography*, IX, 297; Hallman, *op. cit.*, 325; Census of 1790, Queen Annes County.)

hardened. We had a heavy time: I felt much like what I suppose Jonah felt. We were furnished richly with the comforts of life.

Delaware

I came to the dwelling house of my dear friend Judge White (whose death I have already mentioned)—it was like his funeral to me. I learned since I came here, and I think it worthy of observation, that just before he died, unknown to his wife he had showed Samuel, his son,[34] his books, and given directions concerning his house, &c. He then came to his wife, and said, "I feel as I never felt before," and gave certain directions concerning his burial.

Wednesday, 17. I had a solemn season at Dover. I spent the evening with Doctor Abraham Ridgely, in the late dwelling house of his father. In some houses we serve the fathers, not the children; in some the children, not the fathers; and in some we serve both parents and children.

Thursday, 18. I preached at Duck Creek Cross Roads, where there has been a great revival of religion.

Pennsylvania

Friday, 19. I set out for Philadelphia, and came to Whiteclay and Redclay Creeks.[35] I saw my old friend Samuel Hooper once more. I must needs preach, although I had ridden thirty-five or forty miles. Next day I called at Chester, and found my dear sister Withy unwell and in trouble. O may I meet her in heaven at last!

Sunday, 21. I preached in the city of Philadelphia three times, not with the success I would wish. I was exceedingly assisted in meeting the classes, in which I spent three days, and am now of opinion that there is more religion among the society than I expected. I trust both they and myself will remember this visit for days to come. I was also much quickened in meeting the local preachers and leaders, who spoke feelingly of the state of their souls and the work of God. I now go hence to meet new troubles, and to labour while feeble life shall last.

[34] Samuel White (1770–1809) was born in Mispillion Hundred, Kent County, Delaware. He attended Cokesbury College, studied law with Governor Richard Bassett, by whom he was appointed to the United States Senate in 1803 and served until his death in Wilmington, Delaware, 1809. (*Biographical Dictionary of the American Congress, 1774–1927*, 1692; article by Henry Clay Conrad, *Samuel White and His Father, Judge Thomas White. An Almost Forgotten Senator; and his father who was a follower of Asbury in the early days of Methodism.* Historical Society of Delaware, Bound Vol. Nos. 31–40.)

[35] These creeks were in East Marlborough Township of Chester County, Pennsylvania. (*Pennsylvania Gazetteer.*)

Thursday, 25. I rode to Crosswicks.

Friday, 26. Although very poorly I reached brother Brown's.[36] I was happy in this family, and addressed most of them concerning their souls.

New Jersey

Saturday, 27. I came to Elizabethtown, and found brother Morrell (who had been bled and physiced almost to death) on the recovery. My troubles are greater than ever: my body is weak, and my spirits very low. At the request of my friends, I stayed in town until *Sunday*, and was assisted in a manner I least expected, in preaching to about eighty people, from 1 Cor. xv, 58: after sermon I called the society together, and had a melting time in speaking personally to each. I attended the Bowery church in the afternoon; and the minister spoke largely on, "That your faith might not stand in the wisdom of men, but in the power of God."

New York

Monday, 29. I came to New York the new way by Newark bridges, which are well established over Second and Passaic rivers:[37] it is the nearest way to New York, and preserves the traveller from heat in the summer, and cold in the winter; from mosquitoes, and delays by winds, and other incidents. I began meeting the women's classes, and felt happy, and found the Lord was amongst the sisters.

Saturday, July 4. Being the anniversary of Independence, the bells ringing, drums beating, guns firing, and orations on liberty, and equality too, are not forgotten. I see the need of being more watchful among the best of men: a spirit of love exists among the preachers; but we are far from being as spiritual as we ought to be. The Rev. Mr. Ogden was kind enough to present me with his first volume, On Revealed Religion: it contains a soft, yet general answer to the deistical atheistical oracle of the day, Thomas Paine; it is a most excellent compilation, taken from a great number of ancient and modern writers on the side of truth; and will be new to common readers. So far as I have read, I can recommend it to those who wish

[36] See *Journal* entry for June 30, 1794.

[37] The Hackensack and Passaic rivers empty into Newark Bay, and these two broad streams formed serious obstacles in colonial times to communication directly with New York. The New Jersey legislature authorized the erection of bridges over the two rivers on November 24, 1790, and the bridges were completed in 1795. Asbury's friend Uzal Ogden was one of the company of thirty-six persons empowered by the state commissioners to administer the concerns of the bridge franchises, and after incorporation of the board Ogden was named president of the corporation. (Shaw: *History of Essex and Hudson Counties, New Jersey*, II, 1037–43; Gordon, *op. cit.*, 153, 204.)

for full information on the subject. I met the official members of the society and had some close talk on the doctrine and discipline of the Church: I asked if they wished to be Methodists? But how could I suppose anything else, when they had been a society of nearly thirty years' standing?[38]

Sunday, 5. I preached in Brooklyn in the morning, and returned to assist in the sacrament in the afternoon at the new church; I then met the black classes;[39] and preached at half-past six; I closed my day's work by meeting two men's classes.

Monday, 6. I met nine classes; so that I have now spoken to most of the members here, one by one.[40] I left the city in peace, and received of their bounty towards bearing my expenses.

Connecticut

We came to Stamford; where I preached in a private house.

Rode thirty-three miles to Stratford; the prospects here are great as to the fruits of the earth. My body was weak, and my faith still more so; however, I gave them a sermon on John iii, 19–21; and the house was crowded inside and out.

Friday, 10. We had a very warm ride, fourteen miles, to New Haven. I think it as sultry here as it was the tenth of June in Delaware. Nothing would do but I must preach in Doctor Edwards's meeting house;[41] which I did, on these words: "Yea, doubtless, and I count all things but loss for the excellency of the knowledge of Jesus Christ my Lord."

Saturday, 11. I came to Middletown: we had a prayer meeting, and I spent some time in visiting from house to house.

Sunday, 12. Brother Roberts being indisposed, I had to give them two sermons at the farms,[42] and one at the court house.

Monday, 13. We had some life at Middle Haddam. *Tuesday*, 14, preached at New London[43] about six o'clock, where I found most of the preachers present. *Wednesday*, 15, we opened our conference, which consisted of about twenty members, and sat until noon on *Saturday*. We had great peace

[38] Philip Embury had organized the society in his home on Augustus Street in 1766.

[39] There were eight black classes. (*John Street Church Records*, II, 42.)

[40] There was a total of twenty-seven classes in New York, comprising the membership of the two congregations and numbering 600 white and 155 coloured. (*General Minutes* of 1795; Seaman, *op. cit.*, 134.)

[41] Jonathan Edwards, Jr., preached for thirty years in the White Haven Church in New Haven. He had been dismissed in January, 1795, and the pulpit was vacant at the time of Asbury's visit.

[42] South Farms in the southeastern section of the city was and still is an important section of Middletown.

[43] Jesse Lee introduced Methodism into New London, and the first class was formed on October 11, 1793, with eight members. The church was built in 1798, both Lee and Asbury being present at its dedication.

in our conference; but some exercises relative to the externals, arose from the ancient contest about baptism, these people being originally connected with those that are of that line. O! what wisdom, meekness, patience, and prudence are necessary! Our brethren were exceedingly kind; and I hope this conference will be for the good of the people in this place, and thousands besides.

Monday, 20. We took our leave of town, and set off for our respective appointments. Two of our British brethren from the West Indies, Harper and Kingston,[44] who had fled here to save their lives (that is, if possible to recover their health), were with us: I was pleased to see our preachers ready to give their strange brethren a little of the little they had. I came to Norwich, fifteen miles, and preached at eight o'clock, A.M., in the academy (formerly the Separate meeting house). It was a most awful time of heat.

Rhode Island

Tuesday, 21. We rode twelve miles to Plainfield; and after resting and feeding, we came to Coventry,[45] in Providence. My fatigue and indisposition made me glad to get to bed. The people here have made some attempts to improve the state of the roads; and really they need it, for they are properly made up of rocks and stones.

Wednesday, 22. At brother Lippett's[46] I ordained Duncan McCall[47] from Passamaquoddy; who is as one born out of due time. He has been labouring between the British and American boundaries. I consider it fifty hard miles from New London to General Lippett's: we have been the best of three days riding it, through the intense heat; and last year I rode it in one day. I feel a moving towards these people, as though the Lord would get himself a name, and have a people to praise him in this place. I feel myself greatly humbled before the Lord, for the peace and union in our late conference; and the satisfaction expressed by the preachers on receiving their stations.

Thursday, 23. We came in the evening to Providence: when we entered the town, some drunken fellows raised a cry and shout, and made a

[44] Little is known about these two preachers from the West Indies. John Harper was appointed to Boston for the next six months, but his name does not appear in the *Minutes* for the following year. The British *Minutes*, 1812, show that he was received on trial in Ireland in 1786 and appointed to St. Eustatius, West Indies, in 1787. John Kingston was received in 1791 with the notation "not immediately wanted" and assigned to Nevis, West Indies, in 1793.

[45] Coventry is on the route that Asbury probably followed, but it is some distance from Providence.

[46] Probably Christopher Lippett's home.

[47] Duncan McCall was a friend of Jesse Lee and accompanied Lee to the conference. In the *Minutes* for 1795 McCall's name appears for the only time in the list of elders.

sacrifice of the Methodists to hell. Mr. ——[48] is now pastor of, and the Tennant house is shut against us. I wished to ride on, and not to stop in town; but Mr. Robertson, an ancient Englishman, constrained us to turn in with him.

Massachusetts

We dined at Milton; and made it thirty miles to Boston, where I preached twice on the Sabbath (though very unwell), in a room that will hold about two hundred and fifty people. It seemed as if we hardly had either cursing or blessing among the people here. I have no doubt but that if we had a house, we should command a large congregation; but we labour under great inconveniences where we preach at present. I feel myself feeble in body and faint in spirit; yet Christ is mine, and I hope to be his in time and forever. Amen.

Monday, 27. I rode through some rain to Lynn. I was much shut up and distressed in my public exercises. My congregations were large and lifeless. Since I have been in Lynn, I have visited Wood End and Gravesend,[49] met five classes, visited about one dozen families, and talked to them personally about their souls, and prayed with them. I have filled up intervals in reading my Bible, and the second volume of Mr. Wesley's Sermons. O, how I wish our preachers and people to read his Journal, Sermons, and Notes! My body is afflicted, but my soul is serene.

Thursday, 30. I preached on Isaiah lv, 10, 11. *Friday* was an excessively rainy day. My spirits were sunk into dejection. I feel no passion, but grieve and sorrow: to *move, move,* seems to be my life. I now lament that I did not set off with the young men to the Province of Maine. There are some tender, gracious souls in this town, especially among the members of society.

Sunday, *August* 2. Was a very warm, sultry day. I rose in the morning very feeble in spirit, and attended prayer meeting at six o'clock. I preached three times, administered the sacrament, and met two classes, and was not so fatigued as I expected I should have been. I have had some refreshing seasons; and now I bid farewell to Lynn for two years. I rode a solitary way through Malden, Mistick,[50] and North Cambridge; and preached at Waltham, at five o'clock, to a few people: the great rain prevented many from attending. Brother Roberts took an intermittent fever when we were at New Haven, and hath laboured and suffered, sick or well, until he is almost dead. I received from the quarterly meeting held in Fairfield cir-

[48] Probably the Rev. James Wilson, an opponent of Methodism. (See *Journal* entry for July 23, 1793.)

[49] Wood End was in East Lynn. Gravesend is now Glenmere in Lynn. Methodist churches survive in both sections.

[50] Mistick was the present Medford, Massachusetts.

cuit,[51] what I should be glad to receive once a year from every circuit in the Union. It was as follows:—"The preachers of the Methodist Episcopal order who have travelled on this circuit since the last conference, have so conducted themselves that their characters are unimpeachable." Signed by the local preachers, exhorters, stewards, and leaders.

Tuesday, 4. Brother Lee[52] and myself came ten miles to Framingham, where I preached to a simple-hearted people; and although weak in body, I felt enlargement of heart. Here the society appeared to be all tenderness, sweetness, and love. After riding thirty miles to Milford (being an excessive day of heat and hunger), I preached on Isaiah xxxv, 3–6. To my great surprise, whilst I was preaching, brother Roberts, whom I had left sick at Waltham, came in. I was amazed that he should ride thirty miles through such heat, without eating or drinking. It was enough to make a well man sick.

Connecticut

Thursday, 6. We set out for Thompson in Connecticut, whence we came to dear brother Nichols's.[53] If I had not eaten, I could not have stood the labour of thirty miles, and preaching. I found there was religion among this society. The ancient people are stirred up by the Baptists, and the young ones by the Methodists.

Massachusetts

Saturday, 8. We rode twenty-six miles to Wilbraham. I was well-nigh spent, and brother George Roberts was ready to drop on the roadside. I spoke late; the weather was warm; I took but little rest for my body, and my mind was powerfully tried various ways.

Sunday morning, 9. My first subject was the parable of the sower; afterward the sacrament was administered. I thought it a dull time; but others did not think so. I gave them another discourse in the afternoon on, "The promise is to you and to your children." It was a running exhortation, chiefly application. In the evening brother Roberts, though weak in body, gave them a sermon on, "My little children, for whom I travail in

[51] Fairfield Circuit was in Connecticut.

[52] Jesse Lee accompanied Asbury on a part of his journey after the adjournment of the conference at New London. (Thrift: *Memoir of the Rev. Jesse Lee*, with extracts from his *Journal*, 221.)

[53] Captain Jonathan Nichols, an officer of the Revolution, lived at West Thompson, Connecticut, and was a bridge and road contractor. Methodist preaching began in his house this year, and in an upper unfinished room the New England District Conference was held in September, 1796. The house is said to be still standing. A Methodist church was erected nearby in 1797. West Thompson was on the Pomfret Circuit.

birth again till Christ be formed in you." I see but little prospect of good being done, whilst the people are so divided.

Monday, 10. I stopped, and gave an exhortation at Springfield. After a thunder gust, we came on to Agawam. If I accomplish the tour I have in contemplation, it will make about six or seven hundred miles to the city of New York. I was stopped by the rain; but when I cannot do one thing another offers. I could read, write, pray, and plan. I laid out a plan for my travels in 1797; through Connecticut, Rhode Island, Massachusetts, Province of Maine, New Hampshire, Vermont, and New York: making a distance of twelve or fifteen hundred miles. I set out for Williamstown on the banks of Hoosack, on the west borders of Massachusetts. I lodged at sister H.'s. I was well steeped in water, although my cloak saved me, in a good degree, as is frequently the case. My rest was interrupted. To labour hard all the day, and have no sleep at night, ill suit the flesh. Well might St. Paul say, "If in this life only we have hope in Christ, we are of all men most miserable." To labour and to suffer by night and by day, meet reproach, give up father and mother, wife, children, country, liberty, ease, health, wealth, and, finally, sometimes life itself in martyrdom—all this may be required.

Vermont

Friday, 21. We rode in the afternoon into the woods of Bennington,[54] and preached at brother D.'s,[55] and had a melting, comfortable season with about fifty souls. There are sinners, Deists, Universalists, &c., and they all have something to say about religion. I have felt awful for this place and people; but God is able of these stones to raise up children unto Abraham. I feel my soul stayed upon God, although I am in heaviness through manifold temptations.

New York

Saturday, 22. Brother Roberts[56] and myself parted. He went to Pownall and myself to Ashgrove, where we have a society of about sixty members

[54] Since ten days had elapsed after the previous *Journal* entry, when Asbury was at Williamstown, Massachusetts, his point of entry into Vermont is uncertain. Had he passed from Williamstown into the state, he would pave passed through Pownall. This might have been the case. Or he might have gone up the Hoosie River into New York and directly to Bennington.

[55] Probably Obadiah Dunham, a devoted Christian and a member of the Baptist Church. His home was just south of the village of Bennington. (Heaxt: *History of Methodism in Bennington, Vermont*, 13–15.)

[56] George Roberts was the elder of Redding and the four circuits around New York. (See *Minutes*.)

They originated with Philip Embury, who left the city of New York when the British preachers came here.[57] He continued to pursue his purpose of forming societies in the country; but dying in a few years, the society was left, and were without preaching by the Methodists for fifteen years. We have now a neat little chapel here.[58]

Sunday, 23. I had a free, open time, with a few feeling souls, on Luke xi, 1. In the afternoon, I visited a neglected people among the hills, and had an attentive congregation. This day I enjoyed peace of soul, and was happy in Christ. After riding fifteen miles, I found myself at home at this place (Ashgrove). My soul has been much quickened this *Sabbath*, and I find a difference between being amongst saints and sinners.

We came through Cambridge county, now Washington; and passed Argyle,[59] named after Argyle, in Scotland. We came to brother M——'s; we and our horses were quite weary; but it is enough, the Lord is with us. Let this suffice at all times, and in every place. We came through a mere wilderness of swamp: the roots of the white pine, beech, and hemlock were a good deal in our way. We reached Westfield, where is a considerable settlement, and a promising society.

We passed Skenesborough,[60] and turned our course eastward through some rough ground, and came to Hampton township, where we held a quarterly meeting at brother M——'s,[61] in a pleasant vale. We rode through considerable heat, nearly twenty miles, without obtaining any refreshment! I have reason to praise God that I have been able to travel from Lynn to this place; the distance, the way I have come, I compute to be four hundred miles. I am now within a mile of the line of Vermont. There is only one county, in the State of New York, between this and

[57] Embury left New York, in the fall of 1770, after the first clash of the British and the Sons of Liberty in the "Battle of Golden Hill," and settled on a farm at Salem, Albany County, New York, with the Hecks and other Palatinate families. He died there in 1773 and was buried at Ashgrove. His wife moved to Ontario near Prescott. Here Barbara Heck lived. Mrs. Embury married a Lawrence, a relative of Barbara Heck. Mrs. Lawrence and her husband are buried in the Blue Churchyard in the same plot with Barbara Heck. Embury's son helped to start Methodism in that section. (Hurst, *op. cit.*, 20, 21.)

[58] The society at Ashgrove in Washington County, New York, was the first in the present Troy Conference. It was formed by Embury, whose remains were transferred to its cemetery from nearby Cambridge in 1832. The meetinghouse was erected in 1788. (Parks: *Troy Conference Miscellany*, 24, 25.)

[59] Argyle is in Washington County, New York.

[60] Skenesborough is now known as Whitehall. After the Pact of Paris in 1763 Major Philip K. Skene of the British Army bought several large grants and other property rights in the area, amassing at least ten thousand acres of farm land. He applied for and received a royal charter, naming his holdings Skenesborough. After the war Skene went back to England, and New York State confiscated all his property, reselling it in smaller lots, and the name was changed to Whitehall.

[61] This was possibly Philip Mercer, mentioned in *Life of Thomas Ware* as a Methodist leader in this vicinity. Ware was elder of the district in 1795.

Lower Canada. There is a place called Plattsburg,[62] where they have often solicited us to send preachers. I find some similarity between the northern and western frontiers.

Sunday, 30, was a high day: we had sacrament and love feast, and many opened their mouths boldly to testify of the goodness and love of the Lord Jesus. The porch, entry, kitchen, and the lodging-rooms were filled. One soul professed conversion. I find that two hours' close meeting flags the minds of God's children. Many of the people of the world are filled with prejudice because they are shut out.

Sister ——, an ancient woman, and a professor among the Baptists, was sent for by her father to turn the head and heart of her son from the Methodists: but she had grace and sense to know that God had been at work upon his soul; and with tears and prayers wished him God speed. Mr. G——, who had heard great and bad things of the Methodists, was surprised to hear that a son of his died a Methodist, in New York; and still more so, when he was visited by another son, who had joined society in Waltham. When this son came home, the father and family were alarmed, finding that he had met with something that had greatly changed him. After this, the prejudices of the dear old man were dissipated and he came five miles to our quarterly meeting. I rode forty miles. I conclude, that for thirty-five miles of this road there are ten or twelve houses for every mile, including those which extend to the mountains on either side of the road. Notwithstanding the roads are somewhat hilly, they are good for travellers. I laboured under great exercise of mind from various quarters; and my own infirmities of body and mind are neither few nor small.

Wednesday, *September* 2. We had a solemn meeting at Bethlehem, in Ashgrove. *Thursday*, 3, we had a warm-hearted people at R——'s, and a better time than weakness of body or mind could promise. On *Friday*, we came to Lansingburgh,[63] and thence to Troy; at last we got to Coeyman's Patent, weary, sick, and faint, after riding thirty-six miles.

Saturday, 5. We were crowded with people. I suppose we had, perhaps, a thousand at the stone church at Coeyman's Patent; and I felt some life and warmth amongst them.

Sunday, 6. In the morning we had baptism, ordination, sacrament, and love feast; some spoke with life of the goodness of God. I gave them a discourse at eleven o'clock, and then went to bed with a high fever. Brother Roberts pleased, and, I trust, profited the people with a discourse, after I had done.

Monday, 7. I rose very unwell, and had to ride thirty-five or forty miles

[62] Plattsburg is on the west shore of Lake Champlain, about twenty miles south of the Canadian border. Burlington, Vermont, lies across the lake and somewhat south.

[63] Lansingburg is near the confluence of the Hoosic and Hudson Rivers, a few miles above Troy.

through the rain: I came in much wearied, and found a comfortable lodging at Mr. I——'s.

Tuesday, 8. I am somewhat better in body, but clouds and darkness still rest upon my mind.

Thursday, 10. We rode twenty miles to Marbletown (properly so called at present); I preached on Heb. xii, 28, 29. I felt awful; there appeared to be very little devotion among the people. Our southern friends are battered on the subject of slaves, and these are in peace: it will not do; we must be Methodists in one place as well as another.

Saturday, 12. We reached brother Garrettson's;[64] and *Sunday*, 13, I preached at Rowe's chapel. Then returned to Rhinebeck chapel, and preached on Heb. xiii, 5. God once put into brother Garrettson's hands great riches of a spiritual nature, and he laboured much; if he now does equal good according to his temporal ability, he will be blessed by the Lord, and by men.

Tuesday, 15. We made it twenty miles to the wreck of an old Presbyterian meeting house, at Wapping Creek,[65] called the *hollow*; where I gave them a discourse on "Judgment beginning first at the house of God"—and there was some little motion, but the Methodists were not on their own ground.

Wednesday, 16. Brother Roberts gave us a close, good sermon on, My people have committed two evils," &c. I then enlarged on, "My grace is sufficient for thee"; our meeting continued till three o'clock; we got no dinner, and had to ride twelve miles to get to our supper and lodgings. We stopped at Governor Van Courtlandt's,[66] who reminds me of General Russell; we had all we needed, and abundantly more than we desired. Rest, rest, how sweet! yet how often in labour I rest, and in rest, labour.

Sunday, 20. I had a comfortable time at Croton chapel,[67] on Rom. i, 16. I returned to General Van Courtlandt's,[68] and dined with my dear aged friends. Shall we ever meet again? We came to Fisher's, near the White Plains chapel, to hold conference.[69] My soul is kept solemn; and I feel as

[64] The Garrettsons had recently built a commodious house on property in Mrs. Garrettson's estate. She was the former Catherine Livingston, a daughter of Judge Livingston of Rhinebeck, New York. The home was to be known as "Travelers Rest," and all itinerant Methodist preachers were warmly welcomed.

[65] This was Wappingers Falls on Wapping Creek, about ten miles south of Poughkeepsie.

[66] The governor's mansion house was near Croton, twenty-five miles or so south of Wappingers Falls.

[67] This chapel was built on land given by Lieutenant Governor Pierre Van Cortlandt.

[68] This was probably Philip Van Cortlandt, elder son of the Governor. Philip had served with great distinction during the Revolution and had attained the rank of general in the state militia. By this time he had relieved his father of much of the duties involved in the manor estate and resided at the Croton manor house.

[69] This session of conference was appointed for New York, but a very severe epidemic of yellow fever had developed there and the conference was accordingly transferred to White Plains.

if earth were nothing to me; I am happy in God, and not perplexed with the things of this world.

Tuesday, 22. A few of us met in conference; the main body of the preachers not coming in until about twelve o'clock. We went through the business of the conference in three days, forty-three preachers being present. I was greatly disappointed in not hearing the preachers give a full and free account of themselves and circuits. Although we sat ten hours in each day we did not close our business until *Thursday* evening after sitting each night till twelve o'clock.

New Jersey

Friday, 25. We crossed Hudson River twenty-six miles above the city of New York, and came on to the waters of Hackensack; a river that is only thirty miles long and navigable two-thirds of the way:[70] we then came to Passaic River, crossed at Second River, and made out this day to ride forty miles, much fatigued.

Saturday, 26. We rode about thirty-two miles with very little to eat; however, we had the pleasure of seeing the famous Brunswick bridge,[71] which is now nearly finished. It is the grandest of the kind I have seen in America. I was *properly* wearied; and prepared to rest on *Sunday*. I was sorely tried yesterday; more so than I have been these six weeks past.

Monday, 28. We came to Monmouth; we would have gone to Shrewsbury,[72] but time and horses failed us. I learn that the ancient spirit of faith, prayer, and power is taking place in a few places below. I was shocked at the brutality of some men who were fighting, one gouged out the other's eye; the father and son then beset him again, cut off his ears and nose, and beat him almost to death. The father and son were tried for a breach of the peace, and roundly fined; and now the man that hath lost his nose and ears is to come upon them for damage. I have often thought that there are some things practiced in the Jerseys which are more brutish and diabolical than in any of the other States:[73] there is nothing of this

[70] The crossing of the Hudson was probably made at Nyack across the Tappan Zee. Asbury probably crossed the Hackensack River over the "New Bridge" which had been erected before or during the Revolution. He crossed at Second River, now Belleville, via ferry, since the bridge there was only authorized in 1794 and not completed until 1796. (Shaw, *op. cit.*, II, 1041.)

[71] This was the New Brunswick Bridge, built across the Raritan River at the site of the old ford. Asbury had often used the Raritan Landing ferry two miles above Brunswick and even earlier had forded the river on horseback or carriage at the bridge's site.

[72] Shrewsbury was a post town between the Shrewsbury and Nevisink Rivers, twelve miles east of Freehold. Today the town is on Route 35, a short distance from Red Bank.

[73] The "Pineys," inhabitants of the wilderness pine barrens of southern New Jersey, were notoriously quarrelsome and brutish, even bestial. Weygandt tells several stories, similar to those hinted at here by Asbury, but the New Jersey author does not identify the participants by name. (Weygandt: *Down Jersey*, 155–58.)

kind in New England; they learn civility there at least. We rode twenty miles to Emley's church,[74] where the great revival of religion was some years ago. I felt a little of the old, good spirit there still. Thence we journeyed on to Penny Hill,[75] fifteen miles, where I was enabled to speak strong words. Thence I came to New Mills,[76] and gave them an alarming talk on, Judgment beginning at the house of God.

Pennsylvania

Saturday, October 3. I came through the sand to Philadelphia, and on *Sunday* evening I preached on "All seek their own, not the things which are Jesus Christ's." In doing which—

I. I pointed out the things that are Jesus Christ's.

II. How these are to be sought.

III. That men are not to seek themselves wholly, or partially, in the ministry of Christ, but that *self* must be altogether out of the question.

Monday, 5. We opened our conference, and went on with great peace, love, and deliberation, but were rather irregular, owing to some preachers not coming in until the third or fourth day. We made better stations than could be expected, extending from Northampton, in Virginia, to the Seneca Lake.

Friday, 9, we observed as a day of fasting and prayer. I preached at eleven o'clock, on Joel ii, 15–17.

Saturday, 10. Our conference rose.

Sunday, 11. I preached in the morning at the African church, in the afternoon at Ebenezer, and in the evening at St. George's, where, to my surprise, the galleries were filled. I applied, "Knowing therefore the terror of the Lord, we persuade men." I had work enough, being often compelled to digress to call the attention of the wild people.

Monday, 12. After getting a copy of the minutes I came to Chester, and dined with Mary Withy, who hath lived a widow in this house thirty-one years, and hath kept one of the most complete houses of entertainment in America. She hath sold out for £3,000, and is to give place in three weeks.

[74] Emley's Church was near Allentown in Upper Freehold Township, Monmouth County. Samuel Emley was the moving spirit of the church and was the first person to receive and welcome Methodists in Allentown. (Phoebus, *op. cit.*, 152; Gordon, *op cit.* 93.)

[75] Mount Laurel in Burlington County was once called Penny Hill, and Wrightstown in the same county was known as Penny Hill prior to 1834. From the direction of Asbury's itinerary it seems that Wrightstown is the place indicated here. (Letter and map of John W. Zelley, June 4, 1956, Secretary of New Jersey Conference Historical Society.)

[76] New Mills is the present Pemberton. Another village, Birmingham, which was probably absorbed in Pemberton, was formerly called New Mills. (Gordon, *op. cit.*, 104.)

I came late to Wilmington, and preached on Col. i, 10. The great hindrance to the work of God here is the loose walk of professors of religion.

Maryland

Thence, by Thomas Howard's,[77] I proceeded to North East Forge, and lodged with my dear son, D. Sheredine.

Wednesday, 14. We came to Cokesbury. Here we undertook to make an inventory of all the property belonging to Cokesbury college, and found the sum total of the amount to be seven thousand one hundred and four pounds, twelve shillings and ninepence.

Saturday, 17. I came to Baltimore to attend the quarterly meeting; brother Whatcoat and myself filled up *Sunday*, the 18th, and were crowded with people.

Tuesday, 20. Our conference began. We had preachers from the Northern Neck, and what is called New Virginia (Pitt District), and the west of Maryland[78]; about fifty-five in number. On *Friday* night there was a public collection for the assistance of the preachers who were deficient in their quarterage.

Sunday evening, 25. I preached on, "Then shall many be offended, and shall betray one another." As I wished not to be idle I concluded to spend a good part of this week in meeting classes. The Africans of this town desire a church, which, in temporals, shall be altogether under their own direction, and ask greater privileges than the white stewards and trustees ever had a right to claim.

Thursday, 29. Was a very solemn day of thanksgiving: the subject I made choice of was Psalm cxlvii, 20, "He hath not dealt so with any nation." This I applied spiritually—

I. To ourselves as individuals.

II. As it applies to our families.

III. To the society and ministry.

IV. As it applies to the continent.

In the afternoon I preached at the Point, on "In everything give thanks."

Saturday, 31. I left town and came to Elk Ridge, where I found a little time for reflection and prayer.

Sunday, *November* 1. I preached and administered the sacrament on the Ridge. After twenty-three years' preaching here, we have a small society. I dined at the widow Howard's,[79] and had an interview with sister Pue,

[77] Thomas Howard lived in Elkton, Maryland.

[78] Preachers in attendance at this conference came from the Northern Neck, which included the peninsula between the Rappahannock and the Potomac rivers in Virginia; also from the present West Virginia, western Pennsylvania, and eastern Ohio.

[79] This was probably Achsah Dorsey Howard, widow of Dr. Ephraim Howard (1745–88). Mrs. Howard inherited Long Reach near Elkridge. Mrs. Pue was the widow of Dr. Michael Pue.

who appeared to be deeply oppressed with the loss of her valuable husband. It is now more than twenty years since the doctor attended my ministry; and I have to hope was deeply awakened. In the latter part of his life he was much afflicted; he called upon God, and I trust died in peace. I doubt if there hath been a man of his profession of equal skill, continuation, and attention, in the state of Maryland. Mr. John Fletcher, when near his end cried out, "My poor, what will become of my poor?" So the doctor, when on his death-bed, "What will become of my patients?"

Monday, 2. After riding forty miles, I came late in the evening to Georgetown, and found a congregation waiting at the new chapel.[80] Although wearied and unwell, I felt some liberty in speaking; and I am persuaded that good might have been done here if professors had not traded away their characters. It is strange, that people professing no religion look for justice and perfection in all Christians, and forget themselves.

Virginia

Thursday, 5. I reached Faulks. *Friday*, 6, preached at the widow Bombry's[81] to about sixty-six hearers, after riding about sixty-six miles from Alexandria.

Saturday, 7. I rode about forty-two miles, and found a quiet retreat at brother Ellis's. Next day I had about four hundred hearers.

Wednesday, 11. I had about three hundred hearers at Lancaster meeting house. Came in the evening to the widow Diggs's. *Friday*, 13, after preaching to a few people at the widow Woolard's,[82] we set out at one o'clock for Bowles's ferry, and crossed in forty minutes, although it was three miles over: we landed in Essex county, and rode eight miles to brother Mann's, where I preached fifteen years ago.[83]

Saturday, 14. I visited brother L. R. Cole, and spent the day with him and his agreeable wife. Brother Reuben Ellis is certainly married, for the first time; may it be for the glory of God, and the good of his Church, and comfort of the dear man and his wife.

[80] The original building was 30 × 40 feet and stood on a lot on the east side of 28th Street between M and Olive Streets in the District of Columbia. It is now the Dumbarton Avenue Church. (Bryan: *A History of the National Capital*, I, 87, 603; Kirkley: *Centennial Sketches of Methodism in Washington, D.C.*, 22.)

[81] Bombry lived in Westmoreland County, Virginia.

[82] See letters to Nelson Reed, November 13, 1795, and to parents, —— 1795.

[83] Mann's Meeting House was in Essex County, Virginia, twelve miles southeast of Tappahannock. A road marker there states that it was the first in that region; "it was built before 1784 and abandoned about 1880. The site is now occupied by the Macedonia Colored Baptist Church." But there is no evidence from the *Journal* that Asbury was there fifteen years ago or in 1780. (See *Journal* entry for March 11, 1812, where Asbury said he was at Mann's thirty-three years earlier, for which no *Journal* evidence exists.)

Sunday, 15. I preached to some souls within and round the house, with a mixture of rich and poor, tame and wild people, at mother Cowles's! I am amazed at the dear aged woman—the additional labour to which she submits, although now between seventy and eighty years of age, and possessing such strong mental powers!—it is surprising.

Monday, 16. After a rainy morning I rode to Paup's chapel, and had nearly a hundred people. I spent the evening with Mrs. J. Ellis, brother Paup, and brother Perry: I was not so spiritual as I might have been.

Tuesday, 17. Crossed Mattaponi at Frazier's ferry, and Pamunkey at Putney, and came to Colonel Clayton's: the weather was cold, and the wind and hunger were both pinching. We were kindly entertained at P. Davies's: Stephen, his brother, is dead, and hath left the chief of what he had to the Church. He hath appointed me his trustee to dispose of it, and J. Ellis his executor. I feel the burden of the connexion; my only hope is, that the Lord of the harvest will send labourers into *his* vineyard, not *mine*.

Thursday, 19. I preached at Richmond; and the next day came, cold and hungry, to my affectionate, kind, adopted son, J. Harding's, in Petersburg. Here several of the preachers met me, to accompany me to the quarterly meeting in Brunswick. I received an original letter from Mr. Lee,[84] not like what I wrote; so I bid him farewell: I will not give him another opportunity to abuse me; neither shall I lay to heart what he saith to afflict me. I attended the quarterly meeting at Merritt's chapel, and there was some move among the people. I rode to John Paup's,[85] and had some consultation about Ebenezer school.[86]

Monday, 23. I preached at White's chapel, and in the evening came, cold and hungry, to L. Holmes's, in Mecklenburg.

Tuesday, 24. Our conference began at Salem chapel; there were present about fifty members, and sixteen probationers—we had close work, and great harmony in sentiment.

Saturday, 28. Brothers Ansley and Cox[87] preached, and we had a warm, living season.

Sunday, 29, was a great day. I preached on 1 Tim. iii, 15, 16; and there were ten elders and nine deacons ordained. This part of the connexion has

[84] Jesse Lee, who sympathized with James O'Kelley but did not join his schism, was frequently antagonistic to Asbury. (See note under June 24, 1810.)

[85] John Paup was an itinerant preacher from 1786 to 1792.

[86] Ebenezer Academy was located near Merritt's Chapel in Brunswick County, Virginia, and was doubtless the first Methodist school in America. It was founded sometime between 1783 and 1793 and antedated Cokesbury College. Some ruins of the building remain. (Cummings: *Early Schools of Methodism*, 35–43; Clark: *An Album of Methodist History*, 193, 194; Morrison: *Beginnings of Public Education*, quotation from *Mecklenburg Times Star*, July 13, 1917; Duvall: *Methodist Church and Education*, 28; Sweet: *Religion on the American Frontier, the Methodists*, 710.)

[87] S. Ansley was appointed to the Greenville Circuit, and Robert Cox and Joshua Cannon were appointed to Portsmouth. (See *Minutes*.)

regained its proper tone, after being kept out of tune for five years by an unhappy division. We were kindly entertained by our friends and brethren; preachers and people were blest; and we parted in peace.

Monday, 30. I had a few people and several preachers at brother Seward's. The next day at Woolsey's barn (now Drumgoole's chapel)[88] I had a few people, they having had but short notice: here religion appears to be in a low state: I spent the evening with brother E. Drumgoole;[89] his house is not with the Lord, as he prayeth and longeth; yet I trust God hath made an everlasting covenant with the father, well ordered and sure.

Wednesday, *December* 2. I preached at my old friend W. Owen's, whom I first knew at Portsmouth; we had a small house, and a good meeting. In the evening I came to my aged friend Mathew Myrick's; whom I have known these twenty years, although never at his house before.

North Carolina

Monday, 7. I preached at brother Clayton's, near Halifax; and then hasted to brother Bradford's, where we had a small congregation the next day. Yesterday evening William Glendenning stayed here: he talked very boldly to R. W——; alleging that he was free, &c. I expect he will go on without fear or wisdom, until many of the Methodists will not receive him into their houses and hear the abuse of their ministers, people, and discipline.

We crossed Tar River and Town Creek, and came to T. Sheppard's, where we had all things richly to enjoy. I had my trials, and my spirit was greatly afflicted and humbled: I was glad to get alone to pour out my soul unto God.

Saturday, 12. This hath been to me a day of trial and consolation. It is wonderful to see how the people in this country are hid by swamps and creeks.

Sabbath day, 13. We set out in the midst of the rain to Spann's meeting house;[90] I had ten hearers, to whom I preached on Luke xii, 32. We came to brother Spann's, who has sold off his property, and is about to move to the high lands of South Carolina: the reason he assigns is laudable; and

[88] This chapel was a merger of Wolsey's, Drumgooles', Mason's and now Olive Branch. It was in Brunswick County, where Edward Drumgoole lived. (See note below.)

[89] Edward Drumgoole (1751–1835) was converted from Roman Catholicism near Sligo, Ireland, and came to America in 1770. Here he came under the influence of Robert Strawbridge and began preaching in 1773. He was one of the early Methodist leaders in Virginia and North Carolina. He married and located in 1786. His extensive correspondence is at the University of North Carolina. (Sweet: *Religion on the American Frontier, the Methodists*, 123–201.)

[90] Spann's meetinghouse was in Pitt County, North Carolina. Spann soon moved to South Carolina, near the present town of Ridge Spring, where he founded Spann's Church, which is still active.

I think God will be with him. It rained powerfully in the night, which brought me under great exercise about getting along, having been so often stopped by, and dipped in, the rivers and swamps.

Monday, 14. We crossed Neuse River at Whitefield's ferry, the river rising very fast. We passed North East and Goshen bridges, and Bear Swamp; all of which we crossed in safety, though not without fear: my feet were wet, my body cold, and my stomach empty, having had no dinner. I found a good fire, a warm bed, and a little medicine, each necessary in its place. No people make you more welcome to their houses than these: but is Christ welcome to their hearts? I am sensible of the want of more religion among them.

Friday, 18. After riding about twenty miles, I preached at Father V——'s;[91] I felt strangely set at liberty, and was uncommonly happy. Here we left Goshen circuit, and Sampson county.

Saturday, 19. We crossed the south branch of Black River, and came to Elizabethton, about fifty miles above Wilmington: we had a very cold day, and nothing to eat for thirty miles. Brother M'Rea met us near the town and took us to his house; and it was well he did, or we might have been lost in the woods. But the kindness of the people in supplying our wants made up for our toil—Lord, comfort them who comfort us! Here we had a quiet retreat, and spent the *Sabbath* in public and private exercises.

Monday, 21. We set out by sunrise, and had to work our way through the swamps, where I feared being plunged in headforemost. I have lately been much tried several ways; and much comforted. We came down Brunswick county, North Carolina, twenty miles to Norman's, within the line of South Carolina. Cross where you will between the States, and it is a miserable pass for one hundred miles west. I was much led out on Rev. xxi, 6–8. This country abounds with bays, swamps, and drains; if there were here no sinners, I would not go along these roads. I am in want of rest, and should be glad of better fare. O, for patience, faith, courage, and every grace! Sometimes I feel as though I could rejoice to die and go home: but at other times the work of God is in my way, and sometimes my own unworthiness.

South Carolina

Thursday, 24. We came to Kingston,[92] where I preached in an old Presbyterian meeting house, now repaired for the use of the Methodists. I spent the evening with W. Rogers, formerly of Bristol, where our wants were richly supplied: thus, sometimes we abound and at other times suffer want; and we may balance the one with the other.

[91] This was either Vick or Van. Both families were numerous in Sampson County.

[92] Asbury entered Horry County, South Carolina, from Brunswick County, North Carolina, about where the present Long's community is situated.

Christmas day, 25. We set out at six o'clock for Georgetown, and came to Yuahannah ferry, which we crossed and came to Wacamaw River: we were detained at the two ferries about three hours, and rested one, and came to Georgetown[93] about four o'clock in the evening; having ridden thirty-seven miles without eating or drinking, except a lowland hard apple, which I found in my pocket. The vanity of dancing in this place is in a good degree done away, and they have no play-house, and the people are very attentive: I trust that time and patience will bring all things about; that we shall not ride so many hundred miles in vain, and that so many prayers offered up, and tears shed for their welfare, will not be lost. After ten years' labour we have done but little; but if we could station a preacher here, we might yet hope for success. I found brother Joshua Cannon[94] had not laboured in vain; he hath established class meetings among white and black; and the good would have been still greater had prayer meetings been properly kept up. We try to do good, but who among us try to do all the good they can? For myself, I leave no company without fears of not having discharged my duty. Were it not for Jesus, who would be saved? When I have preached, I feel as though I had need to do it over again; and it is the same with all my performances. Brother Benjamin Blanton,[95] my faithful friend, who freely offered himself to go to South Carolina, now my companion in travel, had not preached for a month, so I thought it time for him to begin again, which he did in the evening. I preached on Psalm xii, 1, and on the *Sabbath* I preached on Deut. v, 12–14. In the afternoon the people were attentive and somewhat moved. I find the scene is changed in Georgetown; we have a number of very modest, attentive hearers, and a good work among the blacks. The Methodists begin to stand on even ground with their antagonists.

Monday, 28. We directed our course towards Charleston, and crossed Santee at Lenud's ferry, which is the best I know on the river. In the evening we reached Mr. Compton's: I felt for the man of the house, and was pleased in having the privilege of praying with them, and enjoyed great sweetness therein.

Tuesday, 29. We came to our dear brother Jackson's on Cainhoy River:[96]

[93] The Yuahannah Ferry was crossed just below the junction of the two Pee Dee rivers. The second ferry referred to was over Black River near Georgetown.

[94] Joshua Cannon was the preacher on the Georgetown Circuit. (See *Minutes.*)

[95] Benjamin Blanton, who came with Asbury, remained in South Carolina and was appointed to Charleston. He was later presiding elder in the same area.

[96] There must have been a church at Cainhoy by this time, for it was the seat of the famous Capers family and one of Asbury's favorite stopping places. It was difficult of access except by water, but a highway now reaches the place. A few years later a camp meeting was established there which continued for half a century or more. Only a cemetery, in which rests the body of Bishop Capers' mother, and the ruins of the old church remain. It was on a bluff near a creek and the Wando River. (Betts, *op. cit.*, 482.)

here we had the pleasure of hearing of some revival of religion among the children and domestics of the Methodists.

Wednesday, 30. We reached Charleston, having made it about seventy-four miles from Georgetown, along an excellent road. Here are the rich, the rice, and the slaves; the last is awful to me. Wealthy people settled on the rice lands of Cooper River hold from fifty to two hundred slaves on a plantation in chains and bondage: yet God is able of these stones, yea, of these slaveholders, to raise up children unto Abraham. My soul felt joyful and solemn at the thoughts of a revival of religion in Charleston. I find several young persons are brought into the fold of Christ.

Thursday, 31. Several of the preachers came into the city to conference. We had a melting time at the love feast at brother Wells's.

1796

1796

Asbury and Daniel Hitt arrive at Rehoboth Church in West Virginia

CHAPTER TWENTY-FIVE

South Carolina

Friday, January 1. I gave them a sermon suited to the beginning of the year, and the sacred fire was felt. *Saturday*, 2, we began our conference. *Lord's day*, 3, was a day of extraordinary divine power, particularly at the sacrament; white and black cried and shouted the praises of God—yea,

"Clap your hands, ye people all,
Praise the God on whom ye call."

Monday, 4. We again entered on the business of conference; present, about twenty members and seven graduates.

Tuesday, 5. Continued our business; we have great peace and love—see eye to eye, and heart to heart. We have now a second and confirmed account that Cokesbury college[1] is consumed to ashes, a sacrifice of £10,000 in about ten years! The foundation was laid in 1785 and it was burnt December 7, 1795. Its enemies may rejoice, and its friends need not mourn. Would any man give me £10,000 per year to do and suffer again what I have done for that house, I would not do it. The Lord called not Mr. Whitefield nor the Methodists to build colleges. I wished only for schools—Doctor Coke wanted a college. I feel distressed at the loss of the library.

Thursday, 7, we observed as a day of fasting and humiliation, to seek the blessing of God on the conference. We began, continued, and parted in the greatest peace and union. We concluded to send Jonathan Jackson

[1] See letter to Thomas Haskins, January 11, 1796.

and Josias Randle, alternately, as missionaries to Savannah and the ancient parts of Georgia. *Friday*, 8, most of our brethren took their leave of the city, and I had time for recollection. We have in some cases had to station one preacher where formerly there were two: I trust the cause to God, and he will support it for his own glory; I must look more to him and less to men, whether aged, middle-aged, young, married, or single, or great or small abilities. My mind is variously exercised about staying here. I lament the partiality of the people for and against particular preachers.

Sunday, 10. I gave them a discourse on Hab. ii, 1, 2: "I will stand upon my watch and set me upon the tower, and will watch to see what he will say unto me, and what I shall answer when I am reproved. And the Lord answered me, Write the vision, and make it plain upon tables that he may run that readeth it." At noon brother Henry Hill[2] made an attempt to preach in the street opposite St. Michael's church, but was prevented by the guard; however, it wrought right, for many were led to attend the church in the afternoon and evening meetings: there appears to be great moving one way or another.

Monday, 11. My soul is stayed upon God, momently looking upon him. In reading Mr. Winterbotham, I compared the great talk about President Washington formerly, with what some say and write of him now: according to some he then did nothing wrong; it is now said that he was always partial to aristocrats and continental officers: as to the latter, I ask, Who bought the liberty of the States? the continental officers:—and surely they should reap a little of the sweets of rest and peace: these were not chimney-corner whigs. But favours to many of the officers now would come too late—a great number of them are gone to eternity, their constitutions being broken with hard fare and labour during the war. As to myself, the longer I live, and the more I investigate, the more I applaud the uniform conduct of President Washington in all the important stations which he has filled.

Sunday, 17. My spirit felt awful through the morning: I preached to a full congregation, and had a solemn season; and in the afternoon I preached on Luke viii, 10. *Monday*, 18. I am still employed in reading: I admire the sterling truth contained in Mr. Wesley's writings on divinity.

Thursday, 21. Precious time—how it flies! I was greatly entertained and comforted in spirit in receiving from brother Southerland an account of the great, confirming blessing he hath experienced to his soul. O, that we could receive such accounts from every family! I have written to several of my ancient friends in Philadelphia. I may say of letters, as it was said of silver in the days of Solomon, "I make no account of that:" I suppose I must write nearly a thousand in a year.

[2] The Rev. Henry Hill was from North Carolina. He joined the conference in 1791 and served circuits in both the Carolinas. He was assigned to Charleston the first half of 1796 and to Broad River Circuit the latter half. He located in 1797.

Sunday morning, 24. I was so poorly as to be hardly able to rise from my bed; however, I made out to deliver two discourses in public to large congregations. *Monday*, I wrote, visited, and rode; I read but little. O time, precious time, how swiftly doth it fly!

Wednesday, 27. I have great reason to praise God that I am in a house, and not exposed to the dreadful rains and freshets that have taken place. We learn by late accounts that corn, rice, cattle, bridges, and we know not what, are swept away and destroyed by the late uncommon rains. I feel myself humbled before God, under a sense of my not having been as faithful to him as I might have been. I am rather too much delighted with reading on paper what I have read with my eyes in my travels through the continent.

Sunday, 31. Was much taken up with the work of the Lord: I preached in the morning and afternoon.

Monday, February 1. I have written in the most pointed manner to my dear brethren at Baltimore,[3] to establish prayer meetings in every part of the town. My mind is unhappy; I wish to be gone into the country to be about my Master's work.

We had a prayer meeting; but the spirit of prayer and supplication did not appear to be among the people. I have peace with God; but my soul is in continual heaviness for Zion.

Wednesday, 3. I had near two hundred and fifty of the African society at the love feast held for them in the evening. O, my God, display thy power! I received good news from Jesse Lee concerning the prospect of religion in Boston, Providence, and the District of Maine—that the preachers, societies, and quarterly meetings are lively. My soul at times is in heaviness through manifold temptations. I felt an impression on my mind when at prayer that I felt too much, and might fret myself because of evil doers; I resolve, through grace, to be more resigned to the Lord, and less distressed, lest I should lightly sin against God or myself in unnecessarily injuring my health.

Friday, 5, I spent in reading and writing, and observed it as a day of fasting and prayer. I felt myself under dejection of spirit. Ah! what a dreary world is this! my mind is under solemn impressions—the result of my reflections on God and souls. I will endeavour not to distress myself above measure. If sinners are lost, I cannot save them, neither shall I be damned for them. I was happy last evening with the poor slaves in brother Wells's kitchen, whilst our white brother held a sacramental love feast in the front parlour upstairs. I must be poor: this is the will of God concerning me.

The Methodists have now about ninety thousand members of society in Europe, about seventy thousand in America and the Islands, and about four hundred in Africa.

[3] See letter to John Hagerty, January 30, 1796.

Sunday, 7. We had an awful, solemn season, while I discoursed on the two thieves that suffered with the Lord; and still more so in the afternoon on our Lord's comment on the sixth commandment: it was dreadfully loud and alarming. I was pleased to hear that some were stricken with the power of God. I feel very weak in body, and find that age makes an alteration. But my soul is truly happy in the Lord, and his work is reviving amongst us.

Sunday, 14. I began the solemnity of the day by opening and applying our Lord's comment on the seventh commandment, which is designed to condemn the adultery of the heart. It appears to have been the will of our Lord not to give liberty for a second marriage while a former husband or wife is living. St. Paul undoubtedly understood it so, even when heathen husbands left their wives, or wives left their husbands.

Wednesday, 17. The city now appears to be running mad for races, plays, and balls. I am afraid of being out of my duty in staying here too long: my soul is among the lions; yet Christ is mine, and I trust my supreme desire is, "Holiness to the Lord." My soul longeth to be gone, like a bird from a cage.[4] I have been employed in visiting from house to house, and lament the superficial state of religion among the white people who are called Methodists. I have thought if we had entered here to preach only to the Africans, we should probably have done better.

Sunday, 21. I delivered two discourses on our Lord's Sermon on the Mount, and was loud, long, alarming, and not very pleasing.

Monday, 22. I felt myself indisposed, owing to the exertions of the days past.

Wednesday and *Thursday*, 24, 25. I was employed in putting my thoughts together on the unlawfulness of divorce—of having more than one wife, or taking a second on any consideration while the first is living. I begin to feel comfortable at the thoughts of leaving this city shortly. This makes me fear I ought not to stay here so long.[5] It is true, I have a thousand or twelve hundred hearers, and two or three hundred of these change with the day. My soul possesseth peace, but great unworthiness cleaveth to me. I am apprehensive I injure myself by giving too intense application to reading. In my early days I contracted a habit for this, and I cannot easily give it up.

Sunday, 28. My morning subject was Phillippians i, 8, 9. In the evening I treated on *wolves in sheep's clothing*: some laughed, some wept, and some were vexed. Ah! how I wish to make my escape and be gone! I must pay for this indulgence with pain of mind: I feel for these souls: many of them who have been sitting under my ministry, appear to be more hardened now than when I began first to preach to them; and no wonder, seeing they have so insulted the Spirit of God.

[4] See letter to Mrs. Martha Haskins, February 17, 1796.

[5] Asbury frequently spent around two months in Charleston during the winter.

Wednesday, March 2. For my unholiness and unfaithfulness, my soul is humbled: were I to stand in my own merit, where should I be or go, but to hell? The time drawing nigh when I expected to leave the city, I was visited by my poor Africans, and had their prayers and best wishes. And now, what have I been doing? I have preached eighteen sermons, met all the classes, fifteen in number, written about eighty letters, read some hundred pages, visited thirty families again and again. But who are made the subjects of grace? Such are my impressions, that I am apprehensive God will work more in judgment than in mercy, and that this will be an eventful year to the inhabitants of this place. In the course of my stay I have written more than three hundred pages on subjects interesting to the society and connexion.

Thursday, 3. I left the city; the rain of yesterday and today has made the road extremely wet and muddy; it was in our favour that we came over the Causeway at Ashley River, without swimming. We came in the evening, dripping, to father Eccles's,[6] having ridden thirty-four miles.

Friday, 4. We crossed Edisto River, and came to Island Creek.[7] At a pole-house I talked a while on 1 Chron. vii, 14, and administered the sacrament. My feet were as if they had been steeped in water.

We had to ride three miles for lodgings, hungry, wet, and weary. Since half-past eight yesterday we have ridden upwards of sixty miles. I am now turned fifty years of age, and feel it hard to flesh and blood to go upon the old line, as in former days. God is at work in this place, so that we do not labour and suffer altogether in vain. I was under some difficulties about getting along, owing to the great rains, which have so raised the water-courses that they are impassable. We at length directed our course towards Augusta; with deep wading, by the assistance of brother Moses Black,[8] and by the blessing of Providence, we came to father E——'s, a Lot in Sodom. It is all right that I should come to see these aged people, and preach to the young ones. I am weary, but I will travel on: I only want more of the spirit of faith and prayer. I feel very sensibly for my dear Charleston people; I doubt not but they think of and pity me. My feet have been wet every day, for four days successively; but the kindness of the people helpeth me greatly over these troubles.

Wednesday, 9. Rode twenty-five miles to Chester's.[9] Here I learned Edisto was impassable. If we had not hasted along as we did, we should

[6] Eccles lived at Beech Hill on the Edisto a little below Givhan's Ferry.

[7] Island Creek is now Ireland Creek. Asbury stopped at or near the present Walterboro.

[8] The Rev. Moses Black was born near Charleston and admitted to the conference on trial this year. He was appointed to Edisto Circuit and traveled with Asbury until he reached his appointment. In 1802 he went to Holston and died on the Carter's Valley Circuit in Tennessee on February 3, 1810, at the age of forty.

[9] This Chester must have lived in the upper western edge of Barnwell County and was not the same family that lived between Edgefield and Augusta. (See note under March 1, 1789.)

not have passed it in proper time, and I should have been prevented from visiting Georgia this year also. There are so many water-courses, and so few ferries, that going through this country in any certain time is like a lottery.

Thursday, 10. We sent notice through the neighbourhood, to collect a congregation; so I had the privilege of preaching to a people I had not addressed for six years. O! my soul, how dost thou travail for souls night and day!

Georgia

I crossed W——'s ferry; the point on the south side is washed like a beach, and the house swept away by the late freshets; I saw how the flood had ploughed up the street of Augusta: I walked over the ruins for nearly two miles, viewing the deep gulfs in the main street. I suppose they would crucify me if I were to tell them it is the African flood; but if they could hear me think, they would discover this to be my sentiment. I was honoured with the church to preach in; where I had about four hundred respectable hearers. I have delivered my own soul—it may be once for all. I have ridden about one hundred and ninety miles from Charleston into Georgia; I have attended four meetings; and have not had, in all, above six hundred hearers.

Wednesday, 16. I rode fifteen miles to Whiteoak; I was sick; the house was very open, and the wind blew powerfully. Dying! dead!—unpleasing appearances! We swam our horses across Little River, and had to ride fifteen miles after preaching to get our dinners.

Friday, 18. I was very much outdone before I reached Comb's meeting house, which was very open. I was very warm in preaching. I rode to G——'s in the evening, making it nearly twenty miles; when I came there I was so indisposed, that I was glad to go to bed. Next morning I felt better, and rode to the school at Coke's chapel; where, after preaching, I partially examined the scholars.

Thursday, 24. I had a few wealthy, and I fear, wicked people at Pope's chapel; I preached on our Lord's weeping over Jerusalem. We had deep wading across Long Creek, and made it nearly twenty miles to ——: very kind, but no religion here. Since I have been in Georgia, I have had a blessed time of consolation in my own soul. I must needs go through Petersburg.

South Carolina

I had to ride to Curltail River, and thence to the head of Reedy River,[10] twenty-eight or thirty miles. We got no food for man nor

[10] Curltail River was probably Little River in Abbeville County, and Reedy River was in lower Greenville County at Fork Shoals.

horse until we came to D——'s; I preached to his father twenty-two years ago.

Tuesday, 29. I held forth about an hour and a half on Acts iii, 26. We set out again about two o'clock, and had to ride for our dinner *only twenty miles.* We crossed Muddy and Lick Creeks, Little and Great Bush Rivers.[11] These afforded bodies of excellent land.

Wednesday, 30. We had a meeting of the trustees of Bethel school, and it was agreed it should be a *free school*; and that only the English tongue and the sciences should be taught. I drew up an address on behalf of the school in order to raise three hundred dollars per annum to support a president teacher. I dined with my unshaken friend, William Patridge,[12] an Israelite indeed. He hath all things richly to enjoy, and a good conscience also. He was formerly a travelling preacher amongst us, and laboured for and with us nearly as long as he was able. The weather is warm here as in the month of June to the north. I was so weary with the riding I could not sleep.

Sunday, April 3. A multitude of sinners came together at W. Suber's.[13] I feel myself still faint and feeble, and would not live always.

Monday, 4. I crossed Fair Forest, and came to J. Gist's, where I had to stop and rest. Since I came into South Carolina I have ridden through Newbury, Spartanburg, Union, and Lawrence counties. There is a general complaint of the want of corn in these parts; and no wonder, when we consider the great storm which they have had, and the number of stills in the country: the people here drink their bread as well as eat it. I am so very poorly in body that close study injures me. I crossed Lawson Fork at the high shoals a little below the Beauty Spot. I could not but admire the curiosity of the people—my wig was as great a subject of speculation as some wonderful animal from Africa and India would have been. I had about one hundred people at the meeting house: some came to look at, and others to hear me. We must needs go off without any dinner, intending to ride nearly forty miles to father Moore's, in Rutherford county, (N. C.) After brother M. and myself had preached, we passed the Cow Pens, where Morgan and Tarlton had their fray. We made it nearly twenty-five miles to the Upper Island ford, on the main Broad River; and after travelling until seven o'clock at night were glad to stop at brother S——'s, ten miles short of the place we intended to reach when we set out.

[11] Asbury went through Laurens County and into Newberry County, crossing Mudlick Creek and the Brush rivers.

[12] William Patridge (1754–1817) became a traveling preacher in Virginia in 1780 and went to South Carolina in 1788, serving Broad River and Edisto circuits. He retired in 1791 and lived in Newberry County, where Mount Bethel Academy was located. In 1815 he was readmitted and went to Georgia where he died at Sparta. (Betts, *op. cit.*, 172.)

[13] This was probably Mr. Suber, who lived near Whitmire.

North Carolina

Wednesday, 6. We came to Moore's: I was at a loss how to address myself to these people—it may be for the last time: it was laid on my heart to speak from our Lord's lamentation over Jerusalem. I felt awful among them.

Saturday, 9. We came to Cane Creek, in Burke county. We dined on some peach-pie in the woods. In the afternoon there arose a most dreadful storm of rain, with thunder and lightning: it was very awful; we cried to God for man and beast, and were preserved. We came in about seven o'clock, and were received by T. B. with great kindness.

Monday, 11. We crossed Lovelady's ferry and came to Connell's, where I met with several preachers. After preaching, I was going to administer the sacrament and discovered that what they had provided for wine was in reality brandy; so I desisted. Here I met Doctor B——ll, who is still praying and waiting for the consolation of Israel. I rode a mountainous path six miles to father W——'s, where we dined. Ah! what a round of continual running is my life! Of late, feeble as I am, I cannot help thinking of Cumberland, in Tennessee, and trying to go there: if I must go to Kentucky, I think it is time to go to Cumberland also.

Thursday, 14. We took our departure from Johns River, up the branches of Catawba: on our way we met with a half dozen living creatures, like men and women, who seemed quite pleased with their mountain wedding; they were under the whip, riding two and two as if they would break their necks; one had a white cloth like a flag, and the other a silk handkerchief; when they had spent their fire, they called at a still-house to prime again. I ascended about one mile up a mountain, and came to M. Davenport's: here I feel deep dejection of mind as well as great weakness of body, and as if I could lie down and die; owing, in some measure, I presume, to the great fatigue I underwent in ascending the mountain, which was very steep.

Tennessee

Saturday, 16. We set off at six o'clock, and directed our course up Toe River;[14] thence up the Rocky Creek through the gap of the Yellow Mountain,[15] to the head waters of Doe River;[16] we had to ride till eight o'clock at night. My mind is still under deep depression.

[14] The North Toe and South Toe rivers constitute the headwaters of the Nollichucky. Toe is an abbreviation of the Indian word *Estatoa*. (Price, *op. cit.*, I, 29.)

[15] The gap of the Yellow Mountain was Carver's Gap. (Williams: *Early Travels*, 303.)

[16] The Doe River rises in the mountains of North Carolina and runs into the Watauga at Elizabethton, Tennessee.

Sunday, 17. I preached at Dawe's[17] to about two hundred people; and then met the society, and had a melting season. The milk and water of this country are both as physic to me. I am afraid that such shocks as these will, sometime or other, overset me.

Monday, 18. I rested at Dunsworth's;[18] my body very feeble, and mind under exceeding dejection, with imaginary and real evils.

Tuesday evening, the preachers came in from Kentucky[19] and Cumberland.

Wednesday, 20. Our conference began in great peace, and thus it ended.[20] We had only one preacher for each circuit in Kentucky; and one for Greene circuit in Tennessee.[21] Myself being weak, and my horse still weaker, I judged it impracticable to attempt going through the wilderness to Kentucky; and have concluded to visit Nolachucky. I wrote an apology to the brethren in Kentucky for my not coming, and informed them of the cause.

Monday, 25. On the banks of Nolachucky I parted with our dear suffering brethren, going through the howling wilderness. I feel happy in God. Sinners appear to be hardened, and professors cold; the preachers, although young men, appear to be solemn and devoted to God, and doubtless are men who may be depended upon.

I came to C——'s, where I saw a Baptist minister, who had moved from Georgia to Kentucky. He appeared desirous of returning again. I was told he expressed his fears, that the ministers in Kentucky will be a curse to each other, and the people too. Good religion and such good land are not so easily matched together. We came to D——'s, and had a full meeting. Brother Hill and his aids had a great time on the Sabbath; and I trust the time to favour this people is come.

Sunday, May 1. We came to Acuff's chapel.[22] I found the family sorrowful and weeping, on account of the death of Francis Acuff, who from a fiddler became a Christian; from a Christian, a preacher; and from a preacher, I trust, a glorified saint. He died in the work of the Lord in Kentucky. I found myself assisted in preaching on Ephes. ii, 1, 2. The

[17] Dawes was an early settler on the Watauga. (See Williams: *Early Travels in Tennessee*, 303.)

[18] *Ibid.*

[19] There was a conference at Masterson's Station near Lexington, Kentucky, on the same date, the Rev. Francis Poythrees presiding in Asbury's absence. William Burke, James Campbell, and Joseph Dunn attended the conference in Tennessee.

[20] This conference was again held at Nelson's Chapel. (See notes under May 10, 1788, and April 22, 1795.)

[21] Asbury was able, however, to appoint two men to the Greene Circuit, John Page and Nathaniel Munsey. (See *Minutes*.)

[22] (See note under May 2, 1795.) Francis Acuff died in August, 1795, near Danville, Kentucky, while serving the circuit there. He was only twenty-five years of age. (See *Minutes*, 1796.)

house was crowded, and I trust they did not come together in vain. I was somewhat alarmed at the sudden death of Reuben Ellis,[23] who hath been in the ministry upwards of twenty years; a faithful man of God, of slow, but very solid parts; he was an excellent counsellor, and steady yoke-fellow in Jesus. My mind is variously exercised as to future events—whether it is my duty to continue to bear the burden I now bear, or whether I had not better retire to some other land. I am not without fears, that a door will be opened to honour, ease, or interest; and then farewell to religion in the American Methodist Connexion; but death may soon end all these thoughts and quiet all these fears.

Virginia

Thursday, 5. I came to ——'s; thence to the unmeaning meeting house, and found a wild, wicked people, to whom I preached on Gen. xix, 18. An appointment had been made for me to preach in Abingdon. As I expected there would be no opportunity, as the court was then sitting, I concluded to go off to Clinch,[24] but was informed there would be (by the will of the judges) an adjournment of the court for my preaching. I therefore went and preached at three o'clock, and had the judges, some of the lawyers, and very few of the citizens to hear me. As sentence was passed on a poor criminal this day, and two more were burnt in the hand, I judged I ought to meet the solemnities of the day, and spoke on, "Knowing therefore the terrors of the Lord, we persuade men"; but was shut up in my own mind.

Saturday, 7. I escaped from Abingdon as out of a prison, and rode to Clinch. I passed by Mr. Cummings's.[25] He hath not laboured for naught. Few men have a better house or plantation: but his plea is, "He put his life in his hand"; and so have I, every time I have crossed the wilderness and mountains. I expect a crown for my services. Were I to charge the people on the western waters for my services, I should take their roads, rocks, and mountains into the account, and rate my labours at a very high price. We crossed North Holston and came to Dickenson's, sixteen miles; where we had a congregation of about two hundred people.

Sunday, 8. In the morning I awoke very unwell. I took a few drops of camphorated spirits, Bateman's Drops, and paregoric, and found some

[23] Reuben Ellis died in February, 1796, in Baltimore, where he was stationed. (See *Minutes*, 1796.)

[24] By Clinch, Asbury meant Russell County. (Price, *op. cit.*, I, 239.)

[25] The Rev. Charles Cummings was a well-known Presbyterian preacher in Abingdon and Washington County, Virginia. (Summers: *History of Southwest Virginia*, 747.)

ease, although my headache and fever still continued. I made out to preach to about two hundred people.

Monday, 9. I hobbled over the ridge, through the capital part of Russell county, sixteen miles to Bickley's.[26] These people have lived in peace ever since the death of Benge,[27] the half-blooded Indian warrior, who was shot through the head while carrying off two women. He was a dreadful wicked wretch, who, by report, may have been the agent of death to nearly a hundred people in the wilderness, and on Russell. Here I preached to a few insensible people; and had time to read, write, and sleep in quiet. Yesterday our prayers were requested on behalf of F. Dickenson.[28] This day in the evening brother John Kobler[29] was called upon to perform her funeral solemnities. Perhaps she has been as great a female sufferer as I have heard of. The following account, in substance, was taken from her own mouth, some time ago, by J. Kobler, who performed her funeral rites.

Her maiden name was Dickenson. She was married to a Mr. Scott, and lived in Powell's Valley; at which time the Indians were very troublesome, often killing and plundering the inhabitants. On a certain evening, her husband and children being in bed, eight or nine Indians rushed into the house; her husband being alarmed, started up, when all that had guns fired at him. Although he was badly wounded, he broke through them all, and got out of the house. Several of them closely pursued him, and put an end to his life. They then murdered and scalped all her children before her eyes, plundering her house, and took her prisoner. The remainder of the night they spent around a fire in the woods, drinking, shouting and dancing. The next day they divided the plunder, with great equality; amongst the rest of the goods was one of Mr. Wesley's hymn books; she asked them for it, and they gave it to her; but when they saw her often reading therein, they were displeased, called her a conjurer, and took it from her. After this they travelled several days' journey towards the Indian towns; but, said she, my grief was so great I could hardly believe my situation was a reality, but thought I dreamed. To aggravate my grief, one of the Indians hung my husband's and my children's scalps to his

[26] Charles Bickley lived in the Castlewoods valley of Russell County, Virginia. (See *Journal* entries for April 28, 1790; May 14, 1796; September 24, 1801; Whatcoat's *Journal*, *op. cit.*, April 28, 1790.)

[27] Benge was a notorious half-breed Shawnee Indian who had led many raids against the settlers in the region. In 1796 while returning from a raid with captives he was killed near Big Stone Gap by Lieutenant Vincent Hobbs, who later became a Methodist preacher. (Summers, *op. cit.*, 441–43.)

[28] The woman was Mrs. Scott, née Dickenson. (Price, *op. cit.*, I, 241.) She was probably the daughter of the Mr. Dickenson with whom Asbury stayed on May 7. The Dickensons were numerous in that section of Russell County known as Castlewood.

[29] John Kobler was the elder over the Holston circuits. (See *Minutes*.)

back, and would walk the next before me. In walking up and down the hills and mountains, I was worn out with fatigue and sorrow: they would often laugh when they saw me almost spent, and mimic my panting for breath. There was one Indian who was more humane than the rest. He would get me water, and make the others stop when I wanted to rest. Thus they carried me on eleven days' journey, until they were all greatly distressed with hunger. They then committed me to the care of an old Indian at the camp, while they went off hunting.

Whilst the old man was busily employed in dressing a deer-skin, I walked backward and forward through the woods, until I observed he took no notice of me. I then slipped off, and ran a considerable distance and came to a cane-brake, where I hid myself very securely. Through most of the night I heard the Indians searching for me, and answering each other with a voice like that of an owl. Thus was I left alone in the savage wilderness, far from any inhabitants, without a morsel of food, or any friend to help, but the common Saviour and friend of all: to him I poured out my complaint in fervent prayer that he would not forsake me in this distressing circumstance. I then set out the course that I thought Kentucky lay, though with very little expectation of seeing a human face again, except that of the savages, whom I looked upon as so many fiends from the bottomless pit; and my greatest dread was that of meeting some of them whilst wandering in the wilderness.

One day as I was travelling, I heard a loud human voice, and a prodigious noise, like horses running. I ran into a safe place and hid myself, and saw a company of Indians pass by, furiously driving a gang of horses which they had stolen from the white people. I had nothing to subsist upon but roots, young grape vines, and sweet cane, and such like produce of the woods. I accidentally came where a bear was eating a deer, and drew near in hopes of getting some; but he growled and looked angry, so I left him, and quickly passed on. At night when I lay down to rest, I never slept, but I dreamed of eating. In my lonesome travels, I came to a very large shelving rock, under which was a fine bed of leaves. I crept in among them, and determined there to end my days of sorrow. I lay there several hours, until my bones ached in so distressing a manner that I was obliged to stir out again. I then thought of, and wished for home; and travelled on several days, till I came where Cumberland River breaks through the mountain.

I went down the cliff a considerable distance, until I was affrighted, and made an attempt to go back, but found the place, down which I had gone, was so steep that I could not return. I then saw but one way that I could go, which was a considerable perpendicular distance down to the bank of the river. I took hold of the top of a little bush, and for half an hour prayed fervently to God for assistance. I then let myself down by the little bush until it broke, and I went with great violence down to the bottom.

This was early in the morning, and I lay there a considerable time, with a determination to go no farther. About ten o'clock I grew so thirsty, that I concluded to crawl to the water and drink, after which I found I could walk. *The place I came through, as I have been since informed, is only two miles, and I was four days in getting through it.* I travelled on until I came to a little path, one end of which led to the inhabitants, and the other to the wilderness. I knew not which end of the path to take. After standing and praying to the Lord for direction, I turned to take the end that led to the wilderness. Immediately there came a little bird of a dove, colour near to my feet, and fluttered along the path that led to the inhabitants. I did not observe this much at first, until it did it a second or third time. I then understood this as a direction of Providence, and took the path which led me to the inhabitants. Immediately after her safe arrival she embraced religion, and lived and died an humble follower of Christ.

Saturday, 14. We passed Russell court house, and intended to go to Bickley's, but were met by a most violent storm of rain, thunder, and lightning. We had a most dreadful crack; the fire and scent were like the discharge of a great gun. I was much alarmed for nearly a mile with expectation or fear of what would overtake us. We found shelter from part of the storm in a poor cabin, where some people had stopped on their way to Cumberland. Cold, labour, and being in the rain cause me to feel very unwell.

Sunday, 15. How gladly would I have attended my bed, rather than my meeting; but it was fixed otherwise, and I had to stand in the door, pressed with people, and preach to about three hundred hearers. There was some stir among them. I felt better in soul and body after meeting than I did before. We passed through Wythe county, and rode seventy miles in two days.

Thursday, 19. I was crowded with stupid sinners of various descriptions, to whom I preached on Joshua xxiv, 19: "Ye cannot serve God," &c. It was a matter of surprise, that I not only refused to stay a night, but that I did not eat bread nor drink water in that place.

West Virginia

Friday, 20. We rode forty miles to Indian Creek, about fifteen miles above the mouth. We had no place to dine until we arrived at father Cook's,[30] about six o'clock. If I could have regular food and sleep, I could stand the fatigue I have to go through much better; but this is

[30] This was the father of Valentine Cook, Jr. The Cooks built the large fort on Indian Creek in 1770 near the present Greenville. In 1797 the Cooks built a meetinghouse on their land. Valentine Cook was captured by the Indians when he was a boy. (Bennett, *op. cit.*, 252 ff.)

impossible under some circumstances. To sleep four hours, and ride forty miles without food or fire, is hard: but we had water enough in the rivers and creeks. I shall have ridden nearly one thousand miles on the western waters before I leave them; I have been on the waters of Nolachucky to the mouth of Clinch; on the north, middle, and south branches of Holston; on New River, Green Brier, and by the head springs of Monongahela. If I were able I should go from Charleston (S. C.), a direct course, five hundred miles to Nolachucky; thence two hundred and fifty miles to Cumberland; thence one hundred to Kentucky; thence one hundred miles through that State, and two hundred to Saltville; thence two hundred to Green Brier; thence two hundred to Red Stone, and three hundred to Baltimore. Ah! if I were young again! I was happy to have a comfortable night's sleep, after a hard day's ride, and but little rest the night before. I have now a little time to refit, recollect, and write. Here forts and savages once had a being, but now peace and improvement.

Monday, 23. I rode to Rehobeth chapel, in the sinks of Green Brier, where we held conference with a few preachers. Here I delivered two discourses. *Thursday*, crossed Green Brier River, and had to pass along a crooked and dangerous path to Levin Benton's. My mind is in peace.

Friday, 27. I felt myself very heavy, my mind unprepared for the congregation at Gilboa meeting house, and could not preach with any satisfaction. After meeting the society, I came away much clouded. We came off from brother Crawford's about four o'clock, aiming at the Little Levels; but darkness came on, and we had to climb and blunder over the point of a mountain, in descending which my feet were so squeezed that the blood was ready to gush out of the pores: I could hardly help weeping out my sorrow: at length we came to brother Hamilton's,[31] where the kindness of the family was a cordial, and we went to rest about ten o'clock, and all was well.

Sunday, 29. I was very warm in body and mind at M'Neal's. In the afternoon (contrary to my sentiment and practice on the Lord's day) we took our departure, purposing to reach Morgantown on *Wednesday* evening, in order to attend an appointment made for me on *Thursday*, the second of June. We reached my old friend Drinnon's, who received us gladly, and entertained us kindly. Next day (*Monday*) we opened our campaign through the mountains, following a path I had thought never to travel again. Frequently we were in danger of being plucked off our horses by the boughs of the trees under which we had to ride. About seven o'clock, after crossing six mountains and many rocky creeks and fords of Elk and Monongahela Rivers, we made the *Valley of Distress*, called by the natives Tyger's Valley. We had a comfortable lodging at Mr. White's; and here I must acknowledge the kindness and decency of the family, and their

[31] John Smith lodged at Hamilton's and Hamilton is spoken of as pursuing the Indians with seventy men. (Withers: *Chronicles of Border Warfare*, 245.)

readiness to duty, sacred and civil. Thence we hastened on at the rate of forty-two miles a day. We had to ride four miles in the night, and went supperless to *the Punchins*, where we slept a little on hard lines.

After encountering many difficulties, known only to God and ourselves, we came to Morgantown. I doubt whether I shall ever request any person to come and meet me at the levels of Green Brier, or to accompany me across these mountains again,[32] as brother Daniel Hitt[33] has now done. O! how chequered is life! How thankful ought I to be that I am here safe with life and limbs, in peace and plenty, at kind brother John Stealey's.

Pennsylvania

Thursday, June 2. I gave them a discourse on, "Work out your own salvation with fear and trembling." I had half a dozen preachers and a congregation of serious hearers, and some wept. I was informed of an awful circumstance:—A man, aged seventy years, strangled his own son, to prevent his appearing as evidence against him for theft.

Thursday, 9. We crossed Great Youghiogheny, and came to Connel's Town,[34] where we had a good time. I preached on Acts iii, 26. Sister C——, who professed to find peace six or seven years ago, when I prayed with her, was now sick; I gave her counsel and medicine, and trust I left her better in soul and body.

Saturday, 11. I rode to Uniontown, and after a solemn meeting, I sat in conference with the preachers.[35]

Monday, 13. We left Uniontown, and rode about thirty-five miles, and the next day forty-five to J. Foster's.[36]

Maryland

Wednesday, 15. I came to Oldtown, and preached to a few people, at brother J. J. Jacob's,[37] and the next day rode nearly forty miles to father Funk's.[38]

[32] This was Asbury's eighth trip across the mountains to the region of southwestern Pennsylvania. His last previous trip here had been in 1792, and ill health prevented him visiting the region again until 1803.

[33] Daniel Hitt was presiding elder this year over the four circuits in the region: Clarksburg, Ohio, Redstone, and Pittsburgh. (See *Minutes.*)

[34] Connellsville, Pennsylvania, laid out as a town by Zachariah Connell on March 21, 1793. (Mulkearn and Pugh: *A Traveller's Guide to Historic Western Pennsylvania*, 215.)

[35] This was the fourth and last of Asbury's district conferences held at Uniontown, Pennsylvania.

[36] Mr. Foster lived near Cumberland, Maryland.

[37] (See note under July 21, 1785.) Jacob was a native of Anne Arundel County, Maryland. With two other local preachers, William Shaw and Thomas Lakin, he did much to establish Methodism in the mountainous regions of West Virginia, Maryland, and

Friday, 17. We rode forty-two miles, and were weary enough.

Saturday, 18. I came to brother Samuel Philip's, and was glad to lay me down and rest, having ridden about two hundred miles on uneven roads in five days and a half.

Sunday, 19. I was musing in my own mind how I could best spend the morning of that day. I concluded to call the family into the room, and address them pointedly, one by one, concerning their souls: I did so, and hope it was not in vain. In the afternoon I preached on the twenty-third Psalm.

Tuesday, 21. I preached in Fredericktown[39] at ten o'clock, and at Liberty town at five o'clock.

Wednesday, 22. I had some life at the new meeting house on the Ridge. I borrowed a horse to ride nine miles, and then made out to get to Baltimore. O what times are here! The academy is crowded,[40] they have five teachers, and nearly two hundred scholars. I will now take a view of my journey for some months past. From the best judgment I can form, the distance is as follows: from Baltimore to Charleston (S. C.) one thousand miles; thence up the State of South Carolina two hundred miles; from the centre to the west of Georgia two hundred miles; through North Carolina one hundred miles; through the state of Tennessee one hundred miles; through the west of Virginia three hundred miles; through Pennsylvania and the west of Maryland and down to Baltimore four hundred miles. I was employed in town as usual in preaching and meeting the classes, &c. I continued in town until *Thursday*, 30, and then set off, and came in the evening to Esquire Gough's, our ancient lodging, and was received with their usual kindness.

Friday, *July* 1. Came to Abingdon, and saw the walls of Cokesbury with some pain of mind. We came in the evening to Mr. Josias Dallam's, whose house was the first home I had in these parts. Sister Dallam is worn out with affliction; but her confidence in God continues, and appears to grow stronger.

Saturday and *Sunday*, 2, 3. I attended Cecil quarterly meeting; and

Pennsylvania. Jacob seems to have lived in present West Virginia, but after his marriage he lived in Allegany County, Maryland, near Oldtown. His son, who bore the same name, was the third governor of West Virginia. (Lednum, *op. cit.*, 392, 393; Scharf: *History of Western Maryland*, II, 1458–60; *National Cyclopaedia of American Biography*, XII, 430, 431; *West Virginia Historical Magazine*, January, 1956, article by Lawrence Sherwood.)

38 Father Henry Funk lived in Virginia, five miles from Stovertown.

39 See letter to John Kobler, June 21, 1796.

40 The Baltimore Academy, called by some the second Cokesbury College, opened in a former dance hall in Light Street, May 2, 1796. Fire destroyed the academy and the adjoining Light Street Church on December 4, 1796, one year to a day after a similar fate had befallen Cokesbury College. (Coke, *op. cit.*, 232; Roberts: *Centenary Pictorial Album*, 76, 77; *Federal Gazette and Baltimore Daily Advertiser*, April 30, 1796; Archer: *An Authentic History of Cokesbury College*.)

spent *Monday*, 4th, at Mr. Richard Bassett's; I was so unwell, that if my company had not been entertaining I should have been in bed.

Wednesday, 6. We had a solemn season at Dudley's chapel: it was like a Sabbath.

Thursday, 7. I rode to Choptank (now Greensborough) through excessive heat; Sarah Cook was watching for me, and when I came she could hardly bear my presence; she seemed as deeply affected as if I had been her father, knowing the great affection that subsisted between her deceased father and myself.[41] I am now happy that it is not in me to weep as do others, or I might never wipe my eyes. I preached on Isa. lvii, 18–21.

Sunday, 10. I went to meeting under great heaviness; and there was some among the people. I dined with Wm. Moore, where I prophesied seventeen years ago. How few are left now that heard me then!

Monday, 11. The heat has been for some time, and still is, excessive; I doubt if it be not equal to that in Georgia and the islands. We rode fifteen miles to Quantico chapel; where we had a number of gay people; but it appeared as if they did not understand or even hear what I said. We have reason to praise God for an abatement of the heat of the weather, which, had it continued, would have been insupportable. We had excessive rain, attended with thunder and lightning.

We came to Snow Hill, on Pocomoke River. I called on the weeping widow Bowen, whose late husband, Jepthah, after being the principal in building a house for divine worship, died in peace. Here I met about one thousand people: being unable to command the congregation from the pulpit, I stood in one of the doors, and preached to those who were out of the house.

Delaware

I rode eight miles to the seashore; when we came near we felt the cool sea breeze very powerfully. I lodged with Solomon Evans, whose house I visited sixteen years ago: here are two people above seventy years of age, who have lived together forty-eight years.

Tuesday, 19. We rode forty miles to Lewistown; we stopped to dine near H——'s grand mill seat. My spirits of late keep up greatly, not being subject to depression as heretofore. It cleared away about noon, and gave us the opportunity of riding two miles out of Lewistown, after preaching to the brethren and the Africans. I dined with Mr. Shankland, whose house was the first that was opened to me in this place. We then urged our way up the country, and escaped the rain until we came within two miles of Milford; it then poured down very heavily, and we came in dripping about eight o'clock.

Friday, 22. We had a living love feast: many opened their mouths, but

[41] Sarah Cook was a daughter of Judge Thomas White.

spoke too much of what was past. We had an exceeding great company, to whom I preached on Isaiah lxii, 12. The two following days, *Saturday* and *Sunday*, I attended Dover quarterly meeting; where I suppose we had nearly two thousand people. It was a living, open season: there was great sweetness and love among the brethren.

Monday, 25. About thirty-five minutes before I began meeting, I received the last loving request of our dear brother William Jessop, which was to preach his funeral sermon: I had my difficulties in speaking, and the people in hearing, of a man so well known and so much beloved: he was always solemn; and few such holy, steady men, have been found amongst us. I stopped at Middletown, Wilmington, and Chester, on my way to Philadephia.[42]

Pennsylvania

Thursday, 28. I preached on Psalm xxiii, 24.[43] I have thought that we should preach as if we expected no help from the people; yea, as if we believed that enemies of God and us were in the congregation. I began meeting classes in the city. I had some pleasure in receiving news of a revival of religion in the South; likewise from the Eastern States. But there are great failures among the preachers on account of health, &c., preventing their travelling and standing to the work. Brother Blanton has given me an account of the late fire in Charleston, and says that about five hundred houses are destroyed.

Saturday, 30. I began reading Mr. Fletcher's Portrait of St. Paul: the notes are significant, and show what a minister of the Gospel ought to be, and what he may be through grace.

Sunday, 31. I had some life and more liberty at Ebenezer in the morning at five o'clock: I must needs attend the Second African church; and at half-past seven o'clock, in the great unwieldy house and congregation in Fourth Street, I preached on John i, 17.

Monday, *August* 1. I drew the outlines of a subscription, that may form a part of a constitution of a general fund, for the sole purpose of supporting the travelling ministry; to have respect,

First, To the single men that suffer and are in want.

Secondly, To the married travelling preachers.

Thirdly, To the worn-out preachers.

Fourthly, The widows and orphans of those who have lived and died in the work. And

Fifthly, To enable the yearly conference to employ more married men; and, finally, to supply the wants of all the travelling preachers, under certain regulations and restrictions, as the state of the fund will admit.

[42] See letters to parents, July 29, 1796, and August, 1796.

[43] This psalm has only six verses. There is no indication of the correct passage.

Thursday, 4. I was called upon by the African society in Campington to open their new house, which I did, on Rom. i, 16–18, and had an unwieldy congregation of white and black. Brother Dickins gave a lively exhortation on the new birth.

Friday, 5. Having concluded on the presentation of the subscription, I hasted with it from house to house. After dinner we came to Germantown, where I preached in the academy at six o'clock to a large congregation of women. I lodged once more at the house of mother Steele and her daughter Lusby; having had an acquaintance of twenty-two years.

New Jersey

Sunday, 7. It being rainy in the morning, my congregation was not very large at Trenton. I preached on Isaiah lxii, 10. 1. The charge to the ministry to go through the gates as ministers and Christians. 2. Prepare the way—removing all the difficulties. 3. Cast up the highway—repentance, regeneration, and sanctification. 4. Gather out the stones—wicked ministers and people. 5. Set up the standard—that is, form the Christian church; give the standard of Christian doctrine and experience. In the afternoon I preached on Heb. x, 38. It is a dry time, and we cannot get along: I was sorry I did not preach in the street.

Monday, 8. We directed our course through the Jerseys towards New York; passing through Pennytown,[44] and along an agreeable, well-improved part of the country.

Tuesday, 9. We made our way twenty-five miles to brother McCullough's,[45] near Schooley's Mountain[46]—properly a remnant of the Blue Ridge. After a good meeting at brother McCullough's, we went to lay the foundation of a new meeting house: we sung part of Dr. Watts's hymn on *The Corner Stone*, and prayed. I then had to lend a hand to lay the mighty corner stone of the house: we then sung and prayed, and retired to brother Budd's,[47] an Israelite indeed; my never-failing friend in time, and I hope will be to all eternity.

[44] Pennytown was the present Pennington in Mercer County, New Jersey. It was then a post town.

[45] Colonel William McCullough lived at Hall Mills. On this visit Asbury laid the cornerstone of the meetinghouse, and McCullough renamed the place Asbury in his honor. This was the first town to be so named. (Honeyman: *Northwestern New Jersey*, II, 676; Snell: *History of Warren and Sussex Counties*, 705–8.)

[46] Schooley's Mountain was a section of the mountain chain that ran through northwestern Morris County, New Jersey. From its summit four roads ran north, west, east, and south. (See Carey and Lea's map, 1822; Gordon's *Gazetteer*, 233–34.)

[47] This was probably John Budd, one of a prominent family in southern New Jersey. Asbury stopped with some of them frequently. Budd's Lake, a resort near Hackettstown, called Budd's Pond in Gordon's Gazetteer, was a part of the original Budd property in this area. (See New Jersey Archives, Abstracts of Wills, V, 75, 449.)

Wednesday, 10. I thought it good not to be idle, so I went to Hacketts-town,[48] and preached on, "The promise is to you, and to your children," &c.; we had few people, but a feeling, serious time. Thence we rode to Dover;[49] where we had many people at a short warning: I admired the solemnity of the women; the men appeared to be outdone with the heat and labours of the day.

Friday, 12. We rode twenty miles to brother Dickinson's:[50] he is now an official character among us, and can remember, when he was a child, how godly men came to the house of his father, preaching, praying, and talking about religion, as was the case at my father's house when I was a child.

Saturday, 13, I rode to Elizabethtown, where I preached: the next day I met the classes. Having heard many things of Mr. Austin,[51] many of which were very wild, I went and heard for myself: he explained the 22d chapter of the Revelation of Jesus Christ to St. John, and applied it to the Millennium and reign of Christ upon earth: his foretelling the time and place

[48] Asbury may have preached in Hackettstown in the home of Samuel Pew, where Ezekiel Cooper preached in 1786. Methodist preaching seems to have started here in the home of Obadiah Ayer, perhaps in 1784; an erroneous statement in *Historical Statement on Trinity Methodist Church* gives the date as 1754. A society was formed on December 1, 1832, and a meetinghouse was erected immediately thereafter. (Phoebus, *op. cit.*, 47; Snell, *op. cit.*, 582–86; Shampanore: *History and Directory of Warren County*, I, 1, 15; New Jersey Archives, Abstract of Wills, V, 393.)

[49] It seems likely that Asbury preached at Dover, New Jersey, in a house owned by Sylvanus Lawrence "on the road from Center Grove to Succasunna Plains." It had been a hotel, and town meetings had been held there. (See Alonzo B. Searing's account in Platt's *Dover Dates*, 25, 55.) It is possible that this Lawrence was the person referred to by Asbury on May 16, 1811, as "father Laursnats." This seems to be one of the earliest references to the community under the name of Dover. It is not shown on the Carey and Lea map of 1822, and Platt finds no reference to it earlier than 1798. (Platt, *op. cit.*, 25, 55; *History of Grace Church, Dover*, 1901, 25th Anniversary Bulletin; *Historical Statement on First Methodist Church, Dover*, F. F. Reed; Gordon's *Gazetteer of New Jersey*, 133; 100th Anniversary of Methodism in Dover, First Church Anniversary Program, 1938.)

[50] This was doubtless Brainard Dickinson, one of the founders of Methodism in Chatham, New Jersey. He lived at Cheapside or Washington Place and with Matthias Swaim and Isaac Searles was largely responsible for building a church before 1800. Ezekiel Cooper preached there in 1786. (Hampton: *History of Chatham Methodism*, 8–11; Pitney: *History of Morris County*, I, 303.)

[51] The Rev. David Austin, pastor of the First Presbyterian Church, Elizabeth, New Jersey, from 1788 to May, 1797, was also the author of an excellent series of discourses published in four volumes under the title *The American Preacher*. He became interested in prophetic studies and devoted much time to the discussion of the millennial reign of Christ, predicting the second coming and the end of the world on May 15, 1796. He persisted in such a fanatical course until the presbytery severed his relation with the church in May, 1797. He returned to Connecticut, where he was born, and eventually regained a more balanced attitude on the question because he was later readmitted to the Presbyterian ministry, although for some years his erratic course kept him from the pulpits of his church. (Hatfield: *History of Elizabeth, New Jersey*, 596–603.)

of the coming and kingdom of Christ; General Washington being Zerubbabel, and himself Joshua the high priest, and the ploughing up of a certain field—all this appeared to me like wildness of the brain.

New York

Monday, 15. We rode to New York: whilst crossing the ferry some foolish, wicked people, uttered so many *damns*, that I was a little afraid the Lord would sink the boat: I asked a man if he had any chalk to lend me that I might mark down the curses the company gave us on our passage of thirty or forty minutes. I was taken up in meeting classes and visiting from house to house a good deal of my time in the day, and I frequently preached at night. I read Watson's Apology for the Bible.

Sunday, 21. I went over to Brooklyn, where we have a small society: I had very few hearers except those who came from the city. I administered the sacrament, and we had some life. We then returned to the city, where I preached in the afternoon to about one thousand six hundred people, some of whom were wicked and wild enough. The preachers had pity upon me, and desired me to preach only twice this Sabbath. In my own soul I feel happy, but on account of the Church of God, and poor sinners, awful. It appears as necessary to preach conviction and conversion among our own, as among other congregations. O! when will the Lord appear as in ancient times?

Monday, 22. I met three living classes; several among whom professed perfect love. The weather is excessively warm and dry: people are sickly and dying, especially children; I find my body very weak: preaching at night added to the mosquitoes, causes me to sleep very little.

Wednesday, 24. We have still very great heat: it appears to me to be *unhealthy, judgment weather*: I feel almost spent. I generally walk three or four miles a day, pray ten or twelve times, in the congregation, families, and classes; my sleep is interrupted with pain and heat.

Thursday, 25. I was much fatigued in meeting classes and visiting from house to house; but the Lord was present to bless, which gave me consolation. In the evening we had a full house; I was uncommonly assisted in preaching; and there was much weeping in the congregation. It is impossible to preach to these people till you are well acquainted with them; but here I have no continuing city: next week I go hence.

Sunday, 28. I preached in the morning at the old church; in the afternoon at the new church, on Heb. ii, 3; and in the evening at the old church again, on Rev. iii, 2, 3, besides meeting six classes in the course of the day: in general I have had no extraordinary assistance in preaching of late. Brother Lee[52] preached twice in the north end of Broadway; the congre-

[52] Wilson Lee (1764–1804) was born in Sussex County, Delaware. He was received on trial in 1784 when only twenty years of age and was appointed to Alleghany. He

gation appeared serious and attentive. Notwithstanding the labours of the day were considerable, I was not much wearied. In meeting the society, I observed to them, that they knew but little of my life and labours, unless in the pulpit, family, or class meetings; that they were unacquainted with my labours even in that city, much less could they tell where I had been, and what I had been doing for one year.

Tuesday, 30. I delivered my concluding discourse on Isaiah lvii, 18:—1. The penitent backslider. 2. The Lord hath seen his ways; 3. Healing him; 4. Leading him; 5. Restoring comforts to him. We had some serious, feeling souls at our meeting.

Wednesday, 31. I had a meeting with the leaders in close conference and found it necessary to explain some parts of our discipline to them particularly that of the right of preachers to expell members, when tried before the society or a "select number," and found guilty of a breach of the law of God and our rules; and that if an appeal were made, it should be brought before the quarterly meeting conference, composed of travelling and local preachers, leaders, and stewards, and finally be determined by a majority of votes. I found it also needful to observe there was such a thing as heresy in the Church; and I know not what it is if it be not to deny the Lord that brought them, and the eternity of the punishment of the damned, as is virtually done by the Universalists. *Schism* is not dividing hypocrites from hypocrites, formal professors from people of their own caste; it is not dividing nominal Episcopalians from each other, nominal Methodists from nominal Methodists, or nominal Quakers from nominal Quakers, &c. But *schism* is the dividing real Christians from each other, and breaking the unity of the Spirit. I met the trustees; and after going hither and thither, and being much spent with labour through the day, I gave them a discourse at the new house (in the evening), on Acts xx, 32. My attempt was feeble but faithful.

Friday, *September* 2. I left the city, stopped at father Oakley's,[53] twenty miles from New York, where a few people came together, to whom I preached on Acts iv, 12; and at night I was enabled to take a little rest.

Saturday, 3. Notwithstanding the rain I rode twelve miles to the White Plains quarterly meeting, where I enlarged on Ephes. vi, 13–18; being Paul's exhortation to the use of the whole armour of God. I was in great heaviness through temptation and infirmity of body. I lodged with Elijah Crawford:[54] this house is for God.

Sunday, 4. I was very low, but attended the love feast; I stood in one

served circuits from Kentucky to Massachusetts until 1804, when he was declared superannuate, though only forty years of age. He died suddenly on October 11, 1804, while at prayer with a sick friend. (*Minutes*; Sprague's *Annals*, 91; Bangs, *op. cit.*, I, 300; Seaman, *op. cit.*, 134–35.)

[53] Oakley was an elderly leader of the New Rochelle church.

[54] Asbury frequently stopped at the Crawford home. John Crawford, son of Elijah, established the work at Coeyman's in 1789.

of the windows, and preached very loud to a large congregation, on Heb. xii, 25. There were some feeling, gracious souls present. I was desired to preach in Bedford, but declined it for several reasons. I cannot stand such constant exertions. I have felt very severe pain in one of my shoulders, much like that I experienced after Cecil quarterly meeting. I lodged with brother Davis, where we had the company of one who may be a disciple of mine: I hope to see him yet in the kingdom of grace and glory: should he live to read these lines he will know whom I mean.

Monday, 5. I rode fifteen miles to the widow Banks's, to tarry for a night. My soul is in peace, and Christ is mine; but trouble will come: I am not yet all immortal and at rest; my rheumatic affections are very severe; I was imprudent in making, and my indisposition prevented my attending my appointments.

Connecticut

We came off in the morning for Redding; fed at Ridgefield, and reached my journey's end about one o'clock, about twenty-three miles. On my way I dined with lawyer Smith, and preached at Sanford's, on 1 Peter i, 13–15: in doing which I pointed out,—1. The most leading features that formed the character of the people addressed—elect, begotten again; scattered abroad by persecution and by the ministry of the word; suffering ministers and saints of God: 2. The subject on which they were addressed—to *gird up the loins of their mind*, and hope for great grace when Christ shall appear to overthrow Jewish superstition and heathen idolatry; *obedient children*, to fear, trust in, and love the Lord, and to keep all his commandments—to be holy, according to the nature and will of God, and his great and gracious promises.

Wednesday, 7. We had very bad roads over hills and mighty rocks to Oxford, twenty-eight miles; and after dinner, eight miles more to Derby; where I preached in brother H——'s house to about sixty people, on, "If the righteous scarcely be saved," &c. I felt my pain, but could thank the Lord for all things.

Thursday, 8. Was a day of pain to my body, but peace to my soul. I have been of late attending quarterly meetings, and have felt great heat and colds, and changes of weather. We came to New Haven, where I preached in brother William Thatcher's house, near the foundation of the college; we were crowded, and I was elaborate on Rom. i, 16–18.

Friday, 9. We rode solitary on the sand to Middletown. We dined with Captain Hall, who received us kindly, and entertained us comfortably.

Saturday and *Sunday*, 10, 11. We had many brethren and sisters from distant towns, at the quarterly meeting: here I preached on 1 Peter iv. 12–15, and on Isaiah lxii, 12; and was much at liberty, and a little comforted at the love feast and sacrament. Walking backward and forward tended to fatigue my body as well as speaking. As I thought, the preachers have been very acceptable to the people this year.

Monday, 12. I came to Old Haddam. Here they have built a new meeting house; and there are some gracious souls here. I sensibly felt the effects of heat and the labours of the day. We made it fifteen miles to father John Wilcox's.[55] I conclude, that since I have left New York I have ridden about one hundred and forty miles, and a great part of the way is rough and rocky; my body is full of infirmities, and my soul of the love of God. I think God is returning to this place; and that great days will yet come in New England.

Wednesday, 14. Was an exceedingly warm day. The Episcopal house here is grand indeed. We passed Hadlyme; thence to Millington, where we had many to hear at kind brother P——'s.

Thursday, 15. I had twenty miles to New London. My brethren have given me work enough. I feel like a man of a feeble body, but my soul enjoys a sweet calm and pure love; I cannot seek or desire anything but God. I refused to go into the court house to preach, but we had a gracious season at a dwelling house.

Friday, 16. We came to Poquetanuck, a little town of attentive people: I preached on, "The Son of man is come to seek and to save that which was lost": an aged man cried out, and rising up at the close of the meeting, delivered his testimony: what he is I cannot infallibly say; he spoke in too high terms of me to my face.

Saturday, 17. I came with a heavy burden to Norwich Landing; I held forth in the academy made out of a Separate meeting house: there were few present besides the brethren from other towns; I enlarged on, "If ye be reproached for the cause of Christ, happy are ye, for the spirit of glory and of God resteth upon you; on their part he is evil spoken of, but on your part he is glorified." The persons under sufferings—those who were the friends to, and followers of, Jesus—partakers of the Spirit of God, as a spirit of glory teaching them to believe, to love, and suffer, and give glory to God and Christ.

Sunday, 18. We held our feast of charity at eight o'clock: it was a sweet, refreshing season; several talked very feelingly, among whom were some aged people; many praised God for the instrumentality of the Methodists in their salvation. My spirit felt awful this morning, and my body unwell; however, at the time appointed I began preaching on Romans viii, 6–8. A Universalist had his book and pen, or pencil, I suppose, ready to take down my discourse; I said, "Stop, let that gentleman write"; but it appeared as though his fingers or heart failed him: brother Pickering[56] had

[55] See *Journal* entry for June 13, 1802.

[56] George Pickering was on the Boston and Needham Circuit and had been at Lynn the previous year.

preached a sermon in that house, which had been printed and traduced. Serious impressions appeared to be made on the minds of some of the audience. After spending about four hours in the congregation (including sacrament and love feast), I passed the afternoon in retirement at my lodgings, being unwell. This day I was led out greatly for New England; I believe God will work among this people; perhaps they have not had such a time here for many years: the power of God was present; some felt as at heaven's gate—two or three aged women spoke as on the borders of eternity, and within sight of glory. Cold as the evening was, I was under the disagreeable necessity of riding ten miles; I crossed the Williamantic[57] at Lloyd's bridge, and came in late to brother Fuller's. I was pleased to hear an aged mother (formerly a Separatist) tell the dealings of God with her before her daughter (now brother Fuller's wife) was born.

Monday, 19. We rode through Windham, Scotland, and Abington. After dining at Captain P——'s, we rode on to Thompson; a few of the preachers were present, and we were able to form a conference. We talked together, and rejoiced in the Lord. That evening and the next morning, *Tuesday*, 20, and *Wednesday*, 21, we were closely employed; we had about thirty preachers, some of whom were from the Province of Maine, three hundred miles distant, who gave us a pleasing relation of the work of God in those parts. I delivered a discourse on Acts xxvi, 18, 19, and we ordained seven deacons and five elders. About four o'clock I took my leave of town, and stopped at Eastford, and saw father ——, a solemn saint—lamenting the decline of religion among the Baptists.

Thursday, 22. We rode thirty-five miles to East Hartford, where I gave a discourse to a few, on Zeph. iii, 12, 13. *Friday*, 23, we rode to Waterbury, where I preached in the Separate meeting house[58] at four o'clock. Had we not fallen in with Mr. B., we might have missed our way, and not have reached the place till sunset.

Saturday, 24. We passed along an exceedingly uneven and rocky road through Salem[59] and Oxford; the appointment was not made in the latter place, so we dined on what came to hand. Came on to New Stratford, and thence to the widow B——'s in North Stratford. I have been under great heaviness, and was unwell in body. We have ridden upwards of one hun-

[57] Asbury could not have crossed the Williamantic River on his way up the Shetucket towards Windham. A Connecticut map of 1818 indicates that his probable route was along the road which crosses the Shetucket two miles south of Windham. Lloyd's bridge must have been located at that point.

[58] The Separate meetinghouse was in that part of old Waterbury known as Columbia. Asbury was entertained at the farm home of Amos Hotchkiss nearby. In an address at the Waterbury Methodist Church on June 30, 1889, Anson F. Abbott, a descendant, declared that about a hundred Methodists were entertained on this occasion in 1796 in the Hotchkiss home, barn, cider mill, and other accommodations, and that Asbury made his own tea and ate only the crust of some rye bread.

[59] Salem was the present Naugatuck, six miles south of Waterbury.

dred miles in the last three days; but still I must go on; there is no rest. I attended at Chestnut Hill,[60] and preached on 1 Thess. i, 5: a flatness among these people was very visible. This was the first house that was built for the Methodists in Connecticut, and it is not finished yet.

Monday, 26. We rode along to Fairfield, Norwalk, and arrived at Stamford, about twenty-eight or thirty miles. On our way we stopped to feed our horses, and found a woman that was sick, with whom I talked and prayed. I felt as if I should not preach again in haste, if at all, in Stamford.

New York

We crossed the State line and came to New Rochelle, in the State of New York, twenty-three miles—heavy and hungry. We stopped at Clark's,[61] where I preached on Isaiah lxii, 1, and we were crowded with people. I enjoy peace of mind, but am deeply tempted; yet few minutes pass in which my soul is not engaged in prayer.

Thursday, 29. I preached on Luke xii: "Who then is a faithful and wise servant," &c. I began to confer with the brethren as they came in, and do the business by scraps, as we would come at it. We were in doubt whether some of the preachers would come at all, on account of the rumours of the yellow fever, which still appeared in parts of the city. On *Friday*, we entered fully into our work; and on *Saturday* we concluded our short conference, the preachers being desirous to depart. We had a solemn, peaceable sitting; and so also were our congregations. I preached at our house in John Street on Mark ix, 1: "There be some standing here which shall not taste of death until they have seen the kingdom of God come with power"; but I had little opening.

Sunday, *October* 2. I preached at the house in John Street, on Eph. iv, 11–13, and had great enlargement: the feelings of the people were touched, and my own also, as if it had been the last time, as it probably may be with some of my hearers, if not myself: I could not have been much more moved; it was with difficulty I could continue speaking. In the afternoon, at the new house, there was also a move in the congregation whilst I enlarged on 1 Cor. iv, 10, 11. I ordained in both houses in all eight deacons and seven elders, and was on my feet six hours in the course of this day.

Monday, 3. In the morning the weather had a stormy appearance, so that no passage was to be had at Powles Hook.[62] We were as yet safe on

[60] There are two Chestnut hills in Connecticut. Asbury refers to the locality near Stratford.

[61] Peter Clark, active in the New Rochelle church, lived on the west border of that town near the Post Road on its way to Kingsbridge and New York City.

[62] Powles Hook or Paulus Hook is now Jersey City.

shore, but brothers George Roberts and Jacob Egbert went to Whitehall where they found a boat that would sail, *sink or swim*, for Van Duzer's[63] Landing, upon Staten Island: I did not like the appearance of things, but submitted to go, with a high tide and the wind at N.E. We passed the bay, ten miles over, in the space of an hour: when we were within one mile of the dock the wind shifted to N.W. and blew powerfully: the people on shore were alarmed, and had the skiff ready to take us up, expecting we should fill and sink, or be beaten off and strike the rocks: after some time we secured the boat, landed the men, but left the landing of the horses for better weather. We dined, and rode up to the Blazing Star,[64] greatly against my inclination. At the ferry, the men were unwilling to move, and kept us on the bleak marsh sometime: when they came, they told us in anger, it was at our own risk of men and horses if we ventured. We suddenly turned and went to a friend's house,[65] fed, and dried a little, and then rode twelve miles more, and stopped within a mile of Amboy ferry.[66]

New Jersey

Tuesday, 4. We came to the Ferry; and after being detained about an hour, we made out to get a passage. Here we met with the preachers who had been retarded in their journey by the late storm. I pushed along, weary and unwell, to brother Hutchinson's,[67] and next day, faint though cheerful, we reached Burlington.

Pennsylvania

Thursday, 6. We reached Philadelphia about noon; my mind is in peace, but my body and spirits fail. Here I met my old friend Andrews, from Hartford, in England, after twenty-six years' absence. *Friday* I rested a little, and arranged the minutes for the present year.

Saturday, 8. Was spent in preparing for the ensuing conference.

[63] Van Duzer's Landing was at the Narrows on the cast shore of Staten Island.

[64] The Blazing Star was a noted ferry at Chelsea, the present Travis on the west shore of Staten Island. It is not to be confused with the New Blazing Star Ferry at Long Neck.

[65] This friend was perhaps Nicholas Crocheron, with whom Asbury frequently stopped in this part of Staten Island.

[66] Asbury may have stayed with Mr. Cole or John Marshall, both of whom lived about a mile from the Blazing Star Ferry at Rossville. Both were later contributors to the building fund of Woodrow Church. (Hubbell: *History of Methodism on Staten Island*, 30 31; see Map of Staten Island of Revolutionary War, 1775–83.)

[67] Joseph Hutchinson lived at Milford, or Milfordtown. (See *Journal* entries for September 5, 1792, and October 5, 1788.) Four members of this family became Methodist preachers.

Sunday, 9. At Zoar chapel, the church of the second African society, in Campingtown, I enlarged on "Ye were as sheep going astray, but are now returned to the shepherd and bishop of your souls." In the afternoon, at Ebenezer's, my subject was Psalm lxxxi, 11–16. In the evening in St. George's my discourse was like a storm, from Mark xvi, 19, 20. I observed that Jesus sent out his disciples; when he went to rest, they went to labour. The signs of their mission were miracles, and the signs that followed their ministry, convictions and conversions; the hindrances they had to expect, and the qualifications granted them everywhere; and his not leaving them without witnesses.

Monday, 10. We opened a conference of between forty and fifty preachers; we had great love and great riches also: never before have we been able to pay the preachers their salaries; at this conference we have done it, and had two hundred dollars left for debts and difficulties the preachers had been involved in. I was pleased to hear such wholesome talk by our plain countrymen. I sat with great pleasure and heard George Roberts, on, "We beseech you that ye receive not the grace of God in vain"; as also Joseph Whitby, on, "Feeding the flock of God"; and Joseph Pilmoor, on, "The fountain opened for sin and for uncleanness".

Friday, 14. We set apart as a day of fasting and humiliation, and for ordination. I was pleased to dismiss the conference from their confinement in business, and gave a discourse on, "Humble yourselves under the mighty hand of God." I now felt willing to rest both mind and body. We heard by the newspapers of the arrival of Doctor Coke in the United States.

Saturday, 15. We dined at Chester with my dear old friend Mary Withy, and came in the evening to Wilmington.

Delaware

Sabbath day, 16. The morning was rainy, but we had a few serious people to whom I preached on Rev. ii, 1–7. My soul enjoys sweet peace.

Maryland

Being in haste to get to Baltimore, we rode on the *Sabbath* afternoon to my old friend Solomon Hersey's; of this I am not fond, and where necessity does not compel me, rarely do it. I turned out of the way on *Monday* to preach at Bethel, in the place of Doctor Coke; my subject was, "Let us labour to enter into that rest, lest any man fall after the same example of unbelief." It was a happy season. In the course of the day I rode thirty-five miles and lodged at Northeast.

Tuesday, 18. We rode to Perry Hall, and were entertained with the greatest kindness.

Wednesday, 19. We came to Baltimore, where about a hundred preachers were met for general conference.[68] They agreed to a committee, and then complained; upon which we dissolved ourselves. I preached on, "The men of Issachar that knew what Israel ought to do"; and again on, "Neither as being lords over God's heritage, but being ensamples to the flock": there were souls awakened and converted. No angry passions were felt amongst the preachers; we had a great deal of good and judicious talk. The conference rose on *Thursday*, the 3d of November: what we have done is printed. Bishop Coke was cordially received, as my friend and colleague, to be wholly for America, unless a way should be opened to France. At this conference there was a stroke aimed at the presiding eldership. I am thankful that our session is over. My soul and body have health, and have hard labour. Brother Whatcoat is going to the south of Virginia, brother John M'Claskey is going to New Jersey, brother Thomas Ware to Pennsylvania, and brother Sylvester Hutchinson to New York and Connecticut: very great and good changes have taken place.

Friday, *November* 4. We reached the widow Dorsey's[69] by riding an hour in the night. I took a cold; and a boil on my face makes me uncomfortable.

Virginia

Saturday, 5. We rode twenty miles; and on *Sabbath* morning we came directly to Alexandria. Doctor Coke preached on, "The wise men that came to Jesus": brother Whatcoat and myself exhorted.

Monday, 7. We came to Captain Ward's: he is gone to sea, but his wife made us welcome. *Tuesday*, 8, we rode through *awful* Fredericksburgh to Todd's tavern: men and horses being weak and weary we contentedly stopped.

Wednesday, 9. We came about thirty miles to Ellis's tavern, and there, as well as at Todd's, we were kindly and genteelly entertained at a reasonable expense. The next day we stretched on to Richmond: and who could be kinder and more pleased to see us, and make poor sickly travellers

[68] During this General Conference, Asbury apparently stayed in the home of Nelson Reed, then a pastor in Baltimore. (See Asbury's letter to Reed, November 11, 1796.) Bishop Asbury was to suffer disappointment over Bishop Coke's accepted written proposal to his brethren at the conference, ". . . to labour among them and to assist Bishop Asbury," inasmuch as Coke left America within three months. This conference, which met in the Light Street Church, established the boundaries of six annual conferences. (Ware, *op. cit.*, 222–26; Lee: *A Short History of the Methodists*, 233–48; Colbert, *op. cit.*, II, 117–20. See letter to the British Conference, November 1, 1796.)

[69] This was the widow of Colonel Thomas Dorsey.

welcome, than Mr. Parrott and wife?[70] Here I persuaded Dr. Coke, to rest a day.

Saturday, 12. Brother Whatcoat and myself came to brother Walthall's, near Chesterfield court house. We preached to a few people, refitted a little better, and the next day came to brother Featherston's, where I gave them a short discourse. We dined and came on to Petersburg, and spent the evening at J. Harding's. I was much pained with the boil on my face, and another on my eye. Here I heard Dr. Coke preach, and I gave an exhortation.

Monday, 14. I must needs call and see my old friends, Wood Tucker and wife, and talked a little, prayed, and parted. We then went forward, calling on Richard Graves, an old disciple. Thence to mother Mabry's, in Greensville, where I have often had a comfortable night's lodging.

Thursday, 17. Our conference began at brother Batte's,[71] a most convenient house, and very kind people. We sat in great peace and good order. A few preachers declined travelling. We elected and ordained six elders and nine deacons. The deficiencies of the preachers amounted to upwards of £194 Virginia currency.

Sabbath day, 20. Doctor Coke gave a comment on the twentieth chapter of the Revelation of Jesus Christ by St. John, and then a sermon on Luke xiv, 26: "He that loveth father and mother more than me," &c. I then gave a short exhortation, and ended the service of that pleasant day.

Monday, 21. I visited, perhaps for the last time, mother Mabry, who is aged and swiftly declining. I also visited brothers Batte and Drumgoole, and then rode once more to Robert Jones's, in Sussex county. Here I had a few moments' leisure to write and recollect myself, after being so closely employed in conferences and company.

Tuesday, 22. I preached at Jay's chapel to about one hundred people, with whom I had a comfortable season on 2 Peter iii, 17, 18. I noticed, I. The appellation, *beloved*. II. That of the *wicked*, which I distinguished into three classes:—1. Those that make no profession of religion, and are openly wicked. 2. Those who have been awakened and may have enjoyed religion, but have fallen from it. 3. Those who profess the highest attainments in religion and yet live in known sin:—*the error of the wicked*, infidelity in theory, or practice, or both; which embraces the above-mentioned classes of the wicked—*grow in grace*—to grow in the graces of the Spirit, the knowledge of our Lord and Saviour, now and forever; the glory due to Christ in his kingdom of grace and glory.

[70] The Parrotts and Allens were probably the first Methodists in Richmond. They had been Wesleyans in England. Parrott was not a member but a warm friend of the Methodists. They lived on Main Street, and Mrs Parrott was very active in the society. The Methodists had been preaching in the courthouse and fields until Mrs. Parrott had a barn or storehouse fitted up in the rear of her house. Soon this was filled and they went back to the courthouse. About 1796 Coke started a movement to build a church in Richmond, but this did not materialize until 1799. (Bennett, *op. cit.*, 272–74.)

[71] See *Heads of Families*, 54.

Wednesday, 23. I rode to brother Davis's, about twenty-seven miles. On my way I visited brother Graves and mother. Brothers Pennington, Briggs, and Evans are gone to rest. My soul enjoys much peace, and is big with hope that we shall have a greater work in this district than we have ever yet had. I feel happy among the few ancient disciples who are left. I preached once more at Lane's chapel, and the Lord was with us. My subject was Jer. xxxii, 38, 39. We have lost about twenty members of this society by O'Kelly. We have about forty left.

Friday, 25, was a cold day, but we rode twenty-five miles to brother Joseph Wood's, in Isle of Wight county. Some of our brethren riding on before, called a night meeting, and we were comforted together.

My mind of late hath been in great peace. I am glad I have not contended with those violent men who were once with us. We ought to mind our work, and try to get souls to Christ; and the Lord can give us children, "that we shall have after we have lost our former," that shall say in our hearing, "Give place that there may be room for us to dwell." We had a very *winterly* morning, but we rode to brother Blunt's, where I preached to many people on Zeph. iii, 12, 13. Notwithstanding my name has been so cast out as evil, and my character traduced, I ordained brother Bonner and another brother,[72] after taking from the former a written declaration of his opposition to slavery. My dear aged friends told me their troubles and sorrow, which the divisions in the societies had caused.

Sabbath day, 27. Through hard necessity I rode sixteen miles to brother Cowling's, in Isle of Wight county, and had three rooms in the house filled, and there were some of the coloured people out of doors, notwithstanding the coldness of the weather. My subject was Heb. x, 37–39. I spoke with great rapidity for nearly two hours, administered the sacrament, and ordained brother Powell to the office of a deacon. It was time for me to visit this quarter again lest some should think I was afraid to come. But who hath been at the planting of the gospel in the sixteen United States? Had I none but Virginia to visit I could show myself oftener.

Monday, 28. We crossed a small ferry, and came through Suffolk to brother Jolliff's, twenty-two miles. I had solemn thoughts while I passed the house where Robert Williams[73] lived and died, whose funeral rites I performed. The weather is remarkably cold for the season, the ice being more than an inch thick on the streams. I was amazed to hear that my dear, aged friend, Benjamin Evans (now gone to glory), was converted

[72] John Bonner, who was assistant to William McKendree on the Williamsburg Circuit in 1796, and Archer Moody, who was one of four preachers on the Gloucester Circuit. They were both ordained at the conference of 1796. At this conference Bonner was appointed to Sussex and Moody to Tar River, North Carolina. (*Minutes.*)

[73] Robert Williams was called the first Methodist preacher in Virginia. (See *Journal* entries and notes for June 29, 1775; July 14, 26, 1775; September 26, 1775.)

to the new side, by being told by James O'Kelly that I had offended Mr. Wesley, and that he being about calling me to account, I cast him off altogether. But, *query*, did not James O'Kelly set aside the appointment of Richard Whatcoat? and did not the conference in Baltimore strike that *minute* out of our discipline which was called *a rejecting of Mr. Wesley?* and now does James O'Kelly lay all the blame on me? It is true, I never approved of that binding minute. I did not think it practical expediency to obey Mr. Wesley, at three thousand miles' distance, in all matters relative to Church government; neither did brother Whatcoat, nor several others. At the first general conference I was mute and modest when it passed, and I was mute when it was expunged. For this Mr. Wesley blamed me, and was displeased that I did not rather reject the whole connexion, or leave them, if they did not comply. But I could not give up the connexion so easily, after labouring and suffering so many years with and for them. After preaching at Jolliff's we rode to Portsmouth, and preached in the evening, where we had many people at a short warning. My subjects this day were 1 John i, 3, 4, and Isa. i, 9. We visited Norfolk and preached at noon, *Wednesday*, 30, on 1 Peter ii, 11, 12; at night, on 1 Cor. xv, 58.

Thursday, December 1. I returned to Portsmouth, and preached on 1 Peter v, 10. Thence through damp weather, we rode back to Jolliff's, where we had preaching, exhortation, and sacrament, and the Lord was with us.

North Carolina

Friday, 2. We had a long, cold, hungry ride to Gates county, in North Carolina.

Saturday, 3. We had a blessed season in Colonel Baker's new house, on 1 John iii, 1, 2, 3. I have felt unwell by these changes: sometimes preaching makes me sick, and at other times makes me well. Yesterday we rode nearly forty miles; to-day we laboured, and our horses rested. I feel solemnly given up to God in toil and suffering.

Sabbath day, 4. We rode fourteen miles to Winton, where I preached to an attentive congregation, from town and country, on St. John's Gospel i, 4. I remembered my old friend Boon; I was invited to and most kindly entertained at the house of one of his daughters. So it is, when the dear, aged parents go off, they leave me their children. Thence to Northampton county, twenty-eight or thirty miles, and came in about six o'clock. We had to-day as on *Friday* last, to breakfast about six or seven in the morning, and to dine about the same hour in the evening. My soul hath been in great peace. I rode to see Richard Whitaker and his wife, after several years' absence: I felt truly solemn when I found myself at the old house where the father and mother died. I remember well what passed when I was here last—the distress of the doctor, and his kindness to me in the year 1785.

Tuesday, 6. We had a rainy morning. Crossed Roanoke at Edwards's ferry, and came to Champion's: I resolved to preach, although only a part of two families were present. We dined, and hasted to mother Whitaker's, about twenty-four or twenty-five miles.

Wednesday, 7. We had a very sharp morning. I preached at brother Bradford's, on 1 John iv, 16–18. Yesterday on, "The promise is to you and to your children," &c. I parted with my dear brother Whatcoat, after travelling together about seven hundred miles. It was painful to part, yet I was well pleased he had not to drive the rough way, and that through the rain. In this I loved my brother better than myself. We had a comfortable season at sermon and sacrament this day. I felt myself at home in brother Bradford's family.

Thursday, 8. I came again to the widow Philips's, on Swift Creek; the house was filled—my subject was awful, Amos viii, 11: "Behold, the days come, saith the Lord God, that I will send a famine in the land; not a famine of bread, nor a thirst for water, but of hearing the words of the Lord." I observed—

I. The great and interesting things contained in the word of the Lord.

II. The benefits and blessings communicated by the faithful preaching and hearing, believing and obeying, the word of the Lord.

III. The causes and effects of this famine; deaths, removals, backslidings of ministers and people, and had reference to ancient times. Dreadful effects! the want of means to civilize, moralize, and spiritualize mankind.

I felt differently to-day from what I did yesterday; it was like beating upon a rock; but the Lord can give a blessing. We are greatly blessed with healthy weather.

Friday, 9. We came to Tarborough. They had made a fire in the small apartment of the court house, and I thought it was for preaching, but it was for dancing, and the violin lay on the table. Mr. Clement was kind enough to stop the scene, and we had a serious congregation to hear, to whom I preached on Heb. viii, 9–11. There were two or three houses open to me in town, but I lodged three miles out at brother Toole's.[74] We rode on *Saturday*, 10th, twenty-eight miles, without food or rest for man or horse, until we came to brother Forbes's, Pitt county, where I spent the Sabbath, and preached on Rom. ix, 27. I had many hearers, but it was cold times, both literally and spiritually; my soul was solemn—my body unwell.

[74] Geraldus Toole, a prosperous farmer from Edgecomb County, North Carolina, married the only daughter and oldest child of Dr. John King. Toole became associated with his brother-in-law, Joel King, as a merchant. His Franklin County, North Carolina, home was in Hayesville Township, north of Tar River on Toole's Creek. He died in 1846. (Davis: *Historical Sketches of Franklin County*, 282, 283.)

Monday, 12. I rode to father Barrows's: I was much led out on Heb. iii, 12–14. In those words: 1. Christians are cautioned against a most dreadful end. 2. The means to prevent it; and, 3. The example of backsliders. The end interesting and great—to hold fast the beginning of their confidence. The means—by exhorting one another daily. We rode twenty miles to father Ormond's; the people came before the rain, but had to return home through it; my subject was, "The little flock"; and I had considerable opening. I feel nothing painful, but the want of a revival of religion; my soul feels as if the Lord will yet do wonders among this people.

Wednesday, 14. We rose early, and rode in haste to Cox's ferry, on Neuse River: the weather was damp and chilly. We had very few to hear at the meeting house; it was a day of great trial, and I was beset on every side.

Thursday, 15. We made a forced march of twenty-five miles to Newbern; we had no refreshment for man nor horse. Having an inflammation in one of my ears, and having fasted so long, I was very unwell; but a sermon was expected, and delivered on these words: "Because thou knewest not the day of thy visitation": my hearers were numerous and serious. I had never viewed the situation of this town before: it is the image of Charleston (S. C.), Neuse and Trent have a likeness to Cooper and Ashley rivers. This is a growing place. Our society here, of white and coloured members, consists of one hundred. I every day see and feel the emptiness of all created good, and am taking my leave of all: what is worth living for but the work of God? I wrote to our brethren in the city stations, not to neglect the sick an hour, nor an absentee from class one week: indeed we ought to be always abounding in the work of the Lord; to attend to old and new subjects, to our work, and to every means, like men labouring to find out new means for new difficulties. Should piety, health, and trade attend this Newbern, it will be a very capital place in half a century from this.

Friday, 16. I had great openings on Rom. i, 15–17. I know not when I have visited a place with such pleasing hopes and feelings: I trust there hath been something more than man in this. O! how greatly was my heart knit to these people!

Saturday, 17. I preached at ten o'clock the second part of the same theme, Phil. i, 27. I was exceedingly close on the duties, spirit, and practice of the Gospel. We had to ride fifteen miles to Lee's, upon Trent. I felt solemn and sorrowful at leaving my dear people at Newbern;[75] they wished to give me money, but love is better than gold.

Sunday, 18. We had much rain: but few came to meeting. Finding we had twenty miles to Bryans's, we wished to move to Lemuel Hatches's, who was very kind.

[75] See letter to Mrs. Parker, December 17, 1796.

Monday, 19. We had to ride early: my horse trots stiff; and no wonder, when I have ridden him upon an average, five thousand miles a year for five years successively. I preached on Heb. iii. 7, 8. I felt as if the Lord and his messengers had left this place. My spirit was grieved at the conduct of some Methodists, that hire out slaves at public places to the highest bidder, to cut, skin, and starve them; I think such members ought to be dealt with: on the side of oppressors there are law and power, but where are justice and mercy to the poor slaves? what eye will pity, what hand will help, or ear listen to their distresses? I will try if words can be like drawn swords, to pierce the hearts of the owners.

I have heard by a person from Baltimore, that by means of the weekly society meeting, our people are all on flame: thank God that it came into my heart to recommend it to them! this also shall comfort us in our toil. I have ridden upwards of thirty miles this day.

Tuesday, 20. At the rich lands, but amongst spiritually poor people. I had about thirty hearers, and here are a few precious souls. Father Ballard and family still stand by us. I had some freedom on Heb. iii, 14:—1. Wherein believers are partakers of Christ, past, present, and to come; in wisdom, righteousness, sanctification, and redemption. 2. The beginning of their confidence steadfast to the end, without which they cannot be saved or safe. I described the nature, effects, and fruits of this confidence in God, in Christ, in the Holy Spirit; in Scripture promises, precepts, threatenings, in and of heaven, earth, and hell.

Wednesday, 21. We had a cold ride of about twenty miles to Stone's Bay; where there are a few people (who have been forsaken by the preachers), to whom I preached on Heb. x, 38, 39.

Thursday, 22. I came to Nixons's, on the road to Wilmington; here I found a kind people, but the preachers had left them because they did not immediately join in fellowship. Perhaps I was called this way to feel for souls in and round about Wilmington: if we had men and money, it would be well to station a preacher in such places as Wilmington.

Friday, 23. We had an excessively cold ride through heavy sands to Wilmington: when we came to the town wharf there was neither flat nor ferry; the causeway was under improvement; the only expedient therefore that remained was to cross at Negro Head. We came up the sand hills to Wright's ferry. It was truly cold and very bleak on the water, while in a trifling flat; and I feared one or both the horses would be thrown out of it. We were driving through the woods till seven o'clock, and the weather exceedingly cold; at last we came to Rolks's, on Town Creek. We could not spare ourselves the next day, but came off blowing and hiding our fingers. We passed Lockwood's Folly and Shallot River, and came up to father Gause's, where we met with friendship, fellowship and love, and held meeting on Christmas day, it being the Sabbath.

South Carolina

Monday, 26. We came to Little River, and thence to Kingston,[76] where we lodged with our Mr. W. Rogers, after riding about forty-five miles.

Tuesday, 27. I gave a sermon in the chapel, and on *Wednesday*, 28, rode thirty-seven or forty miles to Georgetown.[77] Here we have nearly one hundred Africans in society, while we have only seven or eight whites, our doctrine being too close, and our discipline too strict. After riding the above distance in the cold, without any regular meal, I was hardly fit for the pulpit at night; however I gave them a talk on "Glory to God in the highest, and on the earth peace, good will towards men." I observed on this, as I had on some former occasions, that the redemption and salvation of mankind by Jesus Christ was the brightest display of the justice, mercy, truth, love, and holiness of God; yet in such a manner as that justice should not destroy, but give glory to mercy; and that mercy should not destroy, but glorify justice and mercy in Christ to sinners—justice in the sufferings of Christ, and in the punishment of incorrigible sinners. The truth of God shineth also—it only belongs to a God to preserve and display all his attributes and perfections: in this plan we may say mercy and truth are met together, righteousness (or justice) and peace have kissed each other; and all the truths of God held sacred: with reverence let it be said, God would no longer be God, to act unlike himself, or to be unjust, unmerciful, or unholy, or untrue, or to swallow up or violate one attribute by exerting another. What should we think of a governor or judge that would pardon all criminals indiscriminately and unconditionally? where would be the exercise of justice?

Thursday, 29. Hearing of a sacramental occasion at Boone's chapel,[78] I rode thirteen miles to attend it; it was up Santee, on the upper branches of Sampit: my subject was "Christ hath once suffered for sins, the just for the unjust, that he might bring us to God." We were entertained elegantly, and with great hospitality, at Mr. Boone's.

Friday, 30. We set out in the rain, crossed Santee (we had a quick passage for once), and rode about fifty miles, and came to brother Jackson's[79] about nine o'clock. Here our rapid march was ended: I rested two days. Serious news from Baltimore—the academy and our church in

[76] Kingston was the present Conway, South Carolina.

[77] As previously Asbury went to Georgetown via the Yauhannah Ferry.

[78] Boone's Chapel was in the Sampit community on Sampit River near the present Andrews in Georgetown County. Its successor is the present Sampit Church, twelve miles west of Georgetown on Highway 17A.

[79] Jackson lived just below Cainhoy. Asbury was following a favorite route via Lenud's Ferry across the Santee at Jamestown.

Light Street, with brother Hawkins's elegant house, all destroyed by fire![80] The loss we sustain in the college, academy, and church, I estimate from fifteen to twenty thousand pounds: it affected my mind; but I concluded God loveth the people of Baltimore, and he will keep them poor, to make them pure; and it will be for the humiliation of the society.

[80] This was the second Cokesbury College fire. The building at Abingdon was destroyed on the night of December 7, 1795, and arson was suspected but never proven. An unsuccessful attempt to burn the college had been frustrated on December 9, 1788. A "second Cokesbury" was then opened in Baltimore on a lot adjoining Light Street Church. Both school and church burned on December 4, 1796, and the college was never rebuilt. A stone from the original structure was placed in the foundation of the American University at Washington. (Tees: *Methodist Origins*, 180–84; Hurst: *History of Methodism*, IV, 391–94; Simpson: *Cyclopedia of Methodism*, 235, 236.)

1797

1797

Asbury at the home of Edward Cox in East Tennessee

CHAPTER TWENTY-SIX

South Carolina

January 1, 1797. Being *Sabbath day*, I lectured on Psalm lxxxiv, and on 2 Cor. v. *Monday*, 2. I came to Charleston,[1] and preached in the evening on Eph. v, 15, 16. *Tuesday*, 3. We began conference, and sat some days six or seven hours. We had pleasing accounts of the growth of religion in Georgia as well as in this State. We had a sermon every evening, and many to hear.

Sunday, 8. My subject was John xiv, 21–23. I do not yet feel myself in the spirit of the work. *Monday*, 9. Our conference rose. We have been blessed with some young men for the ministry. By letter from James M'Cannon, in Baltimore, I learn that our people have had the offer of the Episcopal church, and the English and German Presbyterian churches, until we can rebuild. I began reading the Bible and Winterbotham's View of the United States. We have sent out subscriptions for the Methodist Magazine. The like severity of weather hath not been known here for fourteen or fifteen years; the gardens and oranges appear to be destroyed; the want of moisture may have increased the effects of the frost. I have felt my soul filled with love, for the general union in the ministry, and for the Church: my mind is stayed upon the Lord alone. *Tuesday*, 10. Our dear brethren set out for their circuits. *Wednesday*, 11. In the evening we met the society in the manner I had recommended to the brethren in New York, Philadelphia, and Baltimore. We were much blessed; it was a

[1] Asbury went from Jackson's to Charleston via Clement's Ferry. He again spent two months in the city.

gracious season. Brother Edgar Wells appears to be dying swiftly. I purpose to go out only every other night, as I am called to duty every morning with fifty or a hundred Africans. I lament the wickedness of this city, and their great hatred against us. I spent *Thursday*, *Friday*, and *Saturday* in reading, writing, and visiting the sick.

Sunday, 15. Notwithstanding I had taken medicine on *Saturday*, and was unwell, I preached on John vi, 66–69. We were much crowded; and more so, when Dr. Coke preached in the evening. *Monday*, 16. The remnant of the preachers left the city. I rode up the path, and attended the Doctor to Clement's ferry. At night I met the seeking Africans in Brother Wells's kitchen. This evening I prayed with brother Wells for the last time; he expressed his confidence in God, and freedom from guilty dread and horror.

Tuesday, 17. I was called to the house of brother Edgar Wells, just departed this life. His widow I found in prayers and tears, as also the dear children and servants. We appointed his funeral to be at four o'clock to-morrow. The scene was serious. I learned he wished to see me once more: I visited him every day I could with propriety. It is twelve long year's next *March* since he first received Henry Willis, Jesse Lee, and myself, into his house.[2] In a few days he was brought under heart distress for sin, and soon after professed faith in Christ; since that he hath been a diligent member in society. About fourteen months ago, when there was a revival of religion in the society, and in his own family, it came home to his own soul; he was quickened, and remarkably blest, and continued so to be until his death. His affliction was long and very severe. The last words he was heard to say that could be understood were, that "he knew where he was, that his wife was with him, and that God was with him." He hath been a man of sorrows, and hath suffered the loss of two respectable wives and a favourite son; sustained heavy loss by fire, and was subject to a great variety of difficulties in trade and merchandise. He was one much for the feeling part of religion; a gentleman of spirit, and sentiment, and fine feelings, a faithful friend to the poor, and warmly attached to the ministers of the Gospel. This was a solitary day, and I laboured under uncommon dejection. I preached in the evening, and was in great heaviness.

Wednesday, 18. We committed the dust of our dear brother Wells to the old church burying ground, in Cumberland Street. Doctor Coke performed the funeral rites, and delivered an oration. I also gave a short one. My serious gloom continued.

[2] (See *Journal* entry for February 24, 1785.) Edgar Wells not only received Asbury into his home on the Bishop's first visit, but he became the first Methodist convert in Charleston. He was buried in the cemetery of Cumberland Street Church. The second church on the site was burned during the Civil War, and the Wells grave is now under the foundation of a warehouse. (Chreitzberg: *Early Methodism in the Carolinas*, 72.)

Thursday, 19. We were closely attentive to the notes on the Discipline.

Friday, 20. Visited Mr. Grant, declining swiftly in a consumption. He appeared to be somewhat awakened to a sense of the state of his soul and body.

Saturday, 21. Till noon my heart sinketh, and I am ready to conclude we are not sent to the whites of this place, except a very few; but to the poor Africans. I find this a suffering, holy time.

Sunday, 22. I preached Mr. Wells's funeral sermon, on Rev. ii, 10. I observed, 1. Who it is that speaketh. 2. To whom he was speaking. 3. What might be supposed and granted concerning the angel of the Church—that he had professed the convicting and converting grace of God; that he had suffered poverty, temptation, and persecution. 4. What it is to be faithful to God—to fear him, as also to trust in his providence and grace; faithful to Christ and to the Spirit, to the Church of God, to his family and citizens; faithful unto death, even martyrdom. I gave a brief account of Mr. Wells's life and death. I was exceedingly weak in body and mind before I began preaching, but was considerably liberated. I had a solemn, attentive congregation, and was glad to come home and spend the evening in solitary reading and prayer. I have to meet the African people every morning between five and six o'clock, at my lodging, with singing, reading, exhortation, and prayer.

Monday, 23. We were at work upon our notes on the Discipline.

Tuesday, 24. I was very unwell, yet I must needs preach a little on 2 Cor. vi, 2. My body is weak, and my soul is distressed on account of sinners. I have made out to read the third volume of Winterbotham's General View of our Continent. This I do, because I have some hope of visiting British America before I die.

Wednesday, 25. My mind oppressed and my body afflicted, I was close at work—heart, head, and eyes. No justice for Cumberland Street Methodists. A young Scot shouted in the church, and after he was taken out of the house struck three or four men; no bill was found against him; and we are insulted every night by candlelight.

Thursday, 26. Still unwell. The three following days I was confined to the house with fever. I wrought at our work. O, that it may be for the glory of God and the good of his Church! I have numbered the chapters, and versed Scriptures in it. I am resolved to visit more, if spared to get through this weighty business. Mr. Grant, after three years warning with a consumption, is gone. I trust God had mercy on his soul. Doctor Coke preached in the morning, brother Hill in the afternoon.

Sunday and *Monday*, 29, 30. I consulted a physician, who judged my disease to be an intermittent fever, and such it proved itself. On *Tuesday*, 31, I was taken about two o'clock with a powerful ague, which held me till nearly nine o'clock. I presume it has been working for two weeks. I probably took it by going out at the death of brother Wells. *Wednesday*,

February 1, I took the powders of Columbo after the bilious pills. *Thursday*, 2, my fever did not return. *Friday*, 3. Growing better, I had serious thoughts about going home to God. Of late I have been kept uncommonly happy. My depression of spirits at times is awful, especially when afflicted; that which is deeply constitutional will never die but with my body. I am solemnly given up to God, and have been for many months willing to live or die in, for, and with Jesus.

Wednesday, 8. I was better, and was enabled to read, write,[3] ride, and visit.

Thursday, 9. To-morrow my dear Coke sails for Europe. My mind is in peace, but I am not pleased with such confinement. I now take a decoction of the bark. I am under great obligations to Doctor Joseph Ramsay for his peculiar attention to me in my affliction, without fee or reward for his services. By letter from John Dickins, I learn the work of God greatly revives in New York among the aged people and little children. I have lately read the second volume of Mr. Wesley's Sermons.

Friday, 10. This day Doctor Coke is waiting to sail for Ireland. Strangers to the delicacies of Christian friendship know little or nothing of the pain of parting. Glad tidings of great joy from New York. A second glorious work is begun there, twenty souls converted, a great love feast, and Sabbath evening meeting held until one o'clock in the morning. This news hath given a spring to us in this city.

Saturday, 11. I visited a little.[4]

Sunday, 12. I attended my station, and stood upon my watch-tower. My subject was Eccles. v, 1: "Keep thy foot when thou goest into the house of God."

I. The house of God—the temples, first and second, and synagogues, were called houses of God. A place built for the worship and service of the Lord; the congregation and church.

II. The exercises and ordinances of the house of God: reading and preaching the word of God; prayer and praises; baptism and the Lord's supper. In his temple every one shall speak of his glory.

III. The manifestations that God is pleased to make of himself in his own house to the souls of his people.

IV. How people should prepare for, and behave in, the house of God. To keep their eyes and ears—fix their attention on the Lord and Master of the house.

V. The wicked called fools, and the sacrifice they make. Ignorant of themselves, of God, of Christ, and true religion, and the worship of the Lord, and do not consider it is God, Christ, and sacred things they make light of.

We were full, and I put my strength to the test. In the afternoon, from

[3] See letter to Thomas Coke, February 8, 1797.

[4] See letter to George Roberts, February 11, 1797.

Ezekiel xxxvi, 25–27. I showed the evils God threatened, and prophesied the removal of, by his servant to his nominal professed people, Israel.

I. Their stony heart—their idols and filthiness.

II. The blessings promised and prophesied—a new heart, a new spirit, the indwelling and sanctifying influence of the Spirit.

III. The blessed consequential effects—"I will cause you to walk in my statutes, and ye shall keep my judgments to do them." The law, the judgments of God, because of the penalty annexed—thus saith the Lord to the renewed soul, "Thou shalt have none other gods but me." "Lord," saith the Christian, "I want none other but thee." Saith Jehovah, "Thou shalt not make to thyself any graven image." The pious soul saith, "I will not; the work of my hands cannot save my soul: I will not take thy name in vain. I love thy day—thy love hath written thy law upon my heart, and love to my neighbour engages me to fulfil my duty to him also." "The meek shall inherit the earth," as a sacred charter from the Lord—this is their claim, security, and defence.

I was wearied with the duties of the day, and had only retired to rest when the alarm of *fire* was cried—it proved only to be a kitchen, and by the activity of the people it was soon extinguished.

Monday, 13. I have peace, and am as well in health as I could expect. Bless the Lord, O my soul! I was taken up with handing about a subscription for the new house. Our people appear much afraid to move in this work.

Tuesday, 14. I met the stewards on the subject of the new house.[5] We have adjourned on the question. If materials fall in their price, and if we can secure £400, shall we begin? O we of little faith! It is a doubt if we had fifty in society, and £100 on hand, when we laid the foundation stone of Cumberland Street house, which cost us (including the lot) £1,300. The society has been rent in twain, and yet we have wrought out of debt, and paid £100 for two new lots, and we can spare £100 from the stock, make a subscription of £150, and the Africans will collect £100.

Wednesday, 15. I felt much better, and rejoice in hope of going hence.

Thursday, 16, was a solitary day; my soul was in heaviness, and my body weak. I was employed in writing letters, and reading the Bible with critical attention.

Friday, 17. I thought I would fast, refraining from food till six o'clock; I felt very weak, had a fever and headache, and was glad to go to bed at seven o'clock. I feel pain to be gone, and do not expect much peace of mind, or health of body, until I go to my old solitary country life. I judge that discipline, and the doing away of certain things, have contributed somewhat to the late revival of religion in New York.

[5] The new house was the Bethel Methodist Church, for which a building committee of four persons was named. (Chreitzberg, *Early Methodism in the Carolinas*, 72.)

Sunday, 19. I entered on my duty. I had not an opening to preach, so I made an explanatory discourse on Isaiah lv, 1–7; and it appeared to be of use. My leading heads were,

I. The spiritual blessings held forth in the temporal good things, water, wine, milk. Water to quench the thirst, cleanse, and heal, as to drinking, bathing, &c.; all expressive of the grace of God to our souls—comforting, cleansing, healing. Wine for the sickly, tempted, dispirited ones. Milk for babes.

II. The grand qualifications—thirst and no money; and to come, no merit, no righteousness.

III. The reasoning—"Wherefore do you spend your money," &c.; that is, make great sacrifices for pleasure, and yet are disappointed; such is the case of those who seek after ceremonial righteousness.

IV. His offering Christ.

V. The promise of the increase of the kingdom of Jesus Christ among distant and unknown nations.

VI. *When* they are to come to seek the Lord, viz., "while he may be found."

It was a melting season. In the afternoon I preached on Rom. viii, 31: "What shall we then say to these things; if God be for us, who can be against us?"

I. I viewed the whole chapter. The character and distinguishing marks of the people of God.

II. How he will order himself on the side of his people, in his justice, mercy, truth, power, and love: "If God be for us?"—this is a modest supposition. I observed, he will not aid our persecutors—their help is departed from them; that he sanctified persecution; and sometimes would cut off the enemies of his Church and people; that some were enemies from policy, others from heretical principles, some from enmity of heart; others would think their fathers, mothers, husbands, wives, &c., were misguided and deluded. I stood on my feet about three hours this day, was much wearied and slept but little.

Monday, 20. I was weak—the weather uncommonly warm. I rejoice in hope of leaving the city next *Monday*, if the Lord spareth me.

Tuesday, 21. My mind has been greatly afflicted, so that my sleep has been much interrupted, yet there was a balm for this; a poor black, sixty years of age, who supports herself by picking oakum, and the charity of her friends, brought me a French crown, and said she had been distressed on my account, and I must have her money. But no! although I have not three dollars to travel two thousand miles, I will not take money from the poor. I am very unwell, my soul and body is distressed: ah! that such trifles should affect me. I have read four books of Moses critically.

Wednesday, 22. Was a sorrowful day to me: I am thinking God is teaching me I ought not to stay in this place after this manner: perhaps I shall never stay here again for so long a time. I am kept from sinning, yet not from deep and sore temptation.

Thursday, 23. Brother James King came to town to take the charge in this city as assistant preacher to Benjamin Blanton.[6]

Friday, 24. I began to prepare for my departure hence.

Saturday, 25. My mind is happy in the expectation of leaving this city on *Monday*.

Sunday, 26. I judged it best to be plain and explanatory upon the Lord's supper, 1 Cor. v, 7, 8. Our congregation was large, and the sacramental occasion very solemn. My farewell discourse was on 1 Sam. xii, 23, 24. I observed on the duty of those who have the charge of souls.

I. To pray for them.

II. To teach them the good and the right way; which is to fear the Lord, and serve him in truth, sincerity, and purity of intention.

III. The motives to induce them—the consideration of the great things God hath done for them.

What good have I attempted to do here? I assisted the Doctor in the notes on the Discipline. I have preached every *Sabbath* except two; formed a plan to erect a house in the west end of the city suburbs, to be equal to that in Cumberland Street; I have made peace between a dying man and his brother-in-law, in which two families were concerned; and I cured a poor African's sore leg by applying a poultice of bread and milk.

Monday, 27. I felt a fever, yet rejoiced to leave Charleston. Many came to see me. I have persuaded one person to give up the use of what I feared would be her ruin: she promised she would; if so, all will be well. On my way I felt as if I was let out of prison. Hail! ye solitary pines! the jessamin, the redbud, and dog-wood! how charming in full bloom! the former a most fragrant smell. We reached Monks Corner, and were most agreeably entertained at Mr. Jones's. We came on the next day and had but hard fare till we reached Nelson's ferry[7]: it being a rainy day, the gentlemen were regaling themselves with cards: blunt Frank Asbury asked for dinner, but told them he could not dine upon cards; the cards were very politely put away, and every necessary mark of attention paid: Mr. Gurdine, who commands several ferries on this river, is a complete gentleman. We came off in the rain, and it fell very freely. Through the swamp we had deep wading, and steeped our feet; we wrought along as night came on; and after riding four miles in the dark, dirt, and rain, we came to the widow Bowman's:[8] here I found shelter and was kindly

[6] James King, was transferred from the Seleuda (Saluda) Circuit. Blanton, King, and John N. Jones were appointed to Charleston and Georgetown. (See *Minutes*.)

[7] Nelson's Ferry was near Eutaw Springs.

[8] Mrs. Bowman lived in lower Clarendon County near Manning and Jordan.

entertained. Her husband was a godly, gracious man, and died in the Lord some years ago.

Wednesday, *March* 1. We rested and refitted. *Thursday*, 2. We had a cold day at Gibson's;[9] my subject was 1 John v, 13–15. I was very unwell, under infirmities of body and mind. Thence we rode five miles to Mark Moore's,[10] where I preached on 2 Peter iii, 18, and had a comfortable time.

Friday, 3. We had a dry, cold, hungry, long ride of thirty miles to Richard Bradford's,[11] where I dined, and preached at three o'clock and felt resolved to give them one plain talk on Heb. iii, 7, 8. 1. The voice of God is the Gospel of Jesus Christ as preached by himself. 2. What is comprehended in hearing his voice—attending, believing, obeying. 3. How men harden their hearts—by delays, and by inward and outward sin; the Holy Ghost saith, *To-day*, in the word, in the ministry, in the hearts of men.

Saturday, 4. At Rembert's new chapel[12] I preached on Matt. xi, 28–30, where I had some living sweetness.

Sunday, 5. After love feast and sacrament I preached on 2 Cor. vi, 6–10, but had not much satisfaction. Religion is reviving here among the Africans; several are joined in society: these are the poor; these are the people we are more immediately called to preach to.

Monday, 6. I preached in the court house at Camden, set apart for a meeting house: my subject was, "Knowing therefore the terror of the Lord, we persuade men." 1. I treated on the divine character of Christ, as judge—his perfections, and relation to the persons who are to be tried. 2. The characters to be judged—infidels, sinners, Pharisees, hypocrites, backsliders, believers, true and false ministers: these are to be tried, found guilty, or acquitted; sentenced and punished, or applauded and rewarded. I received a second letter from New York, informing me of the revival of religion there among the aged and young people. I rode fourteen miles to Granny's quarter,[13] a small house among the sand hills; thence eight miles to brother Horton's,[14] whose brother, a Baptist, had lately departed this life; he was blest in his end.

[9] Gibson probably lived near Foreston in Clarendon County.

[10] The Rev. Mark Moore was a supernumerary preacher who lived near Shiloh. Asbury probably at this time secured his services as principal of the new Mount Bethel School in Newberry County; his appointment next year was Broad River Circuit and he served the school for six years.

[11] Richard Bradford lived near Sumter.

[12] This chapel was at Rembert Hall, seat of Asbury's friend Publius James Rembert, twelve miles north of Sumter. Nothing remains of this once-famous estate. (Betts: *History of South Carolina Methodism*, 72.)

[13] The chapel on Granny's Quarter Creek (now Sanders Creek) was perhaps the mother of the present Damascus Church at Westville in Kershaw County.

[14] Horton lived at Hanging Rock in upper Kershaw County. From here Asbury proceeded through Lancaster County to Waxhaw in North Carolina.

North Carolina

Wednesday, 8. We rode thirty-two miles to the Waxhaw, hungry and faint: at Wren's I was led out on, "Let us not sleep as do others." The next day, at quarterly meeting, I preached on Isa. i, 9: there was a noise and shaking. This evening a little circumstance gave me great pain; I broke my skin in two places. We rode on *Friday* and *Saturday* seventy miles. We passed through a large settlement of Presbyterians; Mr. M'Ree,[15] their minister, gave us a kind invitation to lodge at his house; but we wished to cross the river at Martin's ferry,[16] and stay at the widow Featherstone's.[17]

Sunday, 12. We were at Daniel Asbury's. My leg was inflamed by riding, and I found it necessary to poultice it. I sat down and taught the people on, "He that cometh to God must believe that he is, and that he is a rewarder of them that diligently seek him." We had a living meeting in the evening; some souls were greatly blest.

Monday, 13. We rode into Iredell country, thirty-three miles. We were caught in the rain, which threw me into a chill, followed by a fever; in this situation I came to, and preached at brother Fitzgerald's. Between four and five o'clock, brothers Dean and Dyson (Methodists), Hall and Bowman (Presbyterians) had filled my appointment in the preceding part of the day.

Tuesday, 14. I preached at the church in the forks of the Yadkin, on Isaiah xxxv, 1–4. I had to ride eight miles in the rain to Templeton's.

Wednesday, 15. I rode five miles to Mr. Marcis Hoy's, and treated on the *rest that remaineth to the people of God*. In the afternoon I rode twelve miles to father Bruce's, where I found myself at home.

Thursday, 16. We had to ride fifteen miles through the rain to Samuel Oxford's. After preaching on Hebrews ii, 1, we rode eight miles to Paynes's. The weather was very damp: I felt the chill through me. The next morning I was seized with a fever which held me more or less until Sabbath morning, when I preached at Perkins's and Connelly's meeting houses; at the former on Heb. ii, 3, and at the latter on 2 Cor. latter part of the sixth chapter. Here as many as eight preachers came to meet me; some of them one hundred miles. I feel myself very unwell, and am afraid that almost

[15] The Rev. James McRee was pastor of the Steele Creek Presbyterian Church in Mecklenburg County, North Carolina. He lived near Martin's Ferry, the present Withers Bridge. (Douglas: *History of Steele Creek Church*.)

[16] Martin's Ferry was over the Catawba River near present Belmont, North Carolina. (See 1789 map in Alexander: *History of Mecklenburg County*.)

[17] Mrs. Featherstone was probably related to Featherstone Wells, who lived at or near the ferry and is buried there in the Fetherstone-Fite-Wells cemetery. Mrs. Featherstone is doubtless buried there also, as there are numerous unmarked graves and illegible inscriptions.

every rain will bring on a relapse of the fever. My mind of late is much resigned to the will of God; I feel I have nothing here but the Church of God; I would not throw my life away nor hold it back, if the Lord called for it in labouring, travelling and suffering. I conclude I have ridden one hundred miles this week, and the weather has been very uncomfortable, the roads bad, and our lodging in some very open houses; to which I may add my preaching in new and unfinished meeting houses in March, which is a searching, changeable month, especially near the mountains.

Sabbath day, 19. At Connelly's new church I preached on 2 Cor. vii, 1. I only intended to give a short discourse.

Monday, 20. I had but twenty miles to ride to Esquire White's at the Mulberry Grove. Here I left Doctor S. B——l; but death hath now removed him. I still continued to feel feverish and feeble, and thought it needful to take mountain bark.

Tuesday, 21. I preached once more at Johns River; my subject was 1 Cor. i, 24, 25. As I thought it would be my last, I exerted myself until my chill and fever returned: I also administered the sacrament and baptized children.

Wednesday, 22. I set out on my journey for the west; and it had a serious influence on my mind to leave brother Hill behind, who I fear hath a confirmed consumption, and I too so unwell. It began to rain violently before we came to Henley's. I took shelter in a house from the rain, and talked and prayed with a poor woman. We dined at Mr. Henley's, calling at Wakefield only to talk and pray. I cannot well pass by my friends without calling. We hastened across Linville Mountain, which is awfully barren, and came on to Young's Cove. The storm followed us, with thunder, lightning, and rain. We arrived after some of the people were gone; but some returned, and I gave them but a small talk, being very weary in walking down the mountains, and over the rocks.

Thursday, 23. I came to Davenport's. My subject was "Godliness is profitable," &c. Grace in the heart, in all its operations. Bodily exercise for a little time is useful for health—for the present world—for the means of grace. Godliness promiseth everything we can wish for in the present and future life; answering all the purposes of civil, domestic, and Christian life:—justice, mercy, and truth;—every duty and relation; all the joys and all the sufferings of life; all the lawful use of lawful things;—and prepares for the enjoyment of God, Christ, the Eternal Spirit, angels, and glory.

Friday, 24. I was unwell: the clouds were lowering. We had ridden but a mile when the rain began. Brother Jones's house was at hand. Here we stopped two hours, until some of the rain fell to the earth. There was a short cessation, and about half-past twelve o'clock we set out again, rode six miles, and were driven into Mr. Cook's by thunder, hail, and rain. Here we stopped to talk with God and man. Hard necessity made us move forward: the western branch of Toe River, that comes down from the

Yellow Mountain, was rapidly filling; and was rocky, rolling, and roaring like the sea, and we were compelled to cross it several times. When we came to ascend the mountain, we had a skirmish of rain, thunder, and lightning—it was distant—it was mercy. I found hard work to ride where Thomas White had driven his wagon, for which he deserves a place in my journal and a premium from the State. When we had ascended the summit of the mountain, we found it so rich and miry, that it was with great difficulty we could ride along; but I was wrapped up in heavy, wet garments, and unable to walk through weakness of body; so we had it, pitch, slide, and drive to the bottom. We then came upon the drains and branches of Great Toe River. From Fisher's we had to ride through what I called the *shades of death*, four miles to Miller's. Here we had to cope with Toe River, and near the house came into deep water. My horse drove to the opposite bank above the landing, and locked one of his feet in a root, or something like it, but freed himself. At last we made the house; the people received us kindly, and gave us such things as they had. We could only partially dry our garments. We heard heavy tidings of a deep rocky ford yet to be passed in our way across Doe River.

Tennessee

Saturday, 25. We were escorted by three brave young Dutchmen. After riding three miles we began to scale the rocks, hills, and mountains, worming through pathless woods, to shun a deep ford. I thought, ride I must; but no—the company concluded to walk. I gave my horse the direction of himself, under Providence. I had to step from rock to rock, hands and feet busy; but my breath was soon gone, and I gave up the cause, and took horse again, and resolved that I would ride down the hills, although I had not ridden up them. At last (hit or miss, Providence is all) into the path we came, and thence kept down the river and over to Little Doe bearing down the stream. When we had passed the Gap we wished to feed; but the man had no corn to sell. We tried, man and horse, to reach Nathan Davies's; where we arrived, and were made comfortable. I was much spent with the labours of this day. Hearing of the quarterly meeting at Dunworth's, I rode on *Sunday*, 26th, twelve miles, and arrived time enough for me to give them a feeble, yet faithful talk, on Isa. i, 9. I am of opinion it is as hard, or harder, for the people of the west to gain religion as any other. When I consider where they came from, where they are, and how they are, and how they are called to go farther, their being unsettled, with so many objects to take their attention, with the health and good air they enjoy; and when I reflect that not one in a hundred came here to get religion, but rather to get plenty of good land, I think it will be well if some or many do not eventually lose their souls. I was met by our brethren, John Kobler, William Burke, and John Page.[18] I rested on *Monday* and *Tuesday*, to take breath and medicine. I find myself so hardly put to it at times that I can only journalize a little. We concluded, as there are not proper stations on the Cumberland path,[19] it will not do for me to lodge on the ground: the general opinion is against it. We are to try to go to Kentucky next week.

Wednesday, 29. I rode to William Nelson's,[20] and after dinner to Nathan Davies's. *Thursday morning* I was very weak, and have slow but almost continual fevers. I preached with great difficulty in the afternoon, and returned to William Nelson's. This night I felt a total change of mind. The weakness of my body, and the cold and unsettled state of the weather, made me, with the general advice of the preachers present, give up the cause; they also advised me to make the best of my way to Baltimore, and not to ride in the rain. It may be, the Lord intends to lead me in a way I have not yet known; it is perhaps best that I should go with all expedient haste from conference to conference, only stopping at the towns and chief places on *Sabbath days*. Live or die, I must ride. After all the disappointments, perhaps every purpose is answered but one. I have sent brother John Kobler to take charge of Kentucky and Cumberland, by visiting the whole every quarter: brother Jonathan Bird I have stationed in the Holston district. I have written a circumstantial letter to brother Francis Poythress[21] and the Kentucky conference. I have made a plan for the stationing of the preachers, at least those of any standing: and now I will make the best of my way to Baltimore; perhaps there may be some special call for me there: I must, as the burden of meeting the conferences, ordaining, and stationing the preachers resteth on me, save myself. I am peculiarly concerned for the cities: the prosperity of the work of God depends much on having proper men for any and every part of the work.

Friday, 31. It being rainy I rested. *Saturday*, *April* 1. The weather was clear and cold: we set off for brother Charles Baker's. My horse hath the honour of swimming Holston River every time I visit this country.

Sunday, 2. I felt better than I had done since I crossed the mountains. I preached on Acts iii, 26, and was for pushing on again about fifteen

[18] These were leading preachers in Holston and Kentucky. Kobler was elder over the Holston circuits. Burke was on the Guilford Circuit and the next year was sent to Holston Circuit. Page was on the Green Circuit and was sent to the Hinkstone. (See *Minutes.*)

[19] The path was the Wilderness Road over the Cumberlands into Kentucky. Taverns were known as "stations."

[20] See note under May 6, 1788.

[21] Poythress was elder over the Kentucky circuits and was supernumerary the following year. He later suffered mental derangement and received a stipend from the conference until his death in Kentucky. (See note under May 13, 1790. Price: *Holston Methodism*, I, 311–17; McFerrin: *Methodism in Tennessee*, I, 229, 230; Finley: *Sketches of Western Methodism*, 129 ff.)

miles farther, to Edward Coxe's: we got lost, and were an hour in the night.

Virginia

Monday, 3. We made a stretching ride of about forty miles, and were another hour in the night, and came to Michael Halfacre's.[22] I was *properly* outdone, and my fever returned and held me thirty hours.

Tuesday, 4. I reached the widow Russell's:[23] I am scarce able to read, write, sing, or pray; nevertheless, after I had rested, I preached in the evening.

Thursday, 6. We took our way up Walker's Valley;[24] after riding about eight miles my weakness came on, and I was addressed by name and earnestly requested to stop and take refreshment and rest at Mr. M'Carty's; here we were richly provided for: the mother and daughter are most agreeable and kind. After commending ourselves and this affectionate family to God, we came to Benoni Banning's. As I was told, so I found this family—attentively kind: we stopped here *Friday*, *Saturday*, and *Sunday*.

My fever never left me, as I thought, from *Monday* until *Friday* night. I am kept cheerful, but very weak. My diet is chiefly tea, potatoes, Indian-meal gruel, and chicken broth. My reading is only the Bible: I cannot think much, and only write a few letters. I think of my charge, of the conferences, and the Church, and of my dear parents, who will probably outlive me; I must be made perfect through sufferings. I rest in rainy weather, and have to ride from eighty to one hundred and twenty miles in a week. The way we now go we have sometimes to ride thirty miles to get to a house. From the 9th of *April* to the 27th of *May* I have kept no journal.[25] The notes of our travels and troubles taken by Jonathan Bird

[22] See note under May 6, 1788.

[23] See notes under May 3, 15, 1788. In July, 1795, Mrs. Russell had freed her six slaves in an indenture which stated that they had been enslaved "by the wrong doing of man" and she had a conviction of conscience "aided by the power of a good and just God that it is both sinful and unjust, as they are by nature equally free with myself, to continue them in slavery." Francis Preston, her son-in-law, also freed his slaves. (Summers: *History of Southeast Virginia*, 444.)

[24] Walker's Valley is northwest of Walker Mountain, paralleling the "Great Valley of Virginia."

[25] Redford in his *Methodism in Kentucky*, I, 218, quoting "Judge Scott," says that Asbury presided over the conference at Bethel Academy, Kentucky, on May 1, 1797. The long silence of the *Journal* renders the bishop's movements uncertain, but it seems unlikely that he went to Kentucky this year. He had already sent John Kobler to take charge of the work in the whole state and had made the appointments of the preachers and presumably sent the plan to Francis Poythrees, announcing that he would proceed to Baltimore. (See *Journal* entries for April 29.) The Judge Scott mentioned by Redford was the Rev. Thomas Scott, who was a preacher from 1789 to 1795, and later became chief justice of the state of Ohio. His manuscript journals are in the possession of the Rev. Lawrence Sherwood. Scott states that Bishop Asbury was present and presided at

and Joshua Wells, will tell a small part of my sorrows and sufferings. I have travelled about six hundred miles with an inflammatory fever, and fixed pain in my breast. I cannot help expressing the distinguishing kindness of some families where I have been forced by weakness to stop,—Captain Shannon, on Walker's creek; my friend Scarborough, on the sinks of Green Brier; Colonel Moffatt and brother Young, in Augusta: neither can I forget Mr. Lee and Moore; the Harrisons, at Rocktown,[26] and brother and sister M'Williams; Sisters Phelps and Reed, in Winchester and my dear friend, Doctor Tiffin.

Maryland

By a strange providence I was cast upon Eli Dorsey,[27] on Linganore, who nursed me as if I had been his own father.

From the 27th of *May* until *June* 10, no journal. We rode nearly forty miles from Linganore to Baltimore. I lodged at brother Hawkins's retreat, about one mile from the city. I lounged away a week in visiting a little.

Sunday, June 18. I was only able to speak about fifteen minutes. I recover but slowly. The constant resort of the wealthy and poor visiting me, made me much ashamed that they should look after such a worthless lump of misery and sin.

June 25. I met the male members of the society *Sabbath morning*, as I had met the sisters and the official members in the preceding week. I obtained the liberty of the managers of the African academy[28] to congregate the fathers as well as to teach the children. We had nearly five hundred coloured people. Brother Henry Willis preached on Acts vii, 7, and I added a few words. In the afternoon I gave a short exhortation at Mr. Otterbein's church, on Howard's Hill. I am now waiting for the making of a sulky. Thomas Barber, from Birmingham (England), took a

the Kentucky Conference in 1797. On the other hand the Rev. Henry Smith in his *Recollections and Reflections of an Old Itinerant*, page 45, states unequivocally that Asbury was not present. Since Smith attended the conference and there is no evidence that Scott was present, Smith's evidence in conjunction with the evidence of the *Journal* is probably correct. Smith states that all the Holston preachers attended the meeting but "Bishop Asbury was not with us in consequence of affliction." He passed through West Virginia en route to Maryland.

[26] Rocktown was the present Harrisonburg.

[27] To Sarah, the wife of Eli Dorsey, Asbury pays a beautiful tribute. (See *Journal* entry and note for August 8, 1799.)

[28] Because of opposition this building, which was erected on Sharp Street, was changed to a church. This became Sharp Street Memorial Methodist Church. (Hawkins: *The Life and Times of Hon. Elijah Stansbury*, 244; *Methodist Sesqui-Centennial, October, 1934*, 68, 69.)

second likeness of me,[29] at the desire of my mother, to send to England. I am trying to organize the African church. I made interest for the use of Mr. Otterbein's church for *Sabbath*, in the morning and evening for the white people. I have attempted to promote society meetings at Old Town and the west end of the city, either at the Dunker's meeting house or Mr. Otterbein's church. My feelings or my fears premonish me this will be a sickly summer. I visit, dine, and ride out every day; but it is very hard work for me to eat, drink, talk, and do nothing. As I am not a man of the world, the most of the conversation about it is irksome to me. I am taken from house to house, and the brethren wish the pleasure of seeing me, and those who are acquainted with their families will come to see me also.

Monday, *July* 3. I attempted to preach in Doctor Patrick Allison's church, and felt more assisted than I expected.

Tuesday, 4. I was taken in a chariot to Perry Hall, in company with sister Martha Fonerden. I felt the effects of my exertions on the Sabbath, the want of rest, rising early, and riding to Mr. Gough's. In my mind I felt almost as in old times. God hath not left this house. I felt great love to the family in praying for them in the family and in the closet. I had an open and free conversation with Mr. Gough about his soul. I conversed with the servants also, and had freedom in prayer, although I felt weakness of body. I wrote a few letters and read a little in the Bible. The weather is excessively warm.

Saturday, 8. I cannot now, as heretofore, spend ten hours out of sixteen in reading the Bible in English or Hebrew, or other books, or write letters from morning until night. My bow is weak, if not broken; but I have more time to speak to God and souls. *Sabbath day* I performed at Mr. Gough's alone.

Wednesday, 12. I borrowed a servant at Mr. Gough's, and came on to Mr. Daniel Sheridine's house, Northeast Cecil county. Here I borrowed another servant, and on *Friday* I rode to Wilmington (Delaware) and stopped at Allan M'Lane's,[30] now living there.

[29] The first portrait by Thomas Barber for which Bishop Asbury sat in the home of Mr. Hawkins was in the possession of a relative of the artist, J. K. Hand, New York City, in 1939. (Dolliver: *The Story of the Mother Church of American Methodism*, 26.)

[30] Allan McLane (1746–1829) moved from Philadelphia to Kent County, Delaware, about 1774. A colonel in the Revolutionary War, he became a friend of Washington. He was a pioneer Methodist in the present town of Smyrna and upon his removal to Wilmington was long a trustee of Asbury Church, in the graveyard of which he and several members of his family are buried. He was speaker of the Delaware legislature and from 1808 until his death was collector of the port of Wilmington. His home was long a favorite stopping place of Bishop Asbury. (Scharf, *op. cit.*, I, 208; Barratt, *op. cit.*, and photograph, 26; *Centennial Services of Asbury Methodist Episcopal Church, Wilmington, 1889*, 135, 144, 145; *American Heritage*, October, 1956.)

Pennsylvania

Saturday, 15. Warm as it was, I reached Philadelphia: and *Sabbath evening*, 16, I felt free to labour a little, feeble as I was, and enlarged on John xiv, 1. I have great reason to be thankful for my sulky; I should soon be silent without it. I rode to Germantown to see aged mother Steele, and sister Lusby, and found freedom, although I could hardly walk or talk; yet must needs speak to the women of the house about their souls. Dined at brother Baker's retreat, and came back to the city very sick, and went to bed.

New Jersey

Tuesday, 18. I came off to Burlington; and was much grieved to hear my appointments had been made, and not attended in consequence of my illness.

Wednesday, 19. Dined at Crosswick's, at brother Abbott's,[31] once a travelling preacher, now a merchant. We came on to father Joseph Hutchinson's. Here I was almost outdone with excessive heat. I stopped four days, but found it hard work to sit still.

Monday, 24. We came to New Brunswick; dined, prayed, and rejoiced to hear that God had kindled a living fire here, through the instrumentality of a brother from Elizabethtown. We came on to Elizabethtown, forty miles. It was ample labour for man and horse. Here I was sick again.

Tuesday, 25. I rode to Newark, and dined with Mr. Ogden,[32] a steady friend.

New York

After the rain, I came to New York. Here I spent a few painful days, being unable to visit or be visited.[33]

On *Monday* I came to Shotwell's,[34] very unwell; and the next day to Kingsbridge. Here I was compelled by affliction to spend two weeks.[35]

[31] David Abbott was the son of the noted and eccentric preacher Benjamin Abbott. David was converted under Philip Gatch in 1773 and became an itinerant preacher in 1781. After he located, he became a merchant at Crosswicks. (Lednum, *op. cit.*, 326.)

[32] The Rev. Uzal Ogden, formerly of Newton, New Jersey, where Asbury first met him, was at this time rector of Trinity Episcopal Church, Newark. (Atkinson, *op. cit.*, 287, 292.)

[33] See letter to Philip Van Cortlandt, August 29, 1797.

[34] Shotwell was a member of the new church then under construction in the area now known as Greenwich Village. The cornerstone had been laid and work begun, but Asbury does not mention it at this time.

[35] Asbury was doubtless cared for these two weeks at the home of Samuel Berian, close to the western edge of the village. (See *Journal* entry for July 9, 1798.)

I then rode to New Rochelle, and lodged at Mr. Sherwood's.[36] Finding myself swelling in the face, bowels, and feet, I applied leaves of burdock and then a plaster of mustard, which drew a desperate blister. I had such awful sore feet, I knew not but that they would mortify; and only after two weeks was I able to set them to the ground. I took cream of tartar and nitre daily, to cool and keep open the body. I also made use of the bark.

Sunday, September 10. I began to walk once or twice across the room.

Monday, 11. We began our route to Wilbraham.[37] We had not ridden far over the rocks before I was taken very unwell. We stopped at Byram, at father Banks's. I was soon put to bed with a very high fever, that held me through the night. I now began to conclude it was not the will of God I should proceed, and the brethren would not persuade me to go on. Brother Totten[38] returned with me to mother Sherwood's. I have had slight fevers, but expect to rest until about the first of October, which I hope, with riding a little every clear day, will restore me to health.

Thursday, 14. I visited Nicholas Underhill's[39] wife, who is near her trying hour. I hope it was good for me, for her, and for the family. I take a small portion of bark each day, and one-third of a common dose of cream of tartar and nitre, and hope I shall yet be raised up. My mind is stayed upon God; and I hope to be more holy: but I fear I shall never be able to ride and preach as I have done in former days, so as to be more useful. I have now much time to think of and review my whole life.

The kindness of this Sherwood family is great—my dear mamma, and Betsy Sherwood,[40] and Jonathan and Bishop also. If I had not been at home here, what additional distress of mind would have attended me! My friends also were welcome to come and see me. *Sabbath day*, at the widow Sherwood's, I had the pleasure of hearing our brother Matthias[41] make a

[36] The widowed mother, Abigail Sherwood, headed this family, and with her lived two sons, Jonathan and Bishop, as well as a daughter whose name is not recorded. On adjacent property lived another son, Moses, with his wife, Tamer. All members of the family were active in the Methodist group.

[37] The only conference to be held north of Philadelphia in 1797 was scheduled for September 19 at Wilbraham, Massachusetts.

[38] Joseph Totten (1759–1818) was received on trial in 1792. His early appointments were in the area around New York and later at Philadelphia and south Jersey. He was appointed to St. John's in Philadelphia in 1818 but served only a few days, dying suddenly there. (*General Minutes*, 1819; Seaman, *op. cit.*, 135; Warriner: *Old Sands Street Church.*)

[39] Nicholas Underhill was a tavern keeper and active member of the group meeting regularly at Sherwood's. His name stands in the early records as an eminent leader.

[40] Betsy was the wife of Bishop Sherwood. She had some skill in nursing and devoted herself to caring for Asbury during this illness. He mourned her passing when he returned on June 28, 1800.

[41] John Barnet Matthias was received into membership in September, 1790, and became a local preacher of acceptable service. His son, John Jarvis Matthias, became a noted preacher in the next generation. (Seaman, *op. cit.*, 248; *John Street Church Records*, II.)

pointed, profitable, and powerful discourse. It is now eight weeks since I have preached—awfully dumb Sabbaths! I have been most severely tried from various quarters; my fevers, my feet, and Satan, would set in with my gloomy and nervous affections. Sometimes subject to the greatest effeminacy; to distress at the thought of a useless, idle life: but what brought the heavy pang into my heart, and the big tear to roll, that never rises without a cause was, the thought of leaving the Connexion without some proper men of their own election, to go in and out before them in my place, and to keep that order which I have been seeking these many years to establish. My aged parents were dear to me in their advanced age and dependent state: like myself, they have spent what they had to spare for many years, nearly forty, in keeping open doors for the gospel and people of God: this burden hath been laid upon them. I am happy that I can now ride a little every clear day for my better health, and can eat and sleep better. I am left too much alone. I cannot sit in my room all day, making gloomy reflections on the past, present, and future life. Lord, help me! for I am poor and needy; the hand of God hath touched me, and I think Satan *forts* himself in my melancholy, unemployed, unsocial, and inactive hours.

Sunday, 17. I was strongly impressed in my mind months ago that this summer and fall would be marked with heavy afflictions. O Philadelphia! I have had very little faith for that city. I have often remarked the general contempt of the Sabbath; the constant noise of carriages; there is a perpetual disturbance of worshipping assemblies. It is true, one event cometh on the righteous and the wicked; but God will stand to his word—he hath punished, he will punish those that rob him. If report be true, the distress of the Philadelphians is great; three-fourths of the citizens are fled.

Monday, 18. I felt strength of faith and body, as if I should be raised up again. I rode for recreation nine miles. The clouds are dispelled from my mind. O that my future life may be holiness to the Lord—prudent and exemplary to many! I wished to speak to a poor African whom I saw in the field as I went out; and as I came along on my return, he was at a stone wall within eight or nine feet of me. Poor creature! he seemed struck at my counsel, and gave me thanks. O, it was going down into the Egypt of South Carolina after those poor souls of Africans I have lost my health, if not my life in the end. The will of the Lord be done!

Wednesday, 20. I rode about fourteen miles. I met a messenger, who came to desire my presence to-morrow at the funeral of our brother Van Nostrand.[42] I have known him about fifteen years, and had great confidence in the man. He hath laboured as a local preacher, and three years as a travelling one. He had his seals, and I know one. Some will complain

[42] Albert Van Nostrand (1757?–97) served with the British forces during the Revolution. In 1785 he joined the first Methodist class to be established at Searingtown, Long Island. His three years in the itinerancy were served in New Jersey and Westchester County. (*General Minutes*, 1797, 73.)

of his negligence in Elizabeth circuit; but what could the man do? He gave his life, and perhaps caught the cause of his death by bad lodging and riding in cold weather. He told a friend he had settled his temporal and spiritual business: he then slept in peace. Brother Van Nostrand was a native of Long Island. He followed the fortune of King George in the revolutionary war, but soon after peace he joined himself under king Jesus, and fought till he died in a good cause, as a Christian and a minister. I had some unpleasing symptoms, and am ready to conclude I shall linger on to death, or at least never be restored to perfect health. My soul continually cries out, Thy will be done, O Lord!

Thursday, 21. I attended the funeral, and gave an exhortation. I have ridden twenty miles this day, with little rest and no food.

Friday, 22. I rode eight or ten miles. I was touched with the fever.

Saturday, 23. I slept well last night, but waked with a slight fever. I received a letter from Dr. Coke. As I thought, so it is—he is gone from Ireland to England, and will have work enough when he cometh here. The three grand divisions of that Connexion are alarming. It is a doubt if the doctor cometh to America until spring, if at all until the General Conference. I am more than ever convinced of the propriety of the attempts I have made to bring forward Episcopal men:—First, from the uncertain state of my health; Secondly, from a regard to the union and good order of the American body, and the state of the European Connexion. I am sensibly assured the Americans ought to act as if they expected to lose me every day, and had no dependence upon Doctor Coke; taking prudent care not to place themselves at all under the controlling influence of British Methodists. I visited three families, talked and prayed in each, but was rather outdone.

Sunday, 24. At Sherwood's Valley: I had greatly desired to speak to these people, and was much assisted so to do; my subject was 2 Cor. vi. 2. I considered by way of introduction, what character of people they were who are to be the subjects of salvation—the lost, the enslaved, and those that cannot save themselves. First, Christ the author of this salvation; the meritorious, efficient, and moving cause. Secondly, The nature of this salvation—to reach all the misery and guilt of sinners; to save, redeem, and liberate. Thirdly, What bespeaks an accepted time and a day of salvation; to have God, Christ, the Spirit, ministers, means, and people that have religion, say, Behold—now is the day of salvation! I was able to speak fervently and regularly for an hour with great affection. I rejoiced to find that God had raised me up to call poor mourning souls to Christ, and to warn careless sinners. After twenty-six years the Gospel is established in this neighbourhood, at a small distance from this house. I preached at Peter Bonnett's before the war; and after peace was restored, the blessing returned to his widow's house; two of his daughters are in fellowship with us. The widow Sherwood's was the substitute house, after the widow Bonnett went to live at New York: now they are about building a church for the word and worship of God.[43] I am happy to hear, by letters, of a revival of the work in several places in Virginia, as also in North and South Carolina.

Monday, 25. The day was clear, and very warm. I rode up to the Plains, and stopped at Elijah Crawford's. God hath honoured this house. Two young men are going into the ministry out of it. I have ridden nearly twenty miles, and had it not been for the heat, I should have done well.

Tuesday, 26. I wrote a letter to ——, he was under grief and trouble. This day Joshua Wells[44] returned from Wilbraham Conference. Matters were conducted well.

Wednesday, 27. The preachers came up; and *Thursday*, 28, we had a sermon and ordination of deacons. I was employed about three hours, and faint indeed. I rode four miles, and lodged at Morgan's,[45] East Chester: this was an excessively warm day.

Saturday, 30. We rode to New York; a very warm day. I found myself much injured, but was well nursed at the north side of the city. They have a touch of the fever here in George Street.[46]

Sabbath, October 1. We had much rain. Live or die, I preached at the old and new church on Isa. xxxiii, 20, and Deut. xxviii, 9. I had some disagreeable things, and was but ill fitted in body to bear them.

New Jersey

Monday, 2. We rode about twenty-seven miles to Hammond's.[47] My fever rises every night.

[43] Moses Sherwood and his wife had sold to the congregation a good-sized plot very near their house for the price of twenty-five dollars. The first church building was nearly completed but still unfinished. A second building was erected on the site in 1866, the original building having been moved across the street and used as a residence. In 1912 a third structure took the place of the second. (Scharf, *op. cit.*, Quarterly Bulletin of Westchester County Historical Society, October, 1935, II, No. 3; Brochure of 175th Anniversary of Asbury Methodist Church, Crestwood, New York.)

[44] Joshua Wells (1764–1861) was under appointment to New York. He entered the itinerancy in 1789 and served for many years in Virginia, Maryland, Delaware, New York, Pennsylvania and Massachusetts. At the time of his death, when ninety-seven years of age, he was the oldest Methodist preacher. (Stevens, *op. cit.*, III, 111; Seaman, *op. cit.*, 141–42.)

[45] Morgan was a class leader in the New Rochelle church, living across the township line in Eastchester. This may have been the location on lower Troublesome Brook to which Asbury went to preach when at the Sherwood home on other occasions. (Scharf, *op. cit.*)

[46] This is now known as Spruce Street. Joshua Wells was to reside on this street and cared for Asbury there. (Seaman, *op. cit.*, 142 n.)

[47] The distance of twenty-seven miles from New York would indicate a stop at Metuchen in Middlesex County, or that vicinity, even though it is not mentioned in the *Journal*.

Tuesday, 3. We rode thirty miles to Joseph Hutchinson's. I lament most of all that I have not lived in a constant state of prayer. I have had most deep and sore temptations of many kinds, such as I could have hardly thought of in health. I must be tried so as by fire. By reason of the fever in Philadelphia our conference is moved to Duck Creek, in the state of Delaware.

Wednesday, 4. After the storm was over we moved on as far as Crosswicks, and lodged at father Lovell's.[48] I was weak in body but comfortable in mind. I visited three families; called at Hulet Hancock's, and saw my old friend of twenty-six years' membership. I came on to Burlington. Serious times still in Philadelphia. I was very unwell; I had an awful night.

Pennsylvania

Friday, 6. We crossed Dunkes's ferry, and came a rough, crooked way to Germantown. We had a meeting at Dr. Lusby's.

Saturday, 7. We rode over the rocks, after crossing Schuylkill at a ferry, to Chester, and thence to Aaron Mattson's. There is a new house and mill built since I was here; but there is room enough for Christ yet.

Delaware

We rode to Wilmington, where I preached on Psalm xlvi, 1–5.

Monday, 9. We came thirty-eight miles to Duck Creek.

Tuesday, 10. We began conference.[49] I appointed the president elders to take my seat, and I sat alone, because the hand of the Lord was upon me. I was resolved to put out my strength to the last in preaching. My first subject was Isaiah i, 26–28; my second was on Luke xvii, 12; my third 2 Cor. xiii, 11. Great times: preaching almost night and day; some souls converted, and Christians were like a flame of fire. Eleven persons were set apart for elders' and three for deacons' orders.

Friday, 13. We rose. I was much outdone, yet happy. We appointed a standing committee to inspect and direct the press. We read some passages of the notes on the Discipline, and left the remnant to this committee.

[48] Joseph Lovell was a local preacher. (Phoebus, *op. cit.*, 219.)

[49] This was the third session of the Philadelphia Conference to be held in Smyrna. During the session Asbury preached three times and ordained the following: deacons, John Lackey and Joseph Jewell; elders, Hamilton Jefferson and Anning Owen. It was unanimously agreed that Jesse Lee should travel with Asbury. (Colbert, *op. cit.*, 170; Thrift, *op. cit.*, 231; Phoebus, *op. cit.*, 233, 234, 353; Lee: *A Short History of the Methodists*, 251.)

Maryland

Monday, 16. We rode to Bohemia Ferry, twenty miles. Dr. Nicholas Ridgely has sent me plenty of Columbo magnesia, soluble tartar, and bark. I am much grieved that I do not converse more abundantly with God in my own heart and soul. We had great peace. I have not of late, if at any time in these parts, heard such an awful account of fever as we now hear rages in Baltimore city and Point. It is reported that our conference was first moved to Evans's meeting house. I spent the evening at Mr. Richard Bassett's, and lectured upon a chapter.

Tuesday, 17, was a very warm day. We rode from Duck Creek to Northeast. They had managed the matter so as to appoint for me and brother Jesse Lee to preach. I gave them a short sermon, on Gal. v. 7: "Ye did run well; who did hinder you that ye should not obey the truth?" I lodged at Mr. Daniel Sheridine's.

Wednesday, 18. We came to Josias Dallam's.

Thursday, 19. Reached Mr. Gough's. I was comforted in seeing a few of my age who were my spiritual children.

Friday, 20. After all the alarm we came to Baltimore; a blessed rain settled the amazing dust and purified the air.

Saturday, 21. I opened conference, and gave up the presidency to the presiding elders. Returned unwell. Very uncomfortable easterly winds and rainy weather. I mentioned in my speech to the conference the weakness of the episcopacy.

The conference rose on *Friday*, 27. There was great peace, and all the preachers, but myself, satisfied with their stations.

Sabbath day, 22. I preached at Dr. Allan's church the funeral sermon of Martha F. Allison,[50] a Methodist for about twenty-seven years; a class leader; a woman of sense and piety: the subject was John xi, 24–27. We had a crowded house.

Sunday, 29. I opened the new church in Light Street[51] with reading 2 Chron. vii, 12; Psalm cxxxii; Haggai ii, Mark xi. The elders read and

[50] This was Dr. Patrick Allison, pastor of the First Presbyterian Church, and the funeral service was for Martha Fonerden. A notice in the *Federal Gazette* and *Daily Baltimore Advertiser* for October 21, 1797, reads: "The Rev. Francis Asbury will preach the funeral sermon of Mrs. Martha Fonerden at the Presbyterian Church, tomorrow afternoon at 3 o'clock." She was the wife of Adam Fonerden who at that time represented the fifth ward in the city council. Fonerden, once an itinerant preacher, has left an on-the-spot account of the Christmas Conference. His wife had been appointed a class leader in 1792 by Asbury. (See letter to Ezekiel Cooper for October 24, 1797, and its value in correcting the above error in names; Phoebus, *op. cit.*, 237, 238; Hawkins, *op. cit.*, 225.)

[51] This was the second Light Street Church, which replaced the one destroyed by fire the previous December. It did not stand on the exact site of its predecessor but on the southwest corner of Light Street and Wine Alley. (Roberts: *Centenary Pictorial Album*, 76, 77.)

prayed. My subject was Eph. ii, 19–22; and at Old Town I preached on 2 Samuel xvi, 17. I had to preach the funeral sermon of father Gatch[52] on 1 Thess. iv, 13, 14. I observed the pleasing, cheering, and charming manner in which the apostle described the death of the righteous. Sleep—sleep in Jesus; a rest from labour, sorrow, affliction, and pain; happy opening visions of God! Secondly, The hope the pious who are alive have for their pious dead who have had experience, and long continuance in religion, and a comfortable dying in the Lord. Those who have no hope for themselves nor their dead, how awful their sorrow! I feel myself very weak. I dined at Mr. Philip Rogers's.

Tuesday, 31. I went to see the poor orphans; to weep with sister Fonerden's children, and dear Nelly Owings, her daughter also. They had a Nelly Owings baptized for the dead brother and sister Reed, my dear nursing friends: my aged friends brought me their beneficence and tears.[53]

Wednesday, *November* 1. We came off and preached at the widow Dorsey's, on, "If in this life only we have hope in Christ, we are of all men most miserable." We had a solemn assembly. I made a few observations on the hope Christians have of Christ only in this life; if in this life only Christians could have hope in Christ, they would be most miserable. They are denied the sinful pleasures, profits, and honours of the world; subject to great afflictions and persecutions; often deprived of life in ages past; no mercy, no justice, no truth, no love; lastly, that they could never be borne up under such principles and persecutions if it were not for the hope of future rewards: they which have no hope in this or the future world in Christ, are of all men the most wretched and miserable. My horse is a little ungovernable, the weather warm, and myself unwell.

Thursday, 2. I did not preach, but exhorted at Shadrach Turner's:[54] here are five children and a mother for Christ, and for usefulness.

District of Columbia

Friday, 3. We came to Georgetown. I felt very feeble in body, almost ready to faint before we reached Col. Lloyd Bell's: I was glad through

[52] This was Conduce Gatch, husband of Priscilla and father of Philip Gatch (1751–1835). (McLean, *op. cit.*, 5–7; Lee: *A Short Account of the Life and Death of the Rev. John Lee*, 33.)

[53] The punctuation in this passage tends to confuse the relationship of the persons mentioned. Samuel Owings (1733–1803) and Deborah Lynch Owings (1745–1810) had a daughter, Nelly, who was married to Thomas Moale in 1793. All names here refer to Baltimore Methodist families. The Samuel Owings were at Lovely Lane, at Strawberry Alley the Moales were pioneer officials, and at Baltimore Town (Exeter Street) the Fonerdens were active. (See article by William Hamilton in *The Methodist Quarterly*, July, 1856; manuscript copy "Owings, Owens Genealogy" by Mrs. Focke, Maryland Historical Society, Baltimore; Armstrong, *op. cit.*, 18, 89.)

[54] Shadrach Turner lived at Bladensburg, Maryland.

my weakness to be excused from preaching: brother Lee supplied the place. I visited John Long's family; I saw mother Moore after more than twenty years; she is going on to glory. A son of brother Long's was sick, and distressed about his soul, and resolved to seek redeeming grace. We must needs go and view the famous bridge; it is amazing to see the river so contracted that a stone could be pitched over where the bridge stands: this is three miles above Georgetown: from the bridge upwards, there is a good road cut out of the rocks.

Virginia

The rain came on, and we were glad we could find Samuel Adams's, three miles from the bridge: here we were happily sheltered from the weather, and comfortably accommodated. I sent for brother Waters and his wife, and we improved the evening in the way Christians should; in prayer, singing, reading the word, and exhortations.

Sunday, 5. We rode ten miles to Alexandria, and had only time to reach town when the rain came on powerfully. I made a feeble discourse on Isaiah xxxiii, 20. I ordained Thomas Lyell deacon.

Monday, 6. Came out of town late, and judged it best to call at William Bushby's. We had a storm of snow. My mind is dull and my body languid; my only hope is Christ and grace.

Tuesday, 7. We thought it good, as the weather was fine, to stand our course southward: we fed at Colchester, at the new bridge: we were told it would cost eighty thousand dollars. This is a great relief to hasty travellers. We dined on the road, in the woods, on what we brought with us. We got to Dumfries, where court was then sitting: we met several drunken men on the way. I have not seen such sights for many days. We slept at Captain Ward's: they expected us the evening before. I ordained brother Hopkinson deacon.

Wednesday, 8. We came away at eight o'clock, making twelve miles to Stafford court house, breakfasted and fed, and then drove twenty-five miles to the widow Bombry's, where we arrived about six o'clock. The hills were very bad to climb, being much washed and broken: I was ready to be cast away, or overset. My body is still weak, and my mind greatly affected.

Thursday, 9. I had gloomy feelings last night. Riding in the night was very injurious. I feel no evil, unless something like murmuring. When I am so unable to travel and yet go on, probably I do more than God or man requires of me; but the will of the Lord be done! If I suffer or sin in this, he will pardon my weakness.

Friday, 10. We rested at the widow Bombry's: this mother in Israel treated us with every necessary mark of attention. I had an interview with sister Forks and her daughter. I found them still walking in the narrow way.

Saturday, 11. We rode ten miles to Port Royal, and then came on nearly twenty miles to the widow Rouse's,[55] in Essex, where we were kindly and comfortably entertained. We then hastened on to Lersy Cole's; he and his wife were gone to quarterly meeting eight miles down the river, but a pious young sister and housekeeper made us comfortable. We had a storm of wind and rain: when it had blown over, we hasted to the meeting house. I gave a short sermon, on, "No man speaking by the Spirit of God calleth Jesus accursed"; and that, "No man can say Jesus is Lord but by the Holy Ghost." What is to be understood by calling Jesus accursed? To put him wholly out of the question; to expel him from being anything in our salvation; and to say all the unkind things that the Jews said of him. We had to ride five miles to the widow Humby's; here all was kindness and love. We rejoiced to see our much esteemed brethren, Cole, M'Kendree, and Mead, and to hear of a great and gracious work of God.

Monday, 13. We rode to Pace's chapel, where I preached on John xiv, 6, after which we had several exhortations, and the sacrament. We lodged at widow Campbell's: we have been fed by the widows more than Elijah.

Tuesday, 14. We rode to Shackleford's chapel,[56] and held meeting three hours: we had a large and solemn congregation. I preached, although very unwell, on 1 Cor. ii, 12. In the month of July last, the Lord visited this place in mercy, and it is judged thirty souls not only professed to be, but were really converted to God. In speaking today, I showed—Of whom, and of what the apostles wrote: the things freely given them to know as apostles and Christians—redemption, salvation in all its degrees, conviction of sin, repentance for sin, faith, justification, regeneration, sanctification, the resurrection, and glorification; that these things are not communicated by the spirit of the world, but by the Spirit of God. We had a very warm day; we fasted eight hours, and held meeting three, and then rode nearly twenty-four miles, and lodged at ——.

Wednesday, 15, was a snowy day, and very cold: I rode seven miles, cased and curtained up in the carriage. I kept house at brother Bellamy's: it is seven years since I was here. My mind enjoys peace, but my body is languid. I had a severe fever, and found it time to rest. A society of nearly forty here is now increased to one hundred, and it is hoped that nearly five hundred have joined this year in Gloucester circuit. I preached at Bellamy's chapel on Heb. iii, 12, 13: it was an exceedingly cold day, but clear. We rode ten miles to John Ellis's, where we were comforted with kindness, and blessed for one short night. We rose early to go on our way and, behold, who should meet us but Bishop Coke, with a borrowed horse,

[55] This was a Mrs. Rowzie. (Butts: *From Saddle to City, By Buggy, Boat and Railway*, 335.)

[56] This chapel is in King and Queen County, Virginia.

and a large white boy riding behind him on the same horse. We halted, and then agreed he should have brother M'Kendree's horse; but up came John Ellis, and took the Doctor (Coke) home, and brought him in a carriage to quarterly meeting. We stood on our course, and by the time we came to Gloucester ferry, it blew a storm of wind and rain: I had only to turn the chair back to the wind and sit wrapped up. After two hours we crossed the river and rode in haste to John Ellis's, seven miles. We drank, ate, prayed, and came on our way: the day, to one in my state, was very uncomfortable. We rode thirty-two miles this day, and stopped at our dear brother Taylor's, in James City. There are two very good meeting houses built here since I visited these parts; one in James City, and the other in New Kent county.

Saturday, 18. I delivered a feeble discourse on 1 Peter ii, 1, 2. I observed on the *malice*, for some real or supposed injury done; *guile* to hide malice until an opportunity for revenge offers. *Hypocrites*—going beyond our attainments, professing what we do not practice, or not practicing what we profess; *envious* at the excellencies or happiness of others; *evil-speaking*—all these arising from the bad state of the heart, chiefly pride and self-love. *Babes*; not giving them strong food or medicines: *babes*; strangers to malice by want of understanding—and not having a capacity for guile; strangers to hypocrisy; no ideas of envy, not having speech to speak evil. Dr. Coke preached on Luke xii, 14: "For where your treasure is, there your heart is also." We spent a night at the widow Cowling's.

Monday, 20. We rode thirty-one miles to brother Mooring's;[57] I had a thought never more to cross at old Jamestown. But we had a remarkable time after we had embarked: myself and Dr. Coke crossing in a skiff, the horses and carriage came in a large boat; my Bible, which was clothed and bound up in a handkerchief, was accidentally thrown into the river, but the black man snatched it up undamaged. The weather being damp, we rested.

Tuesday, 21. I wrote a small epistle to the official members of Baltimore, and another to Philadelphia, as also a short pathetic letter to my parents. We have ridden little less than four hundred miles in twenty days, and rested one. We had very damp weather.

Wednesday, 22, at brother Bellamy's.[58]

Thursday, 23. I rode about thirty miles to Mr. Briggs's,[59] to see how the preachers would be accommodated, and where the conference would be held: Mr. Briggs was willing to take eight or ten of the preachers, and gave the conference the offer of his hall to sit in.

Friday, 24. I visited my old friends, and wrote to Alexander Mather.

[57] (See letter to parents, November 20, 1797.) Mooring lived in Surry County.

[58] Bellamy lived in Gloucester County. Asbury recrossed the James and York rivers to get to Bellamy's, then crossed them again to get to Briggs's.

[59] Briggs lived in Surry County. (*Heads of Families*, 42.)

My route, which I only guessed at, is now fixed by Norfolk, Portsmouth, Newbern, Kingston, Georgetown, and Charleston,—between five and six hundred miles in little more than a month; sick or well, living or dead, my appointments go on.

Saturday, 25. The conference began their sitting at Lane's chapel. About sixty preachers were present: nine or ten had located; and four or five were added. *Sabbath day* two hours were spent in speaking of the circuits, and for souls.

Wednesday, 29. At noon the conference[60] rose; the business was conducted with despatch, and in much peace. I desired the advice of the conference concerning my health: the answer was, that I should rest until the session of the conference to be held in April, in Virginia.

Thursday, 30. I travelled under much weakness of body to Stith Parham's, at the High-hill store.

Friday, *December* 1. I collected the small remains of strength I had, to read, and hear read my manuscript journal. It was written in such haste that it was very incorrect. I visited Robert Jones's family, and on

Sunday, 3, we had a family meeting: brother M'Kendree preached on faith, hope, and charity,—on faith to me, as I felt the need of its exercise.

Monday, 4. We stopped one night at Matthew Davis's;[61] and the next at Ira Ellis's. Our time was taken up in journalizing; I came off twenty-five miles to Edward Drumgoole's: once or twice I felt on my way thither as if the blood would rise into my mouth. I resolved to give up travelling this winter. Dr. Sims bled me; and there appeared an inflammatory buff on the top. O! to rest—to be idle and dependent—is painful: but if this is to make me perfect, the will of the Lord be done! I sent my papers to brother Lee, who proceeds to Charleston; also my plan and directions how to station the preachers, to brother Jackson. I believed that my going to Charleston this season, would end my life; yet, could I be persuaded it was the will of the Lord, I would go and preach. I cannot bear the fatigue of riding thirty miles in a day. I am much pressed to make my will, lest I should be surprised by death; my mind is greatly calmed and centered in God. I have well considered all the solemnities of death.

Saturday and *Sunday*, 9, 10. We sat melancholy in the house—dumb *Sabbaths*! Dr. Sims read me Mr. Wesley's sermon upon the depth of the riches of the wisdom and of the knowledge of God.

Monday, 11. I was led to meditate on the same subject: "By whom shall Jacob rise?" 1. Jacob,—the Church. 2. Rise to spiritual glory. 3. By whom Jacob hath risen. 4. By whom the Church shall rise—it is a prophetic character of the Church. Jacob—see that man loved by his

[60] See letter to the British Conference, November 29, 1797. Lane's was in Sussex County.

[61] Matthew Davis lived in Greensville County. (*Heads of Families*, 54.) Asbury moved on to Brunswick County, where because of illness he stayed for several months.

mother, hated by his brethren after the flesh, guarded against unlawful marriages, yet had two wives, representing the Jewish and Gentile state of the Church. See his afflictions and persecutions; the danger of being extinct in his family; yet preserved, his children, his piety, his prayers. A type of Christ, and his Church. Jacob, rise! rise, increase in children, in faith, in love, in mercy, in justice, in truth, in zeal, in ministerial gifts, in faithful watchmen. By whom hath the Church risen? By Abel, by Enoch, by Noah, by Abraham, Isaac, and Jacob; by Moses and Aaron, Joshua, and the elders that outlived Joshua; by Joel, by Ruth, by Obadiah, servant of Ahab, by Micah, by Joash, by Jotham, Hezekiah, and his grandson Josiah; and all the prophets; by the great wrestling Jacob; by Jesus and his apostles; by faithful ministers in all ages, nations and societies. We want knowledge to know, and time to mention their names. By whom shall Jacob rise? God will pour out his Spirit in the last days on ministers and people, old men and maidens, young men and children, ministers and members of his Church, magistrates and masters, parents and guardians. He is small: see all the little flock—the holy seed; all the weaknesses, all the apostates and backsliders, all the want of justice, mercy, truth, and true religion: these shall be replaced with opposite characters and graces; all the vacancies of ministers and virtues shall be filled up, and more abundantly supplied in spiritual and heavenly glory, when all shall know the Lord, and be taught of the Lord, and all be righteous, and the knowledge of the Lord shall cover the earth, as the water doth all the deep places of the earth and seas. But by whom shall Jacob rise? I answer, by the wisdom, power, mercy, truth, love, and holiness of God, displayed in a glorious Gospel. I am sure Jacob shall rise by the merit, righteousness, and intercession of Jesus Christ. I answer again, by the operations of the eternal Spirit of God, in its convincing, converting, and sanctifying influences, manifested by the calling and qualifying ministers for the work; that thousands of ministers may go forth, and millions of souls may be brought home by their instrumentality.

Tuesday, 12. Whilst taking a sober, contemplative ride for three hours, I conversed sweetly with God; my mind and body were refreshed with a clear and cold day. I read a few chapters in the book of God. In the evening Mr. James Green Martin came to receive deacon's orders; he brought letters of consolation from Richard Whatcoat and Jesse Lee. Also the wishes of my dear brethren and sisters that waited to see me.

Wednesday, 13. I felt a little better; I rode out, but it was not as comfortable a day as yesterday. The smallest exercise or application to study is too great for me. The doctor pronounces my complaint to be debility. I have taken cider with *nails* put into it, and fever powders, and must take more of the barks.

Thursday, 14. My mind is grieved with the *old sore* in Virginia; but I must bear it patiently. One of our sisters asked me if we would not rebaptize persons that desired it. This put me to thinking and revolving the subject in my mind. I considered that there was neither precept nor example in holy writ to justify our rebaptizing one who had been baptized in the name and form which Christ commanded in Matt. xxviii, 19.

Friday, 15. Was my well day; I took some of the powders, had good nursing, and got rest. I only read the Bible and the Form of Discipline. I write, ride, and talk a little with the women, children, and Africans. My thoughts were led to meditate upon 1 Tim. iv, 16: "Take heed unto thyself, and unto the doctrine; continue in them: for in doing this thou shalt both save thyself and them that hear thee."

I. "Take heed to thyself,"—in religion, as in nature, self-preservation is one of the first laws. Take heed that thy experience in religion and doctrine be sound; that thou hast a good heart, and a good head, and a good life, and a good conversation, ministerial diligence and fidelity in every part of Christian and pastoral duty. Saved already by grace, thou shalt be preserved from all the snares set for thy feet, and not backslide as a Christian minister, but feel persevering, sanctifying, glorifying, and crowning grace.

II. Thou shalt "save them that hear thee," from lukewarmness and backsliding; legality on the one hand, and making void the law through faith on the other; that they profess and possess, live and walk as it becometh the Gospel of Christ.

III. "Continue in them,"—in all the doctrines, ordinances, and duties of the Gospel: the same Gospel, the same ordinances, the same duties which are designed to complete the work in the souls of ministers as Christians, are as needful to continue the work of grace as to begin it; and not only continue, but to finish and bring on the headstone with shouting.

Saturday, 16. I employed myself as much as my health would admit, in reading the Bible and writing such observations thereon as were suggested to my mind.

Sunday, 17. I had to keep house; O dumb day! I am better, yet it is not safe for me to go out such very cold weather. I read the word of God and preached.

Monday, 18. Very little done; I wrote to Dr. Coke, advising against the British brethren going to law with the contentious party about their houses.

Tuesday, 19. I am in a more comfortable state of body and mind, for which I feel thankful. I am taking the bark.

Wednesday, 20. I felt much amended by the bark and rest. It appears to have been the Mount Moriah where Abraham essayed to offer up his Isaac, on which the temple of God was built upwards of eight hundred years thereafter, and before the offering of Christ, nearly or upon the same spot, eight hundred and seventy-two: the types and prophecies are not small arguments for the truth of the Scriptures; for fore-knowledge doth not belong to man—he cannot tell, only by probable conjectures, anything that will befall himself, unless revealed by the spirit of prophecy. The prophecy made by the man of God, 1 Kings xiii, fulfilled by Josiah, 2 Kings xxiii. Between the prophecy and fulfilment a probable space of time of about three hundred and fifty years, completely accomplished in every punctilio, and the prophet's tomb and sleeping ashes taken notice of, the prophet's memory kept, who died a witness to what he said, to seal the truth, and his sleeping bones lying there on the spot: what man, untaught by God, who knoweth all things, could come and foretell such events which should so surely come to pass, without being taught and sent of God?

Thursday, 21. Perhaps we may call this one of the coldest days of this winter. I slept under two double-milled blankets, beside coverlids and sheets, but could not keep warm. This is the fifth season of cold weather we have had in Virginia since the first of November. We have had snow, but this is gone in a day: this excepted, it is cold enough for the north. Strange life for me—to sit and burn myself by the fire, and to be nursed. I feel a small return of health. I have been reading David's Psalms in Hebrew, and the Book of Genesis in the English Bible. I could not but admire the provision made for the heathen nations, civil and barbarous, by Abraham's second marriage, and by Ishmael and Esau's posterity. This attended to according to their names, as traced in the Universal History, we should not wondering ask, Where did this or that nation of people come from? either Indians or Africans. I cannot preach now, only to the family, and when a stranger cometh in.

Friday, 22. I rose in the morning, in some fear lest I had or should say too much on slavery. I made a choice of a verse, 1 Kings xxii, 16: "And the king said unto him, How many times shall I adjure thee that thou tell me nothing but that which is true in the name of the Lord," or Jehovah. I have found relief by taking barks, in strength, in feeling, in breath, and in my breast, and have a hope of being raised up once more.

Saturday, 23. Extremely cold. I am closely confined in my room, but could neither read nor write.

Sunday, 24. It is exceedingly cold still. The pain in my breast is returned; I fear it is immovably fixed more or less until death. Lord, thy will be done! Wearisome days are appointed for me. Brother Edward Drumgoole came in the evening of Christmas day. I am cheered with company and with Christ also. I feel as if the coming year would be marked with displays of Divine power upon the souls of men to whoever may live to see it.

Tuesday, 26. We had open weather and rain. I am so much better in health that confinement is as trying to me as hard labour. I hope, if it pleaseth my God, I shall have health to be of some service to mankind yet. Ah! what is life and all this dull round, but for God and souls!

Wednesday, 27. A falling of snow—very cold. I have taken the bark. This is the ninth day, and I am strengthened; but the wine in the smallest portions makes me feverish, and it is astringent. I feel need of great patience, prayer, and faith.

Thursday, 28. We had hard frost and snow. I am thankful it is rest time with the poor blacks, or many might be frozen to death. Ungrateful man that I am, how am I favoured above millions!

Friday, 29. Extremely cold. Mrs. Selby desired to see me, bad riding as it was, through the snow and ice. I am mending. I prayed for health, and had faith to believe I should recover. I thought if God would spare me I was willing to labour and suffer out my days; but the thought of being useless is most distressing to an active, benevolent mind.

Saturday, 30. I felt weakness of body and dejection of mind; and sometimes I am brought to think of requesting, as Elijah and Jonah did, that I may die. I cannot pray in the family without injury; wherefore should I request to live? O! my God, thy will be done in all things—mine in nothing, but as it pleaseth thee!

Sunday, 31. We had a meeting at my lodging.

Wednesday, 27. A falling of snow—very cold. I have taken the bark. This is the ninth day; and I am strengthened; but the wine in the smallest portions makes me feverish, and it is [illegible]. I have need of great patience, prayer, and faith.

Thursday, 28. We had hard frost and snow; I am thankful it is not with the poor blacks, or many might be frozen to death. Ungrateful man that I am, how am I favoured above millions!

Friday, 29. Excessive cold. Mrs. Selby desired to see me; bad riding as it was, through the snow and ice I am mending. I prayed for health, and had faith, as I believed I should recover. I thought if God would spare me I was willing to labour and suffer out my days; but the thought of being useless is most distressing to an active, benevolent mind.

Saturday, 30. I felt weakness of body and dejection of mind; and sometimes I am brought to think, O, could I die as Elijah, and much [illegible] that I may die. [illegible] without [illegible]; wherefore should I request to live? O, my God, thy will be done in all things—I am nothing but as it pleaseth thee.

Monday, 31. We had a moderate [illegible]

1798

1798 *Asbury and Jesse Lee arriving at Readfield in Maine*

CHAPTER TWENTY-SEVEN

Virginia

Monday, January 1, 1798. Several local brethren were present—Drumgoole, Lane, Moore, Smith, and Phillips. The brethren were lively in religion. I am now taking an extraordinary diet—drink made of one quart of hard cider, one hundred nails, a handful of black snakeroot, one handful of fennel seed, and one handful of wormwood, boiled from a quart to a pint, taking one wine glass full every morning for nine or ten days, using no butter, or milk, or meat; it will make the stomach very sick, and in a few days purge the patient well. I was better in my feelings than I have been since I have been taken ill; but I must flee conversation, grief, and care, with deep and close thinking and composition. I made a small meditation on being free from the ceremonial law. Polygamy, slavery, and such like were never commanded under this dispensation, but only tolerated, and accompanied by strict injunctions to prevent men from running to greater lengths in these practices, as may be seen in Exodus xxi, Leviticus xxv, Deuteronomy xxiv. Polygamy was allowed to prevent general whoredom. Servitude was regulated to prevent slavery and oppression, death, and loss of limbs. If any had asked the Lord on the subject of slavery, as on polygamy, he must have said, Moses, as a man, suffered this, a less evil, to prevent a greater; but it was not so from the beginning of the creation: it is the fall which hath done this, not a holy God. It is man's work, of two evils to choose the least. But God is not tempted of us to evil, neither tempteth he any man. Christians, of two evils should not choose or use either, if they would be like God.

Tuesday, 2.—Now I am brought to the second day of the new year—the last hath been a year of great affliction. I may have travelled about three thousand miles, and have been confined with affliction and weakness six months, adding the single days I have stopped, as well as weeks. In April last I had very little expectation of living until this day. I am now under the exercise to desire life, that I may see the connexion better organized, and be more personally useful.

Wednesday, 3. This is a cloudy day; it is probably snowing north or west. I have a better appetite for food: my mind is greatly agitated at times; but patience shall have its perfect work. I pray, and sometimes I wind and pick a little cotton, and read and write about one hour in the day; but Christ is all! I cannot be inactive: the hardest work I have to do is to do nothing.

Thursday, 4. A proper day for rain! Last evening I had a very high fever; but I am as usual to-day. I read my Bible, and selected those texts which struck my mind, that if ever I should preach again I may use. Joseph said, I fear God; Nehemiah said, he could not oppress the people as other governors had done, because of the fear of God. *Fear of God*, in seekers, in believers, and in those who are sanctified: and the motives to the fear of God. *First*, He is holy; *Secondly*, He is wise; *Thirdly*, He is just; *Fourthly*, He is powerful. If holy, he hath no sin; if wise, he knoweth when we sin; if he is just, he must punish sin; and he hath power to punish it. A man may be *wise*, but not *all-wise*; a man may be just, but not infinite in justice: thus man may be holy, but not holy as God; man may be wanting in wisdom, in power, in holiness, and in justice. In some cases it may not be man's duty to punish, nor in his power—not so with Jehovah. Who will not fear him according to his attributes, and according to his word of threatened vengeance?

Friday, 5. The rain is over; the cloud's scattered and gone; and nature smiling again. I only mourn the oppression I cannot remove.

Saturday, 6. We have open and pleasant weather. It may be, that many have overlooked the prophesies of Jacob in Genesis xlix. We may look for the fulfilment nearly fourteen hundred years after, in the coming of Christ; and about one thousand years after, we shall see in Jeremiah, and Daniel, what Jacob further referred to. It appears that it was the wish of Jacob that his youngest but one, Joseph, should have the birthright, which Reuben, his first-born, had lost by his unnatural incest in defiling his father's bed. Simeon and Levi—we cannot tell whether they had a blessing or a curse for their zeal against folly in Israel; they punished whoredom with cruel murder, and yet we see how Levi's zeal wrought in the case of Cozbi, and the Lord confirmed the priesthood by special grant to him. Joseph's prophecy concerning the Israelites' *exodus* from Egypt was not fulfilled for upwards of three hundred years thereafter. It seemeth that Jacob wished (but Jehovah willed not) that Joseph, and not Judah, should be the ruler, and from him should come the Shepherd, the Stone of Israel, the promised Messiah: see this 1 Chron. v.

Sabbath, 7. My mind is serene and happy. I was comforted in seeing one of the travelling preachers. The physic I have been taking operateth well. O that I may not flatter or elate myself! I can only promise to be more faithful if I have more grace.

Monday, 8. I wrote a long letter to John Dickins upon the manner of expediting his books to the distant parts—viz., the Journals, Sermons, Saints' Rests, Patterns, Hymn Books; and that the Magazine should be our grand circulating medium; only let us have more American Lives and Letters.

Tuesday, 9. The weather is temperate: my mind is much pained. O! to be dependent on slaveholders is in part to be a slave, and I was free born. I am brought to conclude that slavery will exist in Virginia perhaps for ages; there is not a sufficient sense of religion nor of liberty to destroy it; Methodists, Baptists, Presbyterians, in the highest flights of rapturous piety, still maintain and defend it. I judge in after ages it will be so that poor men and free men will not live among slaveholders, but will go to new lands; they only who are concerned in, and dependent on them will stay in old Virginia.

Wednesday, 10. I have some peace and some pain of heart.

Thursday, 11. My mind is exceedingly agitated on my peculiar situation: I feel each day, like a day or a year to me, as it is well or ill employed. Ebenezer Academy[1] is under poor regulations; and what is more than all, some gentlemen of Brunswick county had the confidence and want of propriety to wish to wrest it wholly out of our hands, after we had collected so much money to build it.

Friday, 12. My mind still in pain. I read a chapter each day, and take down those verses that appear to me the most select, and which I have never used before in preaching; they may be of use if ever I should serve the sanctuary again. I have read Kempis and Young.

Saturday, 13. I finished three feeble letters, to Nelson Reed, Henry Willis, and John Harper. I cannot read or write long together. I wind broaches of cotton for diversion and recreation; I will not be idle. The class met at my lodging; and I ventured to give a small exhortation and a prayer.

Sunday, 14. I am still confined; I must try emetic tartar, kill or cure. There is preaching at the chapel, a mile and a half distant, but the weather is such that I cannot go with safety. The inveteracy of my fever was such, that on *Monday*, 15, I was fully resolved to take three grains of tartar emetic, which operated powerfully and brought off a proper portion of

[1] Ebenezer Academy was located in the southern part of Brunswick County, Virginia, between Petersburg and Boydton near Merritt's meetinghouse. It was the first Methodist school in America, being founded sometime between 1783 and 1793, and it antedated Cokesbury College. (Cummings: *Early Schools of Methodism*, 35–41.)

bile: in this I hope for a cure. I must commend the old practice after all; no anti-bilious pill will answer as well in my case and many others.

Tuesday, 16. I read a letter and wrote a letter.

Wednesday, 17. I am weak in body, but some better; I read, wrote, and wrought in winding cotton, as I could not be idle and wholly inactive.

Thursday, 18. I went from the place where I had stayed six weeks, and had received every mark of affection, to brother Dromgoole's, ten miles. I felt at home here also.

Friday, 19. My fever was light last night; but this day I am uncomfortable.

Saturday, 20. Very unwell. I am strangely brought down; Lord, let me suffer with patience; thy will be done! I could not do any thing at my books; but that I might not be wholly idle, I wound cotton broaches among the children.

Sunday, 21. I sat at home reading a little. *Monday*, I am better; my fever is greatly broken. I can only write, and meditate about an hour in a day. I must have some exercise, if it is only women's work.

Tuesday, 23. We had news from the assembly, that the American ambassadors were rejected at Paris. A report prevails that the French were about to invade England with one hundred and fifty thousand men. The British can raise two hundred thousand militia, and two hundred thousand regulars; there may yet be most desperate times—worse than in Julius Cæsar's day. My mind is in peace. We have *winterly* weather; more snow after much rain this day: thank God I have where to lay my head, a little reading and winding of cotton that I may not be quite idle.

Wednesday, 24. Nothing of moment except a few thoughts for Ebenezer school.

Thursday, 25. I employed myself in winding cotton; I cannot think long, read, or write. Rebecca Dromgoole reads for me out of Watts, Allcine, and Baxter's works. I am much tried: the weather is so cold that I must keep in the house.

Friday, 26. Was a gloomy morning to me: nothing but the thoughts of death agitated my mind. It oppresses my heart to think that I live upon others and am useless, and that I may die by inches.

Sunday, 28. A solitary day to me, neither preaching, reading, writing, nor conversing.

Monday, 29. I was employed in revising my journal. I am like Mr. Whitefield, who being presented with one of his extempore sermons taken in short hand, could not bear to see his own face. I doubt whether my journals yet remaining will appear until after my death: I could send them to England and get a price for them; but money is not my object.

Tuesday, 30. I was employed in explaining my manuscript; but am afraid of intense application.

Wednesday, 31. Still engaged in revising my journal.

Thursday, February 1. I rode to Owen's, seven miles, and heard brother Whatcoat, on the "end of the commandment." I had been kept back so long that I was constrained to spend about forty minutes in glossing on the epistle to the angel of the Church of Ephesus; I then commented on what law Paul must have alluded to in 1 Tim. i, 9.

Monday, 5. I took four grains of tartar emetic, and had a large bitter return.

Tuesday, 6. My fever was very light last night. I received a most loving letter from the Charleston conference; there is great peace and good prospects there. I hope to be able to move next week. I have well considered my journal: it is inelegant; yet it conveys much information of the state of religion and country. It is well suited to common readers; the wise need it not. I have a desire that my journals should be published, at least after my death, if not before. I make no doubt but others have *laboured*: but in England, Scotland, and Ireland, and those kingdoms which have been civilized and improved one thousand years, and which are under such improvements, no ministers could have *suffered* in those days, and in those countries, as in America, the most ancient parts of which have not been settled two hundred years, some parts not forty, others not thirty, twenty, nor ten, and some not five years. I have frequently skimmed along the frontiers, for four and five hundred miles, from Kentucky to Green Briar, on the very edge of the wilderness; and thence along Tygers Valley to Clarksburg on the Ohio. These places, if not the haunts of savage men, yet abound with wild beasts. I am only known by name to many of our people, and some of our local preachers; and unless the people were all together, they could not tell what I have had to cope with. I make no doubt the Methodists are, and will be, a numerous and wealthy people, and their preachers who follow us will not know our struggles but by comparing the present improved state of the country with what it was in our days, as exhibited in my journal and other records of that day.

Wednesday, 7. Rain and snow; I am a poor prisoner.

Thursday, 8. We made a visit to Matthew Myrick's, and returned.

Friday, 9. It is very cold weather: I was glad to keep close occupied in reviewing my journal, and writing a few letters. This is a sickly time.

Sabbath, 11. I did not preach; I cannot attend these meeting houses, they are only calculated for summer, or good health. I have hopes of being useful once more. My mind at times is under strong temptations: I cannot bear confinement. Mrs. Selby[2] hath told some persons that she is convinced, by my means, that slavery is sinful. I would say—if so, move heaven with your prayers, and earth with your counsels and solicitations; and never rest till slavery is expelled from the plantation.

Monday, 12. I had appointed to meet the trustees of Ebenezer Academy, at brother Holb's, on the north side of the Meherrin. After some conver-

[2] See *Journal* entry for January 29, 1798.

sation they willingly agreed to address the conference in behalf of Ebenezer Academy for an annual subscription, to make provision for a man at about one hundred pounds a year, who shall keep an English school under our rules, with the worship and the word of God.

Tuesday, 13. I rode to brother Pelham's;[3] here I was at home. I spent my time with the women and children, in winding cotton and hearing them read. My soul was much blessed.

Thursday, 15. The weather is cool and changeable. By letters from the north I find that the book interest is upon a good footing, the fund interest well secured, and great peace reigns amongst the preachers.

Friday, 16. There fell a heavy snow from six to nine and twelve inches deep. I had to keep house. I had but little to say but what would call for weeping, lamentations, and woe. I was a little recreated by hearing Betsy and Nancy Pelham read Doddridge's Sermons to Young People.

Saturday and *Sabbath*, 17, 18. Clear, but cold, and much snow. When I get sick and dispirited, I think, Was I not a bishop, and required by duty, and necessity, and conscience, to do the best I can, I would rather go into some line of business to get my own living, and not lounge about. I feel for those who have had to groan out a wretched life dependent on others—as Peddicord, Gill, Tunnell, and others whose names I do not now recollect; but their names are written in the book of life, and their souls are in the glory of God. I reflected with pain, that we had never reprinted, in America, the life, labours, travels, and sufferings of that great man of God, David Brainerd, of gracious memory; it would be a book well fitted for our poor, painful, and faithful missionaries; none but God and themselves know what they suffer, the minutes of which for one week might fill a volume written by an ingenious pen and feeling heart. The last week I spent in some pain of mind, patience and prayer. It being meeting day at my lodgings, I gave an exhortation to the congregation, having three subjects in view,—First, The excellency of the religion of Jesus: Secondly, The way to come at the knowledge of the hearts of men and women; namely, by their actions: Thirdly, To put no confidence in frames and feelings, whilst people are living in wilful sin, or the neglect of plain, known duty.

Sabbath day, 25. It is such cloudy weather I cannot go out: I wind cotton, hear the children read, and teach them a little grammar. I have, by the help of a scribe, marked the States I have travelled through for these twenty years; but the movements are so quick (travelling night and day), it seems that the notes upon two or three hundred miles are only like a parish and a day—on paper. The understanding reader that could judge the distance would see that I purpose to have the names of the people at whose houses I have preached, or the journal will appear utopian.

[3] Pelham lived in Brunswick County. Some of the family, including Peter, moved to Ohio to be rid of slavery. (Dromgoole's Letters, University of North Carolina.)

March, 4. I can only make a few weak observations. What little pen work I dare do has been in writing a letter to New York. I shall only journalize a little, and never enter deeply into my other subjects. I scorn to be idle; the past week hath been spent in the cotton work with my fingers, and in hearing the children read, and instructing them in the English grammar. I have thought, if we do wrong we rank among the vilest of the vile, as having been more favoured than any others. Many other Churches go upon the paths already trodden two or three hundred years. We formed our own Church, and claim the power of a reform every four years. We can make more extensive observations, because our preachers in six or seven years can go through the whole continent, and see the state of other Churches in all parts of this new world. We of the travelling ministers, who have nothing to mind but the gospel and the Church of God, may and ought to be very useful.

Monday, 5, I class among my weeping days.

I have rested at the comfortable house of my dear friend, Peter Pelham, from *February* 9 till *March* 9, on which day we rode through the heat to Hubland Saunders's, and on *Saturday*, 10, to Ebenezer meeting house, formerly Merritt's chapel. I met a few local brethren; the house was open, and the day warm. I was soon outdone, and sunk into dejection; the pain returned in my breast, and a discharge of blood took place.

Sunday, 11. I sat alone at brother Merritt's house. It was expected I should preach—but ah! woe is me, to be cut off from the happy service of the sanctuary through weakness of body! O Lord, show me wherefore thou contendest with me! I was concerned to bring in better order among the local line of the ministry, by classing them together, and then, being thus classed, by making them take regular stations on Sabbath days. I also appointed them a leader, to meet once in three or six months, to discourse about their souls and families, and the congregation and society they attend.

I am now alone with God the Lord, my only hope! In consequence of riding twenty-five miles, a bad road, and sitting about three hours in conference with the local brethren, in an open house, I am quite overcome. It shows that the main spring in my system is broken or much weakened, so that every feeble attempt I make to do any small service to the Church is very burdensome to myself, and will always give grief and disappointment to my friends, to my dearest and best brethren.

Sunday, 18. I have visited four families in Brunswick, and three in Dinwiddie counties. On *Saturday* I had a close conversation with some of our local ministry: we had great union. I was led to inquire of them the state of their own souls, and the standing of the societies and congregations they attended, and advised them to meet in a conference class once in three months, and deal faithfully with each other, and plan their work. We were happy to find seven out of ten were not in the spirit of practice of slavery. I have made out since *Friday* week to ride about sixty-five miles, and to meet as many of the local brethren as I could call together from Brunswick and Amelia counties. I have in general enjoyed peace of mind, and better health of body, than heretofore. I received a letter from the African preacher and society in Philadelphia, giving me an account of the revival of the work of God in the congregation of the Methodists in this city, amongst both white and black.

Sunday, 25. Since the last sacred day, I have visited seven families. A friend of mine was inquisitive of my trade and apprenticeship—as Mr. Glendenning had reported; as he asked me so plainly, I told him that I counted it no reproach to have been taught to get my own living. My health is somewhat better. I am yet unable to read or write largely; I can pray and praise the Lord a little. I assisted Philip Sands to draw up an agreement for our officiary to sign against slavery: thus we may know the real sentiments of our local preachers. It appears to me, that we can never fully reform the people, until we reform the preachers; and that hitherto, except purging the travelling connexion, we have been working at the wrong end. But if it be lawful for local preachers to hold slaves, then it is lawful for travelling preachers also; and they may keep plantations and overseers upon their quarters: but this reproach of inconsistency must be rolled away. Some of our local preachers complain that they have not a seat in the General Annual Conference. We answer, if they will do the duty of a member of the yearly conference, they may have the seat and privilege of the travelling line. The travelling ministry may complain, We must go at a minute's warning to our circuits, far and near; and attend with the greatest strictness to our appointments and societies. The local preachers go where and when they please; can preach anywhere and nowhere; they can keep plantations and slaves, and have them bought or given by their parents. The local preachers can receive fifty or a hundred dollars per year, for marriages; but we travellers, if we receive a few dollars for marriages, must return them at the conference, or be called refractory or disobedient. Let us not have the grace of our Lord Jesus Christ with respect of persons in ministers, any more than in members—in local preachers, any more than travelling ones. I have done great things this week—I have ridden nearly sixty miles. I heard brother Ira Ellis, on the Second Epistle of John, verse 8: "Look to yourselves, that ye lose not the things ye have wrought; but that ye receive a full reward." Great need there is, in this degenerate day and place, for ministers and people to look to themselves.

Monday, *April* 2. I visited a local preacher, and gave him a plain and patient talk upon slavery.

Tuesday, 3. I attended a sermon and sacrament at brother Pelham's.

Wednesday, 4. Rode fifteen miles to brother Saunders's.

Thursday, 5. Attended a sermon and sacrament, and gave a short exhortation on the purity of the communion. We rode fifteen miles after meeting to brother Drumgoole's; rested *Friday*. *Saturday* we rode eight miles to brother Owens's: brother Whatcoat gave us an excellent discourse, on, "He shall feed his flock like a shepherd": we had two exhortations; mine was feeble. We had a meeting with the local preachers. I returned to brother Drumgoole's the same day. I feel that a little application to thought and bodily exercise is too much for me.

Saturday, 7. I was once more privileged to sit in a serious assembly, at Edward Drumgoole's chapel: I also ascended the sacred stand after brother Whatcoat had given us a very plain, valuable, and useful sermon, properly heard, upon Acts xiv, 38–41.[4] I ventured to give a gloss upon Acts ii, 40.

Sabbath, 8. The last week was memorable for a prodigious falling of rain from *Monday* to *Saturday*. I rode with great weakness to my dear brother Seward's,[5] seventeen miles, and on *Saturday* to Salem, for conference. Sabbath we had an open time.

Monday, 9. We began conference, and ended on *Wednesday* evening: we had three public days. The peace and union of the conference was apparently great: I was assisted to attend.

Thursday, 12. Rode twenty-five miles; the roads very deep and much broken; we stopped at brother Paup's. I am but feeble still, and cannot stand labour as in past days. I have travelled since I left brother Drumgoole's sixty-five miles.

Friday, 13. We came the road to Harper's bridge, over Nottoway River, fifteen miles, to brother Robinson's in Dinwiddie county: this being a byway the path was smooth. I have entered upon a tour of two thousand miles before I may probably see this part of the land again. O! can I perform such a toil? Weakness of body maketh me feel great heaviness of mind. I must think, speak, write, and preach a little; or I may as well give up my station.

Saturday, 14. We rode to Henry Reese's; we have *proper* March weather in April.

Sabbath, 15. I attempted a feeble discourse on 2 Peter iii, 11: "Seeing then that all these things shall be dissolved, what manner of persons ought ye to be in all holy conversation and godliness?" We had a large congregation: our brethren, Dyer, White, and Roper, were ordained deacons. I appointed my dear aged and faithful brother Whatcoat to visit the four districts belonging to the Virginia conference, and wrote my apology as not being able to ride on horseback as heretofore. Notwithstanding my bowels were afflicted and much affected, we left brother Henry Reese's, and rode through dust and deep cut roads thirty miles to Petersburg. I endeavoured to commune with God, but I had great sinkings of heart.

[4] This chapter of Acts has only 28 verses. There is nothing to indicate the correct passage.
[5] Seward lived in the southwestern part of Brunswick County.

Monday, 16. I preached at Petersburg very feebly on 2 Peter iii, 17, 18.

Tuesday, 17. There was a severe frost. We then rode to Richmond: I was very unwell. I went to the court house and made my apology for inability.

Wednesday, 18. Being so unwell and crowded with company, I found it best once more to try for Baltimore: we came only forty miles to Lyon's, in Caroline county.

Thursday, 19. We had a gentle ride to Todd's tavern.

Friday, 20. We crossed the new bridge at Falmouth, and came to Stafford court house to dine, and thence to Ward's at night—thirty-five miles.

Saturday, 21. We came to Colchester to dine, and to William Adams's at night, thirty miles. The roads were nearly as bad as in winter, and amazingly ploughed up with frost and using. The prospects for small grain are bad. We met with a powerful storm, but my carriage kept me dry, and my cloak defended brother Enoch George from damage. This has been a changeable day; heat, wind, rain, and the vast fatigue of bad roads, deep gullies, heavy mire, roots, and hills, bore hard upon me. I heard of brother William Watters's preaching at the Fall church, a faithful funeral sermon.

Maryland

Monday, 23. We reached Shadrach Turner's, and made a rapid ride to the city of Baltimore. I visited until the *Sabbath*, *April* 29. They would publish for me at Old Town meeting house.[6] I made an attempt on Psalm cxxxii, 9: "Let thy priests be clothed with righteousness, and let thy saints shout for joy." I went to the Point and heard a sermon on "Speak evil of no man." I gave a short exhortation, and came home much more comfortable than I expected. Our beautiful house is not ready yet.[7] I fear I tremble in imagination, lest it should have more temporal than spiritual glory.

Wednesday, *May* 2. Our conference began:[8] it was *half-yearly*, to bring

[6] This first reference by Asbury to a meetinghouse in Old Town doubtless was to that erected by the third society formed in Baltimore. Asbury addressed its members in John Deaver's house. (See note under December 23, 1773.) There is strong evidence that as early as 1789 the Methodists had a chapel on Green Street which became the Exeter Street Church. (Griffith: *Annals of Baltimore*, 127; manuscript copy, "A Historical Sketch of Exeter Street Methodist Episcopal Church," Pratt Memorial Library; Hawkins, *op. cit.*, 244.)

[7] This was the second Light Street Church which Asbury was to dedicate the following Sunday, May 6.

[8] Asbury began the presidency of this conference in this new Light Street Church, Baltimore, much improved in health. The nature of the many offences given with their depressing effect upon Asbury is open to conjecture. Reference may be to James O'Kelly as indicated in the *Journal*, July 1–3, 1798. (Tipple: *The Heart of Asbury's Journal* 445.)

on an equality by the change from fall to spring. We had to correct the many offences given at many conferences to one particular man! I pleased myself with the idea that I was out of the quarrel: but no! I was deeper in than ever, and never was wounded in so deep a manner. It was as much as I could bear. I cannot stand such strokes.

Sabbath, 6. We opened the new house.[9] Brothers Lee, Bruce, and Forrest preached. *Monday* and *Tuesday* I visited brother Willis.

Wednesday, 9. I attended the public fast. My subject was: "So the Lord was entreated for the land." I observed: I. That there were special times and seasons in which it becomes our duty, in a most special manner, to entreat the Lord for the Church and the land. II. Who they are who ought to be assembled—every order, the elders and people at large; sanctified—that is, set apart from labour and common service—the bride and bridegroom, the children, the infant offspring. III. Who shall intercede—the priests, the ministers of the Lord: again, if my people which are called by my name shall humble themselves. IV. The special seasons—calamities threatened by God or man, feared or felt, such as sword, famine, or pestilence. V. How we should entreat the Lord—with fasting, prayer, reading, and preaching the word of God; confessing our sins and sorrows, and acknowledging his mercies. The calamities of the Church: idolatry, division, superstition, and backsliding. VI. The happy consequences of God's being entreated—he heareth and answereth, in temporal, and spiritual, and in eternal blessings.

Sunday, 13. I had to go upon my watch tower. My subject in our temple was 1 Kings ix, 6–9. It was observed on the first head of the discourse, What the pious Israelites had professed, experienced, and practiced, namely, the knowledge, worship, ordinances, and service of the true and glorious Jehovah—they and their godly children had an experience of convicting, converting, and sanctifying grace through a promised Messiah; and had pardon of sin, and peace with God. Israelites indeed—enjoying the love of God, and walking in loving, living obedience to all the known commandments of God. Secondly, How they might partially return from following the Lord: and, again, how they might wholly depart from God. Thirdly, The dreadful consequences. In this discourse the parallel was drawn, and a close application made, to the rising generation. Some sentiments were expressed upon the burning of the former house; the probabilities of the latter house also being destroyed, unless defended by the Almighty. At the Point I spoke on the epistle to the angel of the Church of Pergamos. I was thankful that my strength was so great. Our congregations were large and seriously attentive.

Saturday, 19. We rode to Perry Hall, and continued there until the twenty-sixth of the same month. I was not employed. Brothers Philip

[9] See letter to John Kobler, May 6, 1798.

Bruce and John Harper[10] attending me, we read over my transcribed numbers of the Journal. A situation so healthy and agreeable had a good influence upon my body and mind; and the kindness and company of the elders of this house were charming and cheering.

Wednesday, 23. We rode about twenty miles to Deer Creek. I was pleased to find here mother Sarah Watters,[11] aged ninety; her son Henry, sixty; and brother Billy (William) Watters and his wife from Virginia. But, O, how many are dead! And some have fled to the woods, and some gone back to the world. The society is all gone that we had formed here more than twenty years back. A most serious aspect in sight—the fly hath eaten up the grain of the fields. My vegetable diet hath its salutary influence upon my system, much more so than medicine. Could I rest this summer, there would be hope of my health; but I must move and live upon mercy, providence, and grace. Poor Deer Creek! the preachers have left the place for want of hearers; but I had many—and an opening on Romans viii, 26. I saw a few who had followed the Lord more than twenty years ago; they have halted—but I trust they will set out anew. I felt life, and some enlargement upon it. It was a comfortable day.

Monday, 28. I rested on account of rain.

Tuesday, 29. We came to Northeast.

Delaware

Wednesday, we were at Hersey's. *Thursday* we came to Wilmington.

Friday, *June* 1. I preached on Luke xxi, 34–36.

Pennsylvania

Saturday, 2, we rode to Philadelphia.

Sunday, 3, I enlarged on Galatians ii, 20. It was observed, That Christ crucified was the grand subject; next in continuance, the being crucified with Christ. Secondly, "I live; yet not I, but Christ liveth in me"—in communicated grace and life, as ministers and Christians: *to live by faith*, as well as to be saved by faith. *Loved me*, is the feeling experience of gracious souls. I received the probable news of the near approach to, or death of my father. I wrote several letters; and feel abundantly better in my body.

Our conference began on *Tuesday*, and we were closely confined until *Saturday*.

[10] John Harper, with Thomas Lyell and Henry Willis, was stationed in Baltimore. Harper, who arrived from the West Indies late in 1794, was an itinerant until 1803 when he located. (Lee: *History of the Methodists*, 327.)

[11] Mother Sarah Watters was the widow of Godfrey Watters.

Sabbath, 10. I preached on Matt. xxiv, 45–47.

We had close work, but good tempers abounded, and just measures were pursued. I made an attempt to ride to Germantown, but returned; and it was well I did, for I had no sooner discharged the fragments of the conference business, and the stationing of the preachers, than the affairs of the society came in sight respecting the city. I have my difficulties with the government of the preachers; but I have some trouble with the city societies—they wish to have the connexion drafted, and some of the most acceptable preachers to serve them. I made all haste to leave the city, but not until I had met the trustees of the church.

Monday, 11, was not an agreeable morning: we had some rain.

I had a meeting with the trustees. It was granted we should raise a fund, by subscription, to finish the meeting house in Fourth street.

New Jersey

I then came on to Burlington, where preaching being appointed for me, I ventured out at eight o'clock in the evening, that my commission might not totally expire in this place. My subject was Psalm xxxvii, 3. I had an opening on the text, and some consolation in my own mind.

Tuesday, 12. We came to Crosswicks: there were very few at four o'clock; as it was thought it would be most agreeable for me to preach, I made choice of Psalm xxvii, 6, 7; my state of mind was serene. Universal nature is beautiful at this season. I feel the want of a fervent, constant, holy flame, such as has been found in the hearts of martyred saints and favoured souls.

Wednesday, 13. We came to Hutchinson's; and on *Thursday*, to New Brunswick; where I bore my feeble testimony, and drew up a subscription for the purchase of a house for divine worship.[12] On *Friday*, we came to Elizabethtown.

New York

On *Saturday*, 16, to New York: here I received the serious confirmation of the death of my father, aged eighty-four or eighty-five.

Sunday, 17. I preached in the new church on Eccles. i, 1. At the old church, in John Street, my text was 1 Pet. iv, 10: "As good stewards of the

[12] Asbury drew up a subscription for a meetinghouse, thus marking the beginnings of Methodism in New Brunswick, New Jersey. The society was organized the following year, but the church was not built until 1811, preaching being in the courthouse until that date. The brick building was known as Shiloh and stood on Liberty Street on a lot purchased from Queens College, now Rutgers University, for $528.00. (Wall and Pickengill: *History of Middlesex County*, II, 338.)

manifold grace of God." I now feel myself an orphan with respect to my father; wounded memory recalls to mind what took place when I parted with him, nearly twenty-seven years next September; from a man that seldom, if ever, I saw weep—but when I came to America, overwhelmed with tears, with grief, he cried out, "I shall never see him again!" thus by prophecy or by Providence, he hath spoken what is fulfilled. For about thirty-nine years my father hath had the Gospel preached in his house. The particulars of his death are not yet come to hand. I employed the remaining part of this week in visiting, reading, writing,[13] attending preaching and love feast. Brothers Jesse Lee and Joshua Wells were officiating ministers: myself a hearer.

Sunday, 24. I preached in John Street church, from Job xvii, 9: "The righteous also shall hold on his way; and he that hath clean hands shall be stronger and stronger." After tracing the origin of the land of *Uz*, as to be seen in the genealogy of *Nahor*, his son *Huz*; taking H as a prefix in Hebrew—as an article, the Uz. In the genealogy of Esau we find Job's friends as princes and pious philosophers. This is the presumption; Johab the father of Job, or Job *ab*, i.e. father of grief, according to the Hebrew word. It was observed from whom these words came, and under what great afflictions—

I. The difficulties and doubts of the righteous as being against their holding on their way.

II. Their privileges and promises.

III. Clean hands, clean hearts; by renouncing oppression of all kinds, civil, sacred, and domestic—every act of injustice, all bribery, all sinful practices; these shall "add strength to strength": we may see this exemplified in the Old and New Testament saints.

At the Bowery church[14] I preached on the epistle to the angel or bishop of Smyrna. On *Monday* I met the married sisters in the old church.

Tuesday, 26. I heard brother Nichols[15] preach in the new church. I read a little, write a few letters, and visit daily: life appears to be but poorly spent with me. I met the married women in the new church.

Sunday, *July* 1. At the old church I preached from Phil. iii, 18–20. At the north church,[16] in the afternoon, on 1 Cor. ix, 2: I was much heated

[13] See letter to John Dickins, June 18, 1798.

[14] This was the church on Forsyth Street which Asbury had hitherto called the "new church."

[15] Andrew Nichols, then under appointment on Long Island, was received on trial in 1791. After three years on Long Island and Brooklyn he went to New England, locating in 1801. (*General Minutes*; Seaman, *op. cit.*, 140.)

[16] This church was located on Barley Street, the present Duane Street, in the general area of Greenwich Village. The cornerstone had been laid June 26, 1797, for a building 75 × 56 feet, of rough-stone exterior with blue stucco. First called "North" or "Hudson" Church, it later became known as "old Duane Street" church. The congregation and the equity of the property appear in the present church at 13th Street and Seventh Avenue, known as "Metropolitan-Duane Methodist Church."

and rather hurried in preaching. The weather is excessively warm—the children are dying, and probably so will the parents unless God sends rain.[17] I live wholly upon vegetables, and wear flannel.

Mr. O'Kelly hath now published to the world what he hath been telling to his disciples for years. Mr. Hammett was moderate; Glendenning not very severe; but James hath turned the butt-end of his whip, and is unanswerably abusive: the Lord judge between us! and he certainly will in that *day of days*.

Wednesday, 4. This day we had sermons in all the churches of the Methodists. I had a meeting with the officiary at the Bowery church in the afternoon, and gave them a sermon upon 1 Peter v, 2. *Sunday* I preached at Brooklyn, on 1 Peter iv, 17; and in the afternoon at the old church on Rev. iii, 1–5.

[18]My subject at Brooklyn was, "The time is come that judgment must begin at the house of God." In temptation, persecution, discipline, heresy, and schism, the general judgment will begin at the house of God. What shall the end be of them that hear but will not obey the Gospel of God. They shall be judged by the Gospel as having, by their disobedience, forfeited every blessing, and as having brought upon themselves every curse the Gospel threatens—they are as completely damned by this disobedience, as the obedient souls are everlastingly saved by the grace of God.

Monday, 9. We came to Samuel Berian's, at Kingsbridge, and on *Tuesday* to my home at the widow Sherwood's. We have a very neatly built house here[19]; but I was so ill that Jesse Lee and Joshua Wells had to fill my place. Mr. Phillips, of Birmingham, writes thus of my father—"He kept his room six weeks previous to his death; the first month of the time he ate nothing but a little biscuit, and the last fortnight he took nothing but a little spirits and water—he died very happy."

Wednesday, 11. We had to keep indoors[20] on account of rain, and could not attend at White Plains.

Thursday, 12. We were at our kind brother Banks's, upon the banks of Byram River, near the line between Connecticut and the State of New York: my congregation was large, and seriously attentive: my subject was Luke xix, 10.

[17] This condition was preliminary to the appalling outbreak of yellow fever which struck New York later in the month. At no time were the ravages of this dread disease greater than in the summer of 1798. Returning from New England at the end of September, Asbury avoided New York, crossing the Hudson to New Jersey well above the city. (See *Journal* entry for September 24, 1798.)

[18] This paragraph preceded the entry for Wednesday, July 11, in the original *Journal* but it has been moved forward to preserve the continuity of the text.

[19] Asbury had preached in this church in 1797 before it was completed. The church had been dedicated at Christmas, 1797. (See *Journal* entry for September 24, 1797.)

[20] Asbury was probably at the home of Elijah Crawford, where he frequently stopped.

Connecticut

Friday, 13. We rode over the rocks and hills to Stamford. We had a comfortable rain that cooled the air. I find I cannot preach often—I must spare myself or destroy myself.

Saturday, 14. We rode to Joseph Hall's, Poquonock, and made it twenty-eight or thirty miles.

Sunday, 15. I attended the congregation at Elnathan Wheeler's, and feebly administered the word from Acts iv, 12. I had a desire to hear brother Jocelyn[21] in the afternoon; but he addressed me, after his reading, singing and prayer, desiring me to preach: my subject was Phil. ii, 12, 13. I applied the text to believers, seekers, and sinners.

Monday, 16. I rode sixteen miles to New Haven.

Tuesday, 17. We took our departure from New Haven, and came through North Brandford to Durham, twenty miles. The day was gloomy and excessively warm at times. We crossed the rocks and hills to Haddam, and rode after sunset, for nine or ten miles, a most desperate road: this put my strength, courage, and skill to trial, with all my patience, and every spring, and every part of the frame of my carriage; but we came safe to father Wilcox's, where we had many tokens of love shown us, to make rest comfortable.

Wednesday, 18. It rained.

Thursday, 19. At four o'clock, brother Jesse Lee gave a warm, encouraging sermon, from 1 Cor. xv, 58. At the new meeting house (properly West Haddam), where the Methodists are upon free principles, I added a few words; and then began our march to New London. We crossed Connecticut river at Chapman's ferry:[22] we came on without touching the ground sometimes, as the carriage would frequently jump from rock to rock. After riding about thirty-two miles, we reached New London at eight o'clock. James O'Kelly hath told a tale of me which I think it my duty to tell better. He writes, "Francis ordered the preachers to entitle him bishop, in directing their letters." The secret and truth of the matter was this: the preachers having had great difficulties about the appellation of the *Rev.* or *Mr.*, that is, to call a man by one of the Divine appellations, supposing *Mr.* to be an abbreviation of Master ("call no man master upon earth"), it was talked over in the yearly conference, for then we had no General Conference established. So we concluded that it would be by far the best to give each man his official title; as deacon, elder, and bishop: to this the majority agreed. James O'Kelly giveth all the good, the bad, and middling of all the order of our Church to me. What can be the cause of all this ill treatment which I receive from him? Was it because I did not,

[21] The Rev. Augustus Jocelyn was stationed at Middletown, Connecticut.

[22] Chapman's Ferry was probably near Chapman's Falls at East Hadam, Connecticut.

I could not settle him for life in the south district of Virginia? Is this his gratitude? He was in this district for ten years, part of the time in the very best circuits in the district, and then in the district as presiding elder; and there was no peace with James, until Doctor Coke took the matter out of my hands, after we had agreed to hold a General Conference to settle the dispute: and behold, when the General Conference, by a majority (which he called for), went against him, he treated the General Conference with as much contempt almost as he had treated me; only I am the grand butt of all his spleen.

Sunday, 22. I made a feeble attempt at the court house, on 2 Peter iii, 17, 18. I was greatly assisted in mind and body. In the afternoon I preached on Matt. viii, 36–38.[23]

At the foundation of the new meeting house, the frame of which was raised on *Monday*, brother Jesse Lee preached. I was pleased by moving along on a good road, but through an exceedingly warm day, fifteen miles to Norwich. The loss of rest last evening made the heat of this day more burdensome to my poor body. There is a growth of religion in this circuit; but it is ploughing among rocks and stone-walls in a two-fold sense. The society came together, and after myself and elder Lee had exhorted, we had a speaking and living time among the brethren and sisters.

Tuesday, 24. We rode through heat and over rocks twelve miles to brother Lyon's,[24] at Canterbury; this made me feel like Jonah. I was much outdone, having slept but little for two nights: but I was compensated for all in finding the life of religion amongst this people. Brother Lyon is the son of a godly father, who was a Baptist minister; he was imprisoned for truth and religious liberty; the aged man lived until we came: his wife is yet living and loving God. The father was awakened by Mr. George Whitefield's ministry: the son is a man of piety and property.

Rhode Island

Wednesday, 25. We passed Plainfield and Sterling, and came to Coventry, in the State of Rhode Island. They have established turnpikes upon the way to Providence, and greatly reformed the road: but I had to turn out to search for my friends, and the souls of my charge: we computed it twenty-five miles to General Lippett's—such work as I had is not easily told: we came in about eight o'clock. *Thursday*, at General Christopher

[23] This chapter of Matthew has only thirty-four verses. There is no indication as to the correct passage.

[24] Probably Captain Judah Lyon, whose father, Walter Lyon of Canterbury, was a Baptist minister. Judah Lyon built a large tavern house in Muddy Brook Village in 1818. (Larned: *History of Windham County, Conn.*, II, 231, 285, 452.)

Lippett's, I preached on 1 John, i, 7, 8. I rested on *Friday* and *Saturday*, and on *Sabbath day* my subject was Heb. ii, 2. *Monday*, rode twenty-two miles through heat to Warren: we lodged at father Martin Luther's. Here John Hills, from Lewistown, Delaware, liveth—but he is no Methodist; who would have thought this once? Mr. Wilson's book was read to me by brother Lee, particularly those parts in which he finds fault with the Methodists. It appears to be the language of two or three men; who they are I know not: but be they who they may, they are mild without merit; and in some things are very simple, if not silly, about our drinking water. But why, Mr. *Age of Reason*, whoever you are, will you find fault with the question, "Have you always a Bible about you?" Poor divinity, and yet poorer spite.

Tuesday, 31. We came upon Rhode Island; stopped at Matthew Cook's,[25] dined, and then came to our little meeting house, and had a good season on Heb. x, 38, 39. This island is most beautiful in its situation and cultivation; the neat stone square walls, level fields of grass, corn, and barley, sloping to the water, are very pleasing to the eye: salt water prospects are most delightful. Upon the summits of the island you may see from water to water. Here fruit trees, fish, and shell fish abound. The Friends' meeting house is large, and the settlement extensive; and if the Baptists, Moravians, Episcopalians, Friends, and Methodists have any religion, there must be some good people here. Rhode Island is by far the most beautiful island I have seen. I have been very low, and weak, and feverish of late: I can hardly write, think, read, ride, or talk to purpose. It is a little trying to be with people who are healthy, active, and talkative, when you cannot bear a cheerful part with them.

Thursday, *August* 2. I returned to the north-east end of the island,[26] where we have a small meeting house, and some gracious souls. Brother Lee preached last evening at Newport. As I was unwell, I gave my services to brother Hall's[27] family, where I was entertained with every mark of affection: may they, their own and adopted children, be numbered with the saints! I came away in weakness of body, but strength of soul, to the house at the ferry which we came to when we first entered upon the island.

Friday, 3. We preached at Bristol; my subject was, Luke xviii, 7. It was to me a serious comfortable time: what but the mighty power of God and the unceasing cries of his people can help us here?

[25] Matthew Cook was a layman who lived at Portsmouth, Rhode Island.

[26] The northeast end of the island doubtless referred to Portsmouth, to which Asbury returned after having accompanied Jesse Lee to Newport.

[27] Brother Hall must have been Joshua Hall, a Methodist preacher who was at Martha's Vineyard the previous year and was appointed to Providence at the conference soon to be held. He organized the first Methodist society at Newport in 1800. However, the reason for the presence of his family at Newport in 1798 is not plain.

Massachusetts

Saturday, 4. We came through Warren, Swansea, Somerset, Dighton, and Taunton,[28] thirty-two miles: the day was excessively warm; and O! rocks, hills, and stones! I was greatly outdone; no price can pay—there is no purchase for this day's hire but souls. We frequently spend a dollar per day to feed ourselves and horses: I never received, as I recollect, any personal beneficence, no, not a farthing, in New England; and perhaps never shall, unless I should be totally out of cash.

Sunday, 5. I was very unwell in my *viscera.* I attempted to preach on Rom. x, 1–3. I am under deep dejection of mind at times, and distressed above measure with the people—they appear to have so little genuine religion. We hear of a serious mortal fever prevailing in Boston: it is what I have feared would be the visitation of this capital town as in other cities; here also are theatres, sinners, blind priests, and backsliding, formal people, and multitudes who are gospel-hardened. We came to Easton; here we have a new house built. I felt exceedingly weak after riding ten miles; the evening was very warm; I, however, gave them a discourse on 2 Tim. ii, 19, and passed the night in some bodily distress.

Tuesday, 7. I rode twenty-two miles through heat and hunger to Boston: here I spent one night, very unwell in body, and with pains and pleasures of mind, upon account of the preachers and people.

Wednesday, 8. I was advised to retire a few days to Waltham. There is affliction in Boston—the malignant fever.[29] But who can tell the sick that are in the second or third house from his own, in a town or city where it is needful to observe secrecy lest people should be frightened away from their homes, or the country people from bringing food? How many may be buried in the night, without any tolling of bells or funeral solemnity, thrown into a coarse coffin, or a tar sheet! O! a solitary house, and social family; a comfortable table, pure air, and good water, are blessings at Waltham. There is a rumour of the blood-shedding in Ireland. O the trade and plague of war! I pity the old world; I fear for the new—shall we be altogether unpunished? My calculation is that we have ridden three hundred and thirty miles since our departure from New York.

Thursday, *Friday*, *Saturday*, and *Sunday*. At Waltham. I ventured to ride four miles, and preach two sermons—the first on Acts ii, 17, 18; and the second from Rom. x, 1–3. I was much enlarged, and had clear views, and saw and felt for the people.

Monday, 13. We began our march to Lynn, in weakness of body and

[28] Warren was in Rhode Island, but the other communities mentioned were in Massachusetts.

[29] During this year there were two hundred deaths in Boston from yellow fever. (*New York Medical Journal*, October, 1856, 367.)

distress of mind. I gave a discourse late in the evening, on Heb. iv, 9, and that night I slept but little. On *Tuesday* we began our journey for the Province of Maine: we passed through Danvers, Salem, Beverly; thence to Hamilton, where we were kindly entertained by some aged people: dined and hasted along through Ipswich, and thence to Newburyport: here I passed in sight of the old prophet, dear Whitefield's tomb, under the Presbyterian meeting house. His sermons established me in the doctrines of the Gospel more than anything I ever heard or had read at that time; so that I was remarkably prepared to meet reproach and persecution. We crossed Merrimac River and bridge: and came in late to Mr. Merrill's, where we were kindly entertained. Here we were let into the secret of a negotiation with a congregation by Mr. Elias Hull, one of our wonder-workers—I told you so—farewell.

New Hampshire

Wednesday, 15. We entered properly into New Hampshire. We passed Hampton Falls, where the people and priests were about installing a minister into the deceased Dr. Langdon's congregation.[30] We had a dripping morning: we, however, set out and rode about twenty miles to Portsmouth: there is a fever somewhat malignant and mortal here. This is a well fortified town against the Methodists. Mr. Hutchinson and daughter received us with great Christian politeness: being exceedingly outdone with heat and labour, I was easily persuaded to tarry until morning. We crossed Piscataqua River, at the town of Portsmouth, in a flat bottomed boat. I am so weak that the smallest shock shakes me. At Portsmouth there is a strong tide, and this morning we had a heavy fog, so that we could scarcely see the tops of the houses on the other side of the river.

Maine

We came through Old York, father Moody's[31] parish, of whom many tales are told; one of which is worth telling to posterity—it is, that the only salary he received was the prayers of his people. We came on to Wells,

[30] The Rev. Dr. Samuel Langdon, formerly president of Harvard College, had been the Congregational minister at Hampton Falls, New Hampshire, since 1781. He died in 1797 at the age of seventy-five years. He was the first man in New Hampshire to be awarded the degree of Doctor of Divinity, which he received from Aberdeen.

[31] The Rev. Samuel Moody (1675–1747) was the minister of the First Church of Christ (Congregational) at York, Maine. "Father Moody" wrote several books, among them being *Vain Youth Summoned to appear before Bar* and *The Doleful State of the Damned.*

and were kindly entertained at Mr. Barak Maxwell's.[32] I was restless through the night and sleepy and sick through the next day, yet we rode forty miles to Major Enoch Ilsley's,[33] near Portland.

Friday, 17. We passed New Stroudswater,[34] named probably after the old one in Gloucester, in *Old* England. We have ridden since *Monday* morning about one hundred and forty miles; the roads tolerable; the weather extremely warm; and we are amongst strangers.

Saturday, 18. We rode five miles to Presumscut River, and stopped at father Baker's.[35] *Sabbath-day*, I preached in the barn, on, "Now is the accepted time, and now is the day of salvation." Mother Baker was sick, but had a sure confidence in God. Here we have the frame of a good meeting house erected upon a beautiful spot.

Monday, 20. We rode to Gray, and were kindly entertained at Mr. Randall's.[36] I preached to a few in a school house, on Matt. xxiv, 12, 13,—the case with these people, if their love was ever warm.

Tuesday, 21. We came through Gloucester to the widow Roe's. We sat under a shade by the road side, and read ——'s acknowledgment of his fall, in an address to the conference—so candid and apparently contrite never did I hear. My subject at Roe's was Acts ii, 21; the people appeared careless and unfeeling. In the evening there came up a very heavy gust of rain, lightning, and thunder, and I feared for ourselves. Next morning a dead ox was found about one hundred yards from our horses in the same field, and the presumption was he was killed by lightning, as there appeared to be one particular shock directed to that place. O Lord, thou preservest man and beast! My soul was much engaged in prayer.

Wednesday, 22. We rode through the woods to Androscoggin River, thence to Lewistown, where our appointment for preaching had been made at two o'clock, and another at four o'clock. No one attending at two o'clock, we came on to Monmouth.

Thursday, 23. I was at home at brother Fogg's.[37] He and his wife are

[32] Barak Maxwell ran a public house in Ogunquit. He died in 1816 at the age of eighty-four. (Bourne: *History of Wells and Kemebunk*, 783.)

[33] By the help of Major Enoch Ilsley the Methodists in March, 1804, purchased the old Episcopal church on Church and Middle streets in Portland. (Allen and Pillsbury, *op. cit.*, 240.) Stevens, *op. cit.*, 302, calls him "Daniel" Ilsley.

[34] Stroudswater was a village or section of Deering, which is now a part of Portland, Maine. Colonel Westbrook, son of Thomas Westbrook, "built a house at Stroudwater which in conformity to aristocratic usage in England he named Harrow House and probably gave the name to Stroudwater from a village of the same name on the river Frome in England." (Willis: *History of Portland from 1632–1864*, 355.)

[35] Father Baker probably lived near West Falmouth. Asbury doubtless traveled over the old Gray Road from Portland to Gray, and five miles along that road would have brought him to the edge of West Falmouth.

[36] Jesse Lee preached the first Methodist sermon at Gray, Maine, in the home of Mr. Randall on Sunday, November 9, 1794. (*Ibid.*, 302.)

[37] Caleb Fogg lived at Monmouth, Maine.

pious souls; such, with an increase, may they live and die! I had taken cold in crossing the mountain, which was rocky and uneven. I preached in the open meeting house to a congregation of people that heard and felt the word. My subject was Eph. vi, 13–18. I was raised a small degree above my feeble self, and so were some of my hearers. We rode that evening to Hopkins's,[38] in Winthrop, where meeting was appointed in the Congregational house. As the day was damp, and myself sick, I declined; and brother Lee preached, and the people said it was a good time. I found father Bishop,[39] at whose house we stayed; his son and wife exceedingly kind. We breakfasted at our brother Prescott's.[40] This part of the District of Maine is settled with people from the south of Massachusetts, and some from New Hampshire.

Saturday, 25. We had to beat through the woods between Winthrop and Redfield, which are as bad as the Alleghany mountain, and the Shades of Death. We have now laid by our carriage and saddle, to wait until Wednesday next for conference; the first of the kind ever held in these parts, and it will probably draw the people from far and near.

Wednesday, 29. Ten of us sat in conference.[41] Great was our union and freedom of speech with each other.

Thursday, 30, was our great day: it was computed that from one thousand to eighteen hundred souls attended public preaching and ordination. The unfinished temporary state of the gallery was such, that the plank and other parts would crack and break. We had one alarm while ordaining, owing to the people's wish to gratify their curiosity; but no person was killed or wounded. My subject was 2 Cor. iv, 1, 2. It was observed: "*this ministry*," by way of eminence distinguished from the law—the ministry of the Spirit and power, and the word and letter of the gospel. Secondly, The apostolic manner of using the ministry—renouncing the hidden things of dishonesty, not walking in craftiness, nor handling the word of God deceitfully: not seeking either worldly honour, ease, or profit; but by manifestation of the truth commending ourselves to every man's conscience in the sight of God—to sinners of all characters; to seekers, believers, men of tender and scrupulous consciences. Thirdly, The temptations, labours, and sufferings the faithful ministers have to meet with in the discharge of their duties. Fourthfuly, The support they shall have by the mercy and power of God, and fruit of their labours. Fifthly; *We faint not*. A person that fainteth loseth all action; is pale and dispirited: it is a near resemblance of death, and sometimes terminates in death. Unhappy the man who is dead and useless in the ministry!

[38] Peter Hopkins lived at Winthrop.

[39] Nathaniel Bishop was a local preacher of Winthrop.

[40] Sewall Prescott of Monmouth was proprietor of a "public house" which still stands near the site of the old academy.

[41] For an account of this first conference in Maine, held at the present East Readfield, see Allen and Pillsbury, *op. cit.*, 28, 29.

Weary of being shut in one house for some days, I came in the afternoon through the *dreadful swamp* to Squire Sewall Prescott's, at Winthrop. I found a Congregational priest there. Early in the morning I came to Monmouth to breakfast; dined at Lewistown, and lodged at the widow Roe's. The next day (*Saturday*) I came to Gray to dinner; thence to Falmouth, and lodged at Major Ilsley's. I came chiefly alone; I experienced much bodily weakness: my trials are great; the roads are bad, and I fear the families are little bettered by anything I could say or do for them.

Sunday, September 2. I am surprisingly supported, and am gaining strength, notwithstanding the heat of the sun and most desperate roads and rocks. We have come nearly sixty miles in two days. I had it confirmed that the ox was killed by lightning, which was found dead within one hundred yards of our horses. I went to Portland, unexpectedly, upon the *Sabbath day*. I preached in the widow Boynton's[42] back room to about twenty-five persons, chiefly women. My subject was 2 Peter ii, 9. In the afternoon I preached to about double the number, on Phil. iii, 8. I returned *Sabbath evening* to my very kind friend's house, Major Ilsley's.

Monday, 3. We came off in haste, and rode thirty-five miles to Wells. We lodged with Deacon Clarke; a most complete house of entertainment.

Massachusetts

Tuesday. We rode forty-seven miles to Salisbury, near Newburyport.

I passed Hampton and Hampton Falls[43]; at the latter Mr. Whitefield preached his last sermon, and probably caught the cause of his death. I came over Piscataqua bridge, a most admirable piece of architecture; it is double, and the tollgate and tavern stand upon the island: we dined at Greenland,[44] and had great attention paid us. The fever is breaking out again in Portsmouth, and it is awful in Philadelphia; it seemeth as if the Lord would humble or destroy that city, by stroke after stroke, until they acknowledge God. Very serious appearances of this fever are now in New York.

Thursday, 6. Came from Captain Patake's to Lynn; where I preached on *Friday*, from Galatians v, 6–8.

Saturday. We came off with a design to call at Boston: the heat was excessive, and the sun met me in the face, so that I was almost ready to faint in the carriage. I changed my mind, and concluded to come on to

[42] Methodist meetings in Portland, Maine, "were mostly held in Theophilus Boynton's house, now Newbury Street, till 1801, when a school house was obtained." (Allen and Pillsbury, *op. cit.*, 240.)

[43] Hampton and Hampton Falls are in the state of New Hampshire.

[44] Asbury would have passed through Greenland, New Hampshire, before coming to Hampton and Hampton Falls. In making the *Journal* entry he probably had forgotten the proper sequence in which he had passed these towns.

Waltham, and spend another *Sabbath*. I missed my way a little, but came in about seven o'clock, riding since two o'clock twenty miles.

Sunday, 9. I attended the chapel in the morning—my subject was 1 Peter ii, 9, 10; and in the afternoon, at five o'clock, from the 11th and 12th verses of the same chapter: many attended.

Monday and *Tuesday*. We continued at Waltham.

Wednesday, 12. We came on to Weston, where I preached in the new house, a well designed building, on 1 Cor. xv, 58.

Thursday, 13. We rode twenty miles, the way stony and dusty, to Mr. Nicoll's,[45] at Westborough: here five preachers came together. With hard sighs I attempted to preach, and was most remarkably assisted upon Titus ii, 11, 12.

Friday, 14. We rode forty-one miles over very uneven roads; my horse ran away with me, but did me no hurt. We lodged at Mr. Hubbard's, at Brimfield. I was surprised to see the meeting and dwelling houses they have built in this place, and the reforms they have made in the roads, since I came up through this part of the state seven years ago.

Saturday, 15. We came once more to Silas Bliss's, at Wilbraham. We have ridden ninety miles in two days, and I would rather have ridden two hundred in the low level lands of the south of this continent.

Sabbath day. I attended at Wilbraham; my subject was 1 Peter ii, 1–4.

Monday, 17. We came to Springfield to dine, and then rode on, through excessive heat and bad roads, sixteen miles to-day.

Tuesday, 18. We came up to Granville, sixteen miles: it was well that I had help over the rocks and mountains.

Wednesday, *Thursday*, and *Friday*. We sat in conference;[46] about fifty preachers of different descriptions present: ten were admitted on probation. We had many weighty and deliberate conversations on interesting subjects, in much plainness and moderation. Six of us lodged amongst deacon Loyd's kind Congregational people.

Connecticut

Saturday, 22. We began our flight to the White Plains, across the hills and along most dreadful roads for a carriage: we came to Canaan, about

[45] In 1798 to 1802 Fortunatus Nichols, Joseph Nichols, Phineas Hardy, and Shadrach Miller were exempted from paying the parish tax on the certificate of a Methodist elder. (Bates: *History of Westborough, Mass.*, 231.) Asbury was probably entertained by Captain Joseph Nichols. Nichols moved to Shrewsbury in 1804, and Asbury was in his house there on July 18, 1805.

[46] This was the third New England conference. It met in the church on Beech Hill in West Granville. A bronze tablet on a huge boulder now commemorates the occasion. Jesse Lee assisted Asbury, and two eccentrics were present, "Billy" Hibbard and "Crazy" Lorenzo Dow. (Mudge: *History of the New England Conference*, 59, 60.)

thirty-six miles, and lodged by the falls of Housatonick river.[47] Its source is in some ponds and springs N. and S.W. of Pittsfield, Massachusetts, and running through the heart of Connecticut, empties into Long Island Sound at Stratford: it is the second in magnitude to that which gives a name to the State.

New York

Sabbath day, 23. We came on, twelve in company, to Dover, in the State of New York. I should have stopped at Sharon meeting house had we not expected a meeting at four o'clock in Dover. We made this *Sabbath day's* journey twenty-five miles; the weather was very warm, and we had nothing to eat from seven o'clock in the morning until four o'clock in the afternoon. My subject was Heb. xii, 12–14.

Monday, 24. We came through Dutchess county, near the line of the two States, and down the waters of Croton River. We lodged at Webb's, near New Salem. We reached the Plains in about thirty-six miles, and came in about sundown. Most awful times in Philadelphia and New York —citizens flying before the fever as if it were the sword! I now wait the providence of God to know which way to go.

Wednesday, 26. Came to my former lodging, where I lay sick last year: it is still like a home.[48]

Thursday, 27. We attempted to cross North River[49] at Woolsey's ferry, but the wind blew too strong. We visited a kind family, and returned to the widow Sherwood's.[50] We have spent a day, and ridden sixteen miles, and are now where we began. *Friday* we rode twenty miles and crossed at Bull's ferry,[51] six miles above New York: we were about two hours and a half in getting over: after which we rode eighteen miles to Elizabethtown.

New Jersey

Saturday, 29. We rode on to New Brunswick, twenty miles, dined, and then hasted to Milford, twenty-two miles: here we spent the Sabbath day. I preached in the Hutchinsonian chapel:[52] my text was Matt. v, 8. Now we

[47] The falls of the Housatonick River were at the present Falls Village, about five miles south of Canaan, Connecticut. Asbury was on his way to White Plains, New York.

[48] This was the home of widow Abigail Sherwood on the west edge of New Rochelle, New York.

[49] This was the Hudson River.

[50] See letter to the trustees of St. George's Church, September 27, 1798.

[51] Bull's Ferry was across the Hudson at the upper line of present Hudson County, New Jersey. At this time the ferry was operated by Theodore Brower on lease from the Bull family. (Westervelt: *History of Bergen County*, I, 160.)

[52] This was Joseph Hutchinson's at Milford.

meet the tidings of doleful distress from poor Philadelphia—ninety dying in a day; surely God will plead with us! *Monday* I rested.

Tuesday, October 2. I stopped and dined, talked, and prayed with the Joseph Lovell family, at Crosswick's, and came that night to Hulet Hancock's, who is a kind and gracious man.

Wednesday, 3. Called upon James Sterling. This morning the certainty of the death of John Dickins was made known to me:[53] he was in person and affection another Thomas White to me for years past: I feared death would divide us soon: I cannot write his biography here.

Pennsylvania

We came to Germantown: and *Thursday*, twenty-five miles to Daniel Meredith's; where we tarried for a night.

Maryland

Next day we reached Thomson's mill,[54] upon Great Elk: within a mile of this place, while going over a desperate piece of road my carriage turned bottom upwards; I was under, and thrown down a descent of five or six feet: I thought at first I was unhurt, but upon examination I found my ankle was skinned and a rib bone bruised. O, the heat, the fall, the toil, the hunger of the day!

On *Saturday* we rode six miles to Northeast: my bruised side pained me much, my spirits were sad; dark clouds impend over Methodism here.

Sabbath day, 7. I preached in the Northeast church on Heb. xii, 15–17. The substance of my sermon was: 1. A caution against failing to obtain the repenting, converting, persevering, sanctifying grace of God. 2. How some bad principles, persons, and practices were like wormwood, gall, and poison to society. 3. How small the gain, and how great the loss of peace. 4. That some might apostatize beyond the possibility of being restored, and weep hopeless and unavailing tears: I enforced the caution; *looking diligently* to avoid the greatest evil and danger on the one hand, and to secure the greatest good, grace, and glory on the other. *Monday* we rode to the Buck, and dined with a daughter of Sarah Dallam's.[55] We then came on to

[53] See letter to Ezekiel Cooper, October 4, 1798. John Dickins, the book steward, died of yellow fever at Philadelphia on September 27, 1798.

[54] This was possibly the mill of Richard Thompson, located on Big Elk River.

[55] The Buck Tavern, also known as Carson's, was on the post road south of New Castle. This was Elizabeth Smith (1774–1825), daughter of Josias William and Sarah Dallam, who married first Herman Stump and second Abraham Jarrett. (Preston: *History of Harford County*, 217; Silver and Archer; *Genealogical Record of the Stump Family*; Brumbaugh: *Maryland Records*, II, 150.)

Perry Hall: in consequence of the drought this place does not appear a *universal green*, as formerly.

Tuesday, 9. We came to Baltimore: here they have little to boast of but health and trade: the outward building of a society house is going on.[56] I had John Dickins's son[57] with me: we sketched out a few traits of his father's life. For piety, probity, profitable preaching, holy living, Christian education of his children, secret, closet prayer, I doubt whether his superior is to be found either in Europe or America.

Friday, 12. I had an appointment in the new church at ten o'clock. I endeavoured to suit my subject to the season, and to the time of affliction in our towns and cities; it was 2 Chron. vii, 13, 14.[58]

Virginia

Saturday, 13. We rode thirty-two miles to Turner's. Here man and beast beginning to fail, I rested on *Sabbath day*; we had a long ride to Fairfax chapel, where we came in about twelve o'clock. In consequence of my affliction of body and mind I was but poorly prepared to preach; however, I attempted a gloss on 1 Peter ii, 1–3. Here I saw and conversed with my old friend William Watters.

Monday, 15. We came to Alexandria; I preached in the evening on Col. iii, 15.

Tuesday, 16. Brother Lee and John Harper accompanied me; we came through excessive heat and dust, thirty miles, to Ward's.

Wednesday, 17. I came to the widow Conner's, who keeps a decent boarding house: we rode this day about forty miles, having nothing to eat but a little bread and cheese. On *Thursday*, twelve miles to the widow Collins', where we breakfasted between eleven and twelve o'clock, and in our usual manner prayed, and addressed the family about their souls;

[56] The identification of this building is difficult. It might have been the Old Parsonage built near the site of the first Light Street Chapel. On an upper floor was the conference room which beginning with 1800 was for years the meeting place of the Baltimore Annual Conference and other Methodist gatherings. (Roberts, *op. cit.*, 78 ff.)

[57] Asbury Dickins, who had been his father's helper, was doubtless brought along to confer with Ezekiel Cooper whose pastorate in Wilmington had been interrupted that he might assume management of the publishing interests. Asbury Dickins became associated with Joseph Dennie in the publication of *The Portfolio* and later attained high political position in Washington, acting as Secretary of State and Secretary of the Treasury, and at the time of his death Secretary of the Senate. (Buckingham: *Anecdotes Personal Memoirs, and Biographies of Literary Men, Connected with Newspaper Literature, from 1690 to 1800*, II, 195; Phoebus, *op. cit.*, 261–70.)

[58] A continued drought and the ravages of yellow fever along the eastern seaboard had decreased the food supplies and had raised the death rate in Philadelphia and Baltimore to alarming proportions. Asbury's text described the terms under which the Lord "will heal this land." (*Baltimore Telegraph*, December 8, 1798; Toner: *Annals of Medical Progress and Medical Education, Washington*, 1874.)

and then rode on, ten miles, to brother Lyon's. Whilst others leave us, and say much evil of us, these people in Caroline county keep closely to us. I felt very unwell, occasioned, I suppose, by riding so late and early through the excessive heat, dust, and dews.

Friday, 19. We came through the dust, thirty-five miles, to Richmond: here I heard of the death of John Norman Jones, who departed in joy and peace in Charleston; this is the second preacher we have lost in about one year in that city. Likewise of Hickson and Brush, in New York; M'Gee and Dickins, in Philadelphia; and Francis Spry in Baltimore. M'Gee, William Dougharty, J. Brush, Stephen Davis, John Ragen, James King, and John Dickins, died of the malignant fever.

Saturday, 20. I rested in Richmond. I here must record my thanks to my ancient and firm friend, Philip Rogers, for the loan of a horse, when mine was fully worn down, and unable to stand my long and rapid rides.

Sabbath, 21. I preached in the court house, at the east end of the city on 1 John i, 6, 7; and in the afternoon on Rom. x, 13–16. On *Monday*, 22, I preached at Manchester, on Heb. viii, 10, 11; and on *Tuesday* rode to Petersburg by three o'clock, and preached on Heb. iii, 16. I spent the evening with, and slept at Joseph Harding's; it was a renewal of our former friendship. I spent *Wednesday* at Wood Tucker's, in as sweet affection as in ancient times. I exhorted his children to come to Christ.

Thursday, 25. In company with my never-failing friend (as far as man can be so) Richard Whatcoat, I came to Roper's. My horse was taken sick, which detained me a night. On *Friday*, at Henry Reese's, my subject was Matt. vi, 16. I had the pleasure of seeing seven preachers present. On *Saturday*, 27, we had what was much wanted—rain.

Sunday, 28. I rode sixteen miles and preached at Mayes's chapel, lodging at Peter Robinson's. Here I left my carriage and sick horse with brother Mansfield. *Monday*, at Trotter's. *Tuesday*, I met the local brethren; in speaking of our own souls, and the work of God upon others, we were quickened.

Wednesday, 31. At Paup's chapel I preached on Eph. v, 25–27. Brothers Lee and Harper exhorted. The meeting continued until three o'clock. It was a cold day, but a warm meeting. Two or three souls professed to find the Lord in his pardoning grace.

Thursday, *November* 1. It rained. On *Friday* we rode to Benjamin Johnson's. Here we talked over ancient and present times, and of our feelings. The work reviveth in this society, and it is as we wish it to be, and should be. The young people are coming to Christ, and will fill up the places of their parents, who must shortly go to glory. In the evening we came to brother Meredith's. God hath blessed his little son; but we found the father sick.

Saturday, 3. Rode to brother Seward's near Roanoke River, where we designed to keep the Sabbath. I felt the want of a cloak or the carriage.

Sunday, 4. I have peace in my soul, but feel uncomfortable in my body.

Monday, 5. This was a great day; many preachers, travelling and local, were present. My subject was Eph. iv, 11, 12. We had a melting time. Brother Dromgoole and myself wept. His wife and others praised the Lord.

North Carolina

Tuesday, 6. We crossed the Roanoke at Moseley's ferry, and stopped at M'Lane's. Here God is working amongst the people. We came on *Wednesday*, by riding two hours in the night through the woods, to Harris's where I preached on *Thursday*, 8th, from 2 Peter i, 4. On *Friday* we rode to Colonel Edmund Taylor's. *Sabbath day*, at Bank's church, I preached on Heb. vi, 11, 12, and administered the supper of the Lord, and ordained John Whitefield deacon. The church was so very open that we could not be outwardly comfortable. We tried to remedy it, in some measure, by closing up some of the windows with blankets. I lodged at Nathan Norris's, one of my sons in Christ, now a father of children, and a very useful preacher.

Monday, 12. We rode twenty miles to Charles Cannon's; and on *Tuesday*, twenty-five miles to Snipe's. *Wednesday* we forded Haw River, and came through a curious path, for a carriage, to the new meeting house on Hickory Mountain. We dined with Mr. Reeves, an ancient friend of mine, and thence proceeded on to brother M'Master's, a local preacher. We have ridden this day thirty miles.

Thursday, 15. We rode from the upper branches of Rocky River, twenty miles, to Pleasant Garden. When I came to the meeting house, I had little strength of mind or body. We lodged at Daniel Sherwood's. My aged brethren and sisters from Maryland and Delaware rejoiced to see me, a poor, feeble man. They had seen me in better times.

Friday, 16. We rode to Mr. Bell's, on Deep River;[59] thence thirty miles to Wood's, upon Uwharrie River. This day was very warm, and we had exceedingly uncomfortable roads. Going at this rate is very trying; but it will make death welcome, and eternal rest desirable. *Saturday* and *Sunday* at quarterly meeting, my subject was Acts iii, 26. We rode down twelve miles to D. West's, and were benighted, which ill suited me. As we had to travel an unknown road to Henry Ledbetter's, I wished to continue on our journey, and not stop at Hancock; but the people thought and said otherwise, so I stopped, and brother Lee preached; after which I gave a discourse on Acts ii, 39, and came off in haste. D. West escorted me down to the ferry, where we called in vain for the flat. D. West went over, and it was with difficulty that he persuaded the ferryman to come with the boat and take me. It being dark, and the wind blowing very strong and cold, we

[59] See *Journal* entry and note for January 22, 1790,

had hard work in crossing. I told the company so in the morning, but stay I must and preach, or be accounted proud. At Henry Ledbetter's I preached on Heb. x, 23, 24, and at John Randall's,[60] 2 Cor. vi, 1. Brother Jackson had secured for me riding and preaching enough as far as Camden.

Thursday, 22. We recrossed the Pee Dee River at C.'s Ferry, and made it about eighteen miles to Mask's, where I preached on Heb. iv, 1. On *Friday*, at Bethel, on 2 Cor. vi, 11. *Saturday* and *Sunday*, at quarterly meeting, at Jesse's (a coloured man) meeting house, near Webb's Ferry. My subject on *Saturday* was Acts ii, 17, 18, and on *Sabbath day*, 2 Tim. iv, 1, 2. We then rode seven miles to Isaac Jackson's. *Monday*, rode.

South Carolina

Tuesday, 27. Preached and rode twenty-two miles to Mr. Blakeney's, on Thomson's Creek.[61] *Wednesday*, rode to Horton's, and preached on Gen. xxiii, 19. At Crul's meeting house, on *Thursday*, on ——, and at Granney's Quarter,[62] on 2 Cor. xii, 9; and on *Friday* we came into Camden. Brother Lee had gone along on brother Blanton's district.[63]

We have ridden since brother Jackson[64] hath had the command of us, nearly one hundred and fifty miles, from Montgomery, in North Carolina, to Camden, in South Carolina. If I attempt any appointments that brother Lee has gone upon, I must ride one hundred and fifty miles next week to Washington, in Georgia. I have made little or no observation on the way, I have been so unwell. The people are remarkably kind in this country. I preached in Camden on 1 Kings viii, 35, 36. Here we have a beautiful meeting house. It was a time of very severe drought, but I hope this place will yet be visited in mercy. *Monday* we rode to brother James Rembert's and on *Tuesday* I preached there on Heb. vi, 18. Here we seated ourselves for writing until *Saturday*. On *Sabbath day* my subject was Acts iv, 20. *Monday*, we rode to brother Richard Bradford's, and on *Tuesday* to Jack Creek.[65] The changes of weather and lodging affect me much. I called and

[60] See note under February 15, 1785.

[61] Blakeney lived near Pageland on Thompson's Creek. Asbury entered South Carolina at the northwest corner of Chesterfield County.

[62] For Horton and Granny's Quarter in Kershaw County see notes under March 6, 1797. Crul's meetinghouse is unidentified.

[63] Asbury was accompanied by Jesse Lee, who acted as the first secretary of record in the South Carolina Conference. Benjamin Blanton was presiding elder of the Charleston district and at the conference was made presiding elder over all the South Carolina charges. (*Minutes*; Betts: *History of South Carolina Methodism*, 75.)

[64] The Rev. Jonathan Jackson was presiding elder in that section of the conference. He joined the conference in 1789 and located in 1815. In the absence of Bishop Asbury he presided over the South Carolina Conference in 1798.

[65] Jack Creek was in Clarendon County.

preached at Robert Bowman's.[66] On *Friday* we came to Monk's Corner, and on *Saturday* to Charleston. Fasting, and riding through the heavy sands, cause me to feel unwell. I received a *cooling breeze* in a letter from the North. For the first time I opened my mouth upon Psalm lxvi, 13, 14. We have peace and good prospects in Charleston, very large congregations attend the ministration of the word. Brother Harper[67] opened his mission upon, "Thy word have I hid in my heart that I might not sin against thee." In the evening I spoke upon our Lord's lamentation over Jerusalem. On *Christmas day* I preached from Luke ii, 14, and at the new church on Haggai ii, 7.

[66] Bowman lived near Summerton.

[67] The Rev. John Harper was born in England and began preaching under John Wesley. He came to America in 1795 and was stationed in Boston. He went to South Carolina with Asbury and was stationed in Charleston for three years, when he located and settled in Columbia. He was the founder of the Washington Street Methodist Church there and one of the founders of Mount Bethel Academy. (Betts, *op. cit.*, 169.)

1799

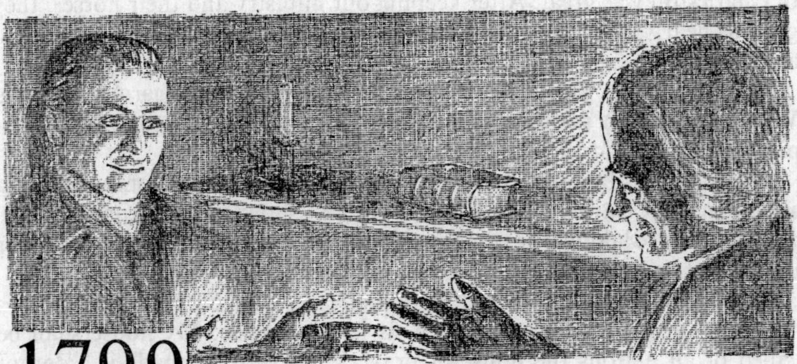

1799

Asbury at the home of William Watters in Northern Virginia

CHAPTER TWENTY-EIGHT

South Carolina

January 1, 1799. Our yearly conference assembled at Charleston. We kept our seats for four days; thirty preachers present. We had great harmony and good humour. I gave a short discourse, addressed to the conference, from Heb. xiii, 17.

I. *Your guides*—consequently governors. These how needful in the night, if there be ignorance in the traveller, and danger in the way, deep pits, wild beasts, or bad men. If it be in the morning, or noon-day, how natural it is to follow a guide; how necessity and fear, upon the part of the traveller, will make him obedient.

II. People are to be led into essential truth, duty, and experience.

III. Ministers are to watch for their souls as they that must give an account—the general and special accountability to God, Christ, and the Holy Spirit, to the ministry, and to the Church, and to all men; they must give an account for the loss of the Christian traveller, if that loss be a consequence of neglect in the guide. The joy faithful ministers have in the prosperity, spirituality, and happiness of the Church; *their grief* or *groaning*, when so far from gaining other souls, they lose some already partially gained; how much the interest of souls is concerned in the prosperity of the ministry. *Pray for us*: the great duty of the flock. *The argument*: We have a good conscience: that this being the case, their prayers might be answered. Live honestly, do our duty faithfully, and take what is allowed us as wages—paying our just debts to souls.

I ordained three elders and seven deacons. The generosity of the people in Charleston was great. After keeping our ministry and their horses, they gave us nearly one hundred dollars for the benefit of those preachers who are in want.

Sabbath day, 6. Very cold, sleet in the streets, and dangerous walking. We had a solemn sacramental season; and a goodly number of "Ethiopians stretched out their hands to the Lord."

Saturday, 12. My time has been chiefly taken up in composing and selecting from Cave's Lives of the Fathers,[1] showing the primitive episcopacy. We are laid up for winter, when it is like summer.[2] I hope to labour upon the Lord's day in the churches, so called.

Sabbath day, 20. I preached at Bethel:[3] my subject was Mark xi, 17: "And he taught, saying unto them, Is it not written, My house shall be called of all nations the house of prayer? but ye have made it a den of thieves." At the old church my subject was 2 Peter i, 16. A group of sinners gathered around the door, and when I took the pulpit they went off with a shout: I felt what was coming. In the evening there was a proper uproar, like old times. I employed the last week in reading, writing, visiting, and attending feasts of charity; one with the white society and the other with the Africans.

Sabbath day, 27. I preached in the morning at Bethel, from Heb. xiii, 20, 21.

I. It was a prayer: as he, Paul, had asked their prayers, he gave them his.

II. "The God of peace": the gracious relation of the Hebrews as reconciled to God.

III. "Brought again from the dead"; when it might be thought, all was lost when Jesus was dead; again he had brought the Hebrews from a state of death in trespasses and sins.

IV. This was more than bringing the apostle to them, although he might be given to them of God to their prayers.

V. "Great Shepherd of the sheep"—all the sheep, Jews and Gentiles. *The Shepherd of the shepherds*; doing *really*, what they, *under-shepherds*, do instrumentally: he seeketh, keepeth, feedeth, and watcheth his ordained flock against those who would steal or kill them, and alienate them from Jesus, or the true fold, and faithful pastors.

VI. "Through the blood of the everlasting covenant": see Exodus xxiv, 3; Moses said, Behold the blood of the covenant, when he sprinkled the people; it is this that meriteth, sealeth, and sanctifieth.

[1] William Cave (1637–1713) was an Anglican divine who was famous for his writings on church history. The work which Asbury was studying was "Ecclesiastici, or a History of the Lives, Acts, Deaths, and Writings of the most eminent Fathers of the Church in the Fourth Century." (*Dictionary of National Biography*, III, 1250–51.)

[2] See letters to Ezekiel Cooper, January 8 and 9, 1799.

[3] Bethel Church was the "new house" for which provision had been made last year and which had now been completed. (See *Journal* entry and note for February 14, 1797.)

VII. "Make you perfect in every good work"—as to the quantity and quality of good works: and,

Lastly, "pleasing to God"—in gracious affections, purity of intention, and uniformity of conduct; and all by the merit and intercession of Jesus Christ. In the afternoon I preached in Cumberland street meeting house on Deut. iv, 9.

Wednesday, 30. Once more, through divine assistance, we left Charleston, and came twelve miles to brother Jackson's[4]; where we rested one day.

Sunday, *February* 3. By riding until ten o'clock in the night, we came, fifty miles, to Mr. Boon's.[5] On *Saturday* I rode alone to Georgetown: we have made it nearly eighty miles from Charleston to this place. I preached on Galatians v, 24–26: First, They that are Christ's in a special spiritual sense: his sheep, redeemed, sought, and saved; his children, bearing his image. Secondly, How they are to be distinguished: they crucify the flesh with the passions and desires thereof; the sinful love of the world, with the sinful fear and joy also. Thirdly, Let us walk in the Spirit, as an evidence that we live in the Spirit. Fourthly, Let us not be "desirous of vain glory"; in forms, ordinances, or any outward appearances of men and things. Fifthly, Let us not by such mean measures "provoke one another," or envy one another. In the afternoon I preached on Isaiah lxvi, 5.

Monday, 4. Was an uncomfortable day; so we did not ride.

Tuesday, 5. We crossed Black River, at Gadsby's ferry: the bridge over one of the natural canals was broken; we had presence of mind to loose the long reins of the bridle: brother Lee put the horse through the ford, and I met him on the other side, and guided him out safe. This day we made it nearly forty miles to W. Rogers's, near Kingston.

Wednesday, 6. We rode in a cold day, thirty miles, to dear brother Hawkins's, upon Little River, crossing Wacawman at Star Bluff.

North Carolina

Thursday, 7. I preached at the meeting house, from Luke iv, 18, 19; and came the same evening to father William Gause's,[6] where I preached, on *Friday*, 8, upon Rom. v, 1–5, we had a living season here. I paid a visit to the sea, and saw the breakers—awfully tremendous sight and sound! but how curious to see the sea gull take the clams out of the sand and bear them up into the air, and drop them down to break them, and then eat the flesh! This I saw demonstrated; and if they fail once in breaking the shell, they will take it up again, and bear it higher, and cast it down upon a hard spot of ground, until they effect their purpose.

[4] See note under December 30, 1796. [5] See note under December 29, 1796.

[6] Gause lived in the southern part of Brunswick County, North Carolina, near the South Carolina line.

We are now in Bladen circuit, Brunswick county, North Carolina. I have travelled nearly four hundred miles in the Southern States, and spent three months therein. We rested on *Saturday*, 9, and on

Sunday, 10, We attended at Shallot church; my subject was Acts xiv, 22. I showed, First, That the souls of the disciples must be confirmed in doctrine, experience, practice, and discipline of the Gospel of Christ in the Church of God. It was observed how plainly these were taught in the oracles of God. I offered some arguments in favour of revelation, to induce a continuance in the substance and exercise of faith through life: through much tribulation entering the eternal kingdom of glory: an object so great is not to be gained without great trials from every enemy, in doing and suffering the whole will of God. The day was so excessively cold, and the house so open, that I was chilled through my whole system. After meeting we rode on to Lockwood's Folly: here are several young converts.

Monday, 11. We came by Town Creck, where I stopped fourteen years ago; but what a change since then! Stephen Daniel and his wife are no more; but their dear children are coming to Christ, to fill up their parents' places.

Sister Daniel was an excellent woman. It seems as though old Brunswick in North Carolina, would be a Methodist county, and that most of the rulers would believe in Christ.

Tuesday, 12. I preached at Sullivan's, on Town Creek, from Gal. vi, 9: the house was crowded with people; there were many children to baptize; but my spirits were sunk, and I had no heart to speak.

Wednesday, 13. We came on to Wilmington; here I was in low spirits still. This town has suffered by two dreadful fires; but the people are rebuilding swiftly. I was so afflicted in body, that brother Lee had to preach two sermons in the church: the people were very attentive.

Thursday, 14. We rode twenty miles to Nixon's;[7] where I preached a little to a little flock, as there was only a half-day's notice. Through this day I have been amazingly dejected, although I am abundantly more happy in constitution and feeling than formerly.

Friday, 15. At Stone Bay: no preaching by the Methodists at this place. We lodged at friend Johnson's: on my last visit I preached here. We made it twenty-seven miles.

Saturday, 16. We rode eighteen miles to Lot Ballard's: here we were at home. It was an excessively cold day; at noon it changed to hail, and terminated in rain. I housed myself; and brother Lee went to the New River chapel to preach to the people.

Sunday, 17. Cold as the day was, and unwell as I felt myself, I could not be absent from the house of God: my subject was Acts iii, 19. The slaves were not permitted to come into the house. We rode to William Bryan's,

[7] Nixon lived in New Hanover County.

at Bryantown, upon Cedar Creek: and on *Monday* we held a meeting at Colonel Bryan's, the father of William.

Tuesday, 19. We were at Trenton court house; and on *Wednesday* at Lee's chapel: my subject here was Micah vi, 6–8. I endeavoured to show, First, that it is still the voice of many, "Wherewith shall I come before the Lord, to enjoy his favour and presence, and bow myself before the high God?" that is, worship him acceptably, as though they would give all they have in the world, no sacrifice should be too great; but men are often great in promise, but defective in performance; they promise much and do little. He hath showed thee, O man! what is good—that is, true religion; the blessed effects and fruits of it—do justly and walk humbly with thy God; see Deut. x, 12; Hosea xii, 6. First, Do justly according to human laws, and the claims and rights of men with men, as it respects continents, kingdoms, or families. Second, Do justice as it concerns the laws of God—as the second table is a claim of justice to obey parents, and not to take men's lives nor their wives; to bear a true witness. Third, Do justly, according to the commandments of Christ, Matt. vii, 12. "Love mercy," as it extends to the souls and bodies of men; this requires more than to do justly to them: "walk humbly with thy God"—feel thy total poverty and universal dependence upon God for all things, spiritual and temporal.

We lodged at Mrs. Knight's, the mother of our dear deceased brother Ahairs, once a travelling preacher amongst us.

Thursday, 21. We came to Newbern, originally settled by Germans, and called after *old Berne*, in Switzerland. For sixteen miles of this road we had heavy rain; but I was well cased up, notwithstanding which I took cold. We have travelled from Charleston three hundred and thirty miles in this our retrograde journey, which we have made longer by frequently turning out of our way.

Saturday, 23. My subjects at Newbern were 1 Peter ii, 11, 12; Heb. vii, 25; 1 Tim. iv, 8. We had very uncomfortable weather. We made some spiritual and temporal regulations, in hopes that matters would work much better in future.

Monday, 25. It was cold to purpose, and we had twenty-four miles to ride to William Cox's, on Neuse, near the mouth of Contentney: here my text was 1 John iv, 16, 17. We hence in a manner fled through the counties of Craven, Lenoir, Glasgow, and Edgecombe.

Tuesday, 26. I did not attend at the Rainbow meeting house[8] in consequence of my illness, the effect of my riding in the cold the day before.

Wednesday, 27. I was comforted in administering the sacrament; after which, as the day was damp, I left brother Lee to finish, and rode along sixteen miles to Seth Spaight's; a deeply distressed man for the loss of his dear wife, who lately departed this life.

[8] The Rainbow meetinghouse was in the northern part of Greene County, North Carolina.

Thursday, 28. We rode thirty-four miles to brother Toole's;[9] the rain poured down upon us on our way, and we had to feed under a pine tree.

Friday, *March* 1. We made out to ride ten miles, to Mr. Hodge's, near Sosson's bridge, upon Fishing Creek; where we were kindly and comfortably entertained.

Saturday, 2. We came to brother Bradford's[10] quarterly meeting: I was glad, after riding sixteen miles through the damp and severe cold, to sit by the fire.

Sabbath day, 3. I preached a little on 2 Cor. iv, 16–18.

Monday, 4. The generally excessive rains having made the Roanoke impassable at the nearest ferry, we had to ride a circuitous route through Halifax, which made it about thirty miles to Richard Whittaker's in Northampton. We had a bad swamp to cross, but I kept out of the water. It was well for me my carriage did not upset in the water, which it was very near doing. To travel thirty miles in such a cold day without fire, and no food, except a bit of biscuit, is serious. We were received gladly by our waiting brethren, Whatcoat, Wanner, and Lambeth.[11] I am of opinion that we have left five hundred miles on the other side of the Roanoke, in all the ground we have ridden over from Charleston, in South, to Halifax, in North Carolina. I went to Rehoboth (a new meeting house), and preached on 2 Cor. ii, 14.

Wednesday, 6. The cold and frost was very severe, and it was with great difficulty we made our way through the swamp from Richard Whittaker's. We rode to St. John's chapel, where brother Lee preached upon Rom. v, 5. The house being open, I was most severely chilled, and unfit for any public service. We lodged at Williford Horton's.[12]

Thursday, 7. We rode to Winton court house; where I preached on Heb. iii, 7. Two-thirds of my congregation were women; perhaps there will be more men when I go there again.

Friday, 8. We rode to Knotty Pine.

Saturday, 9. I preached at Knotty Pine chapel, on Gen. xxiv, 17–19: I was elaborate upon personal and family piety. Here I saw sister Baker; she standeth fast in the liberty wherewith Christ hath made her free, and I hope and believe God will save her children: our souls were mutually blessed.

Sabbath day, 10. At Gates court house[13] many serious people attended:

[9] Gareldus Toole lived in Edgecomb County and was the owner in 1790 of twenty-six slaves. (*Heads of Families*, 55.)

[10] Bradford's was in Halifax County.

[11] Richard Whatcoat was presiding elder over ten circuits in Virginia, North and South Carolina. William Lambeth was on the Greensville Circuit. Wanner does not appear in the *Minutes*.

[12] Williford Horton lived in Hertford County.

[13] Gates Court House was the present Gatesville.

my subject was Heb. vii, 26. I administered the sacrament; and had a solemn, feeling season.

Monday, 11. We rode to Constant's chapel,[14] on one of the branches of Bennett's Creek. The main creek affords a landing at Gates court house, and communicates, after a few miles, with Chowan River. I was made very comfortable in soul and body at Isaac Hunter's;[15] and had a happy meeting with the poor Africans[16] at night.

Tuesday, 12. The coolness of the weather increases. We rode thirty miles to George Sutton's, in Perquimans county.

Wednesday, 13. It both snowed and rained. We had a meeting at a house near Naggshead chapel;[17] where I preached a short sermon from 1 Peter iv, 18. We lodged at J. W——'s, a comfortable house, after a very uncomfortable snowy day.

Thursday, 14. At Nixonton I declined preaching and made an exhortation, after brother Lee had given them a long sermon. It is probably eight years since I came through this circuit, which caused this people to exert themselves in coming out, so that we had a very large congregation.

We have ridden, since we came across Roanoke, one hundred and forty-three miles to John Russell's. We have moved rapidly through Gates, Chowan, Perquimans, and Pasquotank counties: as we pass we have lovely levels, fine white cedar on the rivers, creeks, and swamps, for between six or seven hundred miles: from the low lands in Georgia, to Blackwater in Virginia, it is fine lumber land, but unhealthy in some places.

Friday, 15. It began to rain heavily, but ceased about twelve o'clock; we then rode to a school house, where many attended: my subject was, 1 Peter v, 10. I had the company of several preachers. I then rode on eight miles to brother William Proby's; it was good for me to be there. *Saturday*, 16. I felt greatly depressed in spirit, owing, no doubt, in some measure, to the changeable state of the weather. We crossed the Pasquotank at Sawyer's Ferry: here we were told that we had but seven miles to ride; but we wandered until we made it twelve. We learned that one of the widow Sawyer's daughters was lately committed to the dust; at the gate of the yard we found the mother in tears. As I was not able in body or mind to

[14] Constant's, sometimes called Costen's Chapel, was an Anglican church about one-half mile south of the present Sudbury, Gates County, North Carolina. It was the forerunner of the present Philadelphia Methodist Church, built at Sudbury around 1814. (Bishop Costen J. Harrell.)

[15] Isaac Hunter operated a gristmill on Bennett Creek near Constant's Chapel. His name was on the early membership roll of the chapel, now at Duke University. (See *Journal* entry for March 20, 1801.)

[16] On each of Asbury's visits to Isaac Hunter he mentions the Africans. One-half mile from Sudbury is St. John's African Methodist Episcopal Zion Church, probably the fruit of Asbury's ministry. (See *Journal* entry for March 20, 1801.) (Harrell.)

[17] Nags Head Chapel stood on ground conveyed by James P. Whedbee to the Methodists, and the New Hope Methodist Church now stands on the site. (Winslow: *History of Perquimans County*, 32.)

preach, I gave an exhortation; and after we had dined, we rode ten miles to Samuel Simmons,[18] across the North River swamps, which afford as low and as good land as any part of the beech lands of Cumberland or Kentucky. We swiftly passed through Camden and Currituck counties.

Sunday, 17. I made a feeble effort to preach at Williams's chapel, on James i, 24, 25. Our congregation was large. I returned and left brother Lee to finish. We lodged at brother Brunnell's.

Virginia

On *Monday* we had a violent storm of wind and snow, which lasted until ten o'clock, and we had a bitter ride of nineteen or twenty miles to James Wilson's, at Hickory Ground, in Virginia. I was exceedingly chilled on the way, the snow being from six to seven inches deep, and it blew a heavy cold wind.

Tuesday, 19. I preached at brother Wilson's, from 1 Cor. xv, 58. I sent my carriage for James Morris (formerly with us), afterward an Episcopal minister, and now near death. He expressed great consolation in God, and love to me. He hath a pious wife, who is the mother of nine children. We lodged with John Hodge, who joined the Methodists in early life. I was pleased to find that the elderly Methodists had put their children to trades to learn to work for themselves. I am in hopes the parents will not leave them their slaves, but manumit them—by *will* at least.

Wednesday, 20. At Cuthrell's, near the great bridge, and near Manning's, where we preached before the revolutionary war. On *Thursday* we rode through the rain to Norfolk, where I preached on *Friday*, from Gal. ii, 20: "I am crucified with Christ." Christ crucified: and Paul crucified after the likeness of Christ, and for *Jesus*—crucified to the world in afflictions, hopes, and desires. *I live*—I have had a spiritual birth, and live a spiritual life of faith, love, and holiness; yet not I, as the author of my own birth or life; "Christ liveth in me,"—by his Spirit; "and the life I now live is by faith of the Son of God";—faith of, and faith in, Christ—"who hath loved me, and given himself for me,"—that is, I know and feel my personal and real interest in, and union with, him.

We had a comfortable sacramental season in Norfolk on Easter day; and at Portsmouth, I spoke on James v, 20. Brother Lee preached on Romans ii, 14; 1 Cor. ix, 19–22; 1 Tim. iv, 16.

Monday, 25. We rode eighteen miles to George Walker's, in Princess Anne county, where I, with great labour, preached on Luke xxiv, 46–48. We calculate that we have ridden eight hundred and eighteen miles since we left Charleston.

Tuesday, 26. We came to quarterly meeting at Dawley's meeting house.

[18] Samuel Simmons lived in Currituck County, North Carolina.

The day was cloudy, and myself also. As there were four preachers to attend, I stayed at home. On *Wednesday* there was a most awful storm of rain and wind, which caused us to keep within doors.

Thursday, 28. I rode seven miles to Nimmo's meeting house,[19] where I preached on Heb. ii, 1. The day was excessively cold and the house too. After preaching I rode nineteen miles, having no refreshment for man or horse until we came to James Dawley's, within two miles of Norfolk, about seven o'clock at night. On *Friday* we came into town,[20] and attended quarterly meeting on *Saturday* and *Sunday*. My subject on *Saturday* was Psalm cxxvii, 1, and on *Sabbath day*, James i, 24, 25. I had a painful night after preaching on *Saturday*, having a small ulcer formed in my breast.

At Suffolk I was addressed by two grand-daughters of my dear aged friend, Benjamin Welden, of James City. I dined with Mr. Whitlock, and after the rain was over rode to William Powell's, forty miles from Portsmouth.

Thursday, *April* 4. I must needs preach at Wells's, the *schism* house; the great were there. My subject was 2 Tim. ii, 19. We then rode to William Blunt's. On *Friday* we were at Moody's, and on *Saturday* we came to the house of the widow of Henry Davies. On *Sunday* I preached at Lane's chapel, from 2 Tim. ii, 15, but it was the dividing of blood from my lungs. On the way I ordained two local deacons.

Monday, 8. We rode thirty miles to Jones's chapel. *Tuesday*, *Wednesday*, and *Thursday*, conference sat in great peace and love. As the house was cold, and I was very unwell, I could not attend. I had about two pounds of blood drawn from me.

Friday, 12. We rode to father Nathaniel Lee's,[21] and on *Saturday*, 13, to Frederick Bonner's, where I rested—a solemn *Sabbath*.

Monday, 15. By ten o'clock we came to Petersburg; and then rode on and crossed James River, at Woodson's ferry. We lodged at Keezee's, having ridden thirty-two miles.

Tuesday, 16. We came to Philip Davis's, twenty miles, near Putney, New Kent. I feel low in body, but serene in soul. The brethren in Virginia, in conference, gave it me in charge not to preach until the Baltimore conference. I was willing to obey, feeling myself utterly unable. The houses that we preach and lodge in, in this severe weather, are very open. My breast is inflamed, and I have a discharge of blood.

Wednesday, 17. I rested at brother Davis's; and on

Thursday, 18, Rode to Benjamin Pace's, in King and Queen county:

[19] Nimmo's meetinghouse was in Princess Anne County, and the church there still exists.

[20] See letter to Asbury from Mrs. Baker, March 17, 1799, and Asbury's letter to Alexander M'Caine, March 29, 1799.

[21] Nathaniel Lee, the father of Jesse Lee, lived in Prince George County.

these are gracious and kind souls—God is still working in this place; they have one hundred members in society.

Friday, 19. We rode twenty miles to our dear brother Coles's, in Essex county. We rested on *Saturday*.

Sunday, 21. Attended a meeting at Shephard's; and then rode to the widow Cox's.

Monday, 22. We crossed the Rappahannock, at Layton's ferry, and came to the widow Bombry's, in King George county. We have ridden upwards of sixty miles in two days, through excessively cold weather for the season.

Tuesday, 23. We rode thirty-five miles to Ward's near Dumfries.

Wednesday, 24. This is the great day of election; and there is no small stir in Virginia, about federal and anti-federal men. We rode thirty miles to William Adams's; I was much chilled, and very weary.

Thursday, 25. The general fast day—I attended at Fairfax chapel; Philip Bruce gave a discourse upon those words of our Lord, "And then shall they fast in those days." As I was unable to preach, I gave an exhortation from the subject. I find that very small rest, when joined with comfortable accommodation, gives me great strength of body: by this means I might be restored; but I must keep moving. I was caught in a heavy thunderstorm, from which I took cold, and had a high fever and headache; I rested on *Friday*, at William Watters's. *Saturday*, rode to Alexandria. *Monday* and *Tuesday*, rode to Baltimore.

Maryland

Wednesday, *May* 1. We opened our conference,[22] which sat four days. We had preaching morning and evening. I gave a short exhortation before the sacrament.

Monday, 6. We rode out to Greenwood,[23] Mr. Philip Rogers's country seat, who told me that when I was past labour, there was his house as my own. We asked for new wine; but find the old is better: the fermentation is done.

Tuesday, 7. We rode to Gunpowder Neck; I only exhorted a little, then went on to the bay side.

Wednesday, 8. The wind was high; I declined, but brother Jesse Lee waited, and crossed in an hour. I rode round, and lodged at Josias Dallam's: but dear Sally, his wife, is gone! I walked to her grave.

[22] Concerning this four-day conference held in Light Street Church, Jesse Lee, the traveling companion of Bishop Asbury, writes: ". . . had no great stir of religion, or any very lively meetings."

[23] Greenwood was not far from Collington Square on Collington Avenue between the present Oliver and Hoffman streets. (*Maryland Historical Magazine*, 1949, 197.)

Thursday, 9. I had a disagreeable passage across the Susquehanna. At this ferry, recently, three poor blacks have been drowned. I cannot omit relating a circumstance which took place when I was here last. A very large Negro man, an old ferryman, to whom I talked very faithfully, was drowned. I remember to have told him that if he did not take heed and repent, he might be drowned and damned! the former is certain; the latter is to be feared, as it is reported the Negroes were intoxicated. Doctor William Dallam escaped;[24] and what is remarkable, the boat that saved his life was made of wood taken from his father's plantation. *Thursday evening* I came to Back Creek well wearied.

Friday, 10. We rode to Chestertown—went to meeting; and I exhorted a little.

Saturday, 11. At Churchill church brother Lee preached, and I exhorted. We dined at Mr. Peter T. Causey's, and rode in the evening to brother Chair's.[25]

Whitsunday, 12. At Centreville, after brother Lee had preached, I feebly exhorted upon "Grieve not the Holy Spirit of God." We administered the supper of the Lord: I was weary at the end. I lodged at Thomas Wright's.

Monday, 13. At Tuckahoe a multitude attended; my services were very small.

Tuesday, 14. At Easton a crowd of people attended; here I could say but very little. We crossed Dover Ferry, and rode to William Frazer's, in Caroline county; and on *Wednesday*, 15, held meeting in his dwelling house

Thursday, 16. At Henry Ennalls's I could only gloss upon those gracious words: "Casting all your care upon him, for he careth for you."

Friday, 17. I attended Cambridge quarterly meeting; which was held in a barn: I commented a little upon, "We have not followed cunningly devised fables." Having had but little rest for two or three nights past, I retired with Bartholomew Ennalls, and went on the way to Vienna, to visit Somerset. I rejoiced that Doctor Edward White was standing firm in the grace of God: and that the Lord had blessed the souls of his children.

Saturday, 18. It rained plentifully until ten o'clock. We crossed at Vienna: it was very bad ferrying; the wind being against the tide, it raised high swells in the river. I came that evening to Thomas Garrettson's; we had a very serious congregation at Quantico chapel; I had taken cold

[24] (For photograph of Dr. William Dallam (1778–1859) with note see Lee, Luccock, and Dixon: *Illustrated History of Methodism*, 366.)

[25] The Chairs' home, in which Asbury preached January 2, 1778, was near Centerville, Queen Annes County, probably the same Chairs concerning whom Bishop Coke wrote on December 10, 1784: "This afternoon I went to visit one Mr. Chairs, about two years ago a famous foxhunter, now a leader of a Class, and one of the most zealous men in the country." John Chairs was one of the trustees to whom a lot was deeded June 21, 1794. The present Epworth Church is the outgrowth of the early society. (Hallman, *op. cit.*, 325; Emory: *History of Queen Anne's County*, 233.)

and was very unfit to speak at all. We came to Salisbury, where we rested on *Monday*. Brother Lee preached three times. Here I got bled.

Tuesday, 21. We came to Annamessex. My horse began to sweat, swell, and tremble—and died upon the road. Brother Levin Moore[26] was with me: we put his horse in the sulky, and both of us rode to Samuel Smith's.

Wednesday, 22. I borrowed a horse of Samuel Smith, and crossed Pocomoke, and rode to Littleton Long's, where I gave an exhortation to a few people. It was a very extraordinary legacy of a living friend that put forty-five dollars into my hands; had I not bought a coat I might have had fifty dollars in my pocket; it would have been a wonder for me to have as much money by me; but one hundred or more might be needful to purchase another horse.

Thursday, 23. We rode to Downing's,[27] where I gave a short exhortation, and on *Friday*, 24, we came to John Purnall's;[28] he is gone to his long home. Here I gave up my borrowed horse, and the only alternative was to put brother Hardesty's[29] horse in the sulky, and wedge ourselves with all our baggage together. We rode by Frederick Conner's, and made it nearly thirty miles, through excessive heat, to the widow Bowen's.

Delaware

Sabbath, 26. I preached at the chapel, and rode home with brother William Leister, living in the north end of Worcester county. This day we enter the State of Delaware. I have had great dejection of mind, and awful calculations of what may be and what may never be. I have now groaned along three hundred miles from Baltimore.

Monday, 27. After preaching at Johnson's we rode to the Sound, and lodged at Arthur Williams's,[30] an aged Methodist preacher. I passed the night in great affliction.

Tuesday, 28. We came on to Dagsboro just as the stage was about to set off for Milford. I paid the fare, and sent brother Hardesty along. I called upon William Johnson, a gracious soul. We then came into Milford about eight o'clock, after riding forty-three miles. Here I rested a day.

[26] Levin Moore, an itinerant preacher, 1791–1801, was then en route from Harford Circuit to visit numerous relatives near Laurel, Delaware. Samuel Smith lived near Crisfield, Somerset County, Maryland.

[27] Downing's was in Virginia near the Maryland line.

[28] John Purnall lived near Pocomoke City, Worcester County. At his home Bishop Coke preached during his first visit to America. (Coke, *op. cit.*, 47; Lednum, *op. cit.*, 342; *Maryland, a Guide to the Old Line State*, 441.)

[29] William Hardesty, a traveling preacher, 1792–1801, was in 1799 on the Northampton Circuit. (*General Minutes.*)

[30] Arthur Williams resided near Assawoman Bay, Sussex County. This name appears as one of the trustees of the deed, dated April, 1784, to the land on which the Sound Church was erected. (Scharf: *History of Delaware*, II, 1343.)

Thursday, 30. I must needs ride twenty miles back to Lewes, principally to see the people.

Friday, 31. Returned back to Milford. I had taken cold. I ordained three deacons and exhorted a little.

Saturday, June 1, was a very cold day; we rode to Dover; the crowds of people were painful to me; I ordained two deacons; was confined in meeting four hours, and attempted to preach, but could not.

Sabbath day, 2. After meeting, I rode to Duck Creek Cross Roads, and called at Doctor Cook's to see Thomas White's children. Doctor Anderson, Doctor Ridgeley, and Doctor Needham considered my case; they advised a total suspension from preaching, fearing a consumption or a dropsy in the breast.

Monday, 3. I ordained one person at the Cross Roads, and another at Dickinson's meeting house. I dined with Mr. Moore near the Appoquinimink bridge, and then rode on to Wilmington; we have made forty miles this day. What with labour and fevers my rest is greatly interrupted.

Pennsylvania

Thursday, 6. We held our conference in Philadelphia. I retired each night to *the Eagleworks, upon Schuylkill*, at Henry Foxall's solitary, social retreat.[31] The conference was large, and the business very important. Ezekiel Cooper was confirmed in his appointment by me as our agent in the book concern.[32]

New Jersey

Wednesday, 12. After the rising of the conference I rode to Burlington; and on *Thursday*, 13, to Milford; on *Friday* to Mr. Drake's,[33] near Amboy; and on *Saturday* to New York.

[31] The Eagle Iron Works were located on present 23rd Street and Henry Foxall was one of the owners. He was also a local preacher at St. George's Church. The works were established during the Revolutionary War and were used for casting cannon. Here about 1820 were cast some twenty-two-inch iron pipes, which were the largest ever cast in America up to that date. (Scharf and Westcott: *History of Philadelphia*, III, 225.)

[32] John Dickins had died in the yellow-fever epidemic the previous year and was succeeded by Ezekiel Cooper.

[33] Benjamin Drake, whose home was a regular preaching place, lived at Piscataway in Middlesex County, New Jersey. (Abstracts of Wills, New Jersey Archives, II, 150. See *Journal* entries for June 15, 1800, and August 6, 1804, and letter to Ezekiel Cooper, March 27, 1801; Phoebus, *op. cit.*, 273.)

New York

Sabbath day, 16. I gave a short exhortation in the John street church; likewise in the North River house. It is an unseasonable day for religion; it is time the conference should come; may Almighty God bless and own their labours to the people!

Wednesday, 19. We opened our conference for New York, and all the New England States.[34]

The conference was crowded with work; consequently I had but little rest, and what added to my pain, was brother Shadrach Bostick's lying sick in the next room: heat and haste!

Sunday, 23. We had a charitable day at all the houses, and collected nearly three hundred dollars: but the deficiencies of the preachers were almost one thousand dollars. I attempted to preach a little on Phil. iv, 19; and gave an exhortation at the Bowery church. I met the society at the old church at night. The excessive heat made us wish and haste to leave town.

Monday, 24. Was exceedingly warm; we rode to Sherwood's; but did not get there in time to meet our appointment.

Tuesday, 25. We came to the Plains.

Wednesday, 26. We rode about thirty miles; and came in about ten o'clock at night to Governor Van Courtlandt's, whose wife is a Shunammite indeed.

Thursday, 27. We toiled through the rain over Peekskill mountains to Richard Jackson's,[35] where we lodged, about eight miles from Poughkeepsie. In the night I was taken with a violent pain in my knee. We have travelled over rough roads, and through great heat since we left New York, about one hundred miles. Feverish and full of pain as I was, I attended meeting and gave an exhortation.

Saturday, 29. I rode through heat, twenty-five miles, to Rhinebeck; the pain in my knee subsided. On *Sabbath day* I preached at the school church upon "Grace be with all them that love our Lord Jesus Christ." Brother Jesse Lee gave a sermon on the fruits of the Spirit.

Monday, *July* 1. I rested. My health is somewhat better. I must confess I never felt so great a resolution to resign the general superintendency as I do now; and if matters do not work more to my mind, it is highly probable I shall: my prayers and counsel will be turned this way until next General Conference.

Tuesday, 2. I visited Mr. Sands' family; and on *Wednesday* breakfasted with Mrs. Montgomery at her beautiful retreat. Dined at Mrs. Livingston's

[34] See letter to Wilkins and Ridgly, June 22, 1799.

[35] Richard Jackson was the leader of the Methodist group in and around Lagrangeville in Dutchess County. This had been a Methodist center since 1789, and Asbury frequently stopped there.

EZEKIEL COOPER

on the manor; an aged, respectable mother of many children. The house, the garden, the river view—all might afford much painting for the pen of a Hervey. Brother Garrettson and his agreeable wife attended us.

Thursday, 4. We rode twenty miles to what is called Hudson City; a mere blank.

Friday, 5. Excessively warm: we stopped at Kinderhook,[36] and at Miller's, time enough to hide from a heavy gust; we then came on to Albany: we have ridden thirty-five miles this day. I received a healing letter from Thomas Morrell; but matters will not easily be done away with me: if it were one or two only that were concerned, it would be but little; but it is hundreds, yea, thousands of travelling and local preachers and official men; and thousands of people also.

Saturday, 6. I was awakened at twelve o'clock exceedingly sick, and totally disabled for public service; I was not able to sit up until six o'clock in the evening. I rode two miles out of the city, to Mr. Marks's.

Monday, 8. Rode to Coeyman's landing; and then to the stone chapel; here we have the good news of souls converted at prayer meeting. Rode in the rain and damp six miles to brother Blodgett's, upon Hocketuck,[37] in Albany county and circuit; here also I found the labours of Anning Owings had been blessed in the awakening of some young women. Our congregation was large: I gave an exhortation and a prayer in much weakness of body. We rode back the same evening a few miles to father Waldron's.[38]

Wednesday, 10. I rose at five o'clock, very unwell; but must needs ride in the heat and dust, over hills and rocks, thirty-five miles and came to Crawford's and Dillon's[39] about four o'clock: weary as I was, I could not feel satisfied without prayer and exhortation. We have ridden in three days upwards of sixty miles, and held a meeting each day.

Thursday, 11. We rode nine miles to Cockburn's, in Ulster county:[40] here I gave a small exhortation to a small congregation; it was a day of small things; but it may not be so always.

Friday, 12. I rode fifteen miles to Hurley,[41] and stopped at Cornelius Cole's; no appointments had been made; but we called a meeting in the evening. I rested on *Saturday*, 13, at Marbletown.

[36] Kinderhook was a small community ten miles north of Hudson.

[37] This was a community known as Coeyman's Hollow, six miles up the Hocketuck Creek on a road leading into the mountainous terrain to the west. Blodgett was the first class leader there, and his house stood until well after 1900. (*The Onward Way*, 150th Anniversary Brochure of New York Annual Conference, 72.)

[38] James Waldron was the first Methodist leader at Coeyman's and a trustee of the stone church.

[39] John Crawford established the Coeymans Circuit in 1789, and Robert Dillon built several houses a short distance east of Palenville, New York.

[40] This was a Methodist center near Phoenicia, on Esopus Creek about ten miles west of Kingston.

[41] This was a village about five miles southwest of Kingston, on present Highway 209.

Sabbath day, 14. I was very unwell, and the next day was very warm. I made an attempt to preach on Matt. xxv, 34–36; a marble-hearted congregation as well as Marbletown; and probably will remain so whilst the love of the world predominates: family prayer, class meetings, and prayer meetings are neglected. Brother Lee preached at Hurley in the evening, and I gave a closing exhortation.

Monday, 15. We rode through dust and heat, without refreshment, twenty-five miles to Degoes; here the people of the house seemed all *soul*; we could not leave the place until we had called a meeting.

Tuesday, 16. We rode fifteen miles to Samuel Fowler's, and dined: we then rode on to meet my appointment at Mr. John Ellison's.

Wednesday, 17. Jesse Lee gave an awakening discourse from 1 Cor. xv, 58.

Thursday, 18. We rode over hills and rocks, through heat and with hunger, twenty-eight miles, without stopping until we came to Lazear's,[42] near the Jersey line, Orange county. We have travelled and toiled nearly four hundred miles through this State: weary as I was, I must needs ride five miles farther to Nicholas Simonson's,[43] where I was comfortably entertained.

New Jersey

Friday, 19. We came on to Sussex court house;[44] dined, and pushed on to father Freeman's[45]—no appointments. At night I was taken with great distress in my bowels, which held me two nights and a day.

Saturday, 20. I rode in great pain and heat, hungry and sick, twenty-five miles, to Mr. M'Collock's:[46] how welcome a good house, kind friends,

[42] Cornelius Lazear, Sr., lived at New Milford, New York, and was one of the founders of Methodism there. The ferry was at or near the boundary between Sussex County, New Jersey, and Orange County, New York. (Ruttenber and Clark: *History of Orange County*, 572, 592.)

[43] Nicholas Simonson came from Staten Island and kept an inn at Vernon Village. The house is still standing. Methodism in the community dates from Asbury's first visit in 1787. A society seems to have been formed about the same time at North Vernon, now Glenwood; there was no church building there, however, until 1835, Samuel Simonson then being one of the trustees. (Snell: *History of Warren and Sussex Counties*, 347, 354; Records of Vernon Methodist Church in the New Jersey Historical Society Library, Newark; Hampton: *The Dentons of Vernon Valley*.)

[44] The Sussex County courthouse at Newton was a Methodist preaching place before the erection of a church in 1833. Asbury preached there in August 24, 1784, and on other occasions, and Ezekiel Cooper preached there in 1786. (Phoebus, *op. cit.*, 47; Snell, *op. cit.*, 248; Lytle: *The First Century of Newton Methodism*, 7; Webb: *Historical Directory of Sussex County*, 46; see *Journal* entry for August 24, 1784.)

[45] Andrew Freeman lived at Log Gaol (Jail), now Johnsonburg, which was the county seat of Sussex County before the division of the county. Asbury stopped there on several occasions. (See *Journal* entries for April 25, 1807, and May 14, 1811.)

[46] Colonel William McCullough lived at Asbury in Hunterdon County.

and a cold day! What is the cause of my affliction? Is it the water, or the weather, or my bilious habit? I am at a loss to know.

Sabbath day, 21. At Colonel McCullough's. Having been so unwell for some days past, it was enough for me to exhort a little after Jesse Lee had given them two sermons. I was visited in the evening by John Hanna,[47] an aged, social, Presbyterian minister.

Monday, 22. I rose to ride to James Bryan's, Bucks county, Haycock township, Pennsylvania. We followed Musconetcong Creek[48] to the mouth; we had traced the head branches of it already; it is a most beautiful, useful stream, running through a rich vale into Delaware River, at Hunt's ferry.[49] The weather is warm, and the roads uneven; we had a journey of about thirty miles. We have travelled about sixty-five miles through Jersey, and about five hundred in a month.

Pennsylvania

Wednesday, 24. We rose at three o'clock in the morning, and began our journey at five, over ridges and rocks, twenty-eight miles to Pottsgrove. We did not eat until we came to Coventry. Thirty-six miles is the amount of this day's journey. O heat, drought, and dust!

Thursday, 25. We had a most dreadful time over the mountains to The Forest Chapel; here we found the people much engaged in religion; this was a balm for every sore. We dined at Carberry's and lodged at Abraham Lewis's.

Friday, 26. We rode twenty miles to New Holland, and had a sample of bad roads for a sulky. Here some souls have been brought to Christ. I was exceedingly spent for want of sleep and rest. After five o'clock we rode with elder Ware towards Strasburg; night came on and left me two miles from the place in the woods—in darkling shades, a new cut road, and stumpy path. We came in about nine o'clock, having ridden twelve miles. Thank the Lord for whole bones!

Sabbath day, 28. There was preaching in Thomas Ware's orchard, in Strasburg; we had the respectables of the town, and a large assembly. This place contains, I judge, between sixty and seventy dwelling houses.

Monday, 29. I visited Jacob Boehm's; God hath begun to bless the children of this family The parents have followed us nearly the space of twenty years.

Tuesday, 30. We had a serious earthquake at five o'clock; the earth is

[47] The Rev. John Hanna was prominent as a Presbyterian minister in Sussex County and the area. (Snell, *op. cit.*, 585, 631.)

[48] Musconetcong Creek forms the boundary between the present Warren and Hunterdon Counties.

[49] Hunt's Ferry was at the mouth of the Delaware River and Musconetcong Creek.

growing old; it groans and trembles; which is the necessary consequence of "palsied eld." I visited John Miller's; thence we rode six miles to Martin Boehm's.

Wednesday, 31. We had a comfortable meeting at Boehm's church.[50] Here lieth the dust of William Jessop[51] and Michael R. Wilson.[52] I feebly attempted a discourse upon Heb. vi, 12. In the evening we rode to Abraham Keaggay's,[53] near the mouth of Pequea Creek.[54]

Thursday, *August* 1. After a suspension of rain in some parts, for two, four, six, and eight weeks, we had a gracious moderate rain: on *Friday*, the rain continued quickening, and thus saving the latter fruits of the earth. I rode to Mrs. Elizabeth Wright's. We crossed Conestoga[55] at the mouth of Little Conestoga; we had a very uneven path. Mrs. Wright's family are blessed—all the children profess religion—father and daughter have died in the Lord. Our friends followed us from Pequea.[56] Martin Boehm[57] is all upon wings and springs since the Lord hath blessed his grandchildren; his son Henry is greatly led out in public exercises.

Saturday, 3. We rode to Columbia,[58] formerly called Wright Ferry. The excessive warmth of the sun in crossing the water made me sick. We stopped at Drinnon's; here we met Seely Bunn;[59] he had very late notice

[50] Boehm's Chapel was the first Methodist house of worship in Lancaster County, Pennsylvania. Jacob Boehm, son of Martin Boehm and brother of Henry Boehm, gave the land on which the chapel was built. It is located at Willow Street, Pennsylvania, about five miles south of Lancaster. The plan was furnished by Richard Whatcoat in 1790, and the chapel, measuring forty by thirty-two feet, with galleries, was erected in 1791. It is still in use as an appointment in the Philadelphia Conference.

[51] William Jessop, a native of Sussex County, Delaware, was a traveling preacher from 1784 until his death in 1795. (See memoir, *General Minutes* of 1796.)

[52] Michael R. Wilson was born in Maryland in 1770, was admitted on trial as a traveling preacher in 1796. He traveled the Tioga Circuit in 1796, was not appointed in 1797, and died on April 24, 1798, at Strasburg, Pennsylvania. (See memoir, *General Minutes* for 1798.)

[53] Abraham Keagy was a resident of Strasburg. (See *Journal* entry for August 24, 1800.)

[54] Pequea Creek flows through Lancaster County, Pennsylvania. It enters the Susquehanna at the village of Pequea.

[55] Conestoga Creek flows through Lancaster County into the Susquehanna River at Safe Habor, Pennsylvania. There is a town of Conestoga located southwest of Lancaster, which was named for an extinct tribe of American Indians. (Gordon: *T. F. Gazeteer of the State of Pennsylvania*, 116; Roddy: *Physical and Industrial Geography of Lancaster County*.)

[56] Pequea is a post office in Lancaster County on the Susquehanna River, sixty-two miles below Harrisburg. (*Ibid.*, 340.)

[57] See *Journal* entry for July 3, 1792.

[58] Columbia, formerly called Wright's Ferry, is eleven miles southwest of Lancaster and was first settled in 1726 or 1727 by Robert Barlen, Samuel Blunston, and John Wright, Quakers from Chester County. It was incorporated February 25, 1811. (*Ibid.*, 111.)

[59] Seely Bunn was admitted into full connection in 1794. He was assigned to the Carlisle Circuit in 1799.

of our coming on *Sabbath day*. Seely Bunn preached in Little York and Jesse Lee[60] in the evening. I gave a short exhortation. Twenty miles made our *Saturday's* ride.

Monday, 5. We set off for Maryland: I rode thirteen miles and had my horse fed and shod. We continued on and dined at Littlestown, twenty-five miles, well spent with heat, hunger, and thirst.

Maryland

We then rode on ten miles to Taneytown:[61] the inhabitants here, and hereabouts, are chiefly Germans and Romans. We crossed the Maryland line, and lodged at Bentley's. Next morning we rode on to Jeremiah Browning's, seventeen miles, before we breakfasted.

It may suffice to say my mind hath been kept in great peace; but I have been greatly afflicted and dejected with pain and labour. We have visited six districts since the sitting of the Baltimore conference; and in four out of the six there is a happy revival of religion; on the eastern shore—in New Jersey—Albany—and Pennsylvania: and we hear a rumour of a revival in the northern district of Virginia.

We attempted a meeting at Lewis Browning's[62] at his mill near Woodsboro. In the evening we rode to Liberty, and lodged at Daniel Dorsey's. O, heat! heat! We have ridden twelve miles this day.

Thursday, 8. We held a meeting in the woods near Liberty; the houses were not large enough for our congregation. I visited Eli Dorsey and saw the children of my dear nurse, Sarah Dorsey, and the place where her dust is deposited until the resurrection;[63] O, once lovely features of body and mind! but above all her triumphant death!

Friday, 9. I came eight miles to Edward Owings', where I received every mark of affection I could desire.

Saturday, 10. We rode to Stephen Shermardine's:[64] it was well we had a

[60] Jesse Lee was assigned to travel with Asbury in 1799.

[61] Taneytown is nearly eight miles south of the border in Carroll County, Maryland.

[62] Jeremiah Browning was at this time a resident of Frederick County, the present Carroll County. Later he became a traveling preacher (1802–4). Lewis Browning, probably a kinsman, was an official member of the Federal Circuit.

[63] In the burying ground of the Methodist Church, Linganore, Frederick County, is a gravestone bearing this inscription: "Sacred to the memory of Sarah, wife of Eli Dorsey. Died 1798. June 1797 nursed Bishop Asbury through a serious illness at her home. O, once lovely features of body and mind but above all her triumphant death! Asbury. Erected in 1902 by the Trustees of Linganore Station."

[64] Stephen Shermardine was one of the trustees to whom an acre of land near Pikesville was deeded in 1785 for the erection of Stone Chapel after the dwelling of Joshua Owings had become too small to accommodate the growing congregation. (Hartman: *History of Methodism in Maryland*, 1770–1912.)

short ride of four miles, the weather being so excessively warm. Here we were treated kindly.

Sabbath day, 11. We had a meeting at Fredericktown. I exhorted a little at every one of the above places.

We rode over the Catoctin Mountain to Samuel Philips's, to see his dear wife, who was very low. The people came together, and John Potts[65] gave them a sermon. It was but little I could give them.

Monday, 12. We rode to Joseph Howard's, upon Carroll's manor,[66] where we had a comfortable meeting.

Virginia

Tuesday, 13. We crossed the Potomac at Noland's ferry: the river was so low that those on horseback forded it. I came over with the carriage in the flat. I think of nothing less than the resignation of my office of superintendent at the general conference.

Wednesday, 14. We had a full meeting at Leesburg; many of the brethren and sisters from societies in the country attended; it was the time of court. A company of soldiers collecting attended in good order

Thursday, 15. We rode twenty-eight miles to Charlestown. We had a very rocky, uneven road. We stopped at Key's ferry,[67] and were kindly entertained. *Friday*, at eleven o'clock, we held a meeting in Charlestown and then rode on eighteen miles to Millborough.

Saturday, 17. We had a comfortable rain; after which we rode on four miles to Winchester. *Sabbath day* we held meeting and were about five hours in love feast, preaching, sacrament, and exhortation. I rode home with John B. Tilden,[68] seven miles from town.

Monday, 19. We rode to Stephensburg;[69] here we held meeting. *Tuesday* and *Wednesday*, 20, 21, it rained. We could not be more welcome at any place, or more richly accommodated than we were at Elijah Phelps's.

Thursday, 22. We rode fifteen miles to Lewistown, where we dined, and

[65] John Potts, who traveled from 1796 to 1809, was serving the Frederick Circuit.

[66] Carroll's Manor was a tract of fifteen thousand acres in the Monocacy River valley, west and southwest of Frederick, Maryland. Charles Carroll, although never a resident of the manor, gave it enduring significance with the appendage "of Carrollton" when signing the Declaration of Independence. (Scharf: *History of Western Maryland*, I, 567.)

[67] Thomas Key's ferry was over the Shenandoah River in Jefferson County, West Virginia. Charlestown is also in West Virginia.

[68] This was probably John Milburn, where a meetinghouse was built before 1788. (Smith: *Recollections of an Old Itinerant*.)

[69] A map of 1804 shows Stevensburg, old Newtown, now Stephens City, between Winchester and Chester. On a map of 1809 there is a Stevensburg near Culpepper Court House. The one referred to here is near Winchester. Several places had the same names in Virginia, such as Newtown, New Castle, Staunton, and so on.

then rode on to Pinnell's. O, the rocks, ridges, and gutters, we had to cross at Chester's Gap! I would prefer riding two hundred miles upon the lowlands than seventy to Henry Fry's[70] in Madison.

Friday, 23. We rode twenty miles and dined. We passed Culpepper court house, and came within four miles of Henry Fry's and stopped at a tavern, after riding in great heat and haste. I was sick: from hard labour, want of rest, and want of coffee, my stomach and bowels were greatly agitated. I need much faith and good water.

Saturday, 24. We landed at the mansion, upon the banks of Robertson.[71] Henry Fry may console himself with the last words of David, 2 Sam. xxiii, 1–7. I obtained an extract from Whitby on the Episcopacy of the Early Ages of the Christian Church.

Sunday, 25. We preached at the Springs[72] to about one hundred attentive people. I took a bad cold, and was very unwell.

Monday, 26. We rode between thirty and forty miles to John Lastley's.

Tuesday, 27. We had a crowded audience at the chapel: likewise at M'Gee's, on *Wednesday*; on which day I rode twenty miles and lodged at Richard Ferguson's. *Thursday*, at a new house in the woods, I preached on Psalm lxxxiv, 8; and on *Friday*, 30, I rode eighteen miles to Hezekiah Arnold's.

Saturday, 31, and *Sunday*, *September* 1. I attended quarterly meeting at Davenport's meeting house; and we had large congregations each day; there was a shouting among the people. I attempted to preach upon Hosea xiv, 4. After meeting I was invited to spend a night at Colonel Fountain's.

Monday, 2. At Beaver Creek meeting house[73] we had a lively time. I have travelled, since I came into Virginia, through Loudon, Berkley, Frederick, Shenandoah, Culpepper, Madison, Orange, Louisa, and Hanover counties.

Wednesday, 4. We came to Richmond. Since Friday week we have travelled two hundred miles; to which we may add the labour of our meetings—in common three hours long, and sometimes longer.

James O'Kelly hath sent out another pamphlet, and propounded terms of union himself, for the Presbyterians, Baptists, and Methodists. The Presbyterians must give up their confession of faith. The Baptists, if they open a more charitable door, adult dipping. The Methodists must give up the episcopacy, and form of discipline; renounce the articles of their

[70] Fry formerly lived in Culpepper County. Madison was formed from it in 1792.

[71] Robertson Creek is in the northwestern part of Madison County, Virginia. It is one of the upper tributaries of the Rapidan River.

[72] Rivanna Springs was in Fluvanna County. (See *Journal* entry for September 9, 1800.)

[73] Beaver Creek meetinghouse was the outgrowth of the Sunday school started by Asbury in Thomas Crenshaw's house in 1786 or earlier. The land was bought by Crenshaw and eight other trustees from David Richardson, and the deed was recorded in Hanover County courthouse on June 14, 1791.

religion, and the doctrine of the Trinity. I ask in turn, what will James give up? His Unitarian errors? Did he think the Protestant Episcopalians beneath his notice? I am now more fully satisfied than ever that his book is not worthy of an answer.

Sunday, 8. I left my retreat at John Ellis's;—a most agreeable, social, solitary situation, within two miles of Richmond. I would have preached within the walls of our new house at Richmond,[74] but the excessive rain we have had of late prevented; I was closed up in an upper room. My subject at Manchester was 2 Tim. ii, 19.

Monday, 9. We rode twelve miles to Falling Creek church,[75] where I spoke from Rom. v, 12. There is some small stir about religion here.

Tuesday, 10. We rode twelve miles to Godfrey's, an aged man that stood alone when Mr. O'Kelly made a rent in the society. God hath blessed our labours here; several souls, with his own children are now, brought to God. My subject here was 1 John i, 6, 7.

Wednesday, 11. At Maxey's, my foundation was Matt. vi, 6. I observed First, What things we are directed to pray for: Secondly, The rules to be attended to in prayer—the precepts and example of Christ and the saints: Thirdly, The promise: "Your Father that seeth in secret shall reward you openly."

I put a blister upon my breast. Brother Whatcoat preached at Charity chapel, where we administered the sacrament. We went home with John Hobson,[76] and were treated with every mark of kindness we could desire. On *Friday* I preached at Smith's church, dined at Robert Smith's, and then rode on, in a very warm and dry day, twenty-six miles, to Daniel Guerrant's, and came in a little after eight o'clock in the evening. I have stretched along through Chesterfield, Powhatan, Cumberland, Buckingham, into Prince Edward county; and this whilst enduring a raw and running blister upon my breast, excessive heat, and with very little rest by night or by day: I would not live always: weary world! when will it end?

Saturday, 14. At Lackland's meeting house I preached on 2 Peter ii, 17, 18. And on *Sabbath day* on Psalm cii, 11–14. I felt some special assistance. I lodged at mother Lackland's. The weather was very close and warm. On *Monday* we had a curious ride about the hills of Appomatox river, to Robert Martin's, eight miles.

Tuesday, 17. We rode twenty miles to Mount Pleasant. I put a blister in the morning to my breast;—but I must go to meeting and preach.

[74] The first permanent church in Richmond was built in 1799 at the corner of 19th and Franklin Streets. Thomas Lyell, the pastor, later withdrew and became an Episcopal minister in New York. (Mastin: *One Hundred Years of Richmond Methodism*; Bennett, *op. cit.*, 375–76.)

[75] The Falling Creek church was in Chesterfield County, Virginia.

[76] Maxey's and Charity chapels were in Powhatan County, and John Hobson lived in Cumberland County.

Why? because the Presbyterian minister and some of his flock came to hear me: my subject was Zech. xii, 10.

Thursday, 19. We rode twelve miles to William Spencer's,[77] and had a comfortable meeting in his school house; he keeps a Christian school.

Friday, 20. We came fifteen miles to John Spencer's, near Charlotte court house. We have felt great spiritual affection and fellowship in our meetings this week. Richard Whatcoat attended us through the district with a very sore leg; and myself had a sore breast inside and out.

Saturday, 21. I rested at my hospitable home, that hath been so these twenty years, in Colonel Bedford's day, and now in John Spencer's: these people have not turned me out of doors, by separation, defamation, or reproach; they have made no such return for my love and labours, although some have done it. I could not be quite idle: I read over one number of my journal, and wrote a few letters.

Sabbath day, 22. I had thoughts of staying at home, as there were no less than eight preachers at the quarterly meeting at Taply's; however I concluded to go. I gave an exhortation, and returned the same evening: our meeting was held in a dead place; yet we had a lively time.

Monday, 23. I crossed Staunton River, and rode into Halifax county; we made it thirty miles to Hawkins Landrum's. *Tuesday* we had a large congregation and an affecting time upon the banks of Banister River: here I saw only two persons that I was acquainted with twenty years ago —they were brother Baker and his wife. I lodged at Robert Chappell's.

Wednesday, 25. We rode to Armistead Shelton's, in Pittsylvania, twenty miles: we stopped to dine, pray and feed our horses, at Clement M'Daniels; the roads were much broken in some places, and it was as much as we could perform to reach Shelton's by sunset. My mind is calm —my body in better health.

Thursday, 26. A congregation of from three to five hundred attended Divine worship: religion declines in this society; we advised close class meetings, week-day prayer meetings, with fasting or abstinence. On *Friday* we rode twelve miles to Carter's, where a large company attended; my subject was, "What shall the end be of them that obey not the Gospel of God?"

Saturday, 28. We had to travel a most uneven path up Sandy River to George Adams', twenty miles. *Sunday*, 29. I attended at Watson's meeting house, and preached from Zephaniah iii, 12, 13. I was much assisted, and much wearied by the time I had baptized several children. I visited our brethren, Trayham and Church,[78] from Maryland, who have been Methodists for twenty-five years, and still not weary in well-doing.

[77] William Spencer had located and lived in Charlotte County, Virginia. His *Journal* is the property of the Rev. Robert Pierce of Indianapolis.

[78] Nehemiah Trayham and Jeremiah Church lived in Pittsylvania County, Virginia. (*Heads of Families*, 99.) Watson's was at the present Chatham.

North Carolina

We crossed Dan River at Perkin's ferry, entering North Carolina, and came to John Harris's in Rockingham county,—pious souls from Dorset in Maryland.

By resting at times in this solitary, country life, I have my health better; whilst I am, in some degree, free from the knowledge and care of the Church at large. On *Tuesday*, at Smith's meeting house, I gave a short discourse on Heb. iii, 12, 13. We dined at Martin's, and then came on to father Lowe's: we have ridden but eight miles this day.

At Lowe's meeting house a large congregation attended; I spoke upon Isa. xl, 1. The heat was very painful. I suppose we congregate from three to six thousand souls weekly; thus, if no more, I can say that my travelling hath brought thousands to hear the Gospel, who, probably, would not otherwise have heard it.

Thursday, *October* 3. We rode twelve miles to Covey's in Guilford county; I thought it best to decline preaching for a few days.

Friday, 4. We rode twelve miles to Mrs. Campbell's, upon the south fork of Haw River. We had to work our way through the woods. *Saturday* and *Sunday*, I attended quarterly meeting at Bethel, upon Belew's Creek,[79] where I ordained five deacons,[80] and preached from 1 Tim. vi, 11, 12: we had a gracious time. We have ridden only twenty miles in two days. I lodged at M'Daniel's.

Monday, 7. We rode through Stokes county, and attended meeting at Love's church,[81] which has glass windows, and a yard fenced in. After Jesse Lee, I added a few words on Heb. ii, 1. We then came up to William Jean's, near the Moravian Old Town.[82] We have ridden nearly twenty miles this day. Sitting in meeting so many hours among such a multitude of people, and frequently with a blister on my breast, with the difficulties of driving along broken paths, cause me to be variously tried and comforted.

Tuesday, 8. We held meeting, and had a multitude of Germans present. I improved a little upon 2 Cor. v, 13, 14.

[79] Belew's Creek was in Forsyth County, North Carolina. It was variously spelled Belew's, Beloe's, Beloo's, and Bielu's. (Fries: *Forsyth, a County on the March*, 127.)

[80] One of these deacons was John Coe, two of whose descendants were Albert Buckner Coe and his brother Robert Wood Coe, leaders of the Congregational Church in Boston. The ordination certificate is in the possession of the latter.

[81] Love's Church is at Walkertown in Forsyth County, North Carolina. According to local tradition it was organized in 1791. A deed of 1797 records the transfer of one acre from Thomas and Ann Tucker to James Love, Jr., Edmond and William Jean, Edward Cooley, Robert Fulton, and Archibald Campbell as trustees for the Methodist Church. It was burned in 1947 and at once rebuilt. (Fries, *op. cit.*, 133.) The church is a memorial to James Love.

[82] Old Town was a few miles north of Salem.

Wednesday, 9. We rode through Salem; here they have lately built a very grand church.[83] The day was cloudy; the rain began to fall upon us about a mile from Captain Markland's, on Muddy Creek, where we came after riding seventeen miles.

Thursday, 10. Close housed; about twelve souls attended, notwithstanding it rained powerfully, to whom I lectured on Heb. xii, 1–4. I had an interview with Samuel Kenmish, the Moravian minister, and visited him. *Friday*, 11. At M'Knight's,[84] a very uncomfortable day: thence we rode on to Hardy Jones's, fifteen miles.

Saturday, 12. I said but little at the Academical school house,[85] now a house for God. I went to see Charles Clayton and wife, who were sick.

Sabbath day, 13. Rode thirteen miles to Whitaker's church,[86] where I gave a short sermon, on, "Casting all your care upon Him, for he careth for you." I was both sick and tired.

Monday, 14. We came to Shadrach Dial's, from Delaware, near Choptank, who in his younger days attended my ministry to advantage. I feel, in general, great weakness of body, but great confidence in God, and constant and near access by prayer. We are now upon Cedar and Dutchman's Creeks, in Rowan county.

Tuesday, 15. It rained and we rested. On *Wednesday* we came, twelve miles, to Beal's chapel,[87] where, after Jesse Lee had discoursed upon the word of the Lord as *a fire* and *a hammer*, I added a few words on "Take heed how ye hear," whom ye hear, what doctrine ye hear; hear in faith, with prayer, with application, upon all the truths of God. We dined, and then hasted on eight miles to Prather's, in Iredell county. Directly after crossing Hunting Creek, a little circumstance took place, which, if it had happened in the creek, might have been attended with some disagreeable consequences; it was caused by one of the hooks of the swingle-tree giving way.

At Basil Prather's chapel, I gave my thoughts upon "Ever learning, and

[83] The Home Church was built by the Moravians in 1798 and consecrated on November 9, 1800. It was a commodious brick structure. There are fifteen buildings in the Old Salem section of Winston-Salem, North Carolina, which were erected between 1767 and 1800. (Fries, *op. cit.*, 224.)

[84] McKnight's meetinghouse was near the present Clemmonsville, North Carolina, and was a noted early place of Methodist worship and conference center. (See *Journal* entries and notes for April 13, 1787, and May 10, 1789; Historical Papers of Trinity Historical Association, Secs. 9–13, p. 25.)

[85] Cokesbury School on the Yadkin River in present Davie County, North Carolina, near the residence of Hardy Jones, had been converted to a meetinghouse. (See note under April 2, 1794.)

[86] Whitaker's church was on Dutchman Creek near Brown's mill in Davie County. (Grissom, *op. cit.*, 214; see *Journal* entry for March 21, 1786.)

[87] Beal's Chapel was on Hunting Creek five miles west of present Mocksville, North Carolina.

never able to come to the knowledge of the truth:" I fear this will be the case with many souls.

Thursday, 17. We came up the ridges, between Rocky and Hunting Creeks, eight miles to John Templeton's; over a path no sulky ever went before; my testimony was founded upon James iv, 2, 3.

Friday, 18. We had a very uneasy ride of fifteen miles, on the borders of Surry county, over to Doctor Brown's, in Wilkes county. I feel my mind in great peace and resignation, both as it respects the Church of God, and my own soul. The Presbyterians here are much more friendly with the Methodists now than formerly: I dare not say it is policy; it may be piety.

Saturday, 19. We rode through a damp, and, in the end, a rainy day, twenty miles to George Gordon's, near Wilkes court house: we crossed and recrossed the Yadkin River.

Sunday, 20. This is my American birthday; I have now passed twenty-eight years upon this continent. Do I wish to live them over again? By no means: I doubt if I could mend it in my weakness and old age; I could not come up to what I have done; I should be dispirited at what woud be presented before me.

Monday, 21. We came eight miles to William Trible's.[88] We had an open time at a barren place, and I felt Divine aid in a short improvement on Gal. ii, 19, 20.

Tuesday, 22. We had a serious, laborious ride of thirty miles to William White's, Esquire, upon Johns River, Burke county. In this route we had to cross the Yadkin ten times; Elk and Buffalo, each twice. Twenty miles of the path were good; ten miles uneven, with short hills, stumps, sideling banks, and deep ruts. I have renewed my acquaintance with these rivers; they afford valuable levels, with rising hills and high mountains on each side. The prospect is elegantly variegated. Here are grand heights, and there Indian corn adorns the vales. The water flows admirably clear, murmuring through the rocks, and in the rich lands, gently gliding deep and silent between its verdant banks: and to all this may be added pure air.

Wednesday and *Thursday*, 23, 24. Our quarterly meeting was held at William White's, Esquire, and grand patriarch of this settlement, whose family of children, grandchildren, &c., are numerous, and extensively established here. Jesse Lee sermonized each day. My discourse the first day was, 1 Tim. iv, 12–16: *Let no man despise thy youth.* I. That Timothy should be exemplary to believers, in his words, which formed his conversation; at all times, and upon all subjects,—he that offendeth not with his tongue is a perfect man: *in charity*, love, and beneficence: *in spirit*, the spirit of his mind and temper; purity of heart and intention: *in faith*; justifying, persevering faith; confidence in the sure promises and prophesies of God's word: *attendance to reading*; the word of God in the church, in families, in the closet: *exhortation*; as a gift of God, in which some

[88] William Trible lived in Wilkes County.

excel: *doctrine*; the grand doctrines of the gospel—man's original rectitude—his fall—the atonement—repentance—justification—sanctification—the resurrection—the last judgment, and final rewards and punishments. *The gift that is in thee by prophecy*; it is probable, some person, seeing the piety and simplicity of Timothy, had been moved by the Holy Ghost to prophesy that he would be a faithful minister of Christ;—the laying on of the hands of the presbytery. The eldership—here the apostle mentioneth the eldership; and in the first chapter of the second epistle, sixth verse, the laying on or putting on of his own hands upon Timothy. That Timothy and Titus were apostles, and exercised episcopal powers, is plain: they were instructed concerning bishops, elders, and deacons what characters they should be. Titus was left in Crete, and directed to ordain elders in every city. *Meditate upon these things:* ministers should be men of much meditation and prayer; men of contemplative minds, and ready to give up their mental and bodily powers wholly to the work of the Lord. *That thy profiting may appear to all men*—in all things belonging to thy ministerial and Christian calling. The second day of the quarterly meeting I exhorted.

Friday, 25. We had to cross and recross the Johns River, and man it over the hills. I came to Connelly's, twenty-five miles, and dined about five o'clock. I saw a natural curiosity in the mountains:—an old trunk of a poplar had fallen, and four limbs of it had taken root at proper distances from each other, and had grown to be large trees—from fifty to sixty feet high and eighteen inches in diameter.

Saturday, 26. I stayed at the house, to read, write, and plan a little. I tremble and faint under my burden:—having to ride about six thousand miles annually; to preach from three to five hundred sermons a year; to write and read so many letters, and read many more:—all this and more, besides the stationing of three hundred preachers; reading many hundred pages; and spending many hours in conversation by day and by night, with preachers and people of various characters, among whom are many distressing cases.

Sunday, 27. The morning was damp and cloudy, yet I must needs go to the quarterly meeting, which was held in a very open house. My improvement was the first epistle of John iii, 18–22. The meeting lasted five hours.

Monday, 28. We rode about forty miles, and fed upon the path. We came to Daniel Asbury's, in Lincoln county. I crossed once more at the *Horse Ford*, where I was formerly in danger of being drowned. At that time the river was high, myself weak, the horse I rode low and young, and we went in at an improper place upon the rocks and amongst the falls of the river.

Daniel Asbury, an experienced guide, conducted me across this time; but not without some difficulty. His horse stumbled and wet his feet; and my head began to swim before we got through; and my carriage to pitch over the large stones, and small rocks. I think I bid a final adieu to this ford. If I must try this route again, I am inclined to go by Morgantown, the capital of Burke county.

The winter approacheth—we must hasten South.

Tuesday, 29. In the morning I rested: in the evening I walked out and preached, that the people might both see and hear me; my subject was 1 Thess. ii, 11, 12.

Wednesday, 30. We rode to Williams's chapel; where Jesse Lee preached. I added a few words. We then hastened to the widow Featherston's, on Dutchman's Creek. We have ridden thirty miles this day over very uneven roads. We soon called a meeting after our arrival.

South Carolina

Thursday, 31. We crossed the south branch of Catawba, and soon after passed the line between North and South Carolinas, into York county. In consequence of our wandering out of our way in the Hickory barrens, we made it thirty miles to Alexander Hill's;[89] where we held a meeting. God hath blessed the son and daughter of our host, which is better to him than thousands of gold.

Friday, November 1. We had a strange route of twenty miles to Josiah Smith's, on Broad River, Union county. Here we held a meeting.

Saturday, 2. We came to Woad's Ferry upon Broad, at the mouth of Pacolet River, near a small town called Pinkneyville: thence to Spray's, over Tyger and Hendricks bridge, on the Enoree: we were benighted among the woods. The wagons and waters had made such deep ruts and gullies, that I almost despaired of getting onward, until I thought of the expedient of leaving the carriage, and mounting the horse's back, by which means I was better able to guide him: we came into Colonel Benjamin Herndon's about seven o'clock, where we met brothers Blanton, Black, Norman, and Smith.[90]

On *Sabbath day* I commented upon Romans ii, 16. According to my enumeration I have travelled one hundred and sixty miles in four days.

Monday, 4. I rested.

Tuesday, 5. I rode eight miles to Odell's chapel, Laurens county: it was a damp day, and we had an open house. I lodged at Henry Davies's, a native of Ann Arundel county, Maryland.

[89] Alexander Hill is unidentified. Asbury entered South Carolina near King's Mountain on this his fifteenth tour of the state. Jesse Lee was traveling with him by conference appointment.

[90] Colonel Herndon lived near Whitmire in Newberry County. Benjamin Blanton was the presiding elder of the South Carolina district, Moses Black and Jeremiah Norman were on Broad River Circuit, and Isaac Smith, one of the fathers of South Carolina Methodism, had located in 1796 and was living at Camden.

Wednesday, 6. We came to Zoar chapel; a new, unfinished building,[91] the morning was rainy, yet two or three dozen people attended: we lodged at William Holland's.

Thursday, 7. We rode sixteen miles in haste to attend the funeral of Nehemiah Franks, an aged man, who, we hope, died in the Lord: Jesse Lee preached the funeral sermon; after which I made an improvement upon Joseph's prophecy, Gen. l, 24: "And Joseph said unto his brethren, I die; and God will surely visit you." I made some observations on his typical and gracious character; his early piety, his persecution from his brethren, his scenes of adversity, imprisonment, exposure to death, and slavery; his piety in prosperity and worldly honour; an example for us; how God visited the Israelites, and how he hath visited the people of America.

Saturday and *Sunday*. Quarterly meeting at Bramblet's;[92] I made a discourse upon Titus ii, 3; we had a good season. I only gave an exhortation on the *Sabbath*. We are now at the widow Bramblet's, ten miles from the widow Frank's.

Benjamin Blanton came up with us sick; his famous horse died of the staggers; he reported two hundred and sixty dollars; and he had received from the connexion in four years two hundred and fifty dollars. If we do not benefit the people we have but little of their money: such is the ecclesiastical revenue of all our order.

Monday, 11. We rode, sick, weary, and hungry, through a most barren country. Jesse Lee stopped to preach at Colonel Wolfe's; I rode on to the Tumbling Shoals Ford, upon Reedy River; thence on to William Powell's,[93] upon the banks of Fair Seluda; I came in as usual, sick indeed, after riding thirty miles—jolting over the roots, stumps, holes, and gullies.

Tuesday, 12. Rode five miles to King's chapel;[94] there were six travelling preachers present: the house was very open, and the two sermons and love feast held three hours: I was chilled exceedingly; my subject was Ephesians v, 1–3.

Wednesday, 13. We rode westward sixteen miles, to Warwick Bristoe's, where we held meeting, and then rode to Berry's ford; thence to Thomas Terry's,[95] a Yorkshire Methodist, whom I married seven years ago to Ann W. Dowell, his present good wife, from a Methodist stock on the mother's side in Ireland.

[91] The new Zoar Chapel was on North Tyger in Spartanburg County.

[92] Mrs. Bramlett lived near Woodruff, but in Laurens County. The church is still in existence.

[93] Powell lived near Ware Shoals.

[94] King's Chapel in Laurence County was founded in 1796 by the Rev. James King, who died of yellow fever at Charleston the following year. The church is still in existence near Ware Shoals in Greenwood County.

[95] Bristoe is unidentified. Berry's Ford was in Greenville County. Asbury did not cross the river there but went northward to Terry's at Fork Shoals on Reedy River. Near there, sixteen miles southeast of Greenville, Hopewell Church was formed at an early date.

Thursday, 14. We rode ten miles to the Golden Grove, at Cox's meeting house;[96] my subject was 1 John ii, 20. It is agreed that this is the best society we have in South Carolina: the land here is rich. We lodged at deacon Tarrant's. On *Friday* we crossed Saluda at Wilson's ferry, and rode fifteen miles to Thomas Willingham's, upon the Indian lands.[97]

Saturday, 16. We rode ten miles to Nash's meeting house, in Pendleton county; where I glossed upon Colossians i, 27, 28. I was much affected with the faces and manners of this people. Mr. James Nash is not, nor any of his family, in fellowship with us, but are our most kind friends: we were used in the very best manner, and this was more abundantly acceptable; *friends in need are friends indeed.* We had to preach in an open house; it was a summer's day; we had a love feast and sacrament: my subject was 2 Peter ii, 9; the congregation was very large.

Georgia

Monday, 18. We rode twenty-six miles into the state of Georgia, crossed Rocky River, properly so called, likewise the Savannah at the Cherokee Ford: it was wide, deep, and there were large rocks in it, and I had no guide; however, we came safe to William Tait's[98] in Elbert county. Little did I think I should ever visit Georgia again, much less the frontiers of it. It was a rainy day; but I was kept dry in the *felicity*;[99] not so with brothers Lee and Blanton.

Tuesday, 19. We attended at Tait's chapel,[100] in the Forks: it was a cold day. I gave a short exhortation on Rev. xxi, 7. I passed a night with Charles Tait,[101] formerly of Cokesbury, and was made exceedingly welcome and comfortable.

Wednesday, 20. Rode twenty miles to Coldwater;[102] in a cold day, and held meeting in a cold meeting house, but we had a warm-hearted people. I gave a brief sermon upon Eph. v, 8: "Walk as children of

[96] Cox's meeting house was on Grove Creek twelve miles south of Greenville.

[97] Willingham lived on Indian lands near Pendleton, in the upper part of the present Anderson County. The Cherokee Indian reservation, established in 1766, included what was then Pendleton County and parts of Abbeville and Greenville counties. The Indians later migrated westward.

[98] William Tait was a brother of Charles Tait.

[99] The *felicity* was a kind of buggy or carriage which Asbury was then using.

[100] Tait's Chapel was near the home of Charles Tait, a few miles west of the forks of the Broad and Savannah. The town of Petersburg was in the actual forks.

[101] Colonel Charles Tait lived five miles south of the present Elberton. He became United States Senator in 1809. Georgia tradition says Asbury held the first Georgia conference in his house in 1788. (See note under April 9, 1788.)

[102] Coldwater Meeting House was fifteen miles north of Alberton near Newberg. (See note under April 9, 1788.)

light." We lodged at, and were comfortably entertained by, Ralph Banks.[103]

Thursday, 21. We rode sixteen miles, sometimes through the naked woods, to Redwine's; where we had an unexpected congregation in the solitary woods. I held forth on "The Son of Man is come to seek and to save that which was lost." The house was open, but the people were simple-hearted and very kind.

Friday, 22. We came sixteen miles, to Carroll's meeting house; a new log cabin in the woods. Some of the people of the congregation are from the east and west parts of Maryland. I felt that the Lord was with them. We have the kitchen, house, and chamber all in one, and no closet but the woods.

Saturday, 23. At Park's new cabin chapel, after riding eighteen miles, I exhorted. We lodged at Stephen West Brook's.

Sabbath day. Still at Park's chapel: I preached upon 2 Cor. vi, 1. I doubt if there were ever twice as many crowded in so small a house—some stood upon the benches, and others upon the floor: public and private meeting held five hours. We afterward had to ride ten or twelve miles to lodge at George Christian's. We travelled through Elbert, but mostly in Franklin county. We have crossed about thirteen branches of Broad River. Three of them, which rise near the head branches of Oconee, are large. The land is not very fertile, except what lieth upon the water-courses.

Monday, 25. We were detained by rain in the morning, but set off at nine o'clock, and came in at half-past one, after riding twelve miles to Charles Wakefield's, in Oglethorpe county—so called after the first governor of the state or province. Benjamin Blanton could go no farther, but went to bed with a high fever. I desired Jesse Lee to attend the appointments over the Oconee. We had the appearance of the beginning of winter, and were in a cold cabin, but with kind people.

Tuesday, 26. We came six miles to Cornelius M'Carty's. Here we had to drop anchor again: brother Blanton could go no farther this day; and as there were three of us in company, and one who was well able to do the work, I felt it my duty to do as I would be done by, and have been done by, that is, *to stay and take care of the sick man*.

Wednesday, 27. After brother Blanton had been very ill, and in bed most of his time, I housed him in my carriage, and we proceeded down the Oconee, twelve miles, to Burrel Pope's, after a heavy siege through the woods, from one plantation to another, on brother Blanton's stiff-jointed horse, that I would only ride to save souls, or the health of a brother. Our accommodations compensated for all. I admire the soft soil of

[103] Ralph Banks lived fifteen miles north of Elberton. He was an early Methodist and one authority says the first Georgia Conference met in his house in 1788. The old Coldwater Church is the successor of the class that met in his home. (See note under April 9, 1788.)

Georgia, and it is pleasant to see the people ploughing on the last of November, as if it were the month of April. The weather was very cold on *Thursday* and *Friday*. *Saturday* I rode seven miles up to Hudson's ford, at the mouth of Trail Creek, to have a sight of Oconee River. Jesse Lee visited the forks of the river, and formed a circuit for one preacher. The land upon the river is good. I returned to Henry Pope's.

Sabbath day, December 1. The weather still continues cold. At the new meeting house my subject was Heb. iii, 12–14. There appears to be more wealth than religion here.

Monday, 2. We rode twelve miles, in a very damp day, to the widow Steward's: we had a large congregation for the day and place. The widow's house stands upon a line between Green and Oglethorpe counties.

Tuesday, 3. At Greensborough, in a large meeting house built by and for the Presbyterians, we held meeting. We lodged at William Ufton's. We have travelled in two days about thirty-two miles. The badness of the weather and my constant uneasiness have injured me much: I have spoken very little in public: I drag along exceedingly heavy. It is serious work to be driving through the back settlements, and having open meeting and dwelling houses, in the winter season.

Wednesday, 4. At Burke's meeting house Jesse Lee preached, and I exhorted upon the importance of the ministry, and ordained brother Watts a local deacon. We lodged at John Crutchfield's; where we had a gracious family meeting.

Thursday, 5. We moved along in a cloudy, damp, cold day, fourteen miles to Little Britain, a log pen, open at the top, bottom, and sides: a few people attended: my subject was Matt. vii, 8.

Friday, 6. We rode fifteen miles, through a heavy rain, to Hill's meeting house, upon Long Creek, where six or seven preachers, with a few people attended: my subject was Heb. x, 32. Hope Hull, Josias Randall, S. Cowles, and William Partridge came a long way to see me; we had a family meeting at mother Hill's. It is about twenty years since I first visited this house.

Saturday and *Sabbath day*, 7, 8. We held our quarterly meeting at Mark's meeting house: I had dreaded this appointment. I had some pain and some pleasure. The state of religion is low here. Hope Hull preached on *Saturday* upon Jer. x, 8: we had some signs to show that life had not entirely departed, in the love feast and sacrament. Benjamin Blanton preached *Sabbath day*, from Isa. xxviii, 8, and I gave a gloss upon Joshua xiv, 8: "Nevertheless, my brethren that went up with me made the heart of the people melt; but I wholly followed the Lord my God." In the introduction peculiar atttention was paid to the dealings of God with Israel from the beginning to the end; the influence pious characters had in the case before us, two prevailing against ten; that the well-being of future generations required that a decided tone to the morals, manners, and religious opinions should be given by the first settlers of the country. The weight of the discourse was opened in two divisions: First, what God had done for many Christians; Secondly, Their unfaithfulness and complaints (like the Israelites), and their bad influence upon the camp of Israel, as at the present day.

Monday, 9. We rode twenty miles to Hope Hull's, near Washington, in Wilkes county.

Tuesday, 10, we rested; and on *Wednesday*, 11, I gave a discourse at Coke's chapel upon Gal. vi, 9. The rain began as we closed the meeting. I dined at David Merriweather's, and rode home with Thomas Grant that evening, and was detained on *Thursday* and *Friday* in consequence of a rain.

We have had an exceedingly heavy rain—the Little River was impassable; but I was kindly and comfortably provided for. I lament the state of religion in these new settlements. New lands, new officers and new objects occupy the minds of the peoplc. I invented a continental general plan of movement through the Eastern and Western States, not much short of seven thousand miles.

Saturday, 14. I made an attempt to reach Philips's bridge, but was soon stopped by a creek. Thence we went to a mill-dam, full of holes and rolling stones. I did not choose to risk the overturning of the carriage into the millpond or the creek; so I returned to David Merriweather's, and appointed a meeting at Coke's chapel, and upon the *Sabbath day* gave them a long, weighty talk, upon 1 Cor. vii, 29.

Monday, 16. We had to take the rain and mud upon the Augusta road; the wagons had been detained by high water; men and wagons were very heavily loaded with rum. We rode twenty-four miles, and were kindly entertained at William Shield's.

Tuesday, 17. Rode ten miles to James Allen's, and behold, neither the man nor his wife was at home; the day was far spent, and it was raining, so we stopped.

Wednesday, 18. Before we could get ready to move, it began to rain powerfully. We came down the Augusta road, gouged up by wagons in a most dreadful manner, in consequence of which we were five hours in going twelve miles to Thomas Haine's, upon Uchee. I had great *intestine* war, having eat but little; but here we have all things comfortable. I doubt whether we shall be able to cross Savannah River in five days from this time; the former freshet being increased by latter rains.

Thursday and *Friday* we rested. *Saturday*, 21. We rode to M'Gee's to attend an appointment; but the rain prevented the people from coming.

Sabbath day, 22. We came into Augusta town. I went in the morning to *hear* a sermon, and in the afternoon I *gave* one upon Heb. ii, 1. We have preached several years in this town, but with little success: we want a house of our own here. On *Monday*, 23, the waters were much assuaged.

Augusta town is greatly improved in houses since I was here last. The boat trade from Savannah is very considerable. After waiting an hour on the banks of the river, we crossed, and came in about sunset, after riding twenty-two miles to Cooper's, in the pines.

South Carolina

Tuesday, 24. We came twenty-three miles to Chester's,[104] the best entertainment we could find: it was but for a night.

Christmas-day, 25. We rode twenty-three miles to a *pole* meeting house, near Trotty's; thence ten miles to Jacob Barr's:[105] here I was once more at home.

Thursday, 26. We rode down Edisto River, which was much swelled by the late rains; I dined at Murray's;[106] we then proceeded up the stream to Mr. Hall's: we have ridden twenty-five miles this day.

Friday, 27. We crossed at Fourhold's bridge, which was scarcely passable, the water being deep, and spread out upon the low land nearly three-quarters of a mile.

I came accidentally to my appointment at the Cypress chapel.[107] My text was 1 Tim. ii, 5: "For there is one God, and one Mediator between God and men, the man Christ Jesus." I. The great disproportion there is between a holy God and a fallen mankind. II. The absolute, indispensable necessity of a Mediator in nature and office.

Saturday, 28. I never knew worse roads. I needed one to hold on one side of my carriage to prevent my being overset in the mud. *Sabbath day* I preached in the old church,[108] upon Psalm cxviii, 24, 25. On *Monday* and *Tuesday* we had a little rest.

[104] This Chester family lived in Barnwell County.

[105] "Trotty" (or Trotter) probably lived near Denmark or in that general vicinity. Jacob Barr lived in Orangeburg County.

[106] Murray lived at the present Grover in Dorchester County.

[107] Cypress Chapel was near Ridgeville.

[108] The old church was the Cumberland Street Church, Charleston.

1800

1800

The consecration of Bishop Richard Whatcoat at Baltimore

CHAPTER TWENTY-NINE

South Carolina

Wednesday, *January* 1. We began our conference in Charleston, twenty-three members present. I had select meetings with the preachers each evening, who gave an account of the dealings of God with their own souls, and of the circuits they supplied the past year.

Saturday, 4. After determining by a large majority that our next meeting together (by divine permission) should be in Camden, the conference rose.

Slow moved the Northern post on the eve of New Year's day, and brought the heart-distressing information of the death of Washington, who departed this life December 14, 1799.

Washington, the calm, intrepid chief, the disinterested friend, first father, and temporal saviour of his country under Divine protection and direction. A universal cloud sat upon the faces of the citizens of Charleston; the pulpits clothed in black—the bells muffled—the paraded soldiery—a public oration decreed to be delivered on *Friday*, 14th of this month—a marble statue to be placed in some proper situation. These were the expressions of sorrow, and these the marks of respect paid by his feeling fellow-citizens to the memory of this great man. I am disposed to lose sight of all but Washington: matchless man! At all times he acknowledged the providence of God, and never was he ashamed of his Redeemer: we believe he died, not fearing death. In his will he ordered the manumission of his slaves—a true son of liberty in all points.

Sunday, 5. After the burden of care was thrown off, I again resumed the pulpit; and in order the better to suit my subject to meet the conference, the new year, ordination of elders and deacons, and the General's death, I made choice of Isaiah lxi, 2: "To proclaim the acceptable year of the Lord, and the day of vengeance of our God; to comfort all that mourn."

I. The acceptable year of the Lord.

II. The day of vengeance of our God.

III. To comfort all that mourn.

The congregation was large, decent, and solemn; the ordination was attended with unction from above, and the sacrament with tenderness of heart. At the new church, before the ordination of deacons, Jesse Lee discoursed upon, "The harvest truly is great," &c. After encountering many difficulties, I was able to settle the plan of stations and to take in two new circuits.

Monday, 6. The main body of the preachers left the city. I desired Jesse Lee, as my assistant, to take my horse and his own and visit between this and the 7th of February, Croosawatchie, Savannah, and Saint Mary's (a ride of about four hundred miles), and to take John Garvin to his station:[1] the time has been when this journey would have been my delight; but now I must lounge in Charleston.

Sunday, 12. We have had a week of snow, which made the ways extremely miry. I attended the church in Cumberland street; my subject was 1 Peter i, 17–19. I did not enter, as I wished, into the marrow of the subject.

Monday, 13. Benjamin Blanton left me to attend his charge of preachers' circuits, and to promote the sale of our books, within the limits of the Charleston conference. I have kept no journal from Sabbath to Sabbath. I have been employed in reading and answering letters to different and distant parts of the continent.

Sunday, 19. My subject was 1 Peter i, 6, 7. I have been very unwell since Friday, but as I only attempted to labour upon Sabbath days, I could not stand back from duty; I was greatly assisted in the morning, but much outdone in the afternoon in body and mind.

At intervals Nicholas Snethen[2] read to me those excellent sermons of

[1] John Garvin had been appointed to Savannah and St. Mary's. At this conference Tobias Gibson was appointed to Natchez in Mississippi.

[2] Nicholas Snethen (1769–1845) was stationed at Charleston the previous year and at the 1800 conference was appointed to travel with Asbury. One of the leading preachers of his day, he was called Asbury's "silver trumpet." He was born on Long Island and admitted into the conference in 1794, traveling in Connecticut, Vermont, and Maine before going to South Carolina. He was secretary of the General Conference in 1800 and a member in 1804 and 1812; in the last year he favored the election of presiding elders and declared that he would never attend another General Conference unless by vote of the laity as well as the ministry. He located in 1806 but was readmitted in 1809 and served in Baltimore, Georgetown, and Alexandria. During this period he became

Mr. James Saurin, a French Protestant minister at the Hague; they are long, elaborate, learned, doctrinal, practical, historical, and explanatory.

No journal until *Friday*, 24. I have been unwell in my bowels; C. Patten sent me a decoction of bark, rhubarb, and nutmeg, which helps me much. This week I employed in answering my correspondents in the District of Maine, States of Massachusetts, New York, Jersey, Pennsylvania, and Virginia. On *Thursday* night departed this life Edward Rutledge, governor of South Carolina. He was one of the tried patriots of 1775 and 1776. The Africans gave him a good character for his humanity. On *Saturday*, 25, his dust is to be committed to dust. "I have said ye are gods; but ye shall die like men, and fall like one of the princes."

Sunday, 26. I was under some weakness of body and mind. I attended at the old church, and preached on Romans xii, 9–11. *January* 30th we had another snow. *February* 3d: I have kept no journal for some days. *Sabbath* was a cloudy day, with rain. My sacramental subject was Rev. i, 5, 6. I have had a distressing cold in my head; notwithstanding which I have read much in books, letters, and lives.

Wednesday, 5. I began to relax my mind from writing long letters. I dined with Jesse Vaughan, and afterward visited Mr. Warnack's family, at the Orphan House. There is no institution in America equal to this. Two or three hundred orphans are taught, fed, and clothed, and then put apprentices to good trades.

Friday, 7. Jesse Lee and George Dougherty[3] came to town. The former hath been a route of about six hundred miles; and my poor gray hath suffered for it.

Sunday, 9. I gave my last charge at Cumberland street church, from Rom. xii, 14–18.

Monday, 10. I left the city of Charleston; the day was cold and the roads bad. We came through Broughton swamp. In the evening my carriage got set fast; the second draught, the hook upon the swingle-tree gave way, and I had to take to the mud to fix the traces. At half-past eight o'clock we came to Monk's Corner.

chaplain of the House of Representatives and was later defeated as a candidate for Representative and for the Maryland House of Delegates. He was one of the active opponents of the schismatic movement of James O'Kelly. His strongly democratic principles, however, led him to support the reform movement which resulted in the formation of the Methodist Protestant Church, which he joined. He lived on his farm from 1824 to 1829, then he freed his slaves and settled on the Wabash in Indiana. He again became an itinerant there and continued to preach but was in the supernumerary relation during his last years. (See Freeman: *Francis Asbury's Silver Trumpet*; Simpson: *Cyclopedia of Methodism.*)

[3] George Dougherty was on the Oconee Circuit the previous year and had been appointed to Charleston. A native South Carolinian, he was a notable preacher in the state, and it has been said that his influence on Benjamin Wofford was responsible for the benefaction which founded Wofford College at Spartanburg. Dougherty died in 1807 at the age of thirty-five. (See letter to Dougharty, January 8, 1800.)

Tuesday, 11. It snowed. I was distressed for a wagoner whose horses ran away at the sight of my carriage, and whirled the wagon among the stumps and trees: happily no considerable injury was suffered. We lodged at the widow Turk's, near Nelson's Ferry—an extremely cold night.

Wednesday, 12. We wrought our passage over and through the river and swamp, and as long as we kept the public road it was all swamp. We at length came to Gibson's chapel, where I preached upon James i, 25. We dined at Bowman's,[4] and in the evening held meeting at Mr. Gale's.

Thursday, 13, was a very cold day; it terminated in rain. No meeting at Bradford's.

Friday, 14. We came to Rembert's, where at three o'clock I spoke upon Heb. iii, 3, to a few people. Brother Snethen also gave them a discourse.

Saturday, 15. We came to Camden. The weather is still cold. We stopped to feed at Navy's. We have ridden, since Monday last, one hundred and thirty miles, and my horse would not have been so outdone in two hundred or three hundred miles upon good roads. My soul hath been kept in patience, and much prayer, my body is in great weakness, undergoing disagreeable changes with the weather and my constitutional maladies.

Sunday, 16. At Camden I preached upon 1 Cor. vi, 19, 20. We administered the Lord's Supper. The day was cold for this climate, and but few people attended.

Monday, 17. We rode twenty miles to Horton's; and on *Tuesday*, 18, held meeting there.

Wednesday, 19. We rode forty miles through the sands, and roads made bad by snow and frost. We were travelling as late as eight o'clock in the evening, groping in the dark until a boy guided us along by the blaze of pine wood, to brother Shaw's peaceable dwelling.[5] He was gone to his circuit, but his gracious wife and children were at home.

North Carolina

Thursday, 20. At Jackson's meeting house[6] we had some gracious feelings. After an absence of ten years, I called once more at friend Stephen Pace's.

Friday, 21. We attended a meeting at Anson court house. We had no small congregation at Mr. Cashe's new house. I was kindly entertained at his father's when in Virginia and Tennessee, and now by him. They offered us money, food, lodging, or whatever we wanted. At Threadgill's

[4] Asbury was following a familiar route northward. Bowman lived near Summerton and Gibson's Chapel was nearby. Gale is unidentified.

[5] The Rev. Thomas Shaw had served the Santee and Catawba circuits in 1799 and at the recent conference had been assigned to the Great Pee Dee and Georgetown circuits.

[6] Jackson's meetinghouse was in Anson County, North Carolina.

meeting house Nicholas Snethen preached. We then hasted to Mr. Atkin's. We were compelled to wade Rocky River—the water came into my carriage box.

Sunday, 23. At Randell's church, in Montgomery county, I gave a discourse after brother Snethen, upon 1 Sam. xii, 23.

Monday, 24. We came to Ledbetter's.

Tuesday, 25. Crossed Pee Dee at Tindelsville, and landed at Andersonborough, without any difficulties; but when we came to Williams Ford, across the river, it was impassable; we then changed our course, and took the ridge road, which was open to the Montgomery line; thence we had to guess our way, until we came to Edward Harris's, where we fed, dined, and prayed with the women and children, and then came on we knew not where. As the sun began to decline, we thought it time to look out; to our surprise we saw a Friend's meeting house, as we judged by its form. I then concluded we could not reach Deep River, and we stopped at John Henley's. We had all we wanted but prayer.

Wednesday, 26. I had to pass over heavy hills, rocks, and small runs, and through thick clay: we were concluding when in Charleston, and after we set out, by the excessive cold, that there was snow not far distant. When we came into North Carolina, we found that upon Pee Dec, and Yadkin, and Dcep rivers, the snow had fallen fifteen and eighteen inches deep, and continued nearly a month upon the ground, and had swelled the rivers, and spoiled the public roads. We lodged at Mr. Bell's;[7] having ridden only fifteen miles in two days. We left two appointments on the west side of Uwharrie: so much for that siege. My horse had hard work; my carriage was very loose in the joints by constant and long play; and myself much tired; but I revived when I saw the lawyers going to the Western courts. I thought, if they toiled and suffered for justice and silver, how ought I to labour for truth, and gold that perisheth not, and thousands of people, and hundreds of preachers.

Thursday, 27. I gained a day by the overflowing of Uwharrie, and came to Daniel Sherwood's, in Guilford county, within twenty miles of the track I went down last fall.

Friday, 28. It rained and snowed. I gave an exhortation, and ordained two deacons. We got our horses shod, and then rode to aged William Field's.

Sunday, March 2. We set out early and hasted through deep roads to the Hickory Mountain chapel, not less than twenty-eight or thirty miles. N. Snethen went along, and preached to the people, and brought a few to meet me at friend Reeve's, where we dined about six o'clock.

Monday, 3. We had no small race through Chatham county to Snipe's. We were lost three times before we came to Clarke's ferry, on Haw River, and had to send a boy a mile for the ferryman, and wait nearly a half-hour.

[7] See *Journal* entry and note for January 22, 1790.

Tuesday, 4. A clear, but very cold day. We were treated with great respect at the University, by the president, Caldwell, and the students, citizens, and many of the country people. Brother Snethen preached on, "God forbid that I should glory, save in the cross of our Lord Jesus Christ." When the university is finished, I shall take notice of it. I stopped to baptize some children, and then rode on to Massey's.

Wednesday, 5. We rode to Sihon Smith's; and I gave a lecture in the evening.

Thursday, 6. We came to Raleigh, the seat of government. I preached in the State House. Notwithstanding this day was very cold and snowy, we had many people to hear. I baptized a child, and came that evening to Thomas Proctor's.[8]

Friday, 7. We came to the Union church. Many attended, but the excessive cold penetrated my whole system. We lodged at John Whitefield's.

Saturday, 8. I rode twelve miles through snow to Edmund Taylor's, senior. This week, from *Monday* to *Saturday* at noon, I have ridden one hundred and ten miles. My mind is kept in great serenity. I have spoken every day but this.

Sunday, 9. We have a great sleet. The healthy and the young went to Bank's church. At four o'clock we had a sermon at father Taylor's, on Eph. iv, 3: "Endeavouring to keep the unity of the Spirit in the bond of peace."

I. The end; the unity of the Spirit.

II. The means; there might be a union in interest, in opposition, in sentiment, in ordinances, but not in the Spirit; that this union is a union in experiences by the Spirit; and in the spirits or minds of Christians. The means are set forth in the first and second verses of the same chapter; to walk worthy of their Christian character and calling—disorderly walking breaketh union. "With all lowliness," or every mark of humility. Pride is sure to break union: it hath done it in heaven and paradise. "Meekness": unlawful passion will break union. "Long-suffering": if men will not suffer long from saints and sinners, they will break union with the Church of God.

Monday, 10. I rubbed along, somehow, to Smith's church. The distress I suffered in my bowels was great, and had been so for three days. My misery was so exceedingly great that I set off to leave the place; but my way from the dwelling house lay by the church; the people were collected; I felt better, stepped in, and gave an exhortation. I took *Stoughton's bitters*, and got relief; and then rode on to friend Harris's.

Tuesday, 11. I preached a short discourse on Joshua's resolution, and rode twelve miles to Edmund Taylor's, junior. I felt unwell.

Wednesday, 12. I attended the funeral of sister Broadie; she professed religion three years, lived happy, and died in the Lord. Nicholas Snethen

[8] Thomas Proctor lived in Wake County. (*Heads of Families*, 104.)

preached the funeral sermon, from, "A good name is better than precious ointment; and the day of death better than the day of one's birth." I gave some sentiments on, "God forbid that I should glory, save in the cross of our Lord Jesus Christ."

Virginia

Thursday, 13. We crossed Roanoke at Taylor's Ferry;[9] the river was very full. Hail, ancient Virginia, once more! In little more than four weeks we have ridden nearly two hundred miles in South, and three hundred in North Carolina. We came to Howell Taylor's. N. Snethen preached father Young's funeral, on Isaiah lvii, 1; I could only exhort. We rode home with Samuel Holmes, fifteen miles, and it was well we did.

Saturday, 15, was a stormy day. One of my freinds wanted to borrow or beg £50 of me: he might as well have asked me for Peru. I showed him all the money I had in the world—about twelve dollars, and gave him five: strange that neither my friends nor my enemies will believe that I neither have, nor seek bags of money: well, they shall believe by demonstration, what I have ever been striving to prove—that I will live and die a poor man. At Salem we had a good Sabbath; my subject was Rom. xii, 19–21. Our meeting held nearly three hours.

Tuesday, 18. I preached at William Owens's, on Psalm xxxvii, 39, 40: we had an open, living time.

Wednesday, 19, at Myrick chapel. *Thursday*, 20, at Dromgoole's chapel: Jesse Lee and N. Snethen did the preaching, and I rode home with Peter Pelham:[10] this day's work was riding twenty-five miles. We crossed a bridge like a castle at the Westford Ford.

Friday, 21. We escaped another dreadful rainy day: a prodigious quantity of water fell; we were housed: not a single person came to meeting; but we had a sermon at noon, and one in the family at night.

Saturday, 22. We set out for Sussex, but missed our way; we soon came to an impassable stream; I asked a poor, unintelligible Negro, who lived near? he said, Lewis *Gig*; I recollected Grigg, and we went straight to his house and dined. We then pushed on, and finding the Three Run Creek too deep to cross, took up our lodging at J. Fisher's.

Sunday, 23. We rode fifteen miles to Jones's chapel: I was very unwell, but gave a sermon on Heb. xii, 28, 29: we had three sermons, N. Snethen and Jesse Lee having followed me.

Monday, 24, at Pennington's I spoke on Heb. xiii, 20, 21. As we had reason to believe the river Nottoway was impassable at Allen's bridge, we rode back seven miles to Smith's. *Tuesday* morning we had to ride nearly

[9] Taylor's Ferry was in Mecklenburg County, Virginia. (See map of 1809.)

[10] The Dromgooles and Pelhams intermarried, and some of the family moved to Ohio.

one mile through the water, which was sometimes knee deep, and sometimes up to our horses' sides: after riding seventeen miles, we came to Mr. Briggs's about twelve o'clock; the day was extremely cold, and indicative of snow: we gave two sermons; my subject was 1 Cor. vii, 29, 30.

Wednesday, 26. We gave an exhortation at Lane's chapel; lodged at Philip Davies's; and on *Thursday*, 27, we rode to J. Moody's, twenty-four miles: we crossed Blackwater at Broadwater bridge—it was very deep wading. Brother Snethen preached in the evening.

Friday, 28. At Blunt's chapel: here I was unable to add many words. The probability is, we shall hold conference in this neighbourhood, as the smallpox prevails in Norfolk and Portsmouth, and the people in this settlement have made most generous offers to the preachers, provided they choose to sit in conference here.

Saturday, 29, was a day of settled rain, and we were kept in the house, myself being very unwell.

Sunday, 30. We rode sixteen miles through damp, cold, and cloudy weather, to a meeting house near Everett's bridge,[11] not fit for a horse to stay in: I could not refrain from speaking on Psalm xii, 1: "Help, Lord, for the godly man ceaseth, for the faithful fail from among the children of men." See Isaiah lvii, 1; Micah vii, 2. It was observed, First, What the remaining remnant had to do when the truly pious were taken from the earth:—to be godly; truly gracious souls; faithful—faithfulness the test, and continued proof of such souls: the loss the world and the Church sustained: moral men were valuable; temperate men a loss; friends to liberty and religion a loss;—much more men of sterling piety.

Monday, 31. We passed through Suffolk, and called upon Mr. Cowling, whose pious father is gone to rest since I was here last. After twenty years, I called at Mr. Yerbury's and then came on Isaac Lunsford's. I was very unwell: for some days I have had chills, headache, and bilious symptoms; to this succeeded violent vomiting, and a desperate night.

Tuesday, April 1. We came to William Wright's, on Pig Point,[12] where I preached a little on Heb. x, 29.

Wednesday, 2. At Craney Island[13] chapel: here dreadful havoc hath been made by James O'Kelly; a peaceable society of nearly fifty souls are divided, and I fear in the end some may be destroyed: how he hath done this work we may know by reading his Apology. N. Snethen gave a great discourse on 2 Cor. xiii, 5–7. It is astonishing to hear the falsehoods published against me. I lodged at James Craney's.

[11] Everett's Bridge was on the Western Branch in Isle of Wight County. (See map of 1809.)

[12] Pig Point is in Nansemond County, at the northeast point where Nansemond River flows into Hampton Roads.

[13] When President James Madison declared war against Great Britain in 1812, Augusta County raised a troop and marched to Craney Island. (*Twelve Virginia Counties*, 387. See note under June 29, 1775.)

Thursday, 3. At Jolliff's I read a most gracious account of the work of God on the eastern shore—in Cecil county, Duck Creek, and Dover, in the State of Delaware. I published it in the congregation, reading the letter: my subjects on which I preached were Heb. xii, 15, and Luke xvii, 5.

Friday, 4. We rode to James Taylor's: I was deeply afflicted, probably occasioned by my eating of fish: I exhorted a little, administered the Lord's supper, and then rode twenty miles to Portsmouth, and gave a brief exhortation in the neat, new house. *Saturday* I visited the brethren in Norfolk: they presented me with a plan of a new house, fifty by seventy; and, wonder of wonders! it is to be built on the lot adjoining that on which the old Episcopal church stands!

Sunday, 6. My subject was 1 Cor. xi, 1–5. We administered the sacrament. In the afternoon I exhorted in Portsmouth, but it was an offence to some that I did not preach, weak as I was; and we had to administer the sacrament here also.

Monday, 7. We rode forty miles to William Powell's, in Isle of Wight county: it caused tears and some disappointment, because I did not stop at Suffolk.

Tuesday, 8. We went on to William Blunt's. *Wednesday*, *Thursday*, and *Friday*, we passed in close, comfortable conference. We had great accounts of the work of God in the State of Delaware, and also Franklin circuit in Virginia. We had grace, but no gold, and we wanted one hundred and forty-three dollars of silver to pay the just demands of the preachers to their sixty-four dollars per year. *Friday* afternoon we rode fifteen miles to Mooring's.

Saturday, 12. We rode twelve miles to old Jamestown ferry; we crossed, and had a very good passage, notwithstanding it was a very stormy day at times, with heavy showers: we then rode twelve miles to James City, and lodged at Edmund Taylor's: my company felt the effects of being exposed to the rain: I was safe under a cover, but had as much as I could well bear.

Sabbath, 13. I preached at James City chapel, on Col. iii, 1, 2: we concluded our meeting at two o'clock, dined, and rode sixteen miles to the widow Kerby's. A great hail storm came on a few minutes after we got in.

Monday, 14. After the rain was over, we stood our course to Hampton: we came in about two o'clock. Brother M'Kendree preached the funeral sermon of a little child at three o'clock, myself spoke at five, brother Snethen at seven o'clock. My subject was Phil. iii, 8–10.

Tuesday, 15. We rode back to York. I saw the grave where was buried the effigy of General Washington, at the probable place where Lord Cornwallis delivered up his sword to him. We lodged at brother John Stubbs', in Gloucester.

Wednesday, 16. At Mount Zion, Jesse Lee came in before us, and had begun to preach: I had a headache and fever, so said but little; I had the pleasure of beholding with my eyes the excellent plantation of Mr. Tabb, and of receiving every favour the heart of love and the hand of liberality could bestow. I am *a stranger that tarried.*

Thursday, 17. At Cheese Cake I said a little upon James ii, 5: here is a new house and society. Since I was here ten years ago, my old friend Douglass is gone to his long home.

Friday, 18. We came in haste to Urbanna, fifteen miles. There had been some notice given that there would be preaching here: the court house doors were opened, but not one soul appeared; we paraded upon the green awhile, and then went to the ferry—wind and tide both ahead, a leaky boat, weak hands and oars, heavily loaded in the bow with four horses, and one of them ready to leap out: they cried out to me to put back; after some hesitation, I thought we must go back or to the bottom: after cruising two miles, brother M'Kendree and brother Snethen waited; brother Andrews and myself covered our retreat by riding twenty miles into Essex, and about sunset stopped at the widow Huntley's.

Saturday, 19. We rode fourteen miles to S. Coles's. I judge I have travelled little short of five hundred miles this route, over Virginia; having been in nineteen counties.

Monday, 21. We rode twenty-five miles through a storm of rain to the widow Rowzie's.

Tuesday, 22. We crossed at Port Royal, and came to the widow Bombry's: here we joined brothers M'Kendree and Snethen. *Wednesday*, 23, we rode forty miles to Ward's, near Dumfries, and *Thursday*, 24, to Alexandria, and gave a short discourse on James i, 12. I knew not which was best—to attend the quarterly meeting in Fairfax, or to go to Baltimore; I at length concluded upon the latter.

Maryland

We came through the federal city,[14] and were afterward lost an hour in the woods, and were benighted. We called on the widow of senior John Worthington,[15] and saw the old mansion; we were kindly entertained, and had a comfortable night's rest.

[14] Although as early as 1794 the rising Capital was referred to by the commissioners of the District of Columbia as Washington, the name "federal city" long continued in general use. In May, 1800, it consisted of a total of 372 habitable dwellings. While it is highly probable that itinerants on the Frederick and Montgomery circuits preached to the settlers on the original site of Washington, no such evidence has been found. The pioneer society which formed Dumbarton Church was in Georgetown, and Georgetown did not become a part of Washington legally until 1878. (Clark: *Greenleaf and Law in the Federal City*, 124.)

[15] This was Ann Dorsey Worthington, daughter of Nicholas Dorsey.

Saturday, 26. We came to the city of Baltimore, where I found cause of joy and sorrow.

Sabbath day, 27. I attempted a discourse on James v, 8, 9. Bishop Coke is on his way to this city.

Monday, 28. I visited, and prepared for the arrangement of the preachers at the annual conference for another year. The great accounts of the work of God in various parts are as cordials to my soul. I am persuaded that upon an exact measurement, I have travelled eleven hundred miles from the 10th of February, to the 27th of April: my horse is poor, and my carriage is greatly racked.

Thursday, May 1. We opened our conference,[16] and in three days we concluded our work in peace.

Monday, 5. We came to Baltimore, and *Tuesday*, 6, we opened our General Conference,[17] which held until Tuesday, 20. We had much talk, but little work: two days were spent in considering about Doctor Coke's return to Europe, part of two days on Richard Whatcoat for a bishop, and one day in raising the salary of the itinerant preachers from sixty-four to eighty dollars per year.[18] We had one hundred and sixteen members present. It was still desired that I should continue in my station. On the 18th of *May*, 1800, elder Whatcoat was ordained to the office of a bishop, after being elected by a majority of four votes more than Jesse Lee. The unction that attended the word was great—more than one hundred souls, at different times and places, professed conversion during the sitting of conference. I was weary, but sat very close in conference. My health is better than when we began.

Tuesday, 20. I came to Greenwood (Philip Rogers's), and *Wednesday*, 21, I preached at Patapsco Neck chapel, on Psalm lxxx, 17–19. We called

[16] This session of the Baltimore Annual Conference was held in the Stone Chapel, located about ten miles from Baltimore near Pikesville. In 1862 the original chapel which stood on the same site was replaced by the edifice still in use. In it is the desk used by Francis Asbury. Here Henry Smith was ordained elder. (Smith, *op. cit.*, 348, 349.)

[17] For months before this General Conference convened in Light Street Church, Baltimore, Bishop Asbury in his *Journal*, in private correspondence and conversation, had signified his intention to resign. He explained that his impaired health made him unequal to rapidly increasing episcopal demands. The crisis was met by continuing Asbury, electing Richard Whatcoat (1736–1806) a bishop with equal status, and notifying the English Conference that Dr. Thomas Coke, who was only on loan to them, should be available for American service on demand. (Lee, *op. cit.*, 264–71; Boehm, *op. cit.*, 35–43; Smith, *op. cit.*, 349, 350; Tigert, *op. cit.*, 285, 291; see letter to British Conference, May 9, 1800.)

[18] Because of the number and the quality of itinerants who had been obliged to desist from traveling for want of adequate support, Bishop Asbury was eager to remedy what had become an acute problem. For the first time a General Conference directed increased allowances for preachers and their families, recommended that parsonages be provided and that the support of the bishops should be prorated among the seven annual conferences.

at Tobias Stansbury's,[19] and dined, talked, and prayed with his afflicted wife, who felt her confidence in God. We then came on to Perry Hall, and were received with great openness of heart. Mrs. Gough is, I hope, dying to the world, and living to Jesus. Mr. Gough is most affectionately kind.

Thursday, 22. We came to Gunpowder Neck: bishop Whatcoat preached and I exhorted: I trust the Lord will return to this house. I believe some felt the word this day. We went home with Stephen Watters,[20] once more, after an absence of sixteen years.

Friday, 23. We came to Abingdon: the bricks are fallen down;[21] the probability is we shall not rebuild with hewn stones. My text was Isa. xl, 10: "Behold the Lord God will come with strong hand, and his arm shall rule for him; behold his reward is with him, and his work before him." This text was given me by opening my Bible at the sitting of the General Conference, when I trembled a little for the ark. The people have improved the chapel here; it was not burnt with the college, although it was within twenty yards. We lodged at William Smith's; it is above twenty years since I lodged at his father's house.

Saturday, 24. We were at Bush Forest chapel—the most ancient in this circuit: my subject was Isa. xxxv, 3–6.

Sabbath day. We were crowded, as it was quarterly meeting. I went home with J. W. Dallam: I walked to the grave of my once dear Sally, his former wife.

Monday, 26. I crossed Susquehanna, and came to Northeast: we stopped a night at Howell's;[22] brother Whatcoat preached.

Tuesday, 27. We rode up to Back Creek (a Bethel indeed); at four o'clock, I gave a brief discourse on 1 Cor. vii, 29–31. The people sang and leaped for joy of heart; they have beaten down strong drink, and the power of God is come. We lodged at John Canaan's.[23]

[19] Tobias Stansbury, grandson of Nathan Perigau, lived in a house erected in 1777. It was situated on the old Trapp road, three miles from Baltimore, and was a frequent preaching place of Asbury. (Lee, Luccock, Dixon, *op. cit.*, 223.)

[20] Stephen Watters, son of Godfrey, was a brother to the traveling preachers, Nicholas and William Watters. (See *Journal* entry for February 21, 1774.)

[21] Reference is to the ruins of Cokesbury College, which was destroyed by fire on December 4, 1795. Markers now indicate the foundation of the three-story brick building which was forty by a hundred feet in dimension. The chapel to which Asbury referred is succeeded by the present Cokesbury Church, on or near the same site in Abingdon, Harford County, Maryland.

[22] In the home of Captain William Howell, in or near Northeast, Cecil County, Maryland, Asbury was a frequent guest. In the deed dated October 4, 1794, the name of William Howell appears as a trustee of the new church at Northeast. (Johnston, *op. cit.*, 449.)

[23] John Canaan, usually spelled Carnan by Asbury, is associated with Methodism in Cecil County before 1800. His home was on Bohemia Manor, but his church affiliation is attributed to both Bethel and Bethesda churches. In 1805 he was a trustee of Bethel Church and parsonage. (Johnston, *op. cit.*, 451; Bangs: *Life of Freeborn Garrettson*, 246.)

RICHARD WHATCOAT

Wednesday, 28. At the Manor chapel we had a great time; my soul was divinely refreshed. We lodged at Gov. Bassett's.

Thursday, 29. We came down to Bridgetown,[24] at the head of Chester River. In the evening I lectured upon Luke xix, 44: "Because thou knewest not the time of thy visitation." I gave the people one caution:—I observed, First, What always marked a time of visitation to a people collectively and individually. Secondly, What our Lord must mean by knowing or not knowing this time of visitation; that it was the improving the time for all the valuable purposes designed. Thirdly, The dreadful consequences which will undoubtedly follow the not knowing, not improving a time of visitation; that we might fear that every calamity which might come on us in time was judicial,—and eternal torment. I have been led to meditate upon what are the happy consequences of a revival of religion; pure doctrine, strict discipline, great harmony, love, and life.

Delaware

Friday, 30. We were at Blakiston's chapel: brother Whatcoat preached; I gave a short exhortation; and several of the preachers joined in prayer. I rode in the afternoon into Dover forest, and lodged at Cox's, formerly Lockwood's; but he is gone hence: the people could remember that I had not been in this neighbourhood for fifteen years.

Saturday, 31. I preached at the forest chapel, on Habakkuk iii, 2, and rode to Dover that evening.

Sunday, *June* 1. This was a day to be remembered: we began our love feast at half-past eight; meeting was continued (except one hour's intermission) until four o'clock, and some people never left the house until nearly midnight: many souls professed to find the Lord. In the evening I rode up to Duck Creek, to meet the conference.[25]

Monday, 2. We had sixty-six preachers, all connected with the business of conference: we sat closely six hours each day, until *Friday* 6, when about nine o'clock the conference rose. One hour was spent in public each day; but the people would not leave the house day nor night: in short, such a time hath been seldom known: the probability is, that above one hundred

[24] Bridgetown, the present Millington, was formerly Head of Chester, Kent County, Maryland. Early preaching places were established in the homes of the Ferrells and the William Burtons. (Hallman, *op. cit.*, 317.)

[25] When Bishop Asbury arrived, preliminary services of the Philadelphia Conference in the present Smyrna had been in progress for days. He and Bishop Whatcoat, with others, were guests of George Kennard, a "great business man and a thorough Methodist." At this conference Whatcoat presided for the first time. Jesse Lee was chosen secretary. Accounts agree that for sustained spiritual manifestation few annual conferences have approached this session. (Boehm, *op. cit.*, 44–49; Lee: *The Life and Times of Jesse Lee*, 383.)

souls were converted to God. The stationing of the preachers was a subject that took my attention; it was with the greatest difficulty I could unbend my mind from this one hour, yea, many minutes, by day or night, until I read the plan. I felt myself bound in spirit, and perhaps conscience also, to push on to hold the next *Sabbath* in Philadelphia. Bishop Whatcoat and myself hasted to Wilmington on *Friday*.

Pennsylvania

On *Saturday* we dined with Mary Withy;[26] now raised above her doubts, and rejoicing in God; through her instrumentality a small society is raised in Chester,[27] and she hath fed the Lord's prophets twenty-eight of twenty-nine years. We came onto Schuylkill;[28] and thence to Philadelphia.

Sunday, 8. I preached morning and evening, at Fourth street;[29] now making what it ought to be, and seated properly. I preached at the African church,[30] on 2 Peter iii, 17, 18, and at St. George's, on 1 Peter i, 5–7. I spoke only once at the conference; my subject was Psalm xxix, 9: "And in his temple doth every one speak of his glory"; truly fulfilled at that time and place. Surely we may say our Pentecost is fully come this year, when we recollect what God hath wrought in Edisto in South, and Guilford in North Carolina; in Franklin, Amelia, and Gloucester, in Virginia; in Baltimore, and Cecil, in Maryland; in Dover, Duck Creek, and Milford, in Delaware! My health is restored, to the astonishment of myself and friends. *Monday* and *Tuesday* in Philadelphia.

New Jersey

We rode to Burlington, through excessive heat and dust, in company with Richard Whatcoat and Jesse Lee: the latter wished to preach in the evening and go on in the morning. The Baptist minister had appointed a lecture, and invited brother Lee to take his place: he accepted, and preached an appropriate sermon, on Acts x, 25.

Thursday, 12. I gave a lecture in Burlington on 1 Cor. vii, 29–31: this is an awful place.

Friday, 13. We came through heat and dust to New Mills:[31] we were comforted in God; brother Whatcoat preached; I made a short discourse

[26] See *Journal* entry for July 16, 1773. [27] See *Journal* entry for April 8, 1772.

[28] This was the Schuylkill River, and Asbury probably crossed at Gray's Ferry, now the site of the Gray's Ferry Bridge included in the present limits of the city of Philadelphia.

[29] This was St. George's Church. [30] See *Journal* entry for June 29, 1794.

[31] New Mills is the present Pemberton, New Jersey.

on Heb. x, 32. I wished some to look back to former feelings, duties, experiences, and days. We have ridden above one hundred miles since our departure from Duck Creek.

Saturday, 14. We had to stretch along through Julia, Job's, and Reckla's towns, to Cross Creek.[32] We stopped and fed at Mr. Joseph Lovell's; where we refreshed ourselves for an hour: we then came on to M. Moore's,[33] where I preached on Rom. xii, 1, 2. We then took the road through Allentown, to Joseph Hutchinson's; and came in, weak and wearied, about five o'clock.

Sunday, 15. At Milford, I gave a brief discourse, on Rom. xiii, 11: we attended at Mr. Ely's[34] in the evening; a few souls there appeared to be deeply impressed with religious truth.

Monday, 16. My horse drove heavily; and I did not get in to Brunswick until one o'clock. We had a meeting; and under exhortation many felt the word. We then hasted on to Mr. Drake's,[35] near Amboy, where many were waiting: at five o'clock I gave an exhortation, and I believe it was felt.

New York

Tuesday, 17. We were at Staten Island, where there is a neat meeting house,[36] and as genteel, well-dressed a people as in New York. My subject was Hab. iii, 2. Appearances were rather unfavourable: I was very unwell, and came back to Mr. Drake's the same evening.

Wednesday, 18. We rode in haste to New York; and on *Thursday*, 19, we opened our conference; about forty preachers present. We had some knotty subjects to talk over, which we did in great peace, plainness and love. *Friday* and *Saturday* we were closely confined to business. *Sabbath.* My subject at the old church was Romans xii, 19–21. In my introduction I observed that the text was quoted from Lev. xix, 18, and Proverbs xxv, 21, 22, that it might discover to us what veneration the New Testament

[32] Julia must have been Juliustown in the present Springfield Township. Jobstown was in the same township. Recklesstown was on the "Recklesstown pike" on the road to Shrewsbury in Burlington County. (Woodward and Hageman: *History of Burlington County*, 54; Gordon's *Gazetteer of New Jersey*, 164.) Cross Creek was evidently one of the small tributaries of Black Creek in Fairfield Township, Burlington County. (Gordon's *Gazetteer*, 124.)

[33] Moore lived at Lumberton, near Moorestown. The latter place had been laid out by Thomas Moore in 1772.

[34] John, Richard, Joshua, and William Ely all had farms at Windsor in Middlesex County. (New Jersey Archives, Abstracts of Wills, VII, 75; VIII, 125.)

[35] This was doubtless Benjamin Drake who lived at Piscataway. (See *Journal* entry for June 12, 1799.)

[36] This meetinghouse was the Wood Row (present Woodrow) Methodist Church, built in 1787. (See *Journal* entries for November 7, 1771; September 2, 1791.)

writers had for the Old; and what was required in a believer, under that dispensation. Vengeance is not in our province; we cannot, in civil, much less in sacred causes, be our own judges or jurors: if we must feed an enemy, and not only forgive him an injury, but do him a favour, surely then we ought to love a friend, a Christian, and more abundantly a minister of Christ. This day we made a general collection for the support of the travelling ministry.

Monday, 23. Our conference concluded its sitting. The deficiencies amount to six hundred and ninety dollars: the moneys collected and the draft on the chartered fund, amounted to four hundred and five dollars. A motion was made to move the next yearly conference more into the centre of the work, but it was lost.

Tuesday, 24. I have now a little rest. We have had a mighty stir in the Bowery church, for two nights past, until after midnight; perhaps twenty souls have found the Lord. Bishop Whatcoat preached the ordination sermon in the afternoon at the Bowery church. I have now a little time to unbend my mind from the stations; but still my work is not done. *Tuesday*, *Wednesday*, *Thursday*, and *Friday*, I employed myself in reading, writing and visiting.

Saturday, 28. We left the city; and rode twenty-six miles through heat, and plagued by the flies, to my old home at the widow Sherwood's: but my dear Betsy Sherwood my nurse, is gone, I trust, to glory.

Sabbath day, 29. We had a remarkably cool day, after a great storm of rain and hail. I attempted to preach at Sherwood chapel, on 1 Cor. xv, 34: "Awake to righteousness and sin not; for some have not the knowledge of God. I speak this to your shame." I observed that the apostle, in Rom. xiii, 11; Ephes. v, 14; 1 Thess, v, 6, and in the text, had indicated a sleep which professional and real Christians might fall into—an awful insensibility and inactivity to spiritual things, so as to bring an amazing stupor on all the powers of the soul; so that it would be insensible to righteousness, which is religion—the justifying and sanctifying, and practical righteousness of a gracious, wakeful soul: "Some have not the knowledge of God"; living in sin, neglecting duty, and without the knowledge of God; ignorant of the fear, favour, nature and love of God. Brother Whatcoat and John Wilson both spoke; souls were quickened. In the afternoon, at New Rochelle, brother Whatcoat preached, and I gave an exhortation; many attended. I feel as if there would be a revival of religion in this circuit this year.

Monday, 30. We came to Byram Bridge, and at Banks's[37] we had a crowded house, and a feeling time; the aged people were very attentive.

[37] Byram Bridge was just east of Port Chester, New York, on the boundary between that state and Connecticut. Bryan B. Banks lived on the east side of the river where the old Boston Post Road crossed. (See *Journal* entry for May 22, 1809.)

Connecticut

Tuesday, July 1. In consequence of our circumlocutory motions we have ridden about fifty-five miles since we left the city of New York. We came to Stamford, where brother Whatcoat gave a sermon, on, "The faith and choice of Moses." I had only time to speak a few words, on Luke xix, 44.

Wednesday, 2. We rode on to Norwalk; stopped an hour at brother Day's,[38] and thence rode on to Fairfield. It was a cool day. We had an elegant view: the fields in full dress, laden with plenty; a distant view of Long Island and the Sound; the spires of steeples seen from distant hills—this country is one continuity of landscape. My mind is comforted and drawn out in prayer. We had not time to feed nor rest. It was with some exertions we came in time to Joseph Hall's, at Poquonak. After we got a little refreshment and rest, I gave them a short discourse, on Luke x, 2. Strength and time failed me, and I could not finish and apply as I wished.

Thursday, 3. We came to Stratford, and stopped at brother Elnathan Wheeler's.

Friday, 4. The weather is damp and very warm. We came on to New Haven, where they were celebrating the Fourth of July. I fear some of them have broken good order, and become *independent* of strict sobriety. Bishop Whatcoat preached in the Sandemanian meeting house purchased by the Methodists.

Saturday, 5. We rode through excessive heat, over rocks and hills, to North Bristol, twenty miles. I discoursed with some liberty on Acts xxvi, 18.

Sabbath day, 6. We rode six miles to Ponsett's[39] new meeting house. A revival of religion has begun here; a dozen souls have professed to find the Lord, and several young people are under gracious visitations, and the aged are exceedingly cheered at the prospect. Bishop Whatcoat preached in the morning, and in the evening I made some improvement from 1 Peter ii, 11, 12; after which we administered the sacrament. We were engaged five hours in public exercises: the day was very warm. We have travelled since last Saturday week one hundred and forty miles.

Monday, 7. We rode sixteen miles to Hadley. The day was awfully warm until one o'clock, when a gust came up of wind and rain; we ran from house to house, and escaped being *much wet*; we stopped at Mr. Woods's. *Tuesday* we rode on to New London; twenty miles of the way the roads were exceedingly rocky. My soul was kept in peace, but

[38] Absalom Day was a potter who lived at the "Old Well." He was one of the early local preachers and a local deacon. He died in 1843. (Boehm, *op. cit.*, 240; Hill: *History of Methodism in Norwalk, Conn.*)

[39] Ponsett was a part of the present town of Killingsworth, Connecticut. An Episcopal church there still bears the name of Ponsett.

under great temptations of various kinds. We crossed Connecticut River at Chapman's Ferry, near Old Haddam.[40] Where the roads here are improved they are made for ages, and are much superior to those in the South or West.

Tuesday, 8. Bishop Whatcoat held forth in the new house in New London; his subject was, "With him is plenteous redemption." I gave a discourse upon, "Christ, the author of eternal salvation to all them that obey him."

Thursday, 10. We came on to Norwich Landing.[41] I preached in the neat, elegant Episcopal church, on Acts iii, 26. I felt uncommonly set at liberty: we had a very decent, attentive, well-behaved congregation. From here we hasted on to Norwichtown. Bishop Whatcoat preached. We had a most agreeable ride on the turnpike road, upon each side beautifully smiling with variety and plenty; the stage passed us like a whirlwind.

Friday, 11. We came to Preston, and were kindly entertained at Isaac Herrick's. It was the very height of rye harvest, yet many came together. I was greatly led out on the *great salvation.* I was refreshed in soul and body, and rode on in the evening to Nathan Herrick's. The simplicity and frugality of New England is desirable—you see the woman a mother, mistress, maid, and wife, and in all these characters a conversable woman; she seeth to her own house, parlour, kitchen, and dairy; here are no noisy Negroes running and lounging. If you wish breakfast at six or seven o'clock there is no setting the table an hour before the provision can be produced.

Saturday, 12. We took our departure for Rhode Island through Plainfield. The weather is still excessively warm; the roads sandy, stony, and rocky, notwithstanding the turnpike. We passed Sterling, the last town in Connecticut.

Rhode Island

We wandered a mile or two out of our way, and had to pay for it, by going a cross path: we made it twenty-six miles to General Lippit's.[42] The

[40] There is some confusion at this point. The *Journal* indicates that Asbury rode to New London and then crossed the river at the ferry near Old Haddam. But on this route he would have passed Old Haddam long before he reached New London, crossing the river on the way.

[41] Norwich Landing was originally below the falls at the head of the Yantic basin where Elderkin's Mill was located. Later the name was transferred to the junction of the Yantic and Shetucket rivers. Here a community called Rocky Point or The Landing grew up, which in time became New Chelsea or Chelsea Society. (*History of Norwich*, ch. 21.)

[42] General Christopher Lippit, a Revolutionary officer, lived in Cranston, Rhode Island, about three miles from the village which bears his name. His home was a center for the Methodist preachers, and on quarterly occasions it was said that thirty guests were lodged in his fifteen beds. He sometimes conducted services, removing his boots when he entered the pulpit to be unshod in the presence of God. He was a venerable

general hath built a neat chapel for the use of the Methodist Episcopal Church near his house. I was taken with one of my bilious eruptions through the night.

Sunday, 13. Richard Whatcoat preached in the morning. In the afternoon my subject was Exod. xx, 24: "In all places where I record my name I will come unto thee, and I will bless thee." It was a feeling time: although I was very unwell all the day, I could not stand back from duty.

Monday, 14. We came on our way to Boston, through Providence; here we did not stop—the time is not yet come. We stopped to feed at a house that was not very agreeable to me, and I was glad to come off without dining.

Massachusetts

We came to Deacon Stanley's, at Attleborough, where we took some refreshment, and reached Mr. Guild's, and took lodging.

Tuesday, 15. We came through Wrentham, Walpole, Dedham, and Roxbury to Boston: it was a damp day, with an easterly wind, unfriendly to my breast. As they were about finishing our church we could not preach in it. The new State house here is, perhaps, one of the most simply elegant in the United States. We made our home at Edward Haynes's, late from England, where we had most agreeable accommodations after our toil.

Thursday, 17. We have dry weather. We came through much dust to Lynn.

Friday, 18. We sat in conference; there were twenty-one members present; we had great peace and union.

Saturday, 19. The conference rose, after voting the session of the next yearly conference to be held at Lynn. And now the toil of six conferences in seven months, and the riding of thirteen hundred miles, is over. I found some difficulty in stationing the married preachers.

Sabbath day, 20. We had an elaborate ordination sermon from Matt. ix, 36–38: "But when he saw the multitudes, he was moved with compassion on them, because they fainted, and were scattered abroad, as sheep having no shepherd," &c. There had been a long drought here, and nature seemed as if she were about to droop and die. We addressed the throne of grace most fervently and solemnly, and had showers of blessings. Whilst I was preaching the wind came up and appeared to whirl round to every point, and most gracious rain came on: this I considered as a most signal instance of Divine goodness.

figure with long white hair in braids and his beard carefully arranged. The chapel built by him was abandoned about twenty-five years later because a debt of seventy-two dollars could not be paid. (Miller: *History of the New England Southern Conference*, III, ix, x, 136, 137.)

Monday, 21. We came to Boston, and preached in the Tabernacle, now nearly finished, on Heb. iii, 12–14. We were generously entertained at Edward Haynes's.

Tuesday, 22. Bishop Whatcoat preached in Boston, from Psalm cxvi, 7. *Wednesday* we came thirteen miles to Waltham, where we had a meeting; the subject was Rev. xxi, 6, 7.

Friday, 25. We rode through Weston, where is a grand steeple, porches, and even stalls for the horses; and it is well if they do not make the Methodists pay to support their pomp. O! religion in New England! We came through Needham, Sherburne, and Holliston, and made it thirty miles over Crook's Hills, through excessive heat. We had not time to stop to feed, as we had appointed meeting at Milford, where we arrived a little after one o'clock. I was obliged to let brother Whatcoat ride in the carriage, or I fear he would have fainted; this made me low-spirited, and unfit to answer questions.

Connecticut

Saturday, 26. We had to ride through excessive warmth thirty miles to Thompson's, but we took the day for it: we got to Capt. Jonathan Nicholls's[43] about six o'clock, where we have a house built, and some ground to set our feet upon. I have been of late powerfully tempted, and distressed in mind and body. We had a finely-dressed congregation—a good name is a great matter with these people. O Baxter! are these thy apostate children? Will Methodism ever live in such whited walls and painted sepulchres as these people, who delight to dwell insensible to the life of religion, and closed up in their own formality and imaginary security? We have now returned to the first town in Connecticut.

Sunday, 27. I preached at the new house in Thompson: my subject was Mark viii, 34.

I. I observed the harmony of the evangelists, Matthew and Luke with Mark.

II. That our Lord had given the clusters of the grapes of the promised land in blessings and promises.

III. He had given such demonstrations of his power upon the bodies of men; the dead were raised, the hungry fed, the lepers cleansed, the lame and the blind were restored, the wind and the sea were at his command.

IV. He opened the distinguishing conditions of discipleship; the denial of self in every temper and affection that is evil. They that seek to save their lives by denying Christ, shall lose soul and body; if it is through pride and shame, Christ will not dishonour himself by owning such in the day of judgment.

[43] See *Journal* entry for August 6, 1795.

Bishop Whatcoat preached in the afternoon on, "Acquaint now thyself with him, and be at peace," &c.

Monday, 28. We rode sixteen miles to the north end of Eastford. We have travelled nearly one hundred miles since our departure from Lynn. My subject at Joseph Work's was Matt. v, 11: "Blessed are ye when men shall revile you and persecute you, and shall say all manner of evil of you falsely for my sake." We lodged at Nathan Palmer's. I stopped a few minutes at Mr. Woodward's, in Ashford. We came on to Coventry, twenty miles. We stopped at John Searles's, and were exceedingly well accommodated, both man and horse.

Wednesday, 30. We rode to Mr. Spencer's,[44] in Hartford. My mind is in peace; but I have uncomfortable feelings in my body. Here I met brothers Bostwick and Borrough.[45] We have a house built in Spencertown[46] for the Lord, and now they are building one for the Lord's servants—for the married preachers to live in who are sent to the circuit.

Thursday, 31. Was excessively warm; we made it a little less than thirty miles to Bristol; we stopped to feed our horses, but neglected ourselves. When we came to Samuel Smith's we were nearly outdone by excessive heat and hunger. This day we crossed Connecticut River, and passed the cities of Hartford and Farmington.

Friday, August 1. Freeborn Garrettson came up with us: he attended the funeral of the venerable mother Livingston,[47] who was suddenly and safely called home, aged seventy-eight, removed by a paralytic, and probably it was apoplectic also: perhaps it was about thirty-four years ago that this godly woman was awakened under the first sermon the Rev. Dr. Sadly preached in the Reformed Low Dutch church in New York, as she told me; nor she alone, but six or eight other respectable women. Madam Livingston was one that gave invitation to the Methodist preachers to come to Rhinebeck, and received them into her house; and would have given them more countenance had she been under no other influence than that of the Spirit of God and her own feelings. I visited her one year before her death, and spent a night at her mansion; she was sensible, conversable, and hospitable.

Saturday, 2. We attended the quarterly meeting for Litchfield circuit:

[44] Thomas Spencer lived on Spencer Street in Spencertown, now part of Manchester, Connecticut.

[45] Shadrach Bostwick was the presiding elder. Brother Burrough may have been Banks M. Burrough, who was admitted on trial the following year and assigned to Sussex Circuit in Virginia.

[46] See note under August 31, 1794.

[47] Freeborn Garrettson was the presiding elder in New York. His mother-in-law, Margaret Beekman Livingston, wife of Judge Robert T. Livingston of the New York Supreme Court, had died in June at Kingston, New York. Garrettson's wife was Catherine Livingston, of whom it was said she could have married George Washington but preferred a Methodist preacher. Their home was at Rhinebeck, New York.

my subject was 2 Pet. iii, 17, 18. I had liberty in preaching, and felt some tenderness of heart, and evinced it with weeping eyes.

Sunday, 3. We had a living love feast; some from Waterbury were fervent in spirit, serving the Lord. We had a crowded congregation, a close day, and the house was shut up. In consequence of my breast being weak, I declined speaking in public. Bishop Whatcoat preached, and Freeborn Garrettson exhorted. Our meeting began at eight o'clock in the morning, and continued with a few minutes' intermission, until two in the afternoon; after which we came off, over dreadful roads, twelve miles to Torringford. I was pleased to see a house bought and fixed for brothers Augustus Jocelyn, and Elijah Batchelor,[48] the stationed preachers of the circuit, and their wives. These brethren we left behind to improve in the after part of the *Sabbath*, and quarterly meeting.

Monday, 4. We came on and stopped at Goshen, at Captain Wright's. The people flocked together at a short warning and I gave a discourse on Isa. xxxv, 3–6; after which we dined, and came on across the hills and over dreadful rocky roads to Cornwall, where brother Whatcoat preached in the meeting house, on, "We know that we are of God, and the whole world lieth in wickedness."

Tuesday, 5. We had another tolerable siege over the Housatonic River and hills to Sharon. Here brother Whatcoat preached on, "The Lord knoweth how to deliver the godly out of temptation, and to reserve the unjust to the day of judgment to be punished." I gave an exhortation, and then we came rapidly, fifteen miles, to C. Levie's, in the Nine Partners.

New York

Wednesday, 6. We came to Row's: Bishop Whatcoat preached on 1 John iv, 17. I gave an exhortation: we then came on to Robert Sands's,[49] and lodged all night. We came on to Freeborn Garrettson's new design, upon the Rhinebeck Flats. He hath a beautiful land and water prospect, and a good, simply elegant, useful house for God, his people, and the family. We have ridden between eighty and ninety miles since last *Sabbath*; not less than five hundred and fifty since we departed from New York; and one-third of the roads were rocky and very uneven. I read a book of about five hundred pages, the author of which is a curious writer.

Friday and *Saturday*, 8, 9. We regaled ourselves and horses upon the pleasant banks of the Hudson; where the passing and repassing of boats and small craft, perhaps fifty in a day, is a pleasant sight.

Sunday, 10. We had a sermon, and administered the sacrament at

[48] Augustus Jocelyn was stationed at Redding and Elijah Batchelor at Litchfield. (See *Minutes*, 1800.)

[49] Robert Sands was a brother-in-law of Chancellor Robert Livingston.

brother Garrettson's; and notwithstanding public worship was held at the Dutch Church at the same hour, we had a large congregation. Bishop Whatcoat and myself filled up the service of the day.

Monday, 11. I rested and visited Dr. Tillotson,[50] at his very elegant country seat, beautifully situated. The house is finely set round with trees, and there is a charming view of the North River. I was unwell internally. I must always take great heed to what I eat.

Tuesday, 12. We came through Poughkeepsie—no place for Methodism. We stopped at Elijah Morgan's; brother Thacher[51] was preaching when we came in. We have ridden twenty-five miles this day, and dined in the road upon a watermelon that Mrs. Tillotson was kind enough to give us as we came by her house. I was so unwell, that I had but little appetite for anything else.

Wednesday, 13. We came on twenty-five miles to Cortlandt town,[52] where we saw the aged, venerable pair, the lieutenant governor and his lady: he is in his eightieth, and she in her seventy-eighth year. I had a very rocky ride over the mountains of Peekskill. I have great and sore temptations at times, but God is with me; I trust through grace to overcome them all. We stopped at Warren's;[53] fed, talked, prayed, and refreshed ourselves a little.

Thursday, 14. This day is very warm. I preached at Peekskill town, upon the great salvation. Brother Whatcoat preached at Croton. We lodged at General Philip Van Cortlandt's.

Friday, 15. At the Plains, Richard Whatcoat preached: I gave an exhortation. We then rode on in haste to the widow Sherwood's.

Saturday, 16. We pushed on with great courage, towards New York; but when within six miles of the city my horse blundered twice, and then came down with great force and broke the shaft. I got out, and my horse recovered from his fall. A smith's shop being at hand, the shaft was mended in an hour; and we came into New York and found our service was wanting in the city, there being here only two preachers, and one of them disabled.[54]

Sunday, 17. We had much rain; the streets flowing with water like

[50] Mrs. Tillotson was one of the Livingston sisters, and it was at this home that Garrettson made his first contact in the vicinity in 1789.

[51] William Thacher (1769–1856) was born in Connecticut and converted in Baltimore. He became a local preacher in 1795 at New Haven, Connecticut, where his family was among the founders of Methodism. He held numerous appointments in New York, New England, and Philadelphia, superannuating in 1846 and dying ten years later.

[52] This was the community four miles northeast of Peekskill to which Lieutenant Governor Pierre Van Cortlandt had retired from public life.

[53] Warren lived at Crompond, four or five miles east of Peekskill.

[54] The appointments had been John McClaskey, Jesse Lee, and Sylvester Hutchinson. Lee's appointment was only nominal as to New York, actually covering a wide general assignment he was to pursue. (Lee's *Memoirs*, 273; Seaman, *op. cit.*, 151 n.)

streams. I gave them a sermon at the Bowery church, on, "Who gave himself for us that he might redeem us from all iniquity, and purify unto himself a peculiar people, zealous of good works": and at the old church, John street, I spoke on, "But we are not of them who draw back unto perdition, but of them that believe to the saving of the soul." It appeared most advisable to stay awhile on *Monday*, to have a new shaft put to the carriage.

New Jersey

We landed at Paulus Hook about half-past five o'clock, and pushed on to Newark.

Tuesday, 19. We came off at five o'clock, and reached Brunswick by twelve o'clock, where we dined and rested, and then continued on to Joseph Hutchinson's, at Milford, forty-six miles. We had a pleasant and cool ride for the season.

Wednesday, 20, we came on to Hulet Hancock's.

Pennsylvania

On *Thursday*, 21, reached Philadelphia. I preached at St. George's; and Bishop Whatcoat at the African church.

Friday, 22. We rode to the Valley;[55] it was warm enough. Bishop Whatcoat preached at Daniel Meridith's.[56]

Saturday, 23. We had a *proper* siege up to Sawderstown,[57] and got in by four o'clock. I gave a discourse on Heb. x, 38, 39.

Sabbath day, 24. Bishop Whatcoat preached at Martin Boehm's church,[58] on Psalm lxxii, 16–20. We have now ridden, from *Monday*, one hundred and seventy miles. We lodged at Abraham Keaggay's.[59] Our Dutch Methodists[60] are as kind and more lively than many of the American ones.

Monday, 25. We crossed Susquehannah River at M'Call's ferry;[61] it is narrow, but very deep and rocky. After feeding man and horse, we came on to Sittler's mill, on Muddy Creek. As we were ten miles from the place

[55] See *Journal* entry for February 5, 1781. [56] See *Journal* entry for July 6, 1792.

[57] This was Soudersburg, located about seven miles southeast of Lancaster. It was named after Benjamin and Jacob Souders, who were both Methodists. Benjamin was a local preacher, and the conference of 1804 was held in a private room of his home so that the meetinghouse, built in 1801, could be used for preaching.

[58] See *Journal* entry for July 31, 1799. [59] See *Journal* entry for July 31, 1799.

[60] The name Dutch Methodist was applied to people of German extraction located in Lehigh, Berks, Lebanon, and Lancaster counties, Pennsylvania. They formed the United Brethren and Evangelical churches.

[61] McCall's Ferry in Lower Chanceford Township was one of the most important crossing places over the lower Susquehanna for a century and a half.

we intended to reach, well wearied, and having bad roads before us, we brought to an anchor here for a night. What time I have had to read, write, or journalize, those who know the distance and difficulties that must have attended me through the last week may judge; it would be impossible for me to relate all the workings of my heart, but I trust my soul has been kept in patience and devotion.

Maryland

Tuesday, 26. We came into Maryland:[62] sometimes we had no roads, and at other times old ones that the wagons had left. Thus we bolted and blundered along the rocky rivulets until we came within sight of James Fisher's. The meeting had been appointed at the widow Jolley's:[63] the house was large, and we had no small congregation; they came, some to see and some to hear. I had walked where I feared to ride and it was exceedingly warm; but I took courage when I saw the people: the portion which I gave them was 1 John ii, 24, 25. We had hardly time to eat and breathe, before we had to beat a march over the rocks, eight miles to Henry Watter's, upon Deer Creek. Brother Whatcoat went ahead and preached, and I came on time enough to exhort a little.

Wednesday, 27. I preached at the Forks meeting house (fifteen miles on a carriage road), warm as it was. Brother Whatcoat gave us a good sermon, upon Psa. cxvi, 7: "Return unto thy rest, O my soul"; I exhorted very little. The heat continued. That evening we came with equal difficulties to *Perry Hall*; but the greatest trouble of all was that the elders of the house were not at home[64]: the walls, the rooms no longer vocal, all to me appeared hung in sackcloth. I see not the pleasant countenances, nor hear the cheerful voices of Mr. and Mrs. Gough! She is in ill health, and writes: "I have left home, perhaps never to return." This intelligence made me melancholy. Mrs. Gough hath been my faithful daughter; she never offended me at any time.

Thursday, 28. At *Perry Hall* I preached on Matt. xi, 28–30. I was visited by elders Bruce and Snethen. I heard the Reply to Mr. O'Kelly's Apology,[65] soft and defensive, and as little offensive as the nature of the case would

[62] Apparently Asbury had entered Harford County, Maryland, over little used roads through the hills of York County, Pennsylvania, then known as the "York Barrens." (Brumbaugh, *op. cit.*, II, 163; Preston, *op. cit.*, 266.)

[63] Mrs. John Jolley's husband had been captain of one of the militia companies organized north of Deer Creek in Harford County.

[64] The "elders" were Harry Dorsey and Prudence Gough.

[65] Nicholas Snethen wrote "A Reply to an Apology," which was an answer to James O'Kelly's "The Author's Apology for Protesting Against the Methodist Episcopal Government." The latter was supposedly first published in Pittsburgh and reissued in 1799. (MacClenny: *Life of James O'Kelly*, 178, 179.)

admit. I was invited to town, with the assurance that there was no danger of the fever; but it was very bad at the Point.

Friday evening, 29. I held forth in Light street, on Psalm cxv, 1: "Not unto us, O Lord, not unto us, but unto thy name give glory, for thy mercy and for thy truth's sake." My improvement was the application to Christians. First, To contemplate mercy and truth in the dealings of God to them in the Gospel. Secondly, That they should disclaim all glory to themselves. Thirdly, How the Jehovah God giveth glory to himself and how we should glorify him. Brother George Roberts[66] wrote that they were a thousand strong in Baltimore. That there hath been a work in Annapolis is certain: indeed it begins to be more and more general in the towns, and in the country.

Saturday, 30. We had a most severe ride, nearly twenty miles, to Daniel Elliott's.[67] At St. James's chapel[68] God hath begun to pour out his Spirit; and almost generally through Montgomery and Frederick circuits.

Wilson Lee is all upon the wing in the work; glory! glory! glory! I will not speak of numbers or particular cases without more accurate information, which in my haste I cannot now obtain; but without doubt, some hundreds in three months have been under awakenings and conversions, upon the western shore, District of Maryland.

Sunday, 31. At St. James's chapel I preached on Psalm xxxvii, 39, 40; we had an attentive, solemn sitting, and powerful prayer closed the whole. We dined, and rode on five miles to Henry Hobbs's.[69] The people heard of us, and ran together in the evening. Brother Whatcoat gave a lively discourse upon these words: "Thy children shall be all taught of God." We had a very quickening season. Perhaps six hundred souls, in this district and in Baltimore, have been converted since the General Conference. Harford, Baltimore, Calvert, Federal, Montgomery, and Frederick feel

[66] George Roberts, M.D. (1766–1827), was then stationed at Baltimore and Fell's Point with Thomas Morrell, Philip Bruce, and Nicholas Snethen. (Roberts, *op. cit.*, 89–106.)

[67] Daniel Elliott, whose name appears in the journals of early Maryland circuit riders, was an official member of the Montgomery Circuit. He lived at a place called Delaware Bottom about one mile east of the present St. James Church. In his home were held the services of the society which erected the first St. James Chapel. (Colbert's *Journal*, December 24, 1793; Armstrong: *Old Baltimore Conference*, 509.)

[68] The first St. James Chapel was completed about 1792. It stood about a hundred yards from the present St. James Methodist Church, which is about twenty miles west of Baltimore in West Friendship, Howard County. In the spring of 1957 a new educational building was added to the present edifice which was erected prior to 1892. (Centennial paper read by Judge H. O. Devries, 1892, St. James Church Archives.)

[69] The Hobbs' home was a preaching place as early as 1775. On August 4, 1777, Thomas Rankin rode twenty miles east from Seneca Creek en route to Baltimore to hold a quarterly meeting there. Hobbs' home was then a preaching place on the Frederick Circuit. Griffith locates the residence several miles east of New Market, Frederick County. (Rankin *Journal*, May 3 and November 8, 1775, and August 4, 1777; Griffith: Map of Maryland, 1780 and 1794.)

the flame. *Monday*, we hobbled along to Clarkesburg. On the way dined at Joshua Pigman's. Here I once more saw his brother Ignatius. Art thou he? Ah! But O! how fallen! How changed from what I knew thee once! Lord, what is man, if left to himself! Brother Whatcoat attended the meeting, and the people continued in meeting at Clarkesburg until the morning.

Tuesday, September 2. At the Sugar Loaf, my subject was Luke x, 2–4, compared with Matthew xiii, 16, 17, and 1 Pet. i, 10–12; we were crowded: in the exhortations, prayers, and singing, the power came down, and the work went on until evening. I then rode to Mr. Morton's.[70]

Virginia

Wednesday, 3. We came to Leesburg; some said, go this, and another that way: we made it nearly twenty miles, and were riding six hours, and crossed the Potomac at Conrad's Ferry. Brother George[71] was preaching: Bishop Whatcoat spoke upon, "He that believeth shall not make haste"; but we had to make haste, after I had ordained S. Welsh and Eskridge Hall to the deacon's office. After we had dined, we rode twelve, if not fifteen miles, to the widow Rozzell's: we came in about seven o'clock; and I gave a discourse on 1 Tim. iv, 16. We have travelled about one hundred and fifty miles through Maryland; and we have had bad roads, but have met with good people. My soul hath been agonizing for a revival upon the western shore of Maryland for many years, and now the Lord hath sent it.

Thursday, 4. We came to Rectortown: most distressing roads for eighteen miles. The gentry had made a dinner at a small distance from the town—a kind of green corn feast, with a roasted animal, cooked and eaten out of doors, under a booth. I was greatly wearied with the ride; but was animated while explaining 2 Cor. vi, 1. I then came to Benjamin Hitt's. We have penetrated through Loudon and Fauquier counties in two days.

Friday, 5. We stopped at the court house,[72] and were richly entertained with a breakfast, at Mr. Johnson's: then we rode on to Norman's Bridge, and passed another *old field-feast*, with a race tacked to it. We came to Roger Abbott's, upon Mountain Creek, in the forks of the Rappahannock river; and on

Saturday, 6, to Kobler's; where many attended from different and distant parts: my text was 2 Tim. ii, 15. We pursued our way six miles to the river, and lodged at a widow's house, whose husband died in the Lord a

[70] Thomas Morton conveyed land upon which Sugar Loaf Chapel was erected. He resided in the vicinity of Sugar Loaf Mountain in Frederick County. Between 1801 and 1809 his name appears among the official members living in Montgomery County. (Martz: *The Clarksburg Methodist Church*, 7; Armstrong, *op. cit.*, 509.)

[71] Enoch George was one of the presiding elders over Virginia circuits. (See *Minutes*.)

[72] This was Fauquier Court House.

few years ago. We had an awful *Sabbath day's* journey, through part of Culpepper and Louisa; we came to Ferguson's about half after one o'clock: the people were waiting in the warm sun; the house could not hold them: after a little rest, I cried, *Now is the day of salvation.* We had a hungry ride for thirty miles.

Monday, 8. We rode to Lastley's meeting house, eighteen miles: many people were gone to court—consequently, few at meeting; but the Lord was eminently present whilst I enforced Habakkuk iii, 2.

Tuesday, 9. We rode to Rivanna in Fluvanna county: I have seen the hot, warm, sweet, yellow, red, and now have passed the green springs. When we came within six miles of Magruder's, brother Whatcoat being in the carriage, the hindmost brace gave way: I took hold of a sapling by the road-side, and put it under the body of the carriage, and brother Magruder mounted the horse, and we soon came to his house: that evening the breach was repaired. I took William M'Kendree's horse, and went on fourteen miles, to Richard Davenport's, in Amherst; where we were kindly and comfortably entertained.

Wednesday, 10. We rode twenty miles through heat and over hills, to North Garden, *Tandy Keys*, Albemarle county. I was divinely assisted while I opened 2 Timothy iv, 2. 1. Preach the word. 2. The application of it; that is, reprove, rebuke, exhort; *to time his work*; be instant, in season, out of season;—in the morning, noon, and evening of life;—when it is the winter, spring, summer, and autumn of the Church;—in her pleasing and unpleasing prospects.

Thursday, 11. We rode to New Glasgow, thirty miles; and were entertained most hospitably at Colonel Meredith's.

Friday, 12. We rode to Lynchburg, twenty miles. Samuel Mitchell[73] had dinner provided in town, at Mr. Miller's for the preachers. I preached in the Mason's Hall—a warm day and place, on Titus ii, 12. We then beat along to Samuel Mitchell's, three miles of rude roads.

Saturday, 13. We rode to New London Academy, sixteen miles, now under the direction of Samuel K. Jennings, a local preacher of ours: the institution belongeth to the Presbyterians and Episcopalians. R. Whatcoat preached: I was deprived of my rest the last evening, and very unwell; yet I gave a short discourse in exhortation. We have been going at such an unreasonable rate, that I have not had time to put pen to paper for a week together. Good news from the South District of Virginia: brother Jackson writes, "Two hundred souls have been converted this last quarter; there is a revival in all the circuits but two; and great union among the preachers and people."[74] I am kept in patience, faith, and love.

[73] Samuel Mitchell, brother of Edward Mitchell, had become a local preacher in and around Lynchburg. The Mitchells lived in Bottetourt County. (Bennett, *op. cit.*, 454.)

[74] Jonathan Jackson was presiding elder of the district. His letter was written from the Cumberland Circuit on August 20, 1800, and is printed in Moore: *Pioneers of Metho-*

Sunday, 14. We rode sixteen miles to Liberty, and preached in Bedford court house: I was sick in earnest. When I came up into the crowd, the people gathered around my carriage, as if I had had a cake and cider cart; this sight occasioned a kind of shock, that made me forget my sickness. After alighting, I went immediately to the throng in the court house, and founded a discourse upon Matthew xxii, 5. What great things the Gospel revealeth to mankind. First, The love of God. Secondly, The sufferings, and death, and merits of Christ. Thirdly, The gifts, extraordinary and ordinary, of the Holy Ghost: men make light of all the blessings of God, and of all the miseries and consequences of sin: they not only think lightly of, but are opposed exceedingly to them; "for the carnal mind is enmity against God," and the things of God. I admired the attention and solemnity of the people; many of the men standing in and out of the house the whole time. We rode two miles to brother Patterson's, and dined; and then came on to Blackwell's to lodge.

Monday, 15. We had a heavy march to Fincastle: I rode nine miles to Mr. Ripley's; and then gave up the carriage to William M'Kendree, and took his horse, and came in about ten o'clock. My subject here was Isaiah lii, 7. First, the Gospel;—good tidings of God, of Christ, of the Spirit of grace, of glory:—by comparing temporal with spiritual things, to restore the dead, the blind, the lame, the dumb, the sick, the poor; publisheth peace with God, with conscience, with all men; good tidings of good; the spreading of the work of God: salvation;—from all our sin, misery, and death. Zion, thy God reigneth;—the glory of Christ's kingdom. The feet of the messengers, *beautiful*:—because of their message; their holy walk; their treading the mountains, enduring hardship; their innocence.

We made it forty miles from Liberty to Edward Mitchell's; where we lodged on *Monday*.

Tuesday, 16. We began our route for Holston, by English's Ferry,[75] through Montgomery county. The first day we came to Mrs. Dialley's, upon Roanoke, twenty-eight or thirty miles: the river ridges were very rough: Mrs. Dialley received us with great maternal attention and affection: here I was told of my appointment at Raboue's,[76] ten miles west, over the mountains. It gave me some grief, but it was too late. I was advised not to go Pepper's ferry road.

Wednesday, 17.—We passed Montgomery town and court house among the mountain barrens; we pushed on to Christian's—they are

dism in North Carolina and Virginia, 304. Asbury seems to have misinterpreted the word "but" to mean that the Bertie and Cumberland circuits had not shared in the revival, whereas Jackson meant to convey the idea of "especially."

[75] The correct name of the ferry was Ingles, named for William Ingle, although the map of 1809 shows it as English. (Summers: *Annals of Southwest Virginia*, Index; see State Historical Marker, Montgomery County, 1.4 miles east of Radford.)

[76] This was probably Ralburn's. There is no Raboue's listed in Summers' *Annals*.

British people; we had an acceptable rest for a very warm day. We came to the ferry, and lodged at Draper's[77] (a very quiet house) that night.

Thursday, 18. We came to Wythe court house, a pleasant town of about twenty houses, some neat, and most of them new and painted. We had good accommodations at Mr. Johnson's—both man and horse needed it.

Friday, 19. We began at six o'clock to bend for Holston: it was computed to be forty miles distant. We came in about the going down of the sun at father Carlock's, a German. For two days past we found we could not stop to dine; we rested only to feed our horses. After we cleared the mountains we came upon the perpetual hills. I judge we may charge for one hundred and thirty miles from Edward Mitchell's, in Bottetourt, to Russell's old place upon Holston. We took *Saturday* to refit and write; brother Whatcoat attended the meeting. My mind hath been kept in peace; I had enough to do to drive; I could think but little—only now and then sending up a message to heaven.

Sabbath day, 21. We attended at Carlock's; a very sultry day, and many people were present. My subject was 1 Tim. vi, 2–12. It was judged best we should ride ten miles to Scott's, in order to make Edward Cox's the next day, to attend at Acuff's.

Tuesday, 23. As we came off it began to rain, and that rapidly, with little intermission for two hours; the horsemen were dripping; the roads were so bad that it was with some exertion that I could so shelter myself as not to get wet to the skin in the drowning rain. *Monday*, we passed Abingdon, which is greatly improved.

Tennessee

Breakfasted at Craig's, and then had a pleasant ride to Cox's, but it is excessively warm for the country and season. At Acuff's I talked a little upon coming to the throne of grace. We hasted home with Charles Baker upon Holston. If we have a dry moon and month we may get through the wilderness.

Wednesday, 24. We rested—man and beast. We have ridden sixty miles since Sabbath evening. I am not as patient, dependent, and prayerful as I wish to be. Blountville looks very respectable, and they have built a needful and good bridge at the end of the town. We crossed at Charles Baker's by putting the chaise to two canoes and swimming the horses over Main Holston. The Stubblefield's were upon the north side, so that we were compelled to work through the woods into the road to Snipe's Ferry. We came along eight or ten miles where they had made new cuttings; at last we struck into a new road, and strayed three miles out of our way, we

[77] John Draper was granted a license on November 6, 1798, to keep an ordinary at Draper's Ferry. (Summers, *op. cit.*, 873.)

then returned back two. Now it was that I felt *properly* content to leave my *felicity*, so called, before it came to the wilderness. We made it nearly thirty miles to Ball's mill; we had no time from six in the morning till seven at night to feed man or beast.

Friday, 26. We rode twenty-one miles to Benjamin Van Pelt's,[78] upon Lick Creek; we fed our horses twice, the riders not once! Here I left the horse and carriage, and borrowed a horse to ride to Kentucky. *Saturday*, rode twenty miles across to Holston quarterly meeting at the Stubblefields.[79] I now rode upon horseback, and the rain came on powerfully until we were dripping. I had no cloak but the carriage covering, the rain took shoulders, elbows, and feet; for eight miles it was violent; I had not been so steeped for four years. I washed the wet parts with whisky, and did not take the damage I feared. O thou of little faith, wherefore didst thou doubt? Bishop Whatcoat preached. Our local brethren were loving and lively—brothers Van Pelt, Wells, and Winton.

Sabbath day, 28. We had a good sacramental and speaking time. I preached on Titus ii, 14, and brother M'Kendree from Psalm xi, 2–6. I was led to recollect the loss of time and difficulty met with from Botte-tourt to Holston, one hundred miles; few friends, rough roads, one week lost in riding.

Monday, 29. We began our grand route to Kentucky at eight o'clock. We had to climb the steeps of Clinch about the heat of the day; walk up I could not: I rode, and rested my horse by dismounting at times. We came to Hunt's[80] for the first night. Such roads and entertainment I did not ever again expect to see; at least in so short a time.

Kentucky

Tuesday, 30. We came to Davis's[81] to breakfast, and at night we slept at Ballinger's,[82] upon Cumberland River.

Wednesday, October 1. We came to Logan's[83] and fed: this low and new land is scented; I was almost sickened with the smell. We came to the elder of the Panies's, and lodged.

Thursday, 2. We came rapidly to Job Johnson's, and reached it by riding in the night: now I began to fail.

[78] See letter to John Page, September 26, 1800.

[79] Martin Stubblefield lived in Hamblen County. He was a devout Methodist. (Price, *op. cit.*, II, 77.)

[80] Hunt's Tavern was at Tazewell, Tennessee. (Williams: *Early Travels*, 308.)

[81] Mrs. Davis ran a tavern on the north side of the mountain, where Middlesboro, Kentucky, now stands. (Kincaid: *Wilderness Road.*)

[82] Richard Ballinger's Tavern was at a settlement at the bend of Cumberland River, which later became Barbourville. (*Ibid.*, 196.)

[83] Logan's Station was about forty miles north of Barbourville, Kentucky. (*Ibid.*, 120.)

Friday, 3. We came on to our brother Howard's. We crossed Kentucky River at the mouth of Hickman;[84] it was so low that we forded it with ease. We have travelled in five days one hundred and forty-five miles. I have slept uncomfortably this week.

Saturday, 4. I came to Bethel. Bishop Whatcoat and William M'Kendree preached: I was so dejected I could say little; but weep. *Sabbath day* it rained, and I kept at home. Here is Bethel; Cokesbury in miniature, eighty by thirty feet, three stories, with a high roof, and finished below. Now we want a fund and an income of three hundred per year to carry it on; without which it will be useless. But it is too distant from public places; its being surrounded by the river Kentucky in part, we now find to be no benefit: thus all our excellencies are turned into defects. Perhaps brother Poythress and myself were as much overseen with this place as Dr. Coke was with the seat of Cokesbury. But all is right that works right, and all is wrong that works wrong, and we must be blamed by men of slender sense for consequences impossible to foresee—for other people's misconduct. *Sabbath day*, *Monday*, and *Tuesday*, we were shut up in Bethel with the travelling and local ministry and the trustees that could be called together. We ordained fourteen or fifteen local and travelling deacons. It was thought expedient to carry the first design of education into execution, and that we should employ a man of sterling qualifications, to be chosen by and under the direction of a select number of trustees and others, who should obligate themselves to see him paid, and take the profits, if any, arising from the establishment. Dr. Jennings was thought of, talked of, and written to. I visited John Lewis,[85] who lately had his leg broken; I left him with good resolutions to take care of his soul.

Wednesday, 8. We rode fifteen miles to Shawnee Run, and crossed Kentucky River at Curd's ferry[86]; the river was as low as a stream, and the streams are nearly dried up.

Thursday, 9. I preached on Heb. iii, 12–14, at the new house at Shawnee Run. We had rich entertainment for man and beast at Robert Johnson's.

Friday, 10. We rode to Pleasant Run to John Springer's: it was a very warm day for the season. I had a running blister at my side, yet I rode and walked thirty-two miles. We refreshed ourselves at Crawford's tavern upon the way. We have visited Knox, Madison, Mercer, and Washington counties in this state. It was strongly insisted upon by preachers and people that I should say something before I left Bethel; able or unable, willing or unwilling: accordingly, on *Tuesday*, in the academical hall, I gave a long, temperate talk upon Heb. x, 38, 39.

[84] Asbury crossed the river at the present site of Camp Nelson in Jessamine County, Kentucky.

[85] John Lewis donated the land on which Bethel School was built. Also see note under May 17, 1790. (Redford, *op. cit.*, I, 85.)

[86] Curd's Ferry was at the mouth of Dix River about three miles from Bethel.

Sabbath day, 12. It rained excessively; we were shut up; William M'Kendree met the people. We have had but two Sabbaths to spend in Kentucky, and in both I was prevented by rain.

Monday, 13. We left John Springer's, and came to Lewis Thomas's, fifteen miles; a deep, damp, narrow path; the underwood very wet. Crossed Cartwright and Hardin's Creeks. I gave a short sermon, on, Rom. viii, 9: "If any man have not the Spirit of Christ he is none of his."

I. How we are to know when we have the Spirit of Christ; by the operations, gifts, consolations, and fruits of the Spirit.

II. We are none of his if we are not interested in the offices, if not partakers of the redemption and privileges of Christ.

III. That none can be interested in Christ, who are not partakers of the spirit of Jesus.

My system is greatly affected with the weather; but my soul hath abundant consolation in God. It is plain there are not many mighty among the Methodists in Kentucky. In travelling between two and three hundred miles, I have visited six dwellings besides the academy. At Pleasant Run, October 12, we ordained Joseph Ferguson, and Moses Crame, to the office of deacons.

Tuesday, 14. We began our march for Cumberland. We were told by two persons, that we could not cross the Rolling Fork of Salt River; I judged we could, and as I thought, so it was—we forded it with ease. We came up a solitary path east of the level woods, and struck into the road to Lee's ferry. For ten miles of the latter part of this day's journey, we rode through barrens of hickory, shrub oak, and hazelnut; thirty miles, if not thirty-five is the amount of this day's work; in the morning there was a very great damp, and in the afternoon it was, I thought, as warm as the west of Georgia.

Wednesday, 15. We crossed Green River, the main branch of which riseth near the Crab Orchard. We crossed at the mouth of Little Barren River.[87] We then made a bold push for the Great Barren; dining at Mr. Morrison's,[88] I could not eat wallet provision, but happily for me I was provided with a little fresh mutton at the house, made warm in a small space. Now we have unfavourable appearances of rain; we had bleak, barren hills to ride; which, although beautiful to sight, were painful to sense. The rain came in large and rapid drops for fourteen miles; we were well soaked on all sides. A little after dark we came to Mr. Hagin's, upon Big Barren River; a good house, an excellent fire to dry our clothing, good meat and milk for supper, and the cleanest beds; all this we had. I have paid for this route.

[87] This was in Hart County, Kentucky.

[88] John O. Morrison lived in Barren County, Kentucky. He was the great-grandfather of Dr. Henry Clay Morrison, later president of Asbury College, Wilmore, Kentucky. (Gross: "Prophet on Horseback," Louisville *Courier Journal* magazine, December 5, 1954.)

PLACES VISITED BY

FRANCIS ASBURY

IN

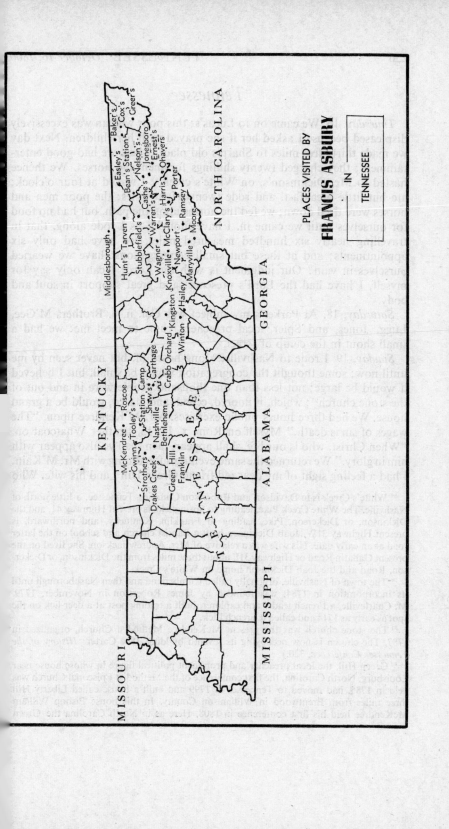

TENNESSEE

Tennessee

Thursday, 16. We came on to Lucas's: this poor woman was excessively displeased because I asked her if she prayed with her children. Next day we made thirty-five miles to Sharp's old place, where we had good entertainment; they charged twenty shillings for men and horses. We thence hasted to Mr. Dickinson's, on White's creek.[89] I waked at four o'clock; ate but little breakfast, and rode twenty-eight miles; the poor men and horses were tired down; we fed the horses upon the path, but had no food for ourselves until we came in. I have thought, as I rode along, that in travelling nearly six hundred measured miles, we have had only six appointments; and at these but small congregations: have we wearied ourselves in vain? Our judgment is with the Lord; I can only say for myself, I have had the Lord's presence, and great support in soul and body.

Saturday, 18. At Parker's my subject was Col. ii, 6. Brothers M'Gee, Lugg, Jones, and Spier, local preachers, came to meet me: we had a small shout in the camp of Israel.

Sunday, 19. I rode to Nashville,[90] long heard of, but never seen by me until now; some thought the congregation would be small, but I believed it would be large; not less than one thousand people were in and out of the stone church[91]; which, if floored, ceiled, and glazed, would be a grand house. We had three hours public exercises. Mr. M'Kendree upon, "The wages of sin is death." Myself on Rom. x, 14, 15. Brother Whatcoat on, "When Christ, who is our life, shall appear, then shall ye also appear with him in glory." We returned the same evening, after dining with Mr. M'Kain. I had a feeling sight of my dear old friend Green Hill[92] and his wife. Who

[89] White's Creek is in Davidson and Robertson Counties, Tennessee, a little north of Nashville. The White Creek Pike, leading to Springfield, is present Highway 41, and the Dickinson, or Dickerson, Pike, leading to Franklin, Kentucky, and northward, is present Highway 31W. Joab Dickinson built a Baptist church and school on the latter road at an early date. His wife was a relative of Mrs. Andrew Jackson. She lived on the present Gallatin Road or Highway 31E about three miles from the Dickinson, or Dickerson, Road and the Joab Dickinson home on White's Creek.

[90] The town of Nashville, originally called Cumberland and then Nashborough until its incorporation in 1784, was founded by James Robertson in November, 1779. M. Charleville, a French trader and explorer, built a trading post at a deer lick on the spot as early as 1714 and called it French Lick.

[91] The stone church was the present McKendree Methodist Church, organized in 1787. The church is now occupying its seventh building. (See Carter: *History of the Tennessee Conference*, 320.)

[92] Green Hill, the local preacher and prominent political figure in whose house near Louisburg, North Carolina, the first conference of the Methodist Episcopal Church was held in 1785, had moved to Tennessee in 1799 and built a house called Liberty Hill three miles from Brentwood in Williamson County. In this house Bishop William McKendree held his first conference in 1808. Here as in North Carolina the Green

would have thought we should ever meet in this distant land? I had not time, as formerly, to go to their house to eat and sleep. We had a night meeting at Mr. Dickinson's.

Monday, 20. We came by Mansker's to Drake's creek[93] meeting house, at the close of a sacramental solemnity, that had been held four days by Craighead,[94] Hodge, Rankin, M'Gee, and Mr. Adair, Presbyterian officiating ministers; we came in, and brother M'Kendree preached upon Jer. iv, 14; after him brother Whatcoat, upon "We know that we are of God": I also spoke; my subject was *the work of God*. Last Sabbath was my birth-day. This will make the thirtieth year of my labours in America.[95] It is supposed there are one thousand souls present, and double that number heard the word of life on *Sunday*.

Tuesday, 21. Yesterday, and especially during the night, were witnessed scenes of deep interest. In the intervals between preaching, the people refreshed themselves and horses and returned upon the ground. The *stand* was in the open air, embosomed in a wood of lofty beech trees. The ministers of God, Methodists and Presbyterians, united their labours and mingled with the childlike simplicity of primitive times. Fires blazing here and there dispelled the darkness and the shouts of the redeemed captives, and the cries of precious souls struggling into life, broke the silence of midnight. The weather was delightful; as if heaven smiled, whilst mercy flowed in abundant streams of salvation to perishing sinners. We suppose there were at least thirty souls converted at this meeting.[96] I rejoice that

Hill home became a notable Methodist center. The original log house stood for nearly 150 years, and its owner is buried in the family cemetery nearby. Liberty Methodist Church in the vicinity is the successor of the society which met at Liberty Hill. (Carter, *op. cit.*, 39–41.) See note under April 19, 1785.

[93] Mansker was a noted frontiersman. (Williams, *op. cit.*, 335.) Drakes Creek meeting-house was in Sumner County about two miles from present Saundersville. The Saundersville Church is probably its successor. (Carter, *op. cit.*, 29.)

[94] Craighead had a school at Spring Hill, which later became the University of Nashville and George Peabody College for Teachers. The present First Presbyterian Church at Nashville grew out of his church at Madison, Tennessee. He founded the Spring Hill Cemetery between Nashville and Gallatin and is buried there.

[95] Asbury's chronology was not strictly accurate. He was born August 20/21, 1745, and reached America on October 27, 1771. (See *Journal* entries for October 27, 1771, and July 16, 1792.)

[96] The meeting at Drake's meetinghouse was one of the earliest of the camp meetings which swept through Kentucky, Tennessee, and other states early in the nineteenth century. They arose under the leadership of the McGee brothers, William, a Presbyterian, and John, a Methodist, James McGready, a Presbyterian of North Carolina, Peter Cartwright, and other evangelists. The Cane Ridge Church in Kentucky, now a church of the Disciples of Christ, was famous as the scene of one of the first and greatest of these meetings. Though started by the Presbyterians, the camp-meeting movement was taken over by the Methodists and became known as a Methodist institution. (The best discussions of the camp meeting are found in Tracy: *The Great Awakening*; Davenport: *Primitive Traits in Religious Revivals*; and the *Autobiography of Peter Cartwright*. See also Clark: *The Small Sects in America*, 90–93.)

God is visiting the sons of the Puritans, who are candid enough to acknowledge their obligations to the Methodists.

We have passed only two counties in the District of Mero:[97] *quiet* Cumberland keeps "the noiseless tenor of his way" through the midst of the settlement; Nashville crowns its lofty bank.

Wednesday, 22. We had a meeting at Richard Strother's,[98] upon a branch of Station Creek, and there were great emotions of tenderness among the people.

Thursday, 23. We came to Edward's. Brother Whatcoat began—I continued upon Matt. xi, 28–30. William M'Gee concluded. We lodged with James Douglas.[99]

Friday, 24. We came to Thomas Blackmore's.[100] Brother Whatcoat, and brother M'Kendree sermonized; the people were not greatly moved; I concluded with prayer.

Saturday, 25. We crossed Cumberland River at Bishop's ferry.[101] What a long solitary river is this! It is probably seven hundred miles upon a line; and near one thousand in its meanderings, before it empties its waters into the Ohio, twelve miles above the mouth of the Tennessee.

We began our quarterly meeting at Elmour Douglas's. Brother Whatcoat preached; brothers M'Kendree and M'Gee exhorted. At the evening meeting there were more shouters than converts; nevertheless the Lord was in the midst.

We have ridden but about sixty-six or seventy miles this week. The country is greatly in want of rain: the large streams are much absorbed; and the people grind their grain with horse mills.

I could not be content to leave the settlement without circumstantial account of the work of God; and I therefore desired John M'Gee to give it me; and I purpose to select such accounts annually, and to read them in the large congregations, and then to have them published.

Sunday, 26. I attempted but little this day in public, except a class on a portion of the word from 2 Peter i, 16. We forded Cumberland River, and came to John M'Gee's.[102] We now began to think seriously upon our

[97] The Cumberland region was sometimes known as the Mero District. (McFerrin: *Methodism in Tennessee*, I, 334.)

[98] Strother lived about seven miles west of Gallatin in Sumner County, Tennessee. Bethel church on Station Camp Creek is still in operation about a mile from the original site. The first Strother's meetinghouse has been moved to the campus of Scarritt College for Christian Workers in Nashville.

[99] William McGee was pastor of Shiloh Presbyterian Church on the Scottsville Road five miles north of Gallatin, Tennessee. His brother, John, was a Methodist. James Douglas lived on Station Camp Creek. Douglas Chapel is still in existence.

[100] Thomas Blackmore lived on the north side of the Cumberland River near Hartsville, Tennessee.

[101] Bishop's ferry was doubtless the ferry at Rome five miles south of Carthage.

[102] John McGee lived between present Gainsborough and Carthage. The river was crossed at the mouth of the Caney Fork near Carthage.

march through the wilderness, and providing food and provisions for man and horse—we took our departure.

Monday, 27. We travelled through rich forests of beech, with rank undergrowth of cane or reed, and arrived at Fort Blount:[103] thence pursuing our way up Flinn Creek, we took the ridge and reached Mrs. Blackburn's, where we lodged, and were well accommodated. This day we have ridden thirty-five miles.

We urged on our way, expecting rain, which overtook us about two o'clock at Flat Rock. We pressed on over Drowning Creek, and the sleepy, discoloured waters of Obey River.[104] About twilight in the barrens we met the Presbyterian ministers, Hall, Montgomery, and Bowman, with whom we rejoiced at the work of God in Cumberland, and then parted. We came on to a place where we found the woods were burning, and finding we had made about forty-five miles we encamped whilst the rain was falling upon us.

Wednesday, 29. We came to the new station at the Crab Orchard,[105] where, although the station was not yet put in order, Mr. Sidnor received us politely, and treated us to tea. Here we found a cabin under the direction of the Cherokee nation, on land they claimed as theirs. We journeyed on to Spencer's Hill, so called because here a man of that name was killed by Indians.[106] Thence we travelled forward to Prospect Hill and the descent to Cumberland Mountain.[107] On our route we experienced a heavy rain. Through damps and mud we pushed forward to Clarke's ferry, upon Clinch, in sight of the fort at South West Point,[108] at the Junction of Tennessee and Clinch rivers, one hundred miles below the mouth of Powels River. We have travelled nearly seventy miles upon land belonging to the Cherokee nation: the soil is generally barren and broken, except where we enter on Cumberland Mountain and the neighbourhood of the new station. This Indian land cuts the state of Tennessee into two parts, passing nearly through the middle, making an indent upon the state of Ken-

[103] Fort Blount was a stockade on the Cumberland River opposite Gainsborough.

[104] The Obey River is in the Carthage area.

[105] Crab Orchard is in Cumberland County near Crossville. The station was the Crab Orchard Tavern which became famous. (Williams, *op. cit.*, 503.) Asbury was proceeding along the route of present Highway 70 to Knoxville.

[106] Thomas Spencer was a hunter and trapper who lived during the winter in a sycamore tree near Gallatin, where a Spencer community still exists. He was a large man, a dead shot, and was killed by Indians near Crab Orchard.

[107] Prospect Hill was probably near the present Ozone in Cumberland County. It is at the top of the Cumberland range, and a few miles eastward is the "descent" into the present town of Rockwood in Roan County. On this first trip through Middle Tennessee Asbury followed the general route of Highway 70 by way of Carthage, Monterey, Crab Orchard, and Kingston to Knoxville and the Holston country. Much of the territory was the domain of the Cherokee Indians.

[108] South West Point was the present Kingston.

tucky on Yellow Creek. We arrived at Mr. Clark's,[109] where we received great entertainment: there was a good fire in the hall, and we were provided with a good dinner, and treated to tea: a fire was also kindled up stairs, at which we dried our clothes; to which may be added excellent lodging in two inner rooms: thus were we within, whilst our horses were feeding to fulness in a grassy valley without. Our kind host rents the land from the Indians at six hundred per annum; himself making the improvements.

Thursday, 30. We rode slowly on to Starr's, twenty-two miles, and had a heavy shower of rain on our way. From *Monday* morning to *Thursday* afternoon we have made one hundred and thirty miles; we have experienced no stoppage by water-courses, and have found the roads of the wilderness, their unevenness excepted, pretty good. And here let me record the gracious dealings of God to my soul in this journey: I have had uncommon peace of mind, and spiritual consolations every day, notwithstanding the long rides I have endured, and the frequent privations of good water and proper food to which I have been subjected; to me the wilderness and the solitary places were made as the garden of God, and as the presence chambers of the King of kings and Lord of lords.

Friday, 31. I gave a long discourse upon the epistle in the office of ordination for deacons, and ordained John Winton[110] in the congregation.

Saturday, November 1. Came twenty miles to Knoxville,[111] of which I had often heard, and which mine eyes now saw. We visited my old friend Greer.[112]

Sabbath day, 2. I preached in the state house on Isa. lv, 6, 7. I was very unwell, but was enabled to bear the heavy cross of public speaking; we had about seven hundred people in and about the house. We came off in haste, intending to make twenty miles that evening; but Francis Alexander Ramsay pursued us to the ferry, franked us over, and took us to his excellent mansion—a stone house: it may not be amiss to mention, that our host has built his house, and takes in his harvest without the aid of whisky.[113] We were kindly and comfortably entertained.

[109] Thomas Norris Clark was a wealthy merchant and planter. (Williams, *op. cit.*, 312.)

[110] John Winton was a local preacher who lived at Muddy Creek, seventeen miles below Knoxville. (Price, *op. cit.*, II, 404.)

[111] The village of Knoxville was the capitol of Tennessee at this time. It was established as the seat of the territorial government in 1792 and named in honor of General Henry Knox, Secretary of War under George Washington. The first legislature of the state met there on March 28, 1796. (Price: *Holston Methodism*, I, 295.)

[112] Joseph Greer was a trader with the Cherokees. (Williams: *Dawn of History in Tennessee*, 348.)

[113] In the pioneer period neighbors frequently assisted each other at log rolling, house raising, and harvesting. These were followed by festive occasions with dinners and alcoholic beverages. Hence the fact that Ramsay was able to harvest his crops on a temperance basis was cause for comment. (Price, *op. cit.*, I, 295, 296.) He was the father of the historian. (Williams: *Lost State of Franklin*, 304.)

Monday, 3. We rode up to M'Cleary's, fourteen miles, where we dined, and pursued our journey to William Blackburn's.

Tuesday, 4. Rode twenty miles up Nolachucky to Benjamin Van Pelt's,[114] where I had left my horse and chaise. In this neighbourhood the land, except a few spots, is little better than barren; nevertheless, good cultivation will make it productive. From the twenty-seventh of last month, the day on which we left the pleasant mansion of our friend Van Pelt, to the day of our return, we rode, I presume, quite six hundred and sixty if not seven hundred miles. Hitherto the Lord hath helped us. We have had twelve proper appointments; two of which (*Sabbath days*) were near failing because of rain.

Wednesday, 5. At Van Town I preached in the new chapel on Luke iv, 18.[115]

North Carolina

Thursday, 6. Crossed Nolachucky at Cureton's ferry, and came to Major Craig's, eighteen miles. I next day pursued my journey and arrived at the Warm Springs,[116] not however without an ugly accident. After we had crossed the Small and Great Paint mountain, and had passed about thirty yards beyond the Paint Rock,[117] my roan horse, led by Mr. O'Haver[118] reeled and fell over, taking the chaise with him; I was called back, when I beheld the poor beast and the carriage, *bottom up*, lodged and wedged against a sapling, which alone prevented them both being precipitated into the river. After a pretty heavy lift all was righted again, and we were pleased to find there was little damage done. Our feelings were excited more for others than ourselves. Not far off we saw clothing spread out,

[114] See *Journal* entries and notes for November 7, 1771; June 28–30, 1790; April 6, 1793; May 12, 1793; March 4, 1800.

[115] Van Pelt's chapel was one of the earliest meetinghouses in the Holston country. It was located on the north side of Lick Creek near the village of Mosheim in Greene County. (Price, *op. cit.*, I, 195–96.)

[116] Warm Springs, the present Hot Springs in Madison County, North Carolina, was discovered in 1778 by Henry Reynolds and Thomas Morgan. The site became a noted resort. Asbury went from Tennessee to North Carolina along the general route of Highway 70 via Hot Springs and Marshall to Asheville. He probably followed what was called the Old Love Road which ran from near Greenville, Tennessee, and along Paint Creek to the French Broad River six miles below Hot Springs. (Arthur: *History of Western North Carolina*, 492.)

[117] The "painted rock" was in present Madison County near the Paint Rock community. It figured in the boundary disputes between North Carolina and Tennessee. Surveyors in 1799 described it as being 107 feet high and stated that in 1790, before it had been defaced by smoke, it had red painted animals, fish, fowls, and men on its face. This was discounted by Arthur, who said the red "paint" seemed to be oxidation of iron ore. (Arthur, *op. cit.*, 47.)

[118] John O'Haver lived in the present Cocke County, Tennessee, near Newport. (Price: *Holston Methodism*, II, 116. See *Journal* entry for October 22, 1808.)

part of the loading of household furniture of a wagon which had overset and was thrown into the stream, and bed-clothes, bedding, &c., were so wet that the poor people found it necessary to dry them on the spot. We passed the side fords of French Broad, and came to Mr. William Nelson's; our mountain march of twelve miles calmed us down for this day. My company was not agreeable here—there were too many subjects of the two great potentates of this Western World—whisky, brandy. My mind was greatly distressed.

Saturday, 8. We started away. The cold was severe upon the fingers. We crossed the ferry, curiously contrived with a rope and poles, for half a mile along the banks of the river, to guide the boat by. And O the rocks! the rocks! Coming to Laurel River, we followed a wagon ahead of us—the wagon stuck fast. Brother O'Haver mounted old gray—the horse fell about midway, but recovered, rose, and went safely through with his burden. We pursued our way rapidly to Ivy Creek,[119] suffering much from heat and the roughness of the roads, and stopped at William Hunter's.

Sabbath day, 9. We came to Thomas Foster's,[120] and held a small meeting at his house. We must bid farewell to the chaise; this mode of conveyance by no means suits the roads of this wilderness; we are obliged to keep one behind the carriage with a strap to hold by and prevent accidents almost continually. I have health and hard labour, and a constant sense of the favour of God.

Tobias Gibson[121] had given notice to some of my being at Buncombe court house, and the society at Killian's in consequence of this, made an appointment for me on *Tuesday*, 11. We were strongly importuned to stay, which brother Whatcoat felt inclined to do. In the meantime we had our horses shod by Philip Smith: this man, as is not unfrequently the case in this country, makes wagons and works at carpentry, makes shoes for

[119] Laurel River, or Big Laurel Creek, and Ivy Creek flow through the present Madison County.

[120] Thomas Foster lived on the Swannanoa River at or near the mouth of Sweeten Creek, afterward called Foster's Mill Creek, about two and one-half miles south of Asheville on the present Asheville–Hendersonville Road. He built the first bridge across the Swannanoa. He was later a member of the House of Commons and the State Senate from Buncombe County. He is buried in the Newton Academy graveyard at Asheville. He made no religious profession, but his daughter, Mrs. James M. Alexander, became an active Methodist. (Grissom, *Methodism in North Carolina*, I, 300; Arthur, *op. cit.*, 153, 154.)

[121] Tobias Gibson was appointed to the Little Pee Dee and Anson Circuit in South Carolina early in 1799. In January, 1800, he was appointed to Natchez, and sometime during the year he made a famous and perilous canoe voyage down the Mississippi and became the founder of Methodism in Mississippi. Jones (*Methodism in Mississippi*, I, 24 ff.) argues that Gibson reached Natchez late in March of 1799, which was nine months before he was officially appointed. If he gave notice of Asbury's presence in Buncombe County, North Carolina, and it was effective as late as November, 1800, it would seem that he must have lingered in the Blue Ridge area for a period before departing for his appointment in Natchez.

men and for horses; to which he adds, occasionally, the manufacture of saddles and hats.

Monday, 10. Visited Squire Swain's[122] agreeable family. On *Tuesday* we attended our appointment. My foundation for a sermon was Heb. ii, 1. We had about eighty hearers; among them was Mr. Newton,[123] a Presbyterian minister, who made the concluding prayer. We took up our journey, and came to Foster's[124] upon Swannanoa—company enough, and horses in a drove of thirty-three. Here we met Francis Poythress[125]—sick of Carolina, and in the clouds. I, too, was sick. Next morning we rode to Fletcher's[126] on Mud Creek. The people being unexpectedly gathered together, we gave them a sermon and an exhortation. We lodged at Fletcher's.

Thursday, 13. We crossed French Broad at Kim's Ferry,[127] forded Mill's River,[128] and made upwards through the barrens of Broad to Davidson's,[129] whose name names the stream. The aged mother and daughters insisted upon giving notice for a meeting: in consequence thereof Mr. Davis, the Presbyterian minister, and several others, came together. Brother Whatcoat was taken with a bleeding at the nose, so that necessity was laid upon me to lecture: my subject was Luke xi, 13.

[122] George Swain was born in Massachusetts in 1763. He settled at the head of Beaverdam Creek near Asheville in 1795, after living in South Carolina and Georgia. He was a ruling elder in the Presbyterian Church, member of the legislature and constitutional convention in Georgia, and postmaster at Asheville. He married a Methodist, Mrs. Caroline Lowrie, who was a sister of Joel Lane, founder of Raleigh, and an aunt of General Joseph Lane, Democratic candidate for Vice President of the United States in 1860. George Swain's son, David L. Swain, was three times governor of North Carolina and president of the University of North Carolina. (Arthur, *op. cit.*, 150, 151, 382, 383; Price: *Holston Methodism*, I, 302.)

[123] The Rev. George Newton, whom Asbury called "almost a Methodist," conducted Newton Academy, once known as Union Hill Academy in Asheville. He lived on Swannanoa River until 1814, when he removed to Bedford County, Tennessee, and became principal of Dickson Academy and pastor of the Presbyterian church at Shelbyville. (Arthur, *op. cit.*, 423, 424.)

[124] Foster's was Thomas Foster.

[125] Francis Poythress, a noted Methodist itinerant, was presiding elder over all the circuits in North Carolina. He later became insane and died in Kentucky.

[126] William Fletcher lived on a tract of land near the mouth of Cane Creek in present Henderson County. He moved to Alabama, but his son, John, born in Virginia in 1783, returned and developed the tract. A community called Shufordville developed there, the name being changed to Fletcher about 1880. (Patton: *The Story of Henderson County*, 35, 36.)

[127] "Kim's Ferry" was probably at the home of Benjamin Kimzey, a Welsh immigrant who lived near the mouth of Mud Creek in the present Henderson County. (Patton, *op. cit.*, 38.)

[128] Mills River is in Henderson County. There is a Mills River community between Hendersonville and Asheville.

[129] Ben Davidson had 640 acres in present Rutherford County. There was a Ben Davidson's Creek and a Ben Davidson community, later Pisgah Forest. (Patton, *op. cit.*, 39; Arthur, *op. cit.*, 204, 214, 217.)

Friday, 14. We took our leave of French Broad—the lands flat and good, but rather cold. I have had an opportunity of making a tolerably correct survey of this river. It rises in the south-west, and winds along in many meanders, fifty miles north-east, receiving a number of tributary streams in its course; it then inclines westward, passing through Buncombe in North Carolina, and Green and Dandridge counties in Tennessee, in which last it is augmented by the waters of Nolachucky; four miles above Knoxville it forms a junction with the Holston, and their united waters flow along under the name of Tennessee, giving a name to the State.

South Carolina

We had no small labour in getting down Saluda mountain.[130] Arriving at father Douthet's[131] on the south branch of Saluda, where, finding myself quite at home, I had leisure to reflect upon our western visitation. On the 16th of September we set out from Bottetourt in Virginia, and on the 14th of November we were in North Carolina, at the foot of the grand mountain division of South Carolina. In this time I presume we have travelled one thousand miles, have had about twenty appointments, not many of which were large; have lodged about twenty nights under strange roofs, or at houses of entertainment; and have expended about fifty dollars.

Monday, 17. Yesterday we rested at father John Douthet's; he is settled in a cove in the midst of the mountains, upon the south branch of the Saluda. Brother Whatcoat made a discourse on Matt. iii, 10. The computation is, that from Charleston to the western line of this State it is two hundred and seventy-five miles; but from the centre-house it is nearer four hundred miles.

My mind is led out for the interest of the Southern and Western conferences: these are quite enough contiguous to enable the preachers to change with each other, but such is the sickly state of the South, in both senses, that we shall probably be under the necessity of locating five or six of our spiritual labourers.

To-day I gave a sermon founded upon Psalm cxlvi, 8, 9, and felt engaged, if the people were not.

[130] Although Asbury had visited South Carolina fifteen times since 1785, this was his first entrance by way of the Holston country and western North Carolina. He went down Saluda Mountain and crossed the South Saluda River at Table Rock in present Pickens (then Pendleton) County about where the Table Rock State Park is now located.

[131] John Douthet came from Maryland and settled on Table Rock Mountain at Douthet's Ford in the present Pickens County. His two sons, James and Samuel, became Methodist preachers. (Betts: *History of South Carolina Methodism*, 86, 132. See *Journal* entry for October 29, 1813.)

Tuesday, 18. We came fifteen miles to Samuel Burdine's,[132] Pendleton county. Here were many wandering people. Brother Whatcoat preached. We administered the Lord's supper. I was very much indisposed, and felt dejection of spirits. Our sister Burdine professeth to have known the Lord twenty years; in her you see meekness, gentleness, patience, and pure love —and cleanliness.

Wednesday, 19. We came to John Wilson's;[133] I gave a discourse on Acts ii, 17, 18; my mind was divinely elevated, but the people did not appear to feel. Yesterday and to-day I am disciplined by keen pain in my breast. To-day Benjamin Blanton[134] met me: he is now a married man; like others of his Southern brethren, after he has faithfully served the connexion about ten years, he talks of locating.

Thursday, 20. At the Grove.[135] We were lost an hour in the woods at setting out, and terribly bewildered in our way to the meeting house; the day was cold, and a beautiful snow lay on the ground. During the public exercises the people felt as at the reading and preaching of Ezra. Brother Whatcoat improved with light and life upon Coloss. i, 21–23.

Through twelve miles of cold and snow we journeyed to Thomas Terry's.[136] Our host was from Gisborough, in Yorkshire; he made us welcome, and gave us dinner about six o'clock. Here I hauled up the chaise—the pleasure of riding in it does not compensate for the trouble and difficulty of getting it along.

As there were few appointments in this State, and as brother Benjamin Blanton agreed to fill them, I thought fit to accompany brother Whatcoat who was under the necessity of going to fill appointments made for him in Georgia.

We have travelled about forty miles since we left father Douthet's near the Table mountain, which on a clear day is a grand sight; the *stool* appears like a great house of freestone; to-day we only saw it through a mist dimly. At the Cove there are but few religious people, and among these few there are disorderly walkers. The Northern rivers, I presume, begin to close for the winter, which, I judge, will be a severe one. On *Friday* I rested and wrote.

Saturday, 22. Rode twenty miles to James Powell's,[137] upon Walnut Creek, Lauren's county.

[132] Samuel Burdine lived near Pickens in the present Anderson (then Pendleton) County, South Carolina.

[133] John Wilson had a ferry over the Saluda River near Piedmont.

[134] Benjamin Blanton was the presiding elder of the South Carolina and Georgia district.

[135] Cox's meetinghouse was at the Golden Grove about two miles above Piedmont toward Greenville. There is still a station on the Southern Railway called Grove Station. Cox's meetinghouse later became Rehobeth and continued until 1897, when it disappeared from the *Minutes*.

[136] Thomas Terry lived at Fork Shoals on Reedy River.

[137] James Powell lived across the river from Ware Shoals in Laurens County.

Sabbath day, 23, was an extraordinary cold day at King's chapel.[138] I began reading at eleven o'clock, and occupied the pulpit one hour and twenty minutes; brother Whatcoat followed for fifty minutes, and brother Blanton succeeded him; to this followed the sacrament—making the public exercises four hours (or thereabouts) of continuance, in a very open building. It may not be amiss to mention that this house for the worship of God was named after James King, who died a martyr to the yellow fever in Charleston. We lodged for the night at W. Powell's. Next day we crossed Main Saluda at Pension's ford,[139] and rode twelve miles to George Connor's, upon Silvador's Purchase.[140]

I had thought our address would move their majesties and the peers of Charleston. Report says they have pumped poor George Dougherty until they had almost deprived him of breath; and John Harper committed the address to the flames before the intendant of the city: I have seen his apology for receiving them.[141]

At George Connor's we had an evening meeting, and considering the coldness of the night, and the shortness of the notice, it was well attended. Brother Whatcoat preached.

Tuesday, 25. We rode to Nathaniel Burdine's[142]—ancient Methodists, who have a son in the ministry.

Wednesday, 26. We came to Hugh Porter's, at the New Design.[143]

[138] King's Chapel was near the Powell home. It was named for the Rev. James King who served the Saluda Circuit in 1796 and died of yellow fever in Charleston the following year at the age of twenty-five. (Betts, *op. cit.*, 101.)

[139] Pension's or Pinson's Ford was below Ware Shoals. Here Asbury and Whatcoat entered the present Greenwood (then Abbeville) County.

[140] George Connor lived near Greenwood in the old Tabernacle Church community, where was later established the Tabernacle Academy of which the famous Dr. Stephen Olin became principal in 1821 and near where Cokesbury School was later founded. The Silvador Purchase or "Jew's Land" was a tract of around 100,000 acres purchased by Joseph Silvador, a wealthy Portuguese Jew of London. Here he proposed to establish a colony of European Jews and just before the Revolution the owner's nephew and son-in-law, Francis Silvador, was sent over to manage the project, but he was killed in an expedition against the Cherokees in 1776, and the management fell to Richard Andrew Rapley. The enterprise failed, and the land was disposed of by Rapley as attorney for Silvador. (Betts, *op. cit.*, 484.)

[141] Northern abolitionists had sent some printed antislavery addresses to the Rev. John Harper, pastor at Charleston. He stored them away, but a copy got into circulation and enraged the people. Harper was brought before the authorities, and he explained the situation and burned the remaining papers. No charge was laid against him, but he was later seized by a mob, from which he escaped. The Rev. George Dougherty, the other preacher, was seized at the prayer meeting the following night and held under the spout of a pump until he was nearly drowned. (Betts, *op. cit.*, 91, 92.) It was later said that Dougherty was assaulted because he had been teaching Negro children. (*Methodist Magazine*, 1828, 349–53.)

[142] Nathaniel Burdine lived near Ninety Six.

[143] Hugh Porter probably lived near the present Callison. He was a prosperous farmer. In 1802 he joined the conference on trial and located in 1807. (See *Minutes*;

Here we called a meeting in the evening; brother Whatcoat spoke—I spoke after him.

Thursday, 27. Sick and weary, we arrived at Daniel Baugh's, whither we were conducted by Mr. Hennington, having lost our way in the woods.

Friday, 28. At Butler's meeting house,[144] fifteen miles—no notice; we therefore pushed on to Captain Carter's[145]; here the girls hasted to call the people to meeting. Brother Whatcoat preached on Ezek. xxxiii, 2. In this neighbourhood the sad apostasy of two professed preachers, and of one or two private members, hath brought reproach on the cause of God and Methodism.

Georgia

Saturday, 29. Came twelve miles through deep sands to Augusta. We have travelled nearly one hundred miles since last Sabbath day: my soul hath been kept in great peace; but I feel the effects of riding a stiff, aged, falling horse, with a sore back, and my saddle is old and worn.

We have a foundation and a frame prepared for erecting, in a day or two, a house for public worship, two stories high, sixty by forty feet; for this we are indebted to the favour of Heaven and the agency of Stith Mead;[146] and what is better, here is a small society.

Augusta is decidedly one of the most level and beautiful spots for a town I have yet seen:[147] it is of ample extent in its plan, well begun, and

Betts, *op. cit.*, 483, 484.) The reference to the New Design is obscure. It may have been a large tract of land south of Silvador's Purchase in lower Abbeville and McCormick counties. This was a Huguenot settlement known as New Bordeaux, which survives as the Bordeaux community near the Savannah River where the John de la Howe School is operated by the state of South Carolina. (See Willson's historial address, 7, and S.C. Legislative Manual, 1950.)

[144] Butler's meetinghouse was between the Little Saluda River and Big Creek in Saluda County.

[145] Captain Carter lived below the present town of Trenton in Edgefield County.

[146] Stith Mead was on the Burke and Augusta Circuit with William Avant. At the conference held at Camden, South Carolina, in January he was made presiding elder of the Georgia District. He was the founder of Methodism in Augusta and elsewhere in Georgia and one of the leading preachers in the state. He was born in Virginia but was brought to Augusta while a lad by his wealthy father, Colonel William Mead, and attended Augusta Academy. He went back to Virginia, where he was converted at a Bedford County camp meeting and joined the conference, traveling seven years there before returning to Augusta, where there was no organized church. His relatives opposed him, and he preached in the home of Ebeneezer Doughty, where he formed a class of six members in 1798. The church being built when Asbury came was on Green Street where St. John Methodist Church now stands. It was the only church in Augusta except St. Paul's Episcopal Church, and Mead's society was the first organized band of Christians there after the Revolution; there seems to have been no regular rector at St. Paul's. (Smith: *Georgia Methodism*, 338–40.)

[147] Augusta was the capitol of the state and had a population of about four thousand. It was founded in 1732 as a fort and trading post for the Cherokee, Uchee, and Chick-

when their intention shall be fulfilled of building a court house, a college, episcopal churches for Methodists and others, it will do credit to its founders and inhabitants.

Sabbath day, 30. Brother Whatcoat preached a most excellent sermon at Mr. Fary's dwelling house upon Ephraim's lamentation. In the afternoon I preached in the church.[148] We thought to have joined the congregations together, but others thought differently. We had the honour of the priest's company, and few of his people attended.[149]

Monday, December 1. We came to Thomas Hayne's, upon Uchee Creek, Columbia county. Brother Whatcoat preached upon Gal. ii, 20. I came off with a close exhortation.

On the following *Tuesday* and *Wednesday* we held a quarterly meeting at White Oak. Brother Whatcoat first officiated. I followed him. We had very cold weather, an open house, and few hearers. We then rode to Joseph Scott's eight miles, through damp, rainy weather. Our host, his children, and grandchildren will, we hope, if they continue faithful, receive the crown of life.

Thursday, 4. I rode, my mind cloudy, and my body cold, to Thomas Grant's, twenty-four miles.

Friday, 5. I humbled my soul before God. To-day I have been occupied in correcting a transcript of my journal, that one had copied for me, who did not well understand my shorthand. The original was written in my great illness, very imperfectly; but when I reflect on my situation at that time, I wonder that it is as well as it is.

Sabbath day, 7. Yesterday and to-day we have quarterly meeting at Coke's chapel, near Washington. Brother Whatcoat preached the first day from Heb. vi, 4–6. I, in my place, gave some account of the work of God, as it had been reported to me during this year. On *Sabbath morning* we had a quickening season at the sacrament. My subject was Heb. xii, 25: "See that ye refuse not him that speaketh." By introduction—The likeness between Christ and Moses in their persons, offices, ministry, and punishment of the disobedient. In doctrine: I. How Christ, speaking by his Gospel, his ministers, Spirit, and miracles of grace. II. That sinners, seekers, saints, and backsliders ought to see to it, that they "refuse not him that speaketh." Lastly: the awful consequences of refusing. Brothers

asaw Indians, and named for the daughter of George II. St. Paul's parish was laid out about 1757, and some missionaries of the Society for the Propagation of the Gospel in Foreign Parts were sent, but in 1782 the Grand Jury pointed out that there was no church in Augusta or Richmond County. It was the first large center in which Methodism was established in Georgia. The first Methodist preachers to visit the town were probably Thomas Humphries and John Major, who perhaps arrived sometime before 1789. (*Ibid.*, 337, 338.)

148 St. Paul's Episcopal Church. (*Ibid.*, 66.)

149 "As there were quite a number of French refugee Catholics from Haiti, it is probable that the priest was a Roman Catholic." (*Ibid.*)

Whatcoat and Hope Hull exhorted; the latter began to feel like his former self. Upon the whole, it was a good meeting, and we humbly hope that good was done. After meeting we were obliged to ride six miles, through the rain, to Thomas Grant's.

Monday, 8. We crossed Little River, and went forward twelve miles, to Thomas Fountain's, in Warren county. We have ridden about ninety miles since Monday week.

Tuesday, 9. We came to Abraham Heath's meeting house upon Long Creek, Warren county. We arrived during the sitting of the court, and had but a small congregation. Brother Whatcoat being unwell, I filled his place. My subject was Heb. x, 31: "It is a fearful thing to fall into the hands of the living God." First, The character of those people who expose themselves to the danger of falling "into the hands of the living God"—such as are described in verses 26 and 29 of the same chapter. Secondly, The character of those, the contrast of the former, who will escape his avenging hand. These do not as the others do. They also attend to the precepts contained in verses 25, 32, 35, 36, and 39. Thirdly, "It is a fearful thing to fall into the hands of the living God,"—that is, to fear and feel the wrath of God forever, having no interest in Christ, and no advocate with the Father, but exposed to infinite justice, and all the threatened wrath of the Almighty.

We crossed Ogeechee at Thweat's bridge, and came to Powelton,[150] a new establishment, in which there is a Baptist meeting house, formerly occupied by Silas Mercer. He is now gone to eternity, but his son filleth his place.

Wednesday, 10. We came to Edmund Butler's in Hancock county. The people had thrown down the old, but had not yet finished their new meeting house.[151] I was therefore under the necessity of standing bareheaded in the open woods, on a very cold day. As I travelled so much, this was thought a light thing for a man like me. Moses Black,[152] after this, brought the people to the dwelling house. We rode home with Alexander King,[153] a brother to the preacher who ended a short but honourable life in the ministry of the Gospel.

Thursday, 11. We were at Burke's meeting house; after which we came dripping to A. Gilmore's. Here brother Whatcoat preached. After which I gave a few words of exhortation, and we then pushed on to William

[150] The Ogeechee is on the border of Warren and Hancock counties, and Powelton is in the northeastern corner of the latter.

[151] Since the meetinghouse in Hancock County was old enough to be replaced, it must have been on the old Richmond Circuit and was founded before the county was set up in 1793. The first missionary came to the county in 1792. (*Ibid.*)

[152] Moses Black was the preacher on the Richmond Circuit. (See *Minutes*.)

[153] The brother was the Rev. James King. (See *Journal* entry and note for November 23, 1800.)

Greaves's. We have lately crossed the chief branches of the Ogeechee and Little rivers.

Friday, 12. Cold as it was we made as far as Thomas Dunn's; and here I gave a short discourse on 2 Tim. iv, 6, 7. We left Dunn's in haste, and continued on twelve miles farther to the widow Hill's, on Long Creek. These last appointments were in Oglethorpe county. They will be the best judges of the severity of the cold, who have ridden seventeen miles before dinner. I met brother Milligan,[154] at brother Dunn's, and should have been pleased to stay there with him, but the situation of his wife subjected us to the risk of being disturbed and driven from our warm lodging at midnight. We have ridden about sixty miles in four days.

Saturday, 13. We came to Mark's meeting house;[155] brother Whatcoat filled the pulpit.

Sunday, 14. We had sacrament and sermon: my subject was Matt. xvii, 5: "This is my beloved Son, in whom I am well pleased; hear ye him." Introduction. These words were in part spoken at his baptism; see Matt. iii, 17; Mark i, 2; Luke iii, 22: that there were three witnesses present to hear, and four had recorded it; to wit, Matthew, Mark, Luke, and Peter. First, the Divine Father acknowledged the sacred and mysterious union—"This is my beloved Son": a relation infinitely above that of angels, of Adam in his primeval standing, and the souls of any regenerated sanctified, or glorified soul, on earth or in heaven—co-equal, co-eternal, and co-essential with the Father. "Well-pleased!"—that is, in the whole of man's redemption by this "beloved Son": "well-pleased"—in his preaching, living, dying—in every part of his official character. "Hear ye him"—Mark and Luke have omitted *ye*. Secondly, The particular characters who should hear him in his word, Spirit, and operations. His ministers should hear him—this was designed in the text, by *ye*: hear him all his sanctified souls; hear him all who are justified; hear him all ye seekers; hear him all ye sinners—hear his awful warnings: all ye backsliders, hear him as Peter heard him, and repent, and turn to him; hear him ye apostates, as Judas, and despair.

We must needs go to the house after preaching, and dine; then we had to cross Broad River, and pierce through the woods, *scratch and go in* the by-paths—wind round the plantations—creep across the newly cleared

[154] Thomas Milligan was one of the three preachers on the Washington and Oconee Circuit. (See *Minutes*.)

[155] James Marks came from Virginia and lived northwest of Washington River. He was one of the early Methodists of Georgia, and his meetinghouse was one of the first churches; Smith says that the first conference in the state was held at his home. (See note under April 9, 1788.) On the Broad farther north lived John Marks, brother of James, a Revolutionary soldier, whose step-son was Meriwether Lewis, private secretary to Thomas Jefferson and one of the leaders of the famous Lewis and Clark expedition to the Northwest. (Bowen: *Story of Wilkes County*, 58.)

ground by clambering over trees, boughs, and fence rails. Thus we made our way fifteen miles to Charles Tait's,[156] in Elbert county.

Monday, 15. We got over Savannah river at Robert Martin's ferry, a few miles above Petersburg.[157] Here I called upon a family I had often visited in Virginia. I found the parents had grown old, and that they had lost some of their children.

South Carolina

We came onward into Abbeville county, and hastened to John Brunner's[158] near the court house; making a ride of thirty miles for the day.

Tuesday, 16. We proceeded to Silvador's Purchase, twelve miles, to hold quarterly meeting for Bush River circuit, at a meeting house near George Connor's.[159]

Wednesday, 17. I attended quarterly meeting. My subject was Philip. i, 27. We spent four hours in the private and public meeting; a number of white and black children were to be baptized, and probably there were persons who thought *it would be better done by a bishop*. After meeting we had a fifteen miles' ride, part of it in the night, crossing Saluda at Child's ferry, wishing to get to John Weeks's,[160] in Lauren's county. Abbeville is a large county, stretching from river to river, and holds better lands than any other in the State. Although Bush River circuit extends through it, there are few Methodists; the most populous settlements being composed of Presbyterians.

Thursday, 18. At John Weeks's, brother Whatcoat sermonized upon Gal. vi, 15.

Friday, 19. It rained. After it had holden up, we rode thirty miles to Benjamin Herndon's,[161] upon the waters of Enoree.

Saturday and *Sunday*, 20, 21. Held quarterly meeting. Brother Whatcoat spoke from 1 Thess. iii, 8; a very profitable improvement. On *Sabbath day* my choice was Acts iii, 22, 23. We continued about six hours at Mount

[156] Colonel Charles Tait lived five miles south of Elberton on Highway 17. According to Georgia tradition Asbury held the first conference there in 1788, and a marker stands on the spot. (See note under April 9, 1788.)

[157] Martin's Ferry was between Calhoun Falls and Lowndesville, South Carolina. The old town of Petersburg lay directly in the forks of the Broad and Savannah rivers. It was once an important place but became practically abandoned and is now covered by the waters of the Clark-Hill Reservoir. (See *Journal* entry and note for April 9, 1788.)

[158] John Brunner lived near Abbeville.

[159] This meetinghouse was between Hodges and Coronaca. It was soon known as the Tabernacle. Just east of the chapel was a little school of which Olin later became principal. (See note under November 23, 1800.)

[160] John Weeks lived near Cross Hill.

[161] Colonel Benjamin Herndon lived near the present Whitmire.

Bethel. I saw one of the members of the General Assembly of South Carolina, who informed me that our address from the General Conference had been read and reprobated; and furthermore, that it had been the occasion of producing a law which prohibited a minister's attempting to instruct any number of blacks with the doors shut; and authorizing a peace officer to break open the door in such cases, and disperse or whip the offenders. But more of this law when I see it.

Monday, 22. We rode to Thomas Hardy's, in the forks of Enoree and Tyger rivers[162]—nine miles.

Tuesday, 23. At Beauford's meeting house, brother Whatcoat performed upon Philip. iii, 14. We went forward twelve miles to Mr. Glenn's[163] at Broad River.

I have had heartfelt sorrow for the Church of God in Philadelphia. No city upon our continent has been more oppressed by divisions in Christian societies: witness the Episcopalians, Presbyterians, German and English, Quakers, Baptists, Scotch Presbyterians, Roman Catholics—and now the Methodists: I have written on this subject to three official characters.

Wednesday, 24. I gave a sermon upon 2 Peter i, 4, at Glenn's chapel,[164] near Broad River: we had an open season and many hearers. At Glenn's Flat, Chester county, Sealley's meeting house,[165] we kept our Christmas. Brother Whatcoat preached on, "The Son of God was manifested to destroy the works of the devil."

My subject was, "Glory to God in the highest; and on earth peace, good will towards men."

We lodged at Robert Walker's, eighty years of age, awakened under Mr. Whitefield in Fogg's Manor—re-awakened at Pipe Creek, and a member of the first Methodist Society in Maryland: he is now living upon Sandy River, South Carolina.[166]

Friday, 26. We travelled a barren path, and came to Alexander Carter's upon Fishing Creek[167]—a journey of about thirty miles, without food for man or beast, and the weather warm to great excess: after our arrival we had a night meeting.

Saturday, 27. After waiting the leisure of the boatmen, we crossed

[162] Hardy did not live exactly in the forks since the Tyger flows into the Broad River several miles above the junction of the Enoree.

[163] Glenn's Ferry was above Carlisle.

[164] Glenn's Chapel was probably on the Chester side of Broad River. James E. and John B. Glenn, both prominent preachers, came from the family which built the chapel; the former was responsible for the conversion of Stephen Olin when Olin was teaching in the Mount Ariel Academy and boarded in the Glenn home. (Betts, *op. cit.*, 174, 175.)

[165] Seally's meetinghouse was several miles east of Chester. Glenn's Flat and Glenn's Ferry may not have been identical.

[166] Robert Walker's Mill was located on Sandy River, several miles southwest of Chester. (See *Mill's Atlas.*)

[167] Carter lived near where Fishing Creek enters the Catawba.

Catabaw at Wade's ferry, and came three miles to a meeting house at Camp Creek,[168] to attend quarterly meeting for Santee and Catabaw circuits. We lodged at John Grymast's, a Methodist, and originally from Ireland.

Sabbath day, 28. Damp morning. I gave a discourse on Eph. vi, 10. Our lodging was at Johnson's.[169]

Monday, 29. We stopped at Georgetown, at Marlow's.[170] Brother Whatcoat preached upon, "Thou wilt keep him in perfect peace whose mind is stayed on thee; because he trusteth in thee." We made eighteen miles' progress this day, and put up with John Horton upon Hanging Rock River.

Tuesday, 30. Came to Camden. I have received several letters from the North: they bring small consolation—"While he was yet speaking there came also another"—murmurs—complaints of partiality—and with this I may console myself in the midst of unremitted and hard travelling and labour. I was presented with a petition from about eighty male members of the society in *the city of brotherly love*, entreating me to do what I had no intention of doing—that was, to remove brother Everett[171] from the city: how, indeed, was this to be done? He and they had acquitted M. Manly of all the charges brought against him, and restored him to membership; the presiding elder had also restored to office three or four elders who had been put out for murmurings and mischiefs, and had ejected the elder stationed in the city, and had filled his place by another—and they had great congregations, great shoutings; and God was with them, and nearly one hundred had joined society. To all this what can we do but say, "Well done, good and faithful servant" and servants! Poor bishop! no money for my expenses. I am afflicted—my life threatened on the one hand, my brethren discontented on the other: true, I received from them a petition dipped in oil and honey; and if I approve, all will be well; but if not, drawn swords may be feared.

[168] Camp Creek meetinghouse was seven miles southwest of Lancaster. It is still in existence.

[169] Johnson lived on Camp Creek, as did Mr. Grymast (or Bermast), with whom Asbury lodged on the night of December 27.

[170] Georgetown was an unidentified community in Lancaster County, not to be confused with the city of Georgetown above Charleston.

[171] The Rev. Joseph Everett was the presiding elder at Philadelphia.

1801

1801 *Asbury misses a Georgetown appointment because of a late ferry*

CHAPTER THIRTY

South Carolina

THURSDAY, *January* 1, 1801. We began our conference with the new year. Sat from nine to twelve o'clock in the forenoon, and two hours in the afternoon; the band meeting was held between the hours of seven and eight. A clerk for the minutes was appointed, and another to keep the journal.[1] We admitted four probationers; re-admitted two deacons to their standing in the travelling connexion, who had left it to locate; located three, to wit, Benjamin Blanton, Josiah Cole, and Llewellin Evans;[2] and re-stationed, Robert Gains, Rufus Wiley, and William West, who had all located themselves in the course of the last year. We had great union: it is true, some talked loud; but I dare not say there was any improper heat. Our sitting continued five days, and we rested one *Sabbath*. We were richly accommodated at Smith's[3] and Carpenter's, and two other houses. We only failed forty-eight dollars in paying all the preachers their demands.

Thursday, 8. Yesterday and to-day I have been busy writing many long letters to my correspondents in the north.[4]

[1] Shipp says Jeremiah Newman was appointed to keep the *Journal*. (*Op. cit.*, 308.)

[2] The loss of preachers through marriage or "family connections" was heavy. Thirty-two preachers located in all the conferences in 1800, among them being Enoch George, who located because of ill health, was readmitted in 1803, and became a bishop in 1816 to succeed Asbury, who died on the road while en route to the General Conference.

[3] The Rev. Isaac Smith, one of the fathers of South Carolina Methodism, located in 1796 and lived in Camden. He was readmitted in 1820. He was the grandfather of the Georgia Methodist historian George G. Smith.

[4] See letters to Stith Mead, January 6 and 8, 1801, and to Ezekiel Cooper, January 7, 1801.

Friday, 9. We came on thirteen miles to Granney's quarterly meeting, and lodged at Anthony Pressley's.

Saturday, 10. I gave a short discourse upon 2 Peter iv, 3, and afterward rode up eight miles to the Hanging Rock.

Sunday, 11. At Horton's meeting house I spoke on Heb. viii, 10, 11.

Monday, 12. On this day we rested, and were busily employed in looking over our books and papers.

I felt deeply affected for the rising generation. Having resolved to catechise the children myself, I procured a Scripture catechism, and began with brother Horton's; to this duty I purpose to attend in every house where leisure and opportunity may permit.

Wednesday, 14. We left Hanging Rock and came to Little Lynch and Flat Creeks, crossing the great branch at McManus's ford; this last is called a creek; but it rises near the Waxaws, and flows about one hundred and fifty miles, mingling its waters with the great Pee Dee below Port's ferry. We had an excessively warm day for the season: the horses and their riders were both fatigued much in riding forty miles in ten hours. Seated upon the sandhills, we dined, at the root of a pine, upon a morsel of bread and bacon; and then remounted and pushed on to Anson in North Carolina.

North Carolina

We sheltered ourselves for the night at Thomas Shaw's,[5] upon Little Thompson's creek.

Thursday, 15. We are still at Thomas Shaw's. What kind of folks am I among—unhappy people! One aged man had shot the constable when about to serve a warrant on him; a second had stabbed another dangerously—their names may go into shades. O sin! O intoxication! when—when will these people be civilized—and all be truly spiritualized.

On *Friday* we attended at Jackson's meeting house; it was a gracious season. Bishop Whatcoat spoke on Isa. xii, 2. We lodged at Stephen Pace's, upon Brown's Creek.

Saturday, 17. We had a meeting at John Mills's; his wife came from Maryland, he from Virginia; the children are coming to Christ. This neighbourhood is visited with a revival of religion.

Sabbath day, 18. We came to Wadesboro after a court week. We held our meeting underneath the court house, within the arches: we had a most delightful day. Bishop Whatcoat spoke with great ingenuity and authority

[5] The Rev. Thomas Shaw lived across the line in Anson County, North Carolina. In 1800 he had been on the Great Pee Dee and Georgetown Circuit, and in 1801 he was on the Little Pee Dee and Anson Circuit. His work was on both sides of the state line, and he doubtless had a home, probably a farm, on the North Carolina side.

upon "The wages of sin is death; but the gift of God is eternal life." My subject was Luke xviii, 27. We lodged at I. Cash's.

Monday, 19. We came to Webb's ferry: the rain drove us under the roof of the widow Williams, where we remained until the storm was over, and then pushed on to James Pickett's, in Richmond county.

Tuesday, 20. I gave a discourse on Amos vi, 1: "Woe to them that are at ease in Zion!" I felt some openings.

I have had many and great exercises of mind respecting men and things, but my soul enjoys great resignation: I take the *bitters* of life as things which medicine my soul, producing caution, humiliation, and sanctification.

Wednesday, 21. We rode ten miles to the Presbyterian meeting house: many attended at a short warning. My subject was Heb. vii, 25. We had a quickening season. After meeting we rode three miles to Rockingham,[6] the seat of justice for the county of the same name. We had been expected at twelve o'clock, hence with this circumstance, and that of court time to boot, we had but few hearers. Meeting was held in the academy, a very commodious house for Divine service. Rockingham stands upon a beautiful eminence, and hath some valuable houses; about twenty families make the inhabitants. We were kindly and elegantly entertained at the house of one who had been one of us, but now is of and in the world.

Thursday, 22. We came to Mark's Creek. I spoke on Heb. iii, 13–15. We had a good season. We lodged with Solomon Rye.

South Carolina

We now descended into South Carolina. Marlborough county presents many interesting views—the saw-mills; the solitary, lofty, long-leaved pines; and the land, though a *barren*, is of the most beautiful kind, and for range for cattle and for timber is very valuable. It was my lot to be speaker, brother Whatcoat had taken so deep a cold he could do nothing. I preached from the parable of the sower.

We continued our journey down Naked Creek, by Robinson's house, mills, and *stills*, and brought up at Turbot Cottingham's, at the Beauty Spot.[7] Notwithstanding all that Methodists, Baptists, and three meeting houses have done, the people are still far from *beautiful* in a spiritual sense. We had no opportunity to send harbingers, we had therefore no appointment.

[6] Asbury was in error when he said Rockingham was the county seat of the county of the same name. It is the county seat of Richmond County. Rockingham County is in the northern part of North Carolina on the Virginia border.

[7] The Beauty Spot was three miles northeast of Bennettsville in Marlboro County, South Carolina.

Saturday, 24. We hasted to James Speers's, at the Three Creeks,[8] where we dined, talked, and commended ourselves to God. That we might make our own appointments at Harris's meeting house[9] we came on to James Harris's upon Muddy Creek. Brother Speers spread the tidings for us far and wide.

This is an unhappy country: it is thinly settled, and many are moving away to Georgia and the Natchez; our societies are small, and the prospect low. Too often, when any rise in their circumstances, they seek for offices, or become slave traders, and much too great to be Methodists.

We have ridden since the commencement of the year one hundred and eighty miles in the Carolinas.

Monday, 26. We rode twenty miles to Bennet Flowers';[10] the men were from home, but the women gave notice of a meeting for the morrow at the old meeting house. After our meeting, about one o'clock, we came off and travelled down to Gaspero Sweet's, Bull Swamp, Liberty county: we sent our host to call a congregation for *Thursday*. We now had time to read and write.

I find reasons enough in my own mind to justify myself against the low murmurs of *partialty* in which some have indulged. We are impartial. We spend as much time in the extremities. We know not Maryland or Delaware, *after the flesh*, more than Kentucky, Cumberland, Georgia, or the Carolinas: it is our duty to save the health of preachers where we can; to make particular appointments for some important charges; and it is our duty to embrace all parts of the continent and union, after the example of primitive times and the first faithful preachers in America.

Thursday, 29. At Sweet's chapel I preached on Rev. xxii, 14, 15. The order, 1. The city. 2. The citizens. 3. Their admission. 4. The characters shut out from the city. I felt light and liberty.

Friday, 30. We came to the Bear Pond's school house,[11] where we had a decent, attentive congregation. I preached on John vii, 16, 17. Introduction.—It was observed that the dispute of the Jews with our Lord about the Messiah, was not if he should be the eternal Son of God, and the adopted son of man, but whether Jesus was that person whom Moses foretold that Church and nation should come, and what manner of person he should be, fifteen hundred years before. The Jews knew where Christ was to be born from Micah v, 2. See also Matt. ii.

Mr. Shacklesford gave us a pressing invitation to dine with him, and treated us with friendship and hospitality. We rode in the evening to Port's ferry.

[8] Three Creeks was near Blenheim.

[9] Harris's meetinghouse was near Brownsville.

[10] Bennet Flowers lived one mile north of Marion.

[11] There was a Bear Pond meetinghouse adjacent to the school. It was originally Sweet's meetinghouse.

Thomas Humphries[12] had been very sick, but was recovering from a perpneumony: it was reported he would die; but I did not feel as if he would die at this time.

Sure nothing could so effectually alarm and arm the citizens of South Carolina against the Methodists as the *Address of the General Conference.* The rich among the people never thought us worthy to preach to them: they did indeed give their slaves liberty to hear and join our Church; but now it appears the poor Africans will no longer have this indulgence. Perhaps we shall soon be thought unfit for the company of their dogs. But who will mourn the loss of the friendship of the world that hath so hated our Lord and Master Jesus Christ?

We have loitered away this month, and have ridden but about two hundred miles.

Saturday, 31. We rested: wrote,[13] and read, upon the solitary unhealthy banks of Pee Dee, in sight of the lofty moss-grown cypress trees and swamps. My soul is in peace; Jesus, Jesus is my all: my soul is love to God, to Christ, his Church, and all souls.

Sabbath day, February 1. We rode six miles to Brittons Neck meeting house,[14] where I preached on Luke xix, 10: "The Son of Man is come to seek and to save that which was lost." What characters were lost—not in a state of salvation: open, profane sinners; those who had sinned away conviction; backsliders; such as were seeking salvation by works; avowed infidels. It was observed that many were lost to men and means; occasioned hindrances themselves, and were prevented by others.

We came to William Williams's, near Little Pee Dee. On *Monday* we were housed by the rain in the forepart of the day: in the afternoon we visited Richard Woodbury, a great man, weighing upwards of three hundred pounds, and as kind as weighty.

Tuesday, 3. We had preaching at William Williams's: there were few people.

Wednesday, 4. We crossed Little Pee Dee at the Potato Bed ferry. Beautiful deep sands, live oaks, lofty pines, palmetto swamps, with intermingled gums and cypresses, variegated by evergreens of bay and laurel, and twining jessamine flinging its odours far and wide around; lawns and savannahs: such is the country, and such the charming scenes through which we have frequently passed in our late rides. We brought up at Richard Green's, near Kingston.[15]

[12] The Rev. Thomas Humphries lived on his plantation on Jeffers Creek four or five miles above Port's Ferry. He joined the conference in 1783 and preached in Virginia, Georgia, and the Carolinas, and located in 1799. He became a prosperous rice planter. (Betts, *op. cit.*, 72.)

[13] See letter to Daniel Hitt, January 30, 1801.

[14] Britton's Neck Church was in the lower part of Marion (then Liberty) County.

[15] Kingston was the present Conway, South Carolina. (See letter to George Roberts, February 4, 1801.)

Thursday, 5. Counsel and conversation with the presiding elders, several long letters to the north and south, and reading, furnished occupation for the day. I received the compilation of Nicholas Snethen, intended as an answer to James O'Kelly: it is well done, and very correctly done, except in a few cases. There was no sharpness at all upon my side with Doctor Coke at Charleston respecting the proposed general conference, which was afterward held (in 1792):[16] I was fully convinced that nothing *else* would finish the unhappy business with O'Kelly; and that did finish it.

Friday, 6. Occupied in reading and writing.[17] The preachers had not yet made out our plan for a forward move. One Sabbath day yet at Kingston, and then we keep along towards the lovely north.

Saturday, 7. I rode to Robert Anderson's,[18] in the Swamps, and met about thirty souls, to whom I spoke on Ephes. ii, 8–10. Returned to Richard Green's.

Sabbath day, 8. At Kingston. A lovely day; but few people—perhaps not more than one hundred, including the coloured folks. My subject was Luke ix, 24. Brother Whatcoat spoke on John iii, 16. It is now sixteen years since I rode, anxious and solitary, through this part of the land; there was scarcely a house to receive me, and no Methodist to bid me welcome; but God hath given us many friends, of some of those whose houses I lodged in; witness the children of Mr. Clark, and of Durant—and their widows also.

We have been obliged to rest on *Thursday*, *Friday*, *Saturday*, *Sabbath day*, and *Monday*, 9th, with Richard Green. Mr. Rogers will not give us an invitation: his kindness towards the Methodists is at an end.[19]

Tuesday, 10. We rode sixteen miles to Kullum's meeting house:[20] it was a cold day, and coming after such warm weather, its severity was the more sensibly felt; about midday it rained powerfully. My subject was Heb. ii, 1. After meeting we rode to father Kullum's, an old Maryland man, from Dorset county. Here I met Benjamin Sellers, a local preacher, and a faithful servant of God.

Wednesday, 11. We went forward to William Norton's,[21] at the Iron Run; a distance of twelve miles, through swampy ground. Brother Whatcoat preached, and ordained brother Sellers a deacon. I spoke from Gal. iv, 19. It was a disagreeable time, the people were trembling with cold.

[16] See note under March 23, 1791.

[17] See letter to Thomas Morrell, February 6, 1801.

[18] Robert Anderson lived seven miles north of Kingston, the present Conway, near the present Poplar Methodist Church.

[19] W. Rogers lived a short distance south of Kingston, the present Conway. He came from Bristol, England. He had entertained Asbury on December 24, 1795, December 26, 1796, and February 5, 1797 (?). The cause of his coldness in 1801 is not known, but it was a temporary matter since he entertained Asbury again on January 11, 1802.

[20] Kullum and Kullum meetinghouse are unidentified.

[21] Mr. Norton lived near the present Loris in Horry County near the North Carolina line.

North Carolina

Thursday, 12. We rode twenty miles to Frinke's.[22]

Friday, 13.—At Ebenezer:—the house was unfinished and the day windy and uncomfortable. Brother Whatcoat and myself held the people nearly three hours. My text was Gal. vi, 14–16.

A Solomon Reeves let me know that he had seen the *Address*, signed by me; and was quite confident there were no arguments to prove that slavery was repugnant to the spirit of the Gospel: what absurdities will not men defend! If the Gospel will tolerate slavery, what will it not authorize? I am strangely mistaken if this said Mr. Reeves has more grace than is necessary, or more of *Solomon* than the name. We lodged for the night at William Gore's.

From this neighbourhood we came to Abraham Bepent's, Brunswick county, North Carolina, fording the Seven-mile Creek, and crossing the Wacamaw River at Loftus's Flat.

We have ridden at least five hundred and fifty, if not six hundred miles, over the hills, barrens, swamps, savannahs, rivers, and creeks of South Carolina.

At Gause's Manor, or more properly *town*, we were pleasantly situated. I had a most solemn visit to the sea beach, which to me was a most instructive sight: the sea reminded me of its great Maker, "who stayeth the proud waves thereof"; its innumerable productions; the diversified features of its shores—the sandhills; the marsh; the palmetto, tall and slender; the sheep and goats frisking in the shade or browsing in the sun: or the eye, directed to the waters, beholds the rolling porpoise; the seagulls lifting and letting fall from high the clam, which, breaking, furnishes them with food; the eagles with hovering wings watching for their prey; the white sail of the solitary vessel tossed upon the distant wave—how interesting a picture do all these objects make!

We preached at William Gause's, the patriarch of the place: his son stood for scribe, and assisted me in making extracts of letters to add to my manuscript.

We visited Charlotte meeting house, named after the river, vulgarly and improperly called *Shalotte*. On our return, I prepared a few long letters for the north.

My mind is in great peace. I lament that I have no access to the poor: our way is strangely closed up at present in consequence of the *Address*. I made my last visit to the sea. I thought upon my friends on the other side the great waters; my voyage to this country; the little probability there was of my ever again seeing my dear mother, or my native land.

[22] Asbury must have entered North Carolina in the present Columbus County, then a part of Brunswick County.

We have had preaching in three or four places: to wit, at Bepent's, in Brunswick county, and at the Manor.

Sunday, 22. We attended a meeting at Lockwood's Folly. I gave a sermon upon 2 Cor. iv, 5. 1. What the apostles of our Lord did *not* preach. 2. What they did preach. 3. The relation of ministers to Christ and to souls. The principles of their service. They sought not their own honour, ease, or interest—they did not make disciples for themselves—they had not wisdom, righteousness, redemption, for souls; nor grace to convict, convert, or regenerate. They preached Christ in his prophetic, priestly, and kingly offices—in his Gospel; in the sacrifice, once offered, of himself—in his Divinity. "Ourselves your servants for Christ's sake,"—his saved, his qualified, his commissioned servants (not slaves)—bound by his word, his grace, his love—not for any worldly consideration, but "for Christ's sake": warning sinners, hypocrites, Pharisees, and backsliders;—comforting mourners; strengthening believers, and urging and inciting to holiness of heart and life. I observed, "servants," yet their rulers; according to Scripture testimony—see Heb. xiii, 17; 1 Peter v, 2.

We were kindly entertained at Mr. Bellon's: the whole family came to the house of public entertainment, eight miles from their dwelling, to make us comfortable.

Monday, 23. Rode to Edward Sullivan's, at Town Creek—eighteen miles.

Tuesday, 24. I preached: my subject was Luke iv, 18. We had a full house. I baptized three adults, and as many children.

Wednesday, 25. We dined with General Smith—there was abundance of hospitality. We came into town. Jeremiah Norman[23] gave us a sermon. Our tabernacle is crowded again: the minds of the people are strangely changed; and the indignation excited against us is overpast: the people see and confess that the slaves are made better by religion; and wonder to hear the poor Africans pray and exhort.

Thursday, 26. I preached, for the first time, in our house, and for the second in Wilmington: my text was found in Acts xxvi, 17, 18. At eleven o'clock we were crowded; and I felt uncommon enlargement. One of the *respectables* came in the name of some of the *reputables* to request that I would preach in the ancient, venerable brick church: I was weak—had spoken long and loud, and was more than ordinarily unwell; but brother Whatcoat was unwell and not able to go out. At four o'clock we had a large and decent congregation—I lectured upon Romans x, 1–4. In the evening, numbers, both white and black, came again to the tabernacle. After Jeremiah Norman had preached, I read, and commented upon two letters respecting the work of God in Delaware, and Cumberland, in the West.

Friday, 27. We came off early and travelled on to Nixon's, through

[23] Jeremiah Norman was on the Bladen Circuit at this time. (*Minutes.*)

dews, damps, and rain—a great part of the way weary, pained, and sleepy, for want of rest. I gave a discourse on Matt. xi, 28–30.

Saturday, 28. About sunrise we hasted away and came to Lot Ballard's at the Rich Lands, New River, about forty miles: we stopped not on the way. I unfortunately left my famous spectacles behind: I had laid them by, overwhelmed with drowsiness, and failed to take them up to read a chapter, as is my custom, except upon such over-doing journeys. We walked our horses at the rate of four miles an hour: my poor nag limped. I thought it was owing to the bad state of his shoes, when, behold, an oyster shell had wedged itself in the hollow of his hoof, near the heel.

Sunday, March 1. At New River I preached on Luke xix, 10. We had a very serious but unaffected congregation.

Joseph Ballard, and his wife Mary Ballard, are gone to rest, after a respectable profession of religion amongst the Methodists, for seventeen or eighteen years. John Perry, a pious soul, formerly of the Baptists, and an official character amongst them, is also gone to his reward. He had backslidden; but was restored among the Methodists, and became a preacher and deacon: he died upon the road, going to an appointment: neither he nor Ballard held slaves—hail, happy souls!

Monday, 2. We had to march down upon Trenton, sixteen miles. The appointed meeting had been transferred to Frederick Argate's, occasioned by the death of his venerable mother, the respectable wife of General Frederick Argate, who had been suddenly called away. This lady justly deserved the great and good character she had for forty years preserved, as a wife, a mother, a mistress, and a friend: to relieve the poor, and to solace the afflicted, gave her pleasure and occupation almost uninterrupted. *Thursday* week she was at meeting—the following, she was a corpse. My subject on this solemn funeral occasion, was 1 Cor. xv, 22: "As in Adam all die, so in Christ shall all be made alive." First, Our union with Adam, and the unhappy consequences. Secondly, Our union with Christ, and the happy consequences. We have already ridden eighty miles from Wilmington.

Tuesday, 3. We came to Jones court house: we had many women, but few men: my text was 1 Cor. vii, 29–31. I suppose I shall not soon prophesy there again—for good reasons.

We went not to see our wealthy friends, but came down to Thomas Lee's, where we held a meeting on *Wednesday* and *Thursday*. My text was Acts xx, 32. Brother Whatcoat spoke from Isaiah lvii, 1; a portion of Scripture very seasonably chosen.

I began to review for this year the preachers and stations. We may perhaps find one preacher for a circuit in the Virginia Conference. I am shocked to see how lightly the preachers esteem, and how readily they leave, the travelling plan. O Lord, by whom shall Jacob arise?

Friday, 6. Rode to Newbern. Brother Whatcoat preached in the evening.

Sabbath day, 8. We had a sacrament in the morning, and brother Whatcoat preached. In the afternoon I made an improvement upon Matt. xvii, 5. I have been rather clouded in mind, and have felt no pleasure in my administrations to-day.

Monday, 9. We rode thirty-seven miles to Washington. In our way we crossed Neuse, swiftly and safely, at West's ferry. At twenty-one miles we stopped to feed—high price and poor fare. We have ridden six hundred and fifty miles towards the fourth thousand since the Carolina Conference. Here Ralph Potts, a Northumbrian (Old England), but American-made Methodist, received us as the angels of God.

Tuesday, 10. I gave a serious talk to more persons than I expected, on Rom. x, 16—a subject well fitted to the state of the people of Washington.

Ralph Potts hath begun a handsome chapel, thirty feet square, and, by the blessing of God, he will finish it without any man's help.

Wednesday, 11. We came twelve miles to Josiah Little's. We called upon brother Floyd by the way. He is sickly. I bless God that this family standeth by us yet. I also called at brother Norris's. At Little's we had many people. Two of our friend Little's brothers are gone from our society. O! the slave trade!—when will it be no more?

Thursday, 12. A dreary ride of thirty miles, without food for man or beast, brought us to Joseph Pippin's.[24] Here we were kindly entertained. Our friend Pippin hath been settled in the Connecta Swamps for twenty years. He hath six children, and about fifteen slaves, and never has had a death in his family. Mercy and miracle! May they praise the Lord!

Friday, 13. At Toole's meeting house, near Tarboro, brother Whatcoat addressed the congregation, upon Zechariah ix, 12. My choice was Isaiah i, 9. I spoke with great heat and rapidity about half an hour. My text was well chosen, if the comment was not well executed. We lodged at Mr. Toole's.

Saturday, 14. Fifteen miles to Prospect chapel—open to all societies. Brother Whatcoat gave a short discourse upon *justification by faith.* My subject was: The love of God and the love of the world contrasted with, and subversive of, each other: according to the degrees, so the effects and fruits of these opposing systems.

Having fourteen miles to Henry Bradford's,[25] we had no time to dine. We took to horse, and came in with the shadows of evening. This morning we breakfasted at seven o'clock, and we now supped at seven—hard preaching and hard riding occupied the intermediate hours.

We have passed rapidly through Edgecombe into Halifax county. O, the awful state of religion in this circuit!

Sabbath day, 15. At Bradford's meeting house, near Fishing Creek, my portion of the word was from Psalm i, 2, 3. I discovered some solemnity

[24] Pippin lived in Edgecombe County, North Carolina.

[25] Henry Bradford lived in Halifax County, North Carolina.

and a few tears. Brother Whatcoat preached on John iii, 17. We rested this Sabbath. We have ridden one hundred and twenty miles in a few days of the past week.

Monday, 16. We were under the necessity of moving to Northampton. It was very warm: we started, and crossed Roanoke river at Pollock's ferry, and arrived at Richard Whitaker's—twenty miles. I was taken very ill with a bilious affection. I had a high fever, and my head and back furnished symptoms of a lowland intermittent. I could not eat, and thought of staying in the house. I changed my mind, and went to Rehoboth chapel. I read the letters giving the accounts of the work of God in the State of Delaware, and in Cumberland. At brother Grant's I took a little water-gruel, and rode on eight miles farther, making twelve miles this day. We lodged at Joseph Pinner's.[26]

Wednesday, 18. We had timely intimation of rain. We started nevertheless, and had the rain, more or less, to Winton, a distance of twenty-five miles. Here we were glad to stop to dry and dine; but no more—ride we must. Gates court house brought us up in the evening. Our ride to-day is little short of forty miles. I preached in the court house, on Titus ii, 11, 12.

Friday, 20. We went forward to Isaac Hunter's,[27] twelve miles. Alas for this place! Five souls of the whites—some poor Africans are seeking the Lord.

Saturday, 21. We came to Newland Creek, twenty-two miles, and lodged at James Spence's.[28] This is a most awful place, and Satan triumphs. *Sabbath day* was cloudy and myself very unwell; but God enabled me to speak with uncommon unction, from John iii, 19–21. "The darkness of the world"—in birth, education, dispensation, practice—the contrary *light* of Revelation; the inspiration of the Spirit; the experience and practice of God's people and ministers:—they came to the *light* to try thereby their conviction, conversion, and sanctification; and as the touchstone of their justice, mercy, truth, and love. "Condemnation"—they are condemned by the word of God, their own consciences, by the people of God—they shall be found guilty in the day of judgment, and be *condemned*—according to the Gospel privileges and light they have lived under and rejected; and they shall *condemn* themselves forever in hell.

We came to M'Bride's.[29] I had a dumb chill, and a sick night.

Monday, 23. We made twenty-two miles to Samuel Simmons's. Our flight has carried us through Pasquotank, Camden, and Currituck counties, in North Carolina, which we shall leave today. My horse enslaves his

[26] Joseph Pinner lived in Northampton County.

[27] Isaac Hunter lived in Gates County.

[28] James Spence lived in Pasquotank County.

[29] Elisha McBride lived in Camden County and in 1790 owned ten slaves. (*Heads of Families*, 17.)

rider. I suffer under severe bodily affliction. I am sorrowful; yet without sinning.

Tuesday, 24. At Currituck, Williams's meeting house, brother Whatcoat preached. I gave a short exhortation; after which we proceeded on to James Wilson's. We have done with North Carolina for the present.

Virginia

Wednesday, 25. Cold and snow. I spoke on Isaiah li, 3. I. The cause of Zion's mourning. "Waste places"—such as had been improved, but forsaken. "Wilderness"—never cultivated: the one representing the Jewish nation; the other, heathen lands. II. "Joy and gladness"—yea, the shouts of the millions of the redeemed of the earth.

Thursday, 26. Brother Whatcoat preached at Cutherall's, near the great bridge.[30] We came through the rain to Hospital Point,[31] and crossed over to Portsmouth. I answered several letters.[32]

Friday, 27.—We had an open time at Portsmouth.

Sabbath, 29. Unwell: my horse also. Preached in Norfolk: my subject, Gal. vi, 9. Returned in the horse-boat through the rain. At three o'clock, I spoke, on, "These shall go away into everlasting punishment, but the righteous into life eternal." The gracious state of heart, and the gracious practice which was manifested by the *righteous*, in their doing all from a principle of love to Christ; and the blessed consequences—"eternal life." Of the *wicked*—their opposite characters and practices, and the effects produced—"everlasting punishment."

Monday, 30. We came to Jolliff's: it was not my day to preach, nor indeed was I well able.

Tuesday, 31. We came in haste to Suffolk. It was my lot to preach in the court house[33] at twelve o'clock. My foundation was 1 Tim. iv, 9, 10. It was with great labour I came through: my cold, loss of voice, and a pain in my breast, were greatly afflictive. We have one good-hearted Methodist, and two very respectable friends here; and the inhabitants, generally, are very catholic—they desire to build a house for us. This town has one grand street, about one hundred houses, and is well situated for trade in lumber, turpentine, tar, and pork, collected from Carolina and parts of this State. We lodged at Richard Yerbury's, an ancient friend of

[30] Great Bridge, on the road from Portsmouth to the North Carolina line, got its name from the bridge which during the Revolution was a causeway through the marsh.

[31] "In Portsmouth stood Fort Nelson (Naval Hospital) built in the Revolution to protect the Norfolk area." (Virginia State Historical Marker K 265.) A naval hospital has stood here for years.

[32] See letters to George Roberts, March 26, 1801, and to Ezekiel Cooper, March 27, 1801.

[33] This was the Nansemond courthouse.

mine from Dinwiddie. He and his wife were the disciples of Mr. Devereux Jarratt. The old prophet, I hear, is dead. He was a man of genius, possessed a great deal of natural oratory, was an excellent reader, and a good writer. From 1763 to 1801 (I think), he was minister of the parish of Bath, in Dinwiddie county, in this State. I have reason to presume, that he was instrumentally successful in awakening hundreds of souls to some sense of religion, in that dark day and time. How he died, I shall probably hear and record hereafter.[34]

Wednesday, April 1. We came to Jethro Hazlett's, near Somerton.[35] The people were lively, and prayed, and praised, and exhorted. I felt the soreness in my breast, and was silent.

North Carolina

After meeting, we came on to Knotty Pine—to the house of mourning for a favourite son. Marmaduke Baker was this day to have gone to Princeton College to finish his education. We hope he is gone to the college of saints and the society of heaven. We have ridden twenty-four miles—faint and feeble.

Thursday, 2. I gave, perhaps, my last talk in Knotty Pine chapel, on 1 Peter iv, 17. We hasted to Winton; benighted in the swamp, which for two miles was overflowed with water. We arrived late at Dr. Laroque's, where we lodged. From Portsmouth hither, we make sixty-five miles. At eleven o'clock brother Whatcoat preached in the court house, from John iii, 16. After preaching, we hasted to Murfreesboro, twelve miles. I preached at N. Vicks's: my text was John iii, 17. Where I laboured I lodged.

Saturday, 4. We came to Edward Sorry's, in Northampton county, dined, and hasted along towards Sterling Boykin's, twenty-eight miles.

Sabbath day, 5. I preached at Concord meeting house, and lodged with Thomas Dupree, a descendant of a Huguenot who fell a martyr to persecution. I felt dejection of spirits and awful feelings for the state of the people. I preached on Heb. ii, 3. I again preached on "Behold the Lamb of God that taketh away the sin of the world": to these exercises were added a sacrament, and the baptism of children. We had a solemn season.

I recollect having read, some years since, Ostervald's Christian Theology: having a wish to transcribe a few sentiments in the work, I met with it, and extracted from chap. 2, page 317, what follows. "Yet it cannot be denied that in the primitive Church there was always a president who presided over others, who were in a state of equality with himself: this is

[34] See note under November 28, 1775.

[35] Somerton is in the south central part of Nansemond County, Virginia, near the North Carolina border.

clearly proved from the catalogues of bishops to be found in Eusebius and others; in them we may see the names of the bishops belonging to the principal Churches, many of whom were ordained whilst the apostles (but especially John) were still living." So far Mr. Ostervald, who, I presume, was a Presbyterian. In Cave's Lives of the Fathers, and in the writings of the ancients, it will appear that the Churches of Alexandria, and elsewhere, had large congregations, many elders; that the apostles might appoint and ordain bishops. Mr. Ostervald, who, it appears, is a candid and well-informed man, has gone as far as might be expected for a Presbyterian. For myself, I see but a hair's breadth difference between the sentiments of the respectable and learned author of Christian Theology, and the practice of the Methodist Episcopal Church. There is not—nor indeed, in my mind, can there be—a perfect equality between a constant president, and those over whom he always presides.

Virginia

Monday, 6. At Malone's chapel I preached on Luke xxiv, 44–48. We lodged at brother Peeple's.

Tuesday, 7. Leaving Jones's, we proceeded on through heavy rain, to Dromgoole's.

Wednesday, 8. Dromyrick chapel[36] had been removed and enlarged for the conferences. *Thursday*, *Friday*, and *Monday* in conference. We had a press of business, but were peaceable and expeditious.[37] Brother Lee preached on *Saturday*; I held forth on *Sunday morning* to an unwieldy congregation indoors, whilst William Ormond preached out of doors, and the poor blacks had their devotions behind the house. My subject was Rom. i, 16: "I am not ashamed of the Gospel of Christ, for it is the power of God unto salvation to every one that believeth." The manifest excellence of the Gospel of Christ in three cases. 1. As a revelation from God, by ancient, and multiplied, and sure prophecy. 2. As it proclaimeth salvation to all the world who will give it that attention and that credence which is given to the reports and to the business of the world. The spiritual and glorious salvation of the Gospel. The power of God displayed upon the rich, the poor, the worldly minded, the worldly wise, and worldly ignorant, and sinners of the deepest dye. Modern ministers and the people of God of the present day should not be ashamed to believe and profess the experience

[36] It seems that with the removal of the church the name was changed to Dromyrick, a combination of the Drumgooles and Myricks who lived in the community.

[37] Bennett gives a partial report of this conference. Jesse Coe, Willie Jones, Meacham Burrows, Jacob Watson, James Chappel, Thomas L. Douglass, and David Hume were admitted on trial. James Talleson had died during the year in Portsmouth of yellow fever, and his clothes had been sent to the conference to be distributed among the preachers. (Bennett, *op. cit.*, 390–91.)

and obey the precepts of the Gospel; not ashamed to suffer for it and support it; not ashamed to claim all its promises; contend for the truth of its doctrines, and the necessity and efficacy of its divinely appointed ordinances.

Monday, 13. We finished our conference, and next day I recommenced my northern march, preaching at Dromgoole's (now Mason's) chapel,[38] whither we had returned. Doctor Smith, on whom I called, took a wart, cancerous in appearance, which had troubled me three months, from my foot.

Thursday, 16. At Mabry's chapel. I paid a visit to an old mother in Israel. I have fevers and feebleness, but a soul entirely swallowed up in God. I preached on Titus i, 16. The characters of those who profess to know God by his works of nature, his providences; yet there are of these who reject his word, who imitate him not in his attributes and perfections, forgetting that we might as well suppose a man without bodily powers and mental apprehensions, as a God without justice, mercy, love, and holiness. Some profess to know God by revelation, yet in works deny him; others profess to know God by revelation and inspiration, yet, like the others, neither fear God, trust in, nor love him, having deceived their own souls; others have fallen from the experimental and saving knowledge of God, yet profess to know God. Lastly, How excellent the character of those who know God, and prove it by their works, and uniformity of tempers and actions, living always in the fear of God, and in an unshaken confidence in his mercy and his truth.

Friday, 17. Ten miles brought us to Saponey Creek. We lodged at the house of Richard Graves's widow. The husband is gone home, having departed in perfect love, after twenty years' profession: he wrote and felt a blessed experience a short time before his death.

Saturday, 18. For thirty years past I have occasionally preached at Stony Creek; I held forth at the chapel on Psalm lxxviii, 5–7. After preaching we hasted on to B. Malone's to dine, and thence to Petersburg, thirty miles.

Sabbath, 19. There had been put forth a printed appointment for me to preach the funeral sermon of the late Rev. Devereux Jarratt, who had lately returned to his rest.

My subject was Matt. xxv, 21: "His Lord said unto him, Well done, thou good and faithful servant: thou hast been faithful over a few things; I will make thee ruler over many things: enter thou into the joy of thy Lord." It was observed, I. That a good servant was only *good* in the relation which his practice and his experience bore to the example and the precepts of his divine Master; that his was Christian goodness—a goodness altogether founded in grace. II. "Faithful servant"—*faithful* to his

[38] This is the present Olive Branch Chapel, which was first called Wolsey's Barn or Dromgoole's and then changed to Mason's.

ministerial character:—he hath a high and just sense of the authority of his Divine Master in the person of God the Father and God the Son; he hath a just respect for the people he is to serve of all characters: the service he is to perform—1st. The preaching of the word. 2d. The administration of the sacrament and ordinances. 3d. Ruling the Church of God. The "talents"—the gift of prayer, preaching, expounding of the Scriptures; and social advice. "Faithful in a few things"—"to be ruler over many things" in the glory of God. The "joy" of Jesus—the *joy* of his redemption and salvation of souls socially and personally, felt and experienced—and lastly, the hearty welcome into glory.

Mr. Devereux Jarratt was settled in Bath Parish, Dinwiddie county, Virginia, in the year 1763, and continued until February, 1801. He was a faithful and successful preacher. He had witnessed four or five periodical revivals of religion in his parish. When he began his labours, there was no other, that he knew of, evangelical minister in all the province! He travelled into several counties, and there were very few parish churches within fifty miles of his own in which he had not preached; to which labours of love and zeal were added, preaching the word of life on solitary plantations and in meeting houses. He was the first who received our despised preachers—when strangers and unfriended, he took them to his house, and had societies formed in his parish. Some of his people became travelling preachers amongst us. I have already observed that the ministry of Mr. Jarratt was successful—I verily believe that hundreds were awakened by his labours; they are dispersed—some are gone to the Carolinas, to Georgia, to the western country—some perhaps are in heaven; and some, it may be, in hell.

The day after, we rode through a cold day to Chesterfield court house, and the next day we came in, dripping, to Richmond: about four o'clock, lame as I was, I walked to the new house, where I spoke to a small congregation from Matt. v, 16.

Wednesday, 22. Although it was excessively cold, occasioned by a fall of snow on the mountains, we took the road, and came as far as Lyon's, in Caroline, about thirty-five miles.

Thursday, 23. By taking the road over Buck's bridge, we crossed Mattapony[39] without difficulty. On our route I saw that beautiful spot, the Bowling Green, improved into a neat village at Caroline court house. We dined at Todd's, and came on to Fredericksburg: here I completely failed, and went to bed, after ordaining William Hughes a deacon. Brother Whatcoat spoke in the new house,[40] which I could only behold with my eyes at a distance. Some years ago Doctor Coke and myself wished to preach, but there was no place; now, the people desired to hear me and could not.

[39] The Mattaponi now unites with Pamunkey to form the York River.

[40] The new church in Richmond had been built in 1799.

Friday, 24. Was a day of rain. Onward we went—Potomac run was passable—Aquia, full enough to catch my dipping foot—hills, and clay, and another swelling stream still between us and Dumfries—arrived at last we borrowed a widow's house and held a meeting; my subject was Luke xix, 10. We were kindly entertained at Cook's.

Saturday, 25. We came on to Alexandria. O the clay! O the insolvent roads!

Sunday, 26. I gave a discourse upon Zeph. i, 12.

I received two letters sent after me, requesting the substance or heads of the sermon preached on the occasion of the late Rev. Devereux Jarratt: I sat down, and as well as I could collect and remember them, hastily arranged my thoughts upon paper, and left the manuscript with Nicholas Snethen to copy.

Maryland

We had some difficulty next day at the ferry, being obliged to wait an hour, which made us too late for meeting in Georgetown.

I visited Captain Lloyd Beal.[41] I also visited Ezekiel King,[42] son of my most dear friend, father King, in Stroud. Can a son of so many prayers be lost? heavy strokes of Providence have afflicted his mind: he hears—he weeps—O that I may yet see him converted!—he desired that I should pray in the family.

Tuesday, 28. We came to Montgomery court house, fifteen miles, where I found a decent, attentive congregation, in a house as well contrived and fitted for religious worship as any I have seen: my subject was Luke xxiv, 45–48.

Jehovah is at work—We have new converts added. We dined at Enoch Busson's,[43] and came on to Joshua Pigman's, twenty-five miles.

[41] Captain Lloyd Beale, or Beall, was a trustee of both the Goshen Meeting House in Montgomery County, Maryland, and of the "new Chapel" in Washington, D.C. Some have identified him also as the Captain Beale who as an officer at Fort Adams and Fort Wolcott was instrumental in the introduction of Methodism in Rhode Island. (Kirkley, *op. cit.*, 23; Bryan: *A History of the National Capital*, I, 275 n., 596 n.; Martz, *op. cit.*, 7; Stevens: *Memorials of Methodism*, 440; *Journal* entry for May 28, 1809.)

[42] Ezekiel King lived between the present Georgetown, D.C., and Rockville, Maryland. If Asbury refers to Stroudsburg, Pennsylvania, he probably was writing about Ezekiel King, a son of Elijah King, who for a time was both a local preacher and an itinerant in the Genesee Conference. (Palmer, *op. cit.*, 204; *General Minutes*, 189–490; Peck: *Early Methodism Within the Bounds of the Old Genesee Conference*, 336, 337.) However, it is possible that Asbury was referring to members of the King family whom he had known in Stroud, England.

[43] Enoch Busson lived between Rockville and Laytonsville, Montgomery County, and in 1793 was among the lot owners in Rockville, then called Williamsburg. (Scharf: *History of Western Maryland*, 740; *Land Record Books*, Rockville, Maryland.) He was a member of the Baltimore Circuit 1801–9.

Wednesday, 29. We had a large assembly at Goshen meeting house: brother Whatcoat preached. We came on that evening to Levin Warfield's.[44]

Thursday, 30. We arrived to dine at Alexander Warfield's, on Sam's Creek, and pushed on to Henry Willis's, on Pipe Creek, where it had been our intention to open conference.[45]

We had about forty members present, and sat on *Friday*, *Saturday*, and *Monday*: on *Tuesday* morning we rose. We had great peace; and good news from several circuits—revivals of religion. I was greatly supported in mind and body. On *Sabbath day* I preached from Matt. xxviii, 18–20. 1. The authority of Christ—his natural, and his Divine right as the co-eternal Son—his right by redemption—his right by family compact, and the delegation of the whole Trinity, to the work of redemption and salvation. 2. The branches of duty appointed to his ministers: to preach the Gospel in all its essential points; to administer the ordinances; and to rule thc Church of Christ. 3. "I am with you"—at all times, and in all places, to support and to give you success as Christians and as ministers. We had six elders present; to wit, William Watters, John Phillips, Solomon Harris, Joseph Stone, John Cullison, and Alexander M'Caine.[46] There was preaching every day and every night. Our own people, and our friends in the settlement were equally kind; and we had rich entertainment. This settlement of Pipe Creek is the richest in the state: here Mr. Strawbridge formed the first society in Maryland—and *America*.[47]

Wednesday, *May* 6. The clouds are gone, and we must move. The

[44] Levin Warfield, a kinsman of Alexander Warfield, married Ann Hobbs in 1779. They resided in Carroll County.

[45] Henry Willis (?–1808), then a supernumerary, and his wife, the former Ann Hollingsworth, daughter of Jesse, lived on a six-hundred-acre farm in Carroll County. The conference met in their spacious home, "Wakefield," on Pipe Creek. (Roberts, *op. cit.*, 45–56; Hough: *Christian Newcomer, His Life, Journal and Achievements*, 53; Warriner: *Old Sand Street Methodist Episcopal Church, Brooklyn, New York*, 76–78.)

[46] William Watters (1751–1827) had been in the itinerant ranks since 1773; John Phillips, who was received on trial in 1784, had been on the Fairfax Circuit; Solomon Harris, five years an itinerant, was on the Alleghany Circuit; Joseph Stone had finished a year on the Frederick Circuit; John Cullison, who traveled 1796–1804, was appointed to the Federal Circuit; Alexander McCaine (1768–1856), to become one of the most prominent founders of the Methodist Protestant Church, was appointed to Fells Point. (*General Minutes.*)

[47] The concluding words of this sentence, "and *America*," have created much discussion. Those who believe that Robert Strawbridge on Sam's Creek in Maryland antedated Philip Embury in New York City accept this entry in the *Journal* as genuine and authoritative. Those who give the priority to New York explain the words "and *America*" either to be an interpolation in a section of the *Journal* which Asbury did not correct or prepare for the press, or point out that as a historian he was sometimes incorrect. (Atkinson: *The Wesleyan Movement in America*, I, 7, 22; Wakeley, *op. cit.*, 163–65; *The Origin of Methodism in America*, Report of the Joint Committee representing the three major branches of American Methodism, 1916; Sweet: *Virginia Methodism*, 46.)

weather has lately been unpleasant. I changed my old horse for a younger and a better. We came to Baltimore in a great storm, but I was not much damped: I sat in George Roberts's house,[48] and received my old friends and all who called to see me.

Sunday, 10. I had an opportunity of speaking in Light Street church, upon Romans i, 16–18. We had an open time and an attentive congregation: I felt that the Lord was amongst the people. In the afternoon, at the Old Town church,[49] I spoke on Romans xvii, 5.[50] In the evening I read the Duck Creek and Cumberland account of the work of God: it would not have been greater labour to have preached. We went to bed at eleven o'clock, slept at twelve, waked at four, and at five mounted and hasted away to Perry Hall to preach at eleven o'clock: my text was Mark ix, 14–29.

Tuesday, 12. At Gunpowder Neck I spoke on Psalm cii, 13; at five o'clock we had a meeting at Abingdon: there is a revival of religion in this circuit. The day is excessively warm: my foot sore—and a high fever. We lodged at William Smith's.[51] Sarah Dallam's eldest daughter, Eliza Stump,[52] professeth conversion, and her daughter Sarah, and little Philip her youngest son also.

Wednesday, 13. I preached once more at Josias W. Dallam's—I could speak with more faith than usual upon Acts ii, 37, for behold! Henry Watters's son, many years insensible to the things of God, was converted!

[48] George Roberts, M.D., who had joined the traveling ministry in 1790, was in 1801 stationed in Baltimore. It is probable that the house he then occupied was retained for a residence, when in 1806 he became a practicing physician in Baltimore. (Stevens, *op. cit.*, II, 440–43; Roberts, *op. cit.*, 89–106; *Journal* entry for August 29, 1800.)

[49] This was the Exeter Street Church erected in 1789. The society traced its origin from the preaching of John King in 1770 and from December 7, 1773, when Asbury preached in John Deaver's home in Old Town. (Hawkins: *The Life and Times of Hon. Elijah Stansbury*, 244; *Journal* entry for April 23–29, 1798.)

[50] Romans has only sixteen chapters. There is no indication what this passage may have been.

[51] This was Colonel William Smith, an officer in the War of 1812, whose home was on the road to Churchville. The Colonel died in 1835, and his four daughters, the Misses Sara, Margaret, Nancy, and Jane, donated the site upon which in 1858 Glenwood Chapel was erected. William and Charles James led in its construction. In 1860 the name was changed to Smith Chapel, which is on the east Harford Circuit of the Baltimore Conference. (Preston: *History of Harford County*, 244–46.)

[52] This was Elizabeth Smith Dallam (1774–1825), a daughter of Josias William and Sarah Dallam. The Dallam home was a Methodist preaching place as early as 1772 when visited by John King and Joseph Pilmoor. Elizabeth married Hermann Stump, whose mother was a descendant of Augustine Hermann, cartographer and founder of Bohemia Manor, Cecil County. Hermann Stump was a brother and a partner of John Stump, leading industrialist of Harford County and builder of "Stafford" on Deer Creek, owned in 1956 by Colonel Buckner M. Creel, Sr. Elizabeth Dallam Stump's second husband was Abraham Jarrett. (Silver and Archer: *Genealogical Record of the Stump Family*, 1891; Pilmoor's Manuscript *Journal*; Preston, *op. cit.*, 217.)

When we parted with Godfrey,[53] he looked after us with wishful, willing eyes and heart; that the dear soul should sit nearly thirty years under the Gospel, unconverted and almost unconcerned—how strange! and should be at last visited and converted—how merciful!

Thursday, 14. Crossed Susquehannah ferry, and came in to meeting at half-past eleven o'clock: the people were waiting; and I gave a short discourse upon Heb. ii, 3. We dined and rode on to Bohemia Manor.

Friday, 15. Brother Whatcoat preached: I gave a short exhortation. We hope that nearly three thousand souls have been added since last conference in the peninsula of Delaware, Maryland, and Virginia.

Saturday, 16. We rode rapidly to the brick meeting house in Kent,[54] a distance not less than twenty-two miles: I was outdone: brother Whatcoat preached upon, "Now we live, if ye stand fast in the faith."

Sunday, 17. We had a love feast for the whites and blacks: there might have been fifteen hundred people. My subject was Psalm cxlvii, 3–5: this was a trying exercise, but I humbly hope it was not all in vain.

We came away, and steered to New Town Chester, fifteen miles, through dust and heat, to keep an appointment made for the night, which held us until after nine o'clock. Fatigue and fever prevented my sleeping.

Monday, 18. We rose at five o'clock, and came off at six, bending our course to Centerville, seventeen miles. Ah! heavily moves this clay. I came in weary and unwell: I spoke on Romans x, 21. I was greatly assisted in mind and body. After meeting I rode to brother Pinard's,[55] where I was glad to lay myself down to rest.

Tuesday, 19. We came off, cool and calm, to Easton. Brother Whatcoat preached: I gave an exhortation. We take a county and a circuit in a day. I can only say, I am kept from murmuring and sinning: but ah! it is like pressing out life with labour: such extraordinary exertions call for great Divine support, for soul and body. O how sweet will be eternal rest to labouring souls! Our prospects are pleasing in Kent, Queen Anne's, and Talbot circuits: souls are added to the Church and to Christ; prejudices fall before the force of truth and power of God.

Wednesday, 20. We came to Bolingbroke: my subject here was Heb. x,

[53] Godfrey Watters lived on Deer Creek, Harford County. He was the fourth born of the seven children of Godfrey and Sarah Adams, among whom were the Methodist preachers Nicholas and William. (Watters: *The Watters Family*, 10, 13.)

[54] This was Dudley's meeting house, originally called Queen Anne's Chapel, near Sudlersville, Queen Annes County. Asbury's location, "in Kent," apparently refers to the circuit rather than the Maryland county of that name. (Lednum, *op. cit.*, 379; see photostat of Official Trustee Meetings from 1794 to 1900 in Maryland Historical Society, Baltimore; manuscript Maryland Genealogical Rec. Com. 1932–33, D.A.R. Library, Washington, D.C.)

[55] It is apparent that Pinard lived in the vicinity of Centreville. Because this is the only mention of Pinard in the *Journal* or in *Methodism in Queen Annes County*, it is probable that this is a corruption of the name of another resident in the vicinity of Centreville.

38, 39. We dined at William Brown's:[56] one of his sons hath found the Lord. A calm and safe passage brought us over Choptank at Ennall's Ferry.

Thursday, 21. In Cambridge we held a meeting in the court house, and had a large, well-behaved congregation to hear: brother Whatcoat spoke on, "To you is the word of this salvation sent." I made the application, "How shall we escape if we neglect so great salvation?"

Friday, 22. We had a long ride to William Frazier's through dust and excessive heat.

Saturday, 23. I preached upon Peter's fall. It was hard to leave loving souls; so we tarried until morning.

I formed a plan for another year, allowing only about twenty days to visit every circuit but Caroline, by one appointment in a circuit and county.

Delaware

Sunday, 24. We came to Choptank, and found that the people had attended the day before, of which we were ignorant, and that no appointment had been made for the Sabbath. It was not light labour to make thirty miles by eleven o'clock; and, worn as I was, I should have failed had not Thomas Foster[57] lent me his carriage.

Monday, 25. Arrived in Dover, we found the people collected at the meeting houses so numerous that they could not be well accommodated: we therefore adjourned to the state house, where I spoke to them from Haggai ii, 5–9. Brother Whatcoat preached at the chapel, and I gave an exhortation—and so ended the great meeting in Dover with us. My mind was somewhat taken up with getting another horse, and he did not please me. I went to Dr. Robert Cook's to see Thomas White's only surviving daughter, and Sarah Cook. I preached at Duck Creek Cross Roads, upon 1 Thess. i, 7–12. I am under some dejection of spirits; yet I know of no cause except bodily infirmity, produced by excessive labour, and speaking long and tolerably loud to large congregations. My foot and my fears are troublesome to me. In the afternoon I must needs go to attend an examination of the children of a school partly under the Methodist direction: I could not have thought the scholars would so greatly improve in so short a time: their improvement reflects honour upon their teacher, a Mr.

[56] William Brown lived in the neighborhood of Trappe, Talbot County, the location of Bolingbroke or Bolingbrook Chapel, later called Lebanon. On two later ocasions, April 16, 1802, and April 27, 1805, Asbury was the guest of Brown.

[57] Thomas Foster (17—-1821) located in 1792 after traveling from 1785 to 1791. He settled on a farm on Cabin Creek, west of Hurlock in Dorchester County, where he built the Foster meeting house and helped in 1799 with its merger with the society which became Washington Chapel and is now the Hurlock Church. Asbury described him as "of the old stamp, and steady." (Lednum, *op. cit.*, 305, 306.)

Hughes, a Methodist from Ireland. The master had provided a medal, but the committee judged it proper to keep it for a future examination. Indeed, the master himself was best entitled to an honorary reward; and this being the general sentiment, a subscription was undertaken for money, to furnish the children each with a small silver piece, and so make them equal—in a free country.

Thursday, 28. At Dickerson's[58] meeting house I preached upon Matt. xxv, 46. We rode home with Benjamin Hersey, at Noxontown mill.[59]

Friday, 29. We were righteous overmuch in riding in such haste and heat, thirty miles, without refreshment; but we had fears for the Philadelphia society. At six o'clock I gave a discourse at Wilmington, on 1 Pet. v, 7: "Casting all your care upon him, for he careth for you." First, We should have no care, as ministers or as Christians, but what is proper—such care as may, with humble confidence, be cast upon the Lord. Second, How we should cast the whole upon the Lord—by faith, by prayer, by patience, and resignation. "That the Lord careth for us" as a God.

Pennsylvania

Saturday, 30. Most excessive heat, through which we rode to conference in Philadelphia.

Sabbath, 31. I preached in Fourth street, on John iii, 19. I was very lame. On *Monday*, *Tuesday*, *Wednesday*, *Thursday*, and *Friday*, I attended the session of conference, but on *Saturday* I remained in my lodgings, and ministered to my sore foot. Our conference was a gracious one. It appeared, as if the preachers were unwilling to elevate their voices lest there should be an appearance of heat or anger; yet with the greatest plainness would they differ from each other, calmly, and in love.

Sabbath, *June* 7. I took up my cross, and stayed quietly in the house with a blister to my foot. We shall see if another operation will be necessary. Minutes and letters took up my attention. We elected and ordained eight deacons, and the same number of elders; on account of my lameness it was done at my lodgings. We were well satisfied in the stationing of the preachers; we received one from Canada, and sent three thither. My soul hath great peace; and although there has been a formidable division threatened, we humbly hope God will overrule it all to his glory.

Wednesday, 10. Doctor Physick[60] applied a caustic to my foot.

[58] Dickerson meeting house, successor to White's Chapel, was east of Townsend, New Castle County.

[59] Noxontown mill was a gristmill established by Thomas Noxon about 1740. It stood on Noxontown Pond which in the days of Benjamin Hersey was a famed milling centre. (Scharf: *History of Delaware*, 1015; Hallman, *op. cit.*, 113.)

[60] Dr. Philip Syng Physick (1768–1837) was the son of Edmund Physick, one of the Penn family agents in America. He attended the Friend's Academy and was graduated

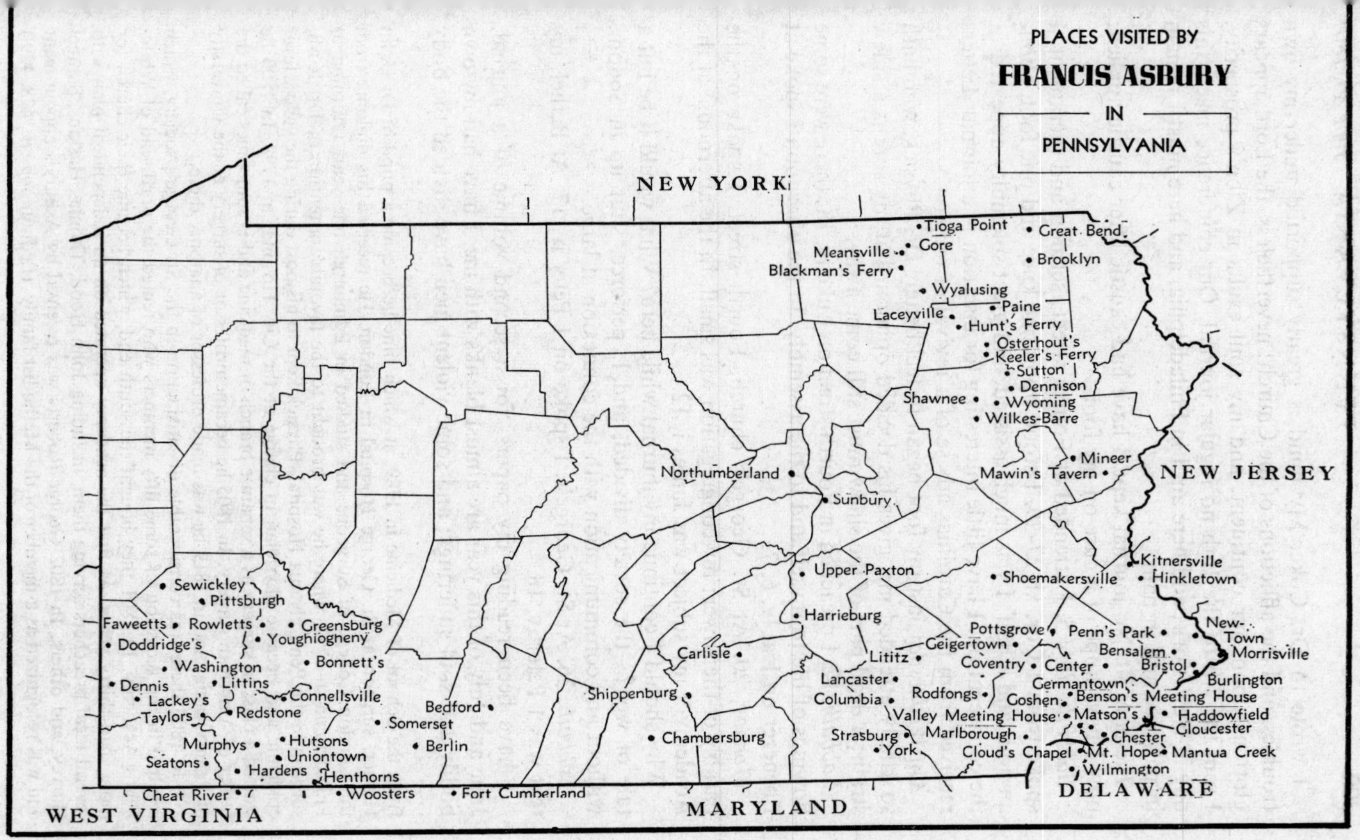
PLACES VISITED BY
FRANCIS ASBURY
IN
PENNSYLVANIA
NEW YORK
NEW JERSEY
DELAWARE
MARYLAND
WEST VIRGINIA
Tioga Point
Great Bend
Gore
Meansville
Brooklyn
Blackman's Ferry
Wyalusing
Paine
Laceyville
Hunt's Ferry
Osterhout's
Keeler's Ferry
Sutton
Dennison
Shawnee
Wyoming
Wilkes-Barre
Mineer
Mawin's Tavern
Northumberland
Sunbury
Kitnersville
Hinkletown
Upper Paxton
Shoemakersville
Harrieburg
Pottsgrove
Penn's Park
New-Town
Morrisville
Geigertown
Bensalem
Carlisle
Lititz
Coventry
Center
Bristol
Burlington
Lancaster
Germantown
Rodfongs
Goshen
Benson's Meeting House
Columbia
Valley Meeting House
Matson's
Haddowfield
Gloucester
Shippenburg
Chester
Strasburg
Marlborough
Chambersburg
York
Cloud's Chapel
Mt. Hope
Mantua Creek
Wilmington
Sewickley
Pittsburgh
Faweetts
Rowletts
Greensburg
Youghiogheny
Doddridge's
Bonnett's
Washington
Dennis
Littins
Connellsville
Lackey's
Taylors
Redstone
Bedford
Somerset
Hutsons
Murphys
Uniontown
Berlin
Seatons
Hardens
Henthorns
Cheat River
Woosters
Fort Cumberland

I wrote to Dr. Coke. My mind is greatly supported under my own troubles, and the afflictions of the Church; nevertheless, the Lord appears glorious upon our continent, and my soul exults in Zion's prosperity. From the 7th to the 16th no regular journal. Our conference meets this day in New York; and here am I in Philadelphia, and here must I remain in patience and in pain.

Tuesday, 30. No journal kept. I have had caustic after caustic applied; now I have hope of a cure on my foot.

Sabbath, July 5. I attended at Fourth street: sermon and sacrament. I spoke from 1 Cor. xi, 27–29. I stood upon one knee and one foot, about an hour and a half. I was much assisted, and great solemnity appeared in the congregation. I have little interesting for insertion in a journal. Letters received from the Carolinas advise of a revival of religion.

On *Wednesday* last my foot began to feel better. Dr. Physick, who hath so kindly attended me, gives his decided opinion that my sore is a sinew strain: a dead part of the sinew must still come away.

Sabbath, 12. I preached in Fourth street on Luke iv, 18: there were some flowings of life to myself and to the assembly. In the afternoon I spoke at Ebenezer on Isa. lv, 6, 7.

Monday, 20. At St. George's church, Fourth street, I spoke on the parable of the sower: my congregation was small. In the afternoon, at the Academy,[61] my subject was James i, 12.

Why should I continue my journal while here? What would it be but a tale of woe?—the society divided, and I, perforce, shut up in Sodom, without any communication with the connexion at large.

Sabbath, 26. At St. George's, I spoke on 1 Peter iv, 17. At Bethel, my text was 1 Peter iv, 18.

I have been reading my papers, for a second volume of a journal. June and July of this year are almost blanks with me. I have had my own bodily and soul sufferings; and some violent men have divided the body

from the School of Medicine in 1789, at which time he became a pupil of Dr. John Hunter, surgeon at St. George Hospital in London. He received his diploma from the London College of Surgeons and studied in Edinburgh one year, returning to Philadelphia in 1792, where he was brought to the favorable attention of Dr. Rush, surgeon in the Pennsylvania Hospital. Physick kept to his post during the yellow fever epidemic and became physician in charge at the City Hospital in 1798. In 1800 he started a class in surgery as a separate branch of medicine and is sometimes called the father of American surgery. In 1805 he became professor of surgery at the University of Pennsylvania, and in 1819 he was made professor of anatomy there.

[61] In 1800 there was considerable dissatisfaction in the St. George's society, which resulted in the secession of some fifty members who rented the north end of Whitefield's Academy. In 1801 they bought the south end, which became their church for more than thirty years. At first the academy operated on an independent plan with several local preachers serving them, including John Hood, Thomas Haskins, Samuel Harvey, and others. In 1802 George Roberts was received by Asbury's appointment and was recognized as a member of the Methodist family. (Lednum, *op cit.*, 428, 429.)

of Christ in the city of Philadelphia—let such answer for it in this, and the world to come.

Friday, 31. After a serious confinement in Philadelphia of two months of trouble and affliction, I took my departure and rode to the Wheatsheaf,[62] where we breakfasted, and thence proceeded to Wilmington, Delaware.

Delaware

I stopped with Allan McLane. I found Mr. Worrel[63] very ill, and addressed him seriously on the concerns of his soul, commending him to God in prayer. After supper we went to John Miller's, in Newport.

August 1. I called upon Mr. M'Intire;[64] we talked, we prayed and rejoiced together in the work of God. I could not pass my old friend Isaac Hersey,[65] without calling. We could with gratitude review the past, and dwell upon the present dealings of the Lord with us as a people, and say, what hath God wrought?

Maryland

Within two miles of North East, the heavens grew big and black with wind and rain: happily for us brother George's house[66] was at hand: there we talked, prayed, and sheltered. Sister Howell is very low and languid. I lodged at Daniel Sheredine's. He has never lost sight of God for twenty-nine years, and now he is united to us.

Sunday, 2. I preached at the chapel opposite the church, so called: my text was Luke vii, 22, 23; we had a living season.

Monday, 3. We came off at six o'clock, and after riding twenty miles,

[62] This was probably an inn located on the Chester–Wilmington Road.

[63] Edward Worrell was long a trustee of Asbury Church, Wilmington, Delaware. On April 29, 1800, he was selected by the male members of the congregation to draft a memorial to the General Conference providing for pecuniary aid to married preachers. (Hanna: *Centennial Services of Asbury Methodist Episcopal Church, Wilmington*, 135, 139, 140, 148.)

[64] William McIntire was a trustee of the Salem Church two miles south of Ogletown, White Clay Creek Hundred, New Castle County, Delaware. He was a half brother of the Rev. John Hersey and entertained Richard Whatcoat on August 18, 1790. (Scharf: *History of Delaware*, I, 937; II, 1083 n.; Sweet, *op. cit.*, IV, 112.)

[65] Isaac Hersey and his wife, Jane, lived four miles west of Christiana, New Castle County. His brothers were Solomon and Benjamin Hersey. (Marine: *Sketch of John Hersey*, 5, 6.)

[66] John George lived two miles east of the town of Northeast, Cecil County. He was a trustee of the Methodist Church when the deed was executed for the building site on October 25, 1794, and during the erection of the house of worship the next year. (Miller: *Cecil County*, 81.)

stopped to take refreshment at Mr. Stump's, in Bush. I spoke a word of consolation to a true daughter of that excellent woman Sally Dallam, now with Christ; it was a time of great family affliction, but the mourner enjoys divine love for her support.

I came on to Perry Hall. Here were things to arrest my attention—out of sixty or seventy servants, many shouting and praising God. My dear Mr. Gough was somewhat unwell, Mrs. Carroll seriously ill,[67] and her mother absent in attendance on old Mrs. Carroll, at the Mount.

I continued at Perry Hall, from *August* 3d to *Saturday* the 15th. An intermittent fever came upon me every morning, and indisposed my stomach: it was with difficulty I could attend to the performance of family and closet duties being much unfitted for reading or writing. I got through a part of Doddridge's Rise and Progress, and some of Young's Night Thoughts. The great engagedness of the African part of the family was delightfully pleasing. Gough Holliday[68] professed to find the Lord, and one or two more of the family appear to be earnestly seeking him. I preached, read, prayed, exhorted and conversed; but it was not much I could do. Our family, when in the chapel, makes a respectable congregation.

Sunday, 16. I spent this day in Baltimore. My indisposition of body was amply compensated by the consolation I felt whilst holding forth upon Matt. v, 8: "Blessed are the pure in heart, for they shall see God."

I. The character of those who by justification are, in a *special* manner, called to be pure in heart; called by promise, by privilege, by duty.

II. The purity of the Gospel in authority, in example, precept and spirit; in its operative influence on the understanding, conscience, intentions, will, hopes, fears, joys, sorrows and affections, producing the sanctification of the soul in a deliverance from all sin.

III. The visions: in what manner the *pure in heart* should see God; they shall see him in his perfections, in his providence, in his works of nature, and the operations of his grace, and they shall see him in his glory!

I had a desire to preach in the market house upon Howard's Hill. I spoke to hundreds, perhaps thousands, upon Luke xiv, 21: "Go out quickly into the streets and lanes of the city, and bring in hither the poor,

[67] Mrs. James Carroll was Sophia, the only child of Mr. and Mrs. Harry Dorsey Gough of Perry Hall. James, to whom she was married in 1787, was the son of Nicholas Maccubbin and his wife, the former Mary Clare Carroll. For assuming his mother's maiden name he inherited a considerable fortune. The granddaughter of James and Sophia Carroll became the wife of Thomas B. Sargent (1805–79) of the Baltimore Conference. (Warfield: *Founders of Anne Arundel and Howard Counties*, 65; *Maryland Historical Magazine*, XXV, 302 ff.; Hansen: *Old Kent*, 150; Smith, *op. cit.*, 201–3.)

[68] Gough Holliday was probably the son of John Robert Holliday, a half brother of Mrs. Harry Dorsey Gough. The latter's mother, born Achsah Ridgely, married first John Robert Holliday for whom Holliday Street in Baltimore is named. (See article by Scharf, "Hampton, Baltimore County, Maryland," *Maryland Historical Magazine* (1948), XLIII, 100 ff.)

and the maimed, and the halt, and the blind." I thought it my duty, and I felt it a delight to sanction what the preachers do in preaching abroad: I wished to do it in Philadelphia, and had appointed it, but some of my brethren made strong objections, and it was abandoned. We have peace, health, and union in Baltimore.

Wednesday, 19. I came from Baltimore to Robert Carnan's, near the Stone chapel. This was a day of great and good news. I heard that eight souls professed to find the Lord at a prayer meeting in the city; twelve souls at Cullison's,[69] in the Barrens, about fifteen days past; and by letters from Thomas Wilkerson and advices from William M'Kendree, forty souls were happily made subjects of converting grace at a late meeting held in Cumberland, Tennessee—this meeting continued from *Saturday* until *Monday*, and there was then no prospect of its concluding soon: the elder was under the necessity of coming away to attend to his other appointments.

I made two visits to a beautiful country seat belonging to Captain Yellott: here is a charming house, fine gardens, and well-improved grounds; but on what lease? Ah, how uncertain are all our earthly enjoyments! My business was with the sick: O, may sweet Sophia find spiritual wisdom, gold tried in the fire, that she may be rich in every virtue and every grace that can adorn the woman, the wife, the mother, the daughter, and the Christian![70]

Thursday, 20. I preached at the Stone chapel at a short notice, to a few serious, respectable people, on 1 John iv, 15–17. I spoke next day at Reisterstown on Isaiah xxxv, 3–6: although the warning was short, it was a day of liberty to me. We dined at Weist's public house,[71] and proceeded on to Henry Willis's, at Pipe Creek: we had the company of Jesse Hollingsworth and James M'Cannon:[72] we felt the heat and feared the rain, but

[69] The Methodist Society held its meetings in the Cullison home in Baltimore County. (*Stewards' Book* of Baltimore Circuit, 1794–1816, Lovely Lane Museum); John Cullison, who in 1801 was stationed on the Federal Circuit, may have been related to this family.

[70] Sophia was a married daughter of Captain Jeremiah Yellott (d. 1811) and Mary Hollingsworth Yellott. Mary was a daughter of Jesse Hollingsworth (1732–1810) and a sister of Mrs. Henry Willis and Francis Hollingsworth. The last mentioned edited the *Journal* of Asbury. (Mary Hollingsworth: *The Hollingsworth Family*, 16, Pratt Memorial Library, Baltimore, Maryland.)

[71] Weist's public house was at Reisterstown. Its owner was Henry Weist, whose wife, Elizabeth, was the daughter of John Reister. (Dixon: *Reisterstown History*, 1869.)

[72] James McCannon (1754–1815), a native of Ireland, was among the first class leaders of Lovely Lane Meeting House. About two blocks distant he operated a tailor shop in which waistcoats were made for Asbury and several of his co-laborers in return for the bishop's consent to sit for his portrait. McCannon was a trustee of Cokesbury College. He had a country home, "Richland," at Medford, Carroll County. (Crook: *Ireland and the Centenary of American Methodism*, 168; James H. Naff, "Recollections of Baltimore," *Maryland Historical Magazine*, May 5, 1910, 118; Wakeley, *op. cit.*, 40–42, 470.)

happily arrived before it fell, at a pleasant shelter and a Christian family. Next day we visited the Sulphur Springs, and rested the body a little.

Sunday, 23. I preached at the Stone chapel on Heb. xii, 25: it was a gracious season. On *Monday* we rested.

Tuesday, 25. We rode to Alexander Warfield's, on Sam's Creek. My mind is variously exercised in my infirm state; but I plainly perceive that I must be made perfect through labour, temptation, and many sufferings in the flesh and spirit.

Wednesday, 26. We visited John Norris's family:[73] here I saw the aged mother of ninety years: she reminded me of my own. I dined with the household of Eli Dorsey—the children of my once dear friend Sarah Dorsey, now no more. At James L. Higgins's I gave a discourse upon 2 Cor. vi, 2.

Thursday, 27. We rode up to Stephen Shelmerdine's.[74]

Friday, 28. At Fredericktown I spoke on Matt. xi, 5, 6. Here I met with Bishop Whatcoat and Sylvester Hutchinson:[75] we formed a plan for our future journeys and labours. They, to visit Maryland by the way of Baltimore and Annapolis, and thence on to Richmond and the towns on the route to Camden in South Carolina, and southward to Georgia; I, in company with Nicholas Snethen, go out to the western conference in Nolichucky, then afterward cross over to the South.

West Virginia

Saturday, 29. The evening brought us to Thomas Keys's, upon Shenandoah. We went by the way of Samuel Phillips's, to see his dear, afflicted wife—perhaps for the last time in this world: God is still gracious to this family. We also saw Harper's ferry, and beheld with satisfaction, the good plain buildings erected there by the United States.

Sunday, 30. At Charlestown I preached under the shady oaks to perhaps fifteen hundred people, upon Heb. x, 39: it was a gracious season—truth had its dominion in some minds. We administered the sacrament. I ordained to the office of deacons, John M'Pherson and Thomas Littleton. I rode home with John Davenport.

[73] The home of John Norris was between Sam's Creek and Frederick. He is listed among the official members of the Frederick Circuit. (Armstrong, *op. cit.*, 508.)

[74] Stephen Shelmerdine (d. 1809), a lieutenant in the Revolutionary War, lived between Liberty and Frederick in Frederick County. He was a trustee of the Methodist Society in Frederick when in 1790 the first lot was bought on West Church Street. (Williams: *History of Frederick County*, I, 457; see note under August 10, 1799.)

[75] Sylvester Hutchinson during his seventeen years as an itinerant ranged from Maryland to New England. In 1801 he was appointed the traveling companion of Bishop Whatcoat. (Stevens, *op. cit.*, III, 457–59; *General Minutes.*)

Virginia

Monday, 31. Reached Winchester. Since I left Baltimore, I suppose I have ridden, by crooks, corners, and straight lines, one hundred and thirty miles. My mind in general has been sweetly stayed upon God.

Wednesday, September 2. We spent this day at Elijah Phelps's[76]—the old place, and it was like old times.

I received an Address from the most respectable citizens of Winchester, praying the continuance of Mr. Snethen to officiate in the ministry amongst them; but it could not be: he was appointed at Baltimore to travel with me, and I could not get another at this time and place to answer as well.

Thursday, 3. We rode through heat and drought to Woodstock. Nicholas Snethen preached upon, "Except ye repent, ye shall all likewise perish." I spoke in the evening on Luke xix, 10: the house was full, and there were people in the street. We lodged at Madera's.

Friday, 4. The weather as yesterday: we nevertheless made thirty miles to Jacob Huster's.

Saturday and *Sabbath day* were spent at Rockingham quarterly meeting, held in Harrisonburg: the brethren were lively in the sacramental meeting. Many came from far, although the heat was very great. N. Snethen preached on *Saturday* upon Rom. xii, 17, and *Sabbath day*, Rom. xii, 1. My subject was 1 Pet. iv, 17. The house could not at all contain the people, we therefore took to the woods; but we failed in shade, and felt some inconvenience in the sun.

Monday, 7. I was very unwell; but I rode. The route led through a fine shade, sixteen miles as computed, but really twenty miles, to William Young's, formerly an elder in the Presbyterian Church. We had a gracious season. Nicholas Snethen preached on John iii, 17. I believe the Lord will work in Augusta county amongst the Presbyterians.

Tuesday, 8. At Moffit's meeting house Nicholas Snethen spoke on 2 Cor. vi, 1, 2. My subject was 1 Pet. v, 7. The heat, augmented by the long drought, was very oppressive to the system: I was very unwell.

Wednesday, 9. At Staunton, Nicholas Snethen preached at eleven o'clock. I preached from Acts iii, 26. Ministers Wilson and Glendie were present. Nicholas Snethen and Philip Bruce held night meeting—heat! heat!

Thursday, 10. We passed Greenville, Fairfield, and came to Lexington to lodge at Shield's: we got here what failed us on the way—good entertainment.

Friday, 11. We rode by the Rockbridge and Springfield, to Pattonsburg,[77]

[76] Elijah Phelps lived near Stephensburg, the present Stephens City, Virginia.

[77] Pattonsburg was in Bottetourt County, Virginia, across the James River from Buchanan. (Summers, *op. cit.*, maps; Map of 1809.)

and thence on to James Tapscote's: I was hungry and unwell, having taken cold by exposure to the evening air.

Saturday, 12. We came to Fincastle. We have made, I presume, one hundred and twenty miles this week; and some rough roads. I have felt suffering faith, and fervent love to God and souls.

Sunday, 13. I preached from 1 John i, 5–7. I had taken cold, attended with a great check to respiration, which made my bodily feelings very uncomfortable.

Monday, 14. We visited Mr. Phillips, a Baptist minister, who received and kindly entertained us: from this fifteen-mile stage we proceeded to Thomas Raborn's, making thirty-three miles for the day. Greatly desired, and much needed, rain came at last.

Tuesday, 15. We preached at Raborn's, brother Snethen and myself, to a very attentive people. I had to excuse my non-attendance at this place last year: the failure was occasioned, first, by my not knowing the distance; secondly, because I was persuaded to take the route by English's ferry,[78] as being the better road for a chaise. After meeting we took up our journey across the Allegheny mountain; but finding after we had ridden nearly ten miles that it was growing late, we turned up towards the sun, and housed for the night with John M'Daniel, upon Tom's Creek. My soul is kept in great peace, and I have grace to bear and suffer, my spirit is calm and pure.

Wednesday, 16. We came to Pepper's ferry[79]—behold me once more on New River!

Thursday, 17. We held a meeting at Pepper's chapel. Nicholas Snethen spoke upon 2 Peter 1, 10. As I was called upon by recommendation to ordain Edward Morgan to the office of a deacon, my subject was 2 Tim. iv, 1, 2. We lodged at Mr. Hance's.

Friday, 18. We stretched along to Thaddeus Cooley's, near Wythe court house, and next day came to Charles Hardy's. My companion's horse fell to-day, and I had scarcely time to reflect upon the probability of its being my turn, when my little mare also came down; but the Lord preserved man and beast.

Sunday, 20. We came over the mountain to Saltville and preached at the widow Russell's. Nicholas Snethen was greatly enlarged, upon Luke xi, 3, 4. I was so feeble, I had but little to say, upon "Behold, now is the day of salvation." I have a partial restoration of health; but the fever returns every morning, added to which, the severe and constant riding, with want of, and generally irregularity of meals, becomes in a great degree a cause of sickness. I was pleased to see our local brethren come forty and fifty miles to visit me. We met with joy, and parted in tears!

[78] This was the ferry operated by William Inglis.

[79] Samuel Pepper's ferry was on New River west of Stoubles Creek and near Dunkard's Bottom in Montomery County, Virginia. (Summers, *op. cit.*, 704, 715.)

Monday, 21. We had to try Clinch mountains—four miles over. I continued on horseback, ascending and descending: my sore-backed, slender-jointed beast wrought it but badly. We made twenty-two miles this day, and happily escaped the showers which fell in the afternoon. We lodged at Francis Browning's.[80]

Tuesday, 22. We had a meeting at Elk Garden meeting house:[81] we felt as if in a stove-room while N. Snethen was speaking, upon, "Work out your own salvation with fear and trembling." I spoke from 2 Peter iii, 17, 18. We dined at Richard Price's.[82] He is now growing very infirm.

Wednesday, 23. We rode to Castle's woods.[83] I was amazed at the goodness of the Lord to this western country generally; and was surprised and gratified to observe the improvements made in Russell county particularly. I was well weary of riding over such an uneven surface as we have lately passed—at the rate of about twenty miles a day, equal to many more on level land.

Thursday, 24. We rested at Charles Bickley's.[84] Nicholas Snethen preached upon Coloss. i, 21, 22. I spoke from 2 Cor. vi, 2: "Behold, now is the accepted time."

Friday, 25. To Copper Creek meeting, fifteen miles. We had mountains, valleys, and rocks, as usual. There was a cabin,[85] but we delivered our testimony in the woods. After meeting, and refreshing our horses with a bite, we pushed on to Moccasin Creek, crossing it nine times in about five miles: the roads were rough as usual, and the fords at the stream, rocks, loose, or sideling and slippery. We lodged at William Lawson's.

Saturday, 26. We wrought down Moccasin to the Gap,[86] where the accumulated waters of the stream have, at some time, apparently burst

[80] Francis Browning went to Russell County, Virginia, from Culpepper County in 1781. He was an ardent Methodist who lived at Elk Garden for seventy years. (Price: *Holston Methodism*, I, 161–62.)

[81] The meeting house at Elk Garden was one of the early churches of Holston. Its successor still stands on the site. (*Ibid.*, I, 159–60.)

[82] Richard Price was the father of John W. Price and the grandfather of the Rev. Richard N. Price, the historian of Holston Methodism. (*Ibid.*, I, 159.)

[83] Castle's Woods was a beautiful valley on Clinch River in Russell County, Virginia. Bickley's Station, home of Charles Bickley, was located there. This frontier settlement had a fort into which the people went for protection against the raiding Indians. Mark Whitaker established a Methodist society there in 1786. (*Ibid.*, I, 164.)

[84] Charles Bickley was one of the early pioneers of Russell County, who lived at Castle's Woods. His descendants still live in Scott County. (Summers: *History of Southwest Virginia*, 67–68; see *Journal* entries and notes for April 28, 1790, May 14, 1796; Whatcoat's *Journal*, *op. cit.*, April 28, 1790.)

[85] The cabin was at the Owens's, frequently referred to by Asbury. It was probably the first church at Owen's Chapel. He lived on Copper Ridge south of the Clinch River and opposite Fort Blackmore in Scott County, Virginia. The last church there was twelve miles west of Castle Woods and was burned about 1930.

[86] Moccasin Gap is about halfway between Gate City, Virginia, and Kingsport, Tennessee.

their way through Clinch Mountain. After recrossing the north branch of Holston, we stopped at John Wadley's, and refreshed man and beast. Our host became our guide, and tripped over the hills with us in the rain, his mare barefoot, and himself without a saddle to ride on, or a great coat to shield him from the weather.

Tennessee

At length we reached Charles Baker's, upon Main Holston, in safety. I began to feel and to fail. I have ridden about one hundred miles in the last four days; the roads equal to any in the United States for badness. My bowels and my poor horse's back are in bad order. How much time we have to read, and write, and pray, those who travel with us may judge.

Sabbath day, 27. I was unwell, and willing to sit still.

Monday, 28. Attended by John Watson, we crossed Holston and Watauga, near the junction, and came to Dungworth's.

Tuesday, 29. I preached upon 2 Tim. iv, 7, 8, and then rode on through Jonesborough to Cashe's.

Wednesday, 30. I spoke on Heb. ii, 1, and hasted on to Ebenezer to attend the conference.

Our brethren in Kentucky did not attend; they pleaded the greatness of the work of God. Twelve of us sat in conference three days; and we had not an unpleasant countenance, nor did we hear an angry word:—and why should it not always be thus? Are we not the ministers of the meek and lowly, the humble and holy Jesus?

Nicholas Snethen gave us two sermons. We ordained on *Friday*, *Saturday*, and *Sabbath day*, and upon each day I improved a little on the duties of ministers. On the *Lord's day* we assembled in the woods, and made a large congregation. My subject was Isa. lxii, 1. On *Friday* and *Saturday evenings*, and on *Sabbath morning*, there was the noise of praise and shouting in the meeting house. It is thought there are twenty-five souls who have found the Lord; they are chiefly the children of Methodists—the children of faith and of many prayers.

North Carolina

Monday, *October* 5. We parted in great love. Our company made twelve miles to Isaiah Harrison's, and next day reached the Warm Springs upon French Broad River.[87]

Wednesday, 7. We made a push for Buncombe court house:[88] man and

[87] Asbury went from Holston to Western North Carolina along the general route taken in 1800. (See note under November 6, 1800.)

[88] Buncombe court house is now Asheville, North Carolina. Buncombe County then extended to the Tennessee, Georgia, and South Carolina lines and covered most of the mountain area of Western North Carolina.

beast felt the mighty hills. I shall calculate from Baker's to this place one hundred and twenty miles; from Philadelphia, eight hundred and twenty miles.

Friday, 9. Yesterday and to-day we rested at George Swain's.

Sabbath day, 11. Yesterday and to-day held quarterly meeting at Daniel Killians's[89] near Buncombe court house. I spoke from Isa. lvii, 6, 7, and 1 Cor. vii, 1. We had some quickenings.

Monday, 12. We came to Murray's[90] upon Mud Creek: here we had a sermon from Nicholas Snethen on Acts xiv, 15. Myself and James Douthet[91] gave an exhortation. We had very warm weather and a long ride. At Major Brittain's[92] near the mouth of Mill's river, we found a lodging.

Tuesday, 13. We came in haste up to elder Davidson's, refreshed man and beast, commended the family to God, and then struck into the mountain. The want of sleep and other inconveniences made me unwell. We came down Saluda River near Saluda Mountain: it tried my lame feet and old feeble joints. French Broad, in its meanderings, is nearly two hundred miles long; the line of its course is semicircular; its waters are pure, rapid, and its bed generally rocky, except the Blue Ridge; it passes through all the western mountains. We continued at John Douthet's[93] on *Wednesday*, and *Thursday* furnished a meeting. Nicholas Snethen spoke upon 1 John v, 10. I spoke also; my subject was Hosea x, 12.

South Carolina

Friday, 16. We reached Samuel Burdine's,[94] sixteen miles. Nicholas Snethen spoke from 1 John v, 4, 5. I followed from Titus ii, 11, 12.

[89] Daniel Killian lived near Asheville, and his home was one of Asbury's famous stopping places. The original log house was torn down in 1901, and many of its logs were used in a tenant house. Asbury frequently preached under a large tree in the yard. Historical markers have been erected there and at a second house built by Daniel Killian not far away. The Asbury Methodist Church continues the society established in the Killian house and contains the chair which Killian made for the use of Asbury.

[90] William Murray kept Murray's Inn on the Howard Gap Road near the present Fletcher, North Carolina. (Patton, *op. cit.*, 39.)

[91] James Douthet was the presiding elder of the Salisbury District, which embraced Buncombe County. The section was on the Swannanoa Circuit.

[92] William Brittain kept a small hotel at the present Flat Rock. (Arthur, *op. cit.*, 493; Patton, *op. cit.*, 101.) Colonel James Brittain, a Revolutionary soldier, was one of a group that bought land in 1852 on which the Methodist church in Hendersonville now stands. Phillip Brittain was among those who bought land in 1826 and erected the Mills River Methodist Church. (Patton, *op. cit.*, 63, 178.)

[93] John Douthet was the father of the Rev. James Douthet. (See note under February 14, 1800. See also Asbury's *Journal* for October 29, 1813.) Asbury had followed his former route to South Carolina by way of Douthet's Ford at Table Rock into Pendleton County.

[94] Burdine lived near Pickens, South Carolina.

Sabbath, 18. Yesterday and to-day we attended quarterly meeting at Salem, near Staunton's ferry, upon Saluda River.[95] Nicholas Snethen's subject was Psalm cxix, 59, 60. I came off with reading a letter containing an account of the revival of religion amongst the Presbyterians and Methodists in Cumberland. On the *Sabbath* Nicholas Snethen spoke upon Luke xiv, 26; the ground I took was John iii, 19, 20. After a shower on *Saturday* it cleared up cold, with the wind from the north-west. The house would not contain our *Sabbath* congregation; they stood in front of the cabin, under whose projecting roof we found shelter from the sun. Our situation was eligible, because the voice was thrown forward, and because we were protected from the wind whilst speaking. James Jenkins[96] followed with a call to backsliders. The people were serious, but I heard of no conversions. We lodged at Henry Parriss's, on the Grove.

Monday, 19. At John Bramblet's, Greensville. After meeting, we rode to Thomas Terry's, upon Reedy River.[97]

Tuesday, 20. Thanks be to God for one night's rest. I calculate that we have ridden eighty miles since we left John Douthet's. O Lord! thou preservest man and beast. We attended a meeting at a Presbyterian vacant house. Nicholas Snethen preached upon Isa. lv, 6. I read James M'Gready's narrative of the work of God in Logan county, Kentucky.[98]

Wednesday, 21. We rode sixteen miles to the widow Bramlett's meeting house.[99] Nicholas Snethen spoke on Matt. v, 3. I followed from 2 Pet. i, 4. We rode four miles to Daniel M'Kee's, where we held a meeting in the evening.

Thursday, 22. We came twenty miles to Caseys.[100] late and lost, and arrived whilst Coleman Carlisle[101] was holding forth. I only read a letter and gave an exhortation. This family (the Caseys) entertained us when we were few in number in these parts.

Friday, 23. We rode ten miles to Bigg's meeting house, and held a meeting. Nicholas Snethen preached from 1 Tim. i, 5; I only exhorted—the wind all the while blowing freely upon my naked head. We kept

[95] Salem Church is now in the suburbs of Greenville. The ferry crossed into Greenville County just below the Easley road.

[96] James Jenkins, known as "Thundering Jimmy" and "Bawling Jenkins," was presiding elder of the South Carolina district and a prominent leader of Methodism in the state. He joined the conference in 1792 and died at Camden on January 24, 1847. He published a valuable autobiography in 1842. (Betts., *op. cit.*, 83; Shipp, *op. cit.*, 232, 233.)

[97] Terry lived at Fork Shoals.

[98] The McGready brothers were among the leaders of the camp-meeting movement which began in Kentucky.

[99] Bramlett's Chapel was across the Enoree in Laurens County near Woodruff in Spartanburg County. It is still in existence and a part of the Woodruff charge.

[100] Casey lived in Union County.

[101] The Rev. Coleman Carlisle was on the Broad River Circuit. For his unjust expulsion in 1794 and his subsequent reinstatement see note under December 30, 1793.

on ten miles to Davis's; here we held an evening meeting: Nicholas Snethen preached, and I exhorted.

Saturday, 24. We had to attend a meeting appointed at Broad River circuit. Nicholas Snethen spoke from 2 Tim. ii, 8. I only exhorted, and read a letter giving an account of the work of God in Kentucky.

We have been working this week from Saluda to Reedy River, down the Enoree, crossing and recrossing through Pendleton, Greensville, Laurens, Spartanburg, and Newbury counties in South Carolina. I cannot record great things upon religion in this quarter; *but cotton sells high.* I fear there is more gold than grace—more of silver than of "that wisdom that cometh from above."

Monday, 26. At Buford's meeting house[102] Nicholas Snethen preached from James i, 4; there was some breathing after life. We lodged at Mr. Hardy's.

Tuesday, 27. At Bethel[103] Nicholas Snethen preached on Heb. x, 32. I afterward gave a discourse. We next day attended a meeting at the widow Coate's, in the Bush River circuit[104]: Nicholas Snethen spoke on Matt. v, 20. I gave a few words on Luke viii, 18. We had an open season; and were made happy at John Myers's,[105] the steward of the circuit.

Thursday, 29. We had a long ride to Edgefield court house, and were kindly entertained at Doctor Fuller's:[106] the town was in great disorder, it being court time.

Friday, 30. We came in haste to Daniel Baugh's: here we met Bishop Whatcoat, Sylvester Hutchinson,[107] who had come along rapidly. At the meeting house, where we spent about three hours, we were joined by Stith Mead, John Garven, and Lewis Mycrel.[108] Now we formed a plan for future labours and travel: it was concluded that Bishop Whatcoat should go from the centre, east to Savannah and St. Mary's; whilst I go west, in Georgia.

[102] Beauford's, or Bluford's, was probably the same as Buford's meeting house between the Tyger and Enoree. It was named for Major Bird Buford. It is no longer in existence. There is a Buford Street Methodist Church at Gaffney in the adjacent county.

[103] This was the Mount Bethel Academy in the Finch Community of Newberry County. (See note under March 19, 1795.)

[104] This was in lower Newberry County. Lewis Myers and Levi Garrison were the preachers on the circuit.

[105] Myers lived in Saluda County.

[106] This was probably Dr. Fuller of Beech Island.

[107] Sylvester Hutchinson had been appointed to travel with Bishop Whatcoat, and Nicholas Snethen had been appointed to travel with Asbury.

[108] Stith Mead was presiding elder of the Georgia District and John Garven was stationed at Augusta. Lewis "Mycrel" must have been Lewis Myers of the Bush River Circuit. The preachers met to plan a strategy. The conference was not scheduled to meet until January 1.

Georgia

Saturday, 31. We came to Augusta. On the *Sabbath day* Nicholas Snethen preached; after which I gave a few thoughts upon, "My house shall be called a house of prayer for all people"; Nicholas Snethen spoke again, in the afternoon, on *the choice of Moses*. Bishop Whatcoat held forth at night. We have a very large and most elegant house in this place,[109] for which we are indebted, chiefly, to the generosity of the inhabitants. Our congregations are most respectable, and very attentive; but I heard of no conversions—the time for this is not yet come.

We have travelled this week one hundred and twenty miles. The season is exceedingly dry. I was made glad to find one who had departed from God for fifteen years, happily restored to the Lord and to myself; his own dear wife and child, and a family of one hundred souls, are also in the enjoyment of religion. Maryland appears as if it would feel the millennium in a few years.

Monday, November 2. We rested in Augusta. In the evening we rode to Mr. Lacey's, and next day travelled on to Columbia, twenty miles, and stopped with brother Allen, a local preacher. We had our brothers Hutchinson and Mead with us.[110]

Wednesday, 4. At Scott's meeting house, upon Little River, Nicholas Snethen spoke on the Pharisee and publican. We came home with Mr. Gatrell. Here we parted with Bishop Whatcoat and his assistant, they directing their course south-west, across the State, and by a circle to Savannah and St. Mary's.

Thursday, 5. We came an hour too late to the Cross Roads: Nicholas Snethen spoke from 1 Tim. iv, 8. I followed from Isa. lxi, 1–3. By riding a little in the rain and evening damps, we arrived at Richard Easter's in Petersburg, at the junction of the rivers, on which are the towns of Lisbon and Vienna in South Carolina. Petersburg is beautifully situated, has about eighty houses, well constructed for stores, and about one hundred buildings in all; they are generally one story in height, well painted, with convenient shed attached.[111] At noon we held a meeting; the day was cold, and the house open. At night I preached in Richard Easter's house on Isa. xl, 31; the people were very attentive.

Saturday, 7. At Thompson's meeting house[112] Nicholas Snethen

[109] This was the church which was in process of construction when Asbury visited Augusta in the previous year. (See *Journal* entry and note for November 29, 1800.)

[110] Sylvester Hutchinson, Whatcoat's traveling companion, and Stith Mead.

[111] (See note under April 9, 1788.) "The people living in Carolina and Georgia at the junction of Broad River with Savannah got such grand ideas in their heads that they named the town Vienna; the Elbert town in the fork, St. Petersburg; the Lincoln County town, Lisbon." (Bowen: *Story of Wilkes County*, 52.)

[112] Thompson's meeting house was located in the southeast part of Elbert County, about ten miles from Petersburg. About 1877 the church was moved about two miles,

preached from Matt. xviii, 19, 20. We also held a meeting on the *Sabbath.*

I suppose we have now travelled twelve hundred miles since leaving Philadelphia. I often have it whispered in my ear, what certain folks are pleased to say of my being an Englishman. How can I help that; I am not ashamed of it. But I am seeking souls, and Zion's glory; heaven is my country.

"There is my house and portion fair,
My treasure and my heart are there,
And my abiding home;
For me my elder brethren stay,
And angels beckon me away,
And Jesus bids me come."

Monday, 9. At Pellum's we had many people, to whom Nicholas Snethen spoke upon Matt. v, 8. We lodged at Captain Blackman's.

Tuesday, 10. Nicholas Snethen spoke at Coldwater[113] on Matt. xi, 28, 29; and next day, at Oliver's chapel,[114] again, upon Psalm lxxxv, 8; I followed with a few words upon 1 John i, 6, 7. We lodged at Stinchecomb's: here I found Maryland people who heard me when children.

Thursday, 12. We came to Redwine's.[115] Here some have been awakened amongst the Methodists, and have joined the Baptists; thus we have laboured, and others reap the fruit.

Friday, 13. At Carroll's meeting house Nicholas Snethen preached from Titus ii, 14. I spoke from Acts xx, 16–18. We have had large, lively meetings. We lodged at Mr. Allen's. Here Nicholas Snethen left me to go and spend five or six weeks in Augusta, at the desire of the citizens; he can be better spared now, as we are near the frontiers, and the congregations are small, and brother Benjamin Blanton is with me.

Saturday, 14. We came to Park's meeting house.[116] Brother Blanton

and a new building was erected and called Bethlehem Church, which is still in use. In the cemetery of Bethlehem Church are buried the remains of around fifty persons which were brought from Petersburg when that town was inundated by the waters of the Clark-Hill reservoir.

[113] Coldwater Church was on the Big Coldwater Creek, twelve miles from the present Elberton. It was near the home of Ralph Banks and was probably erected by him. The Banks home where Asbury sometimes stopped is still standing. It has fourteen large rooms and a cellar. Banks came from Granville County, North Carolina, in 1785

[114] Dionysius Oliver was the founder of Petersburg. Major John Oliver was a Methodist who was converted by Lorenzo Dow. (Bowen, *op. cit.*, 82, 137.)

[115] Jacob Redwine, a Revolutionary soldier, was born in Pittsburgh in 1751. He moved to Elbert County, Georgia, from Montgomery County, North Carolina, and died in Coweta County in 1840. He was largely responsible for the erection of the Redwine Church, which is still in existence, the fourth building on or near the present site.

[116] Park's meeting house was probably built by Henry Park, who was converted in the revivals of John Major and Thomas Humphries in 1786. He lived in the present Elbert County. (Bowen, *op. cit.*, 119.)

spoke on John xii, 35; my subject was Heb. vi, 11, 12. We have travelled about one hundred miles since our entrance into Georgia, passing through parts of Richmond, Columbia, Lincoln, Elbert, and Franklin counties. The evenings and mornings have been cold; the people, however, are extremely kind. I have experienced great sensible enjoyment of God—our cabins and courts, when Jesus is there. In my ministry I have been greatly assisted, but unless I am more temperate in my talk, in tone and time, I shall not be able to manage more than every other day.

In a serious conference with Bishop Whatcoat, Nicholas Snethen, Lyle, Hutchinson, and myself, it plainly appeared, that the best way in future would be to meet at the Virginia conference, and thence continue together to the New York conference; after which, one might go to the east, and the other to the western conference: the bishop who went east, would then visit the Eastern States and the lake country, and thence onward to Pittsburg and the Virginia districts; the bishop who goeth west, will visit over the Blue Ridge, Holston, Kentucky, Tennessee, Georgia, South and North Carolina, to the conferences in the centre of the work: where both will meet again:—in this we all agreed. It was also determined, that each bishop should always have an elder as a travelling companion.

Sabbath, 15. I spoke on Psalm cxlvii, 2–4. Brother Blanton spoke upon *redeeming the time*. We had lodged at Henry Park's. Several persons of the Presbyterian society, upon hearing read Mr. Hodges's letter to me, communed with us.

Monday, 16. We rode to George Christian's. Here we made a stand *at an Ephrata in the woods*, where the logs were laid for a meeting house. My subject was Psalm cxlv, 18–20. On *Tuesday*, my foundation was laid upon Zech. xii, 10. It was the voice of the Lord Jesus: 1st. *How* he was pierced by the house of David, and the inhabitants of Jerusalem—how he is *now* pierced by open sinners, formal and false professors and backsliders 2d. The effects of the outpouring of the Spirit—prayers and sorrows. We lodged at Mr. Walker's, formerly a Presbyterian: his father wishes a more intimate acquaintance with the Methodists, whom he has now heard for the first time. We could not finish our meeting in the woods the second day, being prevented by a storm of wind and rain.

Wednesday, 18. We rode with haste into Jackson—a proper frontier county. We halted at Professor Horton's. I was very unwell, but spoke, after brother Blanton, upon Luke iv, 18, 19. The house and yard held the people. In returning from an upper room, whither I had retired, being slip-shod, I lost my feet, and went from step to step, until the turn stopped me—my back suffered in my fall.

Thursday, 19. We found at Tidwell's a very open house in the woods. I spoke from Acts iii, 26. At Freeman's, next day, we had another open house lately put up, where brother Blanton held forth, upon "the whole head is sick, and the whole heart faint." My subject was Isaiah xxxv, 3–6.

We started, hungry and cold, crossing at Malone's mill, a branch of Oconee, and came to Henry Pope's in Oglethorpe. We have ridden about eighty miles this week of short and cold days. Why should a living man complain?—but to be three months together upon the frontiers, where, generally, you have but one room and fireplace, and half a dozen folks about you, strangers perhaps, and their family certainly (and they are not usually small in these plentiful new countries), making a crowd—and this is not all; for here you *may* meditate if you can, and here you *must* preach, read, write, pray, sing, talk, eat, drink, and sleep—or fly into the woods. Well! I have pains in my body, particularly my hip, which are very afflictive when I ride; but I cheer myself as well as I may with songs in the night—with Wesley's, Watt's, and Stennett's Sight of Canaan, in four hymns. In this country are seen evident traces of a great population, which has some time existed before the present discoverers and settlers of America.

Saturday, 21. Quarterly meeting was held at Pope's meeting house. We had some rain. My text was Matt. xi, 28–30. It was an open time. We lodged at Henry Pope's. Hope Hull came in dripping in the evening, to meet the Lord and his brethren.

Sunday, 22. We had about one thousand people to hear. I came forward again upon Titus ii, 15. Hope Hull and Stith Mead held forth after me. It was an open season. I baptized some adults and infants.

Monday, 23. We went forward to the widow Stuart's, upon the branches of Little River, in Oglethorpe county: we had a cold day, but a blessed meeting which held eight hours; several were converted, and a society was formed, consisting of fifteen souls. I lodged at General John Stuart's.

Tuesday, 24. We had a long ride on a cold day, and arrived at an open house: my subject was, "He that saith he abideth in him, ought himself also so to walk, even as he walked." Our meeting continued three hours, and four souls professed converting grace. I have ridden thirty miles to-day to Wyatt's, hungry and cold. We frequently breakfast at seven o'clock, and dine at six o'clock in the evening.

Wednesday, 25. At Liberty[117] I spoke on Matt, v, 8. I lodged with Joshua Moore: in this family I have served three generations, in Delaware and in Georgia. In Liberty there is life—many souls have been brought to God, even children.

Thursday, 26. My subject at Butler's was Rev. xxii, 14: a cold day this. At Chesnut Level, a beautiful spot, we housed with Mr. Bush: this is an agreeable family, for whom God has worked—and will yet work.

[117] Liberty Chapel and camp ground was in Green County, Georgia, about twelve miles south of Greensboro near the Veazey Road, formerly the Sparta Road. The chapel, or its successor, is still in existence.

Friday, 27. We came to a new house, in Warren county, called Rehoboth, built by the zeal of brothers Fontaine and Randall. I felt enlargement upon 1 Peter v, 7.

Saturday, 28. At Heath's I spoke from Psalm cxxvi, 5, 6; we had an open time. In our crowded house were many brethren and sisters from far. The power of God was present at our night meeting. Georgia promises something great, under the presidentship of Stith Mead; as does also Maryland (west) under that of Wilson Lee. It is of great consequence to have men in the spirit of the work, as president elders of districts.

Sunday, 29. I spoke in the woods at a small distance from the chapel, which the society held in possession: their love feast began at nine o'clock, and held until three o'clock: eight souls are believed to have found peace with God; among whom was a little daughter of Mr. Bush's, about nine years of age. My subject was Isaiah lxii, 6, 7. I was often interrupted by singing and shouting. I was comfortably provided with lodging, at the house of Lawyer Stith's, whither I had been affectionately invited—may my friends find grace here and glory hereafter!

Monday, 30. I called, after fervent and frequent application, upon Mr. Noseworthy: he was once in the possession of religion, and in the exercise of the ministry; but changes and worldly prosperity have wrought an unfavourable change upon him: when in distress he calleth upon God, and wisheth to have the prayers of the servants of God. Lord, save him and his family! We found Smyrna meeting house deserted by removals to other neighbourhoods; but I had an open season upon 1 Corinthians vi, 2. I lodged with James Thweatt.

Tuesday, December 1. At Sparta,[118] after various exercises of mind, I fixed upon 2 Peter iii, 17, 18. Here I saw several acquaintances from Virginia—Jarrattites from Dinwiddie county, amongst whom I was kindly entertained at the house of Mr. Lucas.[119] Whilst I was reading Mr. M'Gready's letter, a Presbyterian-Methodist woman shouted and warned the Spartans to flee from the wrath to come. I lodged with Henry Moss, an old disciple from Virginia.

Wednesday, 2. At Hathorne's, many attended: my subject was Titus ii, 11, 12. We came to Henry Harris's that night.

Thursday, 3. At Harris's meeting house I spoke from Psalm cxlvi, 5–9.

Friday, 4. At new chapel, Williams's swamp, my groundwork was

[118] This was Asbury's first visit to Sparta, then a frontier village not yet ten years old. He probably preached in the court house, as there was no church in the community. The first Methodist preachers in the village were probably those on the Richmond Circuit, and it probably became an appointment when George Dougherty was on the Oconee Circuit in 1799. (Smith: *Georgia Methodism*, 67, 68.)

[119] The Jarrattites were the converts of the Rev. Devereaux Jarratt, evangelical Anglican preacher in Virginia. John Lucas was long a leader of the church in the vicinity. (Smith, *op. cit.*, 68.)

John iii, 16. We were indebted for lodging to D. Davis. Next day we went onward to New Hope, to hold our quarterly meeting. At the close of the week I feel that I fail; the heat of the weather and the want of water—*good water*—I presume to be the cause. We had a noise and a shaking under brother Mead's preaching; but I was unwell and dispirited. We have been travelling in Hancock and Washington counties, and have made about ninety miles this week. I lodged at Richard Burney's; he has a wife and ten living children, the mother of whom appears to be as active as any of the family.

Our love feast began at nine o'clock, and held until three o'clock in the afternoon. Notwithstanding the wind was at north-west, myself and the congregation had to seek an open place in the woods: my improvement was upon Matthew xi, 5, 6. Three souls professed to be converted: they were baptized, and joined the society. I lodged at Jesse Jordan's.

Monday, 7. We came to Father Brett's.

Tuesday, 8. We crossed the stream of Williamson's swamp, the Central Stream and Rocky Comfort; these three streams are the principal branches of the Ogeechee, and make their junction near the seat of government. I preached in the State house[120]: it was an easterly, cold, damp, day: my subject was 2 Cor. v, 19, 20. I dined with Doctor Powell, and housed for the night with Colonel John Lewis.

Wednesday, 9. I preached to a few people in a solitary place amongst the pines, on Luke xi, 13. We dined at Mr. Pollitt's, and came on to Colonel Johnson's.

Thursday, 10. We came to Coxe's meeting house in Burke county[121]—it was an open house, a cold day, and a cold people in the fullest sense of the word.

We came on across Brier and M'Vean's Creek to the Widow Brack's: here I preached a funeral discourse on the occasion of the death of her late husband: my subject was 1 Cor. xv, 56, 57.

Saturday, 12. We came to Augusta, and arrived whilst Nicholas Snethen was preaching. Riding in the cold and writing in the night have occasioned a weakness in my eye.

Sabbath, 13. Ordaining Brothers Joshua Moore and Gilmore to the office of deacons, and assisting at the sacrament, made all my labours for this day. We had an excellent discourse from Nicholas Snethen on Rev. ii, 4, 5. The Lord hath made windows in heaven, and he can do it again, and souls may be converted in Augusta. Here I leave the State of Georgia.

[120] Asbury was now at Louisville, in Jefferson County, then the capital of Georgia. (Smith, *op. cit.*, 68.)

[121] Coxe's meeting house was probably the later Mount Zion Church in the northern part of Burke County. (Smith, *op. cit.*, 68.)

South Carolina

Monday, 14. I found Weatherley meeting house[122] much neater than I expected: my subject here was 2 Cor. iv, 14: "For the love of Christ constraineth us." I know not what beside should move a Christian minister to travel and labour in this country.

Tuesday, 15. Through the rain to Chester's. Next day to Trotter's, where we had damp weather, an open house, and few people. I lodged at Mr. Trotter's.[123]

Thursday, 17. At Jacob Barr's,[124] upon Edisto, I spoke from 2 Tim. iv, 7, 8—few people. In Georgia "I groaned, being burdened"; but my congregations were considerably larger, my rides shorter, and the people abundantly more feeling and fervent than they are here. I have ridden eighty sandhill miles: the weather is very changeable; I feel my old age and infirmities; my eyes and feet are feeble; but, glory to God! I have strong faith for myself and for the prosperity of Zion. Glory, glory, glory to God! Amen!

Saturday, 19. At Cattle Creek[125] my text was Heb. vi, 11, 12. After speaking I read the letters narrative of the work of God. I lodged at Sebastian Fanchesse's[126] and was entertained like a president.

Sabbath, 20. I attended love feast and sacrament, and preached on Matt. xi, 28–30: the people were very still; a few tears were the only signs of feeling which *we* saw. I lodged with Thomas Simpson.

Monday, 21. At the Indian Fields,[127] I spoke from Heb. x, 38; the preachers attended with me, and bore their parts in the religious exercises of the meeting.

Tuesday, 22. We rode in a damp morning to the Cypress, within thirty miles of Charleston:[128] I spoke here on 2 Cor. vi, 1, 2. I felt some opening.

[122] Weatherley meeting house was on Tinker Creek several miles south of Windsor in Aiken County, South Carolina.

[123] Chester lived in upper Barnwell County. Trotter lived near Bamberg.

[124] Jacob Barr lived across the Edisto River in Orangeburg County.

[125] Cattle Creek Church was visited by Asbury as early as 1788. It later became an important camp ground, and both church and camp ground are still in existence about six miles northeast of Branchville in Orangeburg County.

[126] The name of Fanchesse was later corrupted to Funches or Funchess. The daughter of Sebastian, Mary Fanchesse, married a member of the Crum family, and her grandchildren and great grandchildren still reside in Orangeburg County. (Professor Mason Crum, Duke University.)

[127] Indian Fields Church is still active. It is located about half a mile from the original site in Dorchester County on Highway 15 just south of Rosinville. In 1838 the Indian Fields camp meeting was moved two miles farther south, where it still operates as the largest of the old-time camp meetings in the state.

[128] The Cypress meeting house was in lower Dorchester County near Ridgeville on the northwest side of Cypress Swamp near the Berkeley County line. It was an early camp ground and still continues as such on the Ridgeville Circuit. Perhaps Asbury was

Next day I returned to John Moore's[129] and gave a discourse on Heb. ii, 3.

Thursday, 24. The Four Holes is a name given to a river because there are four sinks or holes upon the banks: here, at the White meeting house,[130] I preached on 2 Pet. iii, 18: "But grow in grace." 1. We should have grace planted or sown in our souls. 2. Grow in the habits and exercises of grace. 3. Rules by which we should grow in grace. 4. By what rules we may judge of our growth in grace. I lodged at Jacob Dantzler's.[131]

The Four Holes and Wasmassaw are about eighty miles long; the former, the north—the latter, the central branch of the Edisto River:[132] this settlement was originally peopled by the Dutch Presbyterians: they have declined in language and in religion: the last is reviving in the present rising generation, many of whom have joined the Methodists.

Saturday, 26. We came to Whetstone's meeting house[133] to hold our quarterly meeting: many people attended at noon and at night. I have made a *proper* visit through Edisto, which I had not before done. I find the truth of an observation made by dear John Wesley to Doctor Coke, upon his going to Nova Scotia: the doctor said he did not think highly of the place; "That is because you have never been there," replied Wesley—"when you are there you will think and feel for the people." I have now ridden about seventeen hundred miles upon this tour. I have had close communion with God, and enlargement in preaching the word of life to saints, seekers, and sinners.

Sabbath, 27. Sylvester Hutchinson preached; I only exhorted. As we had seven preachers present, who were on their way to conference, we employed the day and the night in the work. On *Monday* we crossed the Congaree at Hart's ferry,[134] and came to Pickering's; and next day continued on to Camden, crossing Wateree, at English ferry;[135] parts of our route led over deep sands, and all through was barren. I wrote answers to letters.

proceeding to Charleston but turned northward, realizing that the time was short before the meeting of the conference in Camden on January 1.

[129] This probably was John Moorer, which is a prominent name in that section.

[130] White meeting house was in Orangeburg County, southeast of Orangeburg.

[131] The society which met at Jacob Dantzler's was later organized into a church, and by 1815 Jericho Meeting House was standing on land given by Jacob Felkel. It is now Jericho Methodist Church, in the lower part of Calhoun County, the present building having been erected before 1850. A low partition separating the men and women and a slave gallery were removed in 1890, and a porch was added.

[132] Asbury's geography was not entirely accurate. Four Holes flows into the Edisto, but the Wassamaw flows into the Cypress which joints the Ashley.

[133] John Whetstone had a plantation several miles southeast of St. Mathews, towards Lone Star, and Asbury frequently stopped there. The Whetstone Church was succeeded by the Tabernacle Church, located one mile southwest of St. Mathews, and this in turn became the St. Mathews Church.

[134] Hart's Ferry was later known as McCord's Ferry.

[135] The English Ferry crossed the Wateree above Stateburg.

1802

1802 *McKendree and Asbury at Strother's Meetinghouse*

CHAPTER THIRTY-ONE

South Carolina

Friday, January 1, 1802. We opened conference.[1] I gave a discourse upon Isa. lxvi, 1–3. We conducted our business in great peace, and upon the *Sabbath day* were ready for the ordination of seven elders and seven deacons. The members of our conference, with a few others, made up our congregations, to whom we preached at noon and at night each day. Nicholas Snethen spoke on "Many shall run to and fro, and knowledge shall be increased"; and also on the *hidden leaven.* Our finances were low: the married and the single preachers were paid up; but there was no surplus for the children.[2] On *Tuesday* the 5th, we concluded our labours in the greatest harmony. It was thought best to divide South Carolina into two districts; one called Saluda, the other Camden:[3] they were placed under the president eldership of two natives of the State—James Jenkins, and George Dougherty.

[1] This was the sixteenth annual conference. Nicholas Snethen was chosen secretary and served in this capacity for three years. There were now seven conferences in the country, although they were still known as districts. The South Carolina Conference included both South Carolina and Georgia, and a part of North Carolina.

[2] The salaries of the preachers, including the bishops, had been increased to eighty dollars per year; though Asbury opposed the marriage of the preachers, some attempt was made to provide an extra stipend for their children, but this met with small success. Married preachers were frequently forced to leave the itinerancy, and this accounted for the large number of locations reported.

[3] There were actually three districts in the South Carolina Conference. These were the Georgia under Stith Mead, the Saluda under George Dougherty, and the Camden under James Jenkins. (See *Minutes.*)

Wednesday, 6. We rode through heavy damps and dews, twenty miles, to James Rembert's.[4]

Thursday, 7. We made a heavy stretch to Pudding Swamp; but there was no admittance for us at a certain house which shall be nameless: we were as kindly entertained as heart could wish at Mr. Lesesne's;[5] I believe the providence of God led us hither, that preaching might be brought to, and a society formed, at this house.

Friday, 8. We had rain, and came dripping by Kings Tree, and by the lower bridge upon Black River: we were made comfortable, and very welcome at Mr. Miller's.

Saturday, 9. We reached Georgetown. I shall put our pleasures and our pains in a small compass. We were but four days riding one hundred and twenty miles; the weather is like April. I have now made one thousand nine hundred miles. My soul hath been surprisingly stayed upon, and devoted to Jehovah. What South Carolina was, as to Methodism, when I came first to Georgetown, I know; and what it is now, I know: but what may it be thirty years hence?

Sabbath, 10. At Georgetown Nicholas Snethen spoke upon Philippians ii, 1, 2; in the afternoon I spoke upon Galatians vi, 9; at night, Nicholas Snethen again held forth upon "O that they were wise," &c.

Monday, 11. We took the path; dined on the fare we brought with us; and lodged with Mr. Rogers, in Kingston;[6] having made the distance forty-two miles by going somewhat out of the way.

Tuesday, 12. We had between forty and fifty people to hear us in an open house. We lodged at Mr. Wilson's. Next day we crossed Wacamaw at Kingston, came on to Little River,[7] fed at M. Hankin's, and reached Abraham Bessant's, where we housed for the night.

North Carolina

Thursday, 14. Nicholas Snethen came forward in the name of his Master: I followed upon "Consider him that endured such contradiction of sinners against himself, lest you be wearied and faint in your minds." After preaching, we rode on to the house of my once dear friend William Gause, senior; but death had stolen a march upon me—the body of my friend was in the dust, his soul is, I hope and trust, with God.

[4] (See note under March 27, 1788.) Rembert Hall and Rembert's Chapel were prominent Methodist centers about two miles apart.

[5] Lesesne is a well-known Huguenot name in Clarendon County. This member of the family lived in the eastern part of that county.

[6] Kingston was the present Conway.

[7] Little River is in the eastern part of Horry County, two miles from the North Carolina line.

Friday, 15. I visited old Ocean: upon my return I made out a plan for fourteen months' travelling.

Saturday, 16. We attended a meeting at Charlotteville[8] meeting house: Nicholas Snethen spoke upon "Faith, hope, and charity"; I followed on "Let us come therefore boldly, to the throne of grace." We have ridden a solitary, sandy way, about a hundred and ten miles; and in three meetings there were not many more than one hundred souls. O Lord, can these dry bones live? I have been kept in a dependent, praying state of soul. We have the most delightful weather, kind friends, and good entertainment for man and beast. I trust the seed sown in the hearts of some will live and grow to the glory of God, and the good of generations to come to the end of time. I have now filled up two thousand miles of the three thousand I had calculated to be the distance from and back again to Philadelphia; hitherto I have been mightily helped. Glory, glory, glory to the Eternal Trinity in Eternal Unity! We lodged at John Gause's:[9] our host is a local minister, and, I trust, a dear child of God; I hope he never may entail the system of slaveholding upon his posterity.

Sabbath, 17. At Lockwood's Folly meeting house Nicholas Snethen spoke upon a portion of Psalm cxix. I followed from the Epistle General of John iii, 1, 2. It was an exceedingly cold day, and few people. As there were some difficulties in our way, we came off to Town Creek, and housed with Charles Gause: we made our *Sabbath day's* journey thirty miles, and yet had time to dine in the woods.

Monday, 18. Hearing of an appointment for the circuit preachers, we would not lose time, but rode down to New Hope. We both spoke, and then went on to Rolks's,[10] where we lodged for the night.

Tuesday, 19. Could we have crossed the creek to Edward Sullivan's we should have saved ourselves a ride of seven miles round it. Nicholas Snethen went forward upon "Take heed, and beware of covetousness": after him I followed with a warning voice, "Wherefore the Holy Ghost saith, Today, if ye will hear his voice harden not your hearts."

Wednesday, 20. At Wilmington I found matters not altogether as I could wish, neither temporally nor spiritually; in both these relations had the African church been willed to my care; another relation I preserved by the appointment of African stewards. Nicholas Snethen preached on 2 Cor. i, 3, 4. I gave a discourse upon "He that saith he abideth in him ought himself also so to walk," &c. Nicholas Snethen again held forth: his subject was 1 John iv, 4.

[8] Charlotteville was the present Shallotte, North Carolina.

[9] There were six branches of the Gause family in Brunswick County, North Carolina —Benjamin, Charles, Susanna, Bryant, John, Nedam, and William. All of them owned slaves. (*Heads of Families*, N.C., 1790, 189.)

[10] This was probably John Rook, since no Rolks family was listed in Brunswick County or elsewhere. (*Ibid.*)

Friday, 22. We came to Topsail, and dined with Mrs. Campbell, a gracious soul, and so also is her daughter. Thence we went forward to the Widow Spicer's,[11] and arrived about an hour in the night. The sands were heavy, and our horses began to fail greatly.

Saturday, 23. We rode up to New River, where we found Lot Ballard out among the woods, with his own and his father's old mansion moved together. Want of shoes, rest, and food had almost done over my little mare.

Sabbath, 24. Nicholas Snethen spoke upon Rom. viii, 6, 7. I gave an exhortation upon John v, 39, 40. It was not at all agreeable to me to see nearly a hundred slaves standing outside, and peeping in at the door, whilst the house was half empty: they were not worthy to come in because they were black! Farewell, farewell to that house forever!

I have close communion with God. If we spare our lungs, yet must we work our bones and our flesh with riding. We lodged at B. Wilder's.[12] Next day we came along through the rain to Mr. Hargate's,[13] near the head of Trent River.

Tuesday, 26. We arrived in Newbern. Our evening lecture by Nicholas Snethen was upon Psalm li: "Against thee only have I sinned, and done this evil in thy sight." He again spoke on *Thursday*, and on *Friday evening* also: I concluded each meeting with prayer. We were crowded every night. I judged it needful to make some temporal and spiritual arrangements for the society in Newbern—that a travelling preacher shall attend every Sabbath is one. Newbern is a trading, growing town; there are seven hundred or a thousand houses already built, and the number is yearly increased by less or greater additions, among which are some respectable brick edifices; the new court house, truly so; neat and elegant; another famous house, said to be designed for the masonic and theatrical gentlemen: it might make a most excellent church. The population of the town, citizens, and transient persons, may amount to three thousand five hundred or four thousand souls.

Sabbath day, 31. Cold and cloudy. I gave a sermon upon Rom. ii, 7, 8. Nicholas Snethen spoke from Heb. xiii, 16; and in the evening, on 1 John iv, 10, 11. We made a public collection which amounted to nearly sixty dollars; and parted from our brethren, whom we left full of good resolutions to finish the house of God: the African Methodists also were about to build a place of worship. Truly we are encouraged; our own people are stirred up, and judges, counsellors, doctors, and ministers, attended our preaching, and appeared to be pleased: may they be profited, and finally saved!

We had a severe ride to Washington, thirty-five miles, crossing Neuse

[11] Elzey and John Spicer lived in Onslow County, North Carolina. (*Ibid.*)

[12] A Hopkins Wilder lived in Onslow County. (*Ibid.*)

[13] Daniel Hargate lived in Jones County. (*Ibid.*)

and Tar Rivers: near the end of our ride the rain quickened our pace, and drove us in about five o'clock to the hospitable shelter of Ralph Potts (of Alnwick, Northumberland), where we had all things richly to enjoy.

Tuesday, February 2. Considering the inclemency of the day, we had a very respectable congregation to hear us: who can tell what God will do for these people? At our evening meeting many attended: the subject spoken from was Luke xiv, 26.

Wednesday, 3. We came up to ——'s, and stopped awhile, and then pushed on to Brother Perry's:[14] it was a solitary ride. Our host is one of our local ministry in Pitt county. I judged it highly expedient that Roanoke and Pamlico circuits should be divided, and that Washington should have Sabbath preaching every week: it is a growing town of one hundred houses, and there is a good house for public worship.

Thursday, 4. We came to Garratt Toole's plantation; but the bird was flown—our old friend had removed to Franklin county for his health: we stayed with Mr. Davidson, the steward of his estate.

Friday, 5. At Tarboro we held our meeting in the neat new chapel: Nicholas Snethen spoke upon, "This day is salvation come to this house"; the ground work of my discourse was, "My house shall be called a house of prayer for all people": I said but few words. We dined with Mr. Isaac Guion, and lodged with Mr. John Bellamy. We rejoiced in hope that Tarboro and Halifax will yet hear and receive the Gospel: Henry Bradford[15] hath been preaching in the latter, and brother Bellamy in the former with some success. We attended at Prospect Hill. It was an exceedingly cold day, as need be. I only exhorted after Nicholas Snethen had described *the new creature in Christ Jesus*. We fed our horses, and ourselves ate in the woods, and then went forward to Henry Bradford's. My soul is continually stayed upon and comforted in God: but it is not needful to tell all my outward difficulties and inward sufferings: heaven will make up for all—and then we shall know all we wish and wait to know.

Sabbath, 7. Was a very cold and cloudy day: we held our meeting in the dwelling house, and filled both rooms. Nicholas Snethen spoke on 2 Tim. ii, 11–13. My text was 2 Pet. iii, 17, 18.

Monday, 8. We crossed Roanoke at Pollock's ferry, and came to Richard Whitaker's. We had no appointment at Rehoboth, but on *Tuesday* we called a meeting:—Nicholas Snethen spoke on Philippians ii, 5; I followed from Matthew v, 8. At Anthony Moore's[16] we called a meeting, where each of us delivered our testimony, and then rode on to Mr. People's:[17] here the presiding elder made an appointment, by including it with others, but of this there was no notice given, except by our

[14] Shadrach Perry lived in Pitt County. (*Ibid.*)
[15] Henry Bradford, evidently a local preacher, lived in Halifax County. (*Ibid.*)
[16] Anthony Moore lived in Northampton County. (*Ibid.*)
[17] This may have been Drury Peebles, who lived in Halifax County. (*Ibid.*)

coming into the neighbourhood the evening before: we would not neglect our duty, but at Malone's we faithfully, according to the grace and time given, discharged our task and rode on.

Virginia

Brunswick county. We had a cold, damp ride to Matthew Myrick's. On *Friday* we preached at Dromyrick new meeting house: Nicholas Snethen spoke, and I followed: at Wolsey meeting house Nicholas Snethen preached; I only exhorted. I called upon Doctor Simm's, who cut a small wart from my hand and applied the caustic: my right foot was also wounded, by a splinter of lightwood perhaps.

Sunday, 14. We attended at Hickesford, alias Bellfield: in the academy[18] we had a large congregation of the rich and the poor, to whom Nicholas Snethen preached from Deut. xxxii, 29. I also spoke on Luke xix, 10. We lodged at Miss Jenny Fisher's.

Nicholas Snethen preached, I only exhorted at Peter Pelham's: of the children of this family I could say many favourable things—but ah! they are not converted!

Tuesday, 16. At Hobb's meeting house Nicholas Snethen spoke on Rom. viii, 12, 13; my portion of the word was Heb. ii, 3. At Merritt's chapel, Nicholas Snethen spoke on, "Recompense no man evil for evil." I followed on Heb. vi, 11, 12. We rode home with John Easter, and made our ride thirty miles—nearly a day's journey. The inflammation, from the operation on my hand, was attended with pain: I kept it down by bread and milk poultice; and applied spirits of turpentine to assuage the effects of the caustic. We have been received with great affection by our local brethren, Edward Dromgoole, Ira Ellis, H. Saunders, A. Brown, John Easter, and H. Merritt:[19] but the travelling preachers and presiding elders keep at their work; we seldom see them as we travel *two and two*. My soul is very solemn.

On Thursday, at John Easter's, we had many people for the day and place. Nicholas Snethen always speaks first: my text was Heb. xii, 25.

Friday, 19. Was a cold day at Peter Robinson's, Dinwiddie county, yet many attended. I saw my old friend, the weeping widow Jarratt. My text was James i, 22. Henry Reece, John Easter, John Jones, and Samuel S. Stuart, preachers, were present. We had a gracious season.

Saturday, 20. At Maye's meeting house, Nottoway county. I preached from Acts ii, 42. The day was unpleasant. We came back to Peter Robinson's.

[18] This was evidently Ebenezer Academy. Hickesford is now Emporia.

[19] Edward Dromgoole, Ira Ellis, and John Easter had been outstanding traveling preachers before they located. Easter led the great revival of 1787.

Sunday, 21. It began to rain as we set out; we rode into Brunswick again to John Rogers's: he is an old Jarrattite Methodist; a few attended in the dwelling house, to whom Nicholas Snethen first spoke on *the common salvation*; I followed on Heb. ii, 1. We had not a rapid, mountain-like rain and a hard lodging, but a warm house and a good bed—fit for a president: it rained freely in the night—we heard, but did not feel it.

On *Monday* we had a snow storm; yet with a few hours' notice, several came out to Thomas Jordan's—I hope not in vain: my subject was Heb. iv, 15, 16. By computation, we have filled up two thousand five hundred miles to Thomas Jordan's. On *Tuesday* we rested: my hand was inflamed, and the weather was cold.

Wednesday, 24. At Maye's we found a small appointment had been made for the circuit preacher: I spoke upon Matt. xi, 28–30. I sent for Doctor Asa Barnes, who probed the wound in my hand, and prepared a sublimated plaster, which brought on a discharge in twenty-four hours: I give him credit for his skill and friendship.

On our route to Charles Ogburne's [20] on *Thursday*, we crossed Meherrin on a low bridge, whilst the water in places flowed over the planks. Next day I spoke on, "Faith, hope, and charity"; and on *Saturday*, at Zion Chapel, on "Examine yourselves whether ye be in the faith."

Sunday, 28. At Salem.[21]

Monday, *March* 1. We began and held close conference four days;[22] and had preaching each day: Bruce, Lee, Jackson, and Snethen were our speakers; and there was a shaking among the people. Seven deacons and one elder were ordained. I was well pleased with the stations, as far as they went; but Portsmouth, Bertie, Roanoke, Haw River, Guilford, and Salisbury should each have had an additional preacher, if we had them; yea, Petersburg, Hanover, Williamsburg, and Richmond also; but the Lord hath not sent them, and how can we make them? There was great strictness observed in the examination of the preachers' characters: some were reproved before the conference for their lightness and other follies.[23]

Friday, 5. We rode to Peter Wyche's, and next day called upon Jane Fisher on our way to Jones's.

Sabbath, 7. At Jones's chapel I preached on Psalm cxxiv, 1, 2. Ah!

[20] Ogburne lived in Mecklenburg County, Virginia.

[21] Four sessions of the Virginia Conference were held in Salem, near South Hill. The building was burned about 1870. (See State Historical Marker at South Hill.)

[22] At this conference David B. Mintz, James Smith, William Johnson, and Robert Carter were received on trial. Frederickburg was placed on the *Minutes* as a new circuit. (Bennett, *op. cit.*, 393–94.)

[23] Bennett says a "minister was charged with neglecting his appointments and with certain indiscretions and the committee appointed to hear the accusations thought him culpable and directed that one of the bishops should reprove him before the conference." (*Ibid.*, 394.)

where is the Lord God of Elijah—the God who once answered him with power—with fire?

Monday, 8. At Pennington's Nicholas Snethen preached; I only exhorted. We came in haste to Brigg's, to see the children; the dear parents had both died in the space of one week. At Lane's chapel, next day, Nicholas Snethen and myself both preached: my subject was Psalm xlii, 5; it is remarkable that these words are repeated thrice, like Peter's vision.

Wednesday, 10. We came to Joseph Moody's, Isle of Wight county: our appointment had not reached this place. Next day we proceeded to Suffolk, and arrived in the evening at the house of our dear friends, Mr. and Mrs. Yerbury, who received us with great affection. The house was small, and we had a dripping evening, which kept some back: my subject was Exodus xx, 24. Since my last visit they have collected money and materials to build a chapel, which will be shortly raised.

Friday, 12. We rode down, through wet woods and a damp day to Portsmouth, resting and refreshing on our route at David M'Keesy's on the Middle Ground: in the evening, Nicholas Snethen preached on, "For we walk by faith and not by sight." On *Saturday evening* it was my turn; I spoke on James i, 22.

Sabbath, 14. As the wind was high, I thought Nicholas Snethen might as well speak at Norfolk in the morning, and myself at Portsmouth: my text in the afternoon was Matt. v, 8; in the afternoon, "For it is God that worketh in you both to will and to do of his good pleasure." I confined myself to experience; and there was a melting among the people.

Monday, 15. We came to brother Denbigh's, to early dinner; thence proceeded to Suffolk, where I stepped into three houses, and continued on our way to Charles Murphy's to lodge. I felt that I had injured myself by laying by one of my coats too soon.

Tuesday, 16. We called at Michael Murphy's and proceeded on to Blunt's chapel: Nicholas Snethen gave a discourse upon *brotherly love*; I only exhorted, and added a narrative of the work of God: we have made up two thousand six hundred and sixty miles. My mind hath been sweetly stayed upon God at all times and in all places.

Wednesday, 17. We came sixteen miles, to Doctor Bailey's, in Surry county. Nicholas Snethen's horse was taken with a violent colic, and rolled upon the ground in great agony; he was relieved, however, by drenching with sturgeon's oil and clysters. I left the man and horse, and came on to William Birdsong's.

Thursday, 18. I dined at friend Nixon's, where I was kindly entertained; I left my kind host, and came on to Petersburg.

Next day, by appointment, I preached John Lee's[24] funeral sermon; my

[24] John Lee (1770–1801) was the son of Nathaniel and Elizabeth Lee and the brother of Jesse Lee. He was converted in the great revival of 1787 at the age of seventeen and was received as a traveling preacher at the Baltimore Conference in 1788, beginning

text was Philippians ii, 22: "But ye know the proof of him, that as a son with the father, hath he served with me in the Gospel."

I. The excellency of the Gospel. II. The service of the Gospel. III. The proof of Timothy—his pious parents; his education, conviction, conversion, call, and ordination, his ministry; his obedience as a son with a father—in mutual love, in mutual confidence, and mutual services: I showed the excellency of a patriarchal or fatherly government in the Church. I paralleled John Lee's character with Timothy's, in his manner of living, labouring, and death. Nicholas Snethen came up and preached at night. On *Saturday* we arrived at Richmond, and next day Nicholas Snethen preached upon the epistle to the Church of Ephesus. I spoke in the afternoon upon Philip. ii, 12, 13. I had a great crowd of the most impolite, spiritually impolite hearers I have seen for many months: so much for the capital of Virginia.

Monday, 22. We reached Caroline, and the next day, Fredericksburg: here Nicholas Snethen gave a discourse upon the *work of righteousness*—peace; and the effect of righteousness, quietness, and assurance forever. I spoke upon "Seek ye the Lord while he may be found." We started next day for Pohick,[25] and the day after reached William Watters's; here we rejoiced in God together. On *Wednesday evening* there was a thunder-storm, which, clearing up, brought an excessively cold wind on *Thursday*.

Maryland

On *Friday* it snowed most of the day; nevertheless, I rode on seven miles to Henry Foxall's,[26] in Georgetown, where I found a shelter from the

his labors in the Baltimore Circuit. He traveled in New Jersey, New York, and Connecticut, and in 1790 was ordained a deacon and appointed to the New Haven Circuit. However, his health was poor, and upon the death of his mother he returned to Virginia to become a merchant. He died in Wilkes County, North Carolina, on October 6, 1801, where Bishop Whatcoat preached the funeral sermon. Jesse Lee preached another at his home in Virginia, and Asbury preached the third. (Lee: *A Short Account of the Life and Death of the Rev. John Lee.*)

[25] One of the oldest Episcopal churches in Virginia was at Pohick. The building was begun in 1769 and completed in 1774. George William Fairfax, George Washington, and George Mason, vestrymen, were members of the building committee.

[26] Henry Foxall (1760–1823) was a native of the English community in which Asbury was born. He moved from Philadelphia to Georgetown, D.C., in 1800, to be nearer the extensive foundry which he had established one mile north of the latter place. In the Foxall home, 3123 Dumbarton Avenue, Asbury was a frequent guest. Foxall identified himself with Methodism by furnishing a house for a Sunday school which he had sponsored in Georgetown. Among his numerous benefactions was the erection of the first Foundry Methodist Episcopal Church in Washington in recognition of his ordnance plant being unmolested when the British invaded the capital in 1814. Foxall was mayor of Georgetown, D.C., in 1819–21. (Bryan: *A History of the National Capital*, I, 331–33; II, 160 n.; Kirkey, *op. cit.*, 28, 37, 44, 45.)

storm. I have had sore temptations, succeeded by great consolations. The want of good sleep has been a cause of suffering.

Saturday, 27. I made a general start, and a steady ride to Baltimore. On the route I called in to see the widow Shadrach Turner, whom I found rejoicing in the Lord. I fed at Spurrier's tavern;[27] it is now in other hands than formerly.

Sabbath, 28. I had uncomfortable feelings, occasioned by a cold I had taken. Upon my watch-tower in Light Street, I stood and delivered a message on James v, 19, 20. I wrote, and rested until *Thursday* the first day of April, when our yearly conference commenced.[28] We went on with our business smoothly and rapidly, and had preaching each noon and evening in every Methodist house for public worship in the city.[29]

Sabbath, April 4. I administered the word in Light Street from Matt. v, 12: in the new chapel at Fells Point on Isaiah lvi, 7. This is the neatest house, within and without, that we have in Baltimore. Alexander McCaine[30] hath been very attentive to the temporal and spiritual interests of the house and society.

Monday, 5. We had a day of fasting and humiliation for the conference, the continent, and the Church of God; I improved the occasion, and spoke from Acts xiv, 23. I was presented with a new impression of my journal;[31] it is very incorrect: had I had an opportunity before it

[27] Waterloo Inn, successor to Spurrier's Tavern, was located in the present Howard County at the junction of the Northern and Southern Post Road with the Annapolis and Frederick Road. (Warfield: *Pioneers of Anne Arundel and Howard Counties*, 342, 343.)

[28] Of the fifty-four members on the conference roll, forty-four were present. An unusually large class was received, among whom were Robert R. Roberts, a future bishop, and William Ryland, who was six times chosen chaplain of the Congress. For the first time three districts appear grouped under the Baltimore Conference. (Armstrong, *op. cit.*, 130, 131; Stevens, *op. cit.*, III, 400, 401; Elliott: *The Life of the Rev. Robert R. Roberts*, 98–100.)

[29] In 1802 the Methodist churches in Baltimore were Light Street, successor to Lovely Lane; Wilks Street, successor to Strawberry Alley in Fells Point; Exeter Street; Sharp Street, a colored church; and possibly Dallas Street, also colored. (Bibbins: *Methodist Sesqui-Centennial*, 37–40.)

[30] Alexander McCaine, appointed to Fells Point in 1801, had led in the building of Wilks Street Church. (*Ibid.*, 38; Colhouer: *Sketches of the Founders of the Methodist Protestant Church*, 90–119.)

[31] The title of this first copy of Asbury's *Journal* reads: "An Extract from the Journal of Francis Asbury, One of the Bishops of the Methodist Episcopal Church. From January 1st, 1779 to September 3rd, 1780. Printed for Ezekiel Cooper, #118 North 4th Street, near the Methodist Church. 1802." Asbury had consented to publication of parts of his *Journal* on condition that the paper should be of good quality, that he should edit the manuscript and read the proof. He implies that he had been overruled in his wish that the *Journal* should be printed serially rather than in a volume. His disappointment on examining the printed volume indicates that his request had been in a large measure disregarded. (See letter to Ezekiel Cooper, December 31, 1801; see Introduction.)

was put to press, I should have altered and expunged many things; the inaccuracies of grammar, and imperfections of composition incident to the hasty notices of a manuscript journal are preserved in the printed copy. On *Monday evening* the conference rose: all the demands of the preachers were answered; money was advanced towards the purchase of horses; to those who had distant circuits and far to go, donations were made; and nearly two hundred dollars very liberally sent to the Monmouth conference,[32] which is to meet in July next. Within the circling lines of this conference, we report to this sitting an addition to the society of three thousand souls and upwards, besides those who may have died within the last eleven months. John Pawson's letter,[33] and fifty copies of a volume of sermons came safely to hand; his, and other letters, concerning the work of God, I read to my brethren. Whilst in Baltimore, I received an account of the death of my mother, which I fear is true. And here I may speak safely concerning my very dear mother: her character to me is well known. Her paternal descent was Welsh; from a family ancient and respectable, of the name of Rogers. She lived a woman of the world until the death of her first and only daughter, Sarah Asbury: how would the bereaved mother weep and tell of the beauties and excellencies of her lost and lovely child! pondering on the past in the silent suffering of hopeless grief. This afflictive providence graciously terminated in the mother's conversion. When she saw herself a lost and wretched sinner, she sought religious people, but "in the times of this ignorance" few were "sound in the faith," or "faithful to the grace given": many were the days she spent chiefly in reading and prayer; at length she found justifying grace, and pardoning mercy. So dim was the light of truth around her, from the assurance she found, she was at times inclined to believe in the final perseverance of the saints. For fifty years her hands, her house, her heart, were open to receive the people of God and ministers of Christ; and thus a lamp was lighted up in a dark place called Great Barre, in Great Britain. She was an afflicted, yet most active woman, of quick bodily powers, and masculine understanding; nevertheless, "so kindly all the elements were mixed in her," her strong mind quickly felt the subduing influences of that Christian sympathy which "weeps with those who weep," and "rejoices with those who do rejoice." As a woman and a wife she was chaste, modest, blameless; as a mother (above all the women in the world would I claim her for my own) ardently affectionate; as a "mother in Israel" few of her sex have done more by a holy walk to live, and by per-

[32] For an account of the New England Conference session at Monmouth, Maine, which was held in the home of Sewall Prescott, see the *Journal* entries for July 1–4, 1802. For appreciation of help from Baltimore and other donors, see Allen and Pillsbury: *The History of Methodism in Maine*, 66, 67, 74, 228.)

[33] John Pawson (1737–1806) was president of the British Conference in 1793 and 1801, the first person to serve two terms. (Church: *The Early Methodist People*, 7; Hurst: *British Methodism*, III, 1211.)

sonal labour to support, the Gospel, and to wash the saints' feet; as a friend, she was generous, true, and constant. Elizabeth Asbury died January 6th, 1802; aged eighty-seven or eighty-eight years. There is now, after fifty years, a chapel within two or three hundred yards of her dwelling.[34] I am now often drawn out in thankfulness to God, who hath saved a mother of mine, and, I trust, a father also, who are already in glory, where I hope to meet them both, after time, and cares, and sorrows, shall have ceased with me; and where glory shall not only beam, but open on my soul forever. Amen.

Wednesday, 7. I came to Perry Hall. We cannot spend more time with the rich than with the poor; so, being warned by a very fine day, we started, stopped to dine with the Widow Stump, at Bush, and in the evening reached North East. Next day was stormy; but we were safely housed with Mr. Daniel Sheredine.

Saturday, 10. We rode to Back Creek; and on the *Sabbath day*, as we were visited with a gracious rain, I improved on the subject from Isa. lv, 10, 11. At the Bohemia Manor chapel Brother Whatcoat preached in the afternoon from Rev. xxi, 6.

Monday, 12. There were two appointments; one at the new chapel, Cross Roads, and the other at the brick meeting house. Rather than disappoint any, we separated, I taking the former, and Brother Whatcoat the latter. As it was the first time of preaching in the new house, I chose Isa. lxvi, 1, 2. That evening I came on to Chester Town, the wind at east; cold and damp.

Tuesday, 13. We had a rainy day, but we attended the house of God, noon, and night. Our brethren in this town are about to build: by a train of strange persons, providences, and things, they have a place in the public square, where the market house stood: the chapel will be in a line with the Episcopal church; its size, forty by forty-eight.

Wednesday, 14. The morning was very damp. I was not at all prepared for speaking: my subject was Tit. ii, 2. After preaching we rode rapidly down to Dr. Moses D. Allen's: we found the doctor rapidly declining.

Thursday, 15. At Easton I spoke on 1 Peter i, 3–5: Brother Whatcoat preached at night.

Friday, 16. We were at Bolingbroke chapel: it was an exceedingly cold day for the season; I read a little, and added a short exhortation; after which we hasted to Wm. Brown's to dine, and the wind having lulled, crossed Choptank, at Ennall's Ferry. The severity of the weather caused uncomfortable feelings; nevertheless, we greatly rejoiced in the Lord, because of his glorious work, which is spreading along like a moving fire.

Saturday, 17. At Henry Ennall's I spoke on Psa. cxlv, 8–10. I have now

[34] The home of the Asburys still stands on Newton Road and has been declared to be a historic spot by the town council of West Bromwich. The Anglican chapel still stands nearby.

ridden, I suppose, three thousand miles since my departure from Philadelphia on the last of July, 1801.

Sunday, 18. We had a full house at Cambridge. Our new chapel is two stories high; well planned, and neatly finished. After exhortations and sacrament, Bishop Whatcoat preached. Meeting ended, we rode fourteen miles through the rain to Bartholomew Ennall's.

Monday, 19. Rain coming on, we were detained a little; but afterward we rode within two miles of Quantico, arriving too late. We dined at Fletcher's,[35] and rode on to Salisbury, making thirty miles this day. Bishop Whatcoat preached in the evening.

Tuesday, 20. Was *fair time*; yet many attended, and we had a gracious season. My subject was Matt. xxii, 5.

Wednesday, 21. We had a long ride to Annamessex chapel, nearly thirty miles, this day, before we came to our lodgings at Samuel Smith's.[36]

Virginia

Thursday, 22. We rode twenty miles to Downing meeting house, in Accomac county: I spoke upon Psa. lxvi, 16; it was a gracious season. We had only time, and in borrowed carriages rode afterward about twenty miles to Captain Watson's, weary and sleepy, as we had had little rest night or day.

Eastern Shore, Friday, 23. Bishop Whatcoat preached at the meeting house in Diamond Town to a numerous audience. That evening we had to ride twenty miles to Mr. Watts's, upon Chincoteague; but the Lord was in the family, and blessed the people. We have a most pleasing prospect in Accomac: a general revival is going through the county.

Maryland

Next day we had a heavy ride to Snow Hill: our new meeting house not being finished,[37] I preached in the court house to many serious people

[35] This may have been John Fletcher (*d.* 1807), a captain in the Revolutionary War and grandfather of Fletcher Elliott Marine (1821–89), president of the Local Preachers' Association and editor of *The Pioneer*. (Jones: *Revolutionary History of Dorchester County*, 422 ff.) Hallman, however, identifies Fletcher as living two miles north of Quantico, Wicomico County. (*Op. cit.*, 111.)

[36] This was the same Samuel Smith, near Crisfield, Somerset County, from whom Asbury borrowed a horse on May 22, 1799. (See note under date mentioned. See letter to George Roberts, April 21, 1802.)

[37] The deed for a building site purchased from James Martin for forty-five dollars is recorded April 19, 1802. In 1803 a building was erected, and in 1808 Whatcoat Church was incorporated. (Hearne: *One Hundred Years of Methodism in Snow Hill, Maryland*; Hallman, *op. cit.*, 357.)

upon Phil. i, 6. After worship we rode on to Isaac Bowman's,[38] fifteen miles, and lodged at Dr. Wilson's plantation, now in the possession of Mr. White.

Eastern Shore, Sunday 25. We had a great time at Bowen's chapel—there were present about one thousand souls; to whom Brother Whatcoat preached, I read a letter and gave an exhortation. We came on nine miles to Wm. Leicester's[39] that evening.

Delaware

On *Monday* we had to ride to the Sound chapel, where we found a large congregation: the prospect of religion here is good. In the evening we reached Mr. Lacey's,[40] near the head of Indian River, making little short of thirty miles for our day's ride.

On *Tuesday*, Brother Whatcoat went to Lewistown; whilst myself preached at Milford.

Wednesday, 28. I preached at Dover, on Ephes. v, 1, 2; thence I hasted to Duck Creek Cross Roads, where I spoke in the evening.

Thursday, 29. We had a blessed rain; we rode through it to Wilmington, in Judge Bassett's coachee: I was sick, with night-watching and fevers, and a disturbed stomach. I lodged for the night with Allan McLane; my fever rose.

Pennsylvania

Saturday, May 1. On my way to Philadelphia, I called once more upon my old friend Mary Whithy. In the city I found many things I cannot here relate; some pleasing and some painful.

Our conference opened on the first of May. We had an increase of probationers. In two sittings we did not get through the first question: Who are admitted upon trial? We appointed a committee of *five* to manage the temporal concerns, and recommended a day of fasting and prayer to be

[38] Because no Isaac Bowman can be identified in that vicinity, and because a journey of fifteen miles would have brought Asbury near the home of Jephthah Bowen, it seems probable that the transcriber has mistaken the names.

[39] This may have been the William Leicester who lived near Bishop, Worcester County. The only probable reference to him in the county records is the marriage of William Lister (*sic*) and Elizabeth Johnson in 1810. In the baptismal records of Coventry Parish, Somerset County, is William Lister, son of Jesse and Betty Harris.

[40] This was probably Spencer Lacey, whose family was one of fifteen that built the Zoar meeting house several miles north of Millsboro in Indian River Hundred, Sussex County. When this structure, which was incorporated November 5, 1810, fell into disuse, the diminishing congregation united with what is now Gumboro Chapel. (Scharf: *History of Delaware*, II, 1275; Hallman, *op. cit.*, 270.)

observed on the fourth of May, for the conference, the Church in general, and the continent at large. By a hasty calculation, I find I have ridden three thousand three hundred and three miles, from and returning to Philadelphia.

To my happy surprise, George Roberts[41] and John M'Claskey came forward and moved that the brethren of the city who had bought the academy should have the offer of a preacher: the conference at once agreed that the superintendents of the Methodists of the United States should make them an overture upon the best terms; there was but one dissenting voice.

We had great peace throughout the sitting; although there were many things to occupy our thoughts: my mind was taken up in entering the *minutes*; and in making needful changes. After voting the next sitting of our conference at Duck Creek, we rose on *Thursday* the sixth inst.

Sunday, 9. I preached at St. George's upon Rom. xiv, 19, at Ebenezer upon Philip. ii, 12–16, and at Bethel, among the Africans, on Titus ii, 11, 12.

New Jersey

Monday, 10. I had a sudden thought that it would be best to cross at Gloucester[42]; we did so, and had a sudden passage, in a noble boat, to the Jersey shore; we sailed over in eight or ten minutes.

We came on to Clonmell, dined at Robert Newell's,[43] and attended our appointment at three o'clock: Brother Whatcoat made an improvement upon Isaiah xxv, 20, 21.[44] My mind was in an unexpected manner led to John ii, 15. I wake myself: I had probably lost thirty hours in the city.

Tuesday, 11. We rode to Henry Firth's[45] and dined; after which we attended our appointment at Salem.[46] My mind here was overruled on my subject; I made a sudden choice, whilst I was singing a hymn, of 1 Cor.

[41] George Roberts was appointed to the Academy, Philadelphia, this year.

[42] Gloucester, a small town of Gloucester Township, New Jersey, was comprised of a store, tavern, and twenty dwellings. It is not to be confused with the larger post town of Gloucester in Galloway Township. (Gordon's *Gazetteer*.)

[43] Robert Newell of Clonmell, Burlington County, was witness to a number of wills. (New Jersey Archives, Abstracts of Wills, VI, 206, 455; VIII, 266; Lednum, *op. cit.*, 372.)

[44] There are only twelve verses in this chapter of Isaiah, and there is no indication as to what passage this may have been.

[45] The Firths were among Methodist families of prominence in Lower Penn's Neck, an area early cultivated by Benjamin Abbott. Methodism was planted in Quinton's Bridge near Salem in 1781, and the leaders in the society there were Henry Firth and John McLaskey, his brother-in-law. (Lednum, *op. cit.*, 369, 372.)

[46] Historians believe that Salem was the first spot visited and settled by the English emigrants to West Jersey in colonial times. Jacob Mulford and Benjamin Abbott began the Methodist movement there. (Gordon's *Gazetteer*, 231–32; Lednum, *op. cit.*, 371.)

vii, 29–31. We had many serious people at Salem. We returned to Henry Firth's, and lodged there.

Wednesday, 12. We had a blessed rain, but not pleasing to ride through to Humphrey's meeting house at Pittsgrove.[47] Bishop Whatcoat preached upon the *abundant entrance*; I only exhorted upon the seasons, natural and spiritual, and read Mr. Hodges's letter. We lodged at Joseph Newkirk's.[48]

Thursday, 13. We came to Bethel,[49] and I spoke on "Be thou faithful unto death, and I will give thee a crown of life." The rain fell upon us as we rode to Daniel Bates's.[50]

Friday, 14. We rode to Moores Town,[51] and held a meeting at Hugh Hollinshead's.[52] Brother Whatcoat spoke upon "The kingdom of God is not in word but in power"; it was late, and I therefore occupied about fifteen minutes in exhorting against *making light of the Gospel.*

Saturday, 15. In our route to New Mills[53] through the mount, in the hollow, we found the road greatly improved. I have ridden about four hundred towards the four thousand miles. My mind, in general, is kept in great peace. After thirty-one years' acquaintance, William Budd[54] and myself still live; and, I hope, live for God, and to his glory.

Sunday, 16. At New Mills I preached upon Philippians ii, 12–16. We had an open season: the people are in living exercise, and souls are coming home to God.

Monday, 17. Through heavy, continued rain, we came on to Crosswicks. We dined with Mr. Joseph Lovell; and after drying our clothes, about two o'clock went to the meeting house. Here we found a fire and a stove, and warmth and comfort: how different this from visiting an open house in

[47] This was probably John Humphries, who is mentioned in the will of Mary Ronalds of Upper Penn's Neck, Salem County. Pittsgrove is in the limits of present Salem County. (New Jersey Archives, Abstracts of Wills, VI, 334; Gordon, *op. cit.*, 217.)

[48] Families bearing the name of Newkirk are shown as long residing on Upper Alloways Creek, near Pittsgrove, Salem County. (Abstracts of Wills, VI, 289; VII, 167–68; VIII, 278.)

[49] Bethel Church was at Hurffville in Gloucester County and is noted in records of the Steward's Book, Salem Circuit, 1789–1814.

[50] Daniel Bates, of Gloucester Township, Gloucester County, was a leader at Bethel Chapel on the Bethel Circuit. He entertained Ezekiel Cooper at his home in April, 1797. (Phoebus, *op. cit.*, 228.)

[51] Moorestown is in Chester township, Burlington County, New Jersey. Here is located the Zelley House, on Stanwick Avenue, which has the date 1721 on its wall. It is built of red brick and has hand-hewn timbers. The Zelley family has been active in Methodist circles for many years. (Gordon, *op. cit.*, 183; *New Jersey Guide*, 621.)

[52] Hugh Hollinshead, of Chester Township, Burlington County, is identified with the early history of Vincentown Methodism. (*History of Vincentown Methodist Church*, 125th Anniversary Program, May 24, 1953.)

[53] New Mills was the present Pemberton.

[54] William Budd was for many years a local preacher who worked in the South Jersey circuits. He entertained Asbury and other itinerants in his home. (Atkinson, *op. cit.*, 205–6.)

the woods, with wind and rain beating upon you, and sitting in your damp dress and a damp house for three hours, after which you are to ride five or ten miles to a bad lodging, where you are to dry yourself and find comfort if you can!

Tuesday, 18. At Emley's[55] I spoke on Heb. xii, 1, 2; after preaching we rode to Captain Covell's,[56] an old English Methodist sea captain.

At Milford; a cold day and few people. We visited Sylvester Hutchinson,[57] in an afflicted and low state of body.

Thursday, 20. We had a weary ride to New Brunswick: my subject here was Rev. xvii, 14. Next day we came to Benjamin Drake's: Bishop Whatcoat preached to the preachers present—Joseph Totten, William Mills, Henry Clark, to which I add the family, and three others.

New York

Saturday, 22. We came upon Staten Island at the old *Blazing Star*.[58] I called at the mansion of Justice Hezekiah Wright, where I had been entertained, and where I had preached almost thirty-one years past. I was thankful to find Mrs. Wright happy in God, although afflicted in body. Here I saw the third generation rising into accountability: we prayed, and were comforted together. We housed for the night with Joseph Totten, upon the south side.

Sabbath, 23. Nicholas Snethen, who had been on a visit home, came up with us to-day. I had an opportunity of reading his answer to Mr. O'Kelly's *Rejoinder* to his, Nicholas Snethen's, *Reply*.

Whilst at Milford, I read the inscription on the gravestone of Ann Hutchinson,[59] her maiden name was Simpson; she was born upon Long

[56] Emley's Church was at Allentown, Upper Freehold Township, Monmouth County. (See note under September 28, 1795.)

[56] The Covell Hill Cemetery is a historical landmark. Here are buried members of the Mordecai and Hannah Lincoln family, ancestors of President Lincoln. It is located near Clarksburg. (*New Jersey Guide*, 585.)

[57] Sylvester Hutchinson, son of William and nephew of Joseph Hutchinson, was one of four brothers to become preachers and was prominent in New Jersey Methodism around 1790. He left the Methodist Episcopal Church because of differences with Asbury over marriage and later joined the Methodist Protestants, and continued to preach. His name does not appear in the *Minutes* for 1804, and he is reported as located in 1806. (Atkinson, *op. cit.*, 423–33.)

[58] This was the Old Blazing Star Ferry from Perth Amboy to Staten Island at Rossville.

[59] The following remarkable inscription on the headstone of Ann Hutchinson's grave is what Asbury read: "Sacred to the memory of Ann Hutchinson, relict of Wm. Hutchinson, Esq., departed this life, Jan. 4, 1801. Aged 101 years, 9 months and seven days. She was mother of 13 children and grandmother, and great-grandmother, and great-great-grandmother of 375 persons." In a letter from the Rev. H. B. Beegle to the Rev. John Atkinson are these additional comments: "She retained her faculties to the

Island, and married in the country of Middlesex, State of New Jersey. She was the mother of thirteen children, and the great great grandmother of upwards of three hundred children; she died, aged a hundred and one years, nine months, and seven days, in January, 1801. About *eighty*, she *in a great degree* lost her sight—about *ninety*, it returned; her hair changed a few years ago from white to a dark brown. I have seen her, and conversed with her: at this advanced age she did not appear to be weary of the world.

My soul hath been suppressed with deep and sore temptations: it may be thus, that I should not be lifted up at the prosperity of the Church, and increase of ministers and members. I have a variety of letters, conveying the pleasing intelligence of the work of God in every State, district, and in most of the circuits in the Union. Ride on, blessed Redeemer, until all the states and nations of the earth are subdued unto thy sacred sway!

At a meeting house upon Staten Island,[60] at the old Blazing Star, my subject was Matthew xxii, 5. The rain probably deprived us of half of our congregation. After administering the sacrament, we rode in the rain to Nicholas Crocheron's,[61] at the east end: my text here was Acts v, 30–32. Several came forward and joined the society. I have visited upon the island for thirty-one years; and I am pleased to find there is a revival of religion.

New Jersey

Monday, 24. I came to Elizabethtown:—unwell as I had been on the Sabbath evening, and deprived of rest, I was expected to preach at eight o'clock: my subject was Ephes. ii, 10. Wonders will never cease. Nothing would serve, but I must marry Thomas Morrell to a young woman:[62] such a solitary wedding, I suppose, has been but seldom seen—behold father Morrell, seventy-five—father Whatcoat sixty-six—Francis Asbury, fifty-seven—and the ceremony performed, solemnly, at the solemn hour of ten at night!

last, and could see to thread needle, and read without spectacles, when in her 101st year." (Atkinson, *op. cit.*, 432–33.)

[60] This was Wood Row Church, which is today the oldest Methodist church on Staten Island and is located on Woodrow Road, Rossville.

[61] Nicholas Crocheron, who lived in the vicinity of New Springville on the North End, was one of the early supporters of Methodism on Staten Island. His home was always open to itinerants, and in addition to Asbury he entertained John Fountain, Thomas Morrell, Joseph Totten, Nicholas Snethen, and Joseph Crawford. Asbury Church on Staten Island was erected this year. (Morris: *History of Staten Island, New York*, II, 388–89; Bayles: *History of Richmond County, New York*, 520–21.)

[62] Thomas Morrell married Lydia Frazer, daughter of George Frazer of Westfield, New Jersey, on the above date. Morrell was then in his seventy-fifth year. His bride was a woman of deep and uniform piety, who joined the Methodist Church soon after this union was consummated. She died October 11, 1808, leaving three children, one of whom was the Rev. Francis Asbury Morrell. (*New Jersey Conference Memorial*, 18.)

New York

Tuesday, 25. We came to New York, and took up our lodging at Mr. Suckley's.[63]

We advanced toward the completion of four thousand miles for the present year. I have had great exercises in going through rain and continual labour; but have been blessed with great peace by my good and gracious God.

My first public exercise in the city was in the African church,[64]—a very neat wooden house, but by far too small: my text was Ephes. ii, 11–14.

Friday, 28. I spoke in John Street, upon 1 Thess. ii, 4–9.

Sunday, 30. After Bishop Whatcoat had preached, I read letters respecting the great revival of religion, westward and southward; the death of Sarah Hutchinson[65] gave occasion to my preaching her funeral sermon at the Bowery church, in the afternoon. The deceased was the daughter of Frederick Deveau, whose house and family in New Rochelle were the first to receive and welcome the Methodist preachers; and thus became the gate by which we have had such an abundant and permanent entrance into the State of New York: after sitting under the ministry of the Gospel above thirty years, the saint, as I was informed by her sister, Hester Wilson,[66] died very happy in God.

Tuesday, June 1. We opened our yearly conference in John Street meeting house; and continued our labours in great peace and union. We have a large admission of preachers upon trial as travellers: at this conference there are twenty-two; and in six conferences, sixty-three.

[63] George Suckley (1765–1846) was born in England of Methodist parents, received his first class ticket from Wesley, and came to America with Coke. He settled in New York, becoming a merchant of considerable wealth, and immediately identified himself with John Street Church, where he served for many years on the board of trustees. He was later one of the founding trustees of the Wesleyan Chapel on Vestry Street. In 1798 he married Catherine, daughter of John Rutsen of Rhinebeck, New York, and a close friend of Mrs. Freeborn Garrettson. Garrettson died while on a visit to Suckley's home. Suckley was a vice president of the American Bible Society and supported many other charitable and religious institutions. (Wakeley, *op. cit.*, 562–63; Holdich's Memoir of Suckley in *Christian Advocate and Journal*, 1846.)

[64] Negro members of the New York churches began holding separate worship services as early as 1796. Early in 1800 a church was built at the corner of Church and Leonard streets and was dedicated as Zion Church in September of that year. Although inadequate at the beginning, it was not enlarged until 1820. (Seaman, *op. cit.*, 156–57.)

[65] Sarah Deveau is thought to have married Sylvester Hutchinson only a few years before her death, while he was active in the New Rochelle area. However, no reference to this possible marriage is found in records of his life and work. If it was not he, there is no other clue to her husband. (See *Journal* entries and notes for December 10, 1771; June 16, 20, 22, 1773; September 18–22, and November 11, 1774.)

[66] Hester Deveau Wilson was the wife of John Wilson, then one of the ministers appointed to New York. He had particular charge of the Bowery Church, and the parsonage where Sarah died was very near the church. (Seaman, *op. cit.*, 160–61.)

Saturday, 5. We had a day of solemn fasting and prayer for the Church, the conference, the continent, and for the world; upon the eve of which, I preached from 2 Cor. ii, 14, 15, with great plainness, and so much fire as made my earthly tabernacle very restless through the night. John M'Claskey[67] gave us the first sermon upon Joel ii, 15–17.

Sunday, 6. We had a love feast at eight o'clock, preaching at ten o'clock, and sacrament at twelve o'clock: some good shakings went through the house, but there was nothing very signal. The collection for the preachers gave occasion to a sermon, which I must needs preach: it was done upon 1 Cor. xvi, 14. I attended, and read a letter at the Bowery church, where a collection for the same purpose was also made. At six o'clock I preached in the North River church, on Luke xi, 13, and so we closed our labours in the city. But instead of a page, it would require a volume to tell the restless tossings I have had—the difficulties and anxieties I have felt about preachers and people, here and elsewhere—*alternate joy and sorrow*—but I have been supported—I am done: I am gone—New York, once more, farewell!

Monday, 7. We had a very warm, dusty ride to the widow Sherwood's; where we held meeting at four o'clock.

As it appeared to be the wish and will of this conference that I should be at that of Monmouth,[68] I desired Nicholas Snethen to go upon my appointments.

How sweet to me are all the moving and still life scenes which now surround me on every side! The quiet country houses; the fields and orchards, bearing the promise of the fruitful year; the flocks and herds, the hills and vales, and dewy meads; the gliding streams and murmuring brooks: and thou, too, solitude—with thy attendants, silence and mediation—how dost thou solace my pensive mind after the tempest of fear, and care, and tumult, and talk, experienced in the noisy, bustling city! "where will they send me?—to Hampshire—to Rhode Island—to Connecticut—to Canada?" One preacher wishes to go where another dreads to be sent, and smiles at the fears of his more timid brother. "But," say the citizens, "how shall *we* be supplied?—such a one will be too strict, and may put us out of order—a second will not keep the congregations together; and our collections will not be made—a third will not please; because he is not a lively preacher, and we want a revival of religion." Ah! the half is not

[67] John McClaskey (1756–1814) was born in County Derry, Ireland, and came to America after the Revolution. He was converted in Salem, New Jersey, admitted on trial in 1786, and served effectively in New Jersey, Pennsylvania, and Delaware, going to New York in 1799. He died in 1814 while presiding elder of the Chesapeake District. He was a strong personality and an outstanding preacher. (Wakeley, *op. cit.*, 508; Seaman, *op. cit.*, 149; Sprague's *Annals*, VII, 125; *General Minutes*.)

[68] This was the conference appointed to meet at Monmouth, Maine, July 1, 1802. Evidently the preachers did not wish Whatcoat to carry that conference alone with its peculiar problems at the extreme northeastward end of the work.

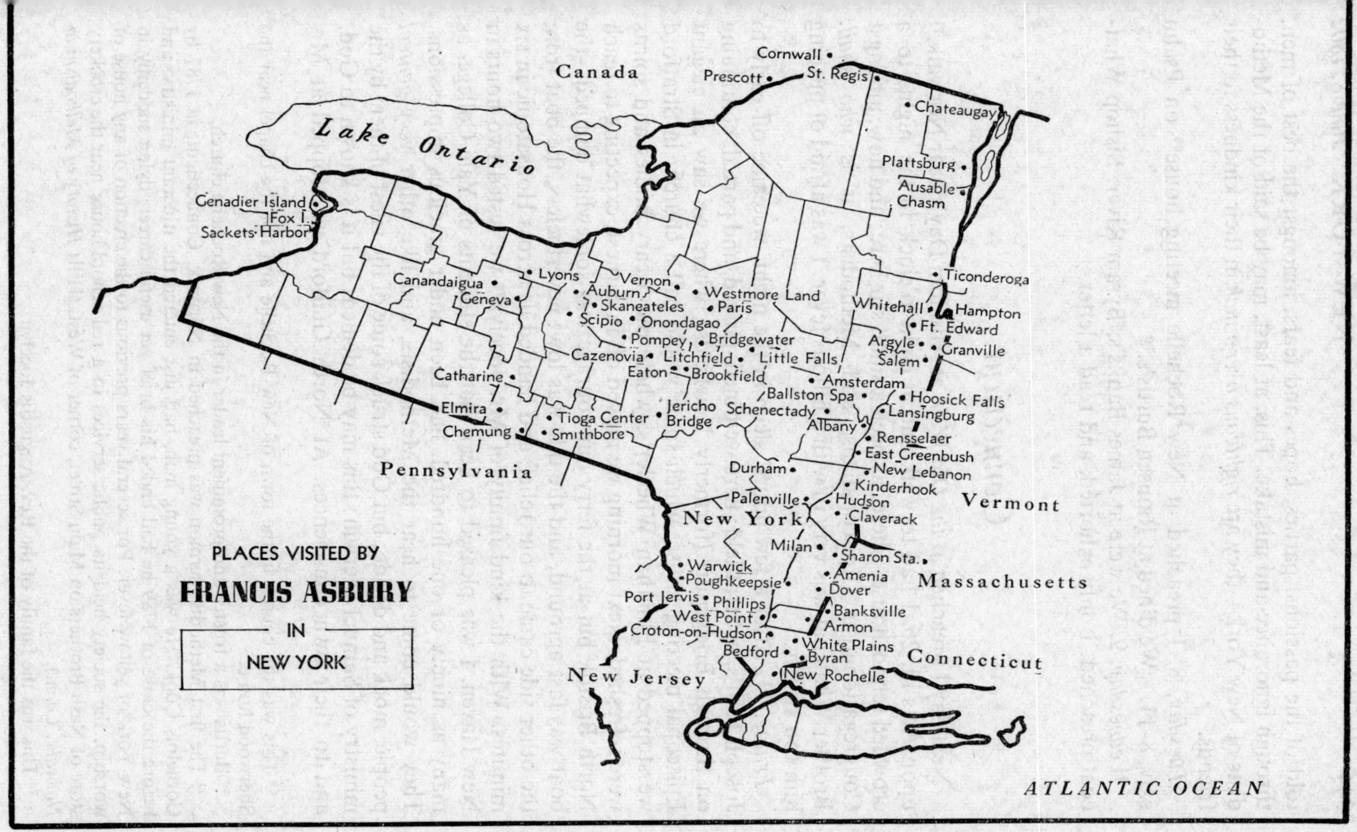
PLACES VISITED BY
FRANCIS ASBURY
IN
NEW YORK
Canada
Lake Ontario
Cornwall
Prescott
St. Regis
Chateaugay
Plattsburg
Ausable Chasm
Genadier Island
Fox I.
Sackets Harbor
Ticonderoga
Whitehall
Hampton
Ft. Edward
Argyle
Granville
Salem
Lyons
Canandaigua
Geneva
Vernon
Auburn
Westmore Land
Skaneateles
Paris
Scipio
Onondagao
Pompey
Bridgewater
Cazenovia
Litchfield
Little Falls
Eaton
Brookfield
Amsterdam
Catharine
Ballston Spa
Hoosick Falls
Schenectady
Lansingburg
Elmira
Jericho Bridge
Tioga Center
Albany
Chemung
Smithbore
Rensselaer
East Greenbush
Durham
New Lebanon
Pennsylvania
Kinderhook
Palenville
Hudson
Vermont
New York
Claverack
Milan
Sharon Sta.
Warwick
Poughkeepsie
Amenia
Massachusetts
Port Jervis
Phillips
Dover
West Point
Banksville
Armon
Croton-on-Hudson
White Plains
Bedford
Byran
Connecticut
New Jersey
New Rochelle
ATLANTIC OCEAN

told of the passions, parties, hopes and fears, amongst the best of men, through ignorance and mistake. This, at least, may be said of the Methodists of New York—they are *righteous over-much* in their kindness to their friends.

Tuesday, 8. I preached at New Rochelle meeting house[69] on Psalm cxlv, 8–11. We dined at Ramsen Burtis's.[70]

Wednesday, 9. We were at James Banks's, Byram River. Bishop Whatcoat preached: I only exhorted, and read a letter.

Connecticut

Next day I preached at *the Old Well*, at Absalom Day's near Norwalk,[71] upon Acts iii, 26. I had to walk out at eight o'clock in the night, to a crowded school house. There has been a small stir here; and now, amongst Congregationalists, Episcopalians, and Methodists, it is *who shall.* Brother Whatcoat was very ill with a bilious fever: I was afraid of pushing him too swiftly.

Friday, 11. After a few hours' sleep in the night, we came off early to Joseph Hall's, in Stratfield: here we dined, prayed, and parted, continuing on through Bridgeport (formerly Newfields), where we saw an elegant Episcopal meeting house, which some would call a church: in Stratford we stopped at Elnathan Wheeler's, where our weary bodies and spirits were refreshed. Next morning we moved off in earnest, expecting to reach North Bristol, but at the ferry our courage was somewhat damped—the boat was fast aground, and the tide was low: nevertheless, the boat from the other side came to our relief, and handed us across Housatonic in six minutes. With the kind family of Mr. Jocelyn[72] we rested two hours in New Haven. I was pleased to hear that the students of Yale College, as many as ninety or one hundred, had been under gracious impressions. They would come to hear the Methodists, and like other *very genteel* people, mock and deride; but God struck some of the vilest of them by the ministry of Samuel Merwin: this may be denied; but it is known to God, and to their own consciences. At North Guilford we stopped at Mr.

[69] This was the church in the town of New Rochelle and not the chapel near the Sherwood home.

[70] Burtis was a trustee and prominent leader in the New Rochelle church.

[71] The first Methodist sermon was preached in Norwalk, Connecticut, in 1787 by Cornelius Cook. He was a young man, had just entered the itinerant ministry, and before the close of 1789 he had ended his brief yet useful career, dying suddenly in New York of yellow fever. For several years previous to the erection of any house of worship, the society held its public services in a red school house near the crockery store of Nash Brothers on Main Street, corner of West. (Hill: *History of Methodism in Norwalk, Conn.*)

[72] This was the family of the Rev. Augustus Jocelyn.

Tallman's,[73] fed, and continued on to Josiah Coan's,[74] where we housed for the night, weak and weary.

Sunday, 13. At West Haddam I preached to a few; there had been no notice. Bishop Whatcoat, feeble as he was, spoke in the afternoon. I read some letters, giving an account of the prosperity of the work of God, south and west. This has been a trying week to body, soul, and spirit: I have made out four hundred and twenty miles, exceedingly rocky and rude. Should I live to be as old as Mr. Wesley, and travel as long as he did, yet shall I never see a Maryland in Connecticut. In West Haddam our people have nearly finished their meeting house: it has a most excellent pulpit, and a neat sanctuary round it, simply enclosed. We lodged with John Wilcox: he is faint, yet faithful; and waiting for the consolation of Israel, in holiness and glory. My soul is like a weaned child, to do and to suffer, to make rest more desirable in pursuit, and more abundantly satisfying in the enjoyment: to say not a word about earthly things, my spirit has been greatly assaulted, and divinely supported in grace, in God, in Christ, in the hope of *rest*, *rest*, *rest*, *eternal rest*.

Monday, 14. We crossed to Connecticut River, and came to Middle Haddam, lodging at Elisha Day's; but it is night in this place:—a little meeting house, a little society, and little religion.

Tuesday, 15. I preached upon Acts viii, 6: "And Philip went down to the city of Samaria, and preached Christ unto them." I inquired *how* the apostles "preached Christ." To sinners the *atonement*; to be apprehended by faith, preceded by repentance: in believers the "hope of glory." It was observed—it appeared, according to the Divine attributes of justice, mercy, truth, and love, that there must be a general provision for all; such as are in God prove it must be so. "Preached Christ" as the anointed of God; a prophet, priest, and king, generally and personally, in his operations of grace. The people were attentive. After preaching, I ordained Jeremiah Stocking a deacon.

Wednesday, 16. We dined at Lyme, and rode on to New London. Brother Whatcoat preached on 2 Cor. vi, 5: the house was crowded, and the young men and boys very disorderly. We lodged at Richard Douglass's.

Thursday, 17. We had a pleasant ride to Norwich—behold! the temple hath been burnt down, and more elegantly rebuilt since I was here. Thus have they made a benefit of a calamity. Bishop Whatcoat preached upon *Christ's love for the Church*: I read a letter and prayed.

[73] Probably Lyman Tallmann, whose name appears in the list of Coast Guard volunteers with the notation that he enlisted on November 14, 1781. (Steiner: *History of Guildford and Madison Connecticut*, 454.)

[74] In 1799 the Methodist Society was formed in the Black Rock District of Madison known as Rockland. A site for the church was granted in 1806 to a group of trustees which included the name of Josiah Coan. (Steiner, *op. cit.*, 389.)

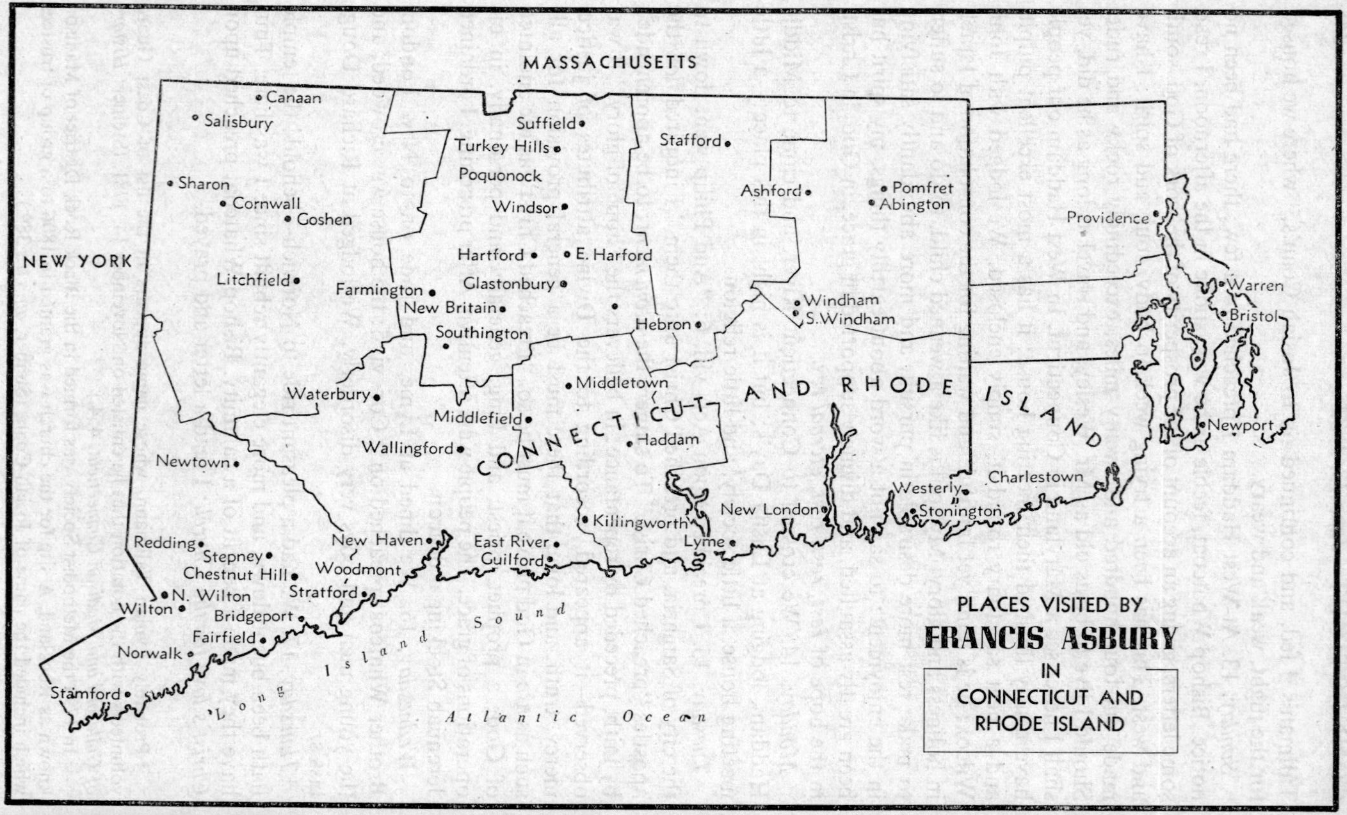
PLACES VISITED BY
FRANCIS ASBURY
IN
CONNECTICUT AND
RHODE ISLAND
MASSACHUSETTS
NEW YORK
CONNECTICUT
AND RHODE ISLAND
Canaan
Salisbury
Sharon
Cornwall
Goshen
Litchfield
Suffield
Turkey Hills
Poquonock
Windsor
Hartford
E. Harford
Glastonbury
Farmington
New Britain
Southington
Stafford
Ashford
Pomfret
Abington
Providence
Warren
Bristol
Newport
Windham
S. Windham
Hebron
Middletown
Middlefield
Haddam
Waterbury
Wallingford
Newtown
Killingworth
Lyme
New London
Westerly
Stonington
Charlestown
New Haven
Woodmont
East River
Guilford
Redding
Stepney
Chestnut Hill
N. Wilton
Wilton
Stratford
Bridgeport
Fairfield
Norwalk
Stamford
Long Island Sound
Atlantic Ocean

On *Friday* we came to Nathan Herrick's, at North Preston: I read some letters, and then preached upon Titus ii, 11, 12: we had an open time. I made two simple propositions:—

I. The operations of grace upon sinners; and

II. The operations of grace on believers, by which they live in self-denial of all evil, and bear the cross, enjoy the life of God, and exercise themselves in Christian temperance, justice, and holiness.

Rhode Island

Saturday, 19. To General Lippet's, at Cranston, twenty-eight miles.

Sunday, 20. I opened the meeting at half-past ten o'clock; then followed the ordination, then the sacrament; after which brother Whatcoat preached upon Eph. iii, 8. My subject was 2 Cor. iii, 11, 12. In my improvement I showed the character and offices of Moses compared with Christ: the glory of Moses and the superior glory of Christ: the letter and spirit of the law, the letter and spirit of the Gospel; and I dwelt largely upon the latter. Plainness of speech, simple and searching; pointed to every case and character. My work was imperfect; I had not time, and perhaps not skill, to finish and properly apply so great a subject. We had four exhortations; and concluded about four o'clock.

Massachusetts

Monday, 21. We dined at Mr. Turpin's[75] in Providence, and came on to Joseph Guild's in Attleborough; making a journey of about twenty-six miles. Next day, after a heavy, hungry, weary, dusty ride, we reached Boston. I closed the labours of the day by a sermon from 1 Peter, and had two Baptist and three Methodist preachers to hear me. It was an open time.

Wednesday, 23. At Lynn I spoke on Hosea x, 12.

Thursday, 24. We reached Marblehead. Brother Whatcoat preached; I gave an exhortation: our audience, chiefly females, nearly filled the room. Mr. Bowler[76] is our good friend (but not a brother), in lending his own

[75] Benjamin Turpin had been a Quaker but forfeited his membership by marrying outside the fold. His home was a kind of headquarters for ministers. He entertained Coke during his visit to Providence in 1804 when the house "was thronged most of the time with Methodists from different parts of the Circuit." (McDonald: *History of Methodism in Providence, Rhode Island*, 35–39.)

[76] James Bowler was greatly pleased with the style and content of the first Methodist sermon he heard preached by Ezekiel Cooper. His house was burned on April 11, 1792, causing him a loss of a thousand pounds, and the house to which Asbury refers was built on Lee Street the same summer. He was a warm friend of the struggling new church. (Candlin: *History of Methodist Episcopal Church, Marblehead, Mass.*)

house, and assisting us largely in building ours for the worship of God.

Friday, 25. We rode round the tomb of that old prophet of the Lord, George Whitefield. We stopped at the sisters Eaton's,[77] in Salisbury, and allow ourselves to have made six hundred and twenty miles. In Newburyport are great improvements, and beautiful houses in and around: as in Boston, everything thrives but religion.

Saturday, 26. At Salisbury brother Whatcoat gave us a lecture on 1 John v, 4.

Sunday, 27. We had a love feast at Jemima Eaton's; a sermon at the meeting house, and administered the sacrament. I spoke on Zech. xii, 10. Brother Whatcoat in the afternoon from 2 Cor. v, 20. Joshua Taylor preached in the evening. It was hard labour, and by no means agreeable to me to preach in other people's houses; to which I may add, that I was under bodily and spiritual infirmity. It is our duty to suffer and to serve: and it is true that we submit to the one, and will, by grace, do the other. We feel the prejudices of the people. They may think we wish to invade their rights; but they are mistaken, for I would rather preach under a tree.

New Hampshire

Monday, 28. We came away in haste to Greenland, breakfasted, resumed our journey, passing through Berwick, and brought up at Deacon Clarke's,[78] in Wells: and thus one day's ride of fifty-one miles brought us across the State of New Hampshire.

Maine

Tuesday, 29. We stopped at Falmouth in the District of Maine; and within sight of Portland. Although we rode thirty miles I was obliged to preach—my subject was 2 Tim. iv, 7.

Wednesday, 30. We had a racking ride of about forty-five miles to Monmouth;[79] our breakfast we took at Gray, and dined with Mr. Bradbury at New Gloucester.

[77] This was probably Jemima Eaton and her sister.

[78] Probably Aaron Clark of the First Parish Congregational Church in Wells. Jesse Lee mentions a "long day's ride to deacon Clark's tavern in Wells" on July 29, 1800. (Bourne, *op. cit.*, 555; Lee's *Journal.*)

[79] Jesse Lee preached the first Methodist sermon at Monmouth, Maine, on October 22, 1793, in the home of Peter Hopkins. Lee weighed around 250 pounds, and he used two horses as he came into Monmouth, one following the other without a lead. (Cochrane: *Our Reasons for Celebrating Today*, prepared for the "Historical Celebration Recalling the Organization in Monmouth One Hundred and Fifty Years Ago.")

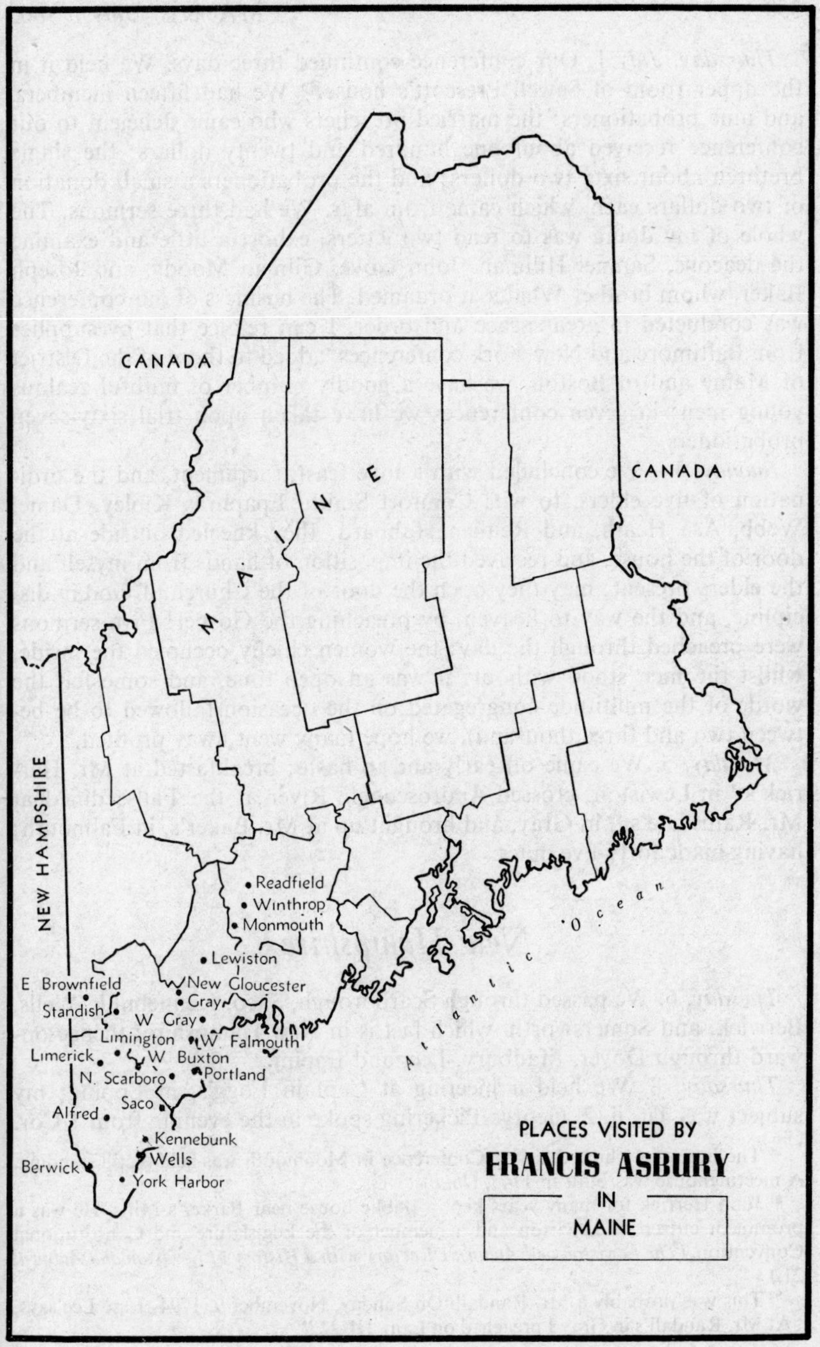
CANADA
CANADA
MAINE
NEW HAMPSHIRE
Atlantic Ocean
Readfield
Winthrop
Monmouth
Lewiston
New Gloucester
Gray
W Gray
W. Falmouth
E. Brownfield
Standish
Limington
Limerick
W Buxton
Portland
N. Scarboro
Saco
Alfred
Kennebunk
Wells
Berwick
York Harbor
PLACES VISITED BY
FRANCIS ASBURY
IN
MAINE

Thursday, July 1. Our conference continued three days. We held it in the upper room of Sewell Prescott's house.[80] We had fifteen members, and nine probationers: the married preachers who came deficient to our conference received about one hundred and twenty dollars; the single brethren about sixty-two dollars; and the probationers a small donation of two dollars each, which came from afar. We had three sermons. The whole of my doing was to read two letters, exhort a little and examine the deacons, Samuel Hillman, John Gove, Gilman Moody, and Joseph Baker, whom brother Whatcoat ordained. The business of our conference was conducted in great peace and order. I can rejoice that by supplies from Baltimore and New York conferences, added to those of the District of Maine and of Boston, we have a goodly number of faithful zealous young men: in seven conferences we have taken upon trial sixty-seven probationers.

Sunday, 4.—We concluded with a love feast, sacrament, and the ordination of five elders, to wit: Comfort Smith, Epaphras Kibley, Daniel Webb, Asa Heath, and Reuben Hubbard: they kneeled outside at the door of the house, and received the imposition of hands from myself and the elders present: may they open the door of the Church of God in discipline, and the way to heaven, by preaching the Gospel! Five sermons were preached through the day: the women chiefly occupied the inside, whilst the men stood without; it was an open time, and some felt the word: of the multitude congregated on the occasion (allowed to be between two and three thousand), we hope many went away profited.

Monday, 5. We came off early and in haste; breakfasted at Mr. Herrick's[81] in Lewiston; crossed Androscoggin River at the Falls; dined at Mr. Ramsdale's,[82] in Gray, and brought up at Mr. Baker's, in Falmouth; having made forty-five miles.

New Hampshire

Tuesday, 6. We passed through Scarborough, Saco, Kennebunk, Wells, Berwick, and Somersworth, which last is in New Hampshire: thence onward through Dover, Madbury, Lee, and Epping.

Thursday, 8. We held a meeting at Captain Fogg's, in Epping; my subject was Tit. ii, 2. George Pickering spoke in the evening from 1 Cor.

[80] The house in which this first Conference in Monmouth was held is still standing. A meetinghouse was built in 1745. (*Ibid.*)

[81] John Herrick for many years kept a public house near Barker's Mills. He was a prominent citizen of Lewiston and a member of the Legislature and Constitutional Convention. (*The Lewiston and Auburn Directory with a History of Lewiston and Auburn*, 21.)

[82] This was probably a Mr. Randall. On Sunday, November 9, 1794, Jesse Lee says, "At Mr. Randall's in Gray I preached on Lam. III:22."

xv, 34. After preaching we rode twelve miles to Hawke.[83] On our route next day to Waltham we passed through Kingston, Plasto, Haverhill, Andover, Wilmington, Woburn, Lexington, and Lincoln, nearly completing another thousand miles. We shall have a great opening in New Hampshire; and a district formed there in a few years.

I crossed New Hampshire from Saybrook to Berwick, a distance of thirty miles, and recrossed from Berwick to Plaistow, a distance of forty miles. The native products of the soil are the spruce, pine, cedar, birch, oak, ash—it is a rich lumber country, well watered, with fine streams for saw mills. The face of the earth is not pleasing; but it is well improved: the prospects for Indian corn are good, the cover fields luxuriant, and the meadows beautiful: the dwellings are handsome, and the meeting houses stand within sight of each other.

Massachusetts

Haverhill bridge engaged my attention. It is thrown across the Merrimack River by three arches; a distance of probably sixteen hundred feet. I also saw the grand canal, designed, principally, to float lumber from the Merrimack to Boston. For about twenty-seven miles they have rocks, and swamps, and hills to wind and labour through; nevertheless, they can draw a raft of great length along, after passing the locks, which admit about seventy feet at a time; they link the disparted fragments together again, and move forward. This navigation will be a vast source of wealth to the country, as well as a great convenience in the passage outward and inward of domestic and foreign products of every species—and it will, doubtless, also be profitable to the company.

Saturday, 10. I rested, fasted, and wrote a little. I have passed so rapidly along, that lately I have had time only for ordinary and common exercises.

Mr. Bemis's[84] family is singularly blessed in four successive generations: elder Pickering's two children, a son called Francis Asbury, and a daughter named Maria, make the fourth.

Sabbath, 11. I spent the *Sabbath* at Waltham. I preached on Matt. vii, 14, and again on Gal. i, 3, 4. My sensations were not very pleasant, and the young people seemed very wild; there was an old drunkard too, who stood up and spoke once and again: perhaps they will behave better the next *Sabbath* I give them.

I feel that fasting at my time of life, if only once a month, brings on such dejection of spirits I can hardly bear up under it. I have had lately two *official cordials*, ironically speaking. They know how to come at me, although four or five hundred miles distant. Lord, help me to do and suffer all I ought to do and suffer for Thee, thy Church, and ministers!

[83] Hawke was the present Danville a few miles from Kingston.

[84] This was Abraham Bemis. (See note under August 5, 1793.)

Monday, 12. We came through Needham. George Pickering stopped to demand the Church rates taken from the Methodists, amounting to one hundred dollars or upwards: this is to pay the Independent ministers, whose forefathers fled from Episcopal tyranny: yet, be it known unto all men, their children's children are risen up and glory in supporting the Gospel *according to law*. Happy the descendants who condemn not themselves by doing that which their ancestors disallowed! We lodged at Mr. Stearnes[85] at Milford.

Connecticut

Tuesday, 13. We came upon the turnpike road through to Thompson. I was told that Mr. Dow,[86] an Independent minister, had relinquished his legal claim of salary, trusting to the *willing minds* of the public, who gave him more by voluntary subscription.

I had to preach at Nichol's meeting house,[87] but being taken with a bilious headache, I said but little: my subject was Heb. iv, 14–16.

Wednesday, 14. I rode to Captain Lyons,[88] in Canterbury: after dinner I continued on over the rocks and hills to Windham. We had a meeting at Robinson's: I was able to preach upon Isaiah lv, 6, 7. Here God had wrought, and the people appeared to be very lively.

Thursday, 15. We scaled the hills and rocks, passing through Lebanon, and stopped at Joseph Bass's. Here will be the beginning of a society.

We came to Hebron. Brother Borroughs[89] attended me. The travelling preachers cannot leave their appointments. At four o'clock in the evening our new house in Hebron was consecrated: the subject on this occasion was chosen from Exod. xx, 24. It was an open time.

Friday, 16. We rode to the city of Hartford, stopping at a brother's house upon Glastonbury[90] hills, and at Mr. Spencer's,[91] and at Squire

[85] It was deemed necessary to organize the Methodist society in legal form. A meeting was called according to law and was held in the North School house on August 28, 1811. David Stearnes was chosen moderator and Pearley Hunt, clerk. (Bragg: *A History of Methodism in Milford, Mass., 1792 to 1948*, xi.)

[86] Daniel Dow, of Thompson, was a Calvinist and a cousin of the famous Lorenzo Dow. (Perrin: *An Epitome History of the Inception of Methodism in North Eastern Connecticut*, 5.)

[87] Nichol's meeting house was near the residence of Captain Jonathan Nichols in West Thompson, Connecticut. (See note under August 6, 1795.)

[88] This was Captain Judah Lyon. (See note under July 24, 1798.)

[89] This was probably Banks N. Borrough.

[90] The Asbury rock in East Glastonbury, which the bishop used as a pulpit, is the silent reminder, as the church there is the active evidence, that Lee and his colleagues were effective when they labored there in the last decade of the eighteenth century. (Ward: *Jesse Lee: Methodist Pioneer, New England Southern Trails*, 15.)

[91] Thomas Spencer lived at Spencertown.

Pitkin's:[92] we talked and prayed (it was all that we could do), and pushed on to Winsted. We lodged with Doctor Lynde.

Saturday, 17. We came up the turnpike road to New Hartford[93] upon the banks of Farmington River.

Sunday, 18. We held quarterly meeting, Litchfield circuit. The *Sabbath day* congregation was small, owing to the rain after the great heat. I spoke from 2 Thess. iii, 1. We had feeling times and hearts, and a living love feast. In heat and in haste, we rode on to Colonel Burrell's, in Canaan, and there lodged.

Monday, 19. We came on to brother Church's, near the Falls of Housatonic River. Our route led us through Salisbury and Sharon, across the line into the State of New York.

At Sharon and at Lewis's we called in. From the eastern to the western line of Connecticut, that is, from Thompson to Sharon, I calculate the distance to be one hundred and thirty miles; it cannot exceed one hundred and forty miles.

New York

At Rhinebeck I made up four thousand miles, and have one hundred in advance towards the fifth thousand I shall have made since the last of July, 1801. Of the little time we have, may be judged by the length of our rides, day after day; yet, at this speed must I go to meet the conferences, and visit the principal societies. My soul is at times greatly drawn out in prayer.

Tuesday, 20. We rested at Traveller's Rest, upon the solitary banks of Hudson, with my dear friends Freeborn Garrettson, and his prudent, pious wife. We have heat, heat, great heat.

Wednesday, 21. I preached upon 2 Cor. iv, 7. It was an ordination sermon at the setting apart of Billy Hibbard[94] to the office of an elder. It is exceeding warm; and the zenith of harvest: yet, we had a congregation.

Thursday, 22. I had to tear myself away from these precious souls: I do believe God dwells in this house (Traveller's Rest). We came on to Fishkill,[95] and fed. A poor intoxicated creature had sense enough left to insult us, and curse the Methodists. After feeding at brother Warren's, we made another push over the hills to Peekskill, and came to Governor

[92] Squire Elisha Pitkin lived at East Hartford.

[93] Asbury must have passed through New Hartford before he reached Winsted unless he retraced his steps, which is unlikely.

[94] Billy Hibbard (1771–1844) was born in Norwich, Connecticut, but reared at Hinsdale, Massachusetts. He was received on trial in 1798 and spent most of his ministry in upper New York State and in New England. He was a man of great drollery, rather eccentric, and particularly effective in troublesome and difficult situations. He died at Canaan, New York. (Seaman, *op. cit.*, 210; Sprague, *op. cit.*, VII, 298–99.)

[95] Fishkill was a town south of Rhinebeck on the east bank of the Hudson River.

Van Cortlandt's. I have received great kindness from this family. We have made forty-eight miles this day.

Friday, 23. I came gently along down, having an admirable view of the North River—the indents and projections of its lofty and beautiful banks. I called on brother Anderson, and was exceedingly well treated. For twenty-two miles we had excessive heat. I came to Captain Requa's[96] by surprise,

FREEBORN GARRETTSON

but I was not therefore made the less welcome. Religion revives in New Rochelle circuit: they have general prayer meetings, and good seasons of grace; that is the way.

Saturday, 24. I came into New York about two o'clock, and escaped heavy rain. My soul hath been sweetly stayed upon God whilst riding alone. I have received a confirmation of the death of my mother, who died January 6, 1802. Of the particulars of her last moments I have received no certain account; but I learn that a certain Mr. Emery has taken

[96] Abraham Requa, of Huguenot descent, was reared in New Rochelle, where as a lad he was influenced by Methodist preaching in the homes of Frederick Deveau and Peter Bonnet. He served with distinction in the American army during the Revolution. In 1796 Captain Requa settled in Yorktown, upper Westchester County, and became an active Methodist in that locality. (Scharf, *op. cit.*, II, 443.)

all her property. I am comforted with good news from several quarters: persecution has ceased in Charleston, and the Africans are growing in grace: our society in Philadelphia becomes more united; and there are good appearances in Old Brunswick circuit, Virginia.

Sabbath, 25. In New York, I preached at the old church, John Street, on Rev. iii, 17–20; at three o'clock, at the Bowery church on Isaiah lv, 6, 7; at the African church at six o'clock in the evening on 1 Thess. i, 5. It rained at times through the day, which prevented more from attending: it was a day of life to me.

Monday, 26. I had to wait in a boat, tormented by heat and flies; still worse for my poor brute, who made an attempt to leap out into the bay; had she been loose, and myself at a distance, poor Jane would probably have been overboard. It came into my mind that we had preached, and should yet preach to little purpose in Newark: this I mentioned to Mr. Richard Leaycraft, with whom I dined in New York, in company with Parson Uzal Ogden: he had thought of building a house; and a small one Parson Ogden thought he might well do himself; and then we might have a church.

New Jersey

I stopped at Mr. Crowell's,[97] in Elizabethtown, and then came on to Mr. Flatt's, Rahway.[98]

Tuesday, 27. I stopped in Brunswick at Benjamin Drake's, and then pushed on, sultry as it was, and made it thirty-eight miles to Joseph Hutchinson's: with his new house, new wife, will he not by and by want a new lease of his life?

Wednesday, 28. I stopped at Crosswick's. I felt *proper* sick; but I was soon relieved by vinegar and water. My friend Hulet Hancock housed me for the night. I found my dear sister Hancock feeble and unwell, but she soon grew better, and at family prayer she praised the Lord with a loud voice.

[97] This was probably Daniel Crowell, who was prominent in Methodist circles at this time. Others of the name who may be identified with Methodism were Samuel Crowell, who lived at Turkey in Essex County, and Captain Thomas Crowell, Jr., and his wife, Esther Crowell. A monument to Captain Crowell's father and mother is found in the First Presbyterian churchyard in Elizabethtown. (Ricord: *History of Union County, New Jersey*, 274; Phoebus, *op. cit.*, 211.)

[98] William Flatt was one of the original members and trustees of the First Methodist Church of Rahway. In 1798 trustees purchased from William Shotwell for fifty dollars a lot on which they proposed to build a house of worship. The deed conveyed the land to Jonathan Oliver and Benjamin Woodruff of Essex County, and William Flatt, Jr., Abraham Storms, and John Marsh of Middlesex County, trustees. Asbury probably preached at Flatt's home on this visit, since a meeting house was not begun until 1806. (Mooney: *Centennial History of Rahway Methodism*, 44–51.)

Thursday, 29. I stopped at Burlington; had a word or two with my friends, and we commended each other to God in prayer.

Pennsylvania

I came on in haste and sickening heat to Mr. Manly's *traveller's rest*,[99] arriving about twelve o'clock. The fever has reappeared in Philadelphia. I hear great times have been known in Dover[100]—above one hundred and fifty souls have felt the operations of Divine grace, at the annual meeting upon the day of Pentecost; and great times also at the Milford[101] quarterly meeting.

I thought to have remained with my friend Manly, and take a short breathing spell; other friends wished to have me in the city, and came to bring me in, but I besought them to let me stay until Sabbath morning.

On *Sunday morning*, according to appointment, I preached for the first time, in the college church (or Academy); my subject was Exod. xx, 24: after sermon we had sacrament: we had seriousness and attention. In the afternoon I preached at St. George's; a gust came up and few attended. In the evening I rode out to Mr. Manly's.[102]

Monday, *August* 2. I took a serious leave, with fears for the health of the city, and a mind impressed with concern for the Church. We were overtaken by rain before we reached Chester. After dinner with Mrs. Withy, I desired Mr. Manly, who had very kindly come with me thus far, to return. I proceeded on to Wilmington (Delaware) through the rain, and lodged with Allan M'Lane.

Maryland

Tuesday, 3. I resumed my journey south, came as far as Isaac Hersey's, dined with him, went on to brother John George's, halted awhile, moved forward again, and brought up for the night with brother Howell, in Charlestown.

Wednesday, 4. I crossed the Susquehannah, dined with Mr. Smith,[103] and reached Perry Hall in the evening. Here my creature consolation was in part gone; Mr. and Mrs. Gough were absent at Bath. Nevertheless, Mrs. James Carroll was here, and not less attentive than her mother.

[99] Mr. Henry Manley was a trustee of St. George's from 1785 and resided at No. 40 Market Street, Philadelphia. This reference is to his country home, of which William Colbert writes in his *Journal* under date of September, 1804.

[100] Dover, Delaware.

[101] Milford, Delaware.

[102] See letter to John Rogers, August 1, 1802.

[103] This may have been the same Smith mentioned in the *Journal* on May 12, 1801.

Last year my soul travailed for her health, and soul's salvation; she is brought to the experimental knowledge of God, and I rejoice over her.

I have one day I can call my own. I write, I read, I think, and refit for the mountains. My mind is in great peace, and has so been kept in all my labours; and my trials, which come from almost every point of the compass, shall be as various winds to waft me to the haven of rest.

Saturday, 7. I came to Baltimore through excessive warmth, and lodged with Emanuel Kent.[104] The wife of our brother Samuel Coate[105] had a daughter born to her, whom I baptized, naming her Sophia.

Sabbath, 8. I preached in Light Street chapel on Rev. ii, 1–5. As the weather was changeable, I had another appointment in the house; my subject was Philippians ii, 14, 15: "Do all things without murmurings or disputings; that ye may be blameless and harmless, the sons of God without rebuke." First, it was observed how Christians are brought into the relation of "sons of God." Second, The duties and privileges of that relation. Third, The purity and sincerity the subjects of this relation are called to experience. Fourth, That "murmurings" either towards God, or good or bad men, ought to be avoided; and perverse "disputings" cautiously guarded against; and in all duties, sufferings, and discipline, true Christian meekness and forbearance should be manifested.

After a thunder gust, the evening cleared away, and became serene. I preached at the Howard's Hill market house at five o'clock, to multitudes of people, from Isaiah lv, 6, 7. And thus ended the duties of the day.

Monday, 9. I rode to Robert Carnan's. Still intense heat. Next day I breakfasted at Charles Carnan's, in company with Nelson Reed and wife, Joshua Wells and James M'Cannon; the evening found me at Henry Willis's, Pipe Creek.

On *Wednesday* I made an improvement on Deut. x, 12. We only had what people could receive notice in the morning. One woman professed to find pardon and peace, and came forward to baptism, presenting her child also.

[104] Emanuel Kent was a tea merchant at 32 Hanover Street, Baltimore. He was a class leader in Light Street Church and a trustee of Cokesbury College. Whatcoat was often a guest in his home. His wife was the former Eleanor Burneston. It is probable that before coming to Baltimore he resided in Queen Annes County where the Town Hundred census of 1776 lists him as the head of a family of six with twenty-three Negroes in his possession. (Brumbaugh, *op. cit.*, II, 200; Armstong, *op. cit.*, 89; Light Street Church Records for 1799.)

[105] Mrs. Samuel Coate, whose husband was stationed at Baltimore and Fells Point in 1802 and 1803, was the daughter of Mrs. Jacob Dulmage, Sr., a sister of Philip Embury. Coate, a native of New Jersey, who had come to Baltimore after four years of work in Canada, is believed to have met his wife among the loyalists in Canada. After four years in the United States he returned to Canada to resume his ministry there. In 1809 he was presiding elder of the Lower Canada District, and the next year he is listed as located. He received ordination in another communion which he abandoned for business pursuits. (Playter: *History of Methodism in Canada*, 55, 64, 65, 101; Carroll: *Case and His Contemporaries*, I, 19–21, 174–77; Stevens, *op. cit.*, III, 195–98).

Thursday, 12. I visited Alexander Warfield's family; and next day came on to James Higgins's, and preached there from 1 Tim. ii, 1–4. On *Saturday* morning I rode over to see Robert Owings's family, and was comforted in finding one of his children, Miranda Evans, professing to have found redemption; may this be a solid work, and an earnest for the whole family. In the evening I went up to Stephen Shelmerdine's. My mind hath been blessed with great consolation. I rejoiced to find the work of God spreading and growing in Frederick circuit, under the ministry of Curtis Williams and Fielding Parker.[106]

Sabbath, 15. At Frederick I once more spoke; my subject was 1 Cor. i, 23, 24. Here then, at last, after more than thirty years' labour, we have a house of worship,[107] and thirty souls, or upwards, in fellowship. In speaking this morning, I had some assistance, and I laboured. Some thoughts passed in my mind of going to the court house steps at five o'clock; but I changed my mind: as there were three preachers in town, to wit, our brothers Curtis Williams, James L. Higgins, and Edward Matthews,[108] I assigned them the duty, in the hope that their superior zeal and faith may be the means of converting some souls to God at the close of the Sabbath.

Monday, 16. We held evening meeting at Samuel Philips's: I spoke from Philippians iv, 6. Sister Philips is gone; she was a daughter of affliction for many years, and died in peace about seven weeks ago: I thought when I saw her last I should see her no more in time. Nicholas Snethen preached her funeral sermon: the text she herself had chosen.

West Virginia

On *Tuesday* we came through heat, and over the hills, to Sheppard's town, Virginia. I found Thomas Boydstone, and Benjamin Boydstone and

[106] Curtis Williams, who spent the years 1795 to 1805 as an itinerant, was serving the Frederick Circuit with Fielding or Fielder Parker. For the latter this was the beginning of five years in the traveling ministry.

[107] It cannot be definitely established when and by whom the first Methodist sermon in Frederick was preached. It is probable that Robert Strawbridge preached there before 1770, and certainly John King was early there. The deed, dated 1790, conveying property to the trustees, is in the possession of Calvary Methodist Church, Frederick. By 1806 it was necessary to enlarge the church to which Asbury refers. (Sweet, *op. cit.* IV, 123, 124; Lednum, *op. cit.*, 20; *History of Calvary Methodist Episcopal Church*, 1930.)

[108] James L. Higgins, who located in 1801, probably had held the relationship of local preacher. Years later Asbury was his guest near New Market, Frederick County. (See *Journal* entry for March 10, 1811.) Although Edward Matthews was appointed to Harford Circuit in 1802, Quinn states that when Asbury visited him that same year on the Winchester Circuit, his traveling companion was Matthews. Matthews, a native of Wales, died in 1834 after thirty-two years in the itinerancy. (Wright: *The Life of James Quinn*, 68, 72; Hedges: *Crowned Victors*, 253, 254.)

his wife, on the road to glory. After thirty years' occasional preaching in this place, we have a small society; and by the purchase of an old academy, a church—*with two chimneys in it*.

Wednesday, 18. I preached on Ephes. ii, 10. Daniel Hitt and Edward Matthews held meetings yesterday evening and this evening. I have formed a plan to go next fall by the way of Chilicothe to Limestone; and so meet the Western yearly conference, should it be held in Kentucky.

Thursday, 19. At Charlestown I preached from 2 Cor. vi, 1; some souls felt the energy of the word. We dined at brother Englishe's, and rode on to John Davenport's to lodge.

Friday, 20. We called at John Millburn's. Next day, at Millburn's meeting house, I spoke upon Hebrews x, 35, 36. We lodged at William Tyler's.

Virginia

On *Sunday*, in the meeting house at Winchester, at eleven o'clock, I preached from Titus ii, 13, 14. We had the sacrament. Many felt, and gave glory to God. In the afternoon, under the shady trees, westward of the town, not a few attended—rulers and people; I read two letters, and preached from Psalm lvi, 16.[109] Mr. O'Kelly having been taken ill in town, I sent two of our brethren, Reed and Walls, to see him, by whom I signified to him, that if he wished to see me, I would wait on him; he desired a visit, which I made him on *Monday*, *August* 23. We met in peace, asked of each other's welfare, talked of persons and things indifferently, prayed, and parted in peace. Not a word was said of the troubles of former times:—perhaps this is the last interview we shall have upon earth. At Elijah Phelp's[110] we rested on *Monday*, and part of *Tuesday*. I have heard of the flight of thousands from the city of Philadelphia; and that all the churches, save the Episcopalian, the Quaker, and the Methodist, are shut up. George Roberts still continues in the city. O my God, keep him and his family alive in the day of pestilence!

Tuesday, 24. At Stephensburg at four o'clock, we held a meeting; my text was 1 John iii, 1–3.

Wednesday, 25, Was a most remarkable day of heat: I rested to refit. Sleep and appetite failed me. Edward Matthews was intended for my companion to the Holston district: but two of the preachers had been sick, and the other was removed; and Frederick and Berkley circuits had been neglected at a time of the greatest prospect of good. We had a com-

[109] There are only thirteen verses in this psalm.

[110] Elijah Phelps lived in the vicinity of Stephensburg. He had been a traveling preacher but was located at this time. His wife, who was somewhat older, was a deeply pious lady and a sensible, well-informed woman. (Bennett, *op. cit.*, 402. See Asbury's letter to Thornton Fleming, August 21, 1802.)

fortable ride to Woodstock, twenty miles: there was a gentle rain, and the weather was pleasant. My mind is freely stayed upon God—my guide in life and death. On *Friday* we rode thirty-three miles to brother J. Huyster's: some rain fell on us, but after we were housed, there came on an awful storm of wind, thunder, lightning, and rain.

Saturday, Sunday, and *Monday*, 28, 29, 30. At Rocktown.[111] On Saturday I spoke in our house on 1 Peter iii, 18. On Sunday, through the progress of the love feast, there was great shaking, and shouting, and weeping and praying: it was thought best not to stop these exercises by the more regular labour of preaching, as most of the persons present were engaged either as subjects or instruments. We accepted the offer of the Presbyterian house, a good shade not being near, and the ground damp, in which I spoke on Zeph. iii, 16, 17: there was great attention, and some tenderness.

Tuesday, 31. The brethren having a wish to continue the meeting another day, I preached on Gen. xxxii, 26, 27. By way of introduction, I made some observations on the peculiar and extraordinary features in the life and character of the patriarch—the blessings of a temporal nature so abundantly bestowed; and the spiritual blessings, rich, Divine, and various, so freely given by the God-man Christ Jesus, with whom he wrestled and prevailed. Jacob is asked his name—he told it: when he was justified his name and his nature were changed; his privileges were increased, and his power enlarged with God and man: he had power with man to stand against their temptations and to do them good—power with God to ask blessings for others, and to receive answers to prayer. It was thought, that in this three-days' meeting, forty or fifty souls were converted or reclaimed, and quickened.

In the afternoon I rode to brother Young's, in Augusta; I was very unwell with a fever and headache, and had a restless night.

At brother Young's, on *Monday*, I spoke on Acts xiii, 26: meeting began at three o'clock, and continued until seven o'clock: there was great praying and shouting. Sister Jones rose up and gave an exhortation: she spoke as if she were going home to glory—I felt it: she reminded me of sister Jones and sister Taylor, those female *flames*, and almost martyrs for Jesus: one of them, I trust, has long been in glory! the other, I believe, is only waiting for her call to eternal rest. I found it was time for me to be off—preaching for four or five days together was enough: I felt weak in my breast.

Wednesday, September 1. We lodged at David M'Nare's; and next day came over the hills, crossing the branches of the Shenandoah, to Brownsburg: night coming upon us, we turned aside to lodge at Andrew Weir's, and were kindly and comfortably entertained.

On *Friday* we passed through Lexington, and being so near, I was willing to gratify my curiosity by a view of the Natural Bridge. I walked down

[111] Rocktown was the present Harrisonburg.

the hill to look at the arch thrown, in a regular ellipsis, about one hundred and sixty feet above a stream, which, in the rainy season, foams and roars beneath: the breadth of the bridge may be sixty feet, and the distance one hundred and sixty feet across. On one side of the road, at the south-east end, large trees are growing. Should I live two years longer I may preach under the arch. We dined at Mr. Huston's, and were honoured as men of the ministry.

Hearing that the circuit preacher was at Morris's, we turned aside and came up—purgatory. On *Saturday* we crossed James River at Pattonsburg, dined at Mr. Lockland's upon Back Creek, and came on to Fincastle.

Sabbath day, 5. I preached upon Matt. xxv, 34–37. My meaning upon the text was, First, To show the *blessedness* of the people of God, as subjects of the kingdom of grace and glory. Secondly, The evidences of their being *blessed* to others, in feeding the hungry, clothing the naked, in a hospitable reception of the stranger, visiting prisoners and the sick, doing good to their souls as well as their bodies: and when the subjects of this love, and mercy, and benevolence, are pious, persecuted saints, the children of God would not hesitate to take them into their houses, or visit them in their distress, although this labour of love might subject themselves to persecution and death. It was observed, that it was not national fellow-feeling, the hospitality of politeness, nor family attachments; no, nor yet the more pure, though too partial affection which one religious society may feel for another, which may be the motive—it is because they are the suffering members of their common Lord—"Ye have done it unto me." The meeting continued four hours, and there was a moving among the people. I lodged at Edward Mitchell's. I drew a plan of a house forty feet long, thirty feet wide, and two stories high, of brick—to be built in Fincastle; two-thirds of the money must be collected before we begin. This, like many more of my good designs, may come to naught.

Monday, 6. We rode to Van Lear's, upon Roanoke, thirty-six miles, and next day crossed New River[112] at Pepper's ferry; weary, yet willing, and my soul in close communion with God. We have good news in this district—the work of God revives in all the circuits.

The season is dry; the streams are consequently—but there is great plenty: O! good Providence—O! ungrateful people.

Wednesday, 8. I preached at Page's meeting house[113] upon Eph. ii, 10. After dinner at Edward Morgan's, I went on to brother Moorehead's:

[112] New River was reached by the explorers Batts and Fallam in September, 1671. The expedition was sent out by Abraham Wood, who lived at Fort Henry, the present Petersburg, Virginia. The river was called Wood's River until its name was changed to New River. There is a State Historical Marker at Radford. Asbury was now in the Holston region.

[113] On September 19, 1795, Alexander Page gave two acres of land to the "Methodist Society on New River waters for a consideration of love." (Summers, *op. cit.*, 936.)

this family fed the Lord's prophets in Rockingham, and the door is still open in the west.

Thursday, 9. We came along to Crockett's[114] and fed, and then hasted through the town[115] and housed for the night at Cattoru's: the father was a native of Germany—a gracious soul; and his children will come into the fold of Christ.

Friday, 10. We came to Charles Hardy's,[116] upon Holston. I found the people praising God. A blessed revival had taken place. Fourteen or fifteen times have I toiled over the mighty mountains, and nearly twenty years have we laboured upon Holston; and lo! the rage of wild and Christian savages is tamed, and God hath glorified himself.

Saturday, 11. I rode to the Salt Works[117]—perhaps for the last time. Alas! there is little *salt* here, and when sister Russell is gone, will there be any left? But, a few miles from the works, up the middle ridge, they have built a meeting house;[118] and there is a revival of religion.

I make my calculation upon four thousand nine hundred miles, from July 30, 1801, to September 12, 1802. If a living man and a Christian might dare to complain ——.

Sabbath day, 12. Sweet peace fills my mind; and glorious prospects of Zion's prosperity cheer my heart: we have not, shall not, labour in vain. Not unto us, not unto us, but to Jehovah be all the glory on earth, and in heaven forever!

Tennessee

Monday, 13. I rode alone to Edward Coxe's, near Shote's ford, upon Holston.

On *Tuesday* and *Wednesday* we rested; and on *Thursday* we rode to Cashe's, near Jonesboro, Tennessee.

Friday, 17. I attended a camp meeting which continued to be held four days: there may have been fifteen hundred souls present. I read an account of the work at the Dover yearly meeting; and of the work of God generally: my text I found in Haggai ii, 4, 5. We had a shaking, and some souls felt convicting and converting grace. The heat, the restless nights, the water, or, it may be, all these combined made me sick indeed. I crossed Nolli-

[114] This was probably Walter Crockett, who lived five miles north of Wytheville. He was appointed clerk of the court for Wythe County in 1790. (*Ibid.*, index.)

[115] The town was evidently Wytheville, Virginia.

[116] Charles Hardy was a located preacher who lived near Wytheville. (Price: *Holston Methodism*, I, 393.)

[117] This was the General Russell home at Saltville, Virginia.

[118] The court records of Washington County for June 28, 1796, show "David Smith and Sarah, his wife, to the Methodist Episcopal Church under the general direction of the General Conference of the Methodist Church, $1.00, 80 square poles on which to erect a meeting house on both sides of the Salt Works Road." (Summers, *op. cit.*, 1315.)

chucky at the fording place of Colonel George Gallespie, who very kindly rode over with me, and held my hand. Main Holston was before me: I came safe over, and stopped with Felix Earnest,[119] making ninety miles this week. I take Fothergill's medicine. I can feel quite resigned to end my days here: thereby, I shall avoid great labours and trials for the coming year.

Sunday, 19. The house at Ebenezer would not hold the people: so, from my stand in the woods, I spoke from Genesis xxxii, 26–28. I was very unwell, but I held out longer than I expected; I also felt that the word was given *me* and applied to the *hearts* of the people.

Monday, 20. I was weak and very unwell. We rode down to Greenville, when I took a little breakfast. It was extraordinary, that a man who was quite a stranger to me appeared very uneasy when he found that we had paid the landlady, it being his wish to bear the expense, and have our money returned to us—his name is Cox. The day was warm. We came on to Little Nollichucky, and lodged at Edward Warren's.[120] I had little rest by night or day.

Tuesday, 21. At Bethel I spoke on Ephesians iv, 1–3. We had a close, sultry day, a small house, and a crowded congregation; an open time, and the triumph of truth.

Wednesday 22. We rode to M'Cleary's, upon French Broad, below the mouth of Nollichucky—between forty and fifty miles.

Thursday, 23. We dined at Francis Ramsay's, and lodged at Knoxville with my old friend Mr. Greer.

Friday, 24. I rode to the Grassy Valley, and next day preached at the quarterly meeting at Muddy Creek.[121] Roan county: my subject was Col. i, 9, 10. On the *Sabbath day* we had sacrament and love feast in the woods. At eleven o'clock I spoke upon John iii, 16. I was unwell; and the congregation were, to appearance, cold and not in the spirit of prayer as I could have wished. I dined with Mr. Ramsay,[122] a Presbyterian minister, at his own house on *Friday*; and he with me to-day at my lodgings: we had quite a Christian interview.

Monday, 27. We made towards West Point,[123] and lodged at Mr. Clark's for the night: in the morning we started in good spirits. We were somewhat shaken in going the old path down Spencer's hill: I walked, fearing every moment a fall for myself or my horse: it was a very noxious evening to me. It was late when we arrived at Obed River, and I imprudently lay too far from our encampment fire, and took a cold, which fixed upon my

[119] Earnest was a local preacher who lived on the Nollichucky River.

[120] Warren lived at Warrensburgh in Hamblen County. Asbury visited him again on October 23, 1809.

[121] This meeting was at the home of John Winton, where one of the early camp grounds was located.

[122] This Ramsay was the brother of Asbury's friend Francis A. Ramsay.

[123] West Point was the present Kingston, Tennessee.

throat. Late the following evening we came into Shaw's, where we lay upon the floor.[124] I was sick indeed.

Thursday, 30. We called at Prim's, and continued on to Doctor Tooley's. My throat worse and worse—I was unable to swallow. Next day we stopped awhile at Blackman's, and proceeded on to James Douglas's.[125] I had an awful night.

Saturday, *October* 2. We rode forward to Station Camp, and found the conference seated.[126] By this time my stomach and speech were pretty well gone. I applied to Mr. William Hodge, and to Mr. William M'Gee,[127] Presbyterian ministers, to supply my lack of public service, which they did with great fervency and fidelity: with great pleasure, and in great pain, I heard them both. I was able to ordain by employing brother M'Kendree to examine those who were presented, and to station the preachers—I hope for the glory of God, the benefit of the people, and the advantage of the preachers. The conference adjourned on *Tuesday*.

Wednesday, 6. I rested. After eight days' suffering of severely acute pain, the inflammation descended to my feet.

Friday, 8. I rested at Shaw's, and bled for the third time, and applied bandages and sugar of lead to my feet.

At Doctor Tooley's I was attacked in the knee with a most torturing pain, attended with a swelling; the use of both my feet I had almost entirely lost before. On *Saturday*, we rode fifteen miles to Prim's. I stopped to rest at Mr. Walton's, at the forks of Cumberland River: here I was treated with great attention and kindness. At Prim's brother M'Kendree preached; I also spoke—my subject was Heb. iii, 7, 8: some wept, and all were attentive. John Watson followed with a warm exhortation.

Monday, 18. We took our departure at five o'clock, and rode to Shaw's, where we got corn in the ear at a dollar per bushel. We continued on until half-past six o'clock, then stopped, struck a fire, and encamped under a heavy mountain dew, which, when the wind shook the trees, fell like rain upon us. Brother M'Kendree made me a tent of his own and John Watson's blankets, and happily saved me from taking cold whilst I slept about two hours under my grand *marquee*. Brother M'Kendree threw his cloak

[124] Asbury was following the Cumberland Trail from the present Rockwood in proceeding from the Holston area to Middle Tennessee. The encampment where the bishop lay upon the ground too far from the fire was evidently near Standing Stone, the present Monterey. Shaw lived near Carthage.

[125] Douglas was a North Carolinian, head of a prominent Methodist family, who lived at the Salem Camp Ground near Gallatin, Sumner County, Tennessee. (McFerrin: *Methodism in Tennessee*, I, 52.)

[126] This was the third session of the Western Conference. It met at Strother's Meeting House on Big Station Camp Creek northwest of Gallatin. (*Ibid.*, 381.)

[127] These ministers were leaders in the Great Revival which started among the Presbyterians but was practically taken over by the Methodists. (*Ibid.*, 341.) Asbury, accompanied by McKendree, was proceeding back to the Holston country of East Tennessee.

over the limb of a tree; and he and his companion took shelter underneath, and slept also. I will not be rash, I dare not be rash in my protestations against any country; but I think I will never more brave the wilderness without a tent.

On *Tuesday*, 19, after riding fifty miles, a part of ninety-three miles in two days, we came about eight o'clock to West Point. An accident, extraordinary in the manner, and desperate in the effect, happened to me. At a rocky run, in attempting to dismount, my horse gave a sudden turn, and swung me against the rocks in the stream—the rude shock to my tender feet made me roar bitterly. My horse was low before, tender-footed, and tired—the hills were steep and rugged, and I was sore by riding—these circumstances combined caused so much pain, that when we came on *Wednesday* to the Grassy Valley, I cast anchor, with a determination to give up Georgia, and go by a straight line to Camden conference, to be held January 1, 1803.

I sent word to James Douthet to explain to the elders of Georgia and South Carolina my situation. I also despatched John Watson to meet brother Snethen, and give him my plan to fulfil the appointments in Georgia—but behold, brother Snethen had had a fall from his horse, and was left lame upon the road! I have been sick for twenty-three days; ah! the tale of woe I might relate. My dear M'Kendree had to lift me up and down from my horse, like a helpless child. For my sickness and sufferings I conceive I am indebted to sleeping uncovered in the wilderness. I passed so quickly along that many people scarcely more than beheld me with their eyes; yet these were witness to my groans; and sometimes *dumb, I opened not my mouth*. I could not have slept but for the aid of laudanum; meantime, my spirits and patience were wonderfully preserved in general, although I was sometimes hardly restrained from crying, "Lord, let me die!" for death hath no terrors, and I could not but reflect upon my escape from the toil and sufferings of another year. I had no sad forebodings of the ills which might befall the Church—it is the Lord's, not mine; nor was I anxious about father or mother—they, I trust are in the paradise of God; nor did I say to myself, what will become of wife and children—these I have not. But what am I to learn from these ills and aches?—"these are counsellors that feelingly persuade me what I am." I am no longer young—I cannot go out as at other times: I must take the advice of friends who say, *spare thyself*. I have ridden about five thousand five hundred miles; and in the midst of all I am comforted with the prospects of the western conference—we have added three thousand members this year; have formed Cumberland into a district, and have sent a missionary to the Natchez.

Sunday, 24. For three days past I have been at John Winton's. By the aid of a chair on which to kneel, I preached at the meeting: my subject was Joshua xxiv, 15.

Monday, 25. I rode through Knoxville, and came to Francis Ramsey's, and by losing ourselves, we increased the distance to thirty-two miles. Next day we gained Justus Huffacre's.[128] I was happy to hear that my lame brother Snethen had gone limping on to attend my appointments in Georgia.

Saturday, 30. We have been at our friend Huffacre's since *Tuesday* last.

Sunday, 31. At Rehoboth upon French Broad, William M'Kendree stood up to speak upon "Blessed is the man that endureth temptation." My text was 2 Tim. iii, 10–12. I ordained Justus Huffacre and James Sullivan deacons. Rain having fallen abundantly, the people had their difficulties in getting home from the meeting.

Monday, *November* 1. The snow being in the mountains, and the wind at west, we had a cold ride to Little Pigeon, Sevier county. At Mitchell Porter's,[129] I spoke to a full house, on 1 Peter v, 10. William M'Kendree followed upon "Godliness is profitable," &c.

Tuesday, 2. We rode through Newport the capital of Cocke county, forded French Broad at Shine's ferry, and came, cold, and without food for man or beast, to John O'Haver's; but O, the kindness of our open-hearted, open-handed friends!

North Carolina

Wednesday, 3. We laboured over the Ridge and the Paint mountain.[130] I held on awhile, but grew afraid and dismounted, and with the help of a pine sapling, worked my way down the steepest and roughest part. I could bless God for life and limbs. Eighteen miles this day contented us; and we stopped at William Neilson's,[131] Warm Springs. About thirty travellers having dropped in, I expounded the Scriptures to them, as found in the third chapter of Romans, as equally applicable to nominal Christians, Indians, Jews, and Gentiles.

Thursday, 4. We came off about the rising of the sun—cold enough. There were six or seven heights to pass over, at the rate of five, two, or

[128] Justus Huffacre was a member of the family which included Michael Huffacre, or "Halfacre," who had entertained previous conferences. Justus lived at Rehoboth near Seven Islands. He was a local preacher and was ordained by Asbury on November 31, 1802. (*Michael Huffacre and His Descendants*, 49.)

[129] This was the first of several visits made by Asbury to the home of Mitchell Porter. He lived three miles south of Sevierville, Tennessee, at the foot of the Great Smoky Mountains, and is buried in Shiloh Cemetery.

[130] Asbury was proceeding to western North Carolina by his usual route by way of Newport and Hot Springs.

[131] The William Neilson with whom Asbury stayed at Warm Springs should not be confused with the William Nelson who entertained the bishop near the present Johnson City, Tennessee. Hale Neilson, a son of William Neilson, lived there in the fifties; he was a "Campbellite," though his family were Methodists. (Price, *op. cit.*, I, 399.)

one mile an hour—as this ascent or descent would permit: four hours brought us at the end of twelve miles to dinner, at Barnett's station;[132] whence we pushed on to Thomas Foster's,[133] and after making twenty miles more, came in about the going down of the sun. On *Friday* and *Saturday* we visited from house to house.

Sunday, 7. We had preaching at Killian's. William M'Kendree went forward, upon "As many as are led by the Spirit of God, they are the sons of God": my subject was Heb. iii, 12, 13. On *Monday* I parted from dear William M'Kendree.[134] I made for Mr. Fletcher's,[135] upon Mud Creek: he received me with great attention, and the kind offer of everything in the house necessary for the comfort of man and beast. We could not be prevailed on to tarry for the night, so we set off after dinner, and he accompanied us several miles. We housed for the night at the widow Johnson's. I was happy to find that in the space of two years, God had manifested his goodness and his power in the hearts of many upon the solitary banks and isolated glades of French Broad: some subjects of grace there were before, amongst Methodists, Presbyterians, and Baptists. On *Tuesday* I dined at Benjamin Davidson's,[136] a house I had lodged and preached at two years ago. We laboured along eighteen mountain miles; eight ascent, on the west side, and as many on the east side of the mountain.

South Carolina

The descent of Saluda exceeds all I know, from the Province of Maine to Kentucky and Cumberland: I had dreaded it, fearing I should not be able to walk or ride such steeps; nevertheless, with time, patience, labour, two sticks, and above all, a good Providence, I came in about five o'clock to ancient father John Douthet's, Greenville county, South Carolina.[137] Here I found myself at home, amongst kind and attentive friends. On the

[132] Barnard, or Barnard's Station, is in Madison County, North Carolina, nine miles south of Hot Springs, and is identified by Price as the Barnett's station mentioned by Asbury. (Price: *Holston Methodism*, I, 396.) Henry Boehm, who accompanied Asbury over this route in 1808, says that Barnett kept a public house; he was an early settler, "quite a character" and "famous as the first man in that part of the country who owned a vehicle with four wheels." (Boehm: *Reminiscences*, 211.) Arthur (*op. cit.*, 46) says Barnett's station "was probably Barnard's old stock stand on the French Broad River, five or six miles below Marshall."

[133] Asbury had lodged with Thomas Foster on November 9, 1800.

[134] William McKendree, presiding elder of the Kentucky district of the Western Conference, had traveled with Asbury from the conference which was held at Strothers meeting house in Sumner County, Tennessee, on October 2. Leaving the bishop at Daniel Killian's near Asheville, McKendree returned to his district.

[135] See note under November 10, 1800.

[136] See note under November 13, 1800.

[137] See notes under November 14, 1800. John Douthet evidently owned land on both sides of the river, in Greenville and Pendleton counties.

Sabbath day I preached at my lodgings, upon Joshua xxiv, 15. Surely the people about here are not the worst in the settlement; and they will mend, and attend the ministration of the word better in future. I have heard of successful meetings which have been held by encampments upon the Catawba, at Morgantown, Swannino, Pendleton, Greenville—in North and South Carolina: ministers of the different denominations had attended: more circumstantial accounts I have not yet been able to obtain. Mr. Newton, a Presbyterian minister, in Buncombe county,[138] appears to be greatly engaged in the spirit of the work. Since my being in this house, for five or six days past, I have been afflicted with painful flatulenceys. Sit still I could not; to read and write I was unable; but I could wind, reel, and pluck out cotton, and thus I employed my fingers. I have now nearly completed the six thousand miles since the last of July of the last year—great and fiery trials; great succeeding consolations. I would here record, that James Lowry,[139] an agreeable, pious youth, rode with me for the last seventy miles. I feel truly grateful to him and to his family: may the same measure of kindness be always meted to him and his, and to all such affectionate young men, and feeling, attentive people!

Tuesday, 16. After resting a day, I lectured in the family, upon Luke xi, 13, and on *Wednesday* left this affectionate household, directing my course to Solomon James's, in the neighbourhood of George's Creek, Pendleton county.[140] I preached the funeral sermon of Polly James, the daughter of my host. Here I met with Major James Tarrant, a local preacher, riding the circuit. We went on to Samuel Burdine's[141] and lodged. I had vainly questioned in my mind the probable cause of the name of *Ninety-Six*—it was this, it seems: During an Indian war, in which there was an expedition against the Keewee towns, it was found by measurement that it was ninety-six miles from that spot to Twelve Mile Creek.[142]

Thursday, 18. I rested and wrote.

Friday, 19. I preached at Samuel Burdine's, on Heb. vi, 12, and pretty fully explained the doctrine of Christian baptism and Christian perfection.

Saturday, 20. I gave a sermon at John Wilson's,[143] in which I treated

[138] See note under November 11, 1800.

[139] James Lowry lived on Big Sandy Mush Creek in Buncombe County. He later became Colonel Lowry, a prominent citizen, and an influential Methodist. He was a half brother of Governor David L. Swain. (See note under November 10, 1800. Also Price, *Holston Methodism*, I, 399–400; Sondley: *History of Buncombe County*, II, 767, 768.)

[140] Solomon James lived at what is now Dacusville in Pickens County.

[141] See note under November 18, 1800.

[142] Both Twelve Mile Creek and Ninety Six got their names from the distance from Keowee, the Indian village located near the present village of Crete in Pickens County and on the Keowee River. Keowee was the Indian capital, and Ninety Six was the British fort and trading post.

[143] At John Wilson's ferry near Piedmont, Asbury crossed the Saluda and went back northward on the eastern side of the river.

largely on the right of persons who were awakened to receive baptism; and also upon the claim of infants to this holy rite of the Church.

Sunday, 21. At Salem[144] upon the Saluda, I preached upon Matt. xxviii, 19, 20. In the *first* general head of my discourse it was considered *who* were to be taught—all, of all nations. *What* these were to be taught—to experience, to do, and to suffer. In the *second, Who* were to be baptized—men, women, children, and infants. The form of the rite—*in the name of the Father, and of the Son, and of the Holy Ghost*: the reasons why, it might be presumed, this form of words was given—because in this solemn exposition of the eternal Trinity in eternal unity, is shown the relations which the Godhead in the three persons bears to our creation, redemption, and spiritual baptism, of which the rite is only the outward and visible sign. The claim of children, it was stated, arose out of the general love and benevolence of God, and the general and universal influences of the Spirit. Baptism, it was observed, was taken from the apostles, and practised in all the primitive, and in all the first reformed Churches throughout the world. Under the third head I tried to explain the nature and the importance of the precious promise, "Lo, I am with you always, even to the end of the world." I went home with James Tarrant, a local preacher; my friend has, for two quarters, filled a travelling preacher's place, and a very acceptable servant he has proved to be.

Monday, 22. I rode to Thomas Terry's, upon the forks of Reedy River.

Tuesday, 23. My mind is occupied in reading, writing, and exercises in prayer, in which I have intimate communication with God. I now feel as if it were my duty to preach more particularly on the subjects of sanctification and baptism.

I have nearly finished my six thousand miles—to God be all the glory! But ah! what small fruit of my labour, since August, 1801. How little do I speak of God and to precious souls! God, be merciful to me a sinner!

Wednesday, 24. At Thomas Terry's I gave an exhortation in the evening on 1 Cor. xv, 58. Next day I went to Nathan Bramlett's.[145] I called to see Mrs. Price, eldest daughter of my once dear old friend, Alexander Leith, formerly of Baltimore. I feel much for those dear children, for whom I have been praying, some twenty, and others thirty years: I think the time long until they are converted. I was made as welcome by the children, I doubt not, as the parents would have made me had they been living and present. In the evening I returned to Mr. M'Kie's.

Sunday, 28. At Bramblet's chapel I spoke on Acts ii, 37–39.

Monday, 29. We had a cold hungry ride of thirty miles to Henry Culvor Davis's, a native of Maryland, and now of Newbury District, South Carolina. The first society we formed at this place declined, and so many removed, few were left; this year they repaired the meeting house;

[144] Salem Church was near Saluda River and is now in the suburbs of Greenville.
[145] Bramlett lived near Woodruff in Laurens County.

and the Lord poured out his Spirit, and nearly one hundred have been added. I found the labours of Lewis Myers and Buddy W. Wheeler had been greatly blest in Broad River circuit, South Carolina.

On *Tuesday*, we had a gracious rain, and cool weather followed. On *Wednesday*, I preached at Odell's meeting house[146] on 2 Cor. xiii, 9. I rode home with Benjamin Herndon. On *Thursday*, at Bethel, I heard Lewis Myers preach on John xvii, 15.

Friday, December 3. I rested, and read, and wrote. I find that excessive riding, in some degree, incapacitates me for the duty of preaching. At Edward Finch's, George Douthet and myself were engaged to put Mount Bethel School in operation: I advised to finish the house for teaching below, and lodging above.

Sunday, 5. At Bethel I spoke on Heb. vi, 1, 2. On *Monday* I rested, and on *Tuesday* passed the day with George Clark, and preached there on 2 Tim. ii, 10–12.

Wednesday, 8. We had the first snow. I was very unwell with a total privation of appetite, accompanied with a high fever.

Thursday, 9. I crossed Tyger River, and came to Major Bird Beauford's.[147] I improved upon 2 Tim. iv, 7, 8. I rode down to Nathan Glenn's, at Broad River: we had a severe season of cold weather, which occasioned very uncomfortable feelings.

Sunday, 12. I was called upon by recommendation to ordain Stephen Shell, John Wallis, and David Owen, to the office of deacons. There were seven of us present who minister in holy things. My subject was 2 Tim. iv, 1, 2: "I charge thee therefore, before God, and the Lord Jesus Christ, who shall judge the quick and the dead at his appearing and his kingdom, preach the word; be instant in season, out of season; reprove, rebuke, exhort, with all long-suffering and doctrine." It was observed of St. Paul, that before finishing his course, he had adopted Timothy, ordained him, and left this charge, a dying charge given by a dying, martyred apostle of the Lord Jesus Christ; and left on record for all who ordain, and all who shall be ordained to the ministry to the end of the world! a charge given as in the immediate presence of God, whose attributes and perfections are great and glorious; "and the Lord Jesus Christ," in his Divine character; and in his important offices and relations to mankind; ministers being his servants, the people his flock, and the word his own eternal word of truth and salvation; who is now, and shall be hereafter, the Judge of all our actions. "Preach the word"—the word of repentance, of faith, of justification, of regeneration, and of sanctification. "Reprove"—there are special uses to be made of the word to convince sinners of all degrees, classes, characters, and modes of faith. "Rebuke"—rebuke backsliders; rebuke errors in practice, and negligence in duty. "Exhort"—exhort souls

[146] Odell's meeting house was in the eastern edge of Laurens County near Whitmire.
[147] Beauford had a meeting house below Carlisle in Union County.

rebuked and convinced, to seek the restoring, preserving grace of God. It was shown how ministers should time their labours, regulating them as favourable or unfavourable seasons would seem to require; and the necessity of preserving the faith and meekness which might enable them to labour "with all long-suffering and doctrine."

Monday, 13. We crossed Broad River at James Glenn's flat; we called upon the aged people, prayed, and came to Benjamin Rowells, Chester District.

Tuesday, 14. I preached at Robert Walker's,[148] upon Phil. ii, 12, 13. I inverted the order of the text,—

I. It is God who worketh in the hearts of sinners, seekers, and believers, "to will and to do of his own good pleasure," which is their personal, present, future, and eternal salvation. See Ezek. xxxiii, 2; Luke xii, 32; Heb. x, 38.

II. That all who desire this salvation should be active in penitence, faith, and regeneration; using every means of grace, and performing every duty connected with holiness here, and preparatory to heaven hereafter.

Wednesday, 15. We rode until evening, and lodged at Mr. Washington's, near the Wateree Creek,[149] which gives the name to the river.

Thursday, 16. Crossed at Chestnut's ferry, and came into Camden. It is but a trifle to ride in this country thirty miles without food for man or beast.

On *Friday*, *Saturday*, and *Sunday*, we had excessively cold weather, and sleet and snow. We held our meeting in Isaac Smith's house,[150] and I preached twice.

Monday, 20. I rode down to James Rembert's upon the head of Black River: I came here that I might enjoy a little solitude, and find time to answer my northern letters. Until *Friday* evening I was pretty well occupied in writing.[151]

Saturday, 25. *Christmas day*. I preached at Rembert's chapel, and on *Sunday* James Patterson spoke on "Enoch walked with God." There is a great change in this settlement; many attend with seriousness and tears. Whenever our preachers gain the confidence of the lowland planters (if indeed that time shall ever be), so that the masters will give us all the liberty we ought to have, there will be thousands of the poor slaves converted to God. The patient must be personally visited by the physician before advice and medicine will be proper; and so it is, and must ever be, with the sin-sick soul, and the spiritual physician. Letters from the north announce very pleasing intelligence of a great work of God in Maryland, and in parts of Virginia.

[148] Robert Walker had a mill on Sandy River several miles west of Chester.

[149] Washington lived in the northeastern part of Fairfield County.

[150] (See note under January 1, 1801.) This meeting was not the annual conference, which was held two weeks later.

[151] See letter to Ezekiel Cooper, December 23, 1802.

Tuesday, 28. Yesterday and to-day I have been busy writing letters. My general experience is close communion with God, holy fellowship with the Father and his Son Jesus Christ, a will resigned, frequent addresses to a throne of grace, a constant, serious care for the prosperity of Zion, forethought in the arrangements and appointments of the preachers, a soul drawn out in ardent prayer for the universal Church and the complete triumph of Christ over the whole earth. Amen, Amen, so be it! I have finished many letters and adjusted some plans. For my amusement and edification, I was curious to read the first volume of my journals. I compared my former with my latter self. It was little I could do thirty years ago; and I do less now.

Thursday, 30. Rode to Camden.[152] On *Friday* I read in public some letters narrative of the work of God.

[152] See letter to George Roberts, December 30, 1802.

1803

1803

Asbury encounters an emigrant train in the "rude hills" of Tennessee

CHAPTER THIRTY-TWO

South Carolina

Thursday, *January* 6, 1803. I wrote three large letters to the north,[1] and put myself in order for travelling. From *Saturday* until *Wednesday* the time was spent in conference, and in public exercises; we had preaching every noon and evening; seven elders and four deacons were ordained. Of preachers, two were admitted, one had located, none were dead, and none were expelled. We had great peace and union in our labours, two days of which were directed to the explanation and recommendation of discipline, as it respects the order of the Church. We have added, in this conference, three thousand three hundred and seventy-one to our number.[2]

Friday, 7. A cold day. We came to Mr. Evans's,[3] on Congaree, thirty miles.

Saturday, 8. We crossed Congaree at Howell's ferry—almost abandoned. The flat was so small, that our horses, had they not been quiet, might have endangered us. It was well we chose this ferry, for we should have had a more roundabout road, and more swamp. We reached John Whetstones's[4] at the end of thirty-three miles, in good time, and were most kindly and comfortably entertained. At the meeting house on the *Sabbath day*

[1] See letter to George Roberts, January 5, 1803.

[2] A considerable revival movement had swept through South Carolina in 1802, and there was a notable camp meeting on the Sandy River Circuit. (Lee: *History of the Methodists*, 293, 294.)

[3] Evans lived near Gadsden in Richland County.

[4] Whetstone lived near St. Matthews.

Nicholas Snethen spoke on 1 Thess. v, 9, 10; my subject was 2 Cor. xiii, 9. Isaac Smith exhorted, George Dougherty prayed, and so we concluded. The cold weather prevented many, yet the house was full, and on the sunny side, without, there were numbers.

Monday, 10. We rode twelve miles to Dantzler's.[5] I have been greatly supported under long rides (by my computation making six thousand miles), and cold, and wet, and sufferings, and privations. My soul is devoted to God. As there are many who preach upon the first principles of the oracles of the Gospel of Christ, I feel it my duty to speak chiefly upon perfection—and above all, to strive to attain unto that which I preach. On *Tuesday* I spoke at the white meeting house on 2 Cor. vii, 1. We lodged at Mr. Winningham's. Next day Nicholas Snethen preached at Cattle Creek.[6] We lodged at Mr. Simpson's. On *Thursday*, at the Indian Fields, I spoke on 1 John iv, 16, 17. We lodged at Moore's: glory to God for a natural and spiritual birth in this family since my last visit! On *Friday*, at the Cypress I only exhorted. Sister Hare is dying of a cancer; but she appears to rejoice exceedingly in God, day and night.[7] On *Saturday* we rode into Charleston. On the *Sabbath day* I preached on Romans v, 20. I was blest in the administration of the word and ordinances. I live in the victory of the grace of God in purity of mind and uprightness of intention.

Tuesday and *Wednesday*, 18, 19, were days made glorious by the visits of the poor Africans who came to visit me: we frequently prayed together.

Thursday, 20. We came to Haddrell's Point; dined at Mr. Pritchard's, rode up to Wappataw, and lodged at Mr. Jones's, where we were well entertained. Next day, it being very stormy and cold, we were compelled to stop at Santee lower ferry.[8]

Saturday, 22. We came to Georgetown—still cold. At the ferry we could scarcely get firewood to keep us warm: we had bad bedding; and I suffered in my body, but my mind was at peace.

Sabbath day, 23. I preached at Georgetown from 1 Tim. iv, 10. Nicholas Snethen preached in the afternoon, and James Mellard in the evening. I visited Miss Dick—Ah! how changed every way!—had I not expected to see her, I might not have known her: I administered the sacrament in her room.

Monday, 24. At Black River chapel I spoke on Matt. vi, 31–33. We crossed the river at Evans's ferry,[9] and lodged at the widow M'Cantry's.

[5] Dantzler lived near White's meeting house in the eastern part of Orangeburg County.

[6] Cattle Creek meeting house was in the eastern part of Orangeburg County also.

[7] Indian Fields, Moore's, Cypress, and Sister Hare were all in Dorchester County on Asbury's route to Charleston.

[8] Asbury left Charleston by a familiar route, crossing to Haddrell's Point (Mount Pleasant). He followed the coast road or the old Kingshighway along present Highway 17 and crossed the Santee at the lower or Myzack's Ferry. Jones lived on that road between Wappetaw and Awendaw.

[9] Evans Ferry crossed Black River near Black Mingo.

Next day I preached at Jenkins's chapel,[10] and after meeting rode up to Port's ferry. We lodged at Thomas Humphries's.[11]

Wednesday, 26. I preached at the Bare Ponds[12] upon Heb. viii, 10, 11. We dined at Mr. Shackleford's, and thence went on to Gaspero Sweet's.

Thursday, 27. Nicholas Snethen preached at Rowell's meeting house:[13] I added a few words on St. Paul's triumphant words in 2 Tim. iv, 7. We lodged at the widow Davis's, a daughter of Mr. Dunham, at whose house I had lodged some years back. I have lived to serve three generations in South Carolina.

Friday, 28. At Wood's meeting house[14] Nicholas Snethen preached: I only glossed a little upon 2 Cor. iv, 3. We lodged at old Mr. Wood's, Marion district.

Saturday, 29. We rode to George Shank's, Marlborough district, upon Great Pee Dee. I have ridden two hundred and sixty miles towards the seventh thousand. My mind hath been very calm: but we have had it so severely cold and the meeting houses are so open between this and Charleston, that I fear the congregations have profited little by the word.

Sabbath, 30. At Harris's chapel,[15] at the head of Catfish, I preached upon Eph. ii, 8. We lodged with Captain Nevell: he and his wife appear to be seeking the Lord.

Monday, 31. We rode a muddy path to Gibson's chapel—*pole* chapel—open as a sieve, and the weather very cold. Nicholas Snethen preached upon Phil. iv, 8. I only added a few pointed, scattering shot in exhortation.

North Carolina

I came off with a very slim breakfast, and then after meeting had to ride on to (*north*) Britain Drake's, Robeson county, North Carolina. Here is a settlement of Scotch, originally: it began in the year 1771; since which time the descendants of these emigrants are chiefly in Cumberland, Richmond, and some in Anson, Robeson, and Bladen counties; and some are over the line south: there is a work of God amongst them, and some

[10] Jenkins' chapel was located near Johnsonville.

[11] The Rev. Thomas Humphries had formerly preached on circuits in Virginia, North Carolina, Georgia, and South Carolina. After fifteen years of itinerant service he located and settled on Jeffers Creek near Port's Ferry on the Pee Dee River in Darlington County, where he continued his work as a local preacher, until his death in 1820. "He lived palatially, was rich as a rice planter, quite popular among the aristocratic, with no discount on his ministry therefor." (Betts, *op. cit.*, 72.)

[12] The Bare Ponds meeting house, formerly called Sweets, was fifteen miles south of Marion.

[13] Rowell's meeting house was near Centenary.

[14] Woods' meeting house was near Sellers.

[15] Harris' chapel was near Brownsville in Marlboro County. After preaching at Gibson's chapel, Asbury proceeded into Robeson County, North Carolina.

living young ministers have been raised up. Perhaps the rebellion of "forty-five" made those people averse to all opposition to *the powers that be*—and they were tories during the American revolution only because they remembered their former failures and sufferings and those of their fathers. The open dwellings, only calculated for warm weather, occasion the people of South Carolina to suffer more, in cold spells, than those of the east or north: let those who doubt this make the trial for one winter. I have felt great lowness of spirits, but a holy resignation in the midst of cold, hunger, thirst, labour, and temptations.

Tuesday, *February* 1. I preached upon the glorious subject of Christian perfection: my text I found in Heb. vi, 1. Next day (*Wednesday*), we had a rainy ride of fifteen miles to Lumberton, which I had not visited for some years. I was present at its foundation and nomination: there are now, I suppose, about twenty families, and a hundred buildings; an academy, which serves also as a church; a very good prison, and a court house, it being the county town of Robeson. Its property is much owing to the navigation of Drowning Creek, down which lumber and other articles are conveyed to Georgetown, and thence frequently the merchandise is sent to Charleston. Nicholas Snethen preached; I only exhorted: Presbyterian ministers, Brown and M'Nare, attended; I had a Christian interview with them, and I learned with pleasure that their labours had been owned and blessed among the Scotch Presbyterians. We lodged at Robert Haille's. We have a small society in this town. Drowning Creek (so called from the drowning of some Indians) is the northeast branch of Pee Dee River; it rises in Cumberland county, North Carolina, is fed by Ten Miles and Great Swamp, passes through Robeson county, flowing about one hundred miles before it mingles with the waters of Pee Dee; at Ford's bridge Little Pee Dee unites with Great Pee Dee, twelve miles below Britain's ferry: the north-west branch of the first-mentioned river flows about the same distance as Drowning Creek, but its navigation is not so good.

Thursday, 3. I preached at Riggins's chapel in a powerful gale of wind; my subject was Acts xi, 23. Daniel Brown gave an energetic exhortation. I ordained William Glover to the office of deacon. After dining at Joseph Riggins's, we went on to Frederick Miller's at Mine Creek. I was very unwell to-day; I could not eat, yet I was compelled to labour under great mental dejection.

Friday, 4. A change for colder weather. We had to ride ten miles to Gray's Creek.

It was my day to preach on *Saturday*, and unwell as I was, I stood up and spoke on 1 Peter iii, 15, to a large congregation of Methodists, Baptists, and people of the world: it was a very cold day. I visited John Newberry, an afflicted man; and his wife, a godly woman.

Sunday, 6. We rode twelve miles to Fayetteville. It was not known whether we were to preach at our own meeting house or in the State house;

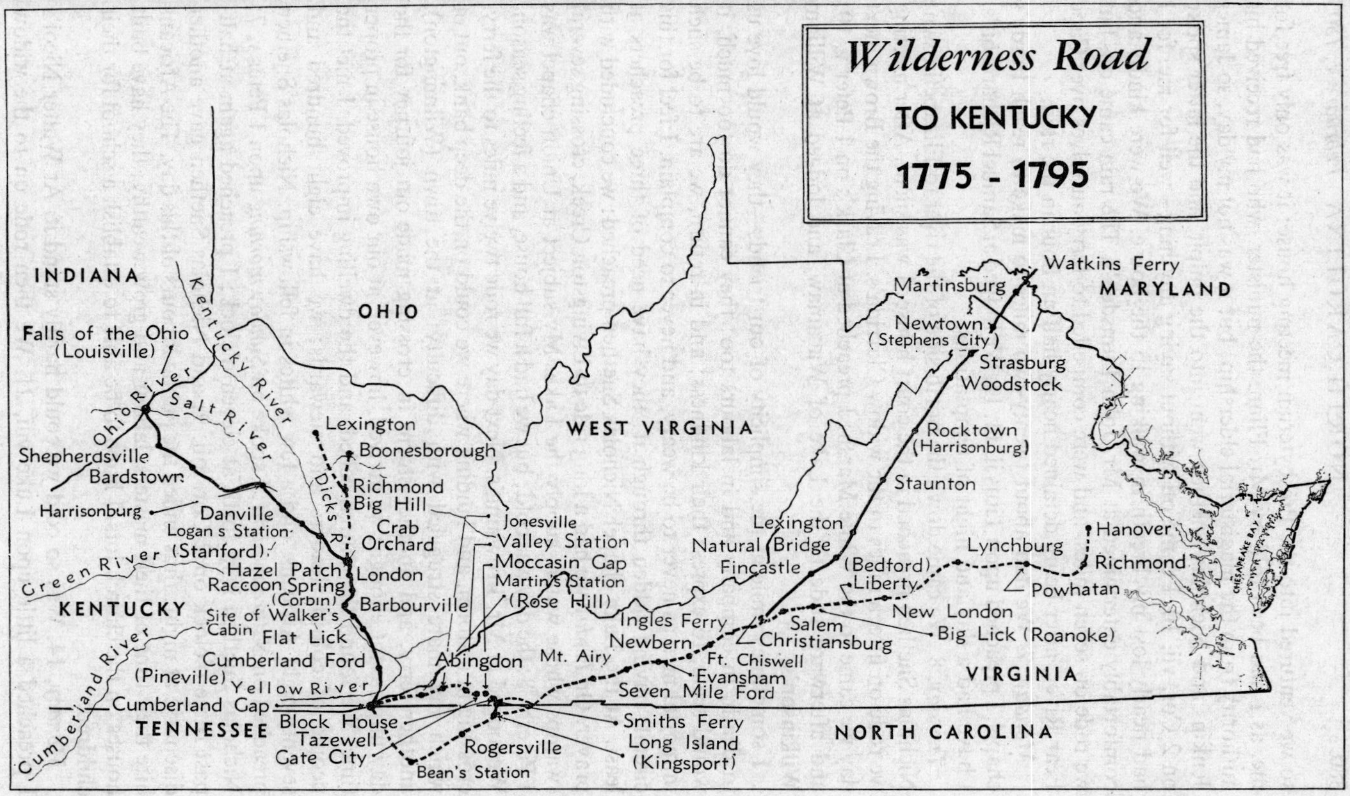
Wilderness Road
TO KENTUCKY
1775 - 1795
INDIANA
OHIO
WEST VIRGINIA
MARYLAND
VIRGINIA
NORTH CAROLINA
KENTUCKY
TENNESSEE
Falls of the Ohio
(Louisville)
Ohio River
Kentucky River
Salt River
Green River
Cumberland River
Yellow River
Dicks R.
Shepherdsville
Bardstown
Harrisonburg
Danville
Logan s Station
(Stanford)
Hazel Patch
Raccoon Spring
(Corbin)
Site of Walker's
Cabin
Flat Lick
Cumberland Ford
(Pineville)
Cumberland Gap
Block House
Tazewell
Gate City
Bean's Station
Rogersville
Lexington
Boonesborough
Richmond
Big Hill
Crab
Orchard
London
Barbourville
Jonesville
Valley Station
Moccasin Gap
Martin's Station
(Rose Hill)
Abingdon
Mt. Airy
Smiths Ferry
Long Island
(Kingsport)
Seven Mile Ford
Evansham
Ft. Chiswell
Newbern
Ingles Ferry
Christiansburg
Salem
Big Lick (Roanoke)
New London
Liberty
(Bedford)
Lynchburg
Powhatan
Richmond
Hanover
Fincastle
Natural Bridge
Lexington
Staunton
Rocktown
(Harrisonburg)
Woodstock
Strasburg
Newtown
(Stephens City)
Martinsburg
Watkins Ferry
CHESAPEAKE BAY

so we ventured into the Presbyterian meeting house: it was only free for me, as I had been told by Mr. Flinn, the minister, who had received his authority from the magisterial eldership; but it was not my day, so James Jenkins and Nicholas Snethen went into the pulpit, and the latter spoke on 2 Cor. vii, 10. I came off without saying anything—well for me, for I had nearly lost my breath in walking to the house. We were kindly and comfortably entertained at Mr. John Lumsden's. The rain came on, but we rode on seven miles, and were compelled to ferry ourselves over Cape Fear River, after being detained nearly half an hour in the rain.

Monday, 7. We had about twenty-two miles to make to reach Purdy's chapel. I preached upon Titus ii, 11, 14. We lodged at Samuel Richardson's. I have had a day and night of temptations.

Tuesday, 8. We came down the north side of the river to Elizabethtown: Nicholas Snethen preached in the court house; I was silent. After meeting we rode on fifteen miles to the widow Clarrida's. Leaving the Brown, next day we came to the White Marsh: I preached at Clark's on 1 Peter v, 10; and afterward rode to the Lake of Wacamaw, and lodged at William Wilkinson's.

I sometimes smile at the simplicity of our friends—they would love us to death, in company and in labours too: they cannot do too much, it would seem, to express their kindness; and in return, we are to be such immortal men as never to be weary, and never to complain. I feel for this circuit, having ridden through it: they have need of three preachers at least. At the Lake chapel Nicholas Snethen preached: we concluded with prayer. On *Friday* we had a long ride to Livingston Creek, crossing several swamps whose waters supply the Lake. My subject at Union chapel was 1 Peter v, 8: the day was cold; but we had a full house, and a feeling season. We lodged at Mr. Browning's. Next day we rode twelve miles to the ferry, crossing in a storm, and landing where we could on the deep bank, out of which my mare struggled with difficulty: at the town (Wilmington), another ferry, and another storm in crossing made our journey for the day unpleasant enough: we arrived, however, at our own house in proper time. We found the church ceiled, and the dwelling improved. I met the people of colour, leaders and stewards; we have eight hundred and seventy-eight Africans, and a few whites in fellowship. Nicholas Snethen preached on *Saturday night*; I spoke on *Sunday morning* upon 1 Peter v, 7; Nicholas Snethen held forth at eleven o'clock; I preached again at half-past three o'clock on 2 Cor. xiii, 9; and Nicholas Snethen gave another discourse at night: thus ended the public labours of this day. The Africans hire their time of their masters, labour and grow wealthy; they have built houses on the church lots. I hope to be able to establish a school for their children.

Monday, 14. Was so cold we could hardly stand it. At Walter Nicol's I preached a little upon Luke viii, 21. We then rode on to the widow

Campbell's, where we held an evening meeting. Next day we must needs ride home with the widow Spicer, living upon the Stump Sound; through hail and wind we went, and little Jane had a shoe on which clogged and made some difficulty. We have been highly favoured hitherto in attending our appointments and having congregations.

Wednesday, 16. Hard necessity compelled us to rest with the widow and the fatherless: we had a mere storm of wind, and hail, and snow.

Thursday, 17. We took a south-west course, through ice, and snow, and frost, and the wind in our faces; and arrived at Lot Ballard's half-past three o'clock; our appointment at the chapel was for twelve o'clock. I conclude I shall have no more appointments between Wilmington and Newbern; there is a description of people we must not preach to; the people of Onslow seem to resemble the ancient Jews—they *please not God, and are contrary to all men.*

Friday, 18. Finding it was but forty-two miles to Newbern, we concluded to push for it. I rose early, ordained J. Wilden to the office of deacon, and started. I had had thoughts of calling at a certain house, but being fearful we had not the time to spare, we stopped and fed on the ground: soon after we met the master of the house, and dropped a hint of our intention of being his guests had time permitted; he did not say "Will you," or "Do call at my house"—farewell! farewell! O unhappy people of Jones, and Trent, and Onslow![16] With a little cake and cheese, and some corn for our horses, we came in fine spirits to Newbern, about six o'clock. On *Saturday* I rested; and Nicholas Snethen preached upon, "He that hath ears to hear, let him hear."

Sabbath day, 20. I preached at seven o'clock upon 2 Peter iii, 14; Nicholas Snethen spoke at eleven o'clock; I held forth at three o'clock on 2 Cor. vi, 2; we were exceedingly crowded. I am grieved for this society; there are more heads than agree well together; want of harmony and want of discipline are too evident: I felt as if I wanted to see them no more until affairs wore a more pleasing aspect.

We set out on *Monday* under some apprehensions that the late rains had swelled the rivers; but we found no difficulties, either at Neuse or Tar rivers. Nicholas Snethen preached at Washington, Beaufort county, on 1 Thess. v, 19, 20; the chapel was crowded. On *Tuesday*, at eleven o'clock, I spoke on Luke viii, 11–15. The want of sleep and other things made me unwell and unpleasant in my feelings. Nicholas Snethen spoke at four o'clock in the evening on Luke xiii, 5.

Wednesday, 23. We rode twenty-two miles, to Williamston, Martin county; I had not been at this place since January, 1792: I find here now about twenty families, and about forty buildings. My subject at the court house was Titus; although greatly outdone by fatigue and heat, I had some openings of mind. I was somewhat surprised to see so many called to-

[16] These were the counties through which Asbury had traveled.

gether by twenty-four hours' notice; and I admired the patience of the people, many of whom were obliged to stand in the lobby of the court house—*a house and a half*. We want a house of our own. John Watts, a local preacher, still keeps his ground as a minister and a Christian, although the Baptists are very numerous here. On *Wednesday* we rode through a very warm, weather-breeding day, twenty-two miles, to Tarboro, and came in about half-past two o'clock. Many came to the new church, and were attentive to hear, whilst Nicholas Snethen preached upon 2 Cor. v, 18–20. I had strength to sit still to-day. We dined at Mr. Ryley's, and were kindly invited to lodge at the widow Tool's, the first which was opened to me in Tarboro. There are in this place about thirty-three families: the people have more trade than religion, more wealth than grace. We have about thirty Africans in fellowship; but no whites. I may notice the bridge; it is 540 feet long, and about thirty feet above the water.

Friday, 25. It rained and hailed; and through the night snowed heavily, and continued to fall on us after we set out until we came to Prospect Hill: we fed, and went on to Henry Bradford's, twenty-five miles. The snow in places was from eight to twelve inches deep; and as my horse was newly shod, he clogged, and kept me in continual fear. On *Saturday* I preached at our host's from 2 Peter 1, 4.

Sabbath day, 27. We came to Halifax. The *rich* had the Gospel preached to them by Nicholas Snethen, from 2 Cor. 16–77; I had to speak a little, and then baptized the children. The respectable sisterhood were very attentive; in short, a more decent, well-bred congregation, need not be. We dined at D. Fisher's, who treated us in a most serious and friendly manner. By guess, I should say there were forty families in Halifax. We were impressed, as if by magic, that the river would rise rapidly; so we crossed at four o'clock, and rode twenty miles, to Seth Peeble's, whom we called from his downy bed to take in poor benighted travellers.

Saturday, *March* 5. Ended our most amicable conference,[17] which began on *Tuesday*. We had preaching each day by Alexander McCaine, Hope Hull, Jesse Lee, Nicholas Snethen, and myself on the last day. We ordained the travelling and local deacons upon *Friday*, and the elders upon *Saturday*.

Sabbath, 6. Nicholas Snethen preached upon 2 Cor. iv, 17, 18; and I followed with an exhortation; and Brother Whatcoat after me. Our stand

[17] The *Minutes* of 1802 show that this session of the Virginia Conference was to be held at Dromgoole's on March 1, 1803. The *Journal* of the conference simply states that it was held at Olive Branch Meeting House. This was the old Wolsey's Barn, later called Dromgoole's, and is presently located at Gasburg in Brunswick County, Virginia. However, the church was moved several miles from its original location to Gasburg. (Bennett, *op. cit.*, 407.) However, if the conference was held in Virginia, Asbury crossed the state line for the sessions and immediately re-entered North Carolina. The night of February 27 was spent with Seth Peebles in Northampton County, North Carolina, and the day after the conference closed, Asbury was entertained by Sterling Boyakin, who also lived in Northampton County. (*Heads of Families*, 72, 73.)

was in the woods; our congregation consisted of about two thousand souls. I was exceedingly pleased with our conference love feast—with its order, solemnity, and life; the testimonies borne appeared to be all given under the immediate impulse of the Spirit of God, both in ministers and members.

Bishop Whatcoat being ill, the burden of the conference labours fell upon me.

Monday, 7. At Concord meeting house I spoke on 2 Cor. vii, 1. We lodged at Sterling Boykin's. I find the *way of holiness* very narrow to walk in or to preach; and although I do not consider *sanctification—Christian perfection*, commonplace subjects, yet I make them the burden, and labour to make them the savour of every sermon. I feel, I fear for my dear low-land brethren—so much of this world's wealth; so much fulness of bread, and idleness, and strong drink. Lord, help!

Tuesday, 8. We rode in the evening to Edward Saurey's. The excessive rains in the morning prevented our attending our appointments, to the sad disappointment of our friends in Murfreesborough—*brethren* we have not, for we have no society there. Next day we had a race of a ride to Winton, twenty-five miles: Brother Snethen preached in the court house at twelve o'clock. We dined at Mr. Bell's, and were generously entertained. Gates court house, twenty miles farther, brought us up for the night.

Thursday, 10. At the court house Nicholas Snethen insisted upon *the one thing needful*. I ordained B. Harrell[18] to the deacon's office: he is a man of good repute, without slaves.

Virginia

As we had two appointments for *Friday*, I preached at Deacon Haslet's, to many people, on 1 Pet. v, 10. We had a consoling, gracious season. Brother Snethen preached at Suffolk.[19] I was surprised to hear that some who had separated from us should have reported that the new meeting house would belong to the bishops, and that they might sell them: these reports were offered by some, not of the connexion, as reasons which prevented their subscribing; and our brethren have therefore determined to build without the aid of others: what our enemies accuse us of intending to do they have already done in some cases, and attempted in others—

[18] The Harrell family was prominent in Gates County, North Carolina. Harrell's Methodist Church was located a few miles north of Gatesville. (Harrell.)

[19] The O'Kellyites were strong in this section. They became the Christian Church after dropping the name Republican Methodists, and this section of Virginia and the adjoining section of North Carolina became their stronghold. Elon College in North Carolina was the college of this denomination, and the church in Suffolk is to this day a very strong church. The Christians later joined the Congregationalists to form the Congregational Christian Church, now United Church of Christ.

Isle of Wight, Mooring's chapel, Wells's chapel, and Major Ben, in building this house within a small distance of the Methodist house, furnish sufficient proofs of their principles and their spirit.

Saturday, 12. I preached at M'Kee's upon Eph. v, 25, 26. We rode to Portsmouth, and I crossed over to Norfolk, where I had an interview with the official members, and ordained George Lee Green to the office of deacon.

Sabbath, 13. I preached in the new house (the best in Virginia belonging to our society): the pulpit is high *with a witness*—like that awkward thing in Baltimore, calculated for the gallery, and too high for that. My subject was Titus ii, 13, 14. At Portsmouth, in the afternoon, I spoke on 2 Cor. vi, 2. Nicholas Snethen preached at Denby's. We had a good passage over the river at Sleepy Hole ferry,[20] and came to Benjamin Powell's; the parents had gone to rest, but some of the children were yet up, and took us in. I felt solemn whilst I looked upon this young race, who make the third generation whom I have served. I ordained their father to the office of deacon, and have preached to their grandfathers, Pinner and Powell, who, with the Collinses, were the three first families that opened their houses to the Methodist preachers in this part of the state.

Tuesday, 15. At Powell's chapel I preached on Rom. xii, 2. In the afternoon Nicholas Snethen held forth at Murphy's chapel on 1 Cor. xii, 27: I concluded the meeting by exhortation. There is a revival of religion in this settlement. Next day, Nicholas Snethen spoke on 1 Cor. iii, 11–15. I feel myself failing and unwell.

Thursday, 17. We rode twenty-five miles to Ellis's chapel. There has been a great mortality in this neighbourhood within the last twenty-six years: only a few of my first female friends are now living. We lodged with the widow of Stephen Andrews.

Friday, 18. We rode to Petersburg, encountering a long, intricate, muddy path; and no food had we, for man or beast, until we came to our friend Joseph Harding's: by erring in our route we made our day's ride thirty-five miles. If my information be correct, the conference congregation meeting continued in the woods until nine or ten o'clock on *Sunday evening*; it held each day from *Saturday* until the *Monday*; and it is believed as many as thirty-five souls professed to find mercy and faith in Christ. By letter from John Pitts, in Fredericksburg, I learn that since he was stationed there, in October last, thirty-five joined the society, which now consists of seventy-three members—Glory, glory be to God!

On *Saturday* Nicholas Snethen preached in Petersburg on 1 John ii, 15–17. On the *Sabbath* my subject was 2 Cor. xiii, 2. We feel the effects of intense labour in the lowlands; our habits were very feverish, and I suffer from a deep cold and oppression on my breast. We contemplate placing a

[20] This was on the Nansemond River, three miles east of Driver. Benedict Arnold crossed there on his return from the Richmond raid in January, 1781.

proper stationed preacher in Petersburg; and the building a new brick church sixty or seventy by forty feet, and two stories high: but this, like many other of our great and good designs, may fall through. Nicholas Snethen preached at four o'clock on 2 Peter iii, 8–10.

Monday, 21. We travelled, very unwell, to Mr. Walthall's, near Chesterfield court house: we rested in part, and then divided our ride to Richmond into a journey of two days: we arrived on *Tuesday*, and I preached at twelve o'clock to many serious people on Titus ii, 10–13. Nicholas Snethen preached at seven o'clock. Next day we came along to Caroline, thirty-five miles. In the morning it rained, and the day was wintry and dreary: we saw the wagons sinking and set fast, for in many places the route was dreadful: we worried through, feeding our horses once, and ourselves not at all. Next day I preached once more at Dickenson's chapel; my subject was Heb. iii, 12–14.

I feel my infirmities, and the labour of my journeys; but my soul is cast upon the Lord in unceasing prayer that God may guide the Church, and give the spirit of wisdom, and love and zeal to our conferences: we only, as we think, want more useful labourers in the vineyard, and thousands will be brought home to God in the cities, circuits, and towns this year. I lodged at the widow Collins's.

Friday, 25. We rode to Fredericksburg and dined, and then pushed on to Stafford court house, making forty miles this day. Next day we gained Alexandria, eating nothing between seven o'clock in the morning and seven at night.

Sabbath, 27. I preached upon John i, 6, 7. John Chalmers spoke in the afternoon, and Nicholas Snethen at night; sermon, love feast, and sacrament held us five hours. God is gracious; the people are lively, and several were admitted into fellowship. On *Monday*, it blew clear and strong, and cold enough: I hardly stemmed the blast, chilly and trembling as I was.

Maryland

I preached at Georgetown on Hebrews iv, 15, 16; it was a quickening time. Brothers Chalmers and Snethen exhorted.

Tuesday, 29. We reached Baltimore, forty-five miles, stopping an hour on our way at the widow Shadrach Turner's. We have travelled about three hundred miles towards eight thousand miles.

April 12. The last *Tuesday*, *Wednesday*, and *Thursday*, in March, were occupied in reading and answering letters,[21] and in making preparations for the conference:[22] its sitting commenced on *Friday*, the first instant,

[21] See John J. Jacob's letter to Asbury, March 21, 1803.

[22] The conference met in Light Street Church with fifty preachers present. There were preaching services daily in Otterbein's church. James Quinn was the sole person to

continuing and ending in great peace: there were sixty-four preachers appointed to their several stations; most of whom were present at the session. Except four hours a day for the transaction of our own business, our time was given to the duties of prayer and the pulpit—we were between the mount and the multitude, and the conference and the congregations large, lively, and serious, to whom we dispensed the word of life at eleven o'clock, at three o'clock, and at night, and we hope and trust much good was done in the name of the Lord Jesus. My subjects were—on the first *Sabbath*, Col. iv, 2, 3; on the second, Titus iii, 9; at Fell's Point, Luke xxiv, 46. The reasons why I did not speak oftener were, First, Because there were many zealous, acceptable preachers present; Secondly, Because I wished to be a man of *one* business, and to have my mind free; and, Thirdly, Because I had neither bodily nor mental strength to preside in the conference, and to take so great a part in my particular duties as its head; to receive the continual applications of so many preachers on so many subjects presented to me at this time; and to fill my place regularly in the pulpit. I paid no visits but to the sick.

It is sufficiently proved that upon our present plan, unless the preachers exert themselves, every conference in the union, except that of Baltimore, will be insolvent in its finances: in the late and last year's conferences they have had a surplus here—they have supported wives, widows and children; and in the present instance have supplied the contingencies of those preachers who have gone to distant parts; besides giving one hundred dollars to the Philadelphia, and as much, each, to the conferences of New York and Boston. I can say, hitherto the Lord hath helped us through deeps, deserts, dangers, and distresses: I have told but a small part of our labours and sufferings—let the great day of eternity reveal the rest! Glory be to the Father, and to the Son, and to the Holy Ghost, forever! Amen!

Yesterday I preached at Gatch's chapel, on 1 Peter v, 10. We then came on to Perry Hall. To-day we have had a meeting here. Brother Whatcoat preached upon Colos. ii, 6. My mind is solemnly stayed upon God.

On *Wednesday*, we parted with the elders at Perry Hall: I had preached on 2 Cor. xii, 9, 10. We rode on to Deer Creek, and halted for the night with Harry Watters.

My mind is in a great calm after the tumult of a Baltimore conference, and the continual concourse of visitors and people to which my duty subjected me: I have felt deeply engaged, and much self-possession; indeed, age, grace, and the weight and responsibility of one of the greatest

receive elder's orders. Christian Newcomer of the United Brethren had come to propose a "plan of operation by which the English and the German brethren could be more united" but to his own regret accepted somebody's advice to defer it until the meeting of the next General Conference. (Armstrong, *op. cit.*, 133–35; Hough, *op. cit.*, 70; Wright, *op. cit.*, 76–78.)

charges upon earth, ought to make me serious. In addition to this charge of the superintendent, to preach, to feel, and to live perfect love! The promise of the year is great—in the fruits of the earth, and in the Church of God: the trees are full of blossoms, and want but rains and sun; and so with us, we want spiritually gracious seasons: Lord, hear, and help, and enlarge, invigorate, sanctify, and bless thine inheritance.

Thursday, 14. We rode to Dublin,[23] upon Deer Creek; and next day I preached upon Heb. iii, 12–14, in a neat chapel, and many attended. After sermon we dined with our brother Evitt,[24] with whom we had lodged, and then rode over the hills of Deer Creek, through a great storm, twelve miles, down to the widow Stump's,[25] at Mount Friendship: J. W. Dallam and three ladies were in company, and I feared for them.

Saturday, 16. Through storms of snow, we pushed on to the ferry, but the water was so low, and the wind so high, we could not cross; we therefore returned to the widow Stump's and rested, and whilst it snowed without, we performed Divine worship within doors in the family. On *Monday* we succeeded better at the ferry, and got over early enough to reach Back Creek, Cecil county, a distance of twenty-eight miles, by ten o'clock, having arrived in time to dismiss the congregation with prayer. We dined at John Carnan's; and after commending his afflicted wife in prayer to God, we rode home with Richard Bassett to Bohemia ferry.

Tuesday, 19. I spoke at the Manor chapel, on 1 Cor. xiv, 15; we had preaching, singing, exhorting, shouting, leaping, and praising God. After meeting, we crossed Bohemia and Sassafras rivers, and housed with Robert Moody.[26] My mind is kept in peace; I only seek to please God, and to serve my fellow men as faithfully and impartially as I can—I cannot accommodate myself to the caprices of every man: what a strange creature should I be were I to suffer myself to exist in such a continual state of transformation as some people's whims might require!

Wednesday, 20. My subject at the new chapel, George Town, Cross Roads, was 1 Tim. iv, 2. We had a living season. Our brethren from Chester Town came to meet us, and to convey us forward with more ease.

[23] It is probable that as early as 1772 Asbury preached in the neighborhood of Dublin, which is three and one-half miles northwest of Darlington in Harford County. The foundations of a church were laid at Greenstone near Bald Frair Road, but the site was abandoned for another in Dublin. This lot was conveyed by Charles Beaver to five trustees in 1800, and it is believed that the church was erected soon thereafter. (*Harford County Directory*, 366.)

[24] This may have been William Evit, who in 1790 lived in Harford County as head of a large household. The marriage of "William Evatt" to Elizabeth Wiley in 1794 appears in the records of Harford County.

[25] This was Elizabeth Dallam Stump, widow of Herman Stump.

[26] Robert Moody (–1815) lived near Galena, Kent County, Maryland. He was formerly of Fells Point, where in 1799 he married Lucretia Butler. He was survived by his wife and daughter. (Kent County Wills; Hallman, *op. cit.*, 117.)

Save me from *parade!* the greatest good-will, and the kindest intentions, will never make it acceptable in my eyes; I choose rather to go on in my own way, though I suffer for it.

The new chapel in Chester Town is elegantly planned: Brother Whatcoat first preached in it. We dined at Solomon Brady's.[27] Blessed be God, there are some still left of this family to show us kindness, and renew the remembrance of kindness shown twenty-five years ago. We came on to Doctor Allen's: he has been strangely kept alive for about seventy years, in many infirmities.

Saturday, 23. I preached at Easton, on 2 Thess. iii, 1. It was a gracious season for preachers and people. I spoke at eleven o'clock; and I advised the brethren to have preaching at three o'clock, and at night. My subjects for the past week have been generally *prayer, and preaching the word.* On the *Sabbath day* we had a love feast: our exercises were closed by my reading the extraordinary accounts I had received of the work of God in the south and west of our continent. Preaching began on Heb. vi, 1, at eleven o'clock, and a more solemn assembly I think I never saw. Brother Whatcoat spoke in the afternoon, and James Moore[28] exhorted clothed with power, and full of love; never was preacher more respected in Talbot than our brother Moore. Doctor Allen's was our lodging place for three nights. It seems as if the whole Peninsula must be *methodised*: twenty-five years of faithful labours, and the consistent lives of our brethren, generally have worn down prejudice; so that many who will not *live* will, nevertheless, when they are sick, send for the preachers, that they may *die* Christians.

Monday, 25. We set out for Dover Ferry, and missing our way, rode an additional twelve miles; arriving, we found it impassable, such was the violence of the weather: we took shelter with Mrs. Dickenson.[29] On *Tuesday* the storm increased; and on *Wednesday* I rode to Cambridge and crossed Choptank. I preached at Cambridge on 2 Cor. vi, 2, and returned to the former residence of Henry Ennalls, deceased.

Thursday, 28. I preached at Foster's chapel[30] on 1 Peter i, 4, and came along to Major Mitchell's, in Caroline:[31] the wind was east, the evening cold, and I unwell. At Denton, I took to bed awhile; we continued on, however, and reached Choptank.

[27] Solomon Brady lived in Chestertown.

[28] James Moore, a traveling preacher (1794–1818), was born in Tyrone, Ireland, in 1760. He was stationed on Queen Anne's Circuit with Thomas Scott in 1803.

[29] Mrs. Dickenson lived near Dover Ferry, Talbot County. Among the heads of families in Talbot County, 1790, the census gives John, Samuel, and Susan Dickenson. Richard Whatcoat refers to one H. Y. Dickenson and his daughter, who lived near Judge Thomas White. (Sweet, *op. cit.*, IV, 84, 85.)

[30] See note under May 24, 1801.

[31] This may have been John Mitchell, who was a captain in the Caroline Militia in the Revolutionary War.

Delaware

On *Saturday* I rode, under great bodily affliction, to Duck Creek town. I was under the necessity of submitting to bleeding, tooth-drawing, and the operation of cathartics. I sat in our conference, held in the Friends' meeting house,[32] four days. We had nearly one hundred preachers, travelling and local, present for the transaction of business. Twelve elders and twelve deacons were ordained. On *Friday* I rode over on a visit to the daughters of Thomas White, Sarah and Anna. I found the children of my once dear friend[33] at Mr. Cook's.

Saturday, *May* 7. I went, very unwell, to Wilmington. Next day (*Sunday*), we had frost and snow. I was very unwell, and kept my room. On *Monday* I attended to the altering of the *minutes*, with Thomas Jones my secretary.

Pennsylvania

Tuesday, 10. We came into the city of Philadelphia: the rain brought on my intermitting fever; yet, unwell as I was, conditional appointments had been made by my friends; but instead of the pulpit, I took to my room. My journey from Baltimore to the city has brought me over about three hundred and fifty miles. *Wednesday*, *Thursday*, *Friday*, and *Saturday*, I remained in Philadelphia, most of the time confined to my room. The spirit of contention and Church divisions adds distress of mind to my bodily afflictions of colds and intermittents. I crept out upon the *Sabbath day*, and preached at St. George's, on 2 Peter i, 5–9; my voice was weak, and some could not hear; but it was a searching sermon and in season.

New Jersey

We set out on *Monday*, and reached Burlington by twelve o'clock: I crossed over and preached in our new house in the solitary town of Bristol.[34] James Sterling[35] and Thomas Ware accompanied me.

[32] The Friends' Meeting House, erected of stone about 1705, stood in Salisbury, Delaware, then a small settlement near the present Smyrna. Of the edifice of this pioneer religious body in Duck Creek Hundred, not a vestige remains save the cemetery. Boehm explains that the Friends' Meeting House was used "so that we could have our own to preach in." Sermons by Bishop Whatcoat and "Black Harry" Hosier were long remembered. (Scharf: *History of Delaware*, II, 1096, 1099; Boehm, *op. cit.*, 88–92.)

[33] The two women were children during the enforced sojourn of Asbury in the home of their parents, Judge Thomas White. (See notes under November 30, 1780, and June 13, 1795.)

[34] Bristol was located in Buck's County, Pennsylvania, about thirteen miles up the Delaware River from Philadelphia. The town was incorporated in 1720. There was a

Tuesday, 17. We rode to Joseph Hutchinson's, and next day came to Elizabethtown and lodged at Mr. Crowell's.

New York

On *Thursday* we reached New York. My weakness continued. Many subjects and persons engaged my thoughts and my attention: but the best of all is God is with me in all my troubles, sharp and strong.

On *Friday* and *Saturday* I did a little in writing, talking, planning, and thinking. I can hear, see, or feel, no more of religion here than there was last year. I signed a memorial for the obtaining in the court a legal claim to £300 left by Miss De Peyster,[36] for the bishops and clergy of the Methodist Church, to be appropriated in the best manner for the good of the society.

Sunday, 22. I preached at the old church, John street, from James iii, 17. I. "The wisdom that cometh from above" is revealed and inspired; it is "pure"—*negatively*: it is not mixed by its Divine Author with that wisdom which is "earthly, sensual, and devilish"; it is not mixed with the policy, or pleasures, or profits of this world; or of sin, which is of hell. The apostle hath written "pure religion," and this it cannot be when mingled with such qualities, all of which spring from men or devils.

II. "The wisdom that cometh from above is pure,"—*positively*; it is pure in conviction, repentance, faith, regeneration, and sanctification: it is the operative principles of grace in the soul, as internally, and externally manifested. It is "peaceable" in relation to God, and all mankind, to the Church, and the world, and the tranquil state of the soul. It is "gentle," soft, amiable in all its administrations, never stormy, or sour, or haughty, or overbearing. "Easy to be entreated," to do and suffer anything that is right and reasonable, for the glory of God, and for the good of our own, and the souls of others. "Impartiality," this is the Christian dress: not bound and pinched by countries, names, forms, and opinions; neither does it envy the rich on account of their riches, nor neglect the poor on account of their poverty. "Without hypocrisy," sincerity is the incontestable evidence of God and man of our possession of the heavenly treasure

small class in Bristol, and Henry Boehm had preached to them in the old Episcopal Church. The Methodists began building a brick edifice, and when the walls were standing but the roof not yet on, Henry Boehm raised a subscription to finish it. It was dedicated on March 12, 1803.

[35] James Sterling was from Burlington, New Jersey.

[36] This was the daughter of Frederick DePeyster, a New York merchant. He had given sixteen shillings to the fund for building Wesley Chapel on John Street in 1769. (Seaman, *op. cit.*, 442.) The amount provided in the will of his daughter has been maintained in the New York Conference and is available for application to necessitous cases among the clergy.

of "that wisdom that cometh from above"; and people may go upon fancies, and be ready to die with raptures, but if they are turbulent, ungovernable, self-willed, and false towards their fellow men, or towards their God, their religion is vain; whatever it may once have been, it is not the gold of the sanctuary now, but a counterfeit, alloyed by a mixture of the *wisdom of this world.*

After Brother Whatcoat had preached in the afternoon, I gave them an exhortation.

Monday, 23. A bread factory caught fire[37] and occasioned a great alarm and bustle; plenty of water, and the great activity of the citizens prevented the flames from spreading.

I rode twenty-two miles to the widow Sherwood's, and preached at four o'clock on Heb. iv, 9–11. Next day we called at Nicholas Underhill's[38] and dined, and exhorted and prayed with the family. At the White Plains I preached on 1 John ii, 15. It was the time of the court's sitting, which, together with a want of information respecting the appointment made for me, caused but a thin congregation. We lodged at Moses Fowler's,[39] and the next day reached Bedford, where brother Whatcoat preached.

Connecticut

On the morrow we reached Reading, passing through Ridgefield, and I preached in Aaron Hunt's house upon Coloss. iii, 12, 13; the text itself is a sermon.

Friday, 27. Finding the road, by information, to be rocky and hilly, we were persuaded to come back to the post road; we therefore directed our course down through Greenfield and Bridgeport to Stratford, and arriving at Elkanan Wheeler's, we were willing to rest: thirty miles of our journey we made without feeding man or beast. My health is better; but the labour of riding, and the inconvenience occasioned by the dust raised by the chaise in advance of us, made me feel a little like Jonah. My soul is often led out after God: my treasure and pleasure in Christ and the service of his Church. The Baptists of Connecticut have sent their petition from the Assembly to the legislature of Connecticut, to the bishops of the Methodist Church, that they may have their aid in obtaining toleration: what can

[37] At 2 A.M. on the morning of May 23 a fire broke out in a large bakehouse on Philipot Street on the estate of J. Pannell. It spread to an adjoining warehouse of W. J. Nicoll, but the blaze was confined to the two buildings. (*New York Morning Chronicle*, May 24, 1803.)

[38] Underhill was a prominent Methodist leader whom Asbury occasionally visited. (See *Journal* entry for September 14, 1797, when Mrs. Underhill was seriously ill.)

[39] Moses Fowler was a leader in the church at North Castle, the present Armonk. Asbury first visited North Castle on June 13, 1787, although he did not then mention Fowler.

we do, and how is it our business? We are neither popes nor politicians: let our brethren assert their own liberties. Besides, who may now be trusted with power? The Baptists are avowed enemies to episcopacy, be the form of Church government as mild as it may; now it seems, popes, as they would otherwise term us, may be useful to them, nor are they too proud to ask for help; but our people will not be pushed into their measures; their bishops have no coercive power of this sort: if the Baptists know not what to do we cannot tell them.

Sunday, 29. We came to Middletown: as it was the hour of devotion, we stepped into the Separate meeting house, and heard a certain Mr. Greaves preach. At five o'clock, brother Whatcoat, after some demurring, was permitted to preach: when he was done, the old woman controverted his doctrine of sanctification. *I told you so.* The work of God revives at New Haven; and Satan's emissaries rage, and those who are *too good to be better*, oppose.

Monday, 30. We crossed Connecticut River at Rocky Hill, and came on to Kelsom,[40] twenty-five miles; I preached at four o'clock on 1 Pet. v, 6–9, and ordained Daniel Burrows a deacon.

Tuesday, 31. We came to Windham, twenty miles, and had some rain. Brother Whatcoat preached. After refreshing ourselves with Mr. Harris and his kind family at Brooklin, we came on through Pomfret, and thence to Thompson, where I preached at four o'clock upon Gal. v, 22–26; and thus ended the labours of *Wednesday*.

Massachusetts

Thursday, June 2. At Milford in Massachusetts, brother Whatcoat preached at five o'clock; and on *Friday* I made at Needham an improvement on 1 Pet. v, 10. On each of the last two days we have travelled thirty miles. I have read some letters giving an account of the work of God at the south[41]: some in our eastern congregations wonder, if they do not believe. Since we left Baltimore we have made seven hundred and twelve miles.

Saturday, 4. We have had a gracious rain. My mind is in peace; but such perpetual motion wearies the flesh, and flags the spirits.

Poor New England! she is the valley of dry bones still![42] Come, O breath of the Lord, and breathe upon these slain that they may live!

[40] This place was doubtless Hebron, which is twenty-five miles from Rocky Hill on the way to Windham. There has never been a Kelsom in Connecticut.

[41] One of these letters was from Stith Mead in Georgia dated April 21, 1803. It is printed in Moore: *Pioneers of Methodism in North Carolina and Virginia*, 222–25. (See Asbury's letter to Charles Atmore in England, June 3, 1803.)

[42] Methodism did not flourish in New England as it did elsewhere. In 1803 the New England Conference reported 22 circuits with 2,941 Methodists, of which 14 were colored. It was by far the smallest of all the conferences. The total membership of the 7 conferences then existing was 104,070 with 22,443 being persons of color.

Sunday, 5. Brother Whatcoat at Waltham spoke upon Heb. viii, 10–12. I dropped a few hints upon Heb. ii, 1–3. We receive good news from the south. We rest, we write, we read, and lay plans for the Boston Conference.

Wednesday, 8. We came through the dust to Boston; and as eighteen members were present, we opened the conference in our chapel.[43] We sat six hours a day for despatch of business; there was preaching at eleven and five o'clock, and in the evening: it was all new, but nothing special appeared.

Saturday, 11. We ordained Joshua Soule and Nathan Emory elders, and Edward Whittle deacon: as our work was done, and we were feeble, we came away to Waltham. It is no time to journalize; but I may remark that we had great peace in our conference, and that we have an increase of five hundred members. I lodged at Mrs. Woodard's, and was kindly and comfortably entertained. The great wants of Boston are good religion and good water. How can this city and Massachusetts be in any other than a melancholy state! worse, perhaps, for true piety, than any other parts of the Union: what! reading priests, and alive? O no! dead, dead, dead, by nature—by formality—by sin!

Sunday, 12. Preached at Waltham chapel on 1 Pet. iv, 18.

On *Monday* I rested, and made ready for the tour to Ashgrove. Long-wanted rain overtook us on our road to Harvard, and we came in dripping to Caleb Sawyer's: here I was pleased with the decency, piety, and simplicity of manners of both parents and children. At a small school house, two miles distant, brother Whatcoat preached. On *Wednesday* we came on to Leominster, twelve miles, and dined at Silas Willard's: at four o'clock I preached on 1 Cor. i, 30. It is in this town we crossed the Nashua River, which empties into the Merrimack.

I will not mention names, but I could tell of a congregation that sold their priest to another congregation in Boston for the sum of one thousand dollars, and hired out the money at the unlawful interest of twenty-five or thirty per cent. Lord, have mercy upon the priest and people that can

[43] The chapel was located in Methodist Alley, a narrow street which ran from North (now Hanover) to Ship Street. In 1829 the name was changed; the chapel was located at what is now 16 Hanover Avenue. The first Methodist class in Boston was formed July 13, 1792, at the present 29 Sheafe Street in the home of Samuel Burrill, a shipsmith. It later moved to the home of James Connor and in September, 1793, to the home of James Ruddock on the corner of White-Bread Alley and Ship Street, now Harris and North Streets. There Asbury preached on July 22, 1794. On August 28, 1795, Jesse Lee laid the cornerstone of the chapel in Ingraham's yard, afterwards Methodist Alley. There were seventy members of the society. The lot cost 22 cents per foot, and the total cost of the chapel was around $1,200, of which $659.07 was raised in the southern states by Jesse Lee and John Hill. (*Memorial History of Boston*, III, 438; Seybolt: *Town Officials of Colonial Boston*; Treasurer's Book, Class Papers, and Steward's Book of the chapel, in the possession of the New England Conference Methodist Historical Society.)

think of buying the kingdom of heaven with money! How would it tell to the south, that priests were among the notions of Yankee traffic?

New Hampshire

Thursday, 16. We came to Ebeneezer Coleburn's,[44] New Hampshire; and I preached upon Titus ii, 11, 12. We had an open time, a baptism, and sacrament. Next day we laboured through extreme heat, and over high hills, to Marlboro and were glad to rest ourselves at Ebenezer Herrick's, opposite the west side of the great mountain called Monadnock. This portion of the State of New Hampshire is full of hemlock swamps; and I question if any part of the Alleghany, south, is more broken: the roads, however, are greatly improved, and there is a turnpike extending from Boston to Keene. The soil, though barren, exhibits, in its abundant productions of grass, oats, barley, rye, and potatoes, what the arm of labour, and habits of economy and industry will do: out-doors there is a well-kept stock of cattle, sheep, and hogs; and in-doors you see plenty of cheese, butter, milk, and fish from the mill ponds, which are wonderfully frequent, producing the finest trout and pike: the people are pictures of health, and appear to be of the old English stamina.

Saturday, 18. We journeyed through the vale and pleasant town of Keene, and climbed along, height after height, towards Walpole; seven miles off, upon the south-west, we turned and came to Westmoreland, and held our quarterly meeting for Chesterfield circuit at Jonathan Winchester's, brother to the famous Universalist of that name. I opened the meeting in a new barn, upon Titus ii, 13, 14. On the *Sabbath* we were crowded from seven o'clock in the morning until three in the afternoon; the wind from the south-east blew in at the door, and it rained withal. Brother Richard Whatcoat and elder Daniel Ostrander preached before, and the young men exhorted after love feast and the sacrament.

Monday, 20. We came over the mighty hills to Chesterfield: here we called upon John Bishop, and at four o'clock a few were got together, to whom I gave a lecture upon Heb. xii, 1–3.

Vermont

Next day we crossed the Connecticut River at Barrett's[45] ferry, and came into the city of Brattleboro, stopping at Joseph Jacob's.[46] We are now in Vermont. The stupendous steeps on each side of the river resemble

[44] Ebeneezer Coleburn was the son of Daniel Coleburn, a Revolutionary soldier. The family lived in Chesterfield, New Hampshire. The Coleburns were numerous in New England, but the only family of Daniel lived in New Hampshire. (*Descendants of Edward Coleburn, 1635–1913*, 60.) [45] *Annals of Brattleboro*, 186.

[46] Joseph Jacob probably lived near East Mount in Guilford, where he owned a lot.

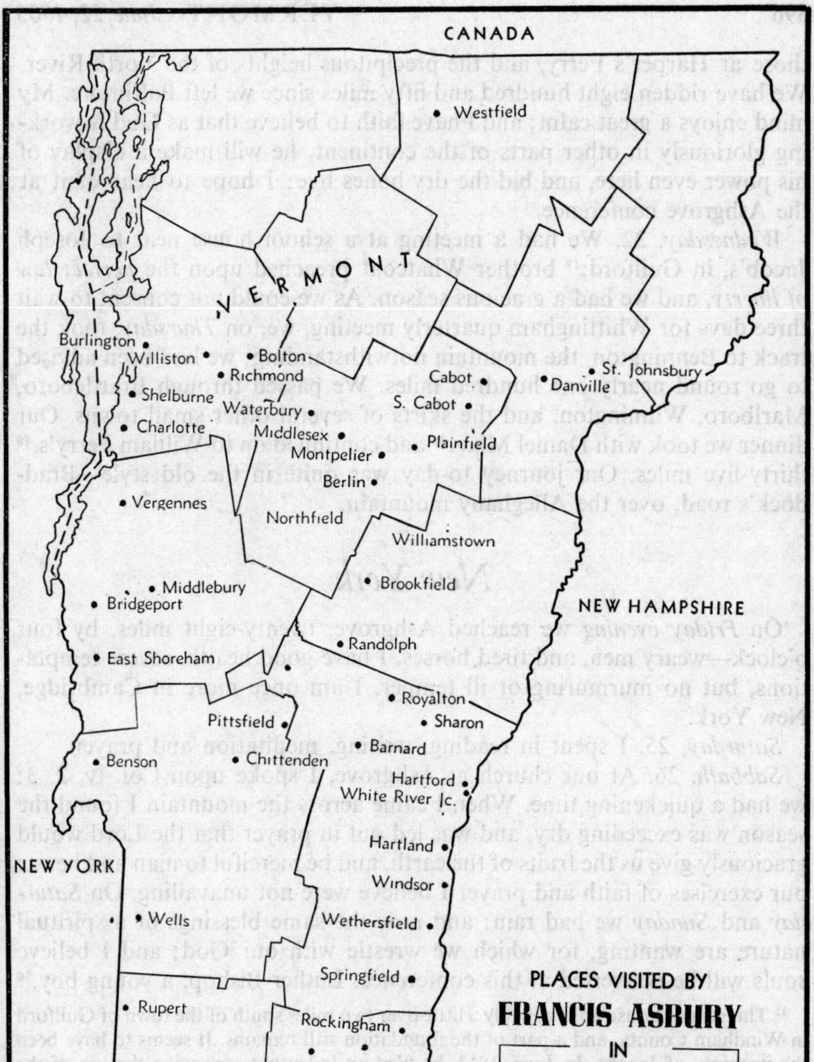
CANADA
VERMONT
NEW HAMPSHIRE
NEW YORK
MASSACHUSETTS
Westfield
Burlington
Williston
Bolton
Richmond
Shelburne
Waterbury
Charlotte
Middlesex
Montpelier
Berlin
Cabot
S. Cabot
Danville
St. Johnsbury
Plainfield
Vergennes
Northfield
Williamstown
Brookfield
Middlebury
Bridgeport
Randolph
East Shoreham
Royalton
Sharon
Pittsfield
Chittenden
Barnard
Benson
Hartford
White River Jc.
Hartland
Windsor
Wells
Wethersfield
Springfield
Rupert
Rockingham
Westminster
Putney
E. Dummerston
Bennington
Wilmington
Brattleboro
Marlborough
N. Pownal
Guilford

PLACES VISITED BY
FRANCIS ASBURY
IN
VERMONT

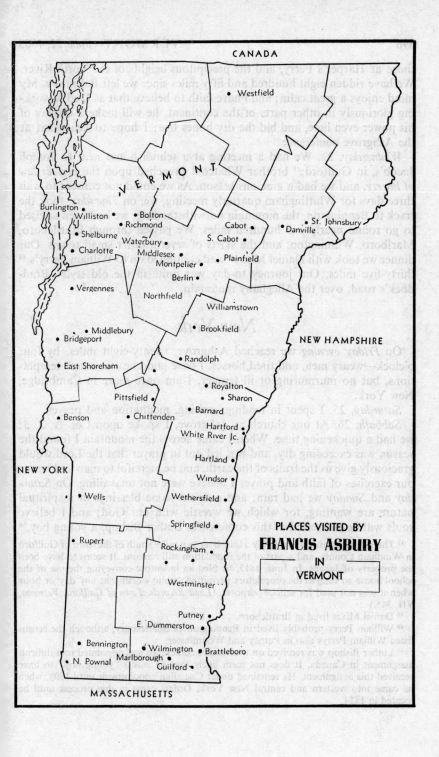

those at Harper's Ferry, and the precipitous heights of the North River. We have ridden eight hundred and fifty miles since we left Baltimore. My mind enjoys a great calm; and I have faith to believe that as God is working gloriously in other parts of the continent, he will make a display of his power even here, and bid the dry bones live: I hope to hear of it at the Ashgrove conference.

Wednesday, 22. We had a meeting at a school house near to Joseph Jacob's, in Guilford;[47] brother Whatcoat preached upon the *perfect law of liberty*, and we had a gracious season. As we could not consent to wait three days for Whittingham quarterly meeting, we, on *Thursday*, took the track to Bennington, the mountain notwithstanding: we had been advised to go round nearly one hundred miles. We passed through Brattleboro, Marlboro, Wilmington, and the skirts of several other small towns. Our dinner we took with Daniel Mixer[48] and continued on to William Perry's,[49] thirty-five miles. Our journey to-day was quite in the old style—Braddock's road, over the Alleghany mountain.

New York

On *Friday evening* we reached Ashgrove, twenty-eight miles, by four o'clock—weary men, and tired horses. I have good health, severe temptations, but no murmuring or ill temper. I am once more in Cambridge, New York.

Saturday, 25. I spent in reading, writing, meditation and prayer.

Sabbath, 26. At our church at Ashgrove, I spoke upon Col. iv, 2, 3: we had a quickening time. When I came across the mountain I found the season was exceeding dry, and was led out in prayer that the Lord would graciously give us the fruits of the earth, and be merciful to man and beast: our exercises of faith and prayer I believe were not unavailing. On *Saturday* and *Sunday* we had rain; and now the same blessings of a spiritual nature are wanting, for which we wrestle with our God; and I believe souls will be converted at this conference. Luther Bishop, a young boy,[50]

[47] This school house was probably a little over two miles south of the town of Guilford in Windham County, and a part of the foundation still remains. It seems to have been the property of Jacobs. In June, 1813, he filed an indenture conveying the use of the school house so long as the proprietors permitted public worship at any day or hour when it was not used for school purposes. (*Land Records, Town of Guilford, Vermont*, VII, 345.)

[48] Daniel Mixer lived in Brattleboro.

[49] William Perry probably lived in Bennington or Shaftesbury, although the census listed William Perrys also in Putney and Westminster.

[50] Luther Bishop was received on trial at this conference and appointed to a difficult assignment in Canada. It does not seem likely that he was a "young boy" to have received this assignment. He remained under Canadian appointment until 1808, when he came into western and central New York. Orders came in due process until he located in 1814.

preached on the *Sabbath day*—and so we will continue every evening until next *Monday* or *Tuesday* week, stroke after stroke with the rod of the Lord, like Moses, until the waters of repentance flow from hearts of rock. On *Monday* brother Whatcoat preached: my subject on *Tuesday* was Rom. ii, 7: we rested at John Baker's.[51] On *Wednesday* the elders did not appear, and I was obliged to hold forth again—my text Psalm cii, 13–17. By deaths and removals,[52] this Ashgrove society is diminished, but there will be a revival at this conference. This is a very eligible place for Albany, New York, Genessee, Pittsfield, and Vermont districts, but the conference ought to be divided between the two old societies of New York and Ashgrove. On *Thursday* I had to preach again.

Friday, *July* 1. We opened our conference at John Baker's in the Holloway, prettily environed with hills, a carpet of green spread beneath, and here and there around us fields clothed with the promise of an abundant harvest. We finished our business on *Tuesday*, public and private: there were nearly seventy preachers and fifty members. On the *Sabbath day*, perhaps, we had two thousand hearers: the house was filled with women, and the men stood without: I stood in the door, and spoke to them from 1 Tim. iv, 11, 12; but I had been overcome by twelve hours a day constant attention to business in the conference, and spoke with pain.

Wednesday, 6. We came to Pittstown,[53] dined with Mr. Follitt, and came on to the Half Moon,[54] thirty miles, and lodged at John Barber's:[55] these two villages increase. On *Thursday* we came through Albany, and stopped to dine at Dole's tavern, three miles beyond: here brother Whatcoat discovered that he had left my coat and my cloak behind: I bore the loss with some patience. Finding we had two hundred miles to reach Trenton, and only six days to accomplish the distance in, we continued on to Blasdale's at Coeyman's Landing: reflecting on this, and the journey of fourteen hundred miles still to Kentucky, and brother Whatcoat's indisposition withal, I felt somewhat moved. On *Friday* we came to John Crawford's,[56] near the Catskill mountains, making thirty-five miles without food for man or beast. On *Saturday* we reached Cole's, at Hurly Town,[57] on Esopus Creek. The drought, and heat, and dust, in nine hundred and ninety miles from Baltimore to this place, made us suffer;

[51] John Baker came from Ireland and settled in Ashgrove in 1786, becoming a strong leader in the Methodist society. (Parks: *Troy Conference Miscellany*, 25–28.)

[52] Among the deaths had been that of Thomas Ashton in 1801, from whose name Ashgrove was derived.

[53] This was a village near Schaghticoke where present Route 40 crosses the Hoosic River.

[54] Half Moon was an inn north of Troy along the present Route 40.

[55] John Barber was a leader in the church at Troy.

[56] John Crawford lived near Palenville.

[57] This town was west of Kingston on the southward road at the crossing of Esopus Creek. Asbury had visited there on July 12, 1799.

but my mind was supported, and my health preserved. At Hurly we called a few attentive people together, to whom I dispensed the word of life on Heb. xi, 25.

Monday, 11. We rose at four o'clock, and came off at six, and at twelve stopped at Mr. Ostrander's[58]: in this happy family we found the son of peace. We came on to New Windsor (through Newburg), to John Ellison's, making forty miles. Were I to listen to the murmurs of people, I might bring myself into dreadful business: feeling my unworthiness, I the more readily forgive their complaints: indeed their censure is far more safe for me than their praise. I have travelled about two hundred miles through the State of New York. By a fair and accurate computation I judge that we have added, exclusive of the dead, the removed, and the expelled, and withdrawn, 17,300. Our total for the year 1803 is 104,070 members: in 1771 there were about 300 Methodists in New York, 250 in Philadelphia, and a few in Jersey; I then longed for 100,000; now I want 200,000—nay, thousands upon thousands.

Tuesday, 12. We rested: but we shall pay for it before we reach Trenton. On *Wednesday*, we started for Warwick, but the tire of the carriage-wheel giving way, we only reached Nicholas Simonson's.

New Jersey

Next day we dined at Sussex court house, and reached Mizner's,[59] on the mountain; next day we came to Asbury Town,[60] between Sussex and Hunterdon counties.

Saturday, 16. We were driven into Jonathan Bunn's,[61] by a blessed rain. On the *Sabbath day*, at Trenton, my subject was 2 Cor. xi, 17.

[58] David Ostrander lived at Plattekill. He was of Dutch ancestry and had served as a major in the Ulster County Militia during the Revolution. He was a leader in the Plattekill Methodist class, and his son, Daniel, entered the Methodist ministry in 1793, becoming an outstanding member of the New York Conference. (Seaman, *op. cit.*, 158–59.)

[59] Adam Mizner was a descendant of the pioneer family which settled in the original Hardwick Township, from which the present Frelinghuysen Township in Warren County was separated in 1848. Mizner lived near the hamlet on the Allamuchy Mountain now known as Warren, but which for many years was called Wiretown. He and his family were among the early Methodists of Tranquility-Allamuchy churches. (Honeyman: *History of Northwestern New Jersey*, II, 787; Snell, *op. cit.*, 684, 738.)

[60] This is the first time Asbury uses the new name of the town which was renamed in 1796 by its chief benefactor, Colonel William McCullough, in recognition of American Methodism's pioneer bishop. The date marks it as the first community in America to be named for Asbury. (Snell, *op. cit.*, 480.)

[61] Jonathan Bunn lived in Hopewell Township in Hunterdon County, New Jersey.

Pennsylvania

Monday, 18. We went forward to Bristol: brother Whatcoat preached; I had spoken at Burlington[62] on Tit. ii, 14.

I must here, in Philadelphia, labour with the pen, and answer letters, and refit for the western conference.

Friday, 22. We left the city. During my three days' stay, I preached once at the Academy. On the Great Valley road[63] we stopped at brother Geiger's,[64] and housed for the night with an exceedingly kind German family by the name of Kenagee.[65] On *Saturday* we found heat, and dust and turnpike gates (twelve in seventy-five miles), as usual.

Sabbath, 24, we spent at Soudersburg. I spoke on Psalm li, 9–12. Here Bishop Whatcoat concluded he must stop, or go on with me and die by inches.[66]

Monday, 25. I passed through Lancaster, called upon John Shainer, upon Little Conastoga, dined at Columbia and preached at three o'clock and then crossed the ferry and reached Henry Strickler's[67] to lodge for the night. We stole a march upon our friends at York, and met them at the court house as they were coming to meet us: we stopped awhile at brother John Lay's,[68] and then came on to brother Pentz's.[69] On *Tuesday* I had a little leisure to write a few letters; and on *Wednesday morning* I preached at the chapel; and in the evening went to James Worley's. On *Thursday* I preached once more at the widow Hollopeter's upon Conewago: since I was here the old man has gone to rest. My mind is under a great calm. I hope this will be a great year of Gospel grace.

Friday, 29. We had a sultry ride to Carlisle. Henry Boehm preached in the evening.[70] Next day, at eleven o'clock, I gave them a sermon from Col. iii, 12–14: in the evening Wilson Lee[71] spoke.

[62] Burlington, New Jersey.

[63] This was the road to Lancaster and the West through Chester County.

[64] Geiger was a member of the Radnor Church. He entertained William Colbert in October, 1797.

[65] There was a family by the name Kaneagy which settled at Kinzer in Lancaster County. Dr. Samuel Kaneagy received his M.D. in 1844, and it is possible that he may have been a child in the home when Asbury visited them.

[66] See letter to Ezekiel Cooper, July 24, 1803.

[67] Henry Strickler lived in Hellam Township near Wrightsville. (Prowell, *op. cit.*, I, 985.)

[68] John Lay was a member of the first board of trustees of the First Methodist Episcopal Church in York, which was incorporated in 1820. (*Ibid.*, 711.)

[69] Hollow Pentz lived a short distance from York. (Boehm, *op. cit.*, 100.)

[70] Henry Boehm traveled only fourteen days with Asbury this trip. When they reached Berlin in Somerset County on August 5, Asbury sent him back to preach to the Germans. Later, from 1808 to 1813, Boehm was Asbury's constant traveling companion. (Boehm, *op. cit.*, 100–101.)

[71] Wilson Lee was admitted in full connection in 1786 and became the presiding elder of the Baltimore District. He was an outstanding early preacher and a great friend of Asbury. (Boehm, *op. cit.*, 103–4.)

On the *Sabbath* we had prayer meeting at five o'clock; James Smith[72] preached at eight o'clock; I spoke on 2 Cor. vi, 2; and Wilson Lee in the afternoon: we had excessive heat, but the people were very attentive. I have read the half of the "Portrait of St. Paul": O inimitable Fletcher—in preaching, writing, in living, and in dying!

Monday, August 1. I came ten miles to a Mr. David Snyder's, near a village called Newville and dined about eleven o'clock: the people gathered together, and I must needs preach to them. We proceeded on to Shippensburgh in haste, and here I again stood up in my Master's name: we had a crowded house, and a sick preacher. There is a meeting house here *on shares* with the Presbyterians and Seceders; the Methodists have one of their own.

On *Tuesday morning*, at four o'clock, we set out to scale the mountains. We passed a little town called Strasburg,[73] and another called Emmitsburg: here we stopped, and I laid myself down upon the floor to rest; intense heat, rugged mountains, and a wasting dysentery almost overcame me. I feel, and have felt thirty-two years, for Pennsylvania—the most wealthy, and the most careless about God, and the things of God: but I hope God will shake the State and the Churches. There are now upwards of twenty German preachers somehow connected with Mr. Philip Otterbein and Martin Boehm; but they want authority, and the Church wants discipline.[74]

Wednesday, 3. We came to David Field's and fed. After prayer, Wilson Lee bade us farewell, and went away to the Fort Littleton quarterly meeting: a rumour had spread that I also was to be there; strange, that they should expect that I would stay one hundred miles in the rear of my appointments for such a purpose; what must I not do to please all the preachers and all the people!

Hard and slowly did we toil up, through intense heat, eight miles of the Sideling Hill;[75] we stopped at a house of entertainment, kept by Mr. Edward Head; the night was very sultry, and my lodging-room very small.

Thursday, 4. We started for Berlin: passing through Bedford and Somerset counties, and crossing the Juniata, we came into pleasant Berlin about sun-set, making a ride of forty miles. We lodged with Squire Johnston; and necessity was laid upon us to speak both in English and German—with the assistance of my travelling companion, Henry Boehm.

[72] James Smith was admitted on trial in 1793. (See *Minutes*.)

[73] This was Upper Strasburg.

[74] This reference is to the rising evangelical movement among the Pennsylvania German people under the leadership of Asbury's friends William Otterbein and Martin Boehm, which became the United Brethren Church.

[75] Sideling Hill was so named because it was so steep that, when the road over it was being built, as many men as could be spared from the work were required to pull on the sidestays, or long ropes, attached to the upper side of the wagons to prevent them from turning over on their sides.

Friday, 5. Forty-two miles over hills and rocks, brought us down upon Connellstown, on the Youghiogeny River, where we lodged with Anthony Banning. I called at the twenty-mile house, and found a daughter of Michael King, a local preacher amongst us whilst living, and now, I trust, a glorified spirit. I think it will be better for me never to ride eighty-two miles in two days again: a wearied mare, just off a journey of thirteen hundred miles, and an old, afflicted man; but God and grace is sufficient. On *Saturday* and *Sabbath* I rested in Connellstown, and preached; my subject was Matt. v, 13. There has been *death in the pot* here, nor do we know that it is yet, or when it will be, out. On our way to Jacob Murphy's, we noticed Colonel Meason's superb stone mansion on Mount Braddock.[76]

Tuesday, 9. At Murphy's barn I spoke on 1 Cor. vii, 29–31. Although much afflicted in my bowels, I felt wholly given up to do or suffer the will of God—to be sick or well, and to live or die at any time and in any place—the fields, the woods, the house, or the wilderness: glory be to God for such resignation! I have little to leave, except a journey of five thousand miles a year, the care of more than a hundred thousand souls, and the arrangement of about four hundred preachers yearly, to which I may add the murmurs and discontent of ministers and people: who wants this legacy? Those who do are welcome to it for me!

Thursday, 11. I dined with the aforesaid Colonel Meason, one of the great men of the west. Next day I came to Union Town, and returned to Jacob Murphy's. On *Saturday* I came to the quarterly meeting; I preached, and we had an open time: at the night meeting it was a shouting time; and our meetings, I believe, were warning times to Union Town. I believe God will yet work in the Redstone settlement; has already begun amongst the Presbyterians.

Tuesday, 16. I rode, twenty miles, to Harry Stephens's, upon Monongahela; weak and afflicted. Next day I attended an appointment made for me at Maple Town; my subject was 2 Tim. iv, 7, 8: many heard and felt. I stayed with Mr. Jackson, on Muddy Creek, for the night.

Thursday, 18. I preached at Sheppard's meeting house upon Rom. viii, 9. I was uncommonly led out upon both my last subjects, and I suppose I had one thousand hearers in the two congregations. After dining we rode

[76] Mount Braddock, just north of Uniontown and the westernmost ridge of the Allegheny Mountains, was the location of the plantation of Christopher Gist, the first white settlement west of the mountains, settled in 1753, and which was an important cause of the French and Indian War. The stone mansion was built in 1802 by Adam Wilson, an English craftsman-architect, for Isaac Meason and is one of the finest examples of postcolonial architecture still standing in western Pennsylvania. Isaac Meason was one of the earliest ironmasters of western Pennsylvania, having established Union Furnace on Dunbar Creek in Fayette County as early as 1792. Jacob Murphy, Meason's son-in-law, and his mother, the widow Ann Murphy, were charter members of the original Methodist society in Uniontown. Mrs. Murphy's home was a favorite stopping place of Asbury and other preachers. (Mulkearn and Pugh, *op. cit.*, 219.)

down the heights of Tenmile, to a town called Frederick; thence to the Quaker settlement, and stopped at Alexander Frew's. Were the grounds not so uneven, and so destitute of springs and streams, I should give the Redstone settlement the preference to almost any in America: the soil is good, the timber lofty, and there is plenty of iron, coal, and limestone; and would the settlers generally do as their Quaker neighbours (the only people here who manure their lands), the soil would never be exhausted. The great promise of fruit has failed. It is mercifully wise in Providence to check our plenty; particularly here: many drunkards will now be kept sober in this distilling country, and I hope some will be converted to God.

Friday, 19. Our camp meeting begins today:[77] the ground chosen was William Jackson's, near the old fort upon the Monongahela; it was upon a beautiful eminence, the great stand was erected, and a second one to the left, concealed by the trees. On *Saturday* I preached to about one thousand hearers; my text was Isa. lv, 12. The Sabbath was wet in the morning, but, clearing away, both stands were occupied, and there might be in the two congregations nearly four thousand people: there was a visible impression made upon many, and we hope fifty souls were converted to God. On *Tuesday* we came away, whilst others were coming to the ground. Thornton Fleming and James Quinn went back and preached. We came to Samuel Hammond's.

Wednesday, 24. At the Forks meeting house I preached on 1 Thess. iii, 1. Whilst we were at dinner at Benjamin Fell's,[78] William Page came in with the agreeable intelligence of a revival at Connellstown. On *Thursday* we crossed Monongahela, at Elizabethtown, and came to William Jones's, and preached to an unexpected congregation: I was unwell, but spoke on Acts ii, 21. A woman, noted for being a mocker, fell down, and cried for mercy, confessing her sins before all the people. Brother Page exhorted, but the people would not disperse until he had given them a sermon under the sugar maple trees: many trembled and wept, if they did not pray. This has been a neglected spot. On *Friday* we rested.[79]

Saturday, 27. We had a dry, sultry ride to Pittsburgh. In the evening William Page preached. In the court house I spoke, on the *Sabbath day*, to about four hundred people; my subject was 1 Chron. vii, 14. I would

[77] This was the first camp meeting which Asbury officially promoted. See his letters to George Roberts in Philadelphia written during this meeting and also his letter of December 2, 1802, to Thornton Fleming.

[78] Benjamin Fell (1739–1811) was a Quaker from Bucks County, Pennsylvania, who moved to western Pennsylvania with his numerous family in 1786. He settled in the "forks of the Yough" where he was neighbor to Edward Teal, whose home was one of the original preaching points of the original Redstone Circuit. The Fells soon became Methodists and donated the land on which the first church of the society was built in 1792. This was the seventh Methodist church in this region. The present stone church, located on the original site and known as "Fells Church," was erected in 1835. (Smeltzer, *op. cit.*, 69.)

[79] See letter to Daniel Hitt, August 26, 1803.

have preached again, but the Episcopalians occupied the house. I come but once in twelve years,[80] but they could not consent to give way for me. It is time we had a house of our own.[81] I think I have seen a lot which will answer to build upon.

Monday, 29. I came down, and crossed at the old fort, the point of confluence of the rivers Monongahela and Alleghany, whence these united waters flow under the appropriate name of Ohio, *beautiful*. I crossed Sawmill and the Chartiers,[82] and passed the lands of General Neville.[83] At John Wrenshall's I found an agreeable hostess, and lovely children.[84] Riding up the road I met an aged Presbyterian, who told me that religion was at a great height in Mr. Wood's congregation—that yesterday under preaching several fell down; he asked my opinion of the work: I replied, that in my judgment, any person who could not give an account of the convincing and converting power of God, might be mistaken; falling down would not do: we agreed in sentiment. I stopped at John Fawcett's, where, although very sick, I preached to a large congregation, at seven o'clock on *Tuesday*; my subject was Matt. vii, 7, 8. I baptized several children. On the same day I rode, weak, faint, and alone, to Washington; it was the time of the court sessions: we had about four hundred people to hear, to whom I spoke on Titus ii, 11, 12. I lodged at John Crouch's: God is in this house.

Wednesday, 31. We rode seventeen miles to Philip Doddridge's, near a new-made town called Middletown; here I preached next day in a new stone house, the first of the kind I have met with in my tour. Although

[80] This was Asbury's second visit to Pittsburgh, the first having been in 1789. The statement "twelve years" must have been an error in copying the original *Journal* as it should be fourteen years.

[81] The Methodist preaching place in Pittsburgh from the time the society started under the leadership of John Wrenshall in 1796 until 1803 was in a large room in abandoned Fort Pitt, which was owned by Peter Shiras, a Methodist. Shiras sold the fort in 1802, and the society met in Wrenshall's and Thomas Cooper's homes until the first chapel was erected in 1810. (Smeltzer, *op. cit.*, 98 ff.)

[82] Sawmill Run and Chartiers Creek flow into the Ohio from the south near the junction of the Monongahela and Allegheny Rivers at the "Point."

[83] General John Neville was a prominent early citizen of western Pennsylvania, commandant at Fort Pitt from 1775 to 1777, an officer who fought in a number of battles of the Revolution in the East, a representative at the Pennsylvania constitutional convention in 1787, and the collector of the excise taxes in western Pennsylvania which precipitated the whiskey insurrection. His mansion at Bower Hill, south of Pittsburgh, the site of which was the occasion of Asbury's observation, was attacked and burned by the whiskey rebels on July 17, 1794. (Mulkearn and Pugh, *op. cit.*, 90–92.)

[84] Smeltzer says this sentence is misplaced and belongs in the paragraph when Asbury was in Pittsburgh. John Wrenshall (1761–1821) was an English Methodist local preacher who emigrated to America in 1794 and established himself as a merchant in Pittsburgh in 1796. He was the founder of Methodism in Pittsburgh, and it was his concern and leadership which enabled the Methodist society there to survive in its early years. (Smeltzer, *op. cit.*, 94–103.)

faint, from heat and a dysentery, I was long and fervent, and the people were attentive.

Friday, September 2. We found a spot and made a pulpit between two sugar maple trees. I was in great pain, so that I did not attend quarterly meeting, which began on *Saturday*, continued until midnight, recommenced on the *Sabbath* with love feast and sacrament, and at eleven o'clock I preached on Eph. vi, 18–20.

I. "The ministry of the Gospel," in redemption and salvation; in what Christ hath done for us, and in what is wrought in us by his Spirit.

II. The duty, nature, and exercise of prayer—for saints, for the ministry, and for the success of the Gospel.

III. That the apostle might be bold as a prisoner and a martyr.

Many things were said of the mysteries of God—creation, the winds, and our own existence in embryo; we have demonstration of these mysteries, and such we also have of redemption, conviction, conversion, sanctification, and the adorable Trinity; and frequent and obvious demonstrations of the power of God and his word *instantaneously* manifested: we do not know *how* these things are, but we know that they do exist.

My indisposition was such, that I felt the people still engaged in worship, much ashamed of the meanness of my performance, however well my hearers may have thought of it: the Lord knew my good intentions, but I saw that the excellency of such sublime and interesting subjects was beyond my reach of thought or expression. The Lord blessed our gathering together, and souls were converted.

West Virginia

Monday, 5. We rode ten miles to John Beck's, near West Liberty. I preached on Acts iii, 26; one soul who had been convicted at our quarterly meeting, professed to find peace with God, and shouted *glory!* with a loud voice. On *Tuesday* I preached near this place to a crowd, at John Spahr's. I came with Reason Pumphrey[85] down the great hill, to the Ohio.

[85] Reason Pumphrey (1735–1812) was probably the first Methodist west of the mountains. He was a Strawbridge convert in Maryland and was accompanied westward in 1772 by Eli Shickle, one of Strawbridge's local preachers. Shickle preached in the camps en route across the mountains and then in Pumphrey's and neighboring log-cabin homes when Pumphrey established his original land claim within the boundaries of the present city of Washington, Pennsylvania, in 1772. In 1786 Pumphrey moved to Beech Bottom on the Ohio River, just below the present city of Wellsburg, West Virginia, where his home became a preaching point on the original Redstone Circuit, and the society raised there became the original Kadesh Chapel congregation when this seventh western Pennsylvania chapel was built in 1788. Pumphrey's location on the Ohio River was doubtless the occasion for early extension of the original Redstone Circuit to the extreme limits of western settlement until the defeat of the Indians of the Northwest Territory. (Smeltzer, *op. cit.*, 38–41.)

Wednesday brought us to Charlestown,[86] the capital of Brook County, situated at the mouth of Buffalo, eighty miles from Pittsburgh. We found the Ohio so low, that the boat of Colonel Lewis,[87] who is going to explore the Mississippi, would not float over the flats.

Ohio

Thursday, 8. I reached Steubenville, and preached on Luke xix, 10. As the court house could not contain the people, we went to a Presbyterian tent; for which, as the "Jews and Samaritans have no dealings" in this country, we must ask pardon. I was invited to dine with Mr. Bazaleel Wells, one of the proprietors of this town, and the rich occupant of a large mansion, which, if rough-cast, would be grand. The rivers and streams were never lower than now. My mind is greatly engaged with God in public and in private; but I feel the power of Satan in these little, wicked, western trading towns.

Friday, 9. At Charlestown I preached in Brook court house, on Joshua xxiv, 19. We came to Nicholas Pumphrey's to lodge in the evening. On *Saturday* we crossed at Pumphrey's ferry, and attended West Wheeling quarterly meeting at Hopewell chapel.[88] I ordained brother Wrenshall[89] to the office of deacon, and then came to the stand, and preached on the *Sabbath day* on 1 Peter v, 10. We had love feast and sacrament. There was a cry raised very soon, and it was with difficulty I could keep the thread of my discourse whilst they were singing and shouting upon the top of the hill. At candle light the cry began again, and continued until the break of day on *Monday morning*: it is judged there were twenty souls converted to God. I came away, keeping up Indian Short Creek to Isaac Meek's, ten miles; on this stream are some of as fine lands as any in America.

Tuesday, 13. We came to Morrison's tavern, twenty miles, our route lying along upon the branches of Short Creek, Wheeling, and Stillwater—the land still fertile. Next day we reached Will's Creek, after riding thirty-seven miles; we were richly entertained at Mr. Beatty's. On *Thursday*

[86] Charlestown is the present Wellsburg, West Virginia, county seat of Brooke County in the northwestern West Virginia panhandle. The town was established in 1791.

[87] Colonel Meriweather Lewis and Colonel William Clark started for the West in 1803. (Gwaltmey: *Twelve Virginia Counties*, 325. For the date see Bakeless: *Lewis and Clark*, 102; Wheeler: *The Trail of Lewis and Clark*, I, 58–61; *American Explorers*, Vol. I.)

[88] Methodism was planted in the former Indian lands of the Northwest Territory across the Allegheny and Ohio rivers between 1799 and 1803. The West Wheeling Circuit was formed in 1802. This is the record of Asbury's first tour across Ohio, though he had taken his "peek into Indian lands" in 1786.

[89] John Wrenshall had been administering the sacraments to the Pittsburgh Society without ordination. Under Asbury's urging he made the eighty-mile journey to the West Wheeling Quarterly Meeting for ordination. This was the first Methodist ordination in the state of Ohio. (John Wrenshall: *Manuscript Journal*.)

morning it rained about two hours; I was damped, and felt a touch of inflammation in my throat. We stopped at Zanesville,[90] and found good entertainment at Mrs. Morrison's.

Friday, 16. We reached John Murphy's, at New Lancaster. Since *Tuesday morning* we have ridden one hundred and twenty miles, over successive and excessively steep hills. My mind has been calm. Daniel and Benjamin Hitt have been my companions. The levels, and on the water-courses the lands, in this state are exceedingly rich,[91] with all the appearances which alluvial soils present. I frequently see the *tumuli* or barrows,[92] such as are seen in the west of Georgia—most probably graves of the aborigines. Jonathan's and Brush Creeks are branches of the Hockhocking: there is fine land on these streams. We are, I judge, six hundred miles from Philadelphia.

On *Saturday*, I preached at John Murphy's, on 2 Peter i, 2. We held a sacramental and social meeting. At eleven o'clock Daniel Hitt preached, and I spoke after him; we had the attention of the people, and we saw some tears, but there was nothing special done. On *Monday* I preached at Edward Teal's[93] once more: this brother I knew in Maryland thirty years ago; he is now settled in Fairfield, near Rush Creek, and has twelve hundred acres of land under his feet, equal to any in the United States: what will not a little enterprise do for a man in this highly-favoured country!

Tuesday, 20. Was a day of settled rain; we sought a shelter at Edward Teal's. Next day, having two appointments, we set out and got bewildered in the woods and lost our way upon Mount Pleasant: we judged it best to take the path to New Lancaster and try to secure our second appointment, at Broad Cole's. After riding about twenty miles, and again missing our way, we came in at three o'clock, and I preached upon Luke xi, 13. I took lodging at Mr. Daniel Van Meeter's. Mr. Van Meeter told me, that a boy had cultivated about twelve acres, which would yield him about

[90] This town was named for Ebenezer Zane. The Zane home was in Wheeling, then in Virginia, and the first Methodist society in Wheeling was established at Zane's while Thomas Scott rode the original Ohio Circuit in 1793. (Thomas Scott, *Manuscript Journal*.)

[91] The early settlement of Ohio was spectacular. No settlement was possible, and land titles could not be granted until 1796. The territory was admitted to the Union on March 1, 1803, with a population of about 100,000.

[92] These were prehistoric Indian mounds, which are numerous in Ohio.

[93] Edward Teal (1737–1822) was converted under Asbury near Baltimore, where he had been a class leader. He moved west to the "forks of the Yough" in western Pennsylvania where Fell's Church is now located and where he opened his home as one of the first preaching places on the original Redstone Circuit. Between 1800 and 1803 he moved on west to the Hockhocking Valley in Ohio, and his leadership there was instrumental in the creating of the Hockhocking Circuit in 1803. His son-in-law, James Quinn, was one of the founding circuit riders and the leading early presiding elder of Ohio Methodism. (Wright: *Life and Labors of James Quinn*, 36–37; Smeltzer, *op. cit.*, 86.)

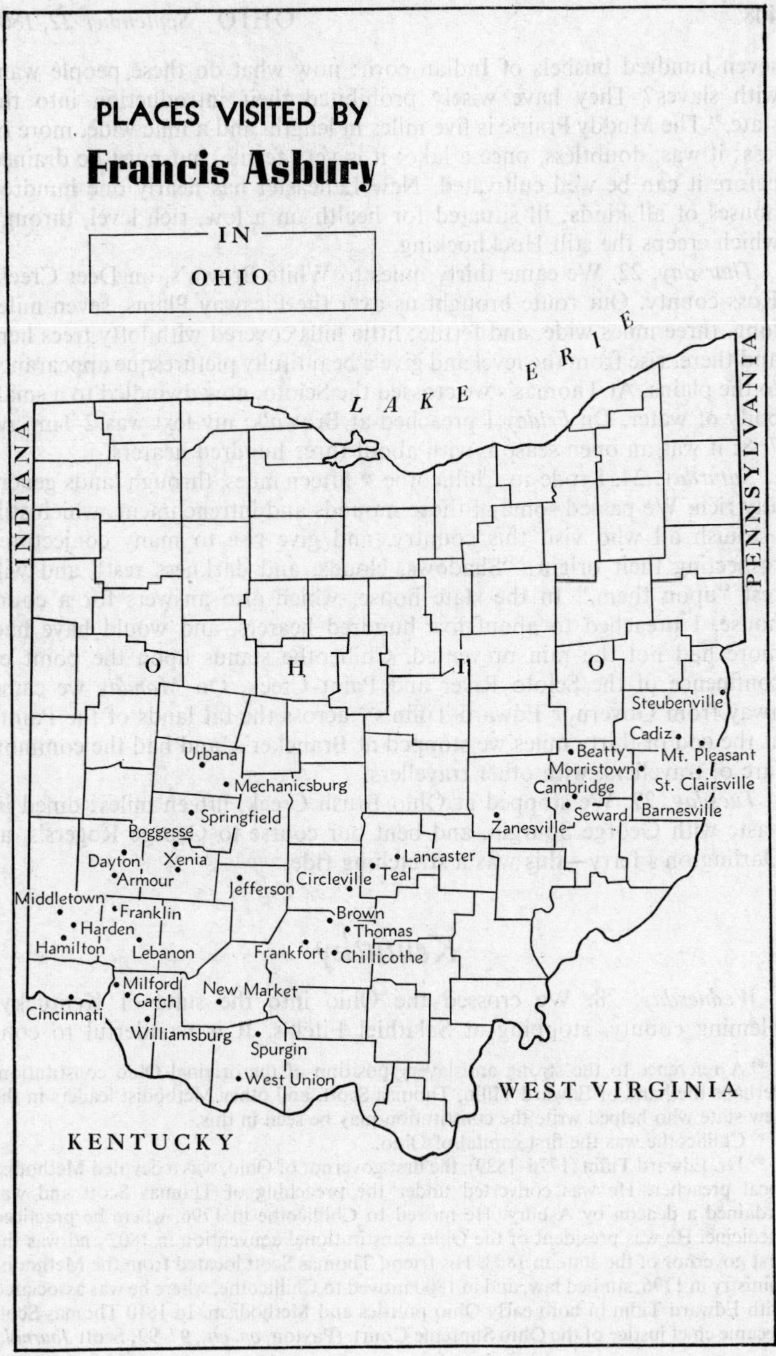
PLACES VISITED BY
Francis Asbury
IN
OHIO
LAKE ERIE
INDIANA
PENNSYLVANIA
OHIO
Steubenville
Cadiz
Beatty
Mt. Pleasant
Morristown
Cambridge
St. Clairsville
Seward
Barnesville
Zanesville
Urbana
Mechanicsburg
Springfield
Boggesse
Dayton
Xenia
Armour
Jefferson
Circleville
Teal
Lancaster
Middletown
Franklin
Harden
Hamilton
Lebanon
Brown
Thomas
Frankfort
Chillicothe
Milford
Catch
New Market
Cincinnati
Williamsburg
Spurgin
West Union
WEST VIRGINIA
KENTUCKY

seven hundred bushels of Indian corn: now what do these people want with slaves? They have wisely prohibited their introduction into the state.[94] The Muddy Prairie is five miles in length, and a mile wide, more or less; it was, doubtless, once a lake: it is very fertile, but must be drained before it can be well cultivated. New Lancaster has nearly one hundred houses of all kinds, ill situated for health on a low, rich level, through which creeps the still Hockhocking.

Thursday, 22. We came thirty miles to White Brown's, on Deer Creek, Ross county. Our route brought us over the Picaway Plains, seven miles long, three miles wide, and fertile; little hills covered with lofty trees here and there, rise from the level and give a beautifully picturesque appearance to the plains. At Thomas's we crossed the Scioto, now dwindled to a small body of water. On *Friday* I preached at Brown's; my text was 2 Tim. iv, 7, 8; it was an open season, with about three hundred hearers.

Saturday, 24. I rode to Chillicothe,[95] fifteen miles, through lands generally rich. We passed some of those mounds and intrenchments which still astonish all who visit this country, and give rise to many conjectures respecting their origin: "Shadows, clouds, and darkness rest" and will rest "upon them." In the state house, which also answers for a court house, I preached to about five hundred hearers, and would have had more had not the rain prevented. Chilicothe stands upon the point of confluence of the Scioto River and Paint Creek. On *Monday* we came away from Governor Edward Tiffin's[96] across the fat lands of the Paint: at the end of thirty miles we stopped at Brancker's, and had the common fare of travellers, with other travellers.

Tuesday, 27. We stopped at Ohio Brush Creek, fifteen miles; dined in haste with George Spurgin, and bent our course to George Rogers's, at Darlington's ferry—this was a stretching ride.

Kentucky

Wednesday, 28. We crossed the Ohio into the state of Kentucky, Fleming county, stopping at Salathiel Fitch's. It is wonderful to con-

[94] A reference to the strong antislavery position of the original Ohio constitution. Perhaps the hand of Edward Tiffin, Thomas Scott, and other Methodist leaders in the new state who helped write the constitution may be seen in this.

[95] Chillicothe was the first capital of Ohio.

[96] Dr. Edward Tiffin (1776–1829), the first governor of Ohio, was a devoted Methodist local preacher. He was converted under the preaching of Thomas Scott and was ordained a deacon by Asbury. He moved to Chillicothe in 1796, where he practiced medicine. He was president of the Ohio constitutional convention in 1802 and was the first governor of the state in 1803. His friend Thomas Scott located from the Methodist ministry in 1796, studied law, and in 1800 moved to Chillicothe, where he was associated with Edward Tiffin in both early Ohio politics and Methodism. In 1810 Thomas Scott became chief justice of the Ohio Supreme Court. (Payton, *op. cit.*, 97–99; Scott *Journal.*)

template the effects of American enterprise exhibited in the State of Ohio: it is but four years since Zane opened the road[97] for the general government through the *wilderness* so lately called, and now there are the towns of Marietta at the mouth of the Muskingum, of about one thousand houses; Cincinnati, containing as many; Hamilton, of five hundred houses: and many others whose names are scarcely fixed.

Thursday, 29. We came through Bourbon county. I crossed Licking River by the Salt Works,[98] and rode thirty-three miles to Benjamin Coleman's, at Mount Gerizim,[99] to attend the Kentucky Conference; this was a heavy ride, without food for man or beast until we reached *home*. On *Friday* we rested.

Saturday, October 1. Barnabas M'Henry preached upon the Divine institution of the *Sabbath*. On *Sunday* I had to preach from a stand in the woods to about two thousand people; my subject was 1 Thess. iii, 1. It was an open time.

Monday, 3. We entered fully upon our conference work; but I had to preach nevertheless. We had preaching every day; and the people continued singing and prayer, night and day, with little intermission. On *Wednesday* the meeting closed. We hope there were twenty souls converted to God, besides five who are reported to have been converted at a family meeting. Our conference ended on *Thursday* the sixth. I had taken cold, but rode twelve miles to Smith's, and was driven by illness early to bed. Next day I rose unwell, and continued my route through Paris, standing upon the fork between Stono and another stream, useful for mills, but apt to be nearly dry in autumn. Paris is the capital of Bourbon county—a growing place of about four hundred houses, some of brick, and a stone meeting house belonging to the Presbyterians. The day was excessively warm, but I made twenty miles to Doctor Hinde's,[100] Clarke county; brothers M'Kendree, Garratt, Douthet, and Granade were with me.

Saturday, 8. I felt my mind devoutly fixed on God. I accomplished two things in conference: viz. 1. Forming the Ohio circuits into a district; 2. Sending two missionaries to Natchez, and one to the Illinois—as the *minutes* of the present year will show.

[97] In 1796 the Federal Government granted Ebenezer Zane the tract of land on the Muskingum River on which the city of Zanesville stands on condition that he open a road across southern Ohio from Wheeling to Maysville, Kentucky.

[98] The Salt Works later became Blue Lick Springs. Daniel Boone made salt there, and he was captured by the Indians near this place in 1788. On August 19, 1782, the famous battle between Kentucky pioneers and Indians was fought near the springs.

[99] Mount Gerizim, or Broadwell, was in Harrison County, Kentucky, three miles from Cynthiana on the road to Ruddell's Mills. The historic church was built of blue ash logs on ground provided by Richard Timberlake, a Presbyterian, and Samuel Broadwell, a Methodist. It was burned in 1825, and a brick church was erected. (Redford: *Methodism in Kentucky*, I, 398.)

[100] Dr. Thomas Hinde was a well-known physician, educated at Oxford. He was the grandfather of Bishop H. H. Kavanagh. (*Ibid.*, I, 371.)

Sunday, 9. At Hinde's chapel, Clarke county, I preached, and thereby paid a debt which I had contracted last year, by sending Nicholas Snethen to preach in my place, by which, it may be, some people were disappointed: my text was 2 Peter i, 4–8. On *Monday* we took the path for Madison, crossing the Kentucky River at Combe's ferry:[101] we put in at Christopher Irwine's. On *Tuesday* we stopped at Wood's—in the woods: his house being unfinished, there were masons, and carpenters, and gentlemen, and riflemen, and whisky topers, besides the gnats and bats, which, ever and anon, flew in and out: we quitted our purgatory upon paying two and a half dollars for three of us.

Wednesday, 12. It rained to-day. We encountered the rocks and hills, on the route to Rock Castle River, and stopped, dripping and willing, at Senior Farris's[102]: here we had fire, food, prayer, a room, and a bed. On *Thursday* we started and reached Richard Ballinger's:[103] our host gave us entertainment *gratis*, and we had prayer at night and in the morning. I think seriously of forming a wilderness circuit: it is high time to begin.

Tennessee

Friday, 14. We came to Hunt's, at Claibornes court house (Taxewell); and next day reached Martin Stubblefield's.[104] What a road have we passed! certainly the worst on the whole continent, even in the best weather; yet, bad as it was, there were four or five hundred crossing the rude hills whilst we were: I was powerfully struck with the consideration, that there were at least as many thousand emigrants annually from east to west: we must take care to send preachers after these people. We have made one thousand and eighty miles from Philadelphia; and now, what a detail of sufferings might I give, fatiguing to me to write, and perhaps to my friends to read! A man who is well mounted will scorn to complain of the roads, when he sees men, women, and children, almost naked, paddling bare-foot and bare-legged along, or labouring up the rocky hills, whilst those who are best off have only a horse for two or three children to ride at once. If these adventurers have little or nothing to eat, it is no extraordinary circumstance; and not uncommon, to encamp in the wet

[101] Combe's Ferry was at Boonesborough. It was the first ferry licensed in Kentucky, being authorized by the Virginia legislature in 1779.

[102] John Farris, Sr., had a tavern at Hazel Patch, about three miles south of London. (Kincaid: *Wilderness Road*, 196.)

[103] Richard Ballinger's tavern was at the present Barbourville, thirty-seven miles from Cumberland Gap. (*Ibid.*, 193. See note under September 30, 1800.)

[104] The Stubblefield brothers, Thomas, Joseph, and Martin, lived at County Line, between Bean Station and Morristown, where there was a church. Martin Stubblefield was later killed by his runaway team in Cincinnati, where he was buried. This has been a prominent Methodist family in the section. (Price, *op. cit.*, II, 76, 77.)

woods after night—in the mountains *it does not rain, but pours*. I too have my sufferings, perhaps peculiar to myself: pain, and temptation; the one of the body, and the other of the spirit; no room to retire to—that in which you sit common to all, crowded with women and children, the fire occupied by cooking, much and long-loved solitude not to be found, unless you choose to run out into the rain, in the woods: six months in the year I have had, for thirty-two years, occasionally, to submit to what will never be agreeable to me; but the people, it must be confessed, are amongst the kindest souls in the world. But kindness will not make a crowded log cabin, twelve feet by ten, agreeable: without are cold and rain; and within, six adults, and as many children, one of which is all motion; the dogs, too, must sometimes be admitted. On *Saturday*, at Felix Ernest's, I found that amongst my other trials, I had taken the itch; and, considering the filthy houses and filthy beds I have met with, in coming from Kentucky Conference, it is perhaps strange that I have not caught it twenty times: I do not see that there is any security against it, but by sleeping in a brimstone shirt:—poor bishop! But we must bear it for the elect's sake. I wrote some letters to our local brethren, and read the book of Daniel while in this house.

Sunday, 23. My soul is tranquil, the air is pure, and the house of God is near; and Jehovah is nearer. At Ebenezer,[105] I preached on James i, 22: "But be ye doers of the word, and not hearers only, deceiving your own selves." By introduction, I collected the words of our Lord, and those of the apostle Paul upon the same subject, and brought them to one point. In opening the subject, I observed, 1. What we are taught in the preaching of the Gospel: First, Christian experience; Secondly, Christian tempers; Thirdly, Christian perfection; Fourthly, Christian duties. 2. General head: How people should hear the word—constantly, seriously; in faith, in prayer; as believing it promises all that is good, and threatens the most dreadful evil. 3. To be doers of the word is to seek for the immediate experience and practice of the word.

On *Monday*, we came off in earnest; refreshed at Isaiah Harrison's,[106] and continued on to the Paint mountain, passing the gap newly made, which makes the road down to Paint Creek much better: I lodged with Mr. Neilson, who treated me like a minister, a Christian, and a gentleman.

North Carolina

Tuesday, 25. We reached Buncombe. The road is mended by changing the direction and bridging the Ivy.

[105] Ebenezer meeting house was in the Earnest community east of Greenville, Tennessee.

[106] Harrison's meeting house was ten miles west of Ebenezer near Greenville, Tennessee.

Wednesday, 26. We called a meeting at Killian's and a gracious season it was: my subject was 1 Cor. xv, 38. Sister Killian and sister Smith, sisters in the flesh, and kindred spirits in holiness and humble obedience, are both gone to their reward in glory. On *Thursday* we came away in haste, crossed Swannanoa at Thomas Foster's, the French Broad at the High Shoals, and afterward again at Beard's bridge, and put up for the night at Andrew Mitchell's: we passed two large encamping places of the Methodists and Presbyterians; it made the country look like the Holy Land.

Friday, 28. We came up Little River, a sister stream of French Broad: it offered some beautiful flats of land. We found a new road, lately cut, which brought us in at the head of Little River, at the old fording-place, and within hearing of the falls, a few miles off of the head of Matthews Creek, a branch of the Saluda: the waters foaming down the rocks with a descent of half a mile, make themselves heard at a great distance.

South Carolina

I walked down the mountain, after riding sixteen or eighteen miles before breakfast, and came in about twelve o'clock to father John Douthet's;[107] once more I have escaped from filth, fleas, rattlesnake's, hills, mountains, rocks, and rivers: farewell, western world, for a while! We are twelve hundred and seventy miles from Philadelphia.

Monday, 31. I rode to Chastaine's,[108] twenty miles, crossing three branches of the Saluda.

Tuesday, November 1. At the meeting house, I spoke on 2 Peter v, 6–9:[109] after meeting we rode away fifteen miles to Wood's[110]; and next day preached at his house, to a lifeless congregation, and came off without dining to John Foster's, twelve miles. In this route I crossed the three branches of Tyger River, and passed through Greenville and Spartanburg counties. My mind hath been in great peace under all my trials, and labours, and troubles. I find that the camp meetings in this State, and in Georgia, have been conducted in great order, and with great success.

Thursday, 3. At Foster's meeting house,[111] I spoke on Matt. v, 12. I had some opening. In the evening, Moses Matthews and G. Dougharty[112] had a lively prayer meeting. I find we have lost Phœbe Wells, Mary Hughs,

[107] Asbury followed his former route from western North Carolina by way of Table Rock Mountain to John Douthet's.

[108] Chastaine lived near Traveler's Rest.

[109] There are only three chapters in this book. The passage may have been 1 Pet. 5:6–9.

[110] Wood lived near Greer.

[111] Foster's meeting house was near Arcadia in Spartanburg County.

[112] Moses Matthews was the preacher on the Saluda circuit, and George Dougharty was presiding elder of the Saluda District.

Eleanor Parker (formerly Owens), and William Hazlewood, members of our society in Charleston: they died of the prevailing fever.

Friday, 4. We re-crossed the branches of Tyger and Enoree rivers, and came along a crippling path to Thomas Terry's, near the Fork Shoals of Reedy River. We have a new frame house, built for worship, on Mount Terry: this has been erected in pursuance of my last year's advice, and by one man. To-morrow we shall open our new house.[113]

Saturday, 5. I spoke on 2 Peter ii, 1, 2. It was a rainy day, but we had a congregation. On the *Sabbath day*, I preached on Isaiah xlvi, 7. I laboured hard—I fear to little purpose: may the seed, sown in great weakness, be raised by the power of God! On *Monday* I rode to the Golden Grove,[114] and preached upon Gal. v, 22–25: it was a cold day, and there were but few people: it is the cotton, corn, and potato harvest. I rode that evening to B. Stanton's, upon Saluda. On *Tuesday*, at Salem, I preached to a few hearers upon Ephes. vi, 13–19. We made James Tarrant's that evening. *Wednesday* brought us to David Dunlap's, and *Thursday*, to Claiborne Brown's.[115] We met people coming from the militia muster, drunk, and staggering along the lanes and paths; these unhappy souls have had their camp meeting and shout forth the praises of the god of strong drink: glory be to God, we have our camp meetings too; of longer continuance, and more and louder shouting of glory, and honour, and praises to the God of the armies of the earth. Go on, ye servants of the Lord; and Thou, mighty Saviour, extend the victories of Gospel grace!

In Laurens county, I passed the Quaker settlement upon Rabun's Creek.

Friday, 11. I rode in haste to Bethel Academy, thirty-five miles. On *Saturday* I rested. On the *Sabbath* I preached at Bethel once more: my text was Mark xiii, 34, to the end of the chapter: after sermon, I rode eight miles to brother Lowe's,[116] amongst the Dutch people, and enforced Heb. iv, 4–16. At Mr. Rolles's,[117] twenty-five miles distant, I had on *Monday* a gracious season whilst expounding Matt. vii, 7–11.

We crossed Contee's ferry on *Tuesday*, and I entered Columbia like an Indian chief; it rained, and I had cast a blanket round me. John Harper[118]

[113] This new meeting house erected by Thomas Terry at Fork Shoals was in Greenville County.

[114] The Golden Grove was two miles north of Piedmont.

[115] James Tarrant lived near Princeton, David Dunlap near Clinton, and Claiborne Brown probably near Cross Hill.

[116] Lowe's was eight miles southeast of Mount Bethel.

[117] Rolles was probably Rawls, a prominent family in Lexington and Richland counties.

[118] The Rev. John Harper was licensed to preach by John Wesley in England. In 1795 he came to America and was stationed in Boston, and in 1799 he was sent to Charleston for three years; locating in 1803, he settled in Columbia and became an outstanding local preacher. He was the founder of Washington Street Church in Columbia and one of the founders of the Mount Bethel Academy. (Betts, *op. cit.*, 169.)

came to meet us and welcome us to his house, where, although the weather was stormy, we held a family meeting, and the rooms were filled with respectable hearers: my choice of a text was singular; it was our Lord's most affectionate words to his broken-hearted disciples when giving notice of his departure from them—John xiv, 18.

Wednesday, 16, was unfavourable; but we took the path manfully for Charleston. After crossing the ferry at Granby the rain came up, and accompanied us to the widow Geiger's; with her we dined, and took it again to John Whetstone's.[119]

Thursday, 17, was a clear, warm day. We dined with the widow Welch and, pursuing our journey, lodged at the widow Hart's;[120] thus we have been cast upon the distinguishing kindness of sisters to her of Sarepta.

Friday, 18. We came to Mr. M'Quinn's,[121] and next day reached Charleston, after riding thirty miles without rest or food for man or beast. I took possession of the new house built for the preachers, near the new chapel.[122]

Sunday, 20. I went once more to Cumberland street house, and had gracious feelings whilst expounding 1 Pet. v, 10. My stay being short, I attended in the afternoon, and spoke upon David's repentance, as recorded in Psa. li, 9–11: this also was a seasonable time, and all were attentive. Brother Kendrick spoke in the new church in the afternoon, and brother Dougharty in the old church at night, whilst the new church was occupied by brother Darley[123]: all this labour was, we hope, not in vain; some appeared to be in distress; who knows what God will yet do for wicked Charleston? I continued a week in Charleston, lodging in our own house at Bethel, receiving my visitors, ministers and people, white, black, and yellow; it was a paradise to me, and to some others.

Sunday, 27. I preached an ordination sermon, upon Gal. i, 15, 16, after which we set apart Bennet Kendrick to the elder's office, to which he had been elected by the Virginia Conference. In the afternoon I gave them my farewell discourse in Cumberland street meeting house, on Eph. iv, 1 2.

Monday, 28. We began our journey to Augusta, on our way dined at Mr. Carr's, in Dorchester, and stopped for the night with Mr. Isaac Perry,

[119] John Whetstone lived seven miles southeast of St. Matthews. Asbury was following the state road which corresponded generally to present Highway 176 toward Charleston.

[120] Mrs. Hart lived near Holly Hill.

[121] McQuinn was probably O'Quinn, a well-known name in Dorchester and Colleton counties.

[122] This new house was the parsonage of Bethel Church, which Asbury was among the first to occupy. The building had been erected but had no furniture. However, Asbury insisted on staying there, and some friends furnished two rooms and the kitchen. (Chreitzburg, *op. cit.*, 82.)

[123] Bennett Kendrick and Thomas Darley were the preachers at Charleston, and George Dougherty was the presiding elder. The new church was Bethel, and the old church was Cumberland Street.

upon Cypress Swamp,[124] by whom we were most affectionately received, and most comfortably accommodated.

Tuesday, 29. We stopped to dine with Captain Kogers, and came on to Spell's; next day to Trotter's. On *Thursday* to Pierce's, Tinker Creek.[125]

Georgia

Friday, December 2. We reached our place of destination. My mind is calm, and hath been kept in a praying frame: I have ridden one thousand six hundred and fifty-four miles by computation since I left Philadelphia. By letter from Philip Bruce, I learn that the work of God has promising appearances in the eastern and western districts of North Carolina; but abundantly more so in the south district of Virginia: at a kind of camp meeting held at Woolsey Barn (but now Ellis's chapel more properly), there have been, report says, one hundred whites, and a number of blacks, converted to God; at Guilford quarterly meeting, thirty, and as many within a short space at Norfolk, brought to Christ: but still larger accounts are received of the work of the Lord in this State; this, however, may be more fully known by reference to Stith Mead's narrative letters on the subject. My lodging in Augusta is with Peter Cantalou,[126] a friend from France.

Sunday, 4. I preached upon Coloss. vi, 2, 3,[127] in the morning; in the afternoon 2 Cor. vi, 2: I had satisfactory openings, but I have not those feelings I enjoyed at Charleston. We have a house here sixty feet by forty; an attentive and large congregation, and seventy members in fellowship: I hope this conference will give us one hundred souls converted.

At Thomas Haynes's, Uchee, we had a house filled; my subject was Colossians ii, 6: it was a feeling season. Next day, at White Oak, I spoke on Heb. xii, 28, 29, to a few; we rode home with Ignatius Few; his eldest son is serious.[128]

Wednesday, 7. We came to Scott's meeting house—an irregular congregation: my text was 1 Cor. xx, 58.[129] The day was gloomy, the preacher sick, and part of the congregation very inattentive. I lodged with Mr.

[124] Carr evidently lived near Summerville, and Captain Isaac Perry lived on the Cypress Swamp in Dorchester County near Ridgeville.

[125] Koger lived in Colleton County, Spell in Bamberg County, Trotter (Trotti) in Barnwell County, and Pierce in Aiken County. This section was formerly in Barnwell County.

[126] Peter Cantalou lived on Ellis Street in Augusta. (Smith, *op. cit.*, 75.)

[127] There are only four chapters in this book. There is no indication as to what the passage may have been.

[128] This son was Ignatius Few (1791–1845), who later became the founder and first president of Emory College.

[129] There are only sixteen chapters in this book. The context does not indicate what the passage may have been.

Gatrell. On *Thursday* it rained; but we wormed through the scratching woods to Mr. Ware's, where I stopped. Brother Stith Mead[130] went to one appointment, and brother Josias Randle[131] to another, with small expectation of meeting many people at either. For myself, let me move which way I may, appointments, or no appointments, I am sure to be brought into business: well, so best.

Friday, 9. Preached at Clendon's chapel, on Romans iii, 2.

I. The characters of "*believers*."

II. The nature and causes of their sleep.

III. The signs of the "time," and the knowledge thereof. That they may be instructed to "awake out of sleep." This was the general plan of my discourse; and we had a gracious season. On *Saturday* I came to Petersburg. The text for to-day was 1 Thess. v, 8, 9.

Sunday, 11. It rained. I spoke in a very open house on Ephes. vi, 18, 19. I lodged at Mr. Oliver's. The face of affairs here is greatly altered for the better; but I expect greater things yet: we have a society, it is true; but we want a house of our own to preach in. On *Monday*, at Thompson's chapel, I spoke on Heb. ii, 3, 4; and had good openings on the text. We lodged with Judge Tait. At Freeman's chapel my subject was Heb. ii, 3, 4: I spoke with liberty. We lodged with Mr. Freeman. *Wednesday* found me at Mark's chapel; my subject was Heb. iii, 14. When brother Mark's house is finished, he hopes to build a chapel, which he means to call Sardis;[132] he is a kind master to his slaves, and hints the probability of his liberating them by will; but he may change his mind before he dies.

Thursday, 15. At Hill's chapel, upon Long Creek, I chose Rom. viii, 1, 2. First, Real Christians are "in Christ Jesus"; and Christ is in believers. See 2 Cor. v, 17: "Therefore if any man be in Christ." Gal. vi. 15: "For in Christ Jesus." Romans viii, 10: "And if Christ be in you." Col. i, 27: "Christ in you the hope of glory." Christ contemplated in this view, must mean the operations of his grace, and the privileges of Christians. Second, What Christians should do, and what they should not do; "not walk after the flesh, but after the Spirit." Third, They that "walked after the flesh" were in a state of condemnation by the law, the word of God, and their own consciences: and, they who "walked after the Spirit" were in a justified state. I showed that condemnation supposed guilt, loss of privileges, and liability to punishment and death; *justification* was present, future, and eternal. After preaching, I took through the rain about twenty miles up to Henry Pope's, upon Long Creek, in Oglethorpe county. I have passed rapidly through Richmond, Columbia, Lincoln, Wilkes, Elbert, and Oglethorpe counties, in Georgia.

I will make a few observations upon the ignorance of foolish men, who

[130] Stith Mead was presiding elder of the Georgia District. (See *Minutes*.)
[131] Josias Randle was on the Little River Circuit.
[132] James Marks called his chapel Asbury. (See note under November 21, 1813.)

will rail against our Church government. The Methodists acknowledge no superiority but what is founded on seniority, election, and long and faithful services. For myself, I pity those who cannot distinguish between a pope of Rome, and an old, worn man of about sixty years, who has the *power given him* of riding five thousand miles a year, at a salary of eighty dollars, through summer's heat and winter's cold, travelling in all weather, preaching in all places; his best covering from rain often but a blanket; the surest sharpener of his wit, hunger—from fasts, voluntary and involuntary; his best fare, for six months of the twelve, coarse kindness; and his reward, suspicion, envy, and murmurings all the year round.

Friday, 16. Rested. Next day, at the chapel, I spoke on 1 Cor. x, 12, 13. The weather was cold, also the people.

Sunday, 18. I stood without doors, fixed my blanket to screen me from the sun, and my cap to shelter me from the wind. I cried in the words of my Divine Master, "Let your light so shine before men, that they may see your good works, and glorify your Father which is in heaven." First, The *light* of your principles and doctrine. Second, The *light* of your experience. Third, The *light* of your tempers. Fourth, The *light* of your practice, that they may see it manifested in virtue and piety, and be converted to God. On *Tuesday*, at Burke's chapel, I spoke upon Gal. vi, 9; we had a full house, a spiritual congregation, and a quickening season: after meeting we were under the necessity of riding in our wet clothes twelve miles to John Stevens's.

Wednesday, 21. Excessively cold. I preached, however, a sermon on 2 Peter i, 4. We came away without feeding man or beast to-day, and bent our course to Mr. Bush's.

Thursday, 22. At Heath's Gap I spoke on Heb. vi, 11, 12: after meeting we went on to Colonel Stith's, at Ogeechee; surely there is a great change here in the heads and members of the family.

Friday, 23. At Sparta, notwithstanding the races, we had a full house at Lucas's retreat. On *Saturday* I rode down to Matthew Harris's. I passed through Warren, Hancock, and Washington; and have ridden by computation nineteen hundred miles from Philadelphia. There are many hindrances to the work of God in this section of the country—some evitable, and some inevitable: amongst the first are Sabbath markets, rum, races, and rioting; of the latter may be enumerated, necessary business (so called); the sudden and severe changes, more peculiar to this southern climate, which affect people powerfully, and against which they have not the protection of warm dwellings—the houses are universally unfinished and open, and the churches and chapels are in no better state. My mind is kept in perfect peace, notwithstanding my daily labours, and my sufferings in exposure to night air, and day damps, and hard fare, and hard lodging.

Monday, 26. At New Chapel I preached; lodged at Jesse Jordan's: at

Walnut Branch chapel I spoke on Romans xiii, 11, 12. We lodged at Mr. Brett's.

On *Wednesday* we had a *proper* storm of rain in the afternoon. Passing through Louisville, we stopped with Mr. Flournoy, a new convert; his wife is amongst the *respectables*[133]—so! On *Thursday* I preached at a new chapel, called Bethel, in the woods, in Jefferson county; my text was Acts xxvi, 17, 18. On *Friday* we rode to Spirit Creek. We had an appointment for *Saturday* at a new chapel, but it rained, and we had few hearers; there being several preachers present, I chose for my text Rom. ii, 21; after meeting we rode thirteen miles to Mr. Beal's, near Augusta. To my surprise I find Bishop Coke is in Augusta before me. I have received letters of consequence from the North.

[133] Mrs. Flournoy was a member of the famous Cobb family. She was noted for her piety, and one of her grandsons became a Methodist preacher. Flournoy was well known, but his religious life did not continue very long. (Smith, *op. cit.*, 75.)

1804

1804

"Oh, New Hampshire, thy perpetual hills and rocks!"

CHAPTER THIRTY-THREE

Georgia

January, 4, 1804. We met for conference: Bishop Coke preached in the morning; and in the afternoon at John's (the old house), Augusta.

On *Monday* we opened our conference in Mr. Cantalou's house. We conducted our business in great harmony, and did it hastily. There was preaching every evening; and the bishops bore their share of ministerial labours. Elders and deacons were ordained. I found little difficulty in stationing the preachers. The conference rose at eleven o'clock on *Thursday*, and I took the road to Swearingen's, eighteen miles.

South Carolina

On *Friday* I reached Williams's; and on *Saturday*, Columbia.[1] *Sabbath day* found me in bed, confined by a deep cold, and an affection of my breast; nature relieved herself. A cold, hungry ride brought us to Camden on *Monday*. I gave Bishop Coke a plan for a journey as far as Boston, before the General Conference.

Saturday, 14. I continued in Camden, occupied in writing answers to Northern letters,[2] and reading Hawies's Church History: this is, perhaps,

[1] Leaving Augusta, Asbury went northeastward along present Highway 25 to Swearingen's, who lived near Trenton, then to the home of Mr. Williams near Monetta, and on to Columbia and Camden.

[2] See letter to George Roberts, January 11, 1804, and to Thomas Sargent, January 14, 1804.

amongst the best I have seen; but his partiality to good old Calvinism is very apparent. I have been unwell; but I am cheered by the glorious prospects of Zion's welfare: I mark this year, 1804, as the greatest that has ever yet been known in this land for religion.

Sabbath, 15. I preached in the morning and afternoon; and James Jenkins[3] in the evening. On *Monday* I rode as far as Mr. Rembert's, on Black River: here I retire to read and write; my body is weak, but my mind is stayed upon God.

Thursday, 19. For three days past I have been reading Hawies: he is concise, elegant enough, and deserves credit for his abridgement of the fathers, purged from their fables; his characters of Whitefield and Wesley are appropriately great; but O, his Calvinism!

Saturday, 21. I preached at Rembert's chapel,[4] and on the *Sabbath day* from Luke xx, 21: "In that hour Jesus rejoiced in spirit, and said, I thank thee, O Father, Lord of heaven and earth, that thou hast hid these things from the wise and prudent, and hast revealed them unto babes; even so, Father, for so it seemed good unto thee."

I. What things they are that are hidden from the wise and prudent: the things of the Gospel, the great things, and the deep things of the Spirit of God, in the Divine operations, and sensations, and affections, and fruits of the Spirit of grace; these are revealed to simple-hearted, ignorant, poor, and unlearned men and women.

II. Why are they hidden from the "wise and prudent"? 1. Because they seek the knowledge of them by their own wisdom. 2. Because they will not submit to the rules of discipleship that they may learn. 3. Because they have chosen the world for their portion, with its riches, honours, and pleasures; and thus living, they cannot learn. 4. Because they will not, cannot part with their darling passions and besetting sins. 5. Because they will not submit to suffer reproach. Jesus rejoiced that his heavenly Father has made foolish the wisdom of this world, so contrary in its spirit to humble faith and holy obedience; and that so many hath been made, and that millions might be made, the subjects of the grace of God—that wisdom which cometh from above. But our Lord did not rejoice in the spiritual ignorance and damnation of "the wise and prudent": he upbraided them for what might have been prevented; and wept, as man, with Godlike love, over Jerusalem.

Monday, 23. Reading, writing, and planning a route and Sabbath labours from now until January, 1805. The ninth volume of Mr. Wesley's Sermons engaged a part of my time.

Tuesday, 24. We braved the weather, keen and freezing, to Pudding Swamp,[5] taking a cold cut in the cold woods: we were well warmed at

[3] James Jenkins was the presiding elder of the Camden District.

[4] See letter to Daniel Hitt, January 21, 1804.

[5] Pudding Swamp was near Turbeville.

Mr. Kissam's; we felt powerfully for the parents and children of this family.

Wednesday, 25. By riding an hour in the night we reached Jane Green's;[6] on our way we found the waters of Black River spread near a mile over the low grounds about the bridge at Kingstree, where we crossed: we dined at Miller's, and baptized a child.

Thursday, 26. At Black River meeting house I spoke to a few souls, on 1 Tim. ii, 1. The weather became cold, but I had good lodging at Mr. Heideger's. This part of the country has a solitary appearance, because the white inhabitants have been much lessened.

Friday, 27. We reached Georgetown. I have suffered in my flesh, and have had "deep waters" of a temporal and spiritual nature to wade through.

If I should die in celibacy, which I think quite probable, I give the following reasons for what can scarcely be called my choice. I was called in my fourteenth year; I began my public exercises between sixteen and seventeen; at twenty-one I travelled; at twenty-six I came to America: thus far I had reasons enough for a single life. It had been my intention of returning to Europe at thirty years of age; but the war continued, and it was ten years before we had a settled, lasting peace: this was no time to marry or be given in marriage. At thirty-nine I was ordained superintendent bishop in America. Amongst the duties imposed upon me by my office was that of travelling extensively, and I could hardly expect to find a woman with grace enough to enable her to live but one week out of the fifty-two with her husband: besides, what right has any man to take advantage of the affections of a woman, make her his wife, and by a voluntary absence subvert the whole order and economy of the marriage state, by separating those whom neither God, nature, nor the requirements of civil society permit long to be *put asunder*? it is neither just nor generous. I may add to this, that I had little money, and with this little administered to the necessities of a beloved mother until I was fifty-seven: if I have done wrong, I hope God and the sex will forgive me: it is my duty now to bestow the pittance I may have to spare upon the widows and fatherless girls, and poor married men.

Saturday and *Sunday*, I rested at Georgetown.[7] I preached in Mr. Hammett's house, now fallen into our hands.[8] Alexander M'Caine attended the afternoon and evening services. The Baptists have built an elegant church, planned for a steeple and organ: they take the rich; and

[6] Jane Green lived in upper Williamsburg County.

[7] See letter to Bennet Kendrick, January 29, 1804.

[8] This was one of the churches erected by the Rev. William Hammett, who led the schism which resulted in the formation of the short-lived Primitive Methodist Church. After Hammett's death in 1803 all of his churches reverted to the Methodist Episcopal Church. (See note under February 11, 1792. See also Betts, *op. cit.*, 65–67.)

the commonalty and the slaves fall to us: this is well. We have about twenty whites, and between three and four hundred blacks in society here. My mind has been deeply tried by my friends who wished me to derange appointments made in two circuits, that one station might be supplied: I do not sport with preachers or people; I judge for the Lord and his Church; I stand in the order of God, as well as the appointment of men.

Monday, 30. We crossed Black River at Evans's ferry, and lodged at Henry Britton's,[9] where we were entertained.

Tuesday, 31. I preached at Jenkin's chapel, on Heb. ii, 3. We dined and came on to Port's ferry, an hour after the setting of the sun.

Thursday, February 2. We crossed Great and Little Pee Dee: over the latter I crossed in a canoe. At Potato Bed Ferry,[10] a forlorn place, we were detained three hours. At Kingston (Conway), brother M'Caine gave us a sermon; and I also gave an exhortation: we lodged at Richard Green's.

Saturday, 4. We came to Hullum's; a curious, fearful road we had—we hardly escaped miring several times. The simple-hearted, poor people have built a house since I was here last. I gave them a sermon, from 2 Tim. iv, 7, 8. After meeting we pushed on to father Hullum's, dined and lodged with William Norton.[11] Brother Benjamin Jones,[12] who had come on Bladen circuit, about ten days back, died upon the road, whether by fits, to which he was subject, or by drowning, we have yet to learn. He was a native of South Carolina, near to Georgetown, a pious, good young man of unblemished life: he had travelled five years, and is now gone to rest. Lord, what is man! Lord, what is life! Let us, let me be also ready!

North Carolina

Monday, 6. We rode eighteen miles to Ebenezer: there were about thirty souls, to whom I spoke, from Titus ii, 13, 14. We came to Pieraway Ferry: I was unwilling to cross: nevertheless, we all got into a small broken flat; and scarcely had we launched, when we upset, and were obliged to back out by wading: had this been in the middle of the river, fifteen feet deep! Lord, thou preservest man and beast! By making three

[9] Evans' Ferry was near Black Mingo, and Henry Britton lived near Poston.

[10] Asbury crossed the Little Pee Dee west of Kingston, the present Conway.

[11] William Norton lived near the present town of Loris, near the North Carolina line. Asbury was proceeding along the route of present Highway 90 toward North Carolina.

[12] Benjamin Jones was admitted on trial in 1801 and had served the Richmond, Charleston, and Bush River circuits. He was appointed to the Bladen Circuit with Hugh Porter at the recent conference. He was subject to apoplexy, and it is supposed that he had an attack and fell into the water of Brown Marsh near the Waccamaw lake, where he drowned in two feet of water. He was about thirty years of age. (See *Minutes*, 1805.)

trips of the horses, men, and baggage, our crazy skiff put us safe over. At the widow Cressett's, we were well entertained.

Tuesday, 7. We rode to little John Gaine's, thirty miles; no food from sun to sun.

Wednesday, 8. We rode to Smithville, so called from General Smith: we rode thirty-three miles through the rain. We lodged at the widow Douyer's, and were plagued with our horses breaking away.

Thursday, 9. Our horses were taken and brought to us. I preached at Smithville, and brother Alexander M'Caine also in a house in the town. This is the old fort Johnson, at the mouth of Cape Fear River: it is partially rebuilt.

Friday, 10. We came to Brunswick, an old town; demolished houses, and the noble walls of a brick church: there remain but four houses entire. I preached at Miss Grimshaw's on 2 Cor. iv, 5; and ordained Nathaniel Bell to the office of deacon. At Edward Sullivan's I found that the cold weather, and hard labour of riding and preaching, began to press me down.

Saturday, 11. At Rork's, at Town Creek, brother M'Caine preached: I also spoke, enforcing, "Be thou faitful unto death, and I will give thee a crown of life." A late camp meeting upon Town Creek has given a revival to religion amongst both whites and blacks. I thought I perceived intimations of this in my last visits. About the going down of the sun we came into Wilmington, faint and feeble.

Sunday, 12. We had nearly one thousand souls, to whom I spoke upon Heb. xii, 25.

Monday, 13. I rested, wrote, and regulated some matters of a temporal nature.

Tuesday, 14. I preached on 2 Pet. ii, 10–12.

Wednesday, 15. We set out, and made Nixon's, at Topsail.

Thursday, 16. Lodged with Lot Ballard, New River.

Friday, 17. Reached Thomas Lee's, Trent River.[13]

Saturday, 18. I preached in Lee's church on 1 Cor. xv, 58; after meeting we had a cold ride to Newbern.

Sunday, 19. I spoke under great heaviness: my subject was Col. iii, 12–16; again in the evening on Ezek. xxxv, 2: my load was thrown off, and we had life springing up in the assembly.

Monday, 20. We moved a subscription to raise one thousand dollars to enlarge and finish the chapel: we have obtained six hundred dollars. Brother M'Caine preached, and there was something of a shout.

Tuesday, 21. I spoke from Heb. iii, 15. Our official brethren were called up in the night to attend two gay females; one had run to call the brethren to pray for her distressed companion, and she also was stricken: they both professed to find the Lord.

[13] Nixon lived in Pender County, Ballard in Onslow County, and Thomas Lee in Jones County.

Wednesday and *Thursday*, 22, 23. We called assemblies in Newbern, and unwieldy congregations came together.

Friday, 24. We took the path to Washington: it was clear and cold: at Neuse Ferry it blew fresh: at Tar River the gale had subsided, and we crossed in comfort.

Saturday, 25. I felt the effects of my long and very cold ride from Newbern: nevertheless I gave them a sermon.

Sabbath day, 26. I spoke at Washington on 2 Cor. v, 11–15. I collected three propositions from the whole.

I. The Gospel is a universal ministration of grace and truth: "we persuade men"—all men, everywhere. This position is proved by the general love of God; the general commission given the ambassadors of Christ; the general atonement; general offers of grace; the general judgment.

II. That consequently, the Gospel must be, in all its administrations, applicable to the cases, consciences, and characters of all; and thus does it behoove the ministers of the Gospel to preach it.

III. It is a ministry of terror: "the terror of the Lord, we persuade men"; it is a ministry of love: the "love of Christ constraineth us."

Monday, 27. At Gardner's bridge I spoke to many hearers, on Luke iv, 18, 19; it was very chilly. In the evening we came to John Watt's; thirty miles to-day, without fire or food, from seven to five o'clock in the evening. On *Tuesday*, being unwell, brother M'Caine officiated for me. "I groan, being burdened": seven conferences to appoint the stations in; to officiate in the General Conference of this year; seventeen States to visit, requiring a ride of five thousand miles at the rate of twenty, thirty, and forty miles a day. O Lord, give me support! for every day, every hour, and every moment is a time of need with me! We rode up to Colonel Samuel Williams's, twenty miles. At Williams's chapel, Taylor's ferry, truly the *great ones* were present to hear, and I preached to them upon the *great salvation*; to little purpose I fear: small fruit of twenty-five years of faithful labours upon the rich lands of Roanoke.

Thursday, *March* 1. After a lonely ride of fifteen miles in the rain, I preached at the widow Ann Whitmell's, near Edward's ferry: we had twenty females, and half as many males to hear. The Baptists go ahead of the Methodists in this settlement: if it be well done, it matters little who does it. My mind is in peace, but my body is weak and in pain.

Friday, 2. After preaching at Whitaker's chapel, on Rev. ii, 10, I ordained Henry Bradford, Benjamin Nevell, and William Lindsay, deacons: it was very cold.

Saturday, 3. I rode twenty miles, crossed Roanoke to Bridges Creek, and lodged at Richard Whitaker's.

Sabbath day, 4, was extremely cold. I preached at Rehoboth chapel, and ordained Richard Whitaker a deacon; we had many more people than I expected; the house was nearly filled with both colours.

Monday, 5. At J. Pinna's my subject was Rom. x, 12. We had excessive snow on *Tuesday*: I ordained E. Everett a deacon. At Montgomery's old house about two dozen souls met me, to whom I spoke on James ii, 6. Twenty miles to-day in the snow, pitch and drive; it was well my mare had no shoes behind to ball her feet.

Thursday, 8. I preached at Wicocon, where I never expected to be again: the windows were open, and the people trembled under the cold, if not under the word. After crossing two ferries, we came to Gates court house, twenty miles: my mind is in peace; but I feel for the people of these low lands: with the exception of a few towns and select places, my ministry amongst them must be near its end. To go around by Norfolk on my route eastward is objectionable for many reasons; and I may find it expedient to bid this part of the country farewell forever.[14]

Friday, 9. At Gates court house I spoke on 1 Cor. vii, 29–31. It was a very cold day: we held our meeting in the house of Daniel Southall: the loss of a favourite child has awfully clouded the day of his prosperity. Ah! hair-hung, breeze-shaken worldly bliss, what art thou!

Saturday, 10. We rode to Edenton, and lodged at a tavern. After nineteen or twenty years, I preached in the court house, and many attended. I dined with Mr. Beesly, a printer, and supped with Mr. Constantine Luton, both Baptists. I found out Caleb and William Manning, nephews of my ancient friend Caleb Manning: these young men want preaching established. I now know why I came to Edenton; that I might feel for the people, and make an appointment of a preacher for them: but we must get a house of worship here of our own.

Monday, 12. At Yawpin chapel I preached on Luke xi, 9–13. I had a very serious, attentive people to hear: I believe God is amongst them.

I called upon Mr. Ross, a Baptist minister of the Gospel, much thought of: I found him in a feeble state of body: we prayed and parted in great affection. We had rain, and night came on before we reached brother Sutton's, twenty-eight miles: we crossed Perquimans upon a floating bridge. My mind is in great peace. To-day Humphrey Wood became my companion in travel.

Tuesday, 13. At Mr. Muller's, at Nags Head, I preached upon 1 Peter v, 10; we had a full house, and the truth was felt; I dined with mother Wood, and lodged with Mr. Samuel Whidbees; were this last family as good as they were kind, they might be perfect.

Wednesday, 14. I spoke on 1 John iii, 1–3, at Nixonton chapel: I had openings, and felt as if God was about to visit this people. In my subject, I showed,

I. The effects manifested by Divine "love" in the fruits produced by it, and the consolations flowing from it.

[14] However, Asbury returned to this area on February 6, 1806, and January 21, 1810. (See *Journal* entries for those dates.)

II. The progress of becoming, and the privileges of being the "sons of God."

III. The evidences furnished by the "sons of God" of their claim to sonship; they "purify themselves" from all sin by humble faith and holy obedience.

IV. The "world"—blind and wretched, "knowing not God," nor the real character of the Eternal Son of God, and mainly ignorant of the hearts, the exercises, the sufferings, the trials, and the heavenly consolations of the "sons of God."

Thursday, 15. At New Begun meeting house I preached, and was filled with my subject: the rich amongst the people came and offered gifts, but we did not receive them: how little do some folks know us! I lodged at Mr. F——'s; a cold night to me in a double sense.

Friday, 16. At the court house in Elizabeth City, Pasquotank county, I preached upon Matt. vii, 7–11: many heard, but few felt. I dined with Mr. Mitchell, a lone Methodist from Cornwall, Great Britain; Lot in Sodom. The site of this place is beautiful for its land and water prospects; and the situation is good for trade. We rode on to Camden, and had to beg a lodging of Mr. Joseph Sandlin, who belongs to the Baptists: these people carry the day here in respectability and numbers.

Saturday, 17. At the widow Capp's we had a small house, but well filled. I enlarged much upon the salvation of the world, including infants and adults of the Christian and heathen world: a Baptist might not think this is a kind return for my night's lodging; but it was the truth. I lodged with Edward Bunnell, from New Jersey.

Sabbath, 18. I ordained Joshua Gambling and Nathaniel Brook, both of Currituck county, deacons in the local line. I baptized Mary Forbush: she had been brought up a Baptist. At Williams's chapel I was very unwell: we had a cold house, and cold people. After meeting I retired to Zachariah Morse's. Eight hundred miles from Augusta, Georgia.

Virginia

Monday, 19. I preached at James Wilson's; *Tuesday* at Cutherell's; *Wednesday* at Portsmouth; *Thursday* at Norfolk; and on *Friday* and *Saturday* I was housed. At a meeting of the women, we laid the foundation of a female charitable society of Norfolk; similar in plan to those of New York and Baltimore, but more liberal: may this live, grow, and flourish when I am cold and forgotten!

Sabbath day, 25. I preached at Norfolk, upon Matthew xxviii, 19, 20; and at Portsmouth, in the afternoon, my subject was 1 Peter ii, 9–12.

Monday, 26. I preached at a new meeting house fourteen miles up the road towards Suffolk: here, after thirty years' labour, first and last, we have a chapel; I named it Ebenezer. At Suffolk, on *Tuesday*, unwell as I was, labour went hard with me: I had an almost total obstruction of perspiration; but a pulpit sweat relieved me in a good degree. My soul is calm.

Wednesday, 28. I preached at Powell's chapel: on *Thursday* at Benn's chapel, Isle of Wight, we had a decent, but not a feeling congregation. After preaching I rode up to William Blunt's. On Good Friday, so called, I preached at Blunt's, and administered the sacrament: I had a cloudy day, and a bad house to speak in. I rode to Joseph Moody's. We drew a plan of a new house, forty by thirty feet, two stories high: but will it ever be built? I doubt it.

Saturday, 31. I preached in an old, abandoned Episcopal church in Southampton[15]: we had an open house, and a cold day. I lodged with Philip Davis. I have made a thirty-miles ride to-day.

Easter day, the first of April, and of the week, found me at Lane's chapel: my subject was Colossians iii, 1–4. We, after meeting, rode fifteen miles to Frederick Pennington's. The time and electioneering increased my congregation on Easter Monday. I lodged at James Rogers's. On *Tuesday*, I preached at Jones's chapel. I feel feeble in body, but confident in mind. I know not if I shall not take leave of week-day appointments: if I do more than preach on the Sabbaths, it will be in towns, or at a called meeting, where I wish to stop.

Wednesday, *April* 4. I preached on 1 Thess. iv, 13–17, at Mabry's chapel, made anew; now sixty by twenty-five feet. I was a preacher here before the first house was built, thirty years ago: first an addition was made, now it is rebuilt in another form, and a gallery added for the blacks. I rode home in the rain with Peter Pelham: here is death temporal, and life spiritual—Thomas Pelham was converted, and is dead since my last visit; and there remain three living children, newborn babes.

Thursday, 5. I preached at the camp meeting house; and on *Friday* at Hobb's chapel; although very weak, I administered the Lord's Supper, after preaching a sermon on Titus iii, 8. I went in the evening to the widow Wyche's.

Saturday, 7. At Wolsey's barn[16] I spoke on 2 Cor. iii, 12; there were few people: we had a stormy day, and a poor, weary preacher. I dined

[15] This was Vick's Old Church, which stood for many years on the north side of the county road, about one and a fourth miles east of Newsoms and only five miles north of the North Carolina line. The church was built in 1768 as a chapel of ease for St. Lukes Parish and was referred to at times as Cypress Swamp Chapel; however, it was built on Simon Vick's land and became better known as Vick's church. It was taken over by the Methodists following a period of disuse after the Revolutionary War and was finally abandoned when its congregation moved into a new building more conveniently situated at Newsoms. (Mason, *op. cit.*, 215.)

[16] See note under November 30, 1795.

with Ira Ellis, and rode up to Edward Dromgoole's. The wife of my old friend is lingering out life.

Sunday, 8. I spoke on 2 Peter iii, 7–11, at the Olive Branch chapel; I am taking leave of the people every visit. I have made up one thousand miles, from Augusta, Georgia, to Brunswick county, Virginia. In old Virginia I have administered the word thirty years.[17] There is a great mortality amongst the aged: our old members drop off surprisingly; but they all, by account, die in the Lord, and in general, triumphantly. Now I have finished my awful tour of duty for the past month. To ride twenty and thirty miles a day; to preach, baptize, and administer the Lord's Supper; to write and answer letters, and plan for myself and four hundred preachers—O Lord, I have not desired this awful day, thou knowest! I refused to travel as long as I could, and I lived long before I took upon me the superintendency of the Methodist Church in America, and now I bear it as a heavy load; I hardly bear it, and yet dare not cast it down, for fear God and my brethren should cast me down for such an abandonment of duty. True it is, my wages are great—precious souls here, and glory hereafter.

Tuesday, 10. Our Virginia Conference began in Mecklenburg county, Salem.[18] We sat six hours a day, and wrought with great application. We had an addition of fifteen preachers, besides two dead, seven located, one expelled; so there was a gain of eight. I liked what was done; only, the preachers' experiences, the state of the work, and the circuits were not given; so we concluded to recommend a session of six days for the next yearly conference, appointed to be held at Edmund Taylor's, North Carolina, March 1, 1805. What I have felt was only known to the Lord; what I have done, was for God and his Church. We have added, after a great mortality, one thousand members to the Virginia Conference bounds.

Saturday, 14. We came away with elders Jackson, George, and Pinnell. On the *Sabbath day* we stopped at John Rogers's, Brunswick county, and I preached from 2 Cor. xiii, 14; after sermon we rode to Peter Robinson's, Nottoway county, fifteen miles.

Monday, 16. We stopped at John Morgan's, Amelia county. Serious times in this family—two sons dead—young men! We put in for the night at Nathan Anderson's, Chesterfield county. Next day a long ride of forty-

[17] This is not quite thirty years since he came to Virginia in 1775. (See *Journal* entry for May 29, 1775.)

[18] After paying all claims, the conference had $85.26 left and divided it among the delegates to the General Conference. They were Philip Bruce, Jesse Lee, Jonathan Jackson, Daniel Hall, Samuel Risher, Joseph Moore, Christopher S. Mooring, Joseph Pinnell, Humphrey Wood, Alexander McCaine, William Allgood, Josiah Phillips, Jesse Coe, John Cox, John Gamewell, Daniel Ross, and John Buxton. William Ormond and Nathan Jarratt had died during the year. The conference sent a Remonstrance and Petition to the General Conference on the matter of slavery. (Bennett, *op. cit.*, 442–48.)

five miles brought us to Elisha Maxey's. We have lately had moderate rides, but heat and dust; our meetings were small, as the people had but partial notice. I ordained Elisha Maxey deacon.

Wednesday, 18. We crossed at Judah's Ferry,[19] upon James River, and came on to Goochland court house, forty-five miles, and lodged with Joseph Perkins. Next day brought us to John Lastley's, Louisa county. On *Friday* we had to be at the hills of Orange and Madison counties, to Robinson River, and once more sheltered under the roof of our brother, Henry Fry. He was labouring under a weakness of his bowels; I gave him Fothergill's recipe. It is thus: one ounce of bark, half an ounce of rhubarb, three nutmegs all boiled together in a gallon, until reduced to two quarts: a wine glass of this to be taken every two hours. On *Saturday* we had a powerful rain; but we were under the lee of a good room. Part of the *Sabbath day* was taken up with a short ride of fifteen miles, to Nicholas Kobler's, Culpepper. I have read John Smith's View of the Last Judgment. I think it elegant and spiritual. *Monday* evening brought us to William Suttle's, in Prince William, thirty-five miles; and on *Tuesday* we reached William Watters's, after a ride of nearly forty miles, without food or rest, as we were disappointed at the place we had expected to get our dinner at. I had heedlessly thrown off my top-coat for a few hours, and caught cold.

Friday, 27. Our conference began in Alexandria. On *Saturday*, I preached in the new chapel. The business of conference was taken up on *Monday* and *Tuesday*, and conducted in great peace.

Maryland

On *Wednesday* we came to Georgetown, D.C., and I visited Wilson Lee, ill with a bleeding of the lungs. We lodged at Biggerly's.[20] On *Thursday* we came to Baltimore.

Monday, *May* 7. Our General Conference began.[21] What was done, the

[19] Judah's Ferry was in Powhatan County. On the other side of the James River the ferry landed near the mouth of Genito Creek in Goochland County. (See old maps.)

[20] This may have been the Baggerly family mentioned in the *Journal* on October 30, 1780. Between 1801 and 1809, John, Peter, and Tyson Baggerly were officials of the Federal Circuit.

[21] There were 107 qualified members present. Morning and afternoon business sessions of three hours each were held in Light Street Church. Of the three bishops present Asbury, Whatcoat, and Coke, the last mentioned engaged most freely in the deliberations. The *Journal* records that Whatcoat spoke once "to recommend the suppression of passion or ill will in debate," which is not the only indication of the tension that attended the revision of the *Discipline*, the question of Dr. Coke's future field of labor, the antislavery agitation, and the transfer of the "book business" from Philadelphia to New York. Although Asbury's tongue was silent, his pen was busy furnishing others with arguments to support his own views on issues before the conference. (See Asbury's letter to Daniel Hitt, January 21, 1804, and to Ezekiel Cooper

revised form of Discipline will show. There were attempts made upon the ruling eldership. We had a great talk. I talked little upon any subject; and was kept in peace. I preached but twice.

Thursday, 24. I came off to Perry Hall, on my way to Soudersburg, to meet the Philadelphia Conference. The Lord did not own the ministerial labours of the General Conference: it was a doubt if any souls were converted; I prayed for hundreds; but God did not answer my prayer.

Pennsylvania

Friday, 25. We came to Jarratt's and dined, and continued on to Benjamin Mannifold's. On the *Sabbath* we crossed the Susquehannah at M'Call's ferry, and came to Martin Boehm's. I preached at Boehm's chapel, and then came away to Soudersburg. The conference opened on *Monday morning*, 28. We had great order. We sat five days and a half. There were one hundred and twenty-five preachers present, whose characters and experiences were brought before us. I preached twice.

Saturday, *June* 2. I rode through the rain to the Valley, twenty-eight miles. On the *Sabbath day* I reached Radnor. Here my little Jane was horned by a cow, and lamed: she is done, perhaps, forever for me; but it may be all for the best. I am unwell, and the weather is bad, but, except my feelings for the poor beast, I am peaceful and resigned. I was able to write, but not to preach on the *Sabbath day*.

On *Monday morning* I desired Isaac James[22] to ride thirty miles, going and coming, and purchase me another little Jane, at eighty dollars; he did so, with great good will. I came to Philadelphia, and found that Richard Allen[23] had bought me a horse for ninety dollars; so I had two, one to sell for sixty dollars: so much for my haste.

while the conference was in session.) Asbury's appraisal three months after the adjournment of the body was as follows: "I think never did a General Conference sit longer with more ado, and do less; and, perhaps the less, the better." (See letter to Daniel Hitt postmarked Shepherds Town, Virginia, August 22, 1804; *General Conference Journals*, I, 47–69.)

[22] Dr. Isaac James (1777–1844) was born in Radnor, Pennsylvania, in a dwelling that had been occupied by three generations of his ancestry. His father's house was the first preaching place of the Methodists in Radnor. Isaac joined the church in 1790, in 1799 was licensed to exhort, and in 1801 was appointed steward of the Chester and Jonesburg Circuit. Five years later he was ordained deacon by Asbury and in 1819 was ordained elder. The great want of good medical advice in his day induced him to study medicine. He attended one course of lectures at the University of Pennsylvania but graduated at the Columbia College, New York. (Ashmead: *History of Delaware County*, *Pennsylvania*, 688.)

[23] Richard Allen, whose parents and their three other children were sold as slaves into Delaware near Dover shortly after his birth, was awakened as a result of the preaching of Freeborn Garrettson. Richard left his master, Stokely, after purchasing his and his brother's freedom, and began to preach, first in Delaware, then into New Jersey,

New Jersey

On *Tuesday* I dined at Burlington, and lodged at H. Hamilton's. *Wednesday* evening brought us to Joseph Hutchinson's; at New Brunswick we dined next day, stopping for the night with Mr. William Flatt, Rahway; and on *Friday* passed through Elizabethtown and Newark, and reached New York.

New York

Saturday, 9. Busy answering letters. On the *Sabbath* I preached in our house in John street, on Heb. x, 23–25; it was an open season.

Monday, 11. We spent some time in social conference with the preachers. To-day, Mr. Thomas Lyell[24] *spoke out* in a letter to me, saying that he wished to be located. I thought that I had discovered his designs, and those of Mr. Dashiell, during the sitting of the General Conference in Baltimore: I am willing that he should belong to the Church people: I believe they have more need of him than the Methodists have. I answered Mr. Lyell, by telling him that I would do what I could to procure him a location at the Boston Conference.

It may suffice to say that our present conference was a happy one, and a conference of great business. We had sermons every day at noon. Fourteen deacons and eight elders were ordained; these last at the Bowery church, where I preached upon 2 Tim. iv, 1–4. By hard labour I read off the stations on *Saturday* night, and our conference sat on *Monday*. We proclaimed a fast, with prayer, for the Methodists, the health of the city, the general Church, and the continent. Nicholas Snethen gave us a melting, nervous discourse on the occasion.

and in 1784 he returned to Philadelphia. In 1786 he was in St. George's Church. He was virtually the pastor, as local preacher on the Philadelphia Circuit, of the First African Church at Sixth and Lombard streets. William Colbert lodged with him during the conference of 1796 and at other times. He declared Mrs. Allen to be the best cook in the country. When the African Methodist Episcopal Church was organized in 1816, Richard Allen became its first bishop. He died in Philadelphia on March 26, 1831. (Scharf and Wescott: *History of Philadelphia*; *Autobiography* of Benjamin Rush; *Journal* of William Colbert.)

[24] Thomas Lyell was received on trial in 1791 and proceeded in the usual course through elders' orders. The notation of his name in the *Minutes* of 1804 is "withdrawn" rather than "located." Very soon after this entry by Asbury, Lyell accepted the rectorship of Christ Protestant Episcopal Church in New York City, located two blocks from the John Street Church. He succeeded Joseph Pilmoor, who returned to Philadelphia. Lyell continued as rector of Christ Church for over forty years and apparently kept up friendly contacts with Asbury and the New York Methodists, since his presence at social gatherings of later conferences in New York is noted. (Seaman, *op. cit.*, 488–89; Greenleaf: *History of the Churches in the City of New York*, 65–67; Sprague's *Annals*, *ad. loc.*)

Wednesday, 20, and the next day, I was kept by a storm within doors; at the widow Sherwood's I wrote letters.[25] I read brother Thacher's answer to Mr. Tagart's book; it is said there is a special call for learned men to the ministry; some may think so, but I presume a simple man can speak and write for simple, plain people, upon simple truths.

Friday, 22. It still continued to rain; but I felt uneasy, and came down three times to move eastward. William Thacher came home and told me Sylvester Hutchinson had brought his horse over the North River, at seven o'clock last night to accompany me. We set off, and called in our way at Mr. Sheet's: we found sister Basling sick.

Connecticut

We dined at Byram, drank tea at Stamford, and lodged with brother Absalom Day at Norwalk; the rain made the ride painful.

Saturday, 23. We rode to brother Elnathan Wheeler's, dined, and rode on to New Haven: we have a good turnpike to travel on, and a good bridge to cross the Housatonic.

Sabbath day, 24. I preached to a few souls in our small house on Heb. iii, 12–14. My chief suffering is from riding: I am under the necessity of riding soft, fearful as I am of worse effects, and my blanket makes me gall sadly; as yet I have been little affected with the piles, thanks to my good God! O, New Haven! thou seat of science and of sin! Can thy dry bones live? Lord, thou knowest! Brother Branch preached this afternoon; and brother Hutchinson[26] at night. I have little leisure to journalize. My soul has constant peace and joy, notwithstanding my labours, and trials and reproach; which I heed not, though it come, as it sometimes does, from the good, when they are not gratified in all their wishes. People unacquainted with the causes and motives of my conduct will always, more or less, judge of me improperly. Six months ago a man could write to me in the most adulatory terms, to tell me of the unshaken confidence reposed in me by preachers and people: behold, his station is changed, and certain measures are pursued which do not comport with his views and feelings: O, then I am menaced with the downfall of Methodism; and my influence, character, and reputation are all to find a grave in the ruins. First, my hill is made so strong that I shall never be moved; anon, O man, thou hidest thy face and changest thy voice, and I must be troubled, forsooth! But I am just as secure as ever, as to what man can do or say. Should this journal ever see the light, those who read it when I am gone may, perhaps, wonder that ever I should have received such letters, or

[25] See letter to Major Van Cortlandt, June 20, 1804.

[26] These persons were Thomas Branch and Sylvester Hutchinson. Both were prominent Methodist ministers in New England during the period.

had such friends: yes, gentle reader; both have been. Whom shall I believe; and whom shall I trust? Why, whom but a good, and true, and never-failing God?

On *Monday the 25th*, we took the path to Durham; here we stopped, as there was room for us in the inn to lodge. On *Tuesday* we passed through Middletown, and found that our brethren were about to purchase a lot on which to build a chapel on a small scale. We rode on to Hebron. I have made four hundred and twenty miles since I took my departure from Baltimore. At Canterbury we lodged at Captain Lyons's: the day's ride brought us through Windham and Scotland.

Friday, 29. We came through Plainfield, Sterling, Scituate, and Coventry, to Cranston; and stopped at General Lippett's.

Rhode Island

Sabbath, July 1. I preached to a few people at Lippett's chapel; my subject was 1 John i, 3–7. It was a gracious season to the speaker and the hearers. Sylvester Hutchinson, my travelling companion, gave them a sermon in the afternoon. I came this way only to hear how the preachers had conducted their work.

Monday, 2. We rode through Providence, dined five miles beyond, and housed with a Mr. Guilds.

Massachusetts

Tuesday, 3. We journeyed through Wrentham and Medfield to Needham, nearly thirty miles, without food or rest for man or beast: we passed Weston, and came into Waltham in the evening. On *Wednesday*, *Thursday*, and *Friday*, I rested; and read and wrote as my failing eyes would permit. My soul is in great peace.

Saturday, 7. A very sultry ride of twenty miles brought us to the pleasant town of Lynn. On the *Sabbath day* I preached upon 1 John iii, 1–3; the state of the society in this town is more pleasing than formerly. Peter Jayne, brought up amongst them, is an acceptable preacher. A house is begun for the preachers to live in. Sylvester Hutchinson preached in the afternoon: I spoke also; and read letters giving an account of the work in the South. O, when shall we see such things in New England!

Monday, 9. We rode to Salem, Beverly, Windham,[27] Hamilton, Ipswich, Rowley, and Newburyport, and so on to Salisbury; we had flies, mosquitoes, heat, dust, and weariness. We lodged at the sisters Eaton.

[27] Windham was the present Wenham.

New Hampshire

Passing through Seabrook, on *Tuesday*, we saw one, once of our despised order, robed in his gown, and sitting in his house like a gentleman, whilst we were beating along like Jonah: well, the *end* is all. Our route carried us through Seabrook, Hampton Falls, Exeter (where is an elegant meeting house), and Epping.

Wednesday, 11. At Epping I preached on Acts xxvi, 18, 19; we had an open time. *Thursday* brought us through Lee, Dover, and Berwick, to Alfred. On *Friday* we passed Doughty's Falls,[28] on the way to Standish, and landed at Buxton.

Saturday, 14. We opened our conference. We admitted and elected nine deacons and two elders. We had preaching on *Friday* and to-day.

Sabbath, 15. We opened by prayer and exhortation, at eight o'clock. At half after ten o'clock I took my stand in the woods, but in about forty minutes the rain fell. There were powerful exercises in the meeting house, until near six o'clock: the Lord appeared; several souls were brought under distress. I trust the fruits of this day's labour will be seen in eternity.

Monday, 16. We had preaching and the ordination in the woods; my subject was 2 Tim. iii, 1–7; it was an open time, and the work of God broke forth upon the right hand and upon the left. On *Tuesday* we hasted the work of the conference and concluded, after appointing our next session at Lynn, July 12, 1805.

Wednesday, 18. It is reported there were fifty souls converted to God: the work continued last night. This morning we took our departure; came to Lymington,[29] crossed Socco River, dined at Doctor Cochran's, and came on through Limerick to Effingham, the first town in New Hampshire, putting up for the night at Lord's tavern. On *Thursday* we passed Ossippee bridge, and came nine miles through the woods. We dined at Night's house, and kept on to Sandwich, rested awhile at William Webster's, and then pushed on to Centre lake and harbour; we had four hours of heavy rain, and rocks, hills, and dales to Chamberlain's. We started away through New Hampton, Bridgewater, and New Chester;[30] dined, and went forward to Alexander and Grafton: we felt willing to stop at deacon Hoyt's for a night. The morning found us under way over the

[28] Doughty's Falls was in North Berwick, Maine. (Atwood: *The Length and Breadth of Maine*, confirmed by the town registers of North Berwick.) There is some confusion in Asbury's account, as elsewhere, probably due to inaccurate memory after the event.

[29] Lymington was eight miles from Standish.

[30] He passed New Chester before reaching Alexandria. In 1819 Bristol was incorporated from parts of Bridgewater and Hill, which was then known as New Chester. (*State of New Hampshire Manual for the General Court*.)

Isinglass hills,[31] which furnish the windows of the country with lights; it was cold to purpose; I could have borne a third coat very well on this *July* 21*st*. We dined at Mr. Haynes's, in Canaan: at a short warning, I spoke to about fifty or sixty souls, on 1 Tim. iv, 7, 8. We came on through Enfield; upon the banks of the pond I saw the settlement of the Shakers. Poor souls!—they have landed where all other sects have landed. O this love of the world! But the Shakers are near the end of the world—they forbid to marry—they are as the angels of heaven! I came to Hanover Town, and lodged at Mr. Hall's. I have travelled, by computation, seven hundred and forty-six miles from Baltimore. O, New Hampshire, thy perpetual hills and rocks! Alas, poor people! Alas, poor suffering preachers!

Sabbath, 22. I preached in the evening at Hanover, on Phil. iii, 8, 9. On *Monday* we came on through Lebanon and Plainfield, and crossed Connecticut River into Vermont, at Hartland.[32]

Vermont

We called at Windsor, a beautiful town upon the river, of about one hundred houses. Mr. Spooner[33] entertained us with pleasure. We passed through Weathersfield and Springfield, and stopped at Rockingham, lodging with Captain Williams:[34] forty miles to-day.

Tuesday, 24. We came in haste to Westminster, to breakfast; this is another pleasant little town; it may have fifty houses. At Putney we found a stream, mills, a store, and a tavern. Passing over a slate ridge, and through Dammerston, we came to Brattleboro which we found a pleasant place, with the advantage of a stream, well employed as a mill power. At Guilford we rested with Mr. Jacobs,[35] from three o'clock in the evening until *Wednesday morning*, at five o'clock, when we took our departure from our host, and from the State of Vermont.

[31] Mica mines are located about halfway on the route from Alexandria to Hanover.

[32] Asbury crossed the ferry in North Hartland, Windsor County, Vermont, at the confluence of the Connecticut and Ottauquechee rivers.

[33] Alden Spooner was the publisher of the Vermont *Journal*, which was printed on the Stephan Daye Press, the first press imported from England. He was an eccentric man and not a church member. (Spooner: *Records of William Spooner of Plymouth, Mass. and his descendants*, I, 157–58.)

[34] This was probably Colonel Jonathan Williams, who lived at Springfield not far from Rockingham. He may have been a captain of the state militia at the time of Asbury's visit. It is said that he built the first hotel on Main Street in Springfield about 1800. (Cutter: *New England Families*, I, 119; Hubbard and Dark: *History of Springfield*, 65, 66.)

[35] This was Joseph Jacob. On Monday, June 21, 1803, Asbury refers to him again. Guilford is not far from Brattleboro, and Jacob's may have been somewhere on the road between the two towns.

Massachusetts

At Greenfield, in Massachusetts, we breakfasted, having passed Barnardston, the first village we entered in the State. We started away again to Deerfield, and Conway, and Ashfield, and Plainfield, and Commington, and Windsor, and Dalton, and Pittsfield, and Richmond, and so out of the State; but I was glad to stop fifteen miles short of Pittsfield, after riding over dreadful hills and rocks forty-five miles: we lodged at a tavern, weary,—weary enough! We took our breakfast with Robert Green, in Pittsfield. Here we crossed the head branch of the Housatonic River.

New York

Thursday, 26. We lodged at David Wager's,[36] in the State of New York. Next day we directed our course through Claverack,[37] and came in to Robert Sands's,[38] Rhinebeck, about five o'clock. My mind hath been cheerfully happy, and mostly in prayer. I was sometimes ready to wish I had no company, and no observations to make, to hinder my constant communion with God. I suffered from hunger, and was skinned several times. Since I left New York, I have spent fifteen dollars, feeding man and beast by the way; and my companions were also obliged to do so. I have seen the sufferings of our preachers, and they have awakened all my sympathies. Seventeen times we dined, fed, or supped at taverns; and well it was we had these to go to, else we had been starved. We have crossed the east and west ends of Massachusetts and New Hampshire, and have ridden about three hundred miles in the State of New York.

Saturday, 28. I preached in the chapel at Rhinebeck, on Psalm cxxvi, 3–6. It was a good beginning of the quarterly meeting. I visited the family of Freeborn Garrettson.

Sabbath, 29. We had our *feast of charity*, and the Lord's Supper followed. I preached in an orchard, upon Matt. xi, 3–6: we had about one thousand hearers. I rested at brother Garrettson's. On *Tuesday* we rode forty miles, to Oliver Ledue's, Fishkill Hook;[39] we called up the family at nine o'clock, and went to rest at half after ten o'clock.

Wednesday, August 1. We rose at five o'clock, and rode, fasting, over the rugged hills of Peekskill and Fishkill; but we were willing to walk at

[36] David Wager was a class leader in the vicinity of Lebanon, just over the state line n New York.

[37] Claverack was a village five miles east of Hudson, New York. Asbury may have tarried with the leader named Booth, whom he mentions under June 4, 1805.

[38] Robert Sands was leader of the church at Rhinebeck, and his wife was a sister to Mrs. Freeborn Garrettson and Chancellor Robert Livingston.

[39] Fishkill was a town on the east bank of the Hudson River opposite Newburgh.

times. We breakfasted with William Likly, from Aberdeen, Scotland; he has been about forty years in the New World. We came on to Esquire Kirby's,[40] and, having dined in haste, pushed on, and came, an hour in the night, to my *home* at the widow Sherwood's. We have ridden fifty miles to-day, over a path so rough and uneven we could not get along fast: this hasty work interrupts that close communion with God my soul longeth after. I have made, I judge, one thousand and fifty miles since I left Baltimore; and there still remain one thousand miles between me and Mount Gerizim, the seat of our conference for the 1st of October next. *Thursday* and *Friday* I devoted to rest, reading, writing, meditation, and prayer. On *Saturday* I came alone to New York.

Sabbath, 5. I preached at the north church, upon Matt. xvi, 24, to the end of the chapter: I felt some opening. At the old house in John street, my subject was 1 Tim. vi, 6–8. New York is the *valley of dry bones.*[41] O, Lord, I lament the deplorable state of religion in all our towns and cities.

New Jersey

Monday, 6. We crossed the river in a calm; but we were dripping by the time we came to Newark; here we rested two hours, then hastened on to Elizabethtown, dined, and kept on to Rahway: the night brought us up at Perth Amboy, with Benjamin Drake.

Tuesday, 7. We had a rainy morning. We have our ancient seasons—plentiful rains and cold weather: this will prevent the fevers. Mr Lyell has engaged with Mr. Pilmore's old congregation, at £450 a year: so, farewell to Tommy Lyell! I hope it may end well. We got as far as Joseph Hutchinson's.

Wednesday, 8. I had a sweet, solitary ride to Hulet Hancock's; the next day found me breakfasting at Burlington; and by two o'clock I had reached Henry Manly's retreat.[42]

Pennsylvania

My mind is devoted to God: I had a pensive letter from Elder John M'Casky, lamenting the death of his son:—but *one*—but only *one*—alas!

[40] Caleb Kirby was a church leader living in the vicinity of present Katonah or Mt. Kisco in the north central part of Westchester County. He gave property for an early church structure. (Scharf, *op. cit.*, I, 627.)

[41] This stricture was addressed to all the churches of the city and not to Methodism alone.

[42] This was probably on the Bristol Road above the Pennypack Creek.

I wrote to Smith,[43] Chandler,[44] and Colbert,[45] presiding elders. I preached once at St. George's, upon Luke xvii, 5; at the Academy, in the afternoon, on 1 Cor. xv, 58.

Monday, 13. I came away from the city to breakfast with sister Withy.

Delaware

I dined with Allan M'Lane, and lodged with John Hersey: forty-five miles to-day.

Maryland

Tuesday, 14. I took breakfast at North East, ordained James Cook a deacon, and came on to Perry Hall; forty-five miles to-day. I found the family of Perry Hall absent; they are gone to Bath.

Wednesday, 15. I rested, being stiff and sore. My poor beast should have had three days to perform that which she has done in two; she shall rest three days in Baltimore: thence to Mount Gerizim,[46] she will have only twenty miles a day, or less, to travel. Next day I came alone to Baltimore: here I remained.

Sabbath, 19. I preached in Light street church; my subject was Luke xiv, 25–27. At three o'clock I preached at Mr. Otterbein's, on 1 Tim. vi, 6–10; this has been an open day with me. I am inclined to think preaching must be in the lanes and streets of the cities:—I advised the preachers to go out to the churchyards; to the sisters I recommended more frequent prayer meetings. I revised the *Revised Form* of the spiritual part of our Discipline:[47] I had long wished to separate the most excellent from the excellent.

[43] James Smith, Sr., was a native of Ireland and was called "Big Jimmy" to distinguish him from Baltimore James Smith and Delaware James Smith. In 1804 he was the presiding elder of the Susquehannah District. He was expelled in 1839.

[44] William Penn Chandler was born in Charles County, Maryland, in 1764. He was converted in 1790 in St. George's Church and admitted on trial in 1797 and into full connection in 1799. In 1804 he was the presiding elder of the Delaware District.

[45] William Colbert was admitted into full connection in 1792. In 1804 he was elder of the Chesapeake District. He married Elizabeth, a daughter of Colonel Jacob Stroud, first settler of Stroudsburg, Pennsylvania. His voluminous journal is a mine of information on Methodism during the period.

[46] This is Mount Gerizim, Kentucky, where Asbury planned to go later.

[47] The recent General Conference authorized the publication of the "Discipline in one volume—in parts." Later it authorized that two thousand copies "of the first or spiritual part . . . be printed as a separate part, for the benefit of the Christian slaves in the South." This was the part that did not include the rules on slavery. (General Conference *Journal*, I, 54, 64, 65; Stevens, *op. cit.*, IV, 182–84.)

Monday, 20. I began my Western tour, bending my course up to Cornelius Howard's,[48] thence to Macklefresh's,[49] and lodged with Alexander Warfield, upon Sam's Creek: the heat was tempered in some measure by a breeze from the West. My appointment at Linganore chapel[50] was not generally known; I preached to a few, and went to dine with Ephraim Howard;[51] we reached friend Shelmerdine's in the evening.

West Virginia

Wednesday, 22. We had showers to brother Reynolds's: we passed through Sharpsburg, and lodged at Shepherdstown.[52] I was informed of a camp meeting held near Charlestown, Jefferson county, at which between sixty and seventy souls professed to be converted to God: the meeting held nine days. On *Thursday* I started, and next day breakfasted with Mrs. Gough, at Bath. I found Mr. Lyell here—his mind deeply engaged with his new design; he was very attentive to me. After resting three hours, I came away to William Dimett's.

Saturday, 25. Starting at six o'clock, I made fourteen miles to Clarke's tavern, to breakfast, through mountain rain and over mountain roads. After a long absence, I came once more to John Jacob's. From him I had the awful account of the awful end of Joseph Cromwell.[53] He had walked backward, according to his own account: three days he lost in drunkenness; three days he lay sick in darkness—no manifestations of God to his soul; and thus he died! We can only hope that God had mercy

[48] Cornelius Howard, a relative of the prominent Baltimore family of that name, is associated with the history of Stone Chapel, Pikesville, Maryland. He furnished the land upon which in 1785 the building was erected and in 1813 had a major part in adjusting the site to include a schoolhouse. In 1787 Howard was appointed a trustee of Cokesbury College and in 1807 a trustee for building the Baltimore Circuit parsonage. (See manuscript Stewards' Book, Baltimore Conference, Lovely Lane Museum, Baltimore; Smith, *op. cit.*, 211; Armstrong, *op. cit.*, 66.)

[49] This may have been Henry McElfresh who lived about two and one-half miles southeast of New Market, Frederick County. From a geographical viewpoint, however, it would seem that reference is to the Macklefresh family who lived in or near Reisterstown. David Macklefresh was licensed to preach by the Baltimore Circuit and recommended to the Baltimore Conference in 1810. John Macklefresh was licensed to exhort in 1812 and to preach in 1813. He located in 1822.

[50] The Linganore Chapel, located in Unionville, Frederick County, is a preaching place of the Washington West District, Baltimore Conference.

[51] Ephraim Howard lived about five miles east of Libertytown, Frederick County. It is probable that he operated Howard's Mill as early as 1794 on the present site of Unionville. He was the leader of a class meeting in his home in 1807. The Ephraim Howards, the Daniel Dorseys, and the Upton Sheradines lived in that community. (Sweet, *op. cit.*, IV, 78.)

[52] See letter to Daniel Hitt, August 22, 1804.

[53] See note under August 25, 1773.

on him. Compare this with what I have recorded of his labours and his faithfulness in another part of my journal. O! my soul, be warned! Brother Jacob preached his funeral sermon, and gave a brief sketch of his life, his fall, and his death. His text was, "Tell it not in Gath, publish it not in the streets of Askelon": how appropriate the choice! I have travelled through great heat: the people are generally sickly; but I have got along one hundred and sixty miles since I left Baltimore; thank the Lord, and kind friends!

Maryland

Sabbath, 26. I had a meeting at Oldtown at four o'clock: my subject was 1 Pet. v, 10; the heat for some minutes was so intense that it appeared as if flesh could scarcely bear it.

Monday, 27. After the rain, J. Jacob rode with me to Joseph Cresap's, upon the north branch of the Potomac. We crossed this water three times, and climbed over the mountain, but not without rain. Now I have left the travelling preachers to mind their own work, and I only make my appointments when I come to the places: the local preachers are my guides, and good guides, and good aids, and good companions they are.

Tuesday, 28. In Cresap's mill I preached upon Hebrews viii, 10–12. We had many people at a short warning.

Wednesday, 29. I was prevented setting out by rain. I made feeble attempts to make peace between two old members of the society: may I have the blessing, and they have the peace—for the good of their children and the society. I came to the Ten Mile house; here I overtook company—a certain Mr. Doyne. We wrought our passage to Tomlinson's, dined, and came on to Simpkins's stand.

Pennsylvania

Next day we breakfasted at the Great Crossings—William Smith's; then on we went to Mr. Slack's—brisk enough to wait upon travellers. At four o'clock we dined. Once more I was compelled to walk down the Laurel Hill. We came into Uniontown about seven o'clock, wearied by the heat and the toils of the day. Brother and sister Thornton Fleming are gone away two hundred and seventy miles to Philadelphia, in search of a cancer doctor: both her breasts are turned black, I understand, and she has a babe of six months to take with her over desperate roads and through heat scarcely supportable: dear souls, what trouble have they in the flesh! The husband is sick in the wife's diseased breast—the fond, anxious wife suffers because she is the cause of his sufferings—and O!

how are all the sympathies of nature in the parents awakened by the sufferings of the poor, solely-wearied babe!

Friday, 31. I ordained at Jacob Murphy's, Mount Braddock, William Page travelling elder.

September 1. I rested, wrote, read, and planned a little. I appointed James Hunter, who has been seven years in the work, president, *pro tempore*, of the Monongahela district, in the absence of Thornton Fleming: he is next to him in standing and reputation.

Sabbath, 2. I rode to Uniontown, and preached upon Matt. x, 37, 38; I also spoke at Murphy's barn, at four o'clock, on Jer. xxxi, 31–33.

I. The "house of Israel" the Jews—the national and Church privileges of that ancient people: the term when applied to professing Christians—their peculiar and important privileges.

II. In what characters God "writes his law upon the heart"—conviction, repentance, faith, and all the evangelical and moral virtues; "Write it in their hearts," in allusion to the "law" written upon tables of stone.

Monday, 3. I visited Colonel Isaac Meason—may it be for his good!

Tuesday, 4. I ordained Andrew Hemphill a deacon, at family prayer, at brother Murphy's. We came in company to the widow Hawthorn's: out of eight children, here are seven subjects of grace. News came after me that Bishop Whatcoat had appeared at Connellsville: as I had failed to come along by Carlisle, he thought I might be sick, or lame, or dead; and that it was time for him to bestir himself.

Wednesday, 5. I came by Bromfield and Geneva, crossed Monongahela River, and stopped with Stephen Gapen, Wayne county,[54] Pennsylvania. The wife of my host was ill, and I was obliged to prescribe: she rested better. I was greatly outdone by walking down the rugged, perpetual hills. Next day I felt stiff and sore.

October 9. After thirty-four days of afflictive illness,[55] I recommence my journal. I have been, during my sickness, at Harry Steven's; kinder souls than this family I could not wish, but there were many of them and others continually coming and going. I had two doctors: but at last was happily left to myself and Charles Conaway. The fever subsided and left a cough. I have not had a more severe attack since I have been in America: the doctor was seldom right and medicines were not to be had, nor indeed, the comfort and alleviations which surround a sick bed in the cities. But the best of all was *God was with us*—God, the glorious Lord, appeared. I was led into the visions of God; I shouted his praise.

Wednesday, 10. We took our departure and came to Mapletown. The

[54] The name "Wayne" County is an error. It should be Greene County, which was set off from Washington County, Pennsylvania, on February 9, 1796. The county was named for General Nathaniel Greene, Revolutionary hero.

[55] This seems to have been a severe recurrence of Asbury's persistent throat malady.

work of God revives. Brother Smalley's daughter has found the Lord. On *Thursday* we came to Jackson's, Carmichaeltown. *Friday* brought us to Crouch's, near Washington, and on *Saturday* we reached Philip Doddridge's.

Sabbath, 14. I preached. Riding brought on a daily fever, and an inveterate cough. Brother Whatcoat being unable to ride at a greater speed than a walk, I exchanged my mare for his horse: we made more speed by this arrangement, but his great beast jolted me in such a manner as I could not have borne in health: I was pressed above measure, so that I despaired of life, or health, or making our journey in this manner. We have lost the Kentucky Conference,[56] and have about eleven weeks for our trip of fifteen hundred miles to Charleston.

West Virginia

We were compelled to spend a week at John Beck's.

Sabbath, 21. Brother Whatcoat preached at West Liberty. From thence we rode to John McCollough's, within a mile of Ohio River: here my fever rose, and I had to quit all hopes of going to the westward: I returned to John Beck's. As I was my own doctor, I resolved to breakfast upon eight grains of ipecacuanha; this cleansed my filthy stomach, and so broke up my disease that a fever of fifty days fled. My cough, nevertheless, is very distressing at night. I have submitted to have a large grinder extracted. Should November prove favourable, I do not yet despair of getting along in time. Brother Whatcoat has been of great service to me: he was still urgent to go on, and he has gone on, wandering alone through the wilderness—I am afraid, in vain:[57] he said he had a *mite*, and it must go. I fear his precious life will go.

Tuesday, 23. My fever abated. I applied a blister, and bled again. I begin to eat and gather strength.

Saturday, 27. The weather has changed greatly—we have the Indian summer.

On the *Sabbath day* a small meeting: and what must I do—go into the woods? The eyes of the preachers were upon me—I was too weak to travel, but not to preach. We had a melting time; it was so unexpected! With some it was the *first* time: with others the *last*, perhaps, they would ever hear me in this part of the country.

[56] The Western Conference was scheduled this year for Mount Gerizim, Kentucky, on October 2. Asbury and Whatcoat were pressing toward it, intending to cross Ohio again, as they had done the year before, when Asbury's illness stopped them. The next scheduled conference was South Carolina on January 1, 1805.

[57] Whatcoat still took the western route, probably to encourage the new work in Ohio.

Pennsylvania

It was so pleasant in the afternoon, I rode down to John Casebeers, an Israelite.

Monday, 29. A summer's day. We rode twelve miles, near to Washington. Here I heard of a suit gained by the Rev. Mr. Birch against the Rev. Mr. M'Cullen: the slander was a charge of drunkenness; the damages awarded thirteen hundred dollars, costs included. On *Tuesday* we gained Joseph Taylor's, near the Old Fort. *Wednesday* we came to Uniontown, seventeen miles.

West Virginia

Thursday, November 1, to the Crossings, twenty-four miles.

Maryland

Friday to Musselman's, thirty miles: and on *Saturday* to Joseph Cresap's to breakfast, making one hundred and twenty-five miles this week: here we rested for the *Sabbath*. It is wonderful to see how Braddock's road is crowded with wagons and pack-horses carrying families and their household stuff westward—to the new State of Ohio, no doubt:[58] here is a State without slaves, and the better calculated for poor, industrious families. O highly-favoured land! I saw the death of Wilson Lee confirmed in the Frederick Gazette: he died at Walter Worthington's, in Anne Arundel county, Maryland. Wilson Lee was born near Lewistown, State of Delaware: he was of a slender habit of body, but active, diligent, and upright in his walk; a pattern of neatness in his habits and attire; and full of gentleness, meekness, and love; his presence commanded respect; his zeal for God was great, and his labours successful, and continually so; few excelled him in the duties of a presiding elder—it is not impossible that the toils of this important office have been too great for his feeble frame. He had been twenty years and ten months in the Methodist Connexion. *Sabbath day* I spoke in Cresap's mill, upon Heb. ii, 2, 3.

After sermon we rode to James Cresap's, near Old Town; notwithstanding what had passed at Cokesbury, he received me as a father—*that matter might have been managed better*. We were to have the boys to become all angels! I sent for brother Jacob and his wife: we breakfasted,

[58] Asbury rapidly returned east via the comparatively easy travel of the main road and went south across West Virginia east of the Blue Ridge. This comment on the teeming migration to the new lands characterizes Asbury's concern for the frontier.

and prayed, and rejoiced in God together. John Hesselius[59] sent me a note of invitation to call and see him: I did so. He reminded me of his respectable father, who took me to his house thirty years ago in the time of my visiting Annapolis, when I was exposed to daily reproach and contempt. I have reason to believe the old gentleman died in the Lord.

West Virginia

Monday, November 5. We forded Potomac about a mile above the south forks, and called in to see mother Pool. We came on to Capon, and lodged at Mr. Largeat's.

Tuesday, 6. We breakfasted at *Quaker* Brown's, and then came on to Winchester.

Virginia

In the evening I preached in George Reed's house; and next day in the house of Elijah Phelps. On *Thursday*, I rested and refitted. My body is in health; my soul established in grace. Sickness has been very common below the mountains, and there are many deaths.

Saturday, 10. The weather has been unpleasant; and our clothing needed improvement and increase: above all, I wished to see Daniel Hitt.[60] My friends were solicitous for my presence at the quarterly meeting at Newtown.[61] On the *Sabbath day* I preached, feebly, upon John i, 50. The Superintendent Bishop of the Methodist Church in America being reduced to two dollars, he was obliged to make his wants known.

Monday, 12. We came to Hand's ferry,[62] went on to Front Royal,[63] or Lucetown; we dined at J. Moore's, and passed over the Ridge, our route leading near the head spring of the north branch of the Rappahannock; we stopped at Justice Clark's. I came in unwell; but the well-ordered

[59] This was the son of John Hesselius, the artist, and of Mary Young Woodward. The latter's first husband was Henry Woodward. The eldest of their four daughters, Rebecca, became the wife of Philip Rogers, prominent Methodist leader in Baltimore and Anne Arundel counties. John Hesselius, Jr., was born either at "Belfield" or at "Primrose" near Annapolis. Summerfield Baldwin, Sr., and his brother, the Rev. Charles Winterfield Baldwin, who through marriage were related to Mrs. Hesselius, were leaders in the Baltimore Conference and benefactors of its institutions. (Warfield, *op. cit.*, 63, 123, 527, 528; *Maryland Historical Magazine*, VLI, 277–79; *Colonial and Revolutionary Lineages of America*, IX, 339–41.)

[60] See letters to Daniel Hitt, November 7 and 10, 1804.

[61] Newtown was the present Stephens City.

[62] Hand's Ferry was just north of Front Royal on Shenandoah River. (See old maps.)

[63] Bennett quotes Henry Smith in reference to Front Royal in 1804: "I have seldom seen so great a time of God's converting power." (*Op. cit.*, 473.)

house and its solitude, the social family and their polite attentions and great kindness, were very consoling: the old folks gave me their room and bed—I was overcome quite—my thoughts and feelings were all gratitude. On *Tuesday* we left our kind-hearted hosts, and took the path to Little Washington and Woodville towns, in Culpepper county, and met with a kind reception and good entertainment. Twenty-eight miles over rough roads, and through cold, enough to make me uncomfortable.

Wednesday, 14. We had not gone above fourteen miles, when the threatening snow began to fall: it made a heavy damp plaster for our garments: we came to Henry Fry's, Robinson River, Madison county. I felt the cold of yesterday's ride, the horses were to be shod, and it was meeting day: so I have reasons enough for resting.

Friday, 16. We rode through Orange to Louisa county: I had a comfortable interview with John Lastley, his good afflicted wife, and serious daughter. On *Saturday* we came on to Joseph Perkins's, crossing the grand branch of Pamunky, at Colonel Norris's five story new mill. The weather is exceedingly pleasant. We had a small congregation called together at a short warning: I spoke from Heb. viii, 10–12; not in vain, I hope.

Monday, 19. We rode through Goochland, crossing James River, at Cartersville—Satan's Ville, I fear—they have rejected the Gospel: Charles Hopkins is their priest—a poor wretch. He was once with us; but when I preached for a suspension of ordinances, and a partial conformity to the ancient Episcopal Church, he raised the cry of Popery: but behold! when there were Churches to supply, and money to be given, there was no Popery. I lodged with Lewis Isbett: I found kind people, and comfortable entertainment. I heard of three camp meetings in Cumberland circuit: one at Charity, one in Buckingham and one in Prince Edward; the first was greatly successful.

Tuesday, 20. We came to Robert Smith's—a very damp day. My mind was greatly engaged with God. On *Wednesday*, through deep damps, we came to David Thompson's, at the upper or west end of Powhatan county. On *Thursday*, we crossed Appomatox at Clement's bridge[64] near a mill and small town of the same name. Our route led through Amelia—solitary Amelia, with its worn-out fields of hundreds of acres, and old houses falling into ruins. We lost our way, wandering without friends or food, from seven in the morning, until seven at night: we made about forty miles, and came, fatigued and hungry to John Ryall's: here we had entertainment good enough for a president.

Friday, 23. We passed Nottoway court house, crossed at the Fall's bridge, where a Morris, owner of a mill and sawmill, finely seated on the stream, gave us food for our horses *gratis*, and unasked: we came to Zachariah Davis's, near Lunenburg court house. On *Saturday* we crossed

[64] This is the present Clementown.

Meherrin at Saffold's bridge: by accident we came to Mr. Warner's, the son-in-law of Samuel Holmes: we were hungry and faint, and the table was soon spread. On the *Sabbath day* I had a local preacher's congregation, to which I discoursed upon 1 Thess. ii, 11, 12.

Monday, 26. We came to Allen Young's: the weather was unusually sultry; my clothing was burdensome. A traveller in this *iron clime*, must feel almost all the climates in the world, with all their extremes; and he must carry with him, all the year, as many clothes as he may *possibly* want but six months of it: in November he may not need a top coat; and yet, if he is wise, he will not be without his cloak in July.

North Carolina

As *Tuesday* was pleasant, the river low, and the wind moderate, I pushed forward to Edward Taylor's, Granville county, North Carolina—twenty-six miles; here I rested to refit. At this point, Joel Smith being unwell, consented to stop, after travelling with me six hundred miles, frequently afflicted and depressed by some peculiarities of both his constitution and country: I wished him to leave me.

Thursday, 29. We came to Edmund Taylor's senior: the aged people were happy, waiting with cheerful patience for the moment which was to change this mortal for an immortal state. On *Friday* we dined at Jesse Carter's, on the banks of Neuse, and crossed the river at the Fish-dam Ford, and put up for the night with Lewis Moore.[65] Our road led us by the home of John Kinsborough, whom we visited: I was pleased to find that *the like precious faith* entailed upon the children, was now enjoyed by the children's children of those *who first trusted in God* thirty years ago.

Saturday, *December* 1. We came to Sihon Smith's, accompanied by Nathaniel Moore. I was glad to house here, and escape the rain. It is a cordial to my spirit to reflect, that although we had but one preacher on that ancient and good circuit of Tar, and that one was a young one, and esteemed by some only of moderate abilities, his labours have been signally blessed: it is true the local brethren helped faithfully; and there were some good seasons at camp meetings. My mind has great peace in God.

Sunday, 2. I preached: my subject was John i, 50. I was chilled for an hour after speaking; a fever succeeded this, and I was very ill through the night.

Monday, 3. I baptized three children of Squire Hinton's. I breakfasted with them. We rode on to the Redfield ferry, upon Haw River.[66] On *Tuesday morning* we breakfasted fourteen miles ahead, with brother

[65] Jesse Carter lived in Granville County and Lewis Moore in Wake County.
[66] The Haw River runs through Chatham County.

Reeves, at the Hickory Mountain. I ordained William Masters a deacon. I dined and lodged with him: God has blest him—his twin sons, converted at the same time, are both called to preach the Gospel. On *Wednesday*, we came away twenty miles, to Bell's house and Mills, to see Alexander M'Caine: we had a night meeting, at which I saw extravagances frequently seen among our people. I believe, nevertheless, that the young people were sincere. On our way to Wiley Harris's, we stopped at Mr. Fuller's to dine. On *Friday* I rode eight miles to breakfast with Ethelred Harris, and came on eighteen miles to John Randle's.[67] On *Saturday* I thought it well to rest. I have ridden, since leaving Baltimore, nine hundred and eighty-eight miles. At Randle's I preached upon Gal. v, 9. In the evening I visited our former brother, my friend Tomkins: he was expelled for selling a slave. The Lord is amongst the coloured people in this family. On *Monday* we lodged at Thomas Shaw's, thirty-five miles distant: his wife still lamented the loss of a dear child.

South Carolina

Tuesday, 11. We reached Lynch's Creek;[68] and next day, twenty-eight miles brought us to Camden: my friends receive me as risen from sickness —tenderly attentive. On the *Sabbath day* Alexander M'Caine[69] supplied my place; on *Friday*, *Saturday* and twice upon the *Sabbath*; this last day, I gave the sacramental discourse upon 1 Cor. vi, 19, 20. Whilst resting, I wrote some letters,[70] and received some persons who wished to converse with me upon the best of subjects. I felt as if we wanted more living religion in the society here.

Monday, 17. I came to James Rembert's, upon Black River, twenty miles. I wish I could be more solitary this week. On *Tuesday* I kept close, that I might finish the short memoirs of Nicholas Watters[71] and Tobias Gibson,[72] both deceased this year.

[67] John Randle lived in Montgomery County, North Carolina.

[68] Asbury and Whatcoat came from Anson County in North Carolina across the northwest corner of Chesterfield County, South Carolina, along a familiar route.

[69] Alexander McCaine was the presiding elder of the Salisbury, North Carolina, District, then in the Virginia Conference. (See *Minutes*.) He was a South Carolinian and was probably traveling with the two bishops.

[70] See letter to Ezekiel Cooper, Autumn, 1804.

[71] Nicholas Watters (1739–1804) was a member of the noted Methodist family of Maryland. There were seven brothers, and William and Nicholas Watters were preachers. Nicholas began preaching in 1776 and served in Maryland, Virginia, Georgia, and South Carolina. He died at Charleston on August 10, 1804. (See *Minutes*, 1805.)

[72] Tobias Gibson (1771–1804) was the founder of Methodism in Mississippi, to which he was appointed in 1800. He was born in Liberty (now Florence) County, South Carolina, and admitted to the conference in 1792. He served circuits in the area, including Holston and North Carolina, until he went to Mississippi. He died at Natchez on April 5, 1804. (See *Minutes*, 1805.)

Wednesday, 19. I preached at Rembert's chapel: we had a cold rain—it chills the people; they cannot hear to profit: my subject was 1 Thess. v, 24: "Faithful is he that calleth you, who also will do it": that is, give you entire sanctification, and persevering grace to the end.

Thursday, 20. We had snow four inches deep: I felt thankful that I had a house, and all things necessary to temporal enjoyment and comfort. Next day it cleared away; my soul is happy in God—purity of heart is my joy, and prayer my delight. I feel as if God would sanctify all the conferences in the South: O may it, in answer to my unceasing prayers, be a great time with the Lord's prophets. It is nine hundred miles from Wheeling on the Ohio, to Charleston, South Carolina: from Baltimore thither, by this route, about twelve hundred miles.

On *Thursday*, *Saturday*, and *Sabbath day*, I rested: Jonathan Jackson[73] preached at Rembert's chapel on *Monday*, and on *Tuesday*, *Christmas day*, I gave them a sermon upon Isa. ix, 6: "For unto us a child is born, unto us a son is given; and the government shall be upon his shoulders; and his name shall be called Wonderful, Counsellor, the Mighty God, the Everlasting Father, the Prince of Peace." A "child," after his human nature; a "son"—of God. "The government shall be upon his shoulders"—upon the shoulder it was that ancient temporal governors carried their badge of office. His "shoulders"—shall be strong enough for the thousands of his faithful ministers, and the millions of his faithful people in his Church militant, who shall confide in his strength. "His name shall be called"—that is, he shall in reality be what he is called. "Wonderful"—that is, a mysterious and miraculous person in his manifestations—in his birth, spiritual and holy; and in his miracles, notable, perfect, and undeniable. "Counsellor"—this may refer to his ministry—his prophetic, priestly, and kingly offices. "Mighty God"—*mighty* in the power of his grace. "The Everlasting Father"—as such, giving life, and life eternal. "Prince of Peace"—giving and preserving *peace* in his kingdom; and thus contradistinguished from temporal princes, who are so generally promoters of war.

Wednesday, 26. We set out for Charleston; the rain overtook us, and we passed Sumter court house dripping. We dined with Mr. Bradford, and pursued our journey, wet as it was: stopping at a house where we might have remained for the night, we were driven off by a drunken madman who went on like a fiend: it was dark, and we had rain above, and mud and water below; the elements appeared to be at war with us: at length Mr. Boyd saw us in our deep distress, and led us to his house, and treated us very kindly. I was wet; I was blistered; I was skinned.

[73] Jonathan Jackson was the presiding elder of the Swannanoa District in North Carolina, then included in the South Carolina Conference. (See *Minutes.*) On January 1, 1798, he presided over the South Carolina Conference in Asbury's absence. (Betts, *op. cit.*, 74.)

Thursday, 27. We came on to contend with Santee at Nelson's ferry, where I once had a *surge* with Hope Hull in company. The mud and mire were bad enough in the road, but O! the swamps! I dipped both feet, yet I came off pretty well: the water was rising; the wind blew fresh; but happily for us, James Jenkins[74] came over in a canoe and brought the flat just as we were ready. We pushed on to Mr. Herrin's, and came in before the sun disappeared.

Friday, 28. We came thirteen miles to Monk's Corner to breakfast; thence to the Ten Mile House,[75] fed our horses, and put off again and reached the city. It may go for one hundred and twenty miles from Rembert's to Charleston.

Saturday, 29. I had to rest indeed: I was sadly sore. Many letters came from various parts, which I answered. Daniel Hall[76] made me glad by his account of the Suffolk camp meeting: in four days they calculate there having been as many hundred converted to God. On the *Sabbath day* I preached at Cumberland street on John i, 50. I feel comforted in spirit: the sitting of this conference will not be in vain in Charleston. Two letters from Philadelphia announce to me that nearly one hundred souls have been converted in the different congregations since October: O, fire of the Lord, come down and consume the fire of contention in that unhappy place! I have a pleasing account also of the success of a camp meeting in New York State.

[74] James Jenkins was presiding elder of the Camden District.

[75] Ten Mile House was a tavern on the road to Charleston where persons taking produce to market could stop at less expense than in the city.

[76] Daniel Hall was presiding elder of the Norfolk District in Virginia.

1805

1805

Governor Tiffin, M.D., treats Asbury's companion Joseph Crawford

CHAPTER THIRTY-FOUR

South Carolina

Tuesday, January 1, 1805. We opened our conference.[1] I preached upon Col. iv, 5: "Walk in wisdom towards them that are without, redeeming the time." To "walk in wisdom towards them that are without" is to purchase the present and future time, both of which are in our power. The highest "wisdom" of ministers is to propound and set forth faithfully, the end and motive of thus "walking." Christians "walk in wisdom" when they earnestly seek perfection by the best and only means; and in the highest "wisdom," when in the possession of all the communicable fulness of perfect love. I preached the ordination sermon of four elders, James Crowder, Henry M. Gaines, James H. Mellard, and Hugh Porter. My body failed a little in these exercises. We had a sacrament, and some singing and tears; but for want of more and closer exhortations, there was nothing special done. The intendant of the city has forbidden our prayer meetings with the blacks before the rising sun; nor must the evening meetings be held later than nine o'clock. The preachers are seriously occupied with the work of the conference; and they are countrymen, and do not speak boldly as they ought to speak; but I believe real good has been, and will be consequent upon the sitting of this conference.

Monday, 7. I attended to the entering of the *minutes*; wrote letters; packed up our stuff for removing; received visits, and bade farewell.

Tuesday, 8. We came off early and in haste, but we were soon checked;

[1] This was the nineteenth session of the conference. The last meeting in Charleston had been in January, 1800.

the causeway was bad, and the flat at the ferry aground: we were three hours getting over. At Andrews's tavern, we had to beg and pray to be taken in for the night; aye, and pay for it too: our supper and lodging were three dollars. Next day, at a lone and slow ferry we waited some time, and lingered on the road: at seven o'clock we came in to Moses Miller's, upon Black River. On *Thursday* we crossed the bridge below Kingstree, and called upon Captain Williams, who took us in, and treated us kindly.

Friday, 11. A cold day. One night at Port's ferry, and away. We have fallen short in our calculations of reaching Lumberton on the *Sabbath day*. On *Saturday* we came up to Robert Dunham's: here brother Whatcoat thought proper to stay a night. My mind has been in great peace. In a day and a half, with lodging, food, and ferries, three of us have spent nine dollars. I will here observe, that we have admitted upon trial eighteen preachers in the Western, and eleven in the Southern, conference; and added two thousand members within the bounds of each, notwithstanding a great mortality, and the constant removal to new lands.

Sabbath, 13. We rode eleven miles to James Ford's, a stage-house, and company: we were kindly treated *gratis*: we gave them our prayers and thanks.

North Carolina

Monday, 14. We came to Mr. Lee's, dined, and came on, lodging at Lumberton, a town of about twenty families. On *Tuesday* we had another cold ride to Fayetteville. At the African meeting house, I preached upon Heb. x, 38, 39: it was a time of feeling; but eleven o'clock was no hour for some folks. I was invited to preach in the State house, but it did not suit my mind at all; the object of our visit was a Methodist congregation and society. Home is home: ours is plain, to be sure; but it is our duty to condescend to men of low estate; and therefore I felt justified in declining the polite invitation of the Rev. Mr. Flinn, to officiate in his meeting house. I must take the road again. O, what sweetness I feel as I steal along through the solitary woods! I am sometimes ready to shout aloud, and make all vocal with the praises of His grace who died, and lives, and intercedes for me. Brother Whatcoat preached at night: I added a few words, a sort of gossiping exhortation.

Thursday, 17. We crossed Cape Fear, dined at Simpson's, and after night stopped at the widow Andres's,[2] a stage house. On *Friday* we had a stormy morning; it paid us off for a time, and then cleared away. We came to Moore's creek: we were so near swimming, I dipped my heels: we stopped at Parker's, dined, and continued on to Negro Head: we had swamps and spring-tides; and behold! one of the bridges in Mr. Mellett's rice field was gone. Well for us, the overseer, one of our sheep, brought

[2] This may have been the widow of John Andres of Bladen County.

a ladder for us to walk upon, and by means of two planks laid together lengthwise, our horses passed over. We asked the housekeeper to let us stay; she consented, little thinking who we were, which, when she discovered, the poor thing was surprised and gladdened: we had a room, and prayed and talked with the blacks, and exhorted them. On *Saturday morning* we crossed North East before sunrise: we came to our own house to breakfast. Our chapel in Wilmington is elegant; sixty-six by thirty-six feet. Brother Whatcoat preached this morning.

Sabbath, 20. I preached on Titus xi, 14.[3] Brother Whatcoat spoke in the afternoon. Our enlarged house was filled with both colours.

Monday, 21. Many attended our meeting, though the weather was severe.

Tuesday, 22, we came on to Top Sail. Brother Nixon and family are preserved in the midst of disease and deaths. Dear Mrs. Campbell is gone home.

Wednesday, 23. We came to Lot Ballard's, forty-one miles. The weather was very cold in the morning, and there was so much ice in the way we could scarcely get along. Brother Whatcoat was afflicted with dysentery and bloody urine. On *Thursday* we rode sixteen miles to the widow Argate's: here is a change; the man is dead: the widow was attentive, and the blacks crowded to prayers.

Friday, 25. We reached Newbern,[4] twenty-six miles. On *Saturday* it rained: we have happily escaped it. We have made two thousand nine hundred and eighty miles since General Conference. We lodged at the widow Jones's; her dear James is gone: he appeared to be as healthy as any man in Newbern: he went off after a few days' illness, of a pleurisy in the breast. Lord, and am I yet alive!

Sabbath 27, was an awful day of cold rain: few attended the worship of God. In my zeal I preached again at night: I exposed myself, and exerted myself.

Monday, 28. We came away through a cold wind to Neuse Ferry: Swift Creek swam us: and the waters of the greater stream floated us across in a tottering canoe, the horses alongside swimming: a twenty-eight miles' ride brought us to the widow Richard's to lodge. Arrived at Tar River we found it was blowing a storm: I was unwilling to cross. The flat was nearly filled with water shortly after we put off: a boat came out to take us up: brother Whatcoat stood midleg in water; I had gained a plank and kept my feet dry; and it was well, as I had a touch of pleurisy, and had discharged blood yesterday evening; we came safe, and praised that God who in deaths oft had delivered us. Brother Whatcoat preached at Washington in the evening.

Wednesday, 30. I preached to a congregation of very unfeeling people. The blacks have no gallery. The whites look upon us with contempt. O, Washington! Washington!

[3] There are only three chapters in this book. The context does not indicate what passage this may have been.

[4] See letter to Daniel Hitt, January 26, 1805.

Thursday, 31. We came to Williamstown. I preached at brother Watts's house; my subject was Rom. v, 1–5. Roanoke was full.

Friday, February 1. We rode up to General Williams's, forty-eight miles from Washington. We must yet go sixty miles out of our way to go by Norfolk; poor men, and weary horses!

Saturday, 2. We stemmed the northwest wind, twenty miles, to cross the awful Roanoke. For a mile and a half from the ferry, the fences were swept away; during the freshet, cattle, and hogs, and some slaves, had been carried off: its proud waves were stayed when we arrived. We rode thirty-two miles to Joseph Penner's, Northampton, without seeing the inside of a house. I was most severely penetrated with cold; and my bowels were disordered. We had snow and cold on the *Sabbath day*, and we were glad to rest. The people came to meeting, and we delivered our testimony.

Monday, 4. The day was excessively cold: the icy, frozen roads endangered limbs and life itself. We kept on. At Murfreesboro we had a meeting at the house of the widow Merideth; I spoke to them from 1 Cor. v, 13–17.[5]

Virginia

Next day, at Sommerton, we had a small meeting in Hazlett's house.

Wednesday, 6. In Suffolk, at the house of Mr. Yerbury, my subject was Rev. iii, 11, 12.

Thursday, 7. I was very unwell; but we pushed on, through water, mud, and mire, to Portsmouth, where we arrived about an hour in the night.

At eleven o'clock on *Friday*, we had a meeting of the official members for business; they unanimously wished to have a stationed preacher: this was a great difficulty last year. Our chapel has been enlarged to sixty feet by thirty; I advised the addition of galleries. As I passed over the bridge to Norfolk, I examined and was pleased with it: it is more upon the Eastern plan of such improvement than any I have seen to the South; it is one thousand one hundred feet long, and thirty wide; the piles coppered to high water mark, to preserve the wood from the worm; and it has a drawbridge; the cost is said to be thirty thousand dollars, and it yields five per cent. to the company. We met the official members of the Norfolk society; here are some difficulties, and more poverty; but the work progresses here as well as at Portsmouth, where the society has grown and prospered under the care of John Potts.[6]

[5] There are only thirteen verses in chapter 5. This may have been II Cor. 5:13–17, which passage Asbury often used.

[6] John Potts was admitted into full connection in 1796 and appointed to the Stafford Circuit. For thirteen years he traveled in Virginia and Maryland, seven of these years being

Sunday, 10. I preached at Norfolk, upon Rom. xiii, 11–14: "That knowing the time," &c. Slumbering, sleeping professors are called, by the signs of the time, to "awake—to cast off the works of darkness," as they would clothes which no longer suited their characters, garments no longer appropriate to their profession, and "to put on the armour of light—the whole armour of God"; to "walk honestly," that is decently—as it becometh the true, consistent, dignified, Christian character, to avoid the sensualities of the world, and the sins and indulgences of the flesh and spirit; to "put on the Lord Jesus Christ," to be dressed, decked, adorned with Jesus Christ, and filled with his Spirit; "to make no provision for the flesh," with the intent of fulfilling its lusts. At Portsmouth I preached upon Luke iii, 6: "All flesh shall see the salvation of God":—

I. The excellencies of this salvation: it is a common salvation, a great salvation, the salvation of God.

II. The nature of this salvation: in its degrees of justification, sanctification, and glorification.

III. The present subjects of salvation—infants and believers. The ample means furnished to all, that they may *see* this salvation—faithful ministers, faithful, consistent, praying professors, and all the holy ordinances of the Church. I was greatly assisted in speaking. I warmly exhorted our friends in Norfolk to build a tabernacle in some part of the town.

Monday, 11. At Joliff's chapel I spoke on an appropriate text, from Isa. xlix, 20; the house is not half large enough. We dined at brother Denbigh's, and came on to the widow Reddick's: she and her sister are both professors.

Tuesday, 12. At Suffolk, brother Whatcoat preached a very appropriate sermon. At Murphy's the work revives; a new house is in preparation: *the place is too strait*: we must *make room for them to dwell*. My subject here was 1 Tim. ii, 3, 4.

Wednesday, 13. Brother Whatcoat preached at Joseph Moody's. God has wrought powerfully at Blunt's and Benn's: they are preparing a large house for worship at the former place. General Wells and family have returned to us: Willis Wells is coming back from following O'Kelly, besides twenty other members who had been drawn away: they profess to have had enough of him. Mr. O'Kelly has come down with great zeal, and preaches three hours at a time upon government, monarchy, and episcopacy; occasionally varying the subject by abuse of the Methodists, calling them aristocrats and Tories; a people who, if they had the power, would force the government at the sword's point. Poor man! The Methodists have but two of their very numerous society members of Congress; and until these democratic times we never had one. I question if, in all the public legislative bodies in the seventeen United States, there are more

in Virginia. He located in 1809. Asbury stayed with Potts in Manchester in 1816 just before preaching his last sermon at Richmond. (Bennett, *Memorials of Methodism in Virginia.*)

than twenty members Methodists. No; our people are a very independent people, who think for themselves; and are as apt to differ in politics (so do the preachers), and divide at the hustings, as those of any other denomination; and surely, they are not seekers of the offices of this world's profit or honour; if they were, what might they not gain in many parts of the United States? Whilst one rails at us, others, who are always fond of fishing in troubled waters, take those who are already in our net; or, hunting on forbidden ground, pick up our crippled game: see what believers their Church is composed of!

Thursday, 14. The rain held us in doubt until eleven o'clock; then we started, and about two o'clock a dreadful storm of thunder, hail, and wind overtook us, and drove us to a house for shelter; here we remained an hour, and then came on to Captain Birdsong's: it blew up excessively cold. O death! death! in the neighbourhood of Ellis's chapel, where we have held conferences too!

Friday, 15. We stopped to feed our horses at a Quaker preacher's, a friend Nixon: we would not eat ourselves, where it was not agreeable we should pray. We found the wind so cold and cutting as we made towards Petersburg, we could hardly bear up against it.

Saturday, 16. Colder still! snow in the North; five and six feet deep in New York. Ice! ice!—awful time!

Sunday, 17. Calm and cold. I preached from Rev. iii, 3–5; the people came very late, and my mind was fettered. I will here take the liberty of inserting the following account:—

A Sketch of the Labours and Travels of Ira Ellis.

In March, 1781, I left my father's house in Sussex county, Virginia, and spent some time with Leroy Cole, in Mecklenburg circuit. This spring and part of the summer I spent mostly with the preachers; and occasionally supplied some vacancies in one or two circuits. About November, I attended a quarterly meeting at Rose Creek chapel, Brunswick circuit; and from thence was sent as a travelling preacher into Mecklenburg circuit, being then about twenty years of age. In April, 1782, I attended the conference held at Ellis's chapel, Sussex circuit. From thence I received an appointment to Pittsylvania circuit, where I continued six months; the six following months I officiated in the Yadkin circuit. In the spring of 1783 the conference was again held at Ellis's chapel, and I received an appointment to Tar River circuit: after spending two quarters there, I spent the remainder of the year in Roanoke circuit. In the spring of 1784, I was stationed in Bertie circuit: six months I laboured there; one quarter in Camden; and the last quarter—excepting the time spent in attending the General Conference, in Baltimore—in Portsmouth circuit. At the conference held in April, 1785, at William Mason's, Brunswick county, I was appointed to Philadelphia circuit: here I continued nearly one year, spending one-third of the time in the city. In the spring of 1786, I was stationed in Dover circuit, in the State of Delaware, and remained one year. The next year I laboured in Kent circuit, on the eastern shore of Maryland: whilst here, I received a letter from Bishop Asbury, informing me that I was stationed for the ensuing year in the city of Charleston, South Carolina. I set out in May, and arrived there, and took my station in July, 1788: except one tour of duty, of about three months, through the district and State at large, I continued here until February, 1790. After this period I was stationed in what was called the middle or centre district of Virginia, lying between James and Rappahannock rivers: in this district I remained, and officiated as presiding elder, until the General Conference held in Baltimore, in November, 1792. James O'Kelly having then withdrawn himself from the Methodist Connexion, I was appointed to succeed him in the south district of Virginia, which station I filled until November, 1795. I then changed my state in life, and became located; and so continue to this day.

Brunswick, Virginia, IRA ELLIS.
Feb. 24, 1805.

The above-named Ira Ellis being about to travel some distance through the United States, on business, Bishop Whatcoat and myself gave him the certificate, of which this is a copy:—

To the Ministers, Members, and Friends of the Methodist Episcopal Church in the United States.

With our Christian salutations we send greeting. Grace, mercy, and peace be multiplied to you, through Jesus our Lord. We have thought it proper to recommend our beloved brother, Ira Ellis, to your pulpits and attentions. One that has travelled fourteen years, extensively, faithfully, and acceptably—nine years he has laboured locally, preserving always a good ministerial and Christian character: he hath filled the various stations among us, having exercised the offices of preacher, deacon, elder, and presiding elder. We give him the recommendation we think his standing and services have merited in our Connexion; he is going upon business of consequence to himself; he may also be as attentive as circumstances will admit to the ministry of the word of God, at all times and places where he can have a congregation. Given under our hands this 22d day of February, 1805.

Brunswick County, FRANCIS ASBURY.
Virginia. RICHARD WHATCOAT.

I desire to render to all their due. Ira Ellis is a man of quick and solid parts. I have often thought that had fortune given him the same advantages of education, he would have displayed abilities not inferior to a Jefferson or a Madison. But he has, in an eminent degree, something better than learning—he has undissembled sincerity, great modesty, deep fidelity, great ingenuity, and uncommon power of reasoning. His English schooling has been good: he is a good arithmetician, and expeditious and ready with his pen: when asked for an account of his travels, he took his pen immediately, and without a recurrence to books or papers, gave it at once; in the conferences and elsewhere, as my secretary, he has been of signal service to me. He is a good man, of most even temper, whom I never saw angry, but often in heaviness through manifold temptations: he is a good preacher too. O, may he finish his life as he hath continued it —faithful, and acceptable, and successful in the travelling and local line! Ira Ellis is married to an agreeable woman, who has made him the father of three beautiful, serious little children.

Monday, 18. We rode away to the high hills, Nottoway, and stopped with Stith Parham; on *Tuesday* we came to Robert Jones's; on *Wednesday* to Peter Pelham's; on *Thursday* to William Ruffin's; on *Friday* to Sterling Ruffin's, where I preached, and then came to Ira Ellis's. On *Saturday* brother Whatcoat preached at the Olive Branch Chapel. We visited Matthew Myrick, who was sick.

Sabbath, 24. I had a most serious talk at the Branch chapel on Rev. ii, 1–5. We lodged at E. Drumgoole's.

Monday, 25. We rode to John Seward's through the rain. William and Sterling are among the *rich*—so called: they had been deistical in their notions; but they appear to be sincere and zealous now. Bishop Coke had been made a blessing to William and his lady. We have passed through Norfolk, Nansemond, Isle of Wight, Surry, Sussex, Prince George, Brunswick, Greensville and Mecklenburg counties.

North Carolina

Tuesday, 26. We directed our course to Salem, chiefly to see sister Taylor, at Howell Taylor's:[7] she is true yoke-fellow to Sally Jones: one is gone to rest, the other, confident in God, is suffering on patiently until she is released from her load of painful affliction. On *Wednesday* we crossed Taylor's ferry, and rode twenty miles to Edmund Taylor's, the seat of the Virginia Conference: we had rain part of the way. We felt a little serious—thinking our elder children and strong sons would leave us by location; and that we should have none but old tottering men, and green, unpractised boys to take care of the plantation: but we have a great

[7] Howell Taylor lived in Warren County, North Carolina.

husbandman, Jesus, and a good God. On *Thursday* made preparations for conference.

Friday, March 1. We opened our yearly conference for Virginia, at Edmund Taylor's,[8] Granville county, North Carolina. We closed our sitting on *Friday evening* following. I have so frequently noticed the affairs of conferences, and they are so common, that I will only observe of this, that we added fourteen preachers, and located four; our business we conducted in great peace, and we had preaching as usual. Our increase is one thousand nine hundred members.

Saturday, 9. We came to John Owens's, and spent an agreeable hour. I was pleased to see sister Owens; she is the daughter of my old good friend, Daniel Grant. We took horse again, and hastened on through the warmth to Doctor R. A. Holland's, making thirty-three miles.

Sabbath, 10. I preached upon Isa. xl, 5. We had many Baptists to hear. It was an open time to me, although I was unwell. Brothers Mead and Bruce exhorted.

Monday, 11. We came away to brother Pate's; and then on to father Chapell's. We lodged with Joel Tucker.

Virginia

Tuesday, 12. We crossed Staunton River at Pannell's ferry. We called at Mr. Old's to warm and feed, and came on to lodge at Henry Brown's, having made thirty miles this day—and very cold it was.

Wednesday, 13. I rested, read, and wrote, whilst brother Mead copied letters narrative of the work of God. We have passed, since conference, Granville, Person in Carolina, and Halifax and Campbell counties in Virginia. I find that nothing so interrupts my communion with God as the cold. I cannot keep my mind fixed, when my whole system seems to be penetrated and stiffened with the cold wind. I suppose this will pass for a very long, hard winter; if the spring is backward, the harvest will be late and full. O, may there be a great harvest of souls gathered in to God!

Thursday, 14. We must needs ride to New London. I felt the cold; the wind gave me an influenza. We had a meeting in Doctor Jennings's house. I spoke on Rev. ii, 8–10.

Friday, 15. We came to Lynchburg: I did not find my body or mind, or the circumstances of the chapel, or the state of the society as I wished. We did not lose time. Brother Whatcoat spoke at night. On *Saturday* I preached upon Eph. iv, 2–6. I was very unwell on the *Sabbath day*. Brother Whatcoat preached, and administered the sacrament. At three o'clock, I was forced to duty by the wishes of the people; I spoke on 1 Cor. vi, 1.

[8] See Asbury's letter to the members of Olive Branch Chapel, March 5, 1805, and his letter to the Virginia Conference, March 8, 1805.

We had about one thousand or fifteen hundred people of the town and country: we lodged with Mr. Wyatt. I felt very willing to move along.

On *Monday* we came to Colonel Meredith's, New Glasgow: we were entertained with great friendship and Christian politeness. We were accompanied hither by Lewis Dawson, whose kind attentions it is proper I should acknowledge. The people being gathered at a short warning, brother Whatcoat gave them a sermon.

Tuesday, 19. Brother James Floyd led us along with as much attention as he would have paid to his parents. We crossed Pine Creek and Tye River, passing Amherst court house. After dining with William Breedlove, we mounted and pursued our way across the rocky ford of Rockfish: we stopped at Benjamin Paine's. God hath wrought amongst the children of these families.

Wednesday, 20. We came to Tandy Kee's; here we found more children coming to Christ. I was pleased and cheered to hear from the local preachers the great things God hath done in this circuit. Brother Mead is coming to preside, and I hope he will have a glorious camp meeting in every circuit in the district. Amherst should, by all means, have another preacher—I hear—I see—I feel. The Baptists are under the whip—straining for victory; Bedford is their stronghold. We shall see. I must be going; although I have a poor, weak, tripping beast; and if she makes a long stumble fifty times a day, I bear it patiently. My mind is in great peace: glory, glory to God!

Thursday, 21. We came to Williams's tavern; dined and passed the elegant seat of Mr. Divers; thence to Ray's ford upon the north fork of James River, called Fluvanna; thence to the north branch of Swift Run: we lodged at Mr. Fretwell's—threescore and ten, and not *born again!* wretched old man! At Stonersville, on *Friday*, we called on Doctor Douglass, formerly a travelling preacher, halted an hour, and made for the waters of Rapidan—Staunton, middle, and south branches: after scaling an arm of the ridge over to Robinson's River (flowing in three branches from the ridge), we came in to lodge with Mr. Glower, a Baptist, who was very hospitable to us. On *Saturday* we reached T. T.'s, upon Hughes's River; and thence continued on to Woodville; thence to Washington, a small town under the south mountain in the west of Culpepper county. We have made one hundred miles of these roads in three days: poor men! poor horses! We are housed with Elias Clark, Esq., near Chester Gap.

Sabbath, 24. Having taken cold in my head, I was very unwell; I was merely forced to preach at Pennell's. On *Monday* we crossed the ridge at Chester Gap, passing the head spring of the north branch of the Rappahannock River. We stopped at Front Royal or Lucetown; I preached at three o'clock; and brother Whatcoat at night. My subject was Rom. xii, 1, 2: "I beseech you, therefore, brethren, by the mercies of God, that ye present your bodies a living sacrifice, holy, acceptable to God, which is your reasonable service. And be not conformed to this world, but be ye transformed by the renewing of your mind, that ye may prove what is that good, and acceptable, and perfect will of God." It was observed, that the apostle's form of address was excellent, and particularly directed to the Christian believers—the subjects of grace. That the people of the "world" who lived in conformity to its manners and maxims, lived in their proper element—"but ye (said our Lord in addressing believers) are not of the world, as I am not of the world, because I have called you out of the world." The apostle had in view one thing, in two parts, namely: the devotion of the whole man, body and soul, to God; without which the man cannot be a Christian, perfect and entire. "Present your bodies a living sacrifice,"—this can only be done by abstaining from all things sinful in practice. We must not only not live in the use of unlawful things, but we must not indulge in the unlawful use of unlawful things: it is lawful to eat, but not to gluttony; it is lawful to drink, but not to drunkenness; it is lawful to be married, but it is unlawful for either husband or wife to idolize the other. We ought to make the faculties of our bodies subservient to the worship and service of God—our eyes to see for God; our ears to hear; our hands to be liberal; our feet to move for God, so as to do or suffer—this is "reasonable service"; and thus occupied, the "mercies of God" excite us properly, and we are "not conformed to this world." That we be "renewed in our minds"—that all the powers of the soul be given in love and service to the Lord; in conviction for indwelling sin, the repentance of believers; in sanctification; persevering grace; perfect love; and the fruition—perfect and eternal glory. We "prove the will of God" by this—to be good—to be "acceptable" to our own souls; and to be "perfect" in our Christian perfection, holiness, and happiness eternal.

Tuesday, 26. We came a rugged path to Elijah Phelps's once more. On *Wednesday* I was busy writing and fitting for conference. Front Royal contains about sixty houses, a Methodist chapel, and academy, a mill, and several stores. We lodged at James Moore's. It was very agreeable to have a home, a room, and everything comfortable for a day or two. Our poor horses needed rest too.

Saturday, 30. We came to Winchester. I ordered a room fitted for conference, with one above the other. On the *Sabbath day* I preached.[9]

Monday, April 1. We opened the Baltimore conference,[10] sitting five days in very great order and peace: on the 5th instant it rose. We had seventy-four preachers present. We had preaching day and night, and some

[9] See letter to Thomas Morrell, April 1, 1805.

[10] The conference met in an upper room in the house of George A. Reid, at the corner of Piccadilly and Braddock Streets, Winchester. Twenty-two were admitted on trial, among them Joseph Corson, whom Bennett quotes. (Bennett, *op. cit.*, 484.)

souls were converted to God. On *Saturday* we came to brother Davenport's.

At Charlestown, West Virginia, my *Sabbath day's* subject was 1 Cor. vi, 19, 20. We lodged with Mr. Key.

Maryland

On *Monday* we reached Fredericktown; on *Tuesday*, Joshua Jones's,[11] Sam's Creek; and on *Wednesday*, 10, came into Baltimore.

I have been greatly supported, but afflicted in my breast and heart; it will not last long. I have made, I calculate, three thousand eight hundred and fifty miles from the 1st of June, 1804, to the 10th of April, 1805. Lawrence M'Combs[12] had refused to take his station; after some alterations were made, he consented to go to Philadelphia. *Thursday* was occupied in writing letters, &c. On *Friday* I preached at Oldtown.

Sabbath day, I preached in Light Street: I had a very heavy congregation: I fear the people are preached to death. In the afternoon I visited the Africans: my subject was Ephes. iv, 1–6. Lord, look upon our city congregations, for they are a valley of dry bones!

Tuesday, 16. I preached at Fell's Point; it was a time to be remembered. I made my escape from Baltimore; low in religion. At Perry Hall I spent a night. The house, spacious and splendid, was newly painted, and the little grandchildren[13] were gay and playful; but I and the elders of the house felt that it was evening with us.

Thursday, 18. We came to North East, and called a meeting; the notice was short; the men were fishing.

Delaware

On *Friday* we reached Back Creek, Delaware. Very warm and dusty. My mind is in great peace. On *Saturday* I was at Duck Creek; and on

[11] Joshua Jones was listed a local preacher of the Linganore Quarterly Conference in 1803. In 1808 he was a steward of the Frederick Circuit. He died September 19, 1830, and is buried in the graveyard of the Bethel Church, near New Windsor. (Scharf: *History of Western Maryland*, II, 895; *Stewards' Book of Frederick Circuit, 1800–46*, Lovely Lane Museum, Baltimore.)

[12] Lawrence McCombs (1769–1836) failed to go to Philadelphia, and his name does not appear in the *General Minutes* for the year 1805. In 1806 he requested a location but re-entered the itinerancy in 1815, in which he continued until his death. In ability and labors this popular preacher was one of the giants of his day. Ezekiel Cooper, however, felt that McCombs was responsible for the regrettable partisan feeling in Philadelphia in 1800. (*General Minutes*, II, 492; Stevens, *op. cit.*, III, 137–40; Warriner, *op. cit.*, 128–32; Phoebus, *op. cit.*, 286–91.)

[13] These were the children of Mr. and Mrs. James Carroll. The latter was a daughter of Mr. and Mrs. Henry Dorsey Gough. (See note under August 3, 1801.)

Sunday evening I preached in Dover state house with very little life: in the morning I had an open time on 2 Cor. vi, 16–18.

Monday, 22. I rode to Milford; on *Tuesday* to Z. Hazzard's;[14] rested, and came on to Lewistown, where we called a meeting, and preached upon Rom. xiii, 11–14: I was assisted greatly and the people were engaged. We lodged at Caleb Rodney's. There may be in Lewistown one hundred and twenty houses, and about eight hundred souls. We came thence to Georgetown, the seat of the courts of justice for Sussex county; containing about forty houses. As the court was in session, we were offered the house, and desired to hold our meeting there: the judges and counsellors attended; and brother Whatcoat spoke, and I followed upon Psalm xli, 10: we had a moving season.

Maryland

Thursday, 25. We came on to Caroline; dined at Caleb Jacob's, and lodged with Thomas Foster. I was gladdened in heart to find that the work of God was progressing in this society.

On *Friday* we came to brother William Frazier's. The fierceness of the wind made Choptank impassable: we had to rest awhile; and need I had, being sore with hard service.

Saturday, 27. We crossed at Dover Ferry, and came through Gaston to Lebanon, lodging at brother William Brown's.

Sunday, 28. I preached at Lebanon chapel,[15] the neatest on this shore; my subject, Isaiah xl, 19, 20. We hasted on to Easton: brother Whatcoat preached; brother Blake gave us lodging.

Monday, 29. We rode forty-three miles through Centreville to Chestertown,[16] to meet the Philadelphia Conference.

Tuesday, 30. We rested and prepared for our work.

Saturday, May 4. On *Wednesday* last our conference began:[17] one day was occupied with the appeal of Caleb Kendall. On the *Sabbath* I was called to duty; I spoke on Luke iii, 4–6: "All flesh shall see the salvation of God."

[14] Although Z. Hazzard is unidentified, he probably was a member of the prominent Hazzard family of Broadkiln Hundred whose progenitor, Coard Hazzard, settled there about 1700. (Scharf: *History of Delaware*, II, 1256; Runk: *Biographical and Genealogical History of Delaware*, 988.)

[15] The Lebanon Chapel in Trappe, Talbot County, is mentioned as the meeting place of a quarterly meeting as early as November 4, 1804. An account of how the chapel received its name is given in the *Journal* of William Colbert, Vols. V and VI, p. 37.

[16] See Asbury's letter to the Onancock Quarterly Conference, May 7, 1805, and the letter to the trustees of the Chartered Fund, May 7, 1805.

[17] The Philadelphia Conference met in the Kent County courthouse in order that the meetinghouse might be used for preaching services. (Boehm, *op. cit.*, 121–23.)

I. The perception; the sense in which this object is seen.

II. By whom? "By all."

III. The provision made for this, and the cause of its operation. The love of God; the general atonement; the general influences of the Spirit; the number of ministers, and the general commission to "preach the Gospel to every creature"; the number of Christians and praying souls. The hinderances that obstruct the universal and efficacious spread of the Gospel; they were diabolical and human. We ordained elders Henry Boehm, James Aikins, James Polemus, John Wiltbank, Asa Smith, and Benjamin Iliff.

Wednesday, 8. The conference rose, after seven days' close labour. We had, as usual, preaching noon and night, and some souls were blessed.

Thursday, 9. We came away to Wilmington, Delaware, and lodged at Collector Allan M'Lane's.

Pennsylvania

Friday, 10. We reached Philadelphia. Eighty miles in two days. Sarah Williams has left £200 to the disposal of Bishop Whatcoat and myself; we ordered its application to the *Chartered Fund.*[18] Thank the Lord! I am happy in the midst of the murmurs of many who are disappointed because I do not meet their strange expectations: O! what a wonder if I walk officially straight, when so many would wish me to incline a little to the right or left, as their whims and fancies would lead!

Saturday, 11. I prayed, read, wrote, and conversed with friends.

Sabbath day, 12. I preached at St. George's chapel, and again in the Academy: this was a gloomy day—in weather, in the congregation, and in my mind.

Monday, 13. I preached in the new house at Kensington;[19] I had light and openings. I was continually in prayer; after breakfast, after dinner, after tea or supper. I visited Doctor Samuel Magaw: his whole system is shattered, but he has intervals of reason; and although he wants the plenitude of witness of justifying and sanctifying grace, he appears to be

[18] At the organization of the Methodist Episcopal Church in 1784, the Preachers' Fund was originated "to provide for superannuated preachers, and the widows and orphans of preachers." The Chartered Fund was established in 1796 for the "relief and support of itinerant, superannuated, and worn-out preachers of the Methodist Episcopal Church in the United States of America, their wives and children, widows and Orphans." All the stock in the Preachers' Fund was thrown into the Chartered Fund, which was incorporated in Philadelphia in 1797. (Simpson, *op. cit.*, 199.)

[19] This church was at Richmond and Marlborough streets in Philadelphia. The original Kensington Methodist Episcopal Church was founded in 1804 and has long been known as "Old Brick." It was a small edifice that was enlarged and finally torn down in 1855. The church built in 1855, which still stands on the site, was the largest building owned by the Methodists in Philadelphia at that time.

full of goodness, full of God: I felt that God was eminently with him: I had confidence and power in prayer for him.

New Jersey

We set out for the East on *Tuesday morning*, and came as far as Trenton; I was unwell with fasting and riding, so brother Whatcoat preached.

Wednesday, 15. At Kingston, fifteen miles, we fed and started, but a storm drove us into Mr. Henry Gulick's: we again set out, but I was afraid of riding in the rain, and turned in under the roof of a Cornish man by the name of John Rule.

Thursday, 16. The roads heavy and damp. We came on to New Brunswick, dined, and reached Benjamin Drake's for the night. Next day, we dined with Thomas Morrell at Elizabethtown, and lodged with Mr. Richard Leaycraft at Newark.

New York

Saturday, 18. We were in New York by eight o'clock. I felt a desire to go to the camp meeting at Mosquito Cove,[20] thirty miles from Brooklyn, on Long Island. Brother Russell took me there. On my journey I felt as if God had been, and would be, and was at camp. We arrived about nine-o'clock. The *Saturday's* exercises continued through the night until near the break of day.

Sabbath morning, 19. I preached to a multitude on Acts ii, 21 ; in the afternoon Michael Coate[21] spoke. The work went on through the whole night. Many precious souls were blessed. On *Monday night* I preached at Brooklyn. I gave them a sermon in John street church in New York on *Tuesday morning*.

Wednesday, 22. We came away to the widow Sherwood's,[22] where I preached: I had a little time to read. In this State the subjects of *succession*, *rebaptizing*, are much agitated. I will tell the world what I rest my author-

[20] This was the present Glen Cove. The camp meeting was directed by William Thacher, elder of the New York District, who the year before had organized and conducted the first camp meeting west of the Hudson River at Carmel, New York, in Putnam County. Asbury refers to this meeting in his *Journal* entry for May 28, 1805.

[21] Michael Coate (1767–1814) was born at Burlington, New Jersey, of Quaker ancestry. He was converted by the Methodists in 1794 and received on trial in 1795, serving difficult appointments in upper New York, New England, and Canada, and was elder of the West Jersey District at the time of his death. His brother, Samuel Coate, served with brilliant success for some time in Canada and then passed into almost total obscurity in England. (*General Minutes*, 1815; Wakeley, *op. cit.*, 517; Seaman, *op. cit.*, 150; Sprague's *Annals*; Barclay, *op. cit.*, I, 181 n.)

[22] See letter to Daniel Hitt, May 22, 1805.

ity upon. 1. Divine authority. 2. Seniority in America. 3. The election of the General Conference. 4. My ordination by Thomas Coke, William Philip Otterbein, German Presbyterian minister, Richard Whatcoat, and Thomas Vasey. 5. Because the signs of an apostle have been seen in me. On *Saturday* I lodged with Nicholas Fisher at the Plains. At the White Plains meeting house on the *Sabbath day* I stood up once more; my subject, 1 Cor. xv, 33, 34. We had some feeling souls to hear; but there is a call for abundantly more. Brother Whatcoat preached at four o'clock. This was a sorrowful day to me; I was in sackcloth.

Monday, 27. I called to see Elder Coleman's wife,[23] who was ill—or expected soon to be. I dined with James Hall.[24] We rejoiced that after sixteen years we were bound heavenward. We crossed Croton to Stephentown, stopping at Thomas Bailey's.[25] I preached at five o'clock.

Tuesday, 28. We made our way across the Peekskill mountains, by Gilead meeting house.[26] We came by the grand encampment where the God of glory appeared last autumn.[27] We lodged with Richard Jackson.

Wednesday, 29, was a day of rest. We called a meeting, and brother Whatcoat preached upon the *perfect law of liberty*. I exhorted. Next day, through an unusually cold north wind, we made a laborious journey to Rhinebeck. We stayed with our brother Robert Sands.

Friday, 31. I read the latter part of Mr. Wesley's Journal. How great and unceasing were his labours; how various, comprehensive, and just are his observation on men, women, modes, manners, doctrines, opinions, authors, and things! I have felt myself strongly urged to pray after every meal, where the families are in the habit of prayer; but I believe there are Methodist households that sometimes fall in my way, who never pray in this way: and is this our poor success, after eighteen years of faithful labours? God be gracious to us, and to such families and unfaithful souls!

Saturday, June 1. Reading closely.

Sunday, 2. I spoke at Rhinebeck chapel, on Joel ii, 28, 29: "It shall come to pass afterward,that I will pour out my Spirit upon all flesh; and your sons and your daughters shall prophesy, your old men shall dream dreams, your young men shall see visions; and also upon the servants and

[23] This was the wife of James Coleman, elder of New Rochelle. Coleman exerted strong religious influence upon Nathan Bangs. (Barclay, *op. cit.*, I, 180, 183.)

[24] James Hall was a leader in the church at North Castle, the present Armonk, in Westchester County. He and Caleb Kirby had built and maintained the church at North Castle despite the fact that they lived five miles to the north. (Scharf, *op. cit.*, II, 627.)

[25] The Methodist society at Stephentown had been organized by Garrettson in 1794. A church building was promptly erected, and Thomas Bailey and Samuel Wilson were among the first trustees. (*Ibid.*, 494.)

[26] Gilead meetinghouse was near present Croton Falls, on the road to Carmel via Brewster.

[27] This was at Carmel, New York, in Putnam County. (See note under May 18, 1805.)

upon the handmaids in those days will I pour out my Spirit." The preacher's mind was somewhat clouded, or he might have better shown.

I. What are the common and extraordinary operations of the Spirit.

II. The subjects of this operation—the children of God, and their children; the "servants" of God, and their servants and slaves; the "old men" of the first generation living, down to the third and fourth; "young, men," gay and forgetful; "young women," giddy and thoughtless; rich and poor.

III. The provision that is made for this—in the love of God, in the death of Christ, in the general grace of God, dispensed by men and means. Brother Whatcoat spoke in the afternoon. It was a heavy day with me; I wearied myself in vain; but my judgment is with my God.

Monday, 3. I rested and read Mr. Wesley's Journal and the last of his Life.

Tuesday, 4. We made, through heat and dust, to Gale's tavern:[28] a plentiful rain afterward drove us into Mr. Booth's, at Claverack. On *Wednesday* we dined at Kinderhook, and lodged with Burtis Goslin, Esq., at Greenbush.[29]

Thursday, 6. On our way to Stillwater, we passed Troy, Lansingburgh, and Waterford, crossing the North River upon a grand bridge. We got within a mile of the camp meeting ground. There is no great shade, nor many tents; but we expect preachers from Canada, Vermont, Massachusetts, Connecticut, New York, and New Jersey.

Friday, 7. We opened our camp meeting exercises in the pine woods at Stillwater. It continued four days and three nights. There were many people, many sermons, many prayers, many sinners, many saints, and little intermission, night or day, of labours and praises. The particulars may be printed.

Tuesday, 11. We came twenty-five miles to Ashgrove, and next day opened conference. On *Tuesday*, the 18th, the conference rose at noon. We had blessed harmony and order; and I never heard less murmuring about the stations, of which there were sixty-two upon the list, and two having no appointments, because of debility. The committee of business, and the committee of addresses, were very attentive to the affairs brought before them, and their labours were highly approved. By allowing the usual provision for the married preachers and their wives (no supplies given for the children), the conference was insolvent seventeen hundred dollars. There were about eight hundred dollars in money, and other things, given to, and given away by, the conference. We had a sacrament and love feast on the *Sabbath*, and I preached: the duty was performed by

[28] Gale's Tavern was located close to the present Clermont on Route 9, midway of the twenty-five miles between Rhinebeck and Claverack.

[29] Burtis Goslin was the town supervisor and Methodist leader at Greenbush, five miles southeast of Renssalaer.

others at other times, as usual; but there were no special marks of good done.

Wednesday, 19. We came to the Falls of Hoosick, and stopped at George Croye's. Here I preached, 1 Cor. ii, 29–31.[30]

Vermont

Thursday, 20. We came through Pownall, in Vermont, to Williamstown, the seat of the college—containing two houses, one, probably sixty by forty feet; the other, one hundred by fifty feet, four stories, of brick. We dined at brother Kinney's, near New Ashford. Thence we came away to Lanesborough, and on to Pittsfield. We have passed through a well-cultivated land of wavy, well-watered surface, roughened with rocks, and broken often enough by hills. We have had two days and nights of heat equal to that of Georgia. Some thunder showers cooled the air, and our ride yesterday was pleasant, though laborious, through Washington, Becket, and Chester, and along upon the headsprings of Agawam River, whose meanders we followed upon a turnpike road, winding amongst the hills of the Green Mountain, equal to any in the West; forty miles brought us to Westfield; and rested at Joel Farnam's.[31] Mr. Knapp[32] invited me to preach in the Congregational temple; but I refused, for sundry reasons valid to myself.

Massachusetts

Sabbath, 23. I attended at a Baptist church. My first subject was Isa. lv, 6, 7. My second Acts xxvi, 18, 19. It was hard labour indeed. I rode home with Nathaniel Phelps, in Tatham.[33] I asked an aged man at the meeting, how many souls were computed to be in the town. Four thousand, was the reply. Not one-fourth of these were at meeting. Here is room! It is a day of feeble things; and I am afraid that some of our friends, instead of boldly facing them, turn their backs upon their enemies; whilst others join

[30] There are only sixteen verses in this chapter. The text does not indicate what passage this may have been.

[31] In 1812 a Methodist class was formed in the center of the town in the house of Joel Farnum, on the corner of Main and Elm streets. Mrs. Farnum was one of the ten original members of the class. Reuben Harris and Thomas Thorpe were the preachers. (Lockwood: *Westfield and Its Historic Influences*, 234, 333.)

[32] Isaac Knapp in 1802 at the age of twenty-nine was ordained and installed as the minister of the Congregational Church of Christ and served for more than thirty years. (Lockwood, *op. cit.*, 234, 333.)

[33] Tatham was a village in what is now West Springfield, Massachusetts. (Massachusetts *Gazetteer*.)

them. Here Ralph Williston[34] was well-known—once so full of fire; and what is he now?

Connecticut

Monday, 24. We set out after mid-day—crossed Connecticut at Enfield, and came on to Ellington, housing with Doctor Steel.[35] Here the Standing Order have built a grand temple to—fame. It is feared there is not in the congregation one soul alive.

Tuesday, 25. I preached in the school house to a few men, women, and children. I went home with Mr. Ostrander[36] at the Square Ponds.[37] I believe Methodism is as low here as true religion: yet there is hope that God will visit New England, as well as every part of the continent, before long. At the Square Ponds meeting house I preached upon Rom. viii, 1, 2. It was an open season—the best time I have had in New England. Several felt. I hope it is a prelude to a revival here. I am resting, writing, and reading our Form of Discipline, and the Jews' Answer to Voltaire.

Saturday, 29. At Tolland quarterly meeting my subject was Jude 20, 21. It was a gracious time. On the *Sabbath* we had love feast and sacrament. I ordained Nathan Fox, John Norris, and James Hyde, deacons. These are some of the first fruits. Tolland revives. We had some living testimonies, and several souls are brought into the Church. At ten o'clock we went into an orchard adjoining the chapel. I spoke on Heb. viii, 10, 11. Brother Ebenezer Washburn's text was, "Blessed are they that hear the word of God, and keep it." Many exhortations followed, and prayers, with power. There was a great cry, and the meeting held without intermission until night.

Monday, *July* 1. We set out to Willington; went on to Mansfield; thence, after dining with Mr. Cyrus Dow, fifteen miles to Thompson. On *Tuesday* we passed through Douglass and Mendon and lodged with Mr. Ball, at Milford.

Massachusetts

Our *Wednesday's* ride brought us through Hopkinton,[38] Framingham, Natick (where we dined with Mr. Jameson), and on to Needham, to lodge. The last two days have brought us through heat (occasionally cooled by

[34] Ralph Williston was a Methodist preacher in the New England area for about seven years. He was then appointed to New York for two years, after which he withdrew from the church and became minister of an Episcopal church in New York.

[35] Elephalet Steele was the Congregationalist minister. (See August 12, 1793.)

[36] Daniel Ostrander was presiding elder of the New London District.

[37] Square Ponds is now Crystal Lake.

[38] Asbury once preached from a tomb in the old burying ground at Hopkinton where the Memorial Hall now stands. (Bragg, *op. cit.*, 1.)

shade) and dust, and the kindness of friends, several miles from the camp ground.

Thursday, 4. I preached at N. W. Bogle's meeting house,[39] on John viii, 30, 31. We stopped *Friday night* at Waltham. On *Saturday* we reached Boston. O heat and dust! I felt like Jonah without his gourd.

Sabbath, 7. I preached in our complete little meeting house, well-filled with hearers, from 1 Cor. v, 7, 8. It was an open time and gracious season. In the afternoon Joseph Crawford spoke upon 1 Tim. i, 15. The word of the Lord appeared to strike like sharp arrows. I feel as if Epaphras Kibby had been faithful in Boston.

Monday, 8. We took the turnpike for Lynn, passing over a bridge three-quarters of a mile long, said to have cost forty thousand dollars. It is rather a causeway, thrown over a marsh—plenty of flies and mosquitoes. I found Peter Jayne in the new house built for the accommodation of the stationed preacher at Lynn. God is moving amongst the people here; they are prepared for the conference.

Tuesday, 9. At Marblehead I spoke on Gal. iv, 20: "I desire to be present with you now, and to change my voice; for I stand in doubt of you." 1. Evangelical men, or apostolic witnesses, may feel a desire to be present with societies at particular times when it is in their power. They will, where this cannot be done, write. 2. That there may be very alarming and doubtful cases and characters in the congregation and Church; such as open sinners, hypocrites, half-awakened souls, backsliders, slothful believers. 3. Changing the voice—using a different method, as to matter and manner of preaching or writing, pointing at the cases and characters which are doubtful. We had another meeting at five o'clock, and then returned to Lynn. I received a letter from Doctor Coke, announcing to me his marraige;[40] and advising me, that he did not intend to visit America again as a visitor, but rather as a sojourner (if at all), could work be appointed him to do. Marriage is honourable in all—but to me it is a ceremony awful as death. Well may it be so, when I calculate we have lost the travelling labours of two hundred of the best men in America, or the world, by marriage and consequent location.

Friday, 12. We had a full conference. Preaching at five, at eleven, and at eight o'clock. Sitting of conference from half-past eight o'clock until eleven, in the forenoon; and from two until six o'clock, in the afternoon: we had great order, and harmony, and strict discipline withal. Sixteen deacons and eight elders were ordained.

Sabbath, 14. We held our meeting in a grove belonging to Benjamin Johnson, a beautiful and sequestered spot, though near the meeting house.

[39] "Deacon" William Bogle lived in Needham (or Weston). He and his wife, Mary, were devoted Methodists and entertained the preachers. (Clarke: *History of Needham, Massachusetts*, 259.)

[40] See Asbury's letter to Stith Mead, July 15, 1805.

My subject was 1 Thess. ii, 6–9. 1. The system of imparting the "Gospel of God"—which is preaching Christ. 2. The doctrines, privileges, precepts, and power of this "Gospel." 3. Apostolical purity of intention, disinterestedness, tempers, manners, labours, and travels. The affection of soul "imparted"—manifested—in preaching and prayer, and bowels of mercies and sympathies. There were many exhortations and much prayer; many must have felt; some were converted: from this day forth, the work of God will prosper in Lynn and its neighbourhood. On *Monday*, the labours of conference, and public religious exercises were continued. On *Tuesday evening* conference rose in great peace. On *Wednesday* I gave them a sermon, and immediately set out to Waltham, twenty miles: wind, heat, dust!

Thursday, 18. We gained Captain Nichols's,[41] Shrewsbury. Wilbraham brought us up on *Friday*. We rested with Abel Bliss on *Saturday*.

Sabbath, 21. At Wilbraham I spoke on 2 Tim. iv, 5–8: "But watch thou in all things," &c. Introduction—the special relation of a spiritual father and son. The time and circumstances peculiar to Paul and Timothy: "Watch, in all things": as a Christian; as a Christian minister or bishop; endure afflictions of mind and body, as a Christian and a minister—endure heat, cold, hunger, thirst, labour, persecution, temptations. "Do the work of an evangelist"—spread the Gospel where it is not, support it where it is. Paul knew he was going by martyrdom: he had "fought a good fight of faith"; and by faith he had "kept" justifying "faith," which some had *made shipwreck of*: the "crown" of justifying and sanctifying, and practical righteousness, was waiting to encircle his triumphant brows—a "crown" thrice radiant with the three degrees of glory. In conclusion I said many things, and with great plainness, urging the necessity of being civilized, moralized, and spiritualized, by the Gospel in the plenitude of its Divine operation. I ordained Luman Andrus an elder, and Urijah Clough to deacon's orders. After two hours' serious labour I retired.

Connecticut

Monday, 22. We came in heat to East Hartford, and lodged with Squire Elisha Pitkins. *Tuesday*, to New Haven: *Wednesday*, to Stamford: *Friday*, to Peter Bonnett's, New Rochelle.

New York

We have ridden two hundred and thirty miles in six days—some of them awfully warm. The earlier fruits and productions of the year have been

[41] Captain Joseph Nichols had moved from Westborough to Shrewsbury in 1804. (Ward: *History of Shrewsbury, Massachusetts, 1717–1829, including a Family Register*, 392. See note under September 13, 1798.)

very abundant; but without a rain, the latter fruits and grain must fail. I took a day to refit clothes, and to write letters. At four o'clock I preached at Rochelle meeting house: the subject suited the state of the town: the men were few, the women many. The Lord was present with us. I lodged under the hospitable roof of the widow Sherwood. On my road hither, I thought I saw what would make a good camp ground:[42] I wrote to the presiding elder,[43] advising him of this circumstance. I am still bent on great designs for God, for Christ, for souls. *Saturday* brought us through excessive heat and dust to New York I would say; but we were barred its entrance by proclamation, having passed through New Haven, afflicted with the yellow fever.[44] I stopped at George Suckley's.[45] Being a little unwell, I made the best use of the day I could by writing letters.

New Jersey

Monday, 29. I preached in our very neat chapel at Second River.[46] We came to Elizabethtown; and on *Tuesday* to Joseph Hutchinson's; and *Wednesday* brought us up at Burlington.

Pennsylvania

Thursday, *August* 1. We found ourselves proclaimed at Philadelphia as at New York. We directed our course to Mr. Henry Manley's seat, in the neighbourhood of the city. I received several letters, from which I learn that there was great order preserved at Duck Creek camp meeting; and that great good was done—three hundred souls were blessed! On *Saturday* I wrote letters. I redeem a day by hard riding for this service. I have bought, for one hundred dollars, a neat little Jersey wagon. On the *Sabbath day* I preached at Germantown, on Isaiah xlix, 1, 2. I returned to Mr. Manley's, and preached at five o'clock, at Mr. Manley's; this day appears to have

[42] This was a wooded area quite near the Sherwood home, in what was then called Phillips Manor rather than New Rochelle, New York.

[43] The presiding elder was William Thacher, who had conducted successful meetings at Carmel and Glen Cove, New York.

[44] Better public-health service with established quarantine now protected New York City from severe epidemics such as it had formerly had.

[45] George Suckley lived in Greenwich Village near the North River Church. This section, although rapidly growing, was not yet technically within New York City as such, and the quarantine did not apply to Asbury there. (See letter to Thornton Fleming, July 28, 1805.)

[46] Prohibited from entering New York City, Asbury crossed the Hudson River to New Jersey by the ferry operating from the foot of present Christopher Street in the Greenwich Village section.

been poorly spent. I am waiting for the minutes of conference, and my little wagon—then away to the West.

Monday, 5. I visited brothers Cook's[47] and Haskins's[48] families; and rested on *Tuesday*.

Wednesday, 7. We set out and reached Radnor. We stopped to dine with brother Gyger, and had a serious time at prayer in his new house, which they are about to move into. We lodged with Daniel Meredith, an old disciple, in the Valley. *Thursday* brought us, through heat and dust, to Soudersburg. Sick on *Friday*, and took medicine. *Saturday*, wrote a great deal.

Sunday, 11. At the chapel at Soudersburg, I preached upon 2 Thess. i, 7–10: "And to you who are troubled, rest with us," &c. 1. The sources of "trouble" to the people of God—temptation, persecution, disorderly walk and backsliding of professors, and the wretched state of sinners. 2. The present and future "rest"—first on earth, and then in glory: the cause—"the Gospel of our Lord Jesus Christ" hath been obeyed by, and hath had its full operation on, "them that believe." 3. The *revelation* "of the Lord Jesus Christ":—the characters of those whom he shall judge, and *take vengeance upon*—ungodly heathens; disobedient hearers of the Gospel. "Vengeance"—for God; for himself; for his insulted Spirit; for the ministers of Christ, and the people of God. "Punished"—their punishment to be beyond the interference of mercy: to be sufferings of body and soul; and these to be eternal. I was considerably assisted; yet I left the subject in an unfinished state, after speaking a full hour.

Monday, 12. We came off with courage, passing through Lancaster still unpropitious to Methodism: seven miles beyond, father Musselman received us with a smiling countenance, a willing hand, and ready mind. We fed, and talked, and sang, and prayed, and parted in the Lord. We crossed Anderson's ferry,[49] the best I know on the river, and came into York. I stopped a day. O! how kind our friends are, at their beautiful retreat: may friend Pentz,[50] and wife, and mother, be blessed of the Lord!

Wednesday, 14. We set out for Carlisle, but I changed my mind and my

[47] This was Alexander Cook. His daughter, Frances B. Cook, married the Rev. J. P. Durbin.

[48] This was Thomas Haskins, who was one of the original editors of Asbury's notes. His first wife, the former Martha Potts, died in 1797, and he later married Elizabeth Richards of New Jersey. He became a member of the Academy (Union) Church and later of St. Thomas Church when it was founded in 1811. (See note under December 8, 1780.)

[49] Anderson's ferry was located at the present site of Marietta, Pennsylvania. (Prowell, *op. cit.*, I, 989.)

[50] Weirich Pentz was one of the founders of the church in York in 1782. The first camp meeting was held in his grove located a short distance southwest of York. (*Ibid.*, 711.)

route to East Berlin[51]: we put up with Isaiah Haars.[52] *Thursday* brought us to Shippensburg, thirty miles. On *Friday* we bent our course towards Pittsburg, over the three mountains,[53] to John Thompson's, in Burnt Cabins Valley.[54] I have moved swiftly, but in my flight have written to five of the preachers. I walked down the mountains, which fatigued me. My soul is at peace; but I have severe trials at times. On *Saturday* we rested, refitted, read and wrote. *Sabbath day*, at Fort Littleton chapel, I spoke upon 2 Cor. iii, 12. We had a feeling, melting season. We lodged with father Ramsay—an exceeding kind people.

Monday, 19. We reached Bedford. At night we had fiddle and flute to enliven our prayers, and assist our meditations. I had but little rest. On *Tuesday* we rode sixteen miles to breakfast. We stopped at Berlin, and I gave them a sermon. *Wednesday* brought us over awful roads to Connellsville,[55] forty-two miles. We were nearly wrecked. A very serious drought prevails west and east: O, we are wicked—we are covetous! we abuse the blessings of abundance, and God in justice withholds. I am indebted to a kind Providence for my good little wagon, and my excellent and active driver—and good preacher too. I am resolved to quit this mountainous, rocky, rugged, stumpy route. It was a mercy of God we were not—men, horses, and wagon—broken in pieces; I praise God now, but I hardly had time to pray then.

The camp meeting begins, to-morrow, at Short Creek, near the Great River.[56] On *Friday* and *Saturday* we laboured onward to Short Creek: I foundered my mare; and had many trials.

Sunday, 25. I preached at the camp ground: it was a moving time. On *Monday* I preached again. It was judged there were five thousand souls present to hear; and that one hundred souls were converted to God.

[51] Berlin, now called East Berlin, located on the Conowago Creek thirteen miles west of York in Hamilton Township, Adams County, must not be confused with Berlin in Somerset County often mentioned in the *Journal*.

[52] Isaiah Haars was the first class leader of Rock Chapel. He lived one-half mile from the church and owned a scythe factory. (Carhart, *op. cit.*, 9.)

[53] The three mountains referred to are Blue Mountain, Kittatinny, and Tuscarora. This trip was made rapidly across Pennsylvania and Ohio into Kentucky, the bishop's schedule calling for him to meet the Western Conference in Kentucky on October 2. Though he mentions Pittsburgh, he did not visit it this year, taking a more direct route.

[54] Burnt Cabins received its name when the cabins of certain adventurers, who had settled on land belonging to the Indians and who had been temporarily driven from them, were burned by Conrad Weiser under the authorization of the county authorities so they could not return.

[55] This was an alternative road, turning south off Forbe's Road near Bedford, Pennsylvania, and known as "The Glade Road." It passed through Connellsville to Brownsville on the Monongahela River where it joined the National road (Route 40).

[56] This was the first camp meeting held on the original Ohio Circuit located in western Pennsylvania and the panhandle of what was then Virginia. It was the direct predecessor of the Castleman's Run Camp Ground to which it was moved in 1815. The "Great River" was the Ohio River.

I purchased a horse; and bent my course through Wheeling, on the banks of the Ohio: we crossed,[57] and in the evening came to Morristown.

Ohio

Friday brought us to Muskingum; *Saturday*, we reached John Murphy's, and on the *Sabbath* I rested with Edward Teel. Joseph Crawford is sick.[58] I have had little rest for six nights past. I have ridden, by computation, sixteen hundred and eighty miles since I left Baltimore.

Monday, September 2. I preached at Richland chapel, on 1 Peter v, 10: the subject was gracious; and so was the season. I find here the children of Methodists, according to the flesh, known elsewhere, and long ago.[59] Jonathan Jackson is married: O thou pattern of celibacy, art thou caught! Who can resist? Our married man was forty years of age: he has taken to wife a Mrs. Roberts—a poor pious widow. Joseph Crawford is very ill. I cannot go on. I have sent sixteen miles for a bottle of wine for him. We started away on *Tuesday*, and came to Judge Vanmeeter's, at the Muddy Prairie, and dined and prayed: brother Crawford still ill of a flux and fever. We stopped at Crouse's mill for the evening. Edward Tiffin's brought us up on *Wednesday*. *Thursday* and *Friday*, brother Crawford could not move on. Doctor Tiffin, the present governor of the State, administered some relief. I was happily employed in reading the Portrait of St. Paul, by the divine Fletcher. I preached at Chillicothe—we have excessive heat. My mind is in great peace.

Saturday, 7. We rode to Deer Creek, and dined with Mr. Davis. The evening found us at White Brown's.

Sunday, 8. I preached in the barn,[60] upon 1 Cor. xii, 8, 9: "My grace is sufficient for thee." A view was taken of the cases, characters, and stations the people of God might be in, and their several relations to each other, as it respected their *duty* to God, to the world, to themselves, and to their brethren. It was attempted to be shown, that in all possible situations arising out of the faithful performance of this duty, the *grace of God* was sufficient for them. The manner in which this grace is to be obtained:—by fervent prayer, three times a day, or oftener; by a diligent use of all the means, and a faithful improvement of the *grace given*.

[57] It was at this point that Asbury entered Ohio.

[58] Joseph Crawford was Asbury's appointed traveling companion.

[59] These were young people whom Asbury had known as children in Methodist homes farther east, especially in western Pennsylvania, and who had emigrated to the new state of Ohio.

[60] About 1805 White Brown erected a large barn on his farm, sixteen miles north of Chillicothe, for the purpose of providing the people a place of worship. For many years this building was used for preaching and other services, and in due time a church was built, known as Brown's Chapel. (*Ohio Archaeological and Historical Publications*, X, 205. See note under August 16, 1778.)

Monday, 9. We missed our path, and went out of our way—we intended for the falls of Paint, and went to Bullskin, twenty miles: we lodged with Michael Hains, who rode with us eleven miles. We passed Franklin, on the way to the town of Newmarket, containing eight cabins. We lodged at Ross's, and were kindly and freely entertained. The roads were heavy; but the wagon was a covering in the heavy rain. The roads were dreadful to Williamsburg, Claremont county. We had a beach swamp, mud up to the hubs, stumps as high as the wagon body, logs, trees:—after all, we came safe. *Wednesday*, we lodged with Levi Rogers—once a travelling preacher, now a physician. We were greatly outdone, but we called a meeting at Williamsburg. Brother Whatcoat preached, and I exhorted. I saw several Jersey friends. On *Thursday* we rode on to Mr. Dimmitt's, on the route to Little Miami: we have made one hundred miles in four days. I was made glad to hear of the revival of the work of God in the new settlements: the local ministry have shared in this labour with the travelling preachers. On *Friday* we came down the east branch of the Little Miami, to Judge Gatch's. On *Saturday* we rested, and I read and wrote. On the *Sabbath day* we held a meeting of four hours at Philip Gatch's:[61] brother Whatcoat's subject was, "Repent and be converted"; Joseph Crawford's, "I am not ashamed of the Gospel of Christ"; and Francis Asbury's, "I have no greater joy than this, that my children walk in the truth." We felt quickened and comforted in God. Our route on *Monday* led through Columbia, and the rich lands of the Miami. William Lives sent one to meet and invite us to his house in Cincinnati; I gave them a discourse upon, "Seek ye the Lord while he may be found," &c.

Kentucky

Next day I called on Elijah Sparks,[62] at Newport, and baptized two of his children. We dined with the widow Stephens. I rejoiced to find that a new circuit had been formed, and there were several growing societies—much of this has been effected by the faithful labours of Benjamin Edge.[63] We passed Grant's Lick, and lodged very comfortably with William

[61] Philip Gatch (1751–1835) was one of the first American-born Methodist preachers. In 1798 he emigrated to the Miami valley of southwestern Ohio where he assisted the Rev. John Kobler in planting Methodism in the region. Gatch was made a magistrate, was a delegate to the Ohio Constitutional Convention, and later was appointed a judge, serving on the bench for twenty-two years. (Stevens, *op. cit.*, IV, 145–47.)

[62] Elijah Sparks was a lawyer and a local preacher. He settled in Shelby County, Kentucky, in the Salt River Circuit but later moved to Newport. (Arnold: *Methodism in Kentucky*, I, 172, 352.)

[63] Benjamin Edge came from Ohio and had joined the conference the previous year and served the Licking Circuit, which he organized with Newport as the main center. He traveled a year with Bishop McKendree and then went to the Virginia Conference. He died at Norfolk on February 10, 1836. (*Ibid.*, I, 291, 292.)

Daniel. On *Wednesday* we reached Joshua Jones's; and next day beat along to Isaac Nevey's—here we were at home. In Kentucky we passed through Campbell, Pendleton, and Harrison counties. Our estimate is one thousand nine hundred and eighty miles from Baltimore to Mount Gerizim.

Friday, 20. We attended at White's chapel; Bishop Whatcoat and myself preached. We dined at brother White's and came through Cynthiana, the capital of Harrison county, to Jonathan Jaques's.

Saturday, 21. At Benjamin Coleman's. On the *Sabbath day*, brother Joseph Crawford and myself had a warm time of it at Mount Gerizim, where we have already held our conference twice. We both preached; we exerted ourselves greatly, and I hope there was good done. We visited Daniel Grigg. I found several of my old friends at this place—among them Colonel Barratt of Alleghany, and his wife; Mrs. Tittle, and some from Baltimore county, and the State of Delaware—and thus our people are scattered abroad; but, thank the Lord! they are still in the fold, and on their way to glory. My own soul is closer and closer united to God.

Monday, 23. I visited John Vernon, an early member of society, at Lewis Afree's, near Duck Creek, State of Delaware. I must look up our old sheep and lambs. On *Tuesday* I went to John Whitaker's, Bourbon county. Joseph Crawford preached at J. Robinson's, on *Wednesday*. I spoke upon 1 Cor. iv, 1–5: "Let a man so account of us as ministers of Christ, and stewards of the mysteries of God." "Of Christ"—for us, and Christ in us. That these "mysteries" are not subjects of reason, but revelation and inspiration—that we must believe them upon Divine testimony. The apostle was not conscious of evil, but he was not his own judge. Men are incompetent judges of what belongs to God and his Spirit; it will be found in the judgment day, that pride, covetousness, and backsliding were the probable cause of the union of heresy and schism. A divinity-doubter was present.

Thursday, 26. I visited Luke Hanson. Next day it rained, and I rested. On *Saturday* I stopped at Madox Fisher's, in Lexington. I was of necessity in our old house on the *Sabbath day*; we could not preach abroad, the weather was damp. My sermon was the echo of my text: "Cry aloud and spare not." Joseph Crawford preached twice. On *Monday* I was unwell, but I rode to Jesse Griffith's, Scott county. On *Tuesday* we rested.

Wednesday, *October* 2. We opened our conference in great peace;[64]

[64] Redford (*Methodism in Kentucky*, I, 464) says the conference met in the home of Jesse Griffith in Scott County, Kentucky. The *Minutes* of the Western Conference, however, say it met in the home of Anthony Houston in the same section, and this is confirmed by Jacob Young, who was present. Houston, who lived in a large stone house a few miles from Mount Gerizim, had two sons, William and Anthony, who were preachers. (Young: *Autobiography*, 163; Arnold, *op. cit.*, I, 295.) At this conference Jesse Head was ordained as a local deacon. Head officiated at the marriage of Thomas Lincoln and Nancy Hanks, parents of Abraham Lincoln. Detractors of Lincoln later

there were about twenty-five members present: six hours a day were steadily occupied with business. The committees of claims and of addresses did much work, and it was done well. I completed my plan for the coming year, and submitted it to the presiding elders, who suggested but two alterations; may they be for the best! On the *Sabbath day* I preached to about three thousand souls. On *Tuesday*, after the rise of conference, I rode to Lexington; and on *Wednesday* to J. S. Hoard's, Jessamine county. I was under affliction of body; but perfect love, peace within, and harmony without, healed every malady.

Our friend Job Johnson gave us a lodging on *Thursday night*; and at Rock Castle chance furnished us with another, such as it was, for *Friday night*,—but we had peace and prayer.

Saturday, 12. We took the path about five o'clock in the morning, and came eighteen miles to dinner at Mr. Freeman's.[65] We reached Johnson's, upon Richland Creek. On the *Sabbath day* we were under the necessity of moving forward slowly, to Ballinger's, where we dined. The evening brought us to Dalton's—crowded with company, but we kept good order.

Monday, 14. Our trouble began. We dined at Davis's; then came on to Jesse Dodson's. *Tuesday morning* was rainy, and the road was bad before we came to, and after we had crossed Clinch River: it was not better than it had been in its native state. Our carriage had nearly upset. I am decided to take the Cumberland path hereafter—at least, until this made and mended road—the worse, perhaps, for making and mending—is in a better condition; the turnpike takes fifty dollars a day, for having made bad worse.

Tennessee

At the Stubblefields we rested a day. We are one hundred and forty miles from Kentucky. Sure I am that nothing short of the welfare of immortal souls, and my sense of duty, could be inducement enough for me to visit the West so often: O, the roads, the hills, the rocks, the rivers, the want of water—even to drink; the time for secret prayer, hardly to be stolen, and the place scarcely to be had! My mind, nevertheless, was kept in peace: I prayed in every house I lodged in, and at almost every place I stopped at. We have heavy rains at present; and another wilderness, bad as this, yet to pass. We meet crowds of people directing their march to the

declared that his parents were never married and that Head was a fictitious character. He lived at Springfield, Kentucky, at the time of the marriage but later became the leading citizen of Harrodsburg, where there is a marker at his grave. His grandson, the Rev. E. B. Head, was for years a member of the Kentucky Conference. (Arnold, *op. cit.*, 296.)

[65] John Freeman operated a tavern a few miles south of London, Kentucky. He later moved to a larger house, which still stands, where Asbury stayed with him on October 8, 1807. (Russell Dyche, London *Sentinel Echo*.)

fertile West: their sufferings for the present are great; but they are going to present abundance, and future wealth for their children: in ten years, I think, the new State will be one of the most flourishing in the Union.

Thursday, 17. We crossed Main Holston, and came into Tennessee, and put into Colonel Conaway's, Little Nolachucky; we rested here on *Friday*. At Moses Ellis's, on *Saturday*, we saw Moses Black[66] and his wife—he about forty, and she fifteen: such are the wise contracts Methodist preachers sometimes make.

Sunday, I felt very unwell from cold taken. We passed Quorton's ferry, upon Great Nolachucky. In crossing the Paint Mountain, on *Monday*, we rode up, and walked down; and I sprained my ankle.

North Carolina

We came into North Carolina,[67] and lodged with Wm. Neilson at the Hot Springs. Next day we stopped with Wilson, in Buncombe. On *Wednesday* I breakfasted with Rev. Mr. George Newton, Presbyterian minister, a man after my own mind: we took sweet counsel together. We lodged, this evening, at Mr. William Fletcher's, Mud Creek. At Colonel Thomas's, on *Thursday*, we were kindly received, and comfortably entertained.

South Carolina

We came into South Carolina[68] on *Friday*, and lodged with Captain Edwards;[69] and on *Saturday*, at Staunton's, Staunton's ferry, Saluda River, Greensville district, we were at home.

Sabbath, 27. At Salem[70] I preached upon Hos. x, 12: "Sow to yourselves in righteousness," &c.

I. The great and glorious end of the coming of the Lord:—"to rain righteousness"—to impart his grace in all its plenitude—to give a right state of heart in justifying, sanctifying, experimental, and practical holiness. "Reap in mercy": when God gives, do you give—do all the good in your power.

[66] Moses Black was serving the Nollichucky Circuit. He was admitted to the conference in 1796 and located in 1806 but was readmitted in 1808. He died while serving Carter's Valley Circuit in Hawkins County, Tennessee, on February 10, 1809. (See *Minutes*; Price: *Holston Methodism*, II, 142.)

[67] Asbury was accompanied by Bishop Whatcoat.

[68] Asbury entered South Carolina from western North Carolina via Saluda Gap on a new toll road along the present Highway 25.

[69] Captain Edwards lived near Greenville City.

[70] Salem Church was between Staunton's and Greenville. It is still active.

II. The means of obtaining this *grace*, and the blessings consequent to its reception and improvement. "Break up your fallow ground"—seek deep conviction. "Seek the Lord"—by repentance and faith in the Lord Jesus Christ. "Rain righteousness upon you"—by justifying grace; humble, holy obedience. The end, everlasting life.

Monday, 28. We proceeded on our way to Georgia, winding along some crooked paths through Pendleton district to Eliab Moore's, upon Rocky River:[71] night came on, and we missed our way into the plantation; I walked up a hill, and called for help, and was relieved. We crossed Rocky River four times on *Tuesday*, and came to Mr. Dunlap's.[72] *Wednesday morning* we rode twenty miles for our breakfast, at Petersburg. We lodged with John Oliver; Joseph Crawford preached two evenings.

Georgia

Friday, November 1. I preached at eleven o'clock on 1 Cor. vi, 19, 20. Instead of building a small convenient house, they have bought an old house and fitted up a room for everybody: this did not please me. I have, for the first time, seen Judge Marshall's Life of Washington;[73] I have read four hundred pages in it. Critics may, for aught I know, find fault (especially on the other side of the water) with the style and general execution of this work; I like both: the early history of the country very properly precedes, and is connected with the life of the great man who has been so justly styled the father (politically) of his country. There is nothing in the work beneath the man of honour; there are no malevolent sentiments, or bitter expressions, derogatory to the character of a Christian. The author deserves credit for the pains he has taken to furnish authorities and authentic records in the notes to his work. If any author has in America, done better than Marshall, it is Belknap,[74] perhaps.

Saturday, 2. I visited Richard Easter, and Judge Tait. On the *Sabbath day* I preached at Thompson's chapel on Ezek. xxxiii, 2; it was an alarming season. Joseph Crawford spoke after me, and we then rode to Mr. Clark's, fourteen miles, and lodged. At three o'clock on *Monday* we held meeting at Mr. Mark's.

Wednesday, 6. We rode to Mr. Pope's, Oglethorpe. I preached at the new chapel; Joseph Crawford preached at General Stewart's.

Thursday, 7. I was sick, and went to bed.

[71] Moore lived between the present Anderson and Williamston.

[72] Dunlap lived near Lowndesville in Abbeville County.

[73] John Marshall's famous five-volume *Life of Washington* was published 1804–7.

[74] The Rev. Jeremy Belknap (1744–98) was the founder of the Massachusetts Historical Society and author of important historical works. His two-volume *American Biography* was published in 1794 and 1798. (*Dictionary of American Biography*, II, 147.)

Friday, 8. We came to Joshua Moore's, upon Shoulder Bone: we were benighted in the woods; the flesh fails, but my mind is in peace.

Saturday, 9. We reached Sparta. The heat was great. From Kentucky to Sparta, five hundred and sixteen miles.

Sunday, 10. I preached: my subject was 1 Pet. iv, 17. Joseph Crawford gave two sermons.

Monday, 11. We came to Matthew Harris's: and next day I preached upon 1 Cor. xi, 30, 31. We drove back to Sparta that evening. I have ridden about fifty miles to preach to about twice as many souls. I would have gone down to the state; but appointments had not been made, and brother Crawford grew very unwell, I judged it proper for him to go through a course of physic, and the weather was cold, and I wanted a coat. I only lamented that I could not see my poor black sheep at Buffalo Creek; but was glad to hear that *Ethiopia still stretched forth the hand* of faith and prayer. I feel very serious about the supplies of preachers for the South Carolina Conference: some are sick, some are settling in life—men of feeble minds. But let the Head of the Church see to his own work—it is not mine. Why should I despond? What was the work thirty-seven years ago, when there were but two local preachers—one in New York, and one in Maryland? Now there are two thousand local, and four hundred travelling preachers.

Friday, 15. We rode to Rehoboth.[75] Next day Joseph Crawford preached on—"The foundation of God standeth sure."

Sunday, 17. Joseph Crawford held forth, and I followed: my subject was 2 Pet. ii, 20, 21: "For if after they have escaped the pollutions of the world," &c.

I. The "pollutions of the world," the sins of the flesh and spirit, by which people are led captive by *the god of this world.*

II. The Gospel method of salvation, by Jesus Christ, "the way of righteousness," justifying, sanctifying, and practical, as set forth in "the holy commandments delivered unto" believers.

III. How persons may be "entangled" and overcome by heresy, schism, and sin.

IV. The last state worse than the first, because they so highly dishonour God, and wound the cause of Christ; and because of the great difficulties attending their recovery; from which causes arise the great danger of eternal perdition.

Monday, 18. At the new chapel at Warrington my subject was Mark xi, 17. Joseph Crawford followed upon Mark x, 9. Next day I preached at Cowles's iron-works.

Wednesday, 20. We reached Augusta.

Thursday, 21. I rested. I preached at Spent Creek on *Friday*.

Saturday, 23. Joseph Crawford took the pulpit. I rode twenty-five miles

[75] Rehoboth meetinghouse was in Warren County. (Smith, *op. cit.*, 67.)

on *Friday*, to preach to twenty-five souls; the appointment had not been made for me.

Sunday, 24. I preached in Augusta.

South Carolina

Monday, 25. I bore up for South Carolina and came to Barnwell court house: I was kindly entertained by Mr. Powers.

Tuesday, 26. We reached Jacob Barr's.[76]

Wednesday, 27. We reached Mr. Perry's;[77] and next day came into Charleston. From Augusta one hundred and fifty miles—heavy rides, and weary men and horses. I was under some dejection of spirits. I have lately read the Life of David Brainerd[78]—a man of my make, such a constitution, and of great labours; his religion was all gold, the purest gold. My eyes fail; I must keep them for the Bible and the conferences.

Friday, 29. Engaged in closest exercises. I do not find matters as I wish: one preacher has deserted his station; and there are contentions amongst the Africans.

Saturday, 30. My soul is deeply oppressed with a heavy sea of troubles.

Sunday, *December* 1. "Still heavy in my heart; still sink my spirits down." At Cumberland street church I spoke upon Rev. vii, 13–17. My two general heads were—

I. The gracious, although afflicted state of God's people in this world.

II. The glorious state of the righteous in heaven.

Our lower floor was nearly filled with communicants, white and black. Do they all indeed "discern the Lord's body?" It will never do for me to record all I fear, hear, and think. At Bethel church I took for my text Rom. xii, 9–12. I observed that the text contained evangelical Christian duties, privileges, promises, and marks, by which we might judge of ourselves as Christians. That if these marks, and this experience, were not upon us and in us, we could not be Christians. Within twenty years I have visited this place, going and returning, at least thirty times.

Saturday, 7. Since *Monday*, amongst other occupations, I have been employed in reading a thousand pages of Mr. Atmore's Memorial,[79] and

[76] Colonel Jacob Barr lived in Orangeburg County.

[77] Perry lived on Cypress Swamp in Dorchester County, near Rubyville.

[78] John Wesley published *An Extract of the Life of the Late Rev. Mr. David Brainerd, Missionary to the Indians* in 1768. There were other editions in 1771, 1793, and 1800. It was really an autobiography edited by Jonathan Edwards, and Wesley added little or nothing of his own. It was probably this publication which Asbury read.

[79] Charles Atmore, a British preacher, in 1802 published a work called *Methodist Memorial*. In the introduction to the appendix he mentioned the remarkable growth of Methodism in America.

Mr. Wesley's Journal: these books suit me best—I see there the rise and progress of Methodism.

I met the members of society, white and black, in small companies in our own house. I gave my advice as to temporals. I recommended the painting of the new, and the enlargement of the old church to eighty feet by forty; to enlarge the preacher's house,[80] and to buy another burying ground. Besides praying regularly after every meal in our own house, I am obliged to go through this exercise many times, daily, with the poor Negroes. I feel that I want to go hence, but not until my God and Guide gives me liberty. I wait to know his will about going to Georgetown, two hundred and thirty miles, before Camden Conference. I wrote a letter to Mr. Atmore, advising of affairs of society and of my own; and counselled him to pursue the good work he is engaged in, and bend all his strength to the Memorial.

Sunday, 8. I was in great heaviness through manifold temptations; yet I preached in Cumberland street in the morning and at Bethel in the afternoon. I was happy, and had great openings. I fear, sometimes, that my commission will wear out amongst one description of people here. Religion of a certain kind must be very valuable, since we spend so much to support it. There must be a prodigious revival in the Independent society[81]—a building of theirs will cost fifty, or, perhaps, one hundred thousand dollars: there is a holy strife between its members and the Episcopalians, who shall have the highest steeple; but I believe there is no contention about who shall have the most souls converted to God.

Monday, 9. Reading and receiving all visitors who came to our house, with counsel and prayer, from room to room, with white and black.

Tuesday, 10. We have goodly weather. God, by his Spirit and his providences, tells us we must set out to-morrow for Georgetown. I doubt if in Charleston we have joined more than one hundred and seventy-eight members of the fair skin in twenty years; and seldom are there more than fifty or sixty annually returned: death, desertion, backsliding: poor fickle souls, unstable as water, light as air, bodies and minds!

Wednesday, 11. We rode to Monk's Corner, and lodged at Mr. Hatchett's.

Thursday, 12. We pursued a blind road to the ferry. We came on to Murray's,[82] and continued along to Mr. Coleman's,[83] a German. Next day

[80] Asbury lodged in the Bethel parsonage while in Charleston. (Betts, *op. cit.*, 112.)

[81] The Independent society was the Circular Congregational Church or the "white meeting house" which Asbury attended on his first visit to Charleston in 1785. (Shipp, *op. cit.*, 164. See note under February 24, 1785.)

[82] Murray's ferry across the Santee was five miles north of St. Stephen. "At James Guerry's near Murray's Ferry the Guerrys, Muchats, Remberts, and several other Huguenot families had fled the persecution and found a safe retreat on the Santee, called the French settlement. At first fervent in religion they declined, the talk about indigo being more common than about religion when they met at church. John Guerry's

we reached Rembert Hall. We had hot weather—man and beast felt the burden.

Some of my northern letters have come in: they bring good news; camp meetings at Albany, New York; at Lebanon, Vermont; in the New Hampshire districts; all successful. But O, the wonders of Doctor Chandler's report![84] He says his authority bids him say, that at Duck Creek camp meeting five hundred souls; at Accomack camp meeting four hundred; at Annamessex chapel, in the woods, two hundred; at Somerset, Line chapel, one hundred and twenty; at Todd's chapel, Dorset, two hundred; at Caroline quarterly meeting, seventy-five; all, all these profess to have received converting grace!

Saturday, 14. I committed the remains of Abijah Rembert[85] to the dust. He was sixty-two years of age, the last sixteen years of which he had been a member of society. He was visited by, and greatly blessed under, the word at camp meeting: in his last illness, he was patient, happy, and confident: he died in the Lord. I was unwell on the *Sabbath day*; but wrote a long letter to Freeborn Garrettson. My soul greatly rejoiceth in the Lord, and exults in the prosperity of Zion. Brother Crawford preached in the morning, and I lectured in the evening in Rembert Hall. On *Monday* I wrote to elders Brodhead[86] and Chandler. This week writing letters and reading Haweis's Church History. By this work I learn it is the author's opinion, that the evangelists were chief, superintending, episcopal men: aye, so say I; and that they prescribed forms of discipline, and systematized codes of doctrine. After the death of the apostles, it would appear that the elders elected the most excellent men to superintend: this course was doubtless the most expedient and excellent. Every candid inquirer after truth will acknowledge, upon reading Church history, that it was a great and serious evil introduced, when philosophy and human learning were taught as a preparation for a Gospel ministry. "Hitherto," says our author, in his observations on the close of the second century, "not a man of eminence for science or letters, had appeared in the Church; all of this time, whose works have come down to us, give thereby no evidence of human attainments—they bear the stamp of simplicity." Yet by these the Gospel had been supported in its purity, spreading it by their labours to the ends of the earth; and these were they who helped to fill the bloody ranks of the noble army of martyrs.

father lamented this and was satisfied that the Methodists had the life and power of godliness. Nearly all the descendants of the above-named persons became Methodists." (Chreitzburg, *op. cit.*, 81, 82; Betts, *op. cit.*, 107.)

[83] Coleman lived between Greeleyville and Manning.

[84] William P. Chandler was the presiding elder of the Delaware District in the Philadelphia Conference, and the circuits mentioned were in his district. (See *Minutes.*)

[85] Abijah Rembert was the father of Colonel James E. Rembert.

[86] John Brodhead was the presiding elder of the New Hampshire District in the New England Conference. (See *Minutes.*)

On the *Sabbath day* I preached a funeral sermon for Abijah Rembert. There is a revival in the society here; so much for camp meetings. I am now in the fortieth year of my labours in the ministry: thirty-four years of this time have been spent in America, counting from October 28, 1771, to October 28, 1805.

On the *Christmas day* I preached at Rembert's chapel: my subject, 1 Tim. iii, 16: "Without controversy, great is the mystery of godliness," &c.

I. I gave a pastoral introduction.

II. A brief explanation of godliness—the knowledge of God in Christ Jesus; confidence in God; love to Him; fear of offending Him. To this were added a few thoughts on the six cases in the text. It was not a pleasant season: *Christmas day* is the worst in the whole year on which to preach Christ; at least to me.

George Dougherty[87] informs me that the wife of John Randle, upon Pee Dee (known by the name of dumb John), died in great peace and joy, after a thirty years' profession of religion amongst the Baptists and Methodists: safe anchorage; clear gains! But I have similar accounts from various parts; my soul triumphs in the triumphant deaths of these saints. Glory be to God!

Thursday, 26. I rested and read; and on *Friday* rode into Camden. I was favoured with a number of letters giving accounts of revivals of religion. *Saturday* employed my pen. *Sabbath day* I preached.

Monday, 30. We opened our conference.

[87] George Dougherty was the presiding elder of the Camden District.

1806

1806

Asbury at the graves of Methodists at Sharptown, New Jersey

CHAPTER THIRTY-FIVE

South Carolina

January 4, 1806. We closed our conference in great peace and order: no murmurs about the stations from preachers or people.[1] Since we came here we have had twenty-six sermons; one of which I preached upon 1 Tim. iv, 12: "Let no man despise thy youth." Brother Whatcoat ordained the deacons. We see no immediate fruit of our labours; but doubtless we shall hear of it, following our many prayers night and day.

Monday, 6. Seven of us came away in company to Mr. Evans's, Lynch's Creek; and next day I parted from brother William M'Kendree, bending my course to Jerningham's, in Anson county, North Carolina.

North Carolina

On *Wednesday* we crossed Well's ferry after waiting an hour: a snow-storm kept with us from Pee Dee to Rockingham; here the people would have assembled, but there was a wedding afoot; this is a matter of moment, as some men have but one during life, and some find that one to have been one too many.

On *Thursday* a cold, cold ride of twenty miles without stopping, was as

[1] This was the twentieth session of the South Carolina Conference. Lovick Pierce and his brother, Reddick, were among those admitted; the former became a notable preacher, and his son was Bishop George F. Pierce.

much as we could well bear; after warming we took the road again, and came to Smith's, twelve miles. This week we have had heat for the first of June; and cold and snow for January.

On *Friday* we reached Fayetteville; putting up with John Lumsden, near the African church. I felt that I had taken a deep cold. I was busy on *Saturday* in answering letters. Joseph Crawford, that he might not be idle, preached to the Africans in the evenings.

Sabbath day, 12. Unwell; nevertheless, I took the pulpit.

Monday morning, we made a start for Wilmington, and came to the widow Anderson's, forty-six miles. Next day we took the round-about way by the bridges, and made forty-five miles: to ride ninety-one miles within day-light, in two days, kept us busy; but we are safe in Wilmington. My affliction upon my breast was great.

Wednesday, 15. We rest. It is very cold; ice in the tubs.

Sabbath day, 19. I preached on that great subject, Coloss. i, 27, 28; we had about fifteen hundred hearers in our house of worship, sixty-six by thirty-three feet, galleried all around. There may be five thousand souls in Wilmington; one fourth of which number, it may be, were present. Joseph Crawford preached in the afternoon and at night. I gave order for the completion of the tabernacle and dwelling-house, according to the charge left me by William Meredith.

Monday, 20. On our way to Newbern we stopped with Mr. Nixon, at Topsail: his house and heart are always open to the faithful ministers of Christ. I have been greatly afflicted with cold, but exceedingly happy in God—I live in love.

On *Tuesday* we had a solitary ride to Lot Ballard's, New River. Hail, prosperity! the chapel shaded; a revival amongst white and black: Lot lives in Jerusalem.

Wednesday, 22. A heavy storm of rain. I rode to Eli Perry's, son of John; here is a son of faith and prayer; I walked with his dear good father —now, I trust, in the paradise of God. I met elder Bruce; all our talk is, What hath God wrought! In Beaufort the Lord hath put forth his power: the whole town seems disposed to bow to the sceptre of the Lord Jesus, after being left and visited again, within the last twenty years, by his faithful ministers.

Thursday, 23. We came into Newbern, twenty-three miles. The prospects here are good. The providence of God was manifested in our preservation to-day. Our horses took fright whilst in the wagon, and went off like fire: they happily struck, and locked a wheel on a poplar; the swingle-tree snapped, no more: less damage, if any, could scarcely have been done.

Saturday, 25. I have read the Jewish Antiquities. I have read Mungo Park's Travels in Africa.[2] Certain parts are so extraordinary, that it

[2] Mungo Park (1771–1806), who secured his surgical diploma at Edinburgh and distinguished himself by his application to botanical science, was sent by the Africa

appeared like a romance. If true, he experienced astonishing hardships. It would seem by this narrative, that the Africans are in a state so wretched, that any sufferings with the Gospel, would be submitted to in preference. But I have my doubts.

Sabbath day, 26. I preached upon Heb. x, 37–39. It was a time and a testimony that was felt.

Monday, 27. It is as pleasant as May: the rivers are very low. We came with great ease to Washington, and lodged one night. Joseph Crawford did not let that awful town go unwarned.

On *Tuesday* we took the road and came to James Williams's, on Tranter's Creek. Griffith Floyd died in the Lord a few days ago. He was a man of affliction, and a man of God—but not a preacher. At the new chapel, I spoke on *Wednesday*, on 1 Peter iii, 14. I was very warm, upon death, the resurrection, judgment, and glory. I visited brother Knowis, and saw sister Hinton and the widow Williams,—on their way to glory.

Thursday, 30. We came very pleasantly to Williamstown. I was afflicted with a severe pain in my foot. On *Friday* I was busy planning; but in pain.

Saturday, *February* 1. We came twenty miles to the widow Williams's, near Taylor's ferry. On the *Sabbath* I preached on Acts xvii, 30, 31: "Now he commandeth all men everywhere to repent."

I. The nature of repentance—the whole of religion.

II. The universality of repentance—all orders, stations, characters, must *repent*.

III. The possibility of, and the provision made for, repentance,—the gift of Christ—the death of Christ—the agency of the Spirit—the preaching of the Gospel—the means of grace.

IV. Necessity of repentance—from the considerations of the fall and our own actual transgressions, a future state and general judgment.

V. The time for repentance—*now*—this Gospel day of grace.

Monday, 3. We lodged at B. Pinner's, on the east side of Roanoke, Northampton county.

Tuesday, 4. We lodged at the widow Meredith's, in Murfreesboro. We crossed Manney's Ferry next day, and came to the widow Baker's, Knotty Pine.

Thursday, 6. I preached at Daniel Southall's, Gates court house: my subject was Rev. iii, 5. I was pleased to see so many come out upon so short a notice; may they overcome! From Camden to Gates court house I compute four hundred and eighty miles.

Friday, 7. We came to Edenton. At Joshua Manning's. *Saturday*, rested, and read, and wrote. I begin to prepare my mind and my papers for the

Association in 1795 to discover the rise and termination of the River Niger. The story of his African travels was a much-read book and was translated into both French and German a year after its publication in English. (*Dictionary of National Biography*, XV, 218–21.)

conference. On the *Sabbath* I preached in the court house, upon 2 Cor. v, 20.

Monday, 10. We started and came rapidly along, calling to see Martin Ross, a Baptist minister, by the way. We lodged with Colonel Hamilton, Elizabeth city.

Virginia

On *Tuesday* we reached James Wilson's, Northwest Woods, Norfolk county. It takes many jolts to ride one hundred miles over rough roads, in two days and a half. I called upon John Hodges: I feel seriously for his soul's welfare. I saw the grave of sister Wilson: these were profitable visits to me.

Friday, 14. Virginia Conference began in Norfolk; progressed peaceably, and ended on *Thursday*. One member opposed all petitions from the people for conference sittings: he also condemned all epistles from the sister conferences, as being too long and pompous, and as likely to make innovations. He dictated an epistle himself by way of sample, to show how epistles ought to be written: the committee of addresses wrote one too; but it was rejected, as being too much like that of the objecting member, whose epistle was rejected as being too much like himself: the conference voted that none should be sent. Strange, that such an affair should occupy the time of so many good men! Religion will do great things; but it does not make Solomons.

We had preaching morn, noon, and night; large congregations, and many souls engaged. We have reason to hope that nearly one hundred souls were under the operations of grace. I ordained two elders, and brother Whatcoat twelve deacons.

We have a rich supply of preachers for every circuit; and an addition of two thousand three hundred and ninety-eight in numbers, exclusive of the dead, expelled, withdrawn, and removed.

Friday, 21. We came away to Suffolk; next day came to General Wells's, Isle of Wight.[3] On *Sunday*, at Blunt's chapel, I spoke on Heb. xiii, 13. It was not a great meeting. I have not had a good night's rest until last night, for the last twenty days; during the sitting of conference, five hours were as much as I could get in the twenty-four. I feel happy in God continually.

Monday, 24. We came to Bernard Major's, Surry county: on *Tuesday* to Petersburg; and *Wednesday* to Richmond: I had no time to preach, but Joseph Crawford gave them a sermon in each place. On *Thursday* we left the capital, and came on to Lyon's, Caroline; on *Friday* got to Fredericksburg.

Saturday, *March* 1. We rode to brother Samford's, Pohick, within

[3] See letter to Mrs. Mary Pilkinton, February 22, 1806.

twelve miles of Alexandria. Cold *for certain. Sunday*, brother Whatcoat preached in the forenoon, and myself in the afternoon, in Alexandria. The cold was great, and the wind piercing.

District of Columbia

On *Monday* we rode to Georgetown (D.C.).

Tuesday, 4. I preached; my subject was, "Godliness is profitable unto all things": it was a feeling, quickening time to myself and others.

Wednesday, 5. I was employed in writing to the missionaries in the Mississippi Territory. Company does not amuse, congress does not interest me:[4] I am a man of another world, in mind and calling: I am Christ's; and for the service of his Church. Some years past, I called at Mr. M.'s, in Calvert county: I acted as I do in all houses: now I have found one of his sons a member of the Georgetown society. Does God always hear prayer, and answer it? If it is in the Spirit's groaning, and in purity of intention, and in faith, doubtless He does.

Maryland

Friday, 7. We set out to Spurrier's—all my old friends are dead or removed. *Saturday* brought us to Baltimore. *Sunday*, at Light Street, my subject was Col. i, 28; at the African church, Col. i, 9–12.

Monday, 10. Rested, wrote, and received friends.

Tuesday, 11. My mind is wholly for God. What hath the Lord wrought, and what is he still doing! Scarcely a letter from any one that does not tell us good news of the work of God, as our yearly letter-book will testify.

Friday, 14. Our conference[5] began in great peace.

[4] This is one of several expressions of Asbury's distrust or disinterest in officeholding on any level. The first session of the Ninth Congress had convened on December 2, 1805. The two Delaware senators were Samuel White, son of Judge Thomas White, and Thomas A. Bayard, son-in-law of Governer Richard Bassett. Robert Wright, a brother of Richard, a trustee of the Methodist Chapel in Centerville, Queen Annes County, was a senator from Maryland. Thomas Worthington, once a student in Cokesbury College and a brother-in-law of Governor Edward Tiffin, a local preacher, was in the Senate. Members of the House from Georgia were David Meriwether, a kinsman of Hope Hull and William W. Bibb, and from South Carolina was Richard Winn. There were others also in the Halls of Congress who, if not Methodists, were from Methodist families. Because at that time many congressmen resided in Georgetown, it seems probable that Asbury visited them.

[5] The conference which met in the second Light Street Church with fifty-eight preachers present considered two proposals for assistance to the ailing Asbury in view

Friday, 21. The stations were read off, and all concluded in great peace: never had we a better conference in Baltimore. An answer was given to Dr. Coke's letter, I fear, in a manner that will not please him. An order was passed that the *answer* should be presented to all the annual conferences. It was also recommended to the annual conferences to consider on the propriety of having a select, delegated Conference: the eastern, western, and southern conferences were counselled to take such measures as they, in their wisdom, might see best, to produce a more equal representation from their several bodies to the General Conference.

On the *Sabbath* (16th), I preached at Fell's Point: my subject, Isaiah lxi, 1: "For Zion's sake I will not hold my peace." Introduction. *Zion*—the interests and welfare of the Church: *Jerusalem*—the interests of the State. General propositions. On what principles we should calculate the true interests of the Church and State—who are concerned—what are the ways and means, and what the instruments to be used for the promotion of their welfare. At Old Town[6] I also gave them a talk: my subject, Psalm li: "Then will I teach transgressors thy ways, and sinners shall be converted to thee." On *Thursday* we had an ordination of elders: I preached on the occasion; my subject was 1 Peter v. 1–4. The work of God went on in all the four congregations, night and day: there might be thirty souls converted; but I hope we had one hundred under the operations of grace. We had nearly ninety members on the conference list, eighty-three of whom were stationed. On *Saturday* I went to Perry Hall, to enjoy a calm after such a storm of labour.

Sunday, 23. I preached at Perry Hall; and after the snow ceased, came away to Josias Dallam's, twenty miles.

Tuesday, 25. We crossed Susquehanna. Calm and cold. Dined at Captain William Howell's at Northeast, and lodged at Mr. Moody's, having called in for a minute at Back Creek:[7] by riding a little in the night, we have made little short of fifty miles today.

Wednesday, 26. I preached at Georgetown Cross Roads. Ah! *there is death in the pot* here. I rode on to Chestertown. On *Thursday* I spoke in

of the failing health of Bishop Whatcoat. Of the seven annual conferences this was the first to approve a plan for calling a special General Conference in May, 1807, to elect an additional bishop and to formulate plans for the creation of delegated quadrennial meetings. The calling of the special conference which required unanimous concurrence was doomed to defeat during the year by action of the Virginia Conference. The Baltimore Conference also declined Dr. Coke's written proposal that the work in America be divided geographically between him and Bishop Asbury for administrative purposes. Thus no relief for the intolerable burden resting upon Asbury was given. New circuits named in the Baltimore Conference were Fells Point, Lycoming, Monongahela, and Staunton. (Bangs, *op. cit.*, II, 178, 179; Lee, *op. cit.*, 310; Armstrong, *op. cit.*, 144, 145.)

[6] This service was in the Exeter Street Church in that section of Baltimore called Old Town. (See *Journal* entry for April 23, 1798.)

[7] For the account of Asbury's first visit at Robert Moody's see *Journal* entry for April 19, 1803. To Methodists familiar with the region Back Creek meant Bethel Chapel.

the new, neat chapel in Kent;[8] and was long and laboured. I visited Carvill Hinson: after a twenty years' separation, we who were left were comforted in God together. I have made twenty-four miles today—feeble, and afflicted with a cold and sore throat, but happy in God. The appointment for *Friday*, at Centreville, was filled by Bishop Whatcoat. After dining with Thomas Wright, I rode on to Mr. Lockerman's. I preached at Easton on *Saturday*; my subject, Rom. xiv, 19: "Let us follow after the things that make for peace," &c. In their estimate of the things of the world, as also of the ceremonials of religion, men will widely differ:—these objects, to a divinely-illuminated mind, are not worth the dispute they frequently occasion. But the things most worthy of all our attention, and our most engaged and diligent following after, are *the things that make for peace*, and promote the soul's edification; and these are the great things of God—the love of God; the death of Christ; the operations of his Spirit; and the deep things of God, respecting sanctification and eternal glory. I stay at Captain Frazer's, Caroline county. My hoarseness is afflictive, but my soul is filled with God.

Sabbath, 30. A very dry season. My mind was greatly engaged for a spiritual rain—and temporal also. The Chesapeake district, so far, is not promising: the people's minds are agitated about stationed preachers, some for and some against. The devil would rather they would do something worse than disagree; but this to him is better than nothing. I only exhorted a little at Frazer's chapel, and after meeting rode home with Thomas Foster—of the old stamp and steady.

Monday, 31. I rode down to Cambridge, and preached at eleven o'clock: my subject Psalm li, 9, 10; I felt assisted.

Tuesday, April 1. We returned to Thomas Foster's. I saw Joseph Everett—feeble but faithful, in patient waiting for his Lord.

Delaware

Wednesday, 2. At Brown's chapel[9] I spoke on 2 Cor. vi, 1: "We then, as workers together with him, beseech you also that ye receive not the grace of God in vain."

I. The Gospel dispensation.

II. The revival of religion.

III. The operations of grace in enabling believers to make advances in the Divine life: this was the grand point urged, to wit: that God giveth grace to prepare for more—grace for grace—convictions for sin that they

[8] For an account of the origin and early history of this preaching place in Kent County, Maryland, see *Journal* entry and note for December 11, 1772, and January 25, 1778.

[9] See *Journal* entries and notes for August 16, 1778, and October 12, 1779.

may repent—repentance that they may believe—justification that they may be convinced of indwelling sin—this convincement will evidence to believers the necessity of sanctification; from whence follow faithfulness unto death, and the crown of glory.

The work of God revives; the chapel will soon be neatly finished: the second generation are filling the house, and joining their labours to what myself and their fathers did in the days of their fathers.

I lodged at brother Davis's.[10] They have built a good chapel at Deep Creek.[11] I exhorted here on *Thursday* after Joseph Crawford had preached. We dined at brother Baker's, and came on to Salisbury, Maryland: here the work revives; Joseph Crawford preached; I was unwell.

Virginia

Friday, 4. We came to William Downing's, Virginia. At Downings chapel I spoke on Rev. ii, 10. After sermon we rode to Accomac and lodged at Mr. Seymour's: here Joseph Crawford preached in the evening.

Sunday, 6. That no time might be lost we started away at eight o'clock in the morning to brother Watts's, twenty-seven miles; my subject was Isaiah xxxiii, 14–16: "The sinners in Zion are afraid," &c. I preached in the court house, Accomac: it was an alarming season. The cold was great; and the winds are high. No rain—it is judgment weather—O Lord, arise!

Maryland

Monday, 7. At Snow Hill my subject was Heb. iii, 12–14. A blessed rain came on before sermon and continued after it.

Delaware

We rode fifteen miles to brother C. Hazzard's, Poplartown, State of Delaware.

Tuesday, 8. We rode forty miles to Broadkilntown:[12] I spoke on 1 Cor. xv, 58.

[10] Father Davis lived east of Federalsburg, Caroline County. His home and that of his son, William, were in the neighborhood of Brown's chapel.

[11] Deep Creek Chapel, built in 1782, was located near Houston's Branch, two miles northwest of Federalsburg, Caroline County. About 1910 services were discontinued, and later the building was destroyed by fire. (Hallman, *op. cit.*, 285.)

[12] By Broadkilntown, Asbury probably was referring to Milton, a name given by legislative action in 1807 to the milling and shipping community known as Head of Broadkiln, seven miles from Delaware Bay, Sussex County. In 1801 subscriptions

Wednesday, 9. I preached at Millford, and then rode on to Dover, and took up father Whatcoat; on the way he was taken with a fit of the gravel, and I was afraid would die. I preached in Dover next day. We afterward rode to Duck Creek Cross Roads in a snow storm. Here the people are all very fervent, and the children praise the Lord: Joseph Crawford preached.[13]

Friday, 11. We came in on as cold a day as one would wish who was fond of extremes, to Wilmington, forty miles. Ah! but I must preach. Well, I gave them a sermon at seven o'clock. The Africans here have a house to themselves, of stone, and equal in size to that of the whites.[14]

Pennsylvania

Saturday, 12, brought us to Philadelphia. From Baltimore, round by the eastern shore hither, has cost us, by computation, five hundred and fifty miles. I have been greatly supported in body and mind; glory be to God

Sabbath, 13. I preached at St. George's upon 2 Peter i, 12–14; at the Academy I spoke on James v, 7, 8. Many of the preachers were already in the city for conference. In the sitting of conference we had so much irregular, desultory work, that we went on slowly. We had sixty-three members present for travelling, besides those to be received in locations, and as supernumerary and worn out. Doctor Coke's letter was answered by a committee of ten preachers.

Monday, 21. Conference rose. Of seventy-six preachers stationed, all appeared to be pleased but two or three; but neither they, nor any one else, can know the difficulties I had to encounter in the arrangement of the stations. Brother Whatcoat was left very ill at Dover—perhaps he is dead. Eight deacons and six elders were ordained. I preached three times. I hope many souls will be converted in consequence of the coming together of this conference—having had great peace in the societies, and sound, sure preaching three times a day.

were taken for a meetinghouse, the erection of which was begun in 1802. The Goshen Church in Milton, several times rebuilt, represents the original congregation. (Scharf: *History of Delaware*, II, 1264; *Delaware, a Guide to the First State*, 415, 416.)

[13] Joseph Crawford (1773–1832) was the traveling companion of Bishop Asbury during 1806. From 1797 to 1822 he was an itinerant in New England and New York, serving two terms also as presiding elder. He was expelled from the church and the ministry in 1822. (Warriner, *op. cit.*, 175–78; *Journals of the General Conference*, I, 265, 347.)

[14] This was Ezion Methodist Episcopal Church, erected in 1805 mainly under the leadership of Jacob Pindergrass, a local preacher. Its congregation was comprised mostly of colored members from Asbury Church. (Centennial Services of Asbury Methodist Episcopal Church, Wilmington, Delaware, 172–77.)

New Jersey

Tuesday, 22. We came to Gloucester Point,[15] and on to Carpenter's bridge;[16] here we have a Quaker Methodist meeting house: I preached upon 2 Peter i, 4; heavy as I was, I had some openings. I visited my old friends Thomas and Margaret Taper. At Sharptown[17] on *Wednesday*—no appointment. I walked to the meeting house; in the burying ground I saw the graves of some of the faithful—amongst these that of John Vanneman,[18] once a travelling preacher. We rode to John Firth's, Salem—no appointment.

Thursday, 24. We returned to William Dilkes's.[19]

Friday, 25. Except a few wandering thoughts, I feel great peace and holiness to God in my soul. I preached at Bethel upon Rom. xii, 1, 2. We lodged at Daniel Bates's. I spoke upon 1 Cor. x, 12, 13. We had a ride of thirty-five or forty miles to-day.

Sunday, 27. I preached at Burlington once more: my subject was 2 Peter iii, 9: "The Lord is not slack concerning his promise," &c. The characters to whom *repentance* is essentially necessary—the unawakened; the unfaithful; the backslidden. The *repentance* of believers—the consciousness of indwelling sin, improved by faith and prayer, is productive of holiness. The gracious will of God is, to furnish means, men, and opportunities, because he *is not willing that any should perish*, until they have a suitable trial. The *coming of the Lord* was his judicial appearing to say, *Depart, ye cursed:* or if understood as some judicial displays of his wrath, his *coming* will not be the less certain because of delay—for one day is as a thousand years, and a thousand years as one day with the Lord.

Monday, 28. I spoke at New Mills on 1 Thess. v, 23. I visited Richard

[15] Gloucester Point was on the Delaware River in Gloucester County, New Jersey, opposite the small hamlet of Gloucester and not to be confused with the city of Gloucester. (Gordon's *Gazetteer*, 149.)

[16] Carpenter's Bridge was earlier identified by Asbury as Mantua. Carpenter's Landing is mentioned by Gordon as a post town of Greenwich Township in Gloucester County "upon Mantua Creek at the head of sloop navigation." In May, 1772, Asbury preached in a "new church" at Carpenter's Bridge, and his note here indicates that the meetinghouse was jointly supported or occupied. Gordon refers only to a Methodist church. (*Ibid.*, 118; Lednum, *op. cit.*, 79–80.)

[17] Sharptown was the site of the Pilesgrove Church. Up to the time of the Revolution the community was called Blessington, the name of the Sharp family's plantation. Gordon says the village contained a schoolhouse which was used occasionally as a church in 1832. The meetinghouse referred to by Asbury must have been outside the village limits, which would accord with his walking to it. (Gordon, *op. cit.*, 236.)

[18] The Vannemans were residents of Lower Penn's Neck. (Lednum, *op. cit.*, 372.)

[19] William Dilkes lived at Hurffville, where Bethel Church was located. Asbury had a twenty-five-mile ride in returning to the Dilkes' home from Salem. Ezekiel Cooper was the guest of Dilkes in April, 1797. (Phoebus, *op. cit.*, 228.)

Swain:[20] there were several preachers, and some others present, and the Lord's supper was partaken.

Tuesday, 29. I preached at Mount Zion,[21] in the woods, near a little town called Egypt.[22] We dined at Fuller Horner's,[23] and rode on to Stephen Barcalow's.[24] We have made nearly forty miles to-day. I enjoy great evenness of mind and life in my labours.

Wednesday, 30. I preached at Lower Freehold. I came home with Simon Pyle.[25] Ah! what a death there is in the Leonard family![26]

[20] The Swain families lived in Northampton Township, Burlington County, and in the vicinity of Tuckahoe, Cape May County, New Jersey. Richard and Nathan Swain were both itinerant preachers. At the time of Asbury's visit Richard doubtless lived at New Mills or at nearby Buddtown; his name does not appear in the *Minutes*, but Nathan had been stationed at Gloucester, New Jersey, by the conference recently held at Philadelphia. Richard Swain died soon thereafter. (Lednum, *op. cit.*, 295; New Jersey Archives, Abstract of Wills, V, 513; VII, 219; VIII, 349; Gordon, *op. cit.*, 443.)

[21] Mount Zion Church stands on an old farm about a mile from the present hamlet of Archer's Corners. Methodism began about 1789 in the log house of Job Horner, who lived on the farm that included the present church site. Joseph Cromwell, in charge of the Trenton Circuit in 1789, is the first recorded Methodist preacher in the locality known as Hornerstown. The original church was built in 1801 and was destroyed by fire in 1837, and the present edifice replaced the first building. In 1950 Mount Zion Church was officially declared abandoned and discontinued by the New Jersey Conference but was placed under the care and maintenance of the nearby New Egypt Methodist Church to be preserved as a Methodist shrine. (Abbot: *History of Old Zion M.E. Church, 1907*; New Jersey Guide, 616–17; New Jersey Annual Conference *Minutes*, 1950.)

[22] New Egypt, today a small agricultural village on Crosswicks Creek, was known as Timmons Mills at the time of the Revolution. The name "Egypt" was given to it inadvertently. General Washington needed grain after the victory at Trenton in 1776, and Benjamin Jones, one of Washington's New Jersey advisers, indicated that he had a large quantity of buckwheat flour and cornmeal stored at the mills. He sent his secretary, Joseph Curtis, to bring the milled grain to Trenton, and when Curtis returned Washington commented, "Joseph has been in Egypt and gotten the corn." The name Egypt stuck until 1845, when the prefix "New" was added. (*New Jersey Guide*, 617.)

[23] Fuller Horner lived between Archer's Corners and New Egypt in the locality known as Hornerstown. Fuller and Joshua Horner in 1838 gave a deed for the property on which Zion Church stands. Job Horner had presented this land to the trustees in 1800 but without a deed. (Abbot, *op. cit.*)

[24] The Barcalows lived at Upper Freehold in Monmouth County, New Jersey. They were closely related to the Polemus family, also identified with Methodism in New Jersey. (New Jersey Archives, Abstracts of Wills, IV, 31; VI, 310–11; VII, 179; VIII, 28, 217.)

[25] Simon Pyle (–1822) had been a traveling preacher. He located in 1792 and made his home in Lower Freehold, Monmouth County, where he had a farm. He married a daughter of Samuel Leonard of Shrewsbury in 1792, and although her parents were members of the Episcopal Church of Shrewsbury, she joined the Methodist communion. Pyle continued as a local preacher after his location, and his home was open to itinerants. Ezekiel Cooper visited him in March, 1796. (Atkinson, *op. cit.*, 390–91; Phoebus, *op. cit.*, 221–22.)

[26] Samuel Leonard, who had received Asbury into his home on numerous occasions, had died in 1790. The Leonard family was held in high regard by the Methodist preach-

Thursday, May 1. I breakfasted with Throckmorton:[27] his loss is his gain—he has lost his birth-right as a citizen of the State, but he has the blessing of God on his soul. I preached at Cheesecake meeting house:[28] here, a people who have a trick of claiming a right to all free meeting houses, had shouldered the Methodists out; *but the earth helped the woman*—the people of the world have built a house for us. We lodged at Mr. Warne's.[29]

Friday, 2. I feel the effects of my toil. I declined preaching in New Brunswick; Joseph Crawford supplied my place. I rode on to Benjamin Drake's.

Saturday, 3. I crossed Long Ferry[30] to Staten Island. It is like winter here: but what cannot the God of nature and of grace do physically and spiritually? I viewed the spot where I first landed on the island in October, 1771: I am alive, and about my Master's work still—Glory! glory!

Sabbath, 4. At the first meeting[31] Joseph Crawford preached, I only exhorted; at the second meeting house,[32] on the north side, I preached: we lodged at Nicholas Crocheron's.

ers. (Phoebus, *op. cit.*, 64, 221; New Jersey Archives, Abstracts of Wills, VII, 136; see preceding note.)

[27] Several Throckmortons lived in the vicinity of Colt's Neck, Shrewsbury, and Mount Pleasant. Asbury later identifies John Throckmorton (April 30, 1809) and James Throckmorton (May 1, 1809), where he was entertained. Job Throckmorton of nearby Freehold is another of the name who had Methodist associations. Colt's Neck, where James and John lived, was originally called Caul's Neck for an early settler. It is today a small village which has become famous as a breeding place for race horses. (*History of Monmouth County*, II, 439–40; Myers: *Story of New Jersey*, IV, 21; Wilson: *The Jersey Shore*, I, 120; New Jersey Archives, Abstracts of Wills, IV, 430; VI, 150, 394; VIII, 263; Phoebus, *op. cit.*, 71, 222; *New Jersey Guide*, 589.)

[28] Cheesequake in Middlesex County takes its name from Cheesequake Creek, which in turn derives its name from the "quaking bogs" along it. The earliest Methodist services were held in a Baptist Church, which was evidently a free church used jointly by the Methodists, Baptists, and Presbyterians. A weather-beaten frame structure still stands on the site where Old School Baptists had a log cabin in which services were held. A cemetery surrounding the present building has stones bearing dates as early as 1798. Services are no longer held in the building, but a tablet relates something of its history. (Wall and Pickersgill: *History of Middlesex County*, 441–43; *New Jersey Guide*, 553–54.)

[29] Thomas Warne had settled at an early date on Mount Pleasant near Cheesequake. Asbury may have stayed with Joshua or Zekiel Warne, both of whom lived at Spotswood on the road toward New Brunswick. (Wall and Pickersgill, *op. cit.*, 441; New Jersey Archives, Abstracts of Wills, VIII, 390.)

[30] Long Ferry was at Perth Amboy, connecting with Rossville, Staten Island. Asbury first landed on Staten Island on November 7, 1771, rather than in October.

[31] This meeting was evidently in Woodrow Church since Asbury was at Rossville at the time.

[32] This second meetinghouse became known as Asbury Church, which is located at New Springville not far from Travis. The first entry in the church records declares: "The Methodist Episcopal Church, in the township of Northfield, and County of Richmond and State of New York, was built in the year of our Lord 1802." An election for trustees was held at the home of Nicholas Crocheron on January 30, 1803, with Crocheron and Richard Merrell presiding over the election. The original trustees were

Monday, 5. I preached at Elizabethtown, and then came on to Newark. After stopping awhile, we moved forward to Second River,[33] and called a meeting at which Joseph Crawford preached. We have a warm day, the harbinger of spring: universal nature seems starting into innumerable forms of promise of the fruitful year—O that it may be so spiritually!

Tuesday, 6. I preached at Belleville, and rode on to New York.

New York

Wednesday, 7. I viewed the ground at Philip's Manor, selected for our camp meeting.[34] I felt as if God would be there, in answer to our prayers for nine months past. In the evening we came to Sherwood's Vale; and at night I went to the camp ground, and looked on at the people, busy clearing the ground, fixing the seats, and building the stand.

Thursday, 8. I rested and wrote.

Friday, 9, began with a storm; but the people came, bringing their tents and baggage weary with walking.

Saturday, 10. The weather cleared.

Sunday, 11. I preached: it was an open season; companies here and there dispersed, kept up the exercise of singing and prayer through the day, and far into the night; the Brooklyn tent was all prayer the greater part of the time. A marquee had been fixed for the preachers; and provisions came in from both town and country, the brethren from both delightfully meeting in worship and affections. On *Monday* the people of the world seemed to make a surrender; there was no longer a necessity for guards.

There were between eighty and one hundred official members present; about one thousand Methodists; and some presumed, about six thousand souls were on the ground at different times: the people were so dispersed, and there was such a continual coming and going, I had no means of judging.

We had great order and great power from the beginning to the end: I judge two hundred souls were made the subjects of grace in its various

James Wood, John Decker, Nicholas Crocheron, Richard Merrell, and the Rev. Elias Price, a local preacher. The present church building was erected in 1849. (Timbrell: *A Century of Church Life, the Centennial History of Asbury Methodist Episcopal Church*; Hubbell: *History of Staten Island Methodism*, 166–93; *Staten Island Advance*, October 8, 1927, article on Asbury Church by Vernon B. Hampton.)

[33] Asbury distinguished Second River from Belleville, or used the older name in this instance, since the two terms were used interchangeably for some years for the same locality.

[34] The New Rochelle camp-meeting ground was located on a wooded tract just west of the Sherwood home. (See *Journal* entry and note for July 26, 1805, when Asbury observed the tract and referred it to William Thacher, the elder.)

operations of conviction, conversion, sanctification, and reclamation. Glory! glory!

Wednesday, 14. We came to New York.

Thursday, 15. I recollected myself and wrote letters.

Friday, 16. The conference commenced its sitting,[35] and rose on *Thursday*. We sat seven hours in each day, in great love, order, and peace. A paper was read, setting forth the uncertain state of the superintendency,[36] and proposing the election of seven elders, from each of the seven conferences, to meet at Baltimore, July 4, 1807, for the sole purpose of establishing the American superintendency on a surer foundation: this subject will be submitted to the consideration of all the conferences.[37] The answer to Dr. Coke's letter,[38] by the conference of New York, was read, to be submitted to all the conferences. I preached three times, and ordained three African deacons. We had preaching in the Park[39] as well as regularly in the meeting houses, and a day of fasting and prayer for the health of the city, the success of our conference labours, and the prosperity of Zion. I was greatly supported and blest. The preachers were, perhaps, never better satisfied with their stations.

Connecticut

Sunday, 25. I preached at New Haven. After meeting I visited sister Thacher,[40] rejoicing in perfect love; perhaps she is near her end. Since the 16th of April, 1805, I have, according to my reckoning, travelled five thousand miles: everlasting glory be to my all-sufficient God!

Monday, 26. I dined at Meriden and lodged at Mr. Pitkin's,[41] East Hartford.

Tuesday, 27. I reached Thompson, forty-five miles, *faint, yet pursuing*.

[35] The conference sat at John Street Church.

[36] Feelings of uncertainty and doubt about the stability of the superintendency were prompted by the illness of Whatcoat and the continuing weakness of Asbury.

[37] Although passed at New York and by some other groups, this proposal was rejected by conferences in the south.

[38] This letter from Coke had announced his marriage, requesting the American conferences to indicate whether they might wish him to return as bishop in that status in life. The ultimate courteous answer was that the conferences thought such status would be unwise for their best guidance. This correspondence terminated Coke's official relationship to American Methodism, the 1807 *Minutes* being the last to present his name as a bishop.

[39] Preaching was held on the Commons, now City Hall Park, where public gatherings were often held.

[40] This was probably the wife or mother of William Thacher, who was prominently identified with the early history of Methodism in New Haven, Connecticut. (Osterveis: *Three Centuries of New Haven, 1638–1639*, 215.)

[41] This was Squire Elisha Pitkin. (See note under June 13, 1812.)

Massachusetts

Wednesday, 28. At Milford, the people, young and old, were on the green; the active playing at ball, the aged and others looking on; it was election day.

Thursday, 29, we dined at Mr. Bogle's, Needham,[42] and rode on to Waltham. A few young people are under the operations of grace here; amongst whom are the two children of George Pickering—my namesake Asbury, aged about ten, and Maria, still younger; and there is a small revival of religion in the district. We rested here on *Friday*, and I preached at night, on Phil. i, 8–11.

Saturday, 31. We have a gracious rain; it was greatly needed. In the evening we rode to Boston.

Sunday, June 1. I preached in Boston: as usual with me in this place, it was an open season; some souls were powerfully moved, myself for one.

Monday, 2. I took a walk to West Boston, to see the new chapel, eighty-four by sixty-four feet. The upper window frames were put in. We came to Lynn at two o'clock. I preached at two o'clock, on Haggai ii, 8. After meeting we rode as far as Marblehead: here Joseph Crawford preached. I find that David Batchelor has been useful in this town; a revival has taken place.

New Hampshire

Tuesday, 3. We came, through dust and heat, to Enoch Sandbourn's,[43] East Kingston, forty-five miles.

Maine

We had a ride of about fifty miles to Old Wells on *Wednesday*. Eight or ten of these we might have saved, had we known the nearest way from Exeter.

Thursday, 5. We came to Portland; Joseph Crawford preached.

Friday, 6. We went towards Buxton, to attend the camp meeting. At two o'clock we came on the ground. There were twenty preachers, travelling and local.

Saturday, 7. I preached; and on the *Sunday* also. Some judged there were about five thousand people on the ground. There were displays of Divine power, and some conversions. Our journey into Maine has been

[42] This was William Bogle. (See note under July 4, 1805.)

[43] "Enoch Sanburn's grandson now owns the old home in which Asbury was entertained." (Williams: article in *The Christian Advocate* (N.Y., March 16, 1916) entitled "Asbury in New Hampshire.")

through dust and heat; in toil of body, and in extraordinary temptation of soul; but I felt that our way was of God.

Monday, 9. We journeyed on through Buxton, Limerick, Parsonsfield, Elfingham, into New Hampshire, stopping at Sandwich, to lodge with Mr. William Webster.

New Hampshire

Tuesday, 10. Through town after town we came to Dorchester, lodging at Deacon Blodgett's. Canaan brought us up on *Wednesday*.

Thursday, 12. We opened the New England Conference, and went through our business with haste and peace, sitting seven hours a day.[44] The New York Conference address respecting the superintendency was concurred in, and the seven elders for this conference elected accordingly. We did not (to my grief) tell our experiences, nor make observations as to what we had known of the work of God; the members were impatient to be gone, particularly the married townsmen.

Sunday, 15. I ordained eleven elders in the woods. At three o'clock I preached in the meeting house; it was a season of power.

Monday, 16. I lodged with John Broadhead.

Tuesday, 17. My labour is great; but I am blessed with a great willingness to duty. We came along through Enfield, Hanover, Lebanon, crossing Connecticut at Lyman's bridge into Vermont, and kept on by Hartford, Sharon, and Royalton.

Vermont

We brought up with Samuel Curtis, upon White's River, for the night. From New Haven to White's River we have made, by computation, four hundred and sixty miles. I have had sufferings in the flesh, but perfect peace of mind.

Wednesday, 18. We reached Barnard. I preached at Thomas Freeman's, on Acts xxvi, 17, 18. Here is a lively, large society. We had a full house at a short warning. Our way on *Thursday* led through Randolph, Brookfield, Williamstown, Northfield, and Berlin. I preached at Samuel Smith's.

Friday, 20. We came upon Onion River, at Montpelier, the contemplated seat of government for the State. I think it eminently well selected; for a site of this kind I know nothing in England or America more suitable. At Palmer's mill[45] I preached, on 1 Cor. i, 30.

[44] In 1806 the New England Conference met in Canaan. There was a grand camp meeting in Robert Barber's woods near the Well's place. (*History of Canaan, New Hampshire.*)

[45] Palmer's Mill may have been at Waitesfield, Vermont, since persons named Palmer resided there.

Saturday, 21. Brought us over the heights of Onion River to Russell's bridge;[46] thence to Bolton and Williston, dining at brother Bradley's.[47] After dinner we rattled along to Burlington, on Lake Champlain. Here I saw a grand college—equal, in exterior, to that of New Haven—a state house, meeting house, and other elegant buildings.[48] We passed Shelbourne into Charlotte, on the lake, and put up with Mr. Fuller.[49] We have made forty miles to-day. I am resolved to be in every part of the work, whilst I live to preside. It will be the best plan to bring on the sessions of all the conferences as early as possible, that there may be time given to all the preachers to go to work in the dawn of spring. The New England Conference should meet about the middle of April, and thus be ready for General Conference.

I feel as if I was fully taught the necessity of being made perfect through sufferings and labours. I pass over in silence cases of pain and grief, of body and mind.

From appearances it would seem no great stretch of imagination to suppose there have been many lakes dried up in this country. Onion River Falls, for instance, must at one time have been a boundary; at this narrow pass, as at Harper's Ferry, on the Potomac, and the French Broad in North Carolina, the weight of waters has broken through the mountain on some day far upward in the history of past ages; they now supply Lake Champlain.

On the *Sabbath* I preached in an upper room at Fuller's, to about four hundred people: my subject was Luke iv, 18, 19; and God bore witness to his own word. Why did I not visit this country sooner? By moving the conferences to an earlier period in the year, it might have been done, and may yet be done: what appeared to me to be impossible, I see now is very practicable. Ah! what is the toil of beating over rocks, hills, mountains, and deserts, five thousand miles a year Nothing; when we reflect it is done for God, for Christ, for the Holy Spirit, the Church of God, the souls of poor sinners, the preachers of the Gospel in the seven conferences, one hundred and thirty thousand members, and one or two millions,

[46] Russell's Bridge was perhaps Rock Bridge, about a mile from Waterbury on the Onion (now Winooski) River.

[47] Among the earliest settlers of Williston are listed two brothers, Elisha and Joseph Bradley. It seems likely that one or the other was Asbury's host. (*Williston, Vermont, a History of the Town, 1763–1913*, 38.)

[48] The University of Vermont was founded in 1791. The first college building was erected in 1801. The state house was probably the courthouse which was erected in 1798. Among the "elegant buildings" was Grassemount on Main Street, which was built by Thaddeus Tuttle in 1804 and is perhaps the finest example of Georgian architecture in Vermont. (*Vermont, a Guide to the Green Mountain State*, 103, 109.)

[49] Ammi Fuller, a Baptist minister, opened his own home for a preaching place to Asbury. In his will he generously devised real estate to the value of five thousand dollars to the Methodist Episcopal Church in the town. (*The Vermont Historical Gazetteer*, 744, 746.)

who congregate with us in the solemn worship of God; O, it is nothing!

Monday, 23. At Vergennes court house, I preached upon Mark i, 15. I had to walk up a great hill, a mile, by the falls of Otter. At Bridport, at six o'clock, I spoke upon Titus ii, 11, 12.

Tuesday, 24. Passing through Shoreham, Benson, and other towns, we came to Hampton church[50] at six o'clock; I gave them a sermon upon Heb. iii, 14–16.

New York

On *Wednesday* we came along by Granville and Salem, down to Cambridge. At six o'clock, at Ashgrove, I preached upon Jude 17 to the end. I have travelled one hundred and fifty miles through New Hampshire; and two hundred and twenty or more, in Vermont. We have sustained more damage than I can tell, by the absence of the preachers, two or three months, at every conference: this is an evil that must be remedied. O! how I felt for the people! this was worse than my incredible toil: help, Lord, for vain is the help of man! Were it not for the aid we receive from the local and official members, the suspensions of the travelling preachers would ruin us. What is to be done? 1. Meet the conferences early. 2. Engage the official members to more engagedness and labour. 3. Let prayer meetings be more frequent. 4. Let all the probationers stay on the circuits; and let all who are recommended stay on the circuits also, until they can be admitted into the Connexion.

Thursday, 26. We came rapidly down the pike road to Pittstown, Housack, Lansingburg, Troy, and Greenbush; on *Friday* through Scodack and Phillipstown, breakfasting at Mr. Bushe's well-conducted stage tavern; and then onward through Lebanon and Canaan, in New York State, and Stockbridge, Old Barrington, and Sheffield, in Massachusetts. On *Saturday* we came into Connecticut, breakfasting at Salisbury: our dinner we took on the Sharon camp ground.[51]

Sabbath, 29. I preached in camp on 2 Cor. vi, 2.

On *Monday* we pursued our route through to Dover, and rested with father Rose awhile; dined, and went on to Salem in New York State, and slept at Franklin, under the hospitable roof of father Howes.

Tuesday, *July* 1. We came to Jeremiah Miller's and dined, and reached Elijah Crawford's at the Plains. We have travelled about five hundred miles in the State of New York. I may remark here, now that I have time to make the remark, that the Lebanon camp meeting was great as to the

[50] Hampton Church was at Hampton, New York, on the Poultney River, six miles south of Fair Haven, Vermont.

[51] Asbury tarried nowhere on this journey. He was striving to reach Bishop Whatcoat before that brave saint found death.

numbers which attended, and great in power. We are now, in many congregations and classes, reaping the fruits of the conference camp meetings, all through the circuit of New Rochelle: and the Sharon camp meeting will equal, in effect, those of the conferences. We have a few refreshing rains; the promise of rich crops of wheat; and abundant spiritual harvests. Glory to God!

Wednesday, 2. We came to New York. I had left my little travelling wagon to be sold at the Plains. On *Thursday* I came on to son Aaron Hunt's:[52] Joseph Crawford came over the ferry with me; when about to part, he turned away his face and wept. Ah! I am not made for such scenes, I felt exquisite pain.

New Jersey

At Newark I lodged with brother Leaycraft: I felt for, prayed with, and spoke to all members of this family.

Friday, 4. Noise, parade, seventeen rounds; and then to breakfast. I stole away quietly from this bustle towards Rockaway.[53] I stopped at brother Shearman's,[54] with brother M'Lenahan[55] and wife. At Turkey[56] chapel I spoke on 1 Cor. xv, 58: it was an open season. When there is a stir amongst the Methodists, other denominations send supplies, if they

[52] Aaron Hunt (1768–1858) was born in Westchester County, New York, and came to New York City after the Revolution, taking employment as a clerk. He was converted at John Street Church, received on trial in 1791, and located in a few years due to poor health. Upon regaining his health in 1800, he was again received into the work, continuing until 1823, when he became supernumerary. At the time of this entry he was resident in the parsonage of the Bowery Church on Forsyth Street. (Seaman, *op. cit.*, 167–69; Warriner, *op. cit.*, 100–108.)

[53] Rockaway was in Morris County, New Jersey, in the narrow valley of the Rockaway River. Asbury did not go into Rockaway but turned off at the Caldwell parsonage on the branch road which led to Livingston and New Providence. (Shaw: *History of Essex County*, I, 185, 186; II, 706, 716, 833, 855, 856; Schumacher: *Somerset Hills*, 122.)

[54] This was probably Abijah Shearman, a local preacher in Morris County. Of the same family was Nathaniel Schurman, a member of the Provincial Congress of New Jersey in 1775. The name is doubtless German, and there were many ways of spelling it. (Shaw, *op. cit.*, I, 36, 300, 338, 469; New Jersey Archives, Abstracts of Wills, VI, 172; Snell, *op. cit.*, 50; Platt, *op. cit.*, 31; Munsell: *History of Morris County, New Jersey*, 42.)

[55] William McLenahan was one of two preachers on the circuit in 1806, the other being David Bartine. McLenahan once received from President Washington a letter commending him for using his influence in favor of peace and the enforcement of law. (Hubbell, *op. cit.*, 44.)

[56] Turkey is the present New Providence in Essex County. Ezekiel Cooper, Thomas Morrell, and Jesse Lee had all visited the area. On this visit Asbury stopped at the home of Stephen Day. Two sons of Stephen and Betsey Wood Day became ministers. They were Edwin A. Day and Benjamin Day. (Gordon, *op. cit.*, 198; Molyneaux: *History of New Providence; a Tale of Three Villages: Bernardsville, Basking Ridge, Mendham*, 18.)

have not a stationed minister: the process is, to hold a week-day meeting, perform a sacrament or a baptism, to place the new convert within the ark of safety; and all is done. Now we may *stand still*, or sit still, *and see the salvation of God!* I rejoiced to hear of the appointment of a camp meeting on Turkey, in August.[57]

Saturday, 5. I came to Germantown,[58] twenty-five miles, through a pleasant, beautiful, fruitful land of hills and vales. The place chosen for the encampment on Turkey I found a handsome height, elegantly sloping to the north. I trust four hundred souls will be converted: may it give new springs and tone to the work of God in the Jerseys!

Sabbath, 6. At Mindurt Farley's I preached upon Gal. vi, 9; in the afternoon again upon Acts xx, 32. I was led out in an uncommon degree. May it be the prelude to better days! My first visit here was during the revolutionary war; now the children of people not then married are born, grown up, and married. After meeting I rode on to Pennington, housing for the night with Jonathan Bunn.

Pennsylvania

Tuesday, 8. I was on the road at five o'clock. The bridge over the Delaware is said to have cost three or four hundred thousand dollars. I reached Manley Hall about four o'clock. From New Haven to Philadelphia, I judge I have made one thousand sixty-five miles, going and returning; and about one thousand eight hundred miles, since I left the Philadelphia Conference: much suffering and much toil: not unto me, but unto thy good providence, O my God, be all the glory! After writing some letters, I preached at Kingston at five o'clock, on Acts xx, 24. On my return, I found a letter from Doctor Chandler, declaring the death of Bishop Whatcoat, that father in Israel, and my faithful friend for forty years—a man of solid parts; a self-denying man of God; who ever heard him speak an idle word? when was guile found in his mouth? He had been thirty-eight years in the ministry—sixteen years in England, Wales, and Ireland, and twenty-two years in America; twelve years as presiding elder, four of this time he was stationed in the cities, or travelling with me, and six years in the superintendency. A man so uniformly good I have not known in Europe or America. He had long been afflicted with gravel and stone, in which afflictions, nevertheless, he travelled a great deal—three thousand miles the last year: he bore in the last three months excessively painful

[57] See *Journal* entries for September 5, 1782; July 14, 1803.

[58] Germantown is the present Oldwick in Hunterdon County. Methodist preaching started there in July, 1782, when Asbury visited Nicholas Egbert and Mindurt Farley. The population was predominantly German and was one reason for Asbury voicing a need for preachers with a knowledge of foreign languages. (Wittwer: *History of Oldwick Methodist Church.*)

illness with most exemplary patience. He died in Dover on the 5th of July, and his mortal remains were interred under the altar of the Wesley Dover church: at his taking leave of the South Carolina Conference, I thought his time was short. I changed my route to visit him, but only reached within a hundred and thirty miles; death was too quick for me.

Delaware

Friday, 11. I came to Wilmington; and on *Saturday* to Northeast.

Maryland

On the *Sabbath* I preached. *Monday* brought me to Perry Hall: and on *Tuesday* I reached Baltimore.

Thursday, 17. Busy writing letters to the South, and to England. I enjoy great peace, and am in the spirit of prayer. On *Friday* I visited three families on Elk Ridge. On *Saturday* I came to brother Riggs's;[59] dined, and went on to Doctor Watters's.[60] I preached at Goshen meeting house. We have, it is said, the greatest drought that can be remembered in this country; the springs seem to be failing everywhere. *Monday* I went to Rachel Hall's,[61] dined, and rode on to Samuel Howard's; here I had a bilious attack, and became quick bed sick.

Tuesday, 22. We have a most blessed, glorious shower of rain. I received it as an answer to prayer. The oats in the fields are unpromising; but the corn looks green, and the people are diligent in ploughing and dressing: a fine example this to Christians; O, how diligently should we labour! The heat is great.

West Virginia

Wednesday, 23. I called upon Joseph Perkins, the superintendent of the U. S. armoury. Here is a factory of stores of instruments of death, taste-

[59] This was probably Edmond Riggs, Jr., who on May 23, 1799, married Jane, daughter of Robert Willson. The Willsons were pioneer Methodists in Montgomery County and were among the founders of Clarksburg Church. (See notes under October 15, 1777, and June 15, 1787.)

[60] This was Dr. Richard Waters (*d.* 1810), a native of Prince Georges County. After serving as a surgeon in the War of Independence, he purchased "Spring Garden," an estate on the road leading from Mechanicsville to Clarksburg, Montgomery County. (Boyd: *The History of Montgomery County*, 102, 103; Bible records from the Bible of Dr. Richard Waters, *Genealogical Records of Maryland, 1943*, 98, D.A.R. Library, Washington, D.C.)

[61] This may have been the Rachel Hall who in 1783 became the wife of Humphrey Godman, Anne Arundel County. (Brumbaugh, *op. cit.*, II, 438.)

fully arranged in the several apartments: there may they remain forever! But will it be so? Alas! no. I was caught in a rain upon the river, the effects of which I felt next day.

August 3. I am here at John Davenport's. I have been sick, and laid up since *Thursday* last. Copious bleeding, emetics, cathartics, and bark have had their turns. The fever, since the day before yesterday, has left me. I have been providentially favoured with a good physician, kind friends, and temperate heat; the Lord hath done this well. I might have been taken amongst strangers, and have had more pain. Rest was wanting; and I may hereafter have better weather for the toilsome journey before me. Happily I laid my hands on *Simpson's Plea for Religion*, in which we have a wonderful and interesting account of good and bad men for three centuries. The author has drawn aside the purple curtains of the Church of Rome, and the black robes of the antichristian Church of England, to lay bare the abuses of bad systems, and the vices of mitred heads: he has raised his warning voice against the corruption of manners and morals in all orders, which will, he predicts, without a speedy reformation, cause the downfall of all ecclesiastical establishments; he has magnanimously renounced his living as a minister, which his conscience would permit him no longer to hold: he said he knew not where to go; but the Lord has taken him to *the Church of the first-born*. O, what a warning is here given to all Churches, to all ministers, to all Christians, and to thee, O my soul! Recollecting I had never preached in the neighbourhood, and feeling a little unwilling to pass another dumb *Sabbath*, we called a solemn assembly, as much as if we had come to the funeral of one of the family; my subject was 1 Kings viii, 35–39. I was rapid for about an hour: they are faithfully warned; let them look to it.

Virginia

Wednesday, 6. I came to Winchester. Wrote to Myles and Dougherty. Report says, that a copy of Dr. Coke's letter was taken by stealth: the British are irritated, and the Americans are not pleased; but they were calm in counsel. I lodged at sister Phelps's.[62]

Thursday, 7. Came to the camp meeting at Crissman's Springs, now Stover's Springs. Necessity compelled them to come here for the sake of the water in this great general drought. I moved on to Stoverstown.

Friday, 8. I breakfasted at Millerstown; rode to Wire's to dinner; and by driving two hours in the night reached Rocktown, or Rockingham,[63] and put up with Mr. Williams. I have travelled fifty miles to-day over rough, rocky roads. I rested my feeble body on *Saturday*.

[62] This was Mrs. Elijah Phelps.

[63] Stoverstown was the present Strasburg, Millerstown was the present Woodstock, and Rocktown, or Rockingham, courthouse was the present Harrisonburg, Virginia.

Sunday, 10. Our house here,[64] forty by forty-five feet, may contain fifteen or eighteen hundred people: now that we have a place of worship of our own, I hope we shall have another revival. I preached the first sermon; my subject, Isa. lvi, 8. We had an open time.

Monday 11. I rested.

Tuesday, 12. I came away to Staunton: I preached in the court house on Isaiah lv, 6, 7.

Wednesday, 13, brought us to Fairfield: I lodged at Mr. Moore's tavern. At Lexington I found Mr. Shield, my host, sick: I prayed with them; it was a time of tenderness. I set out, faint indeed, for Mr. M'Conkey's, a decent house: here I prayed as amongst the Methodists. This excessive delicacy of feeling, which shuts my mouth so often, may appear strange to those who do not know me; there are some houses in which I am not sure that I could speak to my father, were he alive, and I to meet him there—bystanders might have cause to exclaim with wonder, *What a son!*

Friday, 15. I rode fifteen miles and breakfasted with Mr. Topcotts; eleven miles farther brought me to Mr. Thomas's, near the camp ground, at a little town called Amsterdam. I have been afflicted; but this may be for good. Had it not been for the top of the sulky, perhaps, sultry as it was, I should have been obliged to stop: faint and feeble, the kindness of good men, and the affectionate attentions of good women supported me: may a gracious God bless those who were thus made blessings to me! In prayer I have had uncommon life and liberty; but I had not strength to talk as much as I wished about God and religion. On *Saturday* I felt unwell.

Sunday, 17. I ventured to the camp. I preached at eleven o'clock to about three thousand souls: I held on, loud and long; it was the Lord, not I. Notwithstanding matters were not as I could wish, I trust much good will be done.

Monday, 18. I rested at Mr. Thomas's.

Tuesday, 19. I ventured on the camp ground again, and preached at eight o'clock: I was weak and unwell, but was divinely aided, whilst enlarging on Philippians i, 1; may this weighty subject rest on the minds of the preachers, and on none more than the heart of the speaker! I came away with Samuel Mitchell.[65] Friendship and good fellowship seem to be done away between the Methodists and Presbyterians; few of the latter will attend our meetings now: well, let them feed their flocks apart; and let not Judah vex Ephraim, or Ephraim, Judah; and may it thus remain, until the two sticks become one in the Lord's hands.

Wednesday, 20. Being unwell, I rested.

[64] This must have been the frame church with a steeple which was used until the building of Andrew Chapel at Harrisonburg, Virginia, in 1851–52. (Wayland: *Historic Harrisonburg*, 29.)

[65] "Rev. Samuel Mitchell (Methodist) granted license to celebrate the rites of matrimony, August 11, 1795." (Summers: *Annals of Southwestern Virginia*, 462.)

Thursday, 21. We came away through excessive heat to Thomas Barrett's, at the foot of the Allegheny mountain.

Friday, 22, brought us over the rough, rude mountain: they are making a turnpike here. After breakfasting at brother Haymaker's, we came on to Pepper's ferry, sometimes directing our route by chance. Since the twenty-third of May to this day, I believe we have not had a steady rain for six hours together; yet it is a miracle and mercy that the prospects of corn are so good. We rested for the day at Pepper's; and, need we add, weary, men and horses.

Sunday, 24. At Page's chapel[66] I spoke on 2 Chron. vii, 13, 14: it was an awful talk, and the people were alarmed. We dined at Edward Mitchell's, and lodged at Whygler's, that we might lose no time.

Monday, 25. I was in danger of being cast away on my route to Crocket's, but was mercifully preserved: I felt exceedingly grateful that not even the skin of either horse or man was broken: I jumped out of the carriage. Ah! I see that old men will fail in great danger.

Tuesday, 26. We came to Wythe court house, eighteen miles, to breakfast, and reached David Stewart's to lodge.

Wednesday, 27. I came to Charles Hardy's. I have not slept well. I am faint with toil, and excessive heat—like an oven in the afternoon.

Thursday, 28, brought us over the dreadful roads to the Salt Works. The great drought has not prevailed so greatly on Holston, of Tennessee.

Saturday, 30. I preached at the widow Russell's; my hostess is as happy and cheerful as ever.

Sunday, 31. I preached at the Mahanaim meeting house.[67] I once thought we should scarcely ever have a tabernacle of our own in these parts; we have now three in a triangle of eight miles' extent.

Tennessee

Tuesday, September 2. I was weak, but attended the appointment of the stationed preacher, A. Houston: my subject was 1 Thess. v, 12–15: strong in spirit, but feeble in body. Next day I rode thirty miles over to Edward Cox's.[68]

Thursday, 4. I preached at Bethel. I was faint; and felt the effects of sickness and the rough roads. I lodged at the widow Lewis's, on Beaver Creek.

[66] Page's meetinghouse was the oldest Methodist chapel in the Holston. It was built by Edward Morgan on New River one mile north of Radford, Virginia, in 1783 and was later known as Morgan's Chapel. The tract of one hundred acres on which it stood reverted to the original donors. (Price: *Holston Methodism*, I, 77; Martin: *Methodism in the Holston Conference*, 11.)

[67] Mahanaim meetinghouse was a log chapel near Saltville and the home of Michael Huffaker, who gave the land for it. A modern church now occupies the site. (Price, *op. cit.*, II, 78.)

[68] See note under April 28, 1788.

Friday, 5. I felt that I was done, and must lay by awhile.

Saturday, 6. I preached at Charles Helton's, upon Main Holston: weak as I was it was an open time.

Sunday, 7. We crossed Holston at the mouth of Watauga: the Sabbath I do not often employ in travelling—sometimes when I fall in with the circuit preachers. I was very close in my discourse at Dingworth's, on Psalm li, 10–13; the people have sat under a Calvinistic ministry. I lodged at William Nelson's,[69] an ancient home and stand for Methodists and Methodist preaching. I have gone over rough roads, and a wild country, rocks, ruts, and sidelong difficult ways, sometimes much obscured; it was thus I lost my way, and travelled twenty miles farther than I needed.

Monday, 8. Prepared for conference.

Saturday, 13. My bowels for some days past have been much disordered, and I have been otherwise ill; but constant occupation of writing, reading, and praying, has diverted my attention from my sufferings: the medicine taken to-day has done good. I am obliged to avoid the sun as I would a burning fire.

Sunday, 14. I preached at the stand in the woods, brother M'Kendree followed: it was a season of feeling.

Saturday, 20, the Western Conference commenced its sitting, and ended on *Monday*.[70] The Mississippi missionary preachers could not be spared, they thought, from their work, and therefore did not come. We had great peace. There are fourteen hundred added within the bounds of this conference. Of the fifty-five preachers stationed, all were pleased. In unison with the preceding conferences, an answer was given to Dr. Coke's letter. We had preaching at noon and night, and good was done. The brethren were in want, and could not suit themselves; so I parted with my watch, my coat, and my shirt. By order of the conference, I preached a funeral discourse, on the death of our dear friend Whatcoat,[71] from John i, 47–50; there were not far from two thousand people present. If good were done, which I trust and hope, it is some compensation for my sufferings—thirteen hundred miles in heat and sickness on the road; and in the house, restless hours, the noise of barking dogs, impatient children, and people trotting about, and opening and shutting doors at all hours.

North Carolina

Wednesday, 24. We came to Buncombe: we were lost within a mile of Killian's and were happy to get a school house to shelter us for the night:

[69] See note under May 6, 1788.

[70] The conference met at Ebenezer meetinghouse in Greene County, Tennessee. A church still occupies the site. (Price, *op. cit.*, II, 76.)

[71] Bishop Richard Whatcoat died at the home of Richard Bassett at Dover, Delaware, on July 5, 1806.

I had no fire, but a bed wherever I could find a bench; my aid, Moses Lawrence, had a bear skin, and a dirt floor to spread it on.

Friday, 26. My affliction returned: considering the food, the labour, the lodging, the hardships I meet with and endure, it is not wonderful. Thanks be to God! we had a generous rain—may it be general through the continent!

Saturday, 27. I rode twelve miles to Turkey Creek,[72] to a kind of camp meeting. On the *Sabbath*, I preached to about five hundred souls: it was an open season, and a few souls professed converting grace.

Monday, 29. Raining. We had dry weather during the meeting. There were eleven sermons, and many exhortations. At noon it cleared up, and gave us an opportunity of riding home: my mind enjoyed peace, but my body felt the effects of riding. On *Tuesday*, I went to a school house to preach: I rode through Swannanoa River and Cane, and Hooper's Creeks.

Wednesday, *October* 1. I preached at Samuel Edney's.[73] Next day we had to cope with Little and Great Hunger mountain. Now I know what Mills Gap is, between Buncombe and Rutherford: one of the descents is like the roof of a house, for nearly a mile: I rode, I walked, I sweated, I trembled, and my old knees failed: here are gullies, and rocks, and precipices; nevertheless, the way is as good as the path over the Table mountain—bad is the best. We came upon Green River,[74] crossed, and then hobbled and crippled along to Martin Edward's, a local preacher: my host had waited two years; I ordained him to deacon's orders. I feel as if I ought not to preach one sermon without being pointed and very full upon the doctrine of purity.

Saturday, 4. Crossed Green and Broad rivers, to attend a meeting in the woods in Rutherford county.[75] I preached on the *Sabbath*, on Psalm li, 8–11; and on *Monday* at eight o'clock in the morning, on 1 John i, 6, 7—it was a moving season. I made my lodging with brother Driskells on

[72] The camp meeting on Turkey Creek near Leicester in Buncombe County, North Carolina, was started this year and continued for a hundred years. (Price, *op. cit.*, II, 80.)

[73] The Rev. Samuel Edney (1768–1844) was one of the founders of Methodism in western North Carolina. He was born in 1768, licensed to preach in 1791, and ordained by Asbury in 1813. In 1793 he was appointed to the Swannanoa Circuit which covered western North Carolina and a part of Tennessee, and it has been said that he was the first preacher definitely appointed west of the Blue Ridge. After his location he lived at the present Edneyville in Henderson County, where a historical marker has been erected. He married Eleanor (called Nellie) Mills, daughter of William Mills who established Mills Chapel and entertained Asbury in South Carolina. (See *Journal* entry for December 16, 1812.) Samuel Edney and others of the family are buried at Edneyville, and numerous descendants still reside in Henderson County and western North Carolina. The Edneyville Methodist Church is the continuation of the early Methodist society which met at the home of Samuel Edney. (Patton, *op. cit.*, 25.)

[74] Green River flows through present Polk County and into Broad River at the present Rutherford County line.

[75] This meeting was probably held near the present town of Rutherfordton.

Sunday night and on *Monday* at Major George Moore's, twenty miles from the ground.

South Carolina

On *Tuesday*, we came rapidly through a part of Lincoln, to South Carolina, about thirty miles, and lodged at Alexander Hill's; next day stayed with Mr. Fulton.[76] My mind is in constant peace under great bodily exertions. I preached at my host's, upon Matthew xxiv, 12, 13.

Thursday, 9. At the Waxhaw. We crossed Catawba at M'Lenahan's ferry, and came to Robert Hancock's to lodge.[77] We have had a blessed rain. On *Friday* we came to the Hanging Rock—death! death! The death of our friend, Daniel Carpenter, makes a great breach: but he has gone safe. *Saturday*, rain—rest—closely occupied in writing. On the *Sabbath* I preached at the Hanging Rock[78]—few people; but a good season. On Monday I copied the *minutes*. I feel full of God: glory to God! On *Tuesday* I went over to Thompson's Creek, Anson county, to see George Dougharty; but his friends had conveyed him away on a bed.[79] I spent *Wednesday* in reading, meditation, prayer, and Christian converse in Thomas Shaw's family.

Thursday, 16. Rode back to the Hanging Rock: I felt the effects of the ride, as the exercise was somewhat new. I prayed in two out of three families we visited: it seemed to me as if they were cases of life and death. It is the duty of a general officer to be careful of all his men, especially those composing his staff. A drought is the cause of want and affliction: in such seasons we should use humiliation, fasting, penitence, and prayer.

Friday, 17. Closely occupied in writing.[80] On *Saturday*, rode to Camden. I have received a full account from Doctor William P. Chandler,[81] Delaware district, of the work of God from May third to August twenty-fourth. What hath God wrought!

Sunday, 19. I preached upon 1 Cor. xi, 28: "Let a man examine him-

[76] Fulton lived at Tirzah in York County, nine miles west of Rock Hill.

[77] McClenan's ferry was probably east of Rock Hill. Hancock lived in upper Lancaster County in South Carolina. Waxhaw was four miles east. Whatcoat had died, and Asbury had no episcopal colleague on this his twenty-second trip to South Carolina.

[78] Betts says the bishop stayed with John Horton at Hanging Rock as previously. (See *Journal* entries for December 24, 1792; December 26, 1793; March 6, 1797; February 17, 1800.) Daniel Carpenter was another friend there.

[79] From Hanging Rock the bishop detoured northward to Anson County, North Carolina, to see George Dougharty, presiding elder of the Camden District. This prominent preacher was near death with consumption, though he was able to attend the conference at Sparta, Georgia, three months later. He died on March 23, 1807, at Wilmington, North Carolina, and was buried in the African church there. (*Minutes*, 1808; Smith: *Georgia Methodism*, 83.)

[80] See letter to Thomas Haskins, October 17, 1806.

[81] See note under December 12, 1805.

self." After making some general observations on the sacrifice of Abel, of Abraham, and the nature of the passover and the Lord's supper, I enforced the necessity upon sinners, seekers, backsliders, believers, and ministers, *to examine themselves*. In the afternoon, I heard the Rev. Mr. Flinn, and was pleased with him as a Presbyterian minister. Mr. Smilie, a Presbyterian, preached for us in the tabernacle.

Monday, 20. I rode to Rembert Hall, eleven hundred and twenty miles from Philadelphia—in health, and, I trust, in holiness. Glory to God!

Tuesday, 21. Reading closely. *Wednesday*, *Thursday*, *Friday*, and *Saturday*, reading the eighth and ninth volumes of Wesley's Sermons: they wake the powers of my soul. Abstinence and prayer. I feel my mind in great peace, and a stayed trust that the Lord will provide for the South Carolina Conference: let the preachers go, as they have done, to their farms and their merchandize, yet I am greatly confident of the success of the cause of God in these parts.

Sunday, 26. At Rembert's chapel I preached on 1 John iii, 1–3. 1. The manner of *love*—not that of a master, a father, a mother, or a Christian; but *love* of a peculiar character—the *love* of God, demonstrated in Christ for our redemption and salvation. 2. A view of the past, present, future, and eternal state of believers—First, The low estate; Secondly, Adoption, and regeneration, and sanctification; Thirdly, Glorification of soul and body. *Behold*, and wonder whilst ye adore. Lastly: the men of the world know not the *Father*, how then should they know the *children* of God the *Father?*

Monday, 27. I am bound for the city of Charleston. We sought lodging at two houses at Bruton's Lake: we found it at Mr. Martin's.[82] On *Tuesday* we made twenty-five miles to Murray's ferry, instead of fifteen: at Long Ferry, to which we were obliged to steer,[83] we were detained five hours through the swamp; heat, mosquitoes, gallinippers—plenty. We rode twenty miles after sundown to get to Mr. Hatchett's, at Monk's Corner; the family being sick, we went to Mr. Jones's, who kindly entertained us; we made fifty miles to-day, and came to lodgings about ten o'clock at night. On *Wednesday*, we came through heat and heavy roads to Charleston, where we found all things well, and in good order: Lewis Myers is an economist.[84]

Sunday, *November* 2. At Cumberland street church I preached in the morning; and at Bethel in the afternoon.

Monday, 3. Neither unemployed, nor triflingly. If we call for social prayer seven times a day, there are none to complain; the house is our

[82] Bruton's Lake, where Martin lived, was on the upper side of the Santee River in lower Clarendon County.

[83] It seems that Asbury expected to cross Murray's Ferry near St. Stephen but had to move upstream to Long Ferry near Eutaw Springs.

[84] The Rev. Lewis Myers was stationed with Levi Garrison at Charleston.

own, and profane people board not with us.[85] My time is spent in reading, writing, and receiving all who come, whites and Africans: I am sometimes called away in the midst of a letter. God the Lord is here. I am happy that we have finished our new church, and bought an acre of ground; should I live long, I shall see a house in the Northern Liberties of Cooper River.[86] On *Tuesday* I wrote a letter to Dr. Coke, giving a general statement of the late work of God upon our continent.

Sunday, 9. I preached again in Cumberland church, on 2 Cor. iv, 17, 18. I spoke under serious depression of body and mind: in the afternoon I gave them a discourse at the Bethel church, upon Phil. i, 27–30. I have read many pages of Church History, written twelve long letters, preached four sermons, and received all visitors, and spoken to them on the concerns of their souls. *Monday*, 10. It appears that there is a work amongst white and black—some have found the blessing. I received a letter from Daniel Hitt, giving an account of the Long Calm camp meeting, in Maryland:[87] it held from the eighth to the fourteenth of October; five hundred and eighty were said to be converted, and one hundred and twenty believers confirmed and sanctified. Lord, let this work be general!

On *Tuesday* I left my prison, and got as far as Captain Perry's, thirty miles; and next day, by riding two hours in the night, reached Jacob Barr's. On *Thursday* we rode up Edisto to Benjamin Tarrant's, twenty-two miles: next day we reached Weathersby's, twenty-five miles.

Georgia

Saturday brought us to Augusta: we have made a journey of about six days in five, through deep sands.

Sabbath, 16. The morning was cold, and few hearers; my subject was Rom. xiii, 2. *High time* indeed. In the afternoon I spoke again on Heb. xi, 25, 26. I wrote to Daniel Hitt on things sacred. I am grieved to have to do with boys. Hugh Porter[88] had written to this town about a station: and added to the mischief he had formerly done: I shall take care of these youngsters. And behold, here is a bell over the gallery!—and cracked too; may it break! It is the first I ever saw in a house of ours in America; I hope it will be the last.

[85] Asbury was again living in the Bethel parsonage at Charleston.

[86] Northern Liberties was a section of Charleston which now includes Hampstead Park and the old railroad station. The Cumberland Mission was set up there in 1883. (Chreitzberg, *op. cit.*, 90.)

[87] Daniel Hitt (1770–1825) was the presiding elder of the Baltimore District. In 1807 he became Asbury's traveling companion and was book agent from 1808 to 1816. (See *Journal* entry for February 23, 1808.)

[88] Hugh Porter was stationed at Augusta and at the approaching conference was appointed to the Santee Circuit. (See *Minutes.*)

Monday, 17. Pleasant ride to Sindall's, sixteen miles. Here, after the second generation is risen up, we have a revival in Columbia county. By being lost, we made a ride of thirty miles to Thomas Haynes's on *Tuesday*. A few met for prayer: I spoke to them on 1 Peter i, 3–6. On *Wednesday* we rested. At Fountain's, on *Thursday*, I preached on 1 Thess. iv, 13, 14. On *Friday* I rested, wrote, and visited.

Saturday, 22. Rode to the west end of Wilkes county. At Stevenson meeting house we held a three-days' meeting: four travelling, and two local preachers were present. I read the letter from William P. Chandler,[89] in Delaware, and exhorted a little.

Sabbath, 23. I preached on Luke iv, 18: there might be one thousand souls. We hope three were converted, and many quickened—preachers and people. I ordained James Allen a local deacon.

Tuesday, 25. Rained. I kept close; read, wrote, and prayed. A thought struck me that I would take the names and numbers of our congregations in Georgia; this I effected with the assistance of Josias Randall,[90] and found them to be one hundred and thirty; which I calculate to consist of one thousand souls each; so that we preach to one hundred and thirty thousand souls in Georgia—to some of these once in a year, others once in a quarter, others in four, some in two, and by the labours of the travelling and local ministry, to some every week. The return of members for this State will be about five thousand for the present year. It is quite probable we congregate two hundred thousand in each State, on an average; and if to these we add those who hear us in the two Canadian Provinces, in the Mississippi and Indiana territories, it will perhaps be found, that we preach to *four millions* of people. What a charge!

Wednesday, 26. A clear sky—and a soul unclouded. On *Thursday* we rode to Arthur Matthews's, a healthy, decent, serious family, in Warren county. *Friday* brought us to William Hardwick's, Jefferson county.

Next day I preached at Bethel chapel, on 1 Thess. v, 6, 7. I took lodging at Benjamin Bryan's.

Sabbath, 30. We had very cold weather after a rain; the house was badly calculated for the change: my subject was 2 Cor. iv, 2. I lodged at Russell Brown's.

Monday, December 1. Came back to Rehoboth. I have ridden eighty-four miles to attend this meeting at Bethel—to little purpose, I fear, unless for the trial of my own faith and patience: I was greatly chilled in my sys-

[89] William P. Chandler was presiding elder of the Delaware District in the Philadelphia Conference.

[90] Josias Randle (1766–1824) was presiding elder of the Ogeechee District. (See *Minutes*. Also *Journal* entry for December 6, 1799.) He went from Anson County, North Carolina, and was related to "Dumb John" Randle, whose home was one of Asbury's earliest preaching places there. (See February 15, 1785.) There is still a preaching place at or near the old John Randle home. Josias Randle was later a figure in Georgia public life.

tem. On *Tuesday* I read and wrote; and rode through a storm two miles to see Billy Stith. Next day we had rain, snow, and excessively cold weather: I preached upon Rom. xii, 12, 13; there were twelve souls present. On *Thursday* we had our horses shod. The excessive rains and freshets have done damage: the bridges on Ogeechee are generally carried away; so also upon Little River.

Friday, 5. We passed Williams's Creek; and afterward Little River, where the bridge once stood: I lodged at Thomas Grant's, and left a family exhortation.

Saturday brought us along through Washington to Petersburg, thirty-two miles. We fed our horses on the route, though we starved ourselves. I preached at seven o'clock in the evening. Reverend —— Cummins, and Reverend —— Doke, our Presbyterian brethren, were present.

Sabbath, 7. At Tait's meeting house I preached upon Luke xii, 40. It was a very cold day; and the house was so open we had little satisfaction. I visited Charles Tait, a judge; I did not present myself in the character of a gentleman, but as a Christian, and a Christian minister: I would visit the President of the United States in no other character; true, I would be innocently polite and respectful—no more. As to the Presbyterian ministers, and all ministers of the Gospel, I will treat them with great respect, but I shall ask no favours of them: to humble ourselves before those who think themselves so much above the Methodist preachers by worldly honours, by learning, and especially by salary, will do them no good.

Monday, 8. We had cause to rejoice at James Allston's that parents and children love the Lord: the old people have I know for twenty-seven years. I preached here on Monday, on 2 Pet. iii, 2. On *Tuesday* I came to Blackwell's: the widow is my hostess—the former head of the family is gone to rest.

Wednesday, 10. At Ralph Banks's.[91] Where shall we find so healthy and happy a man and wife as we have here? the mother is but thirty-seven, and she has twelve fine children. I was determined to go to the meeting house, excessive as the rain was: we had one woman and thirty men; we rejoiced in God. They have had a camp meeting blessing at Coldwater—the people are lively.

Thursday, 11. We rode twenty miles to James Marks's,[92] Broad River quarterly meeting. Another plentiful and powerful rain. On *Friday* night we held a feeble night meeting. On *Saturday*, at the meeting house, I spoke on Galatians vi, 9; it was penetratingly cold. We held a meeting in James Marks's dwelling-house at night.

[91] Ralph Banks was a prominent Methodist who lived in Wilkes County near Neuberg. One authority says that the first Methodist Conference in Georgia met at his house. (Bowen, *op. cit.*; Smith, *op. cit.*, 60; see notes under April 9, 1788; November 10, 1801.)

[92] See note under November 21, 1813.

Sabbath, 14. At ten o'clock we had prayer meeting. S. Matthews preached at eleven o'clock; and I held forth at twelve o'clock in the open air: I faced the sun, but my glasses saved my eyes. We felt cold enough.

Monday, 15. Rode to Oglethorpe, and put up with Henry Pope. Our thirty miles' ride was made without feeding man or beast. Reaching Athens on *Tuesday*, we had an evening lecture at Hope Hull's.[93] I wished to have crossed the river into Jackson county, but the rain came on and we returned to Blanton's and Pope's. General Clarke and L. Crawford had been dwelling on Indian lands: they and their company, five in all, lodged at Pope's with us; in my presence they restrained their wild, fearless, frontier character, and behaved with great decency and politeness.

Thursday, 18. Great rain. Reading and writing. On *Friday* I visited James Freeman. At Blanton's, on *Saturday*, I spoke on 1 John ii, 15–17. I preached at Pope's church, on Rom. viii, 7–9: elders Stith Mead, Hope Hull, and Moses Matthews were present, and bore a part in the public religious exercises. John, a black man, preached in the evening.

Monday, 22. We rode to General Stewart's. Very warm—like a summer's day. What amazing changes we have in this country! I gave them a sermon. On *Tuesday* we had a night meeting at John Crutchfield's: I spoke on 1 John ii, 1–3: we had a gentle gale of grace. On *Wednesday* we were at liberty. Alas for poor Samuel Mayo, the son of pious John, a local Methodist preacher in England! I have no children to blot my name by drunkenness or murder.

Thursday, 25. Our new chapel at Liberty is thirty by fifty feet. I gave them a sermon in it on 1 Peter iv, 3–5. Lodged at Joshua Moore's. On *Friday* I found Myles Green preaching; I ordained him immediately, and then gave a discourse on Heb. xii, 1, 2. After meeting I came on to Sparta. I received a dozen letters from the north. More good news from Doctor Chandler. The work of God is wonderful in Delaware. But what a *rumpus* is raised! We are subverters of government—disturbers of society—movers of insurrections. Grand juries in Delaware and Virginia have presented the noisy preachers—lawyers and doctors are in arms—the lives, blood, and livers of the poor Methodists are threatened: poor, crazy sinners! see ye not that the Lord is with us?

Sabbath, 28. Prayer meeting at six o'clock. John M'Vean[94] preached at eight o'clock. At twelve o'clock I read the letters narrative of the *great*

[93] Hope Hull (1763–1818), father of Georgia Methodism, located in 1795. He lived at Athens and was one of the leaders in developing the University of Georgia. There was no Methodist church in Athens until 1825, but there was a society which met at Hull's meetinghouse. The customary place of preaching was the college chapel. (Smith, *op. cit.*, 363; Chreitzberg, *op. cit.*, 86, 87; Simpson: *Cyclopedia of Methodism*, 458.)

[94] John McVean was stationed at Augusta and at the conference was appointed to Edisto Circuit in South Carolina. (See *Minutes*.)

work, and preached upon Col. iv, 7, 8. Brother Bennet Kendrick occupied the pulpit at three o'clock; and brother Stith Mead[95] at night.

Monday, 29. We began our conference. The subject of the delegated Conference was adopted, with only two dissenting voices: these members, however, cheerfully submitted, and one of the dissentients was elected a member. All was peace respecting the stations. We had prayer meeting at six o'clock; at eleven, at three, and at seven o'clock at night we had preaching. I was called upon to deliver a funeral discourse for Bishop Whatcoat. On the *Sabbath morning* we had a band meeting in the conference, and I preached in the open air at eleven o'clock; my subject, Mark xvi, 19, 20. From Philadelphia to Augusta I count it one thousand eight hundred and twenty miles, the route we have made. We have fifty travelling preachers in this conference this year, and an increase of one thousand members.

[95] Bennet Kendrick had been at Wilmington and at the approaching conference became presiding elder of the Camden District. Stith Mead had preached in Georgia and was the father of the church in Augusta, but he was now the presiding elder of the Richmond District in Virginia. (See *Minutes*. See also several letters of Stith Mead, property of Edgar A. Potts of Norfolk, Virginia.)

1807

1807

Asbury and Daniel Hitt in peril in the Green Mountains of Vermont

CHAPTER THIRTY-SIX

South Carolina

On *Thursday*, *January* 1, 1807, we set out for Columbia, dining in the woods on our route: it was excessively cold. I preached in Mr. Harrison's house in the evening. Next day we came to Camden. *Saturday* brought us to Rembert Hall. We have been redeeming time by riding two hundred and twenty miles in five days. It has been so cold, I have not been able to pray and meditate as I wished. I must now answer thirteen letters in two days. My body is afflicted, but I am kept in perfect love.

Sabbath, 11. We attended, as was meet, at Rembert's chapel. I gave them a sermon on 1 Chron. xxviii, 9.

Wednesday, 14. We came away to M'Cullom's ferry.[1] I had finished my writing on *Monday* and *Tuesday*. On our way we dined at Woodham,[2] and lodged with Jeremiah Heath. On *Thursday* we crossed Pee Dee, and came to Colonel Bethea's.[3]

North Carolina

Friday brought us through Lumberton, in North Carolina, lodging with Peter Gautier. We found ourselves obliged to ride on the Lord's day, through the cold, to Wilmington, crossing two rivers in a snow and hail

[1] McCullom's ferry was on Lynch's Creek.

[2] Woodham lived in Darlington County.

[3] Colonel Bethea lived in upper Marion, now Dillon, County. Asbury crossed the Pee Dee at Cashua's ferry.

storm. I have ridden four hundred and twenty miles in ten days and a half—cold, sick, and faint: it was as much as I could well bear up under.

Monday, 19. Busy making extracts from letters, and planning for conferences. *Tuesday* occupied as yesterday; in the evening I preached. I feel that God is here. On *Wednesday* brother Kendrick preached. *Thursday*, reading and writing; Joshua Wells preached.

Friday, 23. I preached in the tabernacle, upon Matt. xi, 28–30. It was a time of some quickening. On *Saturday*, reading Wesley's Sermons, first volume; those who feel disposed to complain of the brevity of his Notes, should recollect the wonderful amount and variety of his literary labours, polemical and practical, besides *the care of all the Churches* in three kingdoms.

Sabbath, 25. A *high day* on Mount Zion. At the rising of the sun, John Charles began the worship of the day; he chose for his subject Rom. viii, 1. At eleven o'clock I held forth on Heb. iii, 12–15. I spoke again at three o'clock on Isaiah lv, 6, 7. Stith Mead preached at six o'clock in the evening. O that by any means we may save some! On *Monday* and *Tuesday* still reading Wesley's Sermons: I have completed thirty nearly. On *Tuesday* evening I preached, and it was a serious time.

Wednesday, 28. We took our flight from Wilmington: what I felt and suffered there, from preachers and people, is known to God. At Nixon's, Topsail, I preached on 2 Pet. iii, 14. On *Thursday* I rode forty miles to the Richlands, and preached at Lot Ballard's. *Friday evening* found us at Perry's. *Saturday* brought us to Newbern: we had an awful storm of rain.

February 1. I preached on *Sunday* at eleven o'clock.

Wednesday, 4. We have used great diligence in our conference labours,[4] and have been faithful to the pulpit. I preached to-day on 1 Cor. ii, 5. On the *Sabbath* I preached to the whites, on John iii, 16; and to the Africans, on Eph. vi, 5–8. Much might be said; I will only observe that we have sixty-seven preachers, and have added three thousand one hundred and fifty-nine to this conference bounds; we have, since our sitting here, known that there are twenty whites converted, and as many blacks: these blessings on our labours pay all expenses, reward all toils in the midst of suffering and excessively cold weather.

Monday, 9. I gave them my last discourse on Psalms xxxiv, 15, 16; and next day came away to the widow Williams's. On *Wednesday* at Pinner's. The Roanoke had broken away with its ice. *Thursday* brought us to

[4] It was at this conference that the resolution, begun by the Baltimore Conference, was presented in favor of calling a General Conference of seven delegates from each annual conference to meet in Baltimore in 1807 for the purpose of strengthening the episcopacy. The plan was vigorously opposed by Jesse Lee in the Virginia Conference, and it received only fourteen votes. Since the plan required the vote of all the conferences it was defeated by Virginia's vote. All the other conferences reported in favor. (Bennett, *op. cit.*, 505–9.)

Murfreesboro: I preached upon 1 John iii, 10, 11. It was the day after the celebration of Washington's funeral: many of the *respectables* had come to town on this occasion, and still remained; these attended. I lodged at Doctor Key's.

Virginia

Friday, 13. We came to Suffolk. I had sent on a messenger, and found a congregation, to whom I spoke a few words, on 1 Pet. iii, 10–12. We felt a present God. Brother Yerbury: *as dying and behold he lives*, spiritually. I have time to make but few observations. We have had rain for three days past; bad roads for two hundred miles. Since I left Philadelphia I calculate having travelled two thousand four hundred and forty miles. At Norfolk I preached for them, and at Portsmouth. On *Monday* we came away to General Wells's, Isle of Wight county; and next day called upon Willy Blunt on our way to Birdsong's. *Wednesday* brought us through a *proper* storm to Petersburg: the streets were not easily passable. We lodged on *Thursday night* in Richmond at the house of the widow Tucker: the roads hither had well-nigh mired us. On *Friday* we lodged at William Smith's: these are friends to camp meetings, and gracious souls. A long ride of forty-two miles brought us to Fredericksburg on *Saturday*; we got a little fodder for our horses, and took a cut of dry bread on the cold ground ourselves. My mind enjoys great peace; and yet there are subjects that might disturb it: but I pass them over; I am not fond of hurting the feelings of people.

Sabbath, 22. I preached in the church; and then came away to Aquia Town, sixteen miles, and lodged at Mr. Bailey's. On *Monday* I went over to Sandford's on Pohick; next day the rain followed us to Alexandria: at night I gave them a discourse on Rev. xiv, 12, 13.

Maryland

Wednesday, 25. We crossed over into Maryland at Georgetown (D.C.). Surely the roads are bad! My mind is in great peace. I had to preach a kind of funeral discourse, on the death of Bishop Whatcoat,[5] on *Thursday*: and on *Friday* I came away to Bladensburg. Here I baptized a child, and prayed with the afflicted, and resumed my march eastward through mud and mire, arriving in the night in Baltimore.

Saturday, 28. Snow. I rested and wrote.

[5] Bishop Richard Whatcoat (1736–1806) had died in the home of Richard Bassett, Dover, Delaware, July 5, 1806. For the most complete account of the last illness and death of the bishop, by one who was present, see Boehm, *op. cit.*, 138, 140–43.

Sabbath, March 1. Light Street Chapel; I preached upon Heb. xii, 2. At the African church[6] my subject was Col. ii, 6.

Saturday, 7. Our conference commenced[7] its sitting on *Monday*, and rose this evening. There were a hundred and one members upon the list; eighteen of these were additions made. We sat six hours a day, and did much work in great peace. In the multiplicity of things that necessarily came before me, much must be left in shades; there were few complaints about stations. The increase within the bounds of the Baltimore Conference, is two thousand eight hundred and seventeen members. We had a great deal of faithful preaching. On the *Sabbath* I preached at the Point; and at Light Street I gave them my last discourse. I was in affliction and unwell, but always in peace; God is all in all.

Tuesday, 10. I left Baltimore for Perry Hall.[8] I spent one night with the elders of the house and my old friends Jesse Hollingsworth, and Daniel Hitt, the faithful companion of my travels for three thousand miles. On *Wednesday* we left our kind friends, and came to Bennett's.[9] Next day I preached in brother Howell's house, and came to North East. *Friday* brought us through rain and snow to Georgetown Cross Roads: here we called a meeting in the evening; my subject was 2 Corinthians xii, 9. On *Saturday* we came in to Chestertown; it was damp and cold.

Sabbath, 15. Hail, blessed day! The Sun of Righteousness within us, and the material sun once more gladdens the earth with his beams! Although we have taken five days to come from Baltimore to this place, a distance of one hundred miles, the stage drivers can tell that we have been pretty busy. At Chester I find that unpleasing prejudices have been excited by the publication of a pamphlet on *succession in the Church*; the author is one Kewley, who went from us.[10] In the morning I preached upon Psalm

[6] This reference is probably to the Sharp Street Methodist Episcopal Church (1802–60) which was located on the west side of Sharp Street between Lombard and Pratt streets. Its successor is the Sharp Street Memorial Church, Etting and Dolphin streets, Baltimore. (*Methodist Sesqui-Centennial Souvenir Book,* 68; see note under May 25, 1797.)

[7] Sixty-one preachers attended the session of the Baltimore Conference in Light Street Church. Of most far-reaching effect was the almost unanimous vote to ask the six other annual conferences to give consideration to the "propriety of a selected or delegated General Conference." (Armstrong, *op. cit.*, 146.)

[8] See letter to Daniel Asbury, March 9, 1807.

[9] This was either Elisha Bennett, a trustee appointed to take a deed of land from Nicholas Harding to build a preaching house, or to the home mentioned by Colbert: "I traveled from Thomas Bennett's to Baltimore about 20 miles." (Baltimore Circuit Stewards' Book, 1794–1815; William Colbert's *Journal*, December 15, 1790.)

[10] The book was *An Inquiry into the Validity of Methodist Episcopacy, with an Appendix, containing two original documents never before published by an Episcopalian of the State of Maryland.* John Kewley, the author, was an Irishman and was reared in the Church of Rome. He was converted under the influence of Alexander McCaine and in 1801 was received on trial in the Methodist Episcopal Church. Subsequently he became an Episcopalian but died a priest in the Roman Catholic Church. (Drinkhouse: *History of Methodist Reform,* I, 401, 402.)

xxxiv, 11: "Come, ye children," &c. 1. *Who* are to be taught. 2. *What* they are to be taught. 3. Who are the teachers. 4. The happy consequences of being taught aright, and receiving and practising the instructions given. I spoke again in the afternoon, on Rev. vi, 13, 14. My mind is in perfect peace.

Monday, 16. Came to Centreville, and I preached. After dining with Thomas Wright,[11] the brother of the present governor of Maryland, we came to Easton, and lodged with Mr. Lockerman.[12] On *Tuesday* Daniel Hitt preached; I only exhorted. We met Joseph Everett, who conducted us to William Frazier's to dine. On *Wednesday* we came to Thomas Foster's. I was unwell, and Daniel Hitt preached. We rode on to Cambridge; Daniel Hitt preached in the evening.

Thursday, 19. I took the pulpit at eleven o'clock; it was court time, it was cold, and the notice was short. My subject was 2 Cor. vi, 7: "The word of truth"—the grand doctrines of the Gospel, with special and general application. "The power of God"—in operation upon the souls of the people in numbers and degrees. "Armour of righteousness"—such as described in Ephesians, *helmet of salvation*, and so on. But more fully explanatory of the general subject in its analogy to the justifying and sanctifying operations of grace, and practical righteousness as it respects our relation to God and his Church. We returned to Thomas Foster's.

Friday, 20. At Bethel, Brown's chapel, Daniel Hitt preached, I only exhorted. We dined at father Davis's, and lodged at his son William's. The weather is excessively cold and disagreeably windy. On *Saturday* I preached at Deep Creek, and ordained two local preachers to the office of deacon. The day was unpleasant, and the house open. We dined with Deacon Baker, and then drove to George Parker's, within four miles of Salisbury, for the night. I suffered so much in the last two days, that I could not keep my mind constantly engaged in prayer; this was my grief, but my patience bore me up.

Sabbath, 22. At Salisbury I preached upon Ephes. iv, 1. The Episcopalians have had their day. Our appointment had not been made, nevertheless we preached; Daniel Hitt at eleven o'clock, and at night, and I at three o'clock in the afternoon; and we had people to hear us.

Virginia

Monday, 23. We came to dear William Downing's, Accomack: I came in late and unwell.

[11] Thomas Wright lived at Centreville and was a leader of Queen Annes County in promoting American independence. He was a trustee to whom on June 21, 1794, the lot was deeded on which that same year a chapel was erected. It was the forerunner of the present Epworth Church. Thomas Wright's brother, Robert, was the governor of Maryland 1806–9. (Emory: *History of Queen Anne's County*, 232, 233, 276, 277; see note under June 11, 1795.)

[12] This was probably Theodore R. Lockerman, a prominent citizen of Talbot County.

Tuesday, 24. When I should have gone to preach, I went to bed ill with a bilious colic and fever.

Maryland

We came to Snow Hill on *Wednesday*; my chill and sickness continued, and Daniel Hitt preached. We kept on to Poplartown, and stopped at C. Hazzard's: still unwell.

Delaware

Thursday, 26. We called to see brother Davis: he seemed to be dying by inches in a close room. We stopped at Mr. Clayton's,[13] Dagsboro, in Delaware: from hence we fled with speed to Lewistown, stopped and took coffee. I preached on 1 Thessalonians ii, 11, 12; we had a crowded house and a gracious time.

Friday, 27. At Milford Bishop Whatcoat preached his last sermon, and as I preached here upon 2 Tim. iv, 7, 8, it came as a matter of course to make some observations on his character, labours, piety, and death.

Saturday, 28. I preached in Dover, and the numbers present were so great, that I stood up outside to speak; the wind was cold, and I uncovered. I preached the same day at Smyrna, at four o'clock. I hear many things of the weal and woe of the work of God.

Monday, 30. I gave them a sermon in Wilmington.

Tuesday, 31. Yesterday's excessive cold is explaining itself in a snow storm.

Pennsylvania

Wednesday, April 1. We arrived in Philadelphia.[14]

Friday, 10. Our conference commenced its session on *Thursday* the 2d, and finished to-day. We progressed and finished in great peace. The impeachment, trial, and examination of Richard Lyon[15] took up most of a

[13] This may have been James Clayton, a brother of Dr. Joshua Clayton. He lived at Dagsboro, Sussex County, Delaware, and was the father of John Middleton Clayton (1796–1856), senator, chief justice of Delaware, secretary of state in the administration of President Zachary Taylor, and negotiator of the Clayton-Bulwer Treaty. (Scharf: *History of Delaware*, I, 529.)

[14] See letter to the trustees of the African Methodist Episcopal Church, April 9, 1807, also letter to unnamed brother, April, 1807.

[15] Richard Lyon was admitted on trial in 1797 and into full connection in 1802. Prior to the 1807 session of the conference he was at Smyrna, Delaware, as senior preacher. His appointment in 1807 was in company with John Walker on the Bristol Circuit, Pennsylvania, where he began his ministry. He located in 1808.

whole day: the affair was managed with prudence and impartiality, and, after a patient investigation of the case, it was determined not to give him the charge of a circuit this year. The preachers took their stations very willingly; for aught I know. The excessive labour of the last two days drove me to my bed during the recess of the sitting. Seven deacons and four elders were ordained. I may mention that a short reply was given to Doctor Coke's long letter. On the *Sabbath*, at St. George's, I preached on Rev. ii, 10. The subject of Bishop Whatcoat was incorporated into my discourse at the Tabernacle: my text was Rev. xiv, 13. There was preaching in our houses as usual on conference occasions.

New Jersey

Saturday, 11. I came into Jersey, and lodged with Daniel Bates.

Sabbath, 12. I stood up once more at Bethel, and spoke on Rev. xxii, 14, 15. God hath been in this society—in the last year forty converts were added at one quarterly meeting: the people cease to oppose. We hope there have been three hundred souls converted in one year in this neighbourhood. John Duffield[16] is buried to-day: he had fallen away, but was restored at the last quarterly meeting, and intended to have rejoined the society—we hope he has joined the Church triumphant.

Monday, 13. A great storm of rain located us to the house at William Dilkes's.

Tuesday, 14. Rode to Salem, and preached; I was still very unwell. At Pittsgrove[17] on *Wednesday* I was unable to preach: I rode home with father Early.[18] The widow Ayres,[19] one of the first Methodists in the place, has died in peace.

Thursday, 16. I gave an exhortation and we then came on to Daniel

[16] John Duffield is noted in the New Jersey Archives as a witness to various wills and taking inventory of estates. (Abstracts of Wills, IV, 288; V, 60; VI, 403.)

[17] Pittsgrove is in Salem County, about seven miles from Woodstown. It is probable that Methodism originated in Pittsgrove in a class formed by Philip Gatch in 1773. Benjamin Abbott, who was converted October 12, 1772, averred that there was no Methodist society when he was converted. The class which was formed a short time later was joined by Mrs. Abbott and some of the Abbott children, and Benjamin Abbott was made class leader. (Atkinson, *op. cit.*, 78–80.)

[18] John Early (1738–1828) lived in Gloucester County and was one of the earliest Methodists in New Jersey. He was a native of Ireland and came to America in 1764. By 1770 he had embraced the doctrines of Methodism and served the church for about sixty years. For forty years he was a class leader and steward on the circuit to which he belonged. (Atkinson, *op. cit.*, 25–26; New Jersey Archives, Abstracts of Wills, VIII, 212; Myers, *op. cit.*, II, 11–12.)

[19] This was Susannah Ayres. (See note under October 12, 1786.)

Bates's. At brother Azail Coate's,[20] on *Friday*, I was fit for bed only: Daniel Hitt preached at Lumberton.[21]

Saturday, 18. At New Mills I gave a kind of funeral for Bishop Whatcoat. From Baltimore to this place I count having made six hundred and thirty miles. Sick or well, I have my daily labours to perform. I am hindered from that solitary, close, meditative communion with God I wish to enjoy. I move under great debility. I found old grandfather Budd[22] *worshipping, leaning upon the top of his staff—halting, yet wrestling* like Jacob. Ah! we remember when *Israel was a child*; but now, *how goodly are thy tents, O Jacob, and thy tabernacles* (camp meetings), *O Israel!* Since October, 1771, I have visited Jersey, but never have I seen such prospects: to God the Lord be all the glory!

Sabbath, 19. In the Baptist chapel, Mount Holly,[23] I spoke on Rom. x, 26.[24] I preached at Burlington at six o'clock.

Monday, 20. I gave them a sermon at Trenton; and once more at Hopewell I stood up in my Master's name. We had one hundred souls, but we want more fire: the time will surely come to favour them.

Wednesday, 22. We came to Reading[25]: I spoke to an insensible people upon Acts ii, 21. I may weary myself in vain to heap up spiritual riches, if others will not gather them, and take care of them.

Thursday, 23. At Asburytown I gave them a faithful talk upon Heb. ii, 3, 4. There are about forty houses in or near this village, of all descriptions. In Philip Cummins's[26] kitchen I spoke to a few souls on *Friday*: my

[20] Asahel Coate (1781–1815) lived at Lumberton, a few miles from Mount Holly in Burlington County, and was a class leader there. Boehm mentions two brothers, Michael and Samuel; Michael became a Methodist preacher. Asbury was later to be cared for in a serious illness and nursed back to health in the home of Asahel Coate. (Boehm, *op. cit.*, 419–20; Woodward and Hageman, *op. cit.*, 348; New Jersey Archives, Abstracts of Wills, V, 98; VII, 47; see *Journal* entry for April 25, 1814.)

[21] The *New Jersey Guide* says that the Methodist Church on Main Street in Lumberton was erected on Church Street in 1812 and later moved to its present location. Asbury, who did not preach on this occasion, preached in the church in 1813. (Gordon, *op. cit.*, 171; *New Jersey Guide*, 620.)

[22] This was William Budd, who had welcomed Asbury to New Jersey in 1771.

[23] Asbury's reference to preaching in the Baptist chapel at this time supports the local story that a Mrs. McGowan, converted to Methodism under the preaching of James Rogers in Dublin, had become a resident of Mount Holly, and finding no Methodist society there, had joined the Baptist Church. After the reactivation of the Methodist class she rejoined the Methodists. Methodism had declined in Mount Holly over the past several years, and it appears that this visit of Asbury was responsible for its reawakening. The first Methodist Church in Mount Holly was erected about 1810. (Atkinson, *op. cit.*, 341–43, 366.)

[24] There are only twenty-one verses in this chapter. The context does not indicate what passage this may have been.

[25] Reading was a community in the German-settled portion of Hunterdon County and was named for John Reading, one of the proprietors of West Jersey.

[26] Philip Cummins lived in Vienna, in present Warren County, New Jersey. The

hearers were serious whilst I commented on Luke xi, 9–13. Rough roads, damp weather, and daily preaching, has brought me low: wherever I come, being a stranger, people expect me to speak. O that I could see as great a prospect in East as in West Jersey! *Come, thou south wind, and blow upon this garden!*

Saturday, 25. We came to Andrew Freeman's:[27] our route brought us by the Drowned Lands[28] upon Pequest Creek; this, doubtless, has once been a lake. I preached at Freeman's, and we had a feeling season. About twenty years ago, I once preached at Log Jail church: I spoke once more on the *Sabbath*; my subject was Rev. iii, 20, and I felt some enlargement. Daniel Hitt preached after me, and closed the meeting. We have preached, I suppose, to three thousand people in the Jerseys; and had we had good weather, it is quite probable we should have had six thousand.

New York

Monday, 27. We rode forty miles to lodge near Warwick.

Tuesday, 28. We came to John Ellison's at Windsor.

Wednesday, 29. As we pursued our journey the rain came on whilst at Major David Ostrander's, and we halted. At New Paltz,[29] on *Friday*, we found there was no passage to be had across the river, so we drove six miles down to a new bridge; we dined, and came on to Kingston, or Esopus; here we also were disappointed, so we turned aside to Cornelius Cole's, at Hurley. On *Friday* we made forty miles over desperate roads, and lodged at a tavern, seven miles short of Coeyman's Patent, where the conference was to sit.

Saturday, *May* 2. We met such of the members of the conference as were present.

Sabbath, 3. I preached once more on the subject of the death of our dear departed brother Whatcoat.

Saturday, 9. We concluded our labours. The preachers took their stations with the simple-heartedness of little children. I find two thousand

house in which Bishop Asbury preached is still standing. (Letter to Vernon B. Hampton from Philip G. Palmer, pastor of Vienna Methodist Church, January 7, 1956.)

[27] Andrew Freeman lived in Johnsonburg, formerly known as Log Jail. (New Jersey Archives, Abstracts of Wills, VIII, 397.)

[28] The Pequest River rises in Sussex County and flows through Warren County by a southwest course through Oxford township to the Delaware River. The "Drowned Lands" comprise the marshy lands at Great Meadows not far from Vienna which were reclaimed by engineering enterprise in the last century and today provide thousands of acres of fertile farmland. (Honeyman: *Northwestern New Jersey*, II, 711; Snell, *op. cit.*, 474, 478.)

[29] This town, with many residents of Dutch descent, was twelve miles south of Kingston. Between this point and Kingston the Walkill and Rondout Creeks had to be crossed. Esopus Creek also came in from the west back of Kingston.

and one added to the bounds of this conference. Eighteen preachers and three missionaries. We had much labour, and great peace; and although, from the badness of the weather, we came home every evening through damps and mud, I had more rest than I should have had, had we convened in a city. We had preaching every noon.

Sabbath, 10. I preached at Albany on John iii, 17. I dined with one English family and lodged with another.

Monday, 11. We set out on the turnpike road[30] to brother Carpenter's, dined, and lodged at Cambridge.

Vermont

Tuesday, 12, brought us through Salem; we dined, talked, and prayed at Rupert's:[31] possibly God may save the tavern-keeper. We lodged at Branch's: here we also prayed, but there was a tavern bar: we left, and came to Mr. Hireton's; here the landlady wept and talked, but my faith for the poor woman was not strong. We came to Carpenter's, at Chittenden, and hearing that Z. Andrews's was a home for preachers, we turned aside to tarry for a night.

Thursday, 14. We boldly engaged the Green Mountain, of which we had heard awful accounts. I match it with rude Clinch, or rough Alleghany. We found snow in the gap. A tree was lying across the path; in leading the carriage over, it upset, but sustained little damage. Having dined at Pittsfield, we took fresh courage and proceeded on. When we came to White River we were obliged to lead the horses as they dragged the carriage up the heights, over rocks, logs, and cavings-in of the earth; arrived at the Narrows we found that the bank had given way and slidden down; I proposed to work the carriage along over by hand, whilst Daniel Hitt[32] led the horses; he preferred my leading them, so on we went, but I was weak, and not enough attentive, perhaps, and the mare ran me upon a rock; up went the wheel, hanging balanced over a precipice of fifty feet—rocks, trees, and the river between us; I felt lame by the mare's treading on my foot; we unhitched the beast and righted the carriage, after unloading the baggage, and so got over the danger and difficulty. But never in my life have I been in such apparent danger. O Lord, thou hast saved man and beast! We gladly stopped in Royaltown at brother Ayres's. I have been happy under great temptations and hard labour. In every house, tavern and private, I have prayed and talked; this is part of my mission.

[30] The Turnpike ran north from Albany, east of the Hudson River, through Troy. Asbury had used this road in reverse direction during late June, 1806.

[31] Rupert was a tavern keeper just across the Vermont line, for whom the town of Rupert was named.

[32] Daniel Hitt was Asbury's traveling companion on this trip.

I have two hundred miles before me for the next week—and can I accomplish this labour? what is impossible with me is possible with God.

Friday, 15. We came to Cox's,[33] and next day I preached at Barnard, and had an open season. I ordained five deacons, namely, Carpenter, Currier, Peck, Sterling, and Perkins. On the *Sabbath day* I preached in the woods: my text was 1 Tim. ii, 15. It hailed, and in the afternoon snowed. We had three discourses, in and out of the house, and held a love feast. The work revives in this town.

Monday, 18. We came down White River, and crossed the Connecticut at Lyman's bridge.[34] We have made forty miles to-day.

New Hampshire

Tuesday, 19. We crossed the mountains and came into New Hampshire at Andover,[35] and continued on, dining and praying at Salisbury, to Concord, forty miles: we lodged at Mr. Ambrose's tavern:[36] our host was polite and attentive. We came on *Wednesday* eighteen miles to dinner at Mr. Harvey's,[37] Northwood; then through Durham and Dover, into Berwick, the first town in the district, where we put up for the night.

Maine

On *Thursday morning*, we came sixteen miles to breakfast, but I had taken medicine. We kept on through Kennebunk, Saco, and Scarborough, into Portland: I was unwell, had travelled hard, rising at four o'clock every morning, yet I had to preach here at eight o'clock in the evening. God is here: brother David Batchelor's labours have been blessed. I lodged with Major Illsley, still our great friend.

Friday, 22. We took up our journey through Falmouth to New Yarmouth and stopped at our brother Jabez Bradburg's: we had six hours' rain. It is an awful backward spring, and there is a great scarcity of hay. The wet weather prevents ploughing and seeding. Cold! cold!

Saturday, 23. We lodged with Mr. Dearborn,[38] in Monmouth. We

[33] George Cox (1762–1843) lived at Barnard, Vermont. He was one of the most prosperous citizens and deeply religious. (Cox: *New England Cox Families*, 11.)

[34] Elias Lyman settled at the "Point," or Hartford, Vermont, and built the bridge there about 1790. (Tucker: *History of Hartford, Vermont*, 339.)

[35] Asbury probably meant Hanover, the seat of Dartmouth College.

[36] This tavern was located not in Concord but in Boscawen, a short distance north of the Contoocook River in the village of Penacook. (Williams, art., *The Christian Advocate*, New York, March 16, 1916.)

[37] In 1916 the Harvey House was 183 years old and still in use. (*Ibid.*)

[38] This was Simon Dearborn, with whom he lodged during the conference of 1802.

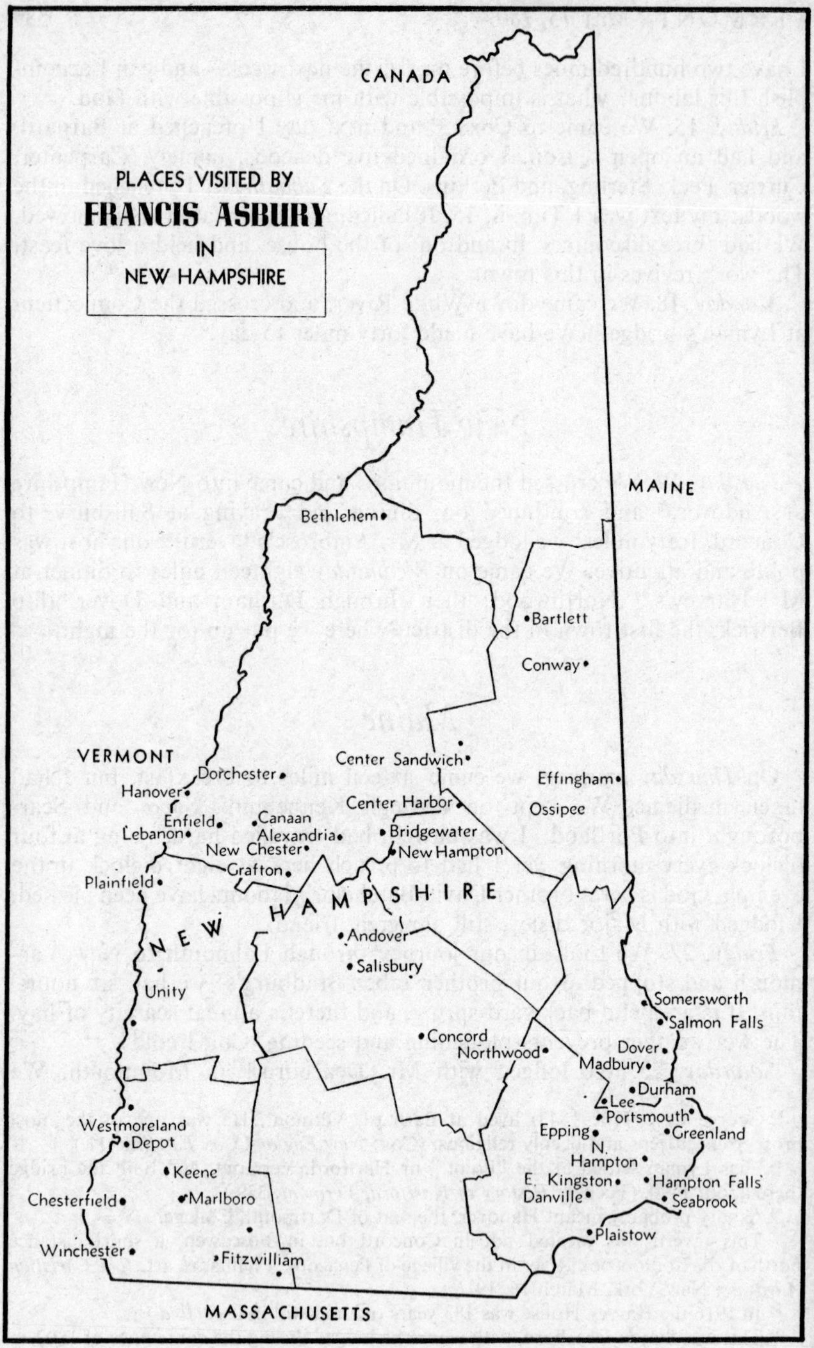
PLACES VISITED BY
FRANCIS ASBURY
IN
NEW HAMPSHIRE
CANADA
MAINE
VERMONT
MASSACHUSETTS
NEW HAMPSHIRE
Bethlehem
Bartlett
Conway
Center Sandwich
Effingham
Ossipee
Dorchester
Hanover
Enfield
Canaan
Lebanon
Alexandria
Center Harbor
Bridgewater
New Hampton
New Chester
Grafton
Plainfield
Andover
Salisbury
Unity
Somersworth
Salmon Falls
Concord
Northwood
Dover
Madbury
Durham
Lee
Portsmouth
Epping
Greenland
N. Hampton
E. Kingston
Danville
Hampton Falls
Seabrook
Plaistow
Westmoreland Depot
Keene
Marlboro
Chesterfield
Winchester
Fitzwilliam

count having made two hundred and thirty miles this week, over *hard* roads in many senses: my work is for God—my reward from him: may I be made perfect through Christian and ministerial trials and sufferings!

Sunday, 24. I preached in Monmouth, on Isa. xxxv, 3–6. At Major Cobb's, where I lodged in Gray, I left my glasses when starting on *Tuesday* morning. On *Tuesday* I preached at Scarborough at five o'clock in the evening, upon Heb. iii, 12–14. We sent forward the preachers to call a meeting in the town of Berwick, in the District of Maine; on *Wednesday* I preached to them, and the people were attentive:—this is the beginning of Methodism in this place.

New Hampshire

Thursday, 28. We dined at Epping, New Hampshire, and came on within six miles of Haverhill. To travel forty miles a day, and be under the necessity of going into *dram* and sin-infected taverns: it is such a journey that teaches us the value of hospitality in the South, and the excellency of Methodism everywhere: how laborious has it been; and expensive; and, it may be, unsuccessful! But my work and my judgement is with the Lord.

Massachusetts

Saturday, 30. At Waltham, I gave them a sermon on 1 Cor. x, 12, 13; several preachers were present. It rained on the *Sabbath*. My Bible and plans for conference stations occupied my mind, and became the devotions of the day.

Monday, *June* 1. Came to Boston. On *Tuesday* we opened our conference, ninety-two preachers being on the list.

Saturday, 6. Our conference rose. There were eight hundred dollars paid; and we were nearly three thousand insolvent. It kept us busy to preach five times a day, ordain fifty-nine to office, and inquire and examine into characters, graces, and gifts, and appoint the numerous stations. I preached on *Wednesday*, and an ordination sermon on *Thursday*, and on *Saturday evening* came away to the town of Lynn. And must I walk through the seven conferences, and travel six thousand miles in ten months?

Sunday, 7. I preached in Lynn, administered the sacrament of the Lord's supper, and came to Waltham. At Westborough I preached on *Monday*, on Luke xix, 10. I lodged at brother Nicholas's. In spite of heat and lameness, we were favoured to reach Wilbraham on *Tuesday*. To Westfield on *Wednesday*, crossing the bridge at Springfield. I am in peace; I dare not murmur, though in pain. I had an interview with a Baptist minister: he started at prayer—he called it talk to any sinner: the answer is, they cannot pray.

Thursday, 11. We crossed the mountain to Pittsfield, thirty-seven miles: we had a violent wind, excessive cold, and I was very lame. Methodism prevails in this quarter: in two societies, two hundred members have been added. A camp meeting is appointed to be held on *Monday* next.

New York

On *Saturday* we made a great ride of forty miles to Waterford,[39] in New York State. I was lame on the *Sabbath*, but I must preach: my subject was John iii, 19.

Monday, 15. Faint, sick, and lame. I made twenty miles to Schenectady,[40] and was entertained at Isaac Johnson's:[41] he is a disciple of Woolman Hickson's,[42] gained by preaching in the streets of Brooklyn, Long Island. I rejoiced to hear that Robert Dillon[43] preached in the market house at Troy. On *Tuesday* it rained, and I rested. *Wednesday* brought us over Yankee Hill[44] to Frank's. We came to Ellwood's on *Thursday*, crossing Schoharie Creek. O fruitful banks of lovely Mohawk! On *Friday* we rode ten miles out of our way, and made a long journey of forty-five miles: we came in at nine o'clock at night to Elijah Davis's.[45] We have travelled one hundred miles up the Mohawk. My feet are much swelled, and I am on crutches; but I have been supported amongst strangers. O that we had two Low Dutch missionaries for the parts of Jersey and York west of the Hudson!

[39] Waterford is a village five miles north of Troy and was an important junction of turnpikes to and from all major directions.

[40] Schenectady is the first city of size west of Albany. The date of first Methodist preaching there is obscure, some thinking Captain Thomas Webb preached there in 1766 and 1767, but he established no class or society and such influence as he may have exerted was dissipated during the Revolution. Garrettson attempted to establish regular preaching, and William Colbert developed the work as part of the Albany District in 1802. The first church was erected in 1809.

[41] Isaac Johnson, an early Methodist leader in Schenectady, had been converted while living in Brooklyn in 1788. His name appears as a member of the class of New York's John Street Church which was made up of Brooklyn residents. He left Brooklyn prior to 1794. (*Records of John Street Church*, II.)

[42] Woolman Hickson had established regular preaching in Brooklyn over the winter of 1787–88, only a few months before his untimely death in the late summer of 1788.

[43] Robert Dillon was under appointment as "missionary within the bounds of New York Conference."

[44] This was in the vicinity of Amsterdam, approximately fifteen miles west of Schenectady.

[45] Elijah Davis was a leader of the church at Utica in Oneida County. Garrettson is said to have preached here just before the turn of the century, the service being held in a dwelling, possibly the residence of Davis.

Sunday, 21. After Ebenezer White[46] had preached in the meeting house, I went into a beautiful grove, where I spoke to about fifteen hundred people, on Colossians i, 28, 29. I ordained three deacons, namely, Stebbens, Parker, and Trueman,[47] and rode to Westmoreland.[48] I retired to B. Hannah's, my feet highly inflamed and painful.

Monday, 22. At B. Holmes's, in Vernon,[49] I preached on Rom. x, 13. Next day I rode to Silas Bliss's,[50] in Cazenovia.[51] On *Wednesday*, on 1 John v, 14, 15; the Lord is with the people. Ten years have I been absent from this kind family; and O! the kindness of all the brethren: I cannot express it, nor my gratitude for the favours shown. I came home to Ebenezer White's. I spoke at brother Nichols's, in Manlius,[52] on *Thursday*; my text was chosen from John xxi, 15–17; it was an open time. I ordained Ebenezer White an elder.[53]

Friday, 26. We came fourteen miles to Onondaga court house; truly we saw gapers enough: my text was John xiii, 17. After taking a cup of tea, we rode to Skaneateles Lake,[54] about sixteen miles in length, and three in breadth, at its widest part. Six more miles brought us to Owasco Lake, about the same size: the outlet of Aurelius River is here. We have had a day's work of forty miles. I am still lame on both feet. Our lodging at Brutus[55] was with B. Upshire. I preached on *Saturday*, in the widow Carpenter's barn: in the afternoon I rode fifteen miles to David Eddy's, in Scipio: here we were quite at home.

[46] Ebenezer White was received on trial in 1802 and into full connection in 1804. His name disappears from conference lists after 1811. His entire ministry was given to this area, known at this time as the Genesee District of the Philadelphia Conference. His current appointment was to the Westmoreland Circuit.

[47] These three were evidently local preachers, as their names do not appear as members of conference.

[48] Westmoreland was approximately ten miles west of Utica and south of Mohawk River.

[49] Vernon was a village ten miles west of Westmoreland.

[50] Asbury had had close relationship with this man and his family at some distant point, though no clue is found as to that location. Bliss seems to have been largely responsible for the rapid and solid growth of the church in Cazenovia.

[51] Cazenovia is located at the southern end of Cazenovia Lake in Madison County. The Methodist work there culminated in the noted Cazenovia Seminary that has prepared many noted ministers of central and western New York State. Boehm says, "It would have been a glorious vision of the future could Bishop Asbury have foreseen the future prosperity of Methodism in Cazenovia and the noble seminary of learning erected there." (Boehm, *op. cit.*, 297.)

[52] Manlius is in Onondaga County, ten or twelve miles northwest of Cazenovia.

[53] The *Minutes* show that White had been voted elder at the 1806 conference. No clue is given as to the reason for delaying the rite of ordination. Asbury occasionally deferred ordination until he could perform the rite at a place of special suitability, in this instance at the person's residence.

[54] With the exception of small Otisco Lake this is the easternmost of the group of lakes southwest of Syracuse known as "The Finger Lakes," so named because of their curious shape.

[55] Brutus is a community about six miles north of the upper end of Owasco Lake.

Sunday, 28. I held forth to about five hundred souls, in Eddy's barn: my subject was Heb. ii, 15, 16: the people were very attentive, but not much affected. Bathing my feet may have done good: they begin to mend. On *Monday* we rode to Milton Methodist meeting house, where I preached to about two hundred souls, on Gal. v, 7, 8. I was faint yet animated, in speaking. We dined with David Hamilton, and came back to Cayuga Lake: this sheet of water is about forty miles long, and four miles wide; it feeds the St. Lawrence.[56] At Samuel Wayburn's I preached on *Tuesday*, and on *Wednesday* we came by Milton to Bailey's where we also had meeting: my subject here was 1 Peter iv, 17; it was a most insensible congregation of about one hundred souls. Daily preaching and daily affliction keep me very low. I feel with sorrow the spiritual death of the people; it brings on great heaviness of body and mind.

Thursday, July 2. We dined at Geneva, on Seneca Lake: the lake is about forty miles in length, and from one to five miles wide. Our entertainer, Mr. Hagley, was exceedingly kind. We rode on to Daniel Dorsey's,[57] late of Liberty, Frederick county, Maryland, now an inhabitant of Lyonstown.[58] This is a great land for wheat, rye, and grass; and the lakes, with their navigation of vessels and boats, and moving scenes, make the prospects beautiful.

Saturday, 4. We were greatly crowded in a small house in Lyonstown:[59] my subject was Matt. xvii, 5. After meeting and dinner, we rode on to the sulphur springs, near Canandaigua,[60] and lodged at the widow Ferguson's.

[56] Cayuga Lake does not flow directly into the St. Lawrence River, but empties into Lake Ontario somewhat south and west of Oswego.

[57] Daniel Dorsey (1757–1823) spent his early life in Frederick County, Maryland, where Asbury knew him first. (See *Journal* entry for August 7, 1799.) Influenced by the success of a friend, John Cole, Dorsey moved to Lyons, New York, late in 1799, and bought over one thousand acres of land just south of Lyons. In 1801 he moved his complete entourage from Maryland, the persons (white and black) numbering over one hundred. He soon attained leadership in the community, serving for years as magistrate and as a member of the state assembly. He became a local Methodist preacher and district steward. In 1810 Asbury and McKendree created the Genessee Conference, holding the organizational session in Dorsey's huge granary. At his death Dorsey was survived by his widow and twelve children. (*Minutes of Central New York Conference*, 1910; Boehm, *op. cit.*, 297.)

[58] Lyons is the seat of Wayne County, New York, located eighteen miles north of Auburn. In 1797 John Cole, local Methodist preacher, delivered the first Christian sermon of any denomination in Lyons, and a congregation was speedily formed. Cole, a convert of Wesley in England, had come to America after the Revolution, settling in Maryland. He moved to New York in 1796 or early 1797.

[59] The first services were held in the homes of Cole, then Daniel Dorsey, and of Richard Jones in the village. In 1802 or 1803 a lot on Broad Street was bought from George Carr, who had built a two-story log house. It was in this building, adapted for worship, that Asbury preached. It is believed to have been the first Methodist building in western New York and was the first stated place of worship in Lyons. (Records of Lyons Methodist Church; *Landmarks of Wayne County*, 247.)

[60] This was probably the present Clifton Springs, fifteen miles southwest of Lyons.

Sunday, 5. I preached to about one thousand souls assembled in White's barn: my subject was 2 Tim. iv, 2: "Preach the word."

I. The primitive qualification, the call and commission to "preach the word"—the Gospel.

II. The right use of the Gospel, to convince, to reclaim the backslidden and disorderly.

III. "Exhort" all characters, "with longsuffering and doctrine." Hear ye him; observe the dignity, eloquence, and power of the speaker. "Doctrine," hear him on this point; hear him all men, of all grades and characters. My congregation was an unfeeling one. Now that my mind is in a great measure lightened of its load of thought and labour for the conferences, I feel uncommon light and energy in preaching: I am not prolix; neither am I tame; I am rapid, and nothing freezes from my lips. I suppose we shall preach to more than ten thousand souls in this district.

Monday, 6. In R. Wrote's barn,[61] fifteen miles from Canandaigua, I preached to about four hundred unyielding souls, on Acts iii, 22, 23.

Tuesday, 7. We passed the lake,[62] sixteen miles long, and one mile wide. At James Stokes's, Ninth Town,[63] I preached in the woods to a more attentive people, on Heb. x, 38, 39.

Wednesday, 8. I preached in the Friends' settlement[64] with some power.

Thursday, 9. At Cresse's. We set out, dining at Dow's, and came to Catharine, at the head of Seneca Lake, thirty miles; the swamps, sloughs, ruts, and stumps made it awful moving. We lodged at Baldwin's tavern.[65]

Friday, 10. We directed our route through Newtown,[66] upon the East Branch of the Susquehanna, to Chemung;[67] rested awhile at Jacob Cresse's, and then passed the narrows of the river, continuing on by Shepherd's mill to Taylor's tavern; it was ten o'clock, and I was fearful of driving farther in the dark.

Saturday, 11. Brought us to the camp meeting on Squire Light's ground:[68] we found it had been in operation two days; God is in the

[61] Wrote's barn was located in the vicinity of South Bristol near the southwest shore of Lake Canandaigua.

[62] This was Keuka Lake, which lies between the southern ends of much larger Canandaigua and Seneca lakes.

[63] Ninth Town is in Bradford township, a few miles east of Keuka Lake.

[64] The lake area of south central New York State had, and still has, numerous communities of Quakers. This was probably in Orange Township, Schuyler County.

[65] Baldwin's tavern was located ten miles south of Catharine, near the present Horseheads in Chemung County.

[66] Newtown was organized in 1792, and the name changed to Elmira in 1826.

[67] Chemung is in the southern corner of Chemung County, New York, near the Pennsylvania border.

[68] Squire Ludowick Light lived at Smithboro, about four miles east of Barton in Tioga County. Methodist preaching began at Barton in 1800, a class being organized in 1805, and another class was formed at Smithboro at Squire Light's at about the same time. At a later date he erected a simple chapel on his property. The camp meeting

camp and with us. I preached on the camp ground, from Matt. xviii, 2: some sots were a little disorderly, but the greater part of the congregation were very attentive; weak as I was, I did not spare myself, my subject, or my hearers. It may be, I spoke to one thousand people. Since the last *Sabbath* we have travelled one hundred and twenty miles; and with good roads and even ground we might have made three hundred miles in the same time. The heights of the Susquehanna[69] are stupendous; the bottom lands very fertile; but this river runs through a country of unpleasing aspect, morally and physically—rude, irregular, uncultivated is the ground; wild, ignorant, and wicked are the people: they have not been wearied by my labours; except the neighbourhood of Lancaster, and by what I may once have done in a visit to Wyoming, they are strangers to them. I am now on my first journey of toil and suffering through Genesee and Tioga.[70]

Sunday, 12. My subject was 2 Cor. v, 20: my congregation may have doubled in numbers to-day; and there were no troublesome drunkards. I feel as if God would own this meeting now, and continue to own it many days, in various families and places. I ordained five worthy men local preachers, namely, Daniel Wilcox, John B. Hudson, Samuel Emmit, John M'Caine, and Nathaniel Lewis,[71] to the office of deacon: had I not made this visit, these men might have waited a long time, or taken a long ride to find me. In the afternoon (*Sabbath*), there was an uproar amongst the people. Some intoxicated young men seated themselves by the women, and refused to move until compelled; they fought those men who came to take them away, and when the presiding elder interfered they struck at him, and one of the guards also, who was helping by order of the constables. There were magistrates (such as they were) to cry peace. The Owego gentry fled away cackling falsehood like wild geese. One Kemp, chief bully, arrested Anning Owen, on *Monday morning*, for the *Sabbath breaking*, drunkenness and fighting of this Kemp and his crew. The presiding elder was charged with having struck Kemp, and then running away; nor was the poor bishop spared—he too had been fighting: it was well for him that he was not on the ground at the time—I was quiet in my room.

referred to by Asbury was the first to be held in this entire area. (Chaffee: *History of the Wyoming Conference*, 776–77.)

[69] This immediate sector appears to have been first visited by William Colbert in 1793. Valentine Cook and John Broadhead followed a few years later, but no society was formed at Nichols, near Smithboro, until 1819. (*Ibid.*, 807.)

[70] From the time he left Chemung until he moved downstream along Susquehanna, Asbury was in Tioga County. Methodist work was begun early in the 1790's, and by 1807 the circuit had over thirty preaching places, covering a travel distance of four hundred miles.

[71] Nathaniel Lewis lived in Oakland Township, Pennsylvania, near Big Bend, where the Susquehanna River makes its sudden and short dip into Pennsylvania, about twenty miles east of Binghamton, New York. He held meetings in many communities of that section (*Ibid.*, 484–85.)

Pennsylvania

Monday, 13. We rode to Tioga,[72] and brother Shippy[73] gave us our dinner. A ride of sixteen miles brought us to Daniel Minier's[74] where we lodged. Tioga Point, at the junction of Chemung and the river, is a pleasant spot.

Tuesday, 14, we came six miles to Judge Gore's:[75] here I preached upon John vii, 17. When we set out on *Wednesday* we found we were obliged to take the carriage over a precipice by hand.[76] The road to the ferry was rough; and behold, the boat was gone, and the bank caved and washed away; a lock upon the wheel, and the assistance of a strap, enabled us to pass the sulky down by hand. Major Gaylord,[77] at Wyalusing, lodged us well and freely.

Thursday, 16. We came eleven miles to breakfast at Sturdevant's;[78] and eleven miles more brought us to Hunt's ferry:[79] after dining at Frosbury's,[80] free and kind, we went on to Newton Smith's,[81] ten miles farther; I ordained my host a deacon in his own house.

Friday, 17. To Sutton's[82] ten miles: the house neat as a palace; and we were entertained like kings, by a king and queen; it was no small con-

[72] Tioga, or Tioga Point, is now Athens, Pennsylvania. (See *Journal* entry for March 10, 1807; *Minutes*, 1807.)

[73] Shippy is mentioned in records at the Spalding Memorial Library at Athens as being a "blacksmith who held Methodist meetings in his house."

[74] Daniel Minier lived two miles south of Tioga, or Athens, on Queen Esther's Flats. (Palmer, *op. cit.*, 75; Spalding Memorial Library records, Athens.)

[75] Judge Obadiah Gore (b. 1744) came to the Wyoming section from Norwich, Connecticut, at the age of twenty. He served in the Continental Army and lost three brothers and two brothers-in-law in the battle of Wyoming. In 1785 he established a store at (New) Sheshequin and was one of the first commissioners of Luzerne County. (*Ibid.*, 156 .)

[76] This precipice was a few miles below Judge Gore's and was known as Breakneck Hill.

[77] Major Justus Gaylord, Jr., a Revolutionary soldier, was an early and prominent settler in the region. He lived on a nine-hundred-acre tract on the north side of Wyalusing Creek. His wife was the widow of Amos York, whose whole family were captured by the Indians, and he was killed; their son, Miner M., became a Presbyterian preacher. (*Ibid.*)

[78] "Old Elder" Samuel Sturdevant was an eccentric Baptist preacher, who lived at Black Walnut Bottom above Meshoppen. His second wife was a Methodist, and members of the family later became Methodists. (*Ibid.*, 41.)

[79] Hunt's ferry was at Mehoopany.

[80] Frosbury was probably Vosburg, who lived at Tunkhannock.

[81] Newton Smith lived at Osterhout.

[82] James Sutton was a Quaker who became a Methodist and a class leader when he married Sarah, the daughter of W. H. Smith, M.D. They lived variously at Wilkes-Barre, Forty Fort, and Exeter. Sutton and Dr. Smith set up the Lackawanna Forge at what became known as Old Forge, Pennsylvania. A daughter, Deborah Sutton, married James Bedford, who became a prominent Methodist in the Wyoming Valley. (*Ibid.*, 61 ff.)

solation to lie down on a clean floor after all we had suffered from dirt and all its consequences. Once more I am at Wyoming. We have wearied through and clambered over one hundred miles of the rough roads of wild Susquehanna. O, the precipitous banks, wedging narrows, rocks, sideling hills, obstructed paths, and fords scarcely fordable, roots, stumps, and gullies!

Saturday, 18. I must take medicine; the preachers wish me to remain in my lodging.

Sunday, 19. I went to the woods[83] and preached and ordained Thomas and Christian Bowman,[84] deacons. Before I got through my discourse the rain came on, and I made a brief finish: the people were attentive. In the afternoon the preachers and many of the people went to a barn; there were showers of rain and thunder whilst service was performing. My first visit to Wyoming was in great toil and to little purpose; I am afraid I shall have no better success now.

Monday, 20. We set out upon a turnpike road; but O, dreadful! I came sliding down a dug road precipice, dark and deep, but safe. About nine o'clock we made Mr. Merwin's[85] tavern: and here were drink, and smoke, and wagoners—*but we closed with prayer*. We came along, early on *Tuesday*, through the Wind Gap,[86] seventeen miles to Heller's,[87] and breakfasted. I took a look at the Moravian town of Nazareth;[88] it may

[83] In these woods near the present Forty Fort was then being erected the old Forty Fort Church which still stands, the oldest in the whole area. It was in use the following year. The one-room structure with high pulpit and box-like pews situated in its cemetery, is seldom used now but is carefully preserved. (Palmer, *op. cit.*, 156, 160.)

[84] The Bowmans had come thirty miles from Briar Creek. Thomas was the grandfather of Bishop Thomas Bowman (1817–1914) of the Methodist Episcopal Church. At this service William Butler knelt beside Asbury and held an unbrella over the bishop to protect him from the rain. The bearing of Asbury during the storm so impressed little Deborah Sutton, who was present with her mother, that it led to her conversion. (*Ibid.*, 157; Peck: *Early Methodism Within the Bounds of the old Genesee Conference*, 155, 156.)

[85] Merwin's tavern was at Merwinsburg, thirty-five miles from Wilkes-Barre. (Palmer, *op. cit.*, 178; see *Journal* entry for August 4, 1811.) Asbury left the Wyoming Valley by way of Wilkes-Barre and over the mountains to the southeast.

[86] Wind Gap is a gap in the Blue Mountain, fourteen miles northwest of Easton, Pennsylvania. The town of Wind Gap is situated on the south side of the dry gap.

[87] Heller's Tavern was located at the southern end of the town of Wind Gap. It was later operated by a Mr. Leibert, whose daughter married a Dr. Keller. Keller converted the building into a residence and office. It is now occupied by Dr. Dreher of Wind Gap as a residence and office.

[88] Nazareth is located in Northampton County, Pennsylvania, on the head of a small branch of Bushkill Creek. The first Moravians had crossed the Atlantic in 1735, and George Whitefield secured their services to erect a large school building for Negro orphans on a five-thousand-acre tract of land in the forks of the Delaware River, which he had named Nazareth. In May, 1740, Peter Boehler led a small band of workers to Nazareth, and in six months they had erected two log buildings. The main building, named "Ephrata" and also known as Whitefield House, is still standing and is used as a Moravian museum. Nazareth was laid out as a town in 1744. (Heller: *History of Northampton County*, 497.)

contain forty houses built in the German taste and style: the brethren's house is a large building of, possibly, one hundred and forty feet in length, and fifty feet in width, with a Dutchified tower like a cupola, in the centre —the whole edifice has the exterior appearance of a college. The land in the vicinity was not so fertile, nor the grounds as highly improved, as I expected to have found them. Seventeen miles farther brought us to far-famed Bethlehem,[89] which I had long wished to see. The stream that runs west of the town[90] is pretty and useful, as it works a machine which raises the water one hundred and fifty feet into two reservoirs, for the use of the inhabitants. We found ourselves at the grand tavern[91] at the north end, the property of the brethren: the house is large, but a plain building: the entertainment good at a dollar a night for man and horse. On the second step of the high grounds on the main street, which begins on the hill above, stand the church buildings: on the east and west are rooms appropriate to the institution, and certainly the west end has a grand appearance. On the same street below stands the brethren's house, one hundred feet front, five stories high, very plain, and much German taste discoverable everywhere; add to this the majestic Lehigh, and you have the most striking features of this celebrated place. But, ah! religion— Reader, I am a Methodist. I asked the young man who managed the tavern, if they ever permitted any minister to preach amongst the brethren; he could not answer—he was a servant, and knew not how to answer. Next day came the master of the ceremonies, the *cicerone* of the establishment, who shows the wonders of the place; I asked him—I was told that on that night there was private worship in the church—the minister must perform *himselbst*. Daniel Hitt and two gentlemen from York, who had given money for the sights shown here for money, went to the church meeting. And what did they see and hear? A man read in German they knew not what, sung and played upon the *four thousand dollar* organ: sermon or prayer they heard not. I doubt much if there is any prayer here, public or private, except the stated prayers of the minister on the Sabbath day. But the brethren have a school for boys at Nazareth, and one for girls at Bethlehem; and they have a store and a tavern; the society have worldly wealth and worldly wisdom: it is no wonder that men of the world,

[89] Late in 1740 the Moravian leaders and Whitefield had some disagreement over doctrine, and the latter dismissed the Moravians from his employ. Bishop David Nitschmann, commissioned by the Moravian Church in the Old World to begin a settlement in Pennsylvania, arrived in America in December, 1740, in time to relieve Moravian troubles. In April, 1741, he bought from William Allen, a five-hundred-acre tract of land at the confluence of Lehigh River and Monocacy Creek, and thus the foundation of the city of Bethlehem was laid. The northern headquarters of the Moravian Church are located at Bethlehem, and some of the original buildings are still standing at the northern end of the hill bridge over the Lehigh River.

[90] This was Monocacy Creek, a tributary of the Lehigh River.

[91] This was the Sun Inn, built in 1758–59. The first inn built in Bethlehem was the Crown, erected in 1745.

who would not have their children spoiled by religion, send them to so decent a place.

Wednesday, 22. We crossed the Lehigh[92] to Allentown,[93] beautifully situated—superior in this respect, perhaps, to Bethlehem. We breakfasted at the end of twelve miles, and came on to Kutztown.[94] On *Thursday* morning we bent our course through Reading;[95] the views of meadows and fields were grand—beautiful. Reading may have two hundred houses, one street in a style of grandeur approaching to that of Philadelphia, as it respects the houses; the rest have much of the German feature. Through Adamstown,[96] where we breakfasted, we came on over rocks and hills to New Holland; here, as at Reading, there are fine new churches for the German Lutherans and the German Calvinists:[97] these are the citadels of formality—fortifications erected against the apostolic itinerancy of a more evangelical ministry. Ah! Philadelphia, and ye, her dependencies, the villages of the State of Pennsylvania, when will prejudice, formality, and bigotry, cease to deform your religious profession, and the ostentatious display of the lesser morals give place to evangelical piety?

At Soudersburg we rested one day. I wrote three letters.

Saturday, 25. We came through Lancaster to Columbia. On the *Sabbath day* I preached in a lot near the river: we may have had seven hundred people; my subject was 2 Cor. v, 14. The missionaries, Boehm and Hunter,[98] were present. On *Monday* I came to Little York. Here I met with Nelson Reed. This week I am occupied in writing about thirty let-

[92] The Lehigh River rises as the result of creeks flowing from the Pocono Mountains in Monroe County. It flows westward into Luzerne County, then generally southward through Carbon County, between Lehigh and Northampton Counties, and then eastward into the Delaware River at Easton.

[93] Allentown is located at the confluence of the Jordan and Lehigh rivers fifty-seven miles north of Philadelphia. It was first settled by the Allen family in 1751 and was laid out as a town in 1762 by James Allen, a son of the chief justice of the province, William Allen. The town was originally named for Judge Allen, who settled in Trout Hall in 1702. When it was incorporated as a borough in 1811, the name was changed to Northampton, but the original name was restored in 1838.

[94] Kutztown is in Berks County, Pennsylvania, on the road leading from Reading to Allentown. It was incorporated in March 1815. (Gordon: *Gazetteer of the State of Pennsylvania*, 226.)

[95] Reading is the county seat of Berks County, on the east bank of the Schuylkill River one mile below the mouth of the Tulpehocken Creek, and was laid out in 1748 by Thomas and Richard Penn. (Gordon, *op. cit.*, 392.)

[96] Adamstown is in Cocalio Township, Lancaster County, Pennsylvania, on the road between Lancaster and Reading.

[97] The German Lutheran immigrants' religious roots were in the Lutheran reformation in Germany; the religious background of the German Calvinists was in the Zwinglian reformation in Switzerland.

[98] At the conference of 1807 Henry Boehm and William Hunter received appointment as "missionaries to Pennsylvania." William Hunter (1755–1833) was born in Ireland and was intimately acquainted with John Wesley, having traveled with him in Ireland. He came to America in 1790.

ters;[99] yet, not unmindful of the word of God and prayer. It is but too manifest that the success of our labours, more especially at camp meetings, has roused a spirit of persecution against us—riots, fines, stripes, perhaps prisons and death, if we do not give up our camp meetings: we shall never abandon them, but shall subdue our enemies by *overcoming evil with good*. What hath God wrought in America! In thirty-six years we find one hundred and forty-four thousand five hundred and ninety in number: in England, after seventy-seven years, they count one hundred and fifty thousand nine hundred and seventy-four: they may have thirty millions of souls in the three kingdoms to labour amongst; and we not more, perhaps, than five millions. Our travelling preachers, five hundred and thirty-six, at present; the rest, local and official, about fourteen hundred; but all these are poor men, and unlearned—without books, money or influence. Not unto us, not unto us!—O, Lord, take thou, the glory!

Saturday, August 1. Constant application whilst here. Reading the Bible and writing about sixty pages of letters found me employment. On the *Sabbath* I preached at eleven o'clock at our chapel in York: I spoke on Coloss. i, 27, 28—short and temperate. We might have about six hundred hearers. In the afternoon I spoke on Coloss. iii, 12, 13: I spoke longer than in the morning. We have the *form* of the *power of goodness*, for we shout, and we stamp, and jump, and are very happy—who but we!—but we are contentious, and mingle and mix, by off-hand marriages, believers with unbelievers, and other things we do: but, for once, I have delivered my own soul. I think it begins to be time for another visitation at York.

I have my paradise at brother Weirich Pentz's; but I have much labour, and some temptations. I now fare sumptuously every day; but O, what is before me?—three thousand five hundred miles before I reach the Georgetown Conference.

Tuesday, 4. I took my leave of my kind friends at Weirich Pentz's, and rode to dinner to George Nailor's:[100] that night we passed under the roof of the widow Hollopeter. On *Wednesday* I preached at Stickle's school house:[101] the room was full, and I spoke for an hour on 1 Peter iv, 10, 11. We came that evening to Lewisberry. O my God, help me in soul and body, through my approaching labours and sufferings! *Thursday* brought us through an obscure town[102] to brother Weaver's;[103] our host and his wife are Germans—in their first love.

[99] See Asbury's letters to Daniel Asbury, July 30, 1807; to Mrs. Mary Tabb, July 30, 1807; to Stith Mead, July 30, 1807; to Jacob Gruber, July 31, 1807.

[100] George Nailor was one of the founders of the church in York and a member of the first board of trustees.

[101] Stickle's schoolhouse, located near Lewisberry, was named after Peter Stickle, one of the organizers of the Lewisberry church.

[102] This was probably Shiremanstown.

[103] Casper Weaver owned a tract of land near Shiremanstown. (Warner and Beer, *op. cit.*, 39.)

Friday, 7. At Carlisle. *Saturday*, occupied in reading Burder's Village Sermons, &c.

Sabbath, 9. I preached upon Gal. v, 7–9; in the afternoon on 2 Cor. iv, 1, 2: my body faint; my spirit fervent. On *Monday*, at Shippensburg, I preached upon 2 Peter iii, 17, 18, and ordained John Davis a deacon: it was very warm, but we had an open season. We lodged with brother John Scott, one of my hearers thirty years ago, in Chester county, now warm in the cause of God. After a heavy rain had passed away on *Monday*, on *Tuesday* we began our mountain toil: we crossed three, dined with the *junior*, and lodged with the *senior* Ramsay: no people need be kinder than were these.

Wednesday, 12. We set out again, and the rain attended us into Bedford. We lodged at the stage house: Mr. Graham, my host, had known me in my early visits—I had preached at his father's: the son was kind as a king could be, and charged us not a cent for our entertainment: in a hundred public houses, possibly, that I have thus stopped at in the year, I have received no such favours. We reached Berlin on *Thursday*, and found friend Johnson and his wife kind indeed.

Friday, 14. We dined and prayed at the Twenty Mile house, and were obliged to stop at an ordinary twelve miles farther—drunken people; but they behaved as well as they could: any port in a storm. On *Saturday* we came on eight miles to breakfast at Anthony Banning's:[104] from thence we rode through Connellsville to Union. We put up with the widow Henthorn, intending to be at the camp meeting. And now I have ridden since I left Baltimore in March, two thousand five hundred miles; and have had, as usual, many a jolt over rocks, and rocks again, on the American Alps, and dangers and difficulties, and a head bruised by the iron rods of my carriage.[105] I have been enabled to suffer patiently pains and sickness for the good of souls.

Sabbath, 16. I ordained, on the camp ground,[106] Dobbins, Fell, and Wakefield,[107] to the office of deacons. I preached on 2 Cor. v, 11: "Know-

[104] Anthony Banning was an itinerant preacher in western Pennsylvania from 1789 to 1791. He married in 1791, located, and lived near Connellsville. He served as Valentine Cook's second and timekeeper in the famous western Pennsylvania debate on Calvinism and free grace between the Rev. Valentine Cook, Methodist, and the Rev. John Jamieson, Presbyterian, on June 12, 1793. (Smeltzer, *op. cit.*, 78–79; Payton, *op. cit.*, 88–89.)

[105] This was Asbury's twelfth trip across the mountains to western Pennsylvania. This reference is to the hardship which he endured in all of his numerous mountain crossings.

[106] The historic first campground was at Jackman's on the Monongahela River where the first camp meeting was held in 1803.

[107] These three men were ordained as local preachers. Their names do not appear in the list of deacons in the *General Minutes*. Peter Fell (1771–1839) was the son of Benjamin Fell for whom the original Fells Church in the forks of the Youghiogheny is named. His brother, John Fell, was admitted on trial in 1796 and served as an itinerant preacher for one year. (Smeltzer, *op. cit.*, 69.)

ing the terror of the Lord." I made two general heads: 1. The Gospel is a general, gracious, persuasive, characteristic ministry; in which the ministers thereof are manifest to God, and to the consciences of their hearers in their characters, their sins, their sayings, ways, &c. 2. The Gospel was armed with terror to the disobedient, impenitent, and to apostates from it. *Knowing the terror of the Lord*—Knowing how God is to be feared—when insulted by disobedience, the Trinity is roused into indignation; every attribute, and all the perfection of Deity is arranged on the side of vengeance and vindictive wrath. There was not a sufficiency of seats for the congregation; but they behaved as well as could be expected; there was nothing vicious seen—no plan of opposition was discoverable. On *Monday* I went to camp again, and spoke upon Matt. v, 46, 47. What the followers of Christ professed more than others; and what God had done for them more than others, as Christians and ministers; that therefore God, the Father, Son, and Spirit, requires more from them than from others. By application—to a variety of cases;—what do ye more than others?

Tuesday, 18. We found our horses had been taken or had strayed away. I read Hervey on the Tombs, and wrote the Station Book.

Wednesday, 19. We set out and came to the Old Fort; crossed the Monongahela, and lodged with Dr. Wheeler:[108] he and his lady are Londoners; and O, how kind they were! How did the salvation of the souls of these kind friends rest upon me! The doctor's mother had been in band society with Mr. Wesley. From six in the morning to seven in the evening of *Thursday*, we made about forty miles, over some rough roads and desperate hills: we wished to redeem time, that we might refit at John Beck's,[109] near West Liberty; so we ate not on the route, though we fed the horses twice. I had had pain of a rheumatic kind for some days.

West Virginia

Friday, 21. Marked letters to transcribe, read, took medicine, and nursed myself. On *Saturday* I preached in Beck's new house, on Philip. ii, 12, 13.

[108] Dr. Charles Wheeler was the first physician of Fayette County, Pennsylvania. He settled near Brownsville about 1780. In 1788 Robert Ayres, who had ridden the Methodist Redstone Circuit in 1786–87, entered the ministry of the Episcopal Church, was ordained at Philadelphia, and was sent back to western Pennsylvania to establish Episcopalianism in Brownsville and vicinity. Dr. Wheeler was a prominent leader in the early establishment of the Episcopal Church in the region, and Ayres made the Wheeler home his headquarters for some time. (Buck: *The Planting of Civilization in Western Pennsylvania*, 338; Robert Ayres manuscript *Journal*.)

[109] The home of Colonel John Beck was an early Methodist preaching and stopping place of the itinerant preachers. It was located near the Pennsylvania-West Virginia line, three miles east of West Liberty in Ohio County, West Virginia. (Payton, *op. cit.*, 135.)

On the *Sabbath* I preached in an excellent stone meeting house, at Short Creek, to about one thousand souls, from 2 Cor. iii, 7, 8.

Ohio

We crossed over into the State of Ohio on *Monday*: and I gave them a sermon in the court house at St. Clairsville.

By hard labour we reached Frankfort on *Tuesday*; thence we made Spears's on *Wednesday*: on *Thursday* came to Densenbury's; on *Friday* to Teal's: in four days and a half we have travelled one hundred and thirty miles—mud, gullies, stumps, and hills. I was sick with an inflammatory sore throat; my trials were great, nature failed, but grace supported. Every family shall know me by prayer. *Saturday* I devoted to rest. I have hastily marked above two hundred hymns, taken from the congregational hymn book, to add to a new American edition, which, I hope, will be as good as any extant.

Sabbath, 30. At the stand on the camp ground near Hockhocking[110] I spoke on Heb. iv, 1: "Let us therefore fear." There were about eight hundred hearers, and it was a time of feeling and solemnity to professors. *Monday* was diligently taken up with my pen, and prayer with my friends: the hymns for a new collection occupied my mind much. My poor mare is worn down, and my carriage is wrecked somewhat, and must be repaired. On *Thursday* we came to New Lancaster: I preached in a schoolhouse on Luke xix, 10. We afterward came on to Mr. Vanmeter's, and just escaped an awful storm of thunder, hail, and rain.

Friday, *September* 4. We came away to Chillicothe: O, the mud and the trees in the path! Reading closely on *Saturday*. In our neat, new house[111] I preached on the *Sabbath morning* to about five hundred hearers, on 1 Peter iv, 17, 18; I spoke about an hour. There are some pleasing and some unpleasing accounts here; some little trouble in the society, but great prospects all around in the country. The sitting of conference will be of God for good to souls: we have been praying the whole year for this. By letters from brothers Mead and Bruce I learn that prospects brighten in old Virginia: they have had blessed meetings.

Monday and *Tuesday*, closely reading. On *Wednesday* we rode to Deer Creek. *Thursday*, *Friday*, and *Saturday* selecting hymns and reading Marshall's Life of Washington, nearly three thousand pages in four volumes: only as a *Life of Washington* can I give it the preference to Gordon's History of the Revolutionary War.

[110] This is Asbury's first reference to a camp meeting in Ohio, this being his third journey across the new state. The circuit on the Hockhocking had been commenced in 1803 under the leadership of Edward Teal, with Asa Shinn as its first preacher. (Smeltzer, *op. cit.*, 86.)

[111] This was the first Methodist church building in Chillicothe.

Sabbath, 13. At the Deer Creek camp ground I gave them a discourse on 2 Cor. vi, 1. In the evening we returned to Chillicothe.

On *Monday*, we opened our conference[112] in great peace and love, and continued sitting day by day, until *Friday noon*. A delegation of seven members was chosen to the General Conference.[113] There were thirteen preachers added, and we found an addition of two thousand two hundred members to the society in these bounds; seven deacons were elected and ordained, and ten elders; two preachers only located; sixty-six preachers were stationed.

Finding my work done, and my carriage sold, I ventured once more to take horse, with a determination to visit the frontier settlements on the Great Miami River. We came away, leaving fifty or sixty preachers at the camp meeting near the seat of conference, and got to brother Waugh's for the night.

Saturday, we reached Hinkstone's to dine, and thence, by riding late, got into Cesarsville, and stopped with Peter Pelham: we have made sixty-five miles from Chillicothe. A great rumour is abroad of an expected Indian war; and many fled for fear; but the report was idle wind. The whole matter was, that about a thousand Indians had assembled upon the frontiers for social, and it may be, religious and moral purposes. General Worthington and Colonel M'Carthy magnanimously offered to take a *talk* and a belt of wampum from the governor to the congregated savages: the ambassadors found peace; and brought in four chiefs as hostages, with assurances that no ill was designed to the whites. It is said there is a prophet risen up among the Indians.

At Frederick Bonner's I preached upon Heb. iv, 1, 2: it was an open season.

Monday, 21. I rested at John Sale's. Busy writing. On *Tuesday* we started away and came to Samuel Hitt's; dined, prayed, talked, and came away to Lebanon: we found the court in session. We lodged at Jeremiah Lawson's. There is now a great talk about the Shakers; they are said to consist of two hundred people: three Presbyterian ministers have joined them; *a heavy declension!*

Wednesday, 23. We bent our course down Little Miami: there are many fine situations for mills on this stream, and the land appears to be, generally, very fertile. We found a lodging with Andrew M'Grew, lately from

[112] As early as 1807 it was becoming a common practice to hold a camp meeting near the seat of the conference session, thereby taking advantage of the assembling of the preachers for a spiritual ministry.

[113] This session of the Western Conference was held at Chillicothe, the first capital of the state of Ohio, and was the first Methodist conference held in that state. It included the preachers of Tennessee, Kentucky, and Ohio. The distance of the conference from Baltimore, where the General Conference of 1808 was scheduled to be held on May 6, caused the adoption of the principle of sending an official delegation before the enactment of the legislation making the General Conference a delegated body.

Baltimore county, Maryland. I preached on *Thursday* at Philip Gatch's, on Heb. iv, 2. On *Friday* we stopped in Cincinnati, and dined with Mr. Farris: Solomon and Oliver Langdon had come on, and were of the company.

Saturday, 26. Rested, read, and wrote. I am young again, and boast of being able to ride six thousand miles on horse-back in ten months; my round will embrace the United States, the Territory, and Canada; but O, childhood, youth, and old age, ye are all vanity! My companions and myself are busy compiling the new hymn book. Our brethren here have built a *proper* little stone house for worship, forty feet by thirty.[114]

Sabbath, 27. I preached at eleven o'clock: many could not get seats. I met the society. I also ordained W. M'Neachan and William Whitaker to the office of deacon. Notwithstanding opposition from more than one quarter, our last camp meeting was successful; the fruit is immediate; and where it is not, it will yet be seen: we live by faith in a prayer-hearing, soul-converting, soul-sanctifying, soul-restoring, soul-comforting God.

Kentucky

Monday, 28. Our morning's ride brought us, hungry and weary, into Kentucky: after refreshing at the widow Stevens's, we pushed on to Grant's Lick,[115] and lodged at John Daniel's. In the morning we came away across the forks, and over the hills of Licking, twenty-eight miles, to sister Ritchie's, a widow indeed. Our evening's ride was dark and rough, along an unknown path to Cynthiana: we stopped at J. Jacques's. I judge we made fifty miles to-day.

Whilst resting on *Thursday* and *Wednesday*, I read Atmore's Memoirs,[116] of about five hundred pages; and I wrote a memoir of George Dougharty.[117] All my occupations, however toilsome, are pleasant when I enjoy God in pure and perfect love.

Friday, October 2. Attended the camp meeting at Mount Gerizim. On *Saturday* I spoke on 2 Tim. ii, 19. On *Sunday* my text was Isaiah xlv, 23. Possibly we had two thousand souls to hear us: there were fifteen tents, and twenty wagons. We had a *Sabbath* love feast and sacrament; and

[114] This was the first Methodist church building in Cincinnati.

[115] Grant's Lick was in Kenyon County, Kentucky.

[116] Charles Atmore was one of Wesley's outstanding preachers in England. Wesley ordained him or "set him apart" for Scotland and named him in the Deed of Declaration as one of the one hundred preachers who should constitute the legal conference. (See Wesley's *Journal*, VIII, 338; Tyerman: *Life and Times of John Wesley*, III, 441, 604.)

[117] George Dougherty was one of the leading preachers in South Carolina. He died on March 23, 1807, at Wilmington, North Carolina, and was buried in the African church there. (See *Minutes*, 1808; Betts: *History of South Carolina Methodism*, 170, 289.)

doubtless there were precious souls converted (report says about thirty) and sanctified. I conversed with Valentine Cook[118] on the subject of a mission; he held back; Ah! how hardly shall they who have families growing up, enter into and keep in the travelling connexion! I came from the camp ground every night to Samuel Brodwell's. My host has put my name upon one of his sons: Lord, put thy new name upon the lad, that he may bear it for generations to come, and to be born!

Monday, 5. We set out, and stopped at Martin Hitt's, took dinner and continued on a dark ride through the woods, to William Burke's,[119] thirty miles. On *Tuesday* we held a hasty meeting at Irvine's, Madison county. *Wednesday* we reached Williams's; *Thursday*, Freeman's;[120] *Friday*, Dorton's; and on *Saturday* came to Peter Huffacre's,[121] Powell's Valley.

Tennessee

Sabbath, 11. I preached on Luke iv, 18. O, when shall this wilderness rejoice? I have perfect peace, but great toil. Since the conference we have travelled three hundred and sixty miles. There is a serious want of water, generally, in the western lands.

Monday, 12. We had a heavy ride to Holston, forty miles. We stopped with Martin Stubblefield.

On *Tuesday* we rested; and it may be allowed, considering our six days' ride through heat, great heat and drought. At night I preached from 1 Thess. iv, 3; and weary and faint as I was, I felt strongly disposed to sing and shout away as loud as the youngest. I have been, and am happy in God.

Friday, 16. We reached Wamping's. I suffered much to-day; but an hour's warm bath for my feet relieved me considerably.

[118] Valentine Cook (1765–1820) was one of the outstanding preachers of the period. He was born in Virginia and educated at Cokesbury College in Maryland. He went to Kentucky in 1798 and the following year became the principal of Bethel Academy. He located in 1800 and devoted himself to teaching and conducting camp meetings and preaching in Lexington, Cincinnati, Pittsburgh, New York, Philadelphia. (Simpson: *Cyclopedia of Methodism*, 253; McTyeire: *History of Methodism*, 448; Redford: *Methodism in Kentucky*, I, 232–46.)

[119] William Burke (1770–1855) of Virginia was sent to the Holston region in 1790. He organized the first society in Ohio at Cincinnati in 1811 and was postmaster there for twenty-eight years. He was suspended by the conference in 1818 and organized an independent church, which flourished awhile and then failed. His standing in the conference was restored by the General Conference in 1836. Burke was a member of the committee which drafted the constitution or the restrictive rules of the church in 1808. (Simpson, *op. cit.*, 146; Arnold: *Methodism in Kentucky*, I, 117, 118; see his autobiographical sketch in Finley: *Sketches of Western Methodism*, 22–56.)

[120] See *Journal* entry and note for October 12, 1805.

[121] Asbury had now entered the Holston area of East Tennessee and Virginia. Peter Huffacre was the son of Michael Huffacre. (See note under May 6, 1788; *Michael Huffacre and His Family*, 67.) Huffacre was originally Halfacre.

North Carolina

On *Saturday* we rode to Killian's.

Sabbath, 18. At Buncombe court house I spoke from 2 Kings vii, 13–15. The people were all attention. I spent a night under the roof of my very dear brother in Christ, George Newton, a Presbyterian minister, an Israelite indeed. On *Monday* we made Fletcher's; next day dined at Terry's, and lodged at Edwards's. Saluda ferry brought us up on *Wednesday evening*.[122]

South Carolina

Sabbath, 25. For three days past I have been busy in seeking appropriate portions of Scripture for the new hymns designed to enlarge our common hymn book. Our journey hither from Chillicothe has brought us through five States. Report says there is an awful affliction in Charleston—the mortal fever! I preached today at Salem[123] on 2 Chron. vi, 29–31; we had a serious time. My mind is kept in great peace: surely, God is love!

At Elijah Moore's[124] on *Monday* I preached on Luke xi, 9, 10: my labour I think is not entirely in vain. On *Tuesday* at Jeremiah Robinson's, we had but twelve souls to hear us: the people are too busy with their fine crops of corn. My body fails, but I have great peace of mind.

Georgia

On *Wednesday* Daniel Hitt[125] preached at John Oliver's:[126] our host has a son-in-law converted at camp meeting. Our preachers have passed by this town, but the Lord will not pass by Petersburg, but will visit precious souls here.

Thursday, to Tait's: here I spoke to a few persons on Rev. iii, 4, 5; and God was with us of a truth. On *Friday* I preached at James Halston's on 1 John i, 6, 7: it was not in vain: both colours filled the house. On *Saturday* we rode to Coldwater.

[122] Asbury again went over Saluda Gap to South Carolina. Terry lived in the upper part of Greenville County near Marietta; he is shown on the old maps and is not to be confused with the Terry at Fork Shoals twenty miles below Greenville.

[123] Asbury had preached at Salem Church on October 27, 1805. (See note under that date.) He doubtless stayed at the Staunton home again.

[124] Moore lived near Lowndesville in Abbeville County.

[125] Daniel Hitt was Asbury's traveling companion this year. (See note under November 9, 1806.)

[126] Major John Oliver, a convert of Lorenzo Dow's, lived in Wilkes County. (Bowen, *op. cit.*, 137.)

Sabbath day, November 1. I preached on 1 John ii, 17: I had help. It is wonderful to see how flush the streams are, and excellent the crops, considering the want of rain for three months past. In the sandy lands the waters do not fail in a drought as they do elsewhere. My soul is happy in God continually. It has been reported to me that at the two camp meetings held, the one in Elbert county, the other in Franklin county, about one hundred souls professed converting grace.

Monday, 2. We came to James Marks's.[127]

Tuesday, 3. Both Daniel Hitt and myself preached.

Wednesday, 4. We were diligently occupied with our projected hymn book.[128] I make it a rule where I stop to pray after every meal.[129]

Thursday, 5. I felt the tears and sorrows of the family when parting. We crossed Webb's ferry into Oglethorpe county, passing through Lexington to James Freeman's; a ride of thirty miles, through wind and rain. James Halston told me that his cousin, Colonel Halston, had unfortunately beaten and killed a pious soldier during the war of the revolution: the Colonel settled in Georgia, and whilst everything seemed to prosper round him, he was one night shot in his bed by one of his slaves; the child which lay in his arms was unhurt.

Friday, 6. We were engaged with our collection of hymns. I preached at Henry Pope's[130] at night: it was a time of power and liberty.

Saturday, 7. We came to General John Stewart's.

Sabbath, 8. Daniel Hitt and myself both preached: we felt the state of the people. O! what necessity is there to urge the doctrine of sanctification in this State!—it is a doctrine almost forgotten here.

Monday, 9. I preached at John Crutchfield's, on 1 Peter i, 4. O, the *precious promises!* We did not speak without a present God. Next day Daniel Hitt preached at B. Bush's. Liberty: there has been a good and gracious work in this society.

Thursday, 12. I was taken ill with an influenza.

Monday, 23. I have been one week sick at Sparta. This evening I arrived, a sick, weak old man, at Mr. Bush's. I took another emetic.

Wednesday, 25. We rode to W. Bonner's. I found it good to stay here and take some more medicine. My complaint is a pleurisy, and deep affection of the breast.

Monday, 30. It was as much as I could this day do to reach Tindall's.

Tuesday, December 1. We came into Augusta.

[127] See note under November 21, 1813.

[128] The hymnbook was published in 1808 by John Wilson and Daniel Hitt, the book agents, at New York. It contained 326 hymns without music and was entitled *A Selection of Hymns from Various Authors, Designed as a Supplement to the Methodist Pocket Hymn-book, Compiled under the Direction of Bishop Asbury and Published by Order of the General Conference.*

[129] Giving thanks *after* the meal became an old custom in South Carolina.

[130] See note under December 9, 1814.

South Carolina

Wednesday, 2. I rode up to Martin Hitt's, on Steven's Creek.[131]

Thursday, 3. We reached Spann's.[132] I judge we have travelled nine hundred miles since the Western Conference. Judge William Stith[133] died at Milledgeville, suddenly, and, I believe, safely called home in peace. The mortality has been very general and very great in these parts. We had a blessed rain in Georgia. The weather and indisposition hold me at Spann's. My soul is happy in God in sickness and in health.

Sabbath, 6. I preached.

Monday, 7. We started away to Fridge's, thirty-six miles. As it was a day of general parade on *Tuesday* at Columbia, I returned to General Hutchinson's. Next day we reached Camden. *Thursday* I preached in Camden.[134] I spent *Friday* at Rembert Hall, reading and writing.[135]

Sabbath, 13. I preached at Rembert's chapel. Mr. Rembert was thrown out of his sulky; but there was no mischief done, except that some old bruises were wakened up. My subject to-day was Matt. xxiv, 45. The *good servant*—in spiritual wisdom, in fidelity, his diligence to perform his duties. The *wicked servant*—backslidden, false, and falsely secure. His *Lord delayeth his coming*—therefore he maltreats his fellow-servants who are better than himself. He is sensual; his portion is hell.

Sabbath, 20. At Rembert's chapel, I spoke, on Deut. v, 29. O that God would visit these people! Last week I have occasionally ridden out for exercise; but I am pretty busy with writing, family duty, and reading. My mind is wholly devoted to God and his work.

Monday, 21. It rained. On *Tuesday* we went to Bradford's.[136] *Wednesday* evening we lodged at Simpson's tavern.[137] On *Thursday* at Monk's Corner.[138] *Friday*, Christmas day, brought us to Charleston. *Saturday* was devoted to reading and receiving visits.

Sabbath, 27. I preached at the old church,[139] on Matt. vii, 21. At Bethel, on Deut. x, 12.

[131] Asbury went from Augusta into South Carolina on December 2. Martin Hitt lived on Stevens Creek in Edgefield County.

[132] Spann lived near Ridge Spring, where he founded Spann's Church, which still stands. He had removed from North Carolina, where he had also built a meetinghouse. See *Journal* entry for December 13, 1795.

[133] Judge Stith, a prominent Georgia citizen, had been a Deist but was converted in a Methodist revival in 1807. Jesse Lee, who had been assigned with two other preachers to Sparta but actually had a roving commission in Georgia, sat by his side singing, "Happy soul, thy days are ended," as he died and preached his funeral in the house of Dr. Thomas Bird. (Smith: *Georgia Methodism*, 84.)

[134] See letters to Nelson Reed, December 10, 1807, and to Daniel Hitt from Nelson Reed, December 10, 1807.

[135] See letter to Elijah Hedding, December 14, 1807. [136] Bradford lived near Sumter.

[137] Simpson's Tavern was in Lower Clarendon County near Summerton.

[138] Asbury crossed Nelson's Ferry to Moncks Corner.

[139] The old church was the Cumberland Street meetinghouse.

1808

1808 *Henry Boehm, McKendree, and Asbury driving in Georgia*

CHAPTER THIRTY-SEVEN

South Carolina

Friday, *January* 1, 1808. Our conference began. We sat six hours a day, had great harmony, and little or no trouble in stationing the preachers. Preaching every noon to the conference and others. In my sermon on *Sabbath day*, at the old church, I took some notice of the life and labours of Bennett Kendrick and George Dougharty.[1] The increase of members in the bounds of this and the Western Conference, for this year, is three thousand seven hundred members; preachers twenty-three.[2]

Wednesday, 6. We rode back to Rembert Hall. Busy writing letters. In the midst of restless days and nights of pain, my mind enjoys great peace. On *Saturday* I rode to Camden.

Sabbath, 10. I preached from 1 Cor. i, 30. I had some openings of mind, but there was little unction in preaching or sacrament. Busy writing letters. On *Monday* after the rain we went up to John Horton's, at the Hanging Rock. We reached Pressley's by chance on *Tuesday*.

[1] Each of these preachers rendered his last service as presiding elder of the Camden District. Dougherty died at Wilmington, North Carolina, on March 23, 1807, and Kendrick died at Edward Crosland's near Marlborough Court House on April 5, 1807. (See *Minutes*, 1808.)

[2] At this conference Matthew P. Sturdevant was appointed as a missionary to the Tombigbee section of Alabama, his circuit being a part of Oconee District in Georgia. He was the first Methoaist preacher in Alabama save for a brief visit by Lorenzo Dow in 1803. (Betts, *op. cit.*, 114.)

North Carolina

Wednesday, 13. We reached Mecklenburg, and stayed with our friend McKamie Wilson, a Presbyterian minister,[3] where we were comfortably and kindly accommodated. On *Thursday* we found the main branch of Rocky River unfordable. We stopped at Squire M'Curdey's.[4] *Friday* brought us through Concord to Savage's. Yesterday was very damp and cold; to-day there is ice, probably an inch thick. On *Saturday* we set out over the frozen roads and stopped at the end of ten miles to breakfast with the Rev. John Brown, a Presbyterian minister in Salisbury: thence we came away to John Hitt's. I have preached to his father and mother, who have now fallen asleep: the grandson, Jacob, son of John, feeleth as if he had a call to preach. In this journey, on the one side I may put down cold, hunger, rain, floods, frost, bad roads, and a lame horse; on the other, prayer, patience, peace, love; the balance is greatly in my favour.

Sabbath, 17. At Hitt's, I gave them a sermon, from Heb. iv, 9. Next day we pushed away, thirty miles, to Charles Clayton's. My spirit is greatly grieved with the ungodly children of this family, particularly one who has fallen from grace. On *Tuesday*, I preached at Joshua Clayton's, on Heb. iii, 7, 8. Joshua Clayton has no children to grieve me. The loving old souls in this house are early Methodists from Maryland. I ordained E. Breyer and Robert Field. We went over to father Doule's, on *Wednesday*. My ride over hard roads, on my poor, lame mare, was a trial to me. We crossed the Yadkin, at Clement's bridge—well-constructed and well-secured. In three hours' notice at Daub's we had a large congregation, to whom I spoke a few words on Rom. xii, 2. We came through Haverstown (having my lame mare shod), to Germantown. Both these villages are small; the first may have thirty families in it, the other about half the number. We lodged at Mr. Ennally's, where we have a small society; the grandfather left us, but the grandson is a preacher in the Connexion. On *Friday* we rode through the rain ten miles to breakfast at Brooks's. Amidst all my little difficulties my soul is very happy in the Lord. The prospects in the highland circuits are very good. On *Saturday* we were water-bound by the Mayo branches. We called a congregation at night. We set out on *Sabbath morning*, and had a most severe ride, crossing the first, second, and third branches of the Mayo river.

[3] The Rev. John McKamie Wilson was pastor of the Philadelphia and Rocky River Presbyterian churches, 1801–31. Both churches survive. The Philadelphia Church dates from 1770 and is at Mint Hill, about twelve miles east of Charlotte. Rocky River Church is a few years older and is in Cabarrus County, fifteen miles northeast of Charlotte and a few miles south of Concord. Wilson lived in Cabarrus County near the Mecklenburg County line between the two churches.

[4] This was Captain Archibald McCurdey, who lived in Mecklenburg County, North Carolina. (*Heads of Families*, 162.)

Virginia

At brother Travis's, in Henry county, we had a congregation at a short warning. I ordained Thomas Piner a deacon. We crossed Smith's river on *Monday morning*, at Reed's ford, bending our course down upon Snow Creek. We stopped with one Herman Cook, a rich man and a kind man.

Tuesday, 26, brought us over Pig river, and forward to Anthony's ford —fearful to the sight. We stopped at Staunton.[5] I endure considerable pain: my beast starts and stumbles. The perpetual changes of weather, and the company sometimes forced upon one on the road is disagreeable; but it is much worse in the cabins crowded with men, women, and children—no place to retire for reading, writing, or meditation: the woods are too cold for solitude at this season. We are weather-bound; I employ my time in reading, writing, praying, and planning. I ordained two deacons. On *Thursday* we set out for Murphy's, on Goose Creek. We visited brothers Leftrich and Wheat, and then made a toilsome march over Little and Big Otter, about thirty miles, to Price's. We arrived late, and it was cold. On *Saturday* we reached Lynchburg.

Sunday, 31. I preached at Lynchburg to about six hundred hearers. I feel paid for all my toil. On *Tuesday* our conference opened.[6] We progressed with great speed, and in good order, preaching each day. I ordained nine elders, nine deacons of the travelling order, and as many local deacons.

Sunday, *February* 7. I preached on 2 Cor. xiii, 5. I was blessed in my soul. The rainy weather and miry roads kept our congregations small and manageable, except on the *Sabbath day*. The people of the town honoured us—they were attentive to hear, and were very kind.

My company came away on *Tuesday*, to Colonel Meredith's, New Glasgow. *Wednesday*, to Key's. *Thursday*, we dined at the widow Key's; and lodged at B. Gillom's. I ordained Nathan Anderson a deacon. On *Friday* we rode twenty-four miles through mire, and a heavy cold rain, crossing the Rapidan, to John Stocksdale's Our host made us comfortable after our toil. By deep wading and plunging through mud, we reached Lott Fry's. I ordained him a deacon. It was the day appointed for preaching. I spoke, and had five preachers and two others to hear me. What will become of the children of this household? I cannot predict much good for either their souls or bodies. I could not willingly rest here on the *Sabbath*, so I came away to John Kobler's, and arrived just as sermon had

[5] This was a small town near the Roanoke River about five miles below the juncture of Goose Creek and the Roanoke River. The branches of Mayo river referred to above are in Patrick County, Virginia.

[6] This session of the Virginia Conference gave a favorable vote to the memorial presented from the New York Conference urging the necessity of constituting the General Conference as a representative legislative council. (Bennett, *op. cit.*, 532–35.)

ended. I ordained D. M'Masters a deacon. *Monday*, brought us to Beshaw's. Next day we got in to father Hitt's. O, the rocks, rivers, mud, frost, hills, cold, and hunger! Possibly, we have ridden seven hundred miles from Charleston in twenty-two days.

Tuesday, 23. For some days we have rested under the roof of Herman Hitt: he is now eighty-six. He has lived to see four generations. He is the head of eighteen families. Three of his sons are preachers, Martin, Daniel, and Samuel, and his grandson William also. I am occupied in reading and writing. I preached at the new house in Rectortown: the wind blew, and it was cold; but we had an open season. I preached to-day to a full house at Mount's. On *Wednesday* we visited the widow Rozsell, and her afflicted children. I called on brother Donaw—weak, but faithful. There is a blessed work of God in the east end of Loudon county. *Wednesday*, I preached at Leesburg. On *Thursday* we came to Doctor Wright's, and thence went on to William Watters's. Here I rested, and read and wrote on *Friday*. We arrived in Alexandria on *Saturday*.

Sunday, 28. I preached on 1 Thess, v, 16–18. It was an open time; I was helped and honoured of God before the people.

District of Columbia

Wednesday, March 2. Our conference began.[7] We laboured diligently, and in great peace. On the *Sabbath* I preached, and ordained deacons: souls have been converted since we are here.

Wednesday, 9. Our conference ended; and I came away to Annapolis.

Maryland

We came into the city about six in the evening; have travelled all day without fire, food, or water. Since the twentieth of this month (1807) we have travelled five thousand miles according to my computation. I rested on *Thursday*, and preached: and next day went to Baltimore: it was excessively cold, but we did not stop on the road. At seven o'clock I preached at Old Town. *Saturday* was a day of rest.

Sunday, 13. I preached at Fell's Point in the forenoon; and at Light Street in the afternoon. I hear, see, and feel many serious things; but I must take care of my own soul: my care is to love, to suffer, and to please God.

Monday, 14. I took a view of our new house;[8] large, and well con-

[7] This session of the Baltimore Conference was held at Georgetown, D.C.

[8] This new house stood on Eutaw Street near Mulberry Street, then on the outskirts of Baltimore. During the approaching General Conference, May 8, Asbury preached

structed. I preached to the African congregation. On *Tuesday* we moved off to Bennett's. *Wednesday noon* found us at Howell's.

Delaware

At night we were in Delaware, at Keagy's.[9] O my soul, rest in God! I am sometimes led to think the whole world will rise up against the pretensions of England to the dominion of the seas. Will Bonaparte conquer the world? He may: but will he govern it, and reign universal emperor over sea and land? No, no, no. Here I rest.

Pennsylvania

I preached in passing through Wilmington on *Friday*, and on *Saturday* we got into Philadelphia. I preached at St. George's twice; at the Academy, at Ebenezer, and at Bethel, African. We sat from *Sabbath* to *Sabbath* in conference; our business was conducted in great peace, but I did not please everybody by the appointments of the stations.

Monday, 28. We set out for the Jerseys, through which we passed swiftly to New York.

New York

We arrived on *Wednesday*, *March* 30; Jersey and York are blest with revivals of religion.[10]

Wednesday, *April* 6. Our conference for New York began in Amenia. On the *Sabbath* I preached in the town meeting house, and ordained seven elders. It was a time of solemnity, and we had nearly fifteen hundred people to hear. This conference is pleasant to me: I am near my work, I am not disturbed by company, and we make good progress with our business.

Wednesday, 13. We rose. I stationed eighty-eight preachers.

the dedicatory sermon. Eight years later the body of the bishop was placed in a vault beneath the pulpit, where it remained until 1854, when it was reinterred in Mount Olivet Cemetery. At the same time the body of Bishop John Emory also underwent similar removal. In 1853 extensive improvements made Eutaw Street Church one of the most commodious and best-equipped places of worship in Baltimore. In 1926 the congregation merged with Mount Vernon Place Church, where in its vestibule the old marker which was above Asbury's burial crypt in Eutaw Street Church may be seen.

[9] This was Abraham Keagy, one of the trustees to whom land was deeded by Robert McFarlin for twenty dollars as a site for the first Salem Meeting House. As early as 1771 Methodist services had been conducted in the home of Isaac Hersey. Twice Salem Church, located about two and one-half miles south of Ogletown, New Castle County, was extensively repaired before it was rebuilt in 1904. (Scharf: *History of Delaware*, II, 937.)

[10] See Asbury's letter to Thomas Coke, March 30, 1808.

Connecticut

We came away to Goshen, twenty miles, and lodged with Mr. Munson, a respectable brother. On *Thursday* we made it thirty-five miles to East Hartford: we lodged with Squire Pitkins. Next day brought us to New London. It was *Good Friday*, and had been appointed a State fast day: I took only a cup of coffee, and a small bit of bread. At father Lattimore's we were kindly received, and comfortably fixed. My two last days' rides were severe; my flesh is not brass, nor my bones iron; but I was in peace and communion with the Father and the Son. On *Saturday* we had a great storm. Confinement indoors gave me an opportunity of preparing papers for the conference.

Sunday, 17. Easter Sunday. I preached in the Baptist meeting house, the Baptists occupied ours; theirs was the larger building, and we had it crowded. Conference sat until *Friday*; we wrought in haste, in great order, and in peace, through a great deal of business. There were seventeen deacons, travelling and local, ordained; and nine elders ordained in the Congregational church, before fifteen hundred or two thousand witnesses. I know not where large congregations are so orderly as in the eastern States. There was a work of God going on during the sitting of the conference. The General Conference hastened our breaking up, the delegates thereto requesting leave to go. There were deficiencies in money matters, but no complaints.

Monday, 25. We came in haste through Milford, Stratford, Bridgeport, and Fairfield, to Stamford, forty-two miles.

New York

On *Tuesday*, a thirty-eight miles' ride brought us into New York: we had very heavy showers on the way. I feel my shoulders eased a little, now that I have met the seven conferences. I have lived to minute five hundred and fifty-two preachers in this country. The increase this short year is seven thousand five hundred in round numbers.

Wednesday, 27. I preached at the African church, and ordained D. Coker and W. Miller.

New Jersey

Thursday, 28. We set out, and reached a place ten miles beyond Brunswick, in New Jersey. On *Friday* we reached Hancock's.

Pennsylvania

Saturday brought us through Burlington to Philadelphia, where we dined, and stopped. At Kensington I preached a *Sabbath* sermon. At the African Zoar I also preached.

Maryland

Monday, *May* 2. We set out and reached Abraham Keagy's, forty-two miles. On *Tuesday* we arrived at Perry Hall: truly we came to the house of mourning; the master is possibly dying. Mr. Harry Dorsey Gough is dead: I saw and touched his dying body. When the corpse was moved to be taken into the country for interment, many of the members of the General Conference walked in procession after it to the end of the town. Harry Dorsey Gough professed more than thirty years ago to be convicted and sanctified: that he did depart from God is well known; but it is equally certain that he was visibly restored: as I was the means of his first turning to God, so was I also of his return and restoration: certain prejudices he had taken up against myself and others, these I removed. In his last hours, which were painfully afflictive, he was much given up to God. Mr. Gough had inherited a large estate from a relation in England, and having the means, he indulged his taste for gardening, and the expensive embellishment of his country seat, Perry Hall, which was always hospitably open to visitors, particularly those who feared God. Although a man of plain understanding, Mr. Gough was a man much respected and beloved: as a husband, a father, and a master, he was well worthy of imitation: his charities were as numerous as proper objects to a Christian were likely to make them; and the souls and bodies of the poor were administered to in the manner of a Christian who remembered the precepts, and followed the example of his Divine Master.

Friday, 6. Our General Conference opened in peace.[11] On *Saturday* one hundred and twenty-nine members took their seats. The new church in Eutaw Street was opened on the *Sabbath day*, and I gave a discourse on the occasion from 2 Cor. iii, 12. On the 26th the conference rose. We have done very little except making the rule for representation hereafter, one member to the General Conference for every five members of the annual conferences; and the electing dear brother William M'Kendree assistant

[11] This General Conference, attended by 129 preachers, elected William McKendree a bishop and permitted Dr. Coke to remain in Europe. Its action to have proportionate representation, with one delegate to each five members in an annual conference, corrected an increasing inequity. (Armstrong, *op. cit.*, 156; Stevens, *op. cit.*, III, 439–54; Boehm, *op. cit.*, 180–84; *Journals of the General Conference*, I, 71–95.)

bishop: the burden is now borne by two pairs of shoulders instead of one; the care is cast upon two hearts and heads.

Friday, 27. Heavy rain and awful thunder. On *Saturday* I visited Samuel Owings of S——.[12] I baptized George Howard's[13] three pretty children. At the request of some preachers in England, and the desire of the General Conference, I sat to Mr. Bruff, who took my likeness in crayons.[14]

Sabbath, 29. I preached at Old Town, and visited the house of mourning. In the afternoon I gave the Africans a talk. I visited a grandson of mother Triplett: her house, in my first and early visits to Baltimore, was my home. The young man's mother, Mary, married one Killen;[15] she died in peace and joy, and I hope the young man will be brought home to heaven and to God. On *Tuesday* I rode up to Daniel Elliott's and preached: it was an open season. At St. James's chapel Doctor Alexander Warfield heard me, who had heard me thirty-six years ago. Ah! I should not regret riding many miles to be the means of converting this dear man to God. I returned to Baltimore. On *Friday* I preached at Gatch's Chapel.

Sabbath, June 5. Harry Dorsey Gough's funeral sermon was preached; there might be two thousand people to hear. George Roberts spoke first on "He that hath this hope in him purifieth himself": my subject was Acts xiv, 22. I spoke long, and was obliged to speak loud that all might hear; my subject was very much a portraiture of Mr. Gough's religious experience and character.

Monday, 6. Bless the day! I escape from a month's location to the

[12] This Samuel was a son of Samuel Owings. The latter was an early Baltimore convert and his wife a leader of a class of women. (See *Journal* entry for March 13, 1774.) Dr. Henry Wilkins married a daughter of the senior Samuel Owings. (Smith, *op. cit.*, 164–65.)

[13] This may have been George Howard, a member of the firm of G. and T. Howard, merchants, located in 1808 at 169 Baltimore Street. There was a George Howard, a son of Captain Brice and Ann Ridgely Howard, the latter connected with the Gough and Carnan families. (Clagett: *Descendants of Matthew Howard of Anne Arundel County, Maryland*, manuscript D.A.R. Library, Washington, D.C.)

[14] In 1808 there were two Bruffs, both clerks, residing in Baltimore. Samuel lived in Holliday Street, and William, employed in the Custom House, lived in Fish Street. The wife of the latter was the former Catharine Ennalls, a sister of Henry Ennalls and of the first wife of Governor Richard Bassett. She was very conspicuous in the great Baltimore revival of 1800. Either Samuel or William Bruff may have been the person to whom Asbury refers, although neither was a professional artist. On Thursday, May 26, 1808, the General Conference in Baltimore voted "that Mr. Asbury be requested by this Conference to comply with a request of our brethren in England to send his likeness over to them to put in their magazines." This was one day before Asbury states that he sat for the Bruff portrait. Because a new likeness of Asbury appeared as a frontispiece to the *Methodist Magazine* (London), 1809, it seems highly probable that this was a reproduction of the Bruff portrait. (It appears in Clark: *Album of Methodist History*, 163.)

[15] John Killen, a merchant, married Mary, a daughter of Mrs. Triplett, on December 21, 1783. (See note under August 5, 1773.)

pleasant fields. Never were my friends more attentive, kind, and affectionate: but ah! the death of religion; in this I die. I preached at Cole's meeting house:[16] feeble as I was, the people waited and heard with patience, and I delivered my own soul. At Reisterstown I gave them a discourse on Romans xii, 1, 2; it was a time of freedom. After dining at Christopher Carnan's[17] I came away to James M'Cannon's, Richland. On *Wednesday* I preached at the stone chapel. I went, next day, to see the wife of William Durbin[18] in her affliction of body and mind: thirty-six years ago I visited this house: I have seen three generations. We dined with Ann Willis and her aged mother Honour Willis:[19] I prayed with them, and embraced the six children, and blessed them in the name of the Lord.

Friday, 10. At Alexander Warfield's[20] on Sam's creek. I am wholly for God. Our fields promise abundant crops; our stores and barns will be filled with the fruits and productions of field and tree while they are starving in Europe. O, sin! O, ingratitude! I spent *Saturday* with Joshua Jones.

Sabbath, 12. At Linganore chapel my subject was Ephes. v, 15, 16. In the afternoon at Liberty new chapel[21] I gave them a short discourse: I was feeble but fervent. I am kept at work by my friends; but they do what they can, Methodists and others, to pay me in affection, in attentions, in honour; Lord, keep me humble and holy! I went to Stephen Shelmerdine's on *Monday*, preached at Frederick on *Tuesday*, and returned to this afflicted family. On *Wednesday*, at brother Martin's, in Frederick, I met

[16] Cole's meetinghouse was at or near Reisterstown. (Colbert's *Journal*, October 17, 1790, and January 22, 23, 1791; Smith, *op. cit.*, 251; Armstrong, *op. cit.*, 155.)

[17] Christopher Carnan was the son of Robert North Carnan and Elizabeth Carnan. In 1802 Christopher married Christiana Sim Holliday, a half sister of Mrs. Harry Dorsey Gough. The father of Christopher Carnan was for more than half a century steward, class leader, and exhorter. The Carnan family was connected with the Ridgelys of Hampton, the family of General Mordecai Gist, the Goughs, and others who early embraced Methodism and lent their influence during a crucial period. Christopher Carnan, who was captain of the Sixth Cavalry and later a colonel in the War of 1812, lived near the Garrison Church. (Smith, *op. cit.*, 179–89; Allen: *The Garrison Church*, 118; *Journal* entry and note for October 30, 1780.)

[18] For an account of William Durbin see *Journal* entry and note for November 17, 19, 1772.

[19] Henry Willis had recently died. Honour Willis was not the mother of the widow but her mother-in-law. (Boehm, *op. cit.*, 189.)

[20] The Warfield homestead was near Bethel Church, New Windsor, Carroll County. Alexander Warfield (1765–1835) married first Elizabeth Woodward and second Jemima Dorsey. He was buried in the churchyard of Bethel Church. (Scharf: *History of Western Maryland*, II, 895, 896.)

[21] The deed for Liberty Church was made March 7, 1808, and called for payment of two hundred pounds current money and an annual rental of three shillings. The trustees were Nicholas Snethen, Joshua Jones, Alexander Warfield, Lewis Browning, Nicholas Randall, Ignatius Davis, and Jonathan Forrest. (Copy in Lovely Lane Museum, Baltimore.)

with my old acquaintance of York, Pennsylvania, the Rev. Mr. Wagner:[22] he is now fifty-eight; it is many years since our first interview; and this may be our last.

Our meeting ended in prayer; and when going, I gave him a book of our discipline, and recommended to his attention the Portrait of St. Paul by John Fletcher: O that all ministers would read it, and labour to impress it upon their hearts, and show a likeness in their lives and labours! After the rain we pressed on to Samuel Philips's. On *Thursday* my companion, Henry Boehm, went to Middletown: I stayed at home, and read. *Friday*, rain. I preached on Rev. iii, 20: brother Boehm also spoke in German. *Saturday* we rode to Hagerstown. Our German brethren of Otterbein's have shouldered us out, but have failed to establish themselves.

Sabbath, 19. I preached on Rom. i, 16. Henry Boehm spoke in the afternoon and at night. Death without; but there are some lively souls in the society. I feel the effect of riding in the heat; but I have great peace. On *Monday* I preached at St. Leger Neale's, and on *Tuesday* at Prather's.[23] The heat and rough roads have brought on a bilious headache. I begin to fail. *Wednesday evening* brought us to Richard Dowler's, at the mouth of Licking.[24] I preached at Hancock on *Thursday*:—the people were very attentive. Alas! no man careth for these people. We were driven by a storm into Squire Yates's[25]; I talked, prayed, dined, and left a book:—Lord, give us this family! At Clark's tavern,[26] on Friday, where I gave a book, and prayed, I did not know that my host was a Romanist—it was all one to me. We lodged with Lenox Martin.[27] On *Saturday* we came to John Jeremiah Jacob's. Ah! *because he saith the old wine is better*. King James used to call for his old shoes—*they fit me best*.

[22] Daniel Wagner was an intimate friend of Otterbein. He entered the ministry of the German Reformed Church in 1771 and held pastorates in York, Pennsylvania, and in Frederick, Maryland. He died at York in 1810. (Drury: *Life of Otterbein*, 189; Hough: *Christian Newcomer, His Life, Journal and Achievements*, 25, 35.)

[23] This was probably James Prather, who lived on the Potomac River five miles west of Williamsport, Washington County. In 1791 he was a justice of the Orphan's Court. Prather's was a preaching place on the Frederick Circuit before 1800.

[24] Licking Creek in Washington County empties into the Potomac River near the present Parkhead. Richard Dowler may have been the husband of the widow Dowler near Hagerstown.

[25] Because there were no church buildings in Hancock prior to 1823, Asbury either was conducting a service out of doors or in the schoolroom of David Neil. He took refuge from the storm in the home of William Yates, a prominent citizen who lived near the town. (Scharf: *History of Western Maryland*, II, 1252, 1255.)

[26] Clark's tavern was located about ten miles west of Hancock near the Potomac River.

[27] Lenox Martin, the brother of Luther Martin, famed Maryland lawyer, was admitted on trial in 1788. Among his appointments were the Talbot and Calvert circuits. He was admitted to the bar of Allegany County, Maryland, in 1791. He married Miss Elizabeth Cresap, a sister of James M. Cresap, and located on a farm three miles from Oldtown, where he died. (*Ibid.*, 1353, 1459.)

Sabbath, 26. We had about four hundred souls at the chapel in Old Town.[28] I spoke on Romans xii, 1, 2: brother Boehm concluded and met the society—it was an open season: hot as it was, we sang and prayed away the day. On our way to Aquila Brown's, Evitt's Creek, on *Monday*, we were glad now and then, to stop and shelter ourselves under the trees from the extreme heat. I gave advice for the body and soul of the wife of my kind host. At the Lutheran church, Cumberland, on *Tuesday*, we had a full house; my subject was 2 Pet. iii, 17, 18. I was very pointed on sinners and backslidden souls. I was expected to dine at only three several houses. Only let me declare myself, and work is soon found for me; a serious adult of forty years, and three children to baptize—one for Bell, one for Aguila Scott, and one for Brown. Brown was a Deist; he is now a brother: many think Bishop Whatcoat's prayers were heard for him. We have Georgia heat. I preached in the chapel at Cresaptown on *Wednesday*. We breakfasted at four o'clock on *Thursday*, that we might climb the Alleghany.

Pennsylvania

Friday, *July* 1. Moved at four o'clock, after breakfasting: at five in the evening we landed at Jacob Murphy's; our twenty-two hours' ride has brought us seventy miles. I have suffered much—I am pained and sore, and poor Jane stumbled so often! But my limbs and my soul are safe: Glory! Glory! We rested on *Saturday*.

Sabbath, 3. I preached at Uniontown, on James v, 19, 20. We started away for the widow Henthorn's, where we spent a solitary *fourth of July* in reading, and draughting conference plans as far as Baltimore. My mind is wholly devoted to God. On *Tuesday* I read Thomas á Kempis, and copied off a list of preachers for the western and southwestern conferences. Brother Boehm preached to the people in English and German: he also preached at Middletown on *Thursday*: I spoke for about half an hour at the widow Stephens's on *Friday*; my subject was 1 Cor. vi, 19, 20. On *Saturday* I read a part of the seventh volume of Wesley's Sermons. Confinement is excessively irksome, but the rain for four days past is tremendous, and I feel my old rheumatic affections. Edward Drumgoole, from old Virginia, is just on his return from a visit westward: he thinks he has seen *an end of all perfection*: and he has been preaching at the camp meetings beyond the Ohio: he thinks forty souls were converted.

Sabbath, 10. At Connellsville I preached in our new house, sixty by

[28] This was the original chapel which was replaced by a frame one in 1812. In 1863 a troop of New York cavalry used the lumber of the chapel for shanties. The present church stands about one mile from its predecessor, the site being marked by an ancient burying ground. (*Ibid.*, 1459.)

forty feet.[29] Brother Boehm spoke in German. The inflammation of my throat I laid aside as well as I could, and spoke on. Page, Doughady and Boehm each added a few words; and so we dedicated the walls of the house of God; the roof was not yet on. On *Monday* I went to Colonel Meason's, and was kindly received in his splendid, useful, good house. I was constrained to put a blister to my ear. At William Ball's new house I spoke on *Wednesday*, to about two hundred people. We were satisfied to stop at the widow Woodfield's at the crossings of Monongahela. One of my feet was inflamed, my blister was running, and the heat was excessive. Brother Boehm preached. I had a conversation with Asa Shinn, respecting a removal to Baltimore. On *Friday* I preached at Taylor's chapel.[30] I visited Doctor Charles Wheeler—risen from a dangerous fall from his horse, and from apparent death. Rested on *Saturday*; I am lame, and sensibly feel the great heat.

Sabbath, 17. With the aid of two crutches I hobbled into meeting at Brownsville, and preached on John iii, 17.[31] I am sorely lame. I dined with Mr. Hogg; a kind, polite English family. On *Monday* I had an awfully severe ride to Chalfant's,[32] and then on to John Brightwell's.[33] I am fairly arrested in my course; my knees and feet are so disabled that I am lifted to bed. I can neither ride, stand, nor walk.

Sabbath, 24. I feel revived this morning; but O, what an awful night of pain! The people gathered in the house, and I taught them from Acts xxvi, 18. I have a clean house, an excellent nurse as any in the country, and kindly attentive people. How am I honoured! Thornton Fleming[34] paid me a visit, and with him came Mrs. Hebert, and a daughter of Edward Bailey, of Amherst, Virginia; these dear souls came sixty miles to see me. I suppose I must get a four-wheeled carriage. *Wednesday* was a serious day, but prepare to move we must—pain and death are nothing when opposed to duty. On *Thursday* we set off to Washington. We had two hours' rain,

[29] This was the first Methodist church building in Connellsville. Methodist preaching there dates back to the organization of the Pittsburgh Circuit in 1788.

[30] Taylor's was the third chapel in this region, having been erected in 1786. Originally called Hawkin's Chapel, from William and Cassandra Hawkins, on whose farm it was built, its name was changed to Taylor's about 1800. It continues today as the Taylor Church of the Pittsburgh Conference and is located on the National Road (Route 40) four miles west of the Monongahela River. (Smeltzer, *op. cit.*, 68.)

[31] This is the first record of Asbury's preaching in Brownsville, Pennsylvania. The town was laid out in 1770, and Asbury in his tour of the region in 1786 made note that a town was being built at the place.

[32] Chads Chalfant sold the lot for the Methodist Church at Brownsville. The deed is dated March 24, 1806.

[33] Asbury spent a week of affliction, apparently from a severe rheumatic attack, at the home of John Brightwell near Fayette City, Pennsylvania. His letter of appreciation to Mrs. Mary Brightwell, under date of March 4, 1809, is characteristic of his gratitude for the courtesies and benefits tendered to him. (See letter.)

[34] Thornton Fleming was presiding elder of the Monongahela District, Baltimore Conference.

but this was not as bad as pain of body. Mr. McFaddin[35] was as loving and kind as need be.

West Virginia

We found a home at John Beck's on *Friday*.[36] *Saturday*, rested.

Sabbath, 31. At Bethel chapel, Short Creek, I gave them a sermon. I spoke in great weakness.

Monday, *August* 1. I preached in the court house at Wheeling. I have great pain. At Colonel Zane's, where I lodged, the aged people were kind indeed.

Ohio

At Newellsville I gave them a discourse. We first stopped at Galbert's on *Wednesday*, and then went on to Moore's: we had a great heat, and I was almost overdone. On *Thursday* we came to Will's Creek to dine, and then rode on. There is a great want of water. I rested well last night, but my case is pretty serious: I am so disabled, that the riding, and the long hills especially, almost make me cry out.

Sabbath, 7. On *Saturday* we visited the camp ground, and returned to Daniel Stevens's. Wyre and Layton, two young preachers, died lately upon their circuits. I preached to-day at Bush Creek, upon 1 Tim. iii, 14–17. I ordained James Watts an elder. It was a solemn time. Some wagoners attempted to sell whisky on the camp ground: we stopped our preaching—the people soon knew how deeply we felt the insult, and they were driven away. Henry Boehm spoke in German. We had about a thousand people to hear. The house where I stayed was much crowded, which ill suited me in my afflicted state. I paid a visit to John Manly, on *Monday*; stayed there to rest and refit. We moved to the widow Taylor's on *Tuesday*; and on *Wednesday* came into Chillicothe. On *Thursday* I preached in the chapel; it was quite comfortable to know that people dropped the scythe and laid by the plane to come to the house of God. Chillicothe has been cursed with apostate Methodist preachers: but if I am not deceived, God will yet do great things here. I was invited to pass a night under the hospitable roof of General Thomas Worthington at Mount Prospect Hall. Within sight of this beautiful mansion lies the precious dust of Mary Tiffin;[37] it was as much as I could do to forbear

[35] Thomas McFaddin lived in Washington, Pennsylvania. (Boehm, *op. cit.*, 195.)

[36] See Henry Boehm's letter to Mrs. Brightwell, July 31, 1808.

[37] Mary Tiffin, wife of Edward Tiffin, was the daughter of Robert Worthington of Berkeley County, West Virginia, and the sister of Thomas Worthington, who succeeded Tiffin in the office of governor of Ohio. (Gilmore: *Life of Edward Tiffin*, 4.)

weeping as I mused over her speaking grave—how mutely eloquent! Ah! the world knows little of my sorrows—little knows how dear to me are my many friends, and how deeply I feel their loss—but they all die in the Lord, and this shall comfort me. I delivered my soul here; may this dear family feel an answer to Mary Tiffin's prayers!

On *Friday* we went to the camp ground at Deer Creek.[38] *Saturday*, rested—damp, rain. The work of God went on night and day, nevertheless. There were twenty-three travelling and local preachers on the ground: perhaps tents and wagons one hundred and twenty-five; and about two thousand people: forty souls professed converting grace. We rested on *Monday*, and on *Tuesday* came up Short Creek. We found the family of Mr. Wood, at the New Purchase, as kind as need be. The prairies have once been, I suppose, lakes of water; they furnish grand and beautiful views still. O, the flies, the heat! We dined at brother Cutler's on *Wednesday* and came on, through Xenia, to Frederick Bonner's, Little Miami; thirty-two miles. I have more than once put the wrong foot foremost in my journeys to the west: the spring will not do because of wet, and deep, and dismal roads: the summer's extreme heat, and the small and the green flies make disagreeable travelling. I make a decree, but not of the Medes and Persians, never, in future, to cross the mountains before the first of September, nor leave Carlisle before the first of October. On *Thursday* I rested. *Friday* at John Sale's. *Saturday*, rested.

Sabbath, 21. At Xenia court house I preached from Colossians i, 28; we had about five hundred souls to hear; it was a searching season. On *Tuesday* left Peter Pelham's, and came to Samuel Hitt's.

Wednesday, 24. I preached at the widow Smith's. On *Thursday* we passed Lebanon, journeying down the Little Miami, calling at Clark's to escape the rain. It cleared away, and we came in haste by Walsmith's mill, to M'Grue's. Camp meeting commenced at Philip Gatch's on *Friday*: here I saw many whom I had not seen for years—how delightful to see our old friends after a separation, and to find them still on the Lord's side! I spoke twice: then much faithful preaching, and we believe much good done: fifty souls professed converting grace. I talk more than is truly spiritual. I rejoice to think there will be perhaps four or five hundred camp meetings this year; may this year outdo all former years in the conversion of precious souls to God! Work, Lord, for thine own honour and glory!

Thursday, *September* 1. I preached at the chapel, Little Miami. We had a full house at a short notice. I was grieved to see an unfeeling man take away a poor widow's horse for debt: but brother Gatchell soon relieved me—he paid the debt, and restored the horse to the distressed woman to be hers for life.

[38] Boehm says: "This campground was near White Brown's and we were entertained by him. He was a nephew of Thomas White of Delaware. Asbury used to preach at White Brown's on the Peninsula as early as 1779." (Boehm, *op. cit.*, 199.)

Friday, 2. Great work in Spain—the old king resigning to his son, and his son outwitted by Bonaparte. The old king is persuaded by the enemy of both to make Murat, duke of Berg, his viceroy. This, I hear, is the news. Ah! the poor Spaniards will have blood to drink. The first victims will be the priests; and the *House of Mercy*, the Inquisition, what will become of it? Is Europe prepared for free governments and freedom in religion? Bonaparte will establish himself for one year; and then he goes, goes, goes. We cried to God yesterday for rain; today we have it in abundance. After one o'clock we came away from M'Grue's to Cincinnati. The waters of the rivers have failed more than I ever knew them before. I read a book to-day, and wrote two letters. I advised the society here to invite the Western yearly conference to hold its session in Cincinnati.

Sabbath, 4. I preached at ten o'clock, in great bodily weakness; the heat was great, and the house was crowded; but I felt sensible of Divine aid. Brother Boehm spoke after me in German. At three o'clock I preached again at brother Lakin's: brother Boehm also spoke at six o'clock in the evening, in English: thus we improved the day. My temptations are hidden, but great. I have need of great strength, for I am greatly responsible. Lord, help me! On *Monday* we had plentiful rain. I rested. I advised the brethren to enlarge the house to eighty feet. On *Tuesday* we took our flight; it was not pleasant travelling. We stopped and dined at Murphy's, and so avoided the rain. At Judge Simms's new improvement, we crossed the Great Miami. We saw the paroquet here as upon Santee River.

Indiana

After crossing White River, we came to Lawrenceburg, the first town in the Indian territory.[39] In this wild there may be twenty thousand souls already. I feel for them. Elijah Sparks[40] received us gladly. We dined with J. Wilson, and stopped at Dickinson's. After beating the shore of the Ohio for two hours, we crossed in a crazy flat, at the mouth of Kentucky river.[41]

Kentucky

On *Thursday* we lodged at the widow Masterson's.[42] I sighed over the heaps of dust raised upon the bodies of her husband and children. Nathan

[39] This tour across the southeastern corner of Indiana was the first and only time Asbury was on the soil of that state. Indiana was constituted a territory on May 7, 1800, and admitted to the Union as a state on December 11, 1816.

[40] Elijah Sparks was a lawyer and a Methodist local preacher. He was a Marylander and a brother of Robert Sparks. (Boehm, *op. cit.*, 205.)

[41] The party crossed the Ohio into Kentucky at the mouth of Licking, or Kentucky, River. (Boehm: *Reminiscences*, 250.)

[42] (See note under May 13, 1788.) Richard Masterson and Sarah Shore were married

Wyre, a promising youth upon trial on the circuit, has been called away; he died with consumption. Ah! what blessed numbers have gone home triumphantly within the last forty years! Surely we may praise the dead, for they died in the Lord. *Friday* brought us through Williamsport,[43] Gallatin, Henry, and Shelby. We brought up with my old friend, Billy Adams, grandson of William, son of Simon. We have ridden about one hundred miles in three days. Our fare has been rough, but sister Lakin, and the preachers who accompanied us, bore the fatigues of the ride very well. I feel for the people of this territory; but we must suffer with them, if we expect to feel for them as we ought: and here are the disadvantages of a local episcopacy—that it cannot be interested for its charge as it should be, because it sees not, suffers not with, and therefore feels not for, the people. On *Saturday*, at Edward Talbot's.

Sunday, 11. At the brick chapel,[44] I spoke on, 1 Cor. xv, 58; a more attentive congregation I have not seen. But, ah me! to pant for breath, and unable to walk, kneel, or stand up straight to preach, makes public speaking serious work to me. Brothers Lakin and Boehm[45] spoke after me. We were about four hours in the house. I see, I feel what is wrong in preachers and people, but I cannot make it right. I saw some dear old friends from Virginia and Maryland. We rested on *Monday* at Edward Talbot's. On *Tuesday* we passed Shelby, and came to Philip Taylor's; the swelling in my feet had returned—I was weary and willing to rest. We called a meeting on *Wednesday*, and I gave them a sermon from 2 Cor. v, 2. Gabriel Mayo received, and kindly entertained us after crossing Salt River. On *Thursday* we hasted away to Joseph Ferguson's, Nelson county. I met Benedict Swope[46] by accident. I knew him at first glance; but he would not have recollected me: it was pleasing to meet after so long an absence; but, ah! how time, and toil, and suffering have worn us down!

in Virginia on July 29, 1784, shortly before they moved to Kentucky to build near Lexington the first Methodist meetinghouse in the state. (Arnold, *op. cit.*, I, 46.)

[43] Williamsport was Port William, the present Carrollton, on the Ohio River at the mouth of the Kentucky.

[44] The Brick Chapel was in Shelby County, Kentucky, about four miles northeast of Shelbyville. It was built under the supervision of William McKendree in 1804 and was the first Methodist meetinghouse in the state to be built of brick. The society there was formed between 1795 and 1800, but meetings were held in homes and a schoolhouse until the chapel was erected. (Redford: *Methodism in Kentucky*, I, 389, 390.)

[45] Benjamin Lakin (1767–1849) was born in Maryland and began preaching in Kentucky in 1794, becoming one of the notable pioneers. At this time he was on the Deer Creek Circuit in the Ohio District. (See Lakin's *Journal* in Sweet: *Religion on the American Frontier, the Methodists*, 202–60.) Henry Boehm (1775–1875) was born in Pennsylvania and was notable as a German preacher. He had been appointed to travel with Asbury. (See Boehm: *Reminiscences, Historical and Biographical, of Sixty-Four Years in the Ministry.*)

[46] Benedict Swope was a member of the Kentucky Constitutional Convention in 1792, representing Lincoln County. (Collins: *History of Kentucky.*)

—one of us, at least. I preached at Ferguson's[47] on *Friday*. We had a warm, heavy ride to Colonel Thomas's, Hardin Creek, Washington county.

Sunday, 18. At the new chapel, I spoke, on 1 John iii, 1–4; it was a time of seriousness. I could not stand—I sat to preach. My kind brethren, M'Kendree and Thompson, came miles to see me. On *Monday* I parted from sister Lakin,[48] wife of Benjamin; so far from being a troublesome companion, she was very useful to me as a nurse and servant for Christ's sake. We crossed the Rolling Fork of Salt River, passed Merder's hill, dined at M'Murry's, and then hasted on to Georgetown, crossed Green River by fording, and stopped at Manoah Lasley's.[49] We have made forty miles to-day. My lame feet were in a poultice; it was unusually warm, but I enjoyed great peace in my soul. I preached at Lasley's. On *Tuesday* we had a full house at sudden warning. Here I saw William Price and family—great joy, as if we were risen from the dead. I preached at Robert Price's, Adam's Creek, upon Coloss. i, 7. David Rice stepped in whilst I was speaking, and when I had closed, withdrew without speaking to me. On *Thursday* we came to Glasgow, where I visited brother Crusenbury, and Henry and Edward Cowell.

Tennessee

Friday evening brought us up at brother Porter's, from Maryland, now of Warren county. On *Saturday* we came in upon the camp with Bishop M'Kendree. On *Sunday* we had preaching as usual, and a gracious rain—in mercy, if not in answer to prayer. We came no farther than Woodard's, twenty-two miles, on *Monday*. On *Tuesday* we passed through Nashville. This town has greatly improved in eight years. There are several valuable houses built, an elegant court house, and a college. We put in at Green Hill's, Williamson county.[50] We have important business here to

[47] Ferguson's Chapel was in Nelson County, Kentucky. It was a log structure erected about 1792 and was probably the second Methodist meetinghouse in the state. It was built by John Ferguson, who went from Fairfax County, Virginia, and was the nucleus of the Salt River Circuit. A brick church was built in 1816. (Arnold, *op. cit.*, I, 71, 179; Redford, *op. cit.*, I, 387.)

[48] "My wife traveled in company with us about 3 weaks, untill we came to Bro. Thomases on Hardens Creek in Kentucky. her strength would not admit of her going any further [so] that she taried in them parts untill my return from Conference." (Lakin's *Journal* in Sweet, *op. cit.*, 230.)

[49] Manoah Lasley lived on Green River not far from Greensburg, Kentucky, and his house was a Methodist preaching place. He was the progenitor of a number of Methodist preachers. (Redford, *op. cit.*, I, 173.)

[50] The Western Conference met at the home of Green Hill, called Liberty Hill, twelve miles from Nashville. This was McKendree's "home conference," where he had been presiding elder, and was the first at which he presided as a bishop. He had been elected

engage our attention; seven districts there are, and a call for eighty preachers.

Saturday, October 1. I began conference. I preached twice on the *Sabbath day*, and again on *Tuesday*. Our conference was a camp meeting, where the preachers ate and slept in tents. We sat six hours a day, stationed eighty-three preachers, and all was peace. On *Friday* the sacrament was administered, and we hope there were souls converted, and strengthened, and sanctified. We made a regulation respecting slavery: it was, that no member of society, or preacher, should sell or buy a slave unjustly, inhumanly, or covetously; the case, on complaint, to be examined for a member by the quarterly meeting; and for a preacher an appeal to an annual conference. Where the guilt was proved the offender to be expelled. The families of the Hills, Sewalls, and Cannon, were greatly and affectionately attentive to us.

Saturday, 8. We came rapidly to Stones River, and thence to Crane's.[51] At the meeting house I preached on the *Sabbath day*, from 2 Pet. iv, 17. I called upon Hardy Hunt. We rose at four o'clock on *Monday*, and started away for Henry Tooley's.[52] The heat is great; we may give it five months' continuance this year. The increase of the Western Conference for the year will be two thousand five hundred. On *Tuesday* we rested and refitted, preparing ourselves to breast the wilderness. The rain caught us on *Wednesday*, and fell on us with little intermission, until we got to our home at Shaw's, in Carthage. On *Thursday* evening I came in very unwell to Johnson's. We had not above fifty travellers in company! At Haily's, next night, we were not so crowded, and did better. There is order observed under this roof. We breakfasted at S. W. Point[53] on *Saturday*, and then hastened on to Winton's; since we left the conference ground, we have made two hundred miles. My sufferings have been great. I had the piles, and pains of body, and sultry weather, crowded houses and rough roads, and bad men for company; but my mind enjoyed great peace, notwithstanding my starting, stumbling horse, that ever and anon would run away with me. I preached on the *Sabbath day* at Winton's chapel, a crowd within and without; the wind prevented our taking the woods. There is a special revival of religion in the society here. After preaching we crossed

at the General Conference at Baltimore in May and had returned to the West by the most direct route. (Boehm, *op. cit.*, 200.) Here McKendree first introduced the "cabinet" of presiding elders as participants in the work of making the appointments of the preachers, a strange and not entirely pleasing innovation to Asbury.

[51] On his way to the Holston country Asbury crossed Stones River and proceeded by way of the present Lebanon and Carthage. "Everywhere the old and the new bishops were objects of interest, and their appearance hailed with joy." (Boehm, *op. cit.*, 209.)

[52] "On Monday we reached Dr. Henry Tooley's. This was a family of note, and their house one of the best of homes. Here we rested and refitted and prepared to climb the mountains and to penetrate the wilderness." (*Ibid.*)

[53] This was the present town of Kingston. (See note under September 27, 1802.)

Holston, and rode ten miles to meet the people at John Saffle's.[54] We started in the rain on *Monday* to Maryville, called upon Mark Moore,[55] and continued to Esquire Black's,[56] and lodged.

Tuesday, 18. Came to Mitchell Porter's,[57] on Pigeon River, *Wednesday*, rain. *Thursday*, rain; we crossed the river twice. I preached at the chapel on Matt. v, 8. On *Friday*, James Riggin came twenty miles, breasting the rains, and plunging through the swollen streams, to see me; he wept over me and bade farewell: but shall we not meet where all tears shall be wiped from all eyes? We started away on *Saturday*, wade or swim, foul or fair, across the east forks of Little and Great Pigeon: the waters were full enough.

Sunday, 23. At O'haver's a camp meeting had been appointed by the preachers and people. Bishop M'Kendree and brother Boehm spoke, as well as brother Blackman and myself. Brother Bowman spoke at night, and some souls were affected. On *Monday* I spoke again; there was a flood of speaking to about three hundred souls, some of whom joined society. It was very cold on the ground. Our party came away to George Wells's.

North Carolina

On *Tuesday* we rode twenty miles to the Warm Springs; and next day reached Buncombe, thirty-two miles.[58] The right way to improve a short day is to stop only to feed the horses, and let the riders, meanwhile, take a bite of what they may have been provident enough to put into their pockets. It has been serious October to me. I have laboured and suffered; but I have lived near to God.

Saturday, 29. We have rested for three days past. We fell in with Jesse Richardson: he could not bear to see the field of Buncombe deserted by militia men, who fire a shot and fly, and wheel and fire, and run again: he is a veteran who has learned to "endure hardness like a good soldier of the Lord Jesus Christ." On the *Sunday* I preached in Buncombe court house, upon 1 Thess. i, 7–10. I lodged with a chief man, a Mr. Erwin.[59]

[54] Asbury was now in the Holston region. John Saffle lived near a small church near Middle Settlement in Blount County. It is the oldest church in that county.

[55] Mark Moore had joined the conference in 1786 and was alternately a local and a traveling preacher until his final location in 1820. At this time he was a local preacher living near Maryville, Tennessee. (Price, *op. cit.*, I, 102.)

[56] Squire Joseph Black lived between Maryville and Sevierville.

[57] Mitchell Porter was a Revolutionary soldier. Asbury frequently visited in his home.

[58] Warm, or Hot, Springs was then in Buncombe County. Asbury's references to Buncombe meant the Buncombe courthouse, or Asheville. On this trip to western North Carolina, Asbury was accompanied by Bishop William McKendree and Henry Boehm.

[59] This was Henry Erwin. He was born in Virginia in 1773 and died in Bedford County, Tennessee, in 1833. He went to North Carolina in 1790 and was a merchant

Henry Boehm went to Pigeon Creek to preach to the Dutch.[60] On *Monday* I went to David Jay's; I thought I was unknown, but the woman of the house, the mother of seven children, quickly told me I had joined her in matrimony to her present husband. Here we met with Daniel Asbury;[61] great news from Georgia, South and North Carolina! Thirty, or forty, or fifty souls converted at camp meetings; but in old Virginia the work is still greater, and brother Bruce's labours have been blessed in an extraordinary manner.

Tuesday, *Wednesday* and *Thursday*, *November* 1, 2, 3, I rested, read, and preached but once. On *Friday* we descended the heights of Cooper's Gap, to our friend David Dickey's;[62] fasting, and the labour of lowering ourselves down from the mountain top, have made us feeble. Bishop M'Kendree preached upon, "Cast not away your confidence." On the *Sabbath* brother Boehm spoke in the morning at eight o'clock; I preached from Matt. xvii, 5; exhortations followed, and brother Boehm ended our Sabbath labours by preaching at night, when there was a considerable move. We came away on *Monday* by Rutherford court house to G. Moore's. At Moore's chapel on *Tuesday* I preached from Colossians ii, 6. Henry Boehm spoke at night: verily we had a shout! Bishop M'Kendree preached at Lucas's chapel upon Little Broad, and we lodged at Lucas's. A ride of forty miles brought us next day to William's, in Lincoln. I preached on *Friday*. My mind hath great peace, but my body is weak. The prospects are reviving and cheering in the South Carolina Conference, and they will grow better every year. On *Saturday* I preached. I ordained Samuel Smith and Enoch Spinks. The *Sabbath day* was windy and cold; I had taken an emetic, and kept the house.

Monday, 14. Rode thirty-three miles, hungry, cold, and sick, to Harrison's,[63] Mecklenburg county.

and innkeeper at Wilkesboro. He was a member of the House of Commons from Wilkes County in 1800 and was the first postmaster of Asheville. (Arthur, *op. cit.*, 153.)

[60] Henry Boehm had left the two bishops at John O'Haver's campground in Cocke County, Tennessee, and had made a detour to preach to the German-speaking people on the Pigeon River of western North Carolina. He preached six times and then hastened to overtake the bishops at the Buncombe courthouse. He spent a night at Barnard's public house in the present Madison County near Marshall (see note under November 2, 1802) where he preached to the family. He failed to overtake the bishops at Asheville but found them at the Rev. Samuel Edney's on Monday, November 2. This date, however, does not agree with Asbury's *Journal*. (Boehm: *Reminiscences*, 210, 211.)

[61] Daniel Asbury (1762–1825) was born in Virginia and became a prominent pioneer preacher in western North Carolina. He was not related to Bishop Asbury. (Grissom: *Methodism in North Carolina*, 278–80.)

[62] Dr. David Dickey, physician and representative in the General Assembly, lived on Maple Creek a few miles west of Rutherfordton. The house is still standing. (Griffin: *Essays on North Carolina History*, 78.)

[63] Harrison Chapel is located five miles south of Pineville in Mecklenburg County, near the South Carolina border.

South Carolina

I came, unwell and taking medicine, to Robert Hancock's, Waxhaw's:[64] I suffer, but it is the will of God. Eighteen hundred miles since leaving Baltimore. I have ordained Robert Hancock a local deacon. We came rapidly to Hanging Rock[65] on *Wednesday*, and next day reached Camden, and lodged with Samuel Matthews.[66]

Sabbath, 20. I preached in the tabernacle in Camden in the morning, and brother Boehm in the afternoon, and Bishop M'Kendree at night.[67] Letters from the presiding elders announce great times in camp meetings.

Monday, 21. This day I renew my covenant with God; to do nothing I doubt is not lawful, and at all times, and in all places to live as if it were my last hour—may God help me so to do! On *Wednesday* I went to the encampment, four miles from the city. Bishop M'Kendree preached.[68] It was very unpleasant weather. I took cold sitting in the stand. *Thursday*, dwelling under curtains: I took an emetic: wrote two letters to elders Soule and Beale, Province of Maine.[69] I am still at Rembert Hall.[70] I

[64] "It was a tremendous task to descend from the lofty mountain. The ascent was rough and fatiguing, but the descent still more difficult. On we went, the bishop preaching every day and several times on the Sabbath till we reached Waxhaw, South Carolina, famous for being the birthplace of Andrew Jackson. Here at this time Bishop Asbury ordained Robert Hancock, who was a respectable local preacher. There were many private ordinations of that kind in those days." (Boehm, *op. cit.*, 212.) The present Hancock community is four miles west of Waxhaw in South Carolina.

[65] Betts says the party lodged as usual with John Horton at Hanging Rock.

[66] The otherwise unidentified Matthews was called Matthis by Boehm. (*Ibid.*, 212.) Moses Matthews was the presiding elder of the Camden district.

[67] Boehm says that immediately after the first sermon Jonathan Jackson, pastor on the Santee Circuit, preached to three hundred colored people "on putting the hand to the plow and looking back." In the love feast one colored brother testified, "I have put my hand to the Gospel plow, and I am determined to plow my furrow clean up to glory." (*Ibid.*, 212, 213.)

[68] This camp meeting was at the Rembert Camp Ground. In addition to the two bishops and Boehm the preachers included Lovick Pierce, James Jenkins, and Morris Mathis (perhaps Moses Matthews). With such a company of preachers the meeting was notable, William Capers calling it one of the best he had ever known. The future bishop was licensed to preach at a quarterly conference held there, and his two brothers, John and Gabriel Capers, were both converted. Their father, who had been estranged by William Hammet, was reconciled to Asbury in a touching manner. (The story is related by Boehm, *op. cit.*, 214, 215, and by Bishop Capers: *Autobiography*, 90.)

[69] Joshua Soule (1781–1867) was a native of Maine and presiding elder of the Portland District. In 1808 he was the author of the plan for a delegated General Conference and principal author of the constitution of the church. In 1816 he was book editor and edited the *Methodist Magazine*. He was elected bishop in 1820 but refused the office because he thought the General Conference violated the constitution by its action providing for the election of presiding elders; he was again elected in 1824 and accepted when the objectionable legislation was rescinded. In 1845 he adhered to the Methodist Episcopal Church, South, because he believed the southern position in opposing the

visited, and preached upon the camp ground; we had an exceeding strong wind, but the people were very attentive. The superintendency had a hut with a chimney in it: there were forty tents and cabins: Bishop M'Kendree was three days and nights on the ground, and there was a powerful work amongst white saints and sinners, and the poor, oppressed, neglected Africans.

Sabbath, 27. At Rembert chapel my subject was Rev. vii, 14–17. Brothers Smith and Boehm followed with energetic exhortations. I felt dejected in mind, and my soul was humbled. I suffer much from ill health, too close application to business, and from having preached in the open air. I filled an appointment made for Bishop M'Kendree at Rembert's. On *Monday* I rode forty-five miles to Mr. Keel's;[71] we crossed Murray's[72] next day, and stopped in the evening at the widow Kennedy's. *Wednesday* we had a heavy ride, and I felt it from top to bottom. Great news!—Baltimore taken fire—Bohemia has a great work—camp meetings have done this: glory to the great I AM!

Sunday, December 4. At Cumberland church we had a sacramental day. I preached at Bethel in the afternoon. We have a great change and a gracious prospect here in Charleston, and in the neighbourhood among both descriptions of people: by our coloured missionaries the Lord is doing wonders among the Africans.

Monday, 5. I am closely employed in reading and writing letters and receiving company: our house is a house of prayer ten or twelve times a day. I read Mr. Wesley's Journal: Ah! how little it makes me feel!—the faithfulness—the diligence of this great man of God!—I cannot meet the classes like him, but I have a daily throng of white and black who apply for spiritual instruction.

Sabbath, 11. I preached in Cumberland street: it was a serious parting time. At Bethel I also gave them a talk in the afternoon: this was a heavy day—I felt the weight of souls. Some may think it no great matter to build two churches, buy three lots, pay fifteen hundred dollars of bank debt, and raise a growing society: this has been done in this Sodom in less than twenty-four years:—O Lord, take thou the glory! We dined in the woods on *Monday*, and made it thirty-two miles to Perry's.[73] On *Tuesday* we

deposition of a bishop without charges or trial was constitutionally sound. He died at Nashville, Tennessee. He with Bishops M'Kendree and McTyeire are buried at Vanderbilt University.

[70] With reference to Rembert, Boehm says, "He lived at a place called Rembert's Settlement; there was a church called Rembert's Chapel, and James Rembert was the honored patriarch." (Boehm, *op. cit.*, 216.)

[71] Keel lived between Manning and Greeleyville near Forreston.

[72] The party crossed Murray's ferry to Monck's Corner and proceeded to Charleston. William Phoebus was one of the preachers there, and Boehm recorded the fact that he had preached in the home of a brother, John Phoebus, on the Eastern Shore of Maryland. (*Ibid.*, 216.)

[73] Captain Perry lived on Cypress Swamp in Dorchester County.

crossed Edisto, dining at Koger's,[74] and came into Benjamin Risher's. Next day, at the Green Ponds chapel,[75] Bishop M'Kendree, brother Boehm, and myself, all spoke. We lodged at Lewis's, niece to one who had first received the Methodist preachers. Next day we called on B. M'Lellan, a preacher, and lodged with Benjamin Tarrant[76]:—O that it was with him as in years past!—once, how holy and innocent! We reached Benjamin Weatherly's[77] on *Friday evening*. Cold, very cold weather.

Georgia

We came into Augusta on *Saturday evening*; we dined in the woods. One disorderly man has given great trouble, and awful Osborn Randall has shot a man!

Sabbath, 18. I preached in Augusta chapel. My flesh sinks under labour. We are riding in a poor thirty-dollar chaise, in partnership, two bishops of us, but it must be confessed it tallies well with the weight of our purses: what bishops! well: but we hear great news, and we have great times, and each western, southern, and the Virginia Conference will have one thousand souls truly converted to God; and is not this an equivalent for a light purse? and are we not well paid for starving and toil?—yes; glory be to God! We came away to Wysing's on *Monday*, and next day toiled through a very heavy rain to the widow Fountain's.[78] We remained *Thursday* and *Friday* in Sparta, and went on *Saturday* to brother Bush's.

Sabbath, 25. *Christmas day*. I preached on John iii, 17. We opened our conference on *Monday*. We had great labour which we went through in great peace. Between sixty and seventy men were present, all of one spirit. We appointed three missionaries—one for Tombigbee, one to Ashley and Savannah, and the country between, and one to labour between Santee and Cooper Rivers. Increase within the bounds of this conference, three thousand and eighty-eight. Preaching and exhortations, and singing, and prayer—we had all these without intermission on the camp ground, and

[74] Koger lived across the Edisto beyond Givhan's in Colleton County. This family sent the first missionary to Brazil in 1881; this was the Rev. James W. Koger (1852–86), who died of yellow fever. His wife was Fannie Smith, sister of Bishop A. Coke Smith.

[75] Benjamin Risher and his Green Pond Church were ten miles up the river between Canadys and Smoaks in Colleton County. The church is still in operation on the Smoaks Circuit.

[76] Tarrant lived in Barnwell County.

[77] Weatherly lived on Tinker's Creek in Aiken County about twenty miles east of Augusta, Georgia. He was the uncle of Lovick and Reddick Pierce. He had been a "Calvinistic sinner" who was distrustful of the preachers and "barely suffered preaching in his house" but was converted near Three Runs in Barnwell County after reading Fletcher's *Checks to Antinomianism*. (Chreitzberg: *Early Methodism in the Carolinas*, 76.)

[78] The Widow Fountain lived in Warren County near Warrenton.

we have reasons to believe that many souls will be converted. The number of travelling and local preachers present are about three hundred. There are people here with their tents who have come one hundred and fifty miles. The prospects of doing good are glorious. We have already added two new circuits, and gained six preachers. There may have been from two to three thousand persons assembled. I preached once: we had finished our conference concerns the evening before.[79]

[79] This twenty-third session of the South Carolina Conference met at Liberty Chapel near Sparta and Milledgeville, Georgia. The sessions were held in the home of Mr. Bush, and the bishops were entertained there. The camp meeting was on the Liberty camp-meeting ground, and Boehm remarked that he "had never thought of attending a camp meeting between Christmas and New Years." William Capers was admitted on trial, though Lewis Myers, presiding elder of the Saluda District and a "strict constructionist," opposed his admission because he lacked one month of having completed his period of probationary church membership. (Boehm, *op. cit.*, 219; Smith: *Georgia Methodism*, 90, 91; Capers: *Autobiography*, 91, 92.)

1809

1809

Henry Boehm, McKendree, and Asbury in Charleston

CHAPTER THIRTY-EIGHT

Georgia

January 1, 1809. We came away on *Monday morning* in haste. We stopped to dine with our friend Doughty in Powelton;[1] this is a stronghold of the Baptists; nevertheless, we have a house to preach in, and a society. We went as far as W. Bonner's to lodge. On *Tuesday* we dined at pleasant Tindall's, and reached Augusta about six o'clock.

South Carolina

A cold rain, and freezing ride brought us on *Wednesday* to Speir's: next day, Arthur's, near Granby:[2] there was an appointment here for a local preacher, and I filled it for him. I ought to record that the good old folks where I lodged gave up their rooms to me. A hard ride on *Friday*, between the hours of eight and five, brought us into Camden. I scarcely have time to make these few brief journalizing remarks.

Sabbath, 8. I preached in our enlarged meeting house in Camden: it was a feeling season—in anticipation of great things here. We came away on *Monday morning* through clouds and a cold rain, twenty-six miles, to brother Woodham's, on Lynch's Creek.[3] I ordained Stephen Thompson a

[1] Powelton was in the northeastern part of Hancock county, fourteen miles from Sparta, Georgia.

[2] Granby was on the Congaree River just below Columbia, South Carolina.

[3] Woodham lived on Lynch's Creek near Bishopsville.

deacon. In crossing Cashua ferry[4] on *Tuesday*, it was a mercy we were not thrown into the water, like poor Hilliard Judge. We were kindly and comfortably lodged by Esquire Neville;[5] my mind most deeply felt for the salvation of this amiable family.

North Carolina

Wednesday, 11, was cloudy and very cold; but we took horse and made it thirty-three miles to Lumberton, and stopped at the widow Thompson's: I am most at home when I am housed with the widow and the orphan. We reached Fayetteville on *Thursday*.[6] My limbs, my patience, and my faith, have been put to severe trial.

I preached in the morning on the *Sabbath*, and Bishop M'Kendree and brother Boehm after. Since *Friday morning* I have been occupied in writing, forming plans, and occasionally reading. I baptized a daughter for Mr. Newby. Eli Perry came fifty-six miles for deacon's orders: I advised him to tell his father, a backslidden Baptist preacher, that he (Eli) would set apart once a month a day of fasting and prayer for his father's restoration.

We set out on *Monday* the solitary path on the north side of Cape Fear, to the widow Andrew's, forty-five miles: we were in the night, and I was very much disordered. *Tuesday* brought us to Wilmington, forty-five miles; again in the night, and by pain extreme. I was compelled to preach on *Wednesday* at eleven o'clock. I gave them a sermon also on *Thursday*. My body is in better health, and my mind enjoys great sweetness and peace. We had morning preaching on *Friday* at five o'clock, to about two hundred souls. We came away afterward, and a ride of twenty miles brought us to the widow Nixon's: the dear old man, her husband, died in Georgia—died in prayer. I gave those present an exhortation and my evening prayers. *Saturday* brought us to New River; and next day, the *Sabbath*, I preached in our enlarged chapel, on 1 Tim. ii, 3, 4. It was unusually warm, and so great a wind at night that it frequently waked me. We were most kindly and comfortably entertained at *Gaius* Rowe's: God is worshipped in this house: O! what a change is here!—the poor Africans, once oppressed, have now great privileges allowed them. We came to Adonijah Perry's[7] on *Monday*: may he follow his father, who followed Christ! Newbern brought us up on *Tuesday*. I preached on *Wednesday*, and it was an open season: God will visit Newbern again. A cold ride brought us to Washington—a disagreeable place to me; but there are souls here, and God can

[4] Cashua Ferry was across the Pee Dee. Boehm says, "We just escaped drowning" at the ferry. (*Op. cit.*, 220.)

[5] Neville lived in upper Marion, now Dillon, County.

[6] See letter to Zachary Myles, January 5, 1809.

[7] Adonijah Perry lived in Jones County, North Carolina. (*Heads of Families*, 144.)

convert and save them. We have a neatly finished house, in which I preached on *Friday* in great heaviness of body—it is a day of abstinence. I spent my *Saturday* at Williams's—a secluded house, and social family.

Sabbath, 29. I preached at Williams's chapel on Habakkuk iii, 2. I felt myself in the spirit of the work. In the evening we had snow and hail. We set out on *Monday* and had a very disagreeable ride through deep swamps and snow. At Williamston I preached to a few people. A ride of thirty-two miles brought us to Tarboro on *Tuesday*.

Wednesday, *February* 1. Opened the Virginia Conference.[8] We had eighty-four preachers present, sixty of them the most pleasing, promising young men; seventeen preachers were admitted; in all the conference there are but three married men. The high taste of these southern folks will not permit their families to be degraded by an alliance with a Methodist travelling preacher; and thus, involuntary celibacy is imposed upon us: all the better; anxiety about worldly possessions does not stop our course, and we are saved from pollution of Negro slavery and oppression.

Bishop M'Kendree preached an ordination sermon on *Friday*. On the *Sabbath* I gave them a discourse on *humiliation before God*. Bishop M'Kendree ordained eight elders, and I thirteen deacons. I suppose we have two thousand souls to hear us in the two churches, and our friends are very attentive to entertain us in their houses, abundantly better than we deserve. Our increase in members, unless we allow for a great waste by death, and loss by removals, is not very encouraging; the *west* and *south* have given more than three thousand each, whereas here it is not three hundred. We are defrauded of great numbers by the pains that are taken to keep the blacks from us; their masters are afraid of the influence of our principles. Would not an *amelioration* in the condition and treatment of slaves have produced more practical good to the poor Africans, than any attempt at their *emancipation?* The state of society, unhappily, does not admit of this: besides, the blacks are deprived of the means of instruction; who will take the pains to lead them into the way of salvation, and watch over them that they may not stray, but the Methodists? Well; now their masters will not let them come to hear us. What is the personal liberty of the African which he may abuse, to the salvation of his soul; how may it be compared?

We adjourned on *Wednesday*, to hold our next session in Petersburg, in Virginia. A general contentment appeared in the preachers with regard to stations. I came away instantly, and had a rapid ride of twenty-eight miles to Mr. Lisiomes, near Edward's ferry, upon Roanoke.

[8] This session of the Virginia Conference, held in Tarboro, North Carolina, received a fraternal message from the prisoners in the penitentiary in Richmond. Stith Mead had been working among them. (Bennett, *op. cit.*, 546–54.)

Virginia

We next day crossed the river, and breakfasted at Pinner's. We lodged with Jesse Battle; forty-three miles to-day. *Friday* brought us to Isaac Lunsford's.[9] We reached Norfolk on *Saturday*, by ten o'clock.

Sabbath, 12. I preached on Psalm xxxvii, 3, 4, and felt liberty and life. Met the society; and preached at Portsmouth. Preached on *Monday*, at the Western Branch; and at night again at Suffolk. I found Richard Yerbury greatly afflicted with the gout; his hands and feet had burst; but he was resigned and patient. On *Tuesday* we came away to General Wells's: his brother Willis Wells, an early Methodist and local preacher, died last year; he died in great peace. He had been led away by the misrepresentations of O'Kelly, but he came back into our bosom. I expected to have found religion more lively in this district; but we are on our lees. I grieved to find that some of the preachers went about visiting instead of being at their work; the spirit of the world, and still worse, *politics*; O, death, death! O Lord God, keep thy ministers faithful! I preached at William Blunt's to a few people who had come through a dark night at a short warning. We had, after meeting, hail and rain. I rode next day, very cold, to Birdsong's, in Sussex, thirty miles in six hours: I have need of patience and courage for the roads and weather. It was exceedingly cold on *Thursday*; nevertheless we reached Petersburg, about forty miles. We lodged at Edward Lee's[10]; Joseph Harding is no more. He joined us in Norfolk in 1772: he was a man of labour and sorrow; meek and benevolent. I had hoped to find religion more prosperous, but I find, except a few places in the district, there is great languor and indifference observable: we hope for better times. We have added fifty probationers in the three conferences —western, southern, and that of Virginia; and have located twenty. Many of these are the most elegant young men I have seen, in features, body, and mind; they are manly yet meek. I preached in Petersburg on *Friday*. After meeting I rode home with John Ryall Bradley, now warm in his first love: he was strangely brought to God. He was alone on a *Sabbath day* and was reading, what he indeed seldom read, his *prayer book*; suddenly he was powerfully struck with keen conviction; he began to pray without book, and with all his might: what followed came of course. At his conversion he had a stud of race horses to part with. We reached Richmond on *Saturday*, and I preached next day in the city; and at Manchester[11] in the afternoon: there is a change here for the better.

Monday, 20. We rode twenty-four miles to brother Cross's; twenty-four miles of heavy roads. I preached at night to a respectable congregation on

[9] Isaac Lunsford lived in Nansemond County, Virginia.
[10] Edward Lee was a brother of Jesse Lee. (Boehm, *op. cit.*, 223.)
[11] Manchester was the present South Richmond.

1 Thess. v, 14. The young men prayed, and there was life and feeling. C. Hines is likely to be an instrument of great good in Hanover circuit. On *Tuesday* we had an uncommonly large congregation for a two hours' notice: bishop M'Kendree preached to them. A forty-five miles' ride, without food for man or beast, brought us in, after being twice lost in the woods, to brother M'Gruder's. We reached Frederick Gilliam's, beyond the Green Mountain, on *Thursday*. We seldom lodge at a house without the company of preachers: we are pleased to see them; but would be better pleased to know they were on their circuits, faithfully at work. On *Friday* we passed Charlottesville within sight of fair Monticello, the seat of Thomas Jefferson. We rested at Daniel Maupin's: his father and mother are gone to rest. We crossed the ridge at Brown's Gap, and came to Port Republic.

Sabbath, 26. I preached upon Acts ii, 21. We found it dangerous riding through snow to Harrisonburg on *Monday*.[12]

Thursday, *March* 2. Our conference opened.[13] *Friday*, *fast day*, we wrought with order and industry, and did much in a little time. There were travelling and local deacons ordained, and we had preaching three times a day.[14]

Sabbath, 5. In the morning we had a general band meeting. I preached; we had German preaching also; and a sermon at night. On *Wednesday* we closed our labours in great peace. We came away on *Thursday morning*, and had a heavy, cold ride of thirty-six miles to Woodstock. We took a by-road on *Friday* to Stephensburg.[15] We called a congregation, who came through frost and snow and mud; and I gave them a talk from 1 Thess. v, 16, 17. There were some unhappy contentions in the society here, but I did not know it, although from my preaching, some of the congregation might well suppose I did; God maketh the mind and the mouth of man. We reached Winchester on *Saturday*, and on the *Sabbath* I gave them a discourse on Habakkuk iii, 2: it was a season of freedom.

West Virginia

An awful storm of snow overtook us on our way to Thomas Key's, where we were made comfortable for the night.

[12] See the letter to the United Brethren, March, 1809, written during this conference; also Newcomer's *Journal*, 119, 126, 141, 154, 159, 164-65, 169, 182.

[13] At this conference the Methodists had contacts with the United Brethren through the Rev. Christian Newcomer, bishop of the United Brethren Church, who attended that conference (1809) as a delegate to seek the union of the two churches.

[14] See letter to Mrs. John Brightwell, March 4, 1809.

[15] This was formerly known as Newtown.

Maryland

We crossed Harper's Ferry on *Tuesday*, and came to Joseph Perkins's; my friend and neighbour has gone to rest. Next day we had deep roads to Fredericktown. I had scarcely sat down when I heard the bells ring; it was an invitation to the people to come and hear me preach; well, go I must. About three hundred people had collected in the German Presbyterian church; they were devoutly attentive. Next day we reached Mr. Helms's, near Patapsco bridge;[16] a number of workmen were deeply attentive whilst I officiated in the family evening devotions. We reached Baltimore on *Thursday*. *Friday* and *Saturday* received letters and visitors. My soul is greatly humbled in this city; I tremble for the ark, and fear my own soul will suffer loss.

Sabbath, 19. At Light Street my subject was 2 Chron. xv, 2. In the evening I preached again upon Hosea vi, 1. On *Monday* we went to the camp meeting near Perry Hall; and I preached in the chapel[17] upon Philippians ii, 12–15. As I rode by the graves of the elders of the Gough family, the image of my dear departed Harry Gough was very present to me. We stopped in our way at B. Bennett's[18]; his prodigal son has enlisted, and gone as a sergeant to New Orleans: the mention of this place kindled strong desires in my mind to send another missionary to that quarter; I wrote to John McClure,[19] presiding elder of the Mississippi district, on the subject. *Tuesday* was cold. We crossed the wide Susquehanna with a gentle breeze. There was no appointment for us, and it was as well thus. On *Wednesday* I preached at John Canaan's, Back Creek; my subject was 1 John iii, 1, 2.

Delaware

I preached at Smyrna on *Thursday*.

We went through the State of Delaware on *Friday*, but there had been no notice given: we, however, gathered a few, to whom we gave a word of

[16] Helms probably lived near the bridge that crossed the north branch of the Patapsco River which forms part of the boundary between Baltimore and Carroll counties. In 1808 the road between Baltimore and Frederick was being improved to meet the Cumberland Road which was to be begun in 1811.

[17] This was evidently Camp Chapel, located near Perry Hall.

[18] Bennett lived in Harford County between the home of Josias Dallam and the Lower Ferry of the Susquehanna River, the present Havre de Grace.

[19] John McClure was admitted on trial at the conference held at Mount Gerizim, Kentucky, October, 1803, and in 1814 was listed a supernumerary of the Tennessee Conference. When Asbury wrote to McClure, the latter was the presiding elder of the Mississippi District, Western Conference. (Redford, *op. cit.*, I, 430, 432; *Journal* entry for September 30, 1803.)

exhortation, and went on to Choptank. I preached on *Saturday* from Luke xii, 40. It is still excessively cold, and we suffer much. After sermon we rode twenty-six miles to Milford.

Sunday, 26. At Milford, my subject was Ezek. ix, 4; very open and alarming time to saints and sinners. On *Monday*, at Barratt's chapel, I preached and baptized some children. I had powerful feelings of sympathy for the children and grandchildren of that holy man in life and death, Philip Barratt. We felt the wind, on our way to Dover, like the piercing of a sword. My dear friends, Governor Bassett and his lady, came nearly forty miles to meet me. I preached in Dover, and baptized James Molison,[20] advanced in life. I have suffered incredibly by the cold in the last hundred and thirty miles: souls and their Saviour can reward me, and nothing else! Lord, remember Francis Asbury in all his labours and afflictions! *Friday* I preached at Keagy's.[21] Brother M'Kendree and father Martin Boehm met me once more, and we greatly rejoiced in God together. In Wilmington I preached on *Thursday*. On *Friday* I spoke at the Bethel chapel,[22] a beautiful new house, about seven miles from Wilmington; brother M'Kendree in the evening.

Pennsylvania

I preached at Matson's chapel; this is a house of much the same kind as the former. I sat down to teach the people, and we had an open season.

Saturday, *April* 1. I forestalled a meeting at Darby; but few attended. I dropped them a few hints on the shortness of time. I suffer by the unusual heat, and by soreness from riding. We came safe into the city of Philadelphia. I found letters from Savannah, Tombigbee, Mississippi, Ohio, and also from the eastward.

Sabbath, 2. At St. George's, my subject was Haggai i, 7. I was fervent. We had a sacrament, and the Lord was present of a truth. On *Monday* we opened our conference in great peace and good order. I preached on *Wednesday*, and it was recollected that I had preached on the same subject, in the same place, in 1771. *Friday* we observed as a day of fasting and prayer. Both elders and deacons were ordained. There was some little difficulty with respect to our money concerns; and some of the members had been rather warm partizans as politicians. This is always wrong for them, let them take which side they please. There was general satisfaction given as to the stations—about eighty-four in the whole. The Philadelphia

[20] Molison is probably an incorrect spelling of Molleston, a familiar Kent County surname. He may have been related to Henry Molleston, governor-elect of Delaware, who died before assuming office in 1819. (Scharf, *op. cit.*, I, 404; II, 1040, 1124, 1145.)

[21] Abraham Keagy married Barbara Boehm, only sister of Henry Boehm. (Boehm, *op. cit.*, 227, 376, 377; note under March 16, 1808.)

[22] This was called Cloud's Chapel until 1799, when the name was changed to Bethel.

Conference has subjected itself to a demand for twelve preachers who have no stations; six are married, and there is a widows' maintenance to be added, an expense of two thousand dollars.

Sabbath, 9. I preached at Kensington chapel, on Habakkuk iii, 2. Here I ordained Jacob Tapsco, and James Champion[23]—both Africans. I gave the congregation at the Academy church an exhortation in the evening. With difficulty we got out of the city of Philadelphia, and ran some risk in crossing the river into Jersey.

New Jersey

I preached at two o'clock at Carpenter's bridge. We lodged with father John Early, twenty-four miles from the city. Here I take a little rest. I am not conscious of indulging or feeling wrong tempers in the mighty work at which I daily labour; but I never wish to meet the conference in the city of Philadelphia again. But possibly my time is short!

On *Wednesday* I preached at Union chapel; it is a neat building, two stories high, forty by thirty-six feet, built on the plan I furnished them. I spent a night with John Abbott,[24] a local preacher. Snow on *Thursday*; I preached at Pittsgrove. Lodged under the roof of Joseph Newkirk. Here I found the children and grandchildren of Susanna Ayars, who first received the Lord's prophets in this town. There was no proper notice of our appointment at Broadneck chapel[25] on *Friday*, so that we had but few people. I lodged at Haywood's.[26] I rode to Cohansey[27] on *Saturday*.

Sabbath, 16. At the chapel, I spoke on Philippians iii, 8: "Yea, doubtless,

[23] These were local preachers of Zoar Church.

[24] John Abbott lived on a plantation in Pittsgrove Township, Salem County, New Jersey, and is cited in the will of Abdon Abit (Abbott). (New Jersey Archives, Abstracts of Wills, VII, 7.)

[25] Broadneck Chapel was in Deerfield Township, Cumberland County, and was one of the places where Benjamin Abbott was instrumental in forming a class. It is one of the two oldest Methodist societies in Cumberland County, Friendship, or Murphy's, being the other. (Atkinson, *op. cit.*, 80; Lednum, *op. cit.*, 207.)

[26] This was doubtless Ephraim Haywood of Deerfield, Cumberland County. In Sarah Filer's will made in 1781 in Deerfield, she left to Ephraim Haywood the "plantation where I live, and the one joining Jeremiah Foster, where Jacob Carns lives, in case he will help support a Presbyterian minister in Deerfield." Benjamin Abbott received a letter "about 1780" from a pious Presbyterian in Deerfield requesting that he come there and preach, which he did. A revival followed and two societies were formed with many Presbyterians joining. (Lednum, *op. cit.*, 297–98; Atkinson, *op. cit.*, 107–12; New Jersey Archives, Abstracts of Wills, IV, 184–85; VI, 143; VII, 34.)

[27] Cohansey was the present Bridgeton. A bridge built across Cohansey Creek about 1716 gave the town the name of Cohansey Bridge, which was later changed to Bridgeton. The chapel in which Asbury preached on this occasion was erected in the latter part of 1807 on land donated by Jeremiah Buck. Cohansey was represented for the first time at a quarterly meeting of the circuit in 1805, and in 1807 the quarterly meeting

and I count all things loss," &c. 1. The object of the apostle's knowledge, *Christ Jesus my Lord.* 2. The nature and degrees of this knowledge in the apostle's own experience. 3. The excellency of this knowledge—a saving knowledge; a life-giving and sanctifying knowledge; it is the spiritual and experimental knowledge of repentance, faith, regeneration, and sanctification, producing a holy life, a triumphant death, a joyful resurrection, and a crown of eternal glory. I had certainly part of a gay congregation. How good is not for me to say; they were serious and attentive. I met the society. Brother Boehm preached in the afternoon. I must needs hold forth again in the evening. I preached, as it was desired, and we had an open season. A heavy ride brought us on *Monday* to Port Elizabeth.[28] I preached on 2 Cor. xiii, 5; it was a searching season. This is a new town, and we have a large house built here: the Baptists are building a grand house. We lodged at Benjamin Fisler's.[29] At Tuckahoe chapel[30] my subject on *Tuesday* was Ephesians iii, 8: I sat down and taught with pleasure. I dined with Nathan Swain: Richard has gone to his rest and reward. The people told me that my time of absence on this path was twenty-five years. I feel the heat and labour, and painful weary nights appointed to me; but God, even my God is with me! I hear of several spots where the work of the Lord is reviving powerfully. At May's Landing, Great Egg Harbour,[31] there was power in the word, whilst I lectured on Heb. xii, 25. We hasted away to Blackman's,[32] to be there at three o'clock, but we

was held for the first time at Cohansey. (Rose: *The Story of the First Methodist Church, Bridgeton*; Ewing: *Information on 150 Years of Methodism in Bridgeton*; Lednum, *op. cit.*, 293; Mulford: *Historic Tales of Cumberland County, New Jersey*, 56.)

[28] Asbury had visited this locality as Morris River in 1786. The large meetinghouse mentioned here is not noted in Gordon's *Gazetteer* in 1834. (Lednum, *op. cit.*, 294; Gordon, *op. cit.*, 220.)

[29] Benjamin Fisler lived on Maurice's River. He was a traveling preacher for a time and died at Port Elizabeth. (Lednum, *op. cit.*, 295.)

[30] Tuckahoe is located ten miles from the Atlantic Ocean. The chapel at Head-of-River was built in the latter part of the eighteenth century. It was dedicated by Benjamin Abbott. (Wilson: *The Jersey Shore*, 290; Gordon, *op. cit.*, 254.)

[31] May's Landing is located on Great Egg Harbor River in Gloucester County. The first Methodist church was built about 1812; its successor being erected in 1848. However a "free church" was built in 1782 and for a while was used by the Methodists, Baptists, Quakers, and Presbyterians. When it passed into the possession of the Baptists, the Methodists had their own church. It was doubtless in this "free church" that Asbury preached. (Wilson, *op. cit.*, 290; Gordon, *op. cit.*, 175; Heston: *Absegami, Heston's Annals*, I, 188.)

[32] The Blackman family has been famous in Gloucester County for generations. David Blackman and Mary, his wife, were the parents of Learner Blackman, a Methodist itinerant who met an untimely end by drowning while crossing the Ohio River in 1815. Andrew Blackman, David's father, was a staunch Presbyterian and gave the land on which the Cedar Bridge meetinghouse in Atlantic County was erected. Zion Methodist Church near Bargaintown was later erected on the same site. (Lednum, *op. cit.*, 295; Heston, *op. cit.*, I, 186; Wilson, *op. cit.*, I, 290; New Jersey Archives, Abstracts of Wills, VI, 46.)

lost our way in the woods,[33] and after riding fifteen miles instead of eight, we arrived at five o'clock. *Tuesday evening* closed rather uncomfortably upon us at a tavern.[34] My spirits were low and my body very feeble. The work of God revives in the society here. Learner Blackman has been raised up from small appearances—possibly, to very considerable consequences. At Absecon,[35] on *Thursday*, I gave them a discourse. We dined in haste at brother Peacock's,[36] and came on to George Peterson's, Pleasant Mills.[37] At the Forks,[38] on *Friday*, I preached in our elegant chapel, on John xii, 38; it was an open time. Whom should I see but dear aged Jesse Chew and wife![39] I went home with friendly William Richards:[40] dear Sarah, his former wife, so often my kind and attentive hostess—I only saw the

[33] This was the country of the Jersey pines, extending northward from the Mullica River. Even today old roads wind their way into pine forests and vanish from disuse and tangling overgrowth. It was probably a white cedar swamp in which Asbury was lost. The cedar swamps were from half a mile to a mile in breadth and five or six miles in length. The straight trunks of the trees, forty or fifty feet high, were crowded together, and the tops were so woven together as to shut out the light of day. (Heston, *op. cit.*, II, 254–56; Boehm, *op. cit.*, 229.)

[34] Asbury and Boehm probably had to stop at one of the famous "jug taverns" of this part of South Jersey. The ruins of these taverns in the forest are marked by overgrown rubble and mossy walls. (Heston, *op. cit.*, II, 254.)

[35] Absecon is an old village in Galloway Township, Gloucester County. It still bears proudly its Indian name "Absegami" and furnishes from among its inhabitants the necessary personnel for nearby Atlantic City's resort operations. (*New Jersey Guide*, 597.)

[36] Joshua Peacock lived in Burlington County, next to Charles Read, who had established the furnace at Batsto in 1766. (Heston, *op. cit.*, I, 159; New Jersey Archives, Abstracts of Wills, VI, 321; VII, 175.)

[37] Pleasant Mills, on the Atsion River and about a mile from Batsto, was called Sweetwater during the Revolution. The church was located midway between the two places. The Rev. Simon Lucas, a Methodist local preacher, preached in the old meeting-house for twenty years or more, until its removal in 1808, and he probably preached in its successor. Lawrence Peterson, probably a brother of George Peterson, was a trustee of the new chapel which Asbury dedicated on this visit. Lawrence Peterson was the grandfather of Charles J. Peterson, author of the Revolutionary story *Kate Aylesford.* Prominently portrayed under other names in this story are members of the Richards family and Simon Lucas, beloved as "Daddy" Lucas. (Heston, *op. cit.*, I, 126, 187; II, 248, 253; Gordon, *op. cit.*, 218.)

[38] Actually four streams come together at this point to form the Mullica River. They are Atsion River, Batsto River, Nescochague Creek, and Mechescatauxin Branch.

[39] Evidently Methodists came from a distance for the dedication of the chapel at Pleasant Mills. Jesse Chew resided at Carpenter's Landing on the other side of the state.

[40] William Richards had been a colonel in the Revolution and was with Washington when Cornwallis surrendered at Yorktown. He undertook the management at Batsto for Joseph Ball, his nephew, in 1784. The Richards manor house at Batsto was a place of hospitality, and they often entertained itinerant preachers. The iron industry declined in this area about the middle of the nineteenth century, and the Batsto estate passed into the hands of the Wharton interests of Philadelphia. The vast area known as the Wharton Tract was purchased by the state of New Jersey for conservation and state park purposes. (Heston, *op. cit.*, I, 159; II, 248–50.)

marble that covered her dust! Some demur was sent by a certain preacher about his station;[41] these things give me more pain than all the labour of the conferences. On *Saturday* I called to see Rebekah Sevior[42] on a sick bed, praising God; she is a true daughter of Sarah Richard. I rode on to Tuckerton[43]—very damp and cold.

Sunday, 23. At Tuckerton my subject was 2 Cor. iv, 2. In the afternoon I preached again. On *Monday* I preached at Waretown.[44] I stayed awhile with Samuel Brown, and then came to Thomas Chamberlain's:[45] I was compelled by uncomfortable feelings to go to rest at six o'clock. At David Woodmansee's,[46] on *Tuesday*, I preached on 2 Tim. ii, 15. On *Wednesday*, after a rain, I set out for Polhemus chapel,[47] where I preached. My friends were exceedingly kind, and I was very sick. I rose unwell on *Thursday*, and took medicine, and set out for Squan River.[48] My host here, Derrick Longstreet,[49] has been married twenty-four years: his wife once had twins, and she has made him the father of sixteen children, all of whom are alive and well. I had a noble congregation here of women and children; the men were generally gone from the neighbourhood, either to the waters or to work. I was seriously unwell. On *Friday*, at Newman's, on Shark River,[50] I had women not a few: I suited my subject to my hearers, and preached from Luke x, 41, 42. Ah! how many Marthas are there, and

[41] See letter to Neal and Burneston, April 21, 1809.

[42] Rebekah Sevior was the daughter of William and Sarah Richards.

[43] Tuckerton was the port of entry for Little Egg Harbor District and situated on a narrow tongue of land projecting into the marsh on Little Egg Harbor Bay. Two Methodist churches were located there in 1834. (Gordon, *op. cit.*, 254.)

[44] Waretown is in Stafford township, Monmouth County, on Barnegat Bay. (*Ibid.*, 256.)

[45] Thomas Chamberlain lived near Waretown. Ezekiel Cooper visited him in 1796. (Phoebus, *op. cit.*, 219.)

[46] David Woodmansee lived in the present area around Lanoka Harbor, formerly called Good Luck and Cedar Creek. Potter's Church was located here, where John Murray established Universalism. The original church was built in 1766 and rebuilt in 1841. Ezekiel Cooper had gone from Waretown to Good Luck in 1796 and "preached there at Mr. Woodmansee's, not in the meeting house." (Phoebus, *op. cit.*, 70, 219; Lednum, *op. cit.*, 362; *New Jersey Guide*, 557.)

[47] Polhemus Chapel was in Shrewsbury Township, Monmouth County. John Polhemus and Joseph Throckmorton are associated in a number of historical documents, making inventory of estates. Others of the name include Tobias, Benjamin, and Joseph; and James Polhemus was received into the Philadelphia Conference about 1800. (Lednum, *op. cit.*, 296–97; Abstracts of Wills, VI, 176, 245, 310, 405, 424; VII, 238, 240.)

[48] This was the Manasquan River, which rises in Freehold Township and flows southeasterly eighteen miles through Howell Township to the Atlantic Ocean. Squan, or Manasquan, is a community with a large summer colony today, and the Manasquan River and Inlet a center for yachting and power boating.

[49] The Longstreet family has had a long and distinguished association with Monmouth County, New Jersey. Samuel and Derrick Longstreet owned land including "rights on Manasquan Beach." (Abstracts of Wills, IV, 256; V, 123, 503; VIII, 404; Lednum, *op. cit.*, 297.)

[50] This was probably Joseph Newman, son of John Newman of Shark River. The family held extensive plantations in Shrewsbury township. Nicholas Vansant refers to

how few Marys! In the afternoon I spoke again at Peter White's.[51] We have meeting twice a day, and sometimes at night; and the prospects are pleasing. The weather is severely cold. I have read Simpson lately—his *Plea for Religion*, how strong! If Simpson is right, the old Church of England has the mark of the *Beast* in her hands at least. Great news! The British Orders in Council are withdrawn, and the American embargo and non-intercourse are forthwith to cease. I fear much that these expected *good times* will injure us:—the prosperity of fools will destroy; therefore affliction may be best, and God may send it, for this is a favoured land: Lord save us from ruin as a people! I rested on *Saturday*.

Sunday, 30. At Long Branch[52] my subject was Acts iii, 26; it was given me to speak strong words—words of God, and from God. At three o'clock I preached in the Episcopal Church at Shrewsbury.[53] I came home with John Throckmorton.[54]

Monday, May 1. No appointment at Mount Pleasant:[55] we came to James Throckmorton's;[56] and thence through New Brunswick to Staten Island.[57]

three preaching places, Newman's Schoolhouse, White's Schoolhouse, and Lower Squankum, which corresponds to Asbury's itinerary. Shark River is a few miles north of Manasquan and was then a millstream with several mills of various types along its course. It flows on its course about six miles into a broad estuary and thence about three miles through Shark Inlet into the Atlantic Ocean. (Lednum, *op. cit.*, 295, 297; Boehm, *op. cit.*, 229; Vansant: *Sunset Memories*, 104; Gordon, *op. cit.*, 236.)

[51] Peter White lived in Shrewsbury Township, Monmouth County. His farm was located in the vicinity of Ocean Grove, a part of present Neptune Township. The famous Ocean Grove Camp Meeting, established in 1869, is on part of the White property. (Gibbons: *History of Ocean Grove, New Jersey*, 12; New Jersey Archives, First Series, Abstracts of Wills, II, 523–24.)

[52] Asbury preached at Long Branch in Monmouth County in what was known as the old Free Church, which was built in 1790 between Ocean Mills and Branchburg and in which all denominations worshiped. The Methodist Church of Long Branch was incorporated in March, 1809, and a building erected later in the year on a lot given by Alexander McGregor. The first preacher in charge was Samuel Budd, and under the presiding elder, Joseph Totten, a camp meeting was held in Brewer's Woods at Squankum which resulted in a great revival. (Lewis: *History of Monmouth County*, 507.)

[53] Christ Episcopal Church is one of the celebrated Queen Anne's churches of which there are several in America, Queen Anne of England having given to each of them a silver communion service. The silver service was given to Christ Church in 1708. The present building was erected in 1765, succeeding an earlier edifice, and is the one in which Asbury preached in 1809. The rector at the time of Asbury's visit was the Rev. John Croes, who had been called by the vestry in 1808 and served the church until 1824. (Mandeville: *The Story of Middletown*, 106; Lewis, *op. cit.*, 342–43.)

[54] John Throckmorton lived along the Navesink River in Monmouth County. (Lewis, *op. cit.*, 55, 64; Mandeville, *op. cit.*, 42–43.)

[55] Mount Pleasant was located on Middletown Creek, ten miles north of Freehold. It is the present Freneau, named in honor of the Revolutionary poet Philip Freneau. (Lewis, *op. cit.*, 487–89, 491; Phoebus, *op. cit.*, 71.)

[56] James Throckmorton evidently lived in the vicinity of Middletown Point, the present Matawan.

[57] See letters to Dr. and Mrs. Coke, May 2, 1809.

New York

We dined at Benjamin Drake's; and supped at Elder Joseph Totten's.[58] I have had great peace of mind; and have been greatly in the spirit of preaching, of faith, and of prayer. God has visited, and will yet powerfully visit Jersey; probably in the last five years, five hundred souls have been converted: Glory to the great I AM! He will bare the arm of his power, and save millions in the world.

I preached on *Wednesday* at the tabernacle[59] on Staten Island: my subject was 1 Peter iii, 15, 16: it was a feeling season: my mind was greatly enlarged. Lodged at Gilbert Totten's.[60] Episcopalians, Presbyterians, Baptists—all upon the stretch to be greatest upon the Island. The Methodists have a stationed preacher; and they have a camp meeting in contemplation.[61] On *Thursday* I preached at the old meeting house: there was some tenderness manifested. On *Friday* I preached in our meeting house at North End.[62] I found brother Nicholas Crocheron in a languid state: I sought to administer consolation to his mind and body. Behold, the Low Dutch have built a church,[63] and the Episcopalians one at the North End near them[64]: there are three local preachers of our order, and a presiding elder; if good be not done, the people must be hardened. I found my old friend Thomas Morrell solitary—his wife is called home. My attention was strongly excited by the steamboat: this is a great invention.[65] Brother M'Kendree preached at Elizabethtown, New Jersey; and I after

[58] Joseph Totten (1759–1818) entered the itinerant Methodist ministry in 1792, being the first from Staten Island to do so, and became a notable preacher in the New York, New Jersey, and Philadelphia areas. He was buried in the churchyard by Woodrow Church, which he helped to establish and where so many pioneers and preachers are buried. (Wakeley, *op. cit.*, 409; Hubbell: *History of Staten Island*, 28, 30–31; Jamison: *A Century of Life—Woodrow Methodist Episcopal Church, 1887*, 14–18.)

[59] This was evidently Woodrow Church, near the village of Rossville.

[60] Gilbert Totten was a brother of Joseph Totten, who also resided on the south side of Staten Island at Bentley, the present Tottenville.

[61] The site of later camp meetings was Bloomfield, on the northwest shore not far from the Asbury Church in New Springville. (Hubbell, *op. cit.*, 179.)

[62] This was the church at New Springville, later named in honor of Asbury.

[63] Asbury here refers to a new brick church built by the Reformed Dutch on the north shore to replace one destroyed by the British during the Revolution.

[64] This was the Episcopalian Trinity Chapel, erected in 1802 with the aid of Trinity Church in New York, and the name was later changed to the Church of the Ascension. It was located on the Shore Road facing the Kill Van Kull, about a mile from the Reformed Dutch church. (Leng and Davis: *Staten Island and Its People*, I, 436–38, 456; Series of Historical Articles—Ecclesiastical History of Staten Island Churches, by Vernon B. Hampton, in Staten Island *Daily Advance*, 1927–29.)

[65] Asbury saw Fulton's steamboat at or near the dock at Elizabethtown Point, where the ferry which he had taken from Staten Island's North Shore also docked. Boehm says both he and Asbury were much excited at their first sight of a steamboat. (Westervelt: *History of Bergen County*, I, 160–61; Boehm, *op. cit.*, 230–31.)

him at six o'clock in the evening. We have a beautiful house here,[66] two stories high, elegantly finished, forty-five by forty feet, and well filled. On *Monday*, I came to New York, where I found letters bringing good news from the south and the west.

On the tenth our conference began, and continued until the fifteenth; about one hundred and twenty preachers present: we had great peace, and good order. We had an ordination of elders at John Street Church on the *Sabbath day*. We had a great deal of faithful preaching. As I wish not to relate the trials met with, I will let everything but what is printed rest in shades: there were some critical cases, but nothing appeared against any member to justify expulsion. There were one hundred and fifteen preachers stationed; and there were few complaints. If I have slumbered five hours per night, it is as much as I have done in the matter of sleep. On *Saturday* I rode, through excessively warm weather, twenty miles, to Jonathan Sherwood's.[67] I retire to sacred solitude, and great and delightful communion with God; but want of sleep comes upon me like an armed man. Hail, holy day! On the *Sabbath* I preached at Sherwood's chapel;[68] afterward at New Rochelle chapel: we had an open season in both congregations. The Quakers are offended because their errors in sentiment and practice are spoken against. But they have a *higher dispensation*. And will this authorize the violation of a positive law of the land, which forbids unnecessary labour on the *Sabbath day?* Will it justify the putting asunder what God has so solemnly joined together, *to wit*, the ordinances of God and the influences of his Holy Spirit? So thought not the eunuch, when Philip, sent by the Holy Ghost, *preached unto him Jesus*. The celebration of the Lord's supper is idolatry, say the Quakers: so thought not Paul, when exhorting the Church of Corinth to the worthy commemoration of our Lord's death and passion, he says, "For I have received of the Lord that which also I delivered unto you." A *higher dispensation!* And had not God already revealed his will before the appearance of George Fox? But hush! the *respectable society of people called Quakers; respectable!* Ah! there is death in that word; "Woe unto you when all men shall speak well of you." I fear what is properly *the reproach of Christ* has long been wiped away from this *respectable people*: O Lord, save thy now despised Methodist children from the praises of the people of the world!

[66] Methodist historians in Elizabeth, New Jersey, do not record a date as early as this. Ricord says that the Morrell Street Church was the only Methodist church within fifty miles, except in New York, and that it was built in 1814 beside a new house which Thomas Morrell erected for himself. The date given by Ricord is obviously in error if it refers to the erection of the church mentioned by Asbury in 1809. (Ricord: *History of Union County, New Jersey*, 274.)

[67] Jonathan Sherwood lived with his widowed mother, Abigail Sherwood, on the western edge of New Rochelle.

[68] The present Asbury Methodist Church, Crestwood, Tuckahoe, stands on the site of Sherwood Chapel.

On *Monday* I dined with B. Banks at Byram Bridge, and then moved on, through heavy thunder showers, to Norwalk.

Connecticut

I had wished them to build a house here, but Mr. G——n had told the Methodists they were poor (poor may they ever be!), and it would ruin them. I gave the good folks a discourse on Rom. xvi, 24.

On *Tuesday* I came to Peck's,[69] Stratford, a faithful friend, and thence on to father Jocelin's,[70] New Haven, weary, and sleepy, and glad to rest. I dined with W. Griffin in Guildford: here is a lot to build a house of worship on, and God will work here. In the afternoon I preached at Jeremiah Miner's, in Killingworth; thence crossing the Connecticut River, came into New London. I have had great temptations, and great consolations. The weather has been extremely warm, and my clothes are too heavy. My horse twice attempted to run away with my chair, so I was obliged to quit it. I must needs preach in New London; I gave them a discourse on 1 John ii, 6. The house was soon filled, and many went away who could not get in: surely the society, and preachers too, have been blind to their own interests, or they would have occupied every foot of ground; but we have never taken advantage of circumstances as they offered in this place, and have lost by our negligence.

Rhode Island

We crossed Narraganset Bay on *Friday*, and came into Newport. Grand house; steeple, pews; by lottery:[71] the end is to sanctify the means; Ah! what pliability to evil!

Sabbath, 28. I preached twice; in the forenoon on Col. ii, 1, 2; 1 John iii, 3–5, in the afternoon: I spoke with difficulty and with little order in my discourses. From New York thus far we have had dust and rough roads, and I have been much tried and greatly blessed. We have ridden two hundred miles in six days.

[69] Thaddeus Peck's was one of the bishop's old stopping places; however, Methodist meetings were held from time to time in the homes of Elnathan Wheeler and Captain John Peck. (Boehm, *op. cit.*, 240.)

[70] This was possibly the father of Augustus Jocelyn.

[71] Lotteries were common in those days, and it appears that some of the leaders in the movement to build a chapel in Newport attempted to raise money by this device. An advertisement of the plan in the *Newport Mercury* of June 5, 1807, said, "10,000 dollars a going for only 5 dollars. Now is the time to make your fortune." However, this scheme for raising money for the chapel was never carried out. Probably it did not receive sufficient support, and the money paid for tickets was refunded to the adventurers. (Davis: *History of the Methodist Episcopal Church in Newport, R.I.*, 35–37.)

Last night we had a tremendous storm of thunder, lightning, and rain. This morning (*Monday*) I visited Captain Beale at Fort Wolcott.[72] I preached to the soldiers on Isaiah lvii, 6, 7; baptized some children; visited the school; prayed with the sick in the hospital; exhorted the poor sinners to turn to God; but I might have said and done more. I saw discipline, order, correctness; it was grand and pleasing.

What changes I pass through! How hardly shall they who travel much keep a constant eye on duty, the cross, holiness, and God!

On *Tuesday* we came to the pleasant town of Bristol. The Methodists here have a house with pews, and a preacher who has not half enough to do: poor work! I gave them a discourse on 1 Cor. xv, 58. I have as much as I can bear in body and mind. I see what has been doing for nine years past to make Presbyterian Methodists. At Warren I lodged with Samuel Childs; his wife is a Shunamite. We had freedom in our meeting here: I preached on Heb. ii, 3.

Massachusetts

Thursday, *June* 1. I had a feeling season at Somerset chapel whilst speaking from 1 Peter iv, 2. Brother Brayton's[73] was my home. Levi Walker has not laboured in vain; but it seemed as if there had been three preachers to do one man's work. There are here two hundred and ninety-one members. We reached Easton, and I was indeed tired; the carriage horse was too wild for me to drive, and the saddle horse started and jolted very much.

We reached Boston on *Saturday*: our route hither from New York has cost us eight dollars for turnpike gates, ferries, bridges, &c.;[74] we called at but one tavern. The family who opened the door for us here is gone; but the house is in the possession of the stationed preachers and their wives.

[72] Fort Wolcott was built by Major L'Enfant of West Point on Goat Island just west of Newport, Rhode Island, in Narragansett Bay. Captain Lloyd Beale was in command of the force at Fort Wolcott. No man could have done more for the struggling Methodist Church at Newport, R.I. In March, 1810, the first meeting of the corporators of this church was held, and Captain Beale presided as moderator. (Davis, *op. cit.*, 25, 26, 33.)

[73] The Brayton family was prominent in Methodist circles. John Brayton was one of the founders of the church at South Somerset, Massachusetts, and his home was a favorite retreat of the preachers. The family became prominent in Fall River, and Brayton Church there was named for them. He was also instrumental in developing Methodism at North Dighton. (Miller: *History of the New England Southern Conference*, I, 60.)

[74] There were tollgates in Massachusetts at intervals of about ten miles. There was an extensive list of toll rates, the fees ranging from three cents per dozen for sheep and hogs to twenty-five cents for four-wheeled carriages drawn by two horses. (Wood: *The Turnpikes of New England*, 58.)

I preached at the old chapel on *Sabbath morning* the 4th, and administered the sacrament. In the afternoon I gave them a discourse in the new chapel; it was an open time of much feeling, and deep attention was paid to the speaker. Had I not spoken sitting, pain and weariness would have prevented my finishing. May the Lord water his own word! I hear of a considerable revival in several places, and that the Lord is bringing out some children to do the work of men; "out of the mouths of babes"—so let it be!

On *Monday* we had a great show; the governor came to town. I reached wretched Waltham dripping wet. I found the four generations in health, and I got (O, how sweet!) a comfortable night's sleep, the first I have had for many nights. How good is rest to soul and body, after hard labour for the good of the souls and bodies of our fellow-men!

Awaking on *Tuesday morning*, I recollected that in the solemn hour of midnight it was strongly impressed upon my mind that I must go by Lynn: this was from God. I preached to a family congregation.

On *Wednesday* I passed through Menotony,[75] Medford, and Malden to Lynn. In the evening I preached. There have been awful times here for two years past; the preachers are a burden—they do not preach evangelically, do not visit families, neglect the classes. I have my load; but leaning to one side: one story is good until another is heard. Our hard going horses brought us through the dust to Marblehead on *Thursday*. I held forth on John viii, 31, 32. Poor David Batchelor is in ill health, and shortly to be bound to a wife: so we go. We rode onwards through a goodly prospect of fine buildings and fine meeting houses. At Beverly my host did not quite understand praying in the daytime.

New Hampshire

At Joseph Weak's in the evening at Greenland. From this unpromising place, and other surrounding towns, God has raised up a society. On *Saturday* I found a happy, simple-hearted society at brother Gardener's.[76] The labours of George Pickering[77] and brother Stevens have raised up, under God, a promising society here.

Sabbath, 11. Henry Boehm[78] spoke at six o'clock, myself at ten o'clock, H. Boehm again at two o'clock, when the holy sacrament was adminis-

[75] Menotony was the present Arlington.

[76] This was probably William Gardner, who lived at Greenland, New Hampshire. He is listed in the manuscript *Vital Statistics of Greenland.*

[77] George Pickering was presiding elder in this section from 1797 to 1801. He seems to have preached the first Methodist sermon in Greenland in 1808. (Cole and Baketel: *History of the New Hampshire Conference*, 140, 141.)

[78] Henry Boehm was Asbury's traveling companion. They preached in Portsmouth and "put up at friend Hutchins." (Boehm, *op. cit.*, 244.)

tered. I gave another discourse in the evening. We had crowded audiences. We returned for the night to Gardener's.

Maine

We passed through Berwick on *Monday morning*, and continuing on, stopped and supped with one Wells. We were here two years ago; we then prayed earnestly for, and with this kind family. It was not a forlorn hope it seems: the young woman who waited on us was brought out last August. We rode on through Kennebunk to Saco. Lodging in a tavern, we were opposed, but persisted in having prayer night and morning. Asa Heath gave us our breakfast and we pushed on to New Gloucester, making about eighty-four miles in the last two days. On *Thursday* we opened our conference,[79] and sat closely at work.

Sunday, 18. I preached to about three thousand deeply attentive people, from Isaiah xliv, 23; it was an open season. We have eighty-two men to do the work, forty of whom compose the conference. I have to lament my want of information respecting both the preachers and the circuits. We have ordained twenty-one deacons and seven elders. We have located eleven elders, readmitted one, and added seventeen preachers upon trial. There is a small increase here, and fair prospects for the future. I am kept in peace.

On *Tuesday* we came away through New Gloucester to Bradbury's. We rested a few minutes at Dennett's, Standish Corner, and rode onwards to Samuel Bachelor's upon Saco; making forty miles for our day's journey. The rain overtook us at Brownfield on *Thursday*, but we continued on, and were most kindly entertained at Samuel Foss's, in Conway.

New Hampshire

On *Friday* I forded Saco: the rest of the company were in a boat. We came through Bartlett to Judge Hall's, and were kindly received. We hasted on to Rosebrook's, supped and went other six miles. O! the rocks, roots, pole-bridges and mosquitoes. We fell asleep about ten o'clock, and sprung up at four o'clock, and were away, without breakfast, towards Bethel;[80] we stopped here awhile. Winding down along a river bank, we came to the bridge and crossed the Connecticut into Vermont, stopping at the widow Sias's, in Johnsbury.[81]

[79] The New England Conference of 1809 met at Monmouth, Maine.

[80] By Bethel the bishop meant Bethlehem.

[81] Mrs. Sias was the mother of Solomon Sias, a prominent Methodist preacher who was publisher of *Zion's Herald* from 1824 to 1827. She lived at Danville.

Vermont

On *Saturday morning* we came away over awful roads, and made about forty weary miles to Danville.

Sunday, 25. In the court house I preached from John vii, 17. I could only speak sitting. From New York to Danville, we compute our ride to have been seven hundred miles: we passed many a fertile hill, and saw many fruitful vales, through which flowed noble rivers. We refit, expecting to fill an appointment for *Tuesday*. At Danville meeting house on *Tuesday*, I attended with two of our preachers: I took a pew near the pulpit, and taught from thence, from Heb. iii, 12–14. The court was in session—the congregations were large nevertheless. I received a polite invitation to preach to the court, but I had no strength and no time for this. We took a bite at the Widow Sias's, and came on to Cabot. Near Joe's Pond,[82] a heavy storm of rain and thunder overtook us and drove us into shelter. I lodged with Mr. Dana. On *Wednesday* our route brought us through Marshfield, Plainfield (exploring to the head of Onion River as we went) to David Parsons, near Montpelier. I preached in the evening. In passing through Montpelier on *Thursday*, we remarked their fine State house worthy of the seat of government of Vermont; to this, the hotel is an appropriate appendage. Our way lay through Middlesex, Waterbury, Richmond, on to Williston, where, about mid-day, a storm overtook us. On *Friday* I preached at Fuller's, on Lake Champlain, from Titus iii, 7, 8. Here I ordained Joseph Sampson, a native of Canada, and sent him a missionary to his countrymen. The day of small things will be great; but the day is not yet come; rather, it is still afar off: patience, my soul! Do I not feel for the lost sheep? Yea, verily.

New York

Sunday, *July* 2. We had this day a crowded audience at Bridport, Vermont. I sleep this night under the roof of Luther Chamberlain, near Ticonderoga Fort.[83] On *Monday* I spoke in Hampton church,[84] on Galatians vi, 7–9.

On *Tuesday* we kept along down Burgoyne's road to Fort Edward.[85]

[82] Joe's Pond was a small pond between West Danville and Walden.

[83] Luther Chamberlain was perhaps a relative of Pamerly Chamberlain, a New York Conference preacher. He lived near the ruins of Fort Ticonderoga. (Boehm, *op. cit.*, 249.)

[84] Hampton is located in the northeast corner of Washington County, New York, very near the Vermont line.

[85] General Burgoyne had found it necessary to create a road for his artillery and baggage for his drive southward from Lake Champlain. In later years the improved road, largely following his line, still bore his name. Today the Champlain Canal and Route 4 parallel the old road, sometimes actually running along its line. (Lossing, *ad. loc.*)

At four o'clock I preached in Doctor Lawrence's store, to about five hundred attentive hearers. It has been serious times for some days past; I feel the effect of riding thirty or forty miles a day, fasting long, and expected to preach every evening. I spoke on Romans viii, 1, at M'Cready's barn.[86] It was an open season, but the flesh suffered. *Thursday* brought us to father Hart's, on Saratoga Lake,[87] to dinner. After refreshing, we went out under a plentiful rain, and mounting our beasts, directed our course away to General Clark's. Here I preached in the bar room, and had life and liberty. We have made nine hundred miles since we left New York, as we compute. There will be an increase of eleven thousand this year. On *Friday* I rest and fast. On *Saturday* I visited Ballston Springs buildings[88]—approximating in elegance to those of Bath in England. The water has a taste of beer, of lemon juice, and of salt of tartar. A ride of about forty miles brought us to Kingsbury in the evening.

Sunday, 9. We took the wood for the shade, and I spoke to about a thousand people, from Matt. xvii, 5: all were attention, and some felt the word. Brother Boehm closed a meeting of three hours' continuance. There were twelve travelling and local preachers present. There is a contention between soul and body. I wish to fast as when young, and when fast day comes, the body has a journey of forty miles to make, perhaps, and do its part of preaching: but Christ is strength in my weakness. At the end of a thirty-miles' ride on *Monday*, I preached in Favill's barn. The young man here is pious, but without great gifts. Great men had passed them in the way to Canada. They were disappointed who hoped to have a meeting house, and congregations, and eminent teachers. Complaints are no new things to us, and I told them we expected such treatment. We tarried a minute at Morale's,[89] Fallstown, and pushed up the turnpike to Caleb Willis's, Deerfield, where I preached. It was an open time. We We passed Utica at the head of the Mohawk. This is a flourishing place, and we shall soon have a meeting house here. Our route brought us through Hartford to Westmoreland, where, at four o'clock, I held forth from John vi, 66, 67. We had a number of travelling and local preachers present. My body is afflicted, and sore with heat, long rides, and labour. I preached in Silas Bliss's barn, in Zanovia, on *Thursday*; we had a profitable meeting. My bed was on the floor at night—it was cooler thus, and I accommodated my friend. Next day I again held forth in a barn in the village of Pompey. Here brother M'Kendree left me to serve alone. The evening brought us up at Paddock's, in Manlius. I lay along the floor, in

[86] McCready lived near Schuylerville, south of Fort Edward.

[87] Saratoga Circuit had been established in 1791. The wide-ranging circuit flourished, but the work in the village lagged until after Asbury's day. (*Troy Conference Miscellany*, 33.)

[88] The medicinal value of this water was known from about 1770 and in Asbury's day enjoyed as great a repute as did the waters of Saratoga Springs to the north.

[89] Morale was a local preacher and leader of the church at Little Falls.

my clothes. There was a lady in the corner, and brother Boehm in bed, *like a gentleman*. The female could not possibly occasion reproach, and so I was persuaded; but I wished I was somewhere else: my fear was not commendable. I rode to Doctor Holland's, Onondaga, on *Saturday*, and preached in the court house.

Sunday, 16. Spoke in the court house at eleven o'clock: we had a full house. Contrary to my usual practice I directed my course away, and brought up at friend Young's, at Auburn. No food or rest to-day. The rain and *Monday morning* finds us at our friend Young's. The New York and New England Presbyterians are labouring to monopolize this country by building meeting houses and other establishments. They will flourish awhile, but a despised and dispersed people will possess the land. O, the terrors of a camp meeting to those *men of pay and show!* In the evening we mounted our beasts in the rain, and came six miles, dripping wet, to Asa Cumming's cabin, twelve feet square.[90] On *Tuesday morning* we were well soaked before we reached David Eddy's. We dried, dined, prayed, and again got in motion and reached Milton, making thirty miles for the day's journey. Lodged at Baker's. We learn there is a revival in this place. We called upon James Egbert on *Wednesday*: he is a child of faith and prayer; I had used his father's house. We had an awful time on *Thursday* in the woods, amongst rocks and trees, living and dead, and prostrate, and barring our way. When we thought the bitterness of death was past, behold the back-water had covered the causeway. A kind soul, one Hathaway, directed us over the point of a hill, and so we got safe along and came to Ludowick Light's.

Pennsylvania

Friday, 21. We were comfortable while resting at Doctor Hopkins's.[91] Arrived at the ferry bank,[92] no boat appeared, so I came back and called a meeting. Since we left Baltimore in April, we have made, we compute, two thousand miles. Such roads, such rains, and such lodgings! Why should I wish to stay in this land? I have no possessions or babes to bind me to the soil; what are called the comforts of life I rarely enjoy; the wish to live an hour such a life as this would be strange to so suffering, so toil-worn a wretch. But God is with me, and souls are my reward: I may yet rejoice, yea, and will rejoice. I might fill pages with this last week's

[90] Asa Cumming was admitted on trial in 1803, progressing to elder's orders in 1807. In 1809 he held the Scipio Circuit, his small cabin being located somewhat north of Scipio village. He was superannuated in 1814. (Boehm, *op. cit.*, 251.)

[91] Dr. Stephen Hopkins lived at Tioga Point, or Athens, Pennsylvania. (Boehm, *op. cit.*, 251; Palmer, *op. cit.*, 167.)

[92] Two ferries crossed the Susquehanna at Tioga Point. Moore's (later Parks') ferry opened in 1785, and the second, at the foot of Ferry Street, opened in 1790.

wonders. We are eighty miles behind our Sabbath appointment.[93] I called at a certain house[94]—it would not do—I was compelled to turn out again to the pelting of the wind and rain. Though old, I have eyes. The hand of God will come upon them: as for the young lady, shame and contempt will fall on her; mark the event. I preached on *Friday* at Tioga Point. We were at Judge Obadiah Gore's by eight o'clock on *Saturday morning*. We took thence through the Narrows,[95] and a late and rough ride brought us to a tavern lodging.[96]

Sunday, 23. We must needs ride to-day. Our route lay through Walnut Bottom,[97] but we missed our way and the preaching of George Lane.[98] A twenty-four miles' ride brought us to breakfast at Otis's. Brother Boehm upset the sulky and broke the shaft. Night closed upon us at Osterout's tavern. Passing along on *Monday*, we stopped to dine with Squire James Sutton. We lodged under the roof of the widow Dennison.[99] On *Tuesday morning* we found the ferry at Wilkes Barre only just passable. Merwin gave us shelter for the night. We have ridden thirty-eight miles to-day, and sore trials have we passed through. On *Wednesday* we rode through the beautiful villages of Nazareth and Bethlehem, and put up for the night at Allentown. Here are gambling sinners. We made a rapid ride of forty-two miles on *Thursday*. On *Friday* a thirty miles' ride brought us to Martin Boehm's.[100] Delightful rest! but it may not be. *Saturday morning* put us

[93] The appointment was the Wyoming Circuit.

[94] This house was probably passed by before the travelers reached Tioga Point. (See Palmer, *op. cit.*, 168 ff., for various contemporary events in the region.)

[95] Boehm says they went through the Narrows on Monday. (*Op. cit.*, 253.)

[96] Any house that lodged travelers was in this period called a tavern although it might be a humble home that did not dispense the liquor for which taverns were noted. (Palmer, *op. cit.*, 33.)

[97] Black Walnut Bottom was a stretch along the Susquehanna, part of which is in the town of Braintrim. In this section Elisha Bibbuis preached, and about 1812 a class was formed in the home of Joshua Keeney. (*Ibid.*, 184.)

[98] George Lane (1784–1859) was senior preacher on the Wyoming Circuit, which extended from Wilkes-Barre to Wyalusing. He was later one of the book agents and as such the treasurer of the missionary society. Because he was able to finance the work by borrowing on his own credit, he was called the "Father of the Missionary Society." (*Ibid.*, 166, 167.)

[99] The widow was Mrs. Nathan Dennison, nee Betsy Sill of Kingston. Her marriage to Colonel Dennison, hero of the Wyoming "massacre," was the first in the Wyoming Valley. The family frequently extended hospitality to the Methodist itinerants. Here Methodism was first introduced by Anning Owen. (*Ibid.*, 111; Boehm, *op. cit.*, 253.)

[100] Martin Boehm (1725–1812) was the father of Asbury's traveling companion, Henry Boehm, and lived on the paternal estate in Conestoga Township, Lancaster County, Pennsylvania. He was expelled by the Mennonites for his friendship with the Methodists and became with Otterbein one of the first two bishops of the United Brethren. At the same time he maintained his connection with the Methodists: a class was formed in his home, a Methodist chapel was built on his land, and he entered his name in the class book. At the time of the visit here mentioned, Boehm was absent, and as Asbury went on to Lancaster, Henry Boehm visited his parents at a camp meeting near

into motion for Lancaster, where we tarried a few minutes, as also at Columbia, and continued on to York, where I preached at six o'clock in the evening.

Sunday, 30. I spoke on "Let your light so shine." I have at least twenty letters to answer, and but one day. *Monday*, company and business enough; and little time to refit. On *Tuesday* at eight o'clock at night I preached in Carlisle. Twice on the road hither we alighted, stopped, talked, ate, and prayed.

Wednesday, August 2. At Shippensburg. I have been simple enough to put plasters too powerful to my knees—they are in blisters; so here is a bishop who can neither stand to preach nor kneel to pray. My body is very feeble, but my soul enjoys perfect love and perfect peace. *Thursday* brought me and my sufferings safe over three mountains to friend John Thompson's. I preached at Fort Littleton, on Heb. iv, 12; we had few hearers, but it was a liberal season. Lodged at the old place, Ramsay's; it is James Hunter's house and home. We must attend to camp meetings, they make our harvest times; the prospects just now are discouraging. On *Saturday* we rode rapidly to Bedford.[101] The hand of God was manifested to-day in saving man and horse from wreck; the danger appeared exceeding great. I had Henry Boehm and James Hunter for my escort. Lodged at Stephenson's. I calculate the distance we have travelled since January 9 to this day, from Georgia to Bedford, Pennsylvania, at three thousand miles. We are generally amongst the poor; too frequently it is a tavern or starvation; many a time and oft the preachers crowd us; and sometimes we are wedged among the people so that we can neither write nor think.

Sunday, 6. I spoke to a very decent congregation on Acts iv, 12. 1. By original and actual transgression, sinners altogether born in sin; lost, as to strength, and wisdom, and righteousness. 2. The character of Christ, the only Saviour; in Deity, in his humanity, suffering, resurrection, ascension, and meditation. 3. The Gospel method of salvation. 4. The work of the ministry. I spoke in the court house by necessity, not choice. There was but one indecorous thing observed; a presiding elder put his feet upon the banister of my pulpit whilst I was preaching; it was like thorns in my flesh until they were taken down. Our host is a kind Yorkshire man. On *Monday* we took the path to Berlin, and had a cool ride. Notice had been given of our coming, and the German Presbyterian priesthood caused the bell to be rung. Brother Boehm preached to them in high Dutch. My rude, rough ride made me more fit for bed than meeting. We encountered a mountain rain on *Tuesday*, which held us thirty miles, and

Morgantown. He overtook the bishop at the home of James Hunter at Fort Littleton, where Asbury was confined with rheumatism. (Hollingsworth in *The Methodist Magazine*, N.Y., VI (June, 1823), 212; *Dictionary of American Biography*, II, 405, 406; Boehm, *op. cit.*, 255.)

[101] See letter to Jacob Gruber, August 6, 1809.

sent us dripping for shelter to a German friend's house. We called a meeting, and our exercises were in German. We gave away religious tracts, German and English.[102] We have disposed of many thousands of these: it is our duty to do good in every possible way.

I preached in Anthony Banning's house on *Wednesday*. I bore a faithful testimony to the truth whilst speaking at Murphy's on Rom. xii, 12. I was unwell and chilly, having received damage by the rain. We learn that a camp meeting will be held at Dr. Wheeler's in expectation of the two superintendents. *Friday*, a day of abstinence: we are halting and refitting at Mrs. Stephens's. On *Saturday* we rode to the old fort. We dined with a Mr. Hogg, a family lately from England, and as kind as the Methodists. Rode to camp, twenty miles:[103] we had eight local preachers, seventy-three tents, perhaps three thousand people. The religious exercises great and constant.

Sabbath, 13. I held forth on 2 Cor. vi, 20.[104] I spoke but once; Bishop M'Kendree four times. I took occasion to be very plain, giving my hearers to understand that frames and feelings would not supply the neglect of family and closet worship, and the duties we owe to each other in society. We began our sacramental feast, but the people broke out into prayer and singing. We came away shortly after. The profligates would not come within our holy limits, but they drank plentifully of strong drink without. It appears that the bishops will hold a camp meeting in every district; we are encouraged so to do: great power was manifested here, and much good was done. I will not say how I felt, nor how near heaven. 2 Sam. xi, 11. This passage came strongly to my mind; I must take the field.

We came away to Brightwell's on *Wednesday*, and I gave them a talk, on Heb. iv. 2. Mary Brightwell, my beloved nurse last year, required my attentions in turn: her sufferings from a bilious colic caused us to rise at midnight; she grew better after solemn prayer on her behalf. My subject at Fell's meeting house, on *Thursday*, at eleven o'clock, was Titus ii, 12, and at Philip Smith's, in the evening, Heb. ii, 7. Want of rest last night, and hard labour to-day, has tried flesh and spirit. I would not dine when invited, fearful of disappointing the congregation at four o'clock; and it was well I did not, for the cross-bar of the sulky broke, and the mending and the rest of the journey just left me time enough and none to spare: the Lord will always direct those who look up with humble dependence. We reached John Wrenshall's, in Pittsburg, on *Friday* evening. The Rev. Mr. Steel offered, unsolicited, in the name of the Presbyterian eldership, their

[102] Boehm says: "We were pioneers in circulating Tracts. The German Tracts were those I had published in Lancaster." (Boehm, *op. cit.*, 256.)

[103] This camp meeting was on Pike Run in Washington County, Pennsylvania. (*Ibid.*)

[104] This chapter has only eighteen verses. The passage may have been 1 Cor. 6:20, which text Asbury used frequently.

large, elegant house, for my Sunday's exercises. I preached at Thomas Cooper's[105] on *Saturday*.

Sabbath, 20. I accepted the offer made, and preached at three o'clock: it was an open time. Could we unite nations and languages, as well as spirits and tempers, we might do great things here. Will the Allegheny and Monongahela ever rise so high as to inundate the point of land on which the town stands—is such a thing impossible?[106] A Baptist family by the name of Plummer received us on *Tuesday*. Young Plummer is sick, a child is sick, and the whole family feel awful. Who will pray with young Plummer when we are gone? the young man is certainly under convictions. Twelve miles brought us to Fawcett's on *Tuesday morning*; I gave them a sermon on Eph. viii, 9.[107] The weather on *Wednesday* was exceeding warm; nevertheless we started for Washington. I spoke in our own house to a goodly congregation as to numbers. The Rev. Mr. Browne was present, and some seceders,[108] as I was told; surely the millennium is approaching! I dined at Mr. M'Fadon's, and came on to Middletown.

West Virginia

We crossed into Virginia, and preached at Brook county court house on the evening of *Thursday*. Our lodging was the stationed preacher's, William Lambdin. My brethren were kind enough to make appointments for me, at least to publish in the public prints more than I had designed. I might murmur at this, and perhaps I do. Well, elders must be better and do more than other men; granted. I can truly say my life is like a daily death. God is my refuge and my reward. I preached on *Saturday* at Beck's.

Sabbath, 27. At Short Creek chapel my subject was 1 Thess. iv, 3. I

[105] The Thomas Coopers, father and son, arrived in Pittsburgh on June 17, 1803, and commenced the brass foundry business in that city. They were Methodists, and Thomas Cooper, Sr., was soon appointed class leader of the Pittsburgh Society. By 1808 Thomas Cooper, Jr., had built a large house on the Monongahela at Smithfield and Water Streets, and the meeting place of the Pittsburgh Methodist Society was moved there from John Wrenshall's house. The first church building of the Methodists was erected in Pittsburgh in 1810. (Smeltzer, *op. cit.*, 100.)

[106] Frequent inundations of Pittsburgh's "Golden Triangle," especially the forty-six-foot flood of 1936, have been the occasion for the system of flood-control reservoirs which now protect the steel metropolis and down-river communities.

[107] This book has only six chapters. The context does not indicate what the passage may have been.

[108] The Presbyterian Church was the dominant denomination on the transappalachian frontier with three main segments of Presbyterianism represented: the Scotch-Irish and two groups of Scots, namely the Reformed Presbyterians and the Associate Reformed Presbyterians, known respectively as "Covenanters" and "Seceders." These two Scottish groups joined in a union consummated at Pittsburgh in 1858 to form the United Presbyterian Church.

contemplate two chapels;[109] one of forty feet square, and the other of fifty feet; the first in Charleston, Alexander Wells to give the lot; and the other in Wheeling, the ground to be bestowed for its erection by Colonel Zane. Our appointment for *Monday* was in Wheeling court house; I spoke with light, and life, and power.

Ohio

The following day (*Tuesday*) brother Boehm spoke at St. Clairsville.

Wednesday, 30. We found the roads disagreeable in the Wills Creek bottoms. While tugging forward, *crack* went the breastband, and *crack* went the shaft; we were two hours in the night, and at last reached Spears's tavern. Next day (*Thursday*) we made eighteen miles to Springfield, where I preached by appointment; we had about four hundred people: I wanted my breakfast, I wanted strength, and I wanted sleep. Brother Boehm preached at Zanesville,[110] named after Colonel Zane, who so kindly entertained us at Wheeling: he is an extraordinary man, and the history of his life strange. The first of the month I rode thirty-five miles to Edward Teel's. Brother Boehm preached *Saturday*.

Sunday, September 3. I preached at Teel's. On *Monday* I spoke in the elegant court house in New Lancaster. We dined with Mr. Tougue, and went forward, sixteen miles, to Laking's: I was weak and weary with riding on horseback, but I had great consolations in God, and a witness of holiness in my soul. We have our difficulties with the married preachers, their wives, and children; but whilst God is with us these difficulties may be well borne. I pray God that there may be twenty camp meetings in a week, and wonderful seasons of the Lord in every direction. I preached on *Wednesday* at the widow Strode's house. Rest on *Thursday*, *Friday*. This is my covenant day. We came twenty miles to Jefferson, and lodged with Mr. Nevill. Doctor Tiffin received us kindly on *Saturday*. After dinner we rode on to Deer Creek, and housed with White Brown.

Sabbath, 10. I preached in my host's barn: my subject was 2 Cor. vi, 1, 2. Brother Lakin added an exhortation, and brother Boehm gave them a discourse. At a late camp meeting I learn that seventy joined society: the prospects are great.

O what a charming view presents itself from Doctor Tiffin's house! but these long talks about land and politics suit me not; I take little interest in either subject: O Lord, give me souls, and keep me holy! Our route

[109] This indicates that it was Asbury's planning which caused the erection of the first Methodist buildings at Wellsburg and Wheeling, West Virginia. The earlier name of Wellsburg was Charleston.

[110] This sermon was in the courthouse, there being no Methodist house of worship in Zanesville at this time. (Boehm, *op. cit.*, 258.)

through the prairies, the weeds as high as our heads on horseback, showed us on *Monday* almost every desirable comfort but pure water. We stopped on the north branch of Paint Creek. At Jacob Cutler's on *Tuesday*, we had an interview with M'Daniel, Flood, and Trader, official men. These and Hunt's settlements are great improved, and the Methodists have increased. Thirteen miles was the extent of our *Wednesday* ride; we stopped at Pelham's.[111] We remain *Thursday* and *Friday*; my study of divinity is Wesley's sermons—I read some of them to-day. As I cannot often meet Bishop M'Kendree, and meeting, we cannot be alone for talk, I wrote a letter of counsel to him.[112] I preached on *Saturday*. I felt solemn whilst dining at Philip Davis's: this is an old Virginia family, and here as brethren and sisters whom I have known, some twenty, others above thirty years. Life is short. We set out for Mad River, and reached Andrew Read's; I gave them a discourse on John iii, 17. I spoke at William Hamar's on *Tuesday*; my subject was Isaiah xxxv, 3–5. There is a serious affliction in the family; I sympathize with them. Dayton is a growing town; we passed through it on *Wednesday*. I found the son of a Methodist from Gunpowder Neck, one Horner, and lodged with him. On *Thursday* we came down Little and Great Miami; the rich lands of these rivers are occupied by New Lights, Shakers, Methodists,—and sinners to be sure. I was glad to stop at Daniel Baker's. I slept about five hours last night: I had excessive labour, a crowd of company, and hogs, dogs, and other annoyances to weary me. I am thankful for a prospect of one night's quiet at John Harden's, near Hamilton, Butler county; preached for them on *Friday*; we had a large and lively meeting. *Saturday* brought us to the descendant of a German. We came on to Milford, Little Miami. Here are folks from most of the eastern States, and of all professions: they have good land, and this rarely makes people any better.

Sabbath, 24. I spoke in the new chapel in Milford: brothers Lakin and Boehm also spoke. I feel the importance of the approaching conference.[113] At brother Gatch's, on *Monday*, I filled up the day in planning, writing, and reading. We visited Andrew Maguire's family. Preached on *Wednesday*; the house was full, and the weather excessively warm: *faint yet pursuing*. My aid is absent amongst the Germans. I lodged at M'Carmut's. *Thursday* I stood up at Columbia, and gave them a talk on Matt. vii, 7–12: the heat was extreme. Fair Cincinnati brought us up. The house here is enlarged and the society has increased. Our brother West is sick and cannot come to the conference; many of our brethren will be absent. *Friday*,

[111] The Pelham family, of which Peter was head, had lived in Greensville County, Virginia, and Asbury visited them there in 1802. Peter Pelham, who married Edward Dromgoole's daughter, moved to Ohio in 1807, and Asbury visited him there in 1808. (Sweet, *op. cit.*, 167; Dromgoole papers at University of North Carolina Library.)

[112] See Asbury's letter to McKendree, September 15, 1809.

[113] This was the 1809–10 session of the Western Conference. It was the first Methodist conference held at Cincinnati and was held there at Asbury's suggestion.

humiliation day. Muskingum district will have four camp meetings. At Kauhaway there were one thousand people present; at St. Clairsville three thousand souls at least; at Rush Creek nearly as many. In Miami district seventeen camp meetings in the year: in Scioto circuit four; Hochhocking two; Deer Creek two; Mad River three; White Water two; Cincinnati two; and White two.

Sabbath, October 1. Brother Blackman preached at nine o'clock, brother M'Kendree at twelve o'clock, and brother Burke at three o'clock: there were, it is judged, three thousand souls on the ground. I may add, that the list may be complete, seventeen camp meetings for Indiana district. I thought it proper to render an account of all I had received, and all I had expended on the road: all *given* away came out of my own pocket. More of camp meetings—I hear and see the great effects produced by them, and this year there will be more than ever.

Sabbath, 8. I preached in the morning; and in the evening I also spoke again by way of exhortation. The conference closed its labours, and the members separated on *Monday*.

Kentucky

My party came away to Carroll's. Next day we stopped with Captain John Sterne, from Stafford, old Virginia. At midnight I called up my fellow-travellers, and set out having an appointment at Mount Gerizim chapel.[114] We arrived in time, and had an ordination, after which I gave an exhortation. Lodged at Whitaker's.[115] Came in haste next day to Martin's meeting house, where I discoursed on Psalm lxxxv, 1–9. We held a conciliatory conference with several of the local preachers, on the subject of the ordination of local elders. On *Friday* Bishop M'Kendree preached, and I also spoke, embracing various subjects in my exhortation. Lodged at Major Martin's.[116] We moved early on *Saturday morning*, breakfasting at Hoskett's, and crossed the Kentucky by fording.[117] Kind

[114] Mount Gerizim Chapel was three miles from Cynthiana. The Western Conference met there in 1803 and 1804. (Arnold, *op. cit.*, I, 184.)

[115] John Whitaker, father of the Rev. Josiah Whitaker, lived between Paris and Cynthiana in Harrison County, Kentucky. Near there was Matheny's meetinghouse, later known as Mount Gilead. (Arnold, *op. cit.*, I, 172; Redford, *op. cit.*, II, 129.)

[116] Martin's meetinghouse, sometimes called Ebenezer, was in Clark County, Kentucky, six miles from Winchester. The society was organized in 1797, and the first log church was erected in 1798. It was named for Major John Martin, a Revolutionary soldier who went from Virginia to Kentucky in 1784. He was a skeptic who was converted by Mrs. Thomas Hinde, wife of the noted Kentucky Methodist and grandmother of Bishop H. H. Kavanaugh. (Arnold, *op. cit.*, I, 188; Redford, *op. cit.*, I, 368 ff.; Boehm, *op. cit.*, 264.)

[117] McKendree and his traveling companion, Thomas Lasley, left the party for the Cumberland section while Asbury and Boehm continued to Holston. (Boehm, *op. cit.*, 265.)

John Bennett's brought us up for the evening. We have stationed about eighty travelling preachers; rejected fourteen; located nine: there is an increase of two thousand three hundred and sixty-six members in this western conference. We have in Mississippi, fifteen travelling and eight local preachers; and three hundred and sixty members: if spared and so directed, I shall see that country and Canada before I die.

Sabbath, 15. I spoke in Bennett's chapel on John iii, 19. I spoke very plainly to a gay congregation. Captain Irvin[118] took me home with him. Our way led through Richmond on *Monday*, and over the Long Hill: we pressed on to Dennis's—any port in a storm. A rough ride of fifteen miles, on *Tuesday morning*, brought us to Howard's: twenty years ago my kind host received me in Georgia. Another rough ride of twenty miles brought us, by moonshine, to Mr. Johnson's, where we were entertained like gentlemen. An early start on *Wednesday evening* gave us advantage of the day, and we came twenty miles to breakfast; we ate, and prayed, and went forward to Mr. White's, where we were comfortably lodged and entertained.

Tennessee

Came away on *Thursday* across Powell's and Clinch Rivers, and reached Cheek's for the night. My health has been, beyond expectation, good: I have travelled on horseback generally. I am continually in prayer; but a certain fiend assaults me without ceasing—this is for my humiliation. *Friday*. I chasten soul and body this day. Our expenses for the last five days have been five dollars thirty cents. We were favoured in two houses, or the sum would have been greater. We crossed Holston at Marshall's ford on *Saturday*. Squire Read has built a neat pine chapel[119] in a short time. We lodged with him.

Sabbath, 22. I gave them a discourse on Rom. xii. 6–20. Pattison, Stier, and Boehm followed:[120] there was also preaching at night.[121] I spoke at Benjamin Van Pelt's chapel[122] on *Monday*. At Warrensburg,[123] next day, my subject was Rom. vi, 1–5. We dined with the elders of the house of

[118] Captain Christopher Irvin was one of the pioneer settlers of Kentucky and a member of the Danville Convention in 1785. (Collins: *History of Kentucky*, I, 354.)

[119] Read's Chapel was built by Phelps Read and was located a few miles south of Marshall's Ford and two miles east of Morristown, Tennessee. (Price, *op. cit.*, II, 122.)

[120] William Pattison was serving the Nollichuckie Circuit, Frederick Stier was presiding elder of the Holston District, and Henry Boehm was Asbury's traveling companion. (See *Minutes*, 1810.)

[121] See letter to Jacob Gruber, October 22, 1809.

[122] Van Pelt's Chapel was on Lick Creek. (See note under May 28, 1790.)

[123] Warrensburg was a village in Greene County, Tennesse. Asbury stayed there on the night of September 20, 1802.

Conway,[124] and lodged with the only son, Thomas Conway. Preached at O'Haver's chapel[125] on *Wednesday*. Dined, and came on to friend Ellis's. We suppose we have made three hundred and forty miles since we left Cincinnati. My mind and body have had no small exercise in bringing my stiff-jointed horse over the rocks, and rough and deep roads. I preached at Harrison chapel,[126] on Gal. v, 7–10; the text is a sermon.

North Carolina

We crossed the French Broad, and fed our horses at the gate of Mr. Hoodenpile:[127] he would accept no pay but prayer; as I had never called before, he may have thought me too proud to stop. Our way now lay over dreadful roads. I found old Mr. Barnard sick:[128] the case was a desperate one, and I gave him a grain of tartar and a few composing drops, which procured him a sound sleep. The patient was very thankful, and would charge us nothing. Here are martyrs to whisky! I delivered my own soul. *Saturday* brought us to Killian's. Eight times within nine years have I crossed these Alps. If my journal is transcribed it will be as well to give the subject as the chapter and verse of the text I preached from. Nothing like a sermon can I record. Here now am I, and have been for twenty nights, crowded by people; and the whole family striving to get round me.

Sabbath, 29. At Buncombe I spoke on Luke xiv, 10. It was a season of

[124] Henry Conway was the head of a notable family. Two of his daughters married sons of Governor John Sevier. (Williams: *Lost State of Franklin*, 303.)

[125] John O'Haver's campground and home in Cocke County, Tennessee, was one of Asbury's favorite stopping places.

[126] Harrison meetinghouse was on the Greene Circuit and was located on the south side of the Nollichuckie near Greenville, Tennessee. (Price, *op. cit.*, I, 140.)

[127] Philip Hoodenpile lived on what was known as Hoodenpile Road, which ran from Hot Springs to the Tennessee line, and he had a contract to maintain a section of this road from Hopewell Hill to Tennessee. In 1796 he had represented Buncombe County in the North Carolina House of Commons, defeating Colonel Thomas Love, founder of Waynesville, largely because of his ability to play the fiddle. In the second race Love charged Hoodenpile with showing contempt for the common people by playing before them with his left hand while he used his right hand before the "quality people." Actually Hoodenpile was left-handed and could not play with his right, but the charge aroused class feeling, and he was defeated and did not again appear in public life. (Arthur, *op. cit.*, 128, 129, 134.)

[128] (For Barnard see note under November 4, 1802.) Henry Boehm, who again traveled with Asbury, says, "The old landlord was very sick and like to die. The bishop, who was a physician when necessary, always carrying medicine with him, gave Mr. Barnett a dose that almost instantly relieved him and he fell asleep. He was so thankful he would receive nothing for our entertainment." He adds that they passed over "mountains, rocks, stumps, trees, streams, awful roads, and dangerous passes" and "crossed to Buncombe, North Carolina, preaching every day." (Boehm, *op. cit.*, 265.) The present Highway 25–70 from Hot Springs to Ashville crosses a range of the Blue Ridge Mountains.

attention and feeling. We dined with Mr. Erwine,[129] and lodged with James Patton:[130] how rich, how plain, how humble, and how kind! There was a sudden change in the weather on *Monday*; we went as far as D. Jay's. *Tuesday*, we moved in haste to Mud Creek, Green River Cove, on the other side of Saluda.

South Carolina

Lodged with kind and pleasant Thomas Edwards.[131] On the first of the month (*November*) we reached Staunton Ferry. We suppose we have ridden five hundred and ten miles since we left Cincinnati; what heights, what hills, what rocks! Lord, thou preservest man and beast! The disagreeable part of this western wandering is the necessity of stopping at night. Ah! how different are the taverns here from the houses of entertainment in the Atlantic States! And the keepers of these poisonous liquor shops—Is there one who fears God and encourages prayer? One or two; the rest are drunkards.

We are at father Staunton's, on the Saluda. Our host is an Israelite indeed, and the wife worthy of such a husband. Here is a society of sixteen souls. I gave a discourse at Salem chapel. It is a cloudy day, well fitted for retreat. I wrote a very long letter to Doctor Coke. We have a quarterly meeting on *Friday*. On *Saturday*, I preached on Luke xviii, 1.

Sabbath, 5. I preached in the open air, because our cabin meeting house was small and open. My subject led me out on the antiquity and truth of Holy Writ; the characters of Moses and Christ, calling the attention to the likeness, but superior excellence of Jesus, at the times of the presence and power of the Almighty, and the more perfect and abundant good produced by this latter manifestation. We had a sacramental feast. On *Monday* we came away, and attended to the mending of our travelling gear. There are no small numbers of the preachers about here married this last year. I have read with satisfaction *The Star in the East*: Lord, hasten the time when all shall know thee! O, Reedy River circuit—spiritually and temporally poor! *Tuesday*, Powell's[132]—I preached. My friend has taken a new wife, and built a new house. His former wife was kind to me; I saw where her remains and those of her daughter lay—they fell

[129] For Erwine see note under November 29, 1808.

[130] James Patton was a leading citizen but not a Methodist. He and his two sons, James W. and John E., were large property owners in Asheville and ran the Eagle Hotel. Patton Avenue is named for them. (Arthur, *op. cit.*, 148, 149.)

[131] Asbury and his party went over Saluda Gap again into Greenville County, South Carolina. Edwards lived near Greenville.

[132] Powell lived near Ware Shoals in Laurens County in the bounds of the Reedy River Circuit of which Osborn Rogers was pastor.

asleep in Jesus. We rode into Abbeville and stopped at George Connor's.[133] Great news—great times in Georgia—rich and poor coming to Christ. At Connor's chapel I spoke, on *Thursday*, on Rom. xii, 1, 2. After sermon I ordained John Stone a local deacon. *Friday*, covenant day. In Edgefield[134] the Baptists are carrying all before them; they are indebted to Methodist camp meetings for this. I preached on opening the new chapel on Luke xix, 9; we had an open time. The Methodists have great success in Camden district; surely there must be some good done—all are on fire, and I feel the flame: God is with preachers and people.

Sunday, 12. I preached to about one thousand people, on Titus ii, 1. The quarterly meeting engaged our attention six hours every day. Our route on *Monday* lay over Bush Creek. This is, or was, a Quaker settlement: the *Friends* have gone to rich lands, unpolluted by slavery—they have formed a settlement in Ohio. I preached in Tranquil chapel[135] on *Tuesday*—God has blessed Stephen Shell's family. Grandmother, who was waiting in great peace for her summons, was called away in August last. I must needs preach at Major's chapel: my subject was *the great salvation*. Lodged with Colonel H. Herndon.[136] O how kind! *Thursday*, rode to Jeremiah Lucas's.[137] I was in heaviness of mind, and suffered in the flesh. Brother Boehm preached in the chapel.

Sunday, 19. I preached to about one thousand souls, standing in the chapel door. The house could not contain the people on any day: some came to see, some to hear, and some felt. We have laboured for three days about six hours a day on our private business. We crossed Pacolet, Thickety, and Broad River,[138] on our way to Josiah Smith's on *Monday*. On *Tuesday* I preached for them, and Boehm and Hill exhorted: it was a gracious season. *Wednesday* we came through York to William Gassaway's.[139] There was heavy snow for about twelve hours.[140] Brother Boehm preached at the dwelling house, and I gave them a sermon in the chapel.

[133] Connor lived across the Saluda near Cokesbury. The meetinghouse there was Connor's Chapel. (Betts, *op. cit.*, 120.)

[134] Edgefield was forty-five miles to the south.

[135] Tranquil Church was about ten miles east of Newberry Court House, a mile above Jallapa.

[136] Colonel Herndon lived near Whitmire.

[137] Jeremiah Lucas probably lived in Laurens County between O'Dell's and Bramlett's Chapel, across the Enoree River from the town of Enoree.

[138] These streams were crossed just below Cherokee Falls.

[139] The Rev. William Gassoway, whom Boehm called a "noble old preacher, universally esteemed," lived at Tirza in York County between York and Rock Hill on a small farm which had been given to him by a friend. He was a member of the conference from 1788 to 1823, and his appointment at this time was Enoree Circuit. (Boehm, *op. cit.* 266; Chreitzberg, *op. cit.*, 88.)

[140] For an interesting account of their experiences in connection with the snowstorm while they were at Gassoway's and the cold at Hancock's, see Boehm, *op. cit.*, 266–70, and Capers: *Autobiography*, 113–15.

On *Friday* we took the road to Waxhaw, and with some difficulty kept the path, and the horses their feet. In about nine hours we made our way, crossed Lenham's ferry, and came in to Robert Hancock's, stiff and chilled.[141] O for patience and courage!

On *Saturday* we attended a congregation of thirty souls.

Sunday, 26. At the Waxhaw chapel I preached to four hundred souls.[142] An exhortation followed, and the sacrament. *Monday*, a cold ride to William Heath's, on Fishing Creek.[143] I met a congregation on *Tuesday*, in a log cabin, scarcely fit for a stable. To my surprise, a number of United States' officers came up; I invited them in: these gentlemen are attached to an establishment at Rocky Mount;[144] they behaved with all the propriety I expected of them. *Wednesday* brought us where a sermon was expected, and I gave them one. I made an acquaintance with a venerable pair—Mr. Buchanan and wife, Presbyterians, and happy in the experience of religion. A brick chapel is building at Winnsboro for the Methodists.[145] We lodged at William Lewis's,[146] but late emerging into light. On *Thursday*, we had a chilly ride of twenty-five miles to Mr. Watson's. It rained excessively on *Friday*, yet I visited James Jenkins, and baptized his child, Elizabeth Asbury Jenkins.[147] We reached Camden on *Saturday*.

Sunday, December 3. I preached in the tabernacle to about five hundred people, and as we had two distinct congregations in the house, I dropped a word of advice to the poor Africans in presence of the whites.

[141] Lenham's ferry crossed the Catawba below Fort Mill. Robert Hancock lived on the South Carolina side though the Waxhaw Community proper was in North Carolina.

[142] The Waxhaw Chapel was near Hancock's. "We reached Waxhaw and put up with Robert Hancock. Almost every prominent Methodist man had a meetinghouse named after him: so we had a 'Hancock Chapel.' " (Boehm, *op. cit.*, 266.)

[143] The party turned back southwestward from the North Carolina border. Heath lived near Fort Lawn.

[144] Rocky Mount was the present Great Falls, west of the Catawba River.

[145] James Jenkins as a local preacher had preached at Wolf Pit near Smyrna and Ridgeway the previous year. He was invited to Winnsboro by the wife of Captain Buchanan, a Revolutionary soldier. Jenkins preached in the courthouse, and Buchanan expressed doubt that a society would be formed. But at a camp meeting near Camden both he and his wife, with Captain Harris and Major Moore, were converted and joined the church. The brick chapel was completed in 1810. (Chreitzberg, *op. cit.*, 130; Betts, *op. cit.*, 118.)

[146] Lewis lived at Winnsboro in Fairfield County.

[147] James Jenkins named the child for his own mother and Asbury. Known as "Thundering Jimmy" and "Bawling Jenkins," he was one of the notable pioneer preachers in South Carolina, having joined the conference in 1792. At this time he had been a local preacher for three years and lived at Camden. His church was Sawney's Creek Meeting House. He joined the conference again in 1812 and was superannuated the following year. He was instrumental in the conversion of Mr. Weatherly, uncle of Lovick and Reddick Pierce, and his home and meetinghouse were the first appointments of the young William Capers, whom he subjected to a rather rigorous "breaking in" process. (See Capers, *op. cit.*, 93–96, 99–101; Shipp, *op. cit.*, 232–37.)

Brother Boehm preached in the evening. On *Monday* I was seriously afflicted in body. In much weakness of flesh, and solemnity of mind, I set out, on *Tuesday*, for Black River. There are great changes in the house where I stopped—my dear old Mary is dead, and there is another wife. On *Wednesday* I saw the third house on Black River[148]—fifty by thirty-six feet. I spoke in an especial manner to Henry Young's Negroes,[149] who were called together for that purpose. At Samuel Rembert's[150] on *Thursday*. My host proposes shortly to remove to Georgia. We preached to a small meeting on *Friday*. Henry Boehm preached on *Saturday* at James Caper's.

Sunday, 10. We had a five hours' meeting. Tarpley and Hobbs prayed[151] after I had preached: some had come to be prayed for. We made a cold, heavy ride of forty-five miles on *Monday*. We reached Kell's tavern in the night. The road was dreadfully ploughed up with wagons; the ferry was wide, and we had the swamp to pass, and dip, dive, and go—we laboured through it: this was our *Tuesday*'s task. *Wednesday evening* brought us rest in Charleston. Where does the cotton go, that arrives in such quantities? To England and France, in spite of the non-intercourse. I am mainly ignorant of these things, and have no wish to be wiser. Our old church is enlarged, and our parsonage completely fitted up. I am busy writing, or occupied with my Bible and Ramsay's History.[152]

Sunday, 17. I preached in Cumberland chapel: I concluded with a close

[148] This was another meetinghouse. It was doubtless on the Henry Young plantation and identical with Russell's Meeting House which became the Bethlehem Church in Bishopsville, South Carolina.

[149] Henry Young's plantation was twelve miles east of Camden on the upper side of Black River in Lee County. Rembert Hall, on the lower side of the river, was several miles away. Henry Young was a local preacher. He died in 1835 at the age of seventy. (Chreitzberg, *op. cit.*, 172.)

[150] Samuel Rembert was probably the son of James Rembert. He moved to Georgia, and Asbury visited him there. (See note under November 30, 1814; Chreitzberg, *op. cit.*, 169, 172.)

[151] Joseph Tarpley was one of the preachers on the Santee Circuit, for which a quarterly conference was being held. Lewis Hobbs was a Georgia preacher; he was admitted in 1808 and in 1811 went as a missionary to Mississippi. John and James Capers exhorted at Rembert's. Both were admitted on trial this year, John going to Sparta in Georgia and James to Santee Circuit. John was William Capers' brother, and James, son of Sinclair Capers, was his cousin. (*Minutes*, 1809, 1810; Betts, *op. cit.*, 234; Boehm, *op. cit.*, 271.) Lewis Hobbs had served Brunswick Circuit and at the ensuing conference was appointed to Union Circuit.

[152] Dr. David Ramsay of Charleston was a noted historian as well as a physician. His two-volume *History of the Revolution of South Carolina* was published in 1785, much of it being from the *Annual Register*. In 1789 he published a two-volume *History of the American Revolution* which leaned even more heavily on the *Register*. He wrote a *Life of George Washington* in 1807 and a three-volume *History of the United States* in 1816–17, and in 1819 he brought out a nine-volume *Universal History Americanized*, of which the former was a part. The work which Asbury read was doubtless Ramsay's two-volume *History of South Carolina* which was published in 1809 and which is still a standard work. (*Dictionary of American Biography*, I, 338.)

application. Bishop M'Kendree came in on *Tuesday*.[153] I received many letters with pleasing accounts from the north. Sarah Dickens once, now Sarah Baker, in Baltimore, has lost her child; and God has converted the mother: is not this another answer to prayer? Father Everitt has gone in glory to glory: God be glorified! Four hundred people attended our ministry on *Friday*. I have eighteen letters to answer, and more are no doubt on their way. We have prayed especially and earnestly for our conference: surely God will hear! It is all peace with preachers and people. On *Saturday* conference set to work in earnest, and in great order. Thomas Glenn's case is a serious one; he is suspended for imprudence, but not for gross immorality.[154]

Sunday, 24. We had a gracious feast of love. I preached at Cumberland in the morning, and at Bethel in the evening. We laboured straight onward *Monday*, *Tuesday*, *Wednesday*, and *Thursday*; *Friday* was set apart for ordination: it was desired that I should preach: it was a season of tears. We came out of Charleston on *Saturday*, and lodged for the night at Mrs. Brian's quarter,[155] with Thomas M'Kendree,[156] who fed us richly. A *Sabbath's* journey brought us to a sick man's house. I prayed with our host, and administered some medicine which procured him ease.

[153] Bishop William McKendree was accompanied by his traveling companion, the Rev. Thomas Lasley. (Boehm, *op. cit.*, 271.)

[154] Thomas Glenn had been on the Sparta Circuit in Georgia. He was not expelled but was not given an appointment. The next year he was sent to the Great Pee Dee Circuit.

[155] Brian's Quarter refers to a community which developed on the Brian plantation. Similarly there was an Orange Quarter in Berkeley County and Granny's Quarter in Kershaw County.

[156] "We were the guests of a brother of Bishop McKendree, who was overjoyed to see us, and treated us in a friendly manner." (*Ibid.*, 273.)

1810

1810

Asbury preaching to the soldiers at Fort Walcott in Rhode Island

CHAPTER THIRTY-NINE

South Carolina

Monday, January 1. The first day of the year 1810, we crossed Potato Ferry.[1] Thomas Lasley was ill, and we stopped at Haydicken's,[2] and gave him medicine: we were compelled to leave him at Blackmingo. Missing our way, we dropped upon Mr. John Graham; he was a Presbyterian, and showed us much kindness. On *Tuesday* we crossed Porter's ferry.[3] I have been unspeakably happy in God to-day. The people of Charleston have been faithfully warned; and it will be seen not many days hence, how God was with the conference. We were kindly entertained on *Wednesday* by Moses Smith.[4] What do the rich do for us but spoil us? Ashpole[5] was deep enough on *Thursday*; we got over in safety, and stopped at Joseph Lee's.

North Carolina

We have had a drop of rain now and then; but there has fallen much all around us. At Fayetteville on *Friday* I was very unwell; but I laboured through five letters.

[1] The party probably proceeded through Jamestown and Lenud's Ferry over the Santee and crossed Black River at Potato Ferry on their way to North Carolina.

[2] "Haydicken" must have resided at or near Black Mingo in Williamsburg County. He is unidentified.

[3] The crossing of the Pee Dee at Port's Ferry took the party into Marion County.

[4] Moses Smith lived near Mullins.

[5] Ashpole is a swamp which drains into the Lumber River above Lakeview near the North Carolina state line.

Sabbath, 7. I preached in our enlarged house in the morning, and Bishop M'Kendree in the evening. We came rapidly next day forty-five miles to the widow Anderson's. At Wilmington I spoke in the new chapel on *Wednesday*: I find the work of God is going on here. We are well in temporals, and a most correct account has been furnished us of all expenditures. I met the African elders, and gave command concerning the parsonage, the painting of the new fences, and the alteration and increase of the benches in the chapel. I recommended the purchase of a grave-yard, and gave a special charge concerning the poor: O, let me ever remember these! A general fast day for the African Churches was appointed. *Thursday* we rode forty-two miles to George Shepherd's.[6] On *Friday* we stopped at Lot Ballard's, for refreshment and prayer, and fled away to Adonijah Penn's: we were an hour in the night. We reached Newbern on *Saturday evening*. I am in unceasing prayer. Erasmus Hill may possibly sell the Gospel for a rich wife, as three or four others have done. Should I say here, And thou, Francis, take heed? Not of this sin.

Sabbath, 14. I preached in the morning: my mind enjoys great peace. Bishop M'Kendree spoke in the afternoon. Our prospects here are not very encouraging. On *Monday* we hasted away across Neuse, at Street's ferry, to Mr. Allen's: we dined and put off again, crossing Swift Creek, and came in after night to the widow Carman's. A hard ride next day, of about fifty miles, brought us to the widow Williams's in the night; rain in plenty. Rose at five o'clock to our day's work; and Joseph Peppins received us, and sheltered us for the night. *Thursday*, up again at five o'clock, and passed through Murfreesborough to Jesse Battle's. Are we riding for life? Nay; but we must not disappoint people; we are men of our words. I feel for others in bad travelling; but little for myself. Our horses are always well fed, and never fail: Lord! thou preservest man and beast, I may truly say. My soul is strong in faith, and constantly engaged in prayer. On *Friday* we crossed Knotty Pine at Manney's ferry; stopped a few minutes at Judith Baker's to talk and pray, and came in to D. Southall's, at Gates court house. It is pleasant, but cold, cold! We proceeded with borrowed horses to Edenton. It is still excessively cold. Lodged with William Hankins.

Sabbath, 21. Snow storm. We had twelve women and six men at the new chapel, and about one hundred Africans. I preached in the evening at Hankins's to about forty women; my subject was a comment on our Lord's conversation with Martha. E. Jones, by providence, has built us a house, and laid the foundation for an African chapel. *Monday* brought cold, and ice, and snow; it was well the horses were rough. We came in safety to Gates. We had dangerous travelling on *Wednesday*: lodged with D. Duke.

[6] George Shepherd lived in Onslow County, North Carolina.

Virginia

On our way to Norfolk we stopped at I. Lunsford's: came into Norfolk after night.

Thursday, closely employed in writing letters.[7] I called the official members together to consult upon the propriety of setting apart a day for fasting, humiliation, and prayer. *Friday*, fasting and humiliation. I gave a brief discourse at the chapel on Joel ii, 12, 13. *Saturday*, read my Bible and Marshall's Life of Washington.

Sabbath, 28. I preached and met the society of both colours: I said many things, and some wept. I gave them a discourse at Portsmouth. Excessively cold on *Tuesday*; I preached at Cox's chapel. In future I will try to hold the meetings in private houses. At Suffolk in the evening; poor Suffolk! On *Thursday* I gave an evening discourse at General Wells's: the house was full. A cold ride brought us to William Blunt's on *Friday evening*. My host's wife and son are in affliction. My flesh complains of cold riding and the labour of preaching; may I be made perfect through sufferings! *Saturday* brought us through rain and snow, without eating or prayer, although we stopped twice, to William Birdsong's. O, how comfortable! and we can pray here.

Sabbath, *February* 4. The day is serene; and so is my soul. I preached at my host's, and at Wright Ellis's. Here were great times thirty years ago; many are fallen asleep, and the children forget God. I felt awful in enlarging amongst these people upon *the great salvation*. I called twice at Blackwater church; shivering, eating a morsel, and praying. Our people preach there with success, and an encouraging society is formed. Lord, increase our faith! On *Monday* we wrought our solitary way through the woods to Allen's bridge: the widow Pennington received us; her husband is dead: she is sick; her children irreligious: O, misery! O, mercy! We went on to James Rogers's, where I gave them a discourse, and spoke as if a thousand had been present. We have passed like a mail through South and North Carolina. I solemnly sympathize with my dear brother Boehm; he has suffered greatly in his journey; an awful cough and fevers: Lord, what is life! Here is William Graves almost gone at fifty-five; Robert Jones, a helpless man at seventy-two, sunk to second childhood: God is with him. A fasting, weary ride, brought us to Petersburg.[8] Our conference began on *Thursday*; and rose on the following *Thursday*. We had, *Friday*, ordination, and preaching in abundance. I gave an answer to an important question; it was, Whether the bishops had a right to form the eighth, or Genesee Conference? as also gave an answer to the Virginia Conference.

[7] See letter to Jacob Gruber, January 26, 1810.

[8] Boehm says they stayed at Sister Harding's in Petersburg. Asbury preached the ordination sermon, and McKendree and Edward Dromgoole also preached. (Boehm, *op. cit.*, 275–76.)

At mid-day we started for Richmond, and arrived after six hours' ride, without stopping. We stopped on our route next day at Caroline court house. A rapid ride through cold and snow brought us to Fredericksburg, forty miles.

Sabbath, 18. I preached to about one hundred souls; a day of feeble things. After meeting the society, I felt a freedom in my mind to travel onwards. We stopped at Suttle's, and our bill was three dollars, without wine or stronger drink. *Monday* came on to Dumfries; where we stopped to visit a sick man and administer the sacrament. Arrived in Alexandria, and housed for the night with brother Sandford. *Tuesday* I preached to a few souls.

District of Columbia

Came to the Federal City[9] on *Wednesday*, and rested three days. Ah, what a world of bustle and show have we here! On *Friday* I preached, though taken with a great hoarseness.

Maryland

We rode on to our brother Kinkey's[10] in Bladensburg. *Saturday* brought us to Baltimore. Fasting to keep down a hoarseness and sore throat.

Sabbath, 25. At Light Street my subject was James iv, 8–11. In the afternoon I spoke at the African house,[11] on 1 Peter v, 5–7. I have had little rest for several nights. I visited Annapolis on *Monday*, and preached for them. The affection of the people is great, and my unworthiness is greater. No rest for *Tuesday*. We crossed, with wind and cold, South River

[9] Federal City was the early name of Washington, D.C. During their visit Asbury and Boehm and possibly McKendree were guests of Henry Foxhall of Georgetown. (*Ibid.*, 277.) The Washington preaching place of both bishops was probably the "Old Tobacco House" occupied by the Methodists from 1807 to 1811. This original barn of Dudley Carroll stood on New Jersey Avenue, south of D Street, and had been for thirty years a place of worship of the Protestant Episcopalians. The new occupants were members of the Greenleaf's Point Society whose place of worship had been in "The Twenty Buildings," South Capitol and N streets. (Ferguson: *Methodism in Washington, District of Columbia*, 30–43.)

[10] The only surname resembling Kinkey is that of Herman Kinkee, a German, who was naturalized in 1720. Zebulon Kankey, a native of Cecil County, near the Sassafras River, who was an itinerant 1792–98, may have been of the same family. (Hallman, *op. cit.*, 73; Stevens: *Memorials of the Introduction of Methodism into the Eastern States*, 302, 303.)

[11] During this visit to Baltimore, Asbury and Boehm were the guests of Mrs. Elizabeth Dickins, widow of the late John Dickins. (Boehm, *op. cit.*, 277.) It is difficult to identify the "African House" inasmuch as at this time Negro congregations occupied both the Sharp Street schoolhouse, transformed into a church, and the Strawberry Alley Chapel.

ferry. I thought of taking down my wallet and eating my morsel of bread under the lee of some favouring tree, when, behold, Colonel Rawlings[12] and Samuel Maccubbin[13] joined us; O, the case is altered! They can now receive a Methodist in their houses. Again in motion; we went, cut and go, through the bleak weather to brother Wood's:[14] here was one of my earliest stands for preaching twenty-eight years ago. *Wednesday*, at the widow Tannehill's,[15] I spoke to a full house. The work of God prospers in this quarter. I lodged once more with mine ancient friend Captain William Weems. O, my jaws and teeth!

Thursday, *March* 1. In West Maryland, we have nine circuits, five stations, twenty-five preachers, one hundred chapels, eleven thousand six hundred and twenty-two members; and perhaps one hundred local preachers. I am kindly and comfortably entertained by Miss Eliza Skinner. A cold *Friday*: we had about four hundred souls at Gray's meeting house: they were deeply serious whilst I expounded 1 Cor. xv, 58. Lodged at the widow Skinner's. I spoke on *Saturday* at Plumb Point to five hundred attentive hearers; after dining with Samuel Essex,[16] we returned to William Weems's. I have a continual pain in my jaws, so that I chew with difficulty. Our labour is not in vain in these parts.

Sunday, 4. I held forth to about one thousand attentive souls in Weems's chapel on "the great salvation." I lodged with David Weems: his wife is in glory, his daughters in the Church, and his sons in the world. On *Monday* we rode fourteen miles through damps and thick woods to Samuel Maccubbin's. I was done over. I blistered for a severe inflammation in the face. *Tuesday morning*, sick and suffering, I rode sixteen miles and filled an appointment at Bicknell's chapel.[17] I hasted on to Baltimore on *Wednesday*. *Thursday*, very sick: I need bleeding and medicine. I was

[12] Gassaway Rawlings (1743–1812) was the father-in-law of Samuel McCubbin and was a property owner of some note. George Wells noted in his *Journal* that McCubbin entertained him and other preachers.

[13] Samuel McCubbin (1763–1838) married Mary Ann, daughter of Mr. and Mrs. Gassaway Rawlings, December 15, 1788. The McCubbin estate, "Brampton", was on South River, Anne Arundel County. (Brumbaugh, *op. cit.*, II, 454; Ridgely: *Historic Graves of Maryland and the District of Columbia*, 9.)

[14] John Woods lived near the head of Rockhold Creek in the present District No. 7, Anne Arundel County.

[15] The Widow Tannehill lived in the northwest corner of Calvert County. When Nelson Reed was on the Calvert Circuit, the James Tannehill home was a preaching place. (Diary of Nelson Reed, June 24, 1781: Colbert's *Journal*, July 18, 1790; Tannehill: *Genealogical History of the Tannahills, Tannehills, and Taneyhills*, 137.)

[16] Samuel Essex lived at Plum Point, Calvert County, Maryland, a village about two miles east of Parran on Chesapeake Bay. Asbury was a frequent guest of Essex. (Art. by S. Paul Schilling in *Calvert Independent Tercentenary Edition*, September 23, 1954; *Journal* entry for March 15, 1813.)

[17] This chapel in Anne Arundel County was named for Thomas Bignall. Asbury used the spelling "Bignal" on October 12, 1793. His reference to the chapel at this time follows that of the census of 1790 in spelling.

scarcely able to sit in conference on *Friday*. Day of fasting and humiliation to all the members. *Saturday*, busy.

Sunday, 11. Bishop M'Kendree preached. We had an ordination. I spoke by way of exhortation. *Saturday*, the conference[18] went forward with order and despatch, and rose at ten o'clock this morning. I rode to Perry Hall.

Sunday, 18. Rode ten miles to the new chapel in Middle River Neck.[19] *I would not ride in the coach.* Will my character never be understood? But gossips will talk. If we want plenty of good eating and new suits of clothes, let us come to Baltimore; but we want souls. A damp and misty *Monday*; but we set out for Henry Watters's. I parted at Deer Creek (Ah, where to meet again!) with aged father Boehm,[20] and my ancient friend Henry Watters. We found the wind fresh from the south in crossing the Susquehanna; but hard toil and a kind Providence brought us safely over, and we came into Northeast hungry and faint. I was mortified for an hour with one who had been expelled from our society. On *Wednesday* I once more preached at Northeast. Bishop M'Kendree exhorted. We hasted away fifteen miles to Bohemia chapel,[21] I spoke to a serious congregation; in the evening once more under the roof of Richard Bassett.[22]

Delaware

Friday, 23. I gave a discourse at Union chapel.[23] On *Saturday* attended the preaching of brother George Pickering[24] at Friendship meeting house.

[18] The conference convened in the conference room of the Light Street Church. Among the twelve admitted on trial was John Wesley Bond, who as Asbury's traveling companion attended him at his death. (Armstrong, *op. cit.*, 159; Boehm, *op. cit.*, 278; Paine: *Life and Times of William McKendree*, II, 249; Hough, *op. cit.*, 126.)

[19] On September 3, 1773, Asbury preached at Asher's in Middle River Neck. Three months later in that same vicinity he visited "Middle River and had the satisfaction of seeing our new house raised and covered in." (*Journal* entry for February 21, 1774.) Apparently the new chapel to which Asbury here refers was the successor to the original meetinghouse. This probably was Ebenezer, three miles from the Philadelphia Pike near Chase's Station. (Hartman: *History of Methodism in Maryland, 1770–1912*, microfilm copy in Library of Congress, Washington, D.C.) The original deed to this chapel is in Lovely Lane Museum, Baltimore.

[20] Martin Boehm (1725–1812) was the father of Henry Boehm. The elder Boehm began as a Mennonite preacher, then joined the Methodists. After expulsion from the Mennonites for excessive zeal he associated himself with the Methodist movement. He served as bishop of the Church of the United Brethren in Christ from 1800 until his death. (Hough, *op. cit.*, 3 n.; *The Methodist Magazine* (*1823*), VI, art. "Notices of the Life and Labours of Martin Boehm"; and 213, funeral oration; Boehm, *op. cit.*, 372–86.)

[21] This was Bethesda Chapel at Bohemia Manor.

[22] See letter to Nelson Reed, March 22, 1810.

[23] Union Church, near Odessa, had as its predecessors White's and Dickerson's chapels. (See note under October 23, 1786.) It was erected on the site of the latter in

I dined with Gideon Emory; his father received me thirty-three years ago.

Sunday, 25. At Smyrna my subject was 2 Chron. xxxii, 25, 26: it was an open time. George Pickering spoke after me. We collected liberally for Boston chapel.[25] I felt solemn while walking in the grave-yard: here moulder my friends of thirty years past. The Africans were serious and attentive in the afternoon whilst I was speaking to them. I wrote letters to the south.[26] My soul is full of confidence in God. On *Monday* I preached at Dover chapel; and next day at Green's chapel.[27] Most of my old friends in this quarter have fallen asleep; but their children are generally with me, and the three generations baptized. We hold in the peninsula, comprising the eastern shore of Virginia and Maryland, and the State of Delaware, about one hundred houses of God; twenty-two thousand nine hundred and thirty-five members; preachers, travelling and local two hundred and thirty-eight. Dined with Philemon Green, and lodged with Andrew Barratt.[28]

At Barratt's chapel, brother Pickering and myself preached. On *Thursday* we had a cold ride to visit two families. O, Milford, there is death in the pot! *Friday*, at Milton, I preached; and also at Lewes on *Saturday*.

Sunday, *April* 1. I preached at Ebenezer. An awful storm prevented the

1848. It was the home church of Bishop Levi Scott (1802–82), whose grave and monument are in the churchyard. (*Delaware, a Guide to the First State*, 345; Hallman, *op. cit.*, 258; Mitchell: *The Life and Times of Levi Scott*; Love: *History of Odessa, 1901*.)

[24] George Pickering (1769–1846), the presiding elder of the Boston District, was a native of Talbot County, Maryland. The General Conference of 1808 had authorized him to solicit funds "in any part of the connection to assist in defraying the enormous debt on the new (Boston) church." His visit to the peninsula was prompted doubtless by the twofold advantage of local pride in Pickering's growing reputation and the backing of Asbury and McKendree, with whom he traveled. (Stevens: *Memorials of the Introduction of Methodism into the Eastern States*, 196–200; *General Conference Journals*, I, 85.)

[25] The chapel, located in "Broomfield's Lane" was the second Methodist place of worship erected in Boston. Even before its dedication, November 19, 1806, indebtedness made its retention by the Methodists appear doubtful. (Mudge: *History of the New England Conference*, 81–83; *Journal* entry for June 18, 1810, about Asbury's letters for aid to five southern Methodist centers; Boehm, *op. cit.*, 290, 291.)

[26] See letter to Lewis Myers, March 24, 1810.

[27] Green's Chapel stood two miles north of Canterbury, Kent County, Delaware. Services held as early as 1777 in neighborhood homes were transferred in 1781 to the new chapel named for Christopher Green, who gave the site. When in 1856 the congregation moved to Canterbury, it took the name Bethesda Chapel but later assumed the name of Canterbury, by which it has ever since been known. (Scharf: *History of Delaware*, II, 1140, 1141; Hallman, *op. cit.*, 236, 239.)

[28] Andrew Barratt (1756–1821) was the son of Philip for whom Barratt's Chapel was named. Admitted to the Kent County, Delaware, bar in 1779, he served his state and county in public office for forty years. (Barratt: *Barratt's Chapel and Methodism*, papers of the Historical Society of Delaware, LVII, 41–44; Conrad: *History of the State of Delaware*, 893.)

attendance of many. I spoke to the Africans in the town; and gave an exhortation in the church, after brother Pickering's sermon; we hope our labours for the day have not been in vain. Brother Pickering spoke again on *Monday*; I added an exhortation. There was a crowd at the Sound chapel on *Tuesday*.

Maryland

We lodged at Robin Davis's. Brother Boehm preached at Martin's chapel: I added a few words. Lodged at William Leister's. At Prideaux's chapel on Sinepuxent, on *Thursday*. Who could well be kinder than the proprietor of this name who gave us the land! I was led to be very plain on *Friday* at Bowen's chapel: there is life here. Lodged at Samuel Porter's,[29] the steward of the circuit; he is a solemn man in his appearance, as an official character ought to be. I have had, in my own spirit and flesh, trials and sufferings and also strong consolations. Paid a visit to William Quinton on *Saturday*.

Sunday, 8. At Snow Hill the rain prevented more from attending than just filled the house. After preaching I met the society, white and coloured: the exercises of the day employed three hours. Lodged with B. Dewer:[30] I spoke to a feeling people at Swan's Cut meeting house.[31] On *Monday* we went on to Hometown. Methodist preachers politicians! what a curse! This is a rude, cold spring, and I feel it sensibly: my jaws are still painful, and I cannot eat hard food. O for faith and patience! *Tuesday morning* I found Bishop M'Kendree had begun meeting. In the evening I preached on Romans viii, 1; it was a very solemn time—doubtless the last with some of us.

Wednesday, 11. I preached at Newtown; we were crowded. This is a flourishing little place, and we have a beautiful little chapel. We came on, and once more visited Samuel Smith:[32] I found him calm and happy in God after strong temptations. I preached at Curtis's chapel to a crowded and attentive house. There is a great change for the better in the morals and manners of all ranks of people in this end of the peninsula, and none

[29] Samuel Porter, a class leader, opened his house for preaching long before there was a Methodist Church in Snow Hill. When in 1802 a lot was acquired, and the next year the predecessor of the present Whatcoat Church was erected, Porter's name appears among the trustees. He was the father of the Rev. John S. Porter. (Boehm, *op. cit.*, 123, 124, 153; Hallman, *op. cit.*, 357.)

[30] Hallman (*op. cit.*, 109) says that Dewer lived in Snow Hill. However, a search of Worcester County records reveals no such name nor one of kindred spelling.

[31] This meeting house was near Swans Cut, a straight or stream that flowed across the Maryland-Virginia boundary below Welbourne, Worcester County. Herman's map of 1673 shows a Swansecut Creek just south of Chincoteague Inlet.

[32] Samuel Smith lived near Crisfield, Somerset County. (See *Journal* entries and notes for May 21, 1799, and April 20, 1802.)

pretend to deny that the Methodists have wrought it. I rode down to Francis Water's,[33] in Potato Neck. They keep me busy: I must preach; I am senior; have been long absent; some never expected to hear me again; possibly, I may never come again: I am reminded that such and such I dandled in my lap: rich, too, thirty years ago, would not let me approach them; now I must visit them and preach to them; and the Africans, dear, affectionate souls, bond and free, I must preach to them. O God, give us the poor! Preached at the chapel on *Friday*: lodged with Stoughton Maddox. On *Tuesday* I had the use of the Presbyterian meeting house:[34] it being court time, we were crowded. After dining I faced a storm of wind in our route to Salisbury.

Sabbath, 15. At Salisbury I preached at Quantico chapel: we held an ordination after sacrament. I met the society, and afterward gave a long exhortation to the Africans. On *Monday* I preached at Ennall's chapel, dined at the widow Ennall's, rode on twelve miles to Cambridge, and lodged with Doctor Edward White. *Tuesday* I gave them a discourse in Cambridge. Called upon George Ward, and rode forward to Thomas Foster's pleasant cottage. On *Wednesday* I had a meeting at Washington chapel: it was a quiet, solemn, and feeling time. I met the society to my great comfort: they are faithful. On *Thursday* we opened the Philadelphia conference at Easton,[35] and went with despatch and great harmony through our usual work. We had preaching as usual, and a camp meeting in the neighbourhood: the stations were read off with much solemnity, and we parted in peace. What a grand and gracious time we have had!

[33] The Water's home was near Quantico, the present Wicomico County, Maryland. Because both father and son were named Francis, and because the latter was finishing his course at the University of Pennsylvania in 1810, the statement of Henry Boehm, who was present, that the call was made upon Francis H. Waters, Esquire, is probably correct. (Boehm, *op. cit.*, 281.) Francis Waters, the son (1792–1868), had a distinguished career as educator and Christian leader. At the age of twenty-six he became the president of Washington College, Chestertown, Maryland, and was president of the organizing convention of the Methodist Protestant Church and subsequently of two of its General Conferences. (Colhouer, *op. cit.*, 182–92; Drinkhouse: *History of Methodist Reform*, II, 493, 494.)

[34] This was the second structure erected in 1765 and stood about seventy-five yards north of the Manokin River, Princess Anne, Somerset County, Maryland. It is claimed that here the Rev. Francis Makemie, earliest apostle of Presbyterianism, erected the first Presbyterian church in America. (Page: *Life Story of Francis Makemie*, 48, 138 ff.; Torrence: *Old Somerset on the Eastern Shore of Maryland*, 244, 245.)

[35] Easton was the scene of Joseph Hartley's confinement in the Talbot County jail from July to October, 1779. His sermons during imprisonment sufficiently strengthened the society to erect in 1787 Ebenezer Church. In 1810 Easton was host to the Philadelphia Conference for the first time. One historian says that this conference "was held in connection with a camp meeting in a beautiful grove, on the western suburbs of Easton." (Todd: *Methodism of the Peninsula*, 49.) However, its regular sessions were held in the second Ebenezer Church, rebuilt in 1790, and were presided over by Bishops Asbury and McKendree. At this conference John Emory, later a bishop, was received on trial. (Boehm, *op. cit.*, 282, 283.)

how kind and affectionate the people! There have been some serious changes of my making:—may I please the Lord, and all men to edification and consolation! We have added nine, located nine, and stationed seventy-four preachers. On *Saturday* we came away at five o'clock to Henry Downs's: my host and his wife are old acquaintances and friends; we met and parted with the feelings of such. I went on and dined with Philip Harrington[36] at Greensboro, another ancient friend: we reached Dover at the end of fifty miles' ride for the day. Bishop M'Kendree preached at night; I followed with a few observations on real discipleship and true friendship to the Lord Jesus.

Delaware

Moved to Keagy's on *Monday*. I preached at Salem chapel[37] on *Tuesday*, the first of the month: on *Wednesday* at the new chapel,[38] and in the evening at the African chapel in Wilmington.

Pennsylvania

After preaching at Bethel chapel, we had a ride through the rain to Mount chapel, and here ended our *Thursday's* labours—I hope they were not in vain; lodged at Aaron Mattson's. *Friday* unwell; the appointment was at four o'clock by information; brother Boehm attended at eleven o'clock, and he was right. At Chester church I preached the funeral of Mary Withy on *Saturday*: she was awakened to a deep inquiry respecting the salvation of her soul whilst I officiated in her house at family prayer: this was in the year 1772, on my first journey to Maryland. She had lived twelve years a wife, forty-four years a widow, and for the last thirty years kept one of the best houses of entertainment on the continent: in her household management she had Martha's anxieties, to which she added the spirit and humility of Mary. Her religious experiences had been chequered by doubts and happy confidence. She slept in Jesus.

We came into Philadelphia late.

Sabbath, May 6. Preached and we had an open time. There are difficulties here; some displeased with their stations.

[36] Philip Harrington lived in Greensboro, Caroline County, a town successively known as Choptank Bridge, Bridgetown, and Greensborough. (Lednum, *op. cit.*, 262; *Journal* entry for January 23, 1778.)

[37] Salem Chapel was erected soon after land was deeded in 1809 by Robert McFarlin, schoolmaster, to a board of seven trustees. The brick church, 30 by 36 feet, was located two miles south of Ogletown, White Clay Hundred, New Castle County, Delaware. (See note under March 16, 1808.)

[38] This new chapel may have been Peniel, erected in 1809, at Newport, New Castle County, Delaware. (Hallman, *op. cit.*, 255.)

New Jersey

I came on to Burlington on *Monday*, and preached for them. *Tuesday*, gave a discourse at New Brunswick, in the court house. *Wednesday*, spoke in the new chapel, Rahway.[39] Lord, what am I?—save me from fainting under my burden! As we came out on *Thursday* a man overtook us, halted George Pickering to tell him he ought to have preached against the iniquity of taking twelve per cent. interest on loans. T. M. and he may preach themselves gray before they will preach the people good.

New York

We are in New York. *Friday*, great times here—two new houses within the year.[40] I preached at old John street: this is the thirty-ninth year I have officiated within the walls[41]; this house must come down, and something larger and better occupy its place. *Saturday*, at the widow Sherwood's. I saw William Blagburne,[42] a member of the British Conference twenty-five years, and well recommended by Doctor Coke and others.

Sabbath, 13. At the White Plains we had a cold, cloudy day, I had Divine help whilst I commented on Heb. vi, 9, 10; I added a word of special exhortation to the Africans. At Nathan Purdy's I was greatly comforted in feeling the life in the members of the little society. The preachers have preserved order and discipline, but the fire has been kept up principally by others of less official importance. At Bedford chapel on

[39] It is not known exactly when the first Methodist church in Rahway, New Jersey, was erected. A deed was given for the premises April 9, 1810, by Dr. Moses Jaques, Jr., and his wife, Susannah, to William Flatt, Abraham Flatt, Jonathan Oliver, Aaron Miller, Anthony Oliver, John Terrill, Peter Britt, and their successors. (Mooney: *History of Rahway Methodism*, 56, 59–60.)

[40] Two small congregations had developed in New York soon after 1800, one worshiping in the house of Samuel Walgrove, where George Suckley was active, and the other meeting in the home of Mrs. Joanna DeGroot. The two groups coalesced to form Bedford Street Church, which was built at the corner of Bedford and Morton streets and dedicated late in 1810. The Bedford Street Church merged in 1913 with the present Metropolitan Temple Methodist Church. The other new church mentioned by Asbury was the Allen Street Church, which was dedicated January 6, 1811. This was a development from the older Bowery Church on Forsyth Street. (Seaman, *op. cit.*, 178–82; Records of Bedford Street Church.)

[41] Asbury first preached at John Street Church on November 12, 1771, soon after his arrival in America. The actual rebuilding, which Asbury deemed necessary, did not occur until 1817, when the chapel was demolished and a more commodious building erected. The present structure is the third to stand on the original site, replacing the 1817 building in 1841.

[42] William Blagburne came from England bearing personal letters from Coke and others but having no formal papers from the British Conference. Problems arose concerning him that were difficult to solve at the conference of 1811 in New York. (See *Journal* entry and note for May 26, 1811; see letter of May 12, 1810.)

Monday; after preaching we came on to Mr. Williams's: I baptized his child, Francis Asbury; may all such be the real children of God! *Tuesday*, a long, cold, hilly, rough ride, brought us by the widow Sandford's to Prince Rowe's: we had a crowded congregation. *Wednesday* we passed a small, but excellent house for our people.[43] I dined with brother Neice, Dover, and preached at Amenia.

Massachusetts

A heavy ride on *Thursday* brought us to E. King's, Egremont: brother Crawford preached, and I added a few warnings on the shortness and uncertainty of life.

Friday, 18. Came through Great Barrington: chiefly of the Anglican Church here. Called at Mr. Steam's—kind and generous; thence by Lenox to Pittsfield. I have found it somewhat difficult to keep my mind in continual prayer whilst travelling these rude, rough, rocky roads. On *Saturday* I indulged in a little rest: wrote some letters.

Sabbath, 20. I opened our solemn assembly at half-past ten o'clock, on Phil. iii, 17–21; there was great heaviness in the congregation. Bishop M'Kendree spoke in the afternoon: his subject was well chosen and well improved. There was also a prayer meeting, and in the Congregational house George Pickering preached. We sat in conference until *Saturday*: amongst the ordinations was that of Stephen Bamford, recommended from Nova Scotia for elder's orders. We have stationed eighty-four preachers, sent two missionaries—one to Michigan, and one to Detroit. There was a considerable deficiency in our funds, which left the unmarried preachers a very small pittance.

Sabbath, 27. Daniel Hitt preached in the morning, and Francis Asbury in the afternoon. We came away on *Tuesday*. On *Wednesday* we crossed the perpetual hills, and were willing to dine and rest a little. After refreshment we proceeded on over the beautiful Connecticut bridge and gained Sunderland for the evening. Lodged at Mr. Leonard's. I resolved to send a missionary among these rude wilds: my feelings are strong towards the souls in the little towns on this route. We reached Northfield in twenty miles' riding, stopped at Mr. Houghton's.

New Hampshire

Reached Chester[44] on *Thursday evening*. Dark, dark!

Friday, June 1. Fasted from six o'clock yesterday until this evening at

[43] This was the chapel at Pawling, New York. (See *Journal* entry for June 6, 1811.)

[44] Asbury meant Winchester, New Hampshire. Henry Boehm in his *Reminiscences* says "On Thursday (1810) reached Winchester and were the welcome guests of Caleb Alexander."

six o'clock. I spent some time in prayer and exhortation at Elias Marble's. *Saturday*, close application to writing[45] and reading.

Sunday, 3. I officiated in the morning, and Henry Boehm in the evening: I think my words pierced the hearts of some like a sword. I neither spared myself nor my hearers. *Monday*, occupied in writing and reading. On *Wednesday* we opened our conference in the Presbyterian church. We had appointed a camp meeting within three miles, where there was preaching three times a day. The ordinary business being gone through, I read off the stations on *Monday*, and closed, as usual, with solemn prayer. There was a work of God manifestly, and opposition rose powerfully: we regretted we could not stay two days more. Although amongst strangers, we were kindly entertained. And shall not our prayers be heard on behalf of these people? yea, verily; and Methodism shall raise Zion from the dust.

Massachusetts

We came away, over bleak rocks and hills, through Fitzwilliam to Winchester. I preached in a new, neat Methodist chapel of our own building. Next day to Waltham; and the day after to Boston. My mind has enjoyed much of God, and great consolation: I only want every minute and moment to be in prayer, mental or vocal.

Sunday, 17. I spoke in the old chapel in the morning, with freedom; in the evening at the new chapel, with less liberty, but there was manifest power in the word. On *Monday* I wrote five letters of supplication to our brethren in Baltimore, Georgetown, Alexandria, Norfolk, and Charleston, for a congregational collection for the use of the new chapel here. Set out, winding my way through the crooked streets of the city, and passed through country villages to Easton. A young brother has lately died here in great triumph. *Tuesday* at Somerset, I gave them a discourse —it was close preaching.

Rhode Island

On *Wednesday*, at Warren, my audience gave me a little of their attention. Our preachers get wives and a home, and run to their *dears* almost every night: how can they, by personal observation, know the state of the families it is part of their duty to watch over for good? We kept on our way to Rhode Island. O, the death, the formality in religion! Surely the zealous, noisy Methodists, cannot but do good here! At Bristol, on *Thursday*, the truth was manifested, whilst I spoke with power to the

[45] See letter to Coke, June 2, 1810.

consciences of the people. The favourite preacher is removed hence,[46] sinners and saints are displeased at this; my labours stand for nothing; I must take my share of reproach. We lodged at a friend's house, and sent our horses to a tavern. I thank them even for this—what are we? *Friday*, humbled ourselves. I preached at Zoar chapel:[47] I spared not, and the truth was felt. Visited T. Barker, and lodged with friend Ayerts. We are on our lees here—no riding of circuits, local preaching, and stations filled in the towns. My soul is bowed down by the consideration of the state of the Church.

Sunday, 24. I have preached three times to-day. I officiated in the evening, because it was observed that at the stated hours people ought to attend their own places of worship, and because I knew there were not a few who were ashamed to be seen going to a Methodist meeting: eight o'clock screened them very well. I indulged a desire I felt to speak to the soldiers of the garrison at Fort Wolcott[48]—there are faithful souls there. Colonel Beall had received orders, and was bidding farewell, to go and take a command in Maryland: I knew not which felt most, but I think the colonel; the soldiers loved him as a father: it was, indeed, a painful parting. *Monday* we set out.

Connecticut

Tuesday evening brought us to New London. I called, on my way, to see Mr. Rogers:[49] we refreshed body and soul by eating, talking, and prayer. I have seen Jesse Lee's History for the first time: it is better than I expected.[50] He has not always presented me under the most favourable

[46] The Rev. Samuel Merwin "was removed at the end of his first year by Asbury and greatly to the disgust of the people whose words of dissatisfaction not always kindly expressed gave the good Bishop great pain." (Upham: *History of the Methodist Episcopal Church, Bristol, R.I.*, 54 A, 55.)

[47] Zoar Chapel was perhaps about two miles from Bristol.

[48] See note under May 29, 1809.

[49] Probably Isaac Rogers, one of those enrolled as the original members of the class formed in New London on October 11, 1793.

[50] Jesse Lee's book *A Short History of the Methodists in the United States*, published in 1810, was the first history of American Methodism. Asbury and Lee were opponents in several administrative matters, and the antagonism between the two men deepened with the years. In 1800 Lee tied with Whatcoat on the first ballot for bishop, and Whatcoat was elected by four votes on the second. Lee is said to have felt that Asbury brought about his defeat, and he later accused Asbury of "electioneering" and discriminating against him in appointments to prevent his election to the General Conference. (See his letter to Asbury, April 10, 1815.) The General Conference of 1808 refused to publish Lee's book because it was deemed to be a "simple and crude narrative" and recommended a "rule to prevent improper publications" and to avoid "that contempt which is poured upon us by improper publications." (*Journal of the General Conference, 1808*, 87, 92.) This action was due to the fact that Asbury did not

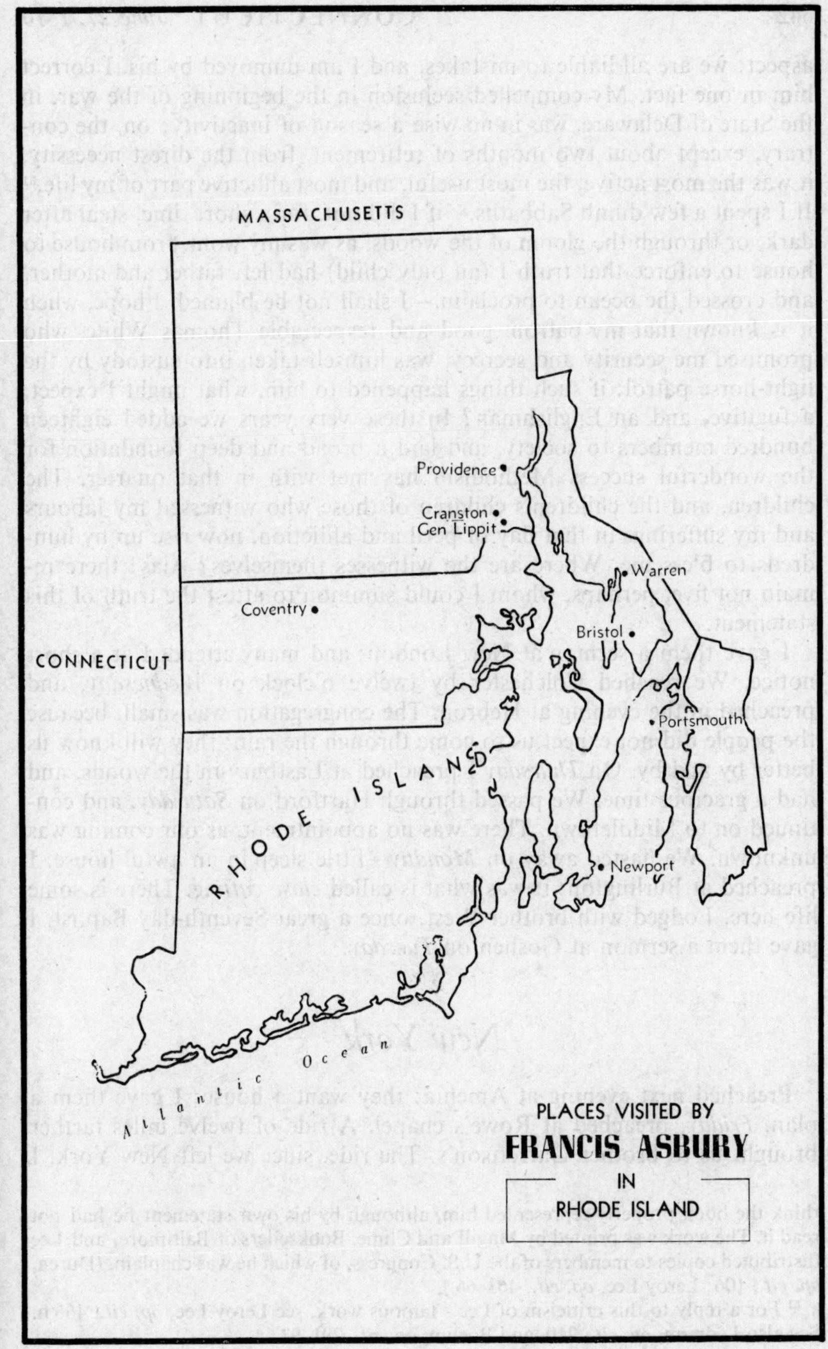
MASSACHUSETTS
CONNECTICUT
RHODE ISLAND
Providence
Cranston
Gen Lippit
Warren
Coventry
Bristol
Portsmouth
Newport
Atlantic Ocean
PLACES VISITED BY
FRANCIS ASBURY
IN
RHODE ISLAND

aspect: we are all liable to mistakes, and I am unmoved by his. I correct him in one fact. My compelled seclusion in the beginning of the war, in the State of Delaware, was in no wise a season of inactivity; on the contrary, except about two months of retirement, from the direst necessity, it was the most active, the most useful, and most afflictive part of my life.[51] If I spent a few dumb Sabbaths,—if I did not, for a short time, steal after dark, or through the gloom of the woods, as was my wont, from house to house to enforce that truth I (an only child) had left father and mother, and crossed the ocean to proclaim,—I shall not be blamed, I hope, when it is known that my patron, good and respectable Thomas White, who promised me security and secrecy, was himself taken into custody by the light-horse patrol: if such things happened to him, what might I expect, a fugitive, and an Englishman? In these very years we added eighteen hundred members to society, and laid a broad and deep foundation for the wonderful success Methodism has met with in that quarter. The children, and the children's children of those who witnessed my labours and my sufferings in that day of peril and affliction, now rise up by hundreds to bless me. Where are the witnesses themselves? Alas! there remain not five, perhaps, whom I could summon to attest the truth of this statement.

I gave them a sermon at New London; and many attended at a short notice. We reached Colchester by twelve o'clock on *Wednesday*, and preached in the evening at Hebron. The congregation was small, because the people did not expect us to come through the rain: they will know us better by and by. On *Thursday* I preached at Eastbury in the woods, and had a gracious time. We passed through Hartford on *Saturday*, and continued on to Middletown. There was no appointment, as our coming was unknown. We hasted away on *Monday*—little sleep in an awful house. I preached at Burlington: it was what is called *close cutting*. There is some life here. Lodged with brother West, once a great Seventh-day Baptist. I gave them a sermon at Goshen on *Tuesday*.

New York

Preached next evening at Amenia: they want a house; I gave them a plan. *Friday*, preached at Rowe's chapel. A ride of twelve miles farther brought us to brother Garrettson's. The ride, since we left New York, I

think the book properly represented him, although by his own statement he had not read it. The work was printed by Magill and Clime, Booksellers of Baltimore, and Lee distributed copies to members of the U.S. Congress, of which he was chaplain. (Duren, *op. cit.*, 106; Leroy Lee, *op. cit.*, 463–66.)

[51] For a reply to this criticism of Lee's famous work, see Leroy Lee, *op. cit.*, 466 n. See also Lednum, *op. cit.*, 210, and Boehm, *op. cit.*, 291–93.

presume to be six hundred miles. Our *ease in Zion* makes me feel awful: who shall reform the reformers? Ah, poor dead Methodists! I have seen preachers' children wearing gold—brought up in pride. Ah, mercy, mercy!

Sunday, *July* 8. I preached in the chapel to a small congregation. *Monday*, crossed the North River, came through Esopus to John Crawford's, hungry enough.

We reached New Durham. We prayed at Runyan's, and gave away books. The people came to hear me: spent with labour and sorrow, how could I preach? I hope the truth was felt. Lodged with father Hubbert.[52] We bent our way up Catskill,[53] and crossed the mountains to Middleburg. Some foolish boys were at cards; we were, however, respectfully treated. I prayed heartily for the family, and gave away some good books, and blessed the household in the name of the Holy Trinity: shall our blessing be lost? We directed our course towards the New Sharon camp meeting. I know not if the people might not starve in the mountains, were it not for the saw-mills and lumber. We came into the camp. On *Thursday*, I preached in the camp in the morning, and Henry Boehm at four o'clock in the afternoon, in German. I took occasion to direct a special exhortation to the members of the quarterly meeting. *Friday*, travelled forward to Cherry Valley,[54] and rested at brother Farley's.[55] Our sister complained that I could not often be seen—she wished to be a few minutes in my company at Trenton; but she was afraid I was crowded. I told her that all who wished to see me might be indulged in the back settlements—a cabin has not always two rooms. At Litchfield I visited the pious and aged Arnolds. Our ride of fifty miles, with abstinence, has made us faint. *Saturday*, through the Eaton of Chenango to Cazenovia—a ride of forty miles. I pray always: prayer is my life.

Sabbath, 15. I preached in Silas Bliss's barn. *Wednesday*. I arrived this evening at Daniel Dorsey's. *Friday*. Our conference began to-day.[56]

Sabbath, 22. Preached at the encampment. *Wednesday*. Conference

[52] Hubbert was a church leader at Livingstonville, six miles above Durham in the southwest corner of Schoharie County.

[53] This was Catskill Creek, which Asbury had followed for miles. Its pass in the northeast sector of the Catskill Mountains makes accessible a route to the north and west of the mountain area.

[54] Cherry Valley was located about five miles west of Sharon campground.

[55] Reuben Farley was received on trial a week later at the organizational session of the Genesee Conference. He was appointed to Scipio, where David Eddy was leader, and located in 1816, having served six years in this general area.

[56] This was the Genesee Conference, which was organized in a large granary on the Dorsey farm. It had sixty-three members, including those on trial, and was divided into four districts, the territory being taken from the Philadelphia and New York conferences. Asbury and McKendree were criticized for forming this new conference, but their action was approved by the New York Conference and by the General Conference of 1812. (Boehm, *op. cit.*, 297–302.)

ended—great order and despatch in business—stationed sixty-three preachers. Came away to Geneva. *Thursday*. Went around Seneca Lake. *Friday*. Bread and water. Came to New Town[57] and stopped at the widow Dunn's a few minutes for prayer, and continued on down to Tioga Point,[58] and housed with Captain Clark.[59]

Pennsylvania

We[60] have made forty-seven miles to-day. *Saturday*. We must needs come the Northumberland road;[61] it is through an awful wilderness. We stopped at Eldred's;[62] they are English, and disciples of Priestley.[63] Alas! Read and prayed in the woods. I leave the rest to God. If the cry of *want of order* came from God, the appointment of the Genesee Conference was one of the most judicious acts of our episcopacy. We stationed sixty-three preachers, and cured some, till then, incurable cases. In the last three days and a half we have ridden one hundred and forty miles: what mountains, hills, rocks, roots, and ruts! Brother Boehm was thrown from the sulky, but, providentially, not a bone broken.

Sabbath, 29. In the wilderness; but God is with us. Wretched lodging, and two dollars! Whilst busy in writing, John Brown[64] came and took us to his cabin. We forded the swollen and rapid streams three times; the Loyalsock was the worst. We have spent the remainder of the day in reading, singing, and prayer. The rains had increased the streams, so that we kept our retreat on *Monday*. *Tuesday*. At the fordings we found drift logs obstructing the way: the stream was very full, and our toil through it great. Two active, bold men, with the aid of a canoe, got us

[57] New Town was the present Elmira, New York.

[58] Tioga Point was the present Athens, Pennsylvania.

[59] Captain Benjamin Clark, a Revolutionary soldier and a Methodist, migrated from Tolland, Connecticut, to Wilkes-Barre, where he was one of the first settlers. He settled in Frenchtown in 1784 and in Ulster a year later. In his home Henry B. Bascomb, who later became a bishop, was converted in 1811. (Palmer, *op. cit.*, 76–77.)

[60] Asbury was now accompanied by Henry Boehm and Anning Owen. (See Boehm's account of the journey in his *Reminiscences*, 303–10.)

[61] The Northumberland Road originated at Harrisburg and ran northward from Northumberland to Tioga Point. (See *Historic Highways of America* and *Old Trails and Roads in Penn's Land*.)

[62] Eldred's tavern was at the present Eldredsville.

[63] Joseph Priestley (1733–1804) an English Presbyterian theologian and sclentist, came to America and settled in Northumberland in 1794. He later became a Unitarian. (See *Columbia Encyclopedia*, 1440; *Dictionary of American Biography*, XV, 223–26.)

[64] John H. Brown, a native of England, was a recluse who lived in Elkland Township on Bear Mountain between Hillsgrove and Lincoln Falls. (See the interesting account in Boehm, *op. cit.*, 305–7.) The name of the recluse seems to have been Bown, although both Asbury and Boehm called him Brown. His descendants still live in the area. ("Now and Then," Muncy Historical Society, Muncy, Pa., VI, 160; XI, 112–13.)

and the horses safe over. Thunder and rain, and an awful mountain, were now before us; but God brought us safe to Muddy Creek.[65] Deep roads and swollen streams we had enough of on our route to Northumberland on *Wednesday*. After waiting two hours at Morehead's ferry,[66] on *Thursday morning*, we got over the Susquehanna, and dined at Ferguson's;[67] these are Methodists lately from Ireland. Lodged at Mr. Folke's.[68] *Friday*, to Middletown.[69] We here broke bread with Doctor Romer,[70] a German, who has translated our Discipline for his countrymen. My friends came in haste and gladness to see me: we prayed and parted, for time was precious. At Lancaster I was unwell. Fifteen letters met me here, and they were to be answered, and I had but a day. I preached in father Boehm's chapel.

Sabbath, August 5. Preached in Lancaster morning and evening. After forty years' labour we have a neat little chapel of our own. *Monday*, away for Columbia, and preached there at twelve o'clock. Came on to Little York, and arrived at seven o'clock in the evening. *Tuesday morning*, rose at four o'clock, and after writing four letters, started away, calling on friends George Nailor and Wall, stopping for the night at friend Casper Weaver's. Reached Carlisle on *Wednesday*; preached in the evening. I drew a plan for a new chapel, seventy by forty-five, of one story: the cost about two thousand dollars. Shall I be able to answer the twenty letters that have met me here? A letter, which I saw, written by one of our preachers, says he has twenty-eight appointments to fill in twenty-five days, besides meeting one thousand seven hundred in classes; it was from Allen Green.[71] *Thursday*. A very warm ride brought us to Shippensburg.[72] Lodged with brother Reid. Preached in our improved chapel. *Friday*,

[65] Muddy Creek empties into the Susquehanna near Watsontown.

[66] Morehead's ferry was between Northumberland and Sunbury.

[67] The Ferguson family lived near present Harrisburg in Dauphin County. David Ferguson was a member of the state assembly 1811–12 and 1813–14.

[68] William Foulks was assessed in Upper Paxtang Township, Dauphin County, in 1777. James Foulks was listed as an ensign in the third battalion in 1790. Evidently this family lived in Paxtang Township, Dauphin County.

[69] Middletown is nine miles southeast of Harrisburg near the juncture of the Susquehanna and Swatara rivers, at which the Pennsylvania and Union canals unite. It was incorporated in 1829. (Gordon's *Gazetteer*, 295.)

[70] Dr. Romer, a native of Switzerland, was educated for the Roman priesthood but became disgusted with the conduct of a corrupt priesthood and did not enter that office. He was awakened by the holy life and deportment of a neighbor widow named Flanagan in Middletown and joined the Methodist Church. He was a Latin as well as a German scholar. Boehm states: "At the request of Bishop Asbury and the Philadelphia Conference, I had the Methodist Discipline translated into German in 1807. I employed Dr. Romer and aided him in the translation." (*Op. cit.*, 179.)

[71] Allen Green was ordained deacon and appointed to the Monongahela Circuit in 1810.

[72] See letter to Zachary Myles, August 9, 1810.

came to Chambersburg.[73] I preached in the court house, though we have a neat little chapel; the word of truth shall not be lost. *Saturday* was awfully warm, and we had a heavy ride over three mountains.[74]

Sabbath, 12. At Fort Littleton chapel I preached; and we administered the sacrament; but as my aid was lame, the labour fell on me: though wearied and sore with travelling, I enjoyed a gracious season. *Monday*. We encountered the steep, rugged path over Sideling Hill; we had heat, rocks, dust, and then rain. Bloody Run is henceforth New Hope. I preached at Barndollar's tavern. The Lord has seven in this family who fear and worship him. This was a very wicked place; but O, what hath God wrought! *Tuesday*, we shod our horses and came away to Bedford. Here it was wished I would stop and preach, but time did not permit. I dined with brother Stevens, and kept on, fourteen miles, to Metzkeffer's. Things in this house were not as they should be: brother Boehm prayed in German. We were well treated. *Wednesday*. We rode eleven miles for our breakfast at Wynn's stone tavern, on the top of the Alleghany; thence to Mrs. Moore's in Somerset. Hard roads, and I am not well. *Thursday*. Our road, in places, was very bad: dined at Indian Creek and reached Connellsville in the evening. I enter my protest, as I have yearly for forty years against this road. Lodged once more under the roof of my dear brother Banning, junior, and christened a child for him. We have ridden, since we left Ontario, five hundred and forty miles by computation. O, what a life is this! My aid is lame, and I am obliged to drive. People call me by my name as they pass me on the road,[75] and I hand them a religious tract in German or English; or I call at a door for a glass of water, and leave a little pamphlet. How may I be useful? I am old, and feeble, and sick, and can do little. I am grieved to find that little, promising Bedford circuit is likely to be injured by one I was afraid would not do his duty; feeble in mind and body, small things are to be hoped from him. And the poor Germans! they are as sheep without a shepherd. Came to the widow Stevens's on *Friday*. *Saturday*, we reached Brownsville, and dined at Mr. Hogg's.

Sabbath, 19. I preached at the camp ground morning and evening: the congregation might have amounted to three thousand souls. There were very wicked people there I learned, who desperately libelled brother M'Kendree and the preachers, and committed other abominable offences. *Monday* I was called on to preach in the morning. I took occasion to give a solemn warning to certain sons of Belial, that they would be watched, and their names published: I felt much, but God was in the truth. I suffered a great deal from hard lodging, and want of fire in the damps of

[73] See letter to Lewis Myers, August 10, 1810.

[74] See letter to Henry Smith, August 11, 1810.

[75] This is an indication of the widespread knowledge of Asbury among the people as he made his annual tours over eastern United States.

the morning. There were about one hundred tents, besides wagons. To-night a watch night. We started away on *Tuesday*. Surely this camp meeting will be remembered in time, and its fruits seen in eternity. On *Thursday* I dined with Benjamin Fell and family: the old pair, about seventy, are patiently waiting for the consolation of Israel. I preached at Philip Smith's at four o'clock, after beating about twenty miles over the hills. *Friday* brought us to Pittsburgh.[76] *Saturday*, O what a prize! Baxter's *Reformed Pastor* fell into my hands this morning.

Sunday, 26. Preached on the foundation of the new chapel[77] to about five hundred souls. I spoke again at five o'clock to about twice as many. The society here is lively, and increasing in numbers. We rose at four o'clock on *Monday*, and started early. I called on Esquire Johnson; his wife is a daughter to my special friend, Barnabas Johnson: how affectionately was I received by old and young! I have seen three generations of this family. We hasted away to Washington; and had heat and hard toil for travelling companions. I gave the good citizens a discourse at five o'clock: the principal members were gone to Short Creek, but others filled their places. Can any one be kinder than my kind host M'Fadden? It is reported that at Short Creek fifty persons were applicants for membership. Three hundred and thirty-five communicants. There were at this camp meeting about fifty tents and forty wagons. I have been reading Fox; his narrative concerning himself and others is truly wonderful.

Ohio

Friday we rode twenty-two miles to Barnesville. I preached in a private house. The Methodists and Friends have a kindly contest for supremacy here. *Saturday*, to James Sherrock's, a local preacher, an Englishman from Lancashire. We went to Leatherwood's Creek.

Sunday, *September* 2. Rested and preached in Queensbury chapel, to a full house convened at a short notice. I was very plain. The prospects are encouraging in Wills's Creek circuit. I can read and think as in years past. My health is good, and I am in perfect peace and love! O, the goodness of God to me! I have journalized very little of my life and exercises, and less of my sufferings; but the Lord knoweth. On *Monday* we had to beat the path to Jesse Waller's. Though feeble and faint, I preached and baptized some children. We had one room to lodge in, plenty of beds, and abundance of food for man and beast. *Tuesday*, we passed many a jolting place, rough with roots of trees and logs: we were willing to stop at Polk's and

[76] See letters to Jacob Gruber, August 25, 1810, and August 26, 1810.

[77] This was the first Methodist house of worship to be built in Pittsburgh, although a society had existed there since 1796. Pittsburgh was now the largest town in the region, having a population in 1810 of 4,768.

take a little food. From hence we were politely conducted to Peter Monroe's. Elder Boehm preached in the house of Mr. Reynolds. *Wednesday*. To my surprise, I was asked to baptize Joseph Asbury Reynolds.[78] We continued on by the Salt Works to Marietta,[79] where I lectured to a few people. *Thursday*, to Mogg's Creek. We tasted neither bread nor water, until we reached father Shumen's, twenty-three miles. We held meeting at night, and I gave them a discourse. *Friday*, to Waterford, and Samuel Miller's fertile soil; but he has, as yet, made little progress in improvement. Here is a family, the grandfather and grandmother of which died in the Lord; so the father and mother promise to do; and the children have begun to live to God: I preached for them and their neighbours.

West Virginia

Saturday. I hear of a camp meeting at Little Kenawha, and must needs go there.[80] After toiling through bad roads and accidents at the ferry to detain us, we are here this *Saturday night* at nine o'clock, safe at the house of the brother of Wilson Lee.[81] Lord, prepare me by thy grace for the patient endurance of hunger, heat, labour, the clownishness of ignorant piety, the impudence of the impious, unreasonable preachers, and more unreasonable heretics and heresy!

Sunday, 9. I preached at the camp twice. Souls were converted, and we hope much good was done. We ordained John Holmes an elder. *Monday*, came away. At B. Wolf's, we gave them Dutch and English sermons. *Tuesday*, preached at the Point Wood's court house, to a large congregation.

Ohio

We lodged at Mr. Browning's, on the other side of the river.[82] On *Wednesday* I preached in a school house on a bluff opposite Blennerhassett's island.[83] Colonel Putnum, son of the renowned general of that

[78] Joseph Asbury was the name of the bishop's father.

[79] This was Asbury's first and only visit to this section of southern Ohio and the adjoining region of West Virginia. The first Methodist circuit in the Muskingum and Little Kenawha valleys was in 1799. (Smeltzer, *op. cit.*, 85.)

[80] This 1810 trip west was the only time that Asbury made four crossings of the Ohio River en route.

[81] Boehm says, "We were the guests of Richard Lee, brother of Rev. Wilson Lee."

[82] Asbury and Boehm recrossed the Ohio River at Belpre, Ohio. (Boehm, *op. cit.*, 316.)

[83] This is the largest island in the Ohio River. Located at the mouth of the Little Kenawha River at Parkersburg, West Virginia, the island was owned for a time by George Washington. A large tract of land on the island was purchased in 1798 by a wealthy Irish immigrant, Herman Blennerhassett. He was an accomplice of Aaron

name, invited me to the house of Waldo, grandson of the old chief: I had a very interesting interview with several revolutionary officers, emigrants to this country, from good old Massachusetts. *Thursday*, we took our departure from the banks of *the beautiful river* (the Ohio), beautiful indeed! How rich the hanging scenery of its wood-crowned hills! Our route was towards and near the Hocking River, a rude, toilsome way: we were glad to stop a moment, and dine at Esquire Rilshure's. We continued on to Burch's, and lodged. I feel the effect of toil in every bone and muscle, but I have great consolations. *Friday*, at camp meeting at Atkins's. I lodged at Barker's. The dear infant died: Ah! what a cry! 'twas a *mother's* cry. *Saturday* I preached in the camp, a humiliation sermon. Mr. Lindley, a Presbyterian clergyman, preached after me. The ground for the camp is beautiful; order is preserved, and there will be good done.

Sunday, 16. We had sinners of all varieties to hear us. I spoke plainly. On *Monday* I preached by special request. Great order has been observed, much good done, and the hearts of many prepared for the future reception of the truth. *Tuesday*, we started away, although I was ill fitted to drive a wilderness road. At Donnelly's, we dined, prayed, and gave away books. *Wednesday* we reached Chilicothe, and put up with our old friend, Doctor Tiffin: I was happy to find him no longer in public life, but a private citizen, respectable and respected, and the work of God revived in his soul. I have preached to many souls in the late camp meetings: Lord, give thy word success! My own soul is humbled and purified: Glory be to God! *Thursday*, I preached at Chilicothe at four o'clock. On *Friday*, engaged in private duties. I paid a visit to my much-esteemed friend, Governor Worthington, at Mount Prospect: he requested me to furnish an inscription for the tombstone of his sainted and much-loved sister, Mary Tiffin; I gave him Luke x, 42, second line to the end. *Saturday*, closely occupied with books and my pen.

Sunday, 23. Preached, and baptized a whole family of Quaker descent: I took occasion to give a lecture on the expediency of this Christian rite, and the duty and additional obligations it imposed upon parents. I spoke again in the evening, and was awfully severe; perhaps too much so. On *Monday* we came away to Samuel Davis's. *Tuesday*, I baptized a child, Thomas Asbury Parvias. *Wednesday*. We have had a hard journey to-day, and after two hours' ride through the woods in the night, we sheltered ourselves under the hospitable roof of Esquire Miranda. *Thursday*, we crossed the Little Miami; dined at Taulman's; and came into Cincinnati oppressed and faint with sickness, excessive heat, and loss of rest. *Friday*, Henry Boehm preached in German: I added an exhortation in English.

Burr in his grandiose scheme of erecting an empire in the West, and most of the treasonable plans were made at Blennerhassett's island estate. (McCartney: *Not Far from Pittsburgh, the Island of Sorrows*, 123 ff.)

Sunday, 30. I preached morning and evening: it was a season of deep seriousness with the congregations. I felt an intimate communion with God; and a great love to the people, saints and poor sinners. *Monday*, met the society. *Tuesday*, we bade farewell to our attentive and affectionate friends in Cincinnati. The great river was covered with mist until nine o'clock, when the airy curtain rose slowly from the waters, gliding along in expanded and silent majesty. We laboured around the rough banks and over the dry ridge of Bank Lick Creek to Barnes's. Alas! for the people—there is a great call for missionaries for Eagle Creek and the Ridge. *Wednesday*, came to Conge's to dine, and stopped at Mubury's to lodge. *Thursday*, to Jesse Griffin's. *Friday*, at rest. Preached for the people. There is a drought prevailing; and the heat is very intense.

Kentucky

Saturday we started away for Lexington, and were well soaked with a glorious shower when about nine miles from the town. Henry Boehm preached.

Sunday, October 7. I preached at eleven o'clock, and gave an exhortation after five o'clock sermon in the evening. *Monday*, reading the best of books, and writing letters. *Tuesday*, at Winchester, Clark county, we stopped at Leroy Cole's.[84] *Wednesday*, busily occupied in my room. *Thursday*, I preached to a very attentive congregation. *Friday*, called at Major Martin's. I have time to-day to complete Mark's Gospel. I mark well that all the Evangelists concur in this;—that the high-priest delivered Jesus to the Roman governor as the Son of God, upon his own confession. *Saturday* I preached at Abraham Cassell's, brother to Leonard Cassell, of Maryland.[85] I learn that Benedict Swope,[86] my old acquaintance, died last winter: he was a man of more than common mind and gifts, and might have been much more useful than I fear he was.

Sunday, 14. At Nicholasville I preached about an hour to Presbyterians, Methodists, and I know not whom.[87] *Monday*. This has been an awful day

[84] Leroy Cole (1749–1830) was born in Virginia and became a traveling preacher in 1777. He was a member of the Christmas Conference in 1784. He located in 1785 and went westward, settling near Lexington, Kentucky, where he became a farmer. He was afterward a member of the Kentucky Conference. (Boehm, *op. cit.*, 322, 323.)

[85] Abraham Cassell, brother of the Rev. Leonard Cassell of the Baltimore Conference, immigrated from Pipe Creek, Maryland, in 1808. He lived near Nicholasville, Kentucky. Boehm preached at his home on Sunday evening. (*Ibid.*, 323.)

[86] Benedict Swope (Schwope) was a preacher of the United Brethren. It was through him that Asbury met Philip Otterbein, minister of the German Reform Church and the founder of the United Brethren in Christ. Otterbein assisted at the consecration of Asbury as superintendent in 1784. (Drury: *A History of the Church of the United Brethren in Christ*, 115, 144.)

[87] A meetinghouse had been built at Nicholasville in 1799. (Arnold, *op. cit.*, I, 176.)

to me—I visited Francis Poythress: "If thou be he—but O, how fallen!"[88]

Tuesday, 16. After a ride of thirty miles, we found comfort and a welcome with Racliff, in Woodford county.

Wednesday, 17. Came by lowly-seated Frankfort. Here are elegant accommodations provided for those who make the laws, and those who break them; but there is no house of God. Lodged with Edward Talbot. *Thursday*, writing. *Friday*, abstaining, praying, and writing. *Saturday*, at William Adams's[89] log chapel I preached to a small assembly.

Sunday, 21. At Shelbyville I preached in the court house: we were crowded. M'Chord, a seceding minister, preached two sermons upon the Deity of the Holy Spirit: he was orthodox, and indulged in some fine flights of eloquence. Elder Wilson spoke in the evening. *Monday*, I preached at Henry Lyon's. Lodged with Mr. Hardin.[90] *Tuesday*, I preached at Philip Taylor's.[91] My mind is in great peace. The Methodists are all for camp meetings; the Baptists are for public baptizings: I am afraid his dippping, with many, is the *ne plus ultra* of Christian experience. *Wednesday*, I rest at Taylor's. Writing and reading. *Thursday*, rode to Joseph Ferguson's, twenty-five miles. *Saturday*. We have spent this day in a visit to the family of Captain Cyrus Talbot: may salvation come in power, and suddenly, to this amiable and interesting household!

Sunday, 28. I spoke at Ferguson's chapel for an hour, and the wind beating on my head; may the word of truth be deeply and long felt! We have an open door set wide to us in Mississippi; the preachers there sent but one messenger to conference—they could not spare more; they keep their ground like soldiers of Christ, and men of God who care for the cause and work of the Lord. Good news from the South—great prospects within the bounds of the South Carolina Conference. *Monday*, we rode rapidly to Philip Taylor's. *Wednesday*, came sixteen miles.

Thursday, *November* 1. Began conference in great peace and good order.[92] *Friday*. Day of humiliation and fasting. I preached in an open

[88] Poythress was living with his sister twelve miles below Lexington. Boehm points out that this reference to Poythress had been misunderstood and had led persons to believe that the noted preacher had fallen into sin, and explains that Poythress was in a state of insanity. (Boehm, *op. cit.*, 323, 324.)

[89] William Adams (1785–1835) was born in Virginia. He was the nephew of William Watters, the first native American traveling preacher. He was taken in childhood to Kentucky and lived near Lexington. He joined the conference in 1814 and continued as a traveling preacher until his death.

[90] Hardin was evidently Mark Hardin, son of Colonel John J. Hardin, who was slain by the Indians. Mark Hardin was registrar of the land office in Kentucky.

[91] Philip Taylor was a Revolutionary soldier who was present at the siege of Yorktown and the surrender of Cornwallis. He went to Kentucky around 1790, where he became a local preacher. Around 1830 he joined the movement which resulted in the formation of the Methodist Protestant Church. (Arnold, *op. cit.*, I, 71.)

[92] This session of the Western Conference was held at the Brick Chapel in Shelby County, Kentucky.

house to a cold auditory. Conference progressed well; there were twenty-six admitted.

Sabbath, 4. Bishop M'Kendree preached; and I finished the meeting with an exhortation. There were elders and deacons ordained in the work. On *Thursday* I preached; speaking long, and with great plainness. We have minuted ninety-five as stationed. There is an increase of four thousand members within the bounds of this conference. I have sold my sulky, and purchased a horse, that I may more easily wind my way through the wilderness to Georgia. The reward of my toils is not to be found in this world. *Friday*, came to Philip Taylor's. *Saturday*, to Springfield Hills—a long, heavy ride.

Sabbath, 11. My mind enjoys great tranquillity. Bishop M'Kendree preached in the morning, the Presbyterians at twelve o'clock, and I spoke in the evening. There have been unpleasant times for the Presbyterians and Methodists; but they are more united now—their ministers appoint meetings for each other. *Monday*, we rode to Manoah Lasley's,[93] on Green River. To Ament's,[94] twenty-five miles. *Wednesday*, twenty-five miles to Gatton's. My body, I find, is still flesh; my mind enjoys great peace.

Tennessee

Thursday, a damp, heavy ride brought us in, about three o'clock, to James Gwinn's.[95] Whilst riding along my soul enjoys sweet and intimate communion with God. The advantages of being on horseback are: that I can better turn aside to visit the poor; I can get along more difficult and intricate roads; I shall save money to give away to the needy; and, lastly, I can be more tender to my poor, faithful beast. *Friday*, rested, fasted,

[93] Manoah Lasley, a local preacher, had immigrated from Virginia in 1795, and lived on Green River near the present Greensburg. His house was a Methodist preaching place. (Redford: *Methodism in Kentucky*, II, 148; Arnold, *op. cit.*, I, 173.)

[94] Gabriel Ament (1760–1850) was born in Germany of Roman Catholic parentage and educated for the priesthood. He came to America, where he was anathematized at Philadelphia in 1789 for renouncing Catholicism. He went to Kentucky in 1790, where he married the sister of Governor Henry Metcalf. At this time he lived at Blue Spring Grove in Barren County, where he kept a tavern. He was an exhorter and class leader, though he spoke English imperfectly. (Redford, *op. cit.*, II, 105–10.)

[95] With advancing age Asbury's *Journal* becomes sketchy. The bishop, accompanied by Bishop McKendree, James Gwinn, and Henry Boehm, had proceeded from Kentucky to Middle Tennessee. James Gwinn was a preacher who lived near Fountain Head in Sumner County, Tennessee. He was a pioneer and was a chaplain in Andrew Jackson's army at the battle of New Orleans. One of his sons, William M. Gwinn, became a member of the U.S. Senate. (McFerrin: *Methodism in Tennessee*, I, 429 ff.; Boehm, *op. cit.*, 325, 326.)

read, wrote letters. *Saturday*, visited James M'Kendree,[96] lately from Virginia.

Sabbath, 18. I rode to Gwinn's chapel[97]—a nice building. Behind it the cabins and the ground make a charming square for a camp meeting. *Monday*, we had a damp, muddy ride to friend Haines's. His wife was surprised—she recollected me. How frequently we find our wandering sheep in travelling! Since I am on horseback my fetters are gone: I meditate. and pray much more at my ease. Lodged with John M'Gee. *Tuesday*, to Dr. Tooley's. *Wednesday*. A ride of thirty miles brought us to Shaw's.[98] *Thursday*, fifteen miles to breakfast at Quarles's; twenty-five miles to supper at Elder Terry's. *Friday*, to the Crab Orchard; thence to Major Hailey's.[99] *Saturday*, to Kingston, thirteen miles; thence to Winton's, twenty miles.

Sabbath, 25. I preached at Winton's[100] in the evening. We have hard labour and suffering; but I dare not complain when I see the wretched fate of the poor Africans in slavery. We pass along so rapidly, that we have only time to pray in the houses we visit; this we have done, *except in one case*. A damp, cold, dreary rough ride brought us very hungry to Joseph Black's,[101] where man and beast were fed, and kindly entertained. *Tuesday*, we came to dinner to father Obadiah Fowler's:[102] and then pushed on to Porter's.[103] Snow most of the day. Glory be to God for the great support both of soul and body I derive from Him! *Wednesday* I rested, and gave them a sermon. The word of truth found its way to the hearts of some. *Thursday*, we were in doubt whether we should take the old or the new route:[104] we took Mahon's road,[105] and got along pretty well,

[96] James McKendree was the brother of Bishop William McKendree. He lived in Sumner County, Tennessee, at this time. Asbury and Boehm lodged at his house. The bishop's father also lived in this section. (Boehm, *op. cit.*, 325–26.)

[97] Gwinn's Chapel was located near the home of James Gwinn.

[98] Asbury and his party were again proceeding to the Holston country along the former route, crossing the Cumberland River at Walton's Ferry. Shaw lived at the present Carthage.

[99] The Hailey home was thirteen miles west of Kingston, Tennessee.

[100] John Winton lived at Muddy Creek, now Martel, four miles from Lenoir City in Loudon County, Tennessee.

[101] Esquire Joseph Black lived near Little River between Maryville and Sevierville in Sevier County, Tennessee.

[102] Fowler lived west of the Little Pigeon River near Sevierville, Tennessee.

[103] Mitchell Porter lived three miles south of Sevierville on the present Highway No. 71, between Sevierville and Gatlinburg, near Porter's Chapel. The place is now called Zion Cemetery.

[104] In previous trips from East Tennessee to western North Carolina, Asbury had gone via the Newport–Hot Springs–Marshall road to Asheville, but this year he took a different route. The "new route" was the Cataloochee Trail, an old Indian trail which leads from Cosby, Tennessee, to Cove Creek, North Carolina, along present Highway 284.

[105] Mahon's road was a new route from near Pigeon Forge on present Highway No.

thirty miles, to the gate:[106] the woman was sick; but the girls of the house were attentive and polite at Mr. Mahon's.

North Carolina

Friday, our troubles began at the foaming, roaring stream, which hid the rocks. At Cataloochee[107] I walked over a log. But O, the mountain—height after height, and five miles over! After crossing other streams, and losing ourselves in the woods, we came in, about nine o'clock at night, to Vater Shuck's.[108] What an awful day! *Saturday, December* 1. Last night I was strongly afflicted with pain. We rode, twenty-five miles, to Buncombe.

Sabbath, December 2. Bishop M'Kendree and John M'Gee rose at five o'clock, and left us to fill an appointment about twenty-five miles off.[109] Myself and Henry Boehm went to Newton's academy,[110] where I preached.

71 to the head of Cosby Creek in Cocke County, Tennessee, where it intercepted the road from Newport to the present Smoky Mountains National Park.

[106] The Mahon home stood at the point referred to as the "gate." It was a toll place. Here Asbury and his party began to ascend the mountain.

[107] The stream crossed was Cataloochee Creek. On its bank the party gave oats to their horses and asked a blessing on their own meal of bread. John McGee drove the horses through the water and Asbury, McKendree, and Henry Boehm crossed on the log. On the North Carolina side they passed through a gate and came to the settlements on Jonathan and Richland creeks. (Boehm, *op. cit.*, 328.) The former was at or near the present Cove Creek in Haywood County, and the latter was probably at the mouth of Richland Creek and Pigeon River a few miles away. They may have followed Pigeon River or gone from Cove Creek up Jonathan Creek through Dellwood Gap and along Richland Creek where it now forms Lake Junaluska, since a better-known trail led that way.

[108] "Vater Shuck" was Father Jacob Shook, who lived on Pigeon River at the present town of Clyde, North Carolina. He was the son of a Dutch immigrant, George Shook (or Shuk), who came to America in 1740. Jacob was born in Northampton County, Pennsylvania, in 1749 and went with his father to Burke County, North Carolina, a few years later. After serving in the Revolutionary War he married Isabella Weitzell and in 1786 settled at the present town of Clyde. Jacob Shook is said to have built the first frame house in the county, and it was a preaching place. The house still stands, considerably enlarged, and the attic room has been preserved with chair and pulpit. Here was formed the first Methodist society in the county, which still survives. A road marker has been erected by the Methodist Historical Society. Jacob Shook died about 1832, and numerous descendants now reside in and near Clyde. At his death he bequeathed a tract of land for a camp-meeting site, and the appointment was long known as Camp Ground. It is now Louisa Chapel, so named for Shook's unmarried granddaughter. It stands on the original camp-meeting property, and its gateway bears the date 1798. (Allen, *History of Haywood County*, 217–27, 593–96.)

[109] McKendree and McGee preached at the home of the Rev. Samuel Edney, at the present Edneyville in Henderson County. The society here is still active. (See note under October 1, 1806.) Asbury and Boehm probably stayed in the home of Daniel Killian. (See note under October 11, 1801.)

[110] For the Rev. George Newton and Newton's Academy see note under November 10, 1800. Asbury loved Newton "not only for his catholic spirit, but his strong resemblance to Bishop Whatcoat." (Boehm, *op. cit.*, 329.)

Brother Boehm spoke after me; and Mr. Newton, in exhortation, confirmed what was said. Had I known and studied my congregation for a year, I could not have spoken more appropriately to their particular cases; this I learn from those who know them well. We dined with Mr. Newton: he is almost a Methodist, and reminds me of dear Whatcoat—the same

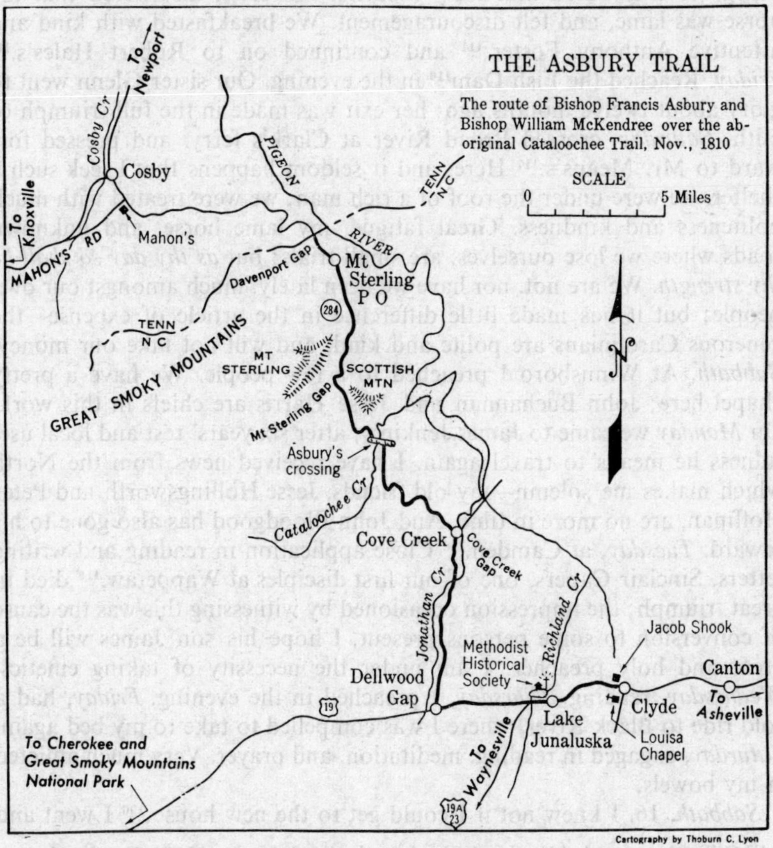

Cartography by Thoburn C. Lyon

placidness and solemnity. We visited James Patton;[111] this is, perhaps, the last visit to Buncombe. *Monday*. It was my province to-day to speak faithfully to a certain person: may she feel the force of, and profit by the truth. *Tuesday*, came thirty-three miles to Murray's at Green River.[112]

[111] For James Patton see note under October 29, 1809.

[112] Green River is between Hendersonville and Rutherfordton, North Carolina. Asbury entered Spartanburg County, South Carolina, about where Chesnee is now located.

South Carolina

Wednesday, 5, rode thirty miles to Rev. James Gilliard's.[113] I found him sick, and prescribed for him. On inquiry into the state of his soul, he expressed his confidence in God. He is alone, with a growing family, and the charge of a hundred and forty families. *Thursday*, discovered that my horse was lame, and felt discouragement. We breakfasted with kind and attentive Anthony Foster;[114] and continued on to Robert Hales's.[115] *Friday*. Reached the Fish Dam[116] in the evening. Our sister Glenn went to glory about twelve months ago; her exit was made in the full triumph of faith. *Saturday*, crossed Broad River at Clark's ferry, and pressed forward to Mr. Means's.[117] Here, and it seldom happens that I seek such a shelter, we were under the roof of a rich man; we were treated with much politeness and kindness. Great fatigue, my lame horse, and unknown roads where we lose ourselves, are small trials; but *as thy day so shall be thy strength*. We are not, nor have we been lately, much amongst our own people; but it has made little difference in the article of expense—the generous Carolinians are polite and kind, and will not take our money. *Sabbath*. At Winnsboro I preached to a few people. We have a pretty chapel here; John Buchannan and Jesse Harris are chiefs in this work. On *Monday* we came to James Jenkin's; after six years' rest and local usefulness he means to travel again. I have received news from the North which makes me solemn—my old friends, Jesse Hollingsworth and Peter Hoffman, are no more in time. And John Bloodgood has also gone to his reward. *Tuesday*, at Camden.[118] Close application in reading and writing letters. Sinclair Capers, one of our first disciples at Wappetaw,[119] died in great triumph; the impression occasioned by witnessing this was the cause of conversion to some persons present. I hope his son James will be a great and holy preacher. I am under the necessity of taking emetics. *Wednesday*, reading. *Thursday*, I preached in the evening. *Friday*, had a cold ride to Black River, where I was compelled to take to my bed again. *Saturday*, engaged in reading, meditation, and prayer. Very much afflicted in my bowels.

Sabbath, 16. I knew not if I could get to the new house;[120] I went and

[113] Gilliard was probably a local preacher who lived near the North Carolina line.

[114] Anthony Foster lived near Arcadia in Spartanburg County, South Carolina.

[115] Hale lived in upper Union County.

[116] Fishdam, near which the Glenn family lived, was the present Carlisle.

[117] Mr. Means lived in Fairfield County.

[118] "Brother Jenkins rode with us to Camden. Father Asbury met a class at night in Brother Mathis' room." (*Ibid.*)

[119] Sinclair Capers was the uncle of Bishop William Capers. (See note under January 11, 1786.)

[120] "On Friday, the 14th, we left Camden and rode to Father Rembert's. Brother William M. Kenneday, Brother Gilman, myself, and several others fixed the seats

was helped of the Lord: the house was filled, and I spoke plainly. On *Monday* I visited Thomas Boone: his father was the first to entertain me at the Lower Santee Ferry. We found our dinner at Henry Young's;[121] I was very ill. *Tuesday*, though ill able to ride, I set out for Camden. *Wednesday*, reading, writing and praying with those who visit me. *Thursday*, came to Columbia. Taylor, of the senate of the United States, lent his house for the session of our conference.[122] We have pleasing letters from York, Genesee, Jersey, Maryland, Virginia, old North and South Carolinas: rich and poor coming to God. Our fund here for special relief amounts to more than we had expected. *Saturday*, our conference began in great order, peace, and love.

Sabbath, 23. I preached, and the truth exhibited its own divine authority. Bishop M'Kendree spoke in the afternoon. We sat seven hours to business in the day, and had preaching at noon and night. *Friday* I was called upon to preach at the ordination of elders: my subject was Heb. iii, 12–14, and was applicable to at least one of them. Conference adjourned this evening: we have stationed about eighty preachers. *Saturday* came away to General Rumph's:[123] God has repaid this family for its kindness to the poor followers of the Lord Jesus: there are four sons and three daughters, gracious souls: two of the sons, Jacob and Christian, are preachers of the Gospel.

Sabbath, 30. I must consult prudence and stay at home to-day—it is stormy and I am sorely attacked in the viscera. On *Monday* we ventured away through rain and hail storms. We made about twenty miles to brother Harley's.

in the new meeting house. We spent the Sabbath there. Father Asbury preached in the morning and William M. Kenneday followed him. I preached in the evening and William Capers exhorted. Bishop Asbury was very much indisposed here for several days." (Boehm, *op. cit.*, 330.)

[121] Thomas Boone, Henry Young, and James Rembert all lived on the upper reaches of Black River.

[122] Colonel Thomas Taylor, United States Senator, was not a Methodist but was friendly. He and his family were in Washington, and he allowed his whole house to be used for the conference and the entertainment of the preachers. "He gave two brethren, Wyth and Williamson, the privilege of moving into his house and entertaining the preachers." (*Ibid.*)

[123] General Jacob Rumph was a wealthy Methodist of Orangeburg County. He had been a general in the Revolution. He was one of the first persons to welcome Asbury to South Carolina. This was the bishop's last interview with him, as the general died in 1811.

1811

1811

Asbury among the "great guns" of the garrison at Kingston in Canada

CHAPTER FORTY

South Carolina

Tuesday, January 1, 1811. On the first day of the new year we rode thirty-five miles to the widow Davis's:[1] I failed greatly in my ride. *Wednesday* came by the new road, crossing the new bridge, forty-five miles, to Charleston.

Sabbath, 6. Preached in Cumberland and Bethel chapels. *Monday* busy in writing letters: sent away fifteen.[2] I preached on *Wednesday*. *Thursday* came away and made thirty-five miles to Mr. Hale's.[3] I was weary, hungry, and sleepy. *Friday*, we crossed Lenud's ferry, and made a ride of twenty-five miles. *Saturday* reached Georgetown. I am always in fetters in this place; and were they to offer me twenty such towns as a bribe I would not visit it again; but I must do my duty without a bribe.

Sabbath, 13. I preached for the people of Georgetown twice. *Monday*, Samuel Dunwody and Thomas Mason[4] set out with us; crossing Black River we came to worthy Samuel Green's—in pleasing manners and sincere friendship an evergreen. We visited his brother Francis[5] and prayed

[1] The Widow Davis lived in upper Dorchester County.

[2] While Asbury was preaching in Charleston, Henry Boehm "attended to some important business for the Book Room, procuring drafts, etc." (Boehm, *op. cit.*, 334.)

[3] Hale lived on the main road between Clement's Ferry, five miles above Charleston, and Lenud's Ferry on the Santee. William Capers established a preaching place there on the invitation of Hale in 1811. (Capers: *Autobiography*, 141.)

[4] Dunwody had been stationed in Georgetown, and Mason had been in Charleston. Their appointments were reversed at the conference just held.

[5] Samuel and Francis Green lived near the present Hemingway or Johnsonville, south of Lynch's River.

in the family, exhorting the Africans. *Tuesday*, reached Port's ferry, and found mother Port keeping house at eighty-seven. Rafts and boats in quantities passing down the Pee Dee. *Wednesday*, made thirty miles to Mr. Newsom's,[6] where we were kindly received and politely entertained. *Thursday*, came early in the day to Priest's, and tarried with him two hours, and then mounted and continued forward to the widow Roland's.

North Carolina

Friday, came to John Martin's, Lumberton, and here I was willing to stay awhile, for the rain and cold had chilled me to the heart. *Saturday*, I am very unwell.

Sabbath, 20. I preached here, possibly for the last time; I spoke in great weakness of body; and having offered my service and sacrifice, I must change my course, and go to Wilmington. I have but a few days to make the one hundred and eighty miles in. I am happy—my heart is pure, and my eye is single—but I am sick, and weak, and in heaviness by reason of suffering and labour. Sometimes I am ready to cry out, *Lord, take me home to rest!* Courage, my soul!

Monday, 21. We began our march, and my suffering from pain in the foot was sore indeed. Came in to Amos Richardson's in the evening. The parents of this man died in peace. *Tuesday*, a ride of thirty miles brought us on to Alexander King's. I baptized this family, of whom the greater part are in society. The old people gave satisfactory evidence of a peaceful end. *Wednesday* we brought a storm into town with us. Wilmington is alive with commerce, and there is no small stir in religion. *Thursday*, brother Boehm preached. *Friday*, it was my duty to preach to-day. I am applied to for the plan of a new meeting house: this is a business of small difficulty; but who is to execute?

Sabbath, 27. I preached in the morning and afternoon. The congregations were large, and I felt my heart greatly enlarged towards them. *Monday*, rose at five o'clock, and moved off pretty soon; we cautioned the ferryman, who had placed his flat so as to be upset; he was obstinate, and would not alter her position: in jumped the horses, over went the skiff; our lives were endangered: the horses reached the opposite shore by swimming, and plunging through the mud got on dry land: our clothes and some of our books and papers were wetted, but not spoiled. We mounted and rode forward to Mount Misery, stopping to dry at Alexander King's: here we dined, and baptized some children. The evening shades closed upon us as we entered under the hospital roof of pious mother Turner, who lodged and fed me at the Wakkamaw Lake twenty-six years ago. *Tuesday*, we pushed on to Amos Richardson's, and thence

[6] John Newsom lived near Mullins.

after dinner to James Purdy's[7]: I preached in the evening. I have been deeply afflicted with an influenza; but God is with me, and supports me. *Wednesday* we had a cold ride to Newberry's: preached to a few people.

Friday, *February* 1. We reached this place this morning. Fayetteville; preaching at night. *Saturday*, I preached.

Sabbath, 3. Preached; our house is too small: preached in the afternoon; we must enlarge our house. I had a rude fall to-day, and it was a mercy that my back was not broken. *Monday*, we came over Cape Fear, lodging at Morgan's, on a solitary road. *Tuesday*, we came into Raleigh.[8] *Wednesday*, I enjoyed some very agreeable interviews with my brethren. *Thursday*. Conference begins this morning.

Sabbath, 10. I preached in the State house to two thousand souls, I presume. We have had, and mean to have, whilst conference is in session preaching three times a day: meeting sometimes holds till midnight. *Saturday*, at ten o'clock we mounted our horses in the rain, and pushed on to Powell's bridge on the Neuse River: we stopped at the house of our friend Samuel Alston,[9] who married the daughter of General Williams: this will hereafter be my stopping place. I believe there was much good done in Raleigh; and we, the preachers, are much indebted to the people for their kindness to us.

Sabbath, 17. I started on my journey this morning, contrary to my usual practice. At Benjamin Sherwood's we stopped a minute, and called the family to prayer. Came at night to Major Taylor's. *Monday*, my kind entertainer and his family made me promises to be henceforth for God; I left them with strong feelings of interest for their welfare. *Tuesday*, we reached Warrington: I must needs preach in William Ruffin's large tavern room.

Virginia

Wednesday, a cold ride to John Seward's, Brunswick county, and next day to Charles Harris's, where we were kindly and comfortably entertained. My old Virginia friends have disappeared from the earth; but it is no small consolation that they have left me their offspring—these are the children of faith and prayer. Witness the Georges, the Booths, and many

[7] James Purdy lived in Bladen County, North Carolina.

[8] Asbury, Thomas L. Douglas, and Henry Boehm stayed with William Glendenning in Raleigh during the sessions of this conference. Glendenning had gone off with O'Kelly and later became a Unitarian. Asbury and McKendree presided over this conference, which had fifty members present. Philip Bruce, Thomas L. Douglass, and John Buxton were appointed a committee to prepare rules to regulate the conference. They again took a collection for the brethren in New England. There were forty-six circuits, and eighty-two preachers received appointments. (Bennett, *op. cit.*, 563–64.)

[9] Samuel Alston lived in Warren County.

others. And God has heard the prayers of the poor Negroes for their masters: surely he is no respecter of persons! Our *Saturday's* ride was cold indeed: kind Mr. Bradley came out to the State road, and took us home with him, and fed us, and warmed us, and lodged us.

Sabbath, 24. I preached in Richmond[10] in the morning. *Monday*, started in storm and snow, and made twenty-five miles, and willingly stopped at Mr. Burroughs's: this family are in their first love. The neighbourhood begins to bow to the sceptre of the Lord Jesus. *Tuesday*, we came on to Todd's. The stage arrived late in the evening, and the passengers would go no farther that night. They were a motley mixture—Georgia speculators, planters, merchants, and gentlemanly, affable Judge Brooke; I was chaplain to the company. *Wednesday*, we were pretty soon laden with thick clay; nevertheless, we got on with speed to Dumfries, and lodged at the widowed house of Mrs. Mason. *Thursday*, reaching Occoquan, I thought I should prefer my dear old friend William Watters's to Alexandria; thither we bent our way and got in before dark.

District of Columbia

Friday, at Georgetown.

Sabbath, *March* 3. I preached for half an hour, and was fervent. At the sacrament took occasion to exhort the society. At three o'clock visited the new house in the city:[11] I preached, though very unwell. I feel great consolation, and perfect love.

Maryland

Monday, preached at Bladensburg. I was surprised to see so many people. On *Tuesday* I preached at Federal chapel.[12] *Wednesday*, a violent

[10] See Asbury's letter to Thomas L. Douglas, February 24, 1811, which sets forth his plan for history "focus."

[11] This first Methodist house of worship erected in Washington stood on Fourth Street between South Carolina Avenue and G Street, S.E. The date of conveyance of the lot was October 5, 1810. The building was of brick with galleries on three sides. The fact that it remained so long unfurnished indicates the heavy financial burden assumed in its erection. Among its nine trustees was Henry Foxhall of Georgetown, in whose home Bishops Asbury and McKendree were guests. The pastor was Beverly Waugh (1789–1858), later a bishop. In 1819 the name Ebenezer was given to the original church. (Ferguson: *Methodism in Washington, D.C.*, 45–66; Boehm, *op. cit.*, 340.)

[12] Federal Chapel, built at the close of the Revolutionary War, stood one-half mile south of Colesville, Montgomery County, Maryland. With the erection of Andrews Methodist Episcopal Church in 1868 and 1869, services were transferred to Colesville. (Scharf: *History of Western Maryland*, I, 758, 759.)

snowstorm. I rode twelve miles to preach at Hopewell[13] to an attentive, respectable auditory. Lodged with Edward Owings. *Thursday*, we have had a trying ride to Goshen chapel.[14] I had a few people to hear me. Lodged at the widow Harris's.[15] I have been blessed in mind, whilst administering the word of truth, but greatly afflicted in body. At Clarksburg, on *Friday*, we had a full congregation, and an open season. *Saturday*, at Hyattstown,[16] the chapel was crowded. It was a very liberal season to the speaker. I have ridden sixteen miles to see brother Willson[17] in his affliction; the family were greatly attentive and kind: the aged people have sat under our ministry for forty years nearly, and have always hospitably entertained our preachers. We came back to Mr. McElfresh's.[18]

Sabbath, 10. I preached at New Market.[19] Many knew me, nevertheless I frequently feel like a stranger in my old home (Maryland); such changes has time wrought! I went home with James Higgins. *Tuesday*, I preached at Liberty. Lodged at Ephraim Howard's:[20] when will this dear family embrace religion? On *Wednesday* I preached at Linganore, and spoke in great plainness. I saw the corpse of our dear sister Jones[21] in the coffin!

[13] In 1726 a grant of three hundred acres, called Hopewell, near the mouth of the Little Monocacy River, Montgomery County, was made. (Scharf, *op. cit.*, I, 652.) As early as 1792 George Wells preached at Hopewell which he located near the residence of Captain Beall, for whose family Beallsville is named. (Manuscript Diary of George Wells, entry for October, 1792, Lovely Lane Museum, Baltimore.)

[14] Goshen Chapel stood three miles south of Woodfield and six miles southeast of Clarksburg, Montgomery County. An abandoned church building occupies the site of the old Goshen meetinghouse. (See note under May 3, 1789.)

[15] This may have been the widow of Cyrus Harris, in whose home William Colbert preached when on the Montgomery Circuit. (Colbert's *Journal*, January 7, 1794.)

[16] In 1804 the congregation of eighteen members at Hyattstown, Montgomery County, erected a log church on land acquired from Mr. and Mrs. Eli Hyatt. Its trustees were Samuel Hobbs, Basil Soper, Charles McElfresh, John Smith, and Joseph Benton. It was in this church that Asbury preached. (Scharf: *History of Western Maryland*, I, 722, 723.)

[17] William Willson married a daughter of John Clark, the founder of Clarksburg in Montgomery County. (See note under June 15, 1783.) He was long a steward of the Montgomery Quarterly Conference. (Armstrong, *op. cit.*, 509.) The father, John Willson, had been a trustee of the Sugar Loaf Chapel in 1788, earliest Methodist house of worship in that region. (Scharf: *History of Western Maryland*, I, 720; Martz: *The Clarksburg Methodist Church*, 7; Boyd: *History of Montgomery County*, 100.)

[18] Henry McElfresh in 1808 lived two and one-half miles southeast of New Market. (See note under August 20, 1804.)

[19] According to Scharf the Methodists erected a log chapel in New Market, Frederick County, before 1800, which served them until it was replaced by a more commodious structure in 1821. However, the *Frederick Circuit Manuscript Stewards' Book* in Lovely Lane Museum, Baltimore, does not list a class earlier than 1804. (Scharf: *History of Western Maryland*, I, 608.)

[20] Ephraim Howard and Upton Sheradine married sisters, who were daughters of Basil Dorsey. (See note under August 20, 1804; Warfield, *op. cit.*, 342, 343.)

[21] This was Annie Jones, wife of Joshua Jones. Mrs. Jones died March 12, 1811, aged thirty-three years. Her grave beside that of her husband, who was a traveling preacher

Thursday, we came to Pipe Creek. I preached for them. Ann Willis[22] is a widow indeed, with six children! Henry Willis—Ah! when shall I look upon thy like again! *Friday*, came through heavy dews to Aquila Garrettson's;[23] halted awhile, and proceeded forward to Providence chapel;[24] here I preached. We dined with friendly Mr. Stockdale, and came on to our brother M'Elfresh's, Reisterstown. O, the *clover* of Baltimore circuit! *Ease*, ease! not for me—toil, suffering, coarse food, hard lodging, bugs, fleas, and certain *et ceteras* besides! *Saturday*, we had a solemn sitting in our chapel at Reisterstown. We called at Ellis Jones's,[25] ancient Methodists; from thence we bent our course over to Charles Carnan's. Here I heard the mournful news of the death of Polly Yellott[26]—gone after her father to paradise.

Sabbath, 17. At the chapel I found preachers in abundance, and a larger congregation than I had expected; as it was an appointment for me, I had the labour to perform. How hardly shall preachers who are well provided for maintain the spirit of religion! But here are eight young men lately married: these will call for four hundred dollars per annum, additional—so we go. *Monday*, preached at Hunt's chapel, and afterward rode into Baltimore. We began our conference[27] in great peace and order on

(1791–97) and who died September 19, 1836, is in the churchyard of Bethel Church. (Scharf, *op. cit.*, II, 895; see notes under April 9, 1805, and June 10, 1808.)

[22] Ann Willis, widow of Henry Willis, and her brother, Francis Hollingsworth, continued to reside in their old homes for several years. *The Engine of Liberty and Uniontown Advertizer*, a Carroll County paper, in the issue of February 3, 1814, carried this notice: "Ann Willis offers her farm of two hundred and eighty-two and a half acres on Sam's Creek, on the road leading from Liberty Town to Baltimore, for sale." The issue of November 25, 1813, advertised the "sale of farming utensils and household goods by Francis Hollingsworth, Little Pipe Creek." (See note under April 30, 1801.)

[23] Aquila Garrettson (1762–1837) was a younger brother of Freeborn Garrettson. From 1791 to 1797 Aquila was an itinerant preacher. (Brumbaugh, *op. cit.*, II, 152.)

[24] The Providence Chapel apparently was near West Friendship in the present Howard County. In 1809 a committee of the quarterly meeting of the Baltimore Circuit was appointed "to inquire into the right of the Methodist Church to a house called 'Providence' and claims upon that house of other people." Evidently the Methodists gained control, for in 1813 it became a preaching place. (*Stewards' Book, Baltimore Circuit, 1794–1816*, Lovely Lane Museum.)

[25] In 1797 Ellis Jones was named a trustee of Reisterstown Church, Baltimore County.

[26] Apparently "Polly" was the pet name for Mary Hollingsworth Yellott (b. 1760), the eldest daughter of Jesse Hollingsworth. Her husband was Jeremiah Yellott, a sea captain of 1776. Polly died at Woodville, Baltimore County, where her father also died in 1810. (Hollingsworth: *The Hollingsworth Family*, 16; note under August 19, 1801.)

[27] The conference, under the presidency of Bishops Asbury and McKendree, convened in Light Street Church with sixty preachers present. Georgetown District was formed. Washington, D.C., became a station. The conference approved a plan for collecting material for a history of Methodism in the United States. The committee of five, selected to devise a plan, submitted one almost identical with that already written by Bishop Asbury. Despite Asbury's incessant urging, the plan failed for want of church-

Wednesday, the 20th, and rose on *Thursday*, the 28th. I took my share of the labour of preaching. What the fruits of our toil have been, and may yet be, the God whom we serve can tell: but we have reasonable grounds of hope that it has not been, nor will yet be, in vain. I preached this morning in Gatch's chapel, and came on to Perry Hall. *Friday*, I preached to about thirty souls in the private chapel at Perry Hall. All, to me, seems yet to be in sackcloth here. *Saturday*, I preached at the Fork meeting house: this is a badly planned building. I dined with Mr. Gorsuch[28]; and called to see the widow Garrettson. She did not at first recognize me.

Sabbath, 31. At Old Bush chapel I preached, and the word was heard and felt. I saw children who now see me for the first time, whose fathers received me forty years ago. Once more to Josias Dallam's.[29] I baptized his little daughter Henrietta Rogers. I visited his son Doctor William, and baptized his son Josias William Dallam.

Monday, *April* 1. Visited my old friend Bennett.[30] There was such a violent storm that we waited for hours before we ventured across the Susquehanna. I preached at North East chapel. *Tuesday*, it is court day at Elkton. I am fitter for bed than the pulpit; but my appointment must be filled, and my sacrifice offered. Eating was not the business of this day. I went to John Carnan's, Back Creek.[31] Here I swallowed a grain and a half of tartar. *Wednesday*, I preached for them at Bethel chapel.[32] I called the society together, and gave them special counsel, and also information respecting the spreading of the work of God. *Thursday*, I preached at

wide co-operation. (Armstrong, *op. cit.*, 161–65; Boehm, *op. cit.*, 340, 341; *Minutes of the Baltimore Conference, 1800–1816*, 191 ff. (See letter to Thomas A. Douglass, February 24, 1811.)

[28] David Gorsuch (1763–1841) was a member of the church at West Liberty near the Mason-Dixon Line, Baltimore County. Earlier meetings of the society were in the Meredith home and later in the Meredith log meetinghouse.

[29] Josias William Dallam (1747–1820) was twice married. His second wife was Henrietta, a daughter of Judge Thomas Jones of Baltimore County, whom he married in 1800. Henrietta Rogers, whom Asbury baptized, was one of five children born to them. "Dr. William," whom Asbury visited, was Dr. William Middlemore Dallam (1777–1859), one of nine children of Josias Dallam and his first wife, Sarah Smith, whom he married in 1770. (See *Manuscript Genealogy of the Dallams*, by Mrs. Dallam Block, Maryland Historical Society, Baltimore.)

[30] Apparently this is that same B. Bennett at whose home Asbury frequently stopped before going to the lower ferry of the Susquehanna River in Harford County. (See note under March 20, 1809.)

[31] In his diary for July 15, 1809, Freeborn Garrettson uses the spelling "Canaan" in describing a visit to his old friend near Elkton, Maryland. (Bangs, *op. cit.*, 246; note under March 20, 1809.)

[32] Bethel Chapel, which was erected in 1780 by the society organized in Thompson's schoolhouse by Richard Wright in 1773. The present Bethel Church is located on the Chesapeake and Delaware Canal, one and one-half miles from Chesapeake City, Cecil County. (Johnston: *History of Cecil County, Maryland*, 440; see note under April 13, 1772.)

Bethesda chapel. It was a rainy day. *Friday*, at Bohemia Cross Roads[33] I preached to a small congregation. We had a time not soon to be forgotten. I dined with Doctor Scott,[34] and came on to James Corse's. *Saturday*, it rained, but it did not prevent two hundred souls from attending at the chapel:[35] it was a time of deep seriousness and feeling. We had nine miles to Chester in a heavy rain; here I also had a congregation.

Sabbath, 7. I preached in Chester, and met the society, white and coloured. I lodged at my son William Burneston's:[36] a few aged *steadies* came to see me, and dine with me, and talk of past times. *Monday*, we had a cold, easterly day, but a considerable congregation to whom I preached. I dined with Daniel Burgess, and rode forward to Thomas Wright's. I find it my duty to convene the societies, and give them my advice, possibly my valedictory. *Tuesday*, I preached in the new brick house at Centreville. Dined with John Brown[37] in company with aged brethren and sisters. Lodged at James Massy's.[38] Methodists are becoming great on this shore: Ah! let them take heed. *The respectable society of people called Methodists.* "Woe unto you when all men shall speak well of you." Save us from this! Never in any past period have we had so much cause to hope or to fear as a society. *Wednesday*, at Wye chapel[39] I preached, and the speaker and the hearers felt seriously and deeply. We dined with John W. Boardley,[40] and hasted on to Easton, lodging with Mr. Lockerman. My mind enjoys great peace and Gospel enlargement; but I am not so ready, upon all occasions to speak to every one who comes into my presence. How precious are their souls, and O, how precious is time! *Thursday*. A day of storms, but I had a respectable congregation to whom I preached at St.

[33] Asbury was at the present Cayots or St. Augustine, Cecil County, Maryland. Previously, perhaps from Perry Hall, Bishop McKendree had left for a preaching mission in Pennsylvania and Henry Boehm to visit his father. Bishop Asbury, therefore, was without their company through the Peninsula and until he reached the Philadelphia Conference. (Boehm, *op. cit.*, 341.)

[34] This is probably Dr. Edward Scott, who in 1808 married Anne Comegys. He lived near Galena, Kent County, Maryland.

[35] This was Dudley's Meeting House or Queen Anne's Chapel, and sometimes referred to merely as "The Chapel." It was near Sudlersville, Queen Annes County. (Emory, *op. cit.*, 568–71; note under October 2, 1783, and May 16, 1801.)

[36] William Burneston lived near Chestertown, Kent County. (Bangs, *op. cit.*, 252; Hallman, *op. cit.*, 107.)

[37] John Brown was a member of the board of trustees to whom the land was deeded by Elizabeth Nicholson on which the first Methodist Church in Centreville, Queen Annes County was erected. The deed bears the date June 21, 1794. (Emory, *op. cit.*, 232, 233.)

[38] About this time James Massey was prominent in the news of Queen Annes County as an office seeker and party stalwart of the Federalists. (*Ibid.*, 344, 441, 442.)

[39] This is Asbury's second reference to preaching in Wye Chapel, Wye Mills, Queen Annes County. (For the first visit see *Journal* entry for November 23, 1789.)

[40] John W. Boardley was active in church and civic affairs in Queen Annes County. He became a local preacher and supplied nearby appointments. (See note under November 26, 1787.)

Michael's. *Friday*. It was a solemn time at Easton whilst I was preaching from Luke xxiii, 26–30, inclusive. I covenanted with General Benson[41] to pray for him every day; he was all feeling whilst I talked with him. I rode to Tuckahoe bridge. Henry Downs, his wife, and myself are nearly all who are left of the early Methodists in this neighbourhood; three and thirty years make great changes on the surface of this world of evanescent existences. *Saturday*, at Tuckahoe chapel, I expounded Acts ii, 21, to a large and serious congregation. We rode twenty miles, through storms, to Joshua Massey's.

Sabbath, 14. A serene day, and my mind is tranquil: I preached at Dudley's chapel. We dined with kind Mr. Elliott, whose father was a benefactor to this chapel. After dinner and prayer we hasted to the head of Chester, where I preached in Mr. Ferrell's house: it appeared as if the whole town came out to hear: lodged at Christopher Spry's.[42]

Delaware

Monday, dined with Mr. Brooke at Middletown, and baptized his child: God was present. I have lately been truly blest in my soul and in my labours. A poor afflicted widow called on me. For what do I live but to do good, and to teach others so to do, both by precept and example? *Tuesday* I preached at Salem, and met the society. It is a day of rest and peace. *Wednesday* I preached at Newport in the forenoon, and at night at Wilmington.

Pennsylvania

Thursday, gave the inhabitants of Darby a discourse, dined at Samuel Lewis's, and came on to the city to meet letters, preachers, and troubles. *Saturday*. We opened our conference to-day.

Sabbath, 21. I preached at Ebenezer and in St. George's chapel.

Monday, 29. Our conference adjourned: there were no complaints, nor grounds for any: there was preaching, as usual, to large congregations, and there were manifestations of the power of God, especially at St. George's. I visited Landreth,[43] at his shrubbery: this is a pious English

[41] For Brigadier General Perry Benson see note under September 11, 1783.

[42] Christopher Spry, a Virginian, was admitted on trial in 1787 and was appointed to the Somerset Circuit, Maryland. After serving appointments on the Peninsula, he labored in New England (1794–96). He returned to Maryland, and following extensive and efficient service as circuit preacher and presiding elder, he located and lived in or near Millington, Maryland. (Stevens: *Memorials of Methodism*, 298, 299.)

[43] David Landreth was born in England in 1758, where he came under the influence of John Wesley in London when he was a young man. He emigrated to Canada in 1781 and settled in Philadelphia in 1783, where he united with St. Paul's Anglican Church. He associated with St. George's Methodists and later united with Ebenezer Methodist

family, Doctor Logan[44] called upon me; he has lately returned from England; he speaks favourably of my nation.

Wednesday, May 1. I preached at Germantown. Doctors Rush[45] and Physick paid me a visit. How consoling it is to know that these great characters are men fearing God! I was much gratified, aye, I ever am, by their attentions, kindness, and charming conversation; indeed they have been of eminent use to me, and I acknowledge their services with gratitude. *Thursday* I preached at Holmesburg:[46] there was a great rain, yet many people attended. We went forward to Mr. Thompson's[47] through the rain, the effects of which I felt in the evening; I preached nevertheless. *Friday*, at Bensalem chapel I preached to a small congregation, dined with father Rodman,[48] and continued forward to Bristol, where I preached in the evening. After forty years of patient labour the work of God has broke forth gloriously in Bucks county,[49] and many doors are now opened to

Church in Southwark. He entertained Asbury at his home in the country (near 22nd and Federal streets, Philadelphia). This country home was the original nursery of the Landreth Seed Company. (*Centennial History of Ebenezer Church*, Southwark, Philadelphia, 51–53.)

[44] George Logan (1753–1821), physician and United States Senator, was the son of William and Hannah Emlen Logan. His grandfather, James Logan, a wealthy merchant in Philadelphia, established in 1728 the family home near Germantown. (*Dictionary of American Biography*, 359.)

[45] Benjamin Rush (1745–1813) was born near Philadelphia and was graduated from Princeton College in 1761. He studied medicine in Philadelphia, London, Edinburgh, and Paris, and became professor of chemistry in 1769. In 1776 he was elected to Congress, and he signed the Declaration of Independence. He married Julie Stockton of Princeton, New Jersey. In 1777 he became physician general of the military hospitals for the Middle Department. Dickinson College is said to have been founded mainly through his influence. He organized the Philadelphia Dispensary in 1785, and in 1787 he was the leading spirit in the founding of the College of Physicians. In 1789 he became the professor of the theory and practice of medicine in the Medical College which was united with the University of Pennsylvania; in 1790 he took the chair in Institutes of Medicine and Clinical Practice, and in 1796 added the chair of the Practice of Physics. He was physician to the Pennsylvania Hospital, the treasurer of the Mint, president of the Society for the Abolition of Slavery, and vice-president of the Bible Society of Philadelphia. (Morris: *Makers of Philadelphia,* 13.)

[46] Holmesburg is in the northeastern part of Philadelphia County on the Bristol Pike. It was built on a portion of the estate of Thomas Holme, surveyor to William Penn; yet the town was named not for Penn's helper but for the descendants of John Holmes, another worthy of the late seventeenth century. (Faris: *Old Trails and Roads in Penn's Land.*) Property was secured for a Methodist church in Holmesburg in 1812. The town is now incorporated in the City of Philadelphia.

[47] This was probably J. Tomlinson, who lived below Bensalem in the upper portion of Philadelphia County.

[48] Joseph Rodman of Bensalem gave a lot on which the church was built in 1810. The Rodman family came from Burlington, New Jersey, and an important member of the family was Dr. John Rodman.

[49] Bucks County was one of the three provincial counties established by William Penn. It extended indefinitely northward of Philadelphia along the Delaware River. It was reduced to its present size by the formation of Northampton County in 1752.

receive us. *Saturday*, I preached at John Bailey's, Marlborough; after meeting we rode on to Mahannon's, at the Swamp,[50] where we had a crowded evening meeting.

Sabbath, 5. I preached under an apple tree. Came into Newtown.[51] The place was crowded with people who came in to see a lady dipped; but she was sick, and the curious were disappointed. At seven o'clock I preached in the court house; this labour shall not be in vain. I lodged with Lawyer Hugh Ross,[52] now a Methodist preacher.

Monday, 6. I preached to a few people at William Wetherill's:[53] toil, toil! Murmuring flesh, be still! Our ride has been through excessive rain to-day.

Tuesday, 7. We started and came to Hinkle's tavern[54] and dined. Went forward to John Purcell's,[55] where I found a crowded house: I preached, and the truth was deeply felt by some. I have proclaimed the truth to many souls lately, and I feel the effect of my labours: my reward is with my God.

New Jersey

Wednesday, 8. Crossed the Delaware,[56] and sat down in Godley's school room[57] and taught the people: my subject was Acts iii, 26.

[50] This reference is probably to the northeastern part of Nockamixon township, the greater part of Bridgeton township, and the northwestern part of Tinicum township, which comprise a large territory colloquially called "The Swamp." (MacReynolds: *Place Names in Bucks County, Pennsylvania*, 369–71.)

[51] At the time of Asbury's visit Newtown was the county seat of Bucks County.

[52] Hugh Ross, son of Thomas and Jane Chapman Ross of Solebury, Pennsylvania, moved to Newtown in 1796. He studied law with his brother John in Easton and on being admitted to the bar returned to Newtown, later going to Trenton, New Jersey, and finally settling in Milford, Pike County, Pennsylvania. He was admitted on trial in the Philadelphia Conference and made junior preacher on the Lancaster Circuit in 1811, but he stopped traveling at the end of the year. (Davis: *History of Bucks County*, III, 81, 82.)

[53] William Wetherill lived in Wrightstown, Bucks County. The preaching in his home was the beginning of the present Penn's Park Church.

[54] Hinkle's Tavern was located in central Northern Plumstead Township. It was operated by Philip Hinkle, formerly of Germantown. (MacReynolds, *op. cit.*, 193, 194.)

[55] John Purcell lived in Lehnenburg, a village in Durham township, Bucks County. The village was founded about 1793 by Thomas Purcell, purchaser of a part of the Durham tract known as Plot No. 12. He built a grist mill and a saw mill. John Purcell was the son of John and Ann Coomb Purcell, and married Mercy Iliff. He died in 1816, leaving eleven children. (MacReynolds, *op. cit.*, 224, 225.)

[56] Asbury evidently crossed the Delaware River at Hunt's Ferry, which is located at the present Riegelsville, Pennsylvania, and the town of the same name in New Jersey.

[57] This was William Godley (1755–1836) who had a school at Hunt's Ferry. He is listed as a teacher at Pittstown, Hunterdon County, about 1832. (*Christian Advocate and Journal*, XI, No. 19, December 30, 1836.)

Thursday, 9. We came to Asbury, and I preached and added a special exhortation. Were it not for the brewing and drinking miserable whisky, Asburytown would be a pleasant place. *Friday*, to James Egbert's.[58] Bethel chapel has been bought and refitted for the Methodists: I preached in it. I am unknown in Jersey, and ever shall be, I presume: after forty years' labour we have not ten thousand in membership.

Saturday, 11. At Philip Cummings's, Sussex county: I preached for them. A damp, cold ride of seven miles brought us to Albertson's.[59]

Sabbath, 12. I preached to a crowded house at Union chapel.[60] Twenty-three years ago I preached here. The Moravian brethren are almost extinct.

Monday, 13. I preached at the stone church.[61]

Tuesday, 14. I preached at father Andrew Freeman's.

Wednesday, 15. I preached at Sussex court house,[62] and felt as if my labour was not in vain: the minds of the people were open for the reception of the truth. We went to Lockwood,[63] and at eight o'clock I preached in Jonathan Hunt's meeting house.[64]

Thursday, 16. We had a heavy ride to father Lawrence's[65] and such

[58] James Egbert lived at Mount Bethel in Mansfield Township, Warren County. Dr. Robert Cummins, a surgeon for the Continental Army in the Revolutionary War, had settled at Mount Bethel, and he induced Egbert to come there in 1790 from Staten Island. Egbert was a tanner by trade and built a tannery at Mount Bethel, from which its owner grew quite wealthy. The first Methodist meetings were held in James Egberts' home as early as 1800. Asbury preached there in 1809 when there was a log meeting-house used by the Baptists. Egbert bought the church from the Baptists, and the Methodist people worshiped in it for a number of years, and it was called Bethel Chapel. In 1845 Egbert built a stone church and gave it to the congregation. The name "Mount Bethel" has remained. (Snell, *op. cit.*, 725, 729; Honeyman, *op. cit.*, II, 726–27.)

[59] Cornelius Albertson lived near the village of Delaware, which is situated along the Delaware River in Warren County. Albertson was prominent in the community, being at various times town clerk, assessor, collector, and a member of the Town Committee. The Presbyterian manse in Delaware is the farmhouse built by Cornelius Albertson. (Snell, *op. cit.*, 626–27; Shampanore: *History and Directory of Warren County, New Jersey*, 24–G.)

[60] Union Chapel was located two miles northeast of Hope in Warren County. Methodism was organized there about 1785, and the log chapel building was erected on the present site in 1810; the present structure was completed in 1856 and dedicated by Bishop Edmund S. Janes. (Honeyman, *op. cit.*, II, 706.)

[61] This was the church at Johnsonburg.

[62] This was Newton, county seat of Sussex County.

[63] Lockwood was a "forge and post office" on Lubber Run, Byram Township, in Sussex County, nine miles south of Newton. (Gordon, *op. cit.*, 169; Snell, *op. cit.*, 461–62; Phoebus, *op. cit.*, 47.)

[64] Jonathan Hunt, of Lockwood, was elected in 1798 one of three judges of appeals at the first town election. A meetinghouse belonging to Hunt is unknown to historians, who omit all reference to such a church. Undoubtedly it was an established preaching place, since Ezekiel Cooper records preaching at Mr. Hunt's in June, 1786. (Snell, *op. cit.*, 464; Phoebus, *op. cit.*, 47.)

[65] This was probably either Sylvanus or David Lawrence, who lived in the Millbrook area of Dover in Morris County. Sylvanus Lawrence's home was established as

another to Morristown,[66] and a third to the Turkey Hills, where I preached. I have met the societies generally.

New York

Sunday, 19. As we were preparing to go to the house of God a dreadful fire broke out, consuming about one hundred houses. I preached to some serious sisters in John Street. I officiated at Greenwich in the new chapel after dinner.[67]

Thursday, 23. Ordained deacons; Bishop M'Kendree preached.

Sabbath, 26. I preached in the African church, as also in the new and in the Bowery church: I met the societies in each place of worship. Father Blagburne's[68] case occupied us two days: he was taken into the Connexion and ordained a deacon, although he brought no recommendation to us from the British or any other conference.

Tuesday, 28. Conference ceased their labours. There was little trouble in the business of appointments: stationed eighty-seven, superannuated two, and supernumeraries five; increase about three hundred. There were three preachers sent to other conferences. Return to thy rest, O my soul! The society in New York has increased; our chapels are neat, and their debt is not heavy: they wish to rebuild John Street Church,[69] and to build a small house at the *Two Mile Stone*.[70] So frequent are the visits of the

a preaching place as early as 1799, and later Methodist services were held in a stone barn on the property of David Lawrence. (Vansant, *op. cit.*, 108–10; Platt: *Dover Dates, a Bicentennial History of Dover, New Jersey*, 54–58; see note under August 10, 1796.)

[66] Morristown is the county seat of Morris County, situated along both banks of the narrow Whippany River, and has been for many years a cultural and social center. Asbury on this visit preached in the Presbyterian Church. The Methodist society in Morristown was organized during the first quarter of the nineteenth century, after Mr. and Mrs. Samuel Bonsall moved from New York to Spring Valley, a section between Madison and Morristown, and opened their home for preaching and class meetings. (Eckman: *History of Morristown Methodist Church*, 1952; *New Jersey Guide*, 283 ff.; Gordon, *op. cit.*, 186.)

[67] On this occasion Asbury was entertained by the elderly widow Mrs. Grice, who with her widowed daughter, Mrs. Ann Tucker, kept a millinery shop on William Street in New York City. (Boehm, *op. cit.*, 344.)

[68] After prolonged debate William Blagburne was received into the New York Conference and ordained deacon at this 1811 session. He served inconspicuously in New York and vicinity until 1815, when his name disappears from the *Minutes* without comment. He returned then to England, where he preached for some years. (Warriner, *op. cit.*, 413–14; Seaman, *op. cit.*, 186; note under May 12, 1810.)

[69] See note under May 11, 1810.

[70] Mileage was measured from the Federal Building at the corner of Wall and Nassau Streets, where Washington was inaugurated and where Asbury had formally presented American Methodism's Address of Congratulaton to Washington. As the Post Road moved northward, the two-mile stone was fixed at the "Forks of the Bowery," almost at the site of the present Cooper Union Institute near the Bible House

people to talk or to do business, that I have not time to think or to pray, scarcely: I bear it all patiently. I preached at the *Two Mile Stone*,[71] and retired to George Suckley's. I resemble my Master in one thing—*I cannot be hid*; they find me out.

Saturday, *June* 1. A very warm ride to Sherwood's. I feel nothing like fretfulness; I am willing to listen patiently, and endure all things.

Sabbath, 2. At Sherwood's chapel I preached, and also to the society at New Rochelle. I was divinely assisted in my labours this day; it is a day of calm and liberty to my soul. *Monday*. Twenty-five miles to Governor Van Cortlandt's, at the mouth of Croton: I preached at four o'clock. It was a day of militia training; this circumstance, and a failure of early notice, gave me a thin congregation. Ah! what need of watchfulness in the houses of the rich, lest we defile our own souls, and more than lose our labour! *Tuesday*, I felt divine liberty whilst preaching at Somers Town.[72] We lodged with Samuel Wilson; wealthy and kind. At Lemuel Clift's,[73] another man of wealth: here I preached on *Wednesday*. On *Thursday* I preached in the new chapel, Pawling Town. We lodged with Captain Pierce, a man of open mind, and generous soul. *Friday*, we took the road to Neice's,[74] dined, and went forward to Amenia. *Saturday*, peace, rest, love.

Sabbath, 9. I preached at George Ingraham's; there were many people, although the morning was rainy. I met the society after some exhortations had been given. There has been, and will yet be a work in this town. They have built a new chapel. Lansford Whiting,[75] appointed to the western

and John Wanamaker's old store. A small rural community had developed at Two Mile Stone, with a Methodist class formed in 1789 by William Valleau, a local preacher, at the home of John Coutant. In 1795 a small house had been occupied on a nearby street, and when the original Wesley Chapel was demolished in 1817, some of the beams were used to enlarge the Two Mile Stone structure. One of these beams, properly identified, rests directly under the pulpit of the present Park Avenue Methodist Church on 86th Street. (Seaman, *op. cit.*, 155, 291.)

[71] On this occasion Asbury preached in an academy located on what is now St. Mark's Place. (Boehm, *op. cit.*, 345.)

[72] In 1808 the name Somers had officially replaced the earlier designation of Stephentown. The change was to create a perpetual memorial to Captain Richard Somers, brilliant and daring young naval officer, who had died in action at the harbor of Tripoli, North Africa. (See *Journal* entry for May 27, 1805, for Asbury's first visit.)

[73] Lemuel Clift was a prominent and wealthy citizen, and one of the founding directors of the early Farmers' and Drovers' Bank of Somers. (Scharf, *op. cit.*, II, 489.)

[74] This Methodist leader was probably the same person mentioned May 16, 1810.

[75] Lansford Whiting (1786?–1811) was received on trial in 1808 and appointed to pioneer work at Plattsburg on Lake Champlain, near the Canadian line. He was ordained deacon at the 1811 conference, at which time he volunteered and was accepted to go to the Western Conference with Bishop McKendree. Going up Hudson River by sloop to pick up his gear at Plattsburg and join McKendree at the Genesee Conference later, he was stricken and removed at Poughkeepsie. The ailment was there diagnosed as smallpox, and he died in great pain on June 5.

circuit, in returning from conference at New York, was taken with smallpox, and died at Poughkeepsie; he was solemn in deportment, and very pious: he has gone to an early crown. How many triumphant witnesses for Jesus have passed away before my eyes, I might almost say, within the last forty years!

Massachusetts

Monday, 10, I preached at Thomas Heywood's: it was a blessed season. Great accommodations in this part of the world: our preachers will do well to take heed. Stephen Sornborger was above his work; so he let another take his station. I read Adam Clarke, and am amused as well as instructed. He indirectly unchristianizes all old bachelors. Woe is me! It was not good that Adam should be alone for better reasons than any that Adam Clarke has given. How will our commentator comment on Isaiah lvi, 3–5; on 1 Corinthians vii, 7, 8, 17, 27, 32, 34? and will he not need great skill to manage well for his purpose Matthew xix, 12? It may be the indispensable duty of some men and women to marry; the necessity, or the peculiarity of circumstances which would impose this as a duty, or only allow it as an indulgence, who is to judge of; the parties themselves? Could they be *out of the body* awhile, we might allow them to be umpires in their own cases. Adam does not seem to take into the account Mrs. Clarke, so much as the wife. Will he always marry as often as the law will allow? *Tuesday*, at Hillsdale chapel I preached and met the society. We lodged at Reed's, an old member from New York. We rode thirty miles to Lenox in Massachusetts, passing Barrington and Stockbridge: I preached at eight o'clock. Here are walls of opposition to be levelled before we can hope for success. Lodged at Mr. Whiting's. *Thursday*, Pittsfield. We have ridden two hundred miles since we left New York, and have preached every day, and the preachers there are hardly starting to their stations; *but they have wives*. I preached in the chapel, and the truth was felt. *Friday* I preached at Lenox in the evening.

New York

Saturday, we came through Bennington to Ashgrove.[76]

Sabbath, 16. I preached in the chapel. Bishop M'Kendree also preached. I also preached at Mr. Nicholas's; our labours shall not all be lost. *Monday*, came on to Salem, and lodged in Wells.

[76] The loop back from Massachusetts and Bennington, Vermont, into New York was for the purpose of meeting Bishop McKendree at Ashgrove. The entire party then went north to Brandon, Vermont, for the New England Conference.

Vermont

Tuesday, 18, to Pittsfield.[77] *Wednesday*, a heavy ride of twenty miles brought us to Barnard's.[78] Here have been many locations, and serious failures of duty. We began our conference on *Thursday*; worked with great expedition, and finished in four days and a half. There was a general fast on *Friday*, and deacons ordained. On the *Sabbath* I preached to about three thousand people—some of them were wild enough. On *Monday* I ordained the elders. George Pickering preached. We disposed of eighty-seven preachers, and each man took his station at once, and without hesitancy, like a man of God. *Tuesday*, we came away, as conference broke up at twelve o'clock. At one o'clock many of those hardy soldiers of the Lord Jesus were already to horse, and their faces set to the wilds, or wherever else their duty call them. On *Wednesday*, we crossed the grand mountain, and came into Middlebury. Here is college-craft and priest-craft. We have a respectable little society of about twenty members, but no chapel: I preached in the court house. I have moved a subscription to build a house sixty-four by forty-four feet, on the lot fronting the college. The Lord will visit Middlebury. *Thursday*, started in a pealing storm for Vergennes.[79] *Friday*, we came to Charlotte, and crossed Lake Champlain to Sable River.

New York

We were welcomed by John Moorehouse. *Saturday*, busy writing, and occasionally reading.

Sabbath, 30. I preached in the new chapel to one thousand souls, I presume; it was a gracious time—the Spirit gave and applied the word. I hastened to Plattsburg[80] to fill an appointment at four o'clock, where I preached in a very commodious tavern room; the word was great by the power of God, although delivered in weakness of body: the heat and the labour almost overcame me. Rode five miles in the evening to Burdock.

Monday, *July* 1. Breakfasted with William Mitchell, and dined with Henrick Johnson. We have made forty-two miles through open woods,

[77] This village of Pittsfield in Vermont is not to be confused with the city of Pittsfield, Massachusetts, mentioned in the preceding paragraph.

[78] Barnard, Windsor County, Vermont, is located ten miles east of Pittsfield. The 1811 session of the New England Conference held here was presided over by Asbury and McKendree. Asbury was entertained by Andrew Stevens. (Boehm, *op. cit.*, 346–47.)

[79] Vergennes is twelve miles north of Otter River on Route 162. The Vergennes Circuit first appears in the *Minutes* in 1798, with Joseph Mitchell and Abner Wood as the preachers. (*Troy Conference Miscellany.*)

[80] The Plattsburg Circuit was organized in 1799 by Alexander McLane, although regular preaching had occurred for some years before that time. Elijah Hedding was there in 1801. The first church building was not erected until 1831.

and over desperate roads.[81] *Tuesday*, dined at French Mills. Heat, heat! At the Indian village,[82] I led my horse across the pole bridge; careful as I was, he got his feet in an opening, and sunk into mud and water; away went the bags—books and clothes wet; and the horse yet fast. We pried with a pole at the stern, and he, by making a desperate effort at the same time, plunged forward, and came out. The mosquitoes were not idle whilst we were busy. We got to the town, and saw their elegant church.[83] At eight o'clock we set sail, and crossed the St. Lawrence by rowing: the river here is three miles wide.

Canada

We rode through Cornwall[84] in the night, and came to Evan Roy's, making forty-four miles for the day's journey. It is surprising how we make nearly fifty miles a day over such desperate roads as we have lately travelled; we lose no time: Ah! why should we—it is so precious! My strong affection for the people of the United States came with strange power upon me whilst I was crossing the line. I suffer much from my lame feet and the great heat; and no small inconvenience because I had not been instructed how to prepare my mind and body for the change I discovered on this side. *Tuesday*, I preached, and again on *Wednesday*: we rode along the banks of the river; they are neatly and pleasantly improved. We dined with Stephen Bailey, and went from thence with brother Glassford, in his calash. I asked him how we were to get out if we upset; his answer was actual experiment: the saplings on the side of the path broke the fall, so that we escaped unhurt. *Thursday*, on the opposite shore they are firing for the fourth of July. What have I to do with this waste of powder? I pass the pageantry of the day unheeded on the other side: why should I have new feelings in Canada? *Friday*, I preached at the German

[81] Asbury's guide over this route was Bela Smith, a member of the Genesee Conference and in charge of the Cornwall Circuit in Canada. Except for his skill and knowledge of the terrain, the journey could not have been made. (Boehm, *op. cit.*, 349.)

[82] This village was called St. Regis for the tribe of Indians located in this general area. They were even then upon a type of reservation, partly in the United States and partly in Canada. At present this reservation, along the St. Regis River, marks the extreme northwest corner of Franklin County, New York.

[83] Boehm says the people were chiefly Roman Catholic and had a large church with a steeple and bell. The parsonage in which the priest lived was built near the bank of the St. Lawrence River. The church was built about the beginning of 1700. (*Ibid.*, 350.)

[84] Cornwall was a growing community on the Canadian bank of the St. Lawrence River, opposite the St. Regis Indian Reservation. For several years Asbury had cherished the hope that he might see Canada and visit the circuits there. Yet it was only by the skill of Bela Smith's guidance and Asbury's own determination and intense effort that this first and only brief journey into Canada was completed.

settlement:[85] I was weak in body, yet greatly helped in speaking. Here is a decent, loving people; my soul is much united to them. I called upon father Dulmadge:[86] and on brother Heck's[87]—a branch of an old Irish stock of Methodists in New York. I lodged at David Brackenridge's,[88] above Johnston. *Saturday*, we rode twelve miles for our breakfast.[89] Reached Elizabethtown. Our ride has brought us through one of the finest countries I have ever seen: the timber is of a noble size: the cattle are well-shaped and well-looking: the crops are abundant, on a most fruitful soil: surely this is a land that God the Lord hath blessed.

Sunday, 7. I rose in pain. We have a large, unfinished house, in which we congregated for love feast at eight o'clock and sacrament: I could not speak long. We had about one thousand souls together. *Monday*, we took the path to Mallory's, where we dined, and continued on to Baldwin's, and from thence to Joel Stone's, at the mouth of Cannoughway Falls. The pain in my foot is so severe that I cannot much enjoy the great kindness of these people. *Tuesday*, a heavy ride brought me to Elias Dulmadge's.[90] My foot is much inflamed, and my whole body disordered. *Wednesday*, I preached in the new chapel at Kingston. I have applied a poultice to my foot: I must do something to hasten a cure, or I shall scarcely reach conference in time. Wrote six letters. Reading—amongst the rest, Mr. Wesley's sermon on, "If the light which is in thee be darkness." If a rich, serious young lady should marry a rich child of the devil,

[85] This community was located near the present Prescott, Ontario, opposite Ogdensburg, New York. Leaders in the group had been colonists in New York, and their young people, including Embury, Heck, Dulmadge, and Detler, had been the core of Methodist beginnings there. In the early 1770's they had moved into either Ashgrove, New York, with Embury, or into this area of Canada with Heck. Asbury preached in their "Matilda Chapel," and Boehm followed him with a sermon in German. (*Ibid.*, 352–53.)

[86] Dulmadge was the only survivor of the original group who had moved from New York City to Canada. He had been active in Wesley Chapel from its inception in 1766 but had probably left New York before Asbury arrived in 1771.

[87] The noted Paul and Barbara Heck, founders with Embury of the New York Society in 1766, had moved to Prescott, Ontario, early in 1770's. The man now visited by Asbury was probably either their son or nephew, as both the elder Hecks had died years previously.

[88] David Brackenridge was a local deacon at the German Settlement. He had preached the funeral sermon for Barbara Heck upon her death in 1804. Her husband, Paul, had died a number of years previously. The Heck family plot and the original headstones are still to be seen in the "Blue Chapel Cemetery" at Prescott. (*Ibid.*, 353.)

[89] Asbury and his companions breakfasted at the home of a Mr. Boyce, a leader of the church at Elizabethtown. (*Ibid.*)

[90] Elias Dulmadge was a son of Father Dulmadge and lived at Kingston, Ontario. He had attended Wesley Chapel in New York when a lad. Asbury remained in his home for almost a week receiving treatment for his badly swollen feet. Boehm kept the bishop's appointments for these days, traveling with Henry Ryan to quarterly meetings at Bay of Quinte and Hay Bay. At the latter place he met John Embury, nephew of Philip Embury of New York. (*Ibid.*, 355.)

she would lose her light; and though she might not be willing to allow that it was extinguished, her pious friends would soon see in her naught but darkness. Why not marry a handsome young Methodist preacher? she would then have something for her money—she would have goodness; for after all, who are good, if not those who practise goodness, and who teach others so to do? But Mr. Wesley meant not this; for he knew, and so do I know, that it would scarcely be good for more than one of the parties: few preachers, if any, have been as holy and useful in after as in former life, who have married rich women; and some have ended in apostasy. I write and read in great pain.

Sunday, 14. I would not willingly be dumb; so I sent round and got a congregation, to whom I preached at the chapel. I met the society, and baptized two children. Alas for us! we want help. I learn from a conversation had with Catherine Detler,[91] that Philip Embury died about two hundred miles from New York:[92] he was much esteemed by his neighbours, and an esquire. He was a descendant of the Palatines who settled in Ireland. Most of those there, and their offspring, have given themselves to the Methodists. He injured himself by mowing, and died somewhat suddenly aged forty-five, greatly loved and much lamented.

New York

Monday, we must away; and leave good houses, grand Roman Catholic church, Episcopal church, and Kingston, with its garrison and great guns. We might go by land, cross three ferries,[93] and travel desperate roads; or we might take the packet for Sacketts Harbour:[94] we chose the latter. A tremendous passage we had. We arrived at two o'clock next day. Here we dined, and set forward in a heavy thunder shower. When we stopped I must preach: I begged it might be at six o'clock in the morning, for my swelled foot was very painful. *Wednesday*. I have passed a night of

[91] Catherine Detler was the daughter of the Detlers who came to America in the early 1760's and who were active in Wesley Chapel, New York, from 1766 to 1770, when they migrated to Canada.

[92] Philip Embury, founder of the New York Society in 1766, had died in August, 1773, thirty-eight years prior to this entry. Asbury had been near Prescott and the "Stone House," home of Barbara Heck which is still extant. She died August 17, 1804. One of her relatives, John Lawrence, married Embury's widow, Margaret; and they are buried in the lot with Barbara Heck at the Blue Church near Prescott. The three names are on the tombstone. Probably Asbury talked with Catherine Detler about Embury's widow, now Mrs. Lawrence, who was living in the community. Philip Embury, Jr., was one of the founders of the church in that community. Philip Embury was buried at Ashgrove, New York.

[93] Short ferries plied from island to island at the head of the St. Lawrence River.

[94] This town in New York State is east of Grenadier Island at the mouth of Black River, which flows into Lake Ontario.

great pain and disquietude, occasioned by my foot and afflicted viscera. I preached at six o'clock, and was blessed in my own soul. We rode on thirty-eight miles to Porter's tavern; where we were well nursed and entertained. *Friday*, sore, lame, weary. I got safe to Paris. My spirit rejoiced with dear Bishop M'Kendree: he nursed me as if I had been his own babe. In all my toils and sufferings, I am thankful that I failed in only one appointment. Well; I have been in Canada, and find it like all stations in the extremities—there are difficulties to overcome, and prospects to cheer us. Some of our labourers have not been so faithful and diligent as we could wish. Doctor Coke says fifteen hundred miles in nine weeks; I may say sixteen hundred miles in sixty days. He writes me that Parliament, by some other act, is about to explain the toleration act, and that the Dissenters have taken the alarm. This is exactly what the Establishment have had for some time; and no marvel; whilst the Methodists are labouring, by night and by day, from village to village, through the whole United Kingdoms. *Saturday*, we opened the Genesee Conference. We passed thirty-eight characters.

Sunday, 21. I preached in the woods at ten o'clock, and again at two o'clock. Bishop M'Kendree, brothers Ostrander, Ryan, Kelsey, and Paddock,[95] also preached. There might be two thousand people, who were very attentive. It is said the wise men in New York Conference have discovered that it will be far better to elect the presiding elders in conference, and give them the power of stationing the preachers. I suppose we shall hear more of this.

Friday, 26. Conference rose. All went on at fair sitting smoothly: the elections came on, and there was some disposition manifested to reject the Canadians and presiding elders. The stations were received in great peace. We have about forty most pleasing young men. There are six hundred and sixty-three on the present minutes. We came away to Bridgewater.[96] *Saturday*, reached New Berlin, and lodged with Matthew Coukin. If the preachers take any specific power, right, or privilege, from the bishops which the General Conference may have given them, it is clear that they dissolve the whole contract.

Sabbath, 28. At Matthew Coukin's. There was no house with a room large enough, so we took to the woods. About five hundred most attentive people listened whilst I expounded 1 Cor. i, 29–31: I was long and loud. My bowels are in a bad state, and I am feverish; but I bless the Lord that

[95] Daniel Ostrander was presiding elder of the Hudson River District. Henry Ryan, who had been with Asbury throughout the Canadian journey, was elder of the Upper Canada District. James Kelsey, elder, was appointed at this conference to Pompey, New York. Benjamin G. Paddock continued on trial at this conference, was appointed to Northumberland, Pennsylvania, on the Susquehanna District.

[96] Bridgewater, on the Unadilla River, was the next township south of Paris, in Oneida County. The party was composed now of Bishop Asbury, Bishop McKendree, accompanied by young Gideon Draper, and Henry Boehm. (*Ibid.*, 360.)

when I cannot stand I can lean upon a table and declare his truth. *Monday*, crossed Jericho bridge over the Susquehanna, four miles below the mouth of Unadilla.[97]

We came in to Samuel Banks's, before a rain began to fall. I feel, very sensibly, the least irregular motion of my horse, whether of start or stumble. I must needs preach. We had about forty men, women, and children to hear us. *Tuesday*, we rode thirty miles. I preached in the evening at eight o'clock, at my host's, Jonas Bush's. We got late to bed. I was in great suffering, but I felt that God is love.

Pennsylvania

Wednesday, we found shelter from the rain under the hospitable roof of Lawyer Catlin.[98]

Thursday, August 1. At brother Paine's I preached and administered the Lord's supper.[99] My right foot is lame. *Friday*, we came along the pleasant banks of Tunkhannock.[100] My lame horse grows worse. We stopped at Dickson's,[101] where I gave ninety dollars for a mare to supply the place of poor Spark, which I sold for twenty dollars; when about to start he

[97] After leaving the Genesee Conference at Paris, New York, Asbury, McKendree, and Henry Boehm went southward along the Unadilla River and then the North Branch of the Susquehanna to Great Bend, Pennsylvania.

[98] Putnam Catlin was born in Connecticut in 1764 and went to Wilkes-Barre, Pennsylvania, after the Revolution, in which he served as a fifer. He practiced law, later becoming a land agent, and at various times lived in Brooklyn, Montrose, and Great Bend. He lived in the last-named place on the occasion of Asbury's visit. Originally the whole area was known as "the big bend" before the present place came into existence. He married Polly Sutton, daughter of James Sutton and a sister of Deborah Sutton Bedford. At eight years of age Polly Sutton and her mother, who were Quakers, were captured by the Indians at the surrender of Forty Fort. The Catlins, who were noted for their hospitality to Methodist preachers, had ten children, the fifth of whom was George Catlin (1796–1872) and who became noted as an artist and author. (Peck: *Early Methodism*, 65, 113; Palmer, *op. cit.*, 91, 142, 178; *Dictionary of American Biography*, III, 574, 575. See note under July 11, 1807.)

[99] Edward Paine (1778–1819) lived at Hopbottom, the present Brooklyn, in Susquehanna County, Pennsylvania, not to be confused with the present Hopbottom four miles away. He was born in Connecticut and went to Pennsylvania in 1809. Originally a Baptist, he became a Methodist class leader and local preacher, and in 1818 he joined the Genesee Conference. He served the nearby Bridgewater Circuit and was drowned in the Susquehanna River while on his way to the conference at Niagara in Upper Canada. Asbury preached and administered the communion in Paine's barn, which still stands in another location. (Peck, *op. cit.*, 152, 306, 322–25; *Life and Times*, 105 ff.; Palmer, *op. cit.*, chs. vi–viii; *Minutes.*)

[100] This stream rose near Great Bend and flows into the Susquehanna at Tunkhannock in Wyoming County, Pennsylvania.

[101] Dickson lived just below the junction of the north and south branches of the Tunkhannock. The community there still bears his name.

whickered after us; it went to my heart—poor slave; how much toil has he patiently endured for me! We rested a few minutes at father Holmes's, on our way to Keeler's ferry.[102] We lodged at father Sutton's.[103] I limped about, sung, talked, and prayed. Dear M'Kendree seemed to be low in spirits. *Saturday*, came on to Kingston, and thence to Wyoming,[104] stopping at Mr. Shoemaker's.[105] We have made a journey of twelve hundred miles since leaving New York. My consolations exceedingly abound in God, though my sufferings be great. The eight conferences have furnished us with twenty-five dollars each, making two hundred dollars; our expenses hitherto are one hundred and thirty dollars.

Sabbath, 4. Preached at the Methodistico-Presbyterian church at Kingston;[106] it was a time of freedom, and words were given me to speak which were felt by preachers and people. I also preached at Wilkes-Barre, and had a liberal season. We were invited to Judge Fell's,[107] and were treated kindly. *Monday* we rode thirty-five miles to Mervin's. My foot is highly inflamed. *Tuesday*, we were compelled to stop at Ritter's,[108] within two miles of Allentown. I was very ill, with a high fever. *Wednesday*, came to Echart's tavern, thirty-five miles. *Thursday*. I wished to rest to-day, because of the inflamed and painful foot, but it might not be. We made twenty-seven miles to Samuel Davis's; and I came in with a high fever. *Friday*, hard labour. We had rain. We reached Martin Boehm's, twenty miles. My flesh is ready to think it something for a man of sixty-six, with a highly inflamed and painful foot, to ride nearly four hundred miles on

[102] The ferry operated by Keeler was a few miles down the Susquehanna from Tunkhannock. "Father Holmes" lived between Dixon and the ferry, probably at or near Tunkhannock.

[103] James Sutton, who moved frequently, doubtless lived on Sutton's Creek opposite Ransom in Exeter Township. (See note under July 11, 1807.)

[104] By Wyoming Asbury probably meant Wilkes-Barre, which was known as Wyoming in the early years. The present borough of Wyoming was not incorporated until 1885; it is north of Kingston and would have been passed before reaching the latter place.

[105] Colonel Elijah Shoemaker was a prominent man in the Wyoming Valley and forebear of a line of distinguished citizens of the area. His wife was the daughter of Colonel Nathan Dennison, a prominent Methodist. (Peck, *op. cit.*, 122 n.; see the account in Boehm, *op. cit.*, 360–62.)

[106] The church was not actually in Kingston but at Forty Fort two miles away. Though other church buildings had been projected, this one, erected in 1807, was the first permanent edifice. It was a joint enterprise of the Methodists and Presbyterians and jointly used by them and some other groups. (Peck, *op. cit.*, 156; Palmer, *op. cit.*, 156, 160. See note under July 19, 1807.)

[107] Judge Jesse Fell of Wilkes-Barre was noted as being the first to use "stone-coal" or anthracite for the heating of buildings, though others had used it in forges. He kept a tavern at the corner of present Washington and Northampton streets, and was at least friendly to the Methodists. (Peck, *op. cit.*, 110–14; Palmer, *op. cit.*, 27, 84, 85; Pearce: *Annals Luzerne County, Pa.*, 368.)

[108] The estate of Thomas Ritter lay on the north bank of the Lehigh River, two miles east of Allentown, Pennsylvania. This is the site of the Rittersville State Hospital.

a stumbling, starting horse, slipping or blundering over desperate roads from Paris to this place in twelve days.

Sabbath, 11. I preached in Boehm's chapel. There is a camp meeting thirty miles distant from hence; but I cannot be there—I have the will, but I want time and strength. *Tuesday*. Yesterday and to-day I have written fifteen letters. I am unspeakably happy in God. *Wednesday*. They will have me away to the camp meeting. John Boehm will take me and bring me back in the carriage. *Thursday*, I preached to about two thousand souls. *Friday*, the heat was excessive; and O, the rocky road, the flies, and my dysentery! I had a high fever, and passed an awful night. I have an appointment to fill this day, *Saturday*. At three o'clock I preached at Strasburg, and returned again to father Boehm's. I take a few glasses of the old man's Rhenish wine to check my bowel complaint.

Sabbath, 18. I lectured at Lancaster on the parable of the sower. I dealt very plainly with my audience, who were deeply attentive. My appointment had been noticed in the public papers of yesterday. Returned in the evening to father Martin Boehm's. *Monday*, I preached at Columbia: I was faint, and the heat excessive. *Wednesday*, I preached at Little York; it was an open time. *Thursday*, we dined in East Berlin, and came on to the twenty-five mile house. *Friday*, reached Chambersburg. Wrote six letters. *Saturday*, very weak indeed.

Sabbath, 25. I preached at our old church, and met the society. I also preached in the Presbyterian church at four o'clock. It has been a day of God to my soul. We are strict on the *Lord's day* in this town—we stop wagons which may attempt to travel through. *Monday*, we kept our faces westward, passing through Campbell's Town[109] and McConnellsburg to Bedford. Jacob Bonnett[110] was exceedingly kind, but strangely shy of our company. *Tuesday*, thirty-one miles to Graft's, *Wednesday* and *Thursday*, at John Bonnett's: there is a great difference in the brothers, in some particulars, but they have kindred spirits. *Friday*, to Millar's, a German descendant, as are most of the families where we stop between Lancaster and Pittsburgh. *Sabbath*, I preached twice. We lodged with John Wrenshall.

Monday, *September* 2. Excessive heat. I rest to-day. Wrote to Doctor Coke, to brothers Hitt, George, Wells, Gruber, Jackson. *Tuesday*, came away, thirty miles to the Cross Roads.

Ohio

Wednesday, at Stubenville: I must needs preach in Basil Wells's fine house; many were present to hear. This place had been well-nigh given up; but behold, now an elegant brick chapel fifty by thirty-five feet, on a

[109] This was the present St. Thomas.
[110] Jacob Bonnett was sheriff of Bedford County.

grand eminence.[111] I heard of a camp meeting ten miles above Jonesville *Thursday*, we passed through Cadiz[112] to father Barrett's, thirty-two miles. *Friday*, a rapid march brought us to Seward's, in Cambridge, on Will's Creek. *Saturday*, came along, through Jonesville, to camp meeting, where I found Bishop M'Kendree. I wet my feet, as I too frequently do in crossing the deep waters; nevertheless, my body is not prostrated, and my mind enjoys great peace.

Sabbath, 8. I preached, and others preached, and there were many exhortations given, and not a few deep and sound conversions. *Monday*, came away, and reached David Swayse's, thirty-three miles from the camp. It became my duty to visit Mr. Williamson: he is alarmed by the great discharge of blood, and wishes to live that he may lament his sins, and reconcile himself to God. *Tuesday*, I preached at Edward Teal's. *Wednesday*, we have rain—in mercy, if not in answer to prayer. We rode to Judge Vanmeeter's the first house that received me on this side of New Lancaster. My mind is greatly given to God. *Thursday*, crossed the Picaway Plains to White Brown's. *Friday*, came on to Wood's; here I rest indeed: how sweet! *Saturday* we came to Pelham's. Betsy Pelham still lives.

Sunday, 15. I preached at the camp meeting; and laboured hard. I availed myself of my situation, to lay a twelve days' plan. *Monday*. There is good done here. I do not like the disposition of some of the ground, and think also that better regulations might be made, and more order kept. *Tuesday*, we have an eclipse. I preached at Union school house. *Wednesday*, to Robert Boggesse's, near Yellow Springs: I preached here to a small assembly, who appeared to be somewhat heavy with sleep. *Thursday*, I preached at Carter's, in Springfield. A general muster of militia made our meeting smaller than it would otherwise have been; but it was a time of strength to the speaker. *Friday*, I preached at Urbana: the house was open, the weather bad, yet I was helped. I saw Colonel Barratt's third son in fellowship: his pious father went in joy and peace—doubtless to glory. He had been thirty years a member of society.

Saturday, 21. Bent our way down Mad River: here is great land. We held a meeting at Lamb's, in New Boston. On my way I called at Ross's, at whose house I had preached on the south branch of Potomac, thirty years ago. Not having eaten since morning, we relished our supper at William Armour's, mouth of Mad River.

Sunday, 22. I preached in the court house at Dayton. We may have

[111] This shows that the first Methodist church building in Steubenville was erected in 1811.

[112] As they came to Cadiz, Ohio, Asbury and Boehm stopped at the home of James Simpson, and the bishop baptized the new son of the household, born June 21, 1811. The son was Matthew Simpson, bishop of the Methodist Episcopal Church from 1852 to 1884. (Crooks: *Life of Bishop Simpson*, 10.)

had one thousand people to hear us. Dinnerless, we came in the evening to Nathan Horner's, and supped and lodged. My skin and flesh complains, but my mind is undisturbed. *Monday*, I preached in a store house in Franklin: I was not at home. I came away with George Hantsberger. Hail solitude, and peace, and plenty! Behold, I had to dig up John Death and his wife[113]—he had, indeed been spiritually so: I found them out without much difficulty: they were old acquaintances on the Monongahela, in early times. *Tuesday*, at Lebanon, I preached and called the society together. We devised the building of a chapel of brick, forty by sixty feet, and one story high. We lodged with M'Greeves: we were hungry and weary, and he was sick—bad enough. Frederick Stier[114] reports that there was a great work of God at Blount camp meeting, in the Holston district; at Lee, at Tazwell, at Washington, at Tennessee, at Green, at Hawkins, at Winton, at Powell's Valley, at Tennessee Valley—at all these there were many souls converted: one hundred and thirty-two joined in communion with the Methodists, besides ten half-breeds. *Wednesday*, after the rain, we made a rapid ride to M'Grew's. *Thursday*, preached at Milford. *Friday*, preached at Oliver Longdon's. *Saturday*, came to Cincinnati.

Sunday, 29. I preached and ordained M. Geohagom, Michael Rouse, J. Voice, D. Anderson, J. Evans, J. B. Finley, Thomas Nelson, S. West, Abraham Cummins, Samuel Hellums, John H. Thompson, John Manley, Francis Travis, John Brown, Abraham Hunt, John Clark, R. Rowe, B. Vanpelt, I. Smith, and Joshua Holland. We have been five days sitting in conference: there has been weighty and critical business before us, but we wrought with industry and good order.

Sunday, *October* 6. I preached; Bishop M'Kendree preached, as did others, and our labour has not been in vain. We occupied the market house as well as the chapel. *Friday*, after a session of ten days, our western conference rose.[115] I had little trouble about the stations—I heard of no complaints. There were one hundred and two preachers; one hundred of whom are stationed: we lack twenty-two. *Saturday*, resting and in prayer.

Sunday, 13. I preached once more in the chapel: it was a farewell warning to the preachers. I met the society, baptized some children, and visited the sick.

[113] Edward Death and his family were members of the society on the original Redstone Circuit that built Robert's Chapel in 1784 or 1785. John Death, son of Edward, had emigrated to the Miami Valley in Ohio.

[114] Frederick Stier was elder of the Holston District in the Western Conference.

[115] This was the final session of the original Western Conference. The General Conference the next spring divided the Western Conference into Tennessee and Ohio conferences. So rapid was the growth of early Methodism in Ohio that only thirteen years from the time of the first organized circuits the ninth conference of American Methodism was organized in the new state.

Kentucky

Monday, we took to horse, and came away to Falmouth, forty-two miles.[116] Our pack horse is lame. *Wednesday*, we came on to Martin Hitt's. *Thursday*, arrived in the night at Colonel Johnson's—a forty miles' ride to-day. *Friday*, a ten miles' ride in the night, added to our day's ride, made fifty miles to Pitman's. *Saturday*, we came in, in an awful storm, to Johnson's.

Sunday, 20. We found the Cumberland rising. We rode twenty-five miles to White's, and rested. *Monday*, to Cheek's. *Tuesday*, to Conway's. It is hard labour, but God is with us. *Wednesday*, to Louisville. *Thursday*, we started at seven o'clock, and came in at seven o'clock in the evening, and have made no great headway. We put up at L. Bostwick's. The work of the Lord hath been manifested here. My afflictions of body are very great—the Lord is pleased to humble me: *perfect through sufferings!* The Lord's will be done! *Thursday*, I preached at Louisville, in great affliction of body; but it was a liberal season: glory be to God for that! *Friday*, a heavy ride to Waynesburg; stopped at Colonel Milton's.[117] It is as warm as July. *Saturday*, after preaching in the old church, I retired to the house of the late Henry Moore, deceased. Wrote a very serious letter to Samuel Dunwoody,[118] on his taking the charge of the Mississippi district. What a field is opened, and opening daily in this New World!

Georgia

Sunday, 27. After twenty years, I preached again in the old church.[119] We had a love feast, and I baptized three persons. The weather was extremely warm. My mind is in perfect peace.

[116] Boehm says the party left Cincinnati on October 14, 1811, and "passed through Kentucky, everywhere preaching the word." (Boehm, *op. cit.*, 365.) Falmouth is in Pendleton County, Kentucky.

[117] Neither Asbury nor Boehm relates details of their trip through Kentucky. The latter says that on Friday evening after dark they came to Rock Castle Bridge and were denied entertainment. They rode seven miles farther and were again denied. This occurred a third time a mile away. Then they met a person who conducted them several miles through the woods to the home of Colonel Milton at Waynesburg, in Lincoln County, "who exhibited a hospitality worthy of patriarchal times." They retired at midnight and were on the road again at five o'clock. (*Ibid.*, 365, 366.)

[118] Samuel Dunwoody had been transferred from Charleston in the South Carolina Conference to the Mississippi District of the Western Conference. Since Tobias Gibson had been sent to Mississippi in 1799, eight circuits had been formed, and there were 639 white and 150 colored members there. (See *Minutes*, 1812.)

[119] Asbury left no record of his route across Tennessee to Georgia. The chronology of the *Journal* is inaccurate and does not agree with Boehm's account. The latter says they reached Athens, Georgia, on Friday, the eighth, and were received by Hope Hull, who had located in 1795 because of his marriage and was living at Athens. On Tuesday, Asbury preached at Bethel Chapel, and Hull and Boehm exhorted. (Boehm, *op. cit.*, 366.)

Monday, 28. We came to Mr. David Lovett's, on Brier Creek, Screven county.

Tuesday, 29. I preached in Blackburn's chapel. Cold, compared with yesterday. Came home with Thomas Thorne.

Wednesday, 30. Came twenty miles to sister King's. My health has somewhat returned. I feel naught but holy desires.

Thursday, 31. I preached at the new chapel. Lodged at Kennedy's. *Friday*, I preached in the Lutheran church. Benjamin Wise, reverend, and some others were present. Brother Boehm gave them a discourse in German. *Saturday*, Savannah.[120]

Sunday, *November* 3. I preached in the Lutheran church. We are about building on a city lot. I hope the time will come to favour us.

Monday, 4. I rest to-day. I went to view the lot. I had two interviews with the Reverend Kollock.[121] I hope when I come again to find a chapel and preacher's house of our own.

Tuesday, 5. Came away, and made a day's journey of forty-two miles. *Wednesday*, reached David Lovett's. *Thursday*, started in the rain. The roads are bad. *Friday*, came to the widow Jarvis's. *Saturday*, reached Augusta.

Sunday, 10. I preached in the forenoon and afternoon, and we had a serious night lecture.

South Carolina

Monday, 11. We rode to Johnson's house of entertainment.[122] *Tuesday*, to Spann's.[123] *Wednesday*, to the widow Hannon's.[124] *Thursday*, to Colonel Hutchinson's.[125]

Monday, 18, the day of my arrival, my knee was stricken with acute rheumatic pain; I applied a strongly-drawing blister, and remained still and quiet. Yesterday I tried a poultice, and I now begin to walk with some ease.

Tuesday, 19. I am something easier to-day. I employ my dumb *Sabbath* and my leisure time as well as I can, and as pain will allow. I have despatched eleven official letters. Hilliard Judge is chosen chaplain to the legislature of South Carolina; and O, great Snethen is chaplain to Congress![126] So; we begin to partake of *the honour that cometh from man*: now is our time of danger. O Lord, keep us pure, keep us correct, keep us holy!

[120] Asbury and Boehm had passed through Effingham County en route to Savannah. (Smith, *op. cit.*, 107.)

[121] Dr. Henry Kollock was the eloquent Presbyterian preacher at Savannah. (*Ibid.*, 114.)

[122] This was probably a tavern at Johnston in Edgefield County, South Carolina.

[123] Spann lived near Ridge Spring in Saluda County.

[124] Mrs. Hannon lived near Lexington.

[125] Colonel Hutchinson lived in Columbia. Asbury spent several days in his home.

[126] Hilliard Judge (1787–1817), a North Carolinian, was in the South Carolina Con-

Monday, 25. We had a serious shock of an earthquake this morning[127] —a sad presage of future sorrows, perhaps. Lord, make us ready!

Thursday, 28. We took to horse, and rode forty miles. It is bitter cold, and we have felt it the more sensibly after being so long housed.

Friday, at Camden, to preside in conference.[128]

Wednesday, *December* 4. I preached before the conference.

Friday, 6. Our conference rose this day.[129] Scarcely have I seen such harmony and love. There are eighty-five preachers stationed. The increase, within its bounds, is three thousand three hundred and eighty. We had a great deal of faithful preaching, and there were many ordinations. I received letters from the extremities and the centre of our vast continent, all pleasing, all encouraging. *Saturday*, rode to brother Henry Young's, on Black River.

Sunday, 29. I preached at Rembert's chapel, and gave an exhortation to the Africans. The society was stayed after meeting, and I exhorted the members. Our labours this day shall not be wholly lost.

Monday, 30. We came away early for Charleston, and made thirty-five miles to Mr. Pendergrass's,[130] where we were well entertained.

Tuesday, 31. Murray's ferry detained us an hour. Down poured the rain. We were glad to stop at Mrs. Kennedy's,[131] and it was no small comfort to be entertained so well.

ference for eight years. At this time he was on the Congaree Circuit but was soon to be appointed presiding elder of the Broad River District. His wife was a sister of Governor Means of South Carolina. He was the first Methodist preacher to be appointed chaplain of the legislature. (Betts, *op. cit.*, 181.) Nicholas Snethen was the first Methodist chaplain of the House of Representatives in Washington. He served in that capacity while he was pastor at Georgetown in the District of Columbia in 1811. (Freeman: *Francis Asbury's Silver Trumpet*, 25.)

[127] This was the New Madrid, Missouri, earthquake of 1811–12. The shock of December 16, 1811, was one of the greatest known earthquakes of history, and it was this shock which Boehm said was felt in Columbia and not the one on the date mentioned by Asbury. Around New Madrid, Missouri, it made the most extensive known change of topography, opening up Reelfoot Lake in Kentucky, changing the course of the Mississippi River, and sank an area of thirty thousand miles from five to fifteen feet deep. The shocks were felt over an area of a million square miles, and the effects are visible today. The best account of the quake was written by Lorenzo Dow. (Boehm, *op. cit.*, 367; Adams: *Dictionary of American History*, II, 181.)

[128] Asbury, McKendree, and Henry Boehm were entertained in the home of Samuel Mathis during the conference. (Boehm, *op. cit.*, 367.)

[129] This conference elected as its representatives to the first delegated General Conference soon to assemble the following: Lewis Myers, Lovick Pierce, Joseph Tarpley, Daniel Asbury, William H. Kennedy, Samuel Dunwoody, James E. Glenn, Hilliard Judge, and Joseph Travis. The session was enlivened by a speech by Lewis Myers against the ordination and admission into full connection of Henry Gramling because he had married. The young preacher was rejected but was admitted later. (*Ibid.*, 368; Smith: *Methodism in Georgia and Florida*, 99, 100; Betts, *op. cit.*, 125; Capers, *op. cit.*, 143, 144.)

[130] Pendergrass lived near Olanta.

[131] The widow Kennedy lived in Berkeley County near Bonneau.

1812

1812 *Asbury arrives at the capitol in Columbia, South Carolina*

CHAPTER FORTY-ONE

South Carolina

Wednesday, *January* 1, 1812.—A steady ride of thirty-eight miles brought us into Charleston. The highways were little occupied by travellers of any kind, which was the more providential to me, for my lameness and my light fly cart would have made a shock of the slightest kind disagreeable. I was anxious also to pass this first day of the new year in undisturbed prayer. *Thursday*, *Friday*, *Saturday*, in reading, meditation, writing and prayer. I do not reject visitors.

Sunday 5. I preached at Cumberland chapel, and met the societies of both colours. I visited the fatherless, and some widows. My mind enjoys peace. In the evening I preached in Bethel chapel. We made our *exodus* from Charleston at eight in the morning. No passage at Clemmon's ferry. We found a lodging with Mr. Brindley: our host has buried one Methodist wife, and is now happy with another. I am consoled to know that our dear departed sister, ever kind to me, died in the Lord. *Tuesday evening*, lodged at the widow Boone's: this family have received Methodist preachers for the last six and twenty years.

Wednesday, 8. We reached Georgetown.[1] I preached in our enlarged chapel on 1 Cor. vii, 29.

[1] At Georgetown the party stopped with William Wayne, the nephew of General "Mad" Anthony Wayne, who had received Asbury on his first visit in 1785. (See note under February 24, 1785.) He was converted by Asbury after having been awakened by reading the writings of John Wesley, and he and his wife were in the first Methodist society at Georgetown. (Boehm, *op. cit.*, 368.)

Thursday, 9. We came away to James Green's, where I preached and then rode over to Francis Green's:[2] here William Capers preached, on "Blessed art thou, Simon Barjona," &c. We took the road on *Friday*, in a driving snow; but missing our path, we got back to James Green's, and there, upon entreaty, consented to stay. We were told on *Saturday morning*, that we could not travel; we tried it nevertheless, and made thirty-five miles in nine hours. The cold was piercing.

Sabbath, 12. No rest for us. We toiled over Pee Dee swamp towards Mary Port's: she had gone to rest. The snow was about a foot deep, and I could not see where they had laid her. We came in to Mr. Newsom's[3] five hours after my time; so I delivered a message to the family: thirty-one miles to-day. On *Monday*, at General Benjamin Lee's, I spoke to a few people.

North Carolina

Tuesday. We dined at Lumberton, and went forward to Mark Russell's, where I spoke to a few people. *Wednesday*, came to Fayetteville. We have had a rude ride of great bodily suffering from Georgetown: but my mind has enjoyed perfect peace, and constant prayer.

Thursday, 16. We made this a sacramental day. What will not perseverance and management do! Here we have built a neat little chapel, costing but twelve hundred dollars, one thousand and fifty of which is paid. *Friday*, we had a cold ride to Amos Richardson's. *Saturday*, thirty miles' riding brought us to King's.

Sabbath, 19. We crossed the river in a storm: at the second ferry it was worse, and we hardly escaped the deep, as it would seem; we arrived, nevertheless, time enough at Mount Zion chapel to bear our testimony from Ephes. v, 14–16: it was open vision. I had, after meeting, a word with the whites and Africans of the society—*plain talk*: Boehm preached in the evening. We were cribbed in our quarters at night—a narrow bed for two; this is no novelty to us. I gave our sister Richards a grant of a lot thirty feet square, in the churchyard. Baptized Captain Cameron's son Alexander. A ride of twenty miles in excessive cold brought us to George Shepherd's hospitable house on *Tuesday*. *Wednesday*, awfully cold: we made twenty miles to S. Ballard's. *Thursday*, another ride of twenty miles brought us to Adonijah Perry's. Our host was sick, and I prescribed for him. *Friday*, a day of abstinence: wrote letters. *Saturday*, we came into New Bern in the rain.

[2] The Green families lived in upper Williamson County. Bishop Capers married the stepdaughter of Richard Green on Black River in Georgetown District. (Capers, *op. cit.*, 147.)

[3] John Newsom lived where Mullins is now located.

Sabbath, 26. I preached morning and evening, and met the whites and Africans of the society. *Monday*. A powerful rain accompanied us to Guilford,[4] twenty-six miles. Here I baptized a Mr. Murphy and his three children. I feel the effects of our damp ride. We called a meeting at Greenville on *Tuesday*, at our sister Brook's: as there were few men present, I adapted text and sermon to the women. We have no chapel here, although we have had a society thirty years. At Mr. Freeman's we dined, talked, and prayed. It began to rain at one o'clock, and we started away to Edward Hall's; we dare not loiter or wait for fair weather. *Thursday*, we halted, concluding to give up Edenton for Tarboro. There are great freshets in the rivers, as we hear. Ah! the ferries! we shall have them, sink or swim. *Friday*, reading, writing, and taking medicine.

Saturday, February 1. I passed the day in prayer, peace, love, and joy.

Sabbath, 2. At Tarboro I preached to a serious, attentive congregation. I preached in the afternoon also at brother Hall's. *Monday*, I breakfasted with Mr. Austin, an English Baptist; his wife with us; my business with him was to charge him most solemnly to hold a perpetual prayer meeting every Wednesday evening in his house. The lowlands about Tarboro bridge are under water. We came thirty miles to Colonel John Whitaker's: here I had occasion to give a solemn and personal testimony, and it was *publicly* given. On *Tuesday* we had a meeting of a few neighbours in Pinner's family. We have made seven hundred miles since we left Camden, through frost, floods, cold, and hunger; poor men, and poor horses! Well, this life is not eternal. *Wednesday*, came to Murfreesboro, dined with the respectable widow Meredith and her children, prayed, and continued forward to Jesse Battle's; a hailstorm overtook us on the way. This house is in affliction.

Virginia

Thursday, reached Isaac Lunsford's, forty miles, visiting an afflicted family on our route. Richard Yerbury has gone from poor Suffolk to the rich inheritance of glory; he was almost a prodigy of affliction and of grace. On *Friday* we held a meeting at Portsmouth, and preached to a full house.

Sabbath, 9. I preached in Norfolk, and met the society.

Monday, 10. Came to Isaac Lunsford's, and thence to Suffolk; what a sickly country is this! I have heard of three deaths in as many days. We had a small meeting at General Wells's widow's: the head of the house

[4] The present Guilford in North Carolina is about two hundred miles from New Bern, the section in which Asbury was traveling at this time. Greenville is about forty-three miles from New Bern, but there is no indication as to the actual place to which Asbury referred as "Guildford."

and his daughter have departed in peace since my last visit. I visited, as is my custom, the graves of the deceased. On *Wednesday* the cold was excessive, and we were right glad to house with Andrew Woodley, who treated us with great kindness. I preached at night at William Blunt's.

Friday, 14. The weather was clear, but chilly. We made twenty-eight miles only, to our friend Birdsong's. I see a providence always over me, and I am always stayed upon God.

Saturday, 15. We came to Bryant's, twenty-five miles, and could go no farther; they put me to bed very unwell. Our host is a disobedient son reclaimed—of Methodist parents. Here are two meeting houses, and the gospel is brought back to the vicinity of Prince George court house, after thirty years' absence. No time was to be lost—I took tartar, and had a serious spell while it lasted.

Sabbath, 16. I rode about a mile and gave a sermon. My breast is sore, and my heart is in pain for Petersburg. *Monday*, I visited my ancient friends, Wood Tucker and wife.

We came to John Bradley's on *Tuesday night*, and preached on Heb. ii, 1–4. *Wednesday*, a muddy ride brought us to town. Our conference began on *Thursday*.[5] The affair of James Boyd and Henry Hardy detained us two days from other business. We shall not station more than seventy-five preachers this year—a less number than last. A charge had been brought against me for ordaining a slave; but there was no further pursuit of the case when it was discovered that I was ready with my certificates to prove his freedom; the subject of contention was nearly white, and his *respectable* father would neither own nor manumit him. I shall mention no names. Old Virginia, because of the great emigrations westward, and deaths, decreases in the number she gives to the Methodists; but new Virginia gains. Doctor Jennings was at conference, and preached often for us, and was much followed. We had little or no trouble about the stations, and conference rose on *Thursday*. I started away and came in great haste to Willis's chapel:[6] the heat was oppressive, and man and beast gladly stopped at the widow Sculley's. Little sleep last night. Let me suffer, and let me labour; time is short, and souls are daily lost.

Sabbath, *March* 1. It blew a cutting wind at northeast, as we made our way towards Roper's chapel,[7] thirty miles distant. I preached some awful truths. *Monday*, I passed a night of great suffering. We came off this morning to James City, and preached in the chapel to many people—we had an evening meeting. Lodged at John Taylor's. *Tuesday*, we came to Williamsburg,[8] where I preached with a full mind, but failing voice.

[5] This conference was held in Richmond, the first to be held in that place. (Bennett, *op. cit.*, 572–75.)

[6] Willis Chapel was in Henrico County. The church was used as a hospital during the Civil War. [7] Roper's Chapel was in New Kent County.

[8] Boehm says they stayed at Brother Ratcliff's in Williamsburg. (Boehm, *op. cit.*, 379.)

Wednesday, we rode near forty miles to breakfast with an English family, the Whitefields; and went forward to lodge with George Hope,[9] a shipbuilder from Whitehaven.

Thursday, 5. I preached in the new brick house, Hampton; ordained Robert Gilliam and brother Evans local deacons. I suffer from a deep cold. On *Friday* I had an opportunity of giving the two families of Lucas and Stubblefield a solemn warning and charge. We crossed the river at Yorktown, now like many other towns, declining in numbers and in wickedness, because of the decrease of trade and strong drink.

Saturday, 7. At Philip Tabb's, Esquire[10]—a great farmer, and a kind and hospitable gentleman.

Sabbath, 8. It rained, and we had two hours in the cold house to utter our testimony. I came home with deacon Bellamy, a witness of the sanctifying power of grace. We rejoiced in God. He handed me Michaelis, which I read. *Monday*, came on to Shackleford's chapel, where I found a few auditors from Gloucester.

Tuesday, 10. To Pace's chapel—I go forward in rain, and in temptation and affliction, and great grief for souls. I find that Michaelis, contrary to Bengelius and Wesley, has left it doubtful concerning the *three that bear witness in heaven*: the doctrine is not the less true.

Wednesday, 11. At Cole's chapel I preached on Luke xiii, 23–25. I dined with father Mann, where, I presume, I preached thirty-three years past;[11] this family cleaves to us, but the Baptists have the rule in Queen Anne[12] and Essex. We must not be envious—we have it, and are getting it, and will continue to get it, if we are faithful, still more abundantly throughout the whole continent. I was happy in spending a night under the roof of a simple-hearted poor man, Billy Carr; he travelled four years, and is now a useful local preacher.

Thursday, 12. I preached at Hobbe's Hole; it was damp and I was cold, but I felt help from God. This labour will go for the Baptists: mother Cox, a Baptist, had appointed a meeting for me, and I gave them a sermon. We sow here, but others reap. On my way to Port Royal, on *Friday*, I expounded a text of Scripture to the family of John Rowzie. *Saturday evening* brought us into poor Fredericksburg.

Sabbath, 15. I preached for them. The Methodists have done great good here: since they began to preach the Baptists and Presbyterians have built

[9] George Hope lived in Hampton.

[10] Philip and Mary Tabb were outstanding people, and Asbury visited their home several times. A son was born shortly after Asbury wrote to her on July 30, 1807. (See *Letters*.) She gave the lot and building for Mount Zion Church, which was located on a hill overlooking Toddsbury estate. The estate is still intact. Members of the Todd family are buried in the Ware Neck Episcopal Church graveyard.

[11] Asbury was not in Virginia in 1779 and did not pass through Essex County in 1780 or 1781. Perhaps he did stop at Mann's in 1782.

[12] Princess Anne County was named for Queen Anne. It was formed in 1691.

meeting houses. Mr. Strebeck has the Episcopal church. We were off on *Monday*, through mud and mist, to Samuel's tavern, twenty miles; here we fed and prayed with the family. At Grigg's I gave a night lecture. I preached at Mrs. Hoe's to a full house on *Tuesday morning*, and went forward to Major Newell's, making a ride of forty-six miles. I called, on *Wednesday*, on my friend Mr. Carter, who has now six children in society: surely the time to favour this family is come. We laboured along to Leesburg, stemming the cold and boisterous northwest. *Friday* and *Saturday* were spent in happy, loving conference.[13] My task it was to ordain sixteen deacons. I preached, so also did brother M'Kendree.

Wednesday, 18. Ordination day for elders; I had declined, not wishing to preach the sermon; but I officiated, and N. Snethen preached. We have had a solemn, loving, peaceful conference. Our labours ended on *Friday morning*, and we separated. Arrived at the ferry, it blew a hurricane. I lifted up my heart in prayer to God. There was in a few minutes a great calm, which all those with me witnessed, but I will not say it was in answer to prayer.

Maryland

We lodged with Ephraim Howard, upon Carroll's manor.

Saturday, 21. We called and dined with our respectable brother Ignatius Davis:[14] Ah! he is rich in property and a young wife! It blew up very cold as we came into Frederick.

Sabbath, 29. Easter Sunday. I was three hours reading, praying, preaching, and meeting the society, white and coloured; it was a day of God and of his power. My congregation chiefly from the country. A cold ride brought us to Liberty; *Monday morning*, I preached for them, and went on to Ephraim Howard's.

Tuesday, 31. We moved forward, calling on brothers Joshua Jones and Alexander Warfield. Lodged under the roof of Nancy Willis. There are many late converts around her: Frank Hollingsworth and his wife,[15] Henry Willis, and a young lady with fifty thousand dollars—can she get and keep religion? I doubt.

[13] This was the Baltimore Conference, which was held at Leesburg, Virginia.

[14] Ignatius Davis (1760–1828) lived near Buckeystown, Frederick County, Maryland. The erection of the first Libertytown Chapel, of which he was a trustee, has been attributed to his effort and generosity. (Scharf: *History of Western Maryland*, I, 568.)

[15] This was Francis Hollingsworth (1774–1826), who was the editor and transcriber of Asbury's *Journal*. He was the son of Jesse Hollingsworth, a pioneer Baltimore Methodist, who led in the erection of Strawberry Alley Chapel. He married Mary Yellott, a daughter of John Yellott. In April, 1812, they with their five children lived on Little Pipe Creek, but it is probable they were spending some time with his widowed sister, Mrs. Henry Willis. (See notes under August 21, 1773, and March 14, 1811.)

Wednesday, April 1. I preached at Joshua Tipton's;[16] this is an ancient friend whom I had not visited for eight years. Henry Boehm preached in German. *Thursday*, dined near Union chapel at Mr. Matthews's,[17] and went forward to Meredith's.

Pennsylvania

Friday, a cold disagreeable ride brought us across the country to Samuel Brinkley's:[18] here I received the first intelligence of the death of my dear old friend Martin Boehm.

Sabbath, 5. I preached at Boehm's chapel the funeral sermon of Martin Boehm, and gave my audience some very interesting particulars of his life. *Monday*, busy writing. *Tuesday*, at Jacob Boehm's: I preached here.

Wednesday, 8. We called on Zeltenright; kinder people need not be: we fed and prayed with them. I went forward and preached at Churchtown,[19] and housed with Owen Brunner. I suffer much in my feet amongst the Germans, and I greatly dislike stoves. We had a blessed meeting on *Thursday evening*.

Friday, 10. Rode to Coventry. We had a full house. Ah! where are my sisters Richards, Vanlear, Potts, Rutter, Patrick, North?[20] At rest in Jesus; and I am left to pain and toil: courage, my soul, we shall overtake them when our task is done! I visited Mr. May.[21] If they wanted the plan

[16] The grave of a Joshua Tipton (1800–53) is in the burying ground of the Methodist Episcopal Church that was erected in 1845 in Hamstead, Carroll County. (Scharf: *History of Western Maryland*, II, 802.) He may have been the son of the Joshua Tipton to whom Asbury refers.

[17] The Union Meeting House was a two-story brick building which was erected in 1760 near the center of the Westminster Cemetery. Until the different denominations erected their own places of worship, it served as a community religious center. For nearly a quarter of a century it was the only Methodist meetinghouse in Westminster. (Lynch: *A Hundred Years of Carroll County*, 30.)

[18] Samuel Brinkley lived about a mile from the home of Martin Boehm. (Boehm, *op. cit.*, 372.)

[19] Churchtown, Lancaster County, Pennsylvania, is located twenty-one miles northeast of the city of Lancaster.

[20] Sister Richards was a granddaughter of Mrs. Grace. It was probably her husband who became one of the founders of the Eagle Iron Works in Philadelphia. (See *Journal* entry for June 6, 1799.) Mrs. Thomas Rutter lived at Nantmeal, near Coventry, where her husband had an interest in the Warwick Furnace. Mrs. North was the wife of Colonel Caleb North, one of the original trustees of the Chartered Fund. He was the partner of Thomas Haskins.

[21] May (1749–1812) married, first, Rebecca, daughter of Thomas and Anna Nutt Potts, and, second, her sister, Ruth Potts. To the first marriage were born two children, Eliza and Rebecca Grace, and to the second were born seven children. The eldest

for their meeting house, here it is—forty by fifty feet. I rejoiced in finding three of sister Rutter's[22] children in the way.

Sabbath, 12. I preached at old Israel Anderson's.[23] Our friend has been in fellowship with us thirty-two years, and has been honoured by missions from his country and district to the legislature and to congress: his family of children are pleasing. Twice only have I ever visited this neighbourhood. *Monday*. Snow and cold.

Tuesday, 14. I preached at Radnor. We dined at B. Gyger's, and slept under the roof of Isaac James. The peace and consolations of God abound towards me.

Wednesday, 15. Came to the city of Philadelphia. We opened our conference in great peace on *Saturday*.

Sabbath, 19. Preached in St. George's in the morning, and at St. Thomas's[24] in the evening. It is a time of peace. We had a solemn time at the ordination of deacons on *Wednesday*. I preached at Union chapel on *Friday*.

Sabbath, 26. I gave them a sermon at Ebenezer in the forenoon, met the society at Union, and ordained, as deacons, Joseph Ingles[25] and John George,[26] venerable and pious men. On *Thursday* all the honours of officiating at the ordinations fell upon me, Bishop M'Kendree being sick. I closed the conference on *Monday* morning. Sister Lusby's[27] lamp is nearly extinct; I visited and prayed with her.

daughter, Eliza, became the wife of Samuel Stevens, who was elected governor of Maryland. Thomas Potts became the rector of the Episcopal Church at Norristown; James, the rector of St. Stephen's Church, Wilkes-Barre, and later of St. Paul's, Philadelphia; Newton received his M.D. and practiced medicine in Holmesburg; and Addison became a lawyer at West Chester. (*History of Chester County*, III, 654–55.)

[22] There were four daughters in the Rutter family.

[23] This may have been Isaac Anderson, of Charlestown and Valley Forge, who was one of the early inhabitants of this section who brought with them religious doctrines to which they adhered strictly. Among the first to accept Methodism in Charlestown were Isaac Anderson and his wife, Mary. Their grandson, the Rev. James Rush Anderson, was a member of the Philadelphia Conference. Isaac Anderson was elected to represent the counties of Lancaster, Chester, and Dauphin in the state legislature. (Lednum, *op. cit.*, 285.)

[24] This was the new meetinghouse on Tenth Street below Market Street. It was an enterprise sponsored by some of the wealthier members of Union Church, Thomas Haskins being one of the prime movers. The enterprise failed as a Methodist church, however, and its building was later used by St. Stephen's Episcopal Church, which now occupies the site with a newer edifice.

[25] Joseph L. Ingles resided on Second Street near Spruce Street in Philadelphia. He was the treasurer of the Frankford and Bristol Turnpike Company. (*Philadelphia City Directory, 1813*.)

[26] John George was a haircloth manufacturer at Chestnut and Fourth streets in Philadelphia. (*Ibid.*)

[27] Elizabeth Lusby was a daughter of Mrs. Steele of Germantown. (See *Journal* entry for January 5, 1796.)

New Jersey

We came away and rode in the afternoon sixteen miles to father Thomas Rodman's. We lodged with Mr. Jacob Snyder at New Brunswick on *Tuesday night*.

New York

Wednesday, a cold ride brought us to New York.

Friday, May 1. Our General Conference began.[28] During the session I saw nothing like unkindness but once, and there were many and weighty affairs discussed. I hope very few rules will be made. We may disquiet ourselves in vain.

Sabbath, 10. At the African church in the morning: I preached also at the Hudson chapel; it was an awful time. A subject before the conference was the question, If local deacons, after four years of probation, should be elected to the eldership by two-thirds of the conference, having no slaves, and having them, to manumit them where the laws allowed it—it passed by a majority. On *Saturday*, a motion was made to strengthen the episcopacy by adding another bishop.

Sabbath, 17. I preached at Brooklyn in our elegant house.[29] After a serious struggle of two days in General Conference to change the mode of appointing presiding elders, it remains as it was. Means had been used to keep back every presiding elder who was known to be favourable to appointments by the bishops; and long and earnest speeches have been made to influence the minds of the members: Jesse Lee, Asa Shinn, and Nicholas Snethen were of a side; and these are great men. Many matters of small moment passed under review, and were regulated. Mr. Shaw, of London, called to see me, and I had seventeen of the preachers to dine with me; there was vinegar, mustard, and a still greater portion of oil: but the disappointed parties sat down in peace, and we enjoyed our sober meal. We should thank God that we are not at war with each other, as are the Episcopalians, with the pen and the press as their weapons of warfare.

Sabbath, 17. At the Two Mile Stone my subject was 1 Peter iv, 6–9. I preached also at Greenwich, and at John Street Chapel. On *Monday* I took an emetic, but I found I could not be sick in quiet, so unceasingly was I pursued by visitors and letters; so I made my escape to George Suckley's and took to my bed. On *Tuesday* I breakfasted with Colonel Few. Some

[28] This was the first delegated General Conference of the Methodist Episcopal Church, with ninety elected representatives attending from the eight annual conferences.

[29] This was the new and larger structure that had recently been completed on the original Sands Street property. This building in later years was called "The Old White Church." (Warriner, *op. cit.*, 15–17; Boehm, *op. cit.*, 396.)

good widows collected above two hundred dollars for the poor preachers in New England States: sister Seney[30] I must make honourable mention of as being very active in this labour of love. We made a peaceable ride of twenty-four miles to mother Sherwood's. I have been kept from sinning, in much patience and affliction.

Wednesday, 20. Came to Eben Smith's; the host kind and attentive; the mother holy and devout: I cannot pass my old friends without a call. I called on Joseph Crawford, and took to my bed: I suffer. In the evening I preached at White Plains chapel in much affliction of body: we lodged at brother Fowler's.

Thursday, 21. Rode to Croton: here I saw once more the elder of ninety-two—much in the enjoyment of God and of himself.

Friday, 22. We halted on our way at Peekskill. I prayed in Burrill's small house.

Saturday, 23. We stopped at Mr. Williams's: I am blessed with patience. I preached on *Wednesday*, and administered the Lord's supper: I am in weakness and fear, and much trembling.

Saturday, *May* 30. I saw our little conventicle in Rhinebeck.

Monday, *June* 1. We halted awhile at Esopus; dined at the widow Scott's. We have had a home here many years: the Lord heard prayer for the father, who died in peace. We lodged at John Crawford's: I suffer from high fevers. On *Tuesday* we rode through the heat, thirty-four miles, to Coeyman's Landing, and preached at six o'clock. The blister at the back of my ears broke on the way. O, for patience and faith! A cold ride brought us to Albany. The Dutch Synod and the Methodist Conference are about to sit here. From the fourth to the tenth we have been occupied in close conference.

Sabbath, 7. I preached in an old house: and we had a gracious season. I gave a solemn exhortation on the spot designated for our new church: the situation is very eligible. *Wednesday*, conference ended its labours. *Thursday*, we rose at five o'clock, and crossed the river: after a ride of five hours in the rain we were willing to stop at Mr. Darling's.

Friday, 12. Came through Shakerstown: if these are children of light, they are wiser in their generation than the children of this world. We took a hasty dinner with Gamaliel Whitney, and came away in the rain to Hawley's. *Saturday*, we dined on our route at Merrill's, and came in to lodge with Squire Pitkin.[31]

[30] Mrs. Seney, a widow, had recently come to New York from Maryland and was very active in Methodist affairs. Her son, Robert Seney (1797–1854), was fifteen years of age at this time. He was received on trial in 1820 and served for thirty years in the Methodist ministry in and near New York. His son, George I. Seney, initiated the organization of the great Methodist Hospital in Brooklyn, providing a large portion of its original endowment. (Seaman, *op. cit.*, 245.)

[31] Hosea Merrill lived at Pittsfield, Massachusetts, and his descendants are still there. Squire Timothy Pitkin lived in East Hartford, Connecticut, where his father, Elisha,

Connecticut

Sabbath, 14. I preached at Glastonbury and met the society. *Monday*, at Hebron we visited three families, and were kindly received by Doctor Huntington, with whom we lodged in Windham. *Tuesday*, we dined in Abington, and lectured to a few people in the evening at John Nichols's. *Wednesday*, a ride of thirty miles brought us to father Balls's, where we lodged; all is not right here.

Massachusetts

Thursday, we dined at Stone's tavern in Framingham; they had nearly been as wild as Indians when we prayed. I have felt sick enough to be in bed. We came to Lynn. I come through great tribulation.

Saturday, 20. Our conference began and progressed in much peace and order. *Thursday*, I gave preachers and people a sermon.

Sabbath, 21. I preached. The chapel, saving the pews and the steeple, is beautiful. We had an ordination. The proclamation of the president of the United States is out, to inform us that there is war between our people and the English people: my trust is in the living God. *Thursday* we came rapidly through a storm of rain to father William Bogle's in Needham; we were well steeped. *Friday*, we took the Worcester road to Brookfield. *Saturday*, we came off at four o'clock, and rode seventeen miles to breakfast at Belcherstown, and continued onward fifteen miles beyond Warner's.

Sabbath, 28. We made a ride of twenty-five miles to Pittsfield. Brother M'Kendree preached at two o'clock; and I ascended the pulpit at six o'clock in the evening. *Monday*, we called on our way at father Spicer's. We have spent on this journey twenty-three dollars. There is a serious division in Pittsfield—about thirty members have withdrawn. They have built a neat house in Lynn; but I am afraid of a steeple; and if they put this foolish addition, it must not be by Methodist order, or with Methodist money—they may pay for their own pride and folly. We have had great peace and order in the New England Conference; but we are poor.

New York

July 1. We came away to Lansingburg. We must stand still and see the salvation of God in these times of trouble.

Sabbath, 5. At Troy I preached and gave an exhortation to the society.

built a house which was called the "Minister's Hotel" because of the owner's hospitality to the preachers. The squire lived where South Meadow Road intersects Second Main Street. (*Pitkin Family Genealogy*, 64, 65.)

At Lansingbury I preached in the evening,[32] but did not feel myself at liberty as in Troy. On *Tuesday* we came through the heat to Beldin's, twenty-two miles; here we had grand entertainment. *Wednesday*, we concluded it best to keep on our way, and miss the camp meeting. We prayed with the family with whom we dined on our route. Came to Little Falls, and were well received and accommodated at Moralle's. It rained, but we continued on to Reuben Mather's. The people gaze and laugh at us as we pass: surely we are men to be wondered at and hated by all but the pious.

Sabbath, 12. We hold our conference in Lyons.[33] Brother M'Kendree preached in the morning, and I gave a discourse in the evening at Westmoreland. We went forward to David Coe's, where I preached at night. My host had entertained me at Middlefield, Connecticut, twenty-two years ago.[34] My mind enters deeply into God, his providence and grace. Consequential W. B. Lacy[35] is married; and why not?—he has left us; and why not? Between Albany and Lynn, and Boston, we have spent thirty dollars and fifty-six cents—a few cents more than the conference furnished for our expenses. On *Saturday* we rode over to our brother Hanna's,[36] from Queen's county, Ireland.

I preached at Bethel chapel, standing on the floor to speak. I was feeble, yet I met the society, baptized a child, and addressed my brethren and sisters on the subject of singing as a part of the worship of God. The solemn fast to be observed on the first Friday in October was not forgotten to be mentioned. I called up the children of my host to read for me, and had a serious conversation with the two eldest, the only son and eldest daughter: the tears witnessed how deeply they felt. We came away to Holmes's on *Monday morning*, and thence to Forbisher's: here we have a chapel. We called a meeting at night at father Doolittle's.

Tuesday, 14. A long ride through Manlius, and calling at Dodge's, brought us into the widow Hocox's neat house. We dined at Hommerman's, in Auburn, on *Wednesday*, and lodged with Eddy, Scipio. On our way we were mocked by some men in a harvest field: this is their glory of

[32] Methodist preaching had begun here rather early, but the first church was not erected until 1810. It was this church in which Asbury now preached. (*Troy Conference Miscellany*, 56.)

[33] This conference had been posted for Niagara but could not be held there because of the War of 1812. Evidently arrangements to hold the conference at Lyons were only now confirmed, hence this entry.

[34] Asbury was not in Connecticut in 1790. However, he had visited Middlefield, Connecticut, on June 11, 1791, "and lodged at the house of a niece of David Brainard." This must have been Coe's, which he mentions here. He was at Middlefield again on July 11, 1794, but mentioned no place of entertainment.

[35] William B. Lacy was received on trial in 1805. He took his station on the Herkimer Circuit in 1812, but after five or six weeks he left his circuit in an unofficial manner. The committee appointed to examine the case agreed that Lacy had attempted to sow discord among the people. (*General Minutes* for 1813.)

[36] Asbury had tarried at this friendly home, while in much suffering, on June 21, 1807.

wickedness: ours is, that the offence of the cross hath not yet ceased. My revenge was prayer that God might convert and save them for Christ's sake.

Sabbath, 19. I preached at Lyon's town. I have been reading Faber; there appears, to my mind, to be more probability in his expositions of prophecy than in those of any other commentator, more especially as it relates to the Jews. We have had a blessed rain. Lord, pardon the sins of an ungrateful and unholy people!

Thursday, *Friday*, and *Saturday* were employed in a very pleasing conference, about thirty members being present: our brethren of Canada were all absent.[37] Elders and deacons were ordained: the increase of members, according to the returns, one thousand.

Sabbath, 26. I preached upon the camp ground. I have been located in Daniel Dorsey's family eleven days; I want to be moving. Had not hostilities existed between us and our neighbours, I should have spent some of this time in visiting the frontiers on Niagara. Our funds allowed us to give forty-nine dollars for the support of each single preacher, one hundred and eighteen dollars for those married and their wives and children. On *Monday* the members of conference communed in the Lord's supper, after which I read off their stations, and we parted in great peace. Through two showers of rain, after dinner, I made my way to Geneva. I lectured in a school house in the evening, from James iv, 8–10. I was directed to forcible and right words.

Tuesday, 28. The heat is excessive, yet we went forward, accompanied by our local brethren. I ordained our brother Goodwin under the trees. We were willing to halt at the invitation of Mr. Thompson to dinner. I felt like Jonah in the sun. We were kindly received for the night by Judge Smith on the Seneca Lake. I die daily. I live in God from moment to moment. My text for *Friday*, 31, the appointed fast-day, was Isaiah lviii, 1: I was weak, but truth was strong. I will leave Newtown this afternoon. There must be a great change here. We came away, after meeting, to Elijah Griswold's: my host is a brand plucked from the burning—strong drink had scorched him forty years. He had a pious son who watched over, and prayed for him; and he himself never closed his doors against the pious. The Lord heard prayer on his behalf, and has entirely delivered him from the love of whisky. I hear of another wonderful emancipation from the slavery of drunkenness.

Pennsylvania

Sunday, *August* 2. We[38] rest at Joshua Kenney's, Black Walnut Bottom.[39]

[37] None of the preachers from Canada appeared at this conference because of the War of 1812.

[38] Henry Boehm was again Asbury's traveling companion. (Boehm, *op. cit.*, 404.)

[39] Black Walnut Bottom was above Meshoppen, Pennsylvania. (See note under July 16, 1807.)

My congregation might amount to one hundred. Our host was a whisky maker; but now it is a house for God. In all my weakness I am kept in perfect peace. Yesterday I visited, conversed, and prayed with Mr. Ourton's family, the wife and mother: the people are serious, but the head is a man of the world. For forty years past we have preached the gospel from the mouth to the branches, and up them, of the great river Susquehanna; the fruit of our labour has begun to appear within the last five years[40]; we shall see it yet more abundant.

Monday, 3. We came away to John Smith's, and continued onward to father Smith's,[41] but came in too late for meeting.

Tuesday, 4. We dined at father Bidlack's,[42] and went forward to Wilkes-Barre. The court was sitting,[43] and a meeting was expected. My subject was "Knowing the terror of the Lord we persuade men." They gave me the court room.

Wednesday, 5. We came along down the turnpike, and rough we found it. Farewell to Merwine's—I lodge no more there; whisky—hell; as most of the taverns here are. Our *Thursday's* ride brought us rapidly to Lehigh; we crossed at the ford, and had little time to admire the beautiful country above and below. The Germans are decent in their behaviour in this neighbourhood; and would be more so, were it not for vile whisky: this is the prime curse of the United States, and will be, I fear much, the ruin of all that is excellent in morals and government in them. Lord, interpose thine arm! Lord, send thy gospel to these Germans![44] We lodge with George Custos, Wyomissing.[45]

Friday, 7. I am still; I abstain. In the evening we had an assemblage of people, and brother Boehm spoke to them in German.

[40] The membership of the Wyoming Circuit had risen from 100 in 1791 to 530 this year. (See *Minutes*.)

[41] "Father Smith" was probably Newton Smith, who lived at Osterhout, Pennsylvania. (See *Journal* entry and note for July 16, 1807.) John Smith probably lived up the Susquehanna River between Osterhout and Tunkhannock.

[42] Benjamin Bidlack (c. 1759–1845), an officer in the Revolution, became an itinerant Methodist preacher in 1799. At the time of Asbury's visit he had located and probably lived in Kingston, Pennsylvania, the home of his wife. (Palmer, *op. cit.*, 92, 98, 99, 123, 198.)

[43] The Luzerne County courthouse on the Wilkes-Barre public square was used for religious services. Asbury preached there on his first visit on July 7, 1793. (See note under that date; Palmer, *op. cit.*, 128.)

[44] Asbury's concern for preaching to the Germans is seen in the fact that he was accompanied by Henry Boehm, the German-speaking preacher, on several tours. It was expressed in Asbury's last letter, written to McKendree from the home of Matthew Myrick in Brunswick County, Virginia, on March 4, 1816. In this letter Asbury suggested that Boehm should be made presiding elder of the Chesapeake District because of his knowledge of the German language. (See that letter in the volume of letters.)

[45] Asbury doubtless referred to Wyomissing, a suburb of Reading. (Plumb: *History of Hanover Township*, 75; Palmer, *op. cit.*, 5, 7, *et seq.*)

Saturday, 8. We visited F. Hyles, on our way to A. T. Brobest's. I feel a deep concern for the Old and New World; calamity and suffering are coming upon them both: I shall make but few remarks on this unhappy subject; it is one on which the prudent will be silent; but I must needs say it is an evil day. I have written many letters of serious warning to our elders.

Sunday, 9. Brother Boehm preached in Dutch. I gave a few words of exhortation to the folks at J. Brobest's, at the Forge; W. Fox exhorted. *Monday*, on our way to Schuylkill[46] we strayed somewhat. Henry Boehm preached at our kind host's, J. Dondor's, a German.

Tuesday, 11. We climbed and laboured over the Furnace hills,[47] to Peter Albie's,[48] a disciple of father Boehm.

Wednesday, 12. We passed through Lititz,[49] a second Bethlehem. What a lovely country we have lately seen! no slaves here. The river Lehigh has three branches, flowing from the Beach or Green Swamp,[50] which cross the Wyoming turnpike to Bethlehem: this beautiful stream, according to my computation, meanders one hundred miles to its mouth, making its way, by disruptive force, as it would seem, through what is called the Gap in the Blue Ridge.[51] *Wednesday, Thursday, Friday, Saturday*, at mother Boehm's, writing, reading, and prayer; these are my occupations and enjoyments.

Sunday, 16. I preached at Souderberg's chapel in the morning; and at

[46] Schuylkill County, Pennsylvania, lies above the Blue Mountain in the east central part of the state.

[47] Furnace Hills was located along the present Highway 322, between Lebanon and Ephrata. In all probability the Cornwall furnaces are responsible for the name.

[48] This was probably Peter Allbright. When George Allbright, who settled in this territory, arrived from Germany, there was a son Peter on the passenger list. Peter, a convert of the Rev. Martin Boehm, was for several years a local preacher among the Methodists. At length he concluded that his call was to the Germans exclusively, and after he had been instrumental in the conversion of many of them, he was recognized as the head of a sect that was at first called "Allbright Methodists." He lived near New Holland, Pennsylvania.

[49] Lititz, a town in Warwick Township, Lancaster County, was begun in 1754, the plan being made by the Rev. Nathaniel Seidel and John Reuter. It was named for a village in Bohemia. The property was owned entirely by the Moravian Brethren, and all its early interests, both religious and secular, were controlled by them. (Ellis and Evans: *History of Lancaster County, Pennsylvania.*)

[50] The Green Swamp was in the northwestern corner of Monroe County. The three creeks are the Bear Creek, the creek that flows out of Brady's Pond, and the Tobyhanna Creek.

[51] The Lehigh Gap is in the Blue Mountain south of Palmerton. The Blue Mountain, so called because of a blue haze that frequently hovers over it, begins at the Delaware Water Gap and continues in a southwesterly direction across the state to the Tuscarora Mountain near Spring Run, Pennsylvania. (Faris: *Old Trails and Roads in Penn's Land.*)

Strasburg at two o'clock; and again at Bethel at six o'clock. *Monday*, we crossed at M'Call's ferry[52] and came to father Jones's.[53]

Maryland

Tuesday, 18. Rode through the rain to John Low's;[54] dined, prayed, and came away to Manchester. We lodged at Rutler's, a Dutch family. *Friday*, we came into the camp.[55] *Monday*, we came to Pipe Creek, and dined with my old friend James M'Cannon. The meeting began yesterday. I preached to a great crowd. What good may be wrought at this meeting, time, and, especially, eternity will show. There were about one hundred tents, and often five thousand people on the ground. In four nights I suppose I have had eight hours' sleep. I was greatly blest at the sacrament. *Tuesday*, dined at Fredericktown; and went forward to Middletown. After forty years' labour, we have a small society in this place. We gave them discourses in English and German in the evening. *Wednesday*, toiling over the South Mountain to Snevely's.[56] On *Thursday* I preached in the neat, new chapel in Hagerstown, to about one hundred hearers; and after meeting visited and tarried for the night with the widow Dowler:[57] our kind hostess is an afflicted woman, unable to walk, yet she enjoyeth much communion with God. On *Friday* we ventured upon the United States' road to Cumberland;[58] dining on our route with Rascer, whom I

[52] McCall's Ferry crossed the Susquehanna River about fourteen miles below Columbia, Pennsylvania.

[53] This was probably Ellis Jones, who was an official member of the Baltimore Circuit. (Armstrong, *op. cit.*, 508.)

[54] The identity of John Low is uncertain. A John Low (1786–1876) of Carroll County served in the War of 1812. Asbury was en route to Manchester, also in the present Carroll County. In 1809 a class was begun at John Low's on the Frederick Circuit.

[55] This camp meeting, which was also the quarterly meeting for Frederick Circuit, was held on land near Enoch Umstead's. This was perhaps the third held on the Frederick Circuit. (*Steward's Book, Frederick Circuit, 1800–1846*, Lovely Lane Museum, Baltimore; Boehm, *op. cit.*, 405.)

[56] The only family with a surname that approaches "Snevely" between South Mountain and Hagerstown is that of Casper Snavely. Between 1780 and 1794 one Snively lived northwest of Williamsport, and one Schnevly lived north of Hagerstown. (Griffith: *Map of the State of Maryland, 1794.*) However, had they in 1812 resided in their same homes, neither would have met Asbury's requirements for location.

[57] The "widow Dowler" was probably formerly married to Richard Dowler, although the Washington County records contain no reference. (For Richard Dowler see note under June 22, 1808.)

[58] Here Asbury uses the popular misnomer for the extension of the road through Hancock to Cumberland which was financed by Maryland banks. The first ten miles of the National Road, authorized by Congress and paid for from federal funds, with Cumberland as its eastern terminus, were completed in 1812. (Hulbert: *Historic Highways of America*, X, 54; Hulbert: *The Paths of Inland Commerce*, 121, 122; Searight: *The Old Pike*, 25–27.)

warned faithfully; as also Thomas Pratt[59] and Major Briscoe,[60] whom we visited, exhorted, and prayed with. *Saturday*, a fatiguing ride, through oppressive heat, brought us fasting to Aquila Brown's.[61]

Sunday, 30. I preached in Cumberland to an attentive people, and went on to Cresaptown, where I also bore my testimony: there might be one thousand people in the two congregations. I have little rest. We came up the mountain, dining at Mussulman's, and going thence forward to Tomlinson's.[62] There was a strange medley of preachers, drovers, beasts on four legs, and beasts made by whisky on two, travelling on the turnpike at one time.

Pennsylvania

Tuesday, September 1. A rude, rough ride, brought us to Clark's, twenty-eight miles. *Wednesday*, we met my friend Judge Vanmeeter, at the bottom of Laurel Hill, with five hundred fat steers from his prairie in Ohio; if he can undertake this labour and perform it cheerfully for the sake of gain, why should I complain of my sufferings? There are very distressing rumours abroad: my mind is fixed on, "Ye are of more value than many sparrows." After losing so much rest, I could have wished to sleep without annoyance from fleas or bed bugs. Two innkeepers on our route, Besoon and Tomlinson, declare against keeping or selling liquid fire: this is great. We moved on *Thursday* to the widow Henthorn's, within a mile of the camp ground. I preached on *Friday* and *Saturday*. The ministry are instructed to be careful to preach to the soldiers, wherever opportunity offers. The Union Volunteers[63] desired a sermon, so I gave a discourse on the ground:[64] my subject was Jer. ii, 13.

Monday, 7. We celebrated a solemn sacrament; a simple-hearted, weeping people, crowded round the table. My soul has been greatly blessed

[59] This may have been the Pratt who kept a tavern on this National Road between Sideling Hill and Polish Mountain. The name of the proprietor has been perpetuated in Pratt's Hollow, Allegany County. (Searight, *op. cit.*, 202.)

[60] Ralph Briscoe (1749–?), a soldier of the Revolutionary War, lived in Hagerstown in 1786.

[61] Aquila Browne (1770–1851) was a local preacher on Allegany Circuit and in 1795 married Sarah Cresap, granddaughter of Thomas Cresap, famous Western Maryland pioneer. Browne later practiced law in Philadelphia. (Cresap: *History of the Cresaps*, 298.)

[62] Jesse Tomlinson (1756–1840) was a Maryland settler west of Cumberland before 1788. Later he operated Tomlinson's Tavern at Little Meadows, three miles west of Grantville, Garrett County. He represented the frontiersman at his best, having served several terms in the Maryland legislature and sending five sons to college. (Scharf: *History of Western Maryland*, II, 1344, 1527, 1528.)

[63] A reference to the recruiting that was going on at this time for the second war with Great Britain.

[64] The Pike Run Camp Ground near Brownsville, Pennsylvania.

during my stay on the camp ground. Good, I doubt not, has been done. I have been pleased by reading, at intervals, Benson's Life of Fletcher. The man of God was worn out before he married; and where else might he have found such a nurse, and helper, and shepherdess in a wife? but, possibly, he would have lived longer had he travelled. Comparing myself with Fletcher, what am I, in piety, wisdom, labours, and usefulness? God be gracious to me!

Tuesday, 8. May I make the best of the remains of life. I presume we had ten thousand at the Liberty camp meeting, and five thousand at the meeting in this neighbourhood of Uniontown. Forty persons came forward to enroll their names in society with us. We came away to George Hogg's: kind as can be; so indeed are the wife and sister. We entered Brownsville on *Wednesday*, and drove to Doctor Wheeler's. Notice of our proposed meeting had not been generally given, and we had not many hearers; perhaps a hundred. I preached in Washington on *Thursday*, on 1 Peter iii, 10–15: it was a solemn time; and indeed there was reason. Samuel Porter,[65] a Presbyterian minister, came to meeting; unable to sit up, he lay down upon the seat: it would appear that he is not long for this world: I lent him Fletcher's Life.

Friday, 11. We had a suffering ride of thirty-two miles to the Stone chapel, on Short Creek. I preached at four o'clock, and there was much feeling in the congregation. I want strength, and food, and rest. We have serious times; it becomes us to be silent, and let God judge the nations, and correct the guilty.

Ohio

Saturday, 12. We directed our route towards the Indian Short Creek camp meeting.

Sunday, 13. We had a solemn meeting. I preached to about three thousand people, as I judge. *Monday*, I was called on to preach; we have had eighty-four tents on the ground, four hundred and fifty communicants, and forty persons have joined us. The work of God was uninterrupted night and day; and we doubt not many precious souls were converted. I shall have travelled six thousand miles in eight months, and met in nine conferences, and have been present at ten camp meetings.

Tuesday, 15. We came away thirty miles to Barnesville, where I delivered my testimony. I suffer for want of rest. The Methodists seem to have almost entire influence in this town. Our chapel is forty by fifty feet.

[65] Samuel Porter was one of the young western Pennsylvania men trained for the Presbyterian ministry by Dr. John McMillan in his Log College on his farm near Canonsburg, Pennsylvania. It is stated that since Samuel Porter "was without means of support Dr. McMillan kindly gave him board and instruction free of expense." (Guthrie: *John McMillan*, 193.)

Wednesday, 16. We came through the heat to Sherrock's, dined, and went forward towards Wills Creek; logs, stumps, ruts, bushes; rough work: we arrived in the night at Waller's.

Thursday, 17. We set out in the rain, and came thirty miles to Zanesville; I retired sick to Spangler's. We have a meeting house here, and at Fairfields. It is a time of trouble on the frontiers; the Indians have killed and scalped some whites, it is said.

Friday, 18. We attended Rush Creek camp meeting. The work of God during the night was awfully powerful. Many Germans present were deeply serious.

Sunday, 20. I preached. The whole night was spent in prayer. We had a sermon on *Monday morning*, and the sacrament followed: there might be two hundred and fifty communicants. I had been unwell, but an emetic, taken on *Saturday night*, prepared me for usefulness. I lodged with Edward Teel, aged seventy-seven. I had known him forty years. On *Tuesday*, we passed through New Lancaster, to Jesse Spurgeon's.

Wednesday, 23. I preached at Stroud's chapel, and we had an open, feeling, gracious season. I find that the mother of my host, Edward Stroud, went safe to rest last April: she was a disciple of ours, and a respectable widow in Israel. I suffer from chills; the nights are cold, and I have been much exposed.

Thursday, 24. We rode over to Judge Vanmeeter's. On *Friday* I preached in the new house in Jefferson; we visited M'Dowell's, and lodged with White Brown on *Saturday*.

Sabbath, 27. I preached; after meeting I gave up and stole to my bed. My rest has been much broken for the last month in various ways, and I am feverish and have the jaw ache. Could I be less earnest when I preach, I might have less bodily suffering; but it may not be. The Ohio Conference[66] sat from *Thursday*, *October* the 1st, to *Wednesday* the 7th; we had great order. The writer of this journal laboured diligently, and was much assisted by the eldership in the business of the stations. He preached three times, was called upon to ordain twelve deacons, and also to ordain elders: upon the last day his strength failed. I want sleep, sleep, sleep: for three hours I lay undisturbed in bed, to which I had stolen on *Wednesday*; but they called me up to read off the stations. I have a considerable fever; but we must move.

Thursday, 8. We made a pretty rapid ride, thirty miles, to Purrey's.

Friday, 9. A morning ride of twenty-two miles brought us over trees,

[66] This, the first session of the newly formed Ohio Conference, was held at Chilicothe. Asbury and Boehm were the guests of Thomas S. Hinde during the conference. Hinde was a local preacher and the author of two series of sketches on early Methodism in the West published in *The Methodist Magazine*. (Boehm, *op. cit.*, 405; Smeltzer, *op cit.*, 83 ff. and 92.)

stumps, and through mud holes to a house of refreshment; we fed hastily, and went into the town of Miranda, thirteen miles farther.

Saturday, 10. We have had rain. We fed on our way, and continued onward through a great storm of thunder, lightning, and rain to Cincinnati. O, let us not complain when we think of the suffering, wounded, and dying, of the hostile armies! If we suffer, what shall comfort us? let us see—Ohio will give six thousand for her increase of members in one new district.

Sabbath, 11. I preached in Cincinnati. We are at low mark here this year; perhaps they will raise the scaffolding for a new house.

Kentucky

We came over to Kentucky on *Monday*, and reached noisy Lexington: there was company enough, and little quiet through the night.

Tuesday, 13. We rode out to the widow Clark's[67] to breakfast. Our ride of twenty-six miles brought us to lodge under the roof of the widow Hall.

Wednesday, 14. We returned to Lexington in the forenoon. The distance gone over in the last two days and a half may be one hundred miles. I preached, but the notice had not been early, and there were few to hear.

I attended Ratcliff's chapel on *Thursday*, and ordained brother Cornelius Ruddle a local elder: he officiated in my place in the pulpit. I preached in the house of his father in 1780: how strangely I often find the lost!

On *Friday* I preached in the representative chamber in Frankfort. I conversed with some of the respectables, and found one who had made one of my company twenty-three years ago in a journey through the wilderness. We reached Edward Talbot's[68] on *Saturday*.

Sabbath, 18. I preached at the brick chapel.

Monday, 19. We rode twenty-four miles to breakfast with James Ward, Goose Creek, Jefferson County, I preached the funeral of his son. Here I saw some of my ancient brethren and sisters, and the children of others of them.

Tuesday, 20. Came to Brunerstown: we had preaching in German and English. We dined with Mr. Conrad's kind family. There are some of Otterbein's and Schwope's people hereabouts. I was called to visit friend Whips in a dropsy. We came down to Baregrass Creek. What is called the Baregrass Settlement is the garden of the State. It is a low, level country, and in wet seasons must be sickly, as it is now. I saw a native of Saxony who had lately arrived, and had joined us. O! what a work has there been

[67] The "widow Clark" was perhaps Mrs. Francis Clark, who lived near Danville, Kentucky. Her husband was the founder of Methodism in the state. (See note under April 10, 1793.)

[68] Edward Talbot was a member of the Brick Church near Shelbyville, Kentucky.

among the Germans, and would more abundantly have been, had they the discipline of the Methodists!

Wednesday, 21. I preached in Louisville at eleven o'clock in our neat brick house, thirty-four by thirty-eight feet. I had a sickly, serious congregation. This is a growing town, and a handsome place, but the falls or ponds make it unhealthy: we lodged at Farquer's.

Thursday, 22. Breakfasted at B. Shaveley's, five miles on our route: we worried and plunged through the deep roads thence towards the Barrens, and happily took the road newly cut through the woods, and found a shelter for the night with a brother Hawkins.

Friday, 23. We came on to Elizabeth, county town of Harden; a little milk, morning and evening, served us for food. We lodged beyond Elizabeth with father Gilliland, whose father and grandfather were killed by the Indians: himself, until lately, has always been a frontier man, and greatly exposed.

Saturday, 24. We set out and reached Mr. Woodson's to lodge.[69] I am greatly supported by God both in body and mind. A prize! a book found in the pocket of Mr. Whits after his death—Baxter's *Poor Man's Family Book*: the old gentleman had a good guide, and doubtless died in peace: I am indebted to the son for this excellent work.

Sabbath, 25. We have an awful storm: preached in Mr. Woodson's house. A Mr. Locke was present; one of the kindest Baptists I have met with. *Monday*, came to Allen's to dinner, and kept on to James Stringfield's.[70] *Tuesday*, we crossed Barren River, rising swiftly. A ride through the rain brought us to Edward Porter's. *Wednesday*, visited David Porter, from Elk Ridge, in Maryland.

Tennessee

Thursday, we rode thirty miles to brother Gwinn's.[71] *Friday*, we came away late to Nashville, stopping on our way to speak to the widow Bowen, the daughter of my ancient friend, the late General Russell; this lady hath three daughters who profess religion: surely we have not prayed in vain.

[69] Mr. Woodson lived in Hart County, Kentucky. Near his house Asbury crossed Green River at the mouth of the Little Barren on October 15, 1800. (See note under that date.)

[70] James Stringfield was the grandfather of the Rev. Thomas Stringfield, friend of Andrew Jackson and a celebrated member of the Holston Conference. (See Price, *op. cit.*, III, 1–49.)

[71] (See notes under November 15 and 18, 1810.) Asbury had passed from Kentucky to Middle Tennessee in a few days, but he does not mention his exact route. Mrs. Bowen was one of General Russell's daughters by his first marriage. His second wife was the widow Mrs. William Campbell. She and General Russell had two daughters. One married Colonel Francis Preston. They lived at Saltville, Virginia.

We found the river high on *Saturday*; Mr. Hobbs, the jailer, kindly took us in; but we are not prisoners, but of hope—but of the Lord.

Sabbath, November 1. I preached in the new, neat brick house,[72] thirty-four feet square, with galleries. Twelve years ago I preached in the old stone house, taken down since to make a site for the state house. The latter house exceeds the former in glory, and stands exactly where our house of worship should by right have stood; but we bear all things patiently. This is a pentecostal day to my soul. Hail, all hail, eternal glory!

Monday, 2. We left our lodging in the jail house, and came away to Green Hill's. *Tuesday*, busy in writing: I conclude that next year we shall visit and hold a conference in Mississippi, if so directed and permitted. *Wednesday*, we had an appointment in the neat little brick house, town of Franklin,[73] upon Harpeth River. After meeting the society, we hasted away to escape the rain; the storm in the night was made awful by the thunder and lightning. We have a brick house in the town, and a frame one five miles out.[74] I find old acquaintances here from Virginia and North Carolina. I preached on *Thursday* to a small congregation at Green Hill's. *Friday*, after meeting at Nashville, we went forward to Benjamin Maxey's;[75] we held a meeting here, and I was expected to occupy the pulpit. We stayed on *Saturday* at the widow Bowen's, on Mansker's Creek.

Sabbath, 8. I preached at Bowen's chapel, baptized a few subjects, and gave three exhortations; I had aid from God. If the Lord means to make us instruments for good, we are wanted here and at Natchez.

Monday, 9. We started away in the rain to James Gwinn's. *Tuesday*, we opened our conference in great peace;[76] forty deacons were ordained, and ten elders; the travelling and local ministry amounts to sixty-two;

[72] This was the second church in Nashville, one of the six forerunners of the present McKendree Church. (See Carter: *History of the Tennessee Conference*, 320, 321.)

[73] This first Methodist church in Franklin, Williamson County, Tennessee, was on East Margin Street, now First Avenue. McFerrin says it was on Water Street, but as it overlooked the river, it was perhaps popularly known as Water Street in pioneer days. (Judge Walter W. Faw; McFerrin: *Methodism in Tennessee*, II, 413.)

[74] This was Ree's Chapel, the present Bethlehem Church. The conference met there the following year. (See note under October 26, 1813.)

[75] Maxey lived in the Long Hollow community north of the present Goodlettsville, Tennessee. He was a brother of the Rev. Bennett Maxey and came from Virginia.

[76] This was the first session of the Tennessee Conference, which had been created when the General Conference in May had divided the Western Conference into the Ohio, or Upper, and the Tennessee, or Lower, conferences. The conference met in the home of a Mr. House at Fountain Head, near Portland. Preaching was in Gwinn's Chapel nearby. Both Bishops Asbury and McKendree were present, though the latter seems to have presided most of the time and the *Journal* was signed by him. The date for the conference had been set for November 1; Asbury says it opened on the tenth, and the *Journal* says it met on the twelfth. The Tennessee Conference was the largest ever organized; it embraced Tennessee, Southern Kentucky, Indiana, Illinois, Missouri, Arkansas, Louisiana, Mississippi, and Alabama. (McFerrin, *op. cit.*, II, 173; Carter, *op. cit.*, 49; Boehm, *op. cit.*, 407.)

the net increase, after allowing for death and removal, two. We came away, after a peaceful close of our labours, on *Tuesday* following, to John M'Gee's, thirty-three miles: *Wednesday*, to Garratt's: *Thursday*, to Gibson's: *Friday*, to Jack's, forty-five miles, arriving in the night. O, the rocks, hills, ruts, and stumps! My bones, my bones!

Saturday, 21. We had a quiet leisurely ride of thirty-one miles to Winton's.[77] Driving my sulky over such roads, and through such uncommon colds, causes me to suffer deeply for the last few days. I am comforted with an increase of eight thousand in the Tennessee Conference. If we meet the Mississippi Conference, as appointed, in November, 1813, we shall have gone entirely round the United States in forty-two years: but there will be other States: well, God will raise up men to make and to meet conferences in them also, if we remain faithful as a people.

Monday, 23. We came through the rain to Knoxville, and lodged with father Wagner, one of Otterbein's men.[78] *Tuesday*, arrived in Dandridge, we drove to Foute's. It is excessively cold. It was my occupation to baptize six of the eight children of our host. *Wednesday*, we crossed French Broad at Seaham's ferry, and forded Pigeon River near its mouth on our way to James Gilliland's;[79] we came into our station for the night almost stiff with cold.

Sabbath, 29. I preached, and so also did Bishop M'Kendree; Henry Boehm exhorted. I found a relief to my cold in a few grains of tartar emetic. God hath wrought upon the vilest of the vile in the fork of Pigeon and French Broad Rivers, and he will yet do wonders.

Monday, 30. We stopped at Michael Bollen's on our route, where I gave them a discourse on Luke xi, 11–13. Why should we climb over the desperate Spring and Paint Mountains when there is such a fine new road?[80]

North Carolina

We came on *Tuesday* a straight course to Barnard's, dining in the woods on our way.

[77] John Winton moved from Pine Chapel in Jefferson County, Tennessee, between Newport and Dandridge, before 1795, and settled on Muddy Creek twenty miles west of Knoxville, where he died on August 2, 1846. (See inscription on his monument in Muddy Creek Cemetery.)

[78] George Wagner, a member of the United Brethren Church, founded by Philip Otterbein, lived where the Macedonia Church in Knoxville now stands. He gave the lot on which that first church was erected in 1809. (Price, *op. cit.*, II, 278, 279.)

[79] James Gilliland lived in Cocke County, Tennessee, and was a member of Zion Church there. (*Ibid.*, I, 140; II, 199.)

[80] The "fine new road" was Philip Hoodenpile's road from the Tennessee line to Hot Springs. (See note under October 22, 1809.)

Wednesday, December 2. We went over the mountain, twenty-two miles, to Killian's.

Thursday, 3. Came on through Buncombe to Samuel Edney's; I preached in the evening. We have had plenty of rain lately. *Friday*, I rest. Occupied in reading and writing. I have great communion with God. I preached at father Mills's.[81]

Saturday, 5. We scaled the mountain—the rise may be a quarter of a mile, the descent much more gradual, and about a mile in length. We had a keen, cold wind, mingled with snow. Green River was full and rapid, but little Fox darted like a fish up the stream: we stopped at Marvill Mills's,[82] chilled indeed.

Sabbath, 6. I preached at Mills's chapel, after meeting we went home with John Mills,[83] White Oak Creek. Ah, John, thy pious, praying mother! think often of her.

South Carolina

Monday, a bitter cold ride of forty miles, brought us to father Francis Watters's.[84] O warm room, and kind old Virginians! Our host has twelve children of eighteen once living.

Tuesday, 8. Came to Broad River. We found Smith's ford[85] deep enough, but Fox turned his fearless breast up the stream, and brought me swiftly and safely through the swell of waters: he is a noble beast. We

[81] William Mills (1746–1834) was one of the leading Methodists of the area. He lived in Henderson County, North Carolina, and Mills River, Mills Gap, Mills Spring, and other places bear his name. He was the son of Colonel Ambrose Mills, who was born in England around 1722 and who lived on Green River in Rutherford County during the Revolutionary War. The father was hanged as a Tory with others in October, 1780, at Biggerstaff's Fields near Rutherfordton after being captured at Kings Mountain. William Mills served as a major under his father in that engagement. William married Eleanor Morris and had two sons, John and Marvill, and five daughters. His daughter Eleanor, or "Nellie," married the Rev. Samuel Edney, pioneer Methodist preacher in the Blue Ridge region. William Mills and other members of his family are buried at Edneyville, and the Methodist church there is the continuation of Mills Chapel which he founded. Members of the Mills family became prominent in North Carolina history and still live in the area. (See note under October 1, 1806; Patton, *op. cit.*, 25; Griffin: *History of Old Tryon and Rutherford Counties*, 37, 38, 69, 79.)

[82] Marvill Mills was a son of William Mills, brother of John and "Nellie," wife of the Rev. Samuel Edney. He lived in Rutherford County, and he and his descendants had a large share in developing Mill Springs in Polk County. (Patton, *op. cit.*, 25.)

[83] John Mills was the son of William Mills and brother of Mrs. Samuel Edney. (See notes under October 1, 1806, and December 3, 1812.)

[84] Asbury and his party followed a familiar route over Saluda Gap into Spartanburg County, South Carolina, where Francis Watters lived.

[85] He probably went by way of Cowpens into Cherokee County to Smith's Ford.

dined in the woods, and stopped at Esquire Leech's;[86] brandy and the Bible were both handed me: one was enough—I took but one.

Wednesday, 9. Came to Winsborough late at night: I cannot easily describe the pain under which I shrink and writhe: the weather is cold, and I have constant pleuritic twinges in the side. In cold, in hunger, and in want of clothing—mine are apostolic sufferings. Jacob Rumph is dead, and so are elder Capers and James Rembert: these were early friends to the Methodists in South Carolina, and left the world in the triumph of faith. We are in Camden.

Thursday, 10. We stay at father Buchanan's: people here give little encouragement to Methodism, but the walls of opposition will fall, and an abundant entrance will yet be ministered to us—the craft of learning, and the craft of interested religion will be driven away.

Friday, 11. A cold ride brought us to Dunkin's. Is not this man a brand plucked from the burning? a reclaimed drunkard! Camp meetings have done this—they do great good, and prosper in the sandhills.

Saturday, 12. We lodged in Columbia with Colonel Hutchinson.

Sabbath, 13. I preached in the legislative chamber, and had the members for a part of my congregation.[87] *Monday*, at the house of the widow of General Jacob Rumph; the father and son both died in the Lord. This house has been open to the Methodists for about twenty-seven years, whether in peace or persecution; Jacob travelled nearly four years;[88] so meek, so mild, diligent, and simple-hearted, so sincerely good. On *Tuesday* we came to father Carr's,[89] a Swiss: here are pious, kind souls. *Wednesday*, came to Stephen Swithen's,[90] within twenty-three miles of Charleston. it remains intensely cold. *Thursday*, my fingers gave out; then the axle-tree gave a crack, seventeen miles from the city. We loaded another, whilst I rode in John B. Glenn's[91] sulky, he and Boehm, with the aid of cushions and bearskins, rode horseback into the city. These are trifles. Ah! we feel —we fear the locations of this conference will be sixteen in number. *Saturday*, our conference began its session in good order.[92]

[86] Squire Leech lived in York County near the present Hickory Grove. Mount Vernon church here is one of the oldest in the county.

[87] Chaplain Hilliard Judge probably made arrangements for Asbury's sermon in the legislative chamber.

[88] Jacob Rumph (1777–1812) was the son of General Rumph who was among the first to open his home to the Methodists. He was licensed in 1802, began to travel in the same year, and entered the conference in 1809. He died in Charleston on September 11, 1812. (*Minutes*, 1813.)

[89] Carr lived near Orangeburg.

[90] Swithen, or Swithin, lived near Ridgeville in Dorchester County.

[91] John B. Glenn had been serving the Ohoopee Circuit in the Sparta District in Georgia.

[92] This was the twenty-seventh session of the South Carolina Conference, the first following the sitting of the first delegated General Conference in New York the previous May. William Capers was ordained elder, and another future bishop, James O.

Sabbath, 20. I preached at Cumberland chapel in the morning, and at Bethel in the afternoon.[93] The presiding eldership and the episcopacy saw eye to eye in the business of the stations: there were no murmurings from the eighty-four employed. *Christmas day* was a day of fasting, and we dined one hundred at our house on bread and water, and a little tea or coffee in the evening. Funds are low; but our Church is inured to poverty, and the preachers may be called *the poor of this world*, as well as their flocks.

Sabbath, 27. I had an opportunity of meeting the society, of both colours, and my exhortations were pointed, and in season. We have, with the increase, about eighteen thousand. What is coming? days of vengeance, or of Gospel glory? We have lost, by locations and other causes, fourteen of the itinerancy.

Monday, 28. Letters—letters to write! We send two missionaries to Mississippi. Religion is not fashionable in Charleston. *Tuesday*, receiving visitors. Our house is a house of prayer. *Wednesday*, we came to Readhammer's.[94]

Thursday, 31. Came to Georgetown:[95] I am now at home here after twenty-nine years of labour. Many letters call my attention: I am happy in God. We hear of a blessed work in James River district—camp meetings

Andrew, was admitted on trial and sent to the "Saltketcher" (Salkehatchee) Circuit. Two additional missionaries were sent to Mississippi, Richmond Nolley and John Shrock. James Jenkins, who had served the Wateree Circuit the past year, located because he was dissatisfied with his appointment, which required a long move. "His wife was in feeble health, and as he had to cut all the wood used, and to put his little son on a horse and walk before him to mill, he was forced to take that action. . . . The good man had as much land as he could cultivate on Lynch's Creek, with an outhouse to live in, given him by James C. Postell, and lived by the labor of his own hands, still preaching without fee, for long, long years." Jenkins wrote his autobiography in 1842 and died at Camden in January 24, 1847. (Chreitzberg: *Early Methodism in the Carolinas*, 146, 147; Betts, *op. cit.*, 83.)

[93] There were three churches in Charleston, but Trinity had been involved in an obligation for eighty dollars which the trustees could not pay. It was released late in 1811, but Capers, who was pastor that year, said "no congregations could be got there." There were three unmarried preachers, and they occupied the Bethel parsonage. There were then three parsonages in the conference, the others being at Georgetown and Wilmington, to which Joseph Travis and William Capers were sent by the conference. (Capers, *op. cit.*, 135; Betts, *op. cit.*, 128–30.)

[94] Readhammer's Tavern was twenty-two miles above Charleston and a few miles below Monck's Corner. Asbury was becoming feebler. As he left Charleston, he "had lost the use of his feet from rheumatism," and Henry Boehm "had to carry him in my arms and place him in a sulky, and then to take him out and carry him into a house or private dwelling, and he would sit and preach. . . . Never was he more feeble, never less able to travel, and yet he would go on. There was only one thing that could stop him—the pale horse and his rider." (Boehm, *op. cit.*, 410.)

[95] Asbury turned to the right or northeastward from Readhammer's Tavern and proceeded by Strawberry Ferry and Jamestown to Georgetown, where he was "at home" in the parsonage.

the great instrument. According to Thomas L. Douglass's[96] account six hundred have joined us. We have also a pleasing account in a letter from Joel Winch, New London district, Bristol, Rhode Island, of a work of God; one hundred have joined, and other converts there were who have joined the Baptists and Episcopalians;—were these stolen from us? *Saturday*, at rest, writing letters.

[96] Thomas L. Douglass was presiding elder of the James River District in the Virginia Conference. (*Minutes*, 1812.)

the great awakening. According to Thomas L. Douglass's[1] account six hundred have joined us. We have also a pleasing account in a letter from Joel Wyatt, New London District, Ipswich, Rhode Island, of a work of God; one hundred have joined, and other converts thirty were who have joined the Baptists and Episcopalians: were these stolen from us? Surely, at most, wanting letters.

[1] Thomas L. Douglass was presiding elder of the James River District in the Virginia Conference. (Journal of 1812.)

1813

1813

June in Connecticut. "Nature is now in all her grandeur and loveliness"

CHAPTER FORTY-TWO

South Carolina

Sunday, *January* 3, 1813. I preached morning and evening. It was a small time—cold, or burning the dead. We have about one thousand blacks, and about one hundred white members; most of them women; the men kill themselves with strong drink before we can get at them. My home in Georgetown is not quite so comfortable; possibly I shall hereafter leave it to better men. *Monday*, it is so cold I have a small fire to write my letters by. *Tuesday*, we took the path to Coachman's, Black River. My evening talk to them was, "Take earnest heed."

Wednesday, 6. I was so lame I stopped at Richard Woodbury's.[1] We held a meeting at two o'clock, and at night. *Friday*, we had a meeting at Collins Woodbury's; I preached in the evening—it was excessively cold, and I was lame.

Sabbath, 10. I preached at Newsom's[2] on Little Pee Dee. *Monday*, a bleak ride brought us to General Lee's. I took an emetic. My foot is much swelled.

North Carolina

Tuesday, I was glad to stay at M'Neil's, in Lumberton. Applied a blister to my foot: Henry Boehm preached. *Wednesday*, came in great pain, and

[1] From Mr. Coachman's the party crossed Black River to Woodbury's, who lived near Poston.

[2] Asbury had proceeded by Port's Ferry to John Newsom's, who lived near Mullins.

very unwell, to B. Russell's. I went to bed in a high fever and a mild medicine. *Thursday*, came on to Fayetteville through a cold, heavy rain. I blistered my foot again. The Lord blesses me with patience.

Sabbath, 17. They carried me into the church. I ordained two deacons and one elder. I failed in strength after preaching, and Rev. Mr. Turner, a Presbyterian, concluded our meeting by prayer. I came home, applied three blisters, and retired in a high fever to bed. A fourth blister completed the work. *Tuesday* and *Wednesday*, closely confined.

Thursday, 21. A bitter cold ride of thirty miles brought us to James Purdy's. I have a high fever, and am in great pain. *Friday*, a heavy ride of thirty-six miles brought us to King's. I anticipate a night of fever and pain. *Saturday*, to Wilmington: there is little trade here, and fewer people; of course there is less sin.

Sabbath, 24. I was carried into the church, preached, and met the society. I preached again in the evening. A bread poultice has procured me a mitigation of pain. Lord, be merciful to me in temporals and spirituals! William Capers is married—he twenty-three, his wife eighteen.

Tuesday, 26. We made a journey of twenty-two miles to the widow Nixon's—a widow of Sarepta, and a mother in Israel. I have a fever, and swelled feet. We had a small congregation. *Thursday*, we took the road in the rain.

Friday, 29. Called a meeting at Mr. Shepherd's. Blessed be God! I have lived to see the third generation of father Ballard. He was the first man that joined us at New River: now his grandson is in the Church, and in Christ. My trials have lately been great. We stemmed the cold wind to Lot Ballard's, eighteen miles. I suffer violent pain in my right foot.

Sabbath, 31. It rained heavily; nevertheless, we held meeting at Richland chapel. I rested above an hour, on my knees, preaching, and in the ordination of Lot Ballard a deacon, and in prayer. We retired from the meeting to G. Rowe's, a son of affliction and consolation in God. We are in a palace—peace, and rich accommodation. Was it with us as in former times, we should be flying north; but we are fast bound by lameness. I have filled all my appointments, and answered the letters received. I neglect not all opportunities of instruction and prayer.

Monday, February 1. Lowering, cold day. *Tuesday*, I preached at Rowe's to about sixty souls. What a land is this of widows; and men sick, dying, and drunken! We came to John Shine's on *Wednesday*; we found his wife ill, and prescribed for her as well as we might. After dinner and prayer, came away to the widow Bryan's. Her husband is dead, and her son sick: we prayed, ventured to prescribe for the diseased subject, and continued onward to Adonijah Perry's.

Thursday, 4. Once more I put on my leather shoes. O, the sufferings I have endured—patiently, I hope! One more warning I gave these people, on Heb. ii, 1–4; it is perhaps the last. I am occupied in marking for reprint about three hundred pages of Baxter. *Friday*, we rode round to Thomas Lee's. *Saturday*, at rest.

Sabbath, 7. We had about two hundred souls, white and black, to hear us. I was two hours preaching, meeting the society, baptizing and ordaining Roscoe Lipsey. I gained a fever and a clear conscience by my labours. Alas! it is the time of Jacob's trouble. *Monday*. I am in Newbern on crutches. *Tuesday*, reading, receiving the visits of presiding elders, and writing letters.

Wednesday, 10. We opened our conference in sister Tenkard's elegant schoolroom: we had great order, great union, and great despatch of business. The increase here in membership this year is seven hundred; but ah! deaths and locations—then the preachers!

Sabbath, 14. I was called upon to preach. *Thursday*, conference rose and we came away, twenty-six miles, to Murphy's. *Friday*, excessively cold. A ride of fifty miles brought us to Edward Hall's. *Saturday*, we started in the rain, crossing Tar River, and driving through the snow driving in our faces: we were glad to stop at James Hunter's; my feet begin to swell again.

Sabbath, 21. Came in to Halifax, calling upon the widow Jones, mother of the Shaker of that name. I preached to a few whom the weather could not keep back. After meeting, and taking food, we directed our course to brother Barratt's. We wished to cross the river whilst the weather would permit: I fly, and a strange flight it is for a sick cripple.

Monday, 22. I halted at James Barratt's, and ordained John Moore, Edward Price, and Edward Drumgoole, one after the other, as they happened to drop in; I lectured in the evening.

Virginia

Tuesday, 23. Came away to Jane Fisher's: here I ordained Thomas Drumgoole. *Wednesday*, I ordained John Comber at Smith Parham's. We found lodgings for the night at Hall's tavern. We passed through Petersburg to Cox's, on the James River. Here flesh failed, and I wished for rest and found it. A heavy ride on *Friday* brought us to Mr. Bleaky's happy family and pleasant mansion. I have looked into Whitehead's Life of Wesley—he is vilified: O, shame!

Sabbath, 28. I preached in Richmond old chapel, gave counsel to the tarrying society, baptized two infants, and ordained John Sullivan and William Whitehead deacons. I spoke again in the afternoon to a congregation made up of the young and the aged. The Presbyterians and Episcopalians are striving to have places of worship.

Monday, *March* 1. Came away to Burrough's. *Tuesday*, came to Carson's ferry, crossed, and kept on to Mrs. Alexander's. After leaving this, we became entangled in the woods, and had a gentle upset, which brought us, without much damage, to the bottom of the hill; a ride of two miles on horseback brought us and our baggage to our lodgings for the night. My mind enjoys great peace; but I am in pain of body, and my legs are swelled.

Wednesday, 3. We were obliged to lie by until the shaft of the sulky was mended. I improved this opportunity of rest to take medicine. I exhorted the family. My mind mourns over the citizens of King George county. O for a Gospel day and work!

Thursday, 4. A desperate plunging of thirty miles through the clay brought us to Dumfries. We stopped at mother Mason's and lectured in the family. *Friday*, to Edward Sandford's.

District of Columbia

Saturday, came to Georgetown, dining with Jacob Hoffman, in Alexandria.

Sabbath, 7. I changed my subject after getting into the church; and I spoke long and plainly. We have news from the English Conference. It has given me an invitation to my native land, engaging to pay the expenses of the visit.

Monday, 8. I sat upon the carpet, reading and writing. William Watters visited me. In the evening I performed the ceremony of marriage, uniting two young people in the house.

Maryland

Wednesday, I visited Doctor Tiffin, baptized his child, Edward Parker Tiffin,[3] and then came on to Bell's chapel,[4] and had here a very respectable

[3] Edward Tiffin (1766–1829) was at the time of Asbury's visit the first commissioner of the General Land Office Bureau under appointment of President Madison. Several years after his arrival in America from England, Tiffin began the practice of medicine in Charles Town, Virginia, now West Virginia. On November 19, 1792, he was ordained deacon by Bishop Asbury. (Original is in the Manuscript Division, Library of Congress.) In 1796 he moved to Chillicothe, Ohio, and played a conspicuous part as speaker of the territorial legislature and president of the Constitutional Convention. He was chosen the first governor of Ohio (1803) and in 1807 was elected to the United States Senate, from which he resigned in 1809. His first wife was a sister of Senator Thomas Worthington. The son whom Asbury baptized was killed in a railway accident in 1853. (*Biographical Directory of the American Congress, 1774–1927*, 1617; Howe: *Historical Collections of Ohio*, II, 500, 501.)

[4] This ancient society is perpetuated in the Camp Springs Church, near Andrews Field, Prince Georges County. It is on the Washington East District, Baltimore Conference.

congregation; but, alas! I was feeble in body and mind. We lodged with brother William Revet. *Thursday*, we visited Colonel Beale,[5] below Piscataway[6]; and here I preached to a very genteel, serious people. *Friday*, I preached at Ford's chapel: the word was not wholly lost. We lodged under the hospitable roof of the widow Ford. *Saturday*, was held a quarterly meeting at Smith's chapel.[7] We preached to a full house. After meeting we were invited to the house of Mr. Somerville.[8]

Sabbath, 14. I suffer extreme pain in one of my limbs, and move with difficulty. A dumb *Sabbath*; but there is no lack of aid. I feel perfect resignation, knowing that it is all for the best. *Monday*, we left our kind host, Captain Somerville,[9] an old revolutionary hero, who lost an arm in the contest. We crossed Patuxent River, and had a cold ride from Lower Marlborough to Samuel Essex's, Plum Point. I am feeble, and have to endure pain and cold, and perform double labour: blessed be God, for the support I receive!

Tuesday, 16. I preached in Child's chapel, and was assisted by Joshua Wells, Henry Boehm, and Henry Smith. We came in, chilled by the cold and rain, to Philip Dorsey's,[10] and lodged there. *Wednesday*, faint and feeble, we took the road to Tannyhill's, and gave a sermon to a small congregation. We lodged with Samuel Wood, who lives where Griffin formerly lived,[11] and has married the widow: here I preached thirty-six years ago.

Thursday, 18. I met about four hundred people at Weems's chapel, to

[5] This may have been Colonel William Dent Beall (1755–1829), an officer of the Revolutionary War and a member of the Order of the Cincinnati. (Newman: *Charles County Gentry*, 260; McQuiston: *The Alexander Beall Family* (Manuscript), 18, D.A.R. Library, Washington, D.C.; Smith. *op. cit.*, 296.)

[6] Piscataway is a village in Prince Georges County, ten miles south of the District of Columbia and three miles southeast of Fort Washington. It is on a creek of the same name.

[7] Smith's Chapel was probably named for Isaac Smith. Henry Smith located it south of Nottingham, near the Patuxent River. (Smith, *op. cit.*, 297.)

[8] This was Thomas J. Somerville (1789–1845.)

[9] This was Captain James Somervell (1758–1815), who lived at "Stokely," Calvert County. He lost an arm at the Battle of Camden in 1780. He married Ann Magruder Truman in 1782. (*Lineage Book*, XLV, 59, D.A.R. Library, Washington, D.C.)

[10] Because there were two Philip Dorseys who lived contemporaneously within riding distance, it is difficult to identify with certainty the family with whom Asbury lodged. The more probable appears to be Philip Dorsey (1759–1818), son of Philip and Margaret, who lived in Calvert County. In 1784 Philip, the son, married Barbara Broome. (*Dorsey Family History.*)

[11] On April 8, 1777, Asbury preached in the home of "Mr. Griffin on the fork of the Patuxent River," which is near the present Priest Bridge. The Samuel Wood-Griffin home was within the bounds of the Smithville Circuit, Washington East District, Baltimore Conference. In 1890 Dr. Thomas M. Chaney located the residence near the Mount Harmony Church, Calvert County. (Snyder: *History of the Smithville Methodist Church, 1840–1940* (Manuscript); Schilling, article, "One Hundred Sixty Years of Methodism," *Calvert Independent Tercentenary Edition*, September 23, 1954.)

whom I preached, and we hope the word was not lost: my congregation was serious and attentive. But, ah! there is death in the pot! will my exhortations to the society do much good? We found our host, William Weems, with an afflicted family.

Friday, 19. We drove through a storm of wind to Lamplin's chapel, and preached to about two hundred attentive hearers. Dined with Doctor Murray's family, and gave them some plain talk. We lodged with Samuel Maccubbin. I was feverish and in pain, and worried through a night of affliction. We have visited Prince George, Calvert, and Anne Arundel Counties; the weather and roads, how unpleasant; and the people, how decently attentive in meeting; and how kind and attentive in their houses! *Saturday*, I housed with my friend Absalom Ridgely, in Annapolis: this amiable family is much favoured.

Sabbath, 21. There was a serious, solemn attention in the congregation, whilst I tried to speak on Colossians i, 27–29. I gave the Africans a sermon in the afternoon. I felt the pain of coughing, and the effects of the blister. *Monday*, came to Sewell's.[12] I preached on James i, 22–24. A heavy ride brought us to Baltimore. I gave an evening to the great Otterbein: I found him placid and happy in God. He says the commentators are mistaken—that the vials are yet to be poured out. *Tuesday*, I had a serious interview with the presiding elders. *Wednesday*, we opened conference,[13] and went forward in our business in great peace and order.

Sabbath, 28. I ordained deacons in the forenoon and preached in the afternoon.

Thursday, *April* 1. Conference rose in great order and peace. I stationed eighty-three preachers. This conference holds, in their several relations, ninety preachers, twenty thousand two hundred and seventy-two members white, and seven hundred and ninety-nine coloured. We came away to Perry Hall: Alas! how solitary!

Pennsylvania

Friday, 2. To Ewen's. *Saturday*, to mother Boehm's. It was necessary to put seventy miles between us and Baltimore before we could write a line: must we always thus *fly away to be at rest?*

[12] John Sewell, Jr. (1761–1817), lived at Sewell's Cross Roads, Indian Landing, at the Head of Severn River. He and his wife, Lydia Baldwin Sewell, were the first to open their home to Methodist preachers in this community. This historic house, "Brooksby Point," in which Asbury often preached and which was the center of Methodist activity in this section of Anne Arundel County, is about one mile from Severn Cross Roads reached by a private road leading from the Generals Highway (Route 175). (Warfield, *op. cit.*, 137–40; Bibbins: *How Methodism Came*, 81.)

[13] Sixty-four preachers were present at the sessions of the conference in Baltimore. A committee comprised of Asa Shinn, Robert R. Roberts, and Beverly Waugh was appointed "to receive and arrange materials from the Presiding Elders and preachers

Sabbath, 4. At Boehm's chapel I expounded 2 Tim. ii, 15. Henry Boehm preached in German; James Norton in English. The society received an exhortation. *Monday*, I wrote a letter to my British brethren, thanking them for their kind invitation to visit them. *Tuesday*, I preached at Strasburg.

Delaware

Wednesday, desperate roads to Newark kept us late. We had about two hundred people to hear us, to whom we spoke upon *the great salvation*.

Thursday, 8. I preached at Salem, and went home to dine with Abraham Keagy. After dinner we went down with Judge Richard Bassett to Bohemia. Spring has at last returned—a treble spring—natural, spiritual, and political. What a winter we have gone through! what weather for five months! what roads!

Friday, 9. We rode down to Smyrna: and preached at night, remembering to exhort the society. I visited sister Davis; near her end: but calm and waiting for deliverance. *Saturday*, went to Dover.

Sabbath, 11. I spoke at Wesley chapel plain words in the forenoon, and I spoke again in the afternoon at Farra's chapel.[14] We dined with Denny,[15] and finding them at the table when we afterward called at Doctor Sykes's,[16] we sat sociably down and ate there also. I called upon Judge Cooper,[17] who is a subject of great affliction: he felt much whilst I prayed with him.

for the composition of the History of Methodism." On Saturday morning Bishop Asbury addressed the conference on "Preachers and Their Wives." Sermons in German were delivered by Jacob Gruber and Henry Boehm in Otterbein's Church. (Armstrong, *op. cit.*, 172, 173; Boehm, *op. cit.*, 413, 414.)

[14] Few names have such a variety of spelling as this one. Asbury has given Farra. The meetinghouse was sometimes called Farries. The historians record John Fairies as having settled there in 1750. Others claim that the first chapel erected in 1780 took its name from the prominent Farrow family. In 1793 Joseph Farrow was a local preacher. The Ferra Meeting House became Bethel Chapel, which is still standing on the main highway north of Cheswold. The Cheswold Church, Kent County, Delaware, perpetuates this ancient society. (Hallman, *op. cit.*, 111, 236; Sweet, *op. cit.*, IV, 720; Scharf: *History of Delaware*, II, 1119.)

[15] In 1816 Thomas Denny and Collins Denny were listed among the large landowners in Little Creek Hundred. A William Denny was a member of the Delaware Legislature from Kent County, 1809–11. (Scharf, *op. cit.*, II, 1118.)

[16] Dr. James Sykes, Sr. (1761–1822) was one of the incorporators of the Delaware State Medical Society in 1789. In 1791 he delivered the anniversary oration. While practicing in Dover he also served in the state legislature for fifteen years and upon the resignation of Richard Bassett in 1801 became acting governor of Delaware. (*Ibid.*, I, 472, 473, 481, 482.)

[17] This may have been Judge Richard Cooper (1755–1818) of Cooper's Corner, Delaware. He was an associate justice of the Delaware courts, 1804–18.

The evening was cold, nevertheless we came away, thirteen miles, to lodge at Purnell's.[18]

Maryland

Monday, 12. A rapid ride brought us to Collins's,[19] in Caroline. I preached at three o'clock, and went home to lodge with Peter T. Causey. *Tuesday*, rode fifteen miles to preach in Frazier's chapel. I preached in the evening at James Harris's. Thomas Foster took us in for the night.

Wednesday, 14. We came to Cambridge.

Thursday, 15. There was an alarm from the enemy,[20] and of course no preaching. We came back to Foster's. I preached in Newmarket, and ordained George Ward to deacon's orders. *Friday*, retired for humiliation and prayer. *Saturday*, I preached at Washington chapel, and ordained Henry Baine a local deacon.

Delaware

We visited Eccleston Brown, now a subject of grace, and lodged with Lemuel Davis, an old disciple.

Sunday, 18. I preached at Brown's chapel, and had a serious, attentive congregation. I preached also in the evening at Bridgeville. What a change is here! the children and grandchildren are left, but few of the first generation. I baptized Daniel Polk's son. *Monday*, to Milford, and preached for them.

Tuesday, 20. I preached in Barratt's chapel, dined at Dover, and slept at Smyrna; making a journey of forty miles.

Wednesday, 21. There was a high wind, and I set out, feeble and faint, and reached Wilmington.[21] I lodged with Governor Bassett. My peace flows

[18] This was probably Thomas Purnall, or Purnell, a local preacher who lived near Felton, Kent County. He was of the family for whom Purnell's Meeting House, erected in 1800, was named. (Hallam, *op. cit.*, 119, 243; Sweet, *op. cit.*, IV, 720.)

[19] Whether this was Edward Collins (Hallman, *op. cit.*, 108) or Abraham Collins near Concord, Caroline County, in whose home the trustees met in 1804 to authorize the purchase of land and the erection of the Concord meetinghouse, is difficult to determine. (*History of Caroline County, Maryland*, by teachers and students, 115, 117.)

[20] On April 10, 1813, Lewes, Delaware, had been bombarded by the British fleet because of the refusal of its citizens to furnish fresh provisions to the ships. English vessels were stationed along the coast to enforce the blockade. Havre de Grace had been burned by Admiral Cockburn.

[21] In Wilmington, John Emory met Bishop Asbury and "by a change made to shelter him from the rain, had the pleasure of riding with him in a chaise a part of the way to this place [Philadelphia]." (Emory: *The Life of the Rev. John Emory, D.D.*, in a letter from Emory to his mother, 66.)

like a river. I suppose we have, in sixteen circuits, ten chapels in each. I preached for the folks in Wilmington.

Pennsylvania

Friday, 23. A heavy ride brought us to Philadelphia.

Saturday, 24. We opened our annual conference, ninety preachers present: much order, and great peace.

Sunday, 25. I preached in the academy chapel in the morning; and at night at St. George's. My congregations were large. We continued in conference until *Saturday*, the first of May. We had speakers in plenty; but peace and union. There is a falling off in numbers, occasioned by locations, and the retirement of the superannuated, and other causes; so that the increase of effective preachers is but two.

Sunday, May 2. I preached at Ebenezer, and exhorted to union; and again at the Tabernacle. I shall throw all the troubles of the times, the Church, and the conference, into shades; nor will I record these tales of woe.

Tuesday, 4. We set out in an easterly storm up the Bristol road, and reached Burlington.

New Jersey

Wednesday and *Thursday*, still raining. Busy writing letters. The increase in six conferences is, in members, twenty-one thousand eight hundred and thirty-four; in preachers seventy-nine; but of these there are only thirty-three travellers. The Baltimore Conference paid up without any charitable dividend. I preached in Burlington on *Thursday*; many attended, although it was damp. Will this place and Trenton ever be famous for vital religion?

Friday, 7. Stormy. I preached at Mount Holly. After meeting, visited William Richards,[22] a friend of ours for many years. His wife and daughter departed in peace, and are gone safe.

Saturday, 8. I preached in Lumberton. Here we have a good house, after forty years' labour. I dined with Mr. Hosea Moore. His mother is a public speaker; yet she attended our Methodist meeting, and told me she found it a blessing to her. We rode to New Mills, to shorten our distance to the city. My mind is greatly in God; but my body is feeble.

[22] William Richards, owner of the famous Batsto Iron Works, was evidently at Mount Holly on the occasion of this visit. In addition to the mansion at Pleasant Mills, which Asbury frequently visited, there was also a Richards residence at Mount Holly, inherited by William Richards from another distinguished bearer of the name who died in 1787. (See *Journal* entry and note for April 16, 1809.)

Sunday, 9. I preached, and it was an open season. We met the society after preaching, and said many things to them.

Monday, 10. Dined at the widow Bunting's,[23] Crosswicks. At Allentown, I preached nearly two hours, and had gracious access to God and to truth. We lodged with John Hughes.[24] I am filled with God.

Tuesday, 11. We came to New Brunswick, thirty miles, and a desperate road. I was weary and faint; yet I went to the meeting house in the evening, delivered my testimony, and retired sick to bed to take medicine.

Wednesday, 12. We came fifteen miles to William Flatt's, Rahway, without breaking bread. I preached in our unfinished house in Bridgetown,[25] at noon; and at Elizabeth, at night. There are distressing accounts from the sea coasts, and from the northwest. God's people must flee to the stronghold of Divine protection.

Thursday, 13. Dined at Newark. Preached at Belleville. *Friday*, preached at Paramus.[26] The rain was abundant; the people, nevertheless, attended. Lodged at Albert Wilson's.

New York

Saturday, preached at Benjamin Sherwood's. We had an open season.

We toiled over the rocky road to Haverstraw, sixteen miles; and I delivered my testimony in great feebleness of body. We lodged with Peter Noyelle. Our host built his house for a tavern, but it was turned into a church. At Philipstown[27] we have an elegant new chapel; I preached in it on *Monday*, and felt liberty in the word.

[23] This was probably Mary Bunting, relict of John Bunting who had died in 1791. She is listed as of Chesterfield Township, Burlington County, in which township Crosswicks is located. (New Jersey Archives, Abstracts of Wills, VIII, 58.)

[24] John Hughes was elected one of the trustees of the church at Allentown on March 29, 1813. (Pitt: *History of the Allentown Methodist Episcopal Church*, 7, 13.)

[25] Rahway was also known as Bridgetown. On July 10, 1812, the trustees passed a resolution the purpose of which was to raise funds sufficient to finish the church. In 1814 another attempt was made to raise money to finish the church, but it was not until two years later that the edifice was completed. (Mooney: *History of Rahway Methodism*, 62–64.)

[26] The Paramus Church is now the Waldwick Methodist Church in the Newark Conference. It dates its beginning to 1791, and the first church trustees were elected in 1797. A church building was erected at that time, and in 1819 a new meetinghouse was built on a lot owned by A. Ackerman. This building stood for more than 120 years, until destroyed by fire in the 1940's. The church has undergone several name changes. In 1863 it was officially named the "Methodist Episcopal Church of New Prospect." And when with changing boundaries it found itself in the village of Waldwick, it assumed that name, by which it is known today. (Manuscript History of the Waldwick Methodist Church; Westervelt: *History of Bergen County*, I, 401–2, 417–18.)

[27] Philipstown was a small community in New York east of the mountains along the east shore of Hudson River. Present Route No. 9 at Nelson Corners is the approximate location.

Tuesday, 18. Came to Richard Jackson's, twenty-five miles. I was required to preach at a minute's warning, as I found an assembly ready. It would seem as if the preachers think they are committing sin if they do not appoint preaching for me every day, and often twice a day. Lord, support us in our labour, and we will not murmur.

Wednesday, 19. A cold, uncomfortable ride brought us to Amenia. We dined with brother Ryder, an ancient disciple and local preacher.

Thursday, 20. We opened the New York Conference in great peace and good order. *Friday*, day of abstinence. I ordained twelve deacons after sermon. My text was 2 Tim. iv, 5.

Saturday, 22. King Gordius had well-nigh been amongst us; but the knots were untied peaceably, and not cut in rashness.

Sunday, 23. Bishop M'Kendree preached. It appeared to me as if a ray of divine glory rested on him. His subject was, "Great peace have they that love thy law: and nothing shall offend them." My subject was Ephes. iv, 1–3. The appearance, manner, and preaching of brother M'Kendree, produced a very powerful effect on Joshua Marsden,[28] a British missionary, who has been present at our conference.

Wednesday, 26. I preached the funeral sermon of Robert Hibbard.[29] He was drowned in the St. Lawrence, on his way to his former circuit. Our conference concluded in peace, and the bishops, upon reading the stations, gave a valedictory address, in which our brethren were assured that the plan of their future labours was deliberately formed, with the aid of the collected and re-collected wisdom of judicious counsel, and in much prayer. We heard no complaint, and there was no appeal.

Connecticut

Friday, 28. We travelled this day ten hours. I preached in the evening in a school house; but had not much freedom. *Saturday*, we made a tedious day's ride to the widow Pease's. In our way we called in to see a sick brother, and prayed with him.

[28] Joshua Marsden was a distinguished member of the British Methodist Conference. He arrived in New York in 1812 looking for passage to England. Being forced to remain in New York, he gave service to the work in New York and vicinity without formally joining the American Conference. (Stevens, *op. cit.*, IV, 186; Seaman, *op. cit.*, 159, 197; Boehm, *op. cit.*, 397.)

[29] Robert Hibbard (1787–1812) was born in Greene County, New York. His parents moved to Amenia, where he grew up and was converted. He was accepted on trial in 1809 and by 1812 was ordained elder, returning to Lower Canada. In October of that year he learned that the preachers of the St. Francis Circuit had failed to take their places because of the war, and he started for that circuit to aid the churches. On October 10, 1812, he was drowned while crossing the St. Lawrence River some distance below Montreal. His body was never recovered. (*General Minutes*, 1813; Boehm, *op. cit.*, 351.)

Massachusetts

Sunday, 30. I preached in Pittsfield. *Monday*, preached at M'Farlan's. Sickness, death, and judicial blindness are the miseries of this part of the world. We called upon John Leland, late from the margin of the grave: we found him pleasant and kind. Hereabouts we scattered some pamphlets on *discipline*, and the supper of the Lord. But baptism is all in all still with them. We avoided controversy.

Tuesday, *June* 1. We have a fine prospect of the Hoosack River, and the Green Mountain, bleak as January. After dinner at Tinney's (kind souls), we descended the precipice, crossing by a slight bridge. We lodged with Deacon Allis: the good Presbyterian officiated for his family; but in the morning we settled the matter, and I prayed.

New Hampshire

Wednesday, 2. We reached Winchester, in New Hampshire, stopping to dine with the nice Websters,[30] in Greenfield. My knee is swelled again. *Like priest*, *like people*, in these parts; both judicially blind. We lodged two nights in Winchester with Caleb Alexander, whose father I followed to the grave. The dust I visited, afterward the widow, and came away. This town is not reformed by Methodist conference or Methodist preaching. We shall direct our course straightforward to New London, to meet our conference there. Studiously employed, *Thursday*, *Friday*, *Saturday*, at brother Marble's.[31]

Sunday, 6. I preached in the morning and afternoon with little freedom. May we not expect increasing days of distress? Methodism in the east is as likely to be anything else as that which it ought to be, unless we have great displays of the power of God, and a strict discipline. We have a gracious rain in mercy, if not in answer to prayer. Knowing the uncertainty of the tenure of life, I have made my will, appointing Bishop M'Kendree, Daniel Hitt, and Henry Boehm, my executors. If I do not in the meantime spend it, I shall leave, when I die, an estate of two thousand dollars, I believe: I give it all to the Book Concern. This money, and somewhat more, I have inherited from dear departed Methodist friends, in the State of Maryland, who died childless; besides some legacies which I

[30] Ezekiel Webster lived in Northfield but was closely connected with Greenfield. He is reported to have been a member of a committee of the court of sessions meeting in Greenfield at the Willard Tavern on March 18, 1812. Asbury notes in his *Journal* that he "stopped at Mr. Houghton's" in Northfield on May 31, 1810. (Thompson: *History of Greenfield*.)

[31] Elias Marble had entertained Asbury on Friday, June 1, 1810, during the session of the conference in Winchester.

have never taken. Let it all return, and continue to aid the cause of piety.

Monday, 7. I preached in Winchester village; a plain discourse.

Massachusetts

Tuesday, came on to Orange, and preached at Asa Lord's. We have had pleasing rains, and nature begins to put on her charms. My mind enjoys a constant serenity, whether labouring or at rest, in ease or in pain. "To me to live is Christ; to die is gain."

Wednesday, 9. We came in haste to Ashburnham, and attended a prayer meeting at the widow Barrell's:[32] I lectured upon Luke xviii, 1. We came to Howard[33] about mid-day. Here are good houses of wood; the country around barren, but partly improved by the cultivation of grass. *Thursday*, was cold. Surely we shall rise in New England in the next generation. I believe, for one, that there has been more true Gospel preaching in the other States, than in the five New England States, after all their boasting. God is my all. I preached in Howard at six o'clock in the evening, plainly and pointedly. Ah! there is death in the pot.

Friday, 11. At Waltham, we stopped, lectured, and prayed; and came away to Needham. Faint, yet pursuing. I endure heat and abstinence, in patience, and in hope.

Saturday, 12. We had a pleasant rain; came away to breakfast, eight miles, in a tavern, praying at the table. Sixteen miles through dust and heat, made us willing to stop for dinner at Easton; and continuing on to Taunton, we sought rest with father Prattson,[34] a Lot in Sodom.

Sunday, 13. We rose at four o'clock, to gain twelve miles for Somerset quarter meeting. I lectured on the Lord's prayer. Dined with Captain Read,[35] and gave an exhortation in the afternoon. I am told there is a revival of the work of God here, and at Warren, and at Bristol. I have difficulties to encounter, but I must be silent. My mind is in God, In New

[32] This was the widow of Luther Barrell, who died of apoplexy in 1806. She died in 1853. Her son, Luther Barrell, Jr., was one of the trustees under whose auspices the Ashburnham and Westminster Methodist societies were merged in 1831. (Stearns: *History of Ashburnham*, 312–13; Haywood: *History of Westminster*, 535–36.)

[33] This should probably be Harvard instead of Howard. (See *Journal* entry for June 13, 1803.)

[34] Asbury probably stayed with the Pratt family, which was prominent in the history of Taunton. No Prattsons are known to have been there at the time. Dier Pratt of Taunton was one of the subscribers to Jesse Lee's *History of the Methodists*. (See page 367 of that book.)

[35] Captain William Read gave the land upon which the South Somerset Methodist Episcopal Church was built. (Miller: *Souvenir History of the New England Southern Conference*, I, 193.)

England we sing, we build houses, we eat, and stand at prayer. Here preachers locate, and people support them, and have travelling preachers also. Were I to labour forty-two years more, I suppose I should not succeed in gettings things right. Preachers have been sent away from Newport by an apostate; so we go. O rare steeple houses, bells! (organs by-and-by?)—these things are against me, and contrary to the simplicity of Christ. We lodge with our brother Brayton.[36]

Monday, 14. We visited the Reeds,[31] senior and junior, and Doctor Winsler[38] and family.

Rhode Island

I preached in Warren in the evening, and lodged with kind Smith Bowen.[39] I preached at Bristol at six o'clock: we did not trouble the people with ourselves or horses. My congregation was large. A pious sister had gone in triumph: we committed her earth to parent earth.

Wednesday, 16. Storm bound. Writing, planning, and reading. *Thursday*, we came in haste, along to Providence. An African gave me his hand in the street, having seen me in New York. George Pickering turned me aside, and presented me to the Governor, Jones,[40] who gave me his hand: we were entertained splendidly. Here are grand buildings; but no chapel for the Methodists. We rode on to Lippett's factories:[41] what a population here is! *Friday*, fast and physic.

Connecticut

Reached Kayser's, in Canterbury. Nature is now in all her grandeur and loveliness. When alone, I am all prayer and praise. *Saturday*, to Colchester, dining with Williams on the route.

Sunday, 20. Brother M'Kendree preached at eleven o'clock; and I in the afternoon. Was it ever known before, that the stations could be ready in four days? Two cases in committee delayed us nearly a day.

Thursday, 24. We rose in peace. Here was an account of the expenditure of six hundred dollars in a charity; and the bishops knew nothing about it: mark! let us have no more fellowship in giving or receiving money. We

[36] John Brayton was one of the first members of the society at South Somerset.

[37] These were doubtless Captain Read and family.

[38] Doctor Winsler was of Swansea.

[39] Smith Bowen lived on Kickamuit Road in Warren, Rhode Island.

[40] William Jones was Governor of Rhode Island from 1811 to 1817.

[41] "Lippett's" factories were owned by General Christopher Lippett, a friend of Asbury and Jesse Lee, whose home was famous for its hospitality to Methodist preachers; he lived at Cranston, now a suburb of Providence.

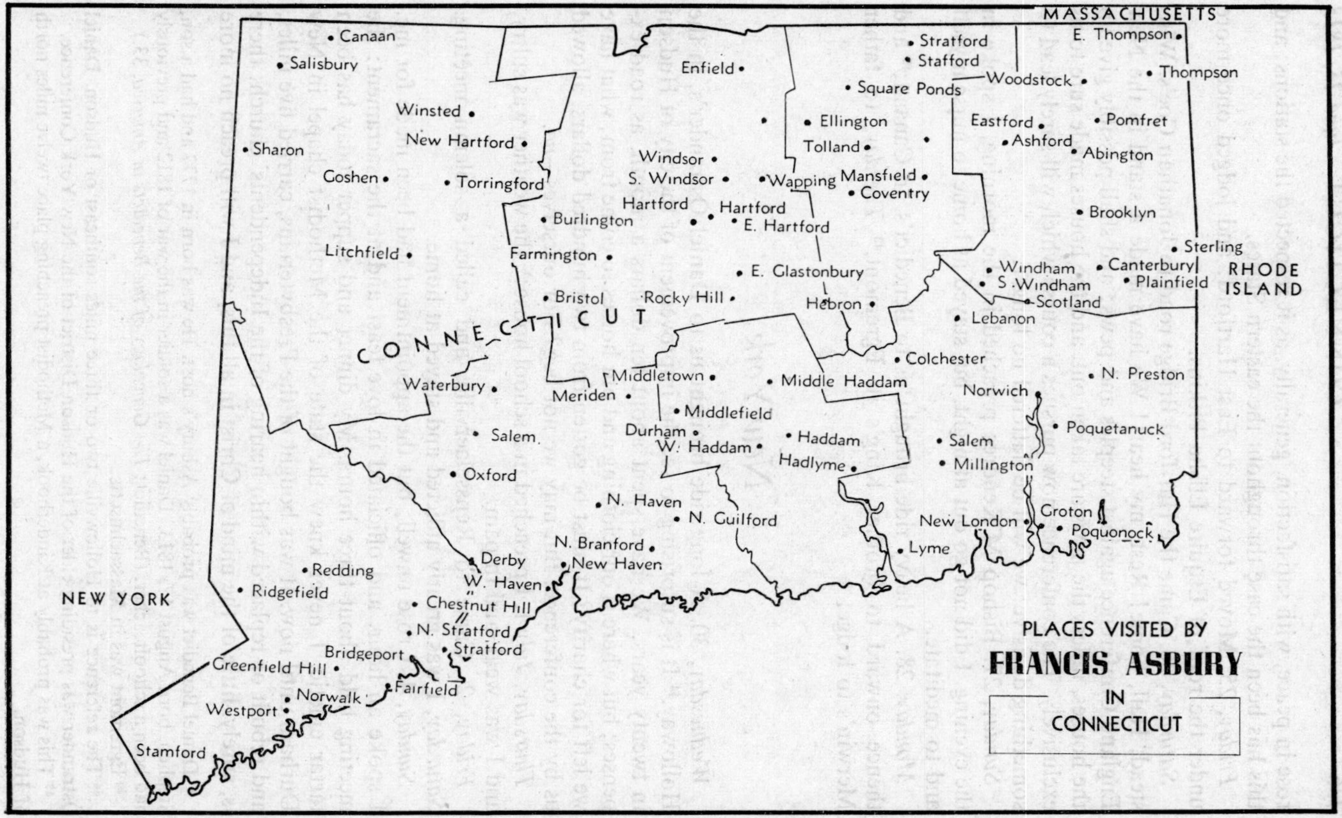

MASSACHUSETTS
RHODE ISLAND
NEW YORK
CONNECTICUT
Canaan
Salisbury
Sharon
Winsted
New Hartford
Goshen
Torringford
Burlington
Litchfield
Farmington
Bristol
Waterbury
Salem
Oxford
Derby
W. Haven
Chestnut Hill
N. Stratford
Stratford
Bridgeport
Redding
Ridgefield
Greenfield Hill
Norwalk
Fairfield
Westport
Stamford
Enfield
Windsor
S. Windsor
Hartford
Hartford
E. Hartford
E. Glastonbury
Rocky Hill
Middletown
Meriden
Middlefield
Durham
W. Haddam
N. Haven
N. Guilford
N. Branford
New Haven
Wapping
Ellington
Tolland
Mansfield
Coventry
Stratford
Stafford
Square Ponds
Hebron
Middle Haddam
Haddam
Hadlyme
Colchester
Lebanon
Salem
Millington
Lyme
New London
Groton
Poquonock
Norwich
Poquetanuck
N. Preston
Windham
S. Windham
Scotland
Canterbury
Plainfield
Sterling
Brooklyn
Eastford
Ashford
Abington
Pomfret
Woodstock
E. Thompson
Thompson
PLACES VISITED BY
FRANCIS ASBURY
IN
CONNECTICUT

rose in peace, with satisfaction, generally, as it respected the stations; and this has been the case throughout the eastern States.

Friday, 25. Moved forward to East Hartford: and lodged once more under the roof of Esquire Elisha Pitkins.

Saturday, 26. Came the Hartford Bridge road to Jonathan Coe's, Winstead. Hail, home! Rest, my heart! We have made a stand in the New England Conference against steeples and pews; and shall possibly give up the houses, unless the pews are taken out, and the houses made sure to us exclusively. The conference now pursues a course which will surely lead to something decisive: we will be flattered no longer.

Sunday, 27. Bishop M'Kendree preached in the morning, I spoke in the evening. I did not go out at night, but stayed at home to nurse myself and to meditate.

Monday, 28. A heavy ride brought us to Benedict's, in Canaan;[42] and thence onward to brother King's in Egremont.[43] *Tuesday*, to father Merwin's to lodge.

New York

Wednesday, 30. A long ride brought us to Daniel Ostrander's, in the Holloway.[44] It is surprising to see the improvement of the city of Hudson in twenty years. We have spent about ten dollars a month, as road expenses; but where is our clothing and our horses to come from; what have we left for charity? It must be gotten from two hundred dollars, allowed us by the conference. But may we not beg? For ourselves—*no*.

Thursday, *July* 1. I preached in a school house:[45] the weather was sultry, and I was weak and in pain.

Friday, 2. Came to Rensselaerville, and called a solemn meeting. *Saturday*, I was greatly afflicted and stayed at home.

Sunday, 4. I rose unwell; but the appointment had been made for me. I spoke an hour, and officiated in love feast and at the sacrament: the meeting held about three hours. My dinner and supper today has been tartar emetic. I never knew the state of the Methodist chapel in New Durham until now. It was bought of the Presbyterians, carried five miles, and rebuilt or replaced within hearing of the Independents' church: there is, surely, little of the mind of Christ in all this, and I will preach no more

[42] Daniel Benedict was probably Asbury's host. He was born in 1777 and had a son, Stephen, born August 17, 1813. Daniel was a soldier in the war of 1812 and previously had been a schoolteacher. (Benedict: *The Genealogy of the Benedicts in America*, 33.)

[43] Egremont was in Massachusetts.

[44] The reference is to Hollowville two or three miles southeast of Hudson. Daniel Ostrander was presiding elder of the Hudson District of the New York Conference.

[45] This was probably at Kinderhook, a Methodist preaching place twelve miles north of Hudson.

in it, if I can avoid it. Should the Methodists have imitated the Low Dutch, who treated them exactly thus in Albany?

Monday, 5. At Sharon; Caukin's, the aged father, is dead. *Tuesday*, a ride through the heavy rain brought us to Springfield.

Wednesday, 7. Came on to Litchfield, and thence to Richards's,[46] a pleasant home.

Thursday, 8. To Westmoreland: in the last two hundred and seventy miles I have suffered much from hunger, heat, and sickness. If we were disposed to stop at taverns (which we are not), our funds would not allow it always when we need refreshment and food; we have not brethren at every place, and the east is not hospitable: Maryland, or the south!

Friday, 9. We opened our conference in peace in our house, sixty by fifty feet; built by the Independents, and bought by the Methodists. We progressed two days in much union and sweetness, having one day the presence and company of our Canadian brethren.

Sabbath, 11. Daniel Hitt preached at nine o'clock. I preached and ordained nine deacons; Bishop M'Kendree ordained six elders, and preached also. We had sermons inside and outside of the house, and in the woods: we might have three thousand souls to hear. Shall our labour all be lost? By sitting in an open, cold house I have taken the influenza.

Tuesday, 13. Our conference adjourned in great peace, and all satisfied with their stations.

Wednesday, 14. Tried medicine. I preached on a short notice at our little chapel at Paris Green. We lodged at Richards's.

Thursday, 15. We had four hours' rain to fall upon us in our eight hours' ride to Brookfield. Brother Pearce[47] was sent in the name of the bishops to communicate to W. B. Lacey[48] what conference had done in his case, and to demand his parchment; the culprit refused to deliver up his credentials in a very peremptory manner: after degrading himself, and despising our authority, it is said he means to be rebaptized.

Friday, 16. We called at our brother Clark's house: our friend and his wife lay in the same grave. We talked and prayed with the grandmother and daughters, one of whom is in society. We have travelled some rugged roads since we left conference, and we have had two hair-breadth escapes for life, both horse and rider, each one. O Lord, thou preservest man and beast! Came to Corkin's. Behold, elder Strait is crooked enough; gone off with things not his own.

[46] Richards was a Methodist leader in Paris, five miles west of Litchfield. Asbury had met McKendree here in 1811, following his journey into Canada.

[47] Marmaduke Pearce was admitted on trial in 1811 and received into full connection at the 1813 conference, when he was appointed to Wyoming, Pennsylvania. Accompanying Asbury to that point, he is sent on this delicate mission.

[48] See *Journal* entry and note for July 12, 1812.

Saturday, 17. A thirty miles' ride brought us[49] to Jericho bridge[50] where the family of Banks generously entertained us.

Sabbath, 18. Bishop M'Kendree stopped to preach; I rode on thirty miles to Brush's. We stopped with a poor family on our route, fed, and prayed with them, and were blest indeed. Next day began our trials. It had rained in the night. We set out and encountered the logs, stumps rocks, and torrents, which came down upon us from the hills above.

Pennsylvania

We put into a house at the Great Bend, and stopped to dine: here I lectured, sung, and prayed with the poor infidels in the house; some stared, some smiled, and some wept. The lady asked me to call again as I passed: yes, madam, on conditon you will do two things; read your Bible, and betake yourself to prayer.

Tuesday, 20. On our way we stopped to visit and pray with the widowed family of our brother Smith, who is called away. As we came into Shawnee[51] the drunkards welcomed us with a dreadful roar. I fail here—my foot is much swelled and very painful.

Thursday, 22. The horse in the sulky has his shoulder swelled. Brother M'Kendree's beast dragged me over a rough path to Bowman's.[52] My face and teeth are in great pain and disorder.

Friday, 23. Great suffering from pain in my face. *Saturday*, I preached, and retired in a high fever to take medicine, and to blister my face. And this is Briar Creek camp meeting! I am alive, however; and some of the good folks of Philadelphia and Jersey have said they should never see Francis again. In the midst of all our suffering and disappointment, God is with us.

Sabbath, 25. I must preach again: my subject was Acts xx, 21. The *testimony* of the ministry—in holiness of life; unwearied labour; in suffering, and in martyrdom. It was the fidelity of this *testifying* which led the first martyrs to the stake; and the unfaithfulness of this *testifying* will lead ministers to hell. *Repentance*—of sinners; of believers; of backsliders;—the difference in their nature. *Faith towards our Lord Jesus Christ*—of seekers of salvation—of believers in sanctification;—in backsliders. I suffer greatly at night.

Monday, 26. We came through the heat, twenty-two miles, to Danville.

[49] Asbury was accompanied by Bishop McKendree and J. C. French. French was his official traveling companion this year.

[50] This was evidently Bainbridge, New York.

[51] The Smith family lived at Tunkhannock. Shawnee is the present Plymouth, Pennsylvania.

[52] Thomas Bowman, an eminent local preacher, was ordained by Bishop Asbury. He was the grandfather of Bishop Thomas Bowman, 1817–1914.

The wife of Daniel Montgomery[53] is my old friend Molly Wallis. Yes, I saw her; but ah! how changed in forty-two years—time has been eighty years at work upon her wrinkled face. We crossed the river to Jacob Gearhart's.[54] My company went to bed, and I sat up helping to hull peas. And am I to preach at six o'clock? be it so. But behold, the saddle horse broke away whilst John French was washing him, and off he went as if Satan drove him.

Wednesday, 28. Our runaway was brought home yesterday at noon. We started at six o'clock, bending our course down the Reading turnpike.[55] We halted at an inn, prayed, and kept forward to Shoemaker's:[56] here we prayed and exhorted in the evening.

Thursday, 29. We bear our trials patiently. John French's sick horse is foundered. Crossed the Schuylkill at Sewey's.[57] We asked for food, and were told the tavern was near. Our money was scarce—we had borrowed five dollars, which will be barely enough, perhaps, to bring us through this inhospitable district. We bent our way along the mountain, stopping at Francis Zellar's, where we were partially welcome. He had a son, a Lutheran priest, who refused to read or pray in the family: Alas! so stupid and so wicked: I would rather be a slave in South Carolina with the gospel and a good master.

Friday, 30. Our saddle horse was stiff enough. We breakfasted richly in Shafferstown[58] for sixty cents—man and beast. We pressed forward to Abraham Bee's, Warwick township.[59] We have great toils and great peace.

Saturday, 31. We halt and limp forward, through Lititz to Lancaster. Happily we met Henry Boehm, who had appointed a meeting at Boehm chapel.

Sabbath, *August* 1. I preached in the forenoon and afternoon. Rest, man and beast! *Monday*, *Tuesday*, and *Wednesday*, busily employed in writing letters, reading, and in prayer. I addressed a valedictory statement

[53] This was probably the brother of General William Montgomery who was one of the founders of Danville and whose son, Daniel, gave it its name.

[54] Jacob Gearhart established a ferry across the river at Danville at an early date. The Gearharts were known as followers of Wesley. (Brower: *A Collection of Historical and Biographical Sketches*, 33.)

[55] The Reading Turnpike runs from Danville, where Asbury had been, to Reading, Pennsylvania.

[56] Shoemakersville is the main village in Perry Township, Berks County, Pennsylvania. As a result of its location at the juncture of Plum Creek with the Schuylkill River, it was early given to industry because of its water powers. Henry Shoemaker, from whom the town derives its name, was one of the first settlers. He built a stone mansion in 1786, which still stands on the north side of Plum Creek about one hundred feet east of the Schuylkill Bridge. (Fox, *op. cit.*, 364.)

[57] This was probably the crossing of the Schuylkill River at Leesburg, Pennsylvania.

[58] Schaefferstown is a village in Heidelberg Township, Lebanon County, eight miles southeast of Lebanon.

[59] Warwick Township is about nine miles above Lancaster.

of my opinion to Bishop M'Kendree, on the primitive Church government and ordinaton; I shall leave it with my papers.

Thursday, we paid a visit to Jacob Boehm. *Friday*, fast day, we went a rough road to the camp meeting, forty-five miles distant.[60] Feeble though I was, the stand was ready for me. I delivered my testimony in great weakness of body. On *Saturday* we had a Sabbath congregation: I preached at three o'clock.

Sabbath, 8. I did not preach a sermon, yet I had often occasion to speak. There was singing and prayer through the whole night; possibly we slept three hours. There were, I suppose, three thousand people on the camp ground, most of them tolerably attentive. Amongst these were some drunkards, but so deeply laden that they could not have done much mischief had they been so disposed. We have gone forty miles out of our way to be here, and to do good; God will bless this coming together of his humble worshippers. Richard Bassett and wife, and sister Bruff, came forty miles to see me. *Tuesday*, the flies plague us. The bridge at Columbia is begun on both sides of the river. We reached Little York.

Maryland

Wednesday, 11. A tiresome ride brought us to our home at the widow Willis's.[61] From the door I saw the tomb of dear Henry Willis. Rest, man of God! Thy quiet dust is not called to the labour of riding five thousand miles in eight months—to meet ten conferences in a line of sessions from the District of Maine, to the banks of the Cayuga—to the States of Ohio, of Tennessee, of Mississippi—to Cape Fear, James River, Baltimore, Philadelphia, and to the completion of the round.[62] Thou wilt not plan and labour the arrangement of the stations of seven hundred preachers; thou wilt not attend camp meetings and take a daily part in the general ministration of the word; and often consume the hours which ought to be devoted to sleep, in writing letters upon letters! Lord, be with us, and help us to fulfil the task thou hast given us to perform! *Thursday*. The Pipe Creek camp meeting begins to-day.[63]

[60] A camp meeting in which the Boehms were interested was near Morgantown, Pennsylvania.

[61] This was Mrs. Henry Willis (1769–1842), a widow since 1808. The grave of her husband, to which Asbury refers, was apparently in the family burying ground visible from "Wakefield," the home in Carroll County. Mrs. Willis was buried in what in 1866 was described as the "old burial ground that belonged to the Methodists, which lies in the rear of what is now called Greenmount Cemetery." (Roberts, *op. cit.*, 55, 56; see note under April 30, 1801.)

[62] Starting in 1800, Bishop Asbury's conference year commenced in the fall of the year with the holding of the session of the Western Conference.

[63] Pipe Creek Camp Meeting, in the general neighborhood of the Willis and McCannon families in Carroll County, was among the first of its kind held in Maryland. Reference

Sabbath, 15. I lectured on the Lord's Prayer, at the camp-stand. We might have three thousand hearers. I have sufficient exercise by riding six miles backward and forward to the ground, and speaking a little. We are told there are between forty and fifty converts, and many professors powerfully quickened; the poor Africans, abandoned by all sects to us, were greatly engaged.

Friday, 20. We started for Ohio, passing through Frederick and Middletown, to Williamsport. Called on father Everhart,[64] and sheltered under his shade from the excessive heat. The old saint has a son and a son-in-law, local labourers. We have encouraging accounts from the encampment near Winchester, Virginia.

Sabbath, 22. Our new chapel here (Williamsport)[65] is too small. I preached to a large congregation on a short notice. I felt that I was commissioned by the anointing of the Holy Spirit: surely the day's labour will not go for nothing.

Wednesday, 25. At Cumberland I preached in the chapel, and ordained John Jeremiah Jacob, Thomas Lakin, and William Shaw, holy men, to the office of elders.

Pennsylvania

A day of toil over the desperate mountains brought us to Brownsville. We have had our trials and afflictions.

Sabbath, 29. I preached strong words from "Examine yourselves"; and after the congregation was dismissed, gave counsel to the society.

Ohio

Wednesday, September 1. We opened our conference[66]—about thirty members present. On *Saturday* deacons and elders were ordained. We

to it may be found in many of the journals of contemporary Maryland Methodist preachers.

[64] Lawrence Everhart (1755–1840) was a local preacher widely known for his heroic exploits during the Revolutionary War and for his ministerial labors in western Maryland. He was the first Methodist preacher ever appointed to Sharpsburg. On his tombstone in the Methodist burying ground, Middletown, Frederick County, were engraved these facts: that "he was ordained a minister of the gospel by Bishop Asbury, A.D. 1808," and that he and a comrade "in the Battle of the Brandywine rescued the wounded Lafayette and carried him two miles to the home of a friend." A daughter was the wife of Colonel Henry R. Smeltzer. (Scharf: *History of Western Maryland*, I, 574, 578; II, 1210.)

[65] Williamsport on the Potomac River, Washington County, was incorporated in 1786. Although the Methodists had a society there as early as the founding of the town, the "new chapel" to which Asbury refers was probably their first house of worship.

[66] This was the second session of the Ohio Conference, held at Steubenville.

have had preaching four times in the day. My mind is at peace, and my body at ease; glory be to thee, O my Creator!

Sabbath, 5. In Bezaleel Wells's grove I may have had one thousand souls to hear me. Bishop M'Kendree preached, and the exercises closed with the sacrament. The people were attentive to hear with much solemnity.

Sabbath, 12. I preached in Chilicothe. We pass on swiftly from tavern to tavern, for we are in great haste, and dare not turn aside to seek our brethren. Mrs. Wells, after painful anxiety, was speedily and happily delivered of a man-child—in answer to prayer, she says; she calls it Francis Asbury. I lament my loss of public labours, especially on the Sabbath: but can I preach more than once a day, constantly engaged, as I am, in conference, in writing answers to letters, and receiving those who come for counsel? Let candid and thinking minds answer.

Tuesday, 14. Reached West Union, with a swelled face, I preached to the people here for the first time; may it not be for the last also? I was turned into another man—the Spirit of God came powerfully upon me, and there was a deep feeling amongst the people.

Kentucky

Wednesday, we came to Limestone,[67] where I consecrated our new house by bearing testimony to the truth of God, on Luke xix, 10. I saw the foundation of our new house in Paris[68] with the more pleasure because of the interesting little history attached to it. An honest brother had failed in business, moved away, recovered his loss, came back, paid his creditors, and moved a subscription to build, and is now building a Methodist chapel.

Sabbath, 19. I preached in our enlarged Ebenezer church, in Clark county.[69] Once more I see Doctor Hinds[70] from the other side the flood, rejoicing in Jesus; he will never again, I presume, put a blister on his

[67] Limestone was the present Maysville, Kentucky. There was a Methodist society there as early as 1800. (Redford, *op. cit.*, II, 285; Arnold, *op. cit.*, I, 176.)

[68] This was the first Methodist chapel in Paris, Kentucky, although a society doubtless was in existence as early as 1797. The first meetings were held in the home of D. B. Flanagan in 1803, and a church was organized in 1805. The building mentioned by Asbury was not completed until 1820, though it was probably in use by 1817. It was a brick building with three hundred seats and a box pulpit with steps on each side. Peter Schwartzfelder, John D. Hearne, and Senator Garrett Davis were the moving spirits in its erection. (Keller and McCann, Sketches in Paris, *Kentucky Methodists*, April 7, 1955; Arnold, *op. cit.*, I, 176.)

[69] The Ebenezer church, near Winchester, had been enlarged in 1810 and was to be still further expanded through the years. The society was formed in 1797, and a log building was erected the following year. (Arnold, *op. cit.*, I, 185.)

[70] Dr. Hinds was the grandfather of Bishop H. H. Cavanaugh. Cavanaugh was born near Ebenezer Church.

wife's head to draw Methodism out of her heart; this mad prank brought deep conviction, by the operation of the Spirit of God upon his soul. His children, some of them, already rejoice with him, having the same joy, and faith, and hope. We came rapidly through Danville to Mulder's. Next day to Thompson's.[71] Next day to Wallis's;[72] and next day to father Bracken's,[73] near the camp ground. What a flight we have had!

Sabbath, 26. I preached in the camp. Our ride from Steubenville has been through pleasant rains, welcome to the before-parched earth. We read the word of God, and prayed in every house in which we stopped. The tavern keepers were kind and polite, as Southern folks should be and as Southern folks ought not to be; they were sometimes two sheets in the wind. O, that liquid fire! The thing I have for some time greatly feared is come to pass—the Creek nation have taken up the hatchet: unhappy people! the whites will take vengeance, cruel vengeance on them for their barbarian warfare on unoffending women and children. O God, save thy people from rage of the heathen!

Tennessee

We came to the Tennessee Conference.[74] I lodged under the hospitable roof of mother Roscoe. Our progress daily was great, and made in great peace and order.

Sabbath, October 3. I preached, and ordained about twenty deacons.[75] We rose on the sixth instant finding very few difficulties objected to the stations. The families in the neighbourhood have not been left unvisited; and we hope our prayers and exhortations will not be in vain to and for the Walkers, the Maxeys, the Saunderses, the Reeses, the Blackmans. Will it be believed that the *races* agitate the public mind notwithstanding the alarms of Indian wars? If in the midst of such terrors the people will not forsake the race-course, why should the people of God neglect to frequent their meetings? in this case they may learn from the example of

[71] William Thompson became a traveling preacher in 1804 and served the Danville Circuit for two years. He then located and lived within its boundary, subsequently going to Ohio and again joining the conference. (*Ibid.*, I, 26, 27.)

[72] This may have been the home of Reuben Wallace, who settled near Campbellsville in Taylor County and remained there until 1833. (*Ibid.*, 354.)

[73] There was a Bracken's meetinghouse as early as 1798 in Bracken County near Brooksville, but this was far from Asbury's location at this time. (*Ibid.*, 182.)

[74] This was the second session of the Tennessee Conference, October 1–7, 1813. It was held at Rees' Chapel, probably the present Bethlehem Church, about six miles from Franklin. (Carter, *op. cit.*, 57, 58; McFerrin, *op. cit.*, 308, 309.)

[75] Bishop McKendree seems to have presided at all sessions except for a brief period when the conference voted on deacon's orders for his brother James. (McFerrin, *op. cit.*, 308.)

sinners. The Tennessee Conference were not willing to let the bishop go to the Mississippi Conference.[76] *Sabbath*, 10. I preached at John M'Gee's.

Sabbath, 17. Last night preached at Porter's chapel. At Marysville,[77] the whole city came out to hear us. Our travels have been through toil, and crowds, and storms. It is our business to read, exhort, and pray, wherever we stop.

Monday, 18. We came away, having first taken an emetic. A thirty miles' ride over unpleasant paths, and through heat, brought us to our lodging for the night with more endurable feelings. I preached at O'Haver's[78] on *Wednesday*, and ordained Joshua West[79] an elder.

North Carolina

We visited the Bolings, the Nelsons, and the Barnets. I feel pleuritic pains in the breast; but they must wear themselves away.

Sabbath, 24. I preached in great weakness. I am at Daniel Killian's once more.

South Carolina

Our ride of ninety miles to Staunton bridge on Saluda River was severely felt, and the necessity of lodging at taverns made it no better.[80]

Friday, 29. On the peaceful banks of the Saluda I write my valedictory address to the presiding elders. At Staunton bridge we rest five days; my horse and his master both disabled. I preached but twice. My leisure has permitted me to read Sellon: I hesitate not to recommend this work to our Book Concern. James, the son of John Douthat, gave me an interesting account of his father:—John Douthat was born in Maryland; left his native place and settled on the Yadkin; became a member of the Methodist society, and was honoured as a class leader, making his house a house of God for the assemblies of his brethren. An infamous woman had found her way into the society, and seduced Douthat away, and he departed from his brethren and from God. Some years after this, the family removed

[76] Asbury always desired to go to Mississippi since Tobias Gibson established Methodism there in 1800, but was never permitted by the conference to do so.

[77] Asbury was now in the Holston country. In the absence of *Journal* entries it may be supposed that he proceeded from the Tennessee conference to Knoxville by his former route. (See *Journal* entries and notes for October 23–29, 1800.)

[78] John O'Haver lived in Cocke County, Tennessee, near the North Carolina line. There was a camp ground at the place. (See note under November 29, 1808.)

[79] Joshua West was a brother of Mrs. Mitchell Porter.

[80] Asbury followed the familiar route over the mountains by way of Table Rock into Greenville County, South Carolina.

to the Table Mountain, Pendleton district: the preachers came to the house, the father was reclaimed, and his two sons, James and Samuel, joined the Methodists, and were useful and respectable travelling preachers; the former labouring twelve, the latter seven years in the ministry. But the elder Douthat had a failing—he was fond of liquor, and indulged himself, and backslid a second time; retaining, nevertheless, his character for strict integrity and his habit of private prayer, occasionally hearing the Gospel. Last summer he fell ill, and came to lie down and die at his son James's; here he became a true penitent, was blest with justifying and sanctifying grace, and slept in peace in the seventy-third year of his age.

Tuesday, November 2. We visited Talliaferro's[81] and went forward to B. Lyon's.

Thursday, 4. Called a meeting at Edward M'Craw's: I spoke with enlargement of mind on Heb. x, 38, 39. We saw Henry Gains, a disciple since 1777; now feeble, but wishing to be faithful unto death. Came forward to Conner's, Abbeville district.

Sabbath, 7. I preached in the tabernacle, on 2 Cor. v, 11. If the people say it was like thunder and lightning I shall not be surprised. I spoke in power from God, and there was a general and deep feeling in the congregation: thine, O Lord, be all the glory! Came home with James Cox.

Monday, 8. I gave an alarming lecture at John Brannon's. There is a serious mortality on the middle and lowlands of South Carolina and Georgia.

Tuesday, 9. We rode through the heat, crossing the Little River to Mr. Shield's, twenty miles.

Georgia

Wednesday, 10. I tried five grains of tartar, and felt the good effects of medicine. We continued on to Petersburg into Georgia. Into what house may I enter without finding two cold professors, and five or ten impious persons? Yet God will favour a righteous cause, though there may be thousands as wicked as fiends.

Sabbath, 14. I preached at Thompson's chapel, and had a pleasant season. We lodged at senator Tait's,[82] and I retired to bed with a fever. Here are two sick families. There is a great drought: these are judgment days. I preached at Peter Oliver's: my host and wife are both sick.

[81] Asbury was on a customary route through Greenville, Pendleton, and Abbeville counties to the Tabernacle Church near Cokesbury where George Connor lived.

[82] Charles Tait (1768–1835) had been a student and instructor in Cokesbury College. He came with his father, James Tait, from Virginia to present Elbert County, Georgia, in 1783. He practiced law with William H. Crawford at Lexington and became judge and U.S. Senator. He moved to Alabama in 1819 and became prominent there. (*Dictionary of National Biography*, XVIII, 274, 275; see note under April 9, 1788.)

Sabbath, 21. I preached in the new chapel at James Mark's—Elbert's—in folly called Asbury.[83] We visited Doctor Bradly, recovering from his affliction; a miracle of grace. We have visited about thirty families. Imprudent man that I am, to take off my flannel, and ride in the damps after sunset! I preached at Sparta, and ordained two deacons. A journey of six days brought us to Savannah: we were careful to leave our testimony and to pray with every family where we stopped. Kind widow Bonnell sent her chaise after me. I must change my mode of travelling, I suppose. I preached twice in the Wesley chapel.[84] This is a good, neat house, sixty feet by forty. I enjoyed great peace. Our chapel cost five thousand dollars: others would have made it cost twice as much, perhaps. We are indebted to Myers and Russell[85] for much of this saving. The Presbyterian Church hath changed its form to Independent—Doctor Kollock must be the same.

Monday, 22. Rode to Mr. Thibeau's plantation: sweet retreat!

South Carolina

Tuesday, we rode forty-six miles to Wainer's. I am again in a chaise: James Russell insisted upon giving me an old gig worth forty-five dollars. We are safe in Charleston, visiting black swamp[86] and some families as we came along. We have had cold, hungry travelling. My mind is holiness to the Lord. We found our family here in health.

Sunday, December 12. I preached in Trinity church: we have it now in quiet possession. I also officiated in Cumberland and Bethel churches.

[83] James Marks and his brother John, who was stepfather of Meriwether Lewis, were prominent Methodists. They lived on Broad River in present Elbert County, Georgia, "between Governor Mathew's and Colonel Johnson's plantations." Asbury's Chapel, built by James Marks, was one of the first meetinghouses in the area. (Gilmer, *op. cit.*, 116; Bowen, *op. cit.*, 58.)

[84] Wesley Chapel, the first Methodist meetinghouse in Savannah, was built by James Russell—at Lincoln and South Broad streets, now Oglethorpe Avenue, in 1812. An erroneous statement in *History of Savannah Methodism* by Haywood S. Bowden (1929) says it was finished in 1815 and dedicated by Asbury on April 24 of that year. On that date Asbury was in Pennsylvania. He was not in Georgia in 1815.

[85] Lewis Myers was presiding elder of the Ogeechee District, and James Russell was pastor at Savannah. This city had been unusually difficult for the Methodists, and Russell succeeded in building the first chapel there in 1812 by cutting and transporting the timber and doing the carpentry work with his own hands, while he cut and sold marsh grass to support himself. He then entered business to free himself from debt and prospered, later becoming bankrupt. (Smith: *Georgia Methodism*, 113–17.)

[86] Black Swamp Church was in lower Hampton County, South Carolina. With advancing age Asbury's *Journal* became increasingly sketchier, but his movements can be traced. From Thibeau Plantation ten miles above Savannah on the Georgia side he crossed the Savannah River and proceeded to Black Swamp and on to Charleston, probably by way of Walterboro, Parker's Ferry, and St. Andrew's Parish on the Ashley River.

The society is not so lively as formerly. In visiting six families I found but two that acknowledge God in his word and worship: Ah, woe is me!

Thursday, 16. We attended the funeral of Doctor Keith, suddenly called away, and greatly lamented by all, especially by the people of colour: he had been twenty-six years a minister of the Independent Church.[87] Most of the clergy of the city were present, and there was great solemnity observed. We had no gloves or scarfs given us: this was well; but I could have wished there had been prayer in the house before the corpse was removed. We lecture morning and evening. We labour to live in and for God; we desire to receive rich and poor, people and ministers; and to consecrate, in the order of faith and prayer, every room and every heart in the house, to God.

Sunday, 19. I preached in Cumberland chapel, in Trinity, and in Bethel. How much good will my ten days' visit do here? I preach, lecture, and pray. I invited the stewards of Bethel, and the trustees of Trinity came to see me on *Tuesday*; we dined and prayed together, and parted in love and peace.

Wednesday, 22. In a cold day we left Charleston, and came thirty miles to preach to preachers at Nichols's.[88] We lodged with Eccles.[89] *Friday*, my mind is in peace in bodily affliction. Weather, roads, swamps—we heed them not. On our way to Black River, we visited many families: O, let me do some good whilst I may! *time is short*.

Thursday, 30. At Rembert's settlement.[90] How my friends remove or waste away! yet I live: let me live every moment to God!

[87] This was the Circular Congregational Church where Asbury had earlier worshiped.

[88] Nichols lived near Summerville.

[89] Eccles lived near Ridgeville.

[90] In reaching the long-cherished Rembert Hall, Asbury had probably proceeded by Holly Hill, Vance, Nelson's Ferry, over the Santee, Summerton, Sumter, and Bradford's.

1814

1814

"Henry Boehm sends me great accounts of the camp meetings"

CHAPTER FORTY-THREE

South Carolina

On the first day of the new year, 1814, I preached at Rembert's chapel. *Sunday, January* 2. I preached in the chapel.

North Carolina

On *Monday* we came away, in company with Myers and Norton,[1] to Fayetteville, one hundred and forty miles, visiting many families in our route.

Friday, 7. I received seven letters: the contents of some of them make me feel serious. We learn that Bishop Coke, with seven young preachers, have sailed for the East Indies.[2] The British Society is poor as well as ourselves, it would appear: this is a good sign. In less than one hundred years, Methodism has spread over three quarters of the globe; and it is now about to carry the Gospel of salvation into Asia. Amen. I am divinely impressed with a charge to preach sanctification in every sermon.

Sunday, 9. We had rain. Bishop M'Kendree preached. I preached on

[1] Lewis Myers was presiding elder of the Ogeechee District, and James Norton was Bishop McKendree's traveling companion this year. (*Minutes.*)

[2] Dr. Coke and his party had set sail for Ceylon on December 30, 1813. On May 3, 1814, before the voyage was completed, he died, leaving his missionary band without a leader. He was buried in the Indian Ocean. (*Wesley and His Successors*, 45–46.)

Isaiah lxiv, 7. We had a spiritual, heavenly, and united conference.[3] There were twenty deacons ordained, eighty-five preachers stationed: twelve have located, and one has died, suddenly; and fifteen are added.

Sunday, 16. I preached. *Thursday*, we came away. On our way we called on Hughes, Shaw, and Saunderson, exhorting and praying with their families. I enjoy great peace of mind.

Sunday, 23. I preached in our chapel, fifty by sixty feet, to a small congregation. Am I not a child, to have been looking for summer? William Glendenning and I met, and embraced each other in peace. I visited sister Perry, the former wife of John King, one of the first Methodist preachers. After all reasonable allowances for drawbacks, we cannot yet tell all the good that was done by our conference in Raleigh, in 1811. We started away northward. Not half a mile from Samuel Alston's[4] we got entangled in the woods. We left the gig in the woods till morning, and found our way by torch light to the house. I preached at my kind host's. On our way to Doctor Brodie's, in Louisburg, we called to dine with our friend Thomas Alston, junior.

Virginia

Sunday, February 20. I am at Norfolk. I have had a serious attack of pleuritic fever, with little intermission of pain until the fifteenth day. I have, during this illness, been moving about amongst the families of the Williamses, the Harrises, the widow Weavers, the Bennetts, and the Merediths; and O! what kindness and nursing. I preached at Henry Williams's, quarter-meeting, and occasionally elsewhere.

Our conference[5] in Norfolk rose on *Tuesday, March* 1. We have been mighty in talk this session. I dare not speak my mind on the state of this place—its Church or its ministry. I endure all things for the elect's sake; and rejoice that peace is again happily restored to the society. Shall we not drop and locate more labourers than we receive? We had a great many sermons preached, as usual; and we have reason to hope souls were converted. I ordained deacons, and assisted my brethren in the ministration of the word.

Tuesday, March 1. We came out of the borough: it was keen and cold to Shoulders hill.

Wednesday, 2. Came to Andrew Woodville's. We reached Richmond on

[3] This was the South Carolina Conference which convened at Fayetteville, North Carolina, on January 12, 1814.

[4] The Alston families lived in Warren County.

[5] This session of the Virginia Conference met in the Masonic Hall in Norfolk with forty-two members in attendance. The circuits were reduced to thirty-seven by uniting some, and seventy preachers received appointments. (Bennett, *op. cit.*, 597–98.)

Saturday. Our journey hither has been through snows and excessive cold; I felt it deeply. We were careful to pray with the families where we stopped, exhorting all professors to holiness.

Sunday, 6. I preached in the old chapel; our labour shall not all be in vain. Doctor Jennings has removed to Richmond; to be useful, we hope, to the society and to himself.

District of Columbia

A journey of suffering by bad roads, and exposure to excessive cold, brought us to Georgetown, Maryland. In the year 1774[6] I first visited Virginia and North Carolina; in the year 1780 I repeated my visit; and since that time, yearly. In the year 1785 I first visited South Carolina and Georgia; and to these States have since paid (except one year) an annual visit, until now (1814). I suppose I have crossed the Alleghany mountains sixty times.

Sunday, 13. I preached in our church in Georgetown, and met the society. We do not labour in vain. My mind is deeply impressed with the worth of souls and value of time.

Maryland

Thursday, 24. Baltimore Conference[7] hath been sitting in great order seven days. My strength and labour was to sit still. I was sick during the whole session: I preached in Old Town, and ordained nine deacons. We have stationed eighty-six members. By request, I discoursed on the character of the angel of the Church of Philadelphia, in allusion to P. W. Otterbein—the holy, the great Otterbein, whose funeral discourse it was intended to be. Solemnity marked the silent meeting in the German Church, where were assembled the members of our conference, and many of the clergy of the city. Forty years have I known the retiring modesty

[6] The *Journal* shows that Asbury came to Virginia first in 1775 and again in 1776. His first trip through North Carolina was in 1780.

[7] This session of the Baltimore Conference was attended by sixty-four preachers and was presided over by Asbury and McKendree. One of Asbury's greatest pulpit efforts of his later years was his tribute to Philip William Otterbein in the latter's church on the closing day of the conference. It is possible that it contained some of the material to be found in the *Methodist Magazine*. (See Asbury's questionnaire submitted to Otterbein, *The Methodist Magazine*, VI (1823), 255, 256.) A regrettable action of the conference was the breaking off of negotiations for a merger with the United Brethren Church. (Hough: *Christian Newcomer, His Life, Journal and Achievements*, 164, 165; Armstrong, *op. cit.*, 173.)

of this man of God; towering majestic above his fellows in learning, wisdom, and grace, yet seeking to be known only of God and the people of God; he had been sixty years a minister, fifty years a converted one.

March 28. I am at Perry Hall, where I have been for three days very ill. The Sabbath was an awful and dumb day. I took an emetic.

Friday, *April* 1. I crossed the Susquehanna. At North East I visited Daniel Sheridan, a son of deep affliction in body, mind, and circumstances. He is one of my spiritual children, and has remained a disciple forty years: we prayed together, and God was with us of a truth.

Delaware

Sunday, 3. I preached in Wilmington. *Monday*, we had great consolation in visiting Mary Withy's children and grandchildren: she, though dead, is yet spoken of. One of these last is in society. I baptized the children of Allan and Lewis McLane:[8] these people have not forgotten the holy living and dying of their mother, nor her early and constant friend, the writer of this journal. Joseph Pilmoor[9] is yet alive, and preaches three times every Sabbath.

Pennsylvania

Philadelphia, *Tuesday*, 5. This is the eve of conference.

Sunday, 10. I preached in the Academy chapel, and at St. George's. Our conference opened and progressed four days in great peace and Gospel order. We doubt not but that souls have been convinced, converted, comforted, and sanctified by the ministry of the word; we had crowded

[8] Dr. Allan McLane (1784–1845) and Louis McLane were the sons of Allan and Rebecca Wells McLane of Wilmington, Delaware. (See note under July 14, 1797.) The former was the first mayor of Wilmington, a surgeon in the War of 1812 and a vestryman in Old Swedes Church. Louis McLane (1776–1857) was a veteran of the War of 1812; a member of the House of Representatives, 1817–27; a Senator from the state of Delaware, 1827; minister to the Court of St. James, 1829; Secretary of the Treasury, 1831; Secretary of State, 1833; president of the Baltimore and Ohio Railroad, 1837–49, and again minister to the Court of St. James. (*National Cyclopaedia of American Biography*, V, 293, 294; Scharf: *History of Delaware*, I, 489; *American Heritage, the Magazine of History*, October, 1956, article by Fred J. Cook, "Allan McLane, Unknown Hero of the Revolution.")

[9] Joseph Pilmoor, then seventy-five years of age, was the rector of St. Paul's Episcopal Church in Philadelphia. The noted early Methodist had returned to England in 1774 and preached there for ten years. He came back to America and in 1785 was ordained in the Episcopal Church and served as rector in Philadelphia until 1793. From that date until 1804 he was rector of Christ Church in New York and then returned to Philadelphia. (*Dictionary of American Biography*, XIV, 609.)

houses, both in the day and at night. The bishops wrote a serious letter to New England, remonstrating on the neglect of family worship.

Thursday, 14. The Philadelphia Conference rose in the spirit, power, and peace of God, in which they had been sitting seven days.

New Jersey

Friday, crossed in a steamboat[10] to the Jersey shore. I am very unwell.

Tuesday, 19. I rode twenty miles from Woodbury[11] to Perkintown,[12] to see the people: we gave an exhortation in great weakness, but the power of truth was felt.

Sunday, 24. I preached at Penns Neck, at Salem, and at Cohansey Bridge. I preached also at Pitts Grove. We may say, that when we are weak, we are strong in the strength of God: yea, Lord, thou art our strength! I preached at Union chapel, and the Lord gave power to his own truth. I preached at Bethel. We had a rainy day, and my flesh failed. I rested at Daniel Bates's, greatly spent with labour. We should have failed in our march through Jersey, but we have received great kindness and attentions, and have had great accommodations. I return to my journal after an interval of twelve weeks.[13] I have been ill indeed, but medicine, nursing, and kindness, under God, have been so far effectual, that I have recovered strength enough to sit in my little covered wagon, into which they lift me.

Pennsylvania

I have clambered over the rude mountains, passing through York and Chambersburg to Greensburg.[14]

[10] This is the first mention of Bishop Asbury's use of the steamboat, which was only five years old, since Fulton's successful trial trip on the Hudson River.

[11] Woodbury is the county seat of Gloucester County, New Jersey, having been established in 1686. Gordon lists a Methodist church there in 1834, describing it as a brick edifice. (Myers, *op. cit.*, III, 471–72; Gordon, *op. cit.*, 265.)

[12] Perkintown is located in Salem County, New Jersey, three miles from Penn's Grove.

[13] Henry Boehm aided in taking care of Bishop Asbury during his severe three-month illness at Sale Coate's home at Lumberton, New Jersey, and asserted that the bishop "never fully recovered from that sickness, and he was physically unfit to go round his diocese again." But here we find the indomitable Asbury traveling rapidly westward as he commenced the round of one of his longest tours. (Boehm, *op. cit.*, 421.)

[14] This entry cannot be accurately dated except by comparison with Henry Boehm's *Reminiscences*. The date next succeeding, July 19, is probably the date of resumption of the *Journal* entries and not the date of resumption of his travels, which must have begun a few days before that to have enabled him to reach York, Chambersburg, and Greensburg, Pennsylvania.

Tuesday, July 19. I would not be loved to death, and so came down from my sick room and took to the road, weak enough. Attentions constant, and kindness unceasing, have pursued me to this place, and my strength increases daily. I look back upon a martyr's life of toil, and privation, and pain; and I am ready for a martyr's death. The purity of my intentions; my diligence in the labours to which God has been pleased to call me; the unknown sufferings I have endured; what are all these?—the merit. atonement, and righteousness of Christ alone make my plea. My friends in Philadelphia gave me a light, little four-wheeled carriage; but God and the Baltimore Conference made me a richer present—they gave me John Wesley Bond for a travelling companion;[15] has he his equal on the earth for excellencies of every kind as an aid? I groan one minute with pain, and shout glory the next!

July 23. Pittsburgh. We have made three hundred and fifty miles since we left Jersey. What roads! It was the mercy of Providence, or we should have been dashed to pieces. My body is, nevertheless, in better health; and my mind and soul happy and confident in God. Glory, glory, glory be to the Triune God!

Monday, 25. We bent our way down the west side of the Ohio to Sewickley;[16] here we were detained two days. John Wesley Bond preached to the people, and I added a few feeble words of exhortation. We having foundered one of our horses, bought a clever little mare for sixty dollars. Crossed Great and Little Beaver. At J. Hemphill's we were told that no person would be more willing for prayer, did business permit—alas! On our way we got fast in a gully: Mr. Lyon, a merchant hereabouts, came up, dismounted in a moment, and sprang to my relief, lifted me out of the carriage, and bore me up the hill: there was something peculiarly engaging in this man's face, whole appearance, and manners.

Friday, 29. We came to Thomas Fawcett's, fasting. "Surely you may stay a night," it was observed. But no—time presses—though sick and feeble, we started away at three o'clock. It might not be: about a hundred yards from the house *crack* went the pole. "It is all for the best," said pious Gilpin, when his leg was broken; and he lived to prophesy in after times and better days, while the execrated Mary, who would have burnt him at the stake, was mouldering in the dust.

Ohio

Sabbath. Brother Bond preached upon a mount crowned with sugar trees. I spoke a few words in exhortation. Had we not chained the wheel,

[15] John Wesley Bond (1784–1817) was a preacher of the Baltimore Conference. He remained with Asbury until the end and was present at the bishop's death.

[16] This is the only time Asbury's route took him north of the Ohio River in Pennsylvania.

we should have gone *souse* into Yellow Creek. *Tuesday*, we had crooked work—we splintered the axle tree, and stopped at the widow Pritchard's. We held two meetings—one at noon, and again at night.

Wednesday, *August* 3. Came to Steubenville. At Bezaleel Wells's we have every accommodation that a president might wish for, with great kindness and polite attentions from all the members of the house. I keep my room, and listen to the storms of wind and rain abroad. My occupations are, reading Saurin, the oracles of God, and prayer. My health is better, although I still cough. I live in patience, in purity, and the perfect love of God. Being disappointed on the Sabbath, I must of necessity meet the people of Steubenville on *Monday*. I preached, and there were those who felt, beside the speaker.

Tuesday, 9. We made a valiant start forwards. It was racking work over Creek Hill. Here *crack* went the bolt; it had been badly mended before. Woe to us had it given way on the last hill. We lodged at Snyder's. I spoke at Cadiz with a feeble voice, and addressed the society after preaching. We rode forward to a brother's, where we found a large family and small house. Within eight miles of Cambridge we were glad to stop: here is a purgatory, if fleas can make one.

Friday, 12. We strove hard to get forward through the heat to Will's Creek. It is as deep as ever, but this is not the first time I have tried it; it is better now, it is said: bad is the best, say I. We reached James Browne's.

Sunday, 14. At Zanesville brother Bond preached, and met about fifty souls in class. I gave an exhortation; it is my first, and may be my valedictory. We have a well-designed house here. This country is in a general state of improvement. *Monday*, to Middletown.

Tuesday, 16. To James Teel's. My infant weakness, and entire dependence upon the aid of others; the excessive heat and rough roads; together with certain *cases* and things, are trying to body and mind: Lord, thou dost, and thou wilt support a worm, and no man! Make me, O Lord, make me perfect!

Wednesday, 17. To Jesse Spurgeon's. *Thursday*, rest. I committed to paper some observations on a book written by B. J. Smith, an elected deacon, against our doctrine, discipline, and administration.

Friday, 19. We came through Circleville. What surprising mounds of earth! Who hath done this? The larger circle must have had water. Stopped at Jeffersonville. *Saturday*, to William M'Dowell's; we found the family sick with the autumnal fever.

Sabbath, 21. I preached at M'Dowell's. *Tuesday*, I preached in great weakness in Chilicothe; but my help was with me; in God will I make my boast. From the 24th to the 30th, we are at senator Worthington's. I pay my mite of worship in this amiable family in great weakness. The kind attentions I receive are greatly beyond my deserts. Mrs. Worthington has taught her boys and girls, servants and children, to read the holy Scriptures, and they are well instructed: I heard them more than one lesson with much satisfaction. O that all mothers would do likewise! I presume the worship of God is kept up in this house, though neither of the heads thereof have attached themselves to any society of professing Christians: doubtless God will bless them, and their children after them. We, ever and anon, halt and listen for dear M'Kendree, but as yet we are without tidings: we are somewhat anxious to see him. *Tuesday*, we came away to Merchant's.

Sabbath, September 4. I made a feeble attempt at Lebanon, on 2 Pet. iii, 14. I also spoke last night. *Tuesday*, we arrived in Cincinnati. There is distress everywhere; in the Church, and abroad in the United States. I have discharged blood in coughing.

Monday, 5. I made an attempt to speak a few words on Philip. ii, 2–5. We have progressed in our conference business very well, although deprived of the presence of the bishops to preside. Bishop M'Kendree had been thrown from his horse, and was severely wounded in the hip and ribs.[17] John Sale presided with great propriety. We lost two days by impeachment of elders; one of whom, in vindicating his character, injured as he thought, had not done it becomingly; there was a more excellent way. The other case was that of Samuel Parker, who had checked the administration of one whom he had employed for a time; these investigations were painful to our feelings, and gave rise to some sturdy debating. On *Friday* I retired to bed with a chill and fever. John Sale finished the plan of the stations from a general draft I furnished him. We closed our labours in peace. One thing I remark; our conferences are out of their infancy: their rulers can now be called from amongst themselves. The dividend of the Ohio Conference was seventy-four dollars to the unmarried, and one hundred and forty-four dollars to the married preachers and their wives. But two hundred dollars were drawn from the Book Concern, and fifty of that sum were returned. I have preached. We lodge at William Lines's. The news has reached us of the descent of the British in Maryland, and the burning of the public buildings at Washington.

Kentucky

Monday, 12. We hasted away, as the river was still rising; night and necessity housed us at Norton's. Next day to Fisher's. We dined in George-

[17] McKendree's accident occurred on July 29, 1814, when the bishops were going from the Genesee Conference at Genoa, New York, to Ohio. No bones were broken, but he was confined to bed for several days and detained for nearly a month. Asbury was too feeble to preside at the Ohio Conference, and John Sale was chosen to do so. Sale had been presiding elder of the Kentucky District and was transferred to the Miami District. (Paine: *Life and Times of Bishop McKendree*, 177; *Minutes*, 1814, 1815.)

town at the Eagle Tavern, and after our meal called the family to prayer: the landlady was a finished lady in her manners, and kind as she was clever; peace, peace, peace, be upon her!

Wednesday, 14. I gave a serious charge to the widow Ratcliffe and her family; the venerable man of the house has gone to rest. *Thursday*, at Edward Talbot's.[18] The gloomy days of J. B——r, B——m, William Burke are over; peace is restored, a society increased, a family blessed with a son a preacher; a house is built, and a society united in Shelbyville:[19] for all these we give glory unto thee, O God!

Friday, 16. To Miller's in haste. *Saturday*, we came through Bardstown to Elizabethton, Hardin county; so called after my serious friend Colonel Hardin.[20] I travelled many miles with brother Hardin towards Lexington, when he was going up to take his command: he was very solemn; a martyr to Indian massacre, I doubt not but that he went to glory. We lodged at the house of Stephen Rawlings, son of Stephen, formerly of Back Creek, Berkley county, Virginia; in 1776 I preached in the grandfather's house.

Sabbath, 25. I preached the funeral sermon of the wife of Stephen Rawlings. In this family of Rawlings, I have officiated for three generations, and have witnessed their profession of religion: may they continue to be in Christ to the latest posterity! We reached M'Gatchin's on *Monday*; it is all love and union here: two of the children have joined the society. The Woodsons, at the ferry, were very friendly: they are Antipedobaptists.

Tuesday, 27. We were kindly entreated to stop by our sister Gatwood, and were well entertained. The dust and heat are oppressive, and I am sick.

Wednesday, 28. At Major Bibb's. Twenty-six years past I was at a brother Williams's, Prince Edward county, Virginia—a brand plucked from the burning.

Thursday, 29. We came upon the camp ground, where we are to hold our conference.[21]

Sabbath, October 2. I ordained about twenty deacons, and gave a sermon and an exhortation. Our encampment cook is brother Douglass.[22]

[18] Edward Talbot was a member of the Brick Church in Shelby County, Kentucky.

[19] The first Methodist meetinghouse in Shelbyville, Kentucky, was erected in 1813. (Arnold, *op. cit.*, I, 176.)

[20] Colonel John J. Hardin's son, Martin D. Hardin, was at this time serving on the northern border in the war against Great Britain. He later became U.S. Senator from Kentucky. Another son of Colonel Hardin was Mark Hardin, who was registrar of the Kentucky land office.

[21] The Tennessee Conference met at the New Chapel, Kennerly's Camp Ground, in Logan County, Kentucky, about ten miles north of Russellville. Philip Kennerly settled there in 1807, and a society was formed in his home soon thereafter. A log church known as Kennerly's Chapel was erected in 1811. (*Ibid.*, 349, 350.)

[22] The Rev. Thomas L. Douglass had been stationed at Nashville and was appointed presiding elder of the Nashville District. (*Minutes*, 1814, 1815.)

We are two hours in the chapel, four hours at the preaching-stand, and then come home. We sit six hours a day in conference. Poor bishops—sick, lame, and in poverty! I had wished to visit Mississippi, but the injury received by Bishop M'Kendree being so great that it is yet doubtful whether he will so far recover as to be present at the South Carolina Conference, I must decline going: I live in God.

Thursday, 6. We closed our labours in great peace and love. The families have been kind to us, but we were much crowded. We have lost members from the society, and gained, perhaps, one preacher in the itinerancy in two years; the local ministry is enriched: may we expect more help? Ah! the labour is too hard, and the wages too low. We cannot, like the Quakers, *take abroad* when we get tired of home, and go feasting about from one rich friend's table to another's, and *bark* or be *dumb*, as the fit may take us. Our discipline is too strict: we cannot leave four or five thousand congregations unsought, like the Church of England, the Presbyterian, Independent, and Baptist Churches. *Go*, says the command; go into all the world—go to the highway and hedges. *Go out*—seek them. Christ came *seeking* the lost sheep. *Seek me out*, says the parson; or advertise and offer a church and a good salary, and I will *seek* you. And is this all these pretenders can do? If we send but one travelling preacher into a four weeks' circuit, we aid him by the labour of our local ministry, good men, and some of them great men.

Tennessee

Sabbath, 9. I would have preached to-day at Fountain Head,[23] but I was bed sick. Thomas Logan Douglass supplied my place. We came away to Doctor Porter's on *Monday*, forty-six miles.

Tuesday, 11. We reached Harvey's, thirty-five miles. The families of Shaw and Walton were visited as we came along. O, the heat, the dust!

Wednesday, 12. We called upon the weeping widow Quarles, whose husband was beaten to death: the supposed murderer, Phillips, is condemned to death; it was a sad scene. Lodged at Terry's, and were pleased with our entertainment.

Thursday, 13. At Holt's, junior; I preached and baptized an infant. Forward we jolted over the turnpike (for which they made us pay a dollar) to Dunlap's.

Friday, 14. We had heat in the extreme to Holt's senior, forty-six miles. *Saturday*, I had a very painful colic. In the families of Holt we have served four generations.

Sabbath, 16. Hearing there was a Presbyterian congregation, we asked to preach and hear: we did both. Mr. Nelson spoke first, and I addressed

[23] Asbury was now in Sumner County, Tennessee, again.

Methodists and others, on John viii, 31, 32: "Ye shall know the truth, and the truth shall make you free." How to know the truth? By continuing under Gospel ministry, and using Gospel means. *Ye shall know the truth* —of the Gospel; feelingly, experimentally, practically. *Make you free.* What the *freedom* wrought consists in. It is an entire deliverance from sin —from its guilt, power, and inbeing. A *freedom* embracing the privileges of pardon, peace, patience, meekness, perfect love, joy on earth, and everlasting glory in heaven. We hasted away, after meeting, to William Cunningham's.[24]

Monday, 17. We came rapidly through Dandridge to William Turnley's:[25] here are kind souls. I was sick, and soon in bed, but John Bond preached for them.

North Carolina

Tuesday, 18. Our ride brought us to Jarratt's, on Pigeon River. O my excellent son, John Bond! A tree had fallen across our way—what was to be done? Brother Bond sprung to the axe fastened under our carriage. mounted upon the large limbs, hewing and hacking, stroke after strike, without intermission, until he had cut away five of them, hauling them on one side as he severed them, so that we passed without difficulty. Is there his equal to be found in the United States? He drives me along with the utmost care and tenderness, he fills my appointments by preaching for me when I am disabled, he watches over me at night after the fatigue of driving all day, and if, when he is in bed and asleep, I call, he is awake and up in the instant to give me medicine, or to perform any other services his sick father may require of him; and this is done so readily, and with so much patience, when my constant infirmities and ill health require so many and oft-repeated attentions! We have had a great drought—I think I never saw the rivers so low. The asthma presses sorely upon my panting breast: Lord, sanctify all my afflictions! The work of God groweth in the neighbourhood; there is a house thirty-five by forty feet built in the fork of Pigeon River. Ought we not to have a Holston Conference,

[24] Asbury had now reached the eastern edge of the Holston country. William Cunningham (Cunnyngham) was a member of the Pine Chapel or Pine Grove community near Dandridge, but later moved to the Seven Islands community between Knoxville and Greenville. He was the father of Jesse Cunnyngham and grandfather of William G. E. Cunnyngham, both noted Methodist preachers, and related to the Turnley and Winton families. (Price, *op. cit.*, II, 401–5.)

[25] William H. Turnley lived between Dandridge and Newport and was a member of Pine Chapel there; he later became a preacher and went to the southwest. His father, George Turnley, long headed the Pine Chapel Society, and his home was a stopping place for the preachers. He became a Methodist in 1791 when his wife, nee Charlotte Cunningham (or Cunnyngham), was put on trial for marrying a man who was not in a society. (*Ibid.*, I, 138–40.)

and unite with the circuits west of the Blue Ridge, Bottetourt and New River, the circuits in North Carolina?

Wednesday, 19. Rode to Bollen's.[26] Behold! Richard Bird came one hundred miles to hasten us to camp meeting away on the bleak hills of Haywood.[27] I was forced by misery to retire to my room and bed at Bollen's; but son John held a meeting and preached.

Thursday, 20. We came by Nelson Spring's[28] to Barnett's gate, for, poor man! some wicked people had burnt his barn; his house escaped. Does Hootenpile pray? I asked. You called upon him; and God did bless the word and prayer to his soul: this was the answer in remembrance he sent me by Richard Bird. We came on the camp ground, *Friday*, 21. *Saturday*, I preached and ordained W. Span and J. Evans deacons.

Sabbath, 23. Ordained two elders, Thomas Bird and Samuel Edney, after preaching. In our tent we contrived a hearth, and had a fire. *Monday*, we visited Richard Bird's.

Tuesday, 25. I preached in the house of the father, Benjamin Bird;[29] there was much feeling manifested. We collected liberally on the mite subscription, to help the suffering ministry. I had for twenty years past wished to visit the Cove; it is done, and I have seen my old, tried friends, dear Richard and Jonah Bird, and William Fulwood, who sheltered me when, during the war of independence, I was compelled to retire to the swamps and thickets for safety.

Wednesday, 26. Our ride brought us to Rutherford's. I paid them as well as I could, for their kindness and attentions, by exhortation and prayer.

Thursday, 27. To M'Hathing's, forty-one miles. Daniel Asbury[30] wished me to take Catawba, above Ladies' Ford, and crossed at the Horse Ford, where a former journal will show my life to have been in danger some years ago. I preached in the evening at Daniel Asbury's, Lincoln county, near Sherwell's Ford. These are kind spirits, who say, "You make your rides too long"; yet they will scarcely be denied when invited to their houses, making my rides longer still; here am I, ten miles out of my way, to see these dear people. And now that limbs, lungs, strength, and

[26] Asbury had stopped at Michael Bollen's on December 30, 1812.

[27] Haywood County was formed from Buncombe in 1809. It extended westward across the Great Smoky Mountains to the Georgia and Tennessee lines.

[28] William Nelson, or Neilson, lived at Hot Springs and conducted an inn there. Asbury stopped with him on other occasions. (See note under November 3, 1802.)

[29] The Birds were prominent Methodists in western North Carolina. Benjamin Bird lived near Old Fort. His son, Jonathan Bird (1764–1848), was admitted to the conference in 1789 and served circuits in North Carolina and Holston until 1797, when he located and settled near his father in McDowell County. (Grissom: *Methodism in North Carolina*, 218.)

[30] Daniel Asbury was presiding elder of the Catawba District of the South Carolina Conference, which included the circuits of Western North Carolina. (*Minutes*, 1814.) He lived in Lincoln County, North Carolina.

teeth fail, I must still go my round of six thousand miles within the year.

Sabbath, 30. I passed a restless, feverish night; yet as I was expected to preach on the camp ground, I discoursed to a large, simple-hearted congregation, on Acts xxx, 32.[31] I sat in the end of my little Jersey wagon, screened by the drawn curtain behind me. It was no common time to either speaker or hearers. We retired after meeting to Jonathan Jackson's.[32] What a rich table was provided! not for me; I retired to bed with a high fever. My spiritual consolations flow from God in rich abundance; my soul rejoices exceedingly in God.

Monday, 31. To Robey's, near Catawba springs.

Tuesday, November 1. I preached to a very attentive people: surely the speaker and hearers felt the power of the word of God. After a hasty dinner, we rode on to Nathan Sadler's, steward of the Lincoln circuit.

Wednesday, 2. I spoke with very unpleasant feelings on Luke xi, 13. We hasted to Featherstone Wells's.[33] Here were all comforts for a sick man; good food, beds, and nursing. This family is blest. Sister Wells[34] is the granddaughter of my ancient friend, father May, of Amelia, and her children are in the way to heaven: here is the fruit of my labours. What a comfort is it to see the fourth generation growing up under our eyes, living in the fear of God, and following in the same path those who are gone to glory!

Thursday, 3. Crossed the north fork of Catawba to Bethesda chapel:[35] the day was damp, and there was a damp upon preacher and people. We went forward to John Dameron's,[36] where I was expected to preach, and I did try, but the people were so wonderfully taken up with the novel sight of the little carriage, and still more of the strange-looking old man who was addressing them, that the speaker made little impression on his hearers. Who neglects me? Not the kind, loving Damerons.

[31] This book has only twenty-eight chapters. There is no indication as to what the passage may have been.

[32] Jonathan Jackson, a well-known preacher in North Carolina, was serving the Lincoln Circuit. (*Minutes*, 1814.)

[33] Featherstone Wells (1769–1853) lived near present Belmont, North Carolina. His grave is in the Featherstone–Fite–Wells cemetery near the Catawba River bridge there. (See *Journal* entry for March 8, 1797.)

[34] Mrs. Willmuth Wells (1765–1818) is buried with her husband at Belmont.

[35] Asbury must have crossed the south fork of the Catawba instead of the north fork. Bethesda Chapel is in Mecklenburg County, about six miles southeast of Gastonia on the New Hope Road. It is still a preaching place. The bishop had gone from the Buncombe area to the Old Fort section of McDowell County and into present Rutherford, Cleveland, Lincoln, and Catawba counties, then turned southward at Sherril's Ford into Mecklenburg County.

[36] John Dameron lived near the Bethesda Chapel and is buried in the cemetery there. He was one of the trustees of the chapel.

South Carolina

We came to John Watson's, Allison's creek,[37] on *Friday*.

Sabbath, 6. At Sardis chapel.[38] The weather was unpleasant. My congregation might have tried my patience. *Monday*, we came to Henry Smith's,[39] an Israelite; he is a native of East Jersey. *Tuesday*, to Winnsboro.

Monday, 7. I am here since last *Tuesday*. I enjoy constant peace and consolation.

Sabbath, 13. I preached at Winnsboro a long discourse on 1 Pet. xiv, 17.[40] *Monday*, to widow Means's. We shall ride about two hundred and twenty miles out of the way to Georgia, but in the way of our duty. *Tuesday*, I preached at Bethel:[41] we hope good was done. Edward Finch, a son of affliction, is still on crutches.

Wednesday, 16. Dined with elder Stephen Shell.[42] Lodged with Frederick Foster. *Thursday*, we had a crowded house at Hopewell chapel:[43] the speaker stood in weakness, but truth came in power to the hearts of the people. Ordained John Molineaux a deacon. Lodged at John Leak's:[44] the master, a local labourer, is gone to his rest and reward.

Friday, 18. Rain. We got bewildered, and were glad to stop with Mr. Morrow,[45] a Presbyterian, who kindly received and entertained us. *Saturday*, we came to Staunton bridge.

Sabbath, 20. Bishop M'Kendree preached and J. W. Bond. I spoke a few words from my carriage: we hope the testimony of three men will be believed. God is with me in all my feebleness. We have visited North Carolina to Catawba, South Carolina; and Fairfield, Newberry, Laurens, and Greenville districts. *Monday* and *Tuesday*, we are at rest at father Staunton's,[46] an active and holy man; an Israelite indeed of seventy-seven years.

Wednesday, 23. We gave an evening lecture at Talliaferro's;[47] the night

[37] This year the aged bishop went into South Carolina through York County, where John Watson lived.

[38] Sardis Chapel was in Chester County north of Chester. It is no longer in existence.

[39] Smith lived near Chester.

[40] This book has only five chapters. The text does not indicate what the passage may have been.

[41] Mount Bethel Church was in Newberry County.

[42] Shell lived near Tranquil Church and Jalopa.

[43] The Hopewell Church was in the present Kinnard Community in Newberry County.

[44] John Leak lived near Clinton in Laurens County.

[45] The Rev. Mr. Morrow lived near Gray Court.

[46] Asbury had now completed a half circle in the northern counties of the state. Staunton lived near Greenville.

[47] The party now turned southward to Georgia, going to Talliaferro's, Mrs. King's, and John Powers's in present Anderson County, to Benjamin Glover's in Abbeville County, and across the Savannah into Georgia near Calhoun Falls.

was damp, and few people attended. Nights of suffering are appointed to me; but God is with us. *Thursday*, rested.

Friday, 25. Rode twenty-five miles to widow King's, Pendleton district. I am reading Saurin's[48] fifth volume: he is great in his way; but it is not Wesley's way, which I take to be *the more excellent way*. *Saturday*, damp, rainy day. I enjoy my private devotions.

Sabbath, 27. It broke away clear for a while, and I took a stand outside of the door, and spoke to the people on Gal. v, 6. *Monday*, to John Power's; here are new disciples, and they are all love. *Tuesday*, to Benjamin Glover's.

Georgia

Wednesday, 30. I preached at Samuel Rembert's:[49] I was feeble, and could not speak with much energy. Here I met with Thomas Asbury, born in Burslem, Stafford, Old England, formerly a member of the British conference. God is gracious to us. Alas! we cannot tell the people of so many things which they do not know, as we can of those which they neither feel nor do. On inquiry of Joseph Tarpley of the work of God in the Ogechee district, of which he is presiding elder, he gave me the following account:—At Little River camp meeting, the number which attended were thought to be three thousand, the converts about thirty. At Appalachee, number attending two thousand five hundred, the converts twenty-five. At Grove camp meeting two thousand attended, the converts might be twenty. At Louisville camp meeting there were scarcely more than one thousand, there might be ten converts. At the Warren two thousand five hundred persons to hear, and but few converts: each camp meeting continued four days.

Saturday, December 3. I preached in Thompson's chapel: the Lord was present. We collected the official brethren into the school-house, where I gave them a talk on the doctrines and discipline of our Church.

Sabbath, 4. I preached at Thompson's chapel. *Monday*, rode from J. Alston's to James Mark's, Elbert county. *Tuesday*, I preached in the chapel: widow Gilmore received us under her roof for the night. *Wednesday*, we reached Prospect, and I preached; the speaker's mind is

[48] James Saurin was an eminent French Protestant preacher who from 1700 to 1705 ministered to French refugees in London at the French Protestant Church in Grey Eagle Street, Spitalfields. John Wesley had a watch night there on September 21, 1750. It was a volume of Saurin's sermons which Asbury read. (Wesley's *Journal*, III, 496 n.; Tipple: *Francis Asbury, the Prophet of the Long Road*, 288; see note under January 19, 1800.)

[49] Samuel Rembert had moved from the noted Rembert settlement twelve miles north of Sumter, South Carolina, to Georgia. This was a numerous family of Asbury's friends. (Chreitzberg, *op. cit.*, 169, 172.)

too strong for his body. It was a sacramental day. *Thursday*, resting at Archibald Pope's. The weather has occasioned me much suffering, notwithstanding the kindness and good dinners of friends, and the convenience of my covered cradle on wheels.

Friday, 9. I preached at Bethlehem to about three hundred souls: the house was unfinished, and damp, and cold. Lodged at the house of the widow of Henry Pope.[50] By letter from John Earley[51] we have great accounts of the work of God at camp meetings in Amelia and Prince Edward.[52] *Saturday*, came to Athens, accompanied by Hope Hull.

Sabbath, 11. Preached in the college chapel;[53] the people were very attentive in that open penance house. The state of things is strangely changed since Doctor Brown[54] has had the presidency: he is a man of piety and order, and will render unto all their due. *Monday*, to Joseph Floyd's, on Appalachee. *Tuesday* I preached at J. Floyd's house: the people appeared somewhat like the preacher, sickly and slender. I ordained Samuel Patallo a deacon, and baptized three children. The lands here are good; but the price paid for quiet possession has been great—sickness, deaths, and murders by Indians.

Wednesday, 14. Rode twenty miles to Nicholas Ware's. When I see mother Steward's children I rejoice. Holy woman! thou didst not believe, and live, and weep, and pray, and die in vain; neither for thyself, nor for thy children, nor thy children's children. Verily, there is a reward for the righteous.

Thursday, 15. To Thomas Scott's; a brand re-plucked from the burning.

Friday, 16. At the new chapel, called after me, I preached, and hope the word of truth was not lost. Lodged at John Turner's.[55] *Saturday* at brother Holt's.

Sabbath, 18. Great rain. Every post almost is a messenger of the tidings

[50] Henry Pope had been a prominent citizen of old Wilkes County. The Popes were numerous there. (Bowen, *op. cit.*, 92.)

[51] John Early was presiding elder of the Meherrin District in the Virginia Conference. At the famous camp meeting in Prince Edward County there were a thousand conversions. (Smith: *Georgia Methodism*, 125.)

[52] The camp meetings were in Prince Edward County, Virginia.

[53] The college was the present University of Georgia, formerly known as Franklin College. Religious services were customarily held in the chapel. Hope Hull had built a log chapel 22 by 24 feet in size and "without a chimney" in Athens in 1804. This was abandoned, and in 1810 a more commodious log chapel known as Hull's Meetinghouse was erected, and this was used until Hull's death. Both Hull and General David Meriwether had moved to Athens, and both taught in the university. Hull was one of the first trustees and founders of the institution. (Wilson: *Methodism in Athens*, 3.)

[54] The Rev. John Brown (1763–1842), a Presbyterian minister, was president of the university from 1811 until 1816.

[55] Asbury was on his way from Athens to Milledgeville. John Turner lived in Hancock County. (Smith, *op. cit.*, 125.)

which ought to make me serious. John M'Claskey is no more.[56] He was a native of Ireland, born in Londonderry—a man of strong mind, a plain but useful preacher, and laboured with us about thirty years. Mother Kent is dead—forty years a subject of grace. My aged friends, Henry and Kesia Moss, have gone to their reward, but they leave me their daughter Freeman to receive me; I trust she will fill her parents' place here, and follow them as they followed Christ. Henry Boehm sends me great accounts of the work of God at camp meetings.

Wednesday, 21. Our conference began and continued until the 27th.[57] There were nearly one hundred characters examined and six admitted upon trial. Twelve are located. Ten elders have been ordained, and twenty-two deacons; eighty-two preachers have been stationed: none are dead, and none have been expelled. I preached at the ordinations, but with so feeble a voice that many did not hear: I had coughed much and expectorated blood. We had great peace, union, and love in our session. *Wednesday*, we rode to Sparta in the afternoon. *Thursday*, we had crowded lodging, and I passed a painful night. *Friday*, to Sweet Water. *Saturday*, to Augusta.

[56] John McClaskey (1756–1814) came to America in 1780. In 1786 he was admitted on trial and preached in Delaware, Pennsylvania, New York, and adjacent states until his death on September 2, 1814. (See *Minutes*, 1815.)

[57] This session of the South Carolina Conference met at Milledgeville, Georgia, which was only ten years old and the capital of Georgia. Stumps were still in the streets, and the Methodist church was still unfinished. It was Asbury's last visit to the state. (Smith, *op. cit.*, 125.)

1815

1815 *Ruins of the Capitol and President's House, Washington, D.C.*

CHAPTER FORTY-FOUR

South Carolina

Sunday, January 1, 1815. I preached at Saterman's house. *Monday*, dined at M'Cleary's, and came on to Ubank's.[1] *Tuesday*, to Button's.[2] O that God may bless my last labours in this family! *Wednesday*, to Koger's.[3] *Thursday*, to Captain Perry's.[4] *Friday*, we had a cold hungry ride of thirty-six miles. *Saturday*, busy writing.

Sabbath, 8. I spoke in much feebleness upon part of Psalm xxxvii, and gave a charge to the society. My labours were followed with much coughing and a restless night. *Monday*, I bled in the arm to relieve the spitting of blood. This place calls for great labour, and I am not fit for it: I must go hence. *Tuesday*, I filled an appointment made for me in Bethel chapel: I was divinely assisted. The care of the societies comes with weight upon my mind. Here are liberal souls at home and abroad: we have added nearly two hundred dollars to our mite subscription. *Thursday*, came to Strawberry Ferry. Grand accommodation at Mr. Lesesne's.[5] *Friday*, to Hale's;[6] we had an appointment here which we knew not of: the people assembled,

[1] Leaving Augusta the bishop rode up Horse Creek Valley to McCleary's and on to Ubanks (Eubanks), who lived beyond Aiken, South Carolina.

[2] Button lived in upper Barnwell County.

[3] Koger lived in Colleton County on the south side of the Edisto.

[4] Captain Perry lived on Cypress Swamp near Ridgeville. On the following day the bishop rode into Charleston for four days of rest.

[5] Asbury crossed the Cooper River at Strawberry Ferry. Lesesne lived near Childsbury. (See note under February 24, 1785.)

[6] Hale lived near the present Bethera.

and I spoke to them. *Saturday*, came to Santee, and crossed the Long Ferry in fifty minutes.[7] Away with the false cant, that the better you use the Negroes the worse they will use you! Make them good, then—teach them the fear of God, and learn to fear him yourselves, ye masters! I understand not the doctrine of cruelty. As soon as the poor Africans see me, they spring with life to the boat, and make a heavy flat skim along like a light canoe: poor starved souls—God will judge!

Sabbath, 15. A sacramental day: I preached and gave a word of exhortation to the society. I cannot preach more than once a day. I wrote two letters, having no other leisure to do it in.

Monday, 16. A great storm without. I glanced at Echard.[8] I find history of the Jews and the Romans, and very little of the pure Church. We have presided in three conferences in seven months. We had planned a ride of one thousand and three hundred miles into Virginia Conference, but Providence forbade it by affliction.

Tuesday, 17. We started away in company with William M. Kennedy, and James Norton,[9] with the last of whom we parted at the ferry over Black River. Lodged with Mr. Rogers[10]—his father has gone to rest. On our route we visited Bethel Durant, and saw his brethren, John and Henry: their simple-hearted, kind father entertained me thirty years ago on my returning from my visit to Charleston.

North Carolina

Wednesday, 18. Crossed the lakes and Waccamaw[11] and got in after eight o'clock to brother Frink's. At William Guse's, I saw my kind mothers in Israel, Guse and Rogers. I continue to expectorate blood. Is it possible that the children of the French Protestant martyrs to the tyranny of Louis XIV, and his bloody priesthood, can ever forget the God of their fathers? Noble, holy men, may God gather in your children to the latest generations!

Friday, 20. A dash of rain stopped us awhile, but we went forward thirty miles to Wilmington. I feel the effect of the damps.

[7] Asbury went by way of Jamestown and Lenud's Ferry to Georgetown.

[8] Laurence Echard (1670?–1730), an English historian and clergyman, published numerous works on history. Among them were his *History of England* in three volumes and an appendix, a five-volume *Roman History*, and *A General Ecclesiastical History*. (*Dictionary of National Biography*, VI, 351.)

[9] William M. Kennedy and James Norton were young preachers who became leaders in the South Carolina Conference. Kennedy had just been appointed presiding elder of the Pee Dee District, and Norton was on his way to the Sandy River Circuit in North Carolina.

[10] Rogers lived at Kingston. He was the son of Asbury's former host at that place.

[11] After crossing Waccamaw Lake the bishop proceeded by way of Little River to Wilmington, North Carolina.

Sabbath, 22. I preached in the chapel. O, wretched appearance of broken windows! It was a sacramental day. Were I a young man, I should not wish to be stationed in Wilmington. Our funds are low here, and our house a wreck.

Monday, 23. We came away to widow Nixon's. *Tuesday*, to Shepherd's. Doctor Lomas has been suddenly called away by death. *Wednesday*, to Lot Ballard's. Shall the Gospel be taken from Goshen? *Thursday*, dined at Joseph Bryan's; lodged at Hardy's. We dashed through Mussel Shell Creek in a swim—it was serious work.

Friday, 27. Dined at Hatch's: our reception kind; and our host is in bed with a leg broken. We reached Newbern in the evening. Here is weeping and lamentations for poor me—the leading characters of the society cannot speak to each other, or of each other, without bringing heavy accusations—yet all very glad to see the bishop.

Saturday, 28. My trust is in a faithful God—he hath never deceived me nor forsaken me. I am scarcely an hour free from pain, and all that I do is in the strength of Jesus.

Sabbath, 29. I preached, and there was a trembling from first to last under the word—but it was with cold. Ah! people hard and dull! John Bond preached three times: possibly in my short exhortation to the society I talked down the tempers of some of the members: Ah! wretched use of liquid fire!

Monday, 30. Cold indeed; my feet suffer. We made twenty-six miles to a house—no wood at the door, and none to cut wood.

Tuesday, 31. A heavy storm took us at Greenville. We put the remains of a poor, pious slave in the ground who had reached one hundred years. Brandy in a cold is like laudanum.

Wednesday, *February* 1. We came twenty-two miles; I was nearly done. Had we followed our first plan, and gone by Norfolk, it would have probably cost me my life. It was time to lower our sails and drop anchor at Edward Hall's, near Tarboro: it is paradise regained for a few days. The weather has been excessively cold, and keenly felt by an old man of seventy, deeply wounded in the limbs, breast, and lungs.

Sabbath, 5. I spoke to a gathering of serious people in Edward Hall's large dining room: the speaker was led to some awful truths. I am occupied in reading, writing, and patching and propping up the old clay house as well as I may: God be gracious to us still!

Monday, 6. We breakfasted with Mrs. Austin. O! the look expressive of the workings of her soul she gave, when in the trying hour she said, "Pray for me!" Shall a Methodist conference assemble, a society be gathered, and a chapel be built in Tarboro? Dined with Exum Lewis and wife: this favoured pair have been renewed and quickened. The house of their father was amongst the first in former days to receive the Methodists, and the children now open their house, and hearts, and hands to them:

may the Lord convert, and own, and bless their children's children to the latest generations! Amen! amen!

Came to James Hunter's at Fishing Creek—a cold ride. I sent for dear Henry Bradford and his wife, and we renewed our covenant with God. *Tuesday*, to Halifax; mother Long would by no means take a *nay*: honourable woman! I gave an evening lecture to some serious souls, and John Wesley Bond exhorted after me with energy.

Wednesday, 8. Crossed Black's ferry to sister Sarah Weaver's.

Virginia

Saturday, 11. We are at Matthew Myrick's, Virginia—to rest the horses, not ourselves. The alarms of the wasting sickness are very serious. I wrote an epistle to Norfolk, and another to Suffolk.

Sabbath, 12. I preached in Dromgoole's house. Doctor Simmons kindly officiated and drew two ounces of blood from my arm. I ordained Edward Dromgoole an elder in the Church of God.[12] Edward Dromgoole was born in Sligo; joined the Methodists in 1770; began to exhort in 1774; travelled in America from 1774 until 1785; since then he has been a faithful local preacher, respected and beloved: he has six children living, two of whom, Edward and Thomas,[13] are local deacons.

Monday, 13. Came away in company with Philip Bruce, John Early, and William Barnes, to Lewis Gregg's, calling on Major Thomas on our route.

Tuesday, 14. A great storm of snow blew for eight miles in our eyes on our way to Sister Holmes's. I saw Francis Hill once more: thirty years has he been a backslider from God: may he be speedily restored! Sister Gregg is sick, and sister Holmes near the last great change. To Ogburn's we went forward twelve miles;—we have seen some of our early acquaintances once more.

Wednesday, 15. To Fennell's, forty miles. Behold, we have a daughter a disciple, in the ancient house of Bedford: the kindness shown to God's people he hath repaid. To father Jude's on *Thursday*, where I was willing to rest, for I felt very ill.

Friday, 17. We came into Lynchburg in great weariness, having dined at Mr. Reed's.

Sunday, 19. I preached in the new, neat brick chapel, forty feet by fifty.

[12] Dromgoole was ordained at Dromgoole's Chapel, in Brunswick County, Virginia, although he was sixty-four years old and had located in 1786. There was no provision for Methodist ordination when he entered the ministry. (See note under January 30, 1774.)

[13] Thomas was the son who had to leave Cokesbury College because he had not done well. He became a splendid Christian and was a credit to the family.

Monday and *Tuesday*, we progressed well in our business.[14] Doctor Jennings preached us a great sermon on, "I am the vine, ye are the branches."

Friday, 24. We ordained elders, and I tried to speak on Phil. ii, 19–22. I failed—I have been almost strangled with an asthmatic cough, and vomiting of blood.

Sunday, 26. I keep the house, and busy myself to organize the stations. Thanks to the God of peace! we are confirmed in the belief that a treaty has been made between the United States and Great Britain.[15] We have ordained twenty deacons and eight elders. Is there not a declination in gifts, as well as members? We settled at seventy-one dollars each man.

Monday, 27. Came away from Lynchburg to Amherst court house, lodging with a local preacher who keeps a public house: may he disappoint all my fears, and exceed all my hopes!

Tuesday, 28. I preached at Meredith's. Shall we have to cross Buffalo, Pine and Tye rivers, after the thawing of the great snow?

Wednesday, *March* 1. Came to S. Garland's, Nelson court house. *Thursday*, to the widow Gentry's.

Friday, 3. As we passed Monticello, a cloud rested upon it: the day was clear. We crossed the north branch of James River, near Charlottesville. Sheltered for the night, under the roof of the widow Gillum. We have had bad roads, and I am feebleness itself. We crossed Rapidan at the Race Ford, and came to my dear John Stockdale's on *Saturday evening*. Hail, rest!

Sunday, 5. We had preaching in the morning, and I spoke a few minutes in the evening; water the seed, O Lord!

Monday, 6. To Henry Fry's.[16] I have passed a painful night—the last in this house, perhaps. *Tuesday*, to Culpepper. *Would I not stay and preach to them?* O, that I were able! to will, is always present with me. We went forward to Rix's. This was a *gentleman* who kept private accommodation; the law being against private entertainment: his bill, in the morning, amounted to five dollars, save two shillings. *Wednesday*, dined at Bashaw's, and lodged at New Baltimore.

Thursday, 9. Came to Fairfax court house, dining on our route at Alexander Wangho's.

[14] This was the business of the Virginia Conference. There was a heavy loss in members, and because of this Asbury asked, "Is there not a declination of gifts as well as members?" The number of appointments was forty-one with sixty-seven preachers. (Bennett, *op. cit.*, 604–6.)

[15] The treaty of peace with England had been signed at Ghent, Belgium, on December 24, 1814. Ratification by Congress occurred on February 17, 1815. For this a day of thanksgiving had been proclaimed.

[16] Henry Fry now lived in Madison County, as Madison was formed from Culpepper County in 1792.

District of Columbia

Friday, to Georgetown. *Saturday*, writing official letters.

Sunday, 12. In the chapel[17] I lectured on a chapter of Hosea. My mind, perhaps, partakes of the weakness of my body—I let fly a few scattering shot; I keep up a kind of running fire with my small-gun sermonizing. Our ranks are thinned, if one hundred have died in the Lancaster, Virginia circuit. I behold the ruins of the capital and the President's house; the navy yard we burned ourselves.[18] O, war! war!

Maryland

Monday, 13. A cold ride brought us to Elk Ridge; and our old friend, widow Honour Dorsey, gave us a shelter and a welcome. *Tuesday*, came in to Baltimore. My kind, inquiring friends, are coming in from morning till night. I am with my old friend the widow Dickins.[19]

Saturday, 18. I preached at the Point. Our conference began on *Monday*, and prudence restrained me to one session per day; perhaps I did not speak officially six times during the continuance of conference. When it

[17] "The small brick building, 30 by 40 feet, one and a half stories high and of very ordinary finish" was enlarged in 1806 to 40 by 60 feet and made two stories in height. This became the Dumbarton Avenue Church, Georgetown, D.C. (Ferguson, *op. cit.*, 166; Bryan: *A History of the National Capital*, I, 603; see note under November 2, 1795.)

[18] The British under command of Admiral George Cockburn and General Robert Ross, having disembarked on the Patuxent River, had put to flight the American forces at Bladensburg, several miles east of Washington. By nightfall of August 24, 1814, the Redcoats entered the defenseless city by the light of the flames of the navy yard, which Secretary of the Navy William Jones had ordered burned. Within an hour only the walls of the two wings of the Capitol were left standing. About eleven o'clock that same night the British moved down Pennsylvania Avenue and applied the torch to the President's house from which President and Mrs. Madison had fled. The official estimate of damage to the building was $334,384. (Elliott: *Historical Sketches of the Ten Mile Square*, 448–76; Williams: *Invasion and Capture of Washington.*)

[19] This was Mrs. John Dickins, the former Elizabeth Yancey of North Carolina. Her husband, the Rev. John Dickins, upon whom Asbury had placed heavy burdens as book steward, had died during the yellow-fever epidemic in Philadelphia on September 27, 1798. When in 1784 Dickins was appointed to Wesley Chapel, New York City, Mrs. Dickins became among the very first women to occupy a Methodist parsonage. Following her husband's death she moved to Baltimore, where in 1835 she died in the home of her son-in-law, Dr. Samuel Baker. Her son, Asbury Dickins (1780–1861) had a distinguished public-service career in Washington, his last office being that of Secretary of the Senate, 1836–61. One of the provisions of Asbury's will reads: "Should Elizabeth Dickins survive me and continue in her widowhood, it is my wish she should be paid during her natural life eighty dollars annually." (See Asbury's will filed in the Hall of Records, Liber 10, Fol. 173, Annapolis, Maryland, and *Letters*, 472; Wakeley, *op. cit.*, 299; Hedges: *Crowned Victors*, 16–19.)

was understood that the ancient superintendent did not attend in the afternoon, the visits to him were renewed. Stationing about eighty-five preachers we found to be no small work. *Friday*, we ordained the deacons in Light Street church. Being *Good Friday*, a fast was appointed, and I spoke a few words on the sufferings of Christ.

Sunday, 26. At Eutaw chapel[20] I spoke upon the apostolic order of things. *Monday*, conference rose. *Tuesday*, I retired to Perry Hall. The stormy, damp weather is hard upon me; but I abound here in comforts above millions: Lord, make me grateful and humble! What a preacher and writer was Samuel Davies![21] His sermons are very Methodistical. We have sent Samuel Montgomery to Montreal, and Samuel Burgess to Chenango district: they have had our counsel, and our prayers.

Sunday, *April* 2. In great weakness, I gave my farewell exhortation at the Fork Chapel.[22] Came back to Perry Hall: all here is solitary to me!

Monday, 3. At Havre de Grace, I see the fourth generation of the Jarratts;[23] but some are still out of Christ. We crossed the ferry in six minutes. At North East chapel I gave them a farewell discourse. I passed a restless night. O, the kindness of the people to a poor sinner saved by grace alone! *Wednesday*, James Smith[24] went forward and preached in the Elk chapel: at one o'clock we came up, exhorted, sung, and prayed. We must attend to our appointments, though we should speak but little, for the people wish to see us: we have lived and laboured so long, that we have become *a spectacle to men*. This place, Elkton, has been founded about fifty years: it may be visited of the Lord in the fourth or fifth generation. The speaker remembered that although the British were all

[20] Eutaw Street Chapel, which Asbury dedicated in 1808, was to become his temporary sepulcher, May 10, 1816. Scarcely more than a year from the date of this farewell sermon, twenty thousand persons marching eight abreast would follow the coffin of the bishop from Light Street Chapel to Eutaw Street Church. (Asbury: *A Methodist Saint, The Life of Bishop Asbury*, 305; see note under March 14, 1808.)

[21] Samuel Davies (1723–61) was a native of New Castle County, Delaware. Licensed to preach, he began the work of a Presbyterian evangelist in Hanover County, Virginia, where he met violent opposition by opponents of religious toleration. He was in sympathy with the Methodists and other evangelicals. In 1758 he was elected to succeed Jonathan Edwards as president of Princeton University, a position he accepted the following year. (*National Cyclopedia of American Biography*, V, 465.)

[22] About 1946 a bronze marker was erected on the inside wall of Fork Church in memory of James J. Baker, first Methodist convert in the city of Baltimore. (See note under June 9, 1776.)

[23] This may have been a descendant of the Jarratt family that resided near Dover, Delaware, to whose home he rode to conduct the funeral of Edward Collins. (See *Journal* entry for December 6, 1780; Hallman, *op. cit.*, 114.)

[24] Of the three Methodist preachers named James Smith who in 1815 were preaching in Maryland and Delaware, one can only guess at an identification. However, the most reasonable selection seems to be that James Smith who was the presiding elder of the Chesapeake District through which Bishop Asbury was traveling. James Smith (1788–1852) was a member of the Philadelphia Conference.

around them,[25] they escaped a visit. In great weakness of body we came on to the comfortable retreat of Nicholas Chambers.[26]

Thursday, 6. Stopped at Bethel, spoke a little and prayed. We dropped anchor at Richard Bassett's, until better weather. *Saturday*, I sent forward John Smith to fill my appointment. My unpleasant cough still cleaves to me. Bohemia Manor was formerly the field in which the Whitefield Methodists, called New Lights, laboured with success; the Wesleyan Methodists are heirs to these, according to the Gospel.

Sunday, 9. We would have attended meeting to-day, but we wished not to ride fourteen miles. We called a meeting at Richard Bassett's, and took occasion to speak of the work of God in the days of the New Lights, sixty years past.

Delaware

Monday, 10. We came away in the rain to Smyrna, stopping by the way at A. Short's:[27] we lodged with Israel Peterson.

Tuesday, 11. At Dover, my dear friends who had not seen me for one and two years visited me, and led me into conversation the whole after noon. It is hard, think they, that we cannot see him; so it might be thought in every place; but do they always remember the hardship they impose on me? So we go.

Wednesday, 12. We came to Camden, the first upon the line of my appointments. I spoke a few words, and came to James's, son of David Owens, my old disciple. We called on James Bateman[28] as we came along.

Thursday, 13. I preached once more at Johnstown: the day had been set apart for a general thanksgiving for peace, and I remembered it in the pulpit. We dined with P. Wells,[29] and rode back to Milford. Dust, fever, and too much company, these are my trials: peace, and perfect love, these are my consolations.

[25] Admiral Cockburn in carrying out the orders of a strict blockade of all American ports had in 1813 sailed up the Chesapeake Bay and among other towns had burned Havre de Grace. Although in close proximity to places invaded by the enemy, Elkton, Maryland, had emerged unscathed. (Paine: *The Fight for a Free Sea*, 185, 186; Scharf: *History of Maryland*, III, 37 ff.)

[26] Nicholas Chambers, Sr., was in 1805 a trustee of Bethel Church and of one of the first parsonages in America at North East. He lived at the head of Long Creek, a branch of Back Creek, near Chesapeake City, Cecil County. (Johnston: *History of Cecil County, Maryland*, 449, 451; Hallman, *op. cit.*, 108.)

[27] Short lived in New Castle County, Delaware, between Bohemia River and Smyrna. (Hallman, *op. cit.*, 120.)

[28] James Bateman (1775–1830) was born at Centreville, Maryland. He became a traveling preacher in 1806 and located in 1814. He had inherited lands on the site of the present Magnolia, Kent County, which he sold in 1818.

[29] Wells lived near the present Greenwood, Sussex County, which was about one mile west of a place then known as Johnstown.

Friday, 14. I preached, and hastened to Frederica, lodging with Andrew Dill:[30] here we saw dear Doctor Edward White, who hath known and followed the Methodists since 1778. I preached at Barratt's chapel, in great feebleness of body. Must I needs dine with Judge Andrew Barratt? "Ah! I know that my father and mother thought more of him, than of any man upon the earth; and well does it become their son to respect him." And is this all? God forbid!

Sunday, 16. I preached in Wesley chapel, Dover, and the truth was felt. *Monday*, after delivering a short exhortation at Smyrna, I rode on to Smith's,[31] Newcastle county.

Tuesday, 18. Reached Wilmington.

Pennsylvania

Wednesday, to Landreth's. *Thursday*, I sat in conference awhile, but became sick. *Friday*, I tried it again. *Saturday*, a chill overcame me, followed by burning heat. I continued at Richard Bowyer's.

Sunday, 23. Instead of filling an appointment, I was taken with a chill, followed by high fever. I have groaned away the whole week. I was lodged beyond the first gate, and few knew where I was: attentions overcome me.

Friday, 28. Feeling no fever, I ventured to whisper a few words: perhaps I shall be able to say something in the new chapel in Tenth street, Philadelphia.

Sunday, 30. At three o'clock I preached in the chapel in Tenth street: what a noble building! *Monday*, *Tuesday*, *Wednesday*, resting at Thomas Haskins.[32]

New Jersey

Thursday, at Trenton.

Friday, *May* 5. We came through bad roads thirty-seven miles, to Mr. Baker's tavern[33]—wearied down. Our host was very attentive, and we had

[30] Andrew Dill lived in Frederica, Kent County, Delaware. In 1812 he deeded land for the church in that place. Benjamin Dill of the same family, a convert to Methodism in 1779 under the preaching of Philip Cox, opened his home that year to the infant society. (Hallman, *op. cit.*, 109, 239; Scharf: *History of Delaware*, II, 998; *Journal* entry for December 8, 1780,)

[31] This is probably that same "Mr. Smith, a strong Churchman," at whose home the bishop had lodged thirty-five years before. He lived near Smyrna, Kent County, but because of its proximity to the New Castle County line, identification is uncertain. (Lednum, *op. cit.*, 347; Hallman, *op. cit.*, 120; *Journal* entry for November 29, 1780.)

[32] Thomas Haskins, member of the Christmas Conference of 1784 and one of the early editors of Asbury's *Journal*, had located and was a merchant in Philadelphia.

[33] Thomas Baker's inn was at Westfield, New Jersey, on the stage route from Trenton and Princeton to Elizabeth. (Van Sickle: *The Old York Road and Its Stage Coach Days*, 60; Hoffman: *The Old Towne, a Brochure of Westfield, New Jersey*.)

prayer in course. *Saturday*, called upon Thomas Morrell. Had an interview with Mr. M'Dowell,[34] the stationed minister of the Presbyterian congregation in Elizabethtown: he is modest and pious. O, for such men in all Protestant Churches!

New York

We drove up to George Suckley's, Greenwich. The weather is most distressing to my feelings.

Sunday, 14. I attended the North church, and gave a discourse—it was something between talking and preaching; yet we had a time of much feeling.

Monday, 15. To Croton, forty miles. The dear aged man, Governor Van Cortlandt, has gone to his rest, having attained to ninety years, and upward.[35]

Tuesday, 16. A twenty miles' painful ride brought us to Warren's tavern,[36] where we were made comfortable. *Wednesday*, to Rhinebeck, forty miles. *Thursday*, to Judge Van Ness's,[37] forty miles—in rain, cold, and suffering. The lady kind; the sister all attention. O, how goodness outshines the vain glories of this world! *Friday*, a cold rain dogged us into Albany. *Saturday*, I paid an hour's visit to my brethren in conference.

Sunday, 21. By vote of conference, I preached the funeral sermon for Doctor Coke[38]—of blessed mind and soul—of the third branch of Oxonian Methodists—a gentleman, a scholar, and a bishop, to us—and as a minister of Christ, in zeal, in labours, and in services, the greatest man in the last century. Poor wheezing, groaning, coughing Francis visited the conference chamber on *Tuesday* and *Thursday*. Although confined to my room,

[34] John McDowell was licensed by the presbytery of New Brunswick in 1804. He married Henrietta, daughter of Shepherd Kollock and sister of the Rev. Henry Kollock. He was an author as well as an outstanding Presbyterian preacher, and was a trustee of the College of New Jersey and a director of the theological seminary at Princeton. (Hatfield: *History of Elizabeth, New Jersey*, 666–69.)

[35] Lieutenant Governor Pierre Van Cortlandt (1721–1814) died on May 1, 1814, at the manor house of his Croton estate. Although a member of the Dutch Reformed Church he was most sympathetic to the Methodists. He gave land and money for the local Methodist meetinghouse, and after 1805 he set aside a grove on his estate for a Methodist camp meeting which he always attended. (*Dictionary of American Biography*, XIX, 164.)

[36] Warren's tavern was probably near Philipstown, above Peekskill on the northern road east of Hudson Highlands.

[37] Judge Van Ness lived at Claverack in Columbia County, New York.

[38] Thomas Coke died on May 3, 1814, on shipboard as he was en route to Ceylon with a party of six missionaries to establish work there. He was buried in the Indian Ocean. His companions continued the journey and founded the mission. (Hurst, *op. cit.*, VII, 44; Simpson, *op. cit.*, 188, 235.)

I was not prevented from entering deeply into the consideration of the plan of the stations: the elders thought I came out well. Alas! what miseries and distresses are here. How shall we meet the charge of seventy married out of ninety-five preachers—children—sick wives—and the claims of conference? We are deficient in dollars and discipline.

Friday, 26. We closed our labours in great peace and union. *Saturday*, we rode out of Albany to brother Spicer's, New Canaan. The bishops here saw eye to eye, with hearts and souls in perfect union.

Massachusetts

Sabbath, 28. I gave an evening lecture. *Monday*, came away through Lebanon to Pittsfield. Elder Case[39] came up to go with the bishop ninety or a hundred miles to Unity, the seat of the New England Conference: the providence was plain; we must part. Came to Chester, thirty-six miles.

Tuesday, 30. To Westfield, and continued on nineteen miles farther. In Wilbraham they think they have had a very general work of God, and an increase of the society: may it grow exceedingly! *Wednesday*, we came on to Leicester greatly outdone.

Thursday, *June* 1. To Needham: there is a revival in several of the societies in this circuit, and a house has been built. Orlando Hinds—his praise is in all the Churches.

Saturday, 3. I am patiently suffering affliction in Boston.

Sabbath, 4. John Wesley Bond attended all day at the chapel. I preached in the evening in weakness and in much trembling.

Monday, 5. We passed towns and villages, making forty miles.

New Hampshire

Wednesday, 7. At Unity, poor Francis was shut up alone as at Albany. George Pickering presided over conference: our business progressed well: I ordained twelve deacons and twelve elders.[40] *Thursday*, rain and snow. We made about twenty-nine miles this day. The taverns in New England are good; good attention and moderate charges. *Friday*, I came very sick to B. Pawlett's.

[39] The Rev. William Case was the presiding elder of the Chenango District of the Genesee Conference.

[40] Bishop McKendree was also ill in Pittsfield, Massachusetts, and Asbury probably ordained the elders in his room while George Pickering conducted the conference. Asbury was being assisted and sometimes carried by John Wesley Bond, and was to die in ten months.

Massachusetts

Saturday, to Cambridge: I must reduce my projected tour of sixteen hundred miles to a straight ride of three hundred and eighty miles to New York, and thence through Philadelphia to Little York, and my son Francis Hollingsworth.[41] As I passed through Ashgrove I preached in the chapel. *Monday*, to Pittsfield. Here we have given up weekly preaching for two sermons a day every other week.

New York

Tuesday, to Troy; *Wednesday*, to Judge Van Ness's; *Thursday*, to Freeborn Garrettson's.[42]

Sabbath, 11. I preached for them; very feeble. *Wednesday*, we started away for Poughkeepsie, lodging in a tavern. *Thursday*, we had a heavy ride over Peekskill Mountains. At the landing I providentially called upon a brother who had been offended, and had withdrawn himself from us; I seriously set life and death before him in a spirit of love and pity.

Friday, 16. Came rapidly to New York, forty-two miles. *Saturday*. I have had company enough.

Sabbath, 18. Attended at Fourth street chapel; my subject, Zeph. i, 12; time was when I could have preached upon this text.

Tuesday, 20. I spoke a few words at the African chapel, both colours being present.

New Jersey

We hasted to Elizabeth that evening. *Wednesday*, to Stephen Barcalow's. *Thursday*, to James Sterling's, Burlington: my old friend has felt a severe shock in his system, but there is some mind, and there is grace yet left.

Pennsylvania

Friday, to Philadelphia; great heat. In the evening rode to Thomas Haskin's.

[41] Francis Hollingsworth was one of the several editors and the final transcriber of Asbury's *Journal*. The family lived near Baltimore, and it is not known that he ever lived in York, Pennsylvania, where Asbury met him on this occasion. (See the statement in the Introduction.)

[42] Freeborn Garrettson and his family lived on a farm at Rhinebeck, New York, where his house still stands. (Bangs: *Life of the Rev. Freeborn Garrettson*, 209–11.) Asbury must have gone from Unity, New Hampshire, across Vermont to Cambridge, New York, and down the east side of the Hudson River to New York City.

Sabbath, 25. I preached in the City Road chapel. *Monday*, we arrived late in the evening at a tavern beyond Downingtown.[43]

Tuesday, 27. Happy at mother Boehm's. A pleasing providence, according to my wishes, had brought Henry Boehm in a few minutes before us. *Wednesday*, I rest a day. Ah! the changes we witness, and the difference of being, in relation to others, I remark in this end of time; to me at least. My long-loved friend, Judge Bassett, some time past a paralytic, is lately restricken on the other side, and suffers much in his helpless state.

Thursday, 29. How the new bridge stretches its pride of length across the wide Susquehanna! Will not the father of eastern waters some day rise in the fury of a winter flood, and tear away this slight fetter which the puny art of man has thrown over him? Columbia bridge is surely a noble work. We came to son Francis Hollingsworth's, Little York. My kind countrywoman gave me up her own room. I tried to preach, but wanted strength: my audience was partly composed of the respectables of the borough, and were no doubt disappointed. I sit seven hours a day, looking over and hearing read my transcribed journal: we have examined and approved up to 1807. As a record of the early history of Methodism in America, my journal will be of use; and accompanied by the minutes of the conferences, will tell all that will be necessary to know. I have buried in shades all that will be proper to forget, in which I am personally concerned; if truth and I have been wronged, we have both witnessed our day of triumph. *Friday*, we came away to Carlisle.

Sabbath, *July* 9. I spoke in the new chapel and the truth was felt. *Monday*, came to Shippensburg. My health is better this hot weather and rough ride. O! how deeply my soul feels for ours, and all Churches; for ours, and all ministers: I smite with my hands, and would lift up my voice like a trumpet: is there not a cause? We lodge with Deacon John Davis: this brother hath been with us in single life; now he hath five sons and a daughter: his eldest, Samuel, is given to God in the ministry, and travels. The old man's heart is still in the work. *Tuesday*. So crowded was the road that we hardly escaped being wedged in the narrows of the mountains on our way to Fannettsburg. Lodged at William Anderson's.[44] *Wednesday*, we came over the third mountain to James Hunter's. My health is much better, and I have lately written more than I had for weeks. We are later in this neighbourhood than last year; so also is the harvest. O, what abundance in our houses, our barns, and in our fields!—"more than we can well manage," cries the husbandman. For peace, liberty, and plenty, O, to

[43] This tavern may have been "The Coach and Four" at Coatesville. Downingtown is located on the Lancaster highway thirty-two miles west of Philadelphia. It was surveyed as early as 1702 for Joseph Cloud, Jeremiah Collett, Robert Vernon, and Daniel Smith, all of whom took up land there. Thomas Downing bought nearly six hundred acres of land there as early as 1739. (Wharton: *In Old Pennsylvania Towns.*)

[44] William Anderson was an innkeeper in Fannettsburg. (Warner, Beers,: *History of Franklin County.*)

grace and to God, what debtors! What man can live to himself amidst the evidences of heavenly, and the enjoyments of social goodness? We could not work ourselves, but we lent our horses to help to hale in the harvest. We left our kind friends to beat across the mountains on *Saturday* and made thirty miles to Bloody Run.[45] The stones of this stream are tinged red as with blood, and the story is, that three men were killed in it by the Indians shortly after Braddock's defeat. My meditations lead me to make some observations on Col. i, 26–28. Colosse was a city of Phrygia, near to Laodicea. Paul had not then visited this Church, yet in apostolic power and authority he wrote them the epistle. And for what purpose? To teach and to exhort. Why, then, not preach as well as write to Churches, in all parts, and in any part of the world, since the end of preaching is instruction and exhortation? O, say the Baptists, this is my Church. O, this is my congregation, says the stationed minister. And must no other ministers preach to these souls? No, says sectarian prejudice; no, says bigoted pride; no, says the wool-shepherd, who is afraid his flock may become too wise for him. "The mystery which hath been hid from ages and from generations." 1. The *mystery* of God the Eternal Son, *hid* till the expiration of four thousand years, *from ages and from generations*; yet not hid from the obedient,—not hid from Abel in the bleeding lamb, from Enoch, from Noah, nor from Abraham; not hid from the Israelites, but typically shown in the passover, the serpent in the wilderness, the release of captives and debtors on the death of the high priest; not hid from Job, from David, nor from Isaiah, who had a fuller manifestation of the glories of that day, whose coming in the order of time should thereafter be fixed by Daniel. *But now is made manifest to his saints*; the Holy Ghost carrying to the soul the conviction of the truth, begetting in obedient, gracious souls this *hope of glory. Christ formed within them the riches of the glory of this mystery*; the only foundation of the hope of everlasting glory; the first moving cause in grace, and the meritorious cause. *Warning* or admonishing *every man*, and *teaching every man*, according to the universal commission in the Gospel. *In all wisdom*: but those who have been taught, and are negligent in *teaching* and giving this *warning*: O, pity, pity, pity that there are such! Do you work faithfully? Continue to do it in the name and by the authority of Father, Son, and Holy Spirit: tell this rebellious generation they are already condemned, and will be shortly

[45] There are several stories of how Bloody Run, now called Everett, received its name. Asbury mentions one here. Another is that following a treaty of peace between the Indians and the settlers, traders began exchanging with the Indians ammunition and weapons for furs. Fearing attacks by the Indians, a group of settlers organized as the "Black Boys" under the leadership of James Smith. When a Philadelphia trader, by the name of Wharton, sent a pack horse team of supplies for the Indians, Smith's band attacked them near Everett. In the fierce conflict which followed it was said the small stream which ran through the settlement was dyed with blood, thus giving the name Bloody Run to the community. (Schell: *The Annals of Bedford County, Pennsylvania*, 20–21.)

damned: preach to them like Moses from Mount Sinai and Ebal, like David—"The wicked shall be turned into hell, and all the nations that forget God"; like Isaiah—"Who amongst you shall dwell with devouring fire? Who amongst you can dwell with everlasting burnings?" like Ezekiel—"O, wicked man! thou shalt surely die!" Pronounce the eight woes uttered by the Son of God near the close of his ministry, and ask with Him—"Ye serpents, ye generation of vipers, how can ye escape the damnation of hell?" Preach as if you had seen heaven and its celestial inhabitants and had hovered over the bottomless pit and beheld the tortures and heard the groans of the damned. *Perfect in Christ Jesus*; in experience, in obedience, in love.

We went up into the little chapel in the state it was, and said a few words to a few people. Lodged at a grand tavern at night, and paid pretty well for our shelter: but I wish not to be under any obligations to tavern keepers. The heat is so great that it requires prudence to avoid its effects. A drover, who had for many days eaten dust like a serpent in following his cattle, broke his leg about seven miles below the town: poor man! it will be well if he saves his life.

Monday, 17. Came into Bedford, overcome with the heat: brother Bond preached.

Wednesday, 19. To Somerset. We found that on the last *Sabbath*, a notice had been politely given of our expected arrival. Many attended at the court house, and the Lord spoke his own truths through a tottering tenement of clay, accompanied with conviction in many minds. William Ross, with whom we lodged, stepped round the town with our mite subscription, and the citizens were liberal.

Thursday, 20. We came across Laurel Hill to the stone mill upon Jacob's creek. We know not what others may think, but we esteem the western Pennsylvania roads to be the roughest on our continent; my poor arms feel them, and will for days to come.

Friday, 21. To John Brightwell's, Freeport. Here we will rest and refit. We left Philadelphia July 3, and have travelled three hundred miles in twelve days.

Sabbath, 23. At Brightwell's I preached upon Galatians iv, 19, 20. The apostle's labour and success at the first. The falling away of the converts —being drawn aside in search of an easier way, or going off to avoid persecution. The fervent desire of the apostle to be with, and to pass a second travail of soul for the whole of religion—inward, practical, and experimental. I spoke about thirty minutes. John W. Bond met the classes. He preached in the afternoon.

Monday, 24. Ordained John Philips, of Union, a local deacon. The heat is such that all flesh seems to groan under it.

Tuesday, *August* 1. Left Brightwell's, fording the Monongahela at Freeport. We ascended the dreadful hills to Briggs's, and saw him and his brother, to whom we failed not to give our parting charge. Briggs is a Marylander, and an ancient Methodist. Down went the fence, and through the flax and corn he conducted us, and onward we toiled to Newkirk's mill—a clean house, and kind souls. We might not stay. Forward we drove up the valley to Rock meeting house, a handsome edifice, and thence along the Williamsport road to Washington.[46] We were lodged like a president at Haslett's. Is it possible? can it be true?—a revival at Steubenville! Not far from two hundred converts there, mostly young people. I rejoice exceedingly. The Book Concern have sent out Horneck—the dagger to the hilt, almost at every stroke. I wrote my valedictory to J. Young.[47] *Wednesday* and *Thursday* at Washington. A Baptist missionary came into town collecting for foreign lands: we labour for those at home. Feeble as I was, the necessity of bearing testimony to the truth pressed upon me. A very unpleasant circumstance had taken place—an illicit intercourse between a lady and gentleman had become public, involving the innocent as well as the guilty in distress; they were members of the Presbyterian Church. Another distressing event in the same Church was talked of. A very respectable merchant and citizen had lost two of his children dying in doubt, and thought to have been somewhat deranged: this visitation fell upon him in a still greater degree. It may be said that he had put himself on the unfavourable side of election; the case was possible, but we cannot say that it was so. I remembered these things when I preached in Washington court house. "The foundation of God standeth sure." This foundation of God, laid for the redemption of mankind, involves their repentance, justification, and sanctification; and its consummation is eternal life. The word to Adam was, Obey, and live. The Gospel-covenant shall stand sure in the wisdom, justice, power, grace, truth, love, goodness, and mercy of God, manifested in the atonement and righteousness of Christ, and the operations of the Holy Spirit, whereby men are made able to repent, believe, and obey. This covenant is conditional to all who hear the Gospel. Because men are unfaithful is the foundation less sure? It is the foundation of God, laid in Christ, and known to the patriarchs

[46] The road from Monongahela to Washington, Pennsylvania, is now Route 31. The earlier name of Monongahela was Williamsport.

[47] Jacob Young was presiding elder of the Ohio District. Young makes the following comment concerning Asbury's presence at his last conference in Ohio, held at Lebanon on September 14, 1815: "The Bishops were both present. Bishop Asbury, in very feeble health, was not able to walk or stand alone. The Rev. John Bond had the charge of him, carried him in his arms like a little child, set him in his carriage when he wished to travel, and took him out in the same way when he wished to stop. . . . He prayed as if speaking to God face to face. While gazing on his pale face my emotions were painful yet pleasant. I saw that Asbury's work was done, and that he was going home to God. He was truly an apostolic man, sent of God on a special mission to these United States. He had done his work, and done it well. Although the Methodist Church had many great and good teachers, she had but one father under God, and that was Francis Asbury." (Young: *Autobiography of a Pioneer*, 317–18.)

and prophets. "Have you heard what Mr. ——, a Presbyterian, has done?" "Have you heard what John Doe and Richard Doe, both Methodists, have done?" "I am done with religion." Have you ever begun with it? Had these people continued faithful, would it have saved you? Have you done with Christ? Do you want to experience, in your own person, the awful certainty of damnation!

As our Baptist brother talked and read letters upon missions to foreign lands, I thought I might help with a few words. I related that a few years past, a London Methodist member, in conversation, had complained to me that the kingdom and the Church had given so largely to support distant missions. I observed in reply, that the Methodist preachers, who had been sent by John Wesley to America, came as missionaries; some of them returned, but all did not. And now, behold the consequences of this mission! We have seven hundred travelling preachers, and three thousand local preachers, who cost us nothing. We will not give up the cause—we will not abandon the world to infidels; nay, we will be their plagues—we will find them herculean work to put us down. We will not give up that which we know to be glorious, until we see something more glorious. Nor will we concede an inch to schismatics and heretics, who say, "Do away your forms, and leave your peculiar doctrines, and we shall show you something better." Show it to us first in the book of God. We are not ignorant of Satan's devices.

West Virginia

Friday, 4. We came away to John Beck's, West Liberty. It is said there were about three thousand people to hear the word last Sabbath at Steubenville: there was great preaching, a great love feast, and sacrament; Bishop M'Kendree was there. I had an interview with R. Brown, and much talk about the work of God, and the necessity of energetic preaching to wake the slumbering generation.

Sabbath, 6. I preached at John Beck's, at four o'clock; my subject was 1 Cor. vii, 28–30. *The time is short.* It might have been true, considering how uncertain persecution then made, and was about more abundantly to make, life, to all the followers of the Lord Jesus; it may be especially true in pestilences, famines, and desolating wars. But the proverbial uncertainty, in all ages and in all lands, of the sublunary things which so deeply engage the thoughts and affections of unthinking mortals, shows the propriety of the apostolic admonition; for verily, in this respect also, *the time is short*.

How many newly married pairs—parents with children, upon whom they have just discovered, in their matured characters and upright conduct, the qualities and virtues which justify all their strength of affection—speculators upon the probabilities and possibilities of fortune, who risk credit and estate to become richer than their fellow-mortals—covetous persons, idolators, who labour and starve to make the golden heap a little higher;—how many of these find that *the time is short*; alas! too short for them! O, sinner, the time is short! Seeker, *the time is short!* strive—agonize to enter in. Backslider, surely to thee *the time is short!* Believers, O remember the time is short! And if you are daily bearing your cross, faithfully combating under the great Captain of your salvation, you will rejoice to remember that *the time is short*. O, joyful consideration to those who have put on the Lord Jesus, and shall love his appearing—*this time* of suffering *is short!*

Monday. Came to Mount Pleasant.

Ohio

Friday, 11. Came to Zanesville. There is a camp meeting now in operation, five miles from this town. We reckon that since the 20th of June, we have passed through New Hampshire, Vermont, New York, New Jersey, Pennsylvania, Virginia, and Ohio, to Muskingum River, making nine hundred miles; two hundred of which ought, in our opinion, to be called the worst on the continent. O, the goodness, providence, and love of God in Christ Jesus to us!

Sabbath, 13. I preached on the camp ground. My subject was 2 Cor. v, 2: "Knowing the terror of the Lord, we persuade men." "The Lord"—that is, the Son of God, in all his attributes and perfections; his offices and character; his perfect Deity in heaven, and humanity on earth; the Maker and Redeemer of mankind; and as their Judge, manifesting his uprightness in the eternal punishment of bad angels and bad men. "Terror of the Lord"—in death, the resurrection, and general judgment. "Terror"—in the recollection of what the sinner had done to offend God, grieve the Holy Spirit—what he had done to bring contempt upon religion and its ministers, and the unoffending followers of the Lord Jesus. "Terror"—in the consideration of the certainty of his punishment being eternal. "Persuade men"—to submit to the conditions of salvation; the use of the means of grace; and to a life of Gospel obedience. "Persuade men"—by all that is desirable in religion, and all that the truly pious enjoy—by all the glories of heaven, and all the horrors of remediless perdition in hell.

By the judgment of charity, we are bound to believe the statement of David Young: that at Kenhawa camp meeting there were twenty-five converts; at Marietta, forty; at Fairfield, twenty-four; at Zanesville, twenty-three. Glory be to our God! now we live, if our people stand fast in the faith.

Sabbath, 20. I preached to a small congregation in the chapel at Chillicothe. There is a camp meeting within nine miles, and some are sick, some dying, and some are dead. My subject was Luke xxii, 61, 62: "And the Lord turned, and looked upon Peter." The Gospels will harmonize here by John, who was witness to the whole. Peter denied thrice; First, to the damsel who kept the door; John having asked leave of the high priest to bring in Peter. Secondly, when the kinsman or cousin of Malchus, whose ear Peter had cut off, witnessed, possibly, by the young man, asked him, "Did not I see thee in the garden with him?" Thirdly, when the conversation is taken up in company with the servants of the high priest, and one of them asks, "Art thou not one of his disciples?" The previous character of Peter may be noticed—a married man, not a youth; forward, ardent, as was seen on many occasions. When faithfully warned, he pledged himself with overweening confidence. His offence was, First, taking unallowed means of defence—like his pretended successors, the popes: Secondly, following too far off: Thirdly, denying his Lord;—the lie, the oath, and their repetition, follow of course. What was the subject of Peter's denial? Did he deny that Christ was the eternal Son of God—the Saviour of the world in all his sacred offices? No: Peter's crime was, that he denied his discipleship; and this is the crime of which so many modern apostates are guilty. Who now deny the Lord? Backsliders, baptized infidels, careless seekers of salvation, slothful believers, and those who have fallen from sanctification by the neglect of the works of mercy, charity, and piety. "The Lord turned, and looked upon Peter." Ah! he was obliged to go out with disgrace; he had entered with honour. But he could not weep and repent in wicked company: no, he sought a solitude—for three days and three nights, it may be. But lo, Jesus sendeth the word of comfort that he may not break his heart: "Go, tell my brethren," said he to Mary Magdalene. Thrice did Peter deny his Lord; and thrice did our Lord question his disciple. "Lovest thou me?" O, how great is the love of God; the love of Christ; the love of the Holy Spirit! redemption is love.

Monday, 21. We visited from house to house with our mite subscription, which seemed to all well pleasing: the citizens were liberal. Hearing that Eleanor W——n was ill, and wished to see me, I delayed not, but went in the evening. When we entered the room, I found her ill indeed; an attack highly inflammatory, accompanied by a deep cough. On *Tuesday* I repeated my visit; and in private examination found that God had shown her the vileness of her nature in a great degree, and that she had received consolation, and only wanted and waited for the Spirit to give assurance of his own work by his witness in her heart. I told her that it was very common for persons to be sure that God had blessed them. O! how her eyes, her face, her tongue spoke! She was an Episcopalian of the English Church. Her mind had been much exercised upon receiving the sacrament: it was administered to her. I find I am about such a feverish, coughing subject as the lady I have been visiting; I coughed nearly the whole night.

Wednesday, 23. We left Chilicothe in the rain. Some folks are fond of railing out against Methodists, taking the worst as a sample; but bad as they are, I would not take the best of the railers without a change in sentiment, in heart, and in manners. Ah! let us take heed that party and politics do not drive out our piety; they do not mingle well. Can it be that Bonaparte is finally overthrown?[48] The time is coming that all kings and rulers must acknowledge the reign of the King of kings, or feel the rod of the Son of God. But will forms do for the United States of America? Foolish people will think they have a right to govern themselves as they please; aye, and Satan will help them. Will this do for us? is not this republic, this land, this people, the Lord's? We acknowledge no other king but the eternal King. And if our great men will not rule in righteousness, but forget God and Christ, what will be the consequence? Ruin.

Saturday, 26. We changed our course, to go to the Mechanicsburgh camp meeting. As soon as we came upon the ground, I felt that God was with the meeting. *Give us a chimney, that we may have fire*: it was done. God was with us, and souls were converted.

Friday, September 1. At John Sale's.

Sunday, 3. I preached on Romans xiii, 12: "The night is far spent." What constitutes the natural *night?* Absence of light, ignorance, insecurity, uncertainty. The Gospel watchman crieth the hours. The Scripture night; from Adam to Moses. The patriarchal stars, and those who preceded them as dim lights, Adam, Abel, Enoch, Noah, Abraham. The moon-light of the law, the Sabbaths, the sacrifices. But this night was about to pass away, although darker just before the dawn of the Gospel day; and it is thus in nature. The Jews had corrupted themselves in religion and in manners. The night of Judaism and Paganism had nearly passed away. When Paul wrote in the year sixty, the Gospel had obtained in Europe, Lesser Asia, Greece, in the city of Rome; and had spread from the Euphrates to the Mediterranean. This *night* has returned occasionally. It came upon the Asiatic Churches because of their unfaithfulness: where once were the Gospel and its martyrs, are now Greek *papas*, and Greek superstitions. From the third to the thirteenth century, the Church of Rome brought darkness upon Europe by prohibiting the Bible, and by the introduction of her own mummeries and idolatries. Philosophy, so called, with Voltaire for its high priest, brought night and destruction upon France; judicially, to avenge on the bloody house of Bourbon the blood of the Protestant martyrs. And would not some of our great men, if they dared, bring a night of infidelity on this land? Who sees them in regular attendance on the house of God? "Let us cast off the works of darkness." Let us not sin in practice. Let us cast off evil tempers, desires, and affections. "The armour of light" (see Ephesians vi, 11–17), perfect faith, perfect hope, perfect obedience, perfect love. On our route we called upon many of our old friends, Buck, Sale, Bonner, Smith, Butler; they treated us like presidents.

Monday, September 4. I have been under the necessity of applying four

[48] The news of Napoleon's defeat at Waterloo, June 18, 1815, had just been received.

blisters for a great inflammation in my face and jaws. I have taken medicine. As a member of the Bible Society in Philadelphia, I have distributed many hundreds of Testaments.[49] We do great things with our mite subscription. John Wesley Bond reads many times in the testaments given to the poor. I have visited the families of Butler, Owens, Beale, Heath, Wright, Fowler, and Davis.

Sabbath, 10. I preached on the camp ground. My subject was Heb. iii, 7, 8: "His voice." What is the voice of God to us; to every case and character? The Gospel of the grace of God, in all its blessings, promises, means, ordinances, doctrines, and precepts. "His voice"—in power, in mercy, in providence, in love. "Harden not your hearts." We may harden our hearts against the former, latter, and present impressions the powerful Gospel may have made upon our hopes, our fears, and our consciences. In what manner? By open, notorious sinning; by secret wickedness; by sinful tempers indulged; by a wilful neglect of Gospel men and Gospel means. The greatness of our rebellion. We sin against the infinite love of God; the infinite merit of Christ; the Spirit of infinite holiness. *To-day*, if ye will hear his voice; *to day*: this is both the true reading and meaning. Not to-morrow; no: it may never come. *To-day*, then, speaker and hearer do all you can for God.

On *Tuesday*, the 12th, we began our journey.

Thursday, 14. Our Ohio Conference began, and all our fears vanished. We have great peace, abundance of accommodation, and comfortable seasons in preaching, noon and night, in the chapel and court house. Great grace, and peace, and success have attended our coming together. We hold in Ohio Conference sixty-eight preachers, sixty-seven of whom are stationed. Ten delegates have been chosen for the General Conference. The settlement with the married and unmarried was made according to the funds, in which the mite subscription aided: the children of the preachers were remembered in the distribution of the funds.

Thursday, we came away to Cincinnati. Bishop M'Kendree and myself had a long and earnest talk about the affairs of our Church and my future prospects. I told him my opinion was, that the western part of the empire would be the glory of America for the poor and pious; that it ought to be marked out for five conferences, to wit: Ohio, Kentucky, Holston, Mississippi, and Missouri[50]; in doing which, as well as I was able, I traced outlines and boundaries. I told my colleague, that having passed the first allotted period (seventy years), and being, as he knew, out of health, it

[49] Asbury was identified with the City Bible Society in Philadelphia before the organization of the American Bible Society.

[50] The General Conference of 1816 did create the Mississippi and Missouri conferences. They became the tenth and eleventh annual conferences. Kentucky became the twelfth when it was created in 1820. Then the General Conference of 1824, only eight years after Asbury's death, brought the number of conferences to seventeen with the creating of Pittsburgh, Holston, Illinois, Maine, and Canada.

could not be expected I could visit the extremities every year, sitting in eight, it might be, twelve conferences, and travelling six thousand miles in eight months. If I were able still to keep up with the conferences, I could not be expected to preside in more than every other one. As to the stations, I should never exhibit a plan unfinished, but still get all the information in my power, so as to enable me to make it perfect, like the painter who touches and retouches until all parts of the picture are pleasing. The plan I might be labouring on would always be submitted to such eyes as ought to see it; and the measure I meted to others, I should expect to receive.

Sabbath, 24. I preached at Lebanon, by request of conference, a memorial sermon for Doctor Coke: my subject was Matt. v, 16: "Let your light so shine before men." The Gospel light, in all its fulness of grace and power, the reflected light of that Light of the world, manifested in faith and in obedience in every grade and class of believers. Ministers should be resplendent like a city illuminated in the night; a great light amidst Churches in darkness and slumber; like Doctor Coke, whose effulgence beamed forth in missions, in labours, in Europe, in America, in the isles of the sea, and in Asia. I took occasion to particularize the abundant labours of this distinguished man of God.

Wednesday, 27. We came rapidly to Cincinnati. *Friday*, Bishop M'Kendree's fractures are all repaired, and bones strong again, I suppose, for he has flown away like a bird with the boys.[51] We must stay and distribute the word of God to the poor, collect a little mite money, and then away, preaching in every town we pass through.

Sabbath, October 1. I preached in the chapel: my subject was Phil. i, 27.

Kentucky

Wednesday, I preached in the court house in Georgetown; my subject Acts xiii, 26: "To you is the word of this salvation sent." *This salvation*; the Gospel, to be sure. Who the author, what the nature, means, conditions, spirituality, and degrees of this salvation. From whom it is sent, by whom, and to whom it is sent. It was sent to Jews first, afterward to the Gentiles, and continued to be sent, and is still sent to the children of men by the written word, by the ministers of that word, and by the influences of the Holy Spirit. The consequences of its reception—eternal life: of its rejection—everlasting damnation. We came into Lexington. My soul is blest with continual consolation and peace in all my great weakness of body, labour, and crowds of company. I am a debtor to the whole continent, but more especially to the northeast and southwest; it is there I usually gain health, and generally lose in the south and centre. I have

[51] For McKendree's accident see *Journal* entry and note for September 5, 1814.

visited the south thirty times in thirty-one years. I wish to visit Mississippi, but am resigned. I preached in Lexington on Zeph. iii, 12, 13: "I will also leave in the midst of thee an afflicted and poor people, and they shall trust in the name of the Lord." The true character of God's people—tempted, grieved, poor in spirit. Their strong confidence in Jehovah; in all his attributes, perfections, promises; in all his sacred offices and near relations to his own people. Well guarded by a supreme love of God, and a love to their fellow-men, this people shall not transgress the law in its word nor in its spirit. Nor shall they deceive; for the deceitful tongue is changed by the grace that changed the deceitful heart. As a flock, their souls shall feed and fatten on the privileges and ordinances of the Gospel, whilst other flocks of the hireling shall starve and be scattered: the flock of God shall be led into green pastures by the Great Shepherd, and they shall lie down, undisturbed by that which shall distress others, assured that they shall never perish, neither shall any be able to pluck them out of his hand.

On *Monday*, 9, we came into the Shakers' town:[52] are these children of light? They are wiser than millions of the children of this world. Well-built houses, two grand gardens—everything well planned for comfort and money. But why should I say any harm of this people, who am, I suppose, the last man in the world to envy or to imitate them?

Tennessee

Tuesday, 10. At James M'Kendree's.[53] Nathaniel Moore has come to take away our sister, Frances M'Kendree:[54] all parties are pleased. *Wednesday*, I took counsel of my elder sons, who advise me not to go to Mississippi this year.

On *Thursday* I officiated at the marriage of Nathaniel Moore and Frances M'Kendree; we believe it is of the Lord—they are a worthy couple, and nearly of an age. We have given away many Testaments to the poor on our route hither, and they were in all cases received with

[52] The Shakers, or United Society of Believers in Christ's Second Appearing, had two communal colonies in Kentucky. One was at Mount Pleasant in Mercer County, and the other was in Logan County near Russellville. Both were popularly known as Shakertown. Asbury's reference here was to the Logan County colony, which was near the Tennessee line.

[53] Dr. James McKendree was the brother of Bishop William McKendree. He lived at Fountain Head in Tennessee. The father, John McKendree, also lived there; he died and was buried there about two weeks later.

[54] Frances McKendree was the sister of James and William McKendree. She was born June 22, 1763, and died near Columbia, Tennessee, January 3, 1835. The bridegroom was a preacher, and the descendants of the couple reside in the section today. (Paine: *Life and Times of William McKendree*, 17, 179, 392.)

thankfulness: we accompany our gifts with prayer and exhortation when opportunities offer.

Sabbath, 15. I attended the funeral of the little son of James M'Kendree, and spoke a few words; James Gwinn spoke on David's words, "I shall go to him, but he shall not return to me." I baptized Frances Elizabeth Mabry. So here have been a marriage, a funeral, and a baptism; and must I be honoured and burdened with them all? Well; make the best of me whilst you have me; it will not be often.

Wednesday, 18. Brother M'Kendree preached a funeral sermon for Mrs. Crabb, daughter of S. Mitchell. I added an exhortation. Our brother Blackman had improved his house and estate. Ah! sad estate of human frailty. The body of the first husband rests in a tomb near the dwelling; the body of the second may yet float in the Ohio.[55] Go, disconsolate sister —thou art prepared to weep for the wretched, for thou thyself knowest what is sorrow of heart! *Thursday*, at Bibb's.

Friday, 20. We opened our conference.[56] *Saturday*, great peace, great order, and a great deal of business done.

Sabbath, 22. I ordained the deacons, and preached a sermon, in which Doctor Coke was remembered. My eyes fail. I will resign the stations to Bishop M'Kendree—I will take away my feet. It is my fifty-fifth year of ministry, and forty-fifth year of labour in America. My mind enjoys great peace and divine consolation. My health is better, which may in part be because of my being less deeply interested in the business of the conferences. But whether health, life, or death, good is the will of the Lord: I will trust him; yea, and will prase him: he is the strength of my heart and my portion forever—Glory! glory! glory! Conference was eight days and a half in session—hard labour. Bishop M'Kendree called upon me to preach at the ordination of elders.

Sabbath, 29. At a little place, called a meeting house, I preached by appointment. The notice given had been short, and rather uncertain, nevertheless many attended—more than was at all expected. We had a feeling time: I spoke awful words.

[55] This reference is obscure. Learner Blackman was one of the outstanding preachers. He had married a widow, Mrs. Elizabeth Elliott, nee Odom, of Sumner County, Tennessee, on June 22, 1813. Blackman was drowned in the Ohio River on June 6, 1815, while crossing the river on a ferry boat at Cincinnati. However, his body was recovered and buried in the rear of the Old Stone Church, afterward Wesley Chapel, in Cincinnati, and since Asbury had so recently been in that city, he must have known the facts. Mrs. Blackman later married Jospeh T. Elliston of Nashville, and in her fine home she entertained the preachers and set aside a "bishop's room" for Bishop McKendree. (Price: *Holston Methodism*, II, 134, 135; Redford: *Methodism in Kentucky*, I, 445–47; McFerrin: *Methodism in Tennessee*, II, 105.)

[56] This was the last conference which Asbury attended. It met at Bethlehem Meeting House, a historic log chapel with eight corners which was located four miles south of Lebanon, Tennessee, and about a mile east of present Highway 70. The Woman's Missionary Society of the Methodist Episcopal Church, South, had its beginning there.

November 1. We came upon the turnpike—a disgrace to the State and to the undertakers, supposing they had any character to lose. It is a swindling of the public out of their money to demand toll on such roads as these. We are told, *Why, they make you pay on the turnpikes to the eastward.* Yes, so they do; and they make them fine roads. *Thursday*, to father Holt's, forty-three miles: we came in two hours after night. This will not do—I must halt, or order my grave.

Saturday, I am very unwell. *Friday*, rest and physic. I felt that keeping three men and four horses three days and four nights, not with my friends but with me, was too great a burden to impose. O, what kindness and attentions I receive!

Sabbath, 5. I declined preaching, being so exceedingly weak. *Tuesday*, we stopped with Wesley Harrison,[57] son of Thomas Harrison, in Harrisonburg; the father was the first man under whose roof I lodged on my first visit to that town: his pious wife, and simple-hearted, pious Robert Harrison, are, I trust, both in glory. I have received a statement from James Axley[58] of the work of God in the different places within his knowledge, at quarter and camp meetings; and it appears there were upwards of one hundred and fifty souls who professed to have found justifying grace: there were powerful rains at some of these meetings to interrupt the preaching, and drive the people from their seats; but the work of God prospered in the tents.

Monday, 6. We came to Captain Hill's—very kind and attentive. *Tuesday*, came to Thomas Harrison's, son of Thomas. *Thursday*, at Boling's, we were greatly annoyed by a brigade of Kentuckians;—can fiends be more wicked? The drunkards kept the house in an uproar.

North Carolina

Friday, at Barnett's, there was a dance—such fiddling and drinking! I delivered my testimony: I am clear from Barnett's blood. A rapid ride brought us to Mills's on *Saturday*.

Sabbath, 12. I attended the quarterly meeting at Samuel Edney's, and bore a feeble, but a faithful testimony to the truth. I have read, with dim

[57] Wesley Harrison lived in Cocke County, Tennessee, about a mile west of Newport. Asbury did not enter the Virginia section of the Holston District on this trip. He doubtless proceeded from Middle Tennessee over his usual route. (Price, *op. cit.*, II, 198.)

[58] James Axley was presiding elder of the Holston District of the Tennessee Conference. He was a "rough ashler" and one of the most notable camp-meeting preachers on the frontier. He joined the Western Conference in 1804 and served in the Cumberland Valley country until he located in 1822. He was a member of the General Conference in 1812 and 1816, and died in 1838. (*Ibid.*, 304–37.)

eyes, Joseph Moore's dialogue; it is not elegant, but argumentative; it seems to have silenced the Baptists.

Sabbath, 19. I preached upon Acts xxvi, 17, 18. Many were the instances of deliverance; they bound him and scourged him, yet had the Jews no power over his life, which they so often sought. And the Gentiles, to whom he was especially sent by the Son of God, what a description is given of their deplorable state! what blindness of mind, ignorance, idolatry, superstition, complicated and unaccountable wickedness! "The power of Satan"—completely in his possession, body, soul, and spirit, in all their powers and passions—in infidelity and impenitence, and under the guilt of actual transgression. Thus Gospel truth and Gospel ministers find sinners; and they must be preached to with energy. And these ministers must be *sent*; and to be qualified for this mission, they must, like Paul, be convinced, convicted, and converted, and sanctified. Like him they must be preserved from the violence of the people; but especially from their indulgences and flatteries. "Turning them from darkness to light, and from the power of Satan unto God." A faithful minister will have these signs to follow him.

I die daily—am made perfect by labour and suffering, and fill up still what is behind. There is no time or opportunity to take medicine in the daytime, I must do it at night. I am wasting away with a constant dysentery and cough.

South Carolina

Monday, 20. At Benjamin Glover's. At Allen Glover's, on *Tuesday*. *Wednesday*, my children will not let me go out.[59]

Thursday, 23. Came to Thomas Child's, near Cambridge,[60] twenty miles. *Friday*. To Doctor William Moon's.[61] *Saturday*. The doctor urges, and I have consented to take digitalis:—O, the powerful expectoration that followed!

Sabbath, 26. I preached, and we had a time of great feeling. *Monday*,

[59] On this his thirty-first and final visit to South Carolina the aged and failing bishop could only sketch his movements. However, he doubtless went from the present Edneyville in western North Carolina through Saluda Gap to Father Staunton's on Saluda River in Greenville County, and then to the homes of the Glovers in Abbeville County near Calhoun Falls. This had been his route on previous occasions.

[60] Cambridge was the present Ninety Six. Betts thinks Asbury was hoping to reach Samuel Rembert's in Elbert County, Georgia; he had removed from Rembert Hall in South Carolina some years previously, and the bishop had visited him in his Georgia home. Asbury had nearly reached the state line when he stopped at Glover's on the previous days. At this point he probably realized his weakness and turned sharply eastward in an effort to reach the seat of the approaching conference at Charleston.

[61] Dr. Moon lived in the southwestern part of Newberry County near Silverstreet.

heavy rain. We came away to Hezekiah Arrington's,[62] a cold, damp ride. *Tuesday*, to the widow Means's[63]; the lady was not at home, but the servants are attentive. John Wesley Bond preached in the kitchen. We try to do good. *Wednesday*, to Sterling Williamson's, thirty miles in eight hours. A damp, rainy day, by no means pleasant to me. *Thursday*, rested. *Friday*, at Columbia.

Saturday, *December* 2. A melancholy and awful scene has been witnessed here. Doctor Ivey Finch, about thirty years of age, in driving a violent horse out of Columbia in his chair, was dashed between the shaft and wheel, and his skull fractured. The unhappy man was the only son of my dear friend, Edward Finch. How many Gospel sermons had he heard, and how many prayers had been offered up for him! I preached on the *Sabbath*. I have passed three nights at B. Arthur's, two at friend Alexander M'Dowell's, and one night at Colonel Hutchinson's. My consolations are great. I live in God from moment to moment. The poor colonel is like myself—broken to pieces. I feel deeply upon my mind the consequence of this charge (Columbia).

Thursday, 7. We met a storm and stopped at William Baker's, Granby.[64]

[62] Arrington lived near Pomaria.

[63] Mrs. Means lived across Broad River near Monticello in Fairfield County.

[64] Granby's Landing and the town of Granby were at the head of navigation of the Congaree opposite Columbia, South Carolina. The town was one mile below the present Cayce. Nothing remains but a stone marker with the inscription "Site of Granby. Laid out in 1735. Seat of Lexington County, 1785–1798. Seat of Lexington District, 1804–1821. Visited by George Washington, 1791." The site was unhealthy, and the town declined as Columbia developed. The year following Asbury's last visit the Granby courthouse was sold and moved across the river, where it became the First Presbyterian Church of Columbia. The father of Woodrow Wilson was later pastor of the congregation when the future President was fourteen years old. The William Baker who entertained Asbury at Granby is unidentified; Elihu Baker, William Baker, and Captain Jesse Baker were among the early settlers in the area. (Green: *History of Richland County*, 21, 64, 109.)

1816

1816 *Burial of Asbury in the buryingground of George Arnold*

CHAPTER FORTY-FIVE

A Short Account of His Death

By Francis Hollingsworth

Here the journal of Bishop Asbury closes. And having followed him through such a laborious and useful, and, very often, suffering life, it is thought the reader would be gratified in following him to his grave, that he might witness the end and final triumph of this apostolic minister of the Lord Jesus. The editors, therefore, take the liberty of subjoining a short account of the last moments of this *great* and *good* man. His character, as it was exhibited in the various relations of life he sustained, we leave to his biographers, who, it is hoped, will soon favour the Christian world with a faithful portrait of Bishop Asbury, both living and dying.

The following sketch of the closing scene of his life is taken chiefly from the minutes of the conferences for the year 1816, the only documents now in our possession from which authentic information, in reference to this subject, can be derived.

It seems that, notwithstanding his extreme debility, which could not be witnessed without awakening the liveliest sensibilities, he flattered himself with the prospect of meeting the ensuing General Conference, which was to assemble in Baltimore on the 2d of May, 1816. In this expectation he was, however, disappointed; the disease with which he was afflicted, terminating in the consumption, made such rapid progress as to baffle the power of medicine, and to prostrate the remaining strength of a constitution already trembling under the repeated strokes of disease, and worn down by fatigue and labour. He appeared, indeed, more like a walking skeleton than like a living man.

His great mind, however, seemed to rise superior to his bodily weakness, and to bid defiance to the hasty approaches of dissolution. Hence, impelled on by that unquenchable thirst to do good, by which he had been actuated for more than fifty years, he continued with his faithful travelling companion, John W. Bond, in a close carriage, to journey from place to place, as his exhausting strength would permit, frequently preaching, until he came to Richmond, Virginia, where he preached his last sermon, March 24, 1816, in the old Methodist church. Previous to his entering upon this last pulpit exercise, perceiving his great weakness of body, some of his friends endeavoured to dissuade him from preaching; but he resisted their dissuasions by saying that he must once more deliver his public testimony in that place: yielding their own tenderness for his temporal welfare, to his desire to proclaim once more the counsel of his God, they carried him from his carriage in which he rode—for he was unable either to walk or stand—to the pulpit, and seated him on a table prepared for that purpose.

Though he had to make frequent pauses in the course of his sermon, for the purpose of recovering breath, yet he spoke nearly an hour with much feeling from Rom. ix, 28: "For he will finish the work, and cut it short in righteousness: because a short work will the Lord make upon the earth." This closed *his* public labours on the earth. The audience was much affected. Indeed how could it be otherwise? To behold a venerable old man, under the dignified character of an ecclesiastical patriarch, whose silver locks indicated that time had already numbered his years, and whose pallid countenance and trembling limbs presaged that his earthly race was nearly finished: to see in the midst of these melancholy signals of decaying nature, a soul beaming with immortality, and a heart kindled with divine fire from the altar of God:—to see such a man, and to hear him address them in the name of the Lord of hosts, on the grand concerns of time and eternity! what heart so insensible as to withstand the impressions such an interesting spectacle was calculated to produce?

After having delivered his testimony, he was carried from the pulpit to his carriage, and he rode to his lodgings.

On Tuesday, Thursday, and Friday, he journeyed, and finally came to the house of his old friend, Mr. George Arnold, in Spottsylvania. It was his intention to have reached Fredericksburg, about twenty miles farther, but the weather being unfavourable, and his strength continuing to fail, he was compelled to relinquish his design, and accordingly he remained under the hospitable roof of his friend, Mr. Arnold. Hearing brother Bond conversing with the family respecting an appointment for meeting, he observed that they need not be in haste. A remark so unusual with him gave brother Bond much uneasiness. As the evening came on his indisposition greatly increased, and gave evident intimations that his dissolution could not be far distant. About three o'clock next morning he observed that he had passed a night of great bodily affliction.

Perceiving his deep distress of body, and anxious to retain him as long as possible on the shores of mortality, his friends urged the propriety of sending for a physician; but he gave them to understand it would be useless, saying, That before the physician could reach him his breath would be gone, and the doctor could only pronounce him dead! Being asked if he had anything to communicate, he replied, That, as he had fully expressed his mind in relation to the Church in his addresses to the bishop and to the General Conference, he had nothing more to add.

About eleven o'clock on Sabbath morning, he inquired if it was not time for meeting; but recollecting himself, he requested the family to be called together. This being done agreeably to his request, brother Bond sung, prayed, and expounded the twenty-first chapter of the Apocalypse. During these religious exercises he appeared calm and much engaged in devotion. After this, such was his weakness, he was unable to swallow a little barley water which was offered to him, and his speech began to fail. Observing the distress of brother Bond, he raised his dying hand, at the same time looking joyfully at him. On being asked by brother Bond if he felt the Lord Jesus to be precious, exerting all his remaining strength, he, in token of complete victory, raised both his hands. A few minutes after, as he sat on his chair, with his head reclined upon the hand of brother Bond, without a struggle and with great composure, he breathed his last, on Sabbath, the 21st[65] day of March, in the year of our Lord 1816, and in the seventy-first year of his age;—after having devoted to the work of the ministry about fifty-five years, forty-five of which were spent in visiting the cities, villages, and wildernesses of North America; during thirty of these he had filled the highly responsible office, and conscientiously discharged the arduous duties of general superintendent of the Methodist Episcopal Church.

His immortal spirit having taken its flight to the regions of the blessed, his body was committed to the earth, being deposited in the family burying ground of Mr. Arnold, in whose house he died. His remains were, by order of the General Conference, and at the request of the society of Baltimore, taken up and brought to that city, and deposited in a vault prepared for that purpose, under the recess of the pulpit of the Methodist church in Eutaw Street. A vast concourse of the citizens of Baltimore, with several clergymen of other denominations, followed the corpse as it was carried from the General Conference room in Light Street to the place prepared for its reception in Eutaw Street; being preceded by Bishop M'Kendree as the officiating minister, and brother Black, a representative from the British to the American Conference, and followed by the members of the General Conference as chief mourners. The corpse was placed

[65] The date here mentioned is an obvious error. Asbury died on March 31.

in Eutaw church, and a funeral oration pronounced by the Rev. William M'Kendree, the only surviving bishop; after which the body of this great man of God was deposited in the vault, to remain until the resurrection of the just and unjust.

It is needless to make reflections here, or to pass encomiums upon his character, not only because it would be anticipating his biography which is now preparing for the press, but because the preceding journal speaks for itself, and loudly proclaims the man deeply devoted to God, exerting all his powers of soul and body to promote "peace on earth and good-will to man"; and who ceased not his labours until compelled by the command of Him who first called him into being. Let those now denominated missionaries read this journal, and learn from the example of its author what it is to "endure hardness as good soldiers of the Lord Jesus."

May that Church which so long enjoyed the services of this eminent minister of the sanctuary, and for whose prosperity he so diligently and conscientiously toiled and suffered, not only cherish a grateful remembrance of his Christian and ministerial virtues, but be long blessed with a succession of ministers who shall make *his* virtues *their* exemplar, and transmit to posterity unsullied those pure doctrines of Christ which *Francis Asbury* so faithfully and so successfully proclaimed.

NEW YORK, *April* 23, 1821.

ASBURY'S LAST JOURNEY

By Elmer T. Clark

It is now possible to supplement the transcriber's brief account and trace Asbury's movements after the ailing bishop closed his *Journal* at Granby, South Carolina. In a vain effort to reach the seat of the approaching conference at Charleston, he proceeded to the home of Mrs. Rumph near Orangeburg courthouse and thence to the home of Squire Eccles on Cypress about thirty miles northwest of Charleston.[1] Here he remained in daily communication with the conference. At this conference "all the remaining members of Mr. Hammet's Church, consisting of a few whites and a considerable number of colored people, returned to our Church."[2]

After the conference McKendree went northward, expecting to meet Asbury at the Virginia Conference. The two bishops never met again. Asbury went northward to John Whetstone's, who lived near St. Matthew's in Calhoun County about seventy miles from Charleston, where it seems that he remained two or three weeks. Here, on January 15, 1816, he dictated to Thomas Mason, who was on the Camden-Santee Circuit, a long letter to Dr. Joseph Benson in England in reply to a letter from the

[1] *South Carolina Christian Advocate*, July 29, 1858, art. by Bishop Andrew.

[2] Paine: *Life and Times of Bishop McKendree*, 179.

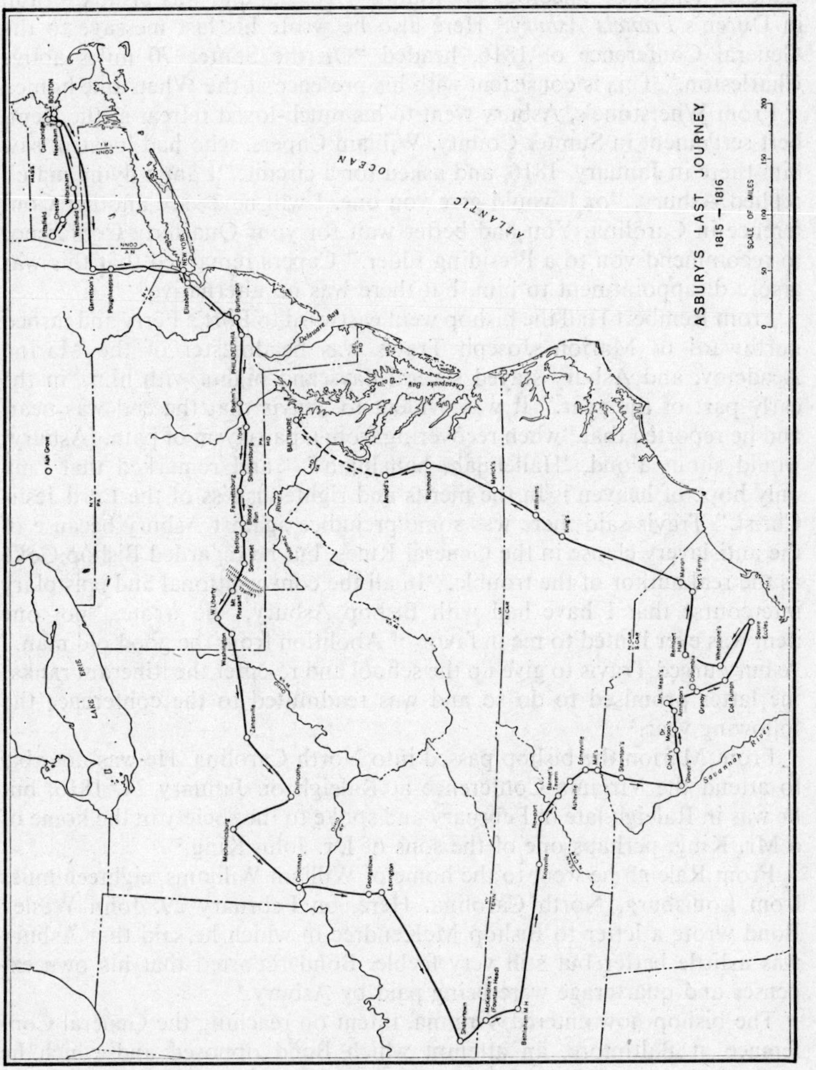
ASBURY'S LAST JOURNEY
1815 — 1816
SCALE OF MILES
ATLANTIC
OCEAN
BOSTON
NEW YORK
PHILADELPHIA
BALTIMORE
Richmond
Cambridge
Pittsfield
Poughkeepsie
Elizabeth
Burlington
York
Bedford
Chillicothe
Cincinnati
Lexington
Georgetown
Knoxville
Columbia
Delaware Bay
Chesapeake Bay
LAKE ERIE

British Conference inviting him to visit England. This important letter was headed "South Carolina" with the date. This document is now in the Candler School of Theology at Atlanta, Georgia, and was printed in full in Duren's *Francis Asbury*.[3] Here also he wrote his last message to the General Conference of 1816, headed "On the Santee 70 miles above Charleston." This is consistent with his presence at the Whetstone home.[4]

From Whetstone's, Asbury went to his much-loved retreat at the Rembert settlement in Sumter County. William Capers, who had located, saw him there in January, 1816, and asked for a circuit. "I am a dying man," replied Asbury, "or I would give you one. I will never see another Conference in Carolina. You had better wait for your Quarterly Conference to recommend you to a Presiding Elder." Capers remarked that this was a sore disappointment to him, but there was no alternative.[5]

From Rembert Hall the bishop went eastward to Port's Ferry and turned northward to Marion. Joseph Travis was headmaster of the Marion Academy, and Asbury stayed several days and nights with him "in the early part of the year." It was evident to Travis that the end was near, and he reported that "when recovering from a paroxysm of pain, [Asbury] would shout aloud, 'Hallelujah, hallelujah!' " and remarked that "my only hope of heaven is in the merits and righteousness of the Lord Jesus Christ." Travis said there was some prejudice against Asbury because of the antislavery clause in the General Rules, but he regarded Bishop Coke as the real author of the trouble. "In all the conversational and epistolary intercourse that I have had with Bishop Asbury," he wrote, "not one item was ever hinted to me in favor of Abolition from the good old man." Asbury urged Travis to give up the school and re-enter the itinerant ranks; the latter promised to do so and was readmitted to the conference the following year.[6]

From Marion the bishop passed into North Carolina. He was not able to attend the Virginia Conference at Raleigh on January 24, 1816, but he was in Raleigh late in February and spoke to the society in the home of a Mr. King, perhaps one of the sons of Dr. John King.[7]

From Raleigh he went to the home of William Williams, eighteen miles from Louisburg, North Carolina. Here, on February 29, John Wesley Bond wrote a letter to Bishop McKendree in which he said that Asbury was a little better but still very feeble. Bond reported that his own expenses and quarterage were being paid by Asbury.[8]

The bishop now entered Virginia, intent on reaching the General Conference at Baltimore, an attempt which Bond opposed and which he realized was impossible. On March 4, 1816, they were at the home of

[3] Pp. 241–55. [4] See these documents in the volume of *Letters*.
[5] Capers: *Autobiography*, 185.
[6] Betts, *op. cit.*, 137, 138; Travis: *Autobiography*, 94–96.
[7] Paine, *op. cit.*, 180. [8] *Ibid.*, 180.

Matthew Myrick in Brunswick County. Bond had not despatched the letter to McKendree, and he opened it to enclose another letter and also one from Asbury himself. These letters dealt mainly with sending missionaries to the German population, and Asbury suggested that Robert R. Roberts, presiding elder of the Schuylkill District, and Henry Boehm of the Chesapeake District should be exchanged because of Boehm's knowledge of the German language.[9]

About the middle of March the feeble old bishop and his traveling companion reached Manchester, now South Richmond, and lodged with an old friend, John Potts. Here he was visited by the Rev. Philip Courtney. Sending Bond to fill "Father" Courtney's appointment, Asbury outlined to the latter a plan whereby the local preachers in a given city might each travel an annual round of the circuit and select one of their number to attend the annual conference.[10]

Entering Richmond, Asbury lodged with the Rev. Archibald Foster, "who lived on Main street, a little above the Market bridge," where he was confined to his room for a week. He sent for Bishop Moore, of the Protestant Episcopal Church, whom he warned against receiving and ordaining a British Methodist preacher whom Asbury regarded as unworthy. He furthermore suggested to Moore that the Episcopalians, who had few churches, should preach in the more numerous but plain Methodist meetinghouses.[11]

A few days later Asbury, unable to stand, was carried into the church at Nineteenth and Franklin streets in Richmond, where he was supported on a table while he preached his last sermon. Then he pushed on at a snail's pace to the home of George Arnold in Spottsylvania County, where he died, as described in Hollingsworth's "short account."

Bishop McKendree was ill with rheumatism in the home of an old friend, Dr. Wilkins, between Baltimore and Philadelphia, when his colleague passed away. Here he received the news by a messenger from John Wesley Bond: "Our dear father has left us, and has gone to the Church triumphant. He died as he lived—full of confidence, full of hope—at four o'clock this afternoon, Sunday, March 31, 1816."[12]

Hollingsworth has told of the interment at Arnold's and subsequent removal of the body to Eutaw Street Church in Baltimore. It rested there until June, 1854, when it was transferred to its final resting place among many other Methodist leaders in Mount Olivet Cemetery in Baltimore.[13]

[9] *Ibid.* 180–82.
[10] Bennett: *Memorials of Methodism in Virginia*, 611.
[11] *Ibid.*, 612.
[12] Paine, *op. cit.*, 182, 297.
[13] Tipple: *The Prophet of the Long Road*, 293–99.

Selected Bibliography

For a complete list of the various works consulted see the references cited in the footnotes

Abbott. *History of Old Zion Methodist Episcopal Church.* New Jersey, 1907.

Allen. *The Garrison Church, Sketches of the History of St. Thomas' Church, Baltimore County, Maryland.* New York, 1898.

———. *Historical Notes of St. Ann's Parish in Anne Arundel County.*

Allen and Pilsbury. *History of Methodism in Maine, 1793–1886.* Augusta, 1887.

Archer. *An Authentic History of Cokesbury College.*

Armstrong. *Old Baltimore Conference.* Baltimore, 1907.

Arminian Magazine. New York, 1789, 1790.

Arnold. *History of Methodism in Kentucky.* 2 vols. Winchester, Ky., 1935.

Asbury, Francis. *Journal of Rev. Francis Asbury.* 1st ed. New York, 1821. 2nd ed. New York, 1852. 3rd printing, 1854.

———. *A Selection of Hymns from Various Authors,* Designed as a Supplement to the Methodist Pocket Hymn-book. New York, 1808.

———. *Causes, Evils, and Cures of Heart and Church Divisions.* Extracted from the Books of Burroughs and Baxter. New York, 1817.

Asbury, Herbert. *A Methodist Saint.* New York, 1927.

Atkinson. *Centennial History of American Methodism.* New York, 1884.

———. *The Beginnings of the Wesleyan Movement in America.* New York, 1896.

———. *Memorials of Methodism in New Jersey.* Philadelphia, 1860.

Atmore. *Methodist Memorial.* Bristol, 1801.

Ayres. *Methodist Heroes of Other Days.* New York, 1916.

Baker. *A Methodist Pilgrim in England.* London, 1951.

Bangs. *Life of Freeborn Garrettson.* New York, 1838.

———. *A History of the Methodist Episcopal Church.* 2 vols. New York, 1839.

Barclay. *History of Methodist Missions.* 3 vols. New York, 1949–57.

Barratt. *Barratt's Chapel and Methodism.* Wilmington, Del., 1911.

———. *Outline of the History of Old St. Paul's Church.*

Bassett. *Concise History of the Methodist Protestant Church.* Pittsburgh, 1882.

Bennett. *Memorials of Methodism in Virginia.* Richmond, 1871.

Betts. *History of South Carolina Methodism.* Columbia, 1952.

Bibbins. *How Methodism Came.* Baltimore, 1945.

Boehm. *Reminiscences, Historical and Biographical, of Sixty-four Years in the Ministry.* New York, 1865.

Bowden. *History of Savannah Methodism.* Macon, 1929.

Bowen. *Story of Wilkes County, Georgia.* Marietta, 1950.

Bragg. *A History of Methodism in Milford, Massachusetts.*

Briggs. *Bishop Asbury.* London, 1879.

Buckley. *A History of Methodism in the United States.* 2 vols. New York, 1898.

Buckley. *Constitutional and Parliamentary History of the Methodist Episcopal Church*. New York, 1912.
Butts. *From Saddle to City by Buggy, Boat, and Railway*. Richmond, 1922.
Candlin. *History of the Methodist Episcopal Church in Marblehead, Massachusetts.*
Carroll. *The Francis Asbury Centennial Volume*. New York, 1916.
Carter. *History of the Tennessee Conference*. Nashville, 1948.
Cathcart. *Historical Address at the Anniversary of Old Rock Chapel.*
Centennial History of Ebenezer Church, Southport, Pennsylvania. Philadelphia, 1890.
Chaffee. *History of the Wyoming Conference*. New York, 1904.
Chreitzberg. *Early Methodism in the Carolinas*. Nashville, 1897.
Church. *The Early Methodist People*. London, 1949.
Clark. *The Methodist Episcopal Churches of Norwich, Connecticut*. Norwich, 1867.
Clark. *An Album of Methodist History*. Nashville, 1952.
———. *The Small Sects in America*. Nashville, 1949.
Clark. *Discourse on the Formation and Progress of the First Methodist Episcopal Church in Lynn, Massachusetts.*
Coke. *Extracts of the Journals of the Late Rev. Thomas Coke*. Dublin, 1816.
Colbert. *A Journal of the Travels of William Colbert*. Typescript in the World Methodist Building, Lake Junaluska, North Carolina.
Cole and Baketele. *History of the New Hampshire Conference*. New York, 1929.
Coles. *Heroines of Methodism*. New York, 1869.
Colhouer. *Sketches of the Founders of the Methodist Protestant Church*. Pittsburgh, 1880.
Conable. *History of the Genesee Annual Conference*. New York, 1876.
Cooper. *Discourse on the Death of Asbury*. Philadelphia, 1819.
———. Calendar of the Ezekiel Cooper Collection of Early American Methodist Manuscripts. Chicago, 1941.
Crook. *Ireland and the Centenary of American Methodism*. London, 1866.
Cummings. *Early Schools of Methodism*. New York, 1886.
Daniels. *Illustrated History of Methodism*. New York, 1887.
Davis. *Historical Sketches of Franklin County, North Carolina*. Raleigh, 1948.
Davis. *History of the Methodist Episcopal Church in Newport, Rhode Island.*
Disosway and Gregory. *Earliest Churches of New York and Vicinity.*
Dix. *A History of the Parish of Trinity Church in the City of New York.*
Dolliver. *Story of John Street Methodist Church*. New York, 1939.
Douglas. *History of Steele Creek Church.*
Drew. *The Life of the Rev. Thomas Coke*. New York, 1818.
Drinkhouse. *History of Methodist Reform and Methodist Protestant Church.* Pittsburgh, 1899.
Dromgoole. Manuscripts at the University of North Carolina. Chapel Hill.
Drury. *History of the United Brethren in Christ*. Dayton, 1953.
———. *The Life of Rev. Philip William Otterhein*. Dayton, 1913.
Du Bose. *Francis Asbury*. Nashville, 1916.
Duren. *Francis Asbury, Founder of American Methodism and Unofficial Minister of State*. New York, 1928.

Duren. *The Top Sergeant of the Pioneers.* Atlanta, 1930.
Duvall. *The Methodist Church and Education up to* 1869.
Eckman. *History of the Morristown Methodist Church, New Jersey.*
Edwards. *Life of John Wesley Childs.* Richmond, 1852.
Elliott. *The Life of the Rev. Robert R. Roberts.* New York, 1844.
Elliott-Binns. *The Early Evangelicals.* Greenwich, 1953.
Emory. *A Defence of "Our Fathers," and of the Original Organization of the Methodist Episcopal Church Against Alexander McCaine and Others.* New York, 1827.
———. *The Life of the Rev. John Emory, D.D.* New York, 1841.
Etheridge. *Life of the Rev. Thomas Coke.* London, 1860.
Ewing. *Information on 150 Years of Methodism in Bridgeton, New Jersey.* New York, 1844.
Ferguson. *Methodism in Washington, D.C.* Baltimore, 1892.
Ffirth. *The Experiences and Gospel Labors of the Rev. Benjamin Abbott.* New York, 1836.
Findlay and Hollingsworth. *History of the Wesleyan Missionary Society.* 4 vols. London, 1921–24.
Finley. *Sketches of Western Methodism.* Cincinnati, 1854.
Fitch. *The Perfect Calendar for Every Day of the Christian Era.*
Freeman. *Francis Asbury's Silver Trumpet.* Nashville, 1950.
Garber. *Romance of American Methodism.* Greensboro, N.C., 1931.
Garrettson. *The Experiences and Travels of Mr. Freeborn Garrettson.* Philadelphia, 1791.
Garsie. *Lives of Eminent Methodist Ministers.* New York, 1859.
Gewehr. *The Great Awakening in Virginia.* Durham, N.C., 1930.
Gilmore. *Life of Edward Tiffin, First Governor of Ohio.* Chillicothe, 1897.
Glendenning. *Life of William Glendenning.* Philadelphia, 1794.
Graham. *History of the Troy Conference.* Albany, 1908.
Gregg. *History of Methodism Within the Bounds of the Erie Annual Conference.* New York, 1873.
Grissom. *History of Methodism in North Carolina.* Nashville, 1905.
Guirey. *History of the Episcopacy.*
Hallman. *The Garden of Methodism.* Wilmington, n.d.
———. *History of Asbury Church.* Wilmington, 1889.
Halterman. *History of Methodism in the South Branch Valley.*
Hampton. *Staten Island's Claim to Fame.* New York, 1925.
———. *Newark Conference Centennial History.* Staten Island, 1957.
———. *History of Chatham Methodism.* New Jersey.
———. *Francis Asbury on Staten Island.*
Hannah. *Centennial Services of Asbury Methodist Episcopal Church, Wilmington, Delaware.*
Hartman. *History of Methodism in Maryland.*
Heads of Families, U.S. Census, 1790.
Hearne. *One Hundred Years of Methodism in Snow Hill, Maryland.*
Heart. *History of Methodism in Bennington, Vermont.*
Hedges. *Crowned Victors.*
Hill. *History of Methodism in Norwalk, Connecticut.*

Hollingsworth. *The Hollingsworth Family.*
Hough. *Christian Newcomer, His Life, Journal, and Achievements.* Dayton, 1941.
Hubbell. *History of Methodism on Staten Island.*
Huffacre. *Michael Huffacre and His Descendants.*
Hurst. *History of Methodism.* 7 vols. New York, 1902.
Hyde. *The Story of Methodism.* New York, 1888.
Jackson. *Lives of Early Methodist Preachers Chiefly Written by Themselves.* 6 vols. London, 1865.
Jarratt. *Life of the Reverend Deveraux Jarratt Written by Himself in a Series of Letters Addressed to the Rev. John Coleman.* Baltimore, 1806.
Jamison. *A Century of Life, Woodrow Methodist Church.* Staten Island.
Jennings. *An Exposition of the Late Controversy in the Methodist Episcopal Church, with Remarks on an Article Entitled Asbury's Life by a Layman.* Baltimore, 1831.
Johnston. *Observations on the Present State of Religion in Cecil County, Maryland.*
Kincaid. *The Wilderness Road.* New York, 1947.
Kirkley. *Centennial Sketches of Methodism in Washington, D.C.* Washington.
Larrabee. *Asbury and His Coadjutors.* 2 vols. Cincinnati, 1854.
Lednum. *A History of the Rise of Methodism in America.* Philadelphia, 1859.
Lee. *A Short History of the Methodists in the United States.* Baltimore, 1810.
Lee. *The Life and Times of the Rev. Jesse Lee.* Richmond, 1848.
———. *A Short Account of the Life and Death of the Rev. John Lee.*
Lee, Luccock and Dixon. *Illustrated History of Methodism.* New York, 1926.
Lewis. *Francis Asbury.* London, 1927.
Liggett. *Methodist Sesquicentennial.* Baltimore, 1934.
Lundy. *Holston Horizons.* Bristol, Tenn., 1947.
Lytle. *First Century of Newton Methodism.*
MacClenny. *The Life of the Rev. James O'Kelly.* Raleigh, 1910.
Mains. *Francis Asbury.* New York, 1909.
Marine. *Sketch of Rev. John Hersey.* Baltimore, 1879.
Martin. *Methodism in the Holston Conferences.* Knoxville, 1945.
Martz. *The Clarksburg Methodist Church,* Maryland.
Mastin. *One Hundred Years of Richmond Methodism.*
McCaine. *History and Mystery of Methodist Episcopacy, the Defense of Truth and Letters on the Methodist Episcopal Church.* Baltimore, 1850.
———. *Letters on the Organization and Early History of the Methodist Church.* Boston, 1850.
McClintock. *History of the Coventryville Methodist Church.*
McFerrin. *Methodism in Tennessee.* 2 vols. Nashville, 1888.
McLean. *Sketch of Rev. Philip Gatch.* Cincinnati, 1854.
McTyeire. *History of Methodism.* Nashville, 1893.
Meade. *Old Churches, Ministers and Families of Virginia.* Philadelphia, 1887.
Meredith. *Jesse Lee.* New York, 1909.
Miller. *Souvenir History of the New England Southern Conference.* Nantasket, Mass., 1897.
Mitchell. *The Life and Times of Levi Scott.*
Mooney. *Centennial History of Rahway Methodism, New Jersey.*

Moore. *Sketches of Pioneers of Methodism in North Carolina and Virginia.* Nashville, 1884.
Mudge. *History of the New England Conference.* Boston, 1910.
Neely. *A History of the Origin and Development of the Governing Conference in Methodism.* New York, 1892.
———. *The Bishops and the Supervisional System of the Methodist Episcopal Church.* New York, 1912.
O'Kelly. *Life of the Reverend James O'Kelly.*
Paine. *Life and Times of Bishop McKendree.* 2 vols. Nashville, 1869.
Palmer. *Heroism and Romance, Early Methodism in Northeastern Pennsylvania.* Saylorsburg, Pa., 1950.
Parks. *Troy Conference Miscellany.* Albany, 1854.
Payton. *Our Fathers Have Told Us; the Story of the Founding of Methodism in Western Pennsylvania.* Cincinnati, 1938.
Peck. *Early Methodism Within the Bounds of the Old Genesee Conference.* New York, 1860.
Peck. *Wyoming.* New York, 1921.
Perrin. *An Epitome History of the Inception of Methodism in Northeastern Pennsylvania.*
Phoebus. *Beams of Light on Early Methodism.* New York, 1887.
———. *Memoirs of the Rev. Richard Whatcoat.* New York, 1828.
Pierce. *Lest Faith Forget: The Story of Methodism in Georgia.* Atlanta, 1951.
Pitt. *History of the Allentown Methodist Church, New Jersey.*
Playter. *History of Methodism in Canada.* Toronto, 1862.
Porter. *Compendium of Methodism.* Boston, 1853.
Price. *Holston Methodism.* 5 vols. Nashville, 1912.
Prince. *The Romance of Early Methodism in and Around West Bromwich and Wednesbury.* West Bromwich, 1923.
Pusey. *The Wilderness Road to Kentucky.* New York, 1921.
Rankin. *The Diary of Reverend Thomas Rankin, One of the Helpers of John Wesley.* Typescript in the World Methodist Building, Lake Junaluska, North Carolina.
Redford. *History of Methodism in Kentucky.* 3 vols. Nashville, 1868.
Reeves. *Methodism in and Around Chester, Pennsylvania.*
Roberts. *Centenary Pictorial Album, Being Contributions of the Early History of Methodism in the State of Maryland.* Baltimore, 1866.
Rose. *The Story of the First Methodist Church, Bridgeton, New Jersey.*
Seaman. *Annals of New York Methodism.* New York, 1892.
Simpson. *Cyclopedia of Methodism.* Philadelphia, 1876.
———. *A Hundred Years of Methodism.* New York, 1876.
Scott. "The Journal of Thomas Scott." Manuscript.
Shipp. *History of Methodism in South Carolina.* Nashville, 1884.
Smeltzer. *Methodism on the Headwaters of the Ohio.* Nashville, 1951.
Smith. *Life and Labors of Francis Asbury.* Nashville, 1896.
———. *History of Georgia Methodism.* Atlanta, 1913.
———. *History of Methodism in Georgia and Florida.* Macon, 1877.
———. *Early Georgia People.*
Smith. *Recollections and Reflections of an Old Itinerant.* New York, 1848.

Snyder. *History of the Smithville Methodist Church, Maryland.*
Sprague. *Annals of the American Pulpit*. Vol. VII. New York, 1861.
Spencer. *Reflections of William Spencer.*
Stevens. *History of the Methodist Episcopal Church in the United States of America.* 4 vols. New York, 1864.
———. *Life and Times of Nathan Bangs*. New York, 1863.
———. *Memorials of the Introduction of Methodism into the Eastern States.* Boston, 1848.
———. *The Centenary of American Methodism*. New York, 1865.
Strickland. *The Pioneer Bishop: Life and Times of Francis Asbury*. New York, 1858.
———. *Life of Jacob Gruber*. New York, 1860.
Summers. *Biographical Sketches of Eminent Itinerant Ministers*. Nashville, 1858.
Sutherland. *Methodism in Canada*. London, 1903.
Sweet. *Men of Zeal*. New York, 1935.
———. *Religion on the American Frontier*. Vol. IV, *The Methodists*. Chicago, 1946.
———. *Methodism in American History*. New York, 1953.
———. *Virginia Methodism*. Richmond, 1955.
———. *Rise of Methodism in the West*. New York, 1920.
Tees. *The Ancient Landmark of American Methodism*. Nashville, 1941.
———. *The Beginnings of Methodism in England and in America*. Nashville, 1940.
———. *Methodist Origins*. Nashville, 1948.
Tevis. *Sixty Years in a School Room.*
Thrift. *Memoir of Jesse Lee.*
Tigert. *A Constitutional History of American Episcopal Methodism*. Nashville, 1894.
———. *The Making of Methodism*. Nashville, 1898.
Tipple. *Francis Asbury, the Prophet of the Long Road*. New York, 1916.
———. *Freeborn Garrettson*. New York, 1910.
———. *The Heart of Asbury's Journal*. New York, 1904.
Todd. *Methodism of the Peninsula*. Philadelphia, 1886.
Townsend, Workman and Eayrs. *A New History of Methodism*. 2 vols. London, 1907.
Tracy. *The Great Awakening*. Boston, 1842.
Tyerman. *Life and Times of John Wesley*. New York, 1870.
Upham. *History of the Methodist Episcopal Church, Bristol, Rhode Island.*
Wakeley. *Heroes of Methodism*. New York, 1856.
———. *Lost Chapters Recovered from the Early History of American Methodism.* New York, 1858.
Ware. *Sketches of the Life and Travels of Rev. Thomas Ware*. New York, 1839.
Warriner. *Old Sands Street Church of Brooklyn*. New York, 1885.
Watters. *A Short Account of the Christian Experiences and Ministerial Labors of William Watters*. Alexandria, Va., 1806.
———. *First American Itinerant of Methodism.*
———. *The Watters Family.*
Wightman. *Life of William Capers, D.D.* Nashville, 1902.

Wilkins. *Family Adviser, or a Plain and Modern Practice of Physic*. New York, 1814.
Wilson. *Methodism in Athens, Georgia.*
Wise. *American Methodists*. Englewood, N.J., n.d.
Wittmer. *History of Oldwick Methodist Church*. New Jersey.
Woodmason. *The Carolina Backcountry on the Eve of the Revolution*. Chapel Hill, 1953.
Wright. *Sketches of the Life and Letters of James Quinn*. Cincinnati, 1851.
Wrenshall. Manuscript Journal of John Wrenshall.
Wesley. *The Journal of the Rev. John Wesley, A.M.* 8 vols. London, 1938.
———. *The Letters of John Wesley*. 8 vols. London, 1931.
Young. *Autobiography of a Pioneer*. New York, 1857.
Young. *A History of the Most Interesting Events in the Rise and Progress of Methodism*. New Haven, 1830.

Illustrations

Maps

Showing Places Visited by Asbury

Index of Sermon Texts

General Index

Date Due